DOLLAR'S VETERINARY SURGERY

GENERAL, OPERATIVE, AND REGIONAL

DOLLAR'S
VETERINARY SURGERY

GENERAL, OPERATIVE, AND REGIONAL

FOURTH EDITION

EDITED BY

J. J. O'CONNOR, M.R.C.V.S.

EXAMINER TO THE ROYAL COLLEGE OF VETERINARY SURGEONS AND TO THE NATIONAL UNIVERSITY OF IRELAND. LATELY PROFESSOR OF SURGERY AT THE VETERINARY COLLEGE OF IRELAND, DUBLIN

CBS

CBS Publishers & Distributors Pvt. Ltd.

New Delhi • Bengaluru • Chennai • Kochi • Kolkata • Mumbai
Hyderabad • Uttarakhand • Nagpur • Patna • Pune • Jharkhand

ISBN: 81-239-0970-5

First Indian Edition: 1980
Reprint: 2001, 2003, 2005

This reprint edition has been authorised by Bailliere Tindall, London

Published by **Satish Kumar Jain** and produced by **Varun Jain** for
CBS Publishers & Distributors Pvt. Ltd.,
4819/XI Prahlad Street, 24 Ansari Road, Daryaganj, New Delhi - 110002
delhi@cbspd.com, cbspubs@airtelmail.in • www.cbspd.com
Ph.: 23289259, 23266861, 23266867 • Fax: 011-23243014

Corporate Office: 204 FIE, Industrial Area, Patparganj, Delhi - 110 092
Ph: 49344934 • Fax: 011-49344935
E-mail: publishing@cbspd.com • publicity@cbspd.com

Branches:

- ***Bengaluru:*** 2975, 17th Cross, K.R. Road, Bansankari 2nd Stage, Bengaluru - 70 • Ph: +91-80-26771678/79 • Fax: +91-80-26771680 E-mail: cbsbng@gmail.com, bangalore@cbspd.com
- ***Chennai:*** No. 7, Subbaraya Street, Shenoy Nagar, Chennai - 600030 Ph: +91-44-26681266, 26680620 • Fax: +91-44-42032115 E-mail: chennai@cbspd.com
- ***Kochi:*** Ashana House, 39/1904, A.M. Thomas Road, Valanjambalam, Ernakulum, Kochi • Ph: +91-484-4059061-65 Fax: +91-484-4059065 • E-mail: cochin@cbspd.com
- ***Kolkata:*** 6-B, Ground Floor, Rameshwar Shaw Road, Kolkata - 700014 Ph: +91-33-22891126/7/8 • E-mail: kolkata@cbspd.com
- ***Mumbai:*** 83-C, Dr. E. Moses Road, Worli, Mumbai - 400018 Ph: +91-9833017933, 022-24902340/41 • E-mail: mumbai@cbspd.com

Representatives:

- Hyderabad: 0-9885175004
- Patna: 0-9334159340
- Jharkhand: 0-9811541605
- Nagpur: 0-9021734563
- Pune: 0-9623451994
- Uttarakhand: 0-9716462459

Printed at:
J.S. Offset Printers, Delhi (India)

PREFACE TO THE FOURTH EDITION

ONCE again the opportunity has arisen to revise this book which has for so long held its place as a standard textbook of operative and clinical surgery for the use of students and practitioners at home and overseas. Evidence of its appreciation abroad has been forthcoming recently in a request for permission to translate the work into a foreign language. It is no easy matter to decide what shall be included and what omitted in a book of this nature, but I trust that the Fourth Edition will continue to serve the veterinary profession, since very great care has been taken with the revision of the text to ensure that it will meet all modern requirements. Attention is drawn to the addition of the new material on the following subjects :

1. Penicillin and the sulphonamide drugs and their uses.
2. A new apparatus for inhalation anæsthesia in small animals.
3. Trilene anæsthesia in small animals.
4. Intravenous anæsthesia in large animals by chloral (also deep narcosis), thiopentone, ether, and " Anavenol."
5. Cyclopropane anæsthesia in ruminants.
6. Blood transfusion.
7. Treatment of fractures by bone pinning.
8. Methods of dehorning.
9. Examination of horses as to soundness.

Other new material will be noticed by those familiar with the book on reading through it, also the introduction of some new illustrations.

As one grows older one feels increasingly conscious of the debt owed to all those colleagues and all those friends with whom one has lived and worked or merely had contact from time to time. It is impossible to acknowledge a debt of this nature individually, but I am most grateful to those who have written to me or spoken to me regarding this book for their kindly assistance, and particularly to Professor J. G. Wright, to whom I am indebted for much of the material on anæsthesia.

J. J. O'CONNOR

From the Preface to the Third Edition

In rewriting Dollar's treatise on Veterinary Surgery my aim has been to abridge the work without omitting any essential detail, to supply deficiencies, and to arrange the matter in a more concise manner and under headings which must greatly facilitate the reader in grasping the salient points of the subject. Abridgment was made possible by:

1. Omitting anatomical descriptions, which can be obtained from works on anatomy.
2. Avoiding the unnecessary repetition of details, such as those of inflammatory symptoms or of the preparation of the site of operation.
3. Arranging matter in an abbreviated fashion under separate numbered headings, thereby obviating the use of several sentences.
4. Omitting references of dubious value or which seemed to obscure rather than throw light on the subject.

Deficiencies have been made good by the introduction of much new material, which will be at once revealed on perusing the book and comparing its contents with those of the original work.

Among the new features introduced into the Second Edition were (1) the addition of the whole of Part I, (2) several articles in Parts II and III, (3) the placing of all the principal operations in one section, rendering them convenient for revision and easy reference for the student when practising on the dead subject.

Notable amongst the material added to the Third Edition are (1) a Section on "Affections of the Skin," (2) a description of anæsthesia by Nembutal, Evipan, and Pentothal, and of epidural anæsthesia in the various animals, and (3) an account of the treatment of fractures by unpadded plaster casts; whilst all existing material has been carefully brought up to date. Many new illustrations have been introduced and a number of old figures which were considered obsolete or unnecessary have been omitted. Expressions of appreciation of the enhanced value of the Second Edition have been received from a number of readers both at home and abroad. It may therefore be justly claimed that in this latest edition the recognised value of the original work has been still further enhanced.

My sources of information include, in addition to the original work, my own experiences, conversations with practitioners, veterinary periodicals, and published works by Cadiot and Almy, Williams (New York), Williams (Edinburgh), Macqueen, Hobday, and Wooldridge. I have given the names of authorities throughout the book where it was possible to recall them. It is obvious that the aspirant to proficiency in clinical and operative veterinary surgery should have a thorough knowledge of anatomy, physiology, pathology, and bacteriology, as all these subjects have an important bearing on surgery. Without a sound knowledge of anatomy it is impossible for the surgeon to operate with confidence or understand many of the abnormalities met with in veterinary practice. Surgical lesions interfere with physiological processes, and are dependent on pathological conditions, many of which are due to micro-organisms.

The student or veterinary surgeon beginning his career should develop his powers of observation and make himself very familiar with the normal habits and characteristics of the domesticated animals and with the anatomy and functions of their various organs. Otherwise he will not be in a position as a clinician to give a competent opinion as to abnormal conditions affecting them.

J. J. O'Connor

Veterinary College,
Dublin,
January 1938.

CONTENTS

PART I

GENERAL SURGERY

CHAPTER		PAGE
I.	INFLAMMATION AND ABSCESSES	3
	I. INFLAMMATION	3
	II. ABSCESSES	7
II.	GANGRENE, ULCERS, SINUS AND FISTULA	13
	I. GANGRENE	13
	II. ULCERS	15
	III. SINUS AND FISTULA	17
III.	WOUNDS AND PHYSICAL LESIONS	20
IV.	TUMOURS AND CYSTS	48
	I. TUMOURS	48
	II. CYSTS	50
V.	AFFECTIONS OF TISSUES	52
	I. SKIN AND SUBCUTANEOUS CONNECTIVE TISSUE	52
	II. BURSÆ	67
	III. MUSCLES	69
	IV. TENDONS	75
	V. SYNOVIAL SHEATHS	79
	VI. ARTERIES	85
	VII. VEINS	91
	VIII. THE LYMPHATIC SYSTEM	95
	IX. NERVES	99
	X. BONES	105
	IX. JOINTS	133

CONTENTS

PART II

OPERATIVE SURGERY

CHAPTER		PAGE
I.	GENERAL CONSIDERATIONS	147
	I. THE CONDITION OF THE PATIENT	147
	II. THE ANATOMY AND NORMAL CONDITION OF THE REGION TO BE OPERATED UPON	147
	III. PREPARATION OF THE PATIENT	148
	IV. THE PLACE AND TIME FOR OPERATION	148
	V. CONTROL OF THE ANIMAL	150
	VI. ANÆSTHESIA	170
	VII. ANTISEPSIS AND ASEPSIS	216
	VIII. INSTRUMENTS, DRESSING AND SUTURE MATERIALS	225
	IX. OPERATIVE TECHNIQUE	228
	X. HÆMOSTASIS	239
	AUTOPLASTIA	245
	PARENTERAL INJECTION OF DRUGS, SERA, OR VACCINES	249
	CAUTERISATION—FIRING.	252
	ARTIFICIAL HYPERÆMIA.	260
	HYDROTHERAPY	261
	DIATHERMY	263
	MASSAGE	263
	ELECTRODIAGNOSIS	264
	ELECTROTHERAPY	264
	FULGURATION	276
	RADIODIAGNOSIS AND RADIOTHERAPY	268
	RADIUM THERAPY	269
II.	OPERATIONS	272

PART III

REGIONAL SURGERY

AFFECTIONS OF THE HEAD	491
AFFECTIONS OF THE EAR	525
AFFECTIONS OF THE EUSTACHIAN TUBE AND OF THE GUTTURAL POUCHES	533
AFFECTIONS OF THE NASAL CAVITIES AND FACIAL SINUSES	541

PAGE

AFFECTIONS OF THE JAWS 555
AFFECTIONS OF THE MOUTH 564
AFFECTIONS OF THE TONGUE 577
AFFECTIONS OF THE PALATE 581
AFFECTIONS OF THE CRANIUM 583
AFFECTIONS OF THE HORNS 588
AFFECTIONS OF THE TEETH 590
AFFECTIONS OF THE NECK 604
DISEASES OF THE LARYNX AND TRACHEA 614
AFFECTIONS OF THE PHARYNX 618
AFFECTIONS OF THE ŒSOPHAGUS 623
AFFECTIONS OF THE WITHERS AND BACK 637
AFFECTIONS OF THE LOINS 642
AFFECTIONS OF THE VERTEBRAL COLUMN AND SPINAL CORD . . 643
AFFECTIONS OF THE CHEST 654
AFFECTIONS OF THE ABDOMEN 661
SURGICAL AFFECTIONS OF THE STOMACH AND BOWELS . . . 684
SURGICAL AFFECTIONS OF THE POSTERIOR PORTIONS OF THE RECTUM AND OF THE ANUS 690
AFFECTIONS OF THE URINARY ORGANS 711
AFFECTIONS OF THE MALE GENITAL ORGANS 740
AFFECTIONS OF THE FEMALE ORGANS OF GENERATION . . . 757
AFFECTIONS OF THE MAMMARY GLAND 770
AFFECTIONS OF THE TAIL 793
AFFECTIONS OF THE LIMBS (LAMENESS) 796
SHOULDER AND ARM 802
ELBOW AND FOREARM 817
KNEE 823
METACARPUS 834
FETLOCK AND DIGIT 856
HIND-LIMB 877
QUARTER 877
STIFLE AND LEG 900
HOCK 917
AFFECTIONS OF THE FEET 943
APPENDIX 1007
INDEX 1018

PART I

GENERAL SURGERY

CHAPTER I

INFLAMMATION AND ABSCESSES

I.—INFLAMMATION

INFLAMMATION is associated with most surgical conditions. It is dealt with in works on pathology, and only requires to be referred to here from a clinical point of view. It is a salutary process by which nature effects repair of damaged tissues. Its intensity varies with the degree of injury to the part. The cause may be—

1. Mechanical (blow, sprain).
2. Physical (excessive cold or heat).
3. Chemical (caustics).
4. Bacterial.

Generally speaking, inflammation due to micro-organisms is more serious than that due to other causes, owing to the destructive local and serious general effects of the toxins of many varieties of bacteria. The severity of septic inflammations is in accordance with the virulence of the causal organisms.

SYMPTOMS.—The symptoms of inflammation comprise—

1. Abnormal heat.
2. Swelling.
3. Redness.
4. Pain.

1. *Abnormal heat* is recognised chiefly by palpation, comparing the temperature of the part with that of a corresponding place on the other side of the body or with the normal temperature of the region.

2. The *swelling* varies according to the nature of the inflammation. It is more marked in vascular than in non-vascular structures, and in loose areolar than in hard tissues.

3. The *redness* is only seen in the non-pigmented skin and is due to the hyperæmia and to extravasation of blood when blood vessels are ruptured.

4. The *pain* varies with the acuteness of the inflammation, the nerve supply of the region, and the tenseness and hardness of the overlying

tissues. It is caused by compression of nerve terminals and probably also by neuritis of the nerves in the affected part.

If the cause of the inflammation be slight irritation, frequently repeated, it will assume a subacute or chronic course in which the four cardinal symptoms mentioned are much less marked than in an acute case. In this form of the condition a comparatively large amount of fibrous tissue is formed, constituting a hard swelling which causes a permanent thickening or induration of the part.

Terminations of Inflammation.—The terminations of inflammation may be—

1. *Delitescence*, in which the inflammation suddenly subsides, owing to its having been very slight.

2. *Resolution.* After the process has been completed the inflammatory exudate becomes reabsorbed, the damaged tissue is repaired by the new formation of fibrous tissue, and the affected part apparently resumes its normal condition, although histologically it is not quite the same as it was before the receipt of the injury.

3. *Suppuration.* In this case pyogenic organisms have been the cause of the condition, setting up an abscess or other form of suppuration, but eventually resolution supervenes, provided that a fatal toxæmia has not ensued.

4. *Gangrene.* Although this is often spoken of as a termination of inflammation, it would be more correctly described as an accompaniment of the lesion, being due to the cause which gave rise to the inflammation, the damage to the affected tissues being so severe that it caused their destruction *en masse*.

5. *Induration.* This has been already alluded to as resulting from chronic inflammation.

The Prognosis of inflammation depends on its nature and the organ or part affected. As already mentioned, the gravity of inflammation of bacterial origin depends on the virulence of the organisms. In no case is the inflammation itself the danger to be feared, but rather the cause of this reaction, the latter being nature's means of effecting recovery.

Treatment of Acute Inflammation

Removal of the Cause.—The only real rational treatment of inflammation is to suppress its cause. If the cause is still operating when the case is presented for treatment, its removal has a marked and rapid effect. Apart from this the treatment has for its object the moderation of the inflammation, chiefly with a view to alleviating the pain and functional disturbance to which it has given rise.

The following forms of treatment are in vogue :

1. *Cold and astringent applications.* These comprise cold compresses frequently renewed, cold-water irrigation, cold baths, or ice or snow and astringent lotions.

This method of treatment is only indicated for slight inflammatory conditions in which the tissues are not threatened with death, which would be accelerated by the use of cold, whose effect is to constringe the blood vessels, thereby diminishing the supply of blood to the region and curtailing the exudation and diapedesis. Astringent lotions may be employed after the application of cold ; they have the same effect, but to a less degree. Cold requires to be applied continuously for hours to produce its good effects.

2. *Warm applications* are indicated in severe inflammatory affections in which the tissues are seriously injured and apt to undergo gangrene. They promote circulation in the damaged region, restoring the blood supply in parts where it has been almost arrested, and thus prevent death of the affected tissues.

They also soften the inflamed structures, thus releasing tension and relieving pain. They may be objected to on the ground that they favour the growth of micro-organisms in parts exposed to infection, but this effect is counteracted by the hyperæmia and phagocytosis which they produce. These applications may be in the form of fomentations, compresses, poultices, or baths at a temperature of 104°–112° F. Medicated poultices are better than ordinary poultices made with linseed meal or bran. " Antiphlogistine " and similar preparations have an excellent effect when used in the form of a thick hot paste covered by a layer of cotton-wool.

3. *Anodyne preparations* such as cocainised vaseline or iodoform ointment made with vaseline are indicated for very painful superficial lesions.

4. *Scarification* of the inflamed tissues may be performed to relieve tension and pain, but it has the objection that it opens the way for infection, which may ensue, with serious consequences, if careful antiseptic precautions are not taken.

5. *Antiseptic applications* are required for septic inflammatory lesions, as exemplified by septic wounds (*vide* Treatment of Wounds).

For the foot and lower part of the limb there is nothing better than the warm antiseptic bath, continued for at least half an hour two or three times a day. In the meantime warm antiseptic compresses are indicated.

6. *Bier's hyperæmic treatment* may be employed with marked effect for inflammatory septic lesions (*vide* Artificial Hyperæmia).

7. *Massage and compression.* *Massage* is effected as described on p. 263. *Compression* is produced by an even layer of cotton-wool covered by a bandage sufficiently tight to create moderate pressure without having an uncomfortable effect. It promotes absorption by supporting the circulation.

Subacute and Chronic Inflammation

Subacute and chronic inflammation may be treated by moist heat, massage, compression, and counter-irritation. Counter-irritation may be effected by rubefacients, blisters, and pustulants, or by the actual cautery, which is a blistering or caustic agent according to the way it is used.

Rubefacients are represented by the well-known liniments, which, however, have a blistering effect when frequently repeated and well rubbed in. They are indicated for comparatively slight subacute inflammation.

Blisters, which may be in the form of a liquid or an ointment, are very effective agents for many chronic inflammatory conditions—*e.g.*, biniodide of mercury, 1 part to 8 parts of lard; cantharides, 1 part to 6 parts of lard, or a mixture of equal parts of these; and other proprietary blisters, such as Wyley's green blister, which is very effective and non-irritating, and therefore indicated for thoroughbred and highly-strung horses, and James's liquid blister. It must be remembered that the application of a cantharides blister over a large area, say more than two limbs, may cause death from absorption of the drug.

Biniodide of mercury blister is largely used, and often has a very beneficial effect, especially in promoting the absorption of inflammatory swellings, including exostoses.

Before applying a blister the hair should be clipped and the skin brushed. The blister should be vigorously rubbed in with the fingers for about ten to twenty minutes, taking care not to allow any of the preparation to come into contact with the hollow of the heel when being applied to the back of the limb, as it will cause cracking of the skin there, followed by inflammation and lameness. After blistering, the horse must be prevented from scratching or rubbing the part, which he is inclined to do owing to the irritation of the blister. For this purpose the horse may be tied up short in the stable, or a cradle, a sidestick, or a "bib" may be applied. A sack of hay between the fore-limbs in contact with the breast, and suspended from the neck and back, prevents the animal rubbing one fore-leg with the other. If any of the foregoing methods is not practicable, the part may be protected with a bandage when it is the lower part of a limb which is involved. If one application of a blister has not had the desired effect, it may be repeated after the acute inflammation caused by the previous one has subsided.

The good effect of a counter-irritant is explained by its converting the indolent chronic inflammation into an acute inflammation whose hyperæmia promotes repair of damaged tissue and is followed by absorption of the persisting chronic inflammatory exudate along with that of the acute inflammation caused by the counter-irritant. Avoid applying a blister in the angles of flexion of the limbs and in the axilla and groin, where it may cause fissuring of the skin.

Pustulants are represented by *setons and rowels.* A seton is a tape smeared with an irritant and passed beneath the skin over the affected part, and left *in situ* for some weeks. It causes purulent inflammation in its track, which has a counter-irritant effect on the deeper tissues. It is not much in vogue nowadays, although it may be very useful for an old-standing chronic inflammatory condition. A rowel is a disc-shaped piece of leather with a hole in its centre and enveloped in tow smeared with an irritant. It is introduced beneath the skin, and left *in situ* for the same period as a seton.

The **actual cautery** is the most powerful counter-irritant for chronic inflammation (*vide* p. 252).

Specific Inflammations

Specific inflammations, such as those caused by the bacillus of malignant œdema, by the anthrax bacillus, and other specific organisms, require special measures, and are dealt with in works on medicine.

II.—ABSCESSES

Abscesses may be classified as—

1. Hot or acute abscesses.
2. Cold or chronic abscesses.
3. Superficial abscesses.
4. Deep abscesses.
5. General abscesses.

Abscesses may occur in any part of the body. They are caused by a breach of surface of the skin or mucous membrane, and the entrance through the breach of pyogenic organisms.

Acute Abscesses

An acute abscess forms after a period of three to five days from the commencement of the infection. It may be said to be composed of a wall (the so-called pyogenic membrane) and contents—the pus. The character of the pus varies according to the tissue involved and the organisms it contains.

If the pus is retained a long time before being evacuated it becomes inspissated, its liquid portion undergoing absorption, while its solid portion becomes caseated, or, if retained for a still longer time, calcified. The wall is at first formed of inflamed tissue, which gradually undergoes softening until the destructive process is arrested by bursting of the abscess. This limiting wall of the cavity forms an obstacle to general infection. It provides the phagocytes which keep the pyogenic organisms in check.

Once the abscess has been opened, the "pyogenic membrane" rapidly granulates and fills up the cavity. The more virulent the organisms the more extensive are their effects. It is seldom, however, that the toxins of the bacteria are sufficient to destroy vessels or nerves that traverse the affected region; they are usually protected by a fibrinous covering which, as a rule, is proof against infection. A severe or fatal hæmorrhage, however, might ensue from erosion of a vessel by the bacterial toxin. If pus cannot escape superficially owing to the presence of resistant tissue, such as an aponeurosis or the horn of the foot, it extends in the direction of least resistance until it finds a means of escape.

An abscess in close vicinity to a joint or visceral cavity may open into it with fatal consequences. An abscess abutting on ligament, tendon or bone may be accompanied by necrosis of these structures, the necrosed tissue remaining *in situ* after the abscess has burst and preventing healing until the dead part is removed. A sub-aponeurotic abscess may burst through the overlying membrane and lead to the formation of two abscess cavities communicating by a narrow opening ("shirt-stud abscess").

SYMPTOMS.—The symptoms of an acute abscess vary according as it is superficial or deep and according to its situation.

The *superficial abscess* is characterised by the symptoms of acute inflammation. It appears as a more or less circumscribed, firm, inflammatory swelling, which is very painful on manipulation. Afterwards the centre of the swelling becomes gradually softer, while its periphery remains firm. Then fluctuation can be detected by pressure with the fingers. If left to itself its centre soon becomes very thin, and the abscess is said to be "pointing." It soon afterwards bursts, allowing escape of more or less of the pus, depending on the situation of the orifice.

There is no febrile disturbance. The deep abscess usually develops under thick layers of tissue, and is first indicated by febrile symptoms. No local manifestations of the condition may be noticed. Attention is usually first drawn by interference with movement or stiffness in the affected part, or perhaps by some œdema in its vicinity. Eventually local symptoms become evident, and when the pus has arrived near the surface the condition assumes the features of a superficial abscess. Such abscesses in the region of important organs like the pharynx, larynx, rectum, or the spinal cord cause serious interference with function.

Diagnosis.—An abscess may possibly be confounded with the following conditions :

1. A *cyst*, whose formation is slower than that of an abscess, is devoid of inflammatory symptoms, fluctuates uniformly throughout, and is not hard at its periphery.

2. A *hæmatoma*, which is formed of coagulated blood and serum, feels somewhat doughy on palpation, may crepitate on pressure, and forms almost immediately after the receipt of an injury. It is not so tense or painful, and does not " point " like an abscess.

3. An *inflamed and distended synovial bursa*, which is recognised by its situation and by careful examination.

4. An *abdominal hernia*. A recent traumatic hernia shows acute inflammatory symptoms which, associated with the hernial swelling, simulate those of an abscess, but careful examination will generally reveal the diagnostic features of a hernia. In any case of doubt an exploratory puncture may be made with a fine trocar and canula, or with an exploring needle.

Treatment.—The treatment of an abscess comprises : (1) Measures to hasten the maturation of the abscess ; and (2) opening the abscess to evacuate its contents. The first indication is effected by the application of either hot fomentations or stupes, or by that of a blister. The latter is quicker in its results, but the former has the advantage of acting as an analgesic.

Opening of an abscess is usually delayed until it is obviously fluctuating. If opened before all the pus is collected in one cavity secondary abscesses may form in the inflamed tissue. In certain cases it is advisable to open an abscess as soon as diagnosed and before the pus has approached the surface—for example, when it is situated in the vicinity of an important cavity or structure to which extension of the suppuration might have serious consequences (peritoneum, joint, etc.).

The abscess is usually opened with a knife, but in certain cases a trocar or thermo-cautery may be used for the purpose. The opening is made at the most dependent part of the region which is fluctuating. The sharp-pointed concave bistoury (Syme's knife) is the most suitable for the operation. It is held like a fiddle bow with the edge directed upwards and thrust boldly into the abscess, a small incision being made in the act of withdrawing the instrument. Before plunging the knife into the cavity the anatomy of the region should be considered, and it should be remembered that vessels and nerves in the part may be somewhat deviated from their normal position by the presence of the abscess. Generally, the incision should be made parallel to the long axis of these structures.

If the tissues be very vascular they may be divided layer by layer to avoid cutting the vessel. The best way however, to open a deep-seated abscess in the region of important vessels and nerves, such as the parotid region, is as follows: (1) Incise the skin. (2) Push a blunt instrument, such as an artery forceps, through the other tissues until it enters the abscess cavity and pus exudes alongside it. (3) Insert a blunt-pointed curved scissors or a forceps into the cavity with its blades or jaws closed, withdraw it with its handles held rigidly apart, thereby pushing aside the tissues and enlarging the opening without endangering the vessels or nerves of the part.

Having opened the abscess, explore its cavity with the finger to ascertain if it contains a foreign body or necrotic tissue, and whether it requires further drainage. The latter may be effected by enlarging the incision downwards if the cavity be shallow, or by making a counter-opening if it be deep.

A counter-opening may be made thus: (1) Insert a blunt sound into the bottom of the cavity, make it bulge the tissues there, and cut down on it with the knife. (2) Insert a sharp-pointed seton needle into the bottom of the abscess, and thrust it through the skin at this point. (3) Take up a fold of skin with a forceps at the level of the depth of the cavity and cut through it with a sharp knife or scissors, and continue the incision into the cavity, making use of the method already described for a deep abscess in a very vascular region.

If a band be felt traversing an abscess cavity, be careful about rupturing it lest it be an important vessel or nerve. It may be a string of fibrin. When a counter-opening has been made, it is desirable to insert a piece of calico or tarlatan bandage or a strip of gauze through the two openings, and tie its ends, for the purpose of keeping the openings patent for two or three days to ensure free drainage. If an abscess cavity is very large, it may be loosely packed with gauze wool or tow or twenty-four hours, thus forming what is known as a tent to keep it walls apart, and prevent their possible adhesion and interference with the complete escape of the pus.

It is customary to irrigate an abscess cavity with an antiseptic lotion after its evacuation, partly to promote the complete removal of its contents and partly as an antiseptic agent. For an ordinary abscess which does not contain any necrotic tissue fixed in its interior this procedure is unnecessary, as its pyogenic membrane is proof against infection. Otherwise it is indicated until the necrotic tissue is separated.

An abscess in a mucous cavity like the pharynx, rectum, or vagina may be opened (1) by thrusting the finger into it when its wall is thin; or (2) by means of a trocar and canula, which, however, has the disadvantage of making a small opening; or (3) by a concealed knife; or (4) by an ordinary sharp-pointed knife enveloped in tow or wool just up to its point to serve as a guard and to afford a sure grip on the instrument.

The thermo-cautery is seldom employed to open an abscess. Its only advantage is that it ensures against hæmorrhage from the tissues through which it passes. Yet it would not be without danger for the division of large vessels which would not be occluded by its effects. It is used at a white heat.

In opening an abscess on a limb, it is important to have the edge of the knife directed upwards, so that, if the animal snatch up the limb suddenly, there will be no danger of the knife penetrating too deeply, with perhaps serious consequences (open joint or sheath, severe hæmorrhage).

A hæmatoma may become purulent from the entrance of pyogenic organisms, and is then spoken of as a hæmorrhagic abscess. It is dealt with as an ordinary abscess.

Cold or Chronic Abscesses

Chronic abscesses show little or no inflammatory reaction. They develop slowly, are painless or slightly painful, and persist for a long time as indurated or cystic swellings. Sometimes they gradually undergo softening, and eventually burst by ulcerating the skin or mucous membrane which covers them. They may be primary or secondary, and local or general.

Etiology.—Primary chronic abscesses usually result from slight and repeated injuries, as may be caused by harness or the shoe, or traumatism of any kind. They occur on the prominences of the limbs and on the ribs as the results of " bed-sores " from constant lying. Secondary local abscesses occur in the course of various local affections (lymphangitis, phlebitis, necrotic lesions, etc.). Secondary general abscesses appear as the result of infectious diseases like strangles, glanders, and tuberculosis. The agent, of course, in all cases which causes the suppuration is pyogenic infection.

Chronic abscesses may also be classified as (1) hard cold abscesses; and (2) soft cold abscesses.

1. A *hard cold abscess* is surrounded by hard fibrous tissue and may contain only a small amount of pus.

2. A *soft cold abscess* has a thin wall, and contains a comparatively large quantity of pus.

SYMPTOMS.—The hard cold abscess may commence with slight inflammatory symptoms which afterwards disappear, or they may be absent from the beginning, so that eventually the lesion assumes more the features of a fibroma than of an abscess.

If the affected region be subjected to a severe injury the abscess may become acute. The soft cold abscess has the appearances of a cyst, except that it may reveal a little abnormal heat and sensibility.

DIAGNOSIS.—Cold abscesses are diagnosed by their situation and by the history of the case. The hard cold abscess may be confounded with a neoplasm, but its evolution is more rapid than the latter and its periphery is less circumscribed. The soft cold abscess is less definite in outline than a cyst. The diagnosis can be confirmed by exploratory puncture.

TREATMENT.—The treatment is on the same lines as that of an acute abscess. A blister may be applied to render the abscess acute and bring the pus nearer to the surface before opening it, but it is generally advisable to open the abscess at once. When very deeply situated, two or more punctures with a narrow-bladed knife may be required before the pus escapes. Even if the pus does not appear immediately, the incision may have the desired effect, the pus afterwards reaching the wound and gaining exit. The thermo-cautery is suitable for plunging into the centre of a hard cold abscess, provided that it is not situated in a dangerous region.

The pus may be inspissated when the lesion is of long standing, and necessitates removal with the fingers or a curette. Drainage must be provided for, as in the case of an acute abscess. Tincture of iodine or other irritant antiseptic solution is indicated as a dressing for the interior of the cavity to promote inflammation and consequent granulation and cicatrisation.

Specific abscesses call for attention to the diseases of which they form a symptom.

CHAPTER II

GANGRENE, ULCERS, SINUS AND FISTULA

I.—GANGRENE

Gangrene in its widest sense means death of a more or less extensive area or volume of tissue. Its strict meaning is death and putrefaction of tissue while attached to the living body. If death of tissue occurs in the absence of infection, the condition is spoken of as necrobiosis (aseptic infarct).

Etiology.—From this point of view gangrene may be divided into two groups :

1. *Gangrene resulting from direct damage to the tissues*, caused by mechanical, physical, or chemical agents, or by bacteria.
2. *Gangrene caused by indirect changes in the tissues.*

1. The organisms which are most frequently the direct cause of gangrene are those of malignant œdema, necrosis, anthrax, and black quarter, and virulent streptococci and staphylococci.

Traumatic gangrene occurs as the result of compression interfering with the nerve and blood supplies of a part, as may ensue from the pressure of harness, or on the prominences of the body from constant decubitus. Burns and frost bite give rise to gangrene, as do also caustic agents. If the dead part in these cases affords a suitable medium for the development of putrefactive organisms, they will soon proliferate therein and set up symptoms of putrefaction. Infiltration of the tissues with certain organic liquids (bile, urine) diminishes the local resistance of the tissues and when they are invaded by virulent bacteria they readily undergo necrosis or gangrene.

2. Gangrene due to indirect alteration of the tissues arises from venous, arterial, or cardiac or nervous affections, or from alterations in the blood. As the result of these conditions the tissues involved are deprived of their nutrition, and consequently lose their vitality. Gangrene is met with as a lesion in various bacterial diseases due to the toxins of the causal organisms.

Clinically gangrene is classified as :

1. Dry gangrene.
2. Moist gangrene.

1. *Dry gangrene* is equivalent to mummification of the tissues, in which the latter become dry and reduced in volume. Owing to the dearth of liquid, putrefaction is practically absent.

2. *Moist gangrene* occurs in tissues rich in liquid. They become disintegrated and liquefied by the action of putrefactive bacteria, giving rise to a blood-stained, very fœtid fluid. The lesion contains volatile odoriferous products and ferments which elaborate soluble poisons, whose absorption into the system causes toxæmia, with more or less serious constitutional disturbance.

Local Symptoms.—The local symptoms of gangrene refer to three periods of the process :

1. The period of death.
2. The period of separation of the slough.
3. The period of cicatrisation.

In dry gangrene the tissues become altered in appearance and diminished in volume. The skin becomes shrivelled, and its hair becomes dry and erect. In moist gangrene the tissues become purple, greenish, or blackish in colour and increased in volume, being engorged with blood and serum. Pain is intense before death of the part supervenes, but after it has occurred the affected region becomes cold and insensitive. The epithelium can be scraped off the skin, which is cold and clammy to the feel. The discharge from the lesion is in the form of a dark red fœtid liquid. A zone of inflammation surrounds the dead area. Soon a line of demarcation forms between the dead and living structures, and the former are eventu lly cast off, provided that the toxæmia was not sufficient to kill the patient.

During this period of separation complications may ensue—for example, secondary hæmorrhage from sloughing of a bloodvessel, or septic synovitis, or arthritis from opening of sheaths or joints. Once the slough has separated, healing of the wound ensues rapidly, except that a portion of hard necrotic tissue like cartilage, ligament, or bone which is slow to separate, remains *in situ* after the soft tissues have fallen away.

Diagnosis.—Diagnosis is generally easy, the symptoms mentioned being characteristic.

Prognosis.—The prognosis depends on the nature of the lesion, which may vary from an insignificant eschar to the sloughing of a large mass of tissue. The condition is dangerous when the toxæmia is severe. It may cause death within twenty-four hours (gangrenous mastitis).

Treatment.—Treatment is directed against extension of the gangrene, hastening separation of the slough and preventing general effects. The chief indications are as follows :

1. *Removal of the cause.* The continuance of the cause of the trouble should be arrested as far as possible.

2. *Scarification.* Scarification with the knife or puncture with the hot iron of the engorged gangrenous tissues may be performed for the purpose of permitting the escape of toxic liquid, and allowing the introduction of disinfectant lotion to counteract the putrefaction. Operation on the diseased tissue is not without danger, as the healthy tissues may be wounded at the same time, allowing the entrance into them of the organisms present in the lesion and leading perhaps to a fatal septicæmia.

It is safer to rely merely on the disinfectant applications and leave the separation of the dead part to nature. In the case of dry gangrene, however, there is no danger in excising the mummified part. The "sit-fast" under the saddle may be pared out. Yet in many cases it is just as well to await the spontaneous separation of the dead tissue. Even here septic complications might ensue from the use of the knife.

3. *Application of an irritant.* An irritant may be applied at the periphery of the dead part to produce increased hyperæmia and phagocytosis, and thus accelerate the separation of the slough either in the case of dry or moist gangrene. If the inflammation be very acute in the vicinity, hot antiseptic applications may be applied to relieve it.

4. *Amputation* of an organ, a limb, or an appendage affected with gangrene may be performed in certain cases.

Otherwise treatment is that described in connection with Septic Open Wounds.

II.—ULCERS

The term "ulcer" means a recent or old superficial wound involving molecular destruction of tissue, and showing no tendency to heal, but that of "ulceration" is often used to mean the same thing, although its true meaning is the process by which the condition is brought about. When a superficial solution of continuity involves only the epithelium, the condition is sometimes spoken of as an erosion.

Etiology.—Ulceration may arise in one of the following ways :

1. Repeated irritation of a wound may cause it to ulcerate—for

example, a wound on the dog's ear or on the tip of its tail, in the angle of flexion of the knee or hock in the horse.

2. Certain conditions associated with infection prevent healing, and thus cause ulceration, such as the presence of a foreign body or necrotic tissue in a wound.

3. Loss of innervation of a part may be followed by ulceration therein, if wounded, for want of the trophic influence of the nerve supply.

4. Impoverishment of the blood supply favours ulceration, so that it is apt to ensue in tissues of low vitality.

5. Specific ulcers occur in the course of specific affections (malignant tumours)—ulcerative lymphangitis, glanders, tuberculosis, etc.

The ordinary ulcer usually follows an open wound. Its cicatrisation is arrested, granulations fail to form, the secretion diminishes and the wound remains stationary, or gradually extends from a molecular destruction of its borders.

SYMPTOMS.—An ulcer has the form of a more or less rounded breach of surface varying in depth in different cases. Its borders may be on a level with the surrounding skin or raised above it, and may be hard or soft. The centre of the lesion may be flat or concave, and may show necrotic spots. In most cases there is a serous, purulent, blood-stained or greyish discharge. Phagedenic ulcers extend rapidly in depth and area, due to a bacterial molecular destruction of the tissues.

DIAGNOSIS.—The diagnosis of an ulcer is easy, but it may be difficult to account for the condition, or say clinically whether it is simple or specific.

TREATMENT.—Treatment comprises:

1. *Removal of the cause.* When due to incessant movement, the part should be immobilised as far as possible. When due to rubbing or scratching by the patient, this should be prevented.

2. *Warm antiseptic fomentations*, stupes, or baths, indicated for painful septic inflammatory ulcers followed by a dressing of iodoform powder or B.I.P.P.

3. *Moderate pressure* with cotton-wool and bandage, which promotes healing when the ulcer has been disinfected.

4. *Astringent or caustic applications.*—These are required when the granulations are excessive or unhealthy, and the cause of the trouble has been arrested.

5. *The use of the thermo-cautery*, which is an excellent agent for destroying unhealthy or callous tissue and promoting normal granulation and cicatrisation.

6. *Excision* of the ulcer by means of the knife. This is the best treatment for a small ulcer in an operable region. After excision the wound is sutured, and it then usually heals by first intention. When the ulcer is situated on bone, curetting of the unhealthy surface is indicated.

7. *Hyperæmic treatment* by Bier's method, an excellent form of treatment (see p. 260).

8. *Specific remedies* for ulcers due to specific diseases.

III.—SINUS AND FISTULA

A *sinus* is a blind purulent tract showing no tendency to heal.

A *fistula*, strictly speaking, is an abnormal opening or passage between a cavity or duct and the surface of the body, or between two cavities or ducts. But the term "fistula" is frequently applied to a sinus. The various forms of fistulæ receive qualifications according to their nature as follows:

1. Complete fistula, which has two openings.
2. Incomplete or blind fistula, with only one opening.
3. Congenital fistula (pervious urachus).
4. Pathological fistula.
5. Purulent fistula.
6. Excretory and secretory fistulæ, etc.

All the foregoing fistulæ will be dealt with as they arise in the systemic portions of the work. It is well, however, to deal here with the blind purulent fistula or sinus.

Purulent Fistula or Sinus

Etiology.—A sinus or blind purulent fistula is usually due to something which maintains a constant purulent discharge from a hollow wound or abscess cavity. The cause may be:

1. *Want of drainage* from a purulent cavity, whereby the infection persists in the tissues, perpetuating the pus formation and absolutely preventing cicatrisation.

2. *The presence of a foreign body or necrotic tissue* in the depth of the lesion, having the same effect as in No. 1.

3. *The existence of a specific lesion* in the tissues—carcinoma, botriomycosis, tuberculosis.

4. Movement of the walls of a sinus or their mechanical separation which also militates against healing.

Symptoms.—The orifice of the sinus may be very narrow and only admit a probe. It may be surrounded by excessive granulations when it is recent, or its borders may be hard and fibrous when it is old.

In old-standing cases the opening may be situated in a depression, due to retraction of the surrounding tissues. There may be more than one opening leading to the centre of the lesion when necrotic tissue is present in its depth.

Cicatrised spots may be seen in the affected region, representing openings that have closed when fresh ones were formed. Exploration of the cavity with a sound or with the finger gives an idea of the depth and extent of the disease. The passage may be tortuous and prevent the probe reaching its bottom. Secondary sinuses may communicate with the principal one. Profuse purulent discharge is an indication of extensive necrosis in the affected part. Liquid injected into the sinus will indicate its capacity, and reveal whether the various orifices communicate.

A sinus may close for a variable time until a new abscess forms and bursts in the vicinity of the former opening, renewing the condition. It is on this account that treatment is sometimes deceptive. The character of the pus varies in different cases. It may be thick or serous, greyish or reddish, and may contain occasionally portions of necrotic tissue. Its odour is usually fœtid. There may be marked inflammatory symptoms associated with the sinus.

TREATMENT.—In general terms the treatment consists in removing or suppressing the cause of the trouble. The measures employed comprise :

1. *Providing for drainage*, when its absence is the cause of the condition, by incising the tract in a downward direction or by making a counter-opening.

2. *The use of liquid or solid caustics* to cause sloughing of the interior of the sinus to its depth, with a view to causing separation of necrotic tissue and removal of the callous lining, when present. It also has the effect of opening up the passage and facilitating drainage. It is often successful.

3. *The application of the hot iron*, which has the same effect as No. 2, but is more powerful in its effects. The instrument must be used with caution, so as not to cause excessive destruction of tissue. It should be rapidly inserted and rapidly withdrawn. This treatment frequently has the desired effect.

It is dangerous to use any caustic agent in the vicinity of a joint or important synovial sheath or cavity on account of the risk of causing sloughing into it.

4. *Operation* to open up the sinus, expose its depth, remove necrotic and callous tissue, and provide for free drainage, careful antiseptic precautions being taken to prevent reinfection of the wound. This is the best method of treatment in well-established cases.

5. *Injection of Bismuth Paste, e.g.*, bismuth subnitrate 33, vaseline 67 or bismuth 30, white wax 5, paraffin 5. Heat the vaseline or wax and paraffin, then gradually add the bismuth while stirring. When the sterilised mixture is sufficiently cool it is injected. Having filled the cavity it is tamponed with gauze until the injection is solidified. The injection is repeated if necessary to keep the sinus full. Several veterinarians have reported success with this treatment. In small animals poisoning might supervene if a large quantitv of bismuth is used.

It is only in cases in which the cavity is lined with atonic granulations and devoid of necrotic tissue that this treatment is indicated. In such cases it has been proved to promote cicatrisation.

6. *Bier's hyperæmic treatment*, which may be employed with advantage for the lower parts of the limbs.

7. *The inoculation of an autogenous* or polyvalent vaccine, which is always indicated in conjunction with surgical treatment in extensive chronic suppurative lesions.

8. *Arrest of movement in the walls of the cavity.* This is often difficult, and may best be effected by opening up one side of the passage so as to convert it into an open wound, thus preventing opposing surfaces from rubbing against each other. This treatment may have the desired effect when the walls of the cavity are rigid and far apart, allowing them to collapse and come into contact.

9. *The use of Penicillin* which is indicated locally and parenterally in a case of obstinate infection where thorough drainage cannot be effected, provided that the causal organism is penicillin-sensitive.

CHAPTER III

WOUNDS AND PHYSICAL LESIONS

WOUNDS

WOUNDS or traumatic lesions may be classified as :

1. *External, open, or exposed wounds*, in which there is solution of the skin and other tissues to a varying depth.

2. *Internal, closed, subcutaneous, or interstitial wounds*, in which there is no solution of continuity of the skin or mucous membrane, but in which the deeper tissues are divided to a varying degree. Both may open into pre-existing cavities.

A wound or traumatic lesion may be said to be composed of a wall and contents. The contents vary with the nature of the injury. They may comprise tissue debris and blood clots, or layers of damaged or destroyed tissue mixed with extravasated blood, lymph, urine, etc., or foreign matter. The wall of the wound contains three zones—viz. :

1. A *central zone* of dead tissue varying in thickness, but always present. It may be so thin that it is imperceptible and not sufficient to interfere with the primary healing of an open wound, or it may involve structures of considerable or great depth and terminate in gangrene.

2. A *stupefied or ischæmic zone*, surrounding No. 1, in which the tissues are reduced in vitality and threatened with death.

3. A *zone of reaction*, surrounding No. 2, characterised by acute inflammation, and actively employed in bringing about repair of the injury.

A. Open Wounds

Open wounds may or may not be accompanied by loss of tissue. They may be caused by mechanical or chemical agents, but are usually due to external violence. They are classified as follows :

1. **Incised wounds** caused by sharp-cutting instruments.

2. **Lacerated wounds,** caused by tearing of the tissues.

3. **Punctured wounds,** caused by pointed bodies, and termed "penetrating" when they extend into a serous or joint cavity.

4. **Contused wounds,** caused by blunt bodies.

5. **Gunshot wounds,** produced by various kinds of firearms.
6. **Poisoned wounds,** containing a poison.
7. **Envenomed wounds,** containing a venom.
8. **Virulent wounds,** containing a virus.
9. **Granulating wounds.**
10. **Ulcerating wounds.**

SYMPTOMS.—The symptoms may be considered as (i) primary and (ii) secondary.

(i.) The *primary symptoms* include *local, remote,* and *general* disturbances. The local primary symptoms comprise hæmorrhage, pain, and gaping of the lips of the wound.

1. *Hæmorrhage.* The amount of hæmorrhage depends on the vascularity of the part and the size of the vessels divided. Parenchymatous tissue bleeds freely, owing to the mouths of the divided vessels remaining patent.

2. *Pain* is always present, but varies considerably according to the amount of innervation in the part. The skin is very sensitive, and wounds therein are accompanied by much more pain than those of muscles, tendons, or mucous membranes. It is intensified by infection of the wound.

3. *Gaping of the lips of the wound.* The gaping of the wound is caused by the mechanical action of the wounding body, and by the contraction or elasticity of the tissues severed. The skin, being very elastic, retracts considerably when incised. In tendons and muscles the separation is slight when the wound is parallel to their fibres, whereas when it is transverse thereto the gaping is very marked.

The amount of separation between the walls of a wound is affected by the amount of movement in the part. It is more marked on the side of extension than on the side of flexion of a joint, and in transverse than in longitudinal wounds. It influences the duration of healing and the size of the cicatrix.

(ii.) The *secondary local symptoms* comprise the phenomena of inflammation or repair or cicatrisation. Healing of the wound may ensue by :

1. *Primary adhesion,* for which the conditions necessary are :

(*a*) Recent or freshened condition of the lips of the wound.
(*b*) Asepsis.
(*c*) Absence of hæmorrhage.
(*d*) Clean-cut edges brought into accurate contact by sutures.
(*e*) A good blood supply to the walls of the wound.

(*f*) An imperceptible layer of dead tissue in the wound.

(*g*) Protection from interference and infection until cicatrisation has occurred.

2. *By second intention* or by suppuration. This ensues after primary healing has failed, or the wound is in such condition that the latter is out of the question. In the course of twenty-four hours inflammation ensues in the wound, and small areas of necrotic tissue form on its surface. Suppuration supervenes, and in a few days the necrotic parts will have separated, leaving the wound with a clean, pink, granulating surface.

The granulations continue to form until they are level with the surface of the skin, when their growth ceases and the epithelium grows in from the periphery to complete the process of cicatrisation. The cicatrix or scar remains permanently devoid of hair follicles and sweat glands, and it is pale from its feeble vascularity. When large, it constitutes a permanent blemish.

3. *By third intention*—that is, by union of granulating surfaces under strict asepsis and with perfect affrontment of the walls of the wound. It rarely supervenes.

4. *By mixed intention*. Some parts of the wound heal by first intention, and other parts by second intention.

5. *Under a scab*. The granulations form under a scab produced by desiccation of the inflammatory exudate. It occurs in superficial wounds.

Remote symptoms are observed in a part more or less removed from the region wounded. They include: (1) *Ecchymosis*, which spreads through fibrous connective tissue to parts remote from the lesion. (2) *Ischæmia* or even *gangrene* of a part supplied by a vessel which has become thrombosed in the wound. (3) *Abscess formation* in the neighbouring lymphatic glands, due to infection that entered through the lymphatic vessels in the wound. (4) *Paralysis* from section of the motor nerve to a part. (5) *Neuritis* extending along the course of a nerve involved in the wound.

General symptoms comprise those of febrile disturbance, and vary according to the degree of toxæmia ensuing. In wounds infected by common organisms they are insignificant.

Prognosis.—Aseptic lesions in normal subjects under natural conditions heal rapidly in every part of the body. Were it not for the risk of infection, open wounds would be harmless lesions and require very little attention. Infection has different consequences, according to its virulence and the region invaded. A debilitated condition of the patient militates against healing, as does also unhealthy surroundings. The possible complications of wounds are dealt with separately.

TREATMENT.—To facilitate description of the treatment of open wounds they may be classified thus:

1. Aseptic wounds.

2. Suspicious wounds which have been subjected to some contamination and which may be more or less septic.

3. Absolutely septic or complicated wounds.

(1) Aseptic Wounds

Probably no open wound in a veterinary patient is absolutely aseptic, but in many cases, although infection is present, its virulence is so slight that it has practically no inhibitory effect on the process of repair. The best example of an aseptic wound is one that has been made surgically with aseptic precautions in non-infected tissues.

In aseptic wounds healing by first intention should be sought for, provided that the conditions necessary for it can be observed (*vide* p. 21). In human surgery portions of appendages completely separated from the body have been successfully replaced by the carrying out of these conditions, and both auto- and hetero-grafting of skin, cartilage, bone, etc., have been done with success by human surgeons. There is little chance of successful grafting in veterinary surgery, owing to the impossibility of keeping animals sufficiently quiet for the purpose.

(*a*) The measures required with a view to obtaining primary healing comprise:

1. **Arresting the Hæmorrhage.**—If the hæmorrhage be considerable it must be arrested at once (*vide* Hæmostasis).

2. **Cleaning and Disinfecting the Skin in the Vicinity of the Wound.**—In the case of an operation this will have been done before the operation. The same procedure should be adopted with an accidental wound, taking care not to soil it during the process (*vide* Operative Technique).

3. **Applying an Antiseptic Lotion to the Wound.**—The wound being practically aseptic, a strong antiseptic preparation which would cause cellular destruction or weaken the reparative powers of the tissues is contra-indicated. Experience has shown, however, that painting the raw surface of the wound with freshly prepared tincture of iodine does not prevent healing by first intention. Eusol and Dakin's solution are reliable applications which do not interfere with the defensive powers of the tissues, but many surgeons maintain that as good if not better results are obtained by the use of normal saline

solution. In veterinary practice the conditions are such that purely aseptic treatment can seldom be assured.

4. **Applications of Sulphanilamide powder to the wound before Suturing.**—It prevents the multiplication of sulphonamide-sensitive bacteria that may have gained access thereto. Its effect has proved markedly beneficial in this respect.

5. **Suturing the Lips of the Wound.**—If the wound be superficial, involving only the skin and subcutaneous tissues, cutaneous sutures will be sufficient; but if the wound be deep and its walls separated to its depth, deep sutures will be required, including the skin and parts beneath, the skin being afterwards sutured separately between the deep sutures. If there be much tension on the lips of the wound, Halsted or quill sutures are indicated (see p. 236). The wound may be of such a nature that saturing is not indicated.

6. **Protecting the Line of Sutures** by an antiseptic sealing topic, such as iodoform and collodion; or gutta percha 10, and chloroform 90. This is unnecessary when a protective dressing is employed. In the latter case a more common practice is to paint the line of sutures with tincture of iodine.

7. **Applying a Protective Pad and Bandage.**—When possible, a dry sterilised pad composed of a thin layer of plain or sulphanilamide gauze next the wound, with cotton-wool or fine tow outside it, should be applied and kept in position by a bandage creating moderate pressure on the part. This protects the wound from outside interference, helps the sutures to keep its lips in apposition, arrests any hæmorrhage that may supervene, and prevents the formation of a space in the depth of the lesion wherein extravasated blood might accumulate and form a medium for the growth of organisms. An antiseptic powder such as sulphanilamide may be dusted over the wound before applying this dressing. If a bandage cannot be applied, the wound may be covered with a veil of cottonwool kept in position by being made adherent to the periphery of the wound by means of vaseline or some other adhesive preparation.

8. **Keeping the Patient at Rest.**—It is necessary to keep the patient and the affected region as quiet as possible, so as not to mechanically disturb the healing process, which requires a period varying from five to twelve days for completion. At the end of this time the dressing should be carefully removed and the sutures cut and taken out. In a region where there is much tension on the sutures and they still give support to the tissues they should be left *in situ* longer. For a considerable time after cicatrisation has been effected it will be necessary

to avoid traction or tension on the cicatrix, otherwise it may rupture owing to the weakness of the embryonic tissue and reopen the wound.

(*b*) If the lips of the wound cannot be brought into contact by sutures treatment consists in :

1. **Irrigating the wound** with a non-irritant antiseptic solution, as mentioned.

2. **Protecting the wound with a dressing** as before, but using in this case an antiseptic ointment or lubricant paste next its raw surface to prevent the granulations growing into the gauze, becoming adherent thereto, and causing pain and hæmorrhage on removal of the dressing. Boric or iodoform ointment made with vaseline, B.I.P.P., or acriflavine emulsion is suitable for the purpose.

3. **Applying an antiseptic powder** daily to the wound, which acts as a desiccant and astringent, and counteracts infection prior to the formation of granulations or subsequently, should the latter be accidentally ruptured. This is indicated where No. 2 is inpracticable.

Sulphanilamide powder should be used on account of its specific effect on certain streptococci. When applied over the entire surface of an exposed wound or when a deep wound is tamponed with gauze impregnated with the drug it frequently has a notable influence in diminishing suppuration and hastening cicatrisation, *e.g.* after rig and ordinary castration or the radical operation for " Fistulous Withers."

Professor J. G. Wright has observed that these good effects are not seen in cattle, whose wounds, apparently, are not subject to contamination by sulphanilamide-sensitive bacteria. When a wound is uniformly granulating, the less it is interfered with the better. It is immune to infection in this condition, and only requires to be protected from irritation, which would cause a breach in its surface or make the granulations flabby and excessive. The application of an astringent powder or white lotion, composed of zinc sulphate ʒvi., acetate of lead ʒi, water Oi has a good effect in keeping the granulations firm and healthy. Should the granulations become excessive or exuberant, the application of a slight caustic is indicated to reduce them *e.g.* powdered zinc sulphate, which is admirably suited for the purpose. When very exuberant swabbing with Formalin 1—40 is more efficacious.

(2) Suspicious Wounds

When the history of the case indicates that a wound otherwise capable of primary healing has been contaminated, the same measures as adopted in class No. 1 may be employed after thoroughly cleaning the wound with the aid of a solution of hydrogen peroxide, and the progress of the case should then be carefully watched. If symptoms of decided acute inflammation supervene in the region of the lesion, accompanied perhaps by febrile disturbance, they indicate that suppuration has occurred in the wound and that the dressing must be removed. In separating the dressing, warm antiseptic lotion should be used to soften it and facilitate its removal without wounding the wound and hurting the patient.

If in the first instance the wound is deep, it should never be sutured throughout its whole extent ; an opening must be left at its lower part to permit of drainage of any discharge that may form. A drainage tube may be left extending to the bottom of the wound beneath the sutures. Healing may occur by first intention in one part of the wound, and by second intention in the other part.

Once the wound has shown evidence of infection by marked inflammation and suppuration, it belongs to the category of septic wounds. The best plan to adopt with all deep suspected wounds is to treat them as septic wounds at once, in order to avoid the danger of septic complications.

(3) Septic Wounds

Treatment must be prompt to check the infecting bacteria before they have had time to multiply and produce their pathogenic effects. The aerobic organisms develop first, and afterwards the anaerobes, when the medium becomes favourable for their growth.

The measures adopted after arresting hæmorrhage, if present, have solely for their object the prevention of pathogenic effects by the bacteria in the wound. The first indication is thorough cleaning of the wound and its vicinity, comprising clipping and shaving the hair from its periphery, painting the surrounding skin with tincture of iodine, the removal of foreign matter, the excision of destroyed tissue, and flushing of the wound with normal saline solution or a solution of hydrogen peroxide or any antiseptic liquid. Having treated the wound in this fashion, different procedures may be adopted according to the nature of the wound or the choice of the clinician—for example :

1. **Excision of the Wound.**—This is a recognised method of treatment in human surgery, as the surest method of removing the reservoir of the virus before it has had time to produce local and general effects. To have the best results it must be done very soon after the receipt of the wound. The resulting wound is treated as an aseptic operation wound. This procedure, however, is not always practicable, and is unnecessarily drastic for the great majority of cases met with in ordinary practice.

2. **The Use of Liquid Antiseptic Preparations,** such as hydrogen peroxide, tincture of iodine, carbolic acid, or cresyl or lysol in 2 to 5 per cent. solution, biniodide or perchloride of mercury 1 in 1,000, eusol (liq. calcis chlorinatæ, ℥xii.; aquæ, ℥lvi.; then add solution of boric acid, ℥xxii.), or Dakin's solution, which may be employed in the form of—

(*a*) *Antiseptic irrigations,* effected by means of a syringe and indicated for deep or sinuous wounds. They have a mechanical and disinfectant action, flushing out septic debris and counteracting the effects of bacteria.

(*b*) *Antiseptic baths,* which are suitable for wounds on the lower parts of the limbs. They have an excellent effect when continued for a long time and frequently repeated. They are employed for at least half an hour, and not less frequently than two or three times daily. They give best results at a temperature of 104° to 112° F. During the intervals between the baths the wounds are covered with moist antiseptic compresses.

(*c*) *Moist antiseptic compresses,* composed of gauze, lint, or cotton-wool or tow applied to the wound and frequently renewed.

(*d*) *Carrel's tube treatment.* This consists in continuous irrigation with Dakin's solution through a system of small rubber tubes 6 mm. in diameter passing through all parts of the wound, which is filled with gauze to support the tubes and absorb the liquid, and keep it in contact with the entire surface of the wound. It is not easily carried out in ordinary practice.

3. **Painting with Tincture of Iodine,** extensively practised nowadays, iodine having the reputation of being probably the most reliable germicide and antitoxic agent. It is by no means infallible in these respects. It is a stimulant to an indolent wound. It is repeated once or twice daily until the wound is clean.

4. **The Use of B.I.P.P.** repeated once daily. It remains in contact with the wound, producing its antiseptic and anodyne effects.

5. **The Application of Eupad,** a mixture of chloride of lime 1 part, and boracic acid 3 parts, which sets free nascent hypochlorous acid when brought into contact with the moisture of the wound, its action being continued for hours. Being in gaseous form, the acid penetrates into the crevices of the wound. It is not always possible to bring it into contact with all parts of the lesion.

6. **The Application of Pure Carbolic Acid** over the whole surface of the wound. It is allowed to remain in contact with it for a minute, and then washed off with alcohol. It has given excellent results where

there was much destroyed tissue doomed to become gangrenous. The wound is afterwards treated with ordinary antiseptic applications—*e.g.*, B.I.P.P.

7. **The use of Penicillin.**—The action of chemical preparations is often disappointing, due to the fact that they destroy leucocytes, the body's own powerful anti-microbic agents, and fail to penetrate the tissues sufficiently to counteract the effects of the pathogenic organisms that have invaded them, so that they may even be more harmful than beneficial. Sir Alexander Fleming has proved this experimentally and reminds us of the futility of their employment during the 1914-18 War, when numerous patients died of septicæmia resulting from septic wounds despite the constant application of the usual wound dressings. It was found that Dakin's solution instilled into wounds every two hours by the Carrel's tube form of treatment lost its potency in 10 minutes. Fleming has stated that penicillin, his own discovery, is the only anti-bacterial agent capable of producing the desired effect because, when administered parenterally, it penetrates the tissues from the blood stream and prevents multiplication of the offending penicillin-sensitive bacteria without damaging the leucocytes or tissue cells.

Its efficacy was demonstrated in the War of 1939–1945, when every severely wounded soldier was injected with penicillin at the base hospital, in transit, and in hospital in England, thus preventing the development of bacteria in the wound before the necessary surgical treatment in the way of debridement and removal of destroyed tissue and foreign matter was carried out. The wound could then be covered and in the case of the limbs immobilised in plaster of paris and left to heal without further interference.

This latter principle was practised with marked success by Trueta during the Spanish Civil War, when he performed excision of septic wounds and then encased the wounded region in plaster of paris, a great improvement on splinting and daily dressings.

Penicillin passes out of the system in about three hours and must therefore be injected subcutaneously or intramuscularly at three-hourly intervals and given in sufficient dosage in order to produce its full effects. See page 224.

8. **Thermotherapy,** by the application of the flame or hot air. The gas flame rapidly passed over a septic wound has an immediate germicidal and stimulating action, and is specially indicated for a very virulently infected lesion. Hot air (500° to 600°C) sterilises the infected area. It requires a special apparatus for its use.

9. **Heliotherapy.**—Exposure of the wound to the direct rays of the sun for a period varying from a quarter to two hours. This acts through the bactericidal power of the violet rays and the heat of the sun. It causes a profuse flow of lymph from the bloodvessels through their dilatation. It operates more quickly than any other form of treatment, and without the intervention of phagocytes. It is not always available, but the lamp may be used to provide the violet rays.

10. **Providing for Drainage** by enlarging the wound downwards or by making a counter-opening is indicated in every case where there is a pocket in the wound in which septic material may lodge. The counter-opening may be kept patent by a seton passed through it and renewed daily.

11. **The Use of the Culture of the Reading Bacillus.**—This was discovered at a hospital in Reading during the First World War. It has the effect of digesting necrotic tissue without producing pathogenic effects. Under its influence the wound cleans up rapidly and the toxic symptoms disappear. It can be obtained from certain laboratories.

12. **The Application of fine Sugar,** highly spoken of by Roe (Cyprus) for septic wounds.

13. **The Use of a Mixture of Honey, Barley Meal, and Olive Oil,** as practised by Luhrs (*Z. Veterinärk.*, **47**, 2) who described it as superior to ordinary antiseptic dressings for deep septic wounds. The mechanism of its action was not discussed.

14. **Aseptic Treatment.**—Cleaning the wound with sterilised water or normal isotonic saline solution (8 or 9 per 1000) and dressing it with sterilised gauze or wool without the use of an antiseptic is advocated by some surgeons on the ground that antiseptics are harmful to the tissues. Experience has shown that antiseptic treatment is preferable for veterinary patients.

Hypertonic salt solutions 15 to 20 per 1,000 or pure seawater at 33 per 1,000 may be used with good effect. When applied to septic wounds they have a cleansing effect and cause destruction of pus cells. They give rise to exudation of organic liquids containing albuminous substances which have to a certain extent a bactericidal effect, acting directly on the bacteria. In 2 per cent. solution they have a retarding effect on the growth of organisms, at 5 per cent. they completely arrest it. In more concentrated solution they have a painful and irritant effect on the skin. They have the disadvantage of producing negative chemiotaxis, that is, repelling the phagocytes, but when isotonic solutions are substituted for them positive chemiotaxis ensues, causing local leucocytosis. So that the wound which up to now had a raw, angry appearance becomes covered with a greyish film formed by living intact polynuclear leucocytes.

15. **Treatment by a Cytophylactic Antiseptic obtained by Electrolysis** (Coquot and Vaslat, *Rec. Méd. vét.*, **110**, 9), performed by a portable apparatus whereby a varying delivery of "electro-serum" from a strong jet to a fine spray is effected by means of a pump and a special nozzle. Its temperature can be controlled by movement of the electrodes.

The "serum" contains 60 to 80 mgms. of oxidising elements, compounds of chlorine and ozone almost in nascent form, in every litre of the liquid.

The solution is neutral. The apparatus has been used successfully at the Alfort Veterinary College. It has proved to be a painless cleanser of deep suppurating and gangrenous wounds, and has been found particularly useful for the treatment of indolent wounds in cats which would otherwise have proved fatal. The time necessary to convert the saline into "electro-serum" with a temperature 98·5° F. or 104° F. is only 30 or 40 seconds.

16. **Serotherapy.**—The application ot normal serum, usually that from the horse, has been proved to have a hæmostatic and leucocytic effect, hastening the process of repair.

The use of a specific polyvalent serum, as recommended by Leclainche and Vallee for infected lesions, in the form of injections or compresses saturated with the serum has the advantages of increasing the defensive powers of the tissues and intensifying phagocytosis. Its results have been described as wonderfully beneficial.

The use of lacto serum, introduced by Dr. Dauvois, a French veterinarian, has proved wonderfully efficacious in the treatment of septic open joints and synovial sheaths, injected so as to percolate through the cavity, and repeated daily, if necessary. It is prepared by adding a tablespoonful of essence of rennet to a pint of fresh milk, aseptically drawn from the udder and previously brought to blood heat (98° F.). The mixture is allowed to cool and strained through muslin, and is then ready for use.

The serum is not antiseptic but is apparently cyto-phylactic, reinforcing cellular resistance and permitting the repair of injured tissue. Many veterinarians, including the present author, have proved its remarkable efficacy.

Whatever treatment has been adopted, it may be discontinued when the wound is uniformly granulating.

17. General Treatment

1. *Blood Transfusion*, indicated for shock or profuse hæmorrhage threatening the life of the patient, or blood poisoning (gas, chloroform, etc.), or for a debilitated subject to reinforce his defensive powers. It is an everyday practice with human patients but so far has not been much in vogue in veterinary practice. Kuhn (*Deuts. tierarztl. Wschr.*, **442**, 50 (1934)) differentiates six separate isolysins in equine blood and states that it is important to determine the groups of the donor and recipient before performing transfusion—done by mixing red blood corpuscles with serum of the recipient. If no hæmolysis occurs transfusion may be proceeded with. The two dangers are hæmolysis and anaphylaxis: the former may follow each and every transfusion of a given blood, while the latter only occurs after a repeated transfusion of blood from the same donor. Kuhn has observed this in cattle but not in horses, and has seen it supervene after a single injection in one cow. Intravenous injection of adrenalin quickly cures the anaphylaxis but has no effect on hæmolysis, which is manifested by general unrest, accelerated respiration, muscular tremors, a rise in temperature, and hæmoglobinuria. This can be prevented by making a trial transfusion of a small amount of blood, 100–200 c.c. If unsuitable, hæmolysis usually appears after a few minutes and recovery follows fairly soon. Rarely hæmolysis does not occur until some days have elapsed. Blood transfusion has been used with success in azoturia in horses, in puerpural hæmoglobinuria in cattle, strangles, purpura hæmorrhagica, acute infections of newborn animals, and in general or severe local infections. Kuhn is referring to direct transfusion without citration. Citrated blood is very valuable in emergency cases of blood loss and toxæmia. There appears to be a high degree of tolerance in horses for citrate solutions. The technique of the transfusion is on the usual lines for performing intravenous infusion. Strict aseptic precautions being observed, a suitable needle with a very sharp point and a short bevel and with rubber tubing attached is made to penetrate the jugular vein of the donor, and sufficient blood is withdrawn into the flask containing the necessary quantity of sodium citrate solution, viz. 10 c.c. of a 2·5 per cent. solution for each 100 c.c. of blood. The blood, without exposure to the air, is introduced slowly, by gravity, into the jugular vein of the recipient. To prevent chilling of the blood before entering the circulation of the recipient it is advisable to have the tube immersed in water a little above body temperature. In the human subject 45 minutes to one hour is allowed for the introduction of 500 c.c. of citrated blood. The apparatus available for the operation whereby the rate of flow of

blood out of and into a vein can be regulated simplifies the procedure. The chief difficulty with the horses is to control his movement, which may cause the needle to slip out of the vein. Blood transfusion is not important in canines. The donor should be in good health and preferably a dog that had recovered from distemper and of the same breed as the recipient. The blood can be taken from the saphena or radial or jugular vein or direct from the heart ; in the latter case brief general anæsthesia may be necessary ; 50 c.c. may be drawn from a cocker into a large syringe containing the proper amount of citrate. The citrated blood is then injected slowly into a vein or heart chamber (lower third) in amounts of 2–4 c.c. per each pound body weight of the recipient and may be repeated as often as necessary. (Prepared citrate solution with directions for dilution may be purchased.)

2. *Dextrose and Saline Injections.*—Normal saline solution containing 10 per cent. glucose may also be used to treat shock and hæmorrhage, introduced at body temperature in amounts up to 4 c.c. per pound body weight. Dextrose may be employed for intravenous nourishment of patients which from weakness or vomiting are unable to retain food. It is immediately assimilated and provides energy very soon after injection. It stimulates the circulation. It is assimilated better if combined with insulin, 1 unit of insulin to every 5 grains of dextrose.

Standard dosage for small dogs is 2 units of insulin in 20 c.c. of 50 per cent. dextrose solution repeated every 12 hours. In severe cases 30–96 c.c. of a 5 per cent. sodium chloride solution plus 20–50 c.c. of glucose and insulin are given intravenously, and 200–500 c.c. normal saline intraperitoneally. The saline solution is used mainly to replace lost fluids. Continued injections of salt solution will produce œdema. This may be prevented by alternating the glucose and saline and using glucose and distilled water. Gum acacia in 6 per cent. solution may also be used to make up blood lost from shock or hæmorrhage. The acacia solution is colloidal rather than crystalloidal and does not as readily produce œdema. The foregoing remarks on intravenous therapy in small animals are taken from an article on " Intravenous Therapy in Small Animals," by Alan C. Second, published in the *Canadian Journal of Comparative Medicine*, February, 1939.

3. *The injection of antitoxic serum or the use of an autogenous or polyvalent vaccine.* The hypodermic injection of antitetanic serum is indicated in every case of a septic wound. In districts where tetanus is common it should be used for every wound. Antistreptococcic serum is advisable for streptococcic infections. For chronic suppurative lesions like poll evil, fistulous withers, and quittor a vaccine is indicated.

4. *The injection of normal saline* solution hypodermically, intravenously, or *per rectum* in cases of profuse hæmorrhage, or where the patient is suffering from shock.

5. *The observance of good hygiene*, including attention to ventilation, drainage, and feeding, and protection from cold.

The absorption of extravasated blood and inflammatory products causes an increased excretion of urea. Consequently nitrogenous food is contra-indicated. Water should be allowed *ad lib.*, and saline laxative and diuretic medicine daily in the drink or mash is useful to promote the elimination of waste and toxic material.

The individual classes of wounds do not require to be dealt with specially, except to refer to some particular features which deserve emphasis.

(1) *Incised* wounds usually present the conditions required for primary healing.

(2) *Lacerated* wounds may have jagged borders, or be clean cut like incised wounds.

(3) *Punctured* wounds are characterised by their great depth compared with their diameter, and when they are septic are particularly dangerous, being prone to complications from the presence of anaerobic organisms owing to the conditions in the wound being favourable to their growth. They may penetrate into important organs or structures. Aseptic punctured wounds are harmless and only require the application of an antiseptic topic to the orifice to prevent the entrance of infection. Septic punctured wounds are first treated by warm antiseptic solutions in the form of irrigations, compresses, or baths. If they fail to respond to this treatment and the inflammatory symptoms increase rather than diminish there is usually a collection of pus or a foreign body in the depth of the wound, and opening up of the lesion is then indicated to provide an exit for the discharge or permit of the removal or escape of a foreign body. Deep punctured wounds caused by septic objects such as stakes of a fence or prongs of a fork or by a picked-up nail should be promptly treated with penicillin injections to prevent the multiplication of anærobic organisms in their depth, *e.g.* the maglignant œdema bacillus or the bacillus of Nicolaïer.

(4) *Contused* wounds have a comparatively thick zone of dead tissue, and are typical examples of contaminated wounds.

(5) *Gunshot* wounds partake of the nature of incised, lacerated, or contused wounds, according to the velocity of the missile and other conditions.

Lesions caused by explosion of shells naturally vary according to the proximity of the victim to the explosion, the amount of shrapnel or shell casing which enters its tissues, and the part of the body wounded.

The lesions are dealt with on general principles. When a bullet is embedded in the tissues it is well tolerated, because it is usually aseptic, provided that it has not undergone a ricochet, when it may have driven some septic material into the wound, which will then evince symptoms of acute inflammation, and refuse to heal until the septic foreign matter is removed.

The surgeon is guided by the symptoms as to whether he will endeavour to remove the foreign body or leave it *in situ*. When a bullet or other wounding substance has entered any part of the body it should be removed at once, if the operation can be done without extensive or deep incisions. But even if a septic foreign body is deeply embedded, it is better to leave it alone until it becomes loose by suppuration and approaches nearer the surface, than to search for it at once by deep incisions.

(6) *Poisoned wounds*. True poisoned wounds contain a mineral or vegetable poison, and thus treatment includes washing the wound to remove the poison, or, in some cases, excision of the wound in order to get rid of the toxic substance.

(7) *Envenomed wounds* contain the venom of some reptile which has bitten the subject. Such wounds are usually situated about lower parts of the limbs, or on the head, lips, or tongue.

Treatment comprises :

1. Arrest of the circulation from the wound towards the heart by the application of a ligature, where possible, on the proximal side of the wound.

2. Washing the wound and compressing it from the periphery towards the centre to flush out the poison.

3. Sucking the wound, which is without danger when the mucous membrane is intact.

4. Cauterisation of the wound with one of the mineral acids or, better, by the hot iron.

5. Irrigation of the wound with liquids which neutralise the venom —chloride of lime 2 per cent., or chloride of gold 1 per cent.

General treatment in the form of diffusible stimulants may be indicated. An antivenom virus may be obtained from the Pasteur Institute, which will prevent death and stop the action of the venom if injected within four hours after the bite. Swarms of bees or wasps and hornets may cause serious lesions by their stings, often causing death in small animals, and sometimes even in large animals. The stings produce acute inflammation characterised by intense agony and consequent excitement of the patients. As well as the external lesions, congestion and inflammation of internal organs supervene.

Treatment is as follows :

1. Disperse the insects by sprinkling water on the patient.

2. Apply alkaline lotions—*e.g.*, solution of ammonia for bee and hornet stings and a weak acid solution for wasp stings.

3. If asphyxia is threatened from inflammatory swelling of the nasal mucous membrane, perform tracheotomy.

4. In grave cases give diffusible stimulants.

(8) *Virulent wounds* are those containing in the wounded tissues the virus of some recognised disease, such as rabies, anthrax, or tuberculosis. The virus is rapidly absorbed, but its effects are only shown after the expiration of its period of incubation.

Treatment is on the same lines as those for envenomed wounds. Ordinary caustics applied to the wound are useless, but the hot iron, if used soon after the infliction of the wound, may have the desired effect. Antirabic vaccine is indicated for wounds inoculated with the virus of rabies.

(9) *Granulation wounds* are characterised by exuberant granulations of an unhealthy nature, being dark red, purplish, or greenish in colour, and often disintegrating, and give rise to a blood-stained discharge, resulting from hæmorrhage from the ruptured embryonic vessels and a serous transudate from the wound. They may undergo caseation or even calcification in a chronic case. They may be found associated with a sinus of long standing.

Granulation wounds of a specific nature, known as granular dermatitis or summer wounds, are met with in hot countries and in the southern parts of Europe (India, Brazil, South of France). They are due to the larvæ of the *Habronema muscæ*, which, after being voided in the fæces of the horse, enter the larvæ of flies which live in horse manure. They develop in the pupa and perfect insect stages of the fly. The latter deposit the larvæ in wounds or abrasions of the horse's skin, where they set up the lesions in question.

Treatment comprises :

1. The administration of vermifuges to horses, the destruction of flies, and the disinfection of manure when of parasitic origin.

2. The usual measures for the treatment of a sinus when it is the cause of the condition.

3. The destruction by caustics of the unhealthy granulations, or, better, their excision by means of the knife or curette.

4. The application of the usual antiseptic dressings for open wounds after the abnormal tissue has been removed.

(10) *Ulcerating Wounds* are dealt with on the same principles as those mentioned for " Ulcers " (p. 16).

B. Subcutaneous Wounds, Contusions

Subcutaneous wounds are of two varieties—viz.:

1. Those in conjunction with which there is a small solution of continuity in the skin and a comparatively extensive wound subcutaneously, as is exemplified in the operation for periosteotomy.

2. Those in which there is no breach in the surface of the overlying skin, and known as contusions or bruises.

Most of the wounds of the first kind are aseptic operation wounds, and being only slightly exposed to infection owing to the small opening in the skin, they are seldom complicated by the entrance of bacteria into the wounded structures beneath.

They require the usual antiseptic precautions to prevent their becoming infected. If they are septic, as is apt to be the case when of accidental origin, they are treated as septic wounds.

Contusions may be classified according to the degree of injury produced—viz.:

1. Contusions of the first degree, characterised by rupture of capillary vessels in the skin and subcutaneous tissues and the formation of ecchymoses.

2. Contusions of the second degree, with rupture of larger vessels and the production of a hæmatoma.

3. Contusions of the third degree, in which there is considerable destruction of tissue, which may undergo gangrene.

SYMPTOMS.—*Contusions of the First Degree.*—The symptoms here are those of slight inflammation. Pain is not very marked. The typical symptoms are only observed in the non-pigmented skin, and are represented by the changes in colour which take place in the part from the time the injury is inflicted until it is healed. They are well seen in the human subject (white) after the receipt of a contusion—*e.g.*, a " black eye."

Contusions of the Second Degree.—Here a pocket of blood or a hæmatoma is formed in the wounded soft tissues. When the blood is extravasated beneath an aponeurotic membrane, it forms a prominent swelling above the level of the surrounding parts. On manipulation it is found to be inflammatory and fluctuating and crepitating, due to the presence of liquid and coagulated blood. If the area involved is small, the symptoms may gradually disappear, owing to absorption of the extravasated blood and the inflammatory exudate ; whereas if it be large the swelling will persist in the form of a cyst after the inflammatory phenomena have disappeared. Should infection gain entrance through some narrow breach of surface, suppuration, or perhaps gangrene, will supervene.

When a region in which a strong aponeurotic membrane is situated undergoes a contusion, inflicted obliquely on the part, an accumulation of serum and lymph forms quickly beneath the skin, due to separation of the latter from the aponeurosis and the consequent rupture of lymphatic vessels and capillary bloodvessels. The swelling in this case is formed mostly of extravasated lymph, there being little coagulated blood in its contents.

The symptoms of this condition are characterised by the formation of a uniformly fluctuating enlargement. The liquid does not completely fill the space beneath the skin, and consequently can be displaced from one part to another by manipulation. For the same reason the swelling has a dimpled appearance at the place not occupied by the liquid. A common site of this lesion is the thigh, buttocks, or forearm. It is usually referred to as a hæmatoma.

Contusions of the Third Degree.—In this case a deep extensive volume of tissues is destroyed, and eventually undergoes gangrene. The history and the appearance of the case indicate the severity of the lesion. There may be evidence of shock or of injury to internal organs, depending on the region affected. A contusion inflicted at the level of a motor nerve often causes temporary paralysis of the muscles supplied by it.

TREATMENT.—*Contusions of the First Degree.*—These are benign affections which undergo resolution, like all slight inflammatory conditions, without any risk of a complication ensuing. They may be treated with cold and astringent applications to arrest capillary hæmorrhage, and thus accelerate recovery. Anodyne ointment may be applied on a painful surface.

Contusions of the Second Degree.—(i.) *When the case is recent*, treatment comprises : (1) Cold-water irrigation ; (2) astringent applications ; (3) the rubbing in of absorbent topics like the preparations of iodine ; 4) massage; (5) compression with a pad and bandage when practicable.

(ii.) *When the case is of long standing*, treatment consists in incising the swelling at a dependent part, evacuating its contents, and treating its lining with an irritant antiseptic solution, so as to cause it to undergo successively inflammation, granulation, and cicatrisation, and thus obliterate the cavity. Collections of lymph may be opened early, as there is no danger from hæmorrhage in connection with them.

Should severe hæmorrhage ensue from the too early opening of a hæmatoma before the ruptured vessels are thrombosed it must be arrested by plugging the cavity.

Contusions of the Third Degree.—Moist warm antiseptic applications are indicated with a view to restore the circulation in the severely damaged tissue and thus ward off gangrene. Should the latter supervene it must be treated as such.

The antiseptic is added to counteract infection that may enter through abrasions on the skin. If the patient suffers from shock the usual treatment for this condition should be adopted (see p. 42).

FROST BITE

The domesticated animals seldom suffer from cold. If deprived of their coats, or insufficiently fed, they are more susceptible to its effects.

Moist cold is more severe in its action than dry cold. The most common sites of frost bite in the horse are the lower parts of the limbs, due to prolonged contact with ice-cold mud. A breach of surface in the integument favours the injurious effects of cold on the tissues beneath. It causes various degrees of dermatitis. Sometimes gangrene supervenes, constituting "gangrenous dermatitis." The gangrene may extend into a joint or important synovial sheath, necessitating destruction of the patient. The toxæmia may be so severe that the animal succumbs to its effects.

TREATMENT is that for inflammation, open wounds, or gangrene, as the case may be.

Antiseptic applications are always indicated where there is breach of surface, to prevent septic complications. To revive a frozen part it should be bathed with lukewarm antiseptic lotion. Hot applications are contra-indicated, as they cause a too sudden reaction, with rupture of the vessels in the congealed region. If an animal be generally affected by exposure to severe cold, it should be rubbed with snow or cold water and given a stimulant internally. On no account should the patient be treated by hot baths or brought into a hot atmosphere, as death is then apt to ensue from thrombosis and embolism and congestion of internal organs

BURNS AND SCALDS

Burns and scalds cause inflammatory or gangrenous lesions, varying in depth and area according to circumstances, and the prognosis varies accordingly. A circumscribed deep burn is less serious than a superficial burn affecting a large area. In the latter case toxic complications may supervene, and cause the death of the subject in the course of a few days or a few weeks after the accident. The smoke of fires may cause fatal laryngitis or broncho-pneumonia.

TREATMENT has for its object the prevention, as far as possible, of septic complications, and the relief of the pain caused by the intense inflammation to which a burn or scald gives rise.

The preparation employed may be :

1. *Tincture of iodine* lightly applied after cleaning the part with sterilised water.

2. *An ordinary antiseptic lotion*, followed by the use of an antiseptic powder.

3. *Saturated solution of picric acid*, which is analgesic and antiseptic. It is used as a lotion, or in compresses covering the part, or as a bath. It has an excellent effect.

4. *Tannic acid* used in the form of a jelly is a very effective application for burns.

5. *An anodyne antiseptic ointment—e.g.*, cocainised vaseline or iodoform ointment.

When vesicles are present they should be punctured to allow the liquid to escape, and thus relieve the acute pain caused by its pressure. Afterwards one of the above-mentioned topics may be employed. The wall of the vesicle should not be removed, as it serves as a protection to the inflamed part beneath.

The following preparation has been highly recommended, and is said to be equivalent to "ambrine," which was used with excellent results during the First World War :

For Burns.

(1) Resorcin	1 part.
(2) Essence of eucalyptus	2 parts.
(3) Olive oil	5 "
(4) Vaseline	25 "
(5) Hard paraffin	67 "

Melt (5) and add (3) and (4). Dissolve (1) in absolute alcohol (the smallest possible quantity), and add to (3), (4), and (5). Allow to cool to 95° F., and then add (2). Naphthol B may replace (1), or (1) may be omitted, and (5) increased to 67·75. Wash with sterile water and dry well. Apply the mixture at 112° F. with a large flat brush. Then put on a thin layer of cotton-wool. Cover this with another layer of the mixture. Finally, a layer of cotton-wool and a bandage. Repeat every twenty-four hours at first, and after a few days, when there is little pus, every forty-eight hours.

When symptoms of toxæmia and general depression supervene stimulants are indicated (strychnine, ether, caffeine hypodermically).

When dyspnœa is severe owing to swelling of the laryngeal mucous membrane tracheotomy is necesssary. Burns caused by acids require the application of an alkali (potass. or sod. carb. soap solution), and those caused by an alkali that of an acid (vinegar). When an animal is very badly burned it should be destroyed at once.

NETTLE STINGS

Very painful dermatitis may be caused in horses and dogs from travelling through or lying in tufts of nettles, the hairs of the leaves penetrating the skin and inoculating into it a caustic liquid. Treatment consists in removing the irritant hairs and bathing the affected parts with a solution of vinegar and an antiseptic lotion. A solution of carbolic acid has an anodyne effect.

COMPLICATIONS OF WOUNDS

The complications of wounds include: (1) Hæmorrhage; (2) Syncope; (3) shock and local shock; (4) traumatic neuralgia; (5) traumatic emphysema; (6) venous thrombosis and embolism; (7) traumatic fever; (8) erysipelas; (9) septicæmia and pyæmia; (10) gas gangrene; (11) tetanus.

1. Hæmorrhage. Traumatic Anæmia

The phenomenon of coagulation of the blood on its escape from the circulatory system or as the result of injury to the cardiac or vascular endothelium is familiar to the student of physiology and need not be described here.

Upon it depends chiefly the process of hæmostasis.

There are agents whose presence in the blood favours its production, the best known of which is calcium.

Some of the other substances which have this effect are (1) Saline solutions, (2) extract of muscle, of kidney, of liver, of thymus, and of heterogeneous blood.

If calcium is absent from the blood it fails to coagulate.

The persistence of hæmorrhage is not always due to the large calibre of the vessels wounded. It may be the result of some defect in the vessel walls or some morbid general condition such as leucæmia or hæmophilia or visceral affections including disease of the liver or heart.

Hæmophilia is not common in veterinary patients, but several authors have reported cases of it in the horse and dog, mostly in the latter.

Traumatic Anæmia results from the loss of a large quantity of blood. When the hæmorrhage is severe, acute anæmia supervenes, the animal being in a state of collapse with gasping respirations, running down pulse, and pallid mucous membranes. Death may follow rapidly from cerebral ischæmia.

Slight repeated hæmorrhages lead to chronic anæmia characterised by pallor of the mucous membranes, feeble heart action, and general debility.

TREATMENT of ordinary traumatic hæmorrhage is described under the heading of Hæmostasis (see p. 239), and it will be sufficient here to refer to persistent hæmorrhage due to lack of coagulants in the blood, or to hæmophilia and to the general or constitutional treatment of severe hæmorrhage, as follows:

1. *The injection of fresh normal horse serum*, the object being to introduce into the circulation of the patient the normal coagulating ferments which it may lack, the doses being 20 to 30 c.c. for large animals, and 4 c.c. to 10 c.c. for small animals.

This treatment has often proved effective in human surgery.

2. *The administration of chloride of calcium* in a draught or in the drink in doses of 3 to 4 drms. for large animals, and 10 grains to a drm. for small animals. This is only of use when the hæmorrhage is due to calcium deficiency.

3. *Lowering the position of the head* in order to avoid or diminish cerebral anæmia.

4. *Performing artificial respiration* when asphyxia is threatened.

5. *Flagellation of the body* to stimulate the circulation.

6. *Hypodermic injection of ether, caffeine, or coramine.*

7. *The intravenous injection of normal saline* (9 per 1,000) or Ringer-Locke's Solution, viz. sodium chloride 9 grms., chloride of potassium 0·42 grms., calcium chloride 0·15 grms., distilled water 1,000 grms. This is indicated when the danger consists more in the insufficiency or mechanical impossibility of the circulation from the diminished volume of blood than in dearth of blood corpuscles.

8. *Rectal injection of normal saline* may be performed instead of No. 7 when facilities are not at hand for the latter. It has an undoubtedly good effect, especially in the large animal, and should always be adopted when a patient is slow to recover after an operation involving much loss of blood.

2. Syncope

Syncope is characterised by sudden stoppage of the heart's action. The patient appears to be dead. The cause may be (1) severe hæmorrhage; (2) reflex action, as may occur during a severe operation.

TREATMENT consists in applying the usual methods of resuscitation, placing the head on a lower level than that of the body, flicking the body with towels, performing artificial respiration, and injecting caffeine, ether, or coramine subcutaneously. When due to loss of blood, a hypodermic, intravenous, or rectal injection of normal saline is indicated.

3. Shock

In this case the movements of the heart and respiration continue, but the patient is unconscious.

TREATMENT is the same as for No. 2.

4. Traumatic Neuralgia

Traumatic neuralgia or hyperæsthesia is of two kinds—viz., (1) primary and (2) secondary neuralgia.

(1) *Primary neuralgia* is manifested by the continuance for an abnormal length of time of the pain caused by the injury. It may be confined to the region of the wound, or extend along the nerves in the vicinity.

(2) *Secondary neuralgia* appears during the period of cicatrisation. It also may be confined to the wound, or be diffused in its neighbourhood.

TREATMENT.—Occurring in a recent wound, treat the latter antiseptically and apply an anodyne preparation. Warm, moist compresses often have an analgesic effect. Secondary neuralgia is treated similarly. When the hyperæsthesia appears in a cicatrix, needle-point firing or deep scarification of the part may be effective. If rheumatism is suspected, salicylate of sodium is indicated.

5. Traumatic Emphysema

This is due to infiltration of the cellular tissue by air, or by gas from the alimentary tract.

It is a common complication of punctured wounds of the respiratory tract (nasal chambers, trachea, etc.). It also follows wounds of the axilla and groin, and of periarticular tissues. The opening and closure of these wounds during movement cause air to be aspirated into the wound and driven through the tissues. After puncturing the rumen in the ox or the cæcum in the horse gas may escape from the alimentary canal and infiltrate the tissues in the vicinity of the wound.

SYMPTOMS.—The condition is recognised by the presence of a soft, circumscribed, painless, crepitating swelling, quite different from that caused by gas gangrene. It is usually harmless. Some local infection may ensue when the case is due to the passage of gas from the digestive tract, owing to some septic alimentary matter being carried by it into the tissues.

TREATMENT is as follows :

(1) *Apply pressure* from the periphery of the swelling towards the wound to expel some of the air or gas. In an ordinary case, however, this is not necessary, for if the case be left alone the air will soon become absorbed.

(2) When the case is due to a wound in the axilla or groin, the main indication is to *keep the patient at rest* after treating the wound in the usual way.

(3) *Enlarging the wound.* In the case of punctured wounds of the respiratory tract, the emphysema is due to the air issuing from the respiratory passage not having a free exit. The indication here is to enlarge the external wound, so that the air may escape instead of infiltrating the tissues.

Traumatic emphysema may become generalised soon after the onset of the condition, and may then cause symptoms of general discomfort and dyspnœa, which, however, soon disappear when the infiltration is arrested.

6. Venous Thrombosis

Venous thrombosis is the result of phlebitis supervening in a vein that has been opened or contused at the site of a wound. The chief danger of the condition is disintegration of the thrombus in the vein, leading to the formation of emboli, whose effects vary according to their size and the degree of sepsis affecting them. When large, they may obstruct the pulmonary artery or the auriculo-ventricular valve and cause sudden death. Septic embolism produces a fatal septicæmia.

TREATMENT.—Apply an antiseptic solution to the wound, and avoid handling it roughly for fear of disturbing the clot and causing embolism. If there seems danger of general infection institute a course of penicillin injections.

7. Traumatic Fever

This is manifested by the symptoms of febrile disturbance, due to the absorption of toxins from the wound caused by the presence of bacteria. The condition, as a rule, is not serious. So long as the patient continues to feed and has a good pulse the prognosis is favourable.

TREATMENT has for its object the counteraction of infection in the wound, by antisepsis.

8. Erysipelas

This is a contagious disease due to a specific streptococcic infection of a wound. Three forms of the malady are recognised—viz. :

1. Cutaneous erysipelas.
2. Phlegmonous erysipelas.
3. Gangrenous erysipelas.

It has been seen in the horse and dog.

1. **Cutaneous Erysipelas.**—Its characteristic features are hidden to a great extent by the hair and the pigment of the skin in the horse. There is a diffuse, hot, painful swelling affecting the skin and spreading rapidly. This may be accompanied by lymphangitis and adenitis. When the horse's lips are affected the whole head becomes enormously swollen. The general symptoms are those of traumatic fever.

2. The **phlegmonous** and **gangrenous** forms are manifested respectively by symptoms of diffuse suppurating lesions and by those of moist gangrene. The febrile disturbance in these forms of the disease is very severe, being characterised by great depression, as well as by other febrile symptoms. Death is a common termination in such cases. The cutaneous variety is generally followed by recovery.

TREATMENT is the same as for septic wounds in general combined with the administration of febrifuge medicine.

9. Septicæmia and Pyæmia

These are characterised by profound depression, the animal's power of resistance being completely overcome. Before the introduction of penicillin both these conditions and gangrenous erysipela were usually incurable, but recovery may now be brought about by the prompt administration of this drug in massive and frequently repeated doses associated with any surgical technique that may be demanded in connection with the wounds.

10. Gangrenous Septicæmia or Gas Gangrene

This is due to the invasion of the wound by the *Vibrion septique* or *Bacillus septicus.* It is not common in the horse, and is rare in the dog, pig, and ruminant. It complicates chiefly deep and tortuous wounds in which the tissues are severely bruised, and from which the air is excluded. The causal organism has a wide distribution, being found all over the world in the soil and in animal excreta. The bacilli are readily killed by the oxygen of the air, but their spores are very resistant and retain their virulence for years in desiccated virulent material, known as septic dust. It is now established that other anaerobic organisms can produce gas gangrene.

SYMPTOMS.—These are local and general.

1. *Local Symptoms.*—These comprise a hot, painful, œdematous swelling surrounding the wound, which spreads rapidly. It has a well-defined, raised border. As the disease advances the centre of the swelling becomes depressed, cold, insensitive, and crepitating. A little later the lips of the wound undergo putrefaction, becoming friable and infiltrated with fœtid gas. If the wound is recent, its surface becomes variegated with greyish and blackish spots, and its recesses contain a fœtid reddish liquid, tissue debris and black blood clots. If the wound has been granulating, its granulations assume an unhealthy appearance, and the ordinary purulent discharge is replaced by a greyish or reddish fœtid liquid.

2. *General Symptoms.*—The general symptoms are those of the most virulent form of toxæmia, a striking feature being the great prostration of the patient. After the fever has reached its height, the temperature gradually falls below normal. Death supervenes in two to four days after the onset of the disease.

TREATMENT.—Once the disease has made its appearance it may be declared incurable. An attempt may be made to stem its course by active antiseptic treatment of the wound on the lines laid down for septic traumatic lesions and for moist gangrene. Dressing with a specific serum and the injection of polyvalent antigangrenous serum are indicated, but probably the best chance of success is the prompt and massive administration of penicillin.

Special precautions should be taken with all deep septic contused wounds to prevent the development of the disease. Dressing such wounds with pure carbolic acid or by continuous irrigation with Dakin's solution or eusol, after cleansing with hydrogen peroxide, constitutes a reliable method of treatment. Here also penicillin is indicated.

Gas may be formed in conjunction with abscesses due to other gas-forming organisms of a less virulent type than the vibrion. They are treated on the usual principles.

11. Tetanus

This disease is fairly common as a complication of wounds in the horse, but comparatively rare in other animals. It is due to an anaerobic organism, the bacillus of Nicolaïer, which multiplies in the wound, elaborating a toxin which becomes fixed in the nerve centres and provokes tetanic convulsions. It is chiefly in deep, dirty wounds, those soiled by mud or fæces and not freely exposed to the air, that the organism of tetanus flourishes. Wounds caused by the harness and the operations of docking and castration are sometimes followed by tetanus. In the cow it occasionally follows parturition.

The disease varies as to the time it makes its appearance after the infliction of the wound. It usually appears on the third to the fifth day, but it may not supervene until the third or fourth week, when the wound is healed. As a rule, the shorter the period of incubation the more acute the disease.

The SYMPTOMS need not be described here, being dealt with in works on medicine. They are very characteristic. The protrusion of the membrana nictitans over the eyeball when the horse's head is tilted upwards is diagnostic.

The PROGNOSIS must always be guarded. The mortality in the horse is about 70 to 73 per cent. It is also high in the ox and dog.

The prevention of tetanus consists in the thorough antisepsis of wounds and the injection of antitetanic serum. The latter should be used as soon as possible after the occurrence of the wound. When used within a few hours after the wound is made it is an absolute preventative

TREATMENT.—There is no specific cure for the disease. Treatment consists in attending to the wound as described (*vide* Septic Wounds), and in injecting large daily doses of antitetanic serum. The latter has no effect on toxin already fixed in the nerve centres, but it prevents the fixation of further doses of the poison. The *Cl. tetani* is susceptible to the effects of penicillin but once the toxin is fixed in the nerves it can have little influence in affecting the course of the disease, as the drug is not antitoxic. In addition to these measures the patient must be kept quiet, and laxative and sedative medicine administered. Slings are advisable if they do not excite the animai ; they enable it to rest and prevent its lying down, which would intensify the spasms and render the prognosis much more grave.

Other conditions that may be included in the complications of open wounds are actinomycosis, actinobacillosis, botriomycosis, bursattee, sporotrichosis, black quarter, anthrax, farcy, tuberculosis, leishmaniosis, since the causal organism may gain entrance through a puncture or breach of surface of the integument of the body. The wounds thus inoculated are in fact *virulent wounds* and must be dealt with as such. The description of these affections belongs for the most part to the domains of medicine, parasitology, and pathology. Consequently they are only mentioned here. It is important that the clinician should be familiar with the external lesions which they produce.

12. Adhesions

It is appropriate to add here some remarks on adhesions between muscles, vessels, and nerves following old-standing lacerated wounds and old sprains. Professor Share Jones (*Vet. Rec.*, May 21, 1932) says that this condition has been overlooked and records cases where severe chronic lameness reckoned incurable were treated successfully by dissecting and separating the adherent structures under the influence of general anæsthesia, a notable instance being a case of a horse with an extensive laceration about 10 inches long on the inner aspect of the forearm and covered by a mass of granulation tissue. It was present for months. The extensor muscles, vessels, and nerves were dissected out in two séances, with the result that the horse was going sound five months afterwards. The animal was kept in slings during treatment.

CHAPTER IV

TUMOURS AND CYSTS

I.—TUMOURS

TUMOURS or neoplasms will only be dealt with from a clinical aspect.

ETIOLOGY.—All sorts of theories have been put forward as to the causation of neoplasms, but so far nothing definite is known in this respect. All animals are subject to tumours, but they are far more common in carnivora than in herbivora. They are more common in the horse and ox than in the sheep, pig, and goat. Generally speaking, tumours more often affect animals in the declining years of life than during youth. This applies chiefly to malignant tumours, and more particularly to carcinoma. Benign tumours—for example, warts—affect principally young subjects. Sarcoma is not infrequently encountered in young adults. Some papillomata are contagious—for instance, those affecting the mouth in the dog. Contagious granulomata, affecting the vagina of the bitch and the prepuce and surface of the penis in the dog, are transmitted from one animal to the other by the act of coitus.

Classification.—Tumours are classified clinically as follows: benign, malignant, solitary, and multiple tumours.

Benign tumours remain local, and do not recur after excision ; they are comparatively slow in growth, the skin does not adhere to them, and they do not ulcerate on their surface.

Malignant tumours develop rapidly, and give rise to secondary tumours in their vicinity and at a distance, the neoplasmic elements being carried by the lymph or blood stream (metastasis). They recur after excision. The skin is usually adherent to their surface, and is frequently ulcerated at their level. The tumour is *solitary* when it is the only one present.

Multiple tumours develop in groups in the same organ or region.

Varieties of Tumours.—The common varieties of tumours met with are papillomata, fibromata, chondromata, myxomata, sarcomata, carcinomata, and lymphadenomata.

Diagnosis.—Papillomata or warts are familiar to everybody, and are easily recognised. Sarcomata and carcinomata generally display features already alluded to, which indicate that they are malignant. When the lymphatic glands in the vicinity are involved, it is a reliable sign that the primary tumour is carcinoma. Sarcoma spreads by the blood stream. Cases, however, occur where immediate diagnosis can only be made by microscopic examination of a section of the tumour.

Prognosis.—Benign tumours are harmless if they are not situated in a region where they interfere with function. They can be successfully excised if situated in a place where operation is possible. Malignant tumours, in the great majority of cases, are incurable. Sarcomata, carcinomata, and lymphadenomata are of this nature. Myxomata often contain sarcomatous elements, and are then malignant.

BENIGN TUMOURS

Treatment.—If benign tumours are not causing trouble and are not unsightly, they may be left alone. Otherwise they may be removed as follows, by—

1. *Ligature.* When the tumour is pedunculated it can be conveniently and effectively removed by the application of a ligature as close to the surface of the body as possible. An india-rubber ligature is best, as it keeps constant pressure on the part, and will not require to be tightened or renewed; but an inelastic material like whipcord or silk usually answers the purpose, and has the advantage of being strong. If the rubber is not stout and of good quality, it may break before having had the desired effect. Even for sessile tumours the ligature has been successfully employed. Antiseptic applications are necessary for the wound caused by the ligature.

2. The *hot iron.* The hot iron is suitable when the tumour is more or less pedunculated, and can be grasped in a retention clam. It has the advantage that it prevents hæmorrhage, and its caustic effect destroys any portion of the tumour that is left and causes it to slough away. It is often employed for papillomata on account of their great vascularity.

3. The *ecraseur.* This may be used for pedunculated tumours like papillomata. If skin has to be severed, it should be incised with a knife and the chain of the ecraseur applied in the incision. It is rather rough usage for this instrument.

4. The *wart enucleator*, in the form of a forceps with excavated jaws with sharp borders. This is very useful for removing warts.

5. *Potential caustics*, such as arsenical paste, nitric or acetic acid, or liquor potassæ. Arsenic is radical in effect. Its action may be too drastic. Salicylic acid ointment has proved very effective for warts.

6. *Excision with the knife*. This consists in carefully dissecting out the tumour with the knife, taking care to cut outside its periphery without encroaching too much on the surrounding parts, to control hæmorrhage, and to observe all the rules of operative technique. Papillomata require excision of the portion of skin on which they are growing to ensure against their recurrence. If merely cut off level with the skin, they will soon grow again. Pedunculated tumours in the mucous cavities, pharynx, vagina, can be readily removed with the ecraseur. Anti-tetanic serum is indicated for ulcerated warts and for all warts before operation for their removal by ligature or other methods.

Malignant Tumours

Generally speaking, treatment of malignant tumours is useless. Methods of treatment that have been tried may be mentioned—viz. :

1. **The Use of Caustics.**—The repeated application of an aqueous alcoholic solution of arsenic has been efficacious for small cancerous lesions confined to the skin (arsenic, 1 ; water and alcohol, 50).

2. **Radiotherapy,** which has had a curative effect in several cases of superficial cancerous tumours in the human subject, but has not been tried on animals. It is painless, and acts only on the neoplasmic cells of the tumour without damaging normal tissue. Curetting the lesion may be associated with it, and increases its efficacy. (See p. 269, Radiotherapy.)

Excision, which must be radical, and performed as far beyond the apparent boundary of the tumour as is practicable. When the nearest lymphatic glands are involved they must also be extirpated.

Notwithstanding wide and deep excision, these tumours grow again. In fact, operation often stimulates their growth, and leads to metastasis where it had not occurred already. When affecting an organ or appendage which can be dispensed with, amputation thereof may effect a permanent cure (penis, tail, limb).

II.—CYSTS

Cysts occur in the form of hollow tumours containing fluid or semi-fluid material, and occasionally solid structures, such as teeth and hair (dentigerous and dermoid cysts). When the contents are liquid the swelling is uniformly fluctuating, and the presence of the liquid can be confirmed by exploratory puncture. Cysts are non-inflammatory and slow in development.

TREATMENT may be as follows :

1. *Puncture and injection.* The cyst is punctured with a trocar and canula to evacuate its contents, and then injected with an irritant liquid such as tincture of iodine or 5 per cent. solution of carbolic acid, to destroy its smooth lining and set up inflammation and granulation, which will lead to obliteration of the cavity. This is not always effective. It may require repetition and prove tedious.

2. *The passage of a seton* through the cyst from above to below, a practical method in large animals which usually proves successful—for example, in a case of hygroma in front of the cow's knee.

3. *Incision with a knife* to release the contents, followed by the application of an irritant as in No. 1. This method often succeeds, but may be slow in effect.

4. *Excision of the cyst* as if it were an ordinary tumour. This is the most satisfactory procedure, care being taken to dissect outside the cyst wall, and not to puncture the latter during the operation. If the cyst were very large, this treatment would involve making a very large wound, and in such a case No. 2 or No. 3 would be a better method to adopt.

In some cases it is preferable to open the cyst before dissecting it out, as for example when it is fairly deep seated and its outline is not distinct.

CHAPTER V

AFFECTIONS OF TISSUES

I.—AFFECTIONS OF THE SKIN AND SUBCUTANEOUS CONNECTIVE TISSUE

THE skin and subcutaneous connective tissue are involved in most superficial surgical affections and are the seat of the external manifestation of many constitutional diseases. Surgical lesions of the skin are dealt with under various headings throughout the work, and those connected with internal diseases are described in text books on medicine, so that it will only be necessary here to allude more or less briefly to the chief cutaneous and subcutaneous affections met with in the lower animals as follows :

(1) Lesions caused by the Harness

These include excoriations, contusions or galls, sit-fasts or areas of dry gangrene which are appropriately dealt with in other parts of the book.

(2) Callosities or Horny Indurations

These may occur in the cow's knee or on the elbow of the large breeds of dogs from repeated injury by contact with the ground and are referred to in connection with bursal affections.

(3) Erythema

Erythema or red eruption is met with in all the domesticated animals, from various causes, including mechanical and chemical irritation which produce it in circumscribed areas, and the action of direct sunlight which gives rise to it in a diffuse form, a sort of sunstroke met with mostly in tropical regions.

The horse is sometimes affected with local erythema in the axilla and groin, caused by exercise when the skin is covered by sweat and dust, the condition being known as intertrigo. It is observed chiefly in fat animals with a fine skin. It is characterised by weeping and acute sensitiveness of the affected parts, and by interference with gait, the limbs being abducted during progression. A similar condition may appear on the cow's udder. A toxic erythema results from the ingestion of certain foodstuffs, including potatoes and brewer's grains, which may be followed by gangrenous dermatitis with patchy sloughing of the skin and general symptoms of toxæmia. The absence of pigment in the skin is a predisposing cause of all forms of erythema.

PREVENTION consists in avoiding the causes mentioned and curative treatment in removing them when still operating, associated with the usual remedies for superficial acute inflammation. Cleanliness of the region followed by astringent lotions and emollient topics is indicated.

(4) Dermatitis

Dermatitis includes:

(*a*) **Moist Eczema,** which is most common in the dog and may be of local or constitutional origin. When of the former nature treatment comprises clipping the hair from the affected region, cleaning it to remove irritant matter and applying a desiccant such as starch, or powdered sulphur, or oxide of zinc, or subnitrate of bismuth, or a mixture of these powders.

Sometimes there is an offensive odour from the lesion which may be counteracted by the use of perfumed toilet powder.

An ointment or paste made with oxide of zinc is often very effective, and when itching is marked a lotion containing a little alcohol and a very small proportion of carbolic acid or a 1 per cent. solution of chloral hydrate may have a soothing effect. Internal treatment is indicated when the cause is constitutional and includes the repeated administration of sulphur, sodium bicarbonate, or arsenical preparations such as Liquor Arsenicalis or Aricyl (hypodermically), the last named being probably the best agent for the chronic form of the condition, used alone or in conjunction with odylene locally and according to instructions issued with the preparation.

Attention must be paid to the diet which may be associated with the cause of the affection, as mentioned in connection with erythema. Cases of constitutional origin may be due to avitaminosis or mineral deficiency and accordingly require to be treated by vitamin-mineral or heliotherapy. Bayer's preparation known as "Murnel," an organic extract with a standardised vitamin H content, has proved efficacious for non-parasitic and non-infectious skin diseases of dogs and cats, *e.g.*, alopecia, eczema of all kinds, intertrigo, paranchyia, and pruritis.

(*b*) **Herpes Zoster** which has been observed in the dog, and characterised by the formation of vesicles associated with erythema on the course of a sensory nerve and accompanied by neuralgia of the latter. It is usually preceded by inveterate scratching. The treatment is that for neuralgia and erythema.

(*c*) **Mud Fever,** a papular form of dermatitis occurring mostly in winter and caused by the irritant action of mud, and affecting chiefly the lower parts of the limbs, below the knee and hock. It is greatly favoured by clipping the legs. The affected part is swollen, somewhat painful, and the site of numerous papules on which crusts form and afterwards separate, leaving small depilated areas. Sometimes the condition extends to the inner aspect of the forearms and thighs. It is not a serious affection, not interfering with work and disappearing in the course of three or four weeks.

TREATMENT consists in washing with mild soap and water, drying, and applying astringent dressings. If the skin is cracked an emollient ointment is indicated.

(*d*) **Cracked Heels** characterised by cracks or fissures in the skin accompanied by inflammation at the back of the pastern, usually due to repeated or constant contact with cold mud or dirty wet litter, or washing the legs and not drying them. The condition causes severe lameness.

It may also result from blister ointment getting into the heel from the skin in the vicinity. If attended to early and treated on general principles by removing the cause, cleaning the affected part, and applying antiseptic ointment, recovery ensues. The following ointment has been found very effective: white lead ʒii., salicylic acid ʒii., carbolic acid ℥i., vaseline 3 lb. When of long standing and the lips of the cracks are callous the application of the hot iron followed by a protective antiseptic dressing brings about healing.

A somewhat similar condition occurs at the back of the knee (mallenders) and in front of the hock (sallenders), but is not so amenable to treatment as the average case of cracked heels. The movement in the angle of the flexion of the joints militates against recovery.

(*e*) **Grease,** a chronic or exudative and hypertrophic dermatitis of the inferior region of the limbs which affects chiefly heavy hairy-legged horses, especially those kept under unhygienic conditions, in dirty, badly-drained stables, or working in muddy places. It seems allied to canker of the foot as regards the conditions which favour its onset and the nature of the lesion. Not infrequently both affections co-exist in the same animal.

The actual cause of the affection is not known. It would appear to be of systemic origin, that is a local manifestation of some defect in the patient's constitution. It is seldom confined to one limb. More frequently two fore or two hind limbs, usually the latter, or all the limbs are affected, which goes to show that it is probably not a purely local disease. Its usual seat is the pastern and posterior aspect of the fetlock. It may extend up to the hock, and rarely it is confined to the latter region.

SYMPTOMS.—The symptoms are well marked. The hair is erect on the seat of the lesion. A greyish liquid exuded from the skin moistens the hair and falls in drops on the hoof and on the ground.

The skin is chronically inflamed and smeared with an offensive purulent discharge. When the disease is well developed vegetations due to hypertrophied papillæ are formed in clusters on the affected area and are known as "grapes." There may or may not be lameness. In cases of long standing the affected region and the greater portion of the limb become greatly thickened from the formation of subcutaneous fibrous tissue, constituting a form of elephantiasis.

PROGNOSIS.—Some cases when attended to early are cured in the course of a few weeks, but when the disease is well established it may be kept in check by suitable applications but cannot be cured. When treatment is discontinued the characteristic features of the condition return.

Exceptionally a similar disease is found affecting the two hind limbs or all the limbs of the ox.

TREATMENT comprises :

1. *Avoiding the conditions* mentioned as predisposing causes.

2. *Warm antiseptic baths* for recent cases, and the application of moist antiseptic compresses in the intervals between the baths.

3. *Astringent or slightly caustic applications* following the treatment in No. 2, *e.g.*, 5 *per cent. solution of a mixture of copper sulphate, lead acetate, and sulphate of zinc* which has proved an excellent preparation for curing or alleviating the disease, arresting the discharge and subduing the inflammatory symptoms. Turpentine applied in the form of a compress after cleaning the region has been recommended by some authors as highly effective. The compress is renewed daily for a while. Then the turpentine is applied without a dressing. Formaline has also been recommended.

Internal treatment consists in the administration alternately of arsenical and iodine preparations.

(*f*) **Contagious Acne,** a contagious non-pruritic purulent dermatitis of the horse characterised by a vesiculo-pustular eruption followed by the formation of crusts or scabs. It is caused by a bacillus. The disease is readily spread by harness, clothing, grooming tools, etc., contaminated with the pus from the lesions.

SYMPTOMS.—A few days after receipt of the infection the eruption appears, the papules and pustules varying in diameter from that of a pea to that of a sixpence. At the centre of the papules the hairs are erect in a tuft. Soon the pustule bursts, giving exit to white pus which afterwards dries into a crust surrounding the tuft of hair. When the crust is detached a pink circular wound covered by fine granulations remains and cicatrises rapidly.

The eruptions may appear in successive crops. If the pustules are irritated the inflammation may become accentuated with thickening of the skin and the formation of subcutaneous abscesses. The back. croup, and shoulder are the commonest sites of the lesions.

PROGNOSIS.—Cure usually supervenes in the course of four or five weeks.

The ox's skin may be infected by the same organism and show the disease in one of two forms, viz. (1) discreet lesions ; (2) confluent and generalised. In the former the pustules are scattered over the trunk, the head, and the upper parts of the limbs. In the latter small abscesses form as in furunculosis.

TREATMENT includes :

1. The usual prophylactic measures for a contagious disease.
2. Separation and destruction of the scabs or crusts.
3. The application of an antiseptic preparation. Painting tincture of iodine on the papules may cut short the progress of the disease by arresting the development of the bacillus.

(*g*) **Horse-Pox** or equine variola which affects chiefly the coronet and hollow of the pastern, but it may also appear on the buccal mucous membrane as contagious pustular stomatitis. It is a benign though very contagious affection which is followed by recovery after the eruption has passed through its various stages of development, but while present (on the limbs) it causes lameness and keeps the horse out of work. It seems to be identical with " heel bug " which is the source of much trouble when it appears in racing stables by interfering with the training of the horses.

TREATMENT consists in taking measures to prevent the spread of the disease to other horses, in dressing the lesions antiseptically, and protecting the affected region with a pad of cotton-wool and bandage after the application of an emollient preparation such as boro-vaseline. B.I.P.P., or acriflavine emulsion.

(*h*) **Cutaneous Ulcers.**—Ulcers may form on the skin from various causes, such as constant irritation or infection of a wounded surface, or a specific disease such as tuberculosis, ulcerative lymphangitis, glanders, or a malignant tumour.

Cutaneous ulcers in the dog and cat must always be considered suspicious of being tuberculous (see p. 61). Treatment is carried out on general principles according to the cause of the lesion.

A serpiginous dermatitis has been observed in certain parts of Western Europe affecting chiefly the cheeks of the horse during the summer and disappearing in the autumn. It appears in the form of "scalded" depilated spots or lines. Its cause is obscure. It has been attributed to bites of insects. It undergoes spontaneous cure, but may be treated with antiseptic anodyne applications such as one per cent solution of carbolic acid or chloral hydrate.

(*i*) **Chronic Purulent Dermatitis of the Dog** is observed almost exclusively in old dogs and characterised by the presence in one or more situations of small bluish-red enlargements, bare on their surface, which on bursting or being opened give exit to a sanguinolent purulent discharge and show no tendency to heal. They are sometimes numerous in the digital region simulating the ordinary digital abscesses or cysts.

TREATMENT.—The lesions may respond to opening and evacuation of the abscesses and application of tincture of iodine, but often they assume the nature of an ulcer or sinus requiring excision of the unhealthy surface or lining. When isolated, this method of treatment is practicable and may be followed by healing by first intention after suturing the wound. Alternatively the diseased tissue may be removed by the action of a caustic preparation, where the affected areas are too numerous for excision.

5. Elephantiasis

This term is applied to a fibrous hypertrophic dermatitis with sclerosis of the skin and subcutaneous connective tissue. It occurs in various situations and in the different species of animals, but is most common in the hind limb of the horse, especially below the hock where it is the result of repeated attacks of lymphangitis. Chronic œdema from any cause leads to it. The circumference and weight of the affected part of the limb may be enormously increased, up to 29 inches and 100 lbs. respectively. Between the attacks of sub-acute lymphangitis to which the patient is subject lameness is absent and the animal is able to work. Treatment to reduce the fibrous thickening is of no avail (see Affections of the Lymphatic System).

In the ox the name *elephantiasis* is given to a constitutional disease associated with (1) tumefaction of the skin of the dewlap, the lower part of the abdominal wall and of the limbs above the knee and hock, and (2) œdema of the muzzle and eyelids, (3) ulcers in the mouth and nose accompanied by a fœtid discharge of saliva. The affected skin may become dry and cracked and devoid of hair. Recent research by Besnoit and Robin have shown that the disease appears to be due to the sarcosporidium which was found in considerable numbers in the affected skin, but all attempts at the experimental transmission of the disease to cattle or other species of animals failed, as did all efforts at treatment.

Scleroderma is a condition peculiar to the pig, and recognised by a circumscribed or diffuse induration of the skin with atrophy of the adipose tissue. It is confined almost entirely to bad thriving, debilitated, thin animals kept under bad hygienic conditions, and may co-exist with chronic rheumatism. It is first noticed in the dorsal region whence it spreads gradually to the lateral and inferior aspects of the body. When extensive or generalised the condition leads to emaciation and cahexia, for which treatment is of no avail.

6. Acne. Folliculitis of Hair Follicles

This is a papulo-pustular eruption due to inflammation of the sebaceous glands and of the hair follicles, affecting all the domesticated animals, but chiefly the horse and dog, and brought about by invasion of the parts mentioned by staphylococci.

The lesion produced may be a simple pustule, or furunculosis—that is, a pustule with a necrotic centre.

In horses recently clipped several pustules may form on the skin beneath the harness. The cut rigid hairs transmit pressure to the hair bulbs, thus setting up inflammation which may be papular or pustular. In the upper part of the neck where the collar rests this condition is often observed and may be complicated by numerous necrotic pustules which render the part so painful that the horse strongly resents its being touched. The papular form of the lesion is characterised by the formation in the integument of nodules varying in size from a millet seed to a pea. When the pustular stage arrives they form little abscesses which discharge a greyish-white pus. They generally appear in clusters, having an area varying in size from a five shilling piece to the palm of the hand.

In the dog acne may be localised or diffuse and affects chiefly the large species with short coats which afford insufficient protection against pyogenic invasion. Its predilection sites are the regions rich in sebaceous glands (the nose, lips, back, sheath, hock, elbow). The constant use of a muzzle favours the occurrence of the lesions by excoriating the parts with which it is in contact. The pustules may be simple, or furuncular, *i.e.*, with a necrotic centre.

TREATMENT consists in removing the predisposing causes of the condition such as offending harness or muzzle, thoroughly washing the affected region with soap and water containing an antiseptic agent, then drying it and smearing it with an antiseptic ointment such as carbolised or boro-vaseline. In a chronic case in the horse with induration of the skin mercurial ointment is probably the best application.

In the dog the treatment is similar to that for the horse, but mercurial and carbolic preparations are avoided in the former for which an ointment made with salicylic acid and lanoline has proved effective after disinfecting the region. Necrotic pustules may require to be incised, to hasten the separation of the " core," and are then treated with tincture of iodine.

7. Furunculosis—Anthrax

These conditions are due also to invasion by the staphylococcus, the lesion produced being in the form of a carbuncle or furuncle, that is, a pustule with a necrotic core.

The term " anthrax " is applied to an agglomeration of these pustules on a piece of skin, associated with severe inflammation, and the formation of sinuses abutting on necrotic centres which soon separate, leaving granulating wounds.

There may be more or less severe constitutional disturbance.

TREATMENT is on the same lines as that advised for acne. Constitutional treatment is often necessary to improve the tone of the system, *e.g.*, the administration of alterative and tonic medicine and a liberal supply of nourishing food. The administration of yeast might give good results in the dog as in the human subject. In obstinate cases a course of penicillin treatment is indicated.

8. Sebaceous Cysts

These have been observed in the horse, chiefly in the false nostril and on the lips and sheath. They are generally of the nature of retention cysts resulting from the accumulation of the secretion of sebaceous glands. Exceptionally they are met with on the buccal mucous membrane where there are no sebaceous glands, and are then due to epidermic inclusions. The size of the cysts varies from that of a hazel nut to that of a tangerine orange. They are round, hemispherical, or somewhat flattened with a central depression, well circumscribed, and vary in consistency, being usually softish, but sometimes vaguely fluctuating, and occasionally of mixed consistency, soft in one part and hard in another.

The contents are composed of epidermic cells and fatty material varying in aspect according to the proportion of its various constituents. It is usually of a caseous or fatty nature, but may be honey-like. As the result of rubbing or traumatism they show evidence of inflammation.

TREATMENT.—The only effective treatment is removal of the lining of the cyst either by the action of a caustic application or preferably by dissecting out its lining, after which primary healing may ensue on suturing the wound.

9. Horny Growths

These have been met with fairly often in the ox and sheep and more rarely in other animals, appearing chiefly on the head but also on the back, flank, abdominal wall, and the limbs without any apparent cause. They vary in length and thickness in different cases and may be smooth or rough on the surface. In some instances they fall off in the course of a few months to be replaced by similar successors, whilst in others they remain permanently.

Another kind of horny formation is that caused by repeated irritation, as on the hygroma in front of the cow's knee.

In some varieties of birds, especially parrots, horny enlargements are occasionally seen about the head, on the trunk, on the limbs, and even on the buccal mucous membrane, due to tuberculosis.

TREATMENT.—The only effective treatment is radical extirpation. Cutting through the structure, even close to the skin, is followed by recurrence of the growth. The piece of skin involved must be removed.

Icthyosis.—This name has been given to a congenital condition affecting only the calf, and consists of a generalised hypertrophy of the epidermis, forming a sort of cover which conceals the hairs and resembles the skin of the crocodile. The affected subjects die within a few days after birth.

10. Tuberculosis

The cutaneous forms of tuberculosis recognised in the human subject comprise :

1. Tuberculous ulcers.
2. Verrucose lesions.
3. Lupus.
4. Scrofular gummæ and cold abscesses.

1. *Tuberculous ulcers* are fairly often met with in the ox, dog, and cat. They are usually a sequel to tuberculosis of a neighbouring lymphatic gland. Occurring on the neck they may be due to auto-infection from the lung through the lymphatic system.

2. The *verrucose or horny lesion* occurs in birds, chiefly parrots.

3. *Lupus* may be either in the form of ulcers or contracted tubercles.

4. The *scrofular* form appears as nodules which undergo caseation and result in the formation of chronic abscesses. These have been

FIG. 1.—TUBERCULOUS ULCER ON THE NECK OF A DOG.

seen in most of the domesticated animals, but chiefly in the dog. Once the disease is diagnosed destruction of the patient is advisable, or alternatively radical removal of the lesion, if practicable.

11. Swamp Cancer

This name has been given to an affection of the skin and subcutaneous connective tissue of the horse met with in marshy districts in the tropical regions of Australia. It is almost identical with the lesion described under the heading of "Leeches," or Bursattee. It appears in the form of confluent granulomata on the lower parts of the limbs and trunk. The disease is contracted by the animal standing in marshes to escape the attacks of flies. The nature of the condition is not known, but some authorities think it is a form of habronemosis.

12. Sporotrichosis

In different countries, but chiefly in South Africa and in Madagascar, a form of mycosis is seen affecting the skin, subcutaneous tissues and the lymphatics of the horse and dog, due to the *Spirotrichum equi*. General debility followed by emaciation and death may ensue, and diagnosis can only be arrived at by laboratory methods. Local antiseptic applications and the administration of novoarsenobenzol have a marked beneficial effect.

13. Bursattee, or " Leeches "

In India and America there is observed in the horse and mule and rarely in the ox a mycosis of the skin characterised by purulent nodules. It is believed to be due to a mycelium. In India it is known as Bursattee and in America as " Leeches." It is generally incurable.

14. Tumours

The skin is involved in all superficial tumours, but some that are confined thereto may be mentioned, including papillomata, dermoid cysts, sarcomata, epitheliomata, and osteomata.

Papillomata or warts or angleberries are referred to in the section on tumours. They are benign growths, but when numerous in the form of clusters, as is often the case in the horse and ox, and situated in regions exposed to injury, they bleed easily, become inflamed and secrete a purulent material which dries on their surface or putrefies, exhaling an offensive odour. In the region of the preputial orifice they may become infiltrated with urine, also causing an offensive odour. They grow more rapidly during the summer and when in groups may then be invaded by maggots. Situated in the axilla and groin they may interfere with and cause pain on movement, and when between the thighs may be ulcerated and painful from rubbing against the opposite limb.

Sometimes they are very widespread, affecting every part of the body except the lower parts of the limbs. The lips, cheeks, eyelids, and ears are common sites and all may be affected at once. Occurring in such large numbers in one animal they would appear to be the result of a diathesis for these growths. There is a good deal of evidence to the effect that there is a hereditary tendency to these tumours. According to the leaflet issued by the United States Department of Agriculture in 1931, warts on cattle are believed to be due to a filtrable virus. This was demonstrated by skin inoculations with wart material which reproduced warts. Infection may be conveyed by rubbing against contaminated posts or buildings.

It is generally admitted that they are contagious. It has often been noticed that secondary tumours formed on parts over which blood from the primary tumour had passed, and warts have appeared on the hands of the veterinary surgeon after operating on clusters of angleberries, and on the hands of the milker after handling teats affected with warts. These secondary warts take a few weeks to two or three months to develop.

There is a contagious form of papillomata affecting the buccal mucous membrane in the dog (see Affections of the Mouth). Like other tumours the etiology of papillomata has not been defined. Microbes found in them have not been proved to be the cause. In young animals, and less frequently in aged animals, warts may disappear spontaneously, but this result is exceptional and never occurs when the growths are large and numerous.

TREATMENT (see Tumours, p. 49). Dermoid cysts are dealt with in the same way as sebaceous cysts. They have similar contents mixed with fine hairs.

Cutaneous and Subcutaneous Sarcomata are occasionally met with. They may be diffused over the whole body and are usually associated with metastatic tumours in the viscera.

Adenomata are rare except in the dog, in which they usually appear in the peri-anal region.

Epitheliomata are fairly common in old dogs, affecting different regions of the skin, including the vicinity of the natural orifices. The lesion commences as a small hard swelling which afterwards gradually increases in size. Later its surface becomes ulcerated, and it persists as an indurated enlargement devoid of pain or slightly painful. There may be lymphangitis in the vicinity, and the neighbouring lymphatic glands may be enlarged.

The growth is malignant, and the best treatment for it is early and radical excision, and even this is not always successful.

Arsenical paste has been successfully employed for recent small circumscribed lesions.

Osteoma, or Ossification of the Skin and Hypodermis.—Some cases of this condition have been recorded as occurring in the horse, less frequently in the ox, and more rarely in other animals, in the form of plaques or small irregular masses of bone in different regions of the body (chest wall, hip, shoulder, fetlock). In the majority of cases they would appear to be the result of injury, *e.g.* by the pressure of harness. Some cases have been recorded in the sow (*Rec. Méd. vét.*, 1935).

Their significance depends on their size and situation. They can be successfully removed when of moderate dimensions.

15. Molluscum Contagiosum

Cutaneous Diphtheria, affecting birds and characterised by the formation on the comb and wattles of small yellowish-grey epithelial tumours varying in size from a millet seed up to a hazel nut, smooth and regular on the surface at first, but afterwards depressed and crusty. They may remain circumscribed or become diffuse, invading the feathered regions, leading in the latter case to emaciation and usually to death.

These lesions often co-exist with those of diphtheria, and immunity to the one affection gives immunity to the other. So that they appear to be a cutaneous form of diphtheria.

16. Parasitic Affections

The larvæ of the Sarcophagus and Lucilus live as parasites on wounds in animals and man. In tropical countries the larvæ of flies may be deposited on the umbilicus of young calves soon after birth, causing a septic inflammatory lesion which usually proves fatal. The use of odoriferous antiseptic solutions is sufficient to prevent or suppress this parasitic invasion.

The Ochromus Anthropophagus may deposit larvæ on the skin of the dog, cat, and goat which develop in the subcutaneous connective tissue. They cause small tumours which disappear rapidly after departure of the parasites, which can be hastened by incision of the swelling.

The subcutaneous connective tissue of the pigeon may harbour the larvæ of the *Hypodectes columbarum* which only cause slightly inflammatory spots.

The Hypoderma Bovis or warble fly deposits its eggs on the skin of bovines, and sometimes on that of the horse and ass, giving rise to the well known warble lesion. Government regulations are in force, compelling the application of dressings to prevent the development of the warble. Departmental leaflets are issued, directing how the regulations are to be carried out.

Filariasis of the Skin.—In the Far East horses are subject to a special affection characterised by the eruption of hæmorrhagic buds varying in size from a pea to a small nut. During the hot season they appear on different parts of the skin, especially on the withers, neck, back, and sides. Fairly tense, painless, and slightly œdematous at their periphery they soon burst and give exit to blood, which agglutinates the hair at their level or forms little streaks of blood in their vicinity. They are caused by the *Filaria multipapillosa* or *hæmorrhagica* which invades the subcutaneous connective tissue. The affection disappears during the cold weather and reappears in the following summer during a period of several years with a gradually diminishing number of lesions as the years pass. Anæmia and perhaps death may supervene when the skin is grossly infested.

The ruptured nodules soon cicatrise as a rule, but sometimes suppuration ensues. Affected horses may remain unworkable for several months. The condition has also been seen in France, Spain, and Italy, not only during hot weather, but also during cool, and less frequently during winter weather.

TREATMENT consists in applying antiseptic topics to the lesions. It might be possible to recognise the filaria after rupture of the "button" and remove it with a forceps. After the parasite has perforated the skin it returns to the connective tissue.

Lesions caused by the larvæ of the *Habronema muscæ* have been considered under "Granulation Wounds" (p. 35).

The embryos of nematodes still undetermined may cause cutaneous lesions simulating urticaria or chronic eczema.

The Filaria Medinensis lives as a parasite on man and sometimes also on the horse, ox, and dog in tropical countries, including South America. Its presence is recognised when it appears under the skin, in various situations, giving rise to the condition known as dracontiasis. The lesion is first an indolent swelling, which afterwards becomes painful and forms an abscess. After evacuation of the pus the worm may be found coiled up in the depth of the wound. On its removal rapid cicatrisation ensues. Prevention consists in filtering or boiling the drinking water.

The Onchocerca Reticulata, or Spiroptera, or Filaria Recticulata.—This parasite invades the subcutis of the horse, ass and dog, giving rise to fibrous nodules situated most frequently on the fore-limbs at the level of the cannon bone and of the knee—they may cause nervous compression and thus give rise to lameness. The parasites may invade the lymphatic vessels, the perivascular tissues, and the articular synovial capsules and the tendon sheaths of the lower parts of the limbs. The only effective treatment is removal of the fibrous enlargements.

In Australian cattle there are found in different regions of the body, but chiefly about the breast and flanks, oval nodules, from a pea to a nut in size, caused by the *Onchocerca gibsoni*.

The filariæ perish a few hours after the death of their host. Infestation may be by the digestive tract or through insect bites. This parasite is the cause of "dropped neck" in Australia (see Affections of the Withers).

Hydatid Cysts.—Echinococcus cysts have been found in the subcutaneous connective tissue in the horse. They sometimes become purulent. The *Cystericus cellulosæ* has been seen in the subcutis in the dog in multiple cysts distributed over the neck, shoulders, chest wall, and back, but none on the limbs. The only effective treatment is complete excision of the cysts.

Coccidiosis.—Coccidia sometimes invade the sweat glands of the pig, causing the formation of cysts of a greyish white to a brown colour about the neck, shoulders, and thighs, for which there is no effective treatment.

Psorospermosis.—Psorosperms sometimes invade the subcutaneous connective tissue in the ox, sheep, goat, and pig, without causing any serious lesion and are thus of no surgical importance.

Sarcosporiodosis.—Sarcosporiodosis has been studied in France by Besnoit and Robin, and is confined to bovines. It gives rise to anasarca and elephantiasis. Its evolution appears in two stages, viz. (1) *Period of invasion*, characterised by fever, œdema of the dependent parts of the body, and petechiæ on the mucous membranes; (2) *Stage of elephantiasis* recognised by a squamous and ridged or folded condition of the skin, and more or less extensive alopecia, the lesions appearing on the dorso-lumbar region, the thighs and head and neck. On the limbs especially, the thickened skin is often bossellated or covered with vegetations resembling those of grease. Microscopic examination of a section of the dermis reveals the presence of numbers of the parasites, round or somewhat oval in shape.

Treatment has proved of no avail.

Mange.—The various forms of mange in the domesticated animals are associated with more or less dermatitis due to the irritation caused by the parasites, accentuated in many cases by rubbing, biting, or scratching the affected parts. Diagnosis is confirmed by isolating the offending mite, and preventive and curative treatment are carried out on the well-known lines adopted for these parasitic affections.

II.—AFFECTIONS OF BURSÆ

There are two varieties of bursæ—viz.:

1. Superficial, atypical, or acquired bursæ situated between the skin and bony prominences. These may be acquired after birth—for example, at the level of exostoses.

2. Deep or typical bursæ situated between tendon and bone, or between tendon and tendon, and always present at birth.

Sometimes the term "bursa" is used in a wide sense, being applied to all synovial sacs, so that the expression "bursal enlargement" may mean a distended bursa, synovial sheath, or joint capsule.

Contusions and Open Wounds of Bursæ do not require special description. When a bursa is opened a sort of synovial liquid escapes, which does not interfere with the healing of the wound.

Acute Bursitis

Etiology comprises contusions, open wounds, infection, and the action of toxins of bacterial diseases, such as rheumatism, influenza, and strangles.

Varieties include (1) dry bursitis; (2) serous bursitis; (3) purulent bursitis. The dry form is transitory. It is soon followed by the serous or purulent form.

Symptoms.—The symptoms are those of acute inflammation combined with distension of the bursa. The swelling is spoken of as an acute hygroma. When pus is present in the sac the condition is virtually an abscess. There is a possibility of the infection spreading to a neighbouring sheath or joint.

Treatment.—The treatment is that for acute inflammation or an abscess, as the case may be. If due to a bacterial disease, the latter requires attention. If rheumatoid, salicylate of soda is indicated.

Chronic Bursitis or Chronic Hygroma

Chronic bursitis may succeed to the acute form, or develop independently as the result of repeated slight irritation. Varieties include cystic, proliferating, fibrous, and hæmorrhagic forms of the condition.

1. **Cystic Form.**—This is the commonest variety. It may be simple or bi- or multi-locular. It contains a variable quantity of a viscid opalescent fluid. Its wall is fibrous, but in cases of long standing it may contain cartilaginous or calcareous material.

2. **Proliferating Form.**—The interior of the sac carries pedunculated or sessile vegetations, which may be infiltrated with cartilaginous or calcareous material.

3. **The Fibrous Form** is practically a fibroma containing a small quantity of fluid in its centre.

4. **The Hæmorrhagic Form** is characterised by the presence of extravasated blood in the bursa, evidently the result of a trauma.

Common examples of the foregoing conditions are "capped elbow," "capped knee," and "capped hock."

SYMPTOMS.—The symptoms are distension or enlargement of a bursa to constitute one of the forms mentioned. In a case that has been long in existence and in which the skin has been subjected to repeated injury, the surface of the latter may be covered with horn or warty-like growths (cow's knee).

The condition may become acute as the result of more severe injury and may suppurate owing to the entrance of infection through some breach of surface. Frequently the lesion does not interfere with function, but merely constitutes an unsightly blemish, which is often difficult to remove.

TREATMENT comprises the following measures :

1. *Removal of the cause.* Suppress, if possible, the irritation which has given rise to the condition. Otherwise other measures will be fruitless.

2. *Cold and astringent applications*, which may be useful when the condition is quite recent.

3. *The application of an absorbent topic or counter-irritant*, which may have a good effect in a comparatively recent case—*e.g.*, tincture of iodine, iodine ointment, biniodide of mercury blister, or Payran's preparation—viz. : hydrarg. biniod., 1 part ; crystalline carbolic acid, 50 parts ; alcohol at 90°, 250 parts, painted on for four consecutive days. This is said to be very efficacious, causing gradual subsidence of the swelling. If not completely cured in four or five weeks, the application is repeated. "Reducine," a proprietary preparation containing Archangel tar, iodine, and potassium iodide, applied every day with a brush until desquamation occurs, often has a good effect.

4. *Needle-point firing*, which may be successful for a chronic bursal enlargement, causing it to reduce greatly in size or disappear altogether.

5. *Aspiration of the contents and the injection of an irritant.* The fluid is removed by a fine trocar and canula, or an aspirating syringe,

and a solution of iodine (tincture) or carbolic acid, 3 to 5 per cent., or perchloride of mercury, 1 in 1,000, is injected (see Chronic Synovitis, p. 83). Compression afterwards with a pad and bandage, where possible, aids this treatment. This procedure is not always quick in its results. It may be associated with No. 4, and the combined measures will be found to be better than either alone. It is worth trying when incision is objectionable—for example, on the point of the hock or in front of the knee in the horse, or on the elbow in the dog. The irritant injection causes inflammation in the bursa, which is followed by granulation, cicatrisation, and obliteration of the cavity.

6. *The passage of a seton* through the bursa from above to below is a very simple and efficacious method of treating bursal enlargements in cattle where scar blemishes are of no consequence. It causes suppurative inflammation, granulation, and cicatrisation of the cavity.

7. *Incision of the bursa* at a dependent part to evacuate its contents, followed by the application of an irritant to its interior, is the best method of treatment for chronic cystic enlargements. It is followed at once by inflammation and cicatrisation. When riziform bodies are free in the bursa, this is the only way of removing them.

The application of biniodide of mercury ointment to the interior and exterior of the cyst after opening it hastens the healing process. If there are vegetations on the lining of the cavity, it should be dissected off.

8. *Excision of the fibrous cyst.* When the enlarged bursa is composed mostly of fibrous tissue, fairly circumscribed, and situated where the formation of a wound and scar is of no great consequence, it may be dissected out and removed as if it were a fibroma. When pedunculated, or even when more or less sessile, it may be removed by means of ligation (capped elbow).

III.—AFFECTIONS OF MUSCLES

Contusions and Open Wounds of Muscles

These are dealt with on general principles.

Ruptures of Muscles

Rupture of muscle is not so common as that of tendon, and sometimes the rupture of a muscle occurs partly in its tendinous and partly in its muscular tissue. Rupture of a muscle may result from excessive contraction thereof, or during its relaxation, in consequence of violent contraction of its antagonist. Want of co-ordination of movement in opposing muscles may lead to rupture of muscular fibres. Fœtal muscles may be ruptured from violent traction during dystokia; slipping, falling, and struggling when cast may be the cause of muscular rupture in adults.

The rupture may be complete or partial. Flat muscles devoid of an aponeurosis give way in their superficial fibres first, and long round muscles with a strong aponeurotic sheath in their central fibres.

SYMPTOMS.—The local symptoms are those of inflammation, associated perhaps with those of a hæmatoma. There is functional disturbance, varying according to the seat of the injury and its gravity. Occurring in the muscles of the limbs, there is severe lameness. Diagnosis of the actual rupture may be difficult.

PROGNOSIS.—Slight ruptures soon heal, and then the inflammatory symptoms and functional disturbance disappear. Extensive rupture of more than one important muscle is incurable. Healing of a muscular wound takes place through the agency of fibrous tissue, and when much of this is formed the muscle is deprived of a good deal of its power.

TREATMENT is chiefly expectant, consisting in resting the patient and applying the usual remedies for traumatic inflammation.

Myositis

ETIOLOGY.—The origin of inflammation of muscle may be (1) *traumatic*, such as an open wound or a contusion; or (2) *infectious*, occurring during the course of some bacterial disease like strangles or influenza; or (3) violent effort causing excessive muscular contraction with rupture of muscular fibres, as may occur from struggling in hobbles.

SYMPTOMS.—The symptoms vary according to the nature of the myositis. Locally they are those of acute inflammation. There is also interference with muscular function, causing stiffness or lameness. In the infectious form of the condition there are symptoms of febrile reaction. Even when of mechanical origin there may be evidence of fever in cases where the lesion is extensive and the pain severe. Chronic myositis may follow the acute form or occur as a primary affection due to the presence of parasites in muscle such as hydatid cysts, psorosperms, actinomyces, botriomyces, or to a foreign body in the tissues, or to some obscure cause. It has often been observed in horse abattoirs localised in certain muscles or more or less generalised.

A progressive ossifying, more or less generalised, chronic myositis has been rarely met with.

TREATMENT comprises: (1) Rest of the patient; (2) giving the usual hospital diet, consisting of soft laxative food; (3) the administration of laxative and diuretic alkaline medicine (soda bicarbonate, magnesium or sodium sulphate, potassium nitrate); (4) the application locally of antiphlogistic remedies, followed later by massage and compression when possible; and (5) the rubbing in of a counter-irritant; or (6) the use of the faradic current to counteract muscular atrophy. Treatment for the chronic form of the disease has no curative effect. It includes counter-irritation and the administration of potassium iodide.

In addition to the above forms of myositis there is the myositis of fatigue affecting the muscles of locomotion, and due to long, tiring journeys or heavy work. The patient shows severe lameness, and the affected muscles are the seat of intense pain and very sensitive on palpation. The symptoms generally disappear after the animal has been rested for a while. The treatment is the same as for the other forms of myositis.

Muscular rheumatism is a specific form of myositis, or perhaps mere myalgia. It is favoured by long exposure to cold and wet, *e.g.*, confinement in damp stables, kennels, or sheds. In the horse it is more likely to ensue when sweating after work. In sporting dogs prolonged work in marshy country may bring it about. It is characterised by pain in the affected muscles and consequent lameness when those of a limb or limbs are involved. Distinguishing features of this disease are: (1) its sudden onset; (2) its fugitive nature, passing from one limb or one part of the body to another, or disappearing altogether for a while and then returning suddenly; (3) febrile disturbance, when several muscles are affected and the case is acute. It may be acute, subacute, or chronic. The chronic form may persist for weeks or months, and then be followed by recovery, or it may continue indefinitely resisting all therapeutic measures. In cattle it is usually of a chronic nature and most commonly affects the shoulder, the dorso-lumbar region, and the limbs, but it is sometimes diffuse or generalised. In the latter case movement of the head and neck and of the limbs causes great pain, the animal standing motionless and reluctant to move. Sheep sometimes suffer from the disease, especially lambs, in which it is characterised by symptoms of lumbago. When several groups of muscles are involved there is general stiffness of the body and limbs; the patient remains lying, or, if standing, avoids movement. In the pig similar symptoms are shown.

In the dog the condition may be more or less generalised, but is more frequently localised in the muscles of the neck, back, loins, or abdomen, and is revealed by symptoms which are much more expressive than in other animals. The affected muscles are hard, tense, and extremely sensitive to pressure, which causes the animal to scream. Functional disturbance according to the muscles affected may be observed—for example, stiffness of the body, extension of the head and neck, interference with mastication and deglutition, great difficulty in rising and moving, constipation and retention of urine on account of the pain caused by defæcation and micturition.

Treatment is as follows:

1. Protect the patient from cold and dampness, and administer a purgative.
2. Rub in a liniment over the affected muscles.
3. Apply an anodyne poultice, such as antiphlogistine, or warm fomentations when the pain is very acute.
4. Administer salicylate of sodium, or quinine, or salol, or potassium iodide, or antifebrine, or colchicum, any one of which, though not a specific, may have some good effect. Salicylate of sodium is probably the most efficacious, but its good effects are not so marked here as in articular rheumatism.
5. Give a hypodermic injection of morphia and atropine in the region of the affected muscles in doses of 4 grs. and $\frac{3}{4}$ gr. respectively in the horse. This has a local sedative effect, but may give rise to general disturbance, excitement, accelerated pulse and respirations, and sweating, which last for twelve to twenty-four hours. Its curative action is often produced after two or three days, or a week at the most. It may be repeated if necessary.

Hæmoglobinuria gives rise to a polymyositis which need only be mentioned here as being generally followed by marked atrophy of the affected muscles.

Muscular Atrophy

Muscular atrophy, as met with in veterinary practice, is usually due either to inactivity of the muscles affected or to their paralysis from [illegible] nerve supply, but it also follows myositis, whether of traumatic or specific origin.

The development of fibrous tissue in muscle following myositis crushes out of existence the muscular fibres in its vicinity, and thus leads to permanent atrophy, as occurs in actinomycosis of the tongue.

Atrophy of muscles is easily recognised. Individual cases of it will be dealt with later.

TREATMENT consists in ascertaining the cause of the condition, and removing it if possible, and adopting some of the following measures when practicable.

1. Massage of the affected region.
2. The application of a counter-irritant—a liniment or blister.
3. Using electrotherapy.
4. Exercising the affected muscles.

Paralysis of Muscles

This will be considered along with affections of nerves.

Spasm of Muscles (Cramp)

Muscular spasm is of two kinds—viz.:

1. Tonic or continuous spasm.
2. Clonic or intermittent spasm.

1. **Tonic Spasm** is exemplified by tetanus.
2. **Clonic Spasm** occurs in chorea and strychnine poisoning.

Tonic spasm of certain muscles is sometimes seen in the horse after severe and prolonged exertion, and is apparently due to reflex action caused by irritation of the nerve terminals in the muscles by the presence there of the effete products of tissue change. It may be seen after a long day with hounds or after a hard day's ploughing, the condition appearing the next morning.

SYMPTOMS.—The muscles affected are bulging and rigid, and the seat of acute pain. The gluteal muscles and those of the thigh are most frequently affected. The limb may be rigid and held in an abnormal position. It may be directed backwards, as in a case of pseudo-luxation of the patella.

TREATMENT consists in—

1. Administering laxative medicine.
2. Applying cold douches and massage, with or without a liniment, to the affected muscles.

The condition soon passes off.

Cramp in Racing Greyhounds

An excellent paper with this title, by Hamilton Kirk, along with an exhaustive discussion thereon was published in the *Veterinary Record*, October 17, 1942, and on it the following remarks are based.

Since the introduction of greyhound racing " Cramp " has beco a common condition in competing dogs. It is mainly sporadic occurrence, but at times it appears to be almost epizootic. The affect dog tails off in the race and in bad cases collapses and has to be carri off the track. Its appearance gives rise to wild allegations of the anim having been interfered with or doped, strychnine being usually th drug suspected, but veterinary surgeons of long experience as official at racing stadiums are agreed that in the majority of cases such inter ference or doping cannot be blamed ; yet they are at a loss to give convincing explanation of the trouble. In mild cases the dog slows down, showing weakness in the hind limbs, which he drags with the front of the digits in contact with the ground. On examination the muscles of the loins and hindquarters are hard, like a board. The dog is distressed and cyanotic, but after rest and massage for 10 to 15 minutes recovers completely. In severe cases the dog falls, struggles, and rolls over, but does not appear in pain, as he does not cry as a rule. The hind limbs are in a state of chronic rigidity and are fully extended.

The ætiology of cramp was discussed under the following headings :

1. Fatigue.
2. Defective heart action.
3. Muscle toxins.
4. Chemical agents.
5. Sodium chloride deficiency.
6. Dehydration.
7. Occupational cramp.
8. Myotania.
9. Exposure to cold.
10. Malpractices.

Although the discussion was very interesting and instructive and many of the theories put forward as to ætiology were plausible, no definite conclusion was arrived at.

There was a general consenus of opinion that skilful training of dogs in its various aspects and their judicious handling on the day of the race had a good deal to do with warding off an attack.

Keeping the animals waiting unduly in kennels or exposed to cold winds, or subjecting nervous dogs to excitement before a race seemed to favour cramp occurring on the track. It is obvious that research is essential to throw more light on the matter.

Tumours of Muscles

Most of the ordinary tumours affect muscles, but one requiring special mention is osteoma, which is occasionally seen in muscular tissue. The cause of it is not always apparent, but it is generally believed to be the result of an injury. The author has seen one in the form of a cyst with a bony wall on the near side of the neck of a thoroughbred yearling. It commenced as a swelling about the size of a hazel nut, and gradually assumed the dimensions of a large fist. It extended into the muscles of the neck in the affected part. It was successfully dissected out. Excision is always indicated.

IV.—AFFECTIONS OF TENDONS

Contusions

Tendons, like other tissues, may be affected with contusions. Probably the flexors of the digit are most frequently involved, the injury being caused by overreaching or interfering in the fore-limbs and by kicking in the hind-limbs. The symptoms are those of contusions in general, except that owing to the feeble vascularity of the structures the symptoms of a hæmatoma are not observed. Treatment is as usual (see p. 37).

Open Wounds of Tendons

The tendons of the muscles of the limbs are often wounded. *Punctured wounds* of the flexor tendons are commonly caused by picked-up nails perforating the plantar aponeurosis, by forks, and by other pointed bodies.

The PROGNOSIS of these punctures must be guarded, their gravity depending on whether infection has reached the wounded tissue. In the latter case serious complications may ensue, characterised by severe purulent inflammation and necrosis of the tendon, which prevents healing until the necrotic tissue is removed. If infection does not ensue, healing is rapid. When one of the large flexor tendon sheaths is involved and becomes affected with purulent synovitis the case is very serious (see p. 80).

TREATMENT is as usual for septic wounds.

Incised or *lacerated* or *contused wounds* of the flexor tendons may be caused in a variety of ways—by the blade of a scythe or of a mowing machine, by barbed wire, or by the shoe when a horse jumps into himself. One or both tendons may be partially or completely divided transversely, and even the suspensory ligament may be severed as well. A tendon may be only partly cut through by the accident, and give way completely afterwards from weight being borne on the limb, or as the result of necrosis of the undivided fibres.

Deformity of the limb supervenes, varying according to the structure involved. If the perforans be completely divided, the toe of the foot will be more or less turned up and the heels will be resting on the ground. If the perforatus or suspensory be severed there will be descent of the fetlock behind, but the corono-pedal joint will not be affected. These characteristic features, however, are not always observed, because the inflammation and consequent pain are so great that the animal does not attempt to put weight on the limb, and when made to move goes on three legs.

When complete section of a tendon occurs, the two ends become more or less widely separated. The upper one, by virtue of muscular contraction, ascends into its sheath, while the position of the lower one is affected by the movement of the joints over which it passes. The intervening space is filled by extravasated blood. If severe infection does not supervene, cicatrisation will take place between the divided ends. The tendinous cells will proliferate and form new tendinous tissue, which, although not as strong as the original tissue, will enable the animal to do useful work again, and in some cases even to win races. It requires a period of two to three months after the accident before the cicatrix is sufficiently strong to permit of work.

Prognosis.—The prognosis depends on the nature of the injury, and whether dangerous infection has got into the wound. Division of an extensor tendon is much less serious than that of a flexor tendon, the former being much more slender and less important. Healing in it usually occurs without trouble, even when there has been loss of tissue, and no functional disability persists.

When two or more of the structures at the back of the cannon bone are severed, the case is more serious than when only one is involved. In the former case perfect recovery is seldom obtained. Necrosis of the wounded structures and purulent synovitis are always to be feared, and when they ensue cure is almost out of the question.

Treatment is summed up in the words "careful antisepsis of the wound in the tendon," associated with measures for keeping the ends of the tendon in as close juxtaposition as possible. Suturing the ends of the tendons is seldom practicable or necessary in the large animals, but it can be readily performed in dogs and other small animals.

When the ends of the severed tendon are close together so that there will be no tension on the threads, ordinary interrupted sutures are suitable, but when some force is required to bring the ends into apposition one of the following recognised methods adopted in human surgery may be employed, silk being the material that is generally used, as catgut might not be able to withstand the strain.

1. Pass the thread obliquely through each end of the tendon, and tie the two ends laterally (Fig. 2 (1)).

2. Pass the needle through the upper end of the tendon near its border from behind forwards, and then close to the opposite border from before backwards. Do the same on the inferior end, but in this case pass the threads successively from behind forwards and then tie them (Fig. 2 (2)).

3. Make two sutures—viz., (1) an affronting suture close to the cut ends; and (2) a suture of support farther away (Fig. 2 (3)).

4. Pass the thread twice through the upper end of the tendon, then bring it back through the inferior end and tie the thread laterally (Fig. 2 (4)).

Afterwards the skin is sutured and provision made for drainage if necessary. Suture of the tendo Achillis has been performed successfully in the dog (Hobday, etc.).

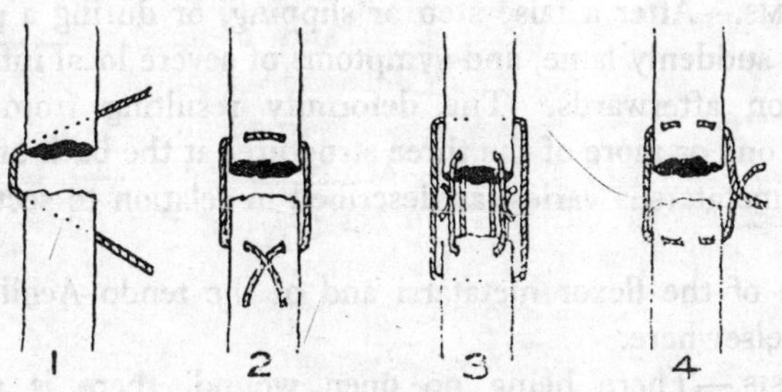

FIG. 2. SUTURE OF TENDONS.

Successful treatment of severed flexor tendons in the horse has been frequently carried out. The constant or repeated application of Dakin's fluid has been found to be reliable in preventing infection of the wound.

To keep the ends as close together as possible in a case of complete section of the flexor tendons, the fetlock must be supported by a projection upwards from the heels of the shoe in the form of a swan's neck, the convexity of the latter being padded and in contact with the fetlock. Slings are indicated if the horse will tolerate them.

Rupture of Tendons

Rupture of tendons occurs chiefly in the lower parts of the limbs, affecting chiefly the flexors of the digit and the suspensory ligament, which may be included with the tendons under this heading. The flexor metatarsi muscle is occasionally ruptured in its tendinous portion.

Predisposing Causes comprise:

1. Natural weakness of the tendon.
2. Weakening of the tendon by some debilitating disease.
3. Working a horse in unfit condition.
4. A tiring race, the rupture occurring towards the end of the race when the muscles are exhausted, and consequently excessive strain is thrown on the tendons.

The exciting cause of flexor rupture is violent over-extension of the fetlock and interphalangeal joints. The seat of rupture varies; it may occur about the centre of the tendon or at its insertion. In the latter case a piece of bone may be torn away with the tendon. The suspensory ligament may be ruptured at its bifurcation or in one of its branches, usually the inner one, or at its point of insertion.

Symptoms.—After a false step or slipping, or during a gallop, the horse goes suddenly lame, and symptoms of severe local inflammation appear soon afterwards. The deformity resulting from complete rupture of one or more of the three structures at the back of the metacarpus or metatarsus varies, as described in relation to section of the tendons.

Rupture of the flexor metatarsi and of the tendo Achillis will be dealt with elsewhere.

Prognosis.—There being no open wound, there is no danger from infection. In all cases union will occur between the ruptured ends by the formation of cicatricial tissue from the connective tissue corpuscles and tendinous cells in the part. Extensor tendons are soon completely repaired in this way, but the healing of ruptured flexor tendons is often imperfect and requires months for its completion. When the gap between the ends is large, great thickening results. If both flexors have been severed, permanent deformity will ensue, the fetlock will be lowered, and the pastern will be very oblique, notwithstanding that cicatricial contraction occurs. When only one of the structures has given way, a fairly good recovery may ensue, rendering the horse fit for light work and occasionally for racing. Rupture of one branch of the suspensory ligament heals well, leaving a thickening which does not cause lameness.

Treatment consists in—

1. Keeping the ends of the ruptured tendon as close together as possible, as indicated already.
2. The application of a supporting pitch or plaster bandage.
3. Keeping the patient at rest, slings being usually indicated to take some of the weight off the limbs, and obviate attempts at lying and rising.

In small animals the ends of the tendon may be exposed aseptically and sutured, with good prospect of success, but perfect healing may ensue without suturing. Suturing would be difficult to carry out in the large animals, and the risk of sepsis supervening is too great to justify its being attempted.

Tendinitis, Tenositis, Inflammation of Tendons

Inflammation of tendons arises from the usual causes, and is dealt with accordingly. The worst form of tendinitis is that resulting from infection, because it is frequently complicated with necrosis of the tendon, involving more or less of its thickness, predisposing it to rupture, and causing constant purulent discharge until the necrotic portion is removed.

Spontaneous separation of the dead tissue seldom occurs, owing to the feeble vascularity of the structure. The infection is likely to spread to one of the large synovial sheaths when a flexor tendon is involved. As a rule, when necrosis affects one of the flexors the case is hopeless.

Treatment in this case is that for a septic wound. Tendinitis resulting from strain or over-distension of a tendon is most commonly met with in connection with the flexor tendons, and will be considered when describing affections of the limbs. This applies also to parasitic tendinitis.

V.—AFFECTIONS OF SYNOVIAL SHEATHS

The gliding of tendons in the limbs is facilitated by the presence of bursæ beneath them, or by synovial sheaths, thecæ, or vaginæ, which completely surround them in certain parts. The sheaths of the flexor tendons are much larger and more extensive than those of the extensors. Consequently affections of the latter are much more serious than those of the former.

Contusions

Contusions of synovial sheaths result from the usual causes, and give rise to traumatic synovitis.

Open Wounds

Open wounds of synovial sheaths are caused in various ways : by violent contact with sharp bodies, by falls, and by punctures with pointed objects. such as forks, nails, and barbed wire.

Symptoms.—The symptoms are those of an open wound discharging synovia, which is recognised by its oily nature and straw-yellow colour. After exposure to the air for a while it forms a yellow coagulum in the wound resembling a pad of fat.

Diagnosis.—When the synovial discharge occurs in the region of a joint it is difficult at first to say whether it is from the synovial sac of the latter or from the tendon sheath at the same level. Probing might help the diagnosis, but is contra-indicated on account of the risk of introducing infection by so doing, even when a sterilised instrument is used, for it might push septic material from the outer part of the wound into its depth.

Treatment.—Generally speaking, the treatment is the same as for ordinary open wounds, and has for its chief object the prevention of infection of the sheath. When infection is excluded, healing of the wound is uninterrupted. The same measures are required as for open joint (*vide* Open Joint).

Purulent Synovitis

Purulent synovitis is the result of an open wound of the sheath and its consequent infection, or it may be due to extension of infection from a lesion in its vicinity.

Symptoms.—The symptoms are those of intense, acute, septic inflammation, and of a synovial fistula discharging clotted and liquid synovia mixed with pus, and usually exhaling a fœtid odour. The sheath is tensely distended, causing a prominent swelling in the region. The local pain is very acute, and in the case of a limb being involved there is extreme lameness, the animal refusing to put any weight on the foot. There is more or less marked traumatic fever.

Diagnosis.—Occurring in the vicinity of a joint, there may be doubt as to whether the latter is the seat of the lesion. However, in a joint the inflammation is all round the articulation, whereas in a sheath it is confined to the limits of the latter. Moreover, the inflammation, lameness, and general disturbance are more marked in articular than in vaginal synovitis.

Prognosis.—Purulent synovitis affecting the great sesamoidean, carpal, or tarsal sheath is a grave condition, because it is very difficult to overcome the infection, which is apt to spread to the tendon, causing necrosis and rendering the case hopeless. It is different with the extensor sheaths, in which the infection can be controlled, owing to their comparatively small area and the slender tendons which pass through them.

In the large flexor sheaths the infection may, in exceptional cases be confined to a portion of the sheath, which is partitioned off from the remainder by adhesions. In this case recovery is likely to ensue. Even when recovery from purulent inflammation in a large sheath supervenes, adhesions may persist between the tendon and sheath, preventing the gliding of the former and causing permanent stiffness.

TREATMENT is on the usual lines for septic lesions. It consists in providing for drainage of the septic contents of the sheath and the introduction of antiseptic or other agents therein to destroy or prevent the multiplication of the causal organisms (see Synoviotomy p. 85).

Drainage is effected by a counter-opening at the lower part of the sheath.

Antiseptic and other agents.—Before the injection of an antiseptic liquid it is advisable to irrigate the sheath with warm boiled water, and to continue the irrigation until the water comes out clear. This mechanically removes most of the septic contents. The antiseptic liquid is then injected. Hydrogen peroxide, pure or diluted, 1 in 4, is an excellent detergent. Its antiseptic effect is not prolonged. Its use should be followed by injection of one of the following preparations :

1. Perchloride of mercury and glycerine, 1 in 1,000.
2. Carbolic acid and glycerine, 3 per cent.
3. A solution of hypochlorous acid.
4. Dakin's solution.
5. Pure or methylated ether.
6. Lacto or other serum (see p. 30).
7. Penicillin solution.

No. 1 is particularly efficacious. The affinity of glycerine for water makes the preparation penetrate into the remotest parts of the sheath ; penicillin, however, is the only drug likely to prove specific for the condition if due to a gram staining organism. It should also be given intramuscularly and repeated at three-hourly intervals, unless a preparation of it which retards its excretion from the blood is used when 24-hourly intervals may be sufficient between its administrations. The injection into the sheath must be repeated three or four times a day.

For the great and small sesamoidean sheaths immersion of the lower part of the limb in an antiseptic foot-bath (1 in 1,000 perchloride of mercury) for the greater part of the day is an excellent method of disinfecting the lesion. No. 5 is described by Cosgrave (Kildare) as having succeeded in a case where lacto serum had failed.

Bier's hyperæmic treatment is always indicated in addition to the other measures. Its efficacy is undoubted. It intensifies nature's method of counteracting infection by increasing leucocytosis and the production of antibodies in the affected part.

When suppuration has ceased, attention must be directed to preventing anchylosis of the tendon in its sheath by massage and regular exercise. When much thickening supervenes, line or needle-point firing may be practised with a view to diminishing it and improving the freedom of movement. It may have some good effect.

Closed Acute Synovitis

Acute synovitis, apart from that resulting from an open wound and infection, is usually associated with tendinitis, and is caused by strain or contusion of the sheath or tendon, or of both.

Varieties of Synovitis.—These comprise :

1. *Dry synovitis.* The serous membrane is congested and deprived of its endothelium, causing a crepitation when the tendon moves in the sheath.

2. *Plastic synovitis*, characterised by fibrinous deposits in the sheath, uniting it to the tendon.

3. *Serous synovitis*, the commonest variety, recognised by an increased formation of synovia, causing more or less distension of the sheath.

SYMPTOMS.—The symptoms are those of acute inflammation in the region of the sheath, associated with distension of the latter, in the serous form of the condition. Lameness is always well marked.

TREATMENT consists in applying the measures recommended for acute inflammation. They comprise : (1) rest ; (2) cold and astringent applications ; (3) hot fomentations or hot compresses ; (4) massage and compression. The inflammation usually subsides gradually, but the distension of the sheath does not always entirely disappear. The treatment required then is that for chronic synovitis or hygromata of synovial sheaths.

Infectious Synovitis

Infectious synovitis occurs during the course of infectious diseases, such as influenza, strangles, pneumonia, rheumatism, and is evidently caused by the toxins of the bacteria. Several sheaths may be affected at once, as well as the synovial capsules of joints.

SYMPTOMS.—The local symptoms are the same as those described in the last section. The animal is very lame, and may lie down more than usual.

TREATMENT is as usual, being directed as far as possible against the causal organism. The trial of a sulphonamide preparation is indicated as well as large doses of sodium salicylate. In some cases this form of synovitis appears as a sequel to an infectious disease after the general symptoms of the latter have disappeared. It is of a rheumatoid nature, disappearing for a while and then returning, or, after being cured in one sheath, attacking another one.

Salicylate of sodium in large doses combined with sodium bicarbonate and warm antiphlogistic applications locally constitute the best form of treatment. The hypodermic or intravenous injection of an appropriate or polyvalent antiserum is indicated.

Chronic Synovitis and Dropsy of Synovial Sheaths

Chronic synovitis or distension of synovial sheaths may be a sequel to acute synovitis, or occur independently without any apparent cause, or as the result of constant hard work. Distension of several sheaths may occur in young horses that have never worked, appearing as a dropsical condition. This is more common in coarse than in well-bred horses.

SYMPTOMS.—Distension of the sheath or sheaths may be the only symptom present. When the condition is of a chronic inflammatory nature, some abnormal heat and evidence of pain may be manifested locally, and lameness may be present when an important sheath is involved. The sheath may contain, in addition to an increased amount of synovia, a variable quantity of riziform bodies, rice-like particles floating in the liquid.

PROGNOSIS.—Synovial distensions appearing in young horses without apparent cause may disappear spontaneously. Other forms are often difficult to get rid of.

TREATMENT.—The form of the condition seen in young unbroken horses may be left to nature for a while, in the hope that it will disappear, as fairly often happens. Otherwise the treatment may be as follows :

1. *Cold applications*, followed by massage and compression with a thick layer or several layers of cotton-wool and a bandage. In comparatively recent cases this may have the desired effect.

2. *Constant pressure* on the distended sheath with cotton-wool and a bandage, as mentioned, or by means of a truss made for the purpose (thoroughpin).

3. *Counter-irritation* by a liniment or blister.

Frequently this acts merely as a " placebo," having little effect in reducing the enlargement

4. *Line firing*, which is often disappointing.

5. *Needle-point firing*. This is often very effective (see p. 256). It is advisable to apply a biniodide blister after the operation. Intense acute inflammation supervenes, accompanied by a copious discharge of synovia from the perforations in the sheath. This ceases in a few days. Months usually elapse before the good effects are noticeable. Then the swelling gradually subsides and may eventually disappear.

6. *Aspiration and injection*. This consists in puncturing the sheath aseptically with a fine trocar and canula or stout hypodermic needle and allowing its contents to escape, or aspirating the latter with an aspirating syringe or an ordinary hypodermic syringe with a rubber tubular connection between it and the needle, and injecting an irritant solution into the sheath. The irritant has the effect, apparently, of causing adhesions between the serous surfaces at the periphery of the sheath, thereby diminishing its capacity and consequently reducing the size of the swelling. It also modifies the vascularity of the serous membrane, and thus curtails the amount of its secretion.

The injection usually employed is tincture of iodine, pure or diluted, in the proportion of 1 part of the tincture to 2 parts of sterilised water. After its introduction into the sheath the latter is massaged for a while to bring the liquid into contact with every part of its interior. Then the liquid, or as much of it as possible, is withdrawn.

Often it is difficult to remove any of the solution after its injection. No harm, however, is done by leaving it in the sheath, even when the pure tincture is used. Other injections that have been utilised are 3 to 5 per cent. solution of carbolic acid, 1 in 1,000 perchloride of mercury, or 1 part of iodoform to 10 parts of glycerine, or Cagny's preparation, which consists of antipyrine, 10; tannin, 10; alcohol at 96°, 100, which the author has used with very good results. The immediate effect of this treatment is to cause acute inflammation in the sheath, characterised by heat, pain, and increased swelling and lameness, and often a rise in temperature up to 105° F. The temperature, however, soon returns to normal, the inflammation gradually subsides, and in favourable cases the original swelling disappears by degrees, showing the good result of the treatment. A large percentage of cures is obtained by this procedure, but two or three months generally elapse before complete reduction of the swelling is effected.

Exceptionally, the swelling becomes so tense that it bursts with an escape of synovia. There is a risk of infection ensuing in this case, but it can be prevented by antiseptic precautions.

The author had such an experience with a case of thoroughpin with intense lameness after the injection, and which recovered after the injection into the sheath of lacto serum, repeated fomenting with a solution of HgI_2 1–1,000, and the application of Glycerine 1 and Hydrarg. perchlor. 16 over the fistulous orifice.

7. *A combination of Nos.* 5 *and* 6 methods of treatment is more effective than either alone.

8. *Synoviotomy*—that is, incising the sheath to enable solid contents (riziform bodies), as well as its liquid secretion, to be removed. This operation is safe for an extensor sheath, in which it is seldom required, but it is a dangerous undertaking in ordinary practice for a large flexor sheath on account of the great risk of septic synovitis and its complications ensuing. It has been performed successfully under aseptic precautions where facilities for such were obtainable.

In the great sesamoidean sheath Professor Williams (New York) incises it in the middle line from its upper to its lower extremity, going through the skin and perforatus tendon, completely evacuates the contents, packs the sheath with gauze saturated with tincture of iodine and covers the part with layers of cotton-wool and bandage. He renews the iodine dressing daily until the lining of the sheath is uniformly granulating, when it is discontinued. The wound is healed, as a rule, within three weeks. The sheath reforms and the horse goes sound. He operates in a similar fashion on the tarsal sheath. He takes extraordinary precautions against infection. This procedure is not to be recommended in general practice. It would be indicated in purulent synovitis of a sheath.

9. *The use of fibrolysin.* Fibrolysin, injected intramuscularly, may be tried when there is great thickening in the wall of the sheath. It may require to be repeated upwards of fifty times to have the desired effect. There are a few reported cases of its efficacy.

VI.—AFFECTIONS OF ARTERIES

Open Wounds and Contusions of Arteries

Arterial wounds may be penetrating or non-penetrating. The latter cause a weak point in the vessel wall predisposing to the formation of an aneurism which, however, is rarely met with from this cause in veterinary practice.

As regards the etiology the wounds may be punctured, incised, contused, or lacerated.

Punctured wounds may be caused in various ways, including the penetration of a spicule of fractured bone or that of a sharp piece of bone swallowed with food.

The carotid has been punctured during the operation of phlebotomy, the posterior radial in that of median neurectomy, and the aorta or one of the iliacs when performing ovariotomy *per vagina.*

The gravity of the wounds depends upon the nature of the wounding body. If the opening in the arterial wall is very narrow it closes spontaneously and no hæmorrhage ensues.

If the wound, although small, is too large to close of its own accord more or less severe hæmorrhage supervenes, which, however, may be arrested spontaneously, especially if the vessel is situated deeply and

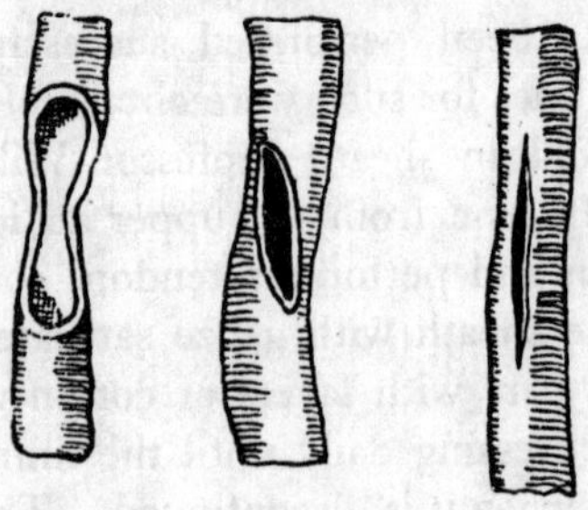

FIG. 3.—WOUNDS OF ARTERIES.

Transverse wound of artery. Oblique wound of artery. Longitudinal wound of artery.

only communicates with the surface of the body by a narrow passage. A thrombus forms round the wound and obliterates the opening in the vessel wall. The outer and inner coats of the vessel may be wounded at different levels so that its lumen does not communicate directly with the exterior, thus favouring hæmostasis by the outer coat covering the opening in the inner coats. In the foregoing cases the circulation continues in the vessel.

Incised wounds may partially or completely sever the artery. Complete section of large vessels soon leads to fatal hæmorrhage, but that of vessels of smaller calibre deeply situated and associated with a narrow wound in the overlying tissues may be followed by natural hæmostasis, a thrombus forming at the level of the section and extending into the vessel as far as the first anastomosing branch. Eventually, in the course of forty or fifty days, the thrombus becomes organised into fibrous tissue by a process of cicatrisation, permanently occluding the vessel. If prior to this taking place the region is subjected to external violence or the force of the circulation is greatly increased the hæmorrhage may recur.

Partial section of vessels may be transverse, oblique or longitudinal. If the oblique or transverse wound is small, spontaneous hæmostasis may occur, as in the case of a punctured wound.

If more than half the circumference of the vessel is involved the lips of the wound gape by virtue of the elastic recoil of the inner and middle coats and the muscular contraction of the outer coat, leaving an opening which favours bleeding. The constant force of the blood stream prevents the formation of an occluding thrombus. Longitudinal wounds are less gaping, and therefore not so dangerous. When an artery is severed by a contusion the inner and middle coats contract and retract within the outer coat, which thus projects as a collapsed tube beyond their level. The conditions here are favourable to hæmostasis, the bruised and roughened vascular walls promoting coagulation of the blood.

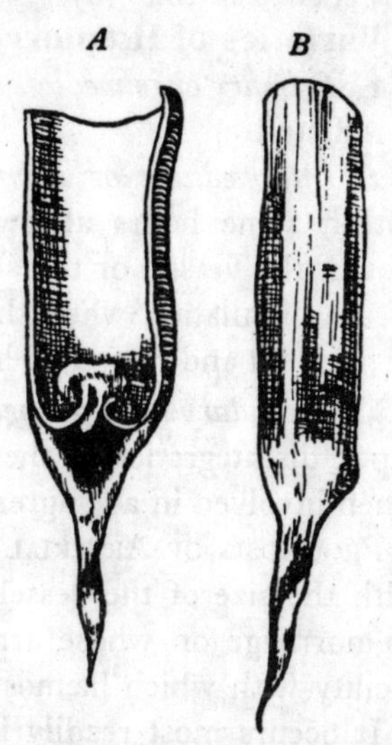

FIG. 4.—TORSION OF ARTERIES. Longitudinal sections showing contraction and retraction of the inner and middle coats and the formation of the thrombus in the vessel.

When an artery is torn across its tunics are stretched and the inner coats give way first and recoil within the outer coat, diminishing the lumen of the vessel, while the outer coat is drawn out in a sort of cap on the end of the severed vessel within which the blood clots to form a coagulum which will be sufficient to arrest the hæmorrhage in a small artery. It is in this way that hæmostasis follows the section of vessels by traction, torsion, and the use of the ecraseur.

Characteristics of Arterial Hæmorrhage are as follows :

1. The blood escapes in a jet whose force increases with its proximity to the heart.

2. The force of the jet increases with each ventricular contraction, so that it appears in jerks or spurts.

3. The blood is bright red.

4. The bleeding is diminished or arrested by pressure on the cardiac side of the wound. When it continues it is due to the distal portion of the artery anastomosing with a collateral branch.

The pulsatile movement of the blood is not marked when the wounded vessel is deeply seated, although a large volume of blood may be escaping.

Ulceration of an Artery.—When an artery is involved in an abscess its walls usually resist the destructive action of the pyogenic bacteria, but when they are unusually virulent the arterial wall may be perforated by a process of ulceration with consequent hæmorrhage whose gravity will vary with the calibre of the vessel. Fatal bleeding has ensued in this way.

Varieties of Hæmorrhage.—These comprise :

1. *Primary or immediate hæmorrhage,* occurring at the time the wound is inflicted.

2. *Intermediary or recurrent or reactionary hæmorrhage,* occurring within some hours afterwards from mechanical disturbance of the clot in the vessel, or the slipping of a ligature or from increased force of the circulation when the animal has recovered from the shock of an accident and the vessel has not been secured by ligation or forceps.

3. *Secondary hæmorrhage,* occurring some days afterwards from the septic disintegration of the clot in the vessel, or sloughing of the latter when involved in a gangrenous lesion.

PROGNOSIS OF ARTERIAL WOUNDS.—The prognosis naturally varies with the size of the vessel wounded, which affects the nature of the hæmorrhage on whose arrest the fate of the patient depends. The facility with which hæmostasis occurs varies in different animals.

It occurs most readily in the dog, and then in the ox, sheep, pig and horse in the order mentioned, the horse being well behind the other animals.

The possibility of recurrent or secondary hæmorrhage must always be borne in mind, and as a precaution against it spontaneous hæmostasis should not be depended upon when vessels of considerable size have been divided.

Spontaneous arrest of hæmorrhage occurs more readily in a vessel that has been severed completely than in one partially severed, as in the latter case the inner and middle coats are prevented from retracting and contracting within the outer coat to favour hæmostasis as described.

TREATMENT OF ARTERIAL WOUNDS.—This is dealt with under Hæmorrhage and Hæmostasis (see pp. 40 and 239).

Rupture of Arteries

Arteries may be ruptured or torn subcutaneously or internally from various causes, including contusions, laceration by the ends of fractured bones, violent effort, such as galloping, jumping, and struggling when cast. Many cases of rupture of the aorta close to the heart, as the result of struggling in hobbles, have been recorded, including one by the author.

SYMPTOMS.—When a superficial artery is ruptured subcutaneously it gives rise to a pulsating hæmatoma beneath the skin, known as a diffuse aneurism. When a large internal artery is ruptured death occurs within a few minutes.

DIAGNOSIS.—The history of the case combined with the symptoms renders diagnosis easy as a rule.

TREATMENT of rupture of a superficial vessel is the same as that for a hæmatoma. When a large internal vessel (aorta, pulmonary artery) is ruptured, treatment is out of the question.

Aneurisms

Aneurisms are not of much clinical interest in veterinary practice. They are practically confined to the mesenteric arteries and the cœliac axis, particularly the anterior mesenteric, where they are the result of the presence of the *Strongylus vulgaris* in the vessels. These aneurisms are very common in the horse, but do not give rise to any clinical symptoms. They are seen in almost every dissecting-room subject. Rare cases of aneurisms on the surface of the body have been recorded.

SYMPTOMS.—An external aneurism is recognised as a pulsating swelling on the course of an artery. The swelling also expands at each pulsation, and this expansion is characteristic. The chief danger of an aneurism is its rupture, with consequent severe or fatal hæmorrhage.

TREATMENT is seldom indicated in veterinary patients. The only satisfactory form of treatment is (1) ligation of the artery above and below the aneurism, or (2) extirpation of the aneurism after ligation, as in No. 1.

Arterio-Venous Aneurism

This is an aneurism resulting from an artery communicating with a contiguous vein, owing to both vessels being wounded simultaneously at the same level, or as the result of a congenital abnormality.

SYMPTOMS.—The condition is manifested by the presence of a pulsating swelling in which a characteristic thrill or tremor can be heard and felt. It has been likened to the hum of a mill, the purring of a cat, etc. The arterial blood is driven by its pulsatile force into the vein. This form of aneurism has been seen in the horse, ox, and dog. In the ox it has been ascribed to castration by torsion, affecting in this case the spermatic artery and vein.

TREATMENT, if required, consists in ligaturing the artery and vein above and below the aneurism, and if the latter is large extirpating it.

Arteritis and Arterial Thrombosis

Arteritis always precedes thrombosis. It is caused by irritation of the arterial endothelium by the presence in the vessel of parasites (sclerostomes) or of bacteria, or perhaps from overstretching of the artery lacerating its lining, as might ensue in the limbs from violent slipping. The endothelium is destroyed on the inflamed area inside the vessel, leaving a roughened surface on which a thrombus is deposited. The thrombus at first only partly occludes the lumen of the vessel, but it gradually increases in size by fresh deposits of fibrin, until it extends up to the first collateral branch and causes complete occlusion.

In veterinary practice the cause is not always evident. The most common seats of arteritis and consequent thrombosis in the horse, giving rise to clinical symptoms, are the termination of the posterior aorta and the commencement of the iliac arteries.

In these cases the blood supply to the hind-limb or limbs, according to the situation of the clot, is sufficient for the muscles in a state of rest, but not when they are active.

Symptoms of Aortic and Iliac Thrombosis

The symptoms of thrombosis at the bifurcation of the aorta are characteristic. The horse is quite normal when at rest, but after being exercised at a trot or a gallop for a variable time, usually five to fifteen minutes, he stops and shows symptoms of distress—viz., anxious expression, increased respirations, and sweating all over the body, except on the hind-limb or limbs involved.

If both limbs are affected, the horse may fall as if paralysed. For a considerable time after the exercise has ceased the pain continues, and the patient may behave as if suffering from colic, lying down and rising, looking round at the quarters, and displaying general uneasiness. When only one external iliac artery is affected, the lameness is confined to the corresponding limb. The veins on the latter are not so prominent as those in the normal limb after exercise. The surface of the affected region is comparatively cold, while the temperature of that of the rest of the body is increased after exertion.

On rectal examination the location of the thrombus can be detected. The vessel is bosselated at its level, and pulsation is absent or feeble on the distal side of it. Sometimes a tremor is felt, due to a thin stream of blood percolating through the thrombus.

PROGNOSIS.—The prognosis is grave, because the case is usually incurable. Stallions, however, sometimes recover sufficiently to be useful at the stud.

TREATMENT.—There is no satisfactory treatment for the condition. The following measures have been tried without definite success :

1. *The administration of potassium iodide.*

2. *Massage of the aorta per rectum.* Möller tried this, and the horse died twenty-four hours afterwards, apparently from embolism caused by fragmentation of the thrombus.

3. *Gradually increasing and frequently renewed exercise* until the symptoms supervene, the idea being to develop in this way the collateral circulation until the animal would be able to render useful service.

Rare cases of thrombosis of the brachial artery have been recorded, with symptoms similar to those just described.

VII.—AFFECTIONS OF VEINS

Open Wounds

Veins are involved in every open wound, giving rise to more or less hæmorrhage. The significance of puncture or section of veins depends on the amount of bleeding which ensues, and on whether pathogenic organisms enter the vessels to set up phlebitis and its possible complications. The methods of dealing with open wounds of veins are described in the chapter on Hæmostasis.

Air Embolism

When a vein of considerable size is opened within the aspiratory sphere of action of the chest or heart, air may be sucked into it with a hissing or gurgling noise. This may or may not give rise to embolism, with symptoms of dyspnœa, which may go on to asphyxia. It is not quite clear how the embolism acts. A feasible theory is that it obstructs the coronary arteries, leading to cardiac anæmia and impotence. Other explanations are that the pulmonary capillaries are blocked with air emboli, and that the right ventricle becomes distended with air and ceases to function.

PREVENTION of air embolism is effected by compressing the proximal ends of divided veins in the regions mentioned.

Treatment, which is not very efficacious, comprises pressure on the vein to expel the air, and the promotion of venous hæmorrhage in the hope that air may escape with the blood.

Phlebitis

Etiology.—The cause of phlebitis may be stated briefly as the entrance of infection into a vein.

The presence of pathogenic organisms in a vein causes roughening of its endothelial lining and consequent thrombosis.

Classification.—Phlebitis has been classified by Hunter as:

1. Adhesive phlebitis.
2. Purulent phlebitis.
3. Hæmorrhagic phlebitis.

In **adhesive phlebitis** the thrombosed vessel is in the form of a hard, resistant cord; the perivenous tissues are œdematous, and pain is evinced along the course of the vein.

In the **purulent form** the inflammatory symptoms are more acute. Little abscesses form along the course of the vein, and on bursting give rise to fistulæ, constantly discharging pus, which may be blood-stained. A probe inserted through one of the fistulæ will enter the vein.

Hæmorrhagic phlebitis is a complication of either No. 1 or No. 2, and due to disturbance of the clot in the vessel, or to purulent disintegration thereof. It is characterised by repeated hæmorrhage, which may be slight or profuse.

Prognosis.—The adhesive form is not serious, except that it leads to permanent obliteration of the affected vessel. The other varieties are more dangerous, inasmuch as death may supervene from hæmorrhage or from septicæmia or pyæmia, due to septic embolism, following breaking down of the clot in the vessel.

Treatment—Adhesive Phlebitis.—The principles of treatment are:

1. *Keeping the affected region at rest* to prevent the extension of the inflammation, and to avoid disintegration of the thrombus.

2. *Using antiseptic applications* for the wound in the vein (*vide* Septic Wounds).

3. *Providing for drainage* from the wound.

4. *Applying a counter-irritant* to the affected region, after the clot has become organised, to stimulate the collateral circulation and promote the removal of œdema from the parts that were drained by the thrombosed vein.

Purulent Form.—The measures to be adopted in this form comprise:

1. *Opening abscesses* as they appear.
2. *Enlarging fistulous orifices.*
3. *Injecting antiseptic lotions* into the vein by means of rubber tubing attached to a syringe.
4. *Opening the suppurating portion* of the vessel at its upper and lower parts, and passing through it by the two openings a seton or a fenestrated rubber tube to ensure free drainage, antiseptic injections being continued until the discharge ceases.
5. *Opening up the septic portion of the vein* and removing its septic contents, as an alternative to No. 4. Care must be exercised in these operations not to break down the clot in the distal portion of the vessel, and give rise to dangerous hæmorrhage or embolism.
6. *Puncturing the suppurating vein* in several places with the actual cautery, in order to make exits for the pus, the hot iron acting at the same time as a germicide. This method has given good results.
7. *Extirpating the purulent vein* by ligaturing it on the distal side of the affected part, cutting it on the proximal side of the ligature, and dissecting it out as far as the suppuration extends. This method is not much practised in veterinary surgery.

Instead of adopting any of the above methods a biniodide of mercury blister, 1 in 8, may be rubbed into the skin over the affected vein, as recommended by Williams of Edinburgh, who described it as a specific remedy for this condition. The writer found it to have a prompt curative effect in an obstinate case of purulent jugular phlebitis.

Hæmorrhagic Form.—In this form measures are required to arrest the hæmorrhage. They comprise:

1. *Plugging* of the wound with antiseptic gauze, and the insertion of sutures through its lips. The sutures and plug are removed after about forty-eight hours.
2. *Ligation* of the vein. The vein is exposed by careful dissection in a healthy part, isolated, and ligatured with aseptic silk or catgut. The cutaneous wound is sutured. Healing by first intention may ensue, but frequently it suppurates as the result of infection from the septic lesion. Antiseptic lotions are applied to the operation wound and to the suppurating part of the vein as described.

The commonest site of phlebitis in the horse is the jugular vein, where it results from infection contracted during, or subsequent to, the operation of phlebotomy. The use of a contaminated fleam will cause it. If the wound in the vein is made transverse to its long axis, or with jagged edges, it will gape and be slow to heal, exposing in the meantime the interior of the vein to infection from the outside, so that faulty procedure of this kind may lead to jugular phlebitis. The general description of the disease already given applies in every detail to jugular phlebitis.

The œdema resulting from the latter appears in the parotid region; it gradually disappears, owing to development of the collateral circulation. It is not advisable, however, to turn a horse out to grass until six months have elapsed after the occurrence of the disease, as the collateral circulation will not be sufficient before this time to prevent swelling of the head in the dependent position during grazing. The obliterated vein can be felt in the jugular furrow as a hard cord, and the absence of blood in the vessel will be demonstrated when an attempt is made to raise the vein by pressure at its level at the base of the neck. Calcareous deposits may form in the clot in the vessel, constituting what are known as phleboliths or blood stones.

Varicose Veins

Varicose veins are not common in veterinary patients, and when they are present they seldom require attention. They are mostly found in the lower parts of the limbs and inferior aspect of the trunk, the following veins being sometimes affected: the radial, cephalic, metatarsal, mammary (cow), and scrotal veins.

In rig castration large varicose veins are often met with in the scrotal region, and are apt to be mistaken for a testicle or epididymis. The distended metatarsal vein in the horse is known as "blood spavin." When varicose veins are wounded, the hæmorrhage is difficult to stop.

Treatment may be required when the varicosities are on the limbs. It includes—

(1) *Compression* by a bandage after the use of cold douches.

(2) *Firing* the skin over the distended vein, to act as a sort of permanent bandage.

(3) The *obliteration method* by the injection into the vein of a substance which will close its lumen and convert the vessel into a sclerosed cord. Quinine hydrochloride-and-urethane appears to be the agent most in favour. It is antiseptic and anæsthetic. About 2 c.c. is sufficient for injection into one vein.

(4) *Ligation* of the vein above and below the swelling, which is seldom performed. If the varicosity be large, it may be then excised. Strict aseptic precautions are necessary. No. (3) is now being employed

with great success in human surgery. It does not require detention in hospital.

Varicose ulcers are extremely rare in veterinary practice, and need not be considered

VIII.—AFFECTIONS OF THE LYMPHATIC SYSTEM

Lymphatic vessels are involved in all open wounds. When large lymph channels are opened, the lymph may be seen to escape as a serous, whitish liquid, which in the region of a joint may be mistaken for synovia, but it is white and less viscid than the latter.

TREATMENT.—The treatment is the same as usual for an open wound. Occasionally the constant and copious discharge of lymph prevents healing of the wound, and then a lymph fistula is produced. The application of a blister generally has the desired effect in this case.

Wounds of lymphatic glands are rarely seen. Sometimes, as the result of infection of a gland, a fistula ensues and necessitates extirpation of the gland. Such cases have been seen in connection with the cervical and popliteal lymphatic glands in the dog.

Lymphangitis

Lymphangitis may be said to be always due to the entrance of pathogenic bacteria into the lymphatic vessels, although the port of entry is not always evident. A very slight, invisible abrasion is sufficient to permit of their entrance. The incubative period of the organisms may be of such duration that the wound through which they passed into the lymph vessels may have closed before the symptoms of the condition appear. The lymphangitis may be acute or chronic, and superficial or deep.

Staphylococci and streptococci are common causes of lymphangitis, while specific forms of the disease are caused by specific organisms, such as farcy, tuberculous lymphangitis, epizootic lymphangitis, and ulcerative lymphangitis. It is important to make a correct diagnosis of the nature of the condition. Microscopic examination of pus from the lesions is therefore indicated with a view to identifying the causal organism. It might be necessary to have it submitted to a biological test before establishing the diagnosis.

Traumatic Lymphangitis.—The most interesting form of the disease from a surgical standpoint is traumatic lymphangitis, which, as already indicated, is due to some breach of surface and consequent infection by pathogenic organisms.

SYMPTOMS.—The commonest seat of the disease is the limbs, especially the hind ones, but it may be seen accompanying wounds on the trunk and head and neck. When affecting a limb, its onset is often very sudden. A horse may be left apparently normal at night, and be found in the morning severely affected, showing severe lameness and intensely acute local inflammation associated with pronounced febrile disturbance, the patient being dull and more or less completely off its feed.

On manipulation of the affected region the corded lymphatics may be felt. Marked pain is evinced on pressure over the lymphatic glands. The whole limb is swollen from the foot to the groin or shoulder, due chiefly to œdema caused by obstruction of the lymph vessels. Sometimes the upper limit of the swelling is marked by an abrupt ridge similar to that seen in connection with purpura hæmorrhagica. A peculiar feature of this form of lymphangitis attacking a posterior limb is that it almost invariably appears after the horse has been resting in the stable for a day or two. For this reason it has been called "Monday morning disease." In a great number of these cases no evidence of a wound or abrasion can be seen.

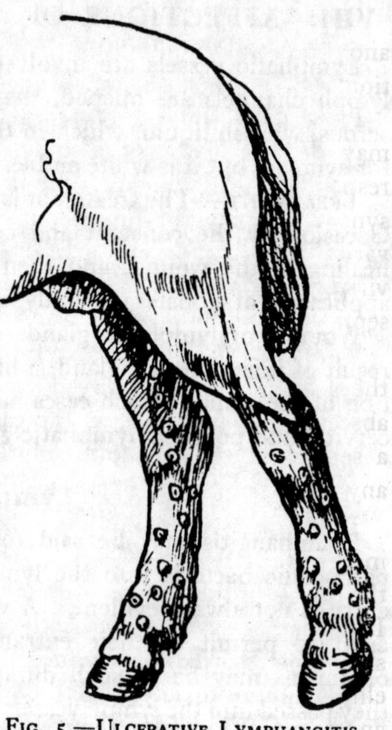

FIG. 5.—ULCERATIVE LYMPHANGITIS.

The following varieties of the disease are recognised: serous, purulent, gangrenous, and septicæmic.

The **serous form** is the most common. It takes the course of an ordinary inflammatory condition, undergoing resolution in a few days, but it may leave a certain amount of thickening in the limb, and when repeated attacks occur, as not infrequently happens, the limb eventually becomes greatly increased in circumference as the result of an accumulation of newly formed fibrous tissue. It is then looked upon as chronic lymphangitis, and the great thickening of the limb is known as elephantiasis.

The **purulent form** is characterised by the formation of abscesses along the course of the lymphatic vessels, containing usually white creamy pus.

The **gangrenous form** is recognised by the presence of gangrenous patches of tissue of varying depth throughout the affected region.

The **septicæmic form** is indicated by the symptoms of septicæmia.

Other complications of lymphangitis that may arise are bursitis and synovitis of tendon sheaths and of joints, owing to the communication between these structures and the lymphatic system.

PROGNOSIS.—The serous form is usually followed by recovery, but may become chronic, as indicated. The purulent form generally responds to treatment. Rarely it is complicated by suppurative synovitis, which is a grave condition. The gravity of the gangrenous variety depends on the extent and depth of the gangrene, and the virulence of the organisms associated with it. When symptoms of septicæmia supervene the case is very grave.

TREATMENT.—The treatment is in accordance with the nature of the lesion, being that already recommended for acute inflammation, abscesses, or gangrene, as the case may be. The condition being of a septic nature, antiseptic solutions are indicated for application to any wound or breach of surface that may be present or suspected.

Internally, the chief indication is the administration of sulphathiozole in frequently repeated doses. It usually has a striking effect in arresting the course of the disease, especially when due to streptococcic invasion. If this is not having the desired effect in a case of septicæmia penicillin should be resorted to. A purgative is usually indicated to promote the elimination of toxic products. Potassium iodide may be prescribed as an absorbent to hasten the reduction of the œdema.

The favourite form of local antiphlogistic treatment is warm fomentations, followed by the rubbing in of a weak liniment, which perhaps acts chiefly by facilitating the massage, which is undoubtedly effective in promoting absorption of the inflammatory exudate. Hot antiseptic baths are most efficacious for local lymphangitis affecting the lower parts of the limbs. There is no satisfactory treatment for chronic lymphangitis associated with the formation of new fibrous tissue.

An attempt may be made with more or less success to ward off this form of the condition by careful attention to the limbs, promptly treating cracks or fissures in the skin or eczematous eruptions, and by keeping the limbs bandaged when the horse is not working. When the case is fairly recent and the thickening is due in great part to the presence of œdema, the application of hypertonic preparations on the skin may be tried with advantage—for example, a saturated solution of common salt or pure glycerine, which have an affinity for water and extract liquid from the subcutaneous tissues by a process of osmosis. Fibrolysin may be tried to reduce fibrous thickening.

Adenitis

Adenitis, or inflammation of a lymphatic gland, is usually the result of the entrance of infection therein. The best example of the condition is the lesion of strangles affecting the submaxillary lymphatic glands. Organisms may pass through the lymphatic vessels without affecting them, and become arrested in the lymphatic glands on their course, setting up there their pathogenic effects.

The commonest microbes invading the lymph glands are streptococci and staphylococci.

The SYMPTOMS are those of acute inflammation or abscess formation in the gland or glands.

TREATMENT is as usual for inflammation and abscesses.

Chronic Adenitis

Acute adenitis may pass to the chronic form, which is characterised by hardness and enlargement of the gland. A group of lymphatic glands affected in this way form one enlarged mass.

SYMPTOMS.—The chief symptoms are enlargement and hardness of the gland. There is little or no evidence of pain.

TREATMENT is of little avail, the abnormal condition of the gland tending to persist. When resolution occurs it is slow to supervene. When any cause of the condition is evident it should be dealt with, such as a septic wound in its vicinity. Counter-irritation may be practised on the gland, the repeated application of tincture of iodine being the favourite form of treatment. Potassium iodide internally may have some good effect.

Specific affections of lymphatic glands, such as glanders, tuberculosis, and malignant growths, are treated in accordance with the recognised recommendations for these conditions.

Tumours of Lymphatic Glands

Primary tumours affecting lymphatic glands are rare, but secondary carcinomatous growths are frequently found in connection with them.

TREATMENT of malignant growths is usually hopeless. It consists in complete extirpation of the affected gland or glands. The superficial lymphatic glands in cattle are often affected with tuberculosis, causing them to assume the nature of tumours. Although it would seem that surgical intervention could be of little use some practitioners maintain that their excision is followed by improvement in the animal's condition (Magee, Hynes, in Ireland).

IX.—AFFECTIONS OF NERVES

Section of Nerves

When a nerve is divided its peripheral end undergoes Wallerian degeneration, the only part left intact being the sheath of Schwann. A sort of neuroma forms on the proximal end and assumes a regenerating function. It becomes joined to the peripheral end by a bridge of cicatricial tissue, which serves as a conductor of regenerated axis cylinders from the proximal to the terminal portion of the nerve, provided that the distance between the two ends does not exceed 2 or 3 inches.

The axis cylinders of the proximal end proliferate, forming numerous new axis cylinders, which, after traversing the cicatricial bridge mentioned, insinuate themselves into the sheath of Schwann and continue to grow for a variable distance, but only a few of them reach the extremity of the degenerated portion of the nerve. Consequently the regeneration of a divided nerve is never complete, and its normal function is never entirely restored.

Immediate union of divided ends of a nerve never takes place even when united by sutures immediately after section. The shorter the distance between them the more readily and quickly does regeneration occur.

The duration of regeneration is, as a rule, from five to six months. Partial restoration of function may ensue before anatomical reconstruction is accomplished, due to nerve impulses being sometimes transmitted through the protoplasm of the peripheral end before it receives axis cylinders.

When a nerve is severed, the part supplied by its distal portion is not always completely deprived of innervation. The latter may still be supplied in an attenuated form through the agency of recurrent filaments from the peripheral end joining other nerves in the vicinity. These recurrent branches do not suffer degeneration along with the affected portion of the nerve to which they belong.

Compression of Nerves

Nerves may be compressed in a variety of ways. Familiar examples of compression of nerves are that of the radial nerve between the shoulder and the thorax, of the facial nerve by the head-collar, and of the obturator by a large fœtus during its forcible delivery through the pelvis.

SYMPTOMS.—The symptoms comprise pain, and paralysis of the muscles involved.

DIAGNOSIS may be difficult without a definite history, except in one of the above cases, in which the symptoms are fairly characteristic.

PROGNOSIS depends on the nature of the compression, whether it is severe or slight, or continuous or temporary.

TREATMENT consists in removing the cause, if possible, and treating paralysis if present.

Contusion of Nerves

ETIOLOGY.—Nerves superficially situated are the most subject to contusions, such as the facial and external popliteal. The effects produced are as usual for contusions in general, and in addition those of more or less interference with the function of the nerve. If the contusion has the effect of rupturing all the fibres inside the neurilemma, the results will be the same as those following section of a nerve. The clinical symptoms are acute pain, which may extend along the course of the nerve, and more or less paralysis or loss of sensation in the muscles involved, depending on the nature of the injury.

TREATMENT.—The treatment has for its object the promotion of the absorption of extravasate and inflammatory exudate which are pressing on the nerve, causing pain and interference with function. It comprises successively warm fomentations, massage, and counter-irritation locally, the administration of potassium iodide internally, and the adoption of other remedies recommended for paralysis, when the latter is present.

Open Wounds of Nerves

Nerves may be affected with punctured, incised, or contused wounds.

SYMPTOMS.—The special symptoms are acute pain at the time the wound is made, paresis or paralysis in the muscles supplied by a motor nerve, and diminished or complete loss of sensation in the part supplied by a sensory nerve. Muscular atrophy and, sometimes, hyperæsthesia ensue later.

TREATMENT.—The only special treatment is immediate suture for completely divided nerves. A very fine needle and thread, a forceps with mouse teeth, and a sharp scissors and scalpel are required for the purpose. Having trimmed the ends of the nerve, they are brought into contact and sutured by one of the following methods :

1. *Direct suture* through the ends of the nerve.
2. *Indirect or perineurotic suture*, passing through the neurilemma only.
3. *Paraneurotic suture*, passing through the surrounding tissue only.

It will be necessary, as far as possible, to keep the affected region in such a position that there will be a minimum of tension on the suture.

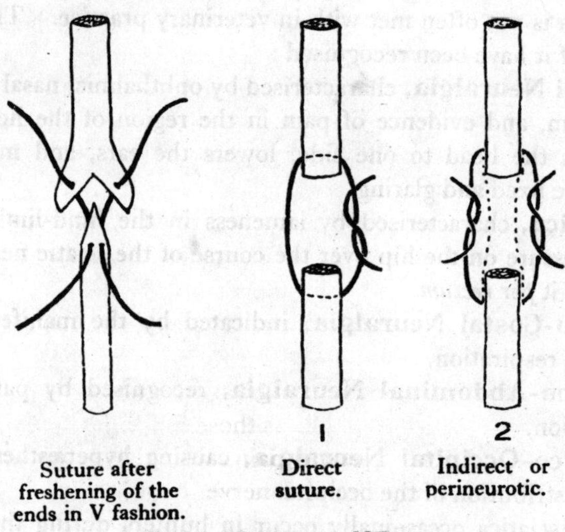

Suture after freshening of the ends in V fashion. Direct suture. Indirect or perineurotic.

Fig. 6.—Suture of Nerves.

Neuritis

Neuritis from a surgical point of view is usually associated with infection through open wounds, and may be spoken of as traumatic neuritis. Otherwise the condition is generally found in connection with rheumatism and other infectious diseases. The chief symptom of traumatic neuritis is pain at the level or along the course of a nerve or nerves—that is, neuralgia.

Treatment consists in applying antiseptic preparations to wounds complicated with neuritis, and in employing analgesic applications, such as hot stupes or fomentations, and anodyne liniments.

Other special forms of neuritis are dealt with in works on medicine (*vide* Neuralgia).

Tumours

Neoplasms affecting nerves are so rarely met with that they are of no practical interest. A few cases of multiple tumours on nerves in different parts of the body have been recorded in the ox. They were seen on post-mortem examination. They had caused neither pain nor interference with function.

Neuralgia

Pain evinced along the course of a nerve or nerves may be the result of an obvious lesion or occur without any apparent cause. In the latter case the condition is merely spoken of as neuralgia.

Neuralgia is not often met with in veterinary practice. The following forms of it have been recognised :

1. **Facial Neuralgia,** characterised by ophthalmia, nasal discharge and ptyalism, and evidence of pain in the region of the head. The horse holds the head to one side, lowers the ears, and may groan. The eyes are fixed and glaring.

2. **Sciatica,** characterised by lameness in the hind-limb, and by pain on pressure on the hip over the course of the sciatic nerve, or by pressure on it *per rectum*.

3. **Dorso-Costal Neuralgia,** indicated by the manifestation of pain during respiration.

4. **Lumbo-Abdominal Neuralgia,** recognised by pain in the lumbar region.

5. **Cervico-Occipital Neuralgia,** causing hyperæsthesia in the region of distribution of the occipital nerve.

Cases of sciatica occasionally occur in hunters during the hunting season, and have been ascribed to the horse contracting a chill when waiting outside the cover. Some obscure cases of lameness, appearing suddenly and disappearing in the same way, are probably due to neuralgia.

DIAGNOSIS.—The diagnosis of neuralgia is not always easy. It may be confounded with acute rheumatism.

TREATMENT is (1) local and (2) general.

1 *Local treatment* comprises the use of—

(*a*) *Moist heat* in the form of hot fomentations, or hot stupes or poultices, including the proprietary preparation antiphlogistine.

(*b*) *Anodyne applications*, such as belladonna liniment.

(*c*) *Counter-irritant* remedies, including stimulating liniments, blisters, and needle-point firing.

(*d*) *A subcutaneous injection* of morphine or atropine locally.

(*e*) *Massage*, which must be light, progressive, and repeated daily.

(*f*) *The electric current.*

The application of a blister on the hip usually has the desired effect for sciatica in the horse.

2. *General treatment* includes the administration of sedative medicine such as potassium bromide, opium, belladonna, chloretone, aconite, and

the injection of morphia, antipyrine, or cocaine. If the patient be debilitated, tonic medicine is indicated—viz., preparations of iron and quinine—and if rheumatism is suspected salicylate of soda must be prescribed.

The operation of stretching the sciatic nerve for the relief of sciatica has not been performed in veterinary practice. It attenuates the transmission of pain without interfering with motility. Alternatively, neurotomy or neurectomy of an affected nerve may be performed when practicable.

Obstinate cases of neuralgia are reported as having been treated successfully by the injection of 90 per cent. alcohol, with the addition of cocaine or stovaine along the track of the affected nerve or nerves. Ionisation with sodium salicylate (2 to 5 per 1,000) is said to have effected a cure where all other measures had failed (see p. 267).

Paralysis

By the term "paralysis" or "akinesis" is meant the loss of power of muscles to contract on receipt of their normal stimulus. Diminution of this contractile power is known as *paresis*.

Loss of sensibility to pain and to touch is termed *analgesia* or *anæsthesia*. This often coexists with paralysis. When the cause of the paralysis is in the muscles it is called myopathic paralysis, and when due to a nervous lesion or phenomenon it is referred to as neuropathic paralysis.

Neuropathic paralysis, as it occurs in animals, is usually the result of some nervous lesion. It is rarely purely functional, as occurs in hysteria in the human subject.

There are various forms of paralysis, including the following:

1. **Local Paralysis,** affecting a single muscle, several muscles of a group, or some groups of muscles.
2. **Hemiplegia,** paralysis of a lateral portion of the body.
3. **Paraplegia,** paralysis of the hind-quarters.
4. **Diplegia** or **Quadriplegia,** paralysis of both sides of an organ or of the four limbs.

Paralysed muscles are usually relaxed, and offer no resistance to passive movement of the part on which they normally act. Rarely they are spasmodically contracted. The origin of the paralysis may be in the brain, the spinal cord, or the nerves.

In many cases the cause of the paralysis is evident from the nature of the symptoms (radial, facial, crural paralysis, etc.). In other cases the diagnosis may be difficult. In examining for paralysis the degree of sensibility, reflex action, and electric contractility is sought for in the affected part.

Sensibility may be increased, diminished, or perverted. It is tested for by pricking with a needle or pin. As a rule, diminished sensibility is found on the same side as the paralysis, but there may be hemiplegia on one side and hemi-anæsthesia on the other side.

Inequality of the pupils and their indifference to light point to lesions of the brain, cervical portion of the cord, or of the sympathetic.

Tendinous reflexes (patella, tendo Achillis) may be normal, diminished, or suppressed. They are diminished or abolished in affections of the centripetal or centrifugal nerves, of the superior or inferior roots of the cord or of the grey matter of the medulla. Lesions affecting the brain or anterior regions of the cord suppress the functions of the moderating centres there, and lead to exaggeration of the reflexes.

Electric contractility is conserved in cerebral and in spinal paralysis when the lesions in the latter case do not affect the inferior horns of the cord.

Diminution of faradic excitability occurs in affections of the nerves and of the inferior horns of the cord. The abolition of this contractility renders the prognosis unfavourable. It is accompanied by loss of the reflexes, and atrophy of the muscles involved soon becomes evident.

Paralysis originating in the peripheral nerves is the form most commonly seen in veterinary patients. It may be limited to a single nerve or be associated with several nerves in the same region. Anæsthesia may accompany the paralysis.

Etiology.—The cause may be mechanical injury, neuritis, hæmorrhage over a nerve leading to pressure thereon, or the toxin of some infectious disease.

Paralysis rapidly produced is usually of mechanical or toxic origin.

Paralysis slow in onset is generally the result of chronic neuritis, or the development of a neoplasm on the course of a nerve.

When the cause of the paralysis is obscure, it may be ascribed to rheumatism without any proof of such being the case.

The Prognosis of paralysis varies according to the cause of the condition, and the importance of the organ or region affected. When it is of apparent rheumatoid origin, recovery is the rule after a few days or a few weeks. Resulting from slight injury, the paralysis may only persist a few days or even a few hours.

The persistence of faradic irritability is a good sign; muscular atrophy is an unfavourable symptom. The longer the duration of the paralysis and the more pronounced the atrophy, the more gloomy the prognosis.

Treatment is directed towards removal of the cause, the stimulation of nervous function, and the prevention of atrophy. The measures adopted may comprise :

1. The *removal of a callus*, a tumour, or a cicatrix compressing a nerve.
2. The *application locally* of a counter-irritant and the administration internally of absorbent medicine, chiefly potassium iodide, to promote absorption of inflammatory exudate pressing on a nerve.
3. The *administration of nerve stimulants*, such as nux vomica internally or strychnine hypodermically, with a view to restoring nervous function. Repeated large doses of arsenic sometimes have an excellent effect.
4. *Massage ; counter-irritation* by liniments, blisters, or firing ; and *exercise*, to prevent muscular atrophy.
5. *Passive movement* of joints to induce the commencement of activity of the paralysed muscles.
6. The *subcutaneous injection* of veratrine ($1\frac{1}{2}$ grains in 75 minims of water), or a solution of common salt, the action of which is to prevent atrophy and promote the restoration of function in the nerves and muscles affected.
7. *Electrotherapy*, when possible, to shorten the duration of the paralysis and prevent muscular atrophy. The galvanic or faradic current is employed. The negative pole is applied on the region corresponding to the trunk of the nerve at a point where it is superficial, and the positive pole on the muscles where the nerve ramifies. The current is continued for four or five minutes daily, or eight to ten minutes every second day. A feeble current must be employed. This method of treatment is undoubtedly efficacious in some instances.
8. The *administration of salicylate of soda* in cases which seem of rheumatoid origin.

Muscular atony is different from paralysis. It is sometimes observed in the foal and calf soon after birth, affecting the extensors of the metacarpus and the digit in the fore-limb and the flexor metatarsi in the hind-limb. Recovery is the rule in these cases. It is accelerated by massage.

X.—AFFECTIONS OF BONES

Contusions

Superficial bones often suffer from contusions varying in gravity according to the severity of the injury and the region affected. The lesion may be practically limited to the periosteum, causing exudation and extravasation beneath the membrane, or the bone itself may be more or less severely bruised, leading to hæmorrhagic centres in its substance and perhaps infiltration of the medulla with blood. Violence inflicted on one side of a bone may cause a fissure on the opposite side.

When the injury is slight it is of no consequence, and is followed by recovery in a few days ; but when it is severe, affecting the bone deeply, acute ostitis supervenes, characterised by well-marked local inflammation, and in the case of a limb pronounced lameness. Febrile disturbance may be observed. It is impossible to say whether a fissure exists as well as the contusion.

Experience has shown that when one of the bones of a limb has been subjected to a severe contusion it is liable to be fractured when the acute inflammation has disappeared and the horse puts weight boldly on the limb, or makes a strong muscular effort. This usually ensues weeks after the occurrence of the accident to the bone. The predisposition to fracture is due to rarefaction of the bone by the inflammation therein, causing a certain amount of decalcification of its structure.

Treatment is on the usual principles for contusions in general. It includes :

1. Complete rest of the patient.
2. Cold and astringent applications to the affected part.
3. Hot fomentations or stupes and counter-irritant topics in the later stages of the inflammation.

When the lameness is severe, it is advisable to put the horse in slings to prevent his lying and rising, and possibly fracturing the weakened bone by so doing.

Prolonged rest is always indicated. A favourite treatment for the condition is the application of a blister to the affected part. It precipitates the inflammatory process, and thus shortens the period of resolution. Apart from this, it has the advantage of enforcing rest of the part by the inflammation it sets up, and of the patient as well.

When the effects of the first blister have passed off, another one is usually applied to continue the enforced rest. Even at the end of five or six weeks after the accident it is necessary to avoid exerting the subject, as the injured bone is not yet consolidated.

Open Wounds

The chief significance of open wounds of bone is that they may become infected, resulting in necrosis, which prevents healing of the wound until the sequestrum separates and causes rarefaction of the bone, predisposing it to fracture. They are treated on general principles.

Fractures

A fracture is a solution of continuity of a bone. Fractures may first be classified as (1) incomplete, in which a part only of the thickness of the bone is broken or the structure is merely cracked; and (2) complete fractures, in which the bone is broken right through its thickness.

Incomplete Fractures

Incomplete fractures include: (1) Curvature of the bone, or greenstick fracture; (2) partial or splintered fracture; and (3) fissure.

1. **Greenstick Fracture** occurs in young animals. The bone, being pliable, curves when it is bent, and may fracture on the convex side after the manner of a green stick.

2. **Partial or Splintered Fractures** are characterised by the separation from the main bone of particles or splinters of bone as the result of direct violence, as may be caused by gunfire.

3. **Fissured Fractures** are represented by longitudinal, transverse, or oblique cracks in a bone without any displacement whatever of the fragments, and are mostly seen in the tibia, radius, and metacarpus as the result of direct violence, and in the pastern as the result of concussion.

Except in the case of the pastern there is always danger of separation of the fragments occurring at a variable time after the accident, usually some weeks afterwards, when the horse is going sound, the condition being then called a "deferred fracture." It has been known to occur two to six months afterwards. Displacement is prevented at the time of the accident by the periosteum and the fascia, which are not ruptured. But these structures give way easily if much weight is borne on the limb.

TREATMENT of these fractures is on the same principles as for complete fractures.

The aim of treatment in fissured fracture is to prevent displacement of the fragments.

Complete Fractures

ETIOLOGY.—The causes of complete fractures are: (1) Predisposing and (2) exciting.

1. **Predisposing Causes.**—These include:

(*a*) Ostitis, necrosis, or caries of the bone.

(*b*) Superficial situation of a bone, exposing it to violence.

(*c*) Slippery roads—for example, during frosty weather, or when they are steam-rolled and tarred—and slippery floors in stables and sheds.

(*d*) General diseases affecting the bones—*e.g.*, osteomalacia and osteoporosis.

(*e*) Advanced age.

2. **Exciting Causes.**—The exciting causes are: (1) External violence (blows, kicks, etc.); and (2) internal violence (muscular action).

(1) *External violence* gives rise to *direct fractures* when the fracture occurs at the point of application of the force, and to *indirect fractures* when it takes place at a site more or less remote from this point, as in the case of fracture of the base of the cranium as the result of a fall on the occipital bone or of fracture of the shaft of the ilium from falling on the external angle.

(2) *Internal violence.* Fractures as the result of excessive muscular action occur in horses during galloping and jumping, and during struggling when cast and fixed for operation.

Classification of Complete Fractures.—Fractures are classified thus:

1. *Single fracture*, when the bone is fractured at one place.
2. *Comminuted* or *multiple fracture*, when the bone is broken into several pieces.
3. *Simple fracture*, when there is no solution of continuity of the skin at the seat of fracture.
4. *Compound fracture*, when there is an open wound of the skin communicating with that in the bone.
5. *Complicated fracture*, accompanied by rupture of an important vessel or nerve, or the opening of a joint or a visceral cavity.
6. *Diaphysary fracture*, affecting the diaphysis of a long bone.
7. *Epiphysary fracture*, involving the epiphysis.

Direction of Fractures.—The direction of the fracture in a bone may be transverse, longitudinal, or oblique. Oblique fractures are the most common, and the form of the fractured surface may be V-shaped or somewhat spiral.

Position of the Fragments.—When the ends of the fragments are fixed in one another by their denticulations, the fracture is *impacted.* When they are overlapping, it is a *riding* fracture. The fragments may also be displaced circumferentially by torsion, or they may be drawn away from one another by muscular action, or they may be bent at various angles.

Changes at Seat of Fracture.—Round the seat of fracture there is more or less damage to the soft tissues, including ruptured vessels and nerves, and lacerated muscles and tendons. There is a varying quantity of extravasated blood between the fragments, depending on the extent of vascular rupture that has taken place.

Healing of Fractures.—In normal subjects nature provides at once for the healing of fractures by the production of embryonic tissue between the broken ends of the bone, which is at first transformed into fibro-cartilage and then into bone, constituting respectively a cartilaginous callus and a bony callus. The latter, when recent, is composed of cancellated bone, which afterwards develops into compact bone. After the callus has been completed and has formed a solid union between the broken parts it diminishes in volume. The greater the amount of separation between the fragments the larger the callus. When the separation has been slight, the callus becomes imperceptible after the lapse of some months. In a long bone the medullary cavity may be re-established.

SYMPTOMS.—The symptoms of fractures comprise :

1. *Pain*, which is always very evident and is accentuated on disturbing the seat of fracture. After the momentary pain caused by the fracture the human patient has a sense of numbness at the seat of injury associated with relaxation of the muscles in the region, persisting for a period of 10 to 20 minutes after the accident, during which time reduction of the fracture can be effected without muscular resistance and with little or no pain to the patient. When this period has passed acute pain is felt and the muscles became contracted.

2. *Inability, as a rule, to bear weight* in the case of a limb. When impacted, some weight may be borne.

3. *Deformity*, due to extravasation of blood, inflammatory changes in the part, and, chiefly, to displacement of the fragments.

4. *Abnormal mobility*, ascertained on manipulating the two ends of the bone, which are then found capable of bending in every direction at the point of fracture.

5. *Crepitation* or *crepitus*, due to the fractured ends grating against one another. It is elicited on manipulation of the fragments in various directions. Sometimes careful examination is required before it can be detected. It may be heard or felt or both. It is different from the crepitation of emphysema, or a hæmatoma, or a synovial bursa (bursitis).

The interposition of a piece of soft tissue between the fragments will prevent crepitation, which is also absent when they are so far apart that they cannot be brought into contact and when they are impacted. It is rarely perceived in fractures of the spinal column. Other special symptoms may be present due to interference with function of different organs.

General symptoms include a rise in temperature of 2° or 3°, and perhaps albuminuria and lipuria.

When examining a part for evidence of fracture, great care must be exercised not to aggravate the lesion by violent or injudicious movement of the fragments, which may cause rupture of vessels or nerves, or other structures, or so increase the damage to the soft tissues that they will undergo gangrene. Moreover, rough handling will cause severe and unnecessary pain to the subject.

DIAGNOSIS is generally easy from the characteristic symptoms mentioned which are present in the majority of fractures. Rare cases of partial epiphysary fractures causing incurable lameness have been met with in which the nature of the condition was only discovered on post-mortem examination. When a fracture is so situated that neither crepitus nor abnormal mobility can be made out the diagnosis is difficult. In all doubtful cases in small animals and in obscure cases in the lower parts of the limbs in the large animals a skiagraph may be taken to confirm the diagnosis.

PROGNOSIS.—The prognosis varies according to circumstances. There is a tendency for healing of fractures to occur in all animals, but it is not always easy, especially in large subjects, to ensure that union of the fragments will occur without deformity that may render the animal useless for work.

Unfavourable conditions for the healing of fractures comprise:

1. *Large size of the subject*, rendering it difficult to reduce and immobilise the fragments.

2. *Indocility of the patient*, whereby the seat of fracture is disturbed and the process of repair interfered with.

3. *Wide separation* of the fragments, rendering it difficult or impossible to bring them into apposition.

On the other hand, healing is favoured by youth, light weight, and lymphatic temperament.

In large animals valuable for stud purposes, the persistence of a deformity, provided that it does not affect the capacity of the pelvis in the female, is of little consequence. Hence treatment should always be attempted in these animals.

For most cases of complete fracture in ordinary horses and large bovines the rule is to advise slaughter on account of the almost insurmountable difficulties encountered in trying to carry out suitable treatment.

Treatment of Complete Fractures

The Horse.—When treatment has been decided upon in the horse the indications are—

1. **Measures to prevent aggravation of the lesion** by movement of the fragments, which might result in serious complications, such as the rupture of important structures by the jagged ends of the broken bone, or the penetration by them of the overlying skin. The animal should be treated at the place where the fracture has occurred, or as close thereto as possible. Before moving the patient a provisional immobilising dressing should be applied, if practicable, to prevent further displacement of the fragments and the possible complications mentioned. This may be composed of rough splints and bandages applied over padding formed by ordinary wool or tow.

If the horse is to be moved a considerable distance, he should be conveyed in a horse ambulance or low float in the standing position, side-to-side movement in the vehicle being prevented by batons of straw packed up on either side of the animal, and to-and-fro movement being obviated by tying the head short with the halter shank, and by having a rope or breeching supporting the buttocks.

2. **Reduction of the fracture.** In rare cases the displacement is practically nil, and then there is no need for reduction.

When the displacement is slight and in the form of bending at the seat of fracture, reduction may be effected in the standing position by having the upper segment of the bone held rigid, while the lower one is brought into line with it. If, however, the displacement is well marked, with more or less riding of the fracture, it will be necessary to cast the patient cautiously, after applying an immobilising dressing, and to administer a general anæsthetic. It might be advisable to produce anæsthesia in the standing position, so that the animal will go down quietly and not struggle after falling. Narcosis or anæsthesia by intravenous administration of chloral hydrate or thiopentone, etc., is indicated to avoid the excitement stage of chloroform anæsthesia.

The procedure then comprises: (1) *Extension and counter-extension*; and (2) *local manipulation.*

Extension is effected by traction by a number of assistants on the distal portion of the limb, parallel to its normal direction, by means of a rope round the pastern.

Counter-extension is produced by traction in the opposite direction by means of a rope applied round the upper part of the limb, or by having this rope made fast to a fixed point. The object of this procedure is to bring the two ends of the fragments on the same level prior to placing them in apposition. When the overlapping of the fragments is well marked it is extremely difficult and often impossible to overcome the displacement, and when it has been overcome it may prove impossible to prevent the fragments reverting more or less to their original displaced position when anæsthesia has passed off, despite the application of the retention dressing.

When the parts of the bone have been drawn far apart by the contraction of attached muscles, it is useless to attempt to bring them together. Pulleys may be used instead of assistants to obtain the necessary power for the purpose of reduction. Steadier traction can be obtained in this way.

Local manipulation is practised by the surgeon to obtain accurate apposition of the ends of the fragments. It also is a difficult and delicate operation, on the success of which a perfect result depends. It is not easy inside a mass of swollen and altered tissues to make sure of the position of the broken ends. The foot must be taken as a guide in providing against rotation of the limb.

It is a question whether reduction should be attempted immediately after the occurrence of a fracture or postponed until local swelling due to immediate inflammatory exudate and extravasated blood has subsided.

It has been proved experimentally on small animals that the more advanced the inflammation in the muscles round the seat of fracture the greater becomes their resistance to reduction. Hence the inference is that the sooner the fracture is dealt with the better, because the inflammation increases in the muscles for some days after the accident has occurred. (See No. 1, p. 109.)

3. **To apply an immobilising dressing,** *i.e.*, to substitute an external for the internal fractured skeleton. It is difficult for many of the complete fractures in the horse to apply a dressing sufficiently secure and rigid to prevent displacement of the reduced fragments. Moreover, there is the trouble of the horse moving about in his stall, even when in slings, which disturbs the formation of the callus, and may fracture it when recent by putting weight on the affected limb before it is fitted to bear it.

The *immobilising dressing* may be composed of—

(1) *Splints and bandages.* Splints may be small boards, or pliable metal, or stout leather softened in hot water so that it can be shaped to the part. Holes are made in the leather to accommodate the bony prominences. When it dries it becomes quite hard, constituting a good serviceable splint.

Splints are not satisfactory for fractures above the knee or hock, as they cannot be effectively applied there, and for fractures below these points plaster of Paris bandages are much more convenient and more efficient. When splints are used, the limb must first be carefully covered with an even layer of padding to protect the soft parts from injury by the splints, and to facilitate the fitting of the latter. Generally speaking, the splints should include the two joints of which the affected bone forms part.

The padding should extend beyond the ends of the splints. The splints are kept in position by strong calico or canvas bandages, reinforced outside by a thin rope coiled round the limb. Splints provided with straps and buckles are very useful, as by this means they can be kept securely in position and tightened at will, the straps being tacked to the outer surface of the splints as recommended by F. Daly (Dublin). This dressing is suitable as a temporary application, as it can be easily removed.

(2) *Splints and bandages associated with some material* which becomes hard on cooling or drying—*e.g.*,

(*a*) *Black pitch*, to which turpentine may be added to lower its melting point and increase its fluidity. A little powdered resin added to it increases the hardness of the dressing.

(*b*) *Black pitch and Burgundy pitch*, of each 1 part, and of Venice turpentine one-half.

(*c*) *Plaster of Paris.* This is used in the form of bandages impregnated with the plaster. The bandage, before application, is immersed in water until bubbles of air cease to escape. It is then rapidly put on. Solidification occurs in about ten minutes. It constitutes a dressing of stony hardness. Splints are unnecessary when this material is used. Plaster of Paris bandages alone are commonly employed for fractures below the knee or hock. It is difficult to adjust them properly above these points, owing to the limb being wider in its upper part, causing the dressing to slip downwards. An adhesive substance, such as pitch, is more suitable here, as it may be applied directly on the skin in the superior region of the limb, thus preventing the downward displacement. Before applying the plaster bandage, the part which is to be covered is enveloped in a perfectly even layer of cotton-wool or wadding to make it uniform in shape, and protect the soft tissues from injury by the hard dressing. It is very important to have the padding evenly distributed, otherwise certain parts will be subjected to excessive pressure, causing great pain and leading, perhaps, to sloughing of the affected part.

It is advisable to first smear the skin with tinct. benzoin co. or Archangel tar, so that the wool will adhere to it and remain in the position in which it was placed until the bandage is applied.

(3) *Plaster of Paris splints and gutters without padding*. An objection to ordinary plaster bandages is that they absolutely conceal the part of the limb to which they are applied, and cannot be disturbed to examine the seat of fracture. To overcome this objection, plaster splints and gutters have been introduced.

The plaster splint is made of tarlatan folded about a dozen times on itself in the form of a band, and impregnated with the wet plaster It is laid longitudinally on the limb, covering the seat of fracture, and made to take the form of the part on which it is placed by the application of a circular bandage. Two to four of these are applied. When they become hard the bandage is removed, and the splints are joined by cords which keep them in position, and can be loosened or tightened at will. They might be employed for fractures of the forearm and leg in the horse and ox, extending from the foot to the shoulder or stifle. Moussu recommends alternate longitudinal and circular plaster bands for fracture of the radius in the bovine, omitting the latter bands at the level of the radial vein to prevent pressure thereon and consequent œdema.

The plaster gutter is made by first cutting out a piece of stuff of suitable length and width by measurements on the sound limb, then imbibing it with the wet plaster, reversing it, and applying it on the fractured limb. It adapts itself exactly to the latter, preventing displacement of the fragments. So far it has not been utilised in veterinary practice, but has found considerable favour with human surgeons.

When the seat of fracture in a limb is much swollen it is useless to apply a permanent dressing immediately, for when the swelling subsides the dressing will become loose and require to be removed. Hence an application which can be readily taken off is indicated in such cases.

(4) Vineburg, Rice, and Brawn (*Canad. Med. Ass. J.*, **53**, 170–171) advise a mixture of 10 per cent. du Pont elvanol and 90 per cent. plaster of Paris to impregnate bandages for use like plaster of Paris bandages and claim the following properties for it :

1. About 50 per cent. stronger and 10 per cent. lighter than plaster of Paris.
2. No contraction or expansion on setting.
3. Setting time 12—15 minutes.

4. Non-toxic, non-irritating.
5. Not friable.
6. Slightly more elastic than plaster of Paris.
7. Porous.
8. It is not resistant to a thorough wetting with water.

(5) *Poroplastic felt*, which consists of felt impregnated with a resinous solution. It becomes quite plastic on immersion in boiling water or on exposure to dry heat, and may be moulded to the shape of the injured part. It becomes hard on cooling, and sets further after some hours. It is porous and permits of transpiration, and is therefore not likely to cause maceration of the skin from retention of the perspiration. Care must be taken that the edges of the material do not turn in and press on the skin and thus cause necrosis thereof.

Dollar has seen excellent results from its use in the setting of fractured limbs in race-horses.

(6) A *charge*, which is made thus: Some tow is chopped into fine particles with a scissors. Some melted pitch is smeared on the skin at the seat of fracture, taking care that it is not scalding hot. The chopped tow is scattered over the pitch. Alternate layers of pitch and tow are formed until a substantial plaster is produced, which has some immobilising effect on the region. This is often employed for fractures of the shoulder and hip, where other dressings are difficult to apply. As the hair grows it tends to push the plaster away from the skin, thus interfering with its effect.

Aids to the immobilising dressing comprise:

1. *Slings*, which enable the horse to rest and prevent his attempting to lie down. They are always indicated in fractures of the long bones of the limbs, but for fractures of the pelvis they are of doubtful benefit.
2. A *sort of sling* for the limb itself, suspending it from the roof of the stable and relieving it of the weight of the dressing.
3. A *special apparatus* in the form of a vertical iron bar with forked branches supporting a framework for the broken limb, serving to immobilise the seat of fracture and to keep the foot off the ground. It is rarely employed.
4. *Making an excavation in the floor* beneath the affected limb to prevent the possibility of its bearing weight and disturbing the seat of fracture.

4. **Suturing and Plating the Ends of the Broken Bone.**— Cutting down aseptically on the seat of fracture, performing direct reduction of the fragments, and uniting them by wire sutures or by steel

plates have been seldom, if ever, performed in fractures of the limbs in large animals. They are done in human surgery in cases where it is impossible to keep the ends of the bone in apposition by other means. This method of treatment is necessary for certain fractures of the premaxilla and inferior maxilla. For the purpose of suturing bone, a drill and fine wire are required. The wire may be of silver, aluminium, bronze, galvanised iron, or platinum. The holes must be drilled at right angles to the fractured surfaces when the latter are oblique, so that when the sutures are inserted no displacement will occur.

The Use of the Stadar Splint or other Form of Bone Pinning.—In 1931 an American veterinary surgeon (Otto Stadar) introduced the now famous Stadar splint, consisting of two pin-bars joined by an extension bar. Each pin-bar is drilled to carry two stainless steel pins inclined at an angle to each other, the inclination giving them a fixed grip in the bone.

The pins are inserted through skin and muscle and transfix the bone, the pins passing obliquely through each fragment. The heads of the two pins are joined by the extensor bar, which is operated by a screw whereby the fragments can be pushed in opposite directions until their ends are in exact apposition, when the bar is fixed. This ensures perfect alignment and immobilisation of the fragments. It is being extensively and successfully used in human surgery. Strict asepsis must be observed in its application.

Full information regarding its use in the dog can be found in a pamphlet entitled "Veterinary applications, Stadar Reduction and Fixation Splint," Directions No. 11437, obtainable from the General Electric X-Ray Corporation, 2012 Jackson Blvd., Chicago (12), Ill., U.S.A.

Bone Pinning.—Apropos of the Stadar Splint the following points on Bone Pinning in Small Animals, taken from a paper with this title read at the Annual Congress of the N.V.M.A. (1949) by Jack O. Knowles, V.M.D. (Miami, Florida), are appropriate.

1. It is an advanced procedure adaptable to the average practice provided that a sterile technique is adopted.

2. *Indications* for the procedure are—

(1) Fractures near the body.

(2) Compound fractures.

(3) Fractures accompanied by extensive soft tissue injury.

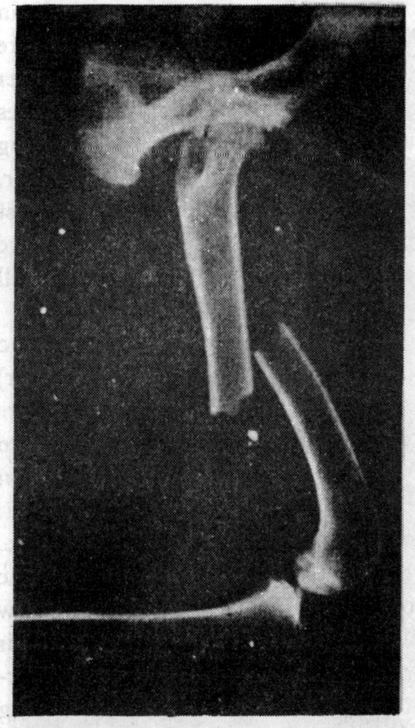

[By courtesy of Victor X-ray Corpn., Ltd.

FIG. 7.—MID-SHAFT FRACTURE OF THE FEMUR WITH GROSS DISPLACEMENT.

[By courtesy of Victor X-ray Corpn., Ltd.

FIG. 8.—THE SAME AFTER REDUCTION AND SPLINTING.

3. *Advantages* of the method are—

(1) Absolute immobilization is applied directly to the fragments.

(2) The limb is in use immediately after repair has taken place, thus ensuring adequate circulation for the consolidation of the callus.

(3) Atrophy of the tissues is also avoided by the absence of the ordinary external immobilising dressing.

(4) Free access to the wound is permitted for treatment.

(5) Tampering with the splint is difficult.

(6) It is a simple matter to test the healing at the time of the removal of the pins and if necessary to reapply the fixing device.

4. *Procedure.*

(1) Employ Nembutal anæsthesia; take an X-ray giving two clear views of the seat of fracture and place them in a double viewing screen for reference during the operation.

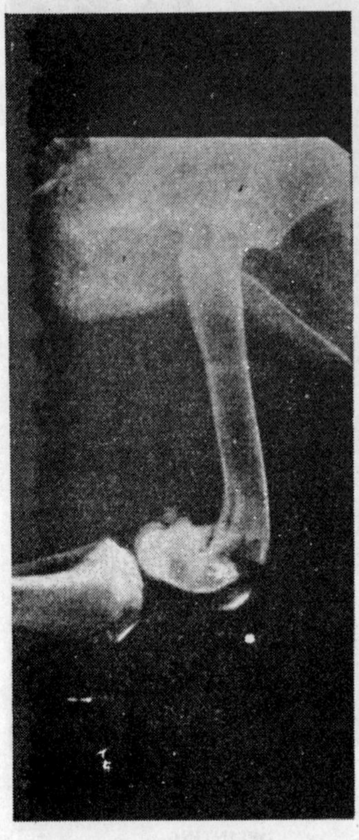

[*By courtesy of Victor X-ray Corpn., Ltd.*

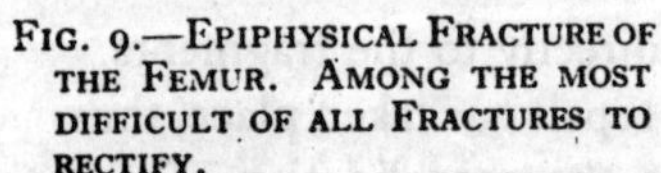

FIG. 9.—EPIPHYSICAL FRACTURE OF THE FEMUR. AMONG THE MOST DIFFICULT OF ALL FRACTURES TO RECTIFY.

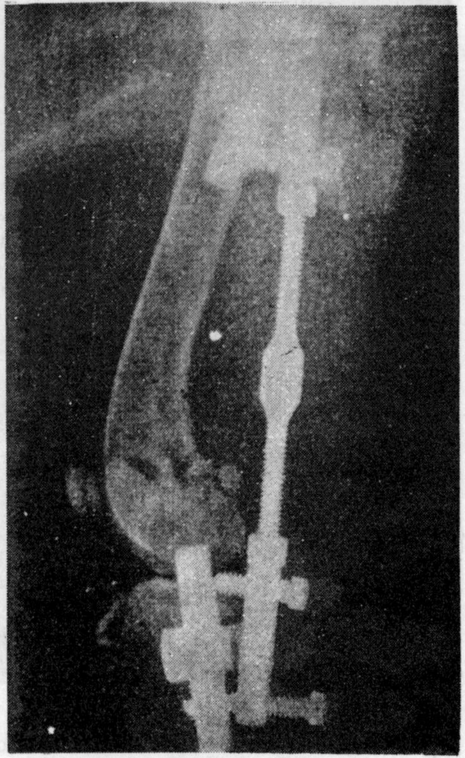

[*By courtesy of Victor X-ray Corpn., Ltd.*

FIG. 10.—THE SAME PERFECTLY SET WITH A STADAR SPLINT. IN THIS CASE THE APPARATUS IS APPLIED DISTALLY TO THE TIBIA.

(2) When repair has apparently taken place, check it with fluoroscopy, make adjustments if necessary, and then take an X-ray.

(3) Take an X-ray during the immediate post-operative treatment to determine the healing process, possible pin displacement, commencing degeneration, etc. This is not necessarily a routine procedure as pin reactions of clinical significance are not anticipated.

(4) The duration of fragment immobilisation is determined by the degree of bony union even in cases where pins have been *in situ* for 8 to 16 weeks.

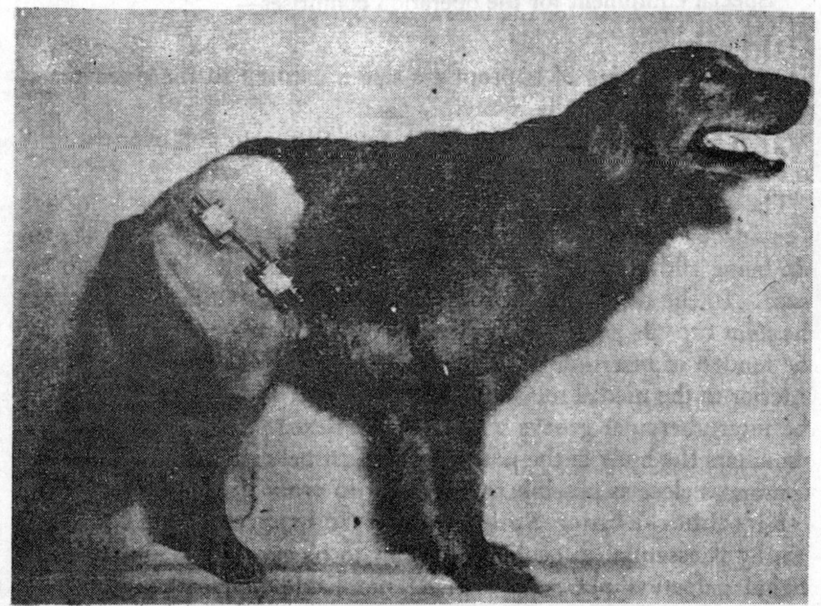

[By courtesy of Victor X-ray Corpn., Ltd.

FIG. 11.—A DOG WEARING THE SPLINT, SHOWING THE ACCESSIBILITY OF ADJUSTMENT NUTS.

(5) Actual operation for the application of the Kirschner-Ehmer Splint comprises the practice of four main principles—

(*a*) Sterilisation, otherwise there may be pin infections, loose pins, gangrene, osteomyelitis, etc.

(*b*) Use of sharp pins to avoid disappointment and discouragement, as dull pins are difficult to insert and, the metal being soft, the point is easily turned under pressure.

(*c*) Penetration of both cortices of the bone by each pin, otherwise they will loosen.

(*d*) Placing the pins at a converging angle clear of the fractured area and of the joints.

Intermedullary Pinning.—This is the most recently developed method of fracture repair. Objections raised to it are bone marrow destruction and the danger of sepsis and of fat embolism, but there is ample evidence to show that these objections are more potential than real. The field for its use is limited. It is suitable for transverse or nearly transverse fractures of the femur, humerus, tibia. It is often easier to apply than the K.E. Splint.

Special equipment for the operation comprises—

(1) Pin handle.

(2) Stimmon pins of appropriate size according to the diameter of the marrow cavity on the X-ray.

(3) A Gordon Extendor and Stockinette Sleeve to pull over the limb to be operated upon.

The site of insertion in the femur is in the trochanteric fossa through a cutaneous incision on the dorsal aspect of the trochanter major, the pin being slid along the medial surface of the trochanter and into the fossa. In the tibia, the pin is inserted with the stifle flexed to tighten the joint capsule and pull it posteriorly. The pin is passed medially to the tendon of insertion of the quadriceps into the tibial tuberosity just anterior to the medial meniscus. In the humerus it is inserted through the intertubercular groove with the joint flexed. In the mandible the pin enters the body at the posterior end just below the angular process, keeping as close as possible to the cortex to avoid the roots of the teeth.

Kirschner-Ehmer Splint for Pelvic Fractures.—Good radiography is essential to enable the splint to be accurately applied, mere digital palpation per rectum being unreliable to ascertain the exact nature of the displacement of the fragments. The use of the splint is the only means of treating successfully pelvic fractures in which the displacement is so marked that spontaneous recovery during complete rest in a confined space is out of the question. Two to four complete sets of splints may be required for proper reduction and fixation. A very important point is to determine what bone or piece of bone is in a normal position and solid and suitable for an " anchor " from which the splint is built. The wing of the ilium is a good point of fixation when available, as is also the tuber ischii.

Proficiency in the practice of bone pinning in the treatment of fractures can only be acquired after repeated experiments on the dead animal and careful perusal of the current literature on the subject including the paper on which the foregoing remarks are based. It remains to be seen, however, whether bone and intermedullary pinning are practicable in the large animals.

Massage and Mobilisation of the Fractured Limb.—Removal of the immobilising dressing occasionally to massage the muscles and mobilise the joints for the prevention of atrophy and anchylosis is not practicable in the large animals, and is not necessary in the majority of cases.

Duration of the Dressing.—It is generally necessary to keep the dressing in position for at least two months in the horse. Although the callus is well formed before this time, it may not be sufficiently consolidated to withstand the force of the body-weight or of strong muscular exertion.

After removal of the dressing the muscles are usually found wasted, and the joints more or less stiff. Lameness persists for a while. Eventually, as the result of exercise, the atrophy and stiffness disappear and the animal goes sound. If a joint is involved in a fracture, the resulting callus usually causes anchylosis.

Separation of the epiphysis may occur in young animals through the cartilage of conjugation. It may be confounded with dislocation. Treatment is the same as for fractures. It is difficult to effect reduction and immobilisation on account of the proximity of the joint.

Complications of Fractures

Complications of fractures include:

1. **Gangrene** of the soft tissues beneath the dressing, owing to the latter being too tightly applied, or to excessive pressure on certain parts. It is favoured by the dressing becoming saturated with moisture, as from exposure to rain.

Except the condition is localised in small areas, it renders the case hopeless. Its occurrence is indicated by discharge appearing at the ends of the dressing and by a foul odour, and by constitutional disturbance if the gangrenous area is large.

Treatment consists in removing the dressing immediately and treating for gangrene, if the case is not too bad. A temporary immobilising dressing must be applied in the meantime.

2. **Faulty Callus Formation.**—Sometimes, owing to poverty of lime salts in the system or to the presence of disease (osteomalacia, rickets), the callus is slow to form. In such a case, except osteomalacia is the cause, generous diet and the administration of phosphates of lime may have some effect.

3. **The formation of a False Joint.**—A false joint is due to the failure of callus formation, the two ends of the bone being united by fibrous tissue or being covered by cartilage and provided with a synovial membrane like a true joint. The false joint may be the result of—

(*a*) Imperfect reduction and immobilisation of the fracture.

(*b*) The interposition of a piece of muscular, tendinous, or aponeurotic tissue between the fragments. There is usually no remedy for this condition in the large animals.

The following measures are recommended, and may succeed in small patients:

1. Rubbing the ends of the fragments together.
2. Scarification of the interfragmentary fibrous tissue.

3. Passing a seton through the false joint.

4. Injecting tincture of iodine or 10 per cent. zinc chloride into the pseudo-arthrosis.

5. Removing a piece of tissue that is intervening between the ends.

6. Bier's hyperæmic treatment, which has often succeeded, but only in cases where there is a fibrous union between the fragments because this tissue is ossifiable.

7. Freshening the ends of the fragments and uniting them by sutures or plates, a favourite method in human surgery.

8. Inserting a rod of bone 3 to 4 inches long, taken from a calf, into the medullary cavity of the two ends, thereby keeping them in position and stimulating ossification.

If a fracture is improperly reduced, resulting in a large callus and deformity of the limb, the bone may be refractured by the hands in a small animal or by osteoclasts and set in the correct position, or osteotomy, which is preferable, may be performed to enable this to be done, as is customary now in the human subject and in small animals. Refracture, however, or osteotomy is not likely to succeed in a large animal, and in any case is only practicable below the elbow or stifle.

When a nerve is compressed by a large callus, causing paralysis or pain, the enlargement may be removed if in an accessible situation. These operations, however, are rarely practised in the large animals.

Fractures in the Dog and Cat

With regard to fractures in the dog and cat, it is only necessary to mention that the prognosis is highly favourable, and to enumerate some of the methods of treatment which are suitable for these animals, other features of the conditions being the same as in the horse. Reduction of the fracture is comparatively easy, and immobilisation of the fragments is on the whole a simple matter.

The following methods of fixing the fragments in position are applicable in these animals :

1. A **plaster of Paris bandage,** suitable for fractures below the elbow and stifle in the medium- and large-sized dogs, but rather heavy for small dogs and cats.

2. A **gum bandage,** suitable for all classes of dogs, but specially indicated for the small varieties and for cats. It takes some hours to solidify, but in the meantime light splints may be applied outside the dressing until the gum becomes hard. The animal does not seem so prone to bite this dressing as that composed of other materials.

3. A **starch bandage,** very suitable for the smaller breeds as an alternative to the gum bandage. It also takes a good while to become solid.

4. **Light splints,** made of thin wood or cardboard or tin, may be used as a temporary dressing, or even as a permanent one.

5. **Pitch** applied between the turns of a bandage answers the purpose for all kinds of dogs, but it is not so clean a dressing as those already mentioned. It is the most suitable application for fractures of the shoulder and hip, because by means of it the bandage can be made adherent to the skin in these regions, and thus prevented from slipping down. For fracture of the shoulder it is advisable to bring the bandage round the thorax and in front of the chest as well as round the limb. Or it may be used in the form of a charge, as described with reference to the horse.

6. **Poroplastic felt** (see p. 115), which is suitable for fractures below the shoulder and stifle. It is rather clumsy for small animals, but makes a useful temporary dressing.

An even layer of cotton-wool, or wadding, or lint must be applied beneath every hard dressing, and extended beyond it above and below.

7. A **Burgess plaster bandage** applied directly on the skin, to which it adheres. It is suitable for fractures of all parts of the limbs, including the hip and shoulder, because it will not slip down. It makes a good immobilising application.

8. An **ordinary adhesive bandage,** which is of the same nature as the Burgess bandage. Both have a rather irritating effect on the skin which cannot be tolerated by some dogs, which consequently bite them off if measures are not taken to prevent their doing so. The hair adheres to the bandage, rendering the removal of the latter painful.

9. **Unpadded plaster cast,** a method of treatment of fractures in man, described by Dr. Lorenz Böhler of Vienna in his work " The Treatment of Fractures " (1936), and afterwards applied to the dog by various veterinary surgeons, including Barrett, Wright, and McCunn, whose experiences in this connection have been published in the *Veterinary Record*, Vols. 48 and 49.

The method consists in effecting immobilisation of the fragments with the joints of the limb in a position midway between flexion and extension, to avoid tension, by the application of an unpadded plaster of Paris cast.

The advantages of this dressing are that—

1. Its pressure is distributed evenly over the whole of the enclosed surface.

2. Many or all of the joints of the limb are permitted to have a certain amount of movement.

3. It favours active movement of the articulation and early support of weight by the limb, thus preventing atrophy of bones and muscles and stiffness or anchylosis of joints.

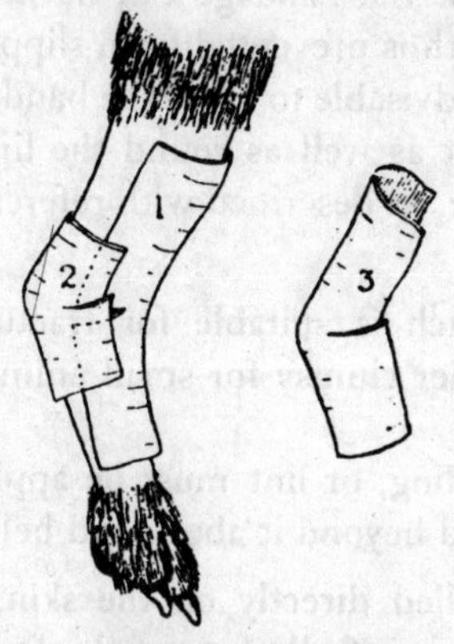

Fig. 12.—Tarsus and Distal End Tibia.

Unpadded plaster casts. (This and Figs. 13, 14, and 15 from Wright's paper, *Vet. Rec.*, Vol. 49.)

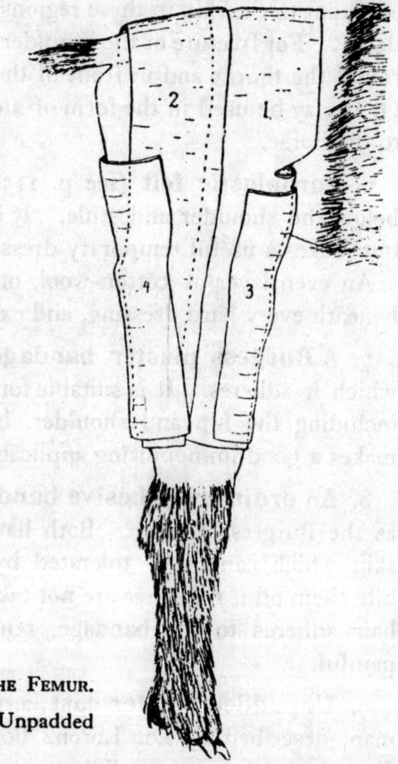

Fig. 13.—Shaft and Lower Third of the Femur.

For shaft and lower third of the femur. Unpadded plaster casts.

Technique.—The plaster is applied in the form of slabs placed longitudinally on the limb. The Cellona plaster of Paris bandages (2, 3, and 4 inches wide and prepared by T. J. Smith and Nephew, Hull) are the most suitable for their formation. The procedure is as follows :

(1) Measure the length of the slab required.

(2) Take a piece of bandage of sufficient length so that when folded four to six times on itself lengthwise it will form a splint or cast of the

required thickness, and roll it on a narrow cylinder of glass or wood and soak it in luke-warm water for a few seconds.

(3) Form the slab on a plate of glass by unrolling the bandage in superimposed layers, adding some water if necessary to ensure that the plaster is well moistened, and pressing the layers together to keep them in close apposition and to remove air bubbles.

(4) Remove the slab by sliding it off the edge of the glass.

(5) Make a sufficient number of slabs which when applied on opposite sides of the limb will completely encircle the latter. A series of short

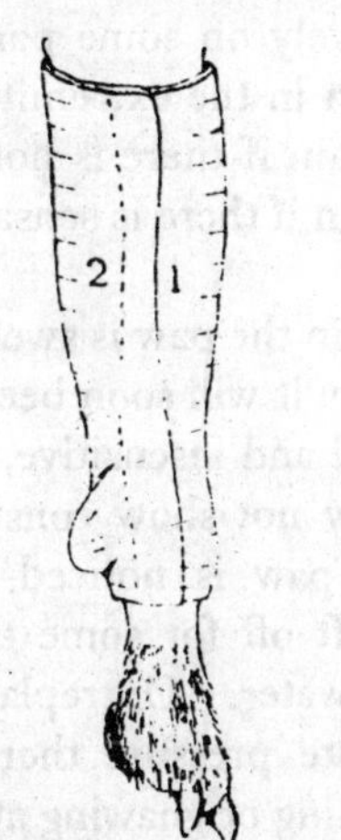

FIG. 14.—PLASTER CAST FOR FRACTURE OF MID-SHAFT RADIUS AND ULNA.

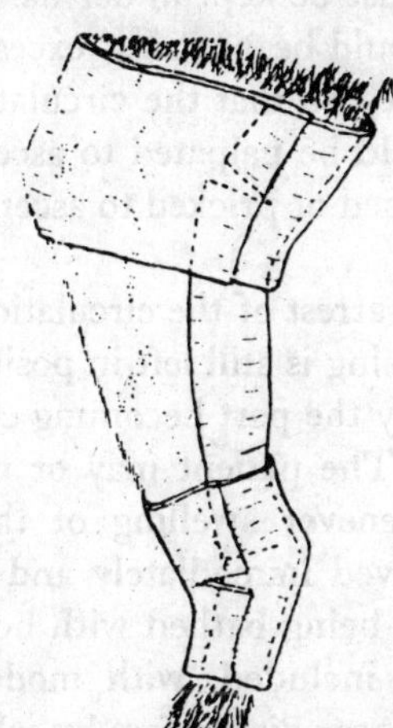

FIG. 15.—PLASTER CAST FOR MID-SHAFT TIBIA WITH "WINDOW."

FIG. 16.—GANGRENE OF THE DOG PAW BY TOO TIGHT BANDAGE.

slabs may be required for wide parts of the limb as they are more easily adapted to the shape of the part.

(6) Before applying the slab wet the hair so that it will more readily imbibe the plaster. If the coat is long it is advisable to shorten it to permit of more accurate adaptation of the slab.

(7) Place the slab in position and carefully mould it to the limb by stroking with the fingers.

(8) Where there is much variation in the thickness of the affected part of the limb the cast should be shaped before putting it in position, and incisions should be made in its edges opposite the joint to allow of correct angulation without creasing the dressing.

(9) Carry out the technique as quickly as possible so that the edges of one slab are not almost dry before applying the next and partly

overlapping one, thereby interfering with the proper setting of the cast.

Although the treatment of fractures by this method has been described as probably applicable to the horse, so far its adoption in veterinary practice has only been reported in connection with the dog.

In all cases (except with regard to the unpadded plaster cast No. 9) the paw must be included in the immobilising dressing, otherwise its circulation will be arrested by the pressure on the upper part of the limb, and it will consequently undergo gangrene if not attended to in time. Precautions must be taken to prevent the patient biting off the dressing and the limb must be kept under daily observation for some time lest the dressing should be pressing excessively on some part or parts of the covered tissues, so that the circulation in the extremity be arrested. The paw should be palpated to ascertain if there is normal heat therein and compressed or pricked to ascertain if there is sensation in the part.

The first indications of arrest of the circulation in the paw is swelling of the latter. If the dressing is still left in position it will soon become gangrenous, recognised by the part becoming cold and insensitive, and by an offensive odour. The patient may or may not show constitutional disturbance. Whenever swelling of the paw is noticed, the dressing should be removed immediately and left off for some time, the paw in the meantime being bathed with hot water. On replacing the dressing the paw is included, with moderate pressure thereon. Whenever the patient evinces discomfort by whining or gnawing at the dressing the latter should be removed and readjusted.

When a false joint supervenes, any of the methods of treatment mentioned on p. 121 may be adopted with a fair chance of success; but the best treatment is to cut down on the seat of fracture, vigorously curette the ends of the fragments and re-apply an immobilising dressing. This procedure usually has the desired effect.

10. **The use of the Stadar Splint or other form of bone pinning or bone plating.** This method is being increasingly and successfully employed in canine practice (see page 116).

Compound Fractures

The open wound in connection with the fracture in the bone may be due to the violence of the accident, or to the end of one of the fragments penetrating the skin, or to sloughing of the soft tissues at the seat of fracture, as the result of severe injury by the force which caused the fracture.

The gravity of the case depends on the severity of the damage inflicted on the bone and other tissues, and the amount of infection that has occurred in the wound. In small animals compound fractures are often caused by the wheels of vehicles passing over their limbs, almost amputating them in some cases, the skin being torn, tendons ruptured, and the bone crushed into numerous pieces. The wound is usually soiled by mud, or dust and hairs.

In bad cases of the nature just mentioned there is no chance of saving the limb, but in ordinary cases, where the tissues are divided without much contusion, the prognosis is nearly as good as in simple fracture with respect to the dog and cat; but in large animals it increases the difficulty of immobilising the fractured bone on account of the necessity of attending to the open wound. Callus formation is more rapid in a compound than in a simple fracture, because in the former the embryonic tissue between the fragments undergoes ossification at once without the formation of a cartilaginous callus.

Treatment consists in:

1. Attending to the open wound.

2. Removing loose spicules of bone devoid of periosteum and bound to undergo necrosis, and cutting off projecting points with a bone forceps.

3. Reducing the fracture as usual.

4. Applying an immobilising dressing with a window opposite the wound to enable it to be kept under observation and to receive suitable treatment. After cleaning the wound with normal saline solution and removing destroyed portions of tissue, performing any necessary debridment, and applying sulphanilamide powder throughout its extent, it may be covered with the plaster of Paris dressing and left undisturbed until healing accurs, provided that the patient evinces no evidence of pain or discomfort or toxæmia. This method of treatment was adopted with marked success during the Second World War. If there is suspicion of serious infection of the wound penicillin should be administered in the usual way.

5. Suturing the ends of the fragments or using the "Stadar Splint," or other form of "bone pinning" or bone plating (see page 116).

In cases of severe compound fractures of the limbs in the dog and cat an attempt should always be made to save the fractured member, provided that its distal portion is not already devoid of vitality. Surprising recoveries sometimes ensue in cases which appeared almost hopeless.

When the wound is kept thoroughly disinfected, sloughing of damaged soft tissues occurs without any complication, leaving a granulating wound which cicatrises rapidly. A portion of the fractured bone may undergo necrosis, but when the sequestrum separates healing ensues. When the injury is obviously irreparable, amputation is indicated. When the condition assumes the nature of a sinus refusing to heal, vigorous curetting of the extremities of the fragments may bring about recovery even after the lesion has been in existence for several weeks.

Fractures in Birds

Fractures in birds are dealt with on the same lines as in other animals. Gum bandages are very suitable as a retention dressing. The escape of air from the interior of long bones causes emphysema at the seat of fracture. If the fracture is compound, the exit of the air from the bone hinders the animal in flight, although the wings are intact.

Ostitis

Ostitis, or inflammation of bone, arises in the same way as inflammation in other tissues. The inflammation is named according to its situation—viz., *periostitis*, affecting the periosteum; *osteoperiostitis*, affecting the periosteum and the bone; *osteomyelitis*, affecting chiefly the marrow in the bone.

Etiology.—The actual causes of any of these forms of ostitis may be a contusion or open wound of bone, or in the case of the limbs, concussion. When an open wound is present, the entrance of micro-organisms aggravates the condition.

When pyogenic bacteria invade the substance of the bone, they set up purulent osteomyelitis. The latter condition is very common in children, affecting chiefly the epiphyses of long bones, and due apparently to pus organisms circulating in the blood selecting these sites for their development. There is no parallel affection in the lower animals.

When septic infection of a bone occurs, necrosis usually ensues.

Inflammation of the bone and periosteum may originate from sprain of ligaments, the condition starting at their points of insertion—*e.g.*, at the pastern and fetlock.

Familiar examples of osteoperiostitis following concussion are splints and "sore shins."

Purulent osteomyelitis is a fairly common condition in the superior or inferior maxilla in the horse and ox, and usually appears as a complication of alveolar periostitis.

Ostitis, as already pointed out, causes rarefaction of the bone, predisposing it to fracture when much of its substance is involved.

Rarefaction is usually followed by gradual sclerosis of the bone.

increasing its power of resistance. This may be merely restitutive or proceed further, causing abnormal condensation of the bone by filling up its canaliculi and Haversian spaces with osseous tissue.

SYMPTOMS.—The symptoms of osteoperiostitis are those of more or less acute or chronic inflammation in a bone, characterised by heat, pain, and swelling, and in the limbs lameness. When the lesion is septic, the inflammatory phenomena are very acute. In chronic cases there may be little local evidence of the condition, except the presence of an ossific deposit. When a limb is affected, lameness is more or less marked. Once an exostosis resulting from osteoperiostitis is completely formed, the inflammation and lameness usually disappear, provided that the bony enlargement does not interfere with the movement of a joint or the play of a tendon.

Purulent osteomyelitis is revealed by the formation of an abscess in the bone, a rare condition in veterinary practice, occurring chiefly in the jaw, as mentioned.

PROGNOSIS.—The prognosis of aseptic inflammatory affections of bone is favourable, the condition running the usual course and terminating in resolution. When sepsis ensues, the prognosis varies according to the severity of the infection and the nature of the complication that may ensue.

TREATMENT is on the usual lines for inflammation, comprising rest, cold, moist heat, massage, and compression for acute and subacute cases, and blistering and firing for the chronic forms. In the suppurative cases drainage for pus must be provided, and antiseptic solutions frequently applied. Caries and necrosis, when present, are treated as described later.

A form of ostitis is met with in animals which appears to be of rheumatoid origin, showing the fugitive and shifting features of this affection, and which responds to the administration of sodium salicylate and potassium iodide. When the acute symptoms have subsided, arsenical preparations are indicated.

Caries

Caries is a gradual molecular purulent destruction of a portion of bone having a tendency to spread rather than undergo spontaneous cure. It is due to pyogenic infection of bone through a breach of surface in the overlying tissues. In the human subject it is usually of tuberculous origin. The os pedis is a fairly common site of the lesion in the horse, as the result of a punctured wound of the foot. It may also affect the dorsal spines in a case of fistulous withers.

SYMPTOMS.—If the bone is superficial, the ulcerated surface is easily recognised, but if deep-seated it is concealed by the soft tissues covering it, and gives rise to the symptoms of a sinus. When a probe is brought against the affected part it can be pushed into the diseased surface, causing a grating noise, serving to distinguish it from necrosis, which is resistant to the probe and sonorous when struck. There may be febrile disturbance due to toxæmia or septicæmia.

PROGNOSIS.—The prognosis is serious on account of the progressive nature of the disease.

TREATMENT is directed towards arresting the progress of the affection, and transforming the centre of the disease into a healthy ordinary wound of bone which will granulate and cicatrise.

This may be effected by:

1. The application of a caustic.
2. Operation.

1. The *use of a caustic* has the effect of transforming the lesion of caries into that of necrosis. The agent used may be the hot iron, a mineral acid, or 10 per cent. zinc chloride. This is a severe and painful method of treatment which does not always have the desired effect.

2. *Operation* consists in removing the diseased portion of the bone by the aid of a sharp curette, which is used to scrape away the diseased osseous tissue until the resistance of the normal bone is encountered and a pink, healthy surface is left. Strict antiseptic precautions must be observed to prevent reinfection of the bone. The operation wound is covered by an antiseptic dressing and cotton-wool. Powdered or crystalline iodoform is a reliable antiseptic dressing to apply to the wound. The dressing is renewed occasionally until the case is cured.

Necrosis

Necrosis of bone is death of a portion of bone *en masse.* It might be called dry gangrene of bone.

ETIOLOGY.—Deprivation of blood supply of a portion of bone will cause that part to lose its vitality. If bacteria are excluded from the affected region, the patient will suffer no ill-effects. This aseptic form of the disease is rarely met with. Practically all the clinical cases are due to infection of the bone through an open wound. Examples of the condition have been seen in the cannon bones, the radius, tibia, lower jaw, ribs, and sternum.

The organisms which most commonly cause necrosis in animals

are staphylococci, streptococci, the bacillus of necrosis, the tubercle bacillus, and actinomycosis. The extent of the necrosis varies in different cases. Frequently it is very slight, affecting only a wafer-like portion of the bone, or causing separation of small particles of it (parcellary necrosis). Exceptionally large portions undergo necrosis. The sequestrum may be exposed or invaginated. In the former case the overlying periosteum has been destroyed, while in the latter case the periosteum remains *in situ*, but separated from the bone in the affected region, over which it forms an encasement of new bone.

Symptoms.—The symptoms are those of a sinus abutting on bone and associated with an inflammatory swelling. A probe passed into the orifice comes in contact with the hard, resistant sequestrum, which is sonorous when struck, and evidently devoid of periosteum. When the sequestrum is invaginated, the overlying bone becomes perforated with holes or cloacæ, through which pus escapes from the necrotic centre. When the sequestrum is loose, it can be made to move by means of the probe or sound passed into the sinus. The swelling is very marked in a case of invaginated necrosis. Functional disturbance may be observed, depending on the part affected.

Prognosis.—The prognosis is more favourable than in caries, because in necrosis there is tendency to spontaneous cure by the elimination of the sequestrum. If the latter is superficial and not invaginated, it may fall away of its own accord after being separated, and then recovery will ensue. But when it is covered by thick layers of soft tissue or imprisoned by new bone it will have no chance of escape, and the suppuration will continue as long as it is present.

Treatment.—The principles of treatment are to (1) hasten the formation of the line of demarcation of the dead part; (2) accelerate the process of separation; (3) counteract infection; and (4) favour the process of repair.

The procedure adopted comprises:

1. The application of ordinary antiseptic solutions to the lesion.

2. The injection of an irritant antiseptic lotion into the sinus, which will have a hyperæmic effect, and thus hasten the process of elimination, such as tincture of iodine.

3. The application of a blister to the region, when practicable, to cause increased phagocytosis, and thus accelerate elimination of the sequestrum in a case where separation is unusually slow.

4. Bier's hyperæmic method when the lower part of a limb is involved.

5. The provision of drainage for the pus from the necrotic centre.

6. The removal of the sequestrum when it is loose, which may be a simple matter, consisting in merely taking it away with a forceps, or may involve cutting through a considerable depth of soft tissue or trephining through the invaginating bone to reach it.

7. Operating to remove the diseased portion of bone instead of awaiting its natural separation. Operation is seldom indicated. It may be done where the necrotic area is circumscribed and can be readily excised—for example, on the summits of the dorsal spines—or when it is feared that infection may spread to some important organ.

In certain cases a 2 to 3 per cent. solution of hydrochloric acid might be employed to decalcify the sequestrum, the following preparation being afterwards applied to digest the decalcified remnant: hydrochloric acid, ♏xvi.; pepsin, ʒss.; distilled water, ℥viii. The patient requires generous diet during the course of the treatment.

Exostoses

Exostoses, or outgrowths on bone, may appear without any apparent cause, or occur as the result of osteoperiostitis. In the latter case they most frequently occur in the vicinity of joints, where they originate as sprain of the ligaments or as an arthritis. Examples of exostoses are represented by splints, spavin, ringbone, etc., which will be dealt with individually.

Rickets

Rickets is a systemic disease of young animals, characterised by a dearth of lime salts in the bones, whereby they undergo deformity as the result of bending or curvature.

Osteomalacia is a similar disease affecting adults, being characterised by the disappearance of the lime salts, as the result of which the bones lose their rigidity and fracture on the slightest provocation.

These diseases belong more to the domain of internal medicine than to that of surgery, and consequently they will not be dealt with here, except to mention some of their characteristic features.

Rickets is common in puppies, affecting chiefly the limbs, and is easily recognised by the deformity they undergo, the joints being enlarged and the long bones curved. Osteomalacia is common in young goats in cities, most frequently affecting the lower jaw, which loses its solidarity, being capable of being bent in various directions and proving powerless for mastication. Rickets tends to improve with time.

TREATMENT.—The treatment of rickets is chiefly constitutional, and comprises giving nutritious diet, administering cod-liver oil and tonic medicine and allowing plenty of exercise in the open air. Violet-ray treatment is indicated for valuable subjects. Osteomalacia is treated on similar lines, but usually without any beneficial result. As a result of it multiple fractures may ensue.

XI.—AFFECTIONS OF JOINTS

Contusions

A contusion of a joint may be simple or accompanied by sprain, dislocation, or fracture. It may be direct or indirect. The former is due to direct violence inflicted on the joint, and the latter to violence transmitted to it through the bones from a point distant from the joint—for example, a contusion of the shoulder-joint may result from a fall on the knees, the articulation being more or less crushed between the scapula above and the radius and humerus below.

SYMPTOMS.—The symptoms are those of acute inflammation in the region of the joint, characterised by heat, pain, and swelling. The synovial capsule may be distended with synovia.

Lameness is more or less severe. The actual amount of damage done to the joint cannot be determined.

PROGNOSIS.—The prognosis must be guarded. Stiffening or anchylosis of the joint is always to be feared.

TREATMENT.—Treatment includes (1) rest of the articulation; (2) the use of antiphlogistic applications; (3) massage and compression of the joint; (4) exercise, when the acute inflammation has subsided, with a view to preventing stiffness or anchylosis.

Immobilisation and compression of the articulation are effected by cotton-wool and a bandage. Where a bandage is not applicable, a blister may be applied instead. Plaster of Paris bandages may be used to compress and immobilise the affected joint. When lameness persists, counter-irritation, blistering, or firing may be practised.

Sprain of Joints

Sprain of a joint results from its movement beyond its physiological limits in the direction of extension, flexion, abduction, or adduction. The joint undergoes a temporary luxation. As a consequence, the articular and periarticular tissues suffer a certain amount of bruising or laceration. The ligaments in particular are subjected to distension. The sprain may occur in various ways: by slipping, falling, or a false step, or by over-exertion.

The changes which occur in and around the joint vary according to the severity of the sprain. The ligaments may have only a few fibres ruptured, or they may be completely severed or torn away from their insertion. The diarthrodial cartilages may be bruised and there is always some hæmorrhage into the synovial capsule, as well as into the periarticular tissues.

Tendons passing over the joint may be overstretched or ruptured. The chief seat of sprain may be anterior, posterior, or lateral; but after a while the inflammation becomes diffuse, and it may then be difficult to locate the exact structure that is principally involved.

Symptoms.—The symptoms are acute local inflammation and severe lameness. Pain is at once manifested on passive movement of the joint, especially in the direction in which the sprain was caused. Pain is also very evident on pressure over the affected region, particularly at the insertion of the sprained ligaments.

The swelling forms quickly. It is due to extravasation of blood, inflammatory exudate, and distension of the synovial capsule. These symptoms are not so obvious in the upper joints of the limbs, where they are covered by layers of muscles. Muscular atrophy may ensue from the extravasation into the joint compressing the nerves there, and thus causing a reflex action which brings about the atrophy.

Prognosis.—The prognosis depends on the severity of the injury to the joint. When the sprain is slight, complete recovery ensues, whereas, if ligaments have been completely ruptured or torn from their insertions, or if the articular cartilages have been crushed, prolonged or permanent lameness will supervene.

Treatment.—The treatment at first is that for aseptic acute inflammation, comprising immobilisation of the joint, cold and astringent applications, followed later by hot moist applications and massage.

The virtues of massage are well known. When the case is chronic, blistering or firing is indicated. During convalescence, regular exercise should be given to prevent adhesions forming in and around the articulation.

Dislocations

A joint is dislocated when the two articular extremities forming it are displaced from perfect contact with one another. The dislocation may be (1) complete, in which the articular ends are in no part in contact with one another; or (2) incomplete, in which they are still partially in contact.

ETIOLOGY.—The cause may be (1) traumatic—that is, direct violence, causing the articular extremities to become separated; or (2) it may be some pathological condition, such as paralysis of certain muscles or arthritis, which favours luxation on slight provocation; or (3) the dislocation may be congenital.

In cases (2) and (3) the condition is hopeless.

Traumatic dislocations are the result of severe violence, and are consequently accompanied as a rule by serious alterations in the articular and periarticular tissues.

SYMPTOMS.—The symptoms are pain, inability to use the limb immobility of the affected joint, and deformity.

The immobility is due chiefly to the mechanical impossibility o free movement of the articular extremities on account of their dis placement. Pain also prevents voluntary movement in the affectec region. Sometimes, however, when all the ligaments, including the capsular ligament, are ruptured, excessive movement can be produced in all directions between the ends of the bones.

Deformity is obvious, due to the displacement: a prominence is observed in an abnormal situation, and a depression may occur where normally there should be a prominence. The limb takes an abnormal direction. The ends of the bones may be actually overlapping. Great inflammatory swelling surrounding a deep-seated dislocation tends to conceal the characteristic features of the condition. A rocking noise, rather than a crepitation, may be obtained on manipulation of the bones, due to the articular ends knocking against each other.

The limb may be shortened or lengthened, according as the bones overlap or are in contact at the periphery of their articular surfaces.

DIAGNOSIS is generally easy from the foregoing symptoms. In contusions and sprains of joints immobility of the articulations is due to pain, and is overcome by anæsthesia, which has no effect in mobilising a dislocated joint. The sharp crepitation of a fracture is absent.

A fracture and a dislocation may coexist. When the case is chronic, atrophy of the muscles acting on the joint supervenes, rendering the ends of the bones very prominent and capable of being mistaken for an exostosis.

PROGNOSIS.—The prognosis varies according to the nature of the dislocation, whether it be accompanied by comparatively slight or serious injury to the surrounding tissues, and on the amount of displacements.

In the large animals reduction may be impossible, and even when it is effected the result may be unsatisfactory, owing to stiffness or anchylosis supervening on cicatrisation of the ruptured ligaments and organisation of the inflammatory exudate inside the joint cavity. If the luxation is not reduced a false joint will be formed, the tissues in the vicinity of the displaced articular extremities undergoing modifications, so as to simulate a true joint, new ligaments, and even a synovial membrane, being formed. The articular ends themselves undergo changes to accommodate them to the new surroundings.

In the ox and dog the new joint may be sufficient to allow the animal to go comparatively sound, and thus prove a satisfactory result, but in the horse it is never good enough to enable the animal to work.

TREATMENT comprises: (1) reduction and (2) retention.

(1) Reduction consists in applying traction in opposite directions on the two extremities of the limb, so as to bring the two articular surfaces on the same level, and then pushing the two articular heads into their normal position.

In small animals these manipulations are easy, but in the large animals they are very difficult. In both cases general anæsthesia is desirable or necessary. It prevents pain and muscular resistance.

In the horse traction is effected by two ropes, one applied at the proximal end of the limb and the other at the distal end. It requires the strength of several men to overcome the displacement. At first, gentle measures should be adopted, so as to avoid further damage to the periarticular tissues; but if these fail, it will be necessary to resort to powerful force. More uniform traction can be obtained by means of pulleys than by several assistants.

In attempting reduction, an effort should be made to return the articular ends in the direction through which the dislocation took place to avoid further laceration of the capsular ligament. When reduction has taken place, a " click " is usually heard, and the normal movement and appearance of the articulation are restored. Perseverance and patience are often required before success is attained. The sooner after the accident that the case is attended to the more easily it is dealt with.

Many cases will be met with where all efforts prove in vain. Then a subcutaneous operation may be performed, known as arthrotomy, to cut fibrous bands which are offering resistance to reduction. The articular head of one of the bones might be resected to enable a useful false joint to be formed, in the dog.

(2) Retention is carried out in the same way as for fractures. Slings

are generally indicated for the horse to help to keep the joint at rest. The joint should not be immobilised for a longer period than is absolutely necessary to prevent recurrence, for fear of stiffness or anchylosis supervening.

The patient should get gentle exercise at the earliest opportunity to promote freedom of articular movement. When the dislocation is complicated by an open wound into the joint, septic arthritis usually follows, rendering the case hopeless. If a fracture accompanies the luxation, a stiff joint will ensue.

Open Joint

Open wounds penetrating into joints give rise to the condition known as "open joint."

The joint may be opened at the time the wound is inflicted at its level, or subsequently from sloughing of a damaged layer of tissue intervening between the base of the wound and the articulation. In the latter case infection of the synovial membrane usually occurs simultaneously.

SYMPTOMS.—The symptoms are those of an open wound at the level of a joint discharging synovia, which is recognised by its pale yellow colour and its oily feel when rubbed between the fingers or in the palm of the hand. In the latter case it forms a soapy lather.

When the joint is moved the synovia flows more copiously. After a while the fluid coagulates to form a yellow clot resembling a piece of fat. A probe passed into the wound would confirm the diagnosis, but there would be danger in doing so of introducing infection into the joint. Hence its use is contra-indicated.

The wound may be punctured, incised, lacerated, or contused. The interior of the joint may be visible when the wound is gaping. When the synovial fistula is recent, there may be little or no evidence of local inflammation, and lameness may be absent. Two to six days may elapse before evidence of infection appears, and it varies in degree according to the virulence of the organisms.

Synovitis only may supervene, which eventually undergoes resolution, or purulent arthritis may ensue, necessitating destruction of the large animal or amputation of the limb in one of the smaller species. The inflammation is indicated by the usual signs of heat, pain, and swelling all round the joint, and in the case of a limb by severe lameness. There is more or less febrile disturbance, according to the amount of toxæmia that has taken place.

Treatment.—The treatment is the same as for open wounds in general, having for its object the prevention of infection, which is the only thing to be feared. Other special indications in connection with " open joint " are (1) to keep the articulation at rest so as to diminish the flow of synovia, and thus lessen its interference with the closure of the fistula ; (2) to produce coagulation of the synovia in the wound, and thereby arrest or diminish its discharge ; and (3) to exercise the joint after the wound has cicatrised to prevent adhesions between the surfaces of the synovial membrane, and consequent limitation of movement in the articulation.

Antisepsis of the wound is carried out on the principles already laid down in the treatment of open wounds. If the wound is extensive and clean cut, it should be sutured throughout the greater part of its extent, an opening being left for drainage at its lower part. Any reliable antiseptic solution may be applied to the wound. Tincture of iodine, Dakin's solution, eusol, perchloride of mercury (1 in 1,000), carbolic acid (2 to 5 per cent.), and lysol (2 per cent.) are amongst those most in favour.

An antiseptic powder should then be applied. It has also a desiccant effect, tending to clog the synovial discharge and thus favour healing. Iodoform or a mixture of iodoform, boric acid, and zinc oxide is very suitable. When possible, a layer of gauze covered by a pad of cotton-wool and a bandage is applied to protect the wound. The following are methods of treatment for which good results have been claimed—viz., the use of—

1. *Perchloride of mercury* (1 *part*) *and glycerine* (16 *parts*) applied above the wound, and allowed to trickle over it. This is an excellent topic.

2. An *antiseptic powder*, as mentioned above, applied repeatedly according as it becomes saturated with discharge, no bandage being employed with this method.

3. *Oil of cloves*, which is antiseptic, and coagulant for the synovia.

4. *Perchloride of mercury powder*, which is a caustic and causes an eschar, under which healing may take place. It is worth a trial in a case in which the fistula is obstinate to heal. It has often been used with success. A danger of it is that it may cause too much destruction of tissues and increase the size of the opening. It is a very old method.

5. The *hot iron* rapidly applied to the walls of the synovial fistula. It has a germicidal and hyperæmic effect which favours cicatrisation. It is not much in vogue nowadays, and requires to be used with great caution.

6. A *blister of biniodide of mercury* (1 in 8) applied over the fistula and its vicinity. This is very useful for an open joint on the upper part of the limb, where a bandage cannot be used, or in any case that is slow in recovering. It has an undoubtedly good effect.

7. *Cold-water irrigation* from a hose-pipe, or a perforated tube applied bracelet-like round the limb above the joint. Many practitioners speak highly of this treatment in association with antiseptic applications.

8. *Steffen's procedure—i.e.*, thoroughly cleaning the wound, irrigating the joint cavity for at least ten minutes with a solution of corrosive sublimate (1 part to 3,000 of water) at body temperature, followed by irrigation with physiological salt solution, the irrigations being continued until the fluid returns clear and free from pus flakes, etc., and then injecting into the interior of the joint the following preparation: Biniodide of mercury, ½ ounce; pure olive oil, 4 ounces; mixed and shaken before using. This is injected slowly, and then the entire joint is enveloped in cotton-wool and suitable bandage or other retaining appliance put on. The dressing is left on for two weeks. Steffen claims that cure is obtained in nine cases out of ten at the end of the period mentioned.

9. *Lacto serum* (see p. 30).

10. *Sulphanilamide and penicillin.*—At present most of the foregoing methods are apt to be relegated in favour of sulphonamides and penicillin used locally and internally as described when dealing with open wounds for the prevention or cure of infection therein.

After healing has taken place, massage or counter-irritation by blistering or firing may be required to reduce periarticular thickening and, along with exercise, to restore freedom of movement to the joint.

Traumatic Arthritis

Traumatic arthritis is the result of septic infection through an open penetrating wound of a joint. It is generally manifested from the third to the fifth day after the occurrence of the accident.

Symptoms.—The symptoms are (1) great swelling of the joint; (2) evidence of great pain on manipulation of the part; (3) synovial discharge from the wound mixed with pus; (4) great lameness when a limb is involved, characterised by inability to bear weight, and by constant shifting of the limb when the animal is standing; (5) extensive swelling in the vicinity of the affected articulation, causing thickening of the whole limb, when it is a joint therein that is diseased.

The general symptoms are indicative of great suffering, the patient having an anxious expression and hurried respirations, and remaining fixed in the one position on account of the pain caused by movement. He may assume the recumbent position, and then lies constantly and often broadside, moaning occasionally with pain and looking round at the seat of the latter. As the disease advances the discharge from the wound becomes more copious and purulent, and emits a very offensive odour. It may be mixed with blood, indicating that the articular cartilages are ulcerated and that the granulations on the ulcers have ruptured, causing hæmorrhage. Traumatic fever is well marked by a high temperature, frequent weak pulse, injected dirty conjunctiva, and inappetence. The animal becomes rapidly emaciated and tucked up.

Bed-sores form on the prominences of the limbs, body, and head from constant recumbency or from resting all the body weight in the slings when the latter are used. If the patient be not destroyed, it will die from exhaustion caused by toxæmia or septicæmia, associated with the great pain of the lesion. The best result that can be hoped for is anchylosis of the joint from fusion of its articular surfaces after removal of the cartilages through ulceration. This, however, is a rare termination, and only occurs, as a rule, in connection with gliding articulations.

TREATMENT.—Once purulent arthritis is established, there is no possibility of curing the condition. Purulent synovitis, involving only the synovial membrane, precedes in many cases septic invasion of the bone and cartilages of the joint, and so long as the latter are intact there is a chance of recovery. This must be the explanation of the exceptional instances of recovery that sometimes occur in cases that appeared hopeless.

The treatment does not differ from that already described for open joint, except that in the case of purulent arthritis opening up the fistula is indicated to enlarge the opening into the joint and provide a free exit for its septic contents. The injection of lacto serum into the joint cavity has given good results in several cases of purulent synovitis which seemed identical with previous cases that had proved incurable by other methods of treatment. Sulphonamides and penicillin are indicated as for aseptic and septic wounds. It may be injected by means of a hypodermic syringe so that it will percolate through the joint cavity. Bier's hyperæmic treatment is indicated where possible. The best treatment in the small animals is amputation when a limb is involved, or excision of the joint when situated elsewhere or as an alternative procedure to amputation. In the ox, affecting one digit, amputation above the diseased joint should be done without hesitation, as it ensures immediate recovery.

Closed Synovitis

Closed articular synovitis is inflammation of a joint occurring apart from an open wound. It may be the result of a contusion, or a sprain, or a dislocation, or infection reaching the articulation by way of the blood stream.

The Symptoms are those of acute inflammation in the region of the joint, which is swollen, hot, and painful. Its synovial capsule is more or less distended with synovia. Severe lameness is present in the case of a limb. At rest, the joint is held in a state of semi-flexion, which corresponds to its greatest capacity, and thus gives some relief. Except the condition is the result of systemic infection, its symptoms are never so severe as those of traumatic arthritis.

Treatment is the same as for external inflammation in general. It comprises rest and the application of antiphlogistic remedies, as described. If the case becomes chronic, with persistent distension of the joint capsule, counter-irritation will be necessary, and if this is not sufficient, aspiration and injection of the synovial capsule may be practised, as described in connection with chronic synovitis.

When the condition is of toxic origin and associated with some bacterial disease, like influenza, pneumonia, etc., its progress depends on that of the disease which it accompanies. The internal administration of large doses of sodium salicylate may be efficacious in such cases, combined with the ordinary local treatment. Penicillin treatment is of course indicated on the ground that the causal organism may be penicillin sensitive.

Articular Rheumatism

Rheumatoid arthritis is fairly common in bovines, carnivora, and swine, but rare in the horse. Its characteristic features are (1) febrile disturbance; (2) several joints being affected at once; (3) shifting of the inflammation from one joint to another; and (4) sudden improvement, followed by relapses.

Treatment consists in protecting the patients from cold and damp, administering sodium salicylate, and adopting local antiphlogistic measures, including the application of anodyne liniments. Treatment is often unsatisfactory. When the case becomes chronic with absorption of the articular cartilages, cure is out of the question.

Post-Partum Synovitis

A form of synovitis most commonly affecting the stifle-joint, and sometimes the knee and hock, is occasionally seen in the cow after parturition, due to toxæmia arising from infection of the genital tract.

Symptoms.—The symptoms are (1) severe lameness; (2) pain and swelling of the affected joint; and (3) febrile disturbance. The condition assumes a chronic course, and after a long time calcareous matter may be deposited in the walls of the synovial capsule.

Prognosis.—The prognosis is unfavourable, as complete cure rarely supervenes and the animal fails to thrive.

Treatments.—Treatment consists in counteracting toxæmia by the usual antiseptic douching of the uterus and vagina and administering a sulphonamide or penicillin according to the nature of the infection. The best results locally seem to have been obtained from needle-point firing or rubbing in pure sulphuric acid. The latter causes a slough which takes three or four weeks to separate and seems hardly justified notwithstanding reports of its efficacy. In bad cases no form of treatment produces a good effect.

Joint Ill

Joint ill or joint evil is the name given to arthritis affecting young animals, and due to infection gaining entrance through the umbilicus before it has become cicatrised. It is a great source of loss to stockbreeders.

Symptoms.—The disease makes its appearance within a few days after birth. Several joints are usually affected at the same time, becoming swollen, hot, and painful, and causing marked lameness. The patient lies almost constantly. Febrile disturbance is evident. The animal becomes dull, refuses to suck, has an accelerated pulse, a rise in temperature, and quickened respiration. After a while abscess formation occurs in the affected joints. In very acute cases death may supervene in twenty-four to forty-eight hours. Occasionally there is only slight constitutional disturbance.

Prevention consists in strict attention to hygiene in connection with parturition, taking every precaution to prevent contamination of the umbilical cord after its rupture. On delivery the fœtus is laid on clean litter or a clean sheet, its umbilical cord ligatured at once with a sterilised ligature (silk or ordinary cord), and severed about an inch below the seat of ligation.

The ligatured cord is dressed with an antiseptic preparation, such as tincture of iodine, after which it may be painted with collodion. A polyvalent serum is also indicated when the disease has already existed on the stud or farm.

TREATMENT.—When the disease is established it usually proves fatal, or if the animal recovers it fails to thrive or remains permanently lame.

Stimulants are indicated, brandy being the best. The swollen joints are treated with hot stupes, or, better, with poultices or antiphlogistine. Sodium salicylate, or salol, and laxative medicine (sulphate of soda) may be given internally. Antistreptococcic or antistaphylococcic serum or a polyvalent serum is indicated. When an abscess is present it is opened, and a free exist made for the pus. The measures mentioned, however, usually prove in vain and the only chance of success when the causal organism is gram positive is the prompt, frequent and massive administration of penicillin.

Gouty Arthritis

Gouty arthritis is sometimes met with in birds, affecting several of the joints, and characterised by a diffuse, soft, painful swelling at the level of the affected articulation. Nodules the size of a pea or a nut form afterwards, and when incised give exit to a whitish material which, on microscopic examination, is found to be composed of crystals of urate of sodium. When left alone, several of these enlargements open spontaneously. There may also be gouty deposits in the viscera. The condition may be confounded with tuberculosis, but is distinguished therefrom by microscopic examination of the discharge.

TREATMENT consists in opening the swellings and the application of tincture of iodine, and in the administration of alkalines, such as bicarbonate of soda.

Dry Arthritis (Arthritis Ossificans or Deformans)

This is a chronic form of arthritis, characterised by a gradual destruction of the articular cartilages and the production of ossific deposits at the periphery of the articular surfaces and in the periarticular fibrous tissue. The condition is met with in the horse, ox, and dog. Common examples of it in the horse are articular ringbone, spavin, and chronic gonitis.

ETIOLOGY.—The cause of the condition is not very clear. It may be traumatic, especially when only one joint is affected. When several joints are involved, it is probably of toxic origin. It is commonly ascribed to rheumatism.

SYMPTOMS.—The symptoms comprise lameness and changes in the form of the joint, which becomes enlarged owing to fibrous thickening and bony deposits in the periarticular tissues and on the ends of the bones. Pain is evinced on passive movement and pressure to the joint, and crepitation may sometimes be detected on flexion and extension of the articulation due to friction between the ulcerated surfaces of the joint.

PROGNOSIS is grave, because the condition is incurable.

TREATMENT is consequently useless. Sometimes a piece of fibrous tissue, fat, cartilage, or bone is found free in a joint affected with the above disease. It may cause no special symptom, or give rise to intermittent phases of intensified lameness. It is a rare condition. Even if diagnosed, there is no object in operating to remove the offending body.

Anchylosis

When the power of movement of a joint is limited or arrested, it is said to be anchylosed. The anchylosis may be (1) complete or (2) incomplete.

(1) **Complete anchylosis** may be due (*a*) to fusion of the two articular surfaces following an attack of arthritis ; or (*b*) to ossification of the periarticular tissues, particularly the ligaments, the synovial membrane and the diarthrodial cartilages being intact.

(2) **Incomplete anchylosis** may be due to adhesions forming between the serous surfaces of the joint capsule, or to fibrous thickening or calcification of the periarticular tissues.

PREVENTION of the conditions has already been considered when dealing with inflammatory affections involving joints.

TREATMENT.—The same measures are required for the treatment of incomplete anchylosis as for its prevention—viz., passive movement of the joint and exercise, associated with frequent massage.

Complete anchylosis is incurable in the large animals. In the dog, if considered worth while, osteotomy may be performed to create a false joint, as is done in human surgery.

PART II

OPERATIVE SURGERY

CHAPTER I

GENERAL CONSIDERATIONS

Proficiency in operative surgery requires careful attention to the following points :—

I. The condition of the patient.
II. The antomy and normal condition of the region to be operated upon.
III. The preparation of the patient.
IV. The place and time of operation.
V. The control of the animal.
VI. Anæsthesia.
VII. Asepsis and antisepsis.
VIII. Instruments and dressing materials.
IX. Operative technique.
X. Hæmostasis.

I.—THE CONDITION OF THE PATIENT

The patient must be carefully examined to ascertain whether it is a fit subject for operation, whether it is debilitated or affected with some condition which renders the operation risk greater than usual, not forgetting in this connection to auscultate the heart and lungs.

The owner should always be warned of the ordinary and extraordinary risks involved and his consent obtained to proceed with the operation. A witness of this transaction may be desirable.

II.—THE ANATOMY AND NORMAL CONDITION OF THE REGION TO BE OPERATED UPON

If the surgeon is not sufficiently familiar with these, he should dissect the part on the dead subject and rehearse on it the operation which he intends to perform. This is the surest way of acquiring efficiency and confidence. By this means he will be able to plan the procedure he is about to adopt, and thus operate without fear or hesitancy.

III.—PREPARATION OF THE PATIENT

This comprises :

1. The **administration of a purgative or laxative** two or three days before the operation to evacuate the bowels and fit the subject for the administration of a general anæsthetic, and in the case of an abdominal operation to facilitate intra-abdominal manœuvres.

2. **Keeping the patient on restricted laxative diet** for two or three days before operating for the same object as No. 1.

Discretion must be used in the observance of Nos. 1 and 2 so as not to weaken the animal thereby.

3. **Cleaning the animal's coat** if it is dirty.

4. **Preliminary preparation of the site of operation**—*e.g.*, clipping the hair or removing the horn in the case of the horse's foot and having it immersed in an antiseptic bath.

IV.—THE PLACE AND TIME FOR OPERATION

1. **The Place for Operation.**—Few veterinary infirmaries outside Veterinary Colleges are provided with an elaborate operating theatre for large animals. When the weather does not permit of operation in the open air it must be performed under cover. In the country the open hay shed can be utilised for the purpose. If space is available in the veterinary surgeon's establishment a suitable inexpensive operating theatre can be erected. The following details of its construction and fittings may be mentioned :

(1) *Dimensions*, 20 × 20 × 10 or 15 feet high are ample dimensions.

(2) *Concrete floor with wide grooves* which will provide a foothold and be easily cleaned, and with surface drainage.

(3) *Smooth cement walls* which are readily washed and disinfected, each being provided with rings at different levels for the fixation of ropes.

(4) *The roof* may be mostly of glass to provide ample light. Strong, narrow steel girders placed edgewise should traverse the theatre for the attachment of ropes or chains and from which a patient may be slung.

(5) *Large windows* so arranged as to give a maximum amount of light, and without ledges on which dust could lodge.

(6) *Sliding doors* exterior to the walls.

(7) *Hot and cold water supply* into an earthenware sink inlet into the wall.

(8) *Suspension electric lamps* capable of being raised or lowered.

(9) *Plugs in the wall* for the use of *portable electric lamps.*

(10) *A radiator inset*, preferably in upper part of wall.

(11) An *adjoining room* for instruments, antiseptic agents, and surgical dressings and sterilising facilities.

Many of the above details may be dispensed with on the ground of economy. The main indication is to have the operating theatre arranged so that it can be easily cleaned and that it contains no ledges where dust can accumulate.

The theatre may be furnished with an operating table, but it is not essential because in places where it is installed it is not often used.

The material on which the animal is to be cast may be a thick bed of clean, long straw at least one foot deep, or, preferably, a leather-covered mattress of about the same depth. To prevent dust rising from the straw it should be damped.

The horse's shoes should be removed before being cast on the mattress.

When the patient is to be thrown in the open a place sheltered from wind and dust should be selected. In the country the best place is a level grass field. Failing this the thick bed of damped straw or perhaps cut long grass or rushes must be used, the latter having the advantage of being free from dust.

The place should be away from ditches, palings, stanchions, glass-houses, etc., into or against which the horse might fall if some hitch occurred in the procedure.

For small animals a properly equipped operating room is very desirable, and can be provided at a moderate cost. It may be furnished with an expensive adjustable operating table, but an ordinary table with a hard, smooth surface of wood or zinc answers the purpose. It may be covered with thick rubber to render it more comfortable for the patient and should be perforated to permit of drainage. In a private house the ordinary kitchen table is quite suitable. It can be covered with a sterilised cloth.

The canine operating theatre should be constructed with a view to strict cleanliness with washable impervious walls and floor, and devoid of shelves or ledges to harbour dust, well lighted and heated in winter, by gas or electric radiation or an oilstove, the latter being very cheap and effective.

All operating requirements should be within easy reach. Instrument cabinets and sterilising accommodation may be installed in the theatre or in an adjoining room.

2. **Time for Operation.**—The operation may be performed at any time of the day, but the morning is preferable to the afternoon,

especially for the large animals, as the patient can then be kept under observation during the greater part of the day and any complication that may arise can be more easily attended to.

V.—CONTROL OF THE ANIMAL

The Horse

Standing Position.—The methods of control in the standing position include the use of :

1. *Blinds* completely covering the eyes. They often have a marked subduing effect on a restive horse during a slight operation or whilst

Fig. 17.—The Blinds. Fig. 18.—Operating Cap or Hood.

the casting tackle is being applied. A cloth fixed to the cheeks of the cavesson or head collar may be used instead of the regular blinds.

2. A *twitch*. The ordinary twitch is so well known that it does not require description. The stick carrying the loop may be long, of medium length, or very short. The long twitch has the advantage that the man holding it is out of the reach of the horse's fore-feet should he strike out with them, but in the majority of cases the twitch of medium length is sufficient and is more convenient and portable.

The short twitch is usually fixed to the cheek of the cavesson, halter, or bridle instead of being held. The usual place where the twitch is applied is the upper lip, but it may also be used on the lower lip, the lower jaw, or the base of the ear. The short twitch is very suitable for young horses. The animal should not be cast on the side on which the twitch is fixed. Another useful twitch is in the form of two cylindrical rods about 1 foot long, joined at one end by a couple of links and having a strap and button at the other end. The upper lip is pinched between them, and it is fixed in position by means of the strap and button. A thin rope may be put on in the form of a noose round the lip behind the twitch and used as a rein for further control.

The leg twitch is a stout piece of rope about 20 inches long in the form of a loop applied to the hind-limb about 4 to 6 inches above the hock, and tightened by twisting with a rod. It is seldom employed, but may be used to control a hind-limb when the animal is cast.

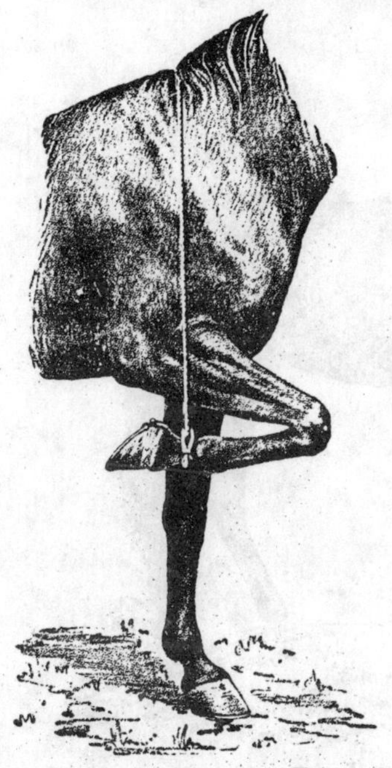

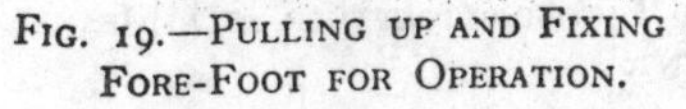

Fig. 19.—Pulling up and Fixing a Fore-Foot for Operation.

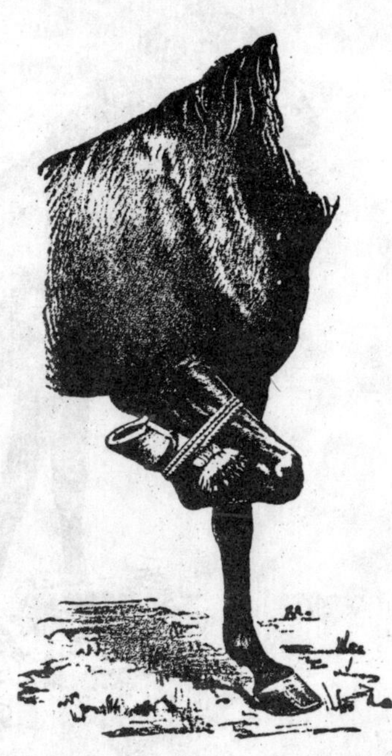

Fig. 20.—Tying up the Fore-Leg.

3. *Holding the horse by the ear or ears.* A tight grip of the base of the ear by a determined man who will not let go is often an effective means of controlling a horse that has a tendency to "go up," especially a colt. Two men, one grasping each ear, are still more effective.

4. *Holding up a fore-foot* with the knee flexed and the hoof grasped by one hand of the assistant while he holds the bridle-rein with the other or steadies himself by catching hold of the mane with his hand. This is a precaution against the operator being kicked.

5. *Strapping up a fore-limb* in the fixed position by means of a

stirrup leather applied round the pastern and forearm or tying them in this fashion with a piece of thin rope. Or the limb may be held in the flexed position by means of a rope passed round the pastern and over the horse's withers.

6. *Side-line*—that is, a rope fixed to a hind-pastern directly, or through the medium of a hobble, passed over the withers, round in front of the breast, and beneath the portion of the rope coming up from the pastern. It is then taken forward. By traction on the

FIG. 21.—FASTENING THE FORE AND HIND PASTERNS TOGETHER AS A MEANS OF RESTRAINT.

rope the hind-foot is carried forward and prevented from bearing weight, thus preventing the horse kicking with the other one. It also serves as a control for dealing with the limb to which it is attached.

A modification of this method, and perhaps more useful, is to double a long rope and by means of it make a noose round the hock, and then bring the two ends over the withers as before. Hock movement is thus prevented and the limb is well controlled.

7. The *side-fetter*—that is, a rope joining the hind and fore pastern of one side, enabling them to be drawn as close together as desired and

rendering them powerless to strike the operator. It is best used in conjunction with two hobbles, being fixed to one and running through the second one and back through the first one. If necessary it can be instantly removed by undoing the running knot by which it is fixed. It is a very useful method of restraint. When the horse fights against it he may fall, but this does not matter if the ground is soft.

8. *Fixing the hind-limb to the tail.* A hobble with a D or preferably with a pulley is applied on the pastern. A rope is fixed to the tail by means of two half-hitches, with a lock of hair turned back between

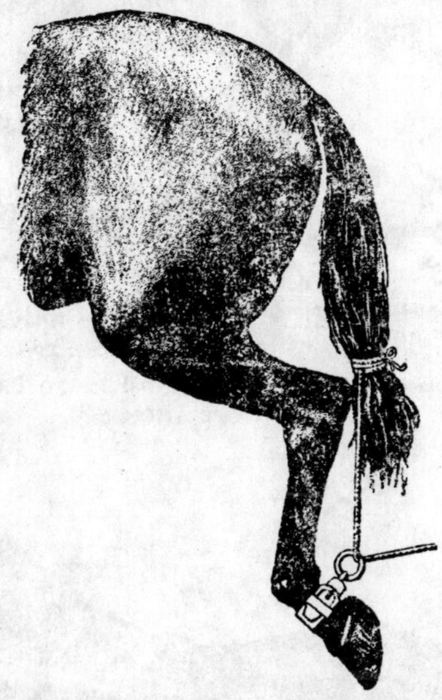

FIG. 22.—PULLING UP AND FIXING A HIND-FOOT FOR OPERATION.

the two hitches to prevent the rope slipping. The rope is then passed through the D or pulley, and by traction upon it the foot is easily lifted from the ground and held in a convenient position for examination or operation. Merely passing the rope round the limb from the outside above the fetlock also answers the purpose.

9. *Service hobbles*, as used on mares during service to prevent the stallion being kicked, may be employed to protect the veterinary surgeon when examining or operating on the pelvic region. No. 7 makes a good service hobble (Fig. 21).

10. *Stocks* or *trevis* are familiar to most horsemen. They are a sort of frame in which the horse is fixed in the standing position, so

that he is powerless to move in any direction. A wide girth prevents his lying down. A foot can be lifted and fixed in a convenient position for dressing or operation. They prove very useful in forges for

FIG. 23.—METHOD OF SECURING THE HIND-LEGS TO PREVENT KICKING DURING OPERATION.

FIG. 24.—THE SIDE-STICK.

shoeing heavy restive horses, and in the veterinary hospital they are almost indispensable for the satisfactory dressing of canker cases. They are also a great help in connection with dental operations in fractious subjects.

11. The *side-stick* and *cradle* are illustrated in Figs. 24 and 25. They prevent the horse biting or rubbing parts of the body which can be reached by the mouth, and are useful to prevent interference with a wound or blistered surface.

FIG. 25.—THE "CRADLE" OR "BEADS."

Cast Position.—There are innumerable ways of casting and fixing horses for operation. The following are some of the best-known methods :

1. *Using an ordinary hemp or cotton rope* such as the ordinary cart-rope found in every farm place. It should be from 30 to 50 feet long and about ½ inch in diameter.

The cotton rope is generally preferred, as it is stronger and less likely to chafe the heels. A very thick rope is clumsy and does not fix the animal securely except it is very soft and pliable, when it answers the purpose admirably, clinging closely to the limb without danger of chafing the skin. The rope may be used as follows :

(*a*) Make a loop in the middle of the rope to fit accurately on the base of the neck, taking care not to have it too big. It dilates with the struggling of the patient. Have the knot on the breast. Apply a rope in the form of a surcingle round the body. (1) Pass the two ends of the neck rope between the fore-limbs and between the body rope and the skin. (2) Pass each rope round the corresponding hind-limb either from within or from without and below the fetlock; (3) beneath the rope coming down from the breast; and (4) through the neck loop from behind forwards. (5) Give each rope to a couple of assistants. (6) Let those on one rope pull forwards and those on the other backwards. (7) When the horse falls have both ropes pulled backwards, and let the man at the horse's head keep it down and extended on the neck.

Having had the hocks flexed as much as possible, fix each limb in the flexed position by means of hitches round the pastern. Fix each fore-limb similarly. This method is suitable for the castration of colts and for other operations on the body. It does not flex the hocks sufficiently for rig castration.

Slight modifications of this method are: (1) tying the neck rope to the back rope at the withers in addition to or instead of passing the two ropes between it and the body; (2) having the knot on the withers instead of on the breast and passing the two ends between the fore-limbs from behind after coming round the hind-limbs, and then through the neck loop, there being no body rope used in this case, as there is no need for it to keep the neck loop from slipping over the head, except the horse struggles violently when the knot may pecome displaced. Of the three methods No. 1 modification is the best.

(*b*) (Fig. 26) Double the rope. Pass the looped end of the double rope round the withers and breast at the upper extremity of the fore-arms and make a bowline knot with the looped end round the other part of the rope at the level of the loins, so that there is a loop formed by a double rope encircling the withers and breast with the knot in the lumbar region. Separate the two ropes behind the knot and pass each round the hind-limb as before (but above the rope coming down from the breast) and through the chest loop from behind. Cast and fix the hind-limbs as in (*a*), and in addition pass each rope a couple of times round the limb above the hock and hitch it again to the pastern, thus keeping the hocks well flexed. Fix each fore-limb in the flexed position by means of a thin piece of rope or stirrup leather passed round the pastern and secured to the chest loop. This is an excellent and simple method of fixing any horse with the hocks perfectly flexed and widely separated in an ideal position for rig castration. It also has the advantages that it causes no pressure on the neck and prevents arching of the spine. When getting the horse down by this method it is best for the assistants on both ropes to pull backwards while the man at the horse's head pulls forward on the lead rope attached to the cavesson so as to prevent the horse walking backwards instead of falling. The horse's head must be pulled to one side down to the ground and

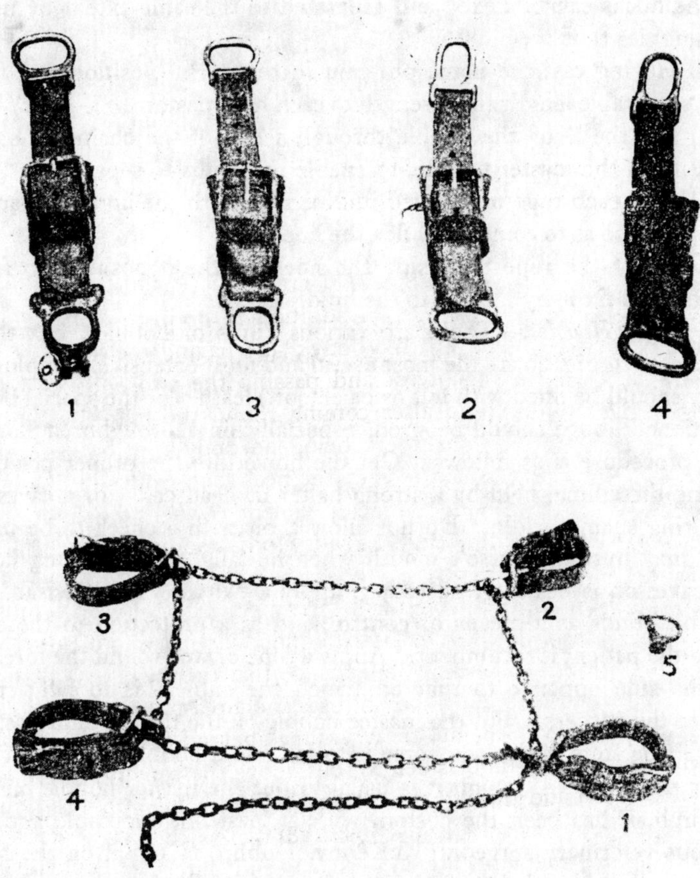

FIG. 26.—THE HOBBLES.

kept there the moment that he falls, otherwise the rope may become disarranged. The horse may first be made to fall by administering chloroform in the standing position and the rope then applied.

For method (*a*) a special rope may be kept for the purpose with an adjustable neck piece spliced to the rope and provided with metal eyes or thimbles to facilitate the gliding of the ropes through it, and rope hobbles with similar eyes may be applied on the hind-pasterns for the passage of the ropes in methods (*a*) and (*b*) to prevent chafing of the skin, or for the same reason special soft leather, double funnel-shaped boots embracing the pasterns, or stable bandages may be used. This precaution is especially necessary in thoroughbred horses.

The hocks can be flexed and separated to the same extent by using the hobbles thus :

(1) Having cast the horse put him in the dorsal position and fix a rope of suitable length and strength to each hind pastern.

(2) Put the D of the hobble through a link of the chain some feet away from the master hobble, to enable the limbs to separate.

(3) Pass each rope mentioned in No. 1 beneath the horse's quarters and pull it so as to completely flex the hock.

(4) Bring the rope up inside the hock of the opposite limb from behind and fix it by hitches to the hind pastern.

2. *Using Hobbles.*—There are various kinds of hobbles, but those illustrated in Fig. 26 are the most useful and most extensively employed. They should be lined with felt or basil (soft) leather or the special boots mentioned above should be used, especially on thoroughbred horses The procedure is as follows : Get the horse into the proper position, having the animal held by a strong halter or head collar or a cavesson or a ring snaffle bridle. Do not allow a bit with a cheek to be used, as it may hurt the horse's mouth when he falls. For a young horse the cavesson is best. If necessary, apply a twitch. It is advisable to put on blinds as a means of control, and as a protection to the eyes when the patient is recumbent. Apply a rope or web round the forearm on the side opposite to that on which the subject is to fall ; pass it over the withers. Put the master hobble on the fore or hind pastern of the side from which the horse is to fall and a hobble on each of the other pasterns. Although it is usual to put the master hobble on the forelimb, it has been the custom with at least one reputable and ingenious veterinary surgeon (McKenny, Dublin) to put it on the hind limb, on the ground that the horse gets a safer fall when the hind limb is the point of fixation of the force. The placing of the hobbles in position (Fig. 28) is made easy by noting that the master hobble No. 1, Fig. 26, and its diagonally opposite hobble (No. 3) have the large or D-shaped iron loop on the long strap while the other two hobbles (No. 2 and No. 4) have it on the short strap (the one carrying the buckle) and that the buckles must be on the outside. Pass the proximal end

of the casting chain or rope through the master hobble from the outside, and then in succession through each of the others back to the master hobble, and fix it there with the screw key. Draw up the slack quietly between the hobbles. Have an assistant in charge of the rope passed behind the withers from the forearm. At a given signal let the assistants

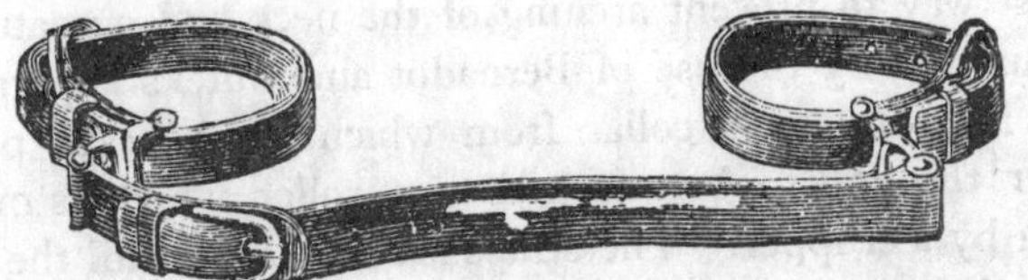

FIG. 27.—CROSS-HOBBLES, OR THIGH AND FOREARM STRAPS.

on the casting rope or chain pull slightly backwards, or forwards if the master hobble is on the hind limb, the man on the other rope or web pull vigorously downwards towards the side of the fall, and let the man

FIG. 28.—THE HOBBLES APPLIED.

in charge of the horse's head push the animal backwards. When the horse is down pull the feet as close together as possible, and maintain them in this position by inserting the D through the link next the hobbles. Have the head kept well extended to prevent arching of the back, and thereby minimise the risk of "broken back" from muscular violence. For the same reason let a man sit on the horse's quarters to prevent as far as possible lateral curvature. A piece of webbing passed round the lower jaw in the interdental space greatly facilitates keeping the head extended, all the pressure being exerted on the chin. When a cavesson is employed, pulling backwards on the leading rein has the same effect.

The best way to prevent arching of the neck and curvature of the spinal column is by the use of Bernadot and Butel's apparatus, consisting of a strong head collar from which stout straps pass backwards over the poll to be attached to a roller which is maintained in position by a crupper. The straps are left loose until the animal is cast, when they are tightened to the required extent. If the horse is a bad kicker, a fore-foot may be fixed up with a Rarey strap or stirrup leather as described, and the animal then cast with three hobbles and made to fall on the side opposite to that on which the fore-limb is strapped up. Doing this is also believed to diminish the risk of fracture of the vertebræ by weakening the *point d'appui*.

Fig. 30 illustrates the Stuttgart method of casting with hobbles. To release the horse when cast with the ordinary hobbles it is only necessary to unscrew the key at the master hobble. It is essential that the casting tackle be of good quality and free from defects which might lead to an accident.

When there is no screw key used the two lower limbs should first be released from the hobbles. When all the limbs are free, the man at the horse's head stands up and holds the reins in the direction in which the animal will rise. If an anæsthetic has been used the animal must be given ample time to recover from it before being induced to get up, otherwise he may stagger and fall and be injured in consequence. If in an awkward position, the latter must be changed before undoing the restraint. A lift at the tail by a couple of men is a great assistance to an old, stiff, or debilitated subject to rise.

Methods of control suitable for individual operations will be described when dealing with the latter.

Cross-hobbles (Fig. 27) are useful for fixing a fore to a hind limb above the knee and hock, and will be referred to again.

Precautions to be taken against injury to the operator and assistants. Novices at the work of casting horses require to be warned as follows:

(1) Avoid getting struck by the horse's hind or fore feet by not standing behind or in front of the animal when applying the casting tackle The man holding the twitch should stand to one side.

(2) When the horse is cast keep clear of the line of movement of the fore and hind limbs. Don't stand in front of or behind the horse

FIG. 29.—THE HOBBLES APPLIED TOGETHER WITH BERNADOT AND BUTEL' APPARATUS FOR THE PREVENTION OF BROKEN BACK.

The strip of webbing passed round the off forearm is intended to afford a purchase when pulling the horse over in the act of casting.

FIG. 30.—METHOD OF CASTING AS ADOPTED AT THE STUTTGART VETERINARY SCHOOL.

when putting the D in the hobbles, but opposite the plantar aspect of the feet and out of their reach.

The operator must not take up his position near the extremities where he may be struck when the horse struggles and extends the limbs, but in front of the breast for operations on the fore limbs and behind the buttocks for those on the hind limbs. When in the latter position beware of being struck by the point of the hock.

(3) Stand close to the dorsal or lumbar region and stretch over the animal's trunk to apply a rope to, or remove a rope from, the pastern, never near the feet where you may be struck by the latter when the patient struggles.

(4) When releasing a horse from hobbles or rope keep all the limbs under control until they are all ready for immediate release, otherwise a person may be struck by the free limb or limbs whilst the others are being released.

(5) When hobbles are being removed refrain from standing in front of or behind the horse in order to avoid being struck by the limbs or by hobbles violently cast off by movement of the limbs when released.

3. *Using an Operating Table or Special Apparatus.*—Operating tables for the horse are not much in vogue, because they are too expensive for the ordinary practitioner and unnecessary for the majority of operations. Even where the table has been installed it is not made use of for every operation necessitating casting.

The chief advantages of operating tables or special fixing apparatus are that they facilitate aseptic operations and render the subjects under control less liable to injury than when cast in the ordinary way. They are, of course, a great convenience to the operator. Restive blood horses are not easily fixed with these special contrivances. A table in the form of a wooden floor which can be raised to a convenient height by means of jacks may be employed, as used at the Royal Veterinary College, London.

A small pit by the side of the casting-bed is very useful, as it enables operations on the feet and lower parts of the limbs to be performed without the inconvenience of assuming the bending position, and thus has to a certain extent the advantages of an operating table.

Mention may be made here of *methods of lifting a horse that is unable to rise.* (1) The following is a well-known method of lifting a horse that is unable to rise, by means of a block and pulley : Take a stout rope about 40 feet long, place its centre part across the back behind the withers, pass the two ends between the fore-limbs from behind cross them in front of the breast ; pass each end backwards

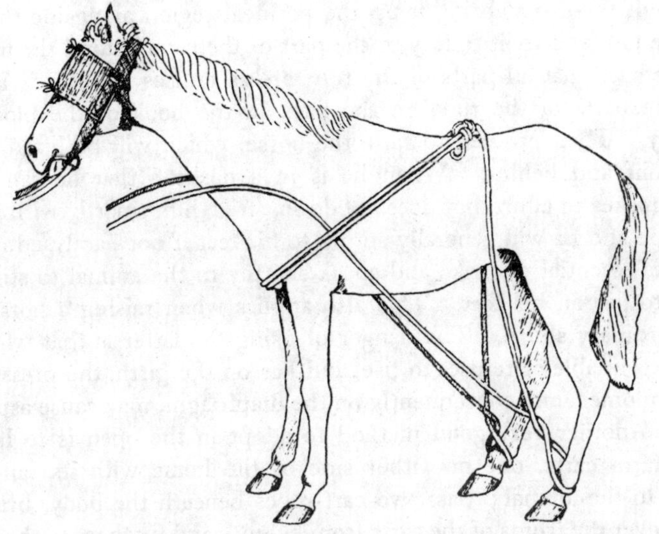

FIG. 31.—ILLUSTRATING (*b*) METHOD OF APPLYING CASTING ROPE.

FIG. 32.—BERNADOT AND BUTEL'S APPARATUS FOR PREVENTION OF BROKEN BACK WHEN CASTING.

over the back to the opposite side; pass it to the inside of the stifle through the groin, bring it up the perineal region alongside the base of the tail, and fix it tightly to the part of the rope behind the withers. Make sure that all parts of the rope are as taut as possible. Include all the parts of the rope on the back in the hook of the block and pulley. Then proceed to raise the horse, which will be lifted evenly in front and behind. When he is in a position that he can stand, if he makes an effort, but does not do so, strike him smartly with a piece of rope and he will generally spring to his feet if not paralysed.

It is essential to strike and speak sharply to the animal to stimulate him to get on his feet. This also applies when raising a horse with the ordinary slings. The danger of using the latter is that when the horse is unable or refuses to rise, and lies on the girth, the pressure on the abdomen, and consequently on the diaphragm, may cause asphyxia.

(2) Another very good method to adopt in the open is to heel up two farm carts, one on either side of the horse with its tail-board close to the animal; pass two cart-ropes beneath the body, bring the ends over the fronts of the carts from behind, and fix them to the shafts, and then pull down the latter, thereby lifting the animal on to its feet.

The Ox

Standing Position.—The methods of controlling the ox in the standing position include:

1. *Holding the beast with the fingers and thumb of one hand in the nostrils, and the other grasping the horn near its tip.* This is sufficient control for slight operations or for the examination of various parts of the body.

2. *Using a bull-holder as illustrated.* This is very useful where No. 1 method is not sufficient.

3. *Using a bull-ring.* Every bull has a ring inserted in its nose below the inferior extremity of the septum nasi. It is made use of to hold or lead the bull when necessary. Too much traction should not be applied to it, as it may tear through the tissues and come away. The bull-leader is used to keep the bull off the person leading it.

4. *A rope applied round the pastern* to hold up a fore-foot for the purpose of examination or operation.

5. A *side-line*, which enables a hind-foot of a quiet animal to be lifted and examined by one man. A rope is passed round the neck and then through the hollow of the hind-pastern. By drawing the two ends together the foot is lifted, and can be examined with one hand while the other hand holds the two ends of the rope.

6. A *kicking-strap*—that is, a strap or piece of rope used to tie the two hind-limbs together above the hocks or above the fetlocks. It prevents kicking.

7. A *twitch* in the form of a rope applied as a surcingle round the

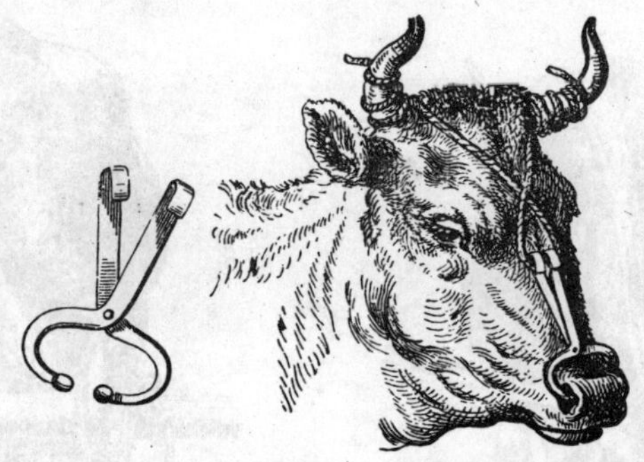

FIG. 33.—BULL-HOLDER.

body, and tightened by twisting it with a rod after the manner of a letter-press. It prevents straining and kicking.

8. *Using a stick to lift a hind-limb.* A stout short pole is passed in front of the hind-limb at the level of the hock, and, being held by

34.—SHOWING THE APPLICATION OF NOSE-RING AND BULL-LEADER.

a man at either end, is taken straight backwards, thereby lifting the foot and holding it in position for operation or examination.

9. *Fixing the hind-limb to a pole*, as in Fig. 36. One end of the pole in this case may be fixed in a hole in a wall or passed between the spokes of the two wheels of a four-wheeled vehicle alongside which the beast is held. The hind-limb may also be lifted backwards by means

of a rope fixed above the fetlock and passed over a beam behind and above the animal.

Cast Position.—The ox may be cast in the following ways :

1. *Using a rope thus* (Figs. 37 and 38) : (1) Take a rope about 40 feet

FIG. 35.—FASTENING A BULLOCK'S HIND-LEGS PREPARATORY TO OPERATION.

FIG. 36.—FASTENING ONE HIND-LEG FOR OPERATION OR SHOEING.

FIG. 37.—CASTING AN OX : FIRST POSITION.

long. Fix one end of it round the base of the horns. Then make a series of half-hitches, one round the base of the neck, another round the anterior part of the trunk, and a third round its posterior part. Tighten all the hitches well, and then pull hard on the end of the rope and the beast will gradually sink to the ground. By this means a heavy bull may be cast by one man. If the animal is polled, the end of the rope may be fixed round the base of the neck or to a head collar and hitched round the body as before. When the rope is fixed to the horns the hitch round the neck may be omitted if in the way of surgical procedure there. When the beast is down, the limbs may be fixed together by a web or rope, or by suitable hobbles. A disadvantage of this method

FIG. 38.—CASTING AN OX: SECOND POSITION

is that the rope may slip backwards during casting and injure the penis in the male, or the mammary gland in the cow.

(2) Fig. 39. Take a rope 40 to 50 feet long, double it, apply its middle part on the middle line of the body on the front part of the withers, cross the two parts of the rope in front of the dewlap, pass them between

FIG. 39.—CASTING THE OX.

the fore-limbs from in front, then over the sides and back, where they are crossed again and passed inside the thighs. Apply traction on the ropes and the animal will fall. The ropes passing between the hind-limbs should be kept well apart to avoid injury to the mammary gland or scrotum.

This method has not the disadvantage mentioned for No. 1 (Fig. 37)

An ox finding difficulty in rising or refusing to rise when in the recumbent position may be made to rise thus :

(1) Place the beast on its sternum with all the limbs flexed and lift the hind-quarters by means of a sack placed beneath them and held by

FIG. 40.—FASTENING A COW FOR OPERATION.

several assistants. If the animal is stimulated it may then get on its feet. Bringing a dog to the vicinity of the beast and making it bark may have this effect.

(2) The methods used for the horse may be adopted (see p. 162).

2. *Making a neck loop on a rope and using it as in the horse*, except that the two parts of the rope are passed above the hocks instead of round the pasterns. The back rope is not necessary in the ox.

3. *Taking two fairly slender ropes or pieces of webbing*, fixing the two fore-pasterns together with one and the two hind-pasterns with the other, leaving a long end in each case, which is passed round the part joining the other two limbs. The two ends are then pulled in opposite directions, thereby drawing all the feet together, when they may be fixed by tying or twisting the two ends. Fig. 40 shows a method of fixing the limbs to a pole after casting.

4. Using hobbles as in the horse but applied above the fetlocks. When a beast with horns is cast, great care must be taken to prevent their being broken by striking the head violently against the ground by having a good man in charge of the beast's head and having a deep layer of straw, which will prevent the horns reaching the ground.

The Sheep

The sheep is easily controlled. It may be fixed in the cast position by first tying each lateral pair of limbs together with a soft thin rope or web, and then uniting the two pairs by a couple of turns of one of the ropes.

The Pig

The young pig is caught by the hind-limb above the hock and held by the ears. The ordinary adult pig is also held by the ears, but the boar requires to have a rope applied in the form of a noose on the upper jaw behind the tusks to enable it to be held under control. A short twitch whose loop is passed round the jaw is very suitable for the purpose. The rope can be passed through a ring above the level of the pig's head, thereby keeping it under complete restraint.

The large boar can be cast by means of small hobbles fitting tightly on the limbs above the fetlocks, or by the method marked No. 3 for the ox (p. 168). The smaller pig may be tied up like the sheep.

The Dog

To catch hold of a wicked dog in a confined place a pole with a loop of rope at the end like a twitch is very useful. The loop is

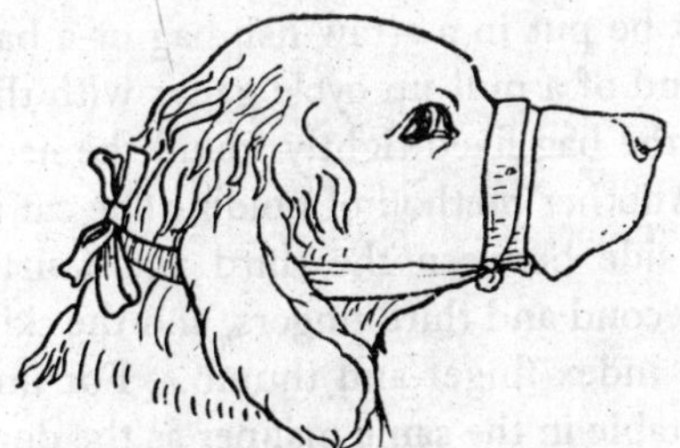

FIG. 41.—TAPE MUZZLE APPLIED TO THE DOG.

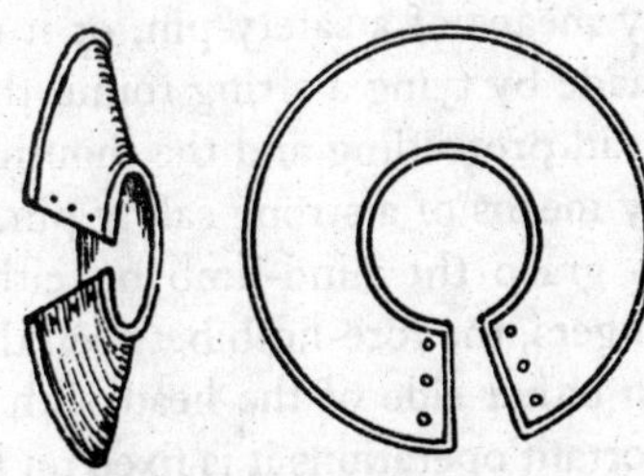

FIG. 42.—ELIZABETHAN COLLAR FOR THE DOG.

passed over the head on to the neck and then twisted by turning the stick, thus getting the animal under complete control. A dose of morphia may then be easily injected to enable any part of the animal to be handled without restraint. A special instrument for catching rabid dogs in France has a long handle, and carries at the end a spring collar which, when pressed on the dog's neck, opens and holds him securely.

The dog is prevented from biting by means of a muzzle in the form of a wide piece of tape passed round the two jaws by two half-hitches, leaving two ends underneath long enough to be passed up behind the ears and fixed there with a bow knot. Another way of fixing it is to bring the two ends up in front over the poll and tie them to the dog's collar. This muzzle is not suitable for short-nosed dogs. For them the ordinary muzzle is best. The Elizabethan collar is useful to prevent the dog reaching parts behind it with its teeth.

The dog may be fixed on a table either in the ventral or dorsal position by means of strong calico strings applied in the form of a noose above the hocks in the hind-limbs, and above the paws in the fore-limbs, pulled taut, and fixed to the legs of the table or to hooks or nails underneath its borders. Or the animal may be fixed similarly with special hobbles on a special operating table, such as Hobday's.

The operating table which can be raised and lowered at will by means of an oil pump and made to revolve or lock as desired is very suitable, but rather expensive.

The Cat

If the cat offers resistance when placed on a table it is best held by grasping the skin at the back of the neck with one hand, and that in the lumbar region with the other, and leaning on it. To prevent its scratching when examining the head it is rolled up in a cloth with the latter closely applied round its neck, and for preference fixed there by means of a safety-pin, or it may be put in a straw fish bag or a bag made by tying a string round the end of a pull-up cycle gaiter with the head protruding and the mouth of the bag fixed tightly round the neck by means of a strong safety pin. Another method of holding the cat is to grasp the hind-limb on either side between the third and fourth fingers, the fore-limb between the second and third fingers, and the skin on either side of the head with the index finger and thumb. For important operations it is fixed on the table in the same manner as the dog.

Complications

In the large animals, and particularly in the horse, complications may occur from casting—for example, breaking the neck, shoulder, pelvis, ribs, or back, or rupturing muscles from falling awkwardly or as the result of violent struggling. The owner should be informed of the possible risks of casting, which can be insured against for a small premium. The veterinarian must take care that no accident occurs through negligence on his part ; for if negligence can be proved, he is responsible for the damage done.

VI.—ANÆSTHESIA

Anæsthesia may be : (1) General, or (2) Local.

Regarding the conditions for which general or local anæsthesia is obligatory in Great Britain the veterinary surgeon should make himself acquainted with the provisions of the Animals (Anæsthetic) Act, 1919 and the amendments thereto.

1. General Anæsthesia

In general anæsthesia the patient is thrown into a profound sleep, during which he is unconscious of pain. It is brought about by the direct action on nerve centres of certain agents. Volatile substances introduced through the respiratory tract are usually employed. They are freely absorbed by the blood circulating in the lungs, whence they rapidly pass to the brain and produce their effect. They cause a series of phenomena in the following order :

(1) Period of excitement.
(2) Period of anæsthesia.
(3) Period of collapse or intoxication.

1. The *period of excitement* is characterised by violent struggling, accelerated respiration and circulation, injected mucous membranes, and dilated pupils. After a while the heart's action slows, respiration becomes easier, more regular, and more extensive, the pupil contracts, excitement diminishes, and sleep commences, the period of anæsthesia being then begun. During the period of excitement respiratory or cardiac syncope or asphyxia from spasm of the glottis may supervene.

2. The *period of anæsthesia* is characterised by suspension of activity in the nerve centres. The excito-motor centres are paralysed, the muscles are relaxed, and the limbs when raised fall inertly. The tail becomes limp and offers no resistance when handled. Respiration is slow, the movements of the chest wall are diminished, but those of the flank are more marked than usual. The heart is accelerated, but the pulse remains regular and full up to the moment when intoxication occurs. The pupils remain contracted and immobile. As sensation is lost in the various regions reflexes cease. The limbs and trunk are first affected, then the organs of sense and those supplied by branches of bulbar origin, and finally those supplied by the sympathetic system. The nasal, buccal, auricular, and genital mucous membranes exhibit reflexes long after other parts have become insensitive.

Certain diseased tissues retain a morbid sensibility even after neighbouring healthy tissues have entirely lost sensation. Inflamed parts especially retain their sensibility long after healthy tissues.

Once established, anæsthesia can be maintained by small doses of the agent employed. Larger doses are dangerous as being liable to induce the third stage of anæsthesia—viz. :

3. The *period of collapse or intoxication*, which is characterised by progressive retardation of respiration and circulation and by sudden dilatation of the pupils. Respiratory movements become

superficial and cease for comparatively long intervals, the heart's action diminishes, and the pulse is small, soft, and irregular. Finally, the medulla becomes intoxicated, respiration is arrested, the heart ceases to beat, and death occurs by respiratory syncope.

With ether the period of excitement is longer and more pronounced than with chloroform. No general anæsthetic is without danger, and every veterinary practitioner who has been in the habit of using it has had a fatality. The heart and lungs should be carefully examined before deciding to administer the anæsthetic to ascertain whether they are functioning normally. If not it should either be withheld or given gradually in minimum doses and with extra care. In all cases the owner should be informed of the risk involved.

Anæsthesia in the Horse

Chloroform produces the most rapid and complete anæsthesia in the horse, and is not dangerous when used with ordinary care. Dollar had only two fatal results in over one thousand cases. The following is a résumé of results obtained by Möller. In a series of 126 cases, the corneal reflex was abolished in an average period of twenty minutes by an average dose of 28 fluid drachms of chloroform; the quantity per unit of body-weight was 1 in 4,000. Anæsthesia usually lasted twenty minutes. Twenty-eight horses received 7½ grains of morphia before administration of the chloroform. In these cases the average quantity of chloroform used was 24 fluid drachms, and the time interval before complete anæsthesia fifteen and a half minutes. Eight horses received a mixture of equal parts of chloroform and ether. The average quantity used was 54 fluid drachms, and the time interval thirty minutes. The chloroform used must be pure and contain no free chlorine, which produces excessive irritation. Adding a little ether to the chloroform and keeping it in yellow bottles with ground stoppers in a cool place prevents its undergoing change.

Procedure—Preparation of the Patient.—If time is available for the purpose, the patient should be fasting for twelve hours before the administration of the anæsthetic, as anæsthesia is then more rapidly and safely produced than when the alimentary tract is replete with ingesta. The heart and lungs should be examined to ascertain if they are normal.

Method of Administration.—Chloroform may be administered in the cast or standing position.

1. **Cast Position.**—Having cast the animal and smeared its nostrils with vaseline, the chloroform muzzle or inhaler is put on.

Varieties of Inhalers.—The following patterns of inhalers have been employed with more or less success :

(1) *Cox's Chloroform Muzzle.*—This consists of a leather tube or cylinder covered with stout canvas which can be drawn together at either end by a strong draw-string. The tube is slipped over the animal's nostrils and into its mouth and strapped securely over the poll. In ponies or yearlings it may be applied over both jaws. A large sponge squeezed out of hot water is impregnated with the desired quantity of chloroform and introduced into the lower part of the muzzle, followed by a small towel of open texture to allow the air to pass freely through it. The towel is not essential. The lower drawstring is then tied. Although this apparatus is not elaborate it answers its purpose very well, and is very widely and successfully employed. The animal inhales and exhales through the chloroform, thereby wasting some of the latter. To avoid this, Brayley Reynolds modified the apparatus by making a perforated metal partition in the centre of the tube provided with a valve which opens during inspiration and closes during expiration, and by making an expiratory valve on each side of the leather cylinder which opens only during expiration. A tube or cylinder made of two or three plies of strong calico and fixed over the poll with a strong calico string loop is almost equally as good as the ordinary Cox's muzzle, and has the advantage of being light and easily put on and hard to shake off.

FIG. 43.—COX'S CHLOROFORM MUZZLE.

(2) The *Carlisle Muzzle*, made of stout leather and open only at its upper end. It is provided with a drawer at its lower end carrying a flat sponge to retain the chloroform. This is separated from the nostrils by a perforated partition. The muzzle covers both jaws. A rim of soft leather on its upper end enables it to fit closely round the horse's muzzle, on which it can be tightened by a strap and buckle. It has the disadvantage that there is not a free current of air passing through the chloroform. It is not much in vogue nowadays. It has been modified by introducing the chloroform through it by means of the apparatus used by Dr. Clarke and Dollar, made on the principle of Junker's apparatus as used in human surgery, in which the glass

bottle is replaced by a copper cylinder about 15 inches in height and 4 inches in diameter, and the glass tubes by large metal tubes about $\frac{3}{4}$ inch in diameter. The blast of air driven by way of the long tube through the chloroform by the aid of a foot bellows passes through the short tube saturated with chloroform vapour, and then through a rubber tube into the muzzle, where the horse inhales it. The principle of this apparatus is better than that of the ordinary Carlisle or Cox's muzzle, as by means of it the animal probably gets a better admixture of air with the chloroform; but Cox's method is simpler and more practicable, and, judging from experience, just as safe.

(3) *Imrie's Muzzle and Inhaler.*—The muzzle portion of this apparatus is similar to the Carlisle muzzle, except that it has a circular opening on the anterior aspect of the cylinder, bordered by aluminium, adapted for attachment of the inhaler, which is a short, stout cylinder of aluminium of about 2 inches internal diameter, with a perforated

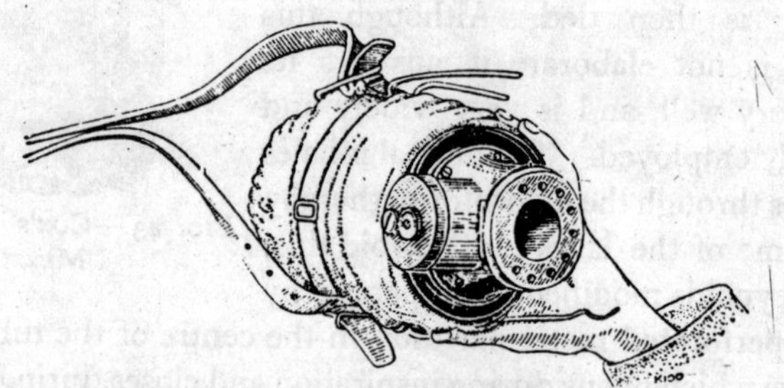

FIG. 44.—IMRIE'S HORSE INHALER.

partition carrying an inhalation valve in the form of a rubber disc on its posterior aspect. There is an expiratory valve on each side of the cylinder. The rim of the external orifice of the cylinder is perforated all round by circular openings capable of being closed or opened by means of a corresponding movable rim applied in front of it, whereby air may be admitted or excluded. The cylinder carries a small chloroform container on its upper aspect which communicates with its interior by a small opening, and through which the chloroform passes from the container on to a small sponge in the cylinder. The outflow of the anæsthetic can be regulated by a screw after the manner of an acetylene cycle lamp. When the horse is standing with the head vertical the inhaler is in front of the muzzle, with its container on its upper aspect. The sponge is impregnated with chloroform when it is introduced, and then more chloroform is allowed to drop from the container until anæsthesia is produced. The muzzle may be used without the inhaler, if desired, by simply introducing a sponge containing the chloroform through the opening on its anterior aspect. This is a very ingenious apparatus which has been used with complete success in hundreds of cases in the standing position by the inventor, Mr. David Imrie, M.R.C.V.S., of Glasgow. The movable parts of the inhaler must be well lubricated or it will go out of order.

Supervision during the Administration of the Anæsthetic.—The effect of the anæsthetic on the patient must be closely watched. It is advisable to have the tongue drawn out through the interdental space, when Cox's muzzle is used and applied over the upper jaw only, secured in this position by a piece of bandage passed in the form of a noose round the organ and attached to the head collar as a precaution against its falling back towards the glottis and partially closing it during the stage of anæsthesia. Nothing should be allowed to interfere with respiration.

When the struggling has ceased the breathing must be carefully watched. If it becomes shallow or intermittent, or if the pulse becomes small, frequent, irregular, or intermittent, the administration of the anæsthetic must be discontinued. When the patient becomes quiet and the tail is comparatively limp, offering little or no resistance when extended, the operation may be commenced. It is not advisable to wait for the corneal reflex to disappear. If the patient wince when the incision is begun, a little more chloroform should be given; although it must be remembered that there may be a reflex response from an incision in certain regions, notwithstanding that the animal is unconscious. Great care must be exercised in giving additional doses of chloroform.

The pupil remains contracted during anæsthesia. Should it become rapidly dilated, it is a sign of bulbar intoxication and imminent syncope. When none of these untoward symptoms appears, anæsthesia can be prolonged for periods of two or even three hours without danger by occasionally administering further small doses of chloroform.

DOSAGE.—The initial dose of chloroform for a yearling or two-year-old is about 1 fluid ounce, and for an adult horse 1½ to 2 ounces. Additional doses of 2 to 4 drachms respectively may be given as required.

Some individuals are more difficult to anæsthetise than others. Occasionally a horse is met with which requires several ounces of chloroform before anæsthesia supervenes. A particular case may necessitate the use of 10 to 14 ounces of chloroform before a prolonged operation is finished.

When the operation is finished and the chloroform apparatus and means of restraint have been removed, the patient should be allowed to remain recumbent until consciousness is completely restored and the tail regains its rigidity. Ten minutes to half an hour may elapse before the animal is fit to rise. If allowed to get up too soon the horse will stagger and fall, and perhaps get into an awkward position or receive serious injury. When shaky after rising, he may be steadied by holding the tail and by supporting the hips on either side.

Fatalities.—Fatal issues result from asphyxia or syncope. Asphyxia occurs during the period of excitation, especially if some closed muzzle like the Carlisle is used. First, breathing stops, and after a short interval the heart's action fails. It may also happen towards the end of anæsthesia when the administration of the agent has been pushed far and is suddenly checked.

Treatment of Threatened Asphyxia comprises: (1) Flicking the chest, face, or lips smartly with a towel or the hand to provoke the reflexes and restore respiration. (2) Artificial respiration effected by a man pressing with all his force by means of his knees on the chest wall in an intermittent fashion, simulating the respiratory movements. (3) Traction on the tongue at intervals of two to four seconds with a view to stimulating the superior laryngeal nerve and respiratory centre. (4) The hypodermic injection of atropine. (5) Dropping prussic acid on the tongue. (6) Inhalation of ammonia held a little distance away from the nostrils.

Cardiac Syncope is indicated by irregularity of the pulse, widely dilated pupils, weak heart's action, and cessation of hæmorrhage, or the escape of a few drops of dark-coloured blood from the incision.

TREATMENT comprises: (1) Lowering the head; (2) artificial respiration; (3) cold douches on the head; (4) smartly slapping the chest wall; (5) a hypodermic injection of ether or strychnine or atropine; (6) intravenous injection of normal saline; (7) giving small doses of prussic acid on the tongue.

2. **Administration of Chloroform in the Standing Position.**—This has been widely practised in recent years. The advantages of it are that:

(1) The risk of injury caused by struggling when cast is eliminated.

(2) As the animal falls from the effects of the chloroform, it is surely anæsthetised when it is down.

(3) The operator is saved the labour and fatigue of overcoming the resistance of the patient when securing him in the cast position.

(4) A wild or wicked horse which cannot be handled or cast can be perfectly controlled by this means.

Disadvantages of the method are that:

(1) More chloroform is required as a rule than in the cast position.

(2) There is a possibility of the animal getting out of control during the excitement period of the anæsthetic, and getting into a dangerous place or striking against some hard, resistant object, or falling on its poll and fracturing the base of the skull.

PROCEDURE.—Cox's muzzle is very suitable for the purpose, and Imrie's apparatus was designed specially for this method of administration. With Cox's muzzle an extra throat leash with a strap from it to a buckle on the inferior aspect of the muzzle prevents the horse shaking it off. It can also be secured by fixing it to the cavesson. The muzzle may be put on the horse in the stable or at the place of operation. A cavesson is the best headgear to use. Having made the muzzle secure, and having a reliable man in charge of the horse, the chloroform is administered. When Cox's apparatus is used, the sponge which has been squeezed dry after saturation with hot water and impregnated with the chloroform is quickly introduced and the draw-string, with the first part of the knot already made with an extra turn of the ends, is rapidly tightened. Instead of the draw-string, it is an advantage to have an india-rubber band fixed by clasps round the lower canvas so as to close the latter automatically after the sponge is inserted, and prevent it from being thrown out by the horse tossing its head, which it is very apt to do. Mr. Fred Daly, of Dublin, has adopted this device and found it a great boon for a very restive horse. The zip-fastener is a rapid means of closing the muzzle, but might fail to act.

The safest place for practising this method is the centre of a field, where there is plenty of room for the horse to move about without getting into a dangerous situation. Nevertheless, it has often been carried out successfully in a confined place—a small yard, or even a loose box.

For a very wicked or restive horse it is advisable to give 1 to 2 ounces of chloral hydrate in the drinking water or mash or by the stomach tube before putting on the muzzle in order to produce a hypnotic effect, the animal having been purposely left without food or drink for at least twenty-four hours. In addition to this, a hypodermic of morphia may also be given. The initial dose of chloroform should be comparatively large—say 1½ to 2 ounces for yearlings and two-year-olds, and 3 to 4 ounces, or even 5 ounces, for big horses. Experience has shown that with large doses in this position there is practically no excitement stage, and the horse gradually becomes dazed, staggers, and falls. A smaller dose is sufficient after administering chloral. A disadvantage of the use of chloral is that the patient may be very slow to rise afterwards or may stagger and fall several times before being able to stand.

When the animal moves he generally shows a tendency to go back but may spring forward. The man at his head should keep him going backwards by chucking the lead or try to keep him within a circle until he falls. When excitement occurs the horse is inclined to rear, and may fall over violently on the poll if the man on the rein does not prevent his doing so by pulling him sharply to one side so that he may fall sideways, or he may be prevented from going up by the man or two or more men pulling on the rein. When the animal gets unsteady on his limbs he may be made to fall by pushing him to one side.

When the patient is down, no further control may be required for an operation of short duration. For castration the patient is allowed to lie on the near side with the upper hind-limb drawn forward to the shoulder. Owing to the large dose of chloroform administered the breathing must be carefully watched after the horse has fallen. It may be necessary to open the muzzle to allow the entrance of more air, or even to take out the sponge for a while.

Thiopentone and Ether Anæsthesia (Intravenous)

Mr. E. O. Longley (*Vet. Rec.*, **62**, 2), has assayed the use of thiopentone (Pentothal sodium) for general anæsthesia in the horse, reporting 26 administrations without misadventure. The injection is made into the jugular vein at an extremely rapid rate, the time for its completion not exceeding 10 seconds. By this means, the concentration in the blood, as compared with the more familiar slow injection-rate, acquires a maximum value, with the result that the effective dose requirement is more than halved, and becomes of the order of $\frac{1}{15}$th to $\frac{1}{10}$th grains per pound of body-weight, according to the condition and size of the animal. He shows that these variations in unit dosage, whereby the dosage requirement in light animals is higher than that in heavy ones and as has long been recognised to be the case (for example in the dog), are explicable in terms of the cardiac output of the animal which, together with the rate of the injection, must govern the dilution of the drug attained as it is injected. The relationship, accordingly, is such that the dosage varies, not as the weight of the animals, but as the cube-root of the body-weight.

The method adopted for the attainment of this high rate of injection is to dissolve the dose, in accordance with these data, in a fixed volume (50 or 100 c.c.) of distilled water, and to inject from a syringe. Connection between needle and syringe is by plastic (polythene) tubing, and the two-way tap described on p. 180 mounts the needle. The needle is inserted into the vein, and the plunger of the syringe then pressed hard to the body of the operator with his left hand, whereupon, when he opens the tap with his right hand, injection follows automatically at the required rate. By this procedure, anæsthetisation is effected single-handed in a period of time not exceeding a minute or two from beginning to end.

The drug takes effect 20 to 30 seconds after injection. Anæsthesia is immediate, the animal falling into lateral recumbency from where it stands, in a matter of a regular 5 seconds from the first sign of action of the drug. No hobbles or other casting tackle or assistance are required and, owing to the instantaniety of the effect and the absence of floundering about or struggle, simultaneous anæsthetisation of the animal may be accomplished in a small area, under cover, such as a loose-box. The anæsthesia lasts, depending on dosage and idiosyncracy, for from 5 to 20 minutes. During the brief recovery period, control at the head, and of the limbs by hitching three of them together with a rope, is recommended because it is best that the animal should remain recumbent until fully ambulatory. The only disadvantage of the method would seem to be the primary cost of the drug, against which may be set the considerable advantages of the convenience and safety of the method, the dispensing with casting tackle and other equipment, and the excellent quality of the anæsthesia.

The same author (*Vet. Rec.*, **62**, 3, 30), has used ether intravenously for anæsthesia in the horse and particularly recommends this as a maintenance anæsthetic after induction of anæsthesia with thiopentone. The ether is in 6 per cent. solution by volume in warm, normal saline (25° to 30°C., not exceeding 30°C.), and is administered in the recumbent animal by gravity-feed ; 120 millilitres of ether are dissolved in 2 litres of ordinary tap water, after the addition of 18 grams of common salt (approximately 1 dram of salt and 1 ounce of ether in 1 pint of water). The anæsthesia has all the familiar features of ordinary inhalation anæsthesia, as with chloroform, but combines the considerable advantages of ether as compared with chloroform, with none of the prohibitive expense attending the use of ether as an inhalation anæsthetic in the horse. The special recommendations claimed for this method are : (1) its great safety, (2) the excellent quality of control of the level of anæsthesia, (3) the non-toxicity of ether as compared with chloroform, (4) obviation of irritation of the respiratory passages by any vapour, (5) economy in the anæsthetic, (6) the great stability of the anæsthesia as compared with inhalation practice, which is particularly useful working single-handed. Used in this way after thiopentone anæsthesia, all physical control of the patient from the beginning to complete recovery of consciousness is unnecessary. Recovery is rapid and without excitement. The dosage for maintenance anæsthesia is upwards of 2 litres of the solution, to be supplemented at intervals as required.

Mr. E. O. Longley urges the use of spear-pointed needles in every case for intravenous work in the large animals, insisting that penetration of the skin is incomparably easier than with the standard pattern. He maintains that these spear-pointed needles should be of the hardest possible steel, instead of the soft steels in traditional use, since it allows of a finer needle for the same bore without loss of strength, and at the same time of a sharper spear-point, which may in fact be given a razor edge on any ordinary oil-stone. He also introduces a considerable improvement on the usual technique of intravenous injection in the large animals by introducing, between the tubing of the delivery apparatus and the needle, the small standard two-way stop-cock in use in human anæsthesia. With this tap appropriately set, on intravenous entry blood escapes freely from the side-arm of the stop-cock, and the tap is then simply turned with the thumb of the hand holding the needle through 90°, to open the channel for injection. By similarly restoring the tap to its first position at any time, reflux of blood, establishing the continued intravenous locus of the needle or for washing it out, as after chloral hydrate, is accomplished without disconnecting. The special advantage of this innovation is that the needle remains in attachment to the apparatus from beginning to end, without the necessity as with other methods of its preliminary and terminal disconnection.

Chloral Narcosis and Anæsthesia in the Horse

Chloral narcosis and anæsthesia in the horse by the intravenous route was practised by several Continental veterinarians in the latter part of the seventeenth century, but was later discontinued owing to the untoward sequelæ which ensued.

Disadvantages of the Method.—(1) Prolonged decubitus, the animal remaining down for one to three hours when recovering from its effects.

(2) In exceptional cases, owing to idiosyncracy, the patient succumbs to its effects. This may occur even when the classical dose of 10 grammes per 100 kilos has not been exceeded.

(3) With a safe dose of the drug the animal is usually only hypnotised,

and when more is administered to induce anæsthesia the patient remains lying much longer than after the hypnotic dose. Moreover, death is then more likely to ensue, while the alternative of administering chloroform to complete the anæsthesia is undoubtedly dangerous.

(4) With the average practitioner there is always the risk of two complications supervening, viz.: (*a*) phlebitis from injury to the intima of the veins by the needle or trocar impinging upon it and from the entrance of infection therein; (*b*) Sloughing of the skin owing to some of the choral escaping subcutaneously, even when ordinary care is taken during its introduction into the vein.

Its use is advocated by some and condemned by other experienced practitioners of the present day. Professor J. G. Wright in a paper published in the *Vet. Rec.*, June 8, 1946, gives his experience of the use of chloral intravenously as a narcotic in 70 horses aged from 6 months to 20 years during a period of 2 years, the dose varying from 5 to 6 grammes per cwt. for light to medium horses and 4·5 to 5 grammes for heavy horses, for a variety of operations. Regarding the value of the method, he states that it affords narcosis of sufficient depth for operations, under local or regional anæsthesia, but is unsatisfactory for general anæsthesia, since the animal remains recumbent too long. He says that it greatly facilitates inhalation anæsthesia, but some authorities believe that it renders the latter more dangerous.

Deep narcosis is characterised by relaxed tail, slow, deep, regular respirations, accelerated pulse, active corneal reflex, and slightly contracted pupil. The animal remains down about one and a half hours and is drowsy for four hours. There may be vigorous struggling during recovery, so that it is advisable to leave the limbs in the hobbles until it is obviously fit to rise. No toxic effects or post-anæsthesia malaise occurred, but in two cases the chloral escaped into the perivascular tissue, without leading to occlusion of the vein.

Marcenax and Lametayer (*Bull. Acad. Vét. Franç.*, 1930) gave records of its use and found that 11 grammes per 100 kilos. body weight produced complete anæsthesia. When 12 grammes were given recovery was delayed too long, in one case until 12 hours afterwards.

Mr. Frank Chambers, writing in the *Vet. Rec.*, **10**, 36, says, "I have on several occasions noticed grave alimentary liver disturbance in horses following the administration of large doses of chloral hydrate."

Mr. A. E. Carey Foster, Epsom, in a communication to the *Vet. Rec.*, September 24, 1946, on the relative advantages of chloral and chloroform anæsthesia relates his experiences on the use of these agents. In

1943 on service in the Central Command, India, under the direction of Colonel C. Stewart, D.D.V.S., he administered chloral to upwards of 2,000 mules for the muteing operation. Not more than 5 per cent. were truly anæsthetised, the remainder being in various stages of narcosis. The dose was 5 to 6 grammes per cwt. body weight of a 10 to 12 per cent. solution. Twelve cases of recovering animals remained recumbent for 15 to 40 minutes, then struggled up, walked a few steps, and dropped dead. For safety he advised leaving the animals recumbent as long as possible and when they rise not to hurry them to move. Although the best technique was practised extravascular injection or leakage of the drug was never eliminated. He concludes that intravenous injection of chloral cannot be recommended for exclusive use in private practice.

In 1944 in the same place about 4,000 animals were anæsthetised with chloroform with an initial dose of ½ to 1 ounce. Only two animals succumbed, thus demonstrating that chloroform is more satisfactory than chloral hydrate. He admits that the former is not a perfect anæsthetic but does not agree that the toxic margin is a "knife edge." He added that chloral by the stomach pump followed by chloroform is not satisfactory, although Professor Mitchell says it is. The author has found this satisfactory in most cases but has had such an unpleasant experience of it in one instance in a thoroughbred horse that he resolved not to make a practice of using it in the future. He would certainly not use chloral intravenously in a valuable blood-horse.

Technique of Intravenous Injection.—Following chiefly the method described by Professor Wright, it is as follows:

(1) It may be administered in the standing or cast position, the former being the more humane as it obviates the fear and struggling caused by throwing the animal, but the latter is better to facilitate the procedure by insuring quietude of the patient while the injection is being made.

(2) Estimate the weight of the horse.

(3) Weigh out the chloral and one-tenth of its weight of sodium chloride and sodium citrate.

(4) Make a 10 per cent. solution of the chloral in tap water and add the two salts.

(5) Sterilise the solution in a litre flask.

(6) Take a hollow needle 6 centimetres long and 2 millimetres bore, preferably with a grip and adaptor with tap.

(7) Inject 2 c.c. of 2 per cent. procaine solution hypodermically.

(8) Have the vein raised by digital pressure or by a noose round the base of the neck.

(9) Make tense the skin with the left hand or take up a fold of it and insert the needle or trocar with the point upwards, parallel and into the vein for a distance of $1\frac{1}{2}$ inches. The trocar is perhaps less likely to impinge on the lining of the vessel than the needle. Hold the instrument firmly in the vein.

(10) When the blood flows release the pressure, fix the tubing to the adaptor and flask, and then lower the flask until the blood passes the window in the tube.

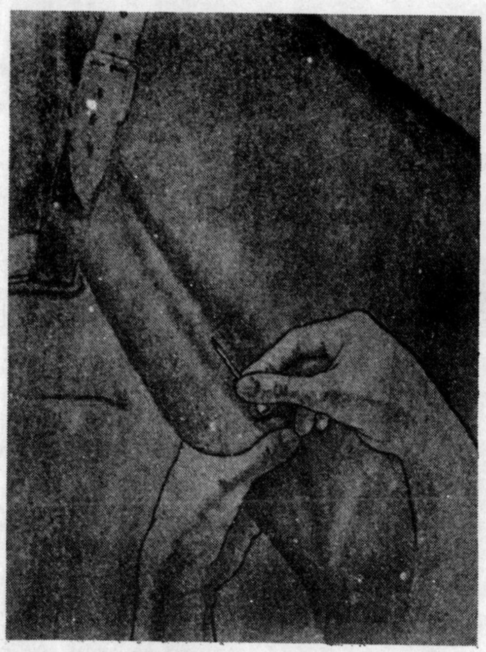

FIG. 45.—INSERTION OF THE NEEDLE INTO THE JUGULAR VEIN OF THE HORSE.

(11) Raise the flask as high as possible and let the solution flow into the vein at the rate of 750 c.c. of the fluid in 4 to 6 minutes. When in doubt about the chloral entering the vein lower the flask to see if the blood passes the window.

(12) When nearly all the solution has been injected lower the flask and allow blood to wash out of the needle all traces of the chlora hydrate as a precaution against some of it passing beneath the skin when the instrument is being withdrawn.

Mr. Norman Gold in a paper published in the *Vet. Rec.*, November 30, 1946, in his remarks on chloral anæsthesia and narcosis in the horse says general anæsthesia by inhalation is most unsatisfactory except as a means of deepening narcosis or light anæsthesia induced by the administration of chloral. The ideal form of anæsthesia is intravenous

Fig. 46.—Intravenous Injection of Chloral Hydrate Solution in the Horse, using the "Simplex" Apparatus.

chloral to the stage of deep narcosis or light anæsthesia supplemented by nerve block anæsthesia where possible; otherwise anæsthesia by intravenous chloral. In some hundreds of cases over a period of 10 years he had only two losses. Prolonged recumbency can be overcome by the injection intravenously of 5 to 6 c.c. pituitrin. A 1 c.c. intra-dermal syringe is useful for injecting the local anæsthetic at the site of venous puncture. He uses 8 to 10 per cent. chloral hydrate solution with 1 per cent. sodium citrate added, in dosage approximately of 5·5 grammes per 50 kilogrammes or 80 grains per pound body weight and is guided in this respect by the animal's reflexes.

The stages of narcosis can be carefully assessed during the introduction of the drug. Higginson's syringe with a glass window between the syringe and the adaptor, is preferable to the flutter valve apparatus for administering the drug. In nervous animals he gives 1 to 1½ ounces of chloral intravenously, in the box, and the animal is then brought out and cast and additional chloral given until deep narcosis or anæsthesia is produced. In the meantime the needle is left in the vein. He sees no advantage in casting the subject before giving the chloral.

Intravenous Anæsthesia by Anavenol

Anavenol is a preparation introduced in 1948–49 by Imperial Chemical (Pharmaceuticals), Ltd., from whose " Veterinary Products " the following description of its use has been obtained. It contains 10 per cent. w/v of B-naphthyethanol finely suspended in a sterile aqueous medium. It has proved highly satisfactory as a short-acting intravenous anæsthetic for horses of all classes and ages for periods up to 30 minutes. The anæsthetia is of an ascending type—the trunk and limbs being affected before the head and neck and special senses.

When injected slowly toxic effects are minimal. Too large or too rapid dosage may unduly increase the heart rate and cause respiratory arrest, when the drug should be discontinued and artificial respiration applied. The Anavenol is rapidly excreted and normal breathing is usually quickly restored.

It is administered in the standing position, the process occupying about 2 minutes at the end of which the animal will become unsteady in the hindquarters and with a step backwards will sink to the ground without excitement or struggling. No restraint of the legs is required. A single injection is sufficient for short operations. Slow injection is essential to avoid toxic effect, the rate of injection being 1 c.c. per second for the average animal, varying in proportion to the body weight, the whole injection taking about 2 minutes. The dose varies between 12 and 25 c.c. per cwt. body weight (0·25 c.c. and 0·55 c.c. per Kilo). Maintenance of anæsthesia longer than 30 minutes can be achieved by an inhalation anæsthetic or perhaps by a further dose of Anavenol. The dose should never exceed 50 c.c. per cwt. body weight (1 c.c. per kilogram).

The preparation is issued in containers of 5·00 c.c. which are designed for direct injection by means of one of the standard types of positive pressure apparatus.

This method of general anæsthesia has not been practised sufficiently often in general practice up to the present to justify its being recommended as a thoroughly safe and effective procedure.

Morphia Narcosis in the Horse

Morphia administered hypodermically, either alone or in conjunction with chloral *per rectum* or *per os*, may have some effect in quieting a restive horse, but as a rule its action in this respect is disappointing. Its dose for the horse is 3 to 7 grains. A larger dose is apt to cause violent excitement lasting for hours. Even a moderate dose sometimes has this effect.

Almy and Desaubry recommend a subcutaneous injection containing morphia hydrochlor. $1\frac{2}{3}$ grains, and neutral sulphate of atropine $\frac{1}{12}$ grain, and distilled water $2\frac{1}{2}$ drachms, to be given half an hour before the administration of chloroform. They claim that when this injection is used less chloroform is required, and anæsthesia is more rapidly induced.

Anæsthesia in the Ox

The ox is a good subject for chloroform. The same precautions are required as in the horse. It may be given in the standing or cast position. The chloroform muzzle must include the upper and lower jaws, as the ox breathes freely through the mouth.

It is important to have the animal fasting for several hours before administering the anæsthetic, as there is danger of regurgitation from the rumen during anæsthesia and passage of alimentary matter into the lungs, setting up foreign body pneumonia. The beast should not be allowed to lie broadside for a long time, as tympany of the rumen may then supervene and lead to asphyxia. The dosage is about the same as for the horse. When the standing method is adopted, comparatively large doses are indicated.

Accidents seldom occur when ordinary precautions are taken, and even when the patient has not been prepared by fasting, which is not always practicable.

J. K. H. Wilde, Tanganyika, in an article in *Vet. Rec.*, June 20, 1942, on general anæsthesia in cattle by chloral hydrate administered intravenously, says that he found 6·36 grammes per cwt. body weight satisfactory for narcosis and that 120 c.c. of a 10 per cent. solution of the drug proved inadequate for surgical anæsthesia. He administered the drug slowly in the standing position. The advocates, in Great Britain, of chloral narcosis and anæsthesia in the horse recommend it with equal confidence in the ox.

Cycloproprane Anæsthesia in Ruminants

R. A. Gregory, Department of Physiology, University of Liverpool, in an article in *Vet. Rec.*, August 2, 1947, describes a successful and satisfactory method of producing general anæsthesia in the ruminant, for experimental surgical operations, by the administration of cyclopropane gas through an intratracheal tube. It eliminates the danger of foreign-body pneumonia liable to ensue during prolonged chloroform anæsthesia given by the ordinary mask, from regurgitation of food from the rumen. With the appropriate apparatus, including a simple laryngoscope, and the aid of a skilled assistant the method appears to be easily practised. It requires pre-anæsthisation by the intravenous injection of nembutal to enable the intratracheal tube to be inserted. The dose of nembutal is not mentioned.

Anæsthesia in the Sheep

Anæsthesia is seldom required in the sheep. Chloroform may be used with safety when carefully administered.

Anæsthesia in the Pig

Chloroform has been used with safety and satisfactory results in the pig. It is administered through a muzzle, including the mouth and nose. The effects of the anæsthetic must be carefully watched as the animal may suddenly succumb to an extra dose if too large.

Chloroform Anæsthesia in the Dog

General anæsthesia is frequently indicated in the dog, chiefly for abdominal operations. The dog is prepared as described for an operation. It may get a little warm milky tea or bovril about two or three hours before administering the anæsthetic. The patient should be allowed to evacuate the bladder before being put on the table, where it is usually fixed in the ventral position until anæsthesia is produced, when it may be changed into the dorsal position if necessary, or the latter position may be adopted from the beginning. There should be nothing to interfere with respiration.

METHOD OF ADMINISTRATION.—Whatever method is adopted, plenty of air must be admitted along with the chloroform.

Open method.—This consists in spreading a piece of lint or cloth over a wire muzzle on the dog, and dropping the chloroform on to the cloth. Or it may be carried out by means of a jam-jar, a piece of cotton-wool containing the chloroform being placed in the bottom of the jar, which is then pushed over the dog's muzzle and held in position until anæsthesia is produced. This acts very satisfactorily when carefully supervised.

Using an inhaler.—Probably the best inhaler for the dog is Hobday's pattern. By this apparatus a current of air is sucked by means of a bellows over the surface of the chloroform contained in a suitable bottle provided with a straight glass tube to let in the air, and a bent glass tube to which the bellows is attached. When the bellows is worked vigorously, air containing about 2 per cent. of chloroform is driven into the mask and inhaled by the patient. It may be necessary to insert into the end of the mask a piece of cotton-wool containing some chloroform until anæsthesia is produced, when it should be taken out and the bellows used to keep the animal under the influence of the anæsthetic. This is a very safe method.

For hospital use, Hobday introduced another pattern of inhaler in which the air containing the chloroform is pumped into the inhaler by an electric motor and by means of which the dose can be accurately graduated.

Anæsthesia must be produced slowly. The time required for the purpose varies from one to two minutes in small dogs to three to eight minutes in larger dogs. During the initial stage of the administration the patient may seem to hold its breath. The respirations must then be allowed to become regular before proceeding further.

The excitement stage is marked by yelping and violent struggling, and often by the involuntary escape of urine and fæces. When anæsthesia is approaching the struggling diminishes, the tail becomes limp, the hind-quarters powerless, and the head can no longer be raised voluntarily. Dilatation of the pupil occurs, and is especially well marked in the cat.

To keep the patient under, small quantities of the anæsthetic are administered from time to time. The animal can be kept under its effect for a considerable time, but it is seldom that a longer period than half an hour is required.

It is a great advantage to have an experienced assistant as anæsthetist. He should watch the respirations carefully. If they should become weak, shallow, or irregular, or suddenly cease, the mask and all restraint must be at once removed and antidotes administered. Convulsive twitching of the extremities is a bad sign, and if the hairs of the coat turn the wrong way it is a sure sign of death.

Restoratives should always be at hand, and the best of these are liquor ammonia and Scheele's prussic acid. Having removed the mask, take the patient quickly into the fresh air, open the mouth, draw out the tongue, and apply on its posterior part a couple of drops of the acid, and then continue traction on it in a jerky fashion. The open mouth of the bottle containing strong ammonia passed fairly rapidly to and fro in front of the nostrils so that the patient may inhale some of its vapour also has a reviving effect. Inhalation of CO_2 is also a good respiratory stimulant and is conveniently provided for the purpose in the form of sparklets. Hypodermic injection of ether,

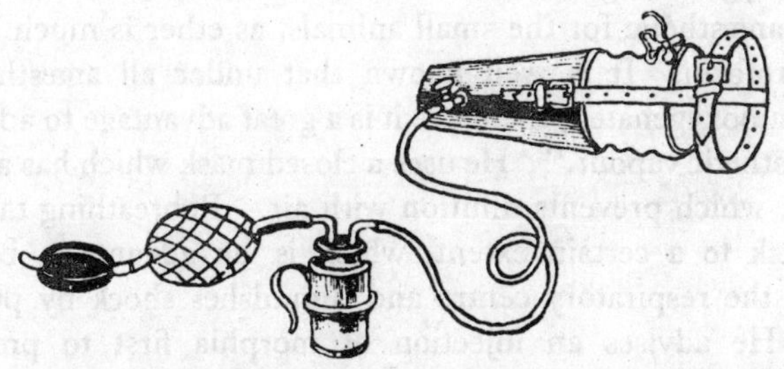

FIG. 47.—HOBDAY'S CHLOROFORM APPARATUS FOR THE DOG.

strychnine, adrenalin, or coramine may be tried. Intracardiac injection of adrenalin has proved effective.

Artificial respiration should also be performed by laying the animal on its right side and expelling the air from the lungs by pressing repeatedly in a short jerky manner on the ribs, which by virtue of their elasticity will then spring up and down, causing the chest to expand and contract as in respiration. The mouth should be kept open and the tongue drawn on at the same time as described. Too much pressure must not be exerted on the thorax for fear of rupturing the liver or the mesenteric artery. When the foregoing methods are successful, signs of recovery are noticed—viz., movement of the jaws, eyelids, head, limbs, and moaning or yelping. The artificial respiration should be continued in unison with the normal respiratory movements until the patient is quite out of danger. Bad signs during the stage of danger are relaxation of the sphincters of the bladder and rectum, stertorous breathing, erection of the hairs of the coat, stoppage of the heart, and no signs of revival after about five minutes' artificial respiration. Attempts at resuscitation, however, should be continued for at least ten minutes.

Ether Anæsthesia in the Dog

Ether is safer than chloroform, but it is too slow in producing anæsthesia, and often seems to have no effect except to cause excitement. A.C.E. (that is, alcohol, chloroform, and ether in the proportion of 1, 2, 3 respectively) or C.E. (chloroform and ether, 1 and 2) is very safe and effective for maintaining anæsthesia in the dog after producing it with chloroform, or for inducing anæsthesia in the cat when an inhaler is used.

Ether and Oxygen Anæsthesia

This method has recently come into vogue for small animals. Mr. E. F. Angler says : (1931) " For the past five years I have used ether and oxygen as a general anæsthetic, and I am now satisfied that it is the safest anæsthetic for the small animals, as ether is much less toxic than chloroform. It is well known that under all anæsthetics the patient is suboxygenated, therefore it is a great advantage to add oxygen to the anæsthetic vapour." He uses a closed mask which has an expiratory valve, which prevents dilution with air. Rebreathing takes place in the mask to a certain extent, which is an advantage, because it stimulates the respiratory centre and diminishes shock by preventing acidosis. He advises an injection of morphia first to prevent (1) physical shock, and (2) psychical shock.

The apparatus comprises a mask, an ether container, and an oxygen cylinder with a Pinson gauge and valve. The ether container is fitted with a rubber cork in which two metal tubes are inserted, one tube extending into the depth of the ether, while the other only extends about ½ inch below the lower surface of the cork. The latter tube is connected to the mask by rubber tubing, while the other tube, immersed in the ether, is connected in a similar way to the oxygen cylinder. The oxygen is turned on slowly at first, and then gradually increased if necessary. When morphia has been given, anæsthesia will be produced in less than one minute, otherwise it will take five minutes. The patient can be kept under the anæsthetic for an indefinite period without any ill-effects. The author has practised this method of anæsthesia for a number of years on numerous occasions without a single death, the subjects being the dog, cat and pig.

A New Apparatus for Inhalation Anæsthesia in Small Animals

The use of mixtures of chloroform and ether has the disadvantage that the more volatile ether evaporates more freely, so that in the course of the operation an ever-increasing concentration of chloroform vapour is in use, which is the precise reverse of what is desirable. A better practice is to induce anæsthesia with chloroform, and maintain it with the safer and less toxic ether, but the change-over is somewhat tiresome to effect with the standard apparatus. Mr. E. O. Longley (*Vet. Rec.*, **59**, 5), has devised an apparatus from simple components which enables the change to ether to be effected by an eighth turn of one tap. The apparatus comprises three glass bottles set in triangular formation on a

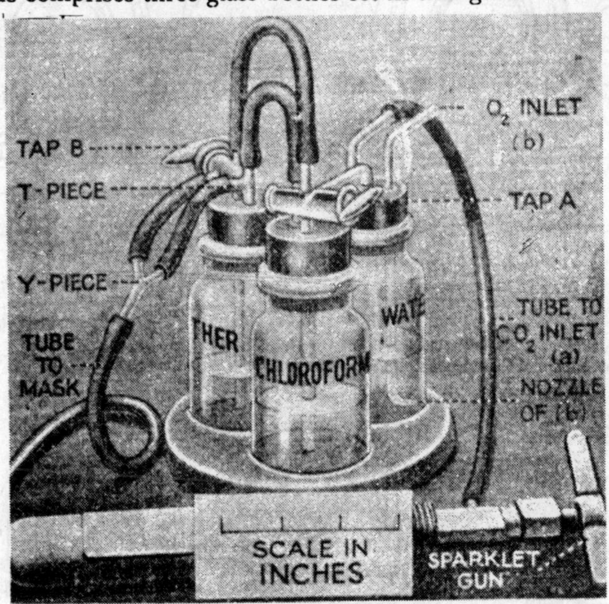

FIG. 48.—LONGLEY'S ANÆSTHESIA APPARATUS.

wooden base, one containing the chloroform, one the ether, and the third water for humidification of the gases.*

The system is fed from a cyclinder of oxygen. With the taps set as shown in Fig. 49, the oxygen bubbles through the chloroform only, and thence on to the mask. This is the setting for induction. If the tap *B* is now turned clockwise through 45° (so that both taps are vertical with their ground-out marker-spots to the right, as in Fig. 51), the oxygen takes the path through the ether only. The change can thus be brought about in a moment and without leaving the animal. At intermediate positions of the tap, the oxygen takes the path through both the bottles (Fig. 50), and mixed ether-chloroform vapour becomes available if

* No matter what mask or other device is employed, oxygen must be kept properly humidified by passing it through water " Hamilton Bailey (1944), *Surgery of Modern Warfare*, p. 138.

desired, without the disadvantage attending the use of mixtures of the liquids. The principle underlying this simple manœuvre is that as chloroform has twice the S.G. of ether, the oxygen, though offered both channels, takes preferentially the path through the lighter ether.

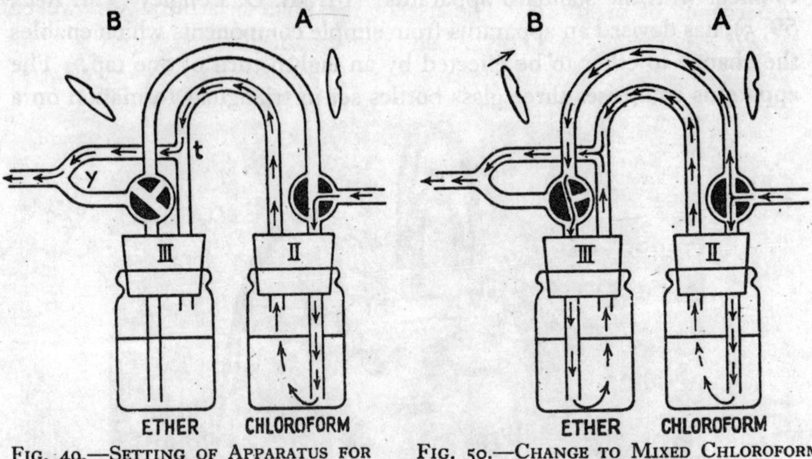

Fig. 49.—Setting of Apparatus for Induction with Chloroform.

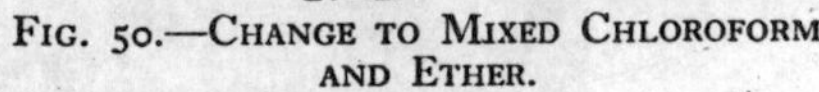

Fig. 50.—Change to Mixed Chloroform and Ether.

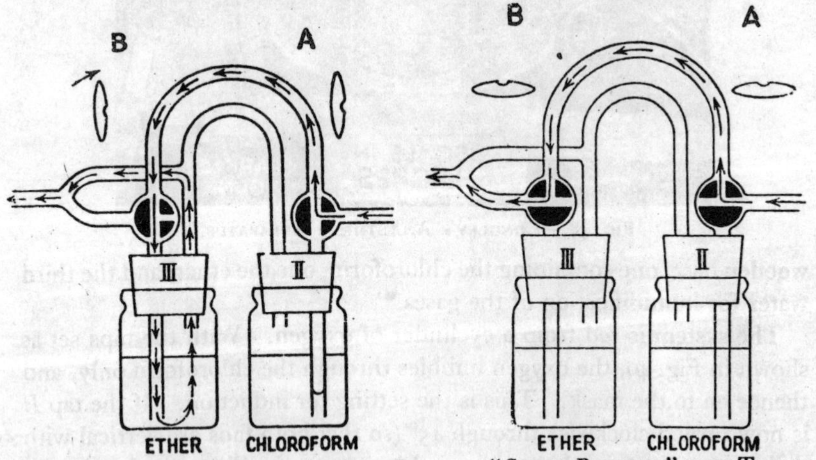

Fig. 51. Change to Ether Only, for Maintenance.

Fig. 52.—"Safety Position," with Through-Channel for Oxygen $\pm CO_2$.

Additional services are available with this apparatus: (1) With both taps horizontal and their marker-spots upwards, as in Fig. 52, a through channel for oxygen only is provided. This of course is the prescription in the event of over-deep anæsthesia or at any other time of difficulty, and with advantage at the conclusion of operations. It is immediately procured by turning both taps anti-clockwise through 90°. (2) The water-bottle is provided with a second inlet, to which a small "Sparklet" CO_2-cylinder may be attached, for the addition of CO_2 to the oxygen. This is desirable during the phase of induction to increase the respiratory function and hence the intake of the anæsthetic, and it is necessary in the emergency of overdose. The use of this inlet is arbitrary, however, and it may remain unconnected and unsealed if desired, since the water acts as an automatic valve closing it to the exterior, when it incidentally constitutes a form of flow-meter for the oxygen input.

Teneril Anæsthesia in Small Animals

FIG. 53.—HENEY'S TRILENE ANÆSTHESIA APPARATUS.

Trilene (trichlorethylene and 0·01 per cent. thymol), a general inhalation anæsthetic used in human surgery, was first employed in small animal practice by Mr. J. W. Heney, M.R.C.V.S., Dublin. He demonstrated the procedure of its administration on a subject to a large meeting in Dublin on November 15, 1946, by an apparatus incorporating Boyle's Bottles (Fig. 53) by which a large number of small animals had been rapidly and safely anæsthetised, recovery taking place after cessation of anæsthesia on the completion of any major operation which was performed.

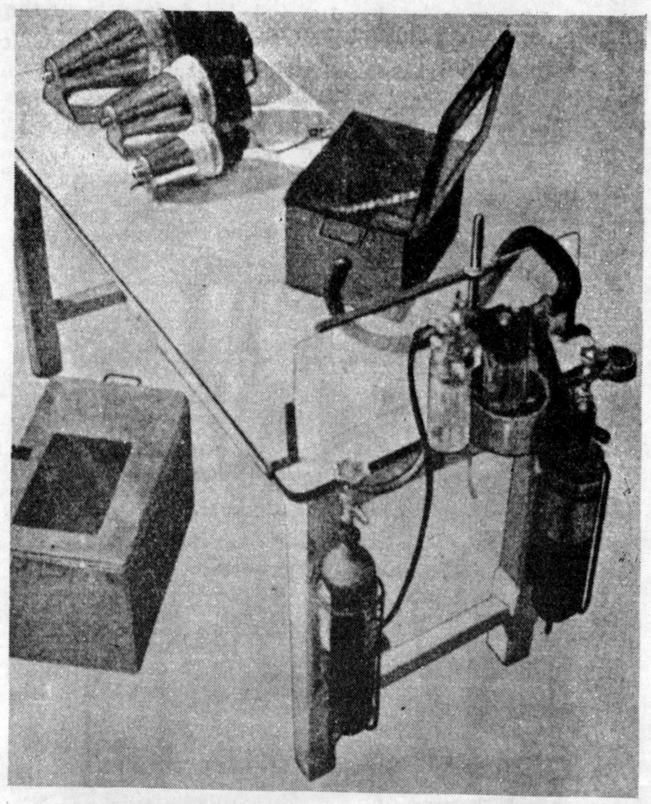

FIG. 54.—HENEY'S APPARATUS WITH ASSORTED MASKS AND THE "CAT BOX."

He has used it on 8,500 cases including dogs, cats, pigs, sheep, and poultry. Out of this number 18 deaths occurred. The anæsthesia is brought about by the passage of oxygen through liquid trilene into a mask or box (Fig. 54). Induction of anæsthesia takes from 2 to 5 minutes depending on the size and condition of the animal. Relaxation is complete and there is little evidence of unpleasant side effects. The depth of the anæsthesia can be usually controlled by the oxygen flow. The time for complete recovery varies from 5 to 30 minutes.

For large dogs (greyhounds, etc.) he advises premedication with seconal, a powder in capsule form, administered 30 minutes beforehand, the dose being 1¼ to 3 grains. He also uses omnopon, nembutal, pethidine, or morphia. It may also be desirable for some of the smaller breeds. He has used trilene for all sorts of operations, including 400 abdominal sections. It may therefore be inferred that it is one of the best and safest inhalation anæsthetics for small animals (*Irish Vet. J.*, January 1947).

Morphia Narcosis in the Dog

In the dog, morphia has a marked effect as a narcotic, producing profound sleep within half an hour after being administered hypodermically. It does not cause anæsthesia, for the patient resents any painful operation done under its influence.

It is extremely useful in canine practice as a means of control for vicious dogs which resent any interference. For operations on the mouth in such animals it is particularly useful. It also has the advantage of keeping a dog perfectly quiet, in a state of sleep, for upwards of twenty-four hours after an operation. Its dose as a narcotic is 1 grain for a terrier to 2 or even 3 grains for a large dog.

If complete anæsthesia is required, chloroform may be administered. It acts more quickly with the morphia than when used alone.

The following solution of atropine and morphia is recommended as an injection prior to the administration of chloroform to the dog. The morphia diminishes excitement and the atropine prevents cardiac syncope.

Hydrochloride of morphia	1½ grains.
Sulphate of atropine	0·8 grain.
Distilled water	2½ fluid drachms.

Doses are 10 minims for small animals, 20 to 40 minims for animals of medium size, and 60 to 80 minims for large dogs. Its effect is produced in twenty to twenty-five minutes, when the administration of the chloroform is commenced.

Anæsthesia in the Cat

The procedure for the cat is the same as that for the dog ; but the cat is more susceptible to the effects of chloroform. A mixture of chloroform and ether acts well in the cat, and is safer than chloroform. One part of chloroform to two of ether has been found to be quite satisfactory. The ordinary A.C.E. mixture may be used.

A common method of anæsthetising the cat is to put it in a box with a glass window on its lid and introduce some chloroform on pieces of cotton-wool dropped into the box. The excitement stage can be observed through the window. When it has terminated, the cat is lifted quickly out of the box and operated upon. This method is often adopted for the operation of castration.

Gray of London has found the jam-jar method of administering chloroform to the cat very safe by taking care to draw the jar slightly away from the animal as soon as it is anæsthetised so that its head rests only on the lip of the jar.

Ether and oxygen, as described for the dog, has proved very safe and satisfactory for the cat. Longley's apparatus would seem appropriate for administering a mixture of chloroform and ether to this animal.

Nembutal intraperitoneally and intravenously has been used with the same success in the cat as in the dog. The median vein of the forearm is the most suitable site for intravenous injection.

Morphia as a narcotic is contra-indicated in the cat as it produces excitement in this animal.

Anæsthesia in Birds

Birds are not good subjects for general anæsthesia. It has been reported that the inhalation of ether is safe after the injection of $\frac{1}{200}$ grain of atropine to prevent cardiac inhibition, but judging from Mr. Heney's remarks "Trilene" would appear to be the best anæsthetic for birds since if a special small mask is employed which does not include the comb and wattles these latter organs will act as a guide to the depth or plane of anæsthesia. He has noted a very definite cyanosis of these appendages in deep anæsthesis of all avians.

Anæsthesia in the Monkey

The monkey is a good subject for chloroform carefully administered.

Avertin Anæsthesia

Avertin introduced in solution *per rectum* causes deep narcotisation in the dog and anæsthesia in the cat.

Since the introduction of nembutal it is seldom employed for these animals, owing to the trouble and time required for the technique of its administration.

Its use has been found disappointing in the horse apart from the fact that the price of the dose required for this animal would be prohibitive. It was brought to the notice of the veterinary profession by Professor Wright, Royal Veterinary College, London (see *Vet. Rec.*, **10**, No. 24).

Avertin.—It is composed of tribrom. ethyl alcohol, CBr_3CH_2OH, was first produced by Wellstätter and Doishberg by yeast fermentation of bromol, and Eichholtz in 1927 studied its pharmacological actions and introduced it into the therapeutics. It occurs as a white crystalline solid with a sharp melting-point of 80° C. It is soluble in water to 3½ per cent. at 40° C., and at this temperature is fairly stable, but at higher temperatures it may split up, yielding hydrobromic acid and dibrom. acetaldehyde. There is also a fluid form comprising tribrom. ethyl alcohol held in solution in amylene hydrate. It is a colourless syrupy liquid with a faint characteristic odour, and is soluble to 3 per cent. by agitating it for three to four minutes in distilled water at 40° C. It volatilises rapidly on exposure. 1 c.c. of fluid avertin = 1 grm. of the solid.

The technique of its use is as follows:

PREPARATION OF THE PATIENT.—Administer a laxative and enema so as to have the rectum empty before injecting the avertin. The enema should be given three hours beforehand, as the presence of fluid in the rectum at the time of injection of the drug greatly reduces its action. Experience has shown that evacuation of the rectum in the cat is unnecessary in the great majority of cases. Food should be withheld for six hours prior to using the anæsthetic, otherwise vomition may ensue.

DOSAGE.—(1) *The Dog.*—0·5 to 0·6 grm. per kilogram body weight.

(2) *The Cat.*—0·3 grm. per kilogram, administered in each case in 3 per cent. solution of distilled water at 40° C. For example, a dog weighing 20 lb. or 9 kilos, would receive 5·4 c.c. of avertin in 180 c.c. of distilled water at 40° C.; and a cat of 10 lb., or 4·5 kilos, 1·3 c.c. in 46 c.c. of distilled water. A small dose of morphia may be given to a nervous or panicky dog about three hours before administering the avertin.

PREPARATION OF THE DOSE.—(1) Agitate the avertin, whether liquid or solid, in the distilled water for five minutes in order to dissolve it.

(2) Test the purity of the injection by adding one to two drops of a 1 in 1,000 solution of Congo red in a clean test-tube to 5 c.c. of the liquid just before administration. (It is necessary to add 2 minims extra to the computed dose and 5 c.c. to the distilled water, for the carrying out of this test.) The resulting colour must be pure orange red. The presence of acidity is indicated by the colour turning blue, and may occur if the temperature of the water is too high.

ADMINISTRATION.—Have the patient held by the tail with the hind-legs raised to the vertical position, introduce a large, lubricated, dog catheter into the rectum, and attach to it a piece of rubber tubing;

take a 50 c.c. glass syringe containing the anæsthetic and inject it slowly through the rubber tube; or, if acting single-handed, adopt the suggestion of Hamilton Kirk, and have the syringe minus the piston held at a convenient height in the fork of a retort stand, after connecting it with the tube and catheter already inserted in the rectum; pour the anæsthetic into the syringe with the right hand, and it will gravitate into the rectum at the required speed, the left hand being employed holding up the patient by the tail.

SYMPTOMS.—The avertin is rapidly absorbed from the colon, and muscular relaxation occurs two to three minutes after injection.

Narcosis appears after five to eight minutes, and is not preceded by any definite period of excitement in the dog; but the cat may show a few convulsive movements of the limbs and bend the head upwards about three minutes after injection. The drug is non-irritant and never causes straining. The onset of deep narcosis is shown by marked muscular relaxation, and even in cases where there is no general anæsthesia the animal is unable to move.

The duration of narcosis varies. In the cat with a dosage of 0·3 it persists for eighteen or more hours. It is more irregular and much more transient in the dog; 0·4 has produced deep narcosis for periods varying from nine minutes to one hour. Young subjects are less susceptible to its effects than adults.

Respirations become slower and shallower, but remain perfectly regular—30 to 40 per minute in the dog and cat.

The *pulse* does not seem to be affected. There is a slight fall in the blood pressure.

There is marked *dilatation of the peripheral vessels*, characterised by decided warmth of the ears, the tip of the nose, and the extremities, and when the nose is non-pigmented it, as well as the visible mucous membranes, becomes bright pink in colour. Hence the patient must be kept in a warm atmosphere to prevent chill.

Action of the pupil.—In slight narcosis, when light and corneal reflexes are present, there appears to be little or no effect upon the pupil; but in deep narcosis, and when reflexes are lost, the pupil in the case of the cat becomes a narrow slit, and in the dog the size of a pin-head.

TOXICITY.—Circulatory collapse can be caused by overdosage. Hence the rules given for dosage must be strictly observed.

Avertin is an excellent painless lethal agent, injected intravenously into the dog or cat, causing death in practically every case within one minute without whine or struggle, the dose being 2–5 c.c.

Nembutal Anæsthesia

Professor J. G. Wright, M.R.C.V.S., of the Royal Veterinary College, London, has been instrumental in popularising the use of nembutal as a general anæsthetic for the dog and cat by recording its effects in a large number of cases. His experience in its use has enabled him to establish a table of approximate dosage for the various sizes of dogs and for cats, whereby it can be successfully and safely employed. According to his publications on the subject he considers it much safer than chloroform, and has estimated that the death-rate following its use is less than 1 per cent. The author has employed it extensively as a general anæsthetic in the dog following chiefly the directions laid down by Wright, and from his experience has formed the opinion that it is the most convenient and, perhaps with the exception of the mixture of ether and oxygen, the safest agent for producing anæsthesia or deep narcosis in the small animal. It is particularly useful for operations about the head, there being no mask in the way.

Kreutzer, in the United States of America, was the first to bring it to the notice of the veterinary profession.

The following remarks on nembutal anæsthesia are based very largely on those made by Professor Wright in his published treatises on the subject.

Composition of Nembutal.—It is composed of sodium-ethyl-methyl-butyl-barbiturate, and occurs as a white crystalline powder freely soluble in water. It is supplied in capsules of 1 grain and 1½ grains.

ADMINISTRATION.—It may be administered:

(1) By the mouth.
(2) Intraperitoneally.
(3) Intravenously.

1. *By the mouth.*—By this route the narcotic action of the drug is more variable than by the other routes. The onset of narcosis takes ½ to one hour, and its duration is at least twelve hours. This method of administration is therefore seldom employed.

2. *Intraperitoneally.*—This is a very convenient and effective method of using the drug. The usual strict aseptic precautions are taken and the injection is made by means of a hypodermic syringe, using a needle size 20 and ¾ to 1½ inches long. It may be introduced through the flank or at the white line, care being taken that the needle penetrates the abdominal wall and is not merely inserted into the sub-peritoneal tissue.

The onset of loco-motor inco-ordination occurs in five to ten minutes and anæsthesia or deep narcosis is reached in about fifteen minutes. The duration of the anæsthesia is one-and-a-half to two hours, after which recovery slowly occurs. Consciousness has generally returned by the fourth to the sixth hour.

Occasionally cases are met with in which the drug is very slow to act, the onset of its action being delayed from one to two hours. It is impossible to account for these cases except to ascribe them to an idiosyncrasy of the patient whereby it is not susceptible to the influence of the agent.

Exceptional instances occur in which although the patient appears to be anæsthetised, by the loss of the power of movement, it whines when the operation is being performed. In cases of this kind complete anæsthesia can be produced by slight inhalations of chloroform or ether.

When the drug is slow in producing its effects the latter last longer than when they appear quickly, their duration being sometimes twenty-four and even thirty-six hours. This slow action is more apt to occur in very fat animals, when it is probably due to the injection being made into the sub-peritoneal fat instead of into the peritoneal cavity. As a rule there is no excitement stage, but exceptionally, especially in the case of the large breeds (greyhounds, wolfhounds), the animal shows prolonged but subdued excitement characterised by whining and slight struggling, although the maximum dose has been used. The careful administration of a small dose of chloroform or ether and oxygen is then indicated.

If a sub-anæsthetic dose is used excitement usually supervenes.

During anæsthesia the pupil is markedly contracted, the pulse is accelerated, and the respirations are of moderate depth and 30 to 40 per minute. Vomition, salivation, or defæcation does not occur. There is congestion of the visible mucous membranes.

Before anæsthesia ensues the animal may sneeze or lick its muzzle, apparently from the effects of the drug. This has been more noticeable in the cat than in the dog. Bulldogs and pekes are not good subjects owing to their difficulty in breathing through the nose. They are apt to succumb during deep anæsthesia from respiratory failure due to mechanical obstruction of the larynx. Animals with cardiac and renal affections have been anæsthetised by this means without ill effects. Extra caution, however, is necessary in the case of debilitated subjects or those suffering from organic affections.

3. *Intravenously.*—By this method anæsthesia is produced as a rule within one minute after completing the injection, whose effects appear

practically immediately, indicated by sudden relaxation of the muscles, inability to hold up the head or move the limbs, and by dropping of the lower jaw. The reflexes continue for a variable time after the patient is apparently profoundly anæsthetised, the animal responding to pinching of the paw between the finger and thumb. Notwithstanding this there may be no response to incision of the tissues and the operation can be proceeded with. The reflexes do not usually persist for more than five minutes.

In exceptional cases the injection is not so rapid in action, and ten to fifteen minutes may elapse before the effects of the nembutal are observed.

In rare instances the drug has little or no effect.

THE SITE OF INJECTION is the recurrent tarsal vein as it passes backwards and upwards on the outside of the leg above the hock, but it may also be made through the median vein in the fore-limb. The latter site is the only suitable one in the cat.

PROCEDURE.—Have the dog held lying on the table on the opposite side, the assistant leaning with one arm on the animal's neck and chest and the hand of the same side holding the front limbs while the other grasps the upper hind-limb in the stifle region, compressing it sufficiently to arrest the circulation in the vein and make it stand out prominently under the skin, where it can be felt rolling beneath the finger. Applying a little xylol to the skin makes the vein stand out more prominently. It is important that the vein should be steadied from rolling when the needle is being introduced. A second assistant may be required to keep the dog steady and hold the leg fully extended so that when the needle has entered the vein it will not be disturbed by movement of the limb and made to penetrate its opposite wall or slip out of the vessel. On the whole it is best to fix the animal with hobbles, or narcotise it with morphia, prior to attempting the injection, especially when short of assistance or when the patient is very restive. In this case an assistant grasps the limb above the stifle with one hand to distend the vein and keep the leg extended, whilst with the other he holds the paw.

Having made the solution in the proportion of 1 grain to 1 c.c. of boiled water, or more concentrated when a large dose is to be given, draw it into the syringe, using a fine, very sharp-pointed needle about $\frac{1}{2}$ to $\frac{3}{4}$ inch long with the syringe attached, and having stretched the skin, if necessary, by pressure with the thumb, make it penetrate the vein with one movement parallel to its long axis, pushing the needle well into the lumen of the vessel. A syringe with the nozzle eccentrically situated facilitates the operation.

The entrance of the vein is indicated by blood intermixing with the clear solution in the syringe when the plunger is slightly withdrawn. Then release the pressure on the vein and inject the liquid slowly, especially the final part of the dose, taking three to five minutes to complete the injection. If blood does not appear in the syringe, or on making the injection a swelling forms under the skin, the needle is not in the vein, and in the latter case the operation must be tried higher up or on the other limb. Even in small terriers this operation is usually easily performed, but occasionally it is difficult, particularly in short-legged dogs, to make the vein stand out sufficiently to ensure penetrating

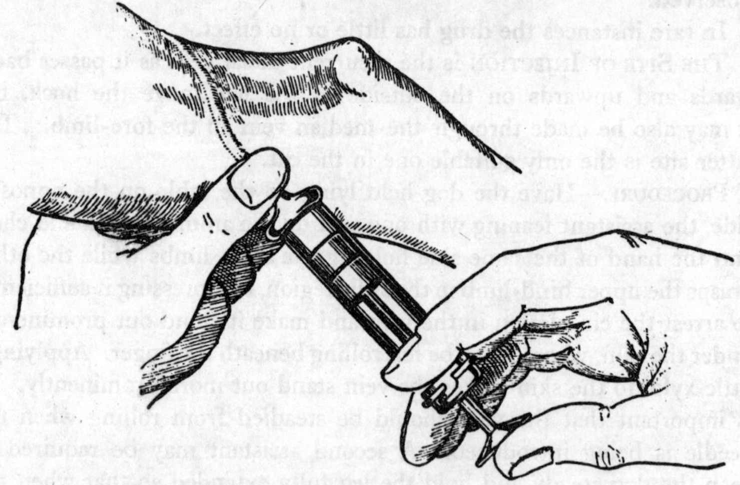

FIG. 55.—INTRAVENOUS INJECTION IN THE DOG, USING THE RECURRENT TARSAL VEIN.
Illustrating the method of holding the needle to the leg.

it with the needle. It is essential that the needle be sharp and preferably of fine calibre, although a needle of comparatively large bore may be successfully employed. Skill in the procedure is acquired by practice.

DOSAGE for the intraperitoneal route. The animal must be carefully weighed in order to compute the correct dose of the drug. The following scale of dosage according to the weight of the animal has been recommended by Wright, and has been confirmed by the author as reliable in most cases.

1. From 10 to 25 lb. in weight, $\frac{1}{4}$ grain per lb. body weight.
2. From 30 to 45 lb., $\frac{1}{5}$ grain per lb. body weight.
3. From 50 to 60 lb., $\frac{1}{6}$ grain per lb. body weight.
4. From 70 lb. upwards, $\frac{1}{7}$ grain per lb. body weight.

For the intravenous route the same scale may be taken as a guide, but must not be followed religiously. This scale is of course only approximately correct. A little more or less than the quantity mentioned in each case may be required, according to the idiosyncrasy of the patient. The dose mentioned under No. 4 may prove too small intravenously. The author found that 14 grains for an Irish wolfhound weighing 91 lb. caused whining and struggling which continued despite the use of a local anæsthetic for the removal of a papilloma from the interior of the concha.

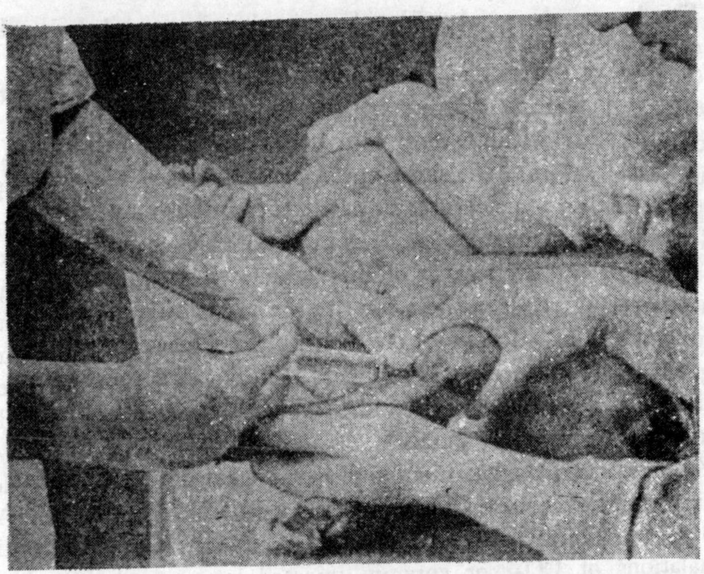

FIG. 56.—ADMINISTRATION OF NEMBUTAL TO THE DOG BY INTRAVENOUS INJECTION, USING THE RECURRENT TARSAL VEIN.

For intravenous injection the calculated amount required is taken up in the syringe and the injection continued slowly until its effects are noticed, and if anæsthesia supervene before all the contents are used the injection is discontinued.

If, on the other hand, the desired result is not obtained within a few minutes an additional dose must be very slowly administered to bring about the stage of anæsthesia, or instead a few inhalations of chloroform or ether may be given. Dissatisfaction occurs when what is considered the maximum dose is injected without unconsciousness ensuing, the veterinarian being in doubt as to giving an additional dose. Subdosage is certainly very unsatisfactory on account of the excitement which may ensue.

Big dogs like greyhounds and wolfhounds are probably the most likely to give trouble in this respect. Perhaps the safest course to adopt in such instances is to complete the anæsthesia with chloroform, a small dose of which is generally sufficient.

Rapid injection of the drug is believed by Wright to interfere with its anæsthetising effect, and to account for some of those cases in which a stage of subdued excitement persists instead of anæsthesia supervening.

This method of administering nembutal is undoubtedly the best when the vein can be readily penetrated.

The dose can be regulated by observing its effects while being slowly injected, which is not possible by the intraperitoneal method.

Care, however, must be exercised with debilitated animals and those suffering from cardiac, respiratory, or renal affections as they may succumb any time within twenty-four hours after administration of the drug, especially dogs of the short-nosed variety—pekes, pugs, and bulldogs—in which it is preferable to produce anæsthesia by inhalation of chloroform or ether and oxygen. An objectionable feature of the action of the drug is the excitement of the patient which sometimes ensues when recovering consciousness four to six hours after its administration, and which lasts for about one hour, the animal crying and throwing itself about in an aimless manner. This occurs most frequently in large dogs, especially greyhounds. When this stage has passed the patient becomes quite normal.

Another disadvantage of nembutal is the want of a reliable antidote to act promptly when collapse is threatened from its effects. Antidotes that are recommended comprise respiratory stimulants such as inhalations of CO_2, or coramin injected intramuscularly, which is more effective. M. L. Morris (*N. Amer. Vet.*, April 17, 1936) writing on nembutal anæsthesia says that " metrazal " (chemically pentamethylenetetrazol) is antagonistic to the barbiturates. It is very soluble in water, easily sterilised by heat without decomposition, stimulates respiratory and vaso-motor centres in the medulla, and appears to stimulate heart muscle directly and reflexly through the medullary centres.

One c.c. given to dogs for respiratory failure under barbiturate anæsthesia has excellent results and may be repeated in two or three minutes. It is a good stimulant in pneumonia.

A hypodermic injection of strychnine has also a good effect. Nevertheless the objectionable features of the drug are insignificant compared with its utility.

Anæsthesia by nembutal followed by the intrathoracic injection of 5 to 10 c.c. of hydrocyanic acid is a humane method of destroying the dog or cat, there being neither cry nor spasm produced by the acid, which causes death within thirty seconds, or alternatively by pouring a little chloroform into the nasal chambers when death will ensue almost immediately.

Nembutal Anæsthesia in the Pig

The pig is a good subject for Nembutal Anæsthesia and the most convenient method of adminstration is by injection into one of the auricular veins on the external aspect of the flap, the vein being raised by pressure with the thumb on the vessel at the base of the appendage (Fig. 57). Wright has found that its use is safe and effective, employing

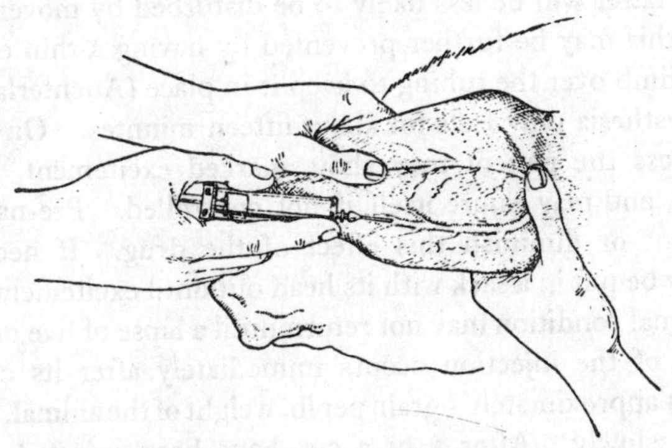

FIG. 57.—INTRAVENOUS INJECTION IN THE PIG, USING THE MARGINAL VEIN OF THE EAR FLAP.
Method of fixing the ear and raising the vein. The syringe and needle are held ready for insertion.

usually a concentration of 1 grain in one c.c. of solution and taking the same precautions as in the dog. He has found that the duration of its effect varies from 10 to 15 minutes for light and 20 to 25 minutes for deep anæsthesia. The average dose is approximately $\frac{1}{7}$ gr. per lb. body weight. Fat animals are more likely to show respiratory distress, and when it appears artificial respiration by prompt intermittent pressure of the chest wall prevents a fatal issue.

The drug may also be given intraperitoneally when its effects are slower in onset and somewhat longer in duration.

Evipan Anæsthesia

Evipan sodium is a soluble salt of a new barbituric acid derivative which on introduction into the circulatory system rapidly produces deep anæsthesia of short duration.

Lindsay Auchterlanie of Nottingham has published his experiences with the drug in 14 cases, and expressed complete satisfaction with its action for operations of short duration.

The patient is prepared in the usual way for general anæsthesia. If thought necessary pre-narcotisation may be effected by morphia or by the Hoffman Roche ampoule containing omnopon $\frac{2}{3}$ grain and scopolamin $\frac{1}{150}$ grain, as used by Auchterlanie (*Vet. Rec.* **14–21**) and Jarman and Abel (*Lancet*, March 10, 1934), the latter being preferred as safer and more certain in action.

Administration is effected by the intravenous route in the same way as described for nembutal. A short, narrow piece of rubber tubing may be used as a connection between the syringe and the needle so that the latter will be less likely to be disturbed by movement of the limb, and this may be further prevented by having a thin elastic band round the limb over the tubing to keep it in place (Auchterlanie).

The anæsthesia only lasts for about fifteen minutes. On recovering consciousness the patient may show marked excitement, staggering, and crying, and may injure itself if not controlled. Pre-narcotisation may prevent or diminish this effect of the drug. If necessary the animal may be put in a sack with its head out until excitement ceases.

The normal condition may not return until a lapse of five or six hours. The effect of the injection occurs immediately after its completion. The dose is approximately $\frac{1}{5}$ grain per lb. weight of the animal. It should be injected slowly. After 2 or 3 c.c. have been injected a pause of thirty seconds should be made before injecting the remainder.

Literature is supplied with both nembutal and evipan, giving a full description of the drugs and their mode of employ. The author has used evipan intravenously in doses of $\frac{1}{2}$ grain per lb. body weight as an agent of euthanasia with excellent results.

Pentothal Anæsthesia

Pentothal sodium, a very short-acting barbiturate, has been recently introduced as a general anæsthetic and has been fairly extensively used as such in human surgery in America. E. E. Sweebe (*Vet. Med.*, **31**, 4), and afterwards J. G. Wright (*Vet. Rec.*, **49**, 2), have described its use in veterinary practice.

Approximate Dosage: $\frac{1}{4}$ grain per lb. body weight for dogs under 20 lb., and $\frac{1}{5}$ grain for those above this weight.

The drug is dissolved in sterile water in the strength of 1 grain to 1 c.c.

Procedure is the same as for the intravenous injection of nembutal. It is important that two to three minutes should elapse during injection.

The symptoms indicating the onset of anæsthesia are the same as those caused by nembutal. The duration of the anæsthesia is ten to twenty minutes.

Complete consciousness returns about thirty minutes after the induction of anæsthesia, but control of movement of the limbs is not quite regained until about one hour afterwards. No untoward after-effect of the drug has been noticed. Pentothal would appear to be a very useful, quick-acting general anæsthetic for operations of short duration in the dog.

Spinal Anæsthesia

Spinal anæsthesia has been introduced for the painless performance of operations in the post-diaphragmatic regions of the body. It is effected by the injection into the subarachnoid space in the lumbar region of the cord of a few c.c. of a solution of cocaine or stovaine or novocaine. It has been used by Mennerat in the dog with complete success.

Novocaine and stovaine have been associated, the former in a 2 to 5 and the latter in a 5 to 10 per cent. solution. The dose for large animals is 8 to 15 grains of either drug, and for dogs $\frac{1}{3}$ grain to 3 grains. Some use tropocaine, others combine strychnine with stovaine. The best anæsthetic solution is a mixture of stovaine and cocaine in the proportion of 3 parts of the former to 1 of the latter. The injection is made by the aid of a fine trocar and canula or a strong hollow needle through the lumbo-sacral space in the different species of animals or through the sixth lumbar intervertebral space in the dog. The method is not much in vogue so far in veterinary practice. (For technique see page 477.)

Epidural Anæsthesia

Epidural anæsthesia seems to have been first introduced by M. A. Siccard (France) about 1901, who described its use in the dog. Since then literature on the subject has been published by numerous veterinarians at home and abroad describing its use in the various domesticated animals. It is only within the last five or six years that it has come into general use in Great Britain and Ireland.

A lucid and exhaustive treatise on the subject by G. B. Brook, D.Sc., M.R.C.V.S., published in series in Vol. 15 of the *Veterinary Record*, has increased its popularity in the latter countries.

It is effected by injecting a local anæsthetic solution into the epidural space at the termination of the spinal cord, where its meninges taper in the form of a cone extending from about the middle of the lumbar region to the middle of the sacrum.

Epidural Anæsthesia in Cattle.—This method of anæsthesia has been more widely practised in cattle than in other animals.

INDICATIONS.—Generally speaking, manipulations and surgical operations upon the posterior abdominal cavity and posterior limbs, in which it has not only the advantage of producing anæsthesia, but also prevents straining, which hampers surgical and manipulative interventions in the posterior abdominal and pelvic regions. Conditions for which it may be successfully employed comprise reduction of prolapsed vagina, uterus, or rectum; surgical intervention upon

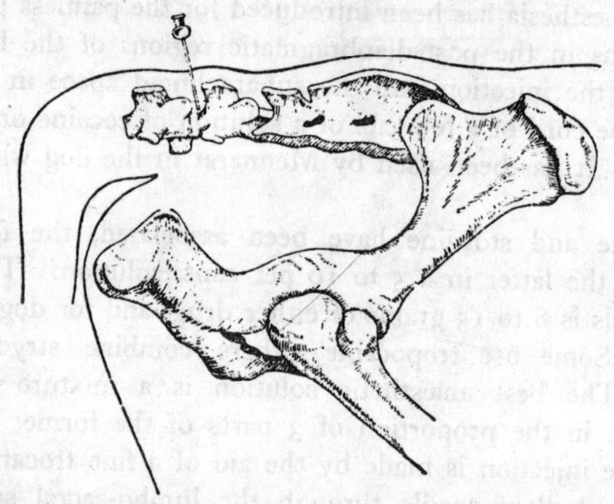

FIG. 58.—EPIDURAL INJECTION IN THE OX.
Insertion of the needle into the first intercoccygeal space.

the vulva, vagina, uterus, rectum, tail, bladder, and urethra; examination of the genital organs in the female, uterine irrigation, correction of fœtal dystokias, examination of and operation on the penis in the bull which protrudes from the sheath owing to relaxation of its retractor muscle.

SITE OF INJECTION.—The interarcual space between the first and second coccygeal vertebræ. It is located by holding the tail in a straight line with the median aspect of the body and moving it up and down, the sacro-coccygeal junction being situated at the point where the movement ceases, and the site of injection immediately behind the eminence representing the first coccygeal spine, in the very evident depression between the latter and the second coccygeal spine, care being taken to keep exactly in the middle line when making the injection as the slightest deviation therefrom will interfere with the procedure.

Anæsthetics employed include:

1. **Procaine** dissolved in physiological salt solution, 0·75 to 1 per cent. strength, recommended by Frank in America; in doses of 20 to 40 c.c., the latter having proved successful for amputation of the udder.

2. **Locadyne and Dulcine,** American preparations in dosage according to directions in the literature regarding them.

3. **Parcaine** (Parsetic), a Parke Davis preparation used by Brooke and others in 2·25 per cent. solution in dosage varying according

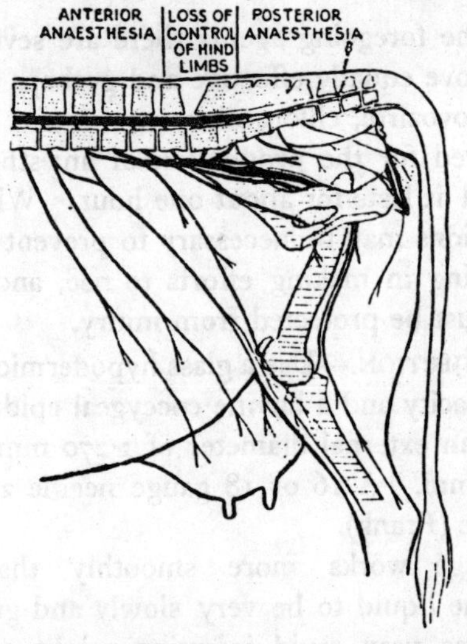

FIG. 59.—EPIDURAL ANÆSTHESIA IN THE COW.
Scheme illustrating the distribution of the spinal nerves involved in posterior and anterior anæsthesia.

to the purpose for which it is employed. If anæsthesia of the hind-limbs is not required and it is desired to keep the animal standing a comparatively small dose is used. The size of the animal has to be considered. For an average-sized shorthorn the animal will probably remain standing with a maximum dose of 15 c.c. which will permit of operations on the tail, rectum, vagina, urethra, and ovaries (ovariotomy), and the performance of embryotomy. For operations on the penis and testicles 55 c.c. for a medium, and 75 c.c. for a large subject may be required, these doses causing the patient to lie down. For anæsthesia of the hind-limbs and mammary gland 110 c.c. will probably be necessary.

4. **Novocaine,** the dose being calculated according to the effect required from 8–15 grains in a 2 to 5 per cent. solution. Lager of Stockholm uses 50 to 60 c.c. of a 1·5 per cent. solution.

5. **Stovaine,** in the same dose as novocaine, in 5 to 10 per cent. solution.

6. **A Mixture of Stovaine and Cocaine,** 3 parts of the former to 1 of the latter, said to be more effective than either alone.

7. **Stovaine Combined with Strychnine,** preferred by some continental authorities.

8. **Ethocaine with Adrenaline** (P. D. and Co.), used by Wright with completely satisfactory results.

In addition to the foregoing agents there are several others which would probably prove equally effective and perhaps more economical, such as novotox, novozirol, chlorocaine.

The time required for the production of anæsthesia is twenty to thirty minutes and it lasts for about one hour. When the patient is recumbent precautions may be necessary to prevent the animal being injured by struggling in making efforts to rise, and in the bull the protruded penis must be protected from injury.

TECHNIQUE OF INJECTION.—Use a glass hypodermic syringe (Record) of 10 to 20 c.c. capacity and a bovine coccygeal epidural needle about 10 cm. long, with an external diameter of 1·270 mm. and an internal diameter of 0·736 mm. A 16 or 18 gauge needle 2 inches long has proved very suitable (Frank).

The glass syringe works more smoothly than an all-metal syringe, allowing the liquid to be very slowly and gradually injected. This is important as very rapid injection might cause death from shock.

Have the animal suitably controlled. Take the usual aseptic precautions, stand on the left side of the patient, insert the needle in the centre of the depression representing the operation site, and push it steadily downwards and forwards at an angle of 60° to the horizontal, keeping exactly in the middle line, until it strikes the bony floor of the canal, having entered for a distance of 1 to 1½ inches with little or no resistance after the skin has been pierced ; inject the fluid slowly, taking one to two minutes for the purpose.

When the needle has entered the space very little force is required to introduce the solution, there being no more resistance than that encountered in the air. The presence of resistance indicates that the space has not been entered.

With reference to dosage there is no consensus of opinion as to the exact dose to be administered in a particular case. The method adopted by Howe (England) to cause protrusion of the penis in the bull (10–12 cwt.) seems commendable, viz., inject 8 to 10 c.c. for a medium-sized bull (10–12 cwt.) and leave the needle *in situ*. If extrusion does not follow give additional increments of 2 c.c. until it takes place. For a large bull commence with 10–12 c.c. Leaving the needle *in situ* does no harm. Occasionally the penis will protrude while the beast is standing, as was experienced by Stinson (England), but as a rule it goes down.

Epidural Anæsthesia in the Horse.—INDICATIONS are comprised under the following headings :

1. *The abolition of expulsive efforts* during foaling without necessarily causing recumbency.
2. *Docking* the adult or the foal.
3. *Ovariotomy*, a preliminary dose of chloral being advisable, since the ovarian nerve supply is not blocked.
4. *Prolonged operations* on the hind limbs or within the abdomen, which can then be conveniently undertaken.
5. Operations on the tail, anus, rectum, vagina, and cervix.

SITE.—According to Cuillé and Chelle the landmarks are as follows : Join the hip joints by an imaginary straight line which intersects the median vertebral line at the level of the sacro-coccygeal junction, immediately behind which the first coccygeal spinous process can be felt. Posterior to this is the depression representing the space between the first and second coccygeal vertebræ. It is the first depression felt by running the finger down the croup on to the tail in the middle line.

It is not easy to locate the site in the heavy draft horse or a fat subject.

CONTROL of a restive highly-strung horse is difficult. The twitch is required for most horses, and a side line or side fetter or service hobbles may be necessary.

If the animal is wicked it may first be hypnotised with chloral, when the injection may be made in the standing position or after casting, if anæsthesia of the hind-limbs is indicated.

The application of a little pure carbolic acid with or without the addition of camphor (4 to 1 of acid) on the skin at the seat of puncture may cause sufficient numbness to prevent the patient resenting the needle, or the skin here may be anæsthetised by the intradermic or subcutaneous injection of a local anæsthetic with a fine intradermic needle.

PROCEDURE is similar to that for the ox. Pass the needle at right angles to the dorsum of the tail held horizontally, inserting it to a depth of about 5 cm. If the tail is left in the drooping position give the needle a slant of 45° with the point forward.

DOSAGE IS NOT DEFINITE and varies according to the size of the horse and the parts to be anæsthetised, as follows for an average-sized horse, using parsetic (Parke Davis):

1. 6 c.c. to affect the tail.
2. 12 c.c. for the vulva, anus, and perinæum.
3. 25 c.c. for the vagina, rectum, bladder, and urethra, for dystokias, and for ovariotomy.
4. 50 to 60 c.c. for the hind-limbs, inguinal region, and posterior abdomen, for foot operations and cryptorchidectomy.

The position of the patient in the recumbent position affects the action of the drug, as it gravitates towards the dependent parts when the patient is recumbent in the lateral posture, instead of being equally distributed in the hind quarters. Raising the latter favours the forward passage of the injected fluid, thus hastening anæsthesia and loss of power in the hind limbs.

Frank (Kansas, U.S.A.) advises the following doses of procaine; (1) for operation on the tail, 10 to 15 c.c. of a 2 per cent. solution; (2) for dystokias, prolapse of the uterus, or other obstetric manipulations, 20 to 40 c.c. of a 1 per cent. solution; (3) for hernia and cryptorchidism, 20 to 40 c.c. of a 2 per cent. solution, causing complete relaxation of the muscles and constituting for these purposes an "ideal form of anæsthesia."

The objection to this form of recumbent anæsthesia is that the animal, being conscious, makes violent efforts to rise, and if not kept under control may seriously injure himself. As the recumbency may last two to three hours the inconvenience of the method is apparent. Failure to induce anæsthesia may result from escape of the solution through unusually patent ventral intervertebral foramina in the sacrum.

Epidural Anæsthesia in the Sheep.—INDICATIONS on the same lines as in the other animals, but fewer in number or more rarely encountered.

SITE.—Where a transverse line joining the summits of the wings of the ilia intersects the mid-vertebral line, about the level of the lumbo-sacral depression between the last lumbar spinal process and the sacral crest, the centre of the depression being the point where the needle is inserted.

PROCEDURE.—Have the patient standing. Insert the needle at right angles to the surface of the tail to a depth of about 5 cm., a distinct sense of resistance overcome being felt when the needle has entered the epidural space. Do not push the needle any farther lest it may enter the subarachnoid space, indicated by the escape of cerebro-spinal fluid through the needle.

DOSAGE.—Wright found that 8 c.c. of procaine gave very satisfactory results in ewes of the Cheviot type.

Epidural Anæsthesia in the Goat.—The procedure is the same as in the sheep, but a smaller dose is required for the goat.

Epidural Anæsthesia in the Pig.—INDICATIONS as in other animals.

SITE.—The lumbo-sacral space which is found by palpating the anterior border of the wings of the ilia, which can be easily felt except in a fat animal, and drawing an imaginary transverse line as mentioned in the sheep, the site of injection being about 1½ inches behind the point where it intersects the median line.

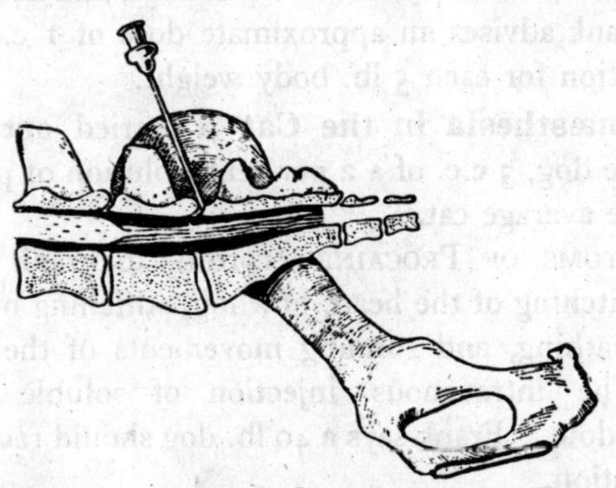

FIG. 60.—EPIDURAL INJECTION IN THE DOG.
The site and direction for insertion of the needle.

CONTROL the animal in the standing position, if possible.

PROCEDURE.—Direct the needle downwards into the epidural space in the usual manner.

DOSAGE.—Frank advises 1 c.c. of a 2 per cent. solution of procaine for each 10 lb. of body weight, and that very fat animals should receive a little less, as they seem to be somewhat more susceptible to procaine poisoning.

He found it the most desirable form of anæsthesia for dealing with scirrhous cord, inguinal hernia, Cæsarean section, monorchidism, etc.

Epidural Anæsthesia in the Dog.—INDICATIONS as mentioned for other animals, including all operations behind the level of the second or third lumbar vertebra; for example, laparotomy, hernia, reduction of hind-limb fractures, excision of anal glands, and obstetrical procedures.

SITE.—The lumbo-sacral space. The depression here may be located by drawing an imaginary transverse line joining the summits of the iliac crests, which usually intersects the vertebral middle line at the level of the summit of the spinous process of the last lumbar vertebra, the point of injection being the centre of the depression behind this spinous process.

CONTROL.—Fix the dog in the lateral position with the hind-limbs bent forward.

PROCEDURE.—Take all aseptic precautions. Stand facing the site of operation with the patient's head to your left. First inject a local anæsthetic subcutaneously and along the track of the needle, and after a while insert the needle into the space, tilting it slightly backwards at an angle somewhat less than 45° from the perpendicular, making it enter for a distance of about ½ inch in small dogs, and about 2 inches in large dogs. Frank advises an approximate dose of 1 c.c. procaine in 2 per cent. solution for each 5 lb. body weight.

Epidural Anæsthesia in the Cat is carried out in the same manner as in the dog, 3 c.c. of a 2 per cent. solution of procaine being sufficient for the average cat.

TOXIC SYMPTOMS OF PROCAINE according to Frank in the dog or cat comprise twitching of the head, howling, stiffening out of the legs, difficulty in breathing, and running movements of the legs. Death may ensue. The intravenous injection of soluble barbital acts as a prompt antidote. Frank says a 40 lb. dog should receive 20 grains in 25 c.c. of solution.

2. Local Anæsthesia

A large number of operations can be done painlessly by the use of local anæsthetics, thereby avoiding the risk of death from general anæsthesia. Local anæsthesia may be produced by:

1. **Cold,** in the form of crushed ice and salt (2 to 1) applied to the part, or ethyl chloride or ether spray projected over the surface. This is not a satisfactory method except for an operation lasting a few minutes or for rendering the skin insensitive prior to making a hypodermic injection.

2. **Cocaine**, which is the most reliable local anæsthetic. It is practically insoluble in water, but its salts are freely soluble. The hydrochloride is most frequently used in solutions of 1 to 10 per cent.; 1 per cent. solution generally has the desired effect, but a 4 per cent.

solution is commonly employed, being safe and surely reliable. Reclus recommends the following formula :

Hydrochloride of cocaine	1½ grains.
Perchloride of mercury	0·03 grain.
Distilled water	2½ fluid drachms.

The perchloride of mercury ensures the solution keeping. A few drops of this solution placed between the eyelids render the superficial layers of the cornea insensitive in three minutes. By repeating the application at two-minute intervals, the cornea, the conjunctiva, and the eyelids are often completely insensitive in less than ten minutes and anæsthesia lasts a quarter of an hour. The pupil dilates, but as a rule the iris is not rendered insensitive unless the injection is made into the anterior chamber. Five or six subconjunctival injections made around the eyeball permit removal of the latter without great pain. The intradermic injection of a solution of cocaine renders the skin of the part insensitive to pain.

It is more frequently injected subcutaneously, when it acts on the subcutaneous tissues as well as on the skin. The procedure consists in injecting the solution at intervals of about 1½ inches along the site of the incision. It takes from ten to fifteen, and sometimes thirty, minutes to show its effect. The irritation caused by the introduction of the hypodermic needle may be prevented by rubbing gently into the spot a mixture of carbolic acid 1 part and camphor 4 parts.

To anæsthetise the lower parts of the fore-limbs, the solution is injected over the plantar nerves. In the hind-limb it is more convenient to inject it over the posterior tibial nerve. It may also be injected over the ulnar, median, and anterior tibial nerves to anæsthetise the regions supplied by them.

Cocaine is toxic for all animals if used in too large doses. The maximum safe dose for the horse may be put at 10 grains, but this amount should be avoided as much as possible. Even after a dose of 5 grains a horse may show marked excitement, characterised by uneasiness, by pricking of the ears, and by a wild look in the eyes.

The dog and cat are very susceptible to the effects of cocaine. The dose for the largest dog should not exceed 2 grains. For medium-sized dogs it is advisable not to use more than ½ grain. For toys about $\frac{1}{10}$ grain may be used. Toxic symptoms in the dog comprise excitement, going round in a circle, and salivation.

The action of cocaine is hastened and its toxicity diminished by the simultaneous injection of adrenalin, which by constringing the blood-vessels of the region prevents diffusion of the cocaine and retards its absorption.

3. **Novocaine,** which is similar in its anæsthetic effect to cocaine, although perhaps not so reliable. It has the advantage over cocaine that it is six times less toxic.

4. **Codrenine,** a solution containing cocaine and adrenaline, having the advantages of a simultaneous injection of cocaine and adrenaline already alluded to.

5. **Parsetic (Procaine),** extensively used, non-toxic and quick-acting.

6. **Eucaine or Benzamine Hydrochloride,** whose action is not quite so prompt as that of cocaine, but more enduring and less toxic. It is particularly useful for dogs, the dose being on an average about 1 grain.

7. **Eudrenine,** which is a combination of eucaine and adrenaline, the solution containing ½ grain of eucaine in 17 minims. It is very convenient, safe, and effective for all animals, and acts more quickly than cocaine.

8. **Quinine and Urea Hydrochloride,** which is non-toxic and very effective. It has the disadvantage that it is very slow in producing its effect, half an hour at least being required for the purpose. On this account it is not in great favour with practitioners, although it has the advantage that its effect lasts several hours.

Other well-known local anæsthetics are: (1) Novozirol, (2) phenolaine, (3) chlorocaine, (4) parkane, all of which are non-toxic and cheaper than cocaine. Phenolaine is claimed to be also antiseptic. They are proprietary preparations which can be obtained ready for use accompanied by descriptive literature.

VII.—ANTISEPSIS AND ASEPSIS

The important part played by pathogenic micro-organisms in surgical affections is well known, and the necessity of counteracting their effects is obvious. There are two methods of doing this—viz., by antisepsis and asepsis. The beneficial effect of the former was first demonstrated by Lister in 1865 when, inspired by Pasteur's work on fermentation, he initiated the use of antiseptic agents in the treatment of open wounds. Lister sought to destroy not only the organisms in and around the wound, but also those in the surrounding air. The great success of the Listerian method rapidly led to its adoption throughout the civilised world. The agent which Lister relied on was carbolic acid in 1 in 20 and 1 in 40 solutions, the former being used for the site of operation, the instruments, and for the wound, the latter for the hands and for rinsing sponges and instruments during the operation. He employed an antiseptic spray to disinfect the atmosphere of the operating theatre.

Asepsis aims at excluding micro-organisms from infection-free tissues by allowing nothing to come in contact with them that has not been sterilised by dry or moist heat, chemical agents being entirely dispensed with on the ground that they are irritant to the tissues, destroying some of their cellular elements or reducing their vitality, whereby their repair is retarded. Even for septic lesions the advocates of asepsis maintain that it is better to rely on flushing the wounds with sterilised water or normal saline solution than to resort to the use of antiseptic preparations. The best results are probably obtained by observing both antisepsis and asepsis when dealing with accidental or surgical open wounds.

The first step in asepsis is strict cleanliness in connection with everything relating to the practice of surgery. The next consists in sterilising every utensil, instrument, and dressing material employed in connection with a surgical operation.

In veterinary practice it is practically impossible in most cases to carry out asepsis sufficiently thoroughly to depend on it alone. Consequently, antisepsis is generally indicated, associated with aseptic precautions as far as they are possible.

It does not follow that because an antiseptic agent is applied to a wound it is sure to exert its effects on all the bacteria therein. Many of the latter may escape through being hidden in interstices or recesses of the wound where the antiseptic solution does not penetrate. Moreover, organisms may be located in the deeper layers of the exposed tissues, where they are not affected by the antiseptic applied on the surface.

Moist heat is more efficacious in destroying bacteria than dry heat. Steam at 212° F. kills most pathogenic microbes, while a dry temperature of 290° to 330° F. is required for the same result. The spores of the tetanus bacillus require a moist temperature of 220° F. to destroy them, and those of anthrax 212° F. All the other bacteria of surgical interest are destroyed at temperatures ranging from 137° to 176° F.

Boiling in water containing 1 per cent. sodium carbonate for ten minutes is sufficient for the destruction of most organisms. It does not give security against certain spores.

Antiseptics

Common antiseptics used in practice may be briefly alluded to. They comprise the following :

Carbolic Acid.—Used in 1, $2\frac{1}{2}$, and 5 per cent. solutions. The 5 per cent. is indicated for instruments, site of operation, and septic wounds, and the 2 per cent. for recent practically aseptic wounds and for rinsing the hands during the operation. The 1 per cent. may be used for mucous surfaces.

Perchloride of Mercury.—The following solution : Sublimate, 1 part ; tartaric acid, 5 parts ; boiled water, 1,000 parts, kills most bacteria, and is suitable for septic wounds. It is rather irritating for recent non-contaminated wounds. Solutions of 1 in 5,000 to 1 in 3,000 may be used for mucous surfaces like the vagina and uterus.

Sublimate is decomposed by alkaline solutions. It is therefore advisable to add a little acetic or salicylic acid to ordinary water used for making the solution. Perchloride of mercury, 1 part, rectified spirits, 1,000 parts, is suitable for disinfecting the surgeon's hands.

Another very useful preparation is : Perchloride of mercury, 1 part ; glycerine, 500 or 1,000. The perchloride of mercury is very poisonous, especially for bovines, hence it must be used with caution in the latter or discarded altogether for them. It should not be used to disinfect metal instruments, as it blackens and tarnishes them, and blunts the edges of knives.

Biniodide of Mercury is a more powerful germicide than the perchloride. One in 10,000 or 20,000 solution is suitable for the ocular and uterine mucous membranes, is non-irritant for the hands or wounds, and does not alter instruments.

Chloride of Zinc in 5 per cent. solution destroys most spores, but is a caustic ; 10 per cent. solution is an effective application for very septic wounds and sinuses.

Dakin's Solution is prepared as follows : In 10 litres of ordinary water there are dissolved 140 grms. of dry carbonate of sodium (or 400 grms. of the crystals) and 200 grms. of chloride of lime of good quality. The mixture is shaken, and at the end of half an hour the clear liquid is siphoned off and then filtered ; 40 grms. of boracic acid are added to the filtrate. It must be employed cold, must not be used in conjunction with alcohol, and must not be kept for more than a week, after which it loses its power. It contains 5 to 6 per 1,000 hypochlorite of sodium. The solution is a powerful bactericide without having any irritant effect on the tissues. It aids the dissolution of necrotic tissue and has hæmostatic properties. Dakin's solution has a widespread reputation as a reliable antiseptic and non-irritant application for open wounds. Its antiseptic power is 100 times greater than that of carbolic acid. Its efficiency, however, seems to be short-lived, for Sir Alexander Fleming has stated that it has been demonstrated that when used in the form of the Carrel tube treatment it lost its potency in 10 minutes.

Hypochlorous Acid, to which the name " eusol " has been given in Great Britain, is prepared thus :

1. Liquor calcis chlorinata (filtered)	..	12 ounces.
2. Water	..	56 "
3. Saturated solution boracic acid	..	22 "

To be mixed in the order given. When Nos. 1 and 3 are kept in stock it can be made at a moment's notice. Its properties and advantages are similar to those of Dakin's solution. It is cheap, non-irritant, and very effective, but not suitable for the immersion of instruments.

Permanganate of Potash is a useful non-toxic antiseptic which owes its efficacy to the oxygen which it gives off. It is non-irritant even for mucous surfaces. It is usually employed in the proportion of 1 in 1,000 distilled water. It decomposes in the presence of organic matter contained in ordinary water. This solution is suitable for all mucous and serous cavities. Ten per cent. solution is used for septic wounds and for the hands. The stain which the solution causes can be removed from the hands by immersing them in a solution of hyposulphite of soda to which a few drops of hydrochloric or sulphuric acid have been added. Permanganate of potash powdered and mixed with boric acid and charcoal in varying proportions forms an excellent dressing for a septic wound. One part of the permanganate to 4 or 8 parts of a mixture of equal parts of boric acid and charcoal is often employed. It is a good application for open joint.

Hydrogen Peroxide is a powerful germicide. Mixed with blood or pus it decomposes with effervescence, and is of considerable value as a disinfectant for sinuses or suppurating cavities, and moreover, is an excellent detergent. Its effects are of short duration.

Iodine is a very active antiseptic ; 1 part in 7,000 destroys both bacilli and their spores. On account of its penetrating power it is the best disinfectant for the skin, and is used for this purpose in the form of the tincture or of a solution in ether or chloroform. The tincture is best when freshly made. Great reliance is laid on it as a disinfectant of a recent wound and a preventative of tetanus. It is not by any means infallible in its action in this respect. The aqueous solution of iodine made by adding 3 parts of the tincture to 1,000 parts of water is efficacious for disinfecting the genital tract in the female.

Iodoform is antiseptic and analgesic. It decomposes slowly, setting free iodine, which acts on microbes and other toxins. Used in large quantity on wounds in adipose subjects, especially dogs, it may be dissolved in part by the fat and cause poisoning.

The following are well-known preparations of iodoform:

1.	Iodoform	7 or 10 parts.
	Ether	100 "
2.	Iodoform	10 "
	Glycerine	100 "
3.	Iodoform	1 or 2 "
	Vaseline	10 "
4.	Bismuth subnitrate	1 part.
	Iodoform	2 "
	Liquid paraffin	Sufficient to make a paste.

No. 4 is known as B.I.P.P., and is widely used for applying to deep wounds after operation. The disadvantages of iodoform are its disagreeable odour, toxic nature, and its price.

Formalin consists of a 40 per cent. aqueous solution of formaldehyde. Diluted with 400 or 500 parts of water it is a useful disinfectant for the hands, seat of operation, and accidental wounds. Strong solutions are irritant and caustic.

Chinosol, a yellow crystalline powder derived from coal tar, and used in the proportion of $\frac{1}{2}$ grain to the ounce of water, is a powerful non-toxic antiseptic. The solution is very readily made from tablets, and is most convenient and efficient for veterinary practice. It temporarily darkens instruments, but does not harm them.

Nitrate of Silver in the form of sticks is a very useful caustic and stimulant for an indolent wound or one covered with soft, unhealthy granulations. The solution of 2 to 4 grains to the ounce is a good astringent eye lotion.

Boric Acid in powder has been widely used as a wound dressing. It is only slightly, if at all, irritant. A saturated solution is soothing and antiseptic for inflamed mucous surfaces.

Creolene, or Jeyes' Fluid, a coal-tar preparation, is extensively employed as an antiseptic and disinfectant. It is cheap, miscible with water and alcohol, very slightly toxic, non-irritant to the hands, does not spoil instruments, is very convenient to use, and is very efficient in its action. The 3 per cent. solution is suitable for the site of operation, the hands, instruments, and septic wounds. Half to 1 per cent. is employed for recent wounds and for flushing the uterus and vagina. The solution is opaque, and hides instruments immersed therein. It also renders them slippery.

Lysol possesses properties similar to those of creolene. Its solution is soapy and very suitable for operations where a lubricant is useful—for example, exploring the inguinal canal in rig castration. The 2 per cent. solution is suitable for disinfecting instruments, especially syringes. One to 2 per cent. solution is suitable for contaminated wounds.

Chloride of Sodium.—Boiled water containing 9 grms. of sodium chloride to the litre is suitable for washing out serous cavities such as the thoracic and abdominal cavities. A 5 to 8 per cent. solution has antiseptic properties. It causes an outpouring of lymph, which acts as a bactericide, but it has the disadvantage that it repels leucocytes.

Magnesium Chloride (Anhydrous) Solution (12 in 1,000) applied as a lotion thrice daily, or used in the form of moist compresses kept in contact with a septic wound, is very highly spoken of by some practitioners. It is non-toxic, cytophylactic, and is said to have a marked effect in favouring phagocytosis (Magee, etc.).

When dealing with grave rebellious lesions it is advisable to vary the antiseptic agents employed, and it may be an advantage to use some of them in combination.

Notwithstanding the foregoing remarks on the virtues of various antiseptic preparations, every veterinary practitioner is aware of their futility in septic lesions, in the absence of surgical intervention to remove dead tissue and foreign matter, and to provide for drainage, and how unnecessary they are when these indications have been carried out. Their disappointing effects are due in great part to their not coming in contact with the bacteria in the recesses of a wound or in the muscle tissue which they have infiltrated and which is a hot-bed for their multiplication owing to its high glycogen content. They are all more or less antagonistic to phagocytic action, and applied to an aseptic wound they tend to retard the healing process. An agent which when left in contact with a recent contaminated, but not yet infected, wound prevents the multiplication of the invading bacteria (bacteriostat) without weakening the natural defences is the ideal topical application, but the most reliable preparation is that which reaches a septic lesion through the blood stream. The recently introduced sulphonamides have these properties in a varying degree for certain bacteria and are specific against hæmolytic streptococci, while penicillin, discovered by Sir Alexander Fleming in 1929, has a marvellous range of usefulness as a bacteriostat acting locally and through the circulation, being specific for several kinds of gram staining organisms on which other agents have no inhibitory effect. Abundance of literature is available from the various drug manufacturers regarding the sulphonamides and penicillin, from which all the necessary information about their properties and uses in veterinary practice can be obtained, *e.g. A Preliminary Review of the Use of Penicillin in Veterinary Practice* (August, 1946), issued by Imperial Chemicals (Pharmaceuticals), Ltd., Alderley Edge, Manchester, and the leaflet issued by the Schenley Laboratories, 350 Fifth Avenue, New York, both of which give full details about the drug. The sulphonamides have been exhaustively dealt with in publications in the *Vet. Rec.*, *e.g.*, by Bazeley, Dec. 13th, 1941 ; A. W. Stapleforth, Jan. 6th, 1945 ; Hamilton Kirk, May, 1945 ; Mary H. Maclay and G. Slavin, June 26th, 1947. Some general remarks, however, may now be made regarding (1) the sulphonamides, and (2) penicillin.

1. The Sulphonamides

The sulphonamides were introduced by Domagk in 1935 in the form of " Prontosil," a red liquid, and its efficacy against streptococci was first proved by Calibrook and Kenny (1936) in the treatment of puerperal fever in women, and that against meningococcal infection in mice by Buttle, Gray, and Stephenson (1936). Eventually the following forms of sulphonamides were produced :

1. Sulphapyridine.
2. Sulphathiazole.
3. Sulphamezathine.
4. Sulphadiazine.
5. Sulphaguanidine.

All of these except Nos. 3 and 5 act more or less similarly and have common features in being rapidly absorbed and rapidly excreted in the urine, their peak concentration in the blood being about the third hour after administration, after which it gradually declines, to disappear between the sixteenth and twenth-fourth hour. It is important that the first dose should be massive to make sure of having an immediate bacteriostatic effect and that it should be followed by three- or four-hourly smaller doses to maintain adequate blood contration until the disease is overcome. Their action is inhibitory, not bactericidal, and they thus allow the natural defences to act untrammelled. They are impotent in the presence of pus, necrotic tissue, and inflammatory effusions and are only specific for certain strains of streptococci and meningococci, having little or no direct influence on staphylococci, only affecting them indirectly in a case of mixed staphylo- and streptococcic infections by leaving the phagocytes free to devote all their attention to the staphylococci. Differences in the potency of the members of the series are given by Stapleforth as follows:

(1) Sulphapyridine and sulphamezathine are bacteriostatic for streptococci, pneumococci, and pasteurella, and not staphylococci.
(2) Sulphathiazole and sulphadiazine affect all four.
(3) Sulphapyridine is said to be more active against streptococci than sulphanilamide.

Sulphaguanidine and sulphamezathine, more so the latter, are slowly excreted with the fæces and therefore do not require such frequent administration as the other members of the group. It is for this reason that they are so useful for intestinal infections by sulphonamide-sensitive bacteria.

The sulphonamides reach all the body fluids, saliva, tears, sweat, and wound exudates. The approximate dosage is as follows:

(1) Sulphanilamide, 1 gramme per 10 pounds body weight.
(2) Sulphapyridine, 1 gramme per 20 pounds body weight or 15 pounds body weight. Some authorities advise that this should be decreased by one-third every two days as a precaution against toxic effects.
(3) Sulphathiazole initial and daily doses of 1 gramme per 20 pounds. Double this for cats and dogs. The daily dose should be divided into rather more doses, given at shorter intervals, owing to the rapid excretion of this drug.
(4) Sulphadiazine in doses similar to (2) and (3). There is a comparatively high blood concentration in this case. Hence watch for toxic symptoms.
(5) Sulphamezathine. The dose is smaller and less frequently repeated than that of sulphanilamide.
(6) Sulphaguanidine from 1 gramme per 20 to 1 gramme per 15 pounds body weight; 1 gramme per 10 pounds body weight gives a concentration of several hundred milligrammes per cent. in the fæces.

The administration of these drugs should not be continued for more than five days, otherwise toxic effects may supervene, characterised by dullness, weakness, and locomotor inco-ordination, and drop in milk yield in cows, and some degree of fever. Diarrhœa is often well marked after taking sulphanilamide. Dermatitis is sometimes observed, especially if treatment is continued for more than seven days—appearing on the nose, udder, and teats in cows.

The most serious symptoms are due to acetylation of the drug causing renal trouble, reported as occurring with sulphaguanidine in calves and pigs, also with sulphapyridine but not with sulphathiazole or sulphanilamide. The symptoms are those of renal colic. The sulphonamides are very slightly soluble in water, from 0·8 per cent. for sulphanilamide (at 25° C.) to 0·01 per cent. for sulphadiazine. They are given by the mouth in solid form or in suspension. For parenteral use there are the sodium salts, which, however, are strongly alkaline and irritant. There is no advantage in using them intravenously or subcutaneously. Well-known solutions are:

(1) Soluseptasine (35 per cent. sulphanilamide).
(2) Soluthiozale (44 per cent. sulphathiozole).
(3) Solupyridine (45 per cent. sulphapyridine).

These are useful when oral administration is difficult.

2. Penicillin

Penicillium occurs as a green mould on bread, jam, apples, and vegetables and as a greenish velvety deposit on leather when left neglected in damp places. *Penicillium notatum* is the variety from which penicillin is made. It is an agent of wonderful potency as a cure for a whole range of diseases against which other preparations, including the sulphonamides, are powerless, and has the great advantages that it has no toxic properties and that its action is not prevented by the presence of pus, dead tissue, or other materials in the tissues.

After its discovery in 1929 by Professor Alexander Fleming of St. Mary's Hospital, London, it was in a very weak and impure state, and for this reason the discovery was dormant until 1939, when Professor Florey (Oxford) concentrated it and brought to light its extraordinary powers. It can now be obtained in any required amount. The drug is very unstable and is destroyed by the gastric juices. It passes out of the body in about three hours. It may be administered intravenously, intramuscularly, or subcutaneously, and may be injected into the serous cavitites, where it is of special use in permitting the great phagocytic activity which exists there to proceed without interruption. The surgeon must do his part in carrying out the proper surgical treatment in connection with any lesion for which it is being employed.

A drawback of penicillin is the frequency with which it requires to be injected to have the best results, but new preparations of the drug are on the market whereby its excretion is retarded and the frequency of administration is reduced, *e.g.*, " Avloprocil " (Imperial Chemical (Pharmaceuticals), Ltd.), a procaine salt of penicillin in simple oily suspension, and a single daily dose of which, it is claimed, is usually adequate for effective penicillin therapy. Each cubic centimetre contains 300,000 units of penicillin and 120 milligrammes procaine base. The dose recommended is 1,000 to 2,000 units per 5 pound body weight administered every 24 hours and in higher doses if the severity of the infection demands it. The special property of " Avloprocil " and similar preparations is that an injection releases the penincillin slowly into the circulation and maintains a demonstrable level of penicillin for at least 18 hours, in most cases for 24 hours.

VIII.—INSTRUMENTS, DRESSING AND SUTURE MATERIALS

Instruments should as far as possible be made entirely of metal and devoid of unnecessary grooves or crevices in which foreign matter may lodge. Very few elaborate instruments are required in veterinary practice. The instruments necessary for the various operations will be mentioned in the description thereof.

Dressing Materials comprise gauze, cotton-wool, lint, tow, and bandages.

Gauze is soft, non-irritant, very absorbent, permits of rapid evaporation, and does not adhere to the wound. It should always be placed next to the wound when the latter is covered by a dressing. It may be obtained in many medicated forms, the best being sulphanilamide gauze.

Absorbent cotton-wool imbibes moisture rapidly, but evaporation from it is very slow. It is used as a protective absorbent dressing for wounds outside gauze. If placed directly on the wound, particles of wool adhere to it and are difficult to remove. Moist cotton-wool is used instead of sponges for mopping up blood during an operation Gauze is better adapted for this purpose, but it is rather expensive for everyday use. Mops of cotton-wool enclosed in gauze may be used.

Lint is a good absorbent, non-irritant material to apply over an open wound, and may be fixed with strings to a part where a bandage cannot be applied.

Tow.—Tow from which the coarse parts have been removed is suitable for surgical purposes as a substitute for cotton-wool, or to supplement the latter as a dressing for a wound. It is too coarse to put next to a raw surface. It is a good absorbent and is cheap.

Bandages are used to keep the dressing in position and to exert on the wound the necessary amount of pressure. They may be composed of calico or tarlatan, or less frequently of cotton or flannel. Tarlatan is the best material for small animals. The usual width of bandages is from 2 to 4 inches, and they may be rolled either by hand or by a roller. Adhesive bandages (Elasto-plast) and tape are very useful for application outside ordinary bandages or plaster of Paris dressing to prevent their displacement or being torn off by the patient, and for keeping dressings in position on different parts of the body by their adhesion to the skin, *e.g.*, wound on the abdominal wall in small animals by applying the bandage round the body over the dressing.

The proper application of bandages is important and requires considerable practice. The bandage should be applied sufficiently tightly not to become displaced and to exert a moderate amount of pressure on the part. It must be remembered that each succeeding turn of the bandage increases its pressure, and that although it may not appear to be tightly applied it may be causing too much pressure. The bandaging of a limb or an appendage should commence at its distal extremity, and each successive turn of the bandage should cover the upper border of the preceding turn without puckering. When the part to be covered is of increasing circumference towards its proximal end it is necessary to fold down each turn of the bandage at a given point, so that the upper edge at this point becomes the lower edge and the inner surface the outer surface. Fig. 61 shows how it is done.

In the dog and cat it is essential to include the paw in every bandage applied on the limb, otherwise it may arrest the circulation therein and cause gangrene of the extremity.

When a knee or fetlock joint in the horse is to be bandaged, the bandage must be applied in a figure-of-eight fashion as illustrated in Fig. 62. A couple of complete turns are first made below the articulation. Then the bandage is brought obliquely upwards, given a complete turn round the limb above the joint, and brought down again in the opposite direction. The oblique turns are continued until the region is adequately covered. Elastic bandages may be used when strong pressure is temporarily required—for instance, for the reduction of an œdematous swelling or for the purpose of arresting hæmorrhage or driving the blood out of a part. It must be employed with caution, and not left on long enough to arrest the circulation in the region. When inflammation ensues after the application of a bandage it is then apt to be too tight, causing discomfort or pain to the patient, and should be readjusted at once.

The materials used for **Sutures** comprise silk, nylon, silkworm gut, cat-gut, kangaroo tendon, and silver or bronze wire.

Silk is most commonly employed in sizes varying from 0 to 14; 0, 1, 3, and 6 are sufficient for most purposes. It is strong, non-irritant, makes a secure knot, and can be sterilised by boiling. It is

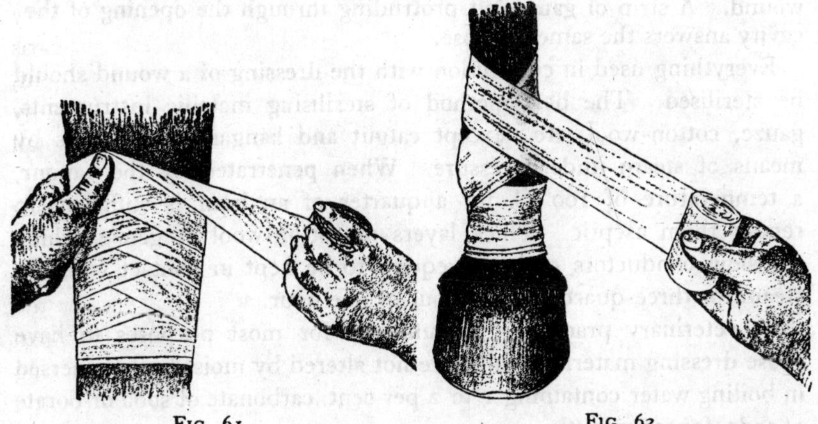

FIG. 61. FIG. 62.

absorbent, and this is a disadvantage, as septic liquid may thus be carried through it to the wound from the surface of the skin by capillary attraction. Silk seldom becomes absorbed if used as a buried suture. It may remain indefinitely in the tissues without causing trouble when aseptic.

Nylon is much in favour now for external buried and internal sutures but the thread must be tied with the " nylon knot," in which the two parts of the knot are made by giving an extra turn to the thread, as is done in the first part only of the " surgical knot," otherwise it is apt to become undone.

Silkworm Gut is smooth, non-absorbent, and strong, and very useful for cutaneous sutures. It is not so likely to cause stitch abscesses as silk, and is not altered by boiling.

Catgut is adopted for buried sutures, as it usually becomes absorbed after performing its function. The rapidity with which it is absorbed depends on its preparation. Different varieties in this respect may be obtained from the makers, sterilised ready for use. It does not withstand boiling.

Kangaroo tendon can be used for the same purposes as catgut. It is absorbable.

Silver and bronze wire are used chiefly for suturing and ligaturing fractured bones.

Drainage Tubes are not much used in veterinary practice. They are made of stout red india-rubber, and are fenestrated for the passage of discharge into their lumen, whence it is conveyed outside the wound. They are fixed in position by a suture at the orifice of the wound. A strip of gauze left protruding through the opening of the cavity answers the same purpose.

Everything used in connection with the dressing of a wound should be sterilised. The best method of sterilising metallic instruments, gauze, cotton-wool, etc., except catgut and kangaroo tendon, is by means of steam under pressure. When penetrated by the vapour, a temperature of 100° C. for a quarter of an hour is sufficient to render them aseptic. Thick layers of cotton-wool or gauze, which are slow conductors of heat, require to be kept in contact with the steam for three-quarters of an hour or one hour.

In veterinary practice it is sufficient for most purposes to have those dressing materials which are not altered by moist heat immersed in boiling water containing 1 to 2 per cent. carbonate of soda or borate of soda, for ten minutes.

The sterilisation of catgut is a prolonged process not likely to be undertaken by the practitioner, as it can be obtained at a moderate price sterilised ready for use in sealed glass tubes.

Ordinary water is more or less contaminated by micro-organisms, and should be sterilised by boiling before being used for making antiseptic solutions.

The autoclave is the best means of sterilising surgical dressings, instruments, and utensils, but it is not available for the average veterinarian.

IX.—OPERATIVE TECHNIQUE

1. Before the Operation

Disinfection of the Hands.—To operate aseptically it is essential to have the hands thoroughly disinfected. This is not easily carried out on account of the number of places where micro-organisms can be concealed and are difficult to reach with disinfectant solutions—viz., the spaces beneath the nails, the folds of the skin, and the orifices of the cutaneous glands. In fact, when the hands have been in contact with septic liquid it is impossible to render them sterile within forty-eight hours. This must be borne in mind when an abdominal operation is being contemplated.

After curetting the nails, the hands and forearms should be washed with soap and boiled water, using a nail-brush. After this it is advisable to wash them with alcohol to remove fatty material, and finally with 1 in 1,000 perchloride of mercury or 2 per cent. creolene or lysol, whose action would be prevented by the presence of fatty matter. Having prepared the hands, they should not be allowed to touch anything that has not been sterilised, and as an additional precaution they should be plunged into an antiseptic solution occasionally during the course of the operation. If they become soiled they must be carefully disinfected again. If disinfection of the hands cannot be relied upon, rubber gloves must be worn. They also serve to protect the surgeon's hands from sepsis when operating on septic tissues. They are particularly indicated if there is an open wound on the hand.

The operator and his assistants should be attired in perfectly clean smocks, with the shirt sleeves rolled up above the elbows or short shirt sleeves. It is also desirable that a mask be worn by the operator and assistants at the operation table to avoid contamination of the wound from the mouth and nose, where streptococci may be dormant. Sterilised protective cloths or towels should be used to cover an extensive area of the skin in the vicinity of the operation site or the whole body except the head in the case of an abdominal operation in a small animal, being fixed in position by forceps for the purpose.

Disinfection of the Instruments.—The usual method of sterilising instruments for veterinary use is by immersion in boiling water containing 1 to 2 per cent. carbonate of soda or 1 to 2 per cent. borate of soda, which prevents alteration of the surface of the instruments. If this method is not convenient, and the operation about to be performed does not necessitate strict asepsis, they may be disinfected by one of the disinfectant solutions already mentioned.

Baths of oil, glycerine, or liquid vaseline raised to a temperature of 120° to 130° C. completely sterilise instruments. The water should be allowed to come to boiling point before putting in the instruments, so as to prevent the possible formation of permanent dark spots on their surface. Metal instruments may also be sterilised by placing them on a metal tray, pouring methylated spirit over them, and then putting a light to the latter. This, however, spoils the edges of knives and scissors. Boiling sharp instruments also blunts them. This may be prevented to a certain degree by enveloping the blades in cotton-wool before putting them into the steriliser.

An ordinary fish kettle is suitable for the sterilisation of most instruments. A more elaborate steriliser is made of copper provided with spirit lamps, which enable it to be used anywhere.

After use the operator should see that his instruments are cleansed with boiling water and thoroughly dried. Gum-elastic instruments are washed in strong alcohol and afterwards in 1 in 1,000 sublimate solution.

Disinfection of the Site of Operation.—In all animals the skin is rich in microbes of different kinds, which are present not only on its surface, but also in its thickness, especially in the epidermis and the ducts of the glands. Hence the necessity of careful disinfection of the skin prior to an operation.

The hair must be clipped and the skin shaved, and a reliable disinfectant applied to its surface. Another method of removing the hair is the application of a paste composed of barium sulphide. Tincture of iodine is the best agent for the purpose of disinfection, as it penetrates into cutaneous crevices and into glandular and follicular openings. When it is to be used, the skin should be dry shaved instead of using a lather, because moisture causes swelling of the epithelial cells, leading to obstruction of the intercellular spaces, the gland ducts, and the hair follicles, thereby interfering with the action of the iodine. If another agent is to be employed, the skin is washed with soap and water after clipping, shaved, rubbed with ether or alcohol to remove fatty matter and then bathed with the antiseptic solution. It is advisible, however, finally to mop the site with normal saline solution to avoid the possible irritant affect on the exposed tissues of the antiseptic agent.

If there be a septic lesion, extra precautions must be taken. An ulcer or sinus should be curetted, and then painted with tincture of iodine, but if the infected area be small the best procedure is to excise it. This is essential if the operation involves opening the abdominal cavity.

A dressing containing perchloride of mercury should not be applied after using tincture of iodine on the skin, as it would result in the formation of the red iodide of mercury, which would have a severe irritant effect.

Tincture of iodine is rather irritating for a fine skin or a mucous surface. The latter should be washed with boiled water or a solution of bicarbonate of soda before applying an antiseptic lotion, in order to remove the mucus which would interfere with the action of the antiseptic.

Tincture of Metaphen (Abbot Laboratories), a recently introduced skin disinfectant, is claimed to be a more powerful germicide than tincture of iodine, and non-irritant. It colours the skin red, temporarily.

Preparation of Requirements

Before commencing the operation the following requirements should be ready:

1. A sterilised tray containing the instruments.
2. A similar tray containing the ligatures, suture thread, and dressing materials.
3. A basin containing antiseptic lotion and pledgets of gauze or wool to serve as sponges.
4. A basin containing antiseptic lotion for rinsing the hands occasionally.

2. During the Operation

During the operation the surgeon takes measures to control hæmorrhage and to observe all the precautions necessary to avoid sepsis and obtain primary healing of the wound when it is possible to bring its lips into contact. He seldom has the advantage of skilled assistance or the equipment of an up-to-date operating theatre, but he may have a trained lay assistant who will help in sponging the blood from the wound, retracting tissues, holding instruments, and applying dressings. The procedure necessary for the various kinds of wounds is described in the section on open wounds.

The disinfection of special parts will be alluded to as they are dealt with in the course of the work.

DIVISION OF TISSUES

Methods of dividing tissue with a minimum of hæmorrhage are described in the section on hæmostasis.

Cutting and Puncturing Instruments: *The Use of Knives, Scissors, and Trocars*.—Knives are of varying form and size. They may be sharp-pointed or blunt-pointed, and the edge may be straight, convex, or concave.

Scissors are also made in various sizes, and may be straight or curved and sharp- or blunt-pointed.

When a deep and bold incision is to be made, the knife is grasped in the full hand after the manner of a dinner-knife or sometimes that of a dagger. For finer work it is held like a fiddle-bow or a pen.

To avoid wounding large subcutaneous vessels and to facilitate cutting the skin where it is relaxed or mobile, a fold of it may be taken up with the fingers or a forceps and the fold cut through. It can also be fixed and stretched with the finger and thumb of the other hand. Deep layers of tissue with important structures beneath must be severed by cutting upwards on a grooved director inserted immediately beneath the layer to be divided.

Dressing or dissecting forceps are necessary for fine dissection. Retractors are often required for holding back tissues to enable the surgeon to operate on deeper parts. Strong, sharp-pronged retractors and forceps are very useful for grasping and holding tissues while they are being excised.

Galvanic and Thermo-Cauteries.—In the galvanic cautery a loop of platinum wire is passed round the tissue to be divided, and after being raised to a bright red heat by the passage of an electric current it is gradually drawn tight. On account of its expense and complexity it is seldom used in veterinary practice. The ordinary actual cautery or one of the auto-cauteries may be used for the division of tissues—for example, Pacquelin's cautery or Déchery's auto-cautery.

Puncture.—A puncture is described by the name, and it may be made with a pointed knife or with a trocar and canula.

The trocar and canula varies in length and diameter according to the purpose for which it is required. The point is usually triangular in shape and made with a slight depression behind, so that when the canula is in position it is flush with the point. Its use will be described in connection with the operations for which it is employed.

The Division of Hard Tissues

The horn of the hoof is cut or reduced by the ordinary farrier's tools. Bones are divided with drills, chisels, saws, and forceps.

The bone is prepared for sawing by removing the periosteum with a periosteotome or a chisel or gouge. The sharp spoon or curette is used for scraping diseased bone or cartilage and removing unhealthy granulation or callous tissues from the walls of sinuses, etc.

The chisel or gouge is used for incisions in bone by striking it with a mallet. Bone forceps are employed for cutting spicules of bone ; they are of different forms and sizes. A trephine is required for the removal of a disc-shaped piece of bone, as in the operation of trephining the facial sinuses.

Illustrations of surgical instruments referred to can be seen in the manufacturers' catalogues.

SUTURES

Methods of Uniting Lips of Wounds

Under certain conditions it is necessary to maintain the lips of wounds in apposition by sutures—for example, in the following cases: (1) Where the other conditions essential for healing by first intention are present (see p. 21); (2) to close the abdominal cavity after performing laparotomy or when it has been opened accidentally; (3) to keep the lips of a deep extensive wound in contact temporarily and thus provide against recurrent hæmorrhage which sometimes ensues when a large wound is left open, although the primary hæmorrhage has been spontaneously arrested; (4) to maintain a plug in a deep wound. Otherwise there is little or no advantage in suturing wounds.

When healing by second intention is about to take place, bringing the edges of the wound together by artificial means has little or no effect in hastening the healing process. When the tension on the threads is great it does more harm than good, because then the edges fail to unite and the sutures cut through the tissues, leaving permanent scars or blemishes in addition to that caused by the wound itself.

Moreover, suturing a septic wound favours complications by preventing the escape of septic discharge, excluding the purifying effect of the air and the sun, and promoting the development of anærobic bacteria.

It is surprising how rapidly extensive wounds cicatrise without the aid of sutures.

Suture Needles

Needles of various forms and sizes are employed. Most of them have the point lancet-shaped and double-cutting. The following are examples.

1. **Curved Needles** in the form of a semicircle, useful for suturing the deep parts or layers of a wound where a straight needle could not be employed.

2. **Half-Curved Needles** in which the anterior half only is curved, and very commonly used for ordinary wounds.

The trouble with semi-curved needles is that they tend to turn when being inserted by the fingers, so that the point goes downwards instead of coming up. To prevent this happening, especially when the tissues are resistant, a needle-holding forceps must be used (Fig. 63). A stout artery forceps answers the purpose.

3. **Straight Needles,** which are the most convenient for suturing cutaneous wounds and thin layers of tissue.

4. **Needles bent** with a convexity or "hump" midway between the point and the eye, forming a *point d'appui* to facilitate pushing them through resistant tissue.

5. **Needles with the proximal end bent** at right angles to the shaft, so as to facilitate insertion.

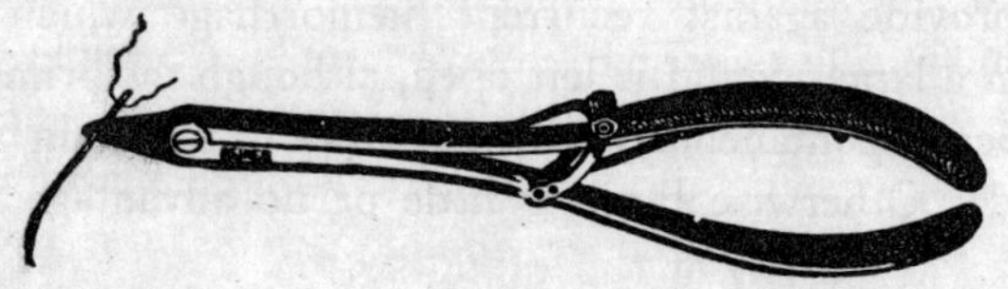

FIG. 63.—NEEDLE HOLDER (REINER'S).

6. **Needles with Handles.**—These are very useful for inserting thick or tape sutures deeply, for the purpose of keeping a large plug in position in a hollow wound—for instance, after operation for poll evil or fistulous withers.

The eye is situated at the point of the needle, and is threaded after inserting the latter.

Numerous devices have been introduced to facilitate threading, without much success.

7. **Milliners' Needles,** the name given to fine needles used for suturing wounds in the hollow abdominal viscera (stomach, intestines, etc.). The best needles for this purpose are prepared ready for use in sealed glass tubes, the thread being fixed to and continuous with the needle.

Varieties of Sutures

Sutures receive different names as follows:

1. **Cutaneous Sutures,** going through the skin only. As a rule there is not much tension on these sutures. They may be inserted about $\frac{3}{8}$ inch from the margin of the wound.

2. **Interrupted Sutures** are separate sutures (Fig. 64), and are those most commonly employed. The needle is held between the fingers and thumb of the right hand, with the thread gathered up in the palm. The edge of the skin is caught with a dressing forceps and held taut while the needle is being inserted. When both borders have been traversed, the needle is placed between the first and second fingers of the left hand and the thread is gathered into the left palm, or more conveniently the thread is cut, leaving ends sufficiently long to tie the knot. A reef knot is then tied to one side of the wound. If there is considerable tension on the cutaneous borders, an extra turn is made on the first part of the knot to prevent its slipping, constituting what is called a *surgical knot*. This is made just tight enough to bring the edges into contact. A common mistake is to make sutures too tight. Protrusion of the subcutaneous tissues between the lips of the wound must be avoided.

FIG. 64.—INTERRUPTED SUTURE.

If the edges of the skin are close together, they may both be grasped between the fingers and thumb of the left hand, while the needle and thread is passed through the base of the ridge thus formed, the knot being made as before. As a rule it is the edges that are brought into apposition, but in certain cases where more secure union is required

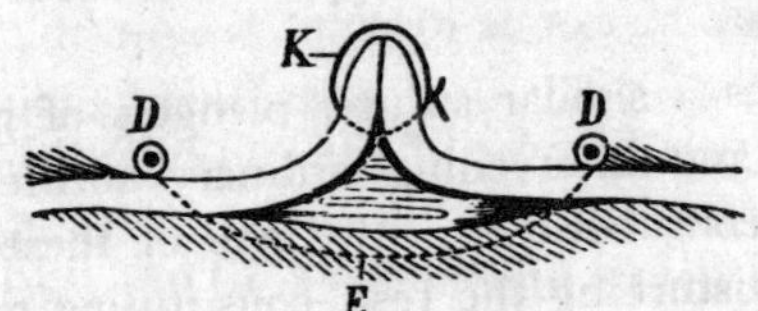

FIG. 65.—METHODS OF SUTURING TO SECURE LARGEST POSSIBLE SURFACE FOR ADHESION.

K, Interrupted suture ; *D, D*, suture of relaxation.

the subcutaneous surfaces may be applied to one another by forming the two borders into a ridge, as just mentioned, and suturing the base with a series of mattress or Halsted sutures, while another series of ordinary interrupted sutures may be inserted through the free borders (Fig. 65).

3. **Sutures of Relaxation, or Tension Sutures.**—When a wound is deep, involving muscular tissue, two series of sutures are required: one inserted at a considerable distance from its lips, going

through the skin and other divided tissues, so as to bring the deep parts of the wound into apposition ; and another series going through the skin only.

The former is spoken of as a *suture of relaxation*, or *tension suture* (Fig. 66), taking the strain off the latter, which may be called a *uniting* or *coaptative suture.*

4. **Quill Suture.**—This is a form of relaxation suture illustrated by Fig. 67, which shows a series of double threads passed across the lips of the wound, with a rod passed through the loops on one side and between the two ends on the other side. It distributes the pressure evenly on both sides of the wound, and prevents the

Fig. 66.—Ordinary Deeply Placed Interrupted Sutures used as Sutures of Relaxation.

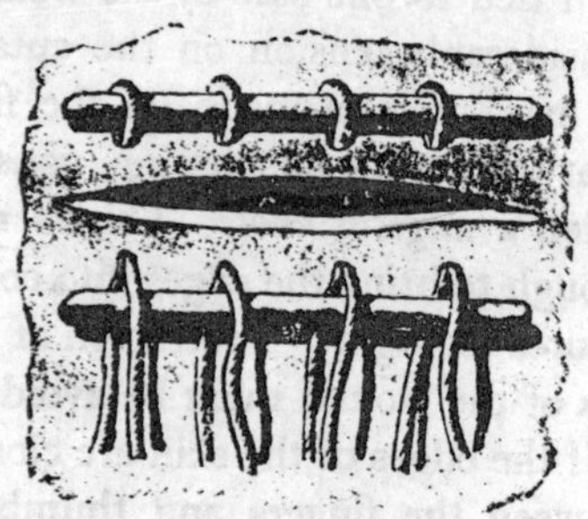

Fig. 67.—So-called "Quilled" Suture.

threads cutting through too soon. A piece of rubber tubing is suitable for a " quill."

Fig. 68 illustrates a similar suture, pledgets of gauze being used instead of quills, and intervening ordinary sutures being inserted through the cutaneous borders. Any one of these sutures may be removed without disturbing the rest, constituting an advantage over the ordinary quill suture.

5. **The Halstead or Mattress Suture.**—In this case, after the needle and thread has traversed the lips of the wound it is brought back again at a variable distance from its point of emergence, and the knot is made parallel to the edges of the wound. It is a good relaxation suture. It is also coaptative.

6. **Continuous or Glover's Stitch.**—This is sufficiently described by the illustration (Fig. 70). It is not much used except as a temporary suture, as for keeping a plug in a wound for a short time. It may be tied as an ordinary knot at either end of the wound, or the two ends of the thread may be tied together in the form of a loop.

7. **Button Suture.**—This is represented by Fig. 69. It is a form of tension suture.

8. **Pin Suture,** also known as the twisted or figure-of-eight suture. It is useful where the edges of the skin are thin and mobile.

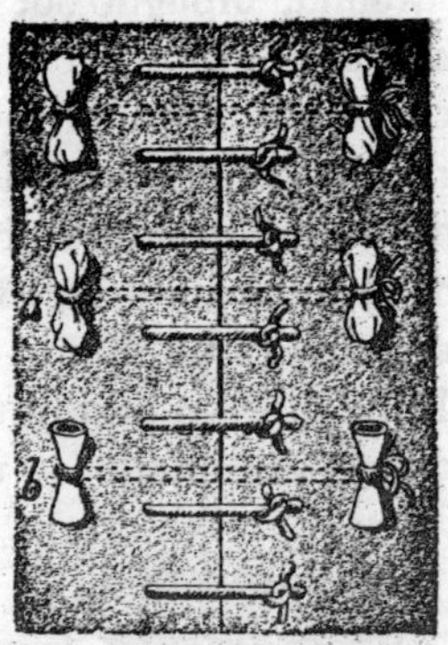

Fig. 68.—Interrupted Sutures combined with Sutures of Relaxation.

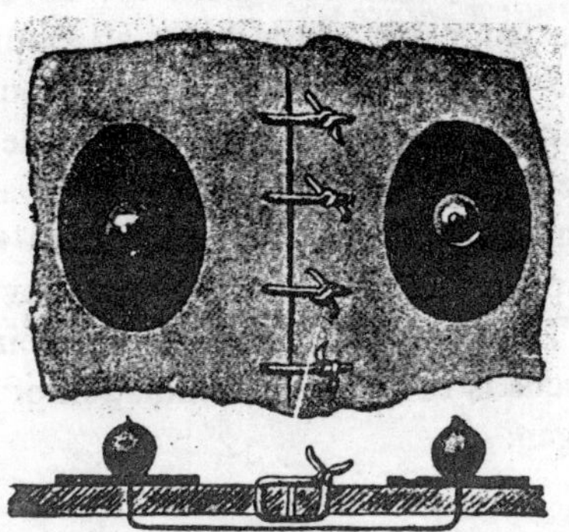

Fig. 69.—Tension Suture in Position.

It keeps them in rigid apposition. It is indicated for wounds of the eyelid, nostril, lip, etc. The pins are usually from 1½ to 2 inches long, ordinary flexible pins answering the purpose. A pin director or grooved needle may be used to facilitate their insertion.

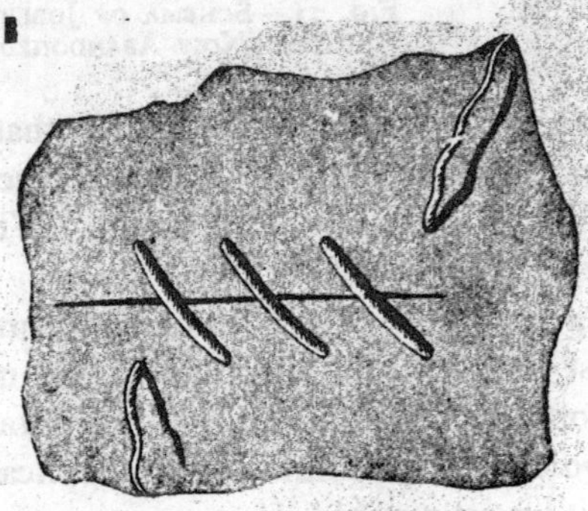

Fig. 70.—Continuous or Glover's Suture.

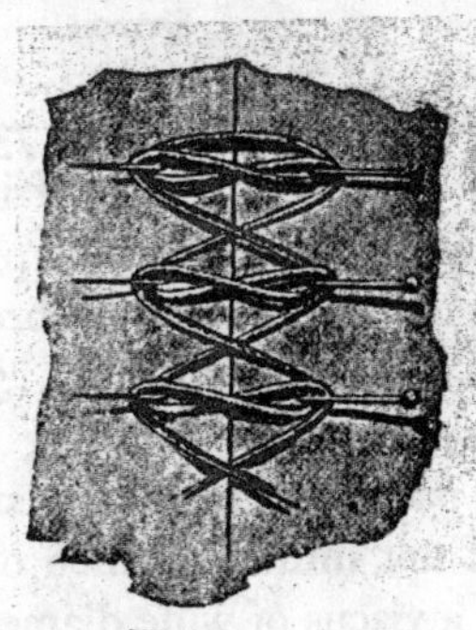

Fig. 71.—Figure-of-Eight or Pin Stitch.

Suture thread is wound round the ends of the pin in a figure-of-eight fashion.

The suture may be made continuous, as in Fig. 71. The thread should not be very tightly applied, lest necrosis of the skin pressed upon ensue.

9. **Bowel Sutures.**—The best bowel suture is *Lembert's* (Fig. 72), made as follows:

A fine milliner's needle furnished with fine silk or catgut thread is inserted through the serous and muscular coats of the bowel at about 1 centimetre from the border of the wound, brought out on the same side of the latter at about 4 to 5 millimetres from its edge, and then given a similar course on the other side. A series of these is inserted $\frac{1}{8}$ inch apart. When the sutures are tied the serous surfaces are brought into intimate contact, and unite more rapidly and securely than cut edges. It is important to have the sutures close together to prevent any leakage from the bowel into the peritoneal cavity.

The object of the suture not going through the mucous coat of the viscus is to avoid contamination of the thread from the interior of the organ.

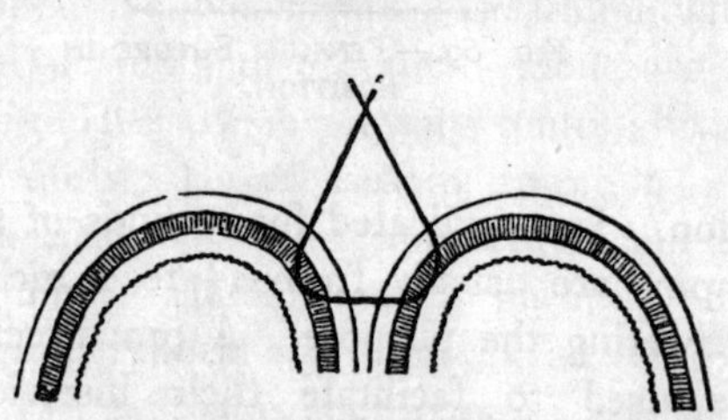

Fig. 72.—Lembert's Bowel Stitch.

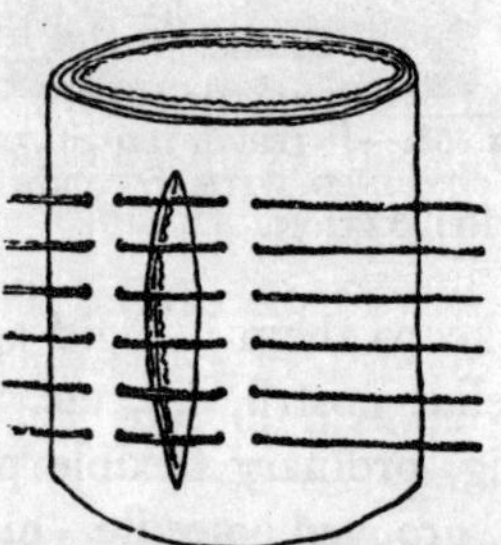

Fig. 73.—Schema of Jobert's Suture (Now Abandoned).

Jobert's suture (Fig. 73) is the same as Lembert's, except that it has the disadvantage of including the mucous coat. In both cases a ridge of tissue is formed projecting into the lumen of the bowel. When the latter is of small calibre, stricture is apt to ensue.

Czerny's suture (Fig. 75) is a double row of Lembert's sutures, the second row burying the first one. In the latter the thread may be passed through the submucous layer of the mucous membrane, but not into the lumen of the bowel. This suture is only applicable for a viscus of wide diameter, as it causes considerable narrowing of the lumen of the organ.

The Lembert suture is indicated for the stomach, uterus, and bladder, as well as for the intestine. It may be interrupted or continuous.

10. **Buried Sutures.**—When superimposed layers of tissue require to be brought together, a separate series of sutures may be used for each layer. Those beneath the surface are called buried sutures. They -e used in suturing the abdominal wall after performing laparotomy.

If the buried sutures remain aseptic they will not prevent healing by first intention, and will either become absorbed or remain encysted according to the material used. But if they become contaminated they will cause suppuration, which will continue until the septic piece of thread is discharged or removed. It may be necessary to incise the skin which has partly healed over them to enable them to be taken away.

Removal of Sutures.—When primary healing occurs, it is completed in five or six days, when the sutures may be removed if they are not still required to give support to a cicatrix subjected to pressure. In an ordinary wound the sooner the sutures are removed after healing

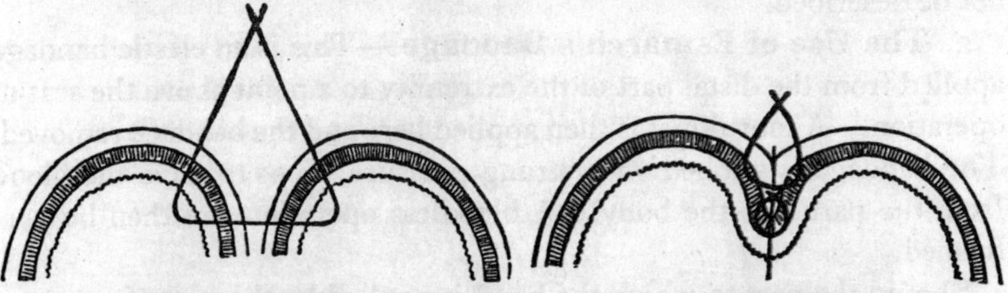

FIG. 74.—SCHEMA SHOWING JOBERT'S SUTURE IN SECTION.

FIG. 75.—LEMBERT-CZERNY BOWEL STITCH.

has occurred the better, as their retention for a longer period may lead to "stitch abscesses," which will result in little scars spoiling the effect of the primary union.

To remove a suture, one end of the thread at the knot is grasped by a dressing forceps and slightly drawn upon to expose the thread beneath the knot, which is then cut with a scissors.

X.—HÆMOSTASIS

The presence of blood during the course of an operation conceals the field of the latter, and its accumulation in the wound afterwards favours the growth of bacteria and prevents primary healing. Hence the importance of its prevention and arrest in operative procedures apart from the danger of death through loss of blood when a large vessel or vessels are severed.

Prevention of Hæmorrhage

Hæmorrhage can be entirely prevented during operations on the limbs, the penis, and the tail by the following methods:

1. **The Use of a Tourniquet.**—The tourniquet is in the form of a band or cord wound tightly round the limb or appendage above the seat of operation for arterial bleeding and below it for venous bleeding,

or in both situations if necessary. An ordinary thick cord or piece of rope, or in an emergency a handkerchief, in the form of a ring slipped over the part and twisted with a rod will have the required effect of compressing the vessels. But the most suitable material for the purpose is a piece of stout rubber gas tubing from 15 to 20 inches long, which is well stretched and tightly wound round the part and fixed with an ordinary knot.

The tourniquet also compresses the nerves, producing a numbing effect and acting to a certain extent as a local anæsthetic. Instrument makers provide special tourniquets, which are not necessary and need not be described.

2. **The Use of Esmarch's Bandage.**—This is an elastic bandage applied from the distal part of the extremity to a point above the seat of operation. A tourniquet is then applied here and the bandage removed. The bandage is applied with strong pressure, so as to drive the blood from the part into the body. A bloodless operation can then be performed.

Should the part to which the band is applied be the seat of a wound the latter should be first covered with a pad and bandage. If the affected region contain a septic lesion, this method of producing artificial ischæmia is contra-indicated on account of the risk of causing a reflux of septic material into the system. For most cases the tourniquet alone is sufficient.

When the operation is completed, the constriction is removed and the bleeding arrested by appropriate measures about to be described. Vessels bleed more copiously than usual after the use of the tourniquet, owing to its causing paralysis of the vaso-constrictors.

3. **Digital Compression.**—Pressure maintained on the chief vessel of supply by the fingers of an assistant or by a blunt object is seldom employed, but may prove useful in certain cases where a large vessel is accidentally wounded until other means are adopted to definitely stop the hæmorrhage.

4. **The Hypodermic Injection of Adrenalin.**—This is useful for the prevention of capillary hæmorrhage. Applied on a mucous surface it has a blanching effect, and is particularly useful for operations on the conjunctiva.

Arrest of Hæmorrhage during and after Operation

Hæmorrhage is slight or absent when an operation is performed by means of the actual cautery, crushing, tearing, blunt dissection, or ligation.

The Thermo-Cautery.—This acts best when used at a dull red heat, the coats of the vessel retracting and contracting, diminishing its lumen, and an eschar forming on its orifice and acting as a plug. At a white heat the vessels are too rapidly severed and imperfectly occluded. The auto-cautery such as the zoo-cautery or the Déchery cautery is very convenient for the purpose.

Crushing.—This method is commonly adopted in veterinary practice by the aid of the ecraseur, of which there are several patterns, the oldest and one of the most reliable being Chassaignac's ecraseur, which is almost exclusively used on the Continent, while Dewar's and Miles's ecraseurs are most widely employed in the United Kingdom and the U.S.A. The former is worked on the ratchet system, and acts somewhat after the fashion of a saw as well as by crushing, while the latter are operated by turning a threaded shaft. In either case the loop of chain

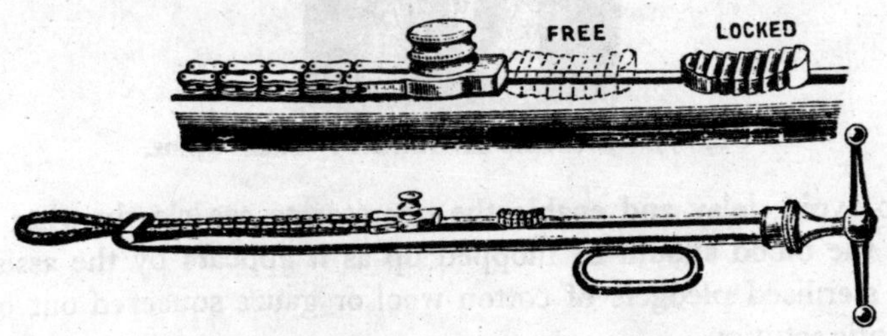

FIG. 76.—PROFESSOR DEWAR'S ECRASEUR.

is gradually tightened on the enclosed tissues, which are severed by degrees without any hæmorrhage. The middle and inner coats of the vessels first give way and retract and contract, while the outer coat is drawn out so that its inner surfaces are pressed into contact, forming a sort of cap over the mouth of the vessel. The more slowly the instrument is operated the more effectively are the vessels occluded.

The various crushing instruments used for the operation of castration act on the same principle as the ecraseur.

Tearing of the tissues is often employed in the removal of tumours loosely attached and situated in the vicinity of important vessels and nerves—for example, in the jugular furrow or the parotid region.

Blunt Dissection.—Blunt dissection is performed by rupturing the tissues by the pressure of a blunt instrument, and is sometimes employed for the isolation of large vessels like the carotid and jugular and for the separation of tumours in contact with important arteries or veins.

Ligation.—The elastic or other ligature is sometimes employed for the removal of tumours, especially when pedunculated.

The above methods of operation are only applicable to a restricted number of cases, the knife being required in most instances.

When the incision is made, blood escapes and more or less conceals the field of operation. Capillary bleeding soon stops spontaneously but to avoid delay and enable the operator to see clearly what he is doing the blood should be mopped up as it appears by the assistant, using sterilised pledgets of cotton-wool or gauze squeezed out of the antiseptic solution.

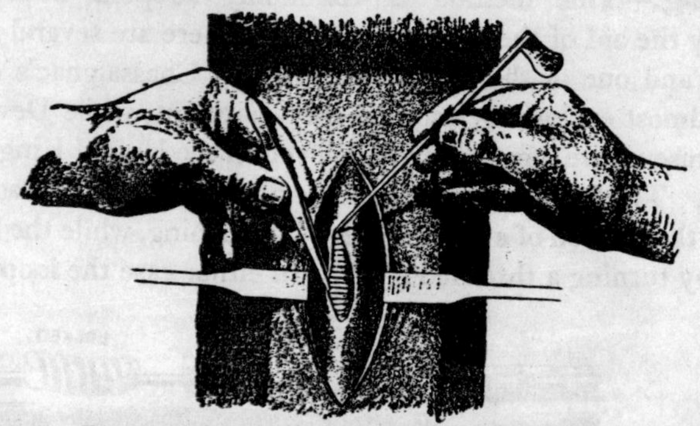

FIG. 77.—LIGATING AN ARTERY: FIRST STAGE.

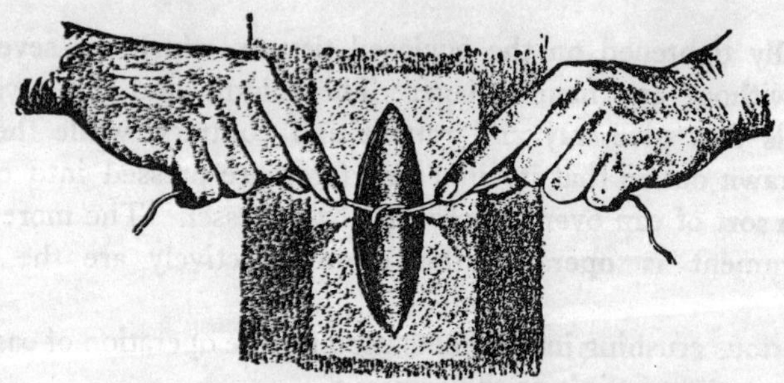

FIG. 78.—LIGATING AN ARTERY: SECOND STAGE.

In operations not requiring delicate dissection slight hæmorrhage may be ignored. When bleeding occurs from important vessels, some of the following methods of hæmostasis must be resorted to:

1. **Digital Compression**, as already described in the prevention of hæmorrhage, may be adopted temporarily until the operation is completed, when some other means is adopted as a permanent hæmostatic.

2. **The Thermo-Cautery.**—This is an effective instrument for arresting hæmorrhage by the production of an eschar which closes the mouths of the bleeding vessels until a coagulum forms therein. It is used at a dull red heat and with a rotary movement to prevent the sere adhering to the iron and becoming separated from the tissues beneath. It must be applied lightly and rapidly, otherwise there will be a too great destruction of tissue, causing a large slough and favouring septic complications. An example of the efficacy of this method is seen in the operation of castration by the hot iron, which is rarely followed by hæmorrhage.

3. **Ligation.**—Ligation of bleeding vessels with silk or catgut, preferably the former, is the surest method of arresting hæmorrhage. When a vessel is divided accidentally, the bleeding end is seized longitudinally with an artery forceps and drawn slightly out of the tissues, and is then ligatured by making one knot with the thread round the forceps, gliding it thence on to the vessel, and tying it securely with a reef knot.

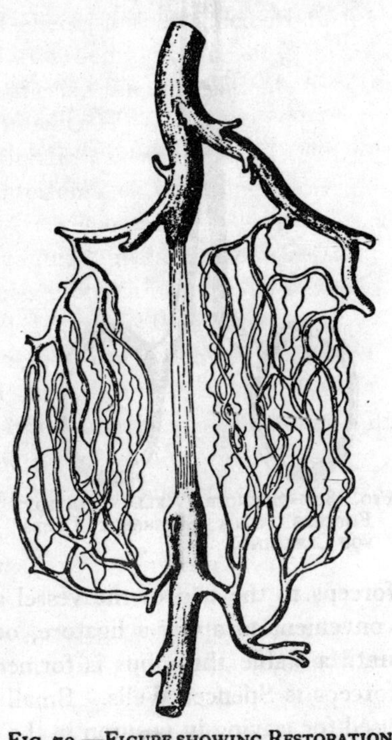

Fig. 79.—Figure showing Restoration of Blood Supply by Collateral Vessels after Ligation of Main Trunk (from a Preparation of the Femoral Artery of a Large Dog Eight Months after Ligation).

When the wound is aseptic the ends of the thread are cut close to the knot, but if it is suspected of infection one of the ends is left protruding through the lips of the wound to enable it to be removed after a few days when it becomes free. If the vessel is seen before being cut, it should be ligatured in two places and cut between the ligatures. Bleeding may occur from the two ends of a divided vessel owing to anastomosis with other vessels.

When an artery is ligatured its inner and middle coats are ruptured at once and retract and contract within the outer coat, partly occluding the lumen of the vessel and affording a rough surface on which clotting readily takes place. The outer coat remains intact for some days, undergoing gradual division by the pressure of the ligature. When the latter is aseptic it either becomes absorbed or remains encysted, the former being the case with catgut and the latter with silk. When an important bleeding vessel cannot be secured in a wound it may be possible to dissect it out in the vicinity and ligate it in its continuity—*e.g.*, the carotid artery—the operation being done aseptically and the wound sutured with a view to getting primary healing. A special forceps is obtainable which ensures the application of a ligature to a severed vessel without including the end of the forceps, the free ends of the jaws being hemispherical.

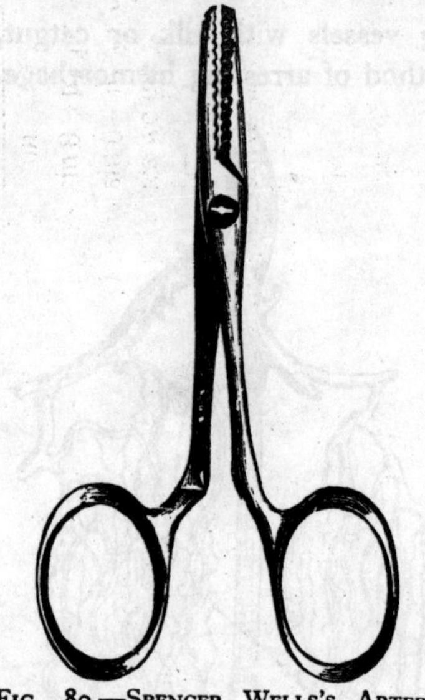

Fig. 80.—Spencer Wells's Artery Forceps (with Separable Limbs for Cleaning).

4. **Torsion.**—Torsion is sufficient to arrest hæmorrhage from small vessels. The bleeding end of the vessel is secured with the artery forceps drawn out slightly and twisted on its long axis several times until a twisted end is left which will not untwist when released.

Torsion may be adopted to sever vessels without hæmorrhage, as in castration by torsion.

Twisting an artery has the effect of rupturing its inner and middle coats, which behave as described in connection with ligation. The outer coat forms a twisted cap closing the orifice of the vessel.

5. **Forcipressure.**— Forcipressure consists in applying an artery forceps to the end of the vessel and leaving it in position until it is convenient to apply a ligature, or for a period of twenty-four hours until a stable thrombus is formed. The best-known type of artery forceps is Spencer Wells. Small " bulldog forceps " are occasionally used for leaving in position in the interior of a wound until the following day. When the forceps is too large to fit inside the lips of the wound it may be left protruding between them until it is safe to remove it—that is, about twenty-four to forty-eight hours afterwards. The handles may be tied together to avoid the danger of the instrument becoming detached.

Compression with the forceps for a few minutes is sufficient to stop bleeding from small vessels.

Crushing of Arterioles difficult to isolate may be performed by a special strong forceps—for example, the intercostal artery may be crushed against the rib.

Plugging or Packing a Hollow Wound.—When hæmorrhage takes place from a hollow wound, it can usually be arrested by packing the cavity with medicated gauze or cotton-wool or fine tow kept in position by sutures. It is generally sufficient to leave the plug in position for twenty-four hours. On removing it, the blood clot should not be disturbed more than is necessary for fear of causing a recurrence of the bleeding. The blood clot will disintegrate and come away afterwards. This method is frequently required after operations. Wounds in veins are dealt with in the same way as those of arteries.

The Application of Styptics to a bleeding wound, such as adrenalin, astringent lotions, tinct. benzoin Co, ice, cold water and very hot water is more or less effective for diffuse hæmorrhage when large vessels are not involved. (See also page 40.)

AUTOPLASTIA

Autoplastic operation is required to bring about union of the borders of a wound in which there has been operative or accidental loss of tissue, whereby its lips are widely separated and a space or opening (when over a cavity like the nasal chamber) or a large amount of cicatricial tissue, constituting a blemish (broken knee) persists.

It may be practised in a recent wound with wide gaping from loss of tissue, but more frequently for a wound already cicatrised, but leaving a large space between its cutaneous borders, occupied by scar tissue, or an opening into a cavity. Examples of where it may be indicated are:

1. Loss of substance in any part of the body, but chiefly where the harness rests, including the whole thickness of the skin, and leaving a hard prominent cicatrix which may be hypersensitive or form a blemish depreciating the value of the animal.

2. Wounds at the level of joints where cicatrisation is hampered by movement and a large scar results, such as those in front of the knee.

3. Lesions in the region of the natural orifices, for example about the lips, where they may lead to more or less interference with prehension and mastication, or the wings of the nostrils, or the eyelids.

4. An opening persisting in one of the air sinuses or the nasal chamber, following a trephining operation.

The principle of autoplastia depends on the possibility of uniting bands of skin displaced from their existing position in the vicinity of the lesion or transported from a region in another part of the same individual. The latter procedure is not practicable in veterinary patients. The method adopted may be displacement by (1) gliding or, (2) traction. The band of skin in the vicinity of the loss of substance may have a pedicle (Indian method), or a wide base (Celse's method). The latter is the method mostly in vogue.

PROCEDURE.—To cover a space resulting from loss of tissue following a pre-existing lesion or the operative removal of tissue, the edges of the wound must be freshened and made even by excising necrotic or damaged or callous tissue. It is often necessary to map out by incisions bands of healthy skin, lined by hypodermis, which are sufficiently large to permit of their suturing without excessive tension and still in continuity with the adjacent tegument by a base which is sufficient to ensure their nutrition. The observation of strict asepsis is an essential condition for primary healing of the sutured wound. Local anæsthesia is indicated. Silkworm gut is preferable to silk as suture material.

The incisions which are required for the mobilisation of the lips of the wound or of the bands of skin which are to be brought into apposition will vary with the form of the lesion thus :

1. **Elliptic and Oval Wound of Small Extent.**—(*a*) It may be sufficient to separate the skin from the borders of the wound for a width of ½ to 1 inch, but excessive tension must be avoided or union will not supervene.

(*b*) If the wound is large it is necessary to make an incision on each side of it at a short distance from its border and parallel to its long axis, and of the same length as the wound, known as an incision of relaxation (Fig. 81 (1)).

(*c*) In a case where (*a*) or (*b*) does not close the breach more mobile bands can be made by curved incisions extending from the extremities of the lesion (Fig. 81 (2)).

2. **Triangular Wound.**—Any of the following methods may be adopted :

(*a*) Make a rectilineal incision prolonging the base of the triangle, mapping out an area of skin which is mobilised so that it can be made, by gliding on the subcutaneous tissue, to cover the wound and be fixed in position by two rows of sutures (Fig. 81 (3)).

(*b*) Make two linear incisions on each side of the base of the triangle, mobilise the two flaps of skin, bring the edges into contact, and unite them by interrupted sutures (Fig. 81 (4)).

(*c*) Instead of straight incisions make one or two curved incisions forming two bands of skin which are dissected and sutured as in the preceding cases (Fig. 81 (5) and (6)).

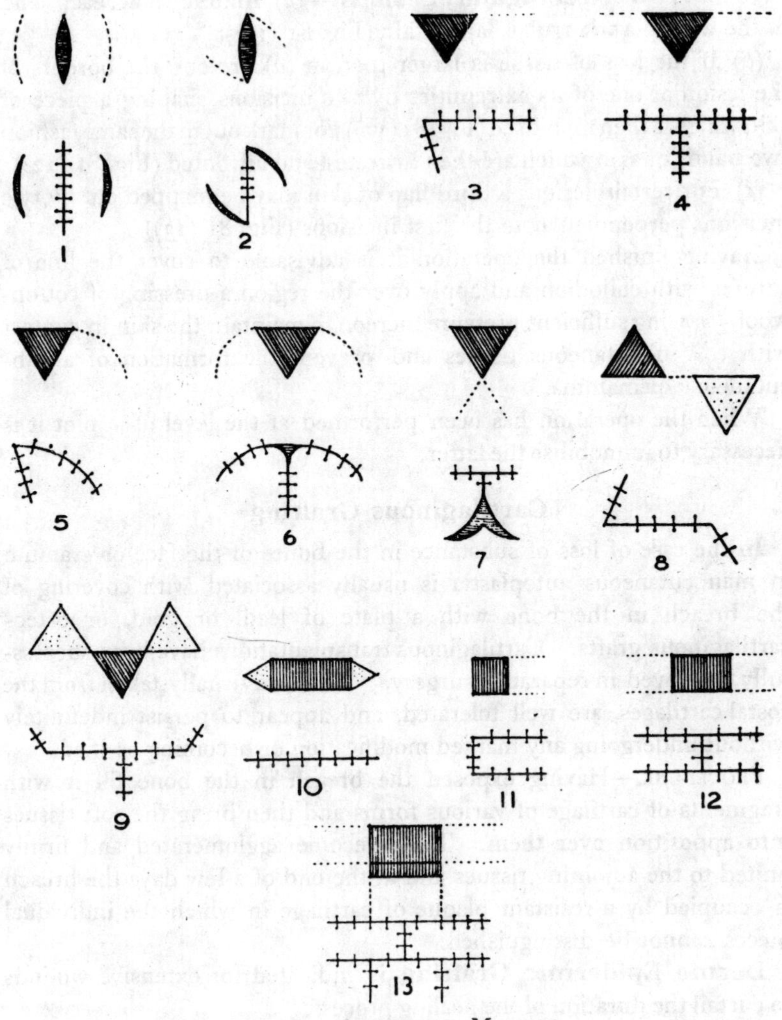

FIG. 81.—AUTOPLASTIC METHODS.

(*d*) Make two incisions, producing the sides of the triangle via the apex, and mobilise the pieces of skin thus delimited so that the sides can be sutured to the base of the triangle (Fig. 81(7)).

(*e*) Make one or two incisions prolonging the base of the lesion, excise one or two triangular flaps of skin whose apex is opposite in direction to that of the triangular lesion, and mobilise the flaps of skin so as to fill the two or three areas of loss of substance (Fig. 81 (8) and (9)).

3. **Narrow Rectangular Lesions.**—(*a*) Map out at each end of the wound a triangular flap of skin (Fig. 81 (10)).

(*b*) If the loss of tissue is larger than in (*a*) prolong the borders of the lesion at one of its extremities by two incisions shaping a piece of skin which is then mobilised (Fig. 81 (11)); or mark out in the same fashion two bands of skin which are then liberated and affronted (Fig. 81 (12)).

(*c*) For certain lesions a third flap of skin may be mapped out by two incisions perpendicular to the first incisions (Fig. 81 (13)).

Having finished the operation it is advisable to cover the line of sutures with collodion and apply over the region a dressing of cotton-wool, exerting sufficient pressure thereon to maintain the skin in contact with the subcutaneous tissues and prevent the formation of a subcutaneous hæmatoma.

When the operation has been performed at the level of a joint it is necessary to immobilise the latter.

Cartilaginous Grafting

In the case of loss of substance in the bones of the face or cranium in man cutaneous autoplastia is usually associated with covering of the breach in the bone with a plate of lead, or gold, or osteo-cartilaginous grafts. Cartilaginous transplantations have been successfully employed in reparative surgery. They are usually taken from the costal cartilages, are well tolerated, and appear to persist indefinitely without undergoing any marked modification or becoming ossified.

PROCEDURE.—Having exposed the breach in the bone fill it with fragments of cartilage of various forms and then bring the soft tissues into apposition over them. They become agglomerated and firmly united to the adjoining tissues and at the end of a few days the breach is occupied by a resistant plaque of cartilage in which the individual pieces cannot be distinguished.

Dermo-Epidermic Grafting is indicated for extensive wounds to curtail the duration of the healing process.

PROCEDURE.—(1) Shave the skin in the affected region and dress it and the wound with ether.

(2) By means of a curette make some outcuts in the granulations of the wound and deposit therein dermo-epidermic grafts 2 to 3 inches in diameter.

(3) Cover the wound with an aseptic dressing of gauze and cotton-wool, the former having been slightly moistened with a solution of sodium chloride (6 per 1,000), and renew the dressing every two or three days.

It is practically impossible to carry out this treatment satisfactorily in veterinary practice, owing to the difficulty in preventing interference with the dressing or keeping it immobile, apart from the difficulty of observing strict asepsis.

PARENTERAL INJECTION OF DRUGS, SERA, OR VACCINES

Indications.—These injections are indicated for various conditions which need not be mentioned here.

Control of the Patient.—No special control is required. A twitch may be used on the horse if very restive, the ox may be steadied by being held by the nose, and the dog may be muzzled.

Procedure

1. **Hypodermic Injection.**—The site having been prepared as for an operation and the syringe sterilised, a fold of skin is taken up with the fingers and thumb at a place where it is loose and not touched by harness, and the needle, held between the first two fingers of the other hand with the thumb on its base, is placed in position at the side of the fold and thrust through the skin by a continuous steady motion. Having a syringe attached to the needle facilitates its insertion.

A fine needle of good quality is the most suitable for ordinary hypodermic injections in the horse or dog, as it is very easily inserted and causes no pain to the patient. This is important to remember in connection with the injection of local anæsthetics in the limbs in the horse, where the use of a comparatively thick needle may cause considerable resistance on the part of the animal and render the procedure difficult. Rubbing into the skin a mixture of pure carbolic acid 1 part to 4 parts of camphor has a numbing effect which prevents the prick of the needle being felt. When injecting a local anæsthetic reinsertion of the needle to extend the field of anæsthesia should be made through the area already anæsthetised, *i.e.*, through the weal caused by the previous injection. There are many patterns of syringes on the market. The " Record " syringe supplied by Messrs. Parke Davis and Co. is very convenient and perfect in its working.

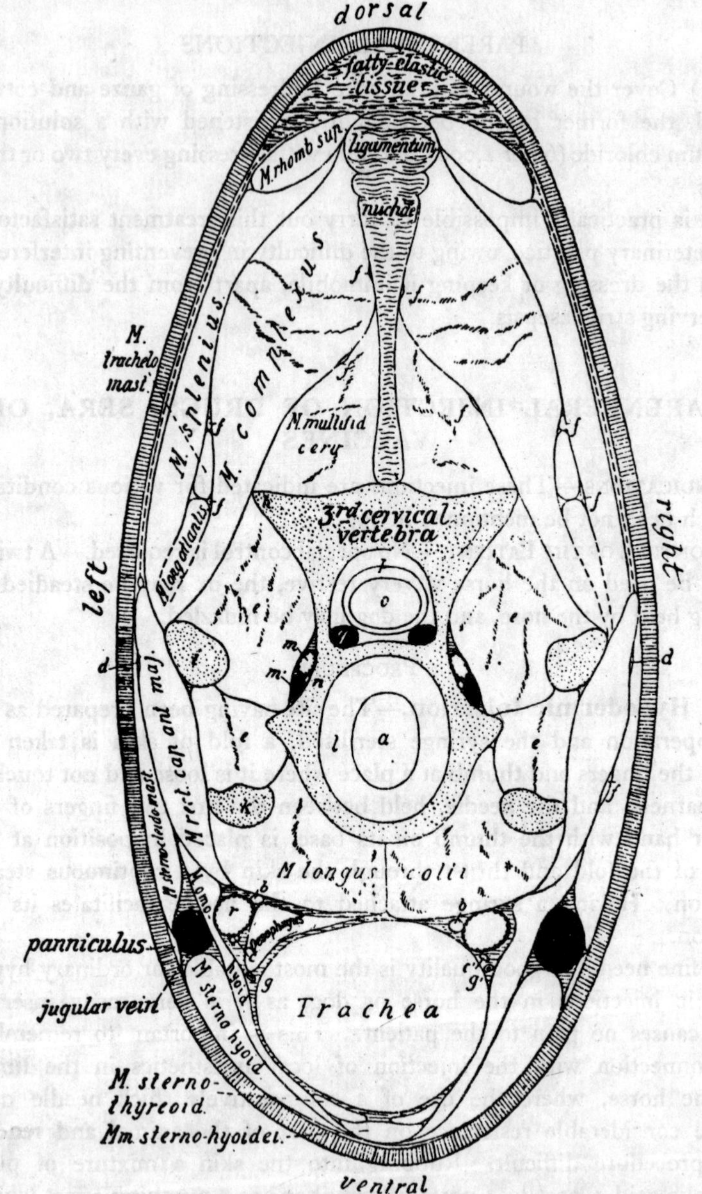

FIG. 82.—TRANSVERSE SECTION OF NECK AT RIGHT ANGLES TO ITS LONG DIAMETER

The section passes through the third cervical vertebra. *a*, Portion of the head of the fourth cervical vertebra; *b*, *b*, vagus and sympathetic nerves; *c*, *c*, recurrent nerves; *d*, *d*, dorsal branches of spinal accessory nerve; *e*, *e*, intertransversales colli muscles; *f*, *f*, muscular twigs of the cervical nerves; *g*, *g*, tracheal lymph duct; *i*, *k*, transverse processes of cervical vertebra; *l*, intervertebral disc of cartilage; *m*, *m*, vertebral artery and vein; *n*, lymphatic nerve twig; *o*, spinal cord; *p*, membranes of the cord; *q*, vessels of the cord; *r*, carotid artery. (After Ellenberger and Baum.)

It must be dismounted and put into cold or warm water when about to be sterilised by boiling, otherwise the glass will break, and when not in use the plunger and barrel should be separated.

If proper precautions are not observed as to asepsis and antisepsis, an abscess may form at the seat of injection.

2. **Intravenous Injection.**—The procedure is the same as for phlebotomy (p. 320), taking care not to allow the needle to impinge on the intima after insertion, which in the case of the injection of a vaccine or chloral hydrate would lead to phlebitis and thrombosis.

The pressure of the thumb or finger of the other hand is sufficient to distend the vein in the horse, but in the ox, on account of its double jugular on each side, it is necessary to make a tight noose round the base of the neck with a thin rope. This may also be used for the horse to leave the two hands free to make the injection. A solid object placed beneath the rope in the jugular furrow facilitates raising the vein in this animal. Intravenous injections in the dog and cat are made through the external saphena and radial vein respectively, as described in connection with nembutal anæsthesia.

3. **Intratracheal Injection.**—Intratracheal injections may be made with an ordinary hypodermic syringe provided with a stout needle, with a large Pravaz syringe, or with Dieckerhoff's syringe, which is used in conjunction with a special trocar and canula. The animal's head is raised, the skin stretched with the fingers of the left hand, and the needle or trocar pushed vigorously between two tracheal rings into the lumen of the tube. The liquid is injected slowly. It may also be pushed through the cartilage, but the needle may then become blocked with the cartilage and require to be cleared. To overcome this difficulty a stout needle with a trifacial point like a trocar and lateral apertures near the point may be used. It is much in favour for the injection of hoose preparations.

4. **Intralaryngeal Injections** are made through the crico-thyroid ligament. They are seldom employed.

5. **Parenchymatous Injections** are made into the substance of glands or other tissues.

A stout needle is inserted into the tissue and the injection is then made with the syringe.

Caustic liquids may thus be introduced into tumours to produce sloughing, or tincture of iodine may be injected into a botriomycotic swelling with a view to killing the organisms therein.

CAUTERISATION—FIRING

Chemical caustics and their actions are dealt with in works on materia medica, and their uses are described in connection with the various conditions for which they are indicated.

Firing, or the application of the actual cautery to the skin, and in some cases to the deeper tissues as well, is the severest form of counter-irritation, and is indicated in deep-seated chronic inflammatory conditions for which other measures have failed or are deemed insufficient.

Varieties of Firing comprise:

1. *Objective firing*—that is, holding a red-hot iron close to the tissues without touching them. It is seldom adopted nowadays, but it has been practised in the past during the rubbing in of a blister, to intensify its effect.

2. *Superficial line firing*, in which the hot iron is applied to the skin so as to form lines therein which go through its superficial layers, just stopping short of passing through its entire thickness.

3. *Superficial point firing*, by which rows of points are made going partly through the skin.

4. *Penetrating point firing*, in which a pointed iron is made to penetrate the skin into the subcutaneous tissues and sometimes into bone.

5. *Needle-point firing*, in which needle points are inserted into various deep tissues, including tendons, ligaments, and bones, and even into synovial capsules.

Control of the Horse.—The operation is most commonly done in the standing position. In the past an anæsthetic was seldom employed, but now its use is obligatory, local or general.

Cocaine or novocaine or eudrenine or other local anæsthetic is injected subcutaneously over the nerves supplying the part to be fired (anterior and posterior tibial and plantar nerves), or into the subcutaneous tissue of the region. Apart from its humane effect in preventing pain, it keeps the patient quiet and greatly facilitates the operation. If, notwithstanding its use, the horse offers resistance, the usual methods of control may be adopted.

To make the horse stand on the limb whilst being fired, it may be necessary to have the other foot lifted by the hand in the case of the fore-limb, or drawn forward by a side-line in the case of the hind-limb.

If the local anæsthetic has not the desired effect, or despite it the horse is uncontrollable, he must be cast and fixed as follows for firing the parts mentioned :

Firing the Flexor Tendons of the Near Fore-Limb

The horse is cast with hobbles on the near side. The two fore-limbs are tied together above the knees by a soft rope or web, a rope is fixed to the under fore-pastern, which is then released from the hobble and drawn forward with the rope so as to make the limb taut and expose it well for the operation. When the inner aspect of the tendons is fired, the horse is turned over and the outer side is done. When the operation is finished, the limb is returned to the hobble and the patient allowed to rise. If both limbs are to be fired, the outer side of the upper limb is done before turning the horse. It is unnecessary to take it from the hobble for the purpose, but it requires to be held straight by a rope applied on the pastern. The fired areas may be protected by a short bandage while the patient is being turned.

Firing the Flexor Tendons of the Near Hind-Limb

A similar method of fixation is employed, the two hind-limbs being tied together above the hocks, and the under hind-limb being released from the hobble and taken backwards.

The object in doing the inner side of the limb first is to avoid rubbing of the fired part on the outside against the ground while the inner side is being done.

Firing the Pastern

The limbs are fixed in the same way as in the last two cases, except that the rope is applied round the hoof instead of on the pastern.

Firing the Inner Aspect of the Hock

The horse is cast with hobbles on the side of the affected limb. The upper hind-limb is drawn forward to the shoulder by means of a rope round the neck, passed between the fore-limbs, round the pastern, and back through the loop on the neck. Local or general anæsthesia may be adopted. Ropes may be used instead of hobbles, and the limbs fixed on the same principles.

PREPARATION OF THE SITE.—The hair is clipped over the part to be fired, and the skin then brushed to remove dandruff. When firing by needle points is about to be performed in an animal with a fine skin, the latter may be shaved and disinfected as for a surgical operation.

1. Superficial Line Firing

The instrument employed may be: (1) *The ordinary firing iron* shown in Fig. 83. Its head is massive, so as to retain the heat, and its firing border is convex, smooth, and rather blunt, so that it will not cut the skin. For operating in the standing position a fairly long handle is an advantage, but for the cast position a shorter handle is more convenient. (2) *The auto-cautery*, such as the zoo-cautery, or Déchery's cautery. The handle of the former contains a reservoir for benzine. Its head is made of nickel, pointed with platinum, which, after being heated, has the peculiar property of remaining hot in the presence of certain vapours.

Its action is started by applying a light to the holes in the head, and it is kept functioning by working a bellows attached to the extremity of the handle for the purpose of pumping in the required amount of

Fig. 83.—Line Firing Iron and Detachable Handle.

air to mix with the benzine vapour. The supply of the latter can be regulated by a stopcock. It is a very good instrument, but has the disadvantage that a bellows has to be used in connection with it.

The Déchery cautery is a more convenient instrument. Its handle contains a reservoir for ether, which is vaporised by heating the head and the part between it and the handle in a spirit or gas flame. The vapour of the ether escapes through a minute hole in the head, where it is ignited and continues to burn, making the part red-hot. This instrument is extensively used at present. Both instruments have the necessary accessories for the various kinds of firing, and full directions for their use are supplied therewith.

Procedure.—When the ordinary iron is to be used it is heated in an ordinary coal fire or in a forge fire, but the best fuel to use for the purpose is charcoal or wood, which will not cause scales to adhere to the iron.

When the iron is ready its head is rubbed lightly with the rasp to remove any scales that may be present, and its edge is rubbed to and fro on a board to ensure that it is smooth. It is applied to the affected part at right angles to the skin, and the lines are made by drawing the instrument towards the operator without much pressure, or occasionally by pushing it from him, as when turning round a part towards the opposite side. A sufficient number of lines is drawn to completely cover the affected area. Their distance apart should be from ½ inch to ¾ inch throughout. The pattern adopted may be horizontal lines, or the herring-bone design with the oblique lines directed upwards, and forwards or downwards and forwards from the back of the limb. Fig. 84 represents various patterns of line firing and point firing, the circular arrangement of the lines being suitable for the shoulder and hip. It is not advisable to have lines intersecting, as the skin may be excessively burnt at the angles of intersection and slough, leaving a blemish. Nevertheless, some practitioners adopt the diamond pattern of firing, in which oblique lines cross one another, forming diamond-shaped spaces.

Fig. 84.—Patterns of Firing.

All the lines are marked lightly at first and then gone over again, beginning at the first one made, until they are sufficiently deep. Three or four times is generally sufficient to retrace the lines with a red-hot iron. The thickness of the skin, the temperature of the iron, and the nature of its edge must be considered in this respect.

Three degrees of cauterisation may be distinguished by the appearance of the base of the lines—viz.: 1. The lines are shallow and contain a few drops of serosity. Their base is a yellowish-brown, the skin is slightly infiltrated, and the epidermis is still adherent. 2. The lines are deeper, their depth is golden yellow, the exudation is more pronounced, and the epidermis is easily separated. 3. The skin is almost cut through, the borders of the grooves tend to separate, and their depth, which is straw-coloured, shows a profuse serous discharge, and sometimes the skin between the lines is covered with phlyctenæ.

No. 2 is the degree of firing aimed at.

2. Superficial Point Firing

An iron with a massive conical head and a blunt point is used. The points are made to the same depth as the lines, and the same distance apart. Succeeding rows of points are made opposite to the interspaces of the preceding row.

3. Penetrating Point Firing

For this the apex of the conical-headed iron is drawn out to a fine point. A certain amount of pressure is applied to the instrument to make it penetrate the skin more readily, otherwise the procedure is the same as in No. 2.

4. Needle-Point Firing

This is performed with needle points of 1 to 2 millimetres diameter. Ordinary needles held in a forceps may be used, but have the disadvantage that they become cool almost immediately after being heated. If the needle is made with a heavy head to retain the heat, the skin

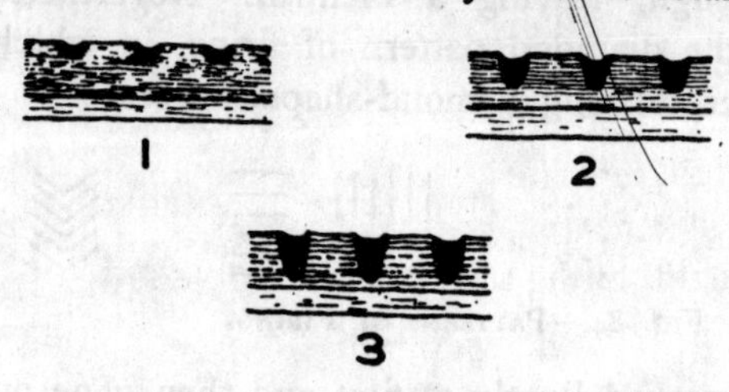

Fig. 85.—Degrees of Cauterisation.
1. Light firing. 2. Moderately deep firing. 3. Deep firing. 4. Penetrating point firing. 5. Needle point firing.

will be burned round the orifice. The best instrument for the purpose is the Déchery cautery.

If the horse remains quiet, the operation may be done in the standing position, but if he is at all restive and moves the limb when the point is applied, the latter bends and requires to be straightened with a forceps.

For parts other than a joint or large synovial sheath the needle is usually inserted two or three times into the same opening, but in the case of the cavities mentioned it should not be introduced more than once into the same orifice for fear of making the hole too large, and thus allowing the entrance of infection. When firing a sheath or joint, it is not advisable to have more than a third of the points penetrating into the organ.

The needle should be quickly inserted and withdrawn, and the punctures made about ½ inch apart. This is the most effective form of cauterisation for deep-seated chronic inflammation.

Crowding the points at a distance of less than ½ inch leads to sloughing.

5. Mixed Firing

To increase the efficacy of line firing, penetrating or needle points may be made between the lines.

Whatever form of firing is adopted, it is usual to apply a blister over the cauterised area after the operation. Biniodide of mercury is the agent recommended after needle-point firing, as it is antiseptic and ensures against any possible risk of infection into the deep tissues. In this case it may be only smeared over the surface. When the firing has been severe, it is not advisable to rub in a blister afterwards, as it would favour sloughing of the skin. Sometimes the vesicant is only applied after some days, when it is seen that the iron has not had sufficient effect, as indicated by the amount of inflammatory reaction. Subsequently, the usual precautions must be taken to prevent the animal rubbing or biting the affected part (see Blisters, p. 6).

Effects of Firing

Superficial Firing.—An acute inflammation with more or less exudation, especially from the lines and points, ensues during the following days. The discharge afterwards becomes dried into yellowish crusts or scabs. Lameness is increased, and the part becomes itchy.

If the inflammation is too severe the skin will have a parchment-like appearance, and clear yellow viscid discharge will appear in the depth of the lines or points, indicating the use of warm antiseptic fomentations to attenuate the inflammatory phenomena.

The dried exudate separates in the course of ten to fourteen days. Its separation is favoured by the application of vaseline or zinc ointment, which also prevents cracking of the skin. If the skin has been divided, granulations will form there and give rise to a bare spot or scar afterwards.

Inflammation also ensues in the subcutaneous tissues, followed by absorption and compression, which constitute the good effects of the operation, the original inflammatory exudate being absorbed along with that resulting from the hot iron, and the cicatricial contraction which follows acting like a permanent bandage, bracing up the tissues.

Penetrating Point Firing.—Here the effects mentioned above are more marked, and the results more beneficial for deep-seated lesions.

Needle-Point Firing.—In this case the ensuing inflammation is very intense, and the patient may show a febrile reaction. When a synovial sac has been penetrated, a synovial discharge will escape from the holes for three or four days after the operation, forming a yellow viscid deposit on the skin. It then dries into a scab, the holes being obliterated. After about twenty days the scab falls off, leaving small pink cicatrices which later become covered by the surrounding hair. The swelling in the region persists for a considerable time.

After-Treatment.—About a fortnight after the operation, daily walking exercise for about half an hour may be given. After another fourteen days the horse may be put to light work, if sound, but when the lesion has been serious, such as sprained tendons, a prolonged rest is advisable. If the season permit, a run at grass for two or three months is indicated.

Accidents occurring during the operation comprise section of the skin with the line firing iron and hæmorrhage from opening of a bloodvessel. The former is not serious when localised, and the latter soon becomes arrested spontaneously, or after compression with a pad and bandage.

Sloughing may ensue from excessive firing. When it seems threatened, warm antiseptic lotions should be applied, and the surface afterwards sprayed with iodoform dissolved in ether (1 in 8).

Tetanus is a possible complication.

Objections to Firing

Notwithstanding what has been said about the good effects of firing, there were—and doubtless still are—veterinary surgeons of high repute and long experience in large horse-practices who condemned firing as lacking the good effects claimed for it and, consequently, as an unnecessary, crude, and cruel method of treatment, doing probably more harm than good, seeing that burned tissues are never as strong as those undamaged by fire. The late Mr. William Hunting, London, recognised as an outstanding expert on affections of horses' limbs and an acute observer, and his partner, the late Mr. R. C. Irving, also a well known authority on horses and their ailments, were strong opponents of firing and asserted that mere rest in a loose box gave much better results. Mr. Hunting demonstrated the truth of this statement by an experiment. He selected twelve horses with "bowed" tendons in both fore limbs and in each case fired the limb which seemed less affected and left the other untreated. After four months' rest they resumed work, and in every case the horses went lame again on the fired leg, whilst the other remained sound. Mr. Irving had many cases, a large number of which were in stallions so badly strained that they were on the point of being destroyed, which he treated by removing their shoes and putting them in loose boxes for six months and always found that their leg or legs became practically normal. He never bought a fired horse, as he found that their legs never became even nearly normal, and, moreover, no foreigner he ever met would buy a fired stallion, and most of the many horses he sold went abroad. Firing a sound limb to make it stronger seems an extraordinary and uncalled-for procedure (*Vet. Rec.*, Oct. 12, 1940).

Firing the Ox

The working ox may suffer from chronic inflammatory conditions indicating the use of the hot iron, which is employed in the same manner as in the horse. The skin of the bovine is thicker than that of the equine, and consequently may be fired somewhat more deeply.

Firing the Dog

The thermo-cautery is seldom applied to the dog, but occasionally it is indicated for chronic inflammatory lesions, *e.g.*, ostitis or arthritis or "track leg." Needle-point firing is generally the most suitable and efficacious form to adopt. Steps must be taken to prevent the dog biting or licking the part by the use of a muzzle or an Elizabethan collar. It is advisable to apply a dressing of gauze and bandage on the fired limb as a further protection, or when the muzzle or Elizabethan collar is not available.

Acid Firing

This term has been applied to the use of strong sulphuric acid as a counter-irritant on the skin instead of that of the actual cautery.

PROCEDURE.—Clip the hair from the part, brush, and wash the skin. Apply the acid by means of a cork in the form of points $\frac{3}{8}$ to $\frac{1}{2}$ inch apart, taking care not to let the acid come in contact with other parts.

Advantages claimed :

1. It is practically painless.

2. There is only slight irritation which does not last longer than fifteen minutes.

3. The superficial nerves are very quickly destroyed so that no local anæsthetic is required, which is a great advantage when operating on the hind limb, *e.g.*, for curb.

4. After acid firing a horse can be hunted, if sound, in ten days; whereas after ordinary firing a rest of three weeks is required.

5. Marked cicatricial contraction ensues from the scars caused by the acid.

6. Blistering is not necessary afterwards, and the horse only requires to be tied up for a maximum period of twenty-four hours, after which the animal shows no inclination to rub the part.

7. Sloughing does not ensue.

Disadvantages :

1. Unsightly scars may be formed, especially if acid is allowed to run down the limb.

2. It is useless for bony enlargements.

3. It produces less deep-seated inflammation than the actual cautery, and is therefore not so effective for lesions in the depth of the tissues.

4. The method is sometimes adopted by laymen, and is an antiquated practice with the Arabs and native Indians.

There seems little or no ground for advising acid firing instead of that by the hot iron, and it is not in favour with the vast majority of veterinary surgeons, yet some owners wish to have it done.

ARTIFICIAL HYPERÆMIA

Bier's Method

This is a therapeutic measure based on nature's method of repair by the phenomena of inflammation—congestion, diapedesis, and phagocytosis. The ordinary procedure is to cause active congestion by moist heat or counter-irritation.

Bier's method is to cause venous congestion in the affected part by the application of a bandage on the proximal end of a limb or appendage sufficiently tightly to almost arrest the venous circulation without causing any obstacle to the arterial flow. Serum and leucocytes are thrown out from the capillaries and exert an antitoxic, germicidal, and anodyne effect on septic lesions.

A stout rubber bandage about 2½ inches wide may be used for the purpose. It is rolled round the limb three or four times, and so disposed that the depth of the part covered is about three times the width of the bandage. As the result of the pressure of the bandage the part below its point of application should become œdematous and perceptibly warmer than normal. When a wound is present, its walls should become hot and congested. The band should never be tight enough to cause pain to the patient. It should be possible to pass the finger fairly easily between the band and the skin. If the constriction is too tight, the animal evinces sharp pain, becomes very uneasy, and may sweat, and the part below swells quickly and is reduced in temperature.

The duration of the compression varies from four to six hours per day, and may be continued for weeks. In man it has been applied for twenty-two hours at a time in severe septic lesions. As the lesion improves, the duration of its application is gradually diminished.

Bier's treatment has been shown both in human and veterinary surgery to have a remarkably beneficial effect on septic lesions which have proved obstinate to other forms of treatment. It is a simple method well deserving of a trial in cases where it is indicated.

In regions where a ligature cannot be applied, cupping may be adopted. A glass from which the air is rarefied by the combustion of a little spirit, or a bit of cotton-wool, or by suction, is placed over the affected part, where it soon causes hyperæmia and an aspiration of serum, or pus in the case of a suppurating lesion, into the vessel. It is never applied for more than ten minutes at a time. Lemire and Ducrotoy in France and McCann in Ireland claim to have had good results from this form of treatment for septic conditions, sinuses, synovitis, etc. So far it is not much in vogue in veterinary practice.

HYDROTHERAPY

The Use of Cold Water

INDICATIONS.—Acute congestion, recent acute inflammation, septic lesions in which there is no danger of death of the tissues from diminished blood supply.

EFFECTS AND METHODS OF APPLICATION.—The normal temperature of the skin is 68° to 86° F., and the temperature of cold water varies from 46·4 to 59° F.

Cold water applied to a part produces a stimulant and sedative effect. It causes vaso-constriction in the skin and subcutaneous tissues, as well as an abstraction of heat and slowing of the process of nutrition.

An anodyne effect is produced in a painful inflammatory lesion as long as the cold application is continued. But when the duration of the latter has been momentary, a reaction sets in having effects opposite to those resulting from the cold—viz., vaso-dilatation with stimulation of local nutrition. Hydrotherapy may be in the form of baths, effusions, lotions, douches, compresses, or continuous irrigation.

The best results are obtained when the water is at a temperature of 59° F. For deep-seated lesions like sprains, water at a lower temperature may be employed, but if it is very cold, it should only be used intermittently. In veterinary practice the water is usually applied directly to the part, instead of being allowed to flow through a coil of rubber or metal tubing laid on the part.

Hot Water

INDICATIONS.—(1) Subacute and chronic inflammations. (2) Recent inflammation after the acute stage has passed. (3) Septic lesions in which the vitality of the tissues is lowered and they are threatened with death, an antiseptic liquid being used in this case.

EFFECTS OF HOT WATER.—These are:

1. *Analgesia*, by softening and relaxing the tissues.
2. *Hyperæmia* and the phenomena which accompany it—viz., exudation, interstitial infiltration, leucocytosis, and when the lesion is septic, phagocytosis.
3. *Reabsorption* of exudate.

METHODS OF APPLICATIONS comprise baths, fomentations, compresses, and poultices, ordinary and medicated (antiphlogistine). The temperature may be gradually raised from 30° to 113° F. or even 122° F. without scalding.

The hot bath is an excellent method of treating inflammatory conditions of the foot or lower part of the limb. When the lesion is septic, an antiseptic agent is added to it. It is very superior to an ordinary non-medicated poultice, which often favours sepsis.

The bath is also very beneficial for inflammation affecting the hind-quarters of the dog, including the pelvis and the abdominal organs. Fomentations and compresses are indicated when baths are not applicable.

At a temperature above 113° F. moist heat diminishes the resistance of the tissues. To have the best results, the hot applications must be frequently renewed, or the temperature of the water maintained by adding, occasionally, more hot water. Even then it is impossible to maintain a local superficial temperature equal to that of the blood. This can only be obtained by the use of the hydrothermo-regulator, which consists of a reservoir in which the water is maintained at a uniform temperature, and from which it is pumped by an electric motor or gas or oil engine into a system of small very flexible tubes disposed in variable fashion over the affected region. By this means a temperature of 107° to 113° F. may be maintained for twelve or twenty-four hours with excellent effect.

Cold and hot applications may be used alternately with good results.

DIATHERMY

Diathermy is the term applied to an improved method for the production of heat in the tissues by the passage through them of modified high-frequency electric currents.

The principle of diathermy is the use of these currents in such a manner that the passage of the current to the body is direct and unbroken. Bi-polar electrodes are employed so that the high-frequency oscillations take a definite course through the body. The current can be applied in such a way that not the smallest muscular contraction is produced through nerve stimulation. This method of employing heat has been used extensively in human surgery for the treatment of arthritis, neuralgia, skin diseases, etc.

In veterinary practice it has been used with success for paralysis in dogs, to assist the healing of wounds, and for the treatment of muscular atrophy associated with nerve injury in the horse, for gangrenous dermatitis in cattle, and for the treatment of catarrh of the genital passages in the sheep, cat, and bitch.

The current may be passed superficially or deeply through the tissues. When a deep action is required a weaker current may be employed, but must be applied for a longer time.

The patient soon becomes accustomed to the use of the current. There is a special apparatus for the production and application of these currents, and instructions are issued with it, describing its use.

Berner describes experiments made with diathermy on the skin of horses (*Z. Veterinärk.*, 46, 254 and 273).

MASSAGE

Massage comprises a series of manœuvres, including :

1. Slight friction.
2. Methodical pressure.
3. Individual compression of muscles.
4. Percussion.

1. **Slight Friction** is performed with the tips of the fingers or the flat of the hand in a centripetal direction. It causes a feeling of warmth, and has a numbing effect, after which more vigorous rubbing may be practised.

The operation disperses exudate and extravasate over a larger area, where it is acted upon by more absorbents and more rapidly removed.

2. **Methodical Pressure.**—This consists in applying firm pressure on the tissues with the pulp of the thumb, or with the fingers, or the heel of the palm, or with the closed fist, so as to act on deep-seated structures.

3. **Individual Compression of Muscles.**—A portion of muscle is seized between the fingers and thumb and manipulated from its insertion towards its origin, compressing and displacing it. It excites contraction and promotes absorption of intramuscular exudate.

4. **Percussion** consists in superficial or deep percussion of the tissues by striking the part perpendicularly with the fingers or the closed hand.

Massage is practised as far as possible in the direction of the venous and lymphatic streams. It is facilitated by smearing the part with vaseline or by using a mild liniment. The operation is usually continued for five to ten minutes at a time. In the case of joints it is associated with passive movement thereof, and with exercise.

When possible, it is advisable to apply compression with cotton-wool and a bandage to the part after massaging it to support the returning circulation and favour the process of absorption. The good effects of massage are universally recognised.

ELECTRODIAGNOSIS, ELECTROTHERAPY

Electricity is employed for the diagnosis of certain nervous and muscular lesions (electrodiagnosis), and in the treatment of different affections (electrotherapy).

Electrodiagnosis

Electricity used in this respect reveals information on the degree of contractility of muscles and on the integrity or alteration of motor nerves. To ascertain the degree of contractility of muscles, the continuous and reduced currents are employed.

It is compared with that in the muscles of a healthy subject, or, in the case of bilateral muscles, with the contractility of those on the normal side.

The positive electrode is usually placed at the level of the spinal cord in the anterior part of the dorsal region for the exploration of the muscles of the fore-limbs and in the lumbar region for the examination of the hind-limbs.

The other electrode is placed on the motor nerves or the muscles to be examined. The excitement is said to be direct when it acts on the muscle itself, and indirect when it acts on the motor nerve.

There is faradic or galvanic hyperexcitability when the muscles of the affected region contract under the action of a current whose intensity is inferior to that which is necessary to produce contraction in similar healthy muscles. There is hypoexcitability when a stronger current is required to produce contraction in the affected than in the normal muscles.

Faradic hyperexcitability and galvanic hyperexcitability usually exist simultaneously in certain lesions of the medulla and in affections which are associated with muscular contraction.

Faradic hypoexcitability denotes an alteration in the motor nerve or in the corresponding muscles, or a simultaneous affection of both. Galvanic hypoexcitability has ordinarily the same signification, but usually indicates an alteration of the motor nerves, resulting from an injury or an affection of the inferior cornua of the cord.

In certain neuromuscular conditions faradic contractility is diminished, and the shocks provoked by the galvanic current are slow or indolent (reaction of partial degeneration). In others, although the faradic contractility is abolished, the galvanic contractility is sometimes exaggerated and sometimes diminished.

The inversion of the formula of muscular contraction under the influence of the galvanic current is also an indication of degeneration. Normally the contraction which occurs at the closing of the current with the electrode placed on the muscle is greater than the contraction which follows opening or interruption of the current. In degeneration, the positive electrode gives stronger contractions than the negative.

The reaction of complete degeneration makes the prognosis very grave. It indicates profound alteration of the structure of the motor nerve. In purely myopathic paralysis there is merely diminution of galvanic and faradic excitability of the muscles.

Electrotherapy

For therapeutic purposes continuous currents (galvanisation), induced currents (faradisation), and high-frequency currents (darsonvalisation) are employed.

Continuous currents are obtained by means of piles. They may also be derived from the ordinary electric supply in cities, provided that a transformer is employed. Hand dynamos do not always supply a current of constant power or intensity. Induced currents are produced by special apparatus, by the aid of which the force of the current can be varied.

The production of high-frequency currents requires an installation comprising an induction bobbin with a condenser and a resonator. Every generator of electricity requires to have connected with it electrodes, an apparatus for current interruption, and a milliamperemeter.

The chief indications for electrotherapy are cases of paralysis and muscular atrophy. The electric treatment of paralysis of medullary or cerebral origin is not undertaken except in small animals.

Galvanic electricity is used for preference. The current should be feeble, and should not cause pain. The electrodes may be placed so that the current traverses the brain or the cord longitudinally from the forehead or from the poll towards the lumbar region, or transversely from one temple to the other, or perpendicularly from the dorso-lumbar region towards the sternum or the abdomen.

Electricity does not seem to have any curative effect on lesions of the central nervous system ; it simply counteracts certain accidents arising from these lesions, especially muscular contractions and trophic troubles.

To act on the limbs, one pole is applied on the spine at the level of the cervical or lumbar thickening of the cord and the other at the extremity of the limb. The current is applied for five to six minutes daily, or at longer intervals.

The treatment of paralysis of peripheral origin following neuritis must act on the affected nerve and on the muscles involved, whether the cause of the neuritis be traumatism or infection. It acts on the nerve to hasten its reparation, and on the muscles to prevent their atrophy.

If the muscles respond to the faradic current it is employed. The positive electrode is placed on the distended part of each of the muscles, and the negative electrode on the course of the nerve at the point of its emergence or where it is superficial. The interruptions should be fairly frequent (thirty to forty per second). The duration of the application should be three to four minutes. If the muscles do not react to the faradic current, the galvanic current is employed.

It is always an advantage to apply friction to the paralysed region with or without the use of a slight irritant.

Electricity may be used to cause penetration of the tissues by medicaments dissolved in water. By the action of the current the molecules of the agents are decomposed into two or several parts formed of atoms, called "ions," of which some charged positively descend the current, and others charged negatively ascend it. The principal substances electrolysed up to the present for therapeutic purposes are sodium chloride, salicylate of soda, iodide of potassium, quinine, zinc, and lithium. The solutions must be prepared with water recently distilled or as pure as possible. The galvanic current is employed. The electrode—positive or negative, according as the active "ion" of the medicament is negative or positive—covered with a thick layer of cotton-wool saturated with the solution, is placed on the region affected and fixed by an elastic bandage in order to ensure close contact with the skin. The other electrode is placed at a point so that the current traverses the region involved. The intensity of the current is gradually increased to a tolerable degree. The séances, lasting ten minutes to half an hour, are repeated every alternate day, provided that the integument remains unaltered.

Electrolysis of medicaments has been used with success in the treatment of different conditions (ulcers, neuralgia, neuritis, rheumatoid arthritis, and gout). The action of the current probably plays a part in bringing about a good effect.

FULGURATION

Fulguration is the employment of electric sparks or flashes, and has been recommended in the treatment of cancer. It is effected by means of high-frequency currents brought to an electrode which, placed at a certain distance from the tumour, projects on to it a series of long flashes. In this way superficial epitheliomata can be treated with success. It is sometimes used after excision of a malignant tumour to eradicate any trace of it that may have been left. Strong flashes 8 to 10 centimetres long are projected on the wound for ten, twenty, or thirty minutes.

The hæmorrhage is immediately arrested, and the surface of the wound becomes blackish-grey, then the pain disappears or diminishes, a copious flow of lymph occurs, and after a few days granulations form, followed by cicatrisation and the production of scirrhous fibrous tissue which englobes the affected part and prevents extension of the disease.

Fulguration has no effect on the cancer cells. It acts solely by the fibrous tissue which results from its effects.

RADIODIAGNOSIS AND RADIOTHERAPY

X-rays are employed for diagnostic purposes and as a therapeutic agent.

Radiodiagnosis

This method of diagnosis depends on the degree of transparency of certain bodies, organs, or lesions to X-rays, and on two properties of the latter—viz. : (1) A physical property whereby the rays which fall on a fluorescent substance sensitise it temporarily and cause it to give off its own light and form images (radioscopy) ; and (2) a chemical property whereby the rays affect photographic plates in the same way as luminous rays, so that impressions can be taken in the same way as photographs (radiography).

Radioscopy permits of the rapid examination of patients and the observation of the functioning of organs—contractions of the diaphragm, cardiac systole, movements of the ribs, etc.

In veterinary practice, both radiography and radioscopy may be employed for the diagnosis of different affections of the limbs and for the location of foreign bodies. They are particularly useful for the diagnosis of—

1. *Fractures* in the vicinity of joints, where manipulation affords uncertain information on account of swelling and separation of the fragments, and of obscure fracture of the bones of the lower parts of the limbs and of the cervical vertebræ in the horse, and of all the bones in small animals. They cannot penetrate the thick muscles of the upper part of the limbs in large animals.

2. *Dislocations*, especially of deep-seated joints like the hip in small animals.

3. *Certain affections of bones*, such as osteomyelitis, separation of the epiphyses, necrosis, and ostitis with sclerosis. In the case of a tumour in the vicinity of a bone, it enables it to be ascertained whether the latter is involved.

4. *Foreign bodies* in the digestive tract or embedded in the tissues.

Radiological examination of the thorax in small animals may be employed to reveal the existence of pleuritic effusion, or of a tumour or inflammatory lesions in the lungs (abscess, consolidation, tuberculosis).

Cinemato-radiography, which has given some interesting results from the point of view of physiology, has not yet been extensively employed for clinical purposes.

The operator requires to protect himself against the injurious action of the X-rays by the use of gloves and of spectacles impervious to these rays.

Radiotherapy

For cutaneous affections, rays of medium penetrating power are employed, while for deep-seated lesions those of great penetrating power are necessary.

Two days are generally allowed to elapse between the applications of this treatment, whose duration varies from a few minutes to half an hour. It is advisable, after adopting the treatment for a while, to suspend it for about a week. Skill and experience are necessary for the operation of X-rays, otherwise serious accidents may happen (erythema, dermatitis, sloughing, falling of the hair and of the nails). By placing a thin metallic plate on the skin, the rays of feeble penetrating power, which cause inflammation of the skin, are arrested, and the penetrating capacity of the other rays is intensified.

Radiotherapy has been used with a certain amount of success in the treatment of neuralgia, neuritis, and pruritus caused by different skin affections, on which it acts by virtue of the analgesic properties of the rays. Their irritant effect is made use of for different lesions of the skin and the superficial tissues (dermatomycosis, ulcers, and malignant muco-cutaneous conditions).

Ringworm and other parasitic conditions of the skin are rapidly cured by X-ray treatment. These rays have a specific action on the cells of neoplasms, which they destroy, whilst leaving the normal tissue intact. Their effects, however, are very superficial, not penetrating beyond a depth of 2 millimetres from the surface.

Coolidge, an American scientist, has invented an ampoule superior to that of Röntgen for the application of X-rays for diagnostic and therapeutic purposes, enabling the quality and quantity of the rays to be easily varied. It emits rays of great penetrating action whose effects are similar to the γ-rays of radium, and which may be used successfully for deep radiotherapy.

RADIUM THERAPY

Radium is related to barium, and belongs to the group of substances known as " radio-active." It is a metal whose salts have been extracted from different minerals, where they are mixed in infinitely small quantity with the corresponding salts of barium.

The chloride and bromide of pure radium, as well as the same compounds of barium, more or less rich in radium, have been used as therapeutic agents, constantly giving off light and heat at the same time as they emit rays comparable to those from the X-ray ampoules.

From the point of view of their biological and therapeutic action, a distinction must be made between the emission of rays and the emanation of gas from the salts of radium. The latter, which can be isolated and collected, is very injurious; mixed with a certain proportion of the inspired air, it causes rapid death in small animals. Hence for therapeutic purposes the salts of radium have been used enclosed in small glass, ebony, or metal receptacles, whose wall arrests the emanation of gas while remaining more or less permeable to the rays.

Although differing in their inherent qualities, the rays emitted by radium and the X-rays produce similar effects. The radium rays are composed of three kinds of rays, designated by the letters α, β, γ. The α-rays, positively electrified, are only slightly penetrating, and are almost completely absorbed and suppressed by the wall of the receptacle containing the radio-active salt. The γ-rays, non-electrified, are much more penetrating than the β-rays, and traverse the wall unbroken; they are vibratory rays, bearing most resemblance to X-rays, but possessing a greater penetrating power than the latter. But the α-rays constitute the strongest part of all the rays emitted, and the proportion of them absorbed is considerable.

It is therefore important to distinguish between the real or potential activity of a given quantity of radium salt free of covering and the degree of activity of the same quantity of the salt enclosed in a container.

The activity of the salts of radium or of barium is calculated by taking for unity that of metallic uranium. It is estimated that the activity of the salts of radium is two million times greater than that of uranium.

Up to the present radium therapy has been practised according to two methods—viz., by the use of composite or global rays and of ultra-penetrating rays. In the former case all the rays of radium come into play except those which are absorbed by the protective covering of the apparatus. This method is chiefly suitable for the treatment of superficial lesions.

In the latter case the rays are filtered through different metals (lead, silver, gold, platinum), whereby about 98 per cent. of them are suppressed.

The application of this method is inoffensive for most normal tissues, even when it is prolonged for twenty-four hours to several days, and it exercises a curative effect on neoplasms and other lesions situated beneath the skin.

Like the X-rays, those of radium possess an analgesic and an irritant action, whose therapeutic applications have been employed for the same affections as those treated by the Röntgen rays. They have been used successfully in the treatment of neuralgia, neuritis, and pruritus due to skin lesions.

It is usual to employ at first rays of feeble intensity, and if they are not effective, ultra-penetrating rays may be employed. In many cases the pain disappears after five or six séances of three to four minutes each.

Their good effect has also been observed in the cure of different affections of the skin and mucous membranes, including progressive lesions like cancer and lupus. They have the advantage that they can be applied in regions where the X-rays could not be used without danger—for example, on certain parts of the face. Moreover, they can be utilised in the interior of cavities (mouth, pharynx, larynx), where it would be difficult or impossible to introduce the ampoules, and may effect a cure there of circumscribed superficial lesions. The action of radium on cancerous lesions is the same as that of the X-rays. It has an elective action on the cancer cells.

An exhaustive treatise on the uses of electricity, X-rays, and radium in veterinary surgery would occupy too much space in a handbook of this kind, and readers anxious for more complete information thereon should consult the current literature devoted thereto, including Hamilton Kirk's articles in his ***Index of Treatment*** on Actino-Therapy, Electro-Therapy, Diathermy, etc.

CHAPTER II

OPERATIONS

OPERATIONS ON THE HEAD AND NECK

1. Opening the Nasal Chambers : Horse

INDICATIONS.—Exploration ; removal of tumours, necrotic turbinated bone, or foreign bodies ; to raise a depressed fragment of bone.

CONTROL.—The operation may be done standing with the aid of local anæsthesia, but it is generally more satisfactory to have the horse cast on the opposite side, with a pillow of hay under the head so placed that the nose will be at a lower level than the poll, to enable blood to escape from the nostrils instead of going back through the posterior nares.

SITES.—1. The outer border of the nasal bone in front of its junction with the premaxilla and extending downwards for a distance of 3 or 4 inches.

2. At a point higher than No. 1, anywhere to one side of the mesial suture between the two nasal bones.

PROCEDURE.—*Site No.* 1.—Make an incision, hugging the nasal bone, going through the skin and subcutaneous tissue into the nasal chamber to the inner side of the false nostril.

Site No. 2.—Remove a disc-shaped piece of skin corresponding in diameter to that of the crown of the trephine. Scrape away the periosteum from the exposed portion of the bone with a curette. Have the centre piece of the trephine projecting slightly beyond the level of its edge, place its point in the centre of the bone, and make it penetrate therein. Work the instrument with a to-and-fro or continuous rotary movement until the resistance is overcome. The isolated disc of bone usually comes away within the trephine when the latter is lifted. If not, prize it up with the point of one of the jaws of the bone forceps and take it away. Should it fall into the chamber, remove it with a forceps. Do not exert much pressure on the trephine or allow it to enter deeper than the nasal bone, otherwise the turbinated bone which lies at a short distance beneath it may be injured and give rise to profuse hæmorrhage.

If necessary, two or more openings may be made at a tangent one above the other, and the intervening spicules of bone broken down with a bone forceps, or after making one trephine opening it may be enlarged by cutting away from its border successive pieces of bone with the bone forceps. The latter is probably the better procedure, being more gradual.

Hæmorrhage is always fairly profuse, and it may be necessary to plug the nasal chamber as follows: Tie a piece of tape to a pledget of cotton-wool, push the wool up the nasal passage to a point above where the bleeding is taking place, and then, holding the string taut,

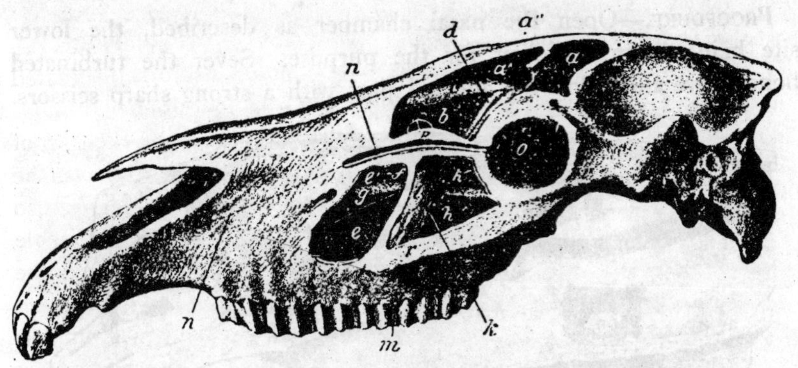

FIG. 86.—LATERAL VIEW OF HORSE'S SKULL: THE FACIAL SINUSES EXPOSED.

a, Posterior portion of frontal sinus; *a'*, anterior portion of same; *a"*, the septum dividing them; *b*, posterior portion of the anterior turbinated bone; *c*, cavity of nostril; *d*, ethmoid bone; *e*, superior maxillary sinus (lower part), which is divided from the upper part *h*, *h* by the thin septum *i*; *e'*, bony plate forming the lateral boundary of the posterior turbinated bone *f*; *g*, infra-orbital canal; *k*, line dividing the upper (thin) from the lower (thick) portion of the septum; *m*, lower margin of the maxillary sinus; *n*, nasal duct; *o*, orbit; *p*, zygomatic ridge.

push in more cotton-wool, or preferably gauze, until the cavity is tightly packed. The protruding string may be tied to the nose-band of the head-collar. Remove the plug the following day, taking care that no wool is left in the nose, and gently irrigate the chamber with a mild antiseptic solution. Continue the irrigation daily until the discharge from the nose has almost ceased.

The artificial opening is kept patent by a plug of gauze until the interior of the cavity assumes a healthy condition.

RESULT.—Usually successful, except when performed for malignant disease, when failure is the rule, owing to the disease not being eradicated. The procedure is similar in the ox.

The Dog

CONTROL.—Fix the dog in the ventral position on the table. Local or general anæsthesia may be adopted.

SITE.—Immediately in front of a perpendicular let fall from the inner canthus of the eye to the median line, and quite close to the latter.

PROCEDURE is similar to that in the horse. A small trephine is used. The opening can be enlarged by clipping off pieces of bone with the bone forceps.

2. Removal of Necrotic Turbinated Bone

PROCEDURE.—Open the nasal chamber as described, the lower site being often sufficient for the purpose. Sever the turbinated bone above and below the affected part with a strong sharp scissors.

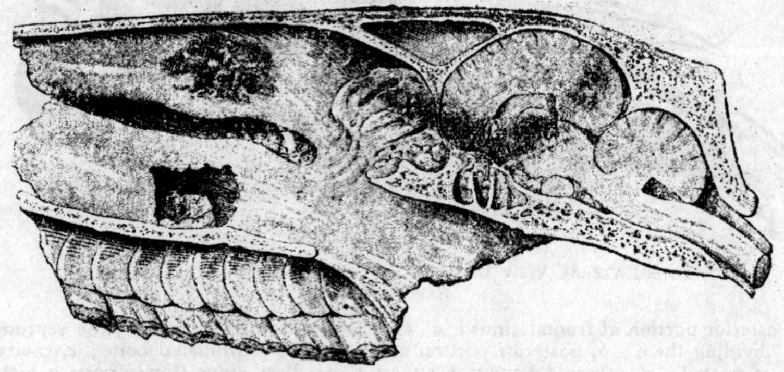

FIG. 87.—NECROSIS OF THE TURBINATED BONES.

Seize the intervening portion with a sharp-pronged retractor, separate it from its attachment, and take it away. Make sure that all the diseased bone is removed.

AFTER-TREATMENT as described in No. 1. Iodoform powder or a mixture of it and boric acid may be insufflated into the affected region once daily as a further antiseptic precaution.

RESULT.—Usually good, the wound healing within a month and the desired effect being obtained.

3. Opening the Facial Sinuses : Horse

INDICATIONS.—Exploration ; pus, a tumour or a cyst in the sinus ; a dental fistula opening therein ; to raise a depressed fragment of bone.

CONTROL.—Merely opening the sinus can be done in most cases in the standing position under the influence of local anæsthesia, but when an important operation is to be performed, the horse must be cast on the opposite side and the head placed on a pillow, as in No. 1.

Frontal Sinus—SITE No. 1.—Take a line joining the middle parts of the roots of the supra-orbital processes, bisect it, and operate in the inferior angle of intersection, or say ½ inch below and to one side of this point. Avoid operating higher for fear of entering the cranial cavity.

SITE No. 2.—The midway point of a line joining the nasal canthus and the mesial suture.

SITE No. 3.—Take a line joining the nasal canthus and the junction of the nasal and premaxillary bones and operate 2½ inches down and 1 inch in front of this line (Craig). This is the lowest part of the sinus when the head is vertical.

Superior Maxillary Sinus—SITE.—About 1½ inches upwards (head vertical) from the lower end of the zygomatic ridge and 1 inch inwards. In the young horse it is well to go a little more upwards to avoid wounding the alveoli of the molar teeth, which are nearer to the surface during youth.

Inferior Maxillary Sinus—SITE.—About 1 inch inwards from the lower end of the zygomatic ridge.

PROCEDURE.—Trephine the bone in the same manner as in No. 1. To extirpate a tumour it may be necessary to remove a large amount of bone. Should a breach consequently remain in the sinus, it may be covered by a piece of leather attached to the bridle.

In a case of pus in the sinuses, the usual procedure is to open the frontal sinus towards its upper part at site No. 1 or No. 2, and the inferior maxillary sinus, and break down the septum between the latter and the superior maxillary sinus, thereby draining all the sinuses and permitting them to be flushed out from above.

In many cases the septum is already removed by necrosis of the piece of bone. When the cavity contains large masses of inspissated pus and pieces of necrotic bone separated from its lining, the lower opening must be made sufficiently large to allow of their complete removal.

There should be sufficient room above and below to admit the finger easily for the purpose of recognising loose pieces of bone. The interior of the sinus may be illuminated by a small electric torch passed in through one of the openings.

On making a cross-section of a skull through the facial sinuses, it will be seen that when the head is horizontal the inferior maxillary sinus is on a higher plane than the superior maxillary sinus, so that the opening in the former does not drain the latter in this position. Nevertheless, the above operation is usually sufficient to effect a cure provided that no necrotic centre is left in the sinus. To obtain more efficient drainage, an opening must be made into the nasal chamber through one of the turbinated bones.

In the case of the frontal sinus the opening is made through the anterior turbinated bone at the level of the lowest part of the cavity next the median line. Locate this spot from the interior of the sinus and then trephine the frontal bone at its level. Through the latter opening make an orifice in the turbinated bone by pushing a blunt instrument through it into the nasal chamber.

To find the exact point at which to puncture the turbinated bone, pass a slightly curved sound or catheter up the nose and operate at the point where it can be felt with the finger inserted into the bottom of the sinus. An alternative method is to trephine the roof of the nasal chamber at its upper extremity and break through the turbinated bone at this point.

With regard to the inferior maxillary sinus, the opening is made through the posterior turbinated bone at the level of the most dependent part of the median compartment of the cavity by thrusting a blunt instrument through it from the sinus. The orifice in the turbinated bone is kept patent by a strip of gauze passed through it and through the sinus and nostril, and fixed in position by tying its two ends. To introduce the gauze, fix it by a couple of hitches to a gum-elastic catheter after passing the latter from the sinus out through the nasal orifice. Renew this seton daily for several days until drainage is no longer required. A hole may be drilled in the solid bone forming the partition between the nasal chamber and the lowest part of the inferior maxillary sinus by means of a special drill. The writer found this latter procedure successful for a thoroughbred yearling with a unilateral congenital accumulation of serous fluid in the sinuses which had no communication with the nasal chamber. The condition did not recur, and the animal became a successful racehorse.

Having completed the operation for empyema of the sinuses, flush them out thoroughly, first with boiled water until it comes out clear, and afterwards with an antiseptic lotion such as potass. permanganate 1 in 1,000, or hydrogen peroxide 1 in 4, or chinosol 1 in 1,000. Hydrogen peroxide is an excellent detergent for the purpose of cleaning out the cavities. Take care not to inject the liquid forcibly, for fear of its entering the larynx and setting up pneumonia, and for the same reason keep the poll well raised during the process.

A good way to irrigate the sinuses is by means of a piece of rubber tubing and a funnel. Antiseptic powder may be insufflated into the sinus through a piece of hose-piping. As a precaution against asphyxia during the operation, some authorities insert a tracheotomy tube before commencing the procedure, but when the head is kept in a proper position this is not necessary.

The openings in the sinus must be kept patent by pledgets of gauze or by pieces of stout rubber tubing inserted through them until the discharge ceases and the offensive odour disappears. The lower orifice should be kept open longer than the upper one.

RESULT.—Usually good, provided that a malignant disease is not present. Cure is generally effected within one month after the operation. Occasionally empyema recurs owing to some necrotic centre remaining in the sinus.

4. Operation for Cystic Condition of the Sinuses: Horses

Occasionally a condition is met with in yearlings in which the facial sinuses on one side of the head are distended with a yellowish non-purulent fluid apparently secreted by the lining of the cavities after the manner of a cyst. There is no nasal discharge, due to closure or absence of the orifice between the maxillary sinus and the nasal chamber. It is a question whether the absence of this opening is the cause or the effect of the cystic condition.

PROCEDURE consists in opening the sinuses as described, evacuating the contents, and making an orifice for permanent drainage through the posterior turbinated bone from the inferior maxillary sinus.

It is advisable to irrigate the cavities for a while with pure tincture of iodine with the object of destroying the secretive power of the lining, assuming that it is of the nature of that of a cyst. Afterwards the use of an astringent lotion is indicated, such as sulphate of zinc in 2 per cent. solution.

RESULT.—Usually good, on the condition that the treatment is continued until the lining assumes a granulating appearance and that a permanent orifice has been made into the nose. Otherwise the condition will recur. Occasionally after trephining the nasal chamber or facial sinus the orifice, when large, refuses to close completely, but it may be made to do so by an autoplastic operation (see p. 245, "Autoplastia").

The Ox

INDICATIONS.—The same as in the horse.

CONTROL.—The operation may be done in the standing or cast position.

Frontal Sinus—SITE NO. 1.—Through the horn about ½ inch above its base, thereby opening the continuation of the sinus into the horn core.

SITE NO. 2.—On a line corresponding to the prolongation of the horn core and about ¾ inch to the inner side of the base of the horn.

SITE NO. 3.—Above a line joining the upper parts of the orbital cavities and immediately on the inner side of the supra-orbital fissure.

The operator should make himself familiar with the disposition of this sinus in the dry skull to avoid the risk of penetrating the brain during the operation.

PROCEDURE is the same as in the horse.

Maxillary Sinus.—The maxillary sinus is single, and does not communicate with the frontal sinus, the latter being drained by several openings into the nasal cavity and the former communicating with the nasal chamber by a slit-like opening.

SITE.—Immediately above the maxillary protuberance in adults, and a width of one or two fingers higher in young subjects.

PROCEDURE.—As in the horse.

In the case of closure of the opening from the sinus into the nose leading to an accumulation of liquid in the former, it will be necessary to make an orifice through the internal wall of the cavity into the nasal chamber.

The Dog

The frontal sinus can be trephined by the landmarks mentioned for the upper site in the horse and for similar conditions.

Maxillary Sinus or Antrum.—This is a small cavity into which projects the alveolus of the fourth upper molar tooth.

INDICATION.—Pus in the antrum, recognised by a fistula therefrom on the face at the level of the root of the fourth upper molar tooth.

PROCEDURE.—The best way to drain the cavity is to extract the tooth mentioned, whose root is usually diseased and the cause of the trouble. Recovery then ensues.

5. Dehorning of Cattle

INDICATIONS.—To enhance the selling value by improving the apparent quality of the beast for fattening, to render it safe to feed cattle loose in straw yards, and when a horn is irreparably injured or affected with an incurable disease.

CONTROL.—The operation can be done painlessly by the injection of a local anæsthetic as follows: Locate the nerve supplying the horn, viz. a branch of the lachrymal running upwards (head vertical) on the temporal muscle close behind the lateral border of the frontal bone, which can be palpated as a bony ridge extending from the orbit to the middle of the base of the horn. Insert the needle immediately behind this ridge about 2·5 centimetres below the horn to a depth of not more than one centimetre, that is almost subcutaneously, thus following the

FIG. 88.—PERINEURAL INJECTION OF THE NERVE TO THE HORN CORE IN THE OX.

directions of Professor T. G. Browne (Dublin), who introduced the procedure from America, where it was first practised by Emmerson. Professor Browne demonstrated its efficacy on many occasions in Great Britain and Ireland and stressed the importance of avoiding deep insertion of the needle, whereby the injection would be made beneath the aponeurosis covering the temporal muscle and thus fail to reach the nerve. In big cattle with massive horns he advises the use of a a second injection about one centimetre behind the first to act on the posterior divisions of the nerve.

PROCEDURE.—Apply the bull-holder in the nose with a rope attached, let one man pull the head well forward by means of the rope, while another twists the head in order to permit the horn shears to be held level by the operator when severing the horn. The second helper stands at the side and reaches under the animal's throat to grasp a horn or ear, and thereby keep the head twisted in the right position. Apply the shears close to the skull so that about an inch of skin will be removed with the horn. When done in this manner the main artery in the stump can be identified and secured with an artery forceps. Rubber bands made from motor tyre tubes may be applied round the horn stumps and poll, if necessary, to arrest hæmorrhage.

Using general anæsthesia it is best to administer chloroform in the standing position, giving a comparatively large dose, so that the animal will quickly stagger and fall, or be easily thrown, and allow the whole procedure to be completed within five minutes.

Other instruments that may be used for the operation instead of the long-handled shears, which is the most convenient, are a fine sharp saw, or a guillotine knife which is made to cut rapidly through the horn by vigorously turning a handle. The use of the saw favours hæmostasis.

There is always considerable hæmorrhage. When the mouth of the bleeding vessel can be seen the latter should be grasped with an artery forceps and twisted or ligatured. As a rule the hæmorrhage soon stops spontaneously. Exceptionally it persists long after the operation, or recurs at a variable time afterwards, and if measures are not taken to arrest it death may ensue. The application of tinct. benzoin Co. has some hæmostatic effect.

After-treatment consists in putting the animals in a field by themselves, and, in summer, applying Archangel tar on the wounds as an antiseptic and a protection against flies.

A possible complication of the operation is the formation of pus in the frontal sinus due to the presence of blood therein and the entrance of infection through the stump of the horn. W. B. Quarmby (*Vet. Rec.*, Sept. 4th, 1948), dealing with the operation of dehorning, describes the application of a tourniquet in the form of binder twine (A) applied round the bases of the horns by means of a clove-hitch and a piece of cord passed beneath the anterior and posterior parts of the hitch near the base of each horn and tied on top (B and C). The tourniquet is left in position for 24 hours after the dehorning operation. There is only slight hæmorrhage (Fig. 89).

N. F. Pollock (*Vet. Rec.*, Sept. 4th, 1948) gives an interesting description of the operation of dehorning of cows and heifers. A rope round the horns is used to draw the animal close to a post, around which the rope is wound twice and then brought round the horns again and given to a man to hold. The muzzle is then put on over both jaws and chloroform is administered with a commencing dose of $1\frac{1}{2}$ ounces. In one to two minutes the beast goes down, the rope being eased if necessary. In this way, with plenty of help, 22 heifers were dehorned in 1½ hours.

PREVENTION OF THE GROWTH OF HORNS.—This may be effected by (1) applying a caustic—usually caustic potash—to the horn end. This is not very satisfactory. J. E. Guthrie (*J. Amer. Vet. Med. Ass.*) reports excellent results on 47 calves by the use of antimony trichloride 28 per cent., salicylic acid 7 per cent., flexile collodion 65 per cent. It was effective in calves aged one to fourteen days. N. F. Pollock (*Vet. Rec.*, Sept. 4th, 1948) corroborated this in the case of shorthorn calves in Norfolk, and says that when the calves are over fourteen days it is necessary to slice the apex of the bud before applying the lotion

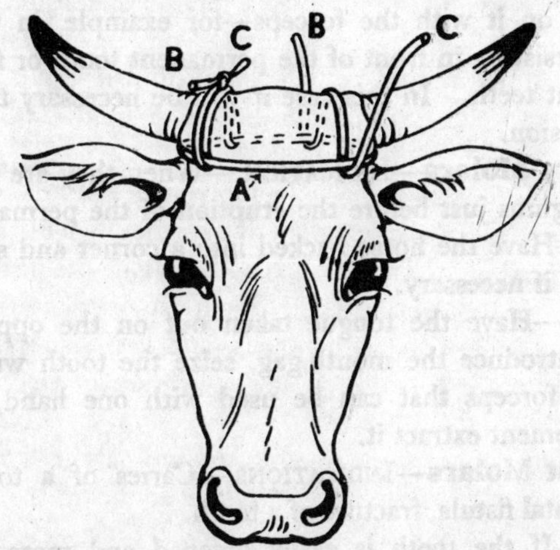

FIG. 89.—QUARMBY'S DEHORNING TOURNIQUET.

(2) using the Cooper Stewart "Hornmaster," an electric apparatus which can be worked off any mains point or from a 12-volt battery. It is quick, humane, and effective in action.

6. Extraction of Teeth : Horse

Temporary Incisors—INDICATIONS.—When the temporary incisors are irritating the gum by remaining *in situ* immediately before the eruption of the permanent teeth, or when they are in an abnormal position interfering with mastication.

PROCEDURE.—Back the horse into a corner or stall, have the tongue held out at one side of the mouth, seize the tooth with a small tooth forceps and wrench it away. When the temporary tooth is in an abnormal situation, and when the permanent tooth does not come up in its track, the milk tooth is firmly fixed in position, and must be dealt with as a permanent one.

Permanent Incisors—INDICATIONS.—When loosened as the result of an injury and there is no chance of their becoming fixed again, or when in an abnormal situation and interfering with mastication.

CONTROL.—If it is possible to grasp the tooth with a forceps, have the horse controlled as in the last case, with the addition, perhaps, of a twitch.

PROCEDURE.—Grasp the tooth as close to the gum as possible with a stout forceps, and, pulling vigorously parallel to its direction with a slight torsion motion, extract it.

Frequently the tooth is in such a position that it is impossible to get a grip on it with the forceps—for example, in the case of a milk tooth persisting in front of the permanent tooth or fixed between two permanent teeth. In this case it will be necessary to remove the tooth by repulsion.

Temporary Molars—INDICATION.—When they are shell-like and irritating the gums just before the eruption of the permanent teeth.

CONTROL.—Have the horse backed into a corner and securely held, using a twitch if necessary.

PROCEDURE.—Have the tongue taken out on the opposite side of the mouth, introduce the mouth gag, seize the tooth with a suitable long-handled forceps that can be used with one hand, and with a vigorous movement extract it.

Permanent Molars—INDICATIONS.—Caries of a tooth, alveolar periostitis, dental fistula, fracture of a tooth.

CONTROL.—If the tooth is easily grasped and more or less loose in its alveolus, it may be extracted in the standing position with the horse securely held in a corner or stall or fixed in stocks, but generally it is necessary, or at least more satisfactory, to have the horse cast on the opposite side and chloroform administered, although the latter is not always necessary.

PROCEDURE.—It must be remembered that the roots of the posterior molars are directed upwards (head horizontal) and slightly backwards, and the anterior ones upwards and slightly forwards, and that as the teeth are extracted by leverage parallel to the direction of their roots, a lever of the first order is consequently indicated for the posterior molars, and a lever of the second order for the anterior molars.

Having the horse in the lateral position when cast, turn the nose upwards so that the head is resting on the poll, have the tongue drawn out on the opposite side of the mouth, insert the gag and have it fixed, or held securely by an assistant.

Recognise the affected tooth and make sure of it before applying the forceps. Introduce the latter and grasp the tooth close to the gums. Fix the jaws of the forceps tightly on the tooth by turning the

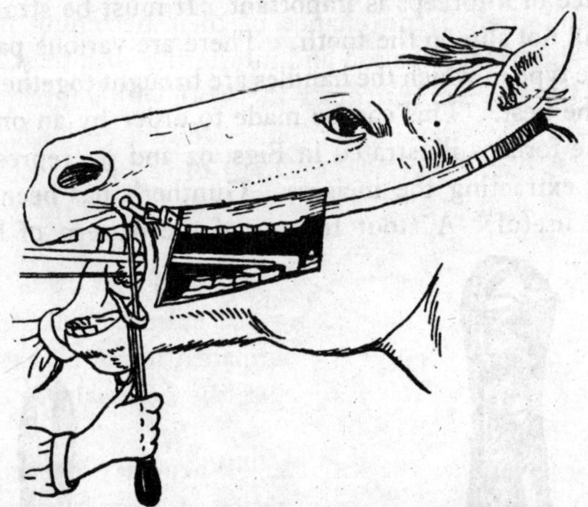

Fig. 90.—Extraction of Inferior Molar Teeth. Forceps Applied with Fulcrum beneath it.

screw between its handles. Loosen the tooth by restricted side-to-side movements of the instrument and by a seesaw movement of the crossbar between the handles; then introduce a square block of wood about

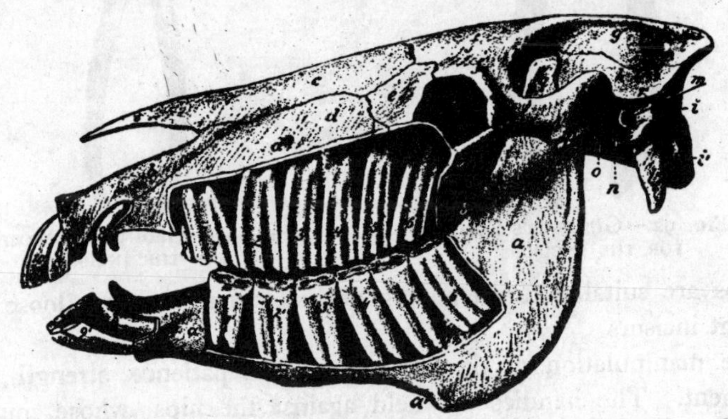

Fig. 91.—Showing the Incisor and Molar Teeth of a Six-Year-Old Horse in Position.

½ inch thick and 2 inches square in a metal frame, continuous with and at right angles to the metal handle as close to the jaws of the forceps as possible, and, using it as a fulcrum, lever the tooth out of the alveolus. This procedure is suitable for a posterior molar, but not so well adapted for an anterior one, for the reason mentioned above. Nevertheless, it usually answers the purpose in the latter case. Once a tooth has been loosened by careful movements, it may be extracted by slight leverage of any kind, or even by direct traction.

The choice of a forceps is important. It must be strong, and made so that it will not slip on the tooth. There are various patterns on the market—the type in which the handles are brought together and fixed by a screw is the best. This can be made to order by an ordinary blacksmith. The forceps illustrated in Figs. 92 and 93 represent the type suitable for extracting the incisors. Günther's has been described as particularly useful. A stout forceps of the pattern of human molar

FIG. 92.—GÜNTHER'S FORCEPS FOR THE INCISORS.

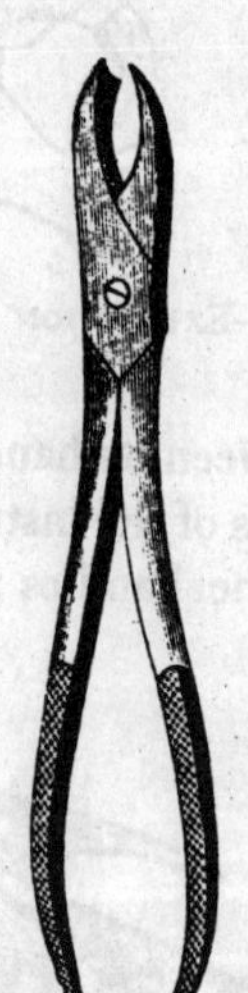

FIG. 93.—ORDINARY FORCEPS FOR THE INCISORS.

forceps are suitable for removing persistent temporary or loose permanent incisors.

The manipulation of the forceps requires patience, strength, and judgment. The handles are held against the hips, whose muscles are utilised to exert the necessary force. Should the patient not be anæsthetised and make violent head movements, they must be followed with the instrument, which, if held rigidly, might fracture the jaw. In a case of alveolar periostitis, the operation is usually easy owing to the tooth being more or less loosened by the disease and its root being generally fairly short, due to the fact that the condition is most common in old horses.

To extract a molar tooth from a sound alveolus in a young horse is almost an impossible task, and if there is an odontoma situated on its root, the operation cannot be performed without causing a fracture of the alveolar walls. Mr. Robert Mitchell, M.R.C.V.S., Sauchiehall Street, Glasgow, has made and can provide a molar tooth extractor for the horse in the form of two strong sharp-edged concave jaws worked on a stout steel rod with a cross-bar handle, for which he claims these advantages :

1. It is operated on quite a new principle and it is outstanding in efficiency
2. When in use there is less bulk of iron in the mouth than with ordinary forceps.

The Ox

INDICATIONS.—The same as in the horse, but they are seldom present.

The operation is carried out in the same manner as in the horse.

The Dog

Temporary Incisors and Canines—INDICATIONS.—When persisting after eruption of the permanent teeth. It is the canines which persist most frequently.

PROCEDURE.—Anæsthesia is unnecessary. Grasp the tooth close to the gum with a suitable forceps, as used in the human subject, and apply traction parallel to the direction of the tooth.

Permanent Teeth—INDICATIONS.—The chief indication for extraction of the permanent teeth, whether incisors, canines, or molars, is alveolar periostitis.

In a case of pus in the antrum, it is necessary to extract the corresponding carnassial tooth.

CONTROL.—General anæsthesia is always desirable when a number of teeth are to be removed or a tooth is firmly fixed in its alveolus. Apart from nullifying pain it keeps the patient quiet. Pentothal sodium is very suitable for the purpose. A vicious dog may be put under the influence of morphia, and thereby be easily controlled. A small dog may be held by an assistant, but a big dog requires to be fixed in the ventral position on the table.

PROCEDURE.—Have the small dog's mouth kept open by two pieces of tape, and that of the large dog by a mouth speculum. Seize the affected tooth close to the gum, and apply traction, combined with a restricted rotary movement, parallel to its long axis. It is only extraction of the carnassial tooth for pus in the antrum that much force is required, the teeth being loose when affected with alveolar periostitis. The extraction of a sound molar or carnassial tooth is almost impossible without fracturing the tooth.

The procedure in the cat is similar to that in the small dog, except that it is generally necessary to have the former fixed on the table.

Regional Dental Anæsthesia in the Dog

INDICATIONS.—(1) *Infra-orbital nerve block.* Any operation on the upper teeth or jaw. (2) *Inferior alveolar nerve block* for tooth operations and for treatment of fractures (wiring, etc.) in the lower jaw.

(1) *Infra-orbital nerve.*—Use a dental or a "Record" syringe with a fine needle about one inch long and with an internal diameter 0·5 to 1·0 millimetre, insert it for a distance of about ½ centimetre along the

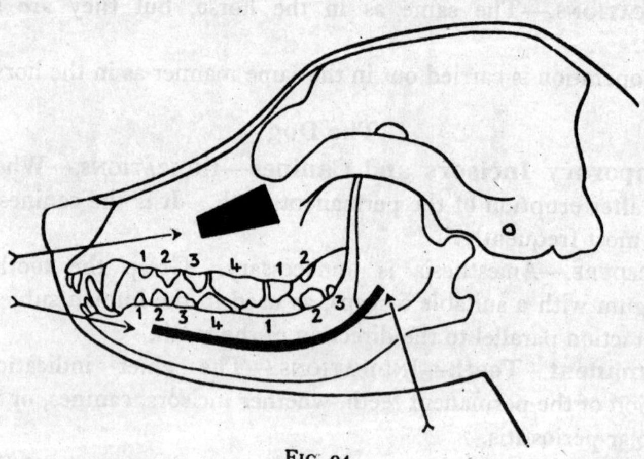

FIG. 94.

ventral part of the canal, *i.e.*, below the nerve, having first made an insensible wheal under the oral mucous membrane. The anæsthesia thus induced should suffice for the extraction of any tooth anterior to and including the carnassial.

(2) *The inferior alveolar nerves.*—The mental foramen can be reached either through the skin or through the mucous membrane, but as it is doubtful whether the whole mandible arcade can be anæsthetised through this site Frank recommends injecting the anæsthetic at the proximal extremity of the mandibular canal, *i.e.*, above the concavity in the lower border of the hinder end of the horizontal ramus, which can be felt from pressure of the finger-tip along the free border of the lower jaw close to the masseter muscle. Use a straight needle about 1½ inches long and one millimetre in diameter and insert it close along

the inner surface of the mandible at the level just mentioned, penetrating to a distance equal to one-half of the vertical height of the ramus measured at the level of the lower carnassial tooth.

When the inferior alveolar nerve is blocked at the point of entry into the mandibular canal all the teeth of the lower jaw in addition to the lower lip and chin can be anæsthetised. To obtain proficiency in practising dental anæsthesia the clinician should make himself familiar

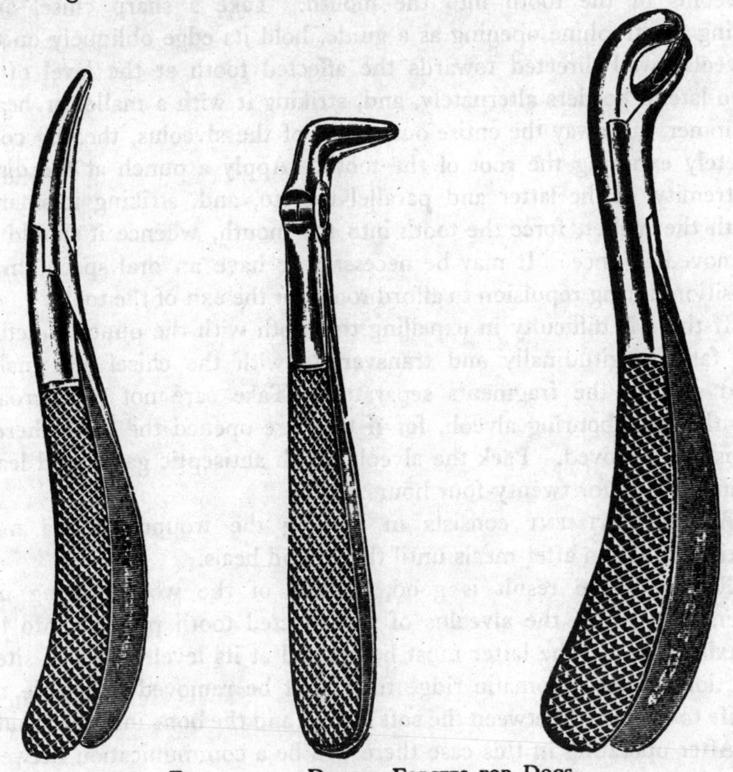

FIGS. 95–97.—DENTAL FORCEPS FOR DOGS.

with the surgical anatomy of the dog's skull and thus be able to make out for himself the correct sites for blocking the nerves in question. (The foregoing is taken from an article by J. T. Edwards in *Vet. Rec.* May 21st, 1932.)

7. Repulsion of Teeth

Repulsion of a tooth is indicated when its removal is necessary and extraction is impracticable owing to the crown being absent or too small to grasp with the forceps, or to the tooth being too firmly fixed in the alveolus or having an odontoma on its root.

Horse

CONTROL.—Cast on the opposite side and have the head resting on a pillow of hay. Administer a general anæsthetic.

PROCEDURE.—Remove a disc of skin at the level of the free extremity of the root of the tooth. Trephine the bone at the same place, exposing the dental fang. Separate the soft tissues from the bone over the alveolus of the tooth into the mouth. Take a sharp chisel and, using the trephine opening as a guide, hold its edge obliquely on the alveolar wall directed towards the affected tooth at the level of its two lateral borders alternately, and, striking it with a mallet or heavy hammer, cut away the entire outer wall of the alveolus, thereby completely exposing the root of the tooth. Apply a punch at the distal extremity of the latter and parallel thereto, and, striking it smartly with the mallet, force the tooth into the mouth, whence it should be removed at once. It may be necessary to have an oral speculum in position during repulsion to afford room for the exit of the tooth.

If there is difficulty in expelling the tooth with the punch, fracture its fang longitudinally and transversely with the chisel and mallet and remove the fragments separately. Take care not to encroach on the neighbouring alveoli, for if they are opened the teeth therein must be removed. Pack the alveolus with antiseptic gauze and leave it in position for twenty-four hours.

AFTER-TREATMENT consists in bathing the wound with a mild antiseptic lotion after meals until the wound heals.

RESULT.—The result is good, healing of the wound being uneventful. When the alveolus of the affected tooth projects into the maxillary sinus, the latter must be opened at its level. At this site a portion of the zygomatic ridge must first be removed to enable the knife to be passed between the soft tissues and the bone into the mouth.

After operating in this case there will be a communication between the mouth and the sinus, and it will be necessary to keep the alveolus plugged with gauze to prevent food material accumulating in the latter until the passage gradually closes.

Occasionally closure fails to occur, and then the patent alveolus must be occluded with gutta-percha, thus: Having cleaned out the sinus, take some gutta-percha, soften it by immersion in hot water, and by means of the fingers of one hand in the sinus and those of the other in the mouth press the gutta-percha into position, spreading it above and below, so that it will not fall out. It will remain *in situ* for years, having the desired effect and causing no inconvenience.

The foregoing procedure applies to all the teeth in the various animals, except that in connection with the incisors in the horse and any of the teeth in the dog the use of the trephine is not required. Moreover, in the case of the horse's incisors and the dog's canines it is unnecessary to go through the skin, it being sufficient to raise the lip, separate the gum from the bone, and then chip away the alveolar wall with the chisel and mallet. Repulsion is the only method that will succeed in taking out sound permanent canine teeth in the dog. When the outer wall of the alveolus has been removed the tooth can be easily extracted with the forceps. The operation is sometimes indicated to make a vicious animal less dangerous.

COMPLICATIONS.—The dangers of operating by repulsion are:

1. *Complete Fracture of the Jaw.*—This is more likely to happen in the inferior maxilla. It is avoided by cautious use of the chisel and punch, taking care not to strike them violently or drive them too far at a time.

2. *Alveolar Periostitis* ensuing in a neighbouring alveolus, due to the latter being accidentally opened during the operation. This accident is avoided by cutting the bone towards the affected tooth, and taking care not to drive the chisel or punch between the tooth and alveolar wall when expelling the former.

8. Extirpation of the Eyeball

INDICATIONS.—Irreparable injury, panophthalmia, malignant disease.

CONTROL.—General anæsthesia is necessary. Hence have the horse cast on the opposite side and the dog fixed in the ventral position.

PROCEDURE—*Method No.* 1.—After bathing the eye with a suitable lotion, take up a fold of conjunctiva with the dressing forceps at the periphery of the cornea and incise it all round the latter. Insert a sharp knife through the incision between the eyeball and the orbital rim at the nasal or temporal canthus, and, encircling the organ, sever all the oblique and straight muscles of the eyeball. Insert a curved scissors behind the orbit and cut through the retractor muscle and the optic nerve. Using the scissors with the blades half open as a lever, remove the eyeball. Insert a piece of gauze into the cavity, and keep it in position by means of a couple of sutures. Remove the gauze the following day. Subsequently bathe the wound with a mild antiseptic lotion until it is granulating, when it will only be necessary to mop away the discharge which appears outside the lids.

RESULT.—Recovery is uneventful provided that malignant disease was not present. There is a slight but constant weep from the mucous membranes still lining the eyelids, constituting a slight disadvantage of this method.

Method No. 2.—Suture the eyelids together with a continuous suture through their free borders. Make an incision through the skin, enclosing the sutured edges. Dissect back the skin to the level of the orbital rim, and then proceed as before to enucleate the eyeball. Suture the cut edges of the skin.

RESULT.—When the wound has cicatrised, the cut edges of the skin will have united, thus leaving no mucous surfaces.

9. Insertion of an Artificial Eye

After extirpation of the eyeball by the first method described, an artificial eye may be inserted when the suppuration has ceased. The best artificial eye is made of gutta-percha, and is shaped to simulate the normal eye. It is composed of a rim and a central piece. The latter constitutes a segment of a sphere or an ovoid. The rim is glided beneath the lids, and the false eye then remains in position, almost defying detection on superficial examination.

To prepare the orbit for its introduction, a temporary artificial eye may be used while the wound is healing, being perforated with openings to permit of the escape of discharge and the injection of antiseptic lotion.

The horse is a better subject than the dog for this operation, as the latter may scratch out the eye with the paw.

Another procedure is as follows: When suppuration has ceased after operation by the first method, disinfect the cavity, freshen the edges of the eyelids and unite them by sutures, and then inject through the nasal or temporal canthus sufficient pure sterilised white paraffin wax to slightly bulge out the eyelids. It is advisable to apply an ether spray immediately afterwards to solidify the wax. This overcomes the deformity caused by a hollow orbital cavity.

10. Dentigerous Cyst in the Temporal Region

This is a congenital condition met with in the horse, and generally first noticed when the animal is about two years old. It consists of a molar tooth growing from the petrous temporal bone, or more rarely from the squamous temporal bone. The cavity containing the tooth has an orifice on the skin near the base of the ear, discharging a little fluid formed by the wall of the cyst.

CONTROL.—Cast and chloroform the horse on the opposite side.

PROCEDURE.—Make an incision in the skin surrounding the fistulous orifice, remove the isolated piece, and expose the tooth *in situ*.

Grip the tooth with a suitable forceps, and endeavour to remove it without using great violence, for fear of fracturing the cranium.

FIG, 98.—PRE-AURICULAR FISTULA DUE TO PRESENCE OF A DENTIGEROUS CYST.

FIG. 99.—TOOTH FROM DENTIGEROUS CYST.

Should this procedure fail to dislodge the tooth, it would be safer to leave it alone than resort to the use of a chisel and mallet to remove it.

RESULT.—It is generally possible to extract the tooth with moderate force without endangering the brain, and then a rapid cure ensues.

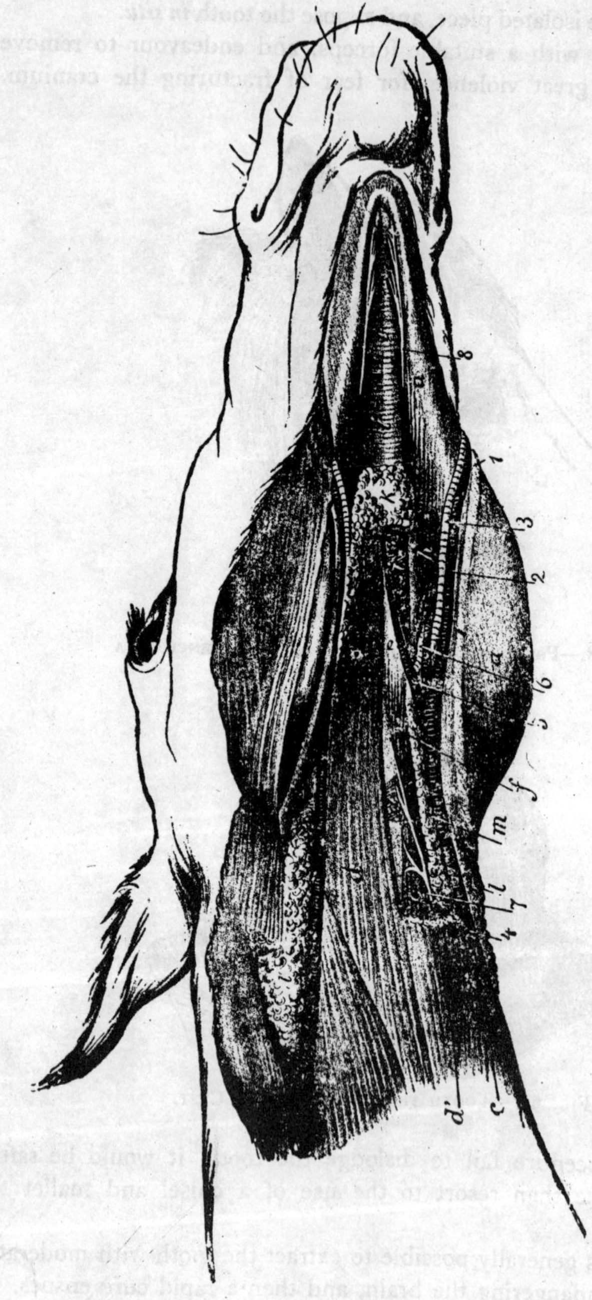

FIG. 100.—INFERO-LATERAL VIEW OF THE LARYNGEAL REGION.

aa, Lower jaw; *b*, panniculus (on the other side it has been completely removed); *cc*, sterno-maxillaris muscle; *d*, sterno and omo-hyoideus (on the other side *d′* it has been removed); *e*, hyoid bone; *f*, hyo-thyroideus; *g*, crico-thyroideus; *h*, digastricus; *i*, mylo-hyoideus; *i′*, myloglossus; *k*, submaxillary lymphatic gland; *l*, parotid gland; *m*, submaxillary salivary gland; 1, Stenson's or Steno's duct; 3, submaxillary artery; 2, 4, submaxillary vein; 5, lingual vein; 6, sublingual artery; 7, branch from the first cervical nerve; 8, mylo-hyoid nerve. (After Ellenberger and Baum.)

11. Amputation of the Conchal Cartilage of the Ear

INDICATIONS.—Extensive necrosis or a malignant tumour affecting the cartilage.

CONTROL.—The operation may be done standing under the influence of local anæsthesia.

PROCEDURE.—Incise the skin round the base of the concha. Excise the latter at its attachment to the external auditory meatus. Arrest the hæmorrhage, and prevent the entrance of blood into the auditory meatus by plugging it with a piece of gauze. Suture the skin round the meatus. Healing occurs without any complication. The tubular portion of the concha may be removed by reflecting the skin therefrom and severing the cartilage from its attachment to the bone and separating it from the upper portion of the cartilage by a transverse incision, thus leaving the greater portion of the ear in position. The writer did this in a case of ossification of this portion of the cartilage associated with chronic suppurative otorrhœa, with good effect in a retriever dog.

Excision of a V-shaped portion of the external part of the tubular portion of the concha is indicated in obstinate chronic otorrhœa, or where there are papillomata in the depth of the external ear round the meatus, the object being to effect good drainage from the affected part, or to facilitate complete extirpation of the papillomatous growth or growths. The epithelia of the skin and lining membrane of the ear unite over the wounded edges of the cartilage, so that no obvious deformity is left after the operation. To remove a portion of the flap of the ear in the dog make a cutaneous semicircular incision on its inner and outer aspects, reflect the skin from the cartilage for a short distance throughout the length of the incisions, so that after cutting through the cartilage the two cutaneous borders can be sutured over its edge. After amputation of the part use interrupted sutures of silkworm gut. Immobilise the ear until the wound is healed.

12. Ligation of Stenson's Duct

INDICATION.—Salivary fistula which has failed to respond to treatment, the idea being to arrest the function of the gland by preventing the outflow of its secretion.

CONTROL.—The operation may be done in the standing position with the aid of local anæsthesia. If necessary, cast the horse on the opposite side and use local or general anæsthesia.

SITE NO. 1.—About the width of two fingers above the border of the horizontal ramus of the lower jaw and ½ inch behind the sub-maxillary artery—that is, just in front of the anterior border of the masseter muscle (the head being horizontal). This site is only practicable when the fistula is on the face, near the buccal opening of the duct.

PROCEDURE.—Make an incision in the skin parallel to the duct. Having exposed the latter, isolate it by means of the tenaculum and apply thereto a silk ligature. Suture the skin. Keep the horse on the pillar reins for a few days to prevent interference with the wound, and give sloppy diet, which will not excite much salivation.

FIG. 101.—PAROTID GLAND AND STENSON'S DUCT (SEMI-SCHEMATIC).

A, Tendon of the sterno-maxillaris ; B, parotid gland ; C, Stenson's duct. The lines D and E should be prolonged. They are intended to point to the facial vein and artery, the latter indicated by the strong cross-shading, the vein being next it towards the left.

SITE NO. 2.—Within about 1 inch behind the posterior border of the vertical ramus of the lower jaw, at the level of the tendon of the sterno-maxillaris, across which the duct passes obliquely downwards and forwards, and where it can be felt by careful palpation with the finger.

PROCEDURE.—Make an incision at the level of the duct, which is recognised on exposure by its faintly pink appearance. Isolate and ligature it, and suture the wound as before.

RESULT.—The wound usually heals by first intention, and the desired effect is generally produced.

Occasionally an abscess forms in the gland subsequent to the operation, but heals after bursting or being opened.

13. Removal of a Salivary Calculus

When a calculus forms in the parotid duct, it may be decided to leave it alone or to operate for its removal.

CONTROL.—As in the last case.

PROCEDURE.—Push the skin upwards at the level of the calculus. Make an incision over the latter into the duct and parallel thereto. Take out the stone, suture the wounds in the duct and skin separately, using a very fine needle and thread for the former. Put the horse on the pillar reins, give him nothing except water for twenty-four hours, and keep him away from the sight of food and of horses feeding, so as to avoid as far as possible a copious secretion of saliva, and thus give the wound a chance to heal by primary union. A hypodermic injection of atropine may be given for the same object.

RESULT.—If the wound does not heal by first intention, a salivary fistula may ensue, which may prove difficult or impossible to close. For this reason the operation is deferred as long as possible, or not undertaken at all.

14. Section of the Infra-Orbital Nerve

INDICATION.—Inveterate shaking of the head in the horse, when all other methods of treatment have failed.

SITE.—Where the nerve can be felt issuing from the infra-orbita foramen.

PROCEDURE.—Make an incision about 2 inches long, commencing just above the foramen and continued downwards over the nerve. Expose the latter completely by dissecting away the connective tissue covering it ; isolate it with the tenaculum and cut it close to the foramen, and then remove about ½ inch of the nerve. Suture the wound and take measures to prevent its being rubbed or interfered with until it heals.

Very strict asepsis is necessary to prevent infection of the wound in the nerve, and consequent neuritis, with great pain to the patient.

RESULT.—Should neuritis supervene, the desired result will not be obtained, and the condition may be aggravated instead of improved It is an operation that should be avoided as far as possible.

15. Opening the Guttural Pouch

INDICATION.—An accumulation of pus or inflammatory exudate or, rarely, food material in the pouch.

CONTROL.—The operation can be done in the standing position with local anæsthesia, but it is generally more convenient for the operator to have the horse cast on the opposite side and anæsthetised. Different methods of opening the pouch have been practised and described, but the following procedure, as adopted by Dieterich, is probably the best.

SITE.—The antero-inferior border of the wing of the atlas.

PROCEDURE.—Make an incision about 3 inches long skirting the antero-inferior border of the wing of the atlas, going through the skin without wounding the parotid gland. Reflect the gland forward by blunt dissection of the loose connective tissue beneath it; have it held in this position by means of a retractor. Break down the areolar tissue to the inside of the mass of muscles formed by the digastricus, stylo-maxillaris, and occipito-styloid until the pale lining of the pouch comes into view. Seize a fold of it with an artery forceps and incise it close to the latter. Enlarge the opening thus made with the fingers, or the jaws of a forceps, and the interior of the pouch will then be quite visible. Evacuate the contents, which may be entirely liquid or partly solid in the form of chestnut-like bodies called chondroids.

To provide better drainage, make a counter-opening in the centre of Viborg's triangle, whose sides are the vertical ramus in front, the tendon of the sterno-maxillaris above, and the submaxillary vein below. Pass a stout metal sound into the pouch and make it bulge the skin in the centre of the triangle, and cut down upon it there. Keep this opening patent for a few days by inserting a strip of gauze through it and the upper opening. Irrigate the cavity gently with a non-irritant antiseptic solution, keeping the poll raised while doing so to avoid the possibility of some of the liquid entering the larynx. Continue the irrigation daily until the discharge has practically ceased.

RESULT.—The operation has the desired effect of evacuating the pouch and relieving the trouble caused by its distension, but the lining may have been so altered by chronic inflammation that it will never resume its normal condition.

In Dieterich's description of the operation he advises, after separating the muscles as mentioned, recognising the angle of bifurcation between the external carotid and occipital arteries by the pulsation in the vessels in the depth of the wound, placing the index finger between them with its dorsum upwards, and puncturing the pouch by pushing a sharp-pointed knife with the edge upwards along the back of the finger into its posterior wall. The method described above is easier and safer.

An alternative procedure is to puncture the occipito-hyoideus muscle parallel to its fibres as shown in Fig. 102.

FIG. 102.—DEEP TISSUES IN THE PAROTID REGION: OPENING THE GUTTURAL POUCH (SEMI-SCHEMATIC).

A, Atlas; B, styloid process of the occipital; C, obliquus capitis superior; D, tendon of the complexus and rectus capitis posticus major (Percivall's complexus minor); E, parotid gland; F, occipito-hyoideus muscle; G, post-auricular artery; H, hyoid bone; J, J, external carotid artery; K, submaxillary artery; L, digastricus; the stylo-maxillaris forms the posterior portion of this muscular mass. The dotted line indicates the point where the occipito-hyoideus is usually punctured.

Whitehouse's Method.—Dr. Whitehouse, of the Glasgow Veterinary College, advises operating as follows: Having the horse anæsthetised and fixed in the dorsal position, make a longitudinal cutaneous incision on the middle line of the under aspect of the neck at the level of the larynx and first two or three rings of the trachea about 3 or 4 inches long. Separate the two subscapulo-hyoideus muscles and break down the areolar tissue to one side of the larynx until the lining of the pouch of the corresponding side is reached. If it is distended it will be easily punctured. If not, it can be grasped with an artery forceps and incised close to the instrument. This method appears to be comparatively simple, and has the advantages of being safe and providing an absolutely dependent orifice.

16. Operation for Poll Evil

INDICATION.—Poll evil—that is, a sinus on the poll due to necrosis of the ligamentum nuchæ, and sometimes of the occiput, atlas, or axis as well.

CONTROL.—Cast and chloroform the horse and have the head resting on a clean sack of hay with the poll projecting over its posterior border.

SITE.—The middle line of the poll from a point in front of the occipital crest to a point behind the posterior limit of the lesion.

PROCEDURE.—Make an incision through the skin and adipose tissue down to the ligamentum nuchæ. Dissect out the latter as far as it is diseased, sever it posteriously to the affected part, reflect it forward, and cut it clean away from its insertion into the occipital crest, leaving the bone smooth. The curette is required to remove traces of it still attached to the bone. Make sure that the sinus and its tributaries are explored to their depth and that no necrotic tissue is left *in situ*. If the bone is ulcerated, curette it until a healthy surface is left. Take care not to penetrate the occipito-atlantoid ligament. Remember that the occipital bone behind the crest represents the bottom of the wound, and no incision is to be made deeper.

The drainage from the wound is not perfect. The occipital crest is an obstacle to it in front. For this reason Professor Williams, New York, makes a groove through the occipital crest extending to its base to provide an escape for discharge down the face. This, however, is not necessary, for recovery ensues without it when all the necrotic tissue has been removed.

The hæmorrhage during the operation is fairly profuse and hampers the surgeon more or less in detecting all the diseased tissue. It is finally arrested by plugging the wound with gauze or wool kept in position by tape sutures inserted by means of a stout needle with a handle. Remove the plug the next day, irrigate the wound with an antiseptic lotion, and then dress it with sulphanilamide or other antiseptic powder or with " B.I.P.P." (*vide* p. 220).

Renew the dressing daily until the wound is uniformly granulating, when it will be sufficient to simply apply the powder or paste or white lotion until cicatrisation is complete.

If a suspicious spot is observed in the wound that was perhaps overlooked during the operation on account of the bleeding, cauterise it by the application of a little powdered corrosive sublimate, which will cause it to slough away after a few days; or in bad cases it is a good plan to cast the horse again after two or three days, to thoroughly explore the affected region, and remove any suspicious tissue that may have been left *in situ*.

RESULT.—Recovery is the rule in the course of six to eight weeks. Only a linear scar remains. There may be a difficulty for some time in lowering the head to graze owing to cicatricial contraction. The animal, however, overcomes this difficulty by bending the knees.

After some time the new tissue stretches and the inconvenience disappears.

A similar procedure is indicated for a chronic bursitis in the region of the poll. Having opened the enlargement from before to behind and exposed the extent of the lining of the cavity, sever the ligamentum nuchæ at the posterior extremity of the latter, excise the anterior portion of the ligament along with the wall of the bursa, and then finish the operation as described above.

17. Laryngotomy

INDICATIONS.—Exploration; to remove a tumour or foreign body; and to perform the operation for roaring.

CONTROL.—The operation may be done in the standing position with the animal backed into a corner or stall with plenty of light in front, the head well extended, and a local anæsthetic injected subcutaneously.

As a rule the cast position is adopted as follows: In the country select a suitable place in a field or paddock near the stable. Avoid the use of dusty straw or hay as an operation bed. It is better to cast the horse on the plain grass. Arrange the position of the patient so that the light will shine into the larynx when it is opened. This is effected by having the posterior end of the body directed towards the point where the sun is situated. Administer chloroform and induce complete anæsthesia before opening the larynx.

SITE.—The middle line of the under aspect of the neck from a point just in front of a line joining the angles of the jaws to the level of the second or third tracheal ring.

Procedure.—Inject about 2 drachms of adrenaline solution intramuscularly in three places along the site of the operation to prevent capillary hæmorrhage. A local anæsthetic may also be injected if profound general anæsthesia is not intended. Make an incision going through the skin and muscles with one or two strokes of the knife. Separate the muscles sufficiently to expose the crico-thyroid ligament. Arrest the hæmorrhage, which is usually slight, owing to the use of the adrenaline. Mop up any blood that is present. Puncture the

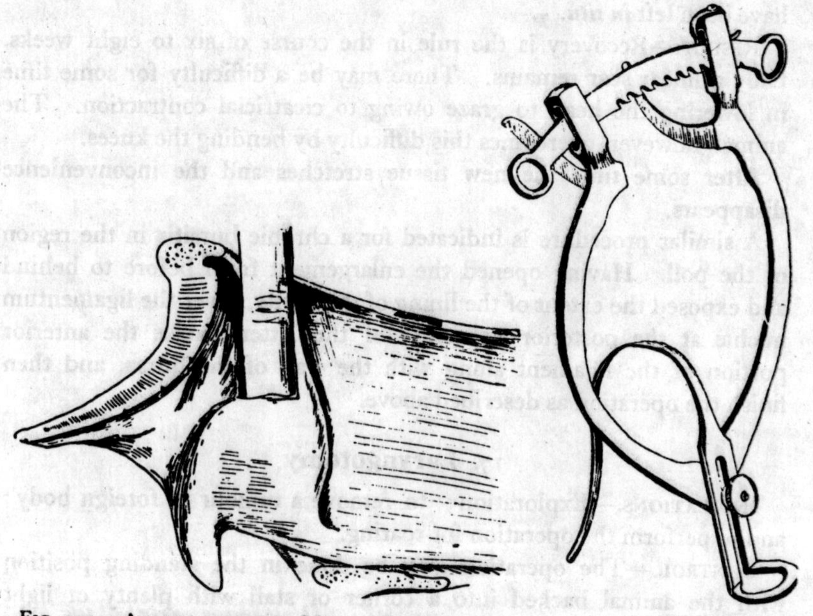

Fig. 103.—Antero-posterior Median Section of the Larynx, showing the Ventricle with Finger Inserted Therein.

Fig. 104. — Williams's Laryngeal Dilator.

crico-thyroid ligament immediately in front of the cricoid cartilage. The air will then escape with a hissing noise. Enlarge the laryngeal opening by continuing the incision up to the body of the thyroid cartilage. Insert the larnygeal dilator, and the interior of the larynx will be visible. If the daylight is insufficient, illuminate the part with an electric torch. Do not introduce any antiseptic lotion into the larynx. If there is considerable bleeding therein, mop up the blood with a pledget of aseptic gauze squeezed out of boiled water and held in a long forceps with one end of the gauze in the hand to prevent the possibility of its falling into the cavity and being aspirated into the trachea. This is seldom necessary during or after the performance of the "roaring operation."

Should the horse commence to move his head owing to the anæsthesia passing off, cover the wound with a layer of gauze and administer a little more chloroform if considered necessary. Take care that the dilator does not tear the larynx where it is in contact with it.

Having done what was necessary inside the larynx, protect the wound with a perfectly clean towel fixed round the neck with a safety

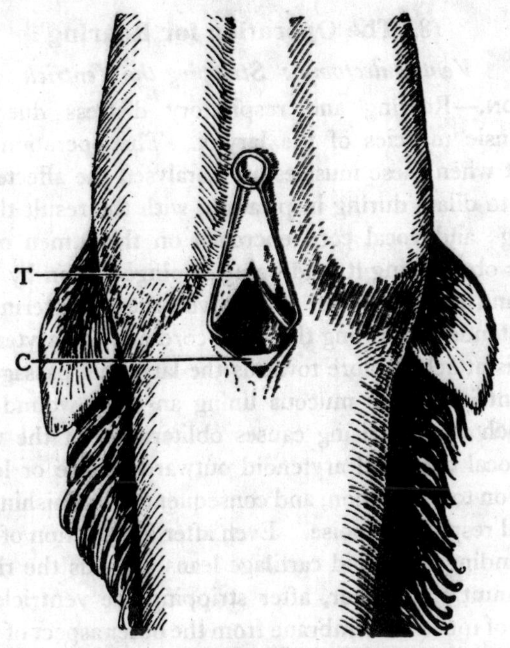

FIG. 105.—LARYNGOTOMY THROUGH THE CRICO-THYROID LIGAMENT. T=body of thyroid; C=cricoid cartilage.

pin, and allow the horse to lie on its side until completely recovered from the chloroform. Then remove the towel and put him in a clean, well-ventilated loose box bedded with good straw. If the litter is dusty it should be damped.

It is advisable to have the food placed at a normal level, so that little stretching of the neck will be required. The hay should not be shaken in the presence of the horse, for fear of hay seeds or dust getting into the larynx. It may be damped.

AFTER-TREATMENT consists in wiping away the discharge from the wound once or twice daily with a piece of cotton-wool soaked in boiled water or in a solution of potassium permanganate (1 in 1,000), care being taken not to allow any liquid to enter the larynx. The discharge may be fœtid, but this is of no consequence provided that the patient's health is normal.

RESULT.—When the operation has not been done for malignant disease, the result is nearly always good as regards the healing of the laryngeal wound. The possible complications that may ensue will be dealt with after the "roaring operation."

18. The Operation for Roaring

Ventriculectomy : Stripping the Ventricle

INDICATION.—Roaring and respiratory distress due to paralysis of the intrinsic muscles of the larynx. The operation is based on the fact that when these muscles are paralysed the affected side of the larynx fails to dilate during inspiration, with the result that the arytenoid cartilage and vocal cord encroach on the lumen of the larynx, more or less obstructing it, and being impinged upon by the incoming air vibrate and cause a noise. Moreover, the air entering the relaxed ventricle distends it, pushing the vocal cord and the arytenoid cartilage to which it is attached more towards the laryngeal passage. By stripping the ventricle of its mucous lining an open wound is produced therein, which on cicatrising causes obliteration of the ventricle and draws the vocal cord and arytenoid outwards, more or less removing the obstruction to inspiration, and consequently diminishing or stopping the abnormal respiratory noise. Even after obliteration of the ventricle the corresponding arytenoid cartilage leans towards the rima glottidis. On this account the author, after stripping the ventricle, removes a narrow strip of mucous membrane from the outer aspect of the cartilage, so as to cause cicatrisation there with a view to consequent drawing outwards of the cartilage.

In over 90 per cent. of cases the disease is confined to the left side of the larynx. Rarely both sides are affected.

PROCEDURE.—Perform laryngotomy as described. Insert the dilator and observe the movement of the larynx. In a case of roaring the affected side of the larynx will be seen to remain stationary, while the other side moves in and out in unison with respiration. If both sides are moving normally, the case is not a laryngeal roarer and the operation is not indicated. The paralysis may be incomplete. Then the laryngeal movements will be comparatively feeble and the operation should be performed.

Although only one side of the larynx may be affected, most operators nowadays strip both ventricles. There is little ground for this procedure except that the apparently normal side might be affected to such a degree that it would cease to function during fast work, although capable of movement during quiet respiration.

Excellent results have been obtained by the unilateral operation, showing that it is sufficient in many cases. The horse, however, seems to suffer no additional ill-effects from the double operation. It may be as well, therefore, to perform it.

To understand the procedure it must be remembered that the

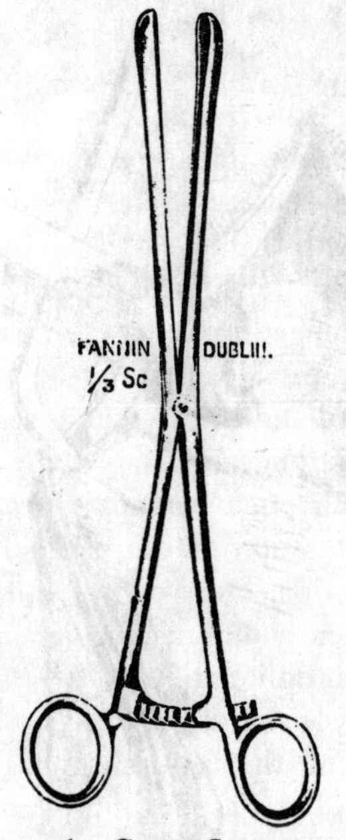

Fig. 106.—Glove Stretcher for Stretching the Ventricle in Roaring Operation.

Fig. 107.—Laryngeal Dilator for Use in Roaring Operation.

horse is on his back, the orifice of the ventricle is looking upwards in the form of an antero-posterior slit bounded inwardly by the vocal cord and the base of the arytenoid cartilage to which the vocal cord is attached, and outwardly by the thyroid cartilage. Anteriorly there is a loose fold of mucous membrane stretching between the arytenoid and a process of the epiglottic cartilage, and enveloping the latter.

The procedure for stripping the ventricle may be as follows:

1. **Separating the Mucous Membrane with the Index Finger.** In order to incise the mucous membrane it must be made tense either by (*a*) grasping the fold of membrane referred to above with a long

spring forceps and stretching it upwards, or (*b*) by introducing a glove-stretcher forceps into the ventricle and stretching it antero-posteriorly.

Take the long-handled special knife with an edge on each side of its point only, and puncture the membrane at the postero-internal aspect of the ventricular orifice, making the incision just large enough to admit the index finger. When operating on the left ventricle, which is on the right side in the cast position, it is more convenient to kneel on the right side of the patient and to use the left index finger.

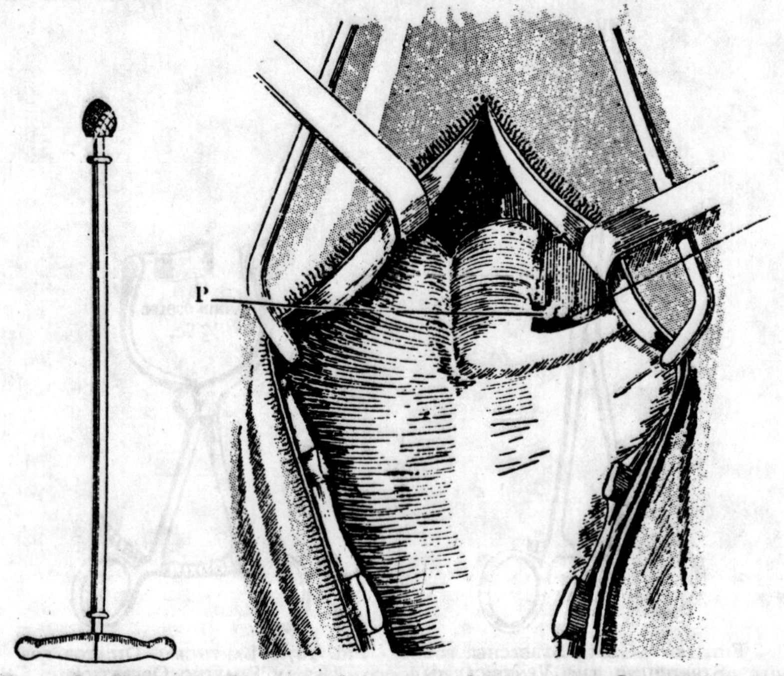

FIG. 108.—BURR FOR ROARING OPERATION.

FIG. 109.—INTERIOR OF LARYNX AFTER STRIPPING OF THE VENTRICLE.

O = orifice of ventricular wound; P = process of epiglottic cartilage.

Pass the finger into the incision in the membrane, and by means of it separate the latter from the ventricular wall. When it is separated push the finger upwards and backwards, and the membrane will be made to protrude like the finger of a glove. It is sometimes possible in this way to bring it out through the external wound and remove it on the finger by cutting it at its attached border. But to avoid the risk of rupturing it by doing this, it is better to grasp the completely separated membrane with the long forceps and make it tense by twisting, to facilitate its excision. Should it prove difficult to get the lining up on the finger, grasp its cut edge with the forceps and hold the membrane taut backwards, thereby facilitating its separation and protrusion. Incise the membrane at its attached border with a special long-handled knife with a short blade and a keen edge, or with a long sharp scissors, taking care not to cut the vocal cord, arytenoid, or epiglottic cartilage. The process of the latter is very apt to be severed if care is not taken to recognise it by its feel and to cut behind it. Having stripped the ventricle, reintroduce the glove-stretcher forceps and stretch it transversely. Grasp the stretched piece of mucous membrane to the outer side of the arytenoid in its centre and cut it on both sides of the forceps, thereby removing a narrow strip thereof. Do not break down the areolar tissue between the arytenoid and the thyroid cartilages, as this would allow the former to fall inwards and possibly cause asphyxia. The other ventricle is stripped from the same or, more conveniently, from the opposite side of the patient.

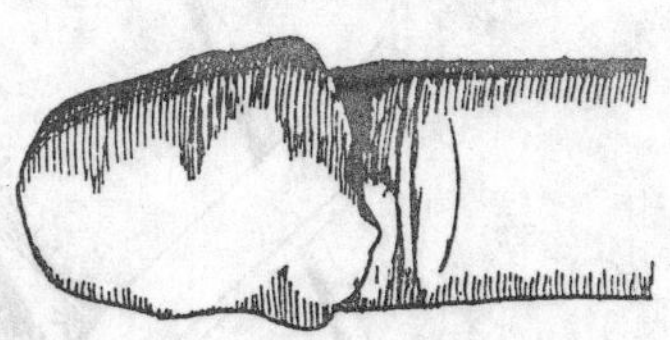

FIG. 110.—MUCOUS MEMBRANE OF VENTRICLE APPLIED ON THE FINGER AFTER ITS REMOVAL.

2. **Using a Burr.**—Made entirely of metal and in the form of a corrugated sphere about the size of a small glass marble with a narrow shaft, about 6 inches long, attached and provided with a cross-handle, by means of which it can be turned inside the canula which encloses it. Introduce the sphere into the bottom of the ventricle, and by alternate rotation and traction on the handle separate the lining, which will come away clinging to the instrument (Fig. 111). Remove the separated membrane by incising it at its fixed periphery. Perform the operation slowly for fear of tearing the mucous membrane before it is completely separated.

This is a simple and effective method. An instrument with a small cylindrical head with corrugations on its circumference also answers the purpose.

The blood from the larynx may be removed as described. There is usually very little present. The after-treatment is that mentioned for laryngotomy. The horse should not be tried for his wind until five or six weeks have elapsed since the operation, otherwise the adhesions might be broken down and the object of the operation defeated. The ventricular wound will be completely cicatrised by this time.

RESULTS.—Usually good, the wound healing without any complication and the desired effect being obtained in the majority of cases. It would be difficult to give the exact percentage of successes.

The degree of success varies. The respiratory noise and distress may completely disappear or the roaring noise may be replaced by a different and less audible noise, which is of no consequence, especially as the staying power of the horse has been restored. In a small percentage of cases there is no improvement of any kind, and in rare instances the horse is worse after the operation, due as a rule to stenosis

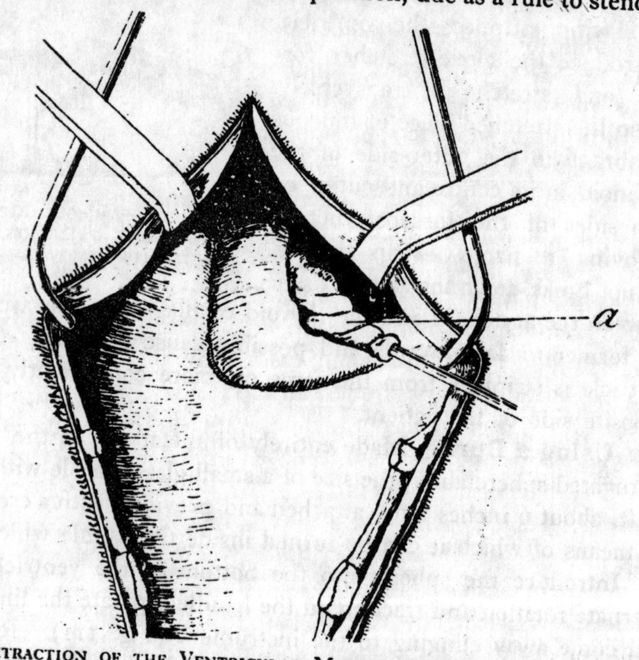

FIG. 111.—EXTRACTION OF THE VENTRICULAR MUCOUS MEMBRANE BY MEANS OF THE BURR.

A mesial incision has been made through the cricoid cartilage and through the epiglottis to enable the interior of the larynx to be seen. *a*, Separated ventricular mucous membrane clinging to the burr.

of the larynx supervening as the result of the excessive development of fibrous tissue at the seat of operation, or of ossification of the larynx. Hobday has estimated the proportion of complete cures at 50 per cent., calculated on some hundreds of cases.

Whatever the proportion of successes may be, it is certainly sufficient in the experience of the author to warrant the performance of the operation in all cases of laryngeal roaring or whistling in valuable hunters and race-horses, especially when associated with respiratory distress. There have been many remarkable recoveries. Proof of its success is afforded by the operator being called year after year to the same districts to perform the operation.

COMPLICATIONS.—Possible complications of the operation comprise:

Œdema of the Larynx.—This may supervene almost immediately after the operation, but it is usually most marked about the third or fourth day afterwards. It is more apt to ensue when both ventricles have been stripped.

SYMPTOMS.—The condition is characterised by dyspnœa, varying in degree in different cases. Rare instances of horses being asphyxiated by it during the night after the operation have been recorded.

The respiration becomes frequent and laboured, with marked heaving of the flanks. The symptoms may gradually or suddenly subside, owing to the œdema disappearing, or the distress may increase and terminate in death, if not relieved.

TREATMENT.—If the case is urgent, give immediate relief by dilating the laryngeal opening with the fingers or by inserting the dilator or a special laryngeal tube. In the absence of the latter, tracheotomy may be performed to prevent asphyxia until the œdema subsides.

When the dyspnœa is not severe, it is only necessary to have the horse kept under observation in case it should become dangerous. This complication is very rare nowadays.

Pneumonia.—Pneumonia due to the entrance of foreign matter through the laryngeal opening has been recorded. It is very rare and usually fatal. Treatment can render little service. It is that for pneumonia.

Stenosis of the Larynx.—In a very small percentage of cases (not more than ½ per cent.) stenosis of the larynx results from the excessive development of cicatricial tissue at the seat of operation. This is more likely to ensue when any of the cartilages have been wounded. It may also be due to ossification and consequent thickening of the larynx. The latter becomes very hard and much enlarged. In either case the calibre of the glottis may be reduced to the diameter of a lead pencil.

SYMPTOMS.—The symptoms are increasing respiratory distress at a variable time after the operation, usually within a year afterwards. The only means of relief for the condition is the insertion of a tracheotomy tube.

Excision of the Vocal Cord.—In addition to stripping the ventricle the centre portion of the vocal cord may be excised with a view to preventing any thickening that might persist from its presence in the form of a slight ridge after closure of the ventricle.

Its removal may also have the effect of allowing the arytenoid cartilage to be drawn more outwards by the cicatricial contraction which follows the stripping operation.

It must be remembered, however, that when excision of the vocal cord alone was done for the relief of roaring it was reported that it proved a failure, due perhaps in some cases to excessive granulation tissue forming at the seat of operation. The possibility of this effect occurring should be borne in mind.

Professor Coquot published an article in the *Receuil de Médicine Vétérinaire*, Vol. XCIII, Nos. 1–2, recording that he has been performing excision of the vocal cord along with ventriclectomy since 1913. He removed from the middle portion of the cord a piece from 10–12 mm. square.

Brayley Reynolds has favoured this procedure in recent years, and reports an increased percentage of successes since he has adopted it in preference to mere stripping of the ventricle. The excision is performed by grasping the vocal cord with a forceps, and severing it on either side of the instrument to the extent mentioned by Coquot.

OPERATION IN THE STANDING POSITION.—By making use of the burr, the stripping operation can be readily done in the standing position under the influence of local anæsthesia, first by subcutaneous injection at the site of operation, and after opening of the larynx, by the application of the agent to the ventricular lining.

Cocaine is the agent usually employed, and when it is used it is necessary to wait about fifteen minutes before it produces its effect on the mucous membrane.

The horse is backed into a stall with plenty of light in front, and the head is raised by passing the reins from the bridle or head collar over a beam above the animal's head.

Professor Williams (New York) demonstrated the standing operation at the International Veterinary Congress, 1914. Since then it has been practised by other operators.

19. Tracheotomy: Opening the Trachea

The operation performed may be:

(1) Permanent tracheotomy.
(2) Provisional or temporary tracheotomy.

(1) *Permanent Tracheotomy*

INDICATIONS.—Any permanent obstruction in the upper respiratory passage, such as inoperable tumours in the nasal chambers, paralysis of the intrinsic muscles of the larynx, instead of ventriclectomy, when a quick result is required, or obstruction in the upper part of the trachea as the result of a fractured ring encroaching on its lumen. The idea, of course, is to facilitate respiration and prevent respiratory distress during fast work or when performing heavy traction.

CONTROL.—Have the horse backed into a stall or corner with plenty of light in front. Inject a local anæsthetic and adrenaline hypodermically at the site of operation; apply a twitch if necessary.

SITE.—The middle line of the under aspect of the neck at the junction of its upper and middle thirds. This site is chosen because it is a convenient place, it is clear of harness, and leaves room for

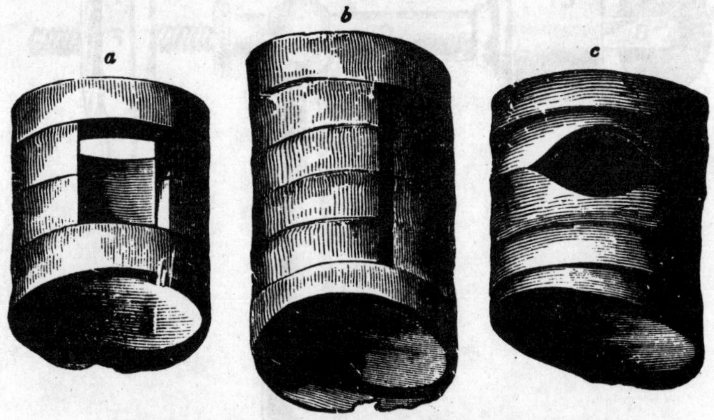

FIG. 112.—METHOD OF PERFORMING TRACHEOTOMY.
a, square opening; *b*, vertical opening; *c*, oval opening. (Hering.)

repeating the operation lower down should stenosis of the trachea supervene.

PROCEDURE.—Stand towards the off side of the horse in front of the neck. Make a longitudinal wound equal in length to the diameter of the flange of the tube to be employed. Separate the muscles and cut through the areolar tissue, completely exposing the trachea. Arrest the hæmorrhage, which may be practically nil or fairly profuse.

Make the opening in the trachea by one of the following methods:

1. *Using McKenny's Tracheotome.*—With this instrument it is practically impossible to make a mistake. It cuts away a semi-disc of cartilage from two adjacent rings, leaving a narrow strip of each ring intact above and below, which prevents their cut ends from turning in to cause stenosis of the trachea. The excised portion of tissue is enclosed in the tracheotome, so that it cannot fall into the larynx. It makes an opening to correspond exactly to Jones's tube.

2. *Using Spooner's Compass Tracheotome.*—This tracheotome is in the form of a compass, one of whose limbs is a knife and the other pointed and provided with a flange. The distance between the two limbs can be fixed, so as to be equal to the radius of the lumen of the tube to be used.

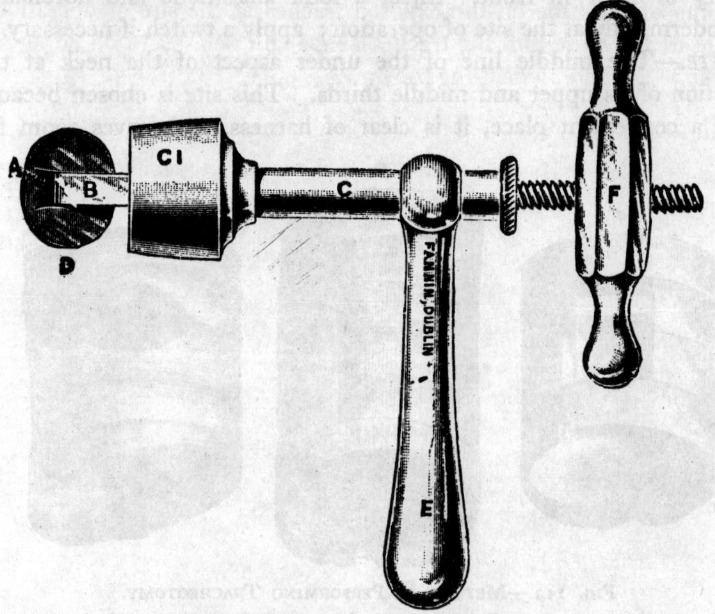

FIG. 113.—MCKENNY'S TRACHEOTOME.

The pointed arm is inserted through the interannular ligament beyond the flange, and the blade is then made to cut out a disc-shaped portion of the trachea, which remains attached to the instrument above the flange.

FIG. 114.—SPOONER'S COMPASS TRACHEOTOME.

3. *Using a scalpel* and proceeding as follows :

Insert the knife into the interannular ligament and partly cut through the upper ring. Introduce one of the jaws of a spring forceps through the incision and grasp the cartilage. Continue the incision round the forceps, thereby excising a semicircular piece from the two adjoining rings without going through the entire width of either ring, and making the opening to correspond to the diameter of the tube to be inserted. It is difficult to make an even circular incision through the cartilage, but it is not essential to do so, as the opening will soon accommodate itself to the tube. To ensure that the diameter of the tracheal opening will correspond to that of the tube, place the plug of the tube on the exposed trachea at the site of operation, and insert the knife into the trachea above and below and on either side of the plug, thereby marking the limits of the circumference of the tracheal opening.

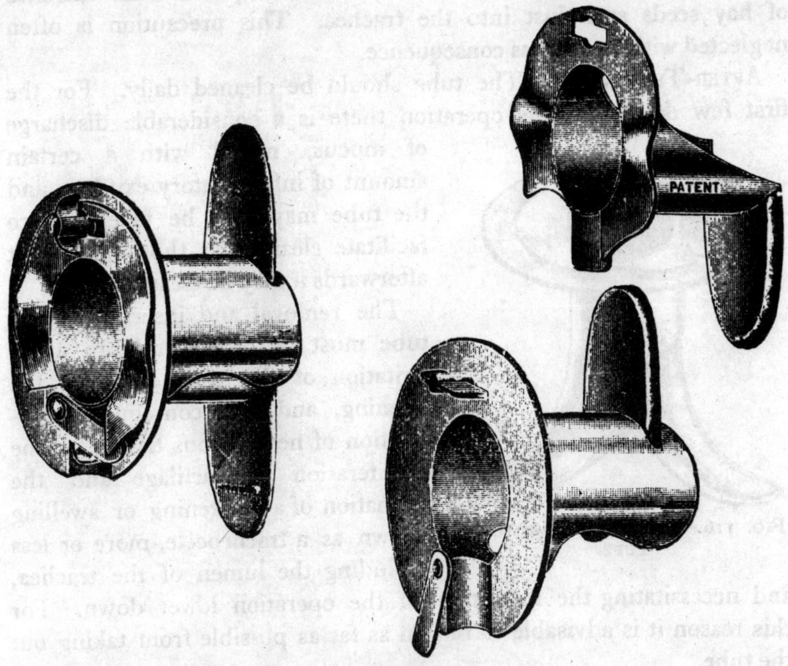

FIG. 115.—COLEMAN'S TRACHEOTOMY TUBE.

McKenny's instrument is the best to facilitate the procedure. Having made the opening, introduce gently the tracheotomy tube, of which there are many different patterns on the market. Coleman's, Jones's, Field's, and Arnold's tubes are well known.

Jones's tube is composed of four parts, an upper and lower, and a central cylindrical portion and a plug, securely joined together by little thumbscrews. Each part is introduced separately in its proper order. It is a very well made and serviceable tube, and is probably the most popular.

Field's tube is composed of two parts, and has the advantage that it is easily inserted or removed. It is very suitable for temporary use.

Arnold's tube is similar to Jones's. Coleman's tube is light, simple, and convenient, and more secure in position than Field's tube.

Young's tube is provided with a valve which closes during expiration and opens during inspiration. It prevents the unpleasant noise caused by expiration through the tracheal opening.

When the horse is in the stable the tube is closed with its own plug, if it has one, or by means of a cork, to prevent the entrance of hay seeds and dust into the trachea. This precaution is often neglected without serious consequence.

AFTER-TREATMENT.—The tube should be cleaned daily. For the first few days after the operation there is a considerable discharge of mucus, mixed with a certain amount of inflammatory exudate, and the tube may then be taken out to facilitate cleaning it thoroughly, but afterwards it may be cleaned *in situ*.

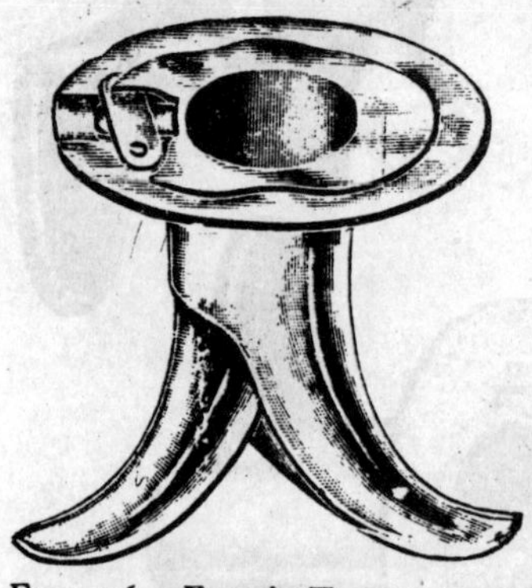

FIG. 116.—FIELD'S TRACHEOTOMY TUBE.

The removal and insertion of the tube must be done gently to avoid irritation of the trachea round the opening, and the consequent production of new fibrous tissue, or the proliferation of cartilage and the formation of a thickening or swelling known as a tracheocele, more or less occluding the lumen of the trachea, and necessitating the repetition of the operation lower down. For this reason it is advisable to refrain as far as possible from taking out the tube.

It is almost a necessity to have a spare tube to be inserted immediately should the other one go out of order, for if the tracheal opening is left without a tube for a few hours it will be difficult to reintroduce it.

The horse should not be turned out to grass wearing a tube, as he might rub it against a fence, and thereby damage the tube and the trachea, and when in a loose box care should be taken that there is no place against which it may be rubbed. If the top part of the door is left open, bars should be placed across it to prevent the horse putting his head over the half-door.

RESULT.—The horse suffers no immediate ill-effects from the operation, and the desired effect of relieving troubled respiration is produced when done for the purpose of racing; it is generally best to perform the operation immediately before the race, so that there will not be time for even slight inflammation to ensue and perhaps interfere somewhat with respiration during fast going, but the objection to this is that some blood and mucus may exude from the tube during the race, and give the impression that operation at this time is not humane.

COMPLICATIONS.—No immediate complication ensues as a rule, although it is possible that pneumonia may supervene from foreign matter gaining entrance through the tracheal orifice; a piece of the separated cartilage may accidentally fall into the trachea and have this effect, but this is a rare occurrence. It is also possible for the blade in McKenny's instrument to break and a portion of it to fall into the tube.

The chief evil effect of tracheotomy to be feared is stenosis of its lumen, due to thickening occurring round the tracheal orifice, as described above when referring to the irritation caused by the tracheotomy tube.

When this sequela occurs, temporary relief may be obtained by excising the thickened part, proceeding thus: Have the horse controlled as for tracheotomy. Inject eudrenine subcutaneously round the part. Grasp a portion of the enlargement with a sharp pronged retractor and hold it while it is being cut away with a strong knife, and continue the operation, using a curette, until the lumen is sufficiently clear.

If the tube has been left out for a while, it may be necessary to proceed similarly to allow of its reinsertion. The urethral dilator (Axe's) has been found useful to dilate the orifice for this purpose, when it is only slightly constricted.

Eventually it is necessary to perform tracheotomy lower down, quite clear of the original site, lest any of the granulation tissue there should spread to the new site. Apart from this taking place the condition may recur, necessitating a third operation, and so on until no room is left for another opening.

Closing the Tracheal Opening.—When a horse or a mare that has been "tubed" is put to the stud, the tube is removed and the opening allowed to close. Sometimes, however, a tracheal fistula persists, owing to the epithelial covering on its edges. To bring about closure it is usually only necessary to pare the smooth edges, when granulations will form and lead to cicatrisation. Should this not be sufficient, an autoplastic operation may be done as follows: After excising the borders of the opening by an elliptical incision, make a longitudinal incision on either side of the opening and about ½ inch therefrom, mobilise the intervening bands of skin by separating them from the subcutaneous tissue, and then unite the edges of the skin over the tracheal opening by interrupted sutures.

(2) *Temporary or Provisional Tracheotomy*

INDICATION.—A temporary obstruction in the upper respiratory passage, such as œdema of the head with encroachment on the nasal chambers, plugging of the latter for the arrest of hæmorrhage, œdema of the larynx, etc.

CONTROL.—The patient may be ***in extremis*** and require no special control, otherwise it is the same as for the permanent operation.

PROCEDURE.—The procedure may be as follows :

1. If the case is urgent, plunge the knife into the trachea, incise two or three rings, and draw their ends apart to allow a free ingress of air into the lungs. The opening may be kept patent by cords passed through the edges of the wound and tied over the neck, or an improvised tube may be used in the form of a piece of hosepipe or other tubing.

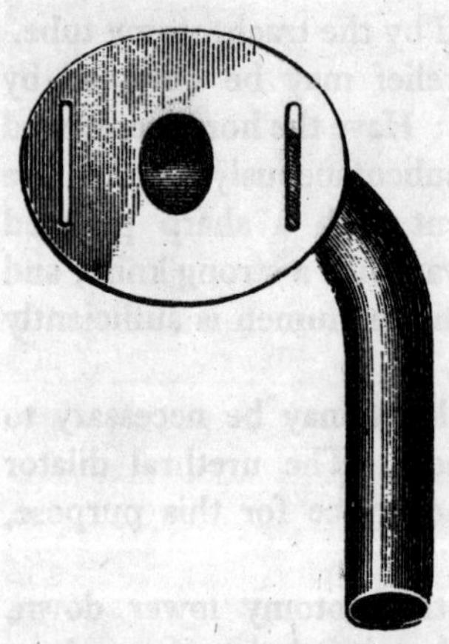

FIG. 117.—BARTHÉLEMY'S CANULA.

2. If there is no immediate danger of asphyxia, an opening may be made between two rings and a special tube with a bent stem flattened from before to behind introduced into the opening, or a larger tube may be inserted through an incision made through two or three rings, or the permanent operation may be performed.

When the case of the respiratory trouble has disappeared the tube is removed. This is ascertained by closing the opening with the hand and noticing the effect on the breathing.

The operation in other animals is similar in every way to that in the horse, and appropriate tracheotomy tubes can be obtained for them.

The ordinary tube used for the horse is too large for a small bovine. It necessitates the removal of too much cartilage, with the result that when the tube is removed the cut rings may fall in and occlude the lumen of the trachea, causing asphyxia. If a large tube is used it should not be removed until the tracheal opening is partly cicatrised, when collapse of the severed rings will not occur.

20. Œsophagotomy : Opening the Œsophagus

INDICATIONS.—To remove an obstruction which cannot be dislodged by other measures, or possibly to cut a stricture in a case of stenosis of the tube.

The Horse

CONTROL.—The operation may be done standing with local anæsthesia, or in the cast position, using local or general anæsthesia, with the horse lying on the off side.

SITE.—At the level of the obstruction or, when the latter is just inside the thorax, at the lower part of the neck, and at the upper

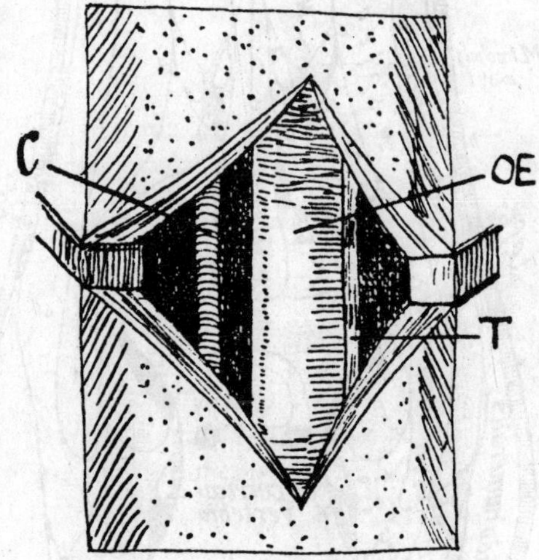

FIG. 118.—ŒSOPHAGOTOMY.

Œ œsophagus ; C, carotid ; T, trachea almost hidden by the œsophagus.

or lower border of the jugular furrow. It is slightly more convenient to operate at the upper border.

PROCEDURE.—Make a longitudinal incision through the skin and subcutaneous tissue sufficiently long to permit of the extraction of the obstruction. If the latter is bulging the œsophagus, it facilitates exposing the latter. If not, break through the areolar tissue down to the trachea, to whose superior aspect the gullet is related in the upper part of the neck, while in the lower part it deviates to the left of that structure.

Taking the trachea as a guide, recognise the œsophagus, pass a blunt instrument transversely beneath it, and thereby expose it

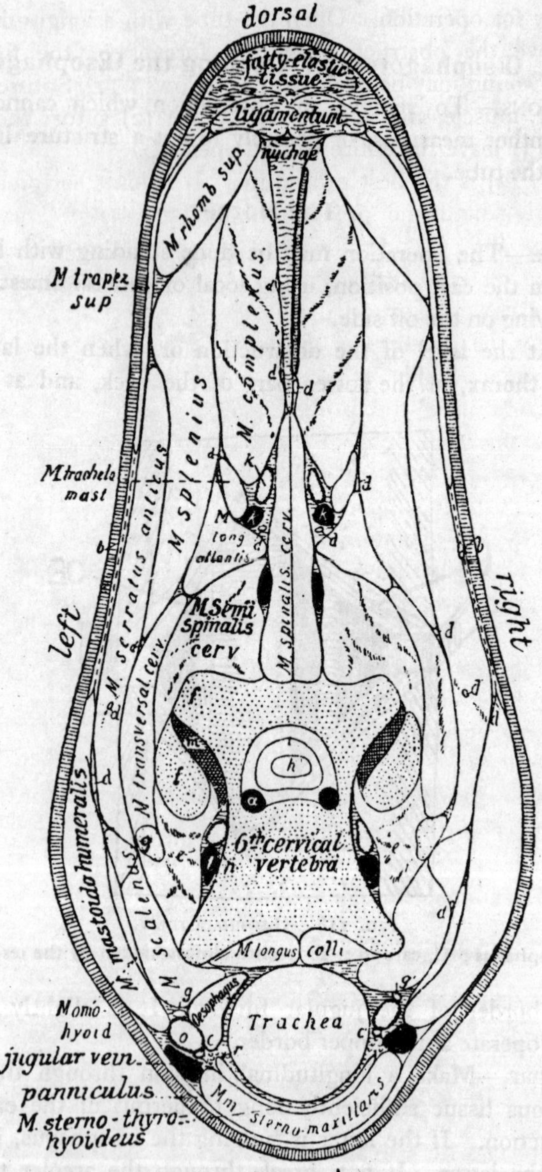

Fig. 119.—Section at Right Angles to the Long Axis of the Neck through the Upper Third of the Sixth Cervical Vertebra.

a, Veins of spinal cord; *b*, branch of spinal accessory nerve; *c*, recurrent nerve; *d*, inconstant nerve twigs; *e*, intertransversales muscles; *f*, *f*, *g*, portions of vertebra; *h*, spinal cord; *i*, its membranes; *k*, *k'*, superior cervical artery and vein; *l*, *l'*, vertebral artery and vein; *n*, branch of the sympathetic; *o*, carotid artery; *p*, jugular vein; *q*, *q*, vagus and sympathetic nerves; *r*, tracheal lymphatic gland.

sufficiently for operation. Open the tube with a longitudinal incision and remove the obstruction with a forceps or the fingers. The operation wound may be dealt with as follows : (1) Suture the mucous membrane, muscle, and skin separately ; or (2) suture the œsophagus only ; or (3) leave the entire wound open.

Probably (2) is the best procedure. It favours early closing of the œsophageal wound and prevents alimentary matter escaping during swallowing, and, leaving the skin unsutured, permits of drainage of any food material that may find its way out between the stitches. Sometimes, however, especially in the dog, a portion of the œsophagus damaged by the pressure of the obstruction has sloughed, rendering suturing impracticable.

In other animals the procedure is on similar lines. The dog and cat are operated upon in the dorsal position under the influence of general anæsthesia or, if dyspnœa is present, of local anæsthesia. The latter is usually sufficient.

RESULTS.—The operation is usually successful, the wound being healed, as a rule, within a month afterwards. Stricture of the œsophagus, however, may ensue after a variable period, due to cicatricial contraction. This is more likely to occur when there has been loss of tissue from sloughing of the œsophageal wall.

The dog is less likely to be affected in this way than other animals, owing to the relatively large calibre and great dilatability of the tube in this animal.

When the œsophageal wound is large and not capable of being sutured, most of the food material swallowed may escape through the opening, and if care is not taken to occlude it during deglutition or to feed the animal through a tube the patient may die of inanition.

21. Phlebotomy, Venesection : Bleeding, Blood-Letting

INDICATION.—As a therapeutic measure in certain constitutional inflammatory conditions in a sthenic subject, such as pulmonary and cerebral congestion, acute lymphangitis, etc., and to obtain blood for laboratory purposes.

The Horse : Jugular Phlebotomy

The operation is most commonly performed on the jugular vein.

CONTROL.—Control the horse standing, using local anæsthesia and applying a twitch if necessary. An anæsthetic is not essential, especially when a fleam or trocar and canula is employed, and in practice it is seldom used.

SITE.—Either side of the neck, but usually the near side at the junction of its upper and middle thirds at the level of the jugular vein.

PROCEDURE.—Cause distension of the vein by applying a cord tightly round the base of the neck in the form of a noose. This acts more readily if a solid object is placed beneath the cord at the level of the vein. The vein may be raised with the pressure of the fingers alone.

1. *Using the Ordinary Fleam on the Near Side.*—Stand on the near side, looking in the same direction as the horse. Have the corresponding eye blindfolded to prevent the horse being frightened by the use of the blood stick. Have the fleam in the left hand, holding the blade between the index finger and the thumb. Place its point on the skin over the middle of the vein, with the edge parallel to the long axis of the latter. Holding it firmly in position, strike it smartly with the blood stick so as to make it penetrate the vein with one stroke, when the blood will flow copiously. To accelerate the escape of the blood, make the horse champ his jaws by putting a stick in his mouth. A couple of gallons of blood may be taken from a horse in robust condition. When sufficient blood has been withdrawn, release the cord and close the cutaneous wound with a pin suture. If the cord is not employed, the middle left finger is used to compress and distend the vein.

2. *Using the Lancet.*—The lancet is seldom used nowadays. It is a very sharp double-edged knife. The procedure is as follows: Having raised the vein, hold the blade between the fingers and thumb and thrust it into the vessel from below upwards. Close the cutaneous wound as before.

3. *Using the Trocar and Canula.*—Take a trocar and canula from $\frac{1}{16}$ to $\frac{1}{8}$ inch in diameter. Having raised the vein, take up a small fold of skin with a stout forceps and incise it completely, close to the forceps, with the point of a sharp knife, making a wound not more than $\frac{1}{2}$ inch long. Push the trocar and canula through the wound into the vessel either upwards or downwards, as seems most convenient. Withdraw the trocar, and the blood will flow through the canula. The trocar and canula can be inserted without incising the skin.

This is the best method for collecting blood for laboratory purposes. It is not so good for producing a therapeutic effect, as the blood flows in a comparatively thin stream. The more rapidly the blood escapes, the greater the depleting effect of the operation.

4. *Using a Hypodermic Needle.*—To adopt this method, insert the needle first through the skin and then into the vein. It is the best method for taking small samples of blood.

After-Treatment.—Put the horse in a place where he cannot rub the wound against anything. Apply a little tincture of iodine gently over and around the wound once daily. Remove the pin carefully after three or four days without disturbing the edges of the wound.

Results.—No untoward result supervenes when the operation has been carefully performed. As regards having a good therapeutic effect, its results are very doubtful. On rational grounds bleeding could not be efficacious in this respect, for the removal of blood from the body deprives it of a considerable amount of its vital power in the form of red and white blood corpuscles and blood serum, all of which are active in defending it against attacks from injurious influences.

Fig. 120.—Bleeding with the Lancet.

The amount of toxic material eliminated from the system in this way in a case of toxæmia could hardly make up for the loss of strength caused by the bleeding. In a sthenic subject, however, the relief of congestion which it causes is beneficial, especially in a case of congestion of the lungs. In some racing circles it is believed to be a preventative of epistaxis, the ground for this belief not being apparent. The author did the operation once with this object in view on the part of the owner, and the epistaxis, which had been frequent during racing, did not recur, at least during the races in which the horse took part soon after the operation. A quart of blood was removed by means of a trocar and canula.

Complications.—Possible complications of the operation are :

1. *Simultaneous wounding of the carotid artery*, indicated by the escape of bright arterial blood in spurts along with the venous flow. Except the opening of the artery is a mere puncture, it will be necessary to quickly isolate and ligature the artery at a lower level, otherwise death will ensue.

2. *The formation of a hæmatoma* beneath the skin at the site of operation. A slight accumulation of blood here is of no consequence.

as it becomes absorbed, but a large collection prevents primary healing and thus predisposes to phlebitis. When it occurs, the wound must be kept open to provide for drainage, and dressed gently once or twice daily with an antiseptic lotion and powder.

3. *Phlebitis*, owing to the entrance of infection into the vessel. This may be the result of want of careful aseptic and antiseptic precautions, or of making an uneven or transverse wound in the vein, whereby it is slow to heal, leaving an opening for bacterial invasion.

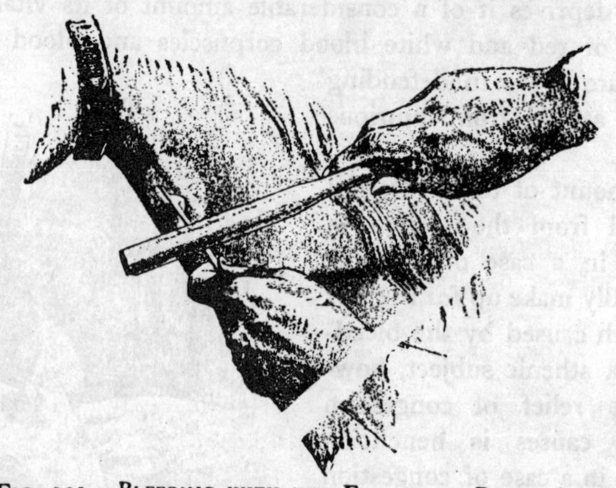

FIG. 121.—BLEEDING WITH THE FLEAM AND BLOOD STICK.

Bleeding from other Veins.—Other veins on which venesection has been performed are the angular vein on the face and the cephalic vein. They are easily opened by means of a lancet or sharp knife. The general effect produced is insignificant, but angular phlebotomy may prove beneficial for cerebral congestion.

The Ox : Jugular Phlebotomy

INDICATIONS.—As in the horse.

CONTROL.—Have the beast securely held by the aid of a bullholder, with the head bent to the opposite side.

PROCEDURE.—It is essential to put a cord round the base of the neck, as described, because there are two jugulars on either side of the neck, and the deeper one cannot be compressed without the use of the cord.

Proceed in the same manner as in the horse. To obtain blood for the laboratory, use a stout hypodermic needle or a fine trocar and canula inserted into the vein after incising the fold of skin held in the forceps, as described above. The skin is thicker than in the horse. Incision of the skin is unnecessary, but it facilitates puncturing the vein.

Mammary Vein.—The mammary vein has been bled from in the cow. The operation, however, is not advisable on account of the risk of phlebitis from the dependent and exposed situation of the vein. It may be opened by the fleam, lancet, or trocar, the last mentioned being the safest.

The angular, auricular, and caudal veins may also be operated upon. The auricular vein is a suitable site for taking small samples of blood.

The Sheep

Jugular phlebotomy is not performed in the sheep, but the angular vein, the median vein on the inner aspect of the forearm, the external saphena vein, or some of the veins of the ear may be opened. It is only necessary to compress the vein on the proximal side of the site of operation to distend the vessel and facilitate its being incised by the lancet or knife or penetrated by a hypodermic needle or trocar and canula.

The Pig

Phlebotomy may be performed on the median, saphena, auricular (see p. 205), or lingual vein. The latter is opened beneath the frænum of the tongue.

The Dog and Cat

Intravenous injection of nembutal is now commonly performed in these animals, otherwise they are rarely subjected to the phlebotomy operation (see Nembutal Anæsthesia, p. 201).

The external saphena and radial veins respectively are the sites adopted.

COMPLICATIONS.—Seldom arise after operation on small veins. Otherwise they are the same as those described already.

Local Bleeding : Scarification

INDICATION.—As a remedy for acute local inflammation or to relieve œdema when very marked. It is seldom advisable.

PROCEDURE.—Make one or more short incisions in the skin, depending on the area affected, and take antiseptic precautions to prevent infection of the wounds. A special instrument, the scarificator, may be used, consisting of a metal box containing several small fleams and the mechanism for working them. It is quite unnecessary.

RESULT.—The operation relieves congestion in an inflamed or œdematous region, but if very careful antiseptic precautions are not taken septic infection may ensue, with more or less serious consequences.

Cupping is another method of withdrawing blood rarely adopted in veterinary practice. The cupping glass is hemispherical. Its centre is pierced by a small hole and carries a short hollow stem, to which a strong rubber ball is fixed. Compressing the ball causes a partial vacuum in the glass, and the consequent suction of blood into it. This is also a method of producing hyperæmia in a part (see p. 261).

22. Transfusion

INDICATIONS.—Severe loss of blood and blood poisoning (gas, chloroform, etc.). Direct transfusion of blood is a difficult and dangerous operation in veterinary patients, and is never advisable.

The same effects are safely obtained by aseptic subcutaneous, intraperitoneal, or intravenous injection of artificial serum at a little above body temperature, the patient being afterwards fed with highly nutritious food (milk, eggs, brandy, etc.) until the normal condition is restored.

OPERATIONS ON THE TRUNK

23. Paracentesis, Thoracis, Thoracentesis, Tapping the Chest

INDICATIONS.—The presence of liquid inflammatory exudate in the chest cavity, causing more or less dyspnœa, or to aid in diagnosis, when this condition is suspected.

The Horse

CONTROL.—No special control is required.

SITE.—*Left side :* The eighth intercostal space, just above the spur vein, and close to the anterior border of the rib, in order to avoid the vessels at the posterior border. *Right side :* The seventh intercostal space. The object in going a space further back on the left side is to avoid the possibility of puncturing the heart. In other words, operate about 9 inches behind the point of the elbow and at the level of same.

PROCEDURE.—Take a trocar and canula about 6 inches long and $\frac{1}{16}$ to $\frac{1}{8}$ inch in diameter. Hold the handle in the hollow of the hand with the tip of the index finger about $1\frac{1}{4}$ inches from its point. Push the skin upwards so that when the puncture is made the wounds in the skin and the chest will not communicate directly, thus minimising the risk of infection from the outside. Push the instrument

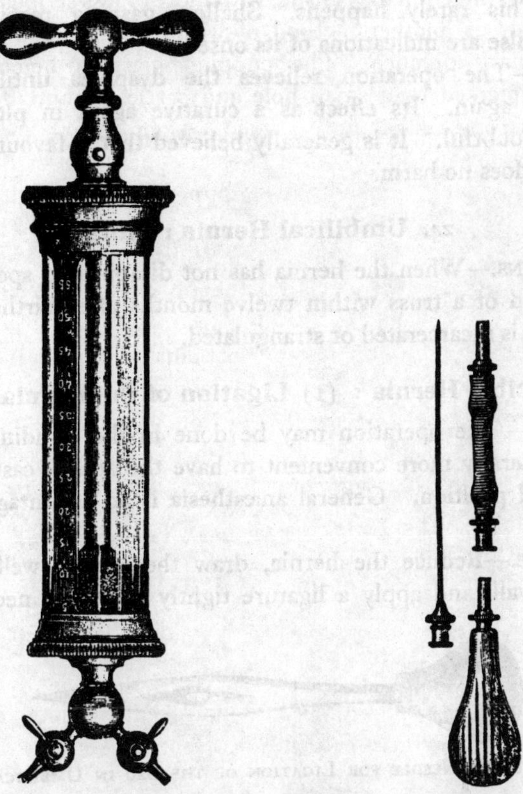

FIG. 122.—DIEULAFOY'S ASPIRATOR, WITH HANDLE FOR INTRODUCING THE NEEDLE AND FLEXIBLE CONNECTION FOR SYRINGE.

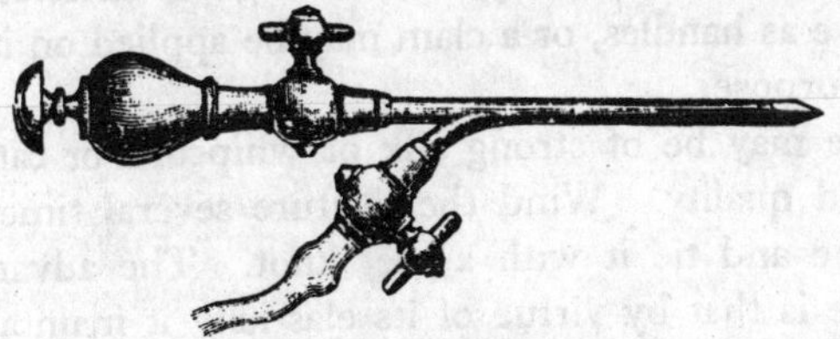

FIG. 123.—SPECIAL TROCAR AND CANULA.
The second limb is provided with a long rubber tube, allowing the instrument to be used as an aspirator.

vigorously into the tissues until a sense of resistance overcome is perceived. Withdraw the trocar, and the liquid will escape through the canula. Allow it to flow until it ceases spontaneously. Should the patient show signs of collapse from the fall in the blood pressure caused by the removal of the fluid, the flow of the latter should be stopped. This rarely happens. Shallow gasping respiration and weakened pulse are indications of its onset.

RESULTS.—The operation relieves the dyspnœa until the fluid accumulates again. Its effect as a curative agent in pleurisy with effusion is doubtful. It is generally believed that it favours recovery. It certainly does no harm.

24. Umbilical Hernia : Horse

INDICATIONS.—When the hernia has not disappeared spontaneously or by the aid of a truss within twelve months after birth, or at any time when it is incarcerated or strangulated.

Reducible Hernia : (1) Ligation of the Hernial Sac

CONTROL.—The operation may be done in the standing position, but it is generally more convenient to have the animal cast and fixed in the dorsal position. General anæsthesia is an advantage, but not necessary.

PROCEDURE.—Reduce the hernia, draw the sac up well from the abdominal wall, and apply a ligature tightly round its neck as close

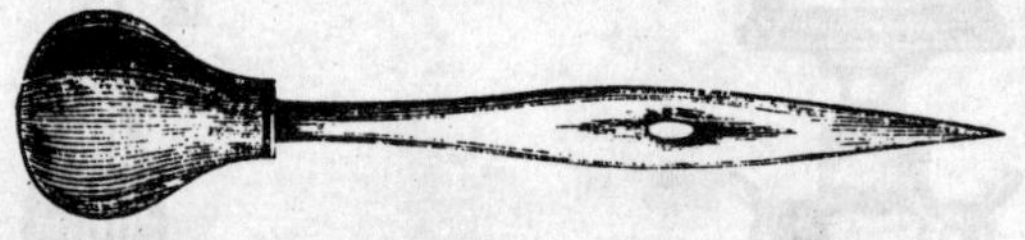

FIG. 124.—KÜHN'S NEEDLE FOR LIGATION OF THE SAC IN UMBILICAL HERNIA.

as possible to the hernial orifice. To facilitate traction on the sac, a loop of silk thread may be passed through it anteriorly and posteriorly to serve as handles, or a clam may be applied on its distal part for the same purpose.

The ligature may be of strong silk or whipcord or catapult india-rubber of good quality. Wind the ligature several times round the neck of the sac and tie it with a reef knot. The advantage of the rubber ligature is that by virtue of its elasticity it maintains constant pressure on the tissues. Yet the results obtained by the non-elastic material leave nothing to be desired. If the india-rubber is not of good quality, it may break before having the required effect.

To prevent the ligature slipping, the neck of the sac may be transfixed by skewers or strong pins or horsehoe nails, one being inserted transversely and another antero-posteriorly or both transversely either before or after performing ligation, usually before it. Care must be taken not to puncture the herniated bowel or to include it in the ligature, by making sure that it is well reduced beforehand. Hold the neck of the sac between the fingers and thumb of the left hand when inserting the skewers or pins, to prevent the hernial contents returning into it. Judgment must be exercised in applying the ligature not to put it on excessively tight, and thus cause, perhaps, too early sloughing of the sac, and consequent prolapse of the bowels.

If the hernial sac is large, a double ligature may be employed thus: Thread a stout needle with the ligature material, leaving the two ends of equal length. Pass the needle and thread transversely and mesially through the neck of the sac close to the abdominal wall, cut the two parts of the thread close to the eye of the needle, intercross them, and ligature the sac in two sections. If necessary, three or more ligatures could be applied in a similar manner.

The necessary procedure in connection with hernia with adhesions, incarcerated and strangulated herniæ, will be dealt with under the heading of the " Radical Operation."

(2) Use of Clams

Instead of a ligature a clam may be applied to the neck of the sac. The procedure is similar to that in connection with ligation. The clam may be of wood, steel, or aluminium.

The wooden clam is light and cheap, and answers the purpose well. It requires to be stout transversely, so as not to buckle when subjected to pressure. The two parts may be joined by cords in the ordinary way, or by means of a thumbscrew at either end, the latter being the preferable form, permitting of any degree of tightness being attained and enabling the clam to be tightened occasionally as the tissue is being cut through.

The parts of the steel clam may be joined by a screw at either end, or by a hinge at one end and a screw at the other, the former pattern being the better, as it permits of more accurate adjustment. It is strong, convenient, and efficient. Its opposing edges are serrated to give them a grip on the tissues. It is comparatively expensive, and may be objected to on the ground that it is heavy, but this is not a serious drawback. The thickness of the steel must be sufficient not to allow of bending, as sometimes occurs when it is thin.

The aluminium clam has the advantage of being light, and is thus suitable for foals, but if much strain is put on it, it is apt to break. The clam is applied longitudinally and as close to the abdominal wall as possible. The best way to ensure this is to apply another clam on the base of the sac, and use it as a handle to draw the sac tensely away from the abdominal wall. When the parts are united by screws, the latter are made as tight as possible with the fingers and thumb, and then given two or three turns with a forceps, the idea being to make sure that the instrument will not become displaced. To guard further against this, it is advisable to transfix the sac on this side of the clam with three or four horsehoe nails or pins or skewers, whose points are then turned downwards.

Combe's clam is of wood with a screw at either end and perforated to allow the passage of needles or ligatures through the sac, and Bordonnat's clam is toothed to give it a grip on the sac. The clam may also be fixed by means of a surcingle round the body. The objection to this is that it may get caught in something.

It is advisable to turn the screws occasionally as the tissue is being severed, but care must be taken not to overdo this, lest the sac may

FIG. 125.—UMBILICAL HERNIA.
Wooden clam applied on the hernial sac.

come away too soon before the hernial ring is closed and allow escape of the bowel.

AFTER-TREATMENT.—After either of the above operations the patient is put into a loose box or, if the weather permit, out on grass and kept under constant observation, for fear he might interfere with the clam, although this is not likely. The site of operation should be painted daily with tincture of iodine or flushed with an antiseptic solution to counteract infection through the wound caused by the clams or ligature. It is advisable to give an injection of antitetanic serum, as tetanus is not an uncommon complication of the operation. Laxative diet is indicated and bulky food should be avoided, as it causes distension of the abdomen and would favour rupture of the recent cicatrix, after separation of the sac, and consequent descent of the intestine, or, instead, cause stretching of the delicate new tissue and recurrence of the hernia, especially if the hernial ring were large. For the same reason violent exertion must be prevented for some months afterwards, until the scar tissue has become strong and resistant.

SUBSEQUENT PHENOMENA.—Whether the clam or ligature be

employed, the subsequent phenomena are the same. The animal may evince slight colic occasionally for a few hours after the operation, but as a rule he seems unconcerned. On the following day inflammatory symptoms appear around the umbilicus, which becomes the seat of a hot œdematous swelling, and the sac becomes cold and purplish. There may be some inappetence and a slight rise of temperature, but otherwise the patient is normal. Towards the fourth day the sac is dead. On about the twelfth or fifteenth day the ligature or clam and the sac fall, leaving a more or less extensive wound and considerable œdema, which gradually disappears. A depression is observed in the position of the umbilicus, but at the end of three or four weeks the wound is completely healed and the umbilical opening is totally obliterated.

Results.—Both methods of operation are usually successful and are equally effective. The employment of clams is more convenient and simpler than that of the ligature, and is nowadays more in vogue. It is undoubtedly the method for choice for ordinary umbilical hernia.

Complications.—Are rare. They comprise too early separation of the sac and descent of the bowel, tetanus, and malignant œdema or other wound infection. Recurrence of the hernia may take place within one year after the operation, but it is very unusual and rarely supervenes at a later period. A second application of the clam may effect a complete cure.

(3) Suture of the Hernial Sac

Having reduced the hernia, grasp the sac with the fingers and thumb as close to the abdominal wall as possible, and, inserting the needle immediately below the thumb, pass a series of interrupted stout Halsted silk sutures across the neck of the sac about ½ inch apart. This brings about adhesion by cicatrisation between the surfaces in contact and consequent closure of the hernial orifice. The empty sac may afterwards undergo atrophy and become obliterated, or persist as a swelling of variable size, which may be excised when the hernial ring is permanently occluded. The advantage of this method is that it is not followed by sloughing of the sac, and the consequent risk of prolapse of the bowels. An objection to this procedure is that infection may possibly spread along the sutures from the skin into the abdominal cavity and cause peritonitis, but experience has shown that this complication is not likely to occur.

Should it be necessary to open the sac or should the hernial orifice be unusually large, proceed in a similar fashion, including the abdominal wall in the sutures, the fingers of the left hand being kept in the abdomen to guide the needle clear of the viscera when inserting the sutures. In this case it is essential to keep an antiseptic compress in contact with the affected part for five or six days until union has occurred in the peritoneal part of the wound.

Radical Operation

INDICATIONS.—Where the sac has to be opened to relieve strangulation or to separate adhesions, or where one of the above methods has failed, or when the hernia is abnormally large.

PREPARATION.—As for laparotomy.

CONTROL.—Cast and fix in the dorsal position with the hocks well flexed and separated and administer chloroform.

PROCEDURE.—Having taken all aseptic and antiseptic precautions, including the application of antiseptic cloths over the feet and hocks, and a window cloth fixed with panel clips over the site of the operation, make an incision through the skin and fibrous covering of the sac over its centre, or at a point where there is no adhesion, parallel to the long axis of the body, from the anterior to the posterior extremity of the swelling. Isolate the delicate peritoneal lining of the sac from its other coats, reduce the hernia, seize this portion of the sac with a long spring forceps, twist it into a cord, and apply a silk or No. 3 catgut ligature (the former being the more secure but having the disadvantage that it does not become absorbed) round its neck as high up as possible; amputate the sac below the ligature, return the stump into the abdomen, freshen the edges of the hernial ring by scraping them with a knife or snipping them with a scissors, and then bring them together with strong interrupted sutures. Shorten the skin, if necessary, to bring the edges into accurate opposition, and then suture it after applying sulphanilamide powder to the wound. Apply the sulphanilamide powder also to the sutured wound, and when the patient rises cover it with an antiseptic pad and bandage. Put the animal in a hygienic loose box and give him the usual hospital diet. Apply a little tincture of iodine to the wound and its vicinity once or twice daily.

Healing by first intention may ensue, but it is not the rule, suppuration sometimes supervening and necessitating removal of the ligature and of the deep sutures, if they do not come away with the discharge. It may be necessary to incise the skin which has healed over them to gain access thereto. This method is seldom adopted in veterinary practice owing to the difficulty in dissecting out the delicate peritoneal sac intact. It is generally modified by removing the whole sac and suturing the parietal wound as in laparotomy, after freshening its edges, or the modified Degive's method is adopted for preference.

Hernia with Adhesions

When adhesions are present, the peritoneum must be incised to permit of their separation, which may be effected by the fingers if recent, or by careful dissection if old. If their separation is impossible in the latter case, the peritoneum may be cut round the adherent portion, which is then returned with the bowel. If it is the omentum that is involved, the adherent portion may be excised.

Incarcerated Hernia

If the hernia cannot be reduced owing to distension of the herniated loop of intestine with gas or liquid, it may be tapped to diminish its volume, and then reduction may be possible. Otherwise it will be necessary to open the peritoneal sac by taking up a fold of it in an artery forceps and cutting it horizontally close to the instrument, and then enlarging the wound by incising it on a director, to permit of direct manipulation of the hernial contents.

It may be possible in this way, with or without the aid of taxis or traction on the bowel *per rectum* by an assistant, to effect reduction. If not, pass the left index finger or a hernia director between the contents and the hernial ring, and then pass a blunt-pointed knife flatwise along the finger or director, and when it has cleared the stricture turn its edge towards the latter and cut it slightly so as to enable the contents to be returned. Having done this, proceed as in an ordinary case.

Strangulated Hernia

When the hernial contents are strangulated the procedure is the same as for incarceration, except that more care is required in manipulation of the bowel on account of its more or less damaged condition due to the arrest of its blood supply. When the case is advanced, it is advisable to proceed at once to relieve the constriction by incision of the hernial ring instead of trying first direct or rectal taxis on the bowel.

In all cases where the hernial sac has been opened it is essential to have the patient completely anæsthetised, lest it may make a sudden effort and cause prolapse of the bowel.

Results.—When the radical operation has been performed without opening the peritoneal sac there is no danger of peritonitis ensuing, and it is therefore usually a complete success. Even when the sac has been opened the same result is usually obtained, provided that careful precautions have been taken to prevent sepsis and that the bowel has not been weakened by strangulation, or that its peritoneal surface is not already infected by micro-organisms which have passed through its devitalised walls from the intestinal tract.

When general symptoms of toxæmia have appeared before the operation is performed, indicating that peritonitis has already supervened, and when the bowel is in a gangrenous condition the case is hopeless.

It may be said that it is useless in a case of necrosis of the herniated intestine to resect the necrotic part and perform enteroanastomosis.

When the case is *in extremis* there is no object in operating, and if the operation is performed the operator may be blamed for the cause of death.

Degive's Method

In 1894 Degive introduced a method of treatment which he said was superior to all others.

PROCEDURE.—Open the sac at about its centre to an extent sufficient to admit the first two fingers of the left hand. Pass a stout, slightly curved needle with a handle, about 10 inches long altogether, through the lips of the anterior half of the ring, going through the skin, abdominal wall, and peritoneum, guiding it clear of the abdominal viscera by means of the fingers in the abdomen. Pass another needle of the same kind in the same way through the posterior part of the ring. Apply a clam between the needles and the abdominal wall, screwing it as tightly as possible with the fingers, and then screwing it a little more with stout forceps. When the clam has been secured, withdraw the needles and insert in their stead pins or skewers or horseshoe nails as described. This procedure has the effect of turning the edges of the hernial ring outwards and bringing the serous surfaces into close contact and maintaining them there until they become united. Owing to the way the clam is applied a portion of the abdominal wall all round the ring is included in it, and sloughs away along with the sac. Its place is taken by scar tissue, an imperfect substitute for the original specialised resistant structures. The fact is that, except for the closure of the hernial opening, the wall of the abdomen is on that account weakened instead of strengthened by this operation. It predisposes to recurrence of a much larger hernia through rupture of the extensive cicatrix. This unpleasant sequel is not, of course, the rule, but it has occurred sufficiently often, judging from reported cases, to make one hesitate about performing it, although tempted to do so, the procedure is so expeditious. The writer has had success with it in every case except one, in which the hernia recurred and was four times the size of the original one ; but the colt in this case was turned out too soon after the operation. In all the recorded cases of failure the ring of the recurrent condition was much larger than that of the primary one. The recurrence usually appears some months after apparent cure has been accomplished.

An essential for the success of this operation is to keep the animal housed and on concentrated diet for at least two months afterwards. It is courting failure to put the patient at liberty in the field and allow the abdomen to become distended with grass or bulky food of any kind.

Modifications of the Degive Method.—1. In a case where the sac must be opened and it is considered undesirable to include the abdominal wall in the clams, the needles may be passed through the neck of the sac, inserting them at some distance from the edges of the ring, to ensure the sac being well drawn out from the abdominal wall and the clams being applied as closely as possible to the latter, between it and the needles.

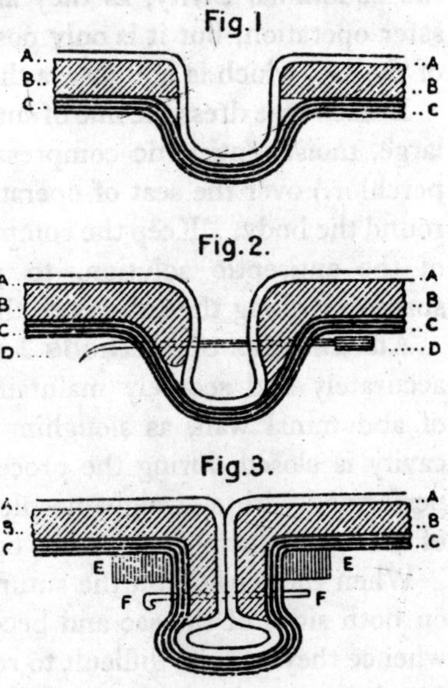

FIG. 126.—SCHEMA ILLUSTRATING DEGIVE'S OPERATION FOR UMBILICAL AND VENTRAL HERNIÆ.

A, Serous ; B, musculo-aponeurotic ; and C, cutaneous coats of the hernia ; D, the special needle in place ; E, E, clam ; F, F, nails. The three figures show the successive stages of the operation.

2. Proceed exactly as described for the Degive method until the needles are inserted, and then apply the metal clams just tight enough to keep the serous surfaces in contact. Insert a series of Halsted or mattress sutures through the ridge of tissue on this side of the clam close to the latter and about ½ inch apart. Then remove the clam. Make the ridge of uniform height by cutting away the higher part of it, skin and fibrous tissue, and unite the cut edges of the skin by ordinary interrupted sutures.

Although no sloughing occurs by this method, it will not ensure against recurrence in the case of a large hernial opening with much tension on its borders, except great care is taken to reduce the abdominal pressure to a minimum.

3. Isolate the peritoneal sac as in the radical method, ligature and remove it, and then proceed as in No. 2, inserting the needles through the skin and muscles only, not through the peritoneum. There will be no danger in this case of infection extending along the sutures to the abdominal cavity, as they are outside it. This procedure is the safer operation, but it is only possible when the peritoneum forms part of the sac, which is not always the case in a ventral hernia.

In each case dress the line of sutures with tincture of iodine. Apply a large, moist, antiseptic compress (saturated with 1 in 1,000 hydrarg. perchlor.) over the seat of operation, secured in position by a bandage round the body. Keep the compress saturated by frequent applications of the antiseptic solution, to prevent the possibility of infection spreading along the sutures to the abdominal cavity.

Advantages of Methods 2 and 3.—(*a*) The lips of the ring are accurately and securely maintained in contact; (*b*) there is no loss of abdominal wall, as sloughing does not occur; (*c*) the abdominal cavity is closed during the process of suturing, which can be rapidly performed with a straight needle; (*d*) there is no danger of prolapse of the bowel during or after the operation.

When the tension on the sutures is great, they cut through the skin on both sides of the sac and become embedded in the deeper tissues, whence they may be difficult to remove. This is more likely to be the case in connection with a ventral hernia, and the condition is then apt to recur.

25. Inguinal and Scrotal Hernia : Horse

Indications.—When the hernia has persisted after one year old, when it appears in an adult animal, and in all cases of incarceration or strangulation of the hernial contents.

1. Reducible Hernia—Control.—Cast, anæsthetise, and fix the patient in the dorsal position, with the hocks well flexed and separated, so as to dilate and expose well the inguinal region.

Procedure.—Proceed as in the covered operation for castration. Incise the skin and dartos, exposing the tunica vaginalis without cutting it. Enucleate the latter up to the external inguinal ring. Reduce the hernia and apply a clam on the spermatic cord, including the tunica vaginalis, and as close to the external inguinal ring as possible. It is advisable to give the cord a half twist before applying the clam. A short, metal, slightly curved clam may be used. It has the advantage that it can be pushed up high on the cord and the disadvantage that it may become embedded in the tissues and be difficult to remove. A comparatively long wooden castration clam whose ends are outside the scrotal wound is just as effective and is easily removed.

A ligature may be employed instead of a clam, and is preferred by some operators on the ground that it can be applied further up

FIG. 127.—INCOMPLETE INGUINAL HERNIA.

The figure shows the position of the inner abdominal ring and the course of the external pudic artery.

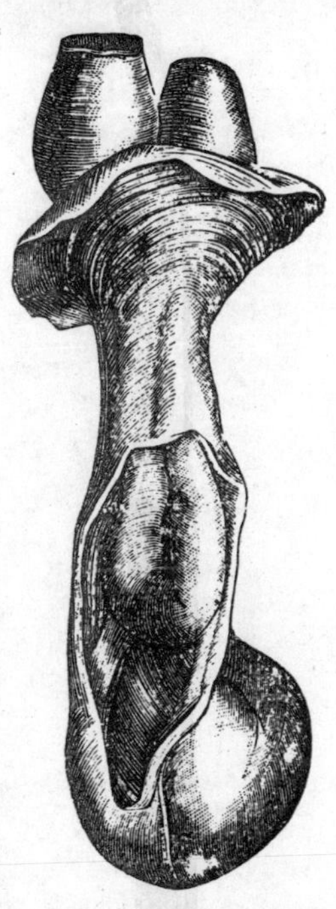

FIG. 128.—INGUINAL HERNIA OF THE HORSE (HERING).

on the cord, thus more effectively closing the neck of the sac; but it has the serious objection that it frequently becomes septic, and may prove a source of infection along the cord to the peritoneal cavity. Moreover, it may not come away readily, and may be difficult to remove. It prevents healing of the wound as long as it is *in situ*. One end may be left long to facilitate its removal, but doing this favours contamination of the thread. Gold, dealing with this operation (*Vet.*

Rec., Nov. 30th, 1946), transfixes the neck of the tunica vaginalis sac, after rotating it, with a No. 3 catgut ligature applied as high up as possible, cuts the sac 1 inch beneath the ligature with a curved scissors,

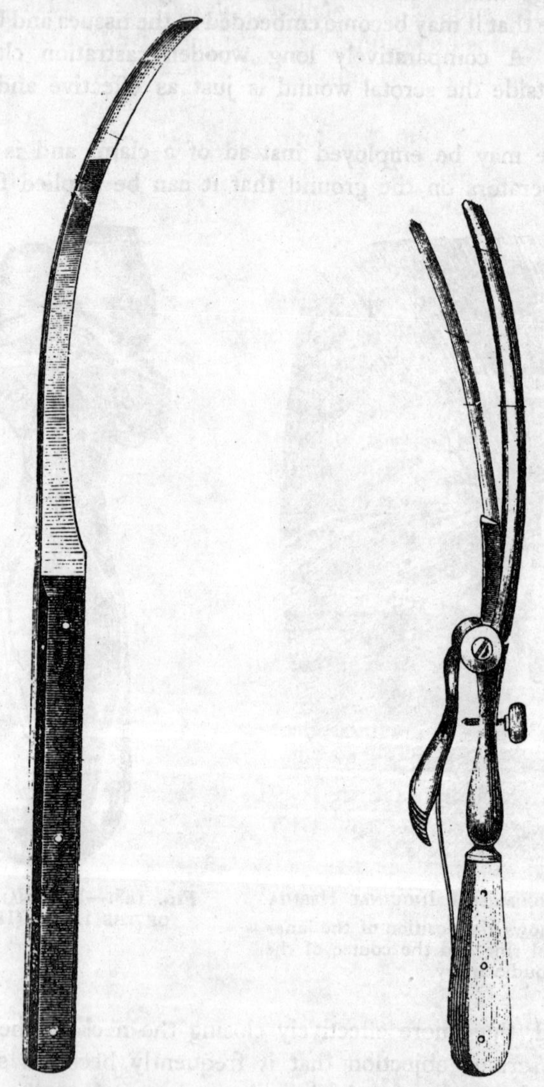

FIG. 129.—HERNIOTOME. FIG. 130.—HERNIOTOME.

and packs the cavity with 2 ounces of sulphanilamide, and says that the scrotal wound may or may not be sutured. The advantages he claims for the ligature over the clam are that there is little or no swelling and that the wound heals practically by first intention. The use of the ligature is certainly more in accordance with modern surgical methods and more humane than that of the clam.

When the subject is a stallion, cut off the testicle about ½ inch below the clams or ligature; apply some B.I.P.P. to the wound.

The clam may be left in position until it falls off in the course of nine to twelve days, or it may be taken off at the end of a week. In the meantime an antiseptic lotion should be splashed on the wound and its vicinity once or twice daily.

One or two injections of antitetanic serum are advisable after the operation.

RESULTS.—Complete recovery is the rule. There is practically no complication to be feared except some serious form of wound infection, which is very unlikely to ensue when ordinary aseptic and antiseptic precautions have been taken.

2. **Strangulated Inguinal Hernia**—CONTROL.—As in No. 1, making sure in this case to have the inguinal region well dilated and the patient profoundly anæsthetised.

PROCEDURE.—Have the feet and hocks and operation site covered with sterilised cloths, to prevent contamination of the wound. If the case is very recent, an attempt may be made after anæsthesia has been produced to reduce the hernia by cautious local manipulation, assisted by rectal taxis performed by an assistant. If it fails, proceed as follows: Make an incision carefully through the skin and dartos over the centre of the swelling from before backwards, exposing, but not cutting, the tunica vaginalis. Enucleate the hernial swelling enclosed in the tunica vaginalis by reflecting the other envelopes up to the external inguinal ring.

In some cases the tunica vaginalis is found ruptured. If not, take a small fold of it in an artery forceps posteriorly and incise it horizontally close to the instrument. Insert a grooved director forwards through the opening, and incise the membrane on it to the same extent as the other coverings. The hernial contents and, in the stallion, the testicle will now be exposed, and seen to be more or less altered according to the duration of the strangulation; a fibrinous deposit is always present. Another careful attempt may be made by direct and rectal taxis to reduce the contents, but it should not be continued for long for fear of damaging further the already weakened and injured bowel. If the latter is distended with liquid or gas, its volume may be diminished by capillary puncture, taking care not to contaminate the wound by the escaping material. Bathing the parts with warm, sterile, normal saline solution is beneficial in favouring reduction and promoting resolution.

Having decided that the hernial contents are fit to be returned by their showing no evidence of necrosis, let an assistant apply traction on the testicle or cord so as to bring the seat of stricture more within

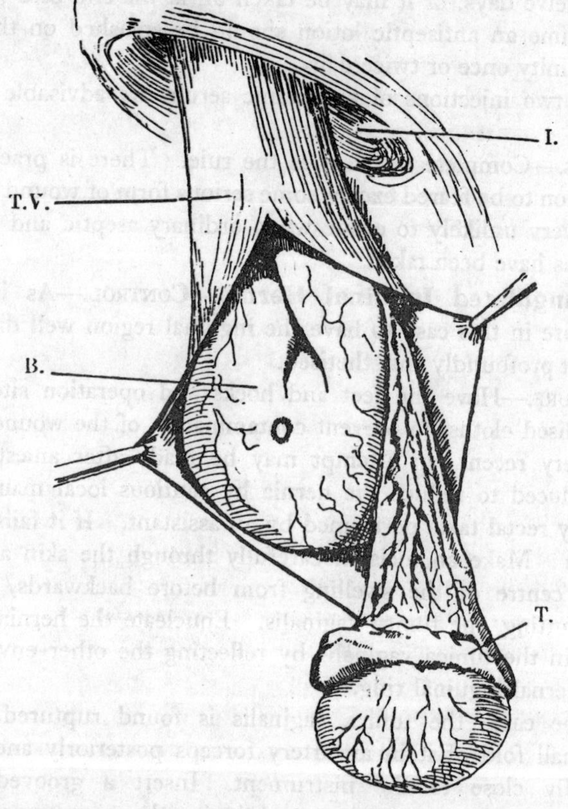

FIG. 131.—STRANGULATED INGUINAL HERNIA.

I., External inguinal ring ; T.V., tunica vaginalis ; B., bowel ; T., testicle.

reach, and then insert the finger or a hernia director between the bowel and the constricted part. Pass the blunt-pointed straight knife flatwise along the finger or director beyond the stricture, turn the edge towards the latter in an outward and forward direction away from the position of the posterior abdominal artery, and make a very limited incision in the neck of the sac (kelotomy).

If the incision is too large it will involve the cremaster muscle and the hernial contents, when being returned, may pass through it instead of going into the abdomen, constituting false reduction. It is usually easy to effect reduction after releasing the stricture. If not, it may be facilitated by taxis *per rectum*, traction and pressure being always applied parallel to the direction of the inguinal canal.

If the bowel is ulcerated or affected with a small area of necrosis, the ulcer or necrosed patch may be depressed by dimpling the bowel wall at its level and shutting it off from the peritoneal cavity by means of a double row of Lembert sutures inserted on either side of it and tied across it, a procedure which is preferable to cutting out the affected part and then suturing, as the viscus is opened in this case and contamination from its lumen is apt to supervene.

When the omentum is irreducible it may be amputated. If the bowel is gangrenous the case is hopeless. After effecting reduction, apply the clam as before. Penicillin is indicated with a view to counteracting any infection that may have taken place.

RESULTS.—When the operation has been done early, before the vitality of the bowel has been weakened and its walls invaded by micro-organisms from its lumen, it is usually successful. But if the patient is already overcome by toxæmia, indicated by a weak, frequent pulse, dirty injected conjunctiva, and profound depression, the operation will be of no avail. Gangrene will have already occurred in this case.

Operation to Preserve the Testicle

INDICATION.—This is indicated in the case of a valuable stud animal.

1. **Reducible Hernia**—PROCEDURE.—Make an incision at the level of the outer aspect of the external inguinal ring, exposing the tunica vaginalis, which is not incised. Reduce the hernia. Draw a fold of the tunica vaginalis out through the wound, and include it in a couple of interrupted sutures inserted through the lips of the wound, the object being to constrict the neck of the sac formed by the tunica vaginalis, and thus prevent recurrence of the hernia. A Danish veterinarian informed the writer that he had done this operation successfully in the horse. It would not, however, appear to be certain of success, and would always involve the risk of possible peritonitis, so that in a case of reducible hernia it would probably be better to leave well alone.

Care must be taken not to constrict the orifice of the sac too much, as it might have a strangulating effect on the testicle and favour infection by curtailing the blood supply.

2. **Strangulated Hernia**—PROCEDURE.—Having exposed the tunica vaginalis at the level of the external inguinal ring, as described, incise it and introduce the finger or a grooved director through the opening thus made beneath the stricture. Pass a knife along the finger or director and cut the stricture. Reduce the hernia, and finish the operation by excising a portion of the tunica vaginalis and suturing the wound therein and that of the skin separately. This procedure does not ensure against recurrence of the hernia.

26. Ventral Hernia

INDICATIONS.—When the hernial ring is of moderate dimensions and the rupture is not situated close to the costal cartilages. Experience has shown that when the hernial ring is very large—exceeding, say, 6 inches in diameter—the hernia frequently recurs within some months after operation, owing to stretching of the cicatrix; and that even in the case of a small hernia immediately behind the costal cartilages the same obtains, due to the tension on the borders of the opening caused by the respiratory movements.

CONTROL.—As for umbilical hernia.

PROCEDURE.—The hernial sac in ventral hernia is not always so well defined as in umbilical hernia, and consequently the ligature or clams cannot be applied in the ordinary way so satisfactorily in the former as in the latter case. The metal clam, when properly applied, has the desired effect. To facilitate its application close to the abdominal wall the modified Degive method No. 1 is indicated (p. 331).

The radical operation may be performed instead of using the clam.

The peritoneum may be ruptured as well as the muscles, in which case there is no peritoneal lining in the sac; consequently, the operation then consists merely in suturing the edge of the hernial ring and the skin by separate series of interrupted sutures.

The method mentioned for umbilical hernia, in which Halsted sutures are passed through the skin and muscles at the borders of the hernial orifice, may also be employed.

The modification (No. 2) of the Degive method is very suitable for a large hernia, in which it would be difficult to approximate the lips of the hernial ring by ordinary sutures. When the hernia is not close to the costal cartilages, but in the proximity of the sheath or mammary gland, this method of operation has a good chance of success. The author succeeded with this procedure in a ventral hernia near the udder in a brood mare with foal at foot.

After-Treatment.—It is important to insist on long rest and to avoid over-distension of the abdomen for some months after the operation.

27. The Ox

The methods recommended for hernia in the horse can be adopted in the ox when operation is considered necessary—for example, when strangulation is present or the condition is interfering with the animal's thriving.

28. Scrotal Hernia in the Pig

Scrotal hernia is very common in the pig, appearing in the form of a more or less voluminous swelling masking the testicle in the perineal region.

Operation is performed in the same way as in the horse, but a comparatively larger cutaneous wound is required in the pig owing to the inguinal ring being farther forward from the seat of the hernia. It is important to continue the incision forwards so as to get opposite to the external inguinal ring, and thus ensure complete reduction of the hernia before applying the ligature on the cord enclosed in the tunica vaginalis. If this precaution is not taken and the ligature applied below the level of the hernial orifice the thin hernial sac will rupture above the ligation and allow escape of the bowel.

A clam may be used instead of a ligature in the large boar.

In suck pigs with a small hernia it is usually sufficient to suture the scrotal wound after castration, but it is safer to do the covered operation, using a ligature on the covered cord.

29. Umbilical Hernia : Dog and Cat

Indications.—When the hernia has persisted after puppyhood, and in all cases of incarceration or strangulation of the hernia.

Preparation.—As usual for an abdominal operation, the patient being deprived of solid food for twenty-four hours previously.

Control.—Fix the animal in the dorsal position on a table and administer a general anæsthetic.

Procedure.—Perform the radical operation as described for the horse, isolating and ligaturing the peritoneal sac, amputating it on this side of the ligature, and suturing the abdominal wall and skin separately with interrupted sutures, employing silk for the former and the same or silkworm gut for the latter. A simpler procedure and just as effective is to remove the entire sac and finish the operation as for laparotomy.

30. Inguinal Hernia

In the male the operation is the same as in the horse, except that a ligature is always employed instead of a clam. An antiseptic solution is applied to the wound once daily until the ligature cuts through and comes away. When a catgut ligature is used and the cutaneous wound sutured, healing by first intention may ensue.

If it is required to preserve the testicle the operation is more delicate, and is performed as already described (p. 337).

31. In the Bitch

The operation performed is similar to that adopted for umbilical hernia.

PROCEDURE.—Have the bitch in the dorsal position on the table and administer a general anæsthetic. Make a short antero-posterior incision in the centre of the swelling through the skin and mammary gland, exposing the peritoneum without cutting it. Enucleate the peritoneal portion of the sac by careful dissection, taking care not to tear it, but cutting close to it, remembering that it gets narrower towards the external inguinal ring, so as to avoid making an unnecessarily large wound, which in a toy dog might be sufficient to cause its death from shock. Grasp the distal portion of the sac in a large forceps and twist it on its long axis, thereby causing reduction of the hernial contents and forming the sac into a cord. Ligature the latter as close to the external inguinal ring as possible, and amputate it on this side of the ligature.

If the inguinal opening does not seem sufficiently closed by the ligature, insert a couple of sutures through its borders, but as a rule these are not necessary and moreover are difficult to insert safely. Apply sulphanilamide powder to the wound, suture the skin, and paint the line of sutures and the vicinity with a little tincture of iodine.

There is usually a cavity beneath the skin preventing primary union. In this case remove a couple of the sutures on the following day to provide for drainage. Dress the wound daily with an antiseptic solution until the ligature and sutures, if any, have separated. If the edges of the skin can be brought into accurate opposition without leaving an " espace mort " beneath it, healing by first intention should ensue.

Incarcerated and Strangulated Inguinal Hernia in the Bitch.—The procedure here is the same as that described for strangulated umbilical hernia, except that rectal taxis is not possible in the small animals. One or both horns of the uterus usually form the hernial contents in the bitch, and the organ may or may not be pregnant In a case of pregnancy at full term, where it is desired to save the pups and preserve the bitch for breeding, perform Cæsarean section and remove the pups, and then reduction is usually easy.

When the uterus is not gravid, or even when it is and the bitch is not required for the stud, perform partial or complete hysterectomy, according as only one or both uterine horns are involved in the hernia. This is the simplest and most expeditious procedure.

When the bladder forms the hernial contents reduction is impossible without incising the hernial orifice even after complete evacuation of the organ when distended from constriction of its neck.

RESULT.—When the operation is performed early, before gangrene has supervened, recovery is the rule. The writer had a case in which the herniated horn of the uterus alone was pregnant. He amputated this horn, and the animal made a good recovery and gave birth to living offspring from the remaining horn after a subsequent service. The increased intervention required when the bladder forms the contents renders the prognosis less favourable.

32. Gut-Tie, Pelvic Hernia, in the Ox

INDICATION.—When other methods of treatment have failed to release the bowel from its herniated position.

CONTROL.—Cast and anæsthetise the beast on its left side.

PROCEDURE.—Perform laparotomy in the right flank. Pass the hand into the abdomen, engage the fingers in the hernial opening alongside the intestine, and endeavour to rupture the cord or border of the ring so as to release the constricted bowel. If this fail, introduce a hooked knife with blunt point, such as Anker's scalpel (Fig. 132), and cut the stricture. Finish as for laparotomy.

FIG. 132.—ANKER'S GUARDED KNIFE FOR PELVIC HERNIA.

RESULT.—When done before necrosis of the bowel has supervened recovery usually ensues.

33. Perineal Hernia

INDICATIONS.—Operation is not indicated except incarceration of the bladder or intestine supervenes, causing symptoms of pain and interfer ingwith micturition or defæcation, because it is often difficult or impossible to operate successfully owing to the absence of a peritoneal sac and the consequent impossibility of closing the hernial passage.

CONTROL.—The subject is usually a dog, male or female, which is fixed on the table in the ventral position and given a general anæsthetic.

PROCEDURE.—Reduce the hernia, raising the hind-quarters if necessary to facilitate the process. Enucleate the peritoneal sac, if present, ligature it as far forward as possible, amputate it behind the ligature, and suture the skin. To prevent the bladder or bowel tending to return into the peritoneal cul-de-sac it is advisable to perform cystopexia or rectopexia, according as bladder or bowel forms the contents.

Perform laparotomy in the median line when the bladder is involved, and in the corresponding flank when it is the rectum that is herniated. Bring the bladder or portion of the bowel that is to be fixed to the level of the parietal wound, and make it fast there by means of a series of sutures passing through its serous and muscular coats, and through the peritoneal and muscular layers of the edges of the operation wound, thus closing the deep part of the latter at the same time. Suture the skin in the ordinary way. This operation will be of little use if the hernial passage cannot be obliterated.

Death from peritonitis is apt to supervene when the abdominal cavity cannot be properly closed for want of a serous lining to the hernial sac.

Forssell (*Berl. tierarztl. Wschr.*) in 1937 described his method of operating for this conditions in male dogs. Having reduced the contents, he closed the hernial ring by means of catgut sutures, using a small curved needle, the first row being put in as deeply as possible in the pelvis and followed by further rows of sutures, each row burying the preceding one. Careful suturing is necessary to avoid wounding branches of the internal pudic artery and vein. The skin wound was closed by stainless wire sutures (diameter of wire 0·2 millimetre), the twisted ends of each suture lying between the edges of the wound. He was successful in eight cases out of ten treated. The secret of success seems to be the number of buried sutures that can be employed. He has frequently inserted as many as thirty in effectively closing the ring.

34. Laparotomy, Abdominal Section, Cœliotomy

INDICATIONS.—Exploration of the abdominal cavity and operation on some of the organs therein.

PREPARATION.—When the case is not urgent, prepare the patient by giving it a purgative a few days previously, and keeping it on laxative concentrated diet until the day of the operation, when it should be fasting from the night before. It is very important to have the volume of the abdominal viscera reduced as much as possible in order to facilitate intra-abdominal manœuvres.

Horse

CONTROL.—Cast, anæsthetise, and fix in a suitable position according to the site of the operation.

SITES.—(1) The flank; (2) the inguinal region; (3) the anterior wall of the vagina.

PROCEDURE—*The Flank Method.*—The left flank is usually chosen owing to the right side of the abdomen being occupied by the large bowel. Having the animal on its right side and taking all aseptic and antiseptic precautions, including the application of a sterile cloth over the trunk and quarters with an opening opposite the site of operation (cœliotomy cloth), make a vertical (in standing position) cutaneous incision, commencing a little below the external angle of the ilium and continued downwards for a distance of 5 or 6 inches. Incise the abdominal muscles to the same extent, dividing the internal abdominal oblique in the direction of its fibres to favour closure of the wound afterwards. Arrest the hæmorrhage. Puncture the peritoneum at the lower extremity of the wound with the finger or a blunt instrument, or, perhaps better, take up a small fold of it in a forceps and incise it horizontally close to the latter. Enlarge the peritoneal wound on the fingers or a director or between the open jaws of a large forceps, held beneath the peritoneum, to the same extent as that in the other tissues.

Intra-Abdominal Manœuvres.—These must be made with the strictest attention to asepsis, without rough handling of the viscera, and as expeditiously as possible. Mechanical injury and long exposure to cold of the serous membrane predispose to peritonitis, as does also the use of irritant antiseptic solutions. Care must be taken not to allow prolapse of the intestine, and, with this point in view, complete anæsthesia is maintained until the abdominal opening is closed. A sudden movement of the patient may cause several feet of the small intestine to escape.

Suture of the Abdominal Wound.—The abdominal wound may be sutured by :

1. One series of sutures through skin, muscles, and peritoneum
2. Two series of sutures, one through the muscles and serous membrane and another through the skin.
3. Three series of sutures, the peritoneum, muscles, and skin being sutured separately.
4. One series of sutures through the skin only.

For the flank method in the horse No. 4 answers the purpose, as there is no tension on the wound, and the separated muscular fibres come into contact automatically. It has the advantage that there will be no trouble from deep stitches becoming contaminated.

When No. 1 is adopted, wire sutures are recommended, as absorption of septic material from outside cannot occur through them to infect the peritoneum. This method is seldom adopted. It does not ensure accurate apposition of the deeper layers of tissue, and establishes a communication between the surface of the skin and the abdominal cavity. No. 2 is the method most in vogue. No. 3 is quite unnecessary, and prolongs the procedure too much.

Before suturing apply some sulphanilamide powder on the wound, and when it has been sutured use the same powder externally or paint it with tincture of iodine. An antiseptic pad and bandage round the body may be applied, but it is not necessary and is difficult to keep in position.

AFTER-TREATMENT.—Put the horse in a comfortable hygienic box and protect him from cold. Give the usual hospital diet. Paint the wound and its vicinity lightly once daily with tincture of iodine.

RESULTS.—Considerable inflammation with surrounding œdema appears about the wound during the days following the operation. When the latter has been carefully performed on a healthy subject recovery is the rule, but if the operation has been done for a septic condition inside the abdominal cavity, or the latter has become infected during the procedure, peritonitis will ensue, and its symptoms will be evident within a week afterwards, being characterised by depression, dull abdominal pain, loss of appetite, tense abdomen, a frequent weak pulse, and a rise in temperature. The pulse is the best guide as to the condition of the patient. A high temperature need not cause alarm if the pulse is fairly full and regular and does not exceed sixty, and the patient continues to feed. When peritonitis is suspected or if the nature of the case suggests the possibility of its supervening a course of penicillin treatment should be adopted.

Healing by first intention may ensue, but sometimes the deep sutures become contaminated and cause constant suppuration until they come away with the discharge or are removed. It may be necessary to incise the skin which has closed over some of them to effect their removal.

Inguinal and Vaginal Sites.—Operation through these sites will be dealt with under the heads of Rig Castration and Ovariotomy respectively.

The Ox

The operation is practically the same in the ox as in the horse. The right or left flank is chosen according to the nature of the operation, and the other sites mentioned may also be adopted. The peritoneum in the bovine is less susceptible to infection than in the equine.

The Pig

The pig is a good subject for laparotomy when in normal health. The flank and linea alba are the two sites for the operation.

The Sheep

The site of operation is the flank.

The Dog

Preparation of the patient is important, as described under "Operative Technique." The bladder should be evacuated before the patient is put on the table. A delicate or toy dog should get a little milk or Bovril a couple of hours before the operation. Careful attention to the preparation of the site is essential. It is advisable to do the rough part of it the day before. In winter the operating room should be artificially heated, or alternatively hot-water bottles should be placed alongside the patient.

CONTROL.—Have the patient fixed in the dorsal or lateral position on the table according to the site chosen, and carefully anæsthetised. The operation may be done under morphia and local anæsthesia, but not so satisfactorily, as the patient may nevertheless struggle and hamper the operator.

SITES.—The sites are (1) the linea alba, and (2) the flank. The white line is a convenient site for most abdominal operations, and is not very vascular. Its dependent position favours prolapse of the bowel should the sutures become undone, but otherwise this accident is not likely to happen, as the weight of the abdominal contents in the dog is insignificant. The part of the white line chosen depends on the organ to be reached—*e.g.*, (*a*) midway between the umbilicus and the xiphoid cartilage for the stomach; (*b*) immediately behind the umbilicus for the ovaries, uterus, and kidneys; (*c*) just in front of the pubis for the bladder. The incision may be actually on the white line or immediately to one side of it. The advantage of the former is the slight hæmorrhage which ensues and of the latter the vascularity of the part which promotes rapid healing of the wound.

In the male the incision behind the level of the preputial orifice must be made to one side of the sheath.

PROCEDURE.—Cover the whole of the patient's body and the operation table in its vicinity with a sterilised calico cloth fixed to the skin by towel forceps, and having an opening opposite the operation site. Make the incision carefully through the skin and subcutaneous fat, exposing the abdominal muscles. Incise the muscles to the same extent, taking care not to penetrate the abdomen and perhaps wound the bladder, which is very easily punctured if distended. Perforate the peritoneum with a grooved director and enlarge the wound thereon with a knife, or by means of a sharp, straight, blunt-pointed scissors, taking care not to snip the bowel with the latter.

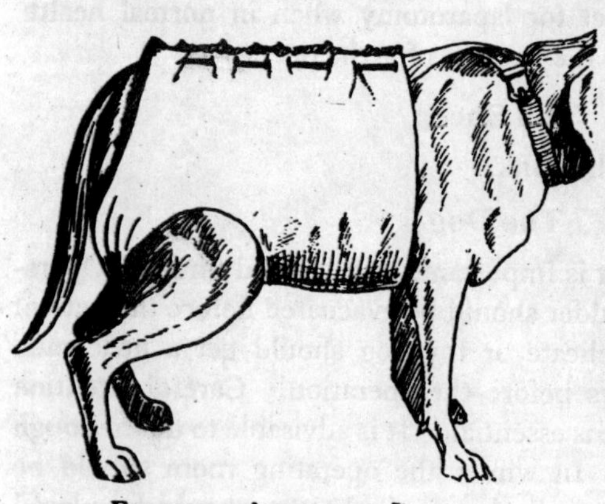

FIG. 133.—ABDOMINAL BANDAGE.

Having completed the intra-abdominal operation, suture the parietal wound by two series of interrupted sutures, one through the peritoneum and muscles and the other through the skin. If troubled by the intestines protruding during the process, insert a layer of lint or gauze in the abdomen beneath the wound, and leave it in position until the wound is three-quarters sutured, and do not forget to remove it.

Making the first series of sutures is facilitated by having the edges of the wound lifted upwards by a loop of silk passed across the wound at either commissure, or by means of a straight, blunt hook passed beneath either of its extremities, as advised by the late Sir Frederick Treves. When this is done, a straight needle can be passed horizontally through the tissues, thereby obviating the trouble caused by a curved or semi-curved needle turning in the fingers when being inserted.

Before closing the cutaneous wound apply a little sulphanilamide powder. Paint the line of sutures and the vicinity with tincture of iodine. Protect the wound with a sterilised pad and bandage, the latter being in the form of a piece of calico fixed by stitches along the back. This is not necessary if the patient is kept afterwards in a kennel with a clean boarded floor without bedding or covered with newspaper, and in the dog it cannot be applied over the sheath. When healing by first intention does not ensue, the cause is contamination of the deep sutures which then act as septic foreign bodies, causing a purulent discharge which persists until they are removed. Their removal is troublesome and a source of pain or discomfort to the patient. This trouble can be avoided by adopting the Double Loop Removable Suture (Fig. 134) for the closure of the abdominal wound, as described some years ago in the *British Medical Journal*, and advocated by Mitchell of Edinburgh. It is performed by passing the needle and thread through the lips of the wound in the following order, viz., through:

1. The skin only, near one commissure of the wound and on its proximal side;
2. the muscle and peritoneum on the distal side about ½ inch from the edge of the wound;
3. the peritoneum and muscle on the proximal side;
4. the muscle and peritoneum on the proximal side about 1 inch from the point of emergence in the longitudinal direction;
5. the peritoneum and muscle on the distal side;
6. the skin only, from within outwards on the proximal side, about ¼ inch away laterally from the point where the needle was first inserted.

Put in the second suture before tying the first one. Three such sutures are sufficient for a wound 4 to 5 inches long.

Draw on the two ends of the thread sufficiently to bring the muscular edges of the wound into apposition, and tie them over a piece of round catapult rubber after the manner of a quill suture.

Having thus closed the deep part of the wound, bring the edges of the skin together with ordinary interrupted sutures. Silkworm gut is the most suitable material for the loop sutures. The latter are easily removed after seven to ten days by cutting the thread and drawing on it. If it is tight it may be left for twenty-four hours to slacken before removing it.

AFTER-TREATMENT.—Put the patient in a perfectly hygienic kennel, which in winter must be artificially heated. Give only liquid diet for a few days, milk being the most suitable. Apply a little diluted tincture of iodine to the wound and its vicinity once or twice daily, if not protected by a dressing. When the wound is aseptic the patient does not interfere with it, but when it is irritated by infection he may gnaw at it and remove some of the superficial and deep sutures, allowing escape of the intestines. This must be guarded against, although it is a rare occurrence. The animal must not be allowed to over-exert itself, and cause, perhaps, rupture of the recent cicatrix and escape of the bowels.

RESULT.—Recovery without complication is the rule in a subject not affected with any disease, and healing by first intention is common when the operation has been carefully performed and the wound protected from infection afterwards.

COMPLICATIONS.—Descent of the omentum or bowel, or both, may ensue under the circumstances mentioned. When the omentum only protrudes, recovery usually ensues when the soiled portion is cut away and the wound resutured. It is not wise to remove normal omentum, as it has been shown to perform an important function in attracting foreign matter in the abdomen and circumscribing it, and preventing infection therefrom being diffused throughout the peritoneum. It has been called the scavenger of the peritoneal cavity. If only a portion of the bowel is prolapsed and is attended to early before it has become soiled, a fatal issue may be avoided. Otherwise peritonitis and death are very apt to supervene.

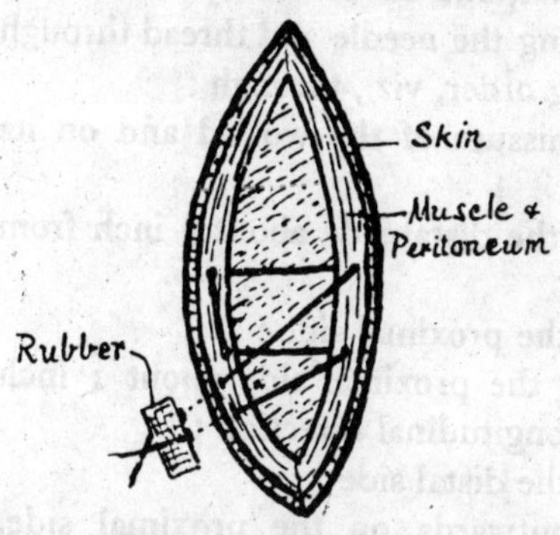

FIG. 134.—DOUBLE LOOP STITCH FOR ABDOMINAL WALL.

Peritonitis is a rare complication, except the accident just mentioned has occurred. Unless it is localised, it usually terminates in death. Treatment is of little or no avail. Should it result from the escape of intestinal contents following perforation of the bowel, washing out the peritoneal cavity with warm normal saline solution may be tried, but it is not likely to succeed. When infection of the peritoneal cavity is feared or has supervened the administration of penicillin intravenously and intraperitoneally is indicated and may have the desired effect.

Death from shock may take place within twenty-four hours after the operation, especially in a delicate subject. When the patient is threatened with collapse, a stimulant is indicated in the form of a hypodermic injection of coramine, ether, caffeine, or atropine, or a subcutaneous injection of normal saline or glucose saline.

The Cat

The cat is dealt with in the same manner as the dog.

35. Gastrotomy

Gastrotomy is not practicable in the horse, and in the ox it is only performed on the rumen, as a rule.

Rumenotomy—INDICATIONS.—Impaction of the rumen; hair, balls, or other foreign body therein or in the reticulum.

CONTROL.—The operation may be done standing, under the influence of paravertebral nerve block as practised by Farquharson in America, the nerves involved being the thirteenth thoracic, and the first, second, and third lumbar, and the directions being as follows: Taking the usual aseptic precautions and having prepared the sites of puncture proceed thus:

(1) Trace the last rib upwards to its head and at a point 2 inches from the middle line insert a strong 4-inch needle through the skin until the point is felt to come in contact with the head of the rib, then withdraw it slightly and direct it backwards until the point is felt behind the rib and inject 20 c.c. of a local anæsthetic (" parsetic ") in various directions by altering the course of the needle, thus infiltrating a fairly large area.

(2) Repeat the procedure in the cases of th. first, second, and third lumbar vertebræ except that here the lumbar transverse processes are encountered by the point of the needle, which is then withdrawn slightly and redirected until the point is felt at the posterior border of the process. In the case of the third lumbar nerve 5–10 c.c. of the local anæsthetic are sufficient, as the nerve only gives a cutaneous branch to the posterior part of the area.

After the lapse of 10 to 12 minutes, if the injections have been made correctly, the whole area of the flank would be desensitised. Gold in his paper (*Vet. Rec.*, Nov. 30th, 1946) from which the foregoing remarks have been taken, says that he administers 1 ounce of chloral prior to making the injections for the purpose of keeping the animal quiet during the procedure, the animal being securely held with its right side against a wall and a kicking-strap applied above the hocks if considered necessary. Legally the operation should be done under general anæsthesia which, however, is not necessary, regional anæsthesia having the desired effect when properly performed.

PROCEDURE.—Perform laparotomy in the left flank, exposing the rumen. Suture the latter to the abdominal wall by a couple of Halsted sutures on either side of the wound. Puncture the rumen with a

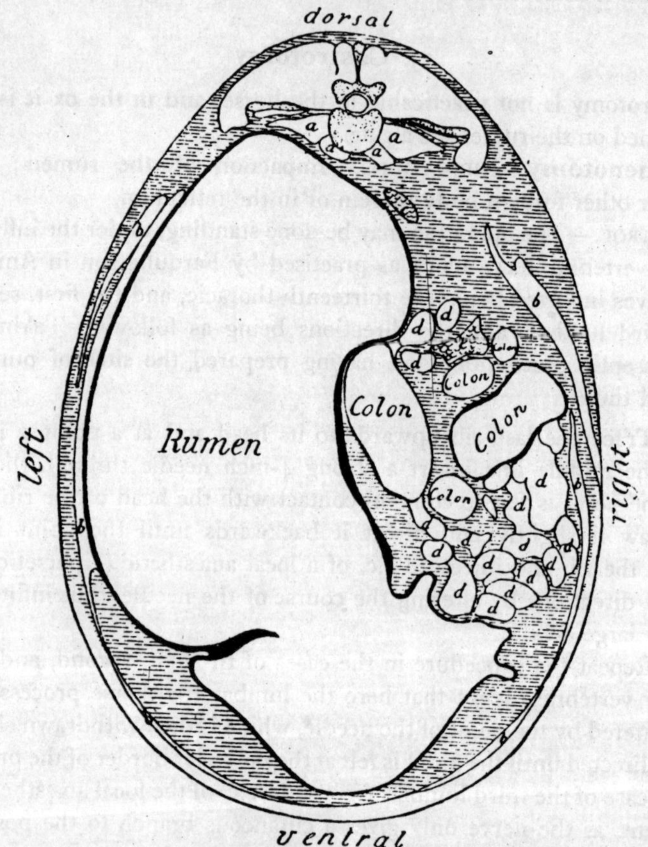

FIG. 135.—VERTICAL SECTION OF THE OX'S BODY, SHOWING RELATIVE POSITION OF RUMEN AND OTHER ORGANS.

a, Lumbar muscles ; *b*, abdominal muscles ; *d*, glands ; *e*, portion of the pancreas. (After Ellenberger and Baum.)

trocar and canula to allow of the escape of gas and avoid its causing an outrush of ingesta when the organ is incised, leading to soiling of the borders of the wound and of the exposed peritoneum. Before incising the rumen insert the end of a sterilised cloth in the lower commissure of the parietal wound and fix it in position by towel clips to prevent contamination of the peritoneal cavity from escaping gastric contents. Before opening the rumen Gold draws a portion of it outside the wound in the abdominal wall and has it held there by four tapes passed through the peritoneal and muscular coats, two above (anterior and posterior) and two below (anterior and posterior) while being incised. Incise the rumen in the direction of the parietal wound and remove one-half or two-thirds of the gastric contents by means of the hand or a ladle, or a suitable vessel. If a foreign body, which is usually a piece of cloth, is present in the rumen, remove it. If a foreign body is to be removed from the reticulum, introduce the hand and arm, which may be clothed in a rubber glove and sleeve, into the rumen and pass it downwards and forwards into the reticulum, where a careful search of each cell may be necessary before finding the foreign body, which may be concealed in an accumulation of sand. It is advisable to complete the search in one exploration to avoid the risk of contamination by reintroduction of the arm. Experience has shown that when the operation has been done for impaction it is better not to suture the gastric wound, but to leave the rumen fixed by sutures to the abdominal wall. A gastric fistula ensues and persists for a while, but eventually closes. Remove the parieto-gastric sutures after a few days, when the rumen has become adherent to the abdominal wall, otherwise the after-treatment consists in cleaning the vicinity of the wound.

When the intervention has been for the removal of a foreign body without impaction, it is usual to suture the rumen by Lembert's method and to finish as for laparotomy. Gold, having finished " exploration " of the reticulum in his operation for traumatic reticulitis and having cleaned the peritoneal surface of the rumen with sterilised swabs, closed the gastric wound with a continuous catgut Lembert suture, commencing at the inferior commissure, so as to minimise the risk of escape of rumenal contents, and he brought the muscular and cutaneous lips of the parietal wound into apposition by one series of interrupted tape sutures passing through skin, muscles, muscles skin, and back through the edges of the skin close to the line of incision, so that when the sutures are tied (not until all the sutures have been inserted) the edges of the skin incision will be everted, thereby bringing the subcutaneous portions into apposition and eliminating dead space.

Result.—The patient usually withstands the operation well, but may fail to thrive afterwards, owing to chronic indigestion and tympanites supervening from interference with the trituratory movements of the rumen because of its adhesion to the abdominal wall. If the animal is in a state of exhaustion when the operation is performed, death is apt to follow.

Sheep and Lamb

Rumenotomy is performed in the same way in the sheep, but is seldom indicated.

Gastrotomy on the fourth stomach is sometimes indicated in the young lamb to remove a wool-ball obstructing the pylorus, but it is seldom of economic value, as the lamb does not thrive afterwards, although the operation has been successfully performed.

PROCEDURE.—Administer a general anæsthetic, perform laparotomy on the median line in front of the umbilicus, draw the stomach to the wound, open it longitudinally without allowing any of the contents to escape into the abdomen, remove the obstruction, suture the gastric wound Lembert fashion, and finish as for laparotomy.

The Dog

INDICATIONS.—To remove a foreign body from the stomach or from the lower end of the œsophagus.

PROCEDURE.—Perform laparotomy between the xiphoid cartilage and the umbilicus. Take measures to prevent escape of gastric contents into the peritoneal cavity. Draw a portion of the stomach through the wound and surround it by warm sterile lint or gauze. Pass a loop of fine silk through the serous and muscular coats at either end of the future incision to serve as handles to hold up the organ. Incise the viscus parallel to its long curvature. Search for the foreign body and remove it with a forceps; suture the gastric wound by Lembert's method. A double row of Lembert sutures may be inserted to ensure complete closure of the wound. Finish as for laparotomy.

AFTER-TREATMENT.—Give only liquid diet for ten days after the operation, milk being the most suitable.

RESULT.—Good when performed before the patient has become exhausted from inanition and vomiting.

36. Van der Kaay's Operation for Chronic Gastric Tympany in the Ox

INDICATION.—Chronic gastric tympany preventing the animal from thriving, the operation being performed in the late spring before the beast is put to grass.

PROCEDURE.—Have the animal fixed in stocks or otherwise controlled in the standing position. Use a local anæsthetic. Make a short vertical incision, at the site for puncturing the rumen, into the peritoneal cavity exposing the organ. Suture the rumen to the abdominal wall above and below and on either side of the wound by a Halsted stitch. Cover the wound with an antiseptic dressing and wait for a few days until adhesion has occurred between the rumen and the abdominal wall. Then incise the rumen and suture each lip of the gastric wound to the corresponding lip of the parietal wound, thus leaving a permanent gastric fistula through which gas will escape according as it is formed.

RESULT.—Professor Dr. Van der Kaay of Utrecht is reported to have got excellent results, the beasts thriving and putting on flesh rapidly after being put to grass. The operation was brought to the notice of the writer by Dr. Fourie, Onderstepoort (S. Africa).

37. Enterotomy

INDICATIONS.—To remove an intestinal obstruction due to a calculus, a swallowed foreign body, or impacted intestinal contents.

PROCEDURE.—The procedure is the same in all animals. Perform laparotomy, draw the affected portion of bowel outside the wound, surround it with warm sterile lint or gauze. Incise the bowel longitudinally on the side opposite to the mesenteric attachment. Remove the obstruction without contaminating the peritoneum. Suture the intestinal wound Lembert fashion, and finish as for laparotomy.

AFTER-TREATMENT.—As for gastrotomy.

RESULT.—The operation has been rarely performed in the horse and has proved fatal in most cases. Successful removal of intestinal calculi, however, has been reported by Félizet. Recovery is the rule in the dog when performed early, before toxæmia has supervened (see Laparotomy). Stenosis of the intestine may supervene at a variable time afterwards from cicatricial contraction at the seat of operation.

38. Enterectomy

INDICATIONS.—Necrosis of a portion of bowel, irreducible invagination, and tumours of the bowel wall.

PROCEDURE.—As for enterotomy, until the affected portion of bowel is drawn outside the abdominal opening. Then push the intestinal contents up and down away from the seat of obstruction, and prevent their return by clamping the bowel at some distance from the proposed line of section. The clamp may be the fingers and thumbs of an assistant, or a piece of rubber compressed with an artery forceps, or a metal clamp. The objection to the last mentioned is that it may bruise the bowel wall, thereby diminishing its defensive power and enabling bacteria to pass through it from the lumen of the intestine to the peritoneal cavity.

Map out a triangular piece of mesentery with its base corresponding to the portion of bowel to be removed. Ligature the arteries of supply thereto, taking care not to occlude any vessel supplying a part of the intestine other than that to be removed. Excise this portion of mesentery along with the affected part of the bowel, using a sharp, straight scissors for the purpose. Bring the two ends of the bowel into apposition and unite them by a series of Lembert sutures, or by some anastomosing device such as Murphy's button. Before suturing, invert the edges of the posterior end and insert the anterior end into it. It is difficult to keep the ends in position when suturing. The difficulty may be overcome by introducing into each end of the bowel a hollow cone shaped out of a turnip, a thread being inserted longitudinally through the wall of the cone above and below from its narrow end, where it is arrested by a knot. When the ends of the bowel are in apposition, the threads are brought out through the intestinal wall a short distance from the cut edges and the anterior and posterior threads are tied, thus keeping the parts fixed while the sutures are being inserted. Care is taken to have the knots of the two threads covered by the other sutures to prevent infection through them from the lumen of the bowel.

It is sufficient to say that Murphy's button is composed of two parts, between which the ends of the bowel are compressed into apposition with the serous surfaces in contact all round, there being a passage through the centre of the button for the intestinal contents. After some time the portion of bowel compressed separates, leaving the button free to be passed out with the fæces, adhesion having occurred between the serous surfaces at the periphery of the line of separation

Each part of the button is first fixed in position by a purse-string suture going through the serous and muscular coats, and the two parts of the button are then fixed together by a clasp in its interior. On seeing the button the mechanism is easily understood.

It is not very suitable for a bowel of narrow lumen like that of the dog or cat, as it may cause obstruction. Moreover, it favours stricture of the bowel owing to the depth of the ridge formed in its circumference at the site of operation. Otherwise it is an extremely useful device, enabling entero-anastomosis to be effectively and quickly performed.

French, of New York, has devised an ingenious method of uniting the ends of the bowel in the dog thus: Take two plain hairpins; compress each with a forceps just in front of the bend so as to bring its two limbs close together. Put each hairpin riding on the bowel, with one limb across where the mesentery is attached, at the two places where the bowel is to be severed. Compress the two limbs of each pin with a spring forceps so as to make it act as a clamp (Fig. 136). Resect the affected portion of bowel and the triangular piece of mesentery. Bring the two cut ends of the bowel into contact, and fix them there by tying the two hairpins together on each side

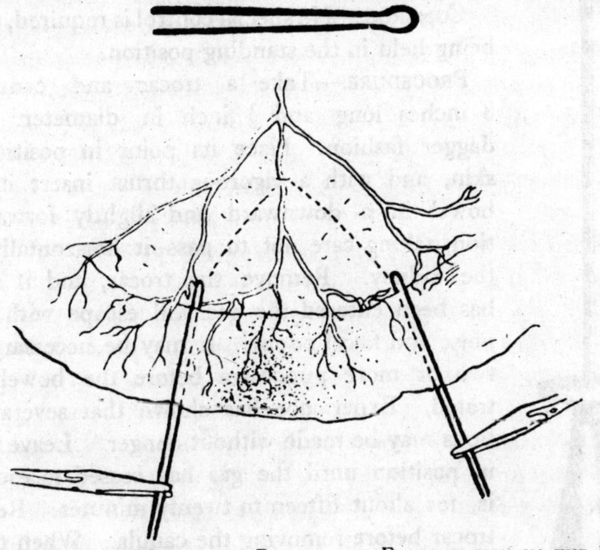

Fig. 136.—Hairpin Method of Performing Enterectomy in the Dog.

of the bowel. Insert a series of Lembert sutures, burying the limbs of the hairpins. After suturing cut each hairpin at its bent part and remove each limb separately. Close the openings, left after extracting the hairpins, by Lembert sutures, making sure that the serous surfaces are turned in. The hairpins serve the dual purpose of clamps and of holding the bowel in position while suturing. This method has proved quite successful in experimental cases in the hands of Mr. French, five out of six cases recovering.

Result.—Enterectomy may be said to be a hopeless operation in the horse. Even in the dog its chance of success is very remote when performed on gangrenous bowel or in an animal already intoxicated by bacterial poisons.

39. Puncture of the Bowel : Tapping

INDICATION.—Intestinal tympany which has failed to respond to medical treatment, or prior to the latter in a bad case.

Puncture of the Cæcum.—This is the bowel most frequently tapped.

SITE.—The right flank at a point equidistant from the external angle of the ilium, the last rib, and the transverse processes of the lumbar vertebræ, or at the highest point of the swelling.

FIG. 137.—FRIEDBERGER'S INTESTINAL TROCAR FOR HORSES.

CONTROL.—No special control is required, the animal being held in the standing position.

PROCEDURE.—Take a trocar and canula about 8 inches long and $\frac{1}{8}$ inch in diameter. Hold it dagger fashion. Place its point in position on the skin, and with a vigorous thrust insert it into the bowel in a downward and slightly forward direction, taking care not to pass it horizontally towards the kidney. Remove the trocar, and if the bowel has been entered the gas will escape with a hissing noise and fæcal odour. It may be necessary to make two or more punctures before the bowel is penetrated. Experience has shown that several perforations may be made without danger. Leave the canula in position until the gas has ceased to escape—that is, for about fifteen to twenty minutes. Reinsert the trocar before removing the canula. When taking out the instrument, press on the skin with the fingers and thumb round the flange of the canula to prevent its separation from the subcutaneous tissue and the formation of a space into which infection might gain entrance and give rise to an abscess. Paint the wound with tincture of iodine. A very small incision may be made in the skin to facilitate inserting the trocar and canula, but it is not advisable.

Puncture of the Colon—SITE.—(1) Each side of the white line below the inferior extremity of the last four ribs at about 30 to 40 centimetres from the umbilicus, or a little higher, about 20 centimetres below the external angle of the ilium. (2) To enter the sternal flexure 5 to 10 centimetres behind the xiphoid cartilage. (3) To enter the pelvic flexure, make the puncture *per rectum*.

PROCEDURE.—For (1) and (2) as described.

For No. 3.—Evacuate the rectum, introduce the instrument with the point hidden inside the canula, place it against the distended bowel, and then thrust trocar and canula into the lumen of the latter.

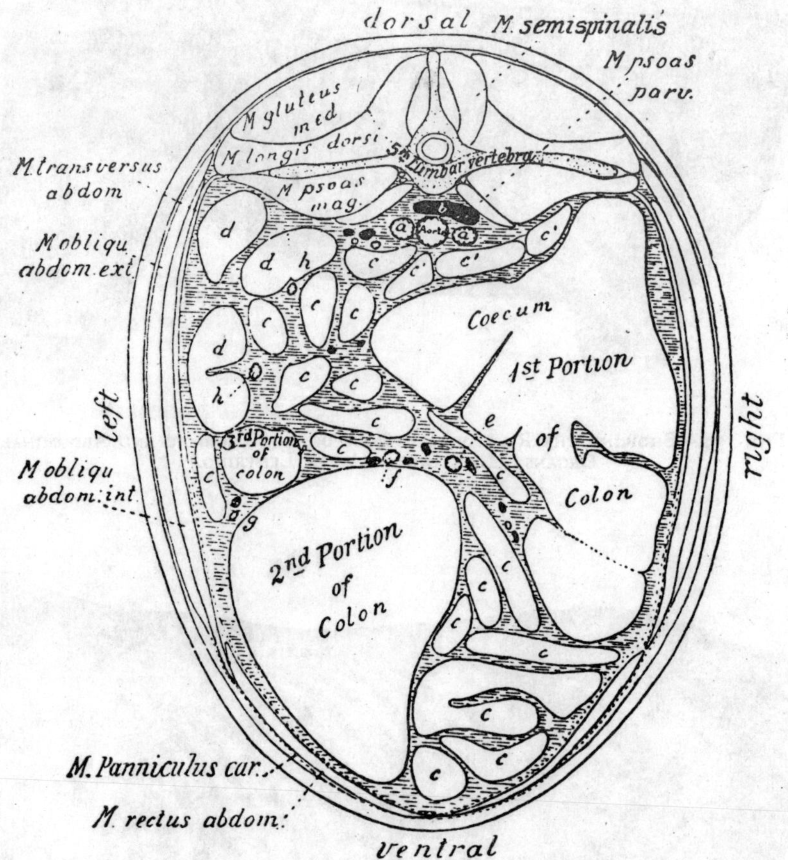

FIG. 138.—VERTICAL SECTION OF THE HORSE'S BODY BETWEEN THE LAST RIB AND EXTERNAL ANGLE OF THE ILIUM.

a, Femoral artery; *b*, posterior vena cava; *c* and *c'*, loops of small intestine; *d*, rectum; *e*, colic artery; *f*, inferior colic artery; *g*, superior colic artery; *h*, arteries of the rectum; *i*, ureter. (After Ellenberger and Baum.)

When a horse is in the recumbent position in the throes of colic, the operation may be done without making the patient rise. If the left flank is distended with gas, it may be punctured in the most prominent part. Both flanks may be punctured if necessary.

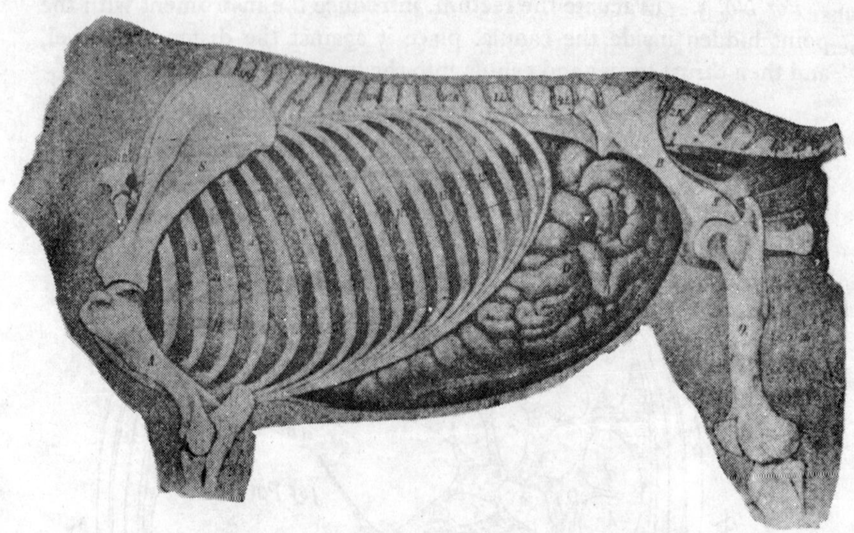

FIG. 139.—SHOWING THE RELATIVE POSITIONS OF THE THORACIC AND ABDOMINAL ORGANS: LEFT SIDE. (AFTER LEISERING.)

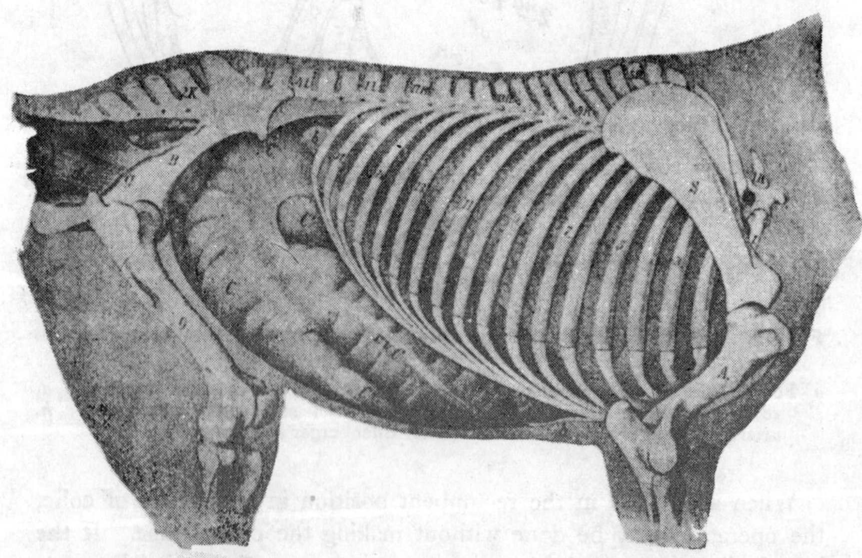

FIG. 140.—SHOWING THE RELATIVE POSITIONS OF THE THORACIC AND ABDOMINAL ORGANS: RIGHT SIDE. (AFTER LEISERING.)

RESULT.—All the foregoing operations are practically harmless when done with due observance of asepsis, and frequently have a very beneficial effect in tympanitic colic. Puncture through the right flank

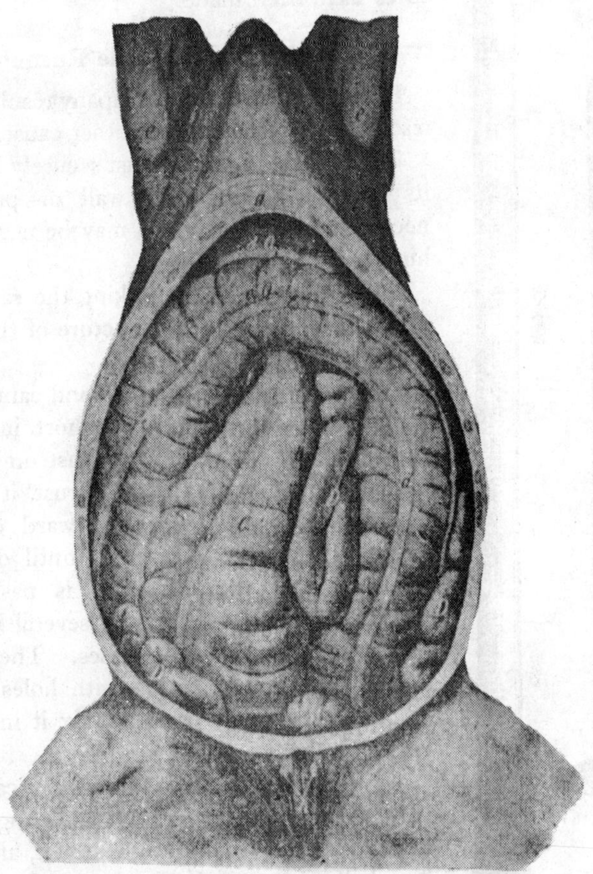

FIG. 141.—ABDOMINAL ORGANS SEEN FROM BELOW.

C, Cæcum ; *r.v.C*, first portion of colon ; *v.Q*, suprasternal flexure ; *l.v.C*, second portion of colon ; *d.Q*, diaphragmatic flexure ; *D*, loops of small intestine ; *M*, loops of floating colon.

is the method most in vogue. Rectal puncture is much in favour with some practitioners.

COMPLICATIONS.—Possible complications are :

1. *Subcutaneous emphysema* from infiltration with gas from the alimentary tract round the site of operation ; not a serious condition.

2. *Abscess formation* from infection of the cutaneous wound, which responds to treatment in the usual way.

3. *Peritonitis*, rare even when several punctures have been made.

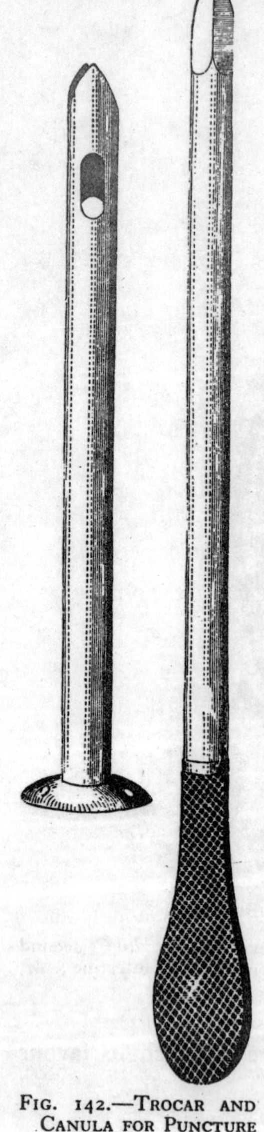

FIG. 142.—TROCAR AND CANULA FOR PUNCTURE OF THE RUMEN.

40. Puncture of the Rumen

INDICATION.—Gastric tympany resulting from œsophageal obstruction or other cause.

CONTROL.—Have the beast securely held with its right side against a wall or paling. If necessary, a kicking-strap may be used on the hind-limbs.

SITE.—The left flank, taking the same landmarks as mentioned for puncture of the cæcum in the horse (page 356).

PROCEDURE.—Take a trocar and canula about ½ inch in diameter, make a short incision in the skin, place the point of the instrument in the centre of the wound, and thrust it into the viscus in a downward and forward direction. Leave the canula in position until danger of recurrence of the condition is past, which may be from half an hour to several hours, or even some days in certain cases. The pavilion of the canula is provided with holes through which tapes may be passed to fix it in position round the body.

In the absence of a trocar and canula the rumen may be opened by inserting a long-bladed, sharp-pointed knife into it, and giving it a half-turn on its long axis to make the opening patent. A piece of stout tubing of any kind may be introduced alongside the knife to act as a canula. Medicament may be poured through the canula into the stomach.

RESULT.—The operation is almost harmless, and always has the desired effect of relieving the distension and preventing asphyxia, to which it may give rise.

COMPLICATIONS.—The possible complications are those mentioned in connection with puncture of the bowel in the horse. Adhesion of the rumen to the abdominal wall may ensue from a local peritonitis occurring round the seat of operation, interfering more or less with the function of the rumen and leading, perhaps, to chronic indigestion. Considerable inflammation may supervene at the site of operation, but it subsides without complication.

The Sheep

The sheep may also require the operation, which is performed with a narrow trocar and canula similar to that used in the horse. It is not so good a subject as the ox, and may succumb to the procedure, which, however, may be imperative to prevent asphyxia.

The Dog

Seldom indicated, but when the bowel is distended with gas it may be punctured with a fine trocar and canula with, at least, temporary good effect.

41. Castration : Emasculation, Gelding, Cutting, Neutralising

Castration means the removal of the essential organs of generatior in the male or female, but in veterinary practice the term is almost exclusively confined to the male, the term ovariotomy or ovariectomy, or oöphorectomy being applied to the female.

The Horse

Indications.—To render the horse docile and capable of control in the presence of mares ; in case of malignant disease or irreparable injury of the gland ; and in connection with the operation for scrotal hernia.

Age.—The operation is usually performed at one year old. The testicles may not have descended into the scrotum until this time. Operation at an earlier period might interfere with the development of the animal. Nevertheless, castration of foals (including thoroughbreds) is now being advocated by certain practitioners, for example Murnane and Howard in Ireland, who say that from their experience of the operation at this age it is quite successful and has no effect in retarding the development of the foal, whereas the operation on yearlings or older colts is more risky from the point of view of accidents and complications. In England cart colts are not castrated as a rule until two years old. The operation may be required in the adult—for example, in the racehorse, when it is found that he is not suitable for the stud, or in any horse which has proved a failure at the latter. The age has little bearing on the success of the operation.

SEASON.—The most suitable season for operating is the late spring or the autumn, but any time will do provided that the patient is protected from severe weather. Operation should be avoided when east winds prevail and when the flies are busy. It is well to operate in the morning, so that the horse can be kept under observation during the day.

CONDITION OF THE SUBJECT.—The horse should be in perfect health and not in contact with animals suffering from any infectious disease or lesion. To operate on a debilitated colt or horse is courting disaster.

ENVIRONMENT.—This should be hygienic. On no account should the horse be placed in dirty surroundings prior to, during, or after the operation. The ideal place for operating is the green field in the open country. Do not operate if there is any contagious disease like strangles or influenza about the place.

PREPARATION OF THE SUBJECT.—Colts should be handled before the time for operation, and should be fasting from the previous evening. They should be carefully inspected to ascertain if they are normal before deciding to operate, whether the testicles are in the scrotum, or a scrotal hernia is present, etc. Wild colts that have not been handled before may sweat profusely from fear and struggling when being controlled. Some careful practitioners refuse to operate in such cases on the ground that a " chill " may supervene and endanger the life of the colt. As a rule, however, sweating has not this effect. It is advisable to use antitetanic serum in districts where tetanus is common.

CONTROL.—The animal may be controlled in the standing or cast position.

Standing Position.—Have the horse backed into a corner in a yard or loose box, or into a stall, and a twitch applied. As a rule, this is all the control that is required. It is not desirable to have a forefoot lifted, as it increases the tendency of the patient to lie down when the testicle is grasped or the scrotum incised, thereby hampering the operator. As a rule, even the thoroughbred horse remains perfectly quiet during the operation. An exceptional case offers determined resistance, gets out of control, and has to be cast. The animal rarely attempts to kick, but a very wicked one may do so, and instances of the operator having a leg broken or badly injured by a kick have occurred.

PROCEDURE.—Paint the scrotum with tincture of iodine. Stand on the near side opposite the flank. Grasp the off testicle and hold it firmly in the left hand. Take the castrating knife in the right hand and incise the scrotum boldly from before backwards from the anterior to the posterior extremity of the gland, releasing the latter with one stroke of the knife. A slightly hooked knife is suitable, as it ensures cutting through all the envelopes at once. If the testicle is small and difficult to hold, it may be grasped in a narrow steel clam applied outside the scrotum. Having released the testicle, it may be difficult to get at the cord, owing to the animal's bringing the stifle in the way of the operator. To overcome this difficulty the cord may be severed from the opposite side where the horse does not advance the leg.

The cord may be severed in a variety of ways, the following being suitable instruments for the purpose: the ecraseur, the emasculator, and the wooden clams, each of which has its advocates. The emasculator is probably the instrument most in vogue at present. When it is used, the non-vascular part of the cord is first cut backwards with the knife, but the whole cord may be included in the instrument, especially in a small animal. When employing the ecraseur, some operators release the two testicles first and then include both cords in the chain to divide them. The clams are applied in the usual way, as described later.

Advantages of the Standing Method.—(1) It is quick, the operation being usually completed within five minutes; (2) all the risks of casting are avoided—excessive sweating, fractured limbs or back, etc.; (3) owners like it.

Disadvantages.—(1) Risk of injury to the operator; (2) general anæsthesia cannot be employed. The latter objection may be overcome to some extent by injecting a local anæsthetic deeply into the gland through a long slender needle.

The standing method is extensively practised, especially by lay castrators in England.

The Cast Position.—A method much in favour nowadays is to administer chloroform standing and allow the animal to fall from its effects. When the horse is down on its left side, it is generally sufficient to draw the upper hind-limb forwards to the shoulder by means of a rope or web round the neck and pastern. But it is safer to control both hind-limbs with the casting rope in case the patient might not be completely anæsthetised.

The administration of chloroform in the standing position is indicated for the adult thoroughbred stallion, who is apt to fracture the back or rupture some of the adductor muscles of the thigh from violent struggling after being cast. A dose of chloral hydrate and morphia is also indicated immediately before taking out the horse.

The alternative procedure is to cast with the rope or hobbles and administer chloroform, and then fix the horse in the lateral or dorsal position. The latter is the more convenient, but requires more assistance for the purpose. General anæsthesia is not obligatory, but should be induced on humane and scientific grounds.

When hobbles are used for the lateral position, the upper (off) hind-limb is released from the hobble and drawn forwards to the shoulder, as mentioned above, while for the dorsal position a back strap or rope is applied to keep the hocks flexed.

PROCEDURE.—Take strict aseptic and antiseptic precautions. The simplest and most effective method of disinfecting the site of operation is to paint it with tincture of iodine. Operate on the near testicle first. Get up the testicle by means of the two hands, one in front

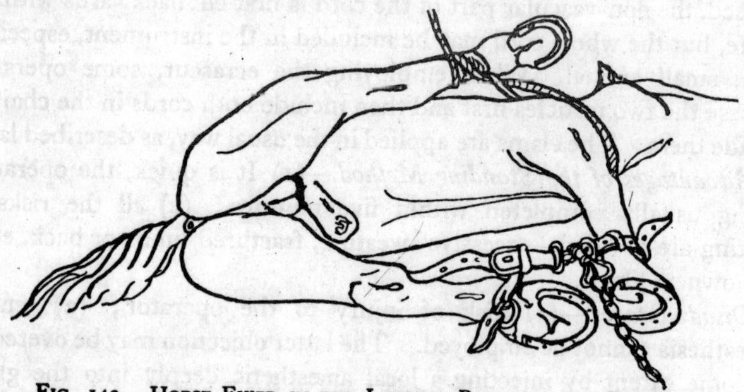

FIG. 143. HORSE FIXED IN THE LATERAL POSITION FOR CASTRATION.

and the other behind, between the extended fingers and thumbs. Grasp the cord firmly with the left hand above the epididymis, making the skin over the gland as tense as possible. Take the knife in the right hand, and with one bold incision from the anterior to the posterior extremity of the organ release the latter. It may require more than one incision to open all the envelopes if the first one is not bold or the knife not very sharp. The testicle may be cut into in the process, but this is no harm.

The testicle may be so small that it is impossible to grasp it through the scrotum. In this case take up a transverse fold of skin over it, hold one end of it with the left fingers and thumb, and let an assistant hold the other end with an artery forceps, and then incise it. It will now be easy to enucleate the testicle enclosed in the tunica vaginalis, and to incise the latter, exposing the gland. Or the skin might be stretched with the fingers and thumb and then incised, but the former method is safer, as it ensures against wounding any large veins that may be present under the skin. Take care not to soil the wound or to handle it more than is necessary. Remove the testicle by any of the following instruments.

1. *The Emasculator.*—Cut the non-vascular (posterior) part of the cord above the level of the epididymis with the knife, or, preferably, use the emasculator to sever both parts separately, thereby preventing

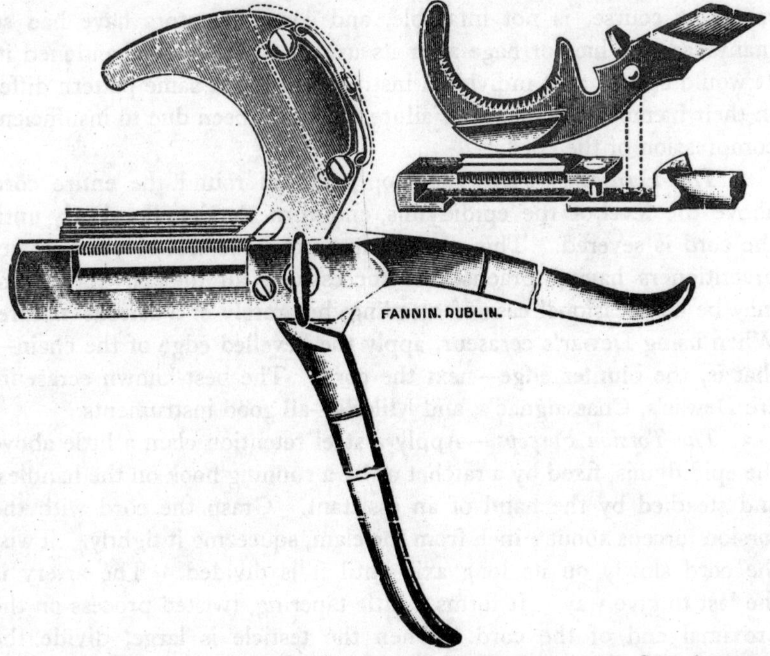

FIG. 144.—HAUSEMANN AND DUNN'S ASEPTIC EMASCULATOR WITH SELF-ADJUSTING AUXILIARY CRUSHER.

any possible hæmorrhage from the artery to the cord or other small vessel supplying its posterior part. When crushing the vascular portion, squeeze the jaws tightly and maintain the pressure for at least twenty or thirty seconds. Then release the pressure for a moment and give the cord a final determined squeeze. This is particularly important in the adult stallion. It is an advantage to have a little antiseptic lubricant smeared on the jaws of the instrument to prevent the cord adhering thereto after being crushed—*e.g.*, creosote 2 drachms, terebene 8 ounces, white vaseline oil 1 pint, which may also be poured into the scrotal wound. There are various forms of emasculators, including Hausemann and Dunn's (Chicago), the " Reliance Castrator," and the French pattern. The instrument most in favour now in England and America is Hausemann and Dunn's. When properly used, it is absolutely hæmostatic. The writer has found all the instruments mentioned quite reliable for animals of all ages, including thoroughbred stallions.

Castration by the emasculator has become very popular within recent years on account of the very expeditious and efficient manner in which the operation can be performed by this means. The instrument, of course, is not infallible, and some operators have had so many cases of hæmorrhage after its use that they have abandoned it. It would appear as if individual instruments of the same pattern differ in their hæmostatic effects. Failure may have been due to insufficient compression of the cord.

2. *The Ecraseur.*—Place the loop of chain round the entire cord above the level of the epididymis, and turn the handle slowly until the cord is severed. This method has stood the test of years, many practitioners having practised it successfully all their lives. There may be an occasional case of bleeding, but rarely of a serious nature. When using Dewar's ecraseur, apply the bevelled edge of the chain—that is, the blunter edge—next the cord. The best-known ecraseurs are Dewar's, Chassaignac's, and Miles's—all good instruments.

3. *The Torsion Forceps.*—Apply a steel retention clam a little above the epididymis, fixed by a ratchet or by a running hook on the handles, and steadied by the hand of an assistant. Grasp the cord with the torsion forceps about ½ inch from the clam, squeezing it tightly. Twist the cord slowly on its long axis until it is divided. The artery is the last to give way. It forms a little tapering, twisted process on the proximal end of the cord. When the testicle is large, divide the posterior part of the cord with the knife or serrated scissors, or, better, with an emasculator, if available. There are various patterns of torsion forceps, but they are all probably equally effective. Robertson's and Williams's are known to be very reliable in Great Britain and Ireland.

Open the clam slowly to ascertain if there is bleeding from the vessel. It is wise to give the cord a good squeeze with the clam before removing it, so as to crush the cord as well, and thus help in the hæmostatic process. Should the patient not be under chloroform, avoid traction on the clam during struggling, for fear of rupturing the cord, an accident which has happened in this way.

Torsion of the cord has been extensively and successfully practised It is a very reliable method of castration.

4. *Wooden Clams.*—Apply the clams from before backwards on the cord above the epididymis. Squeeze them tightly together with the forceps for the purpose and fix the two open ends together by means of a leather or metal ferrule, or by strong cord. Cut off the testicle about ½ inch on this side of the clams or level therewith. Dressed clams are usually employed, the preparation generally used being perchloride of mercury in fine powder mixed with tar or starch paste

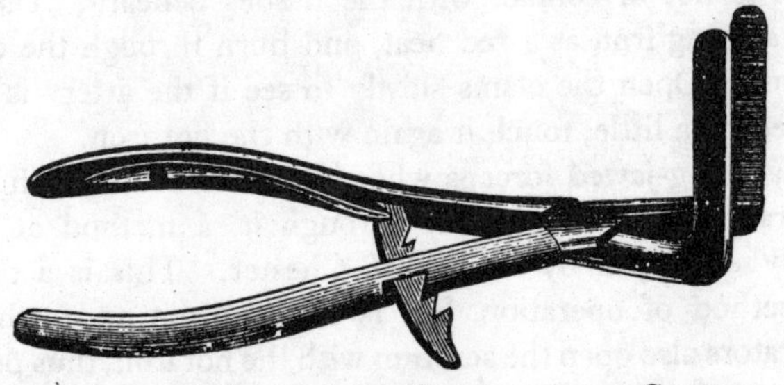

FIG. 145.—ROBERTSON'S FORCEPS FOR TORSION OF THE CORD, AS ADOPTED BY MÖLLER.

or gum arabic, and smeared in a thin layer and allowed to dry over the opposing surfaces of the clams. It is caustic and germicidal.

The clams can easily be made from ash wood, but it is more convenient to procure them prepared and ready for use. Barrett's clams are extensively employed and suit the purpose admirably. They are supplied with a leather ferrule, the two fixed ends being united as usual with cord.

The clams are usually left in position for twenty-four hours. To

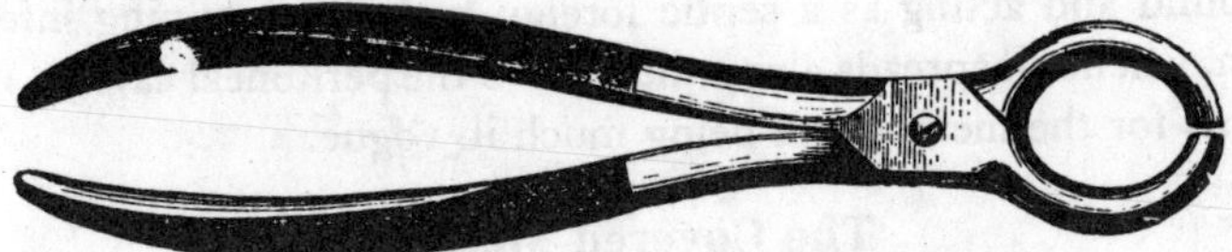

FIG. 146.—FORCEPS FOR CLOSING WOODEN CLAMS.

remove them, have the horse controlled by a twitch, stand on the near side opposite the flank, cut away any portion of the cord that is protruding below the clams, divide the cord uniting the anterior ends of the clams, open out the latter, and remove them.

This is a very safe method of castration for horses of all ages, but it has the following objections : (1) It prolongs the pain of the operation until after the clams have been removed, and pain is caused by their removal ; (2) it necessitates a second visit to the patient ; (3) it is a crude, primitive procedure practised by the travelling gelder ; (4) it favours schirrous cord if the horse is cut proud, owing to the end of the cord being held exposed outside the scrotum.

5. *The Thermocautery.*—Apply a steel or a box-wood retention clam on the cord above the epididymis. The advantage of the latter clam is that it does not conduct the heat, but this is immaterial, as the instrument is not in contact with the tissues beneath. Use an iron similar to a firing iron at a red heat, and burn through the cord close to the clams. Open the clams slowly to see if the artery is bleeding. If it is bleeding a little, touch it again with the hot iron.

A special long-jawed forceps whose jaws are made red-hot may be used to grasp the cord and sear through it, a method at one time successfully employed by Storrar of Chester. This is a thoroughly reliable method of operation, but is troublesome and rather crude. Some operators also open the scrotum with the hot iron, thus performing a bloodless operation. A certain amount of dead tissue is always left in the wound, but, judging from experience, it produces no ill-effects.

6. *The Ligature*, which may be applied : (*a*) on the entire cord ; (*b*) on the anterior and posterior parts of the cord separately ; (*c*) on the vascular part of the cord only.

Method (*c*) is the simplest and answers the purpose, the posterior cord being severed with the knife or emasculator. Ligation is an ideal means of preventing hæmorrhage, but experience has shown that it is more apt to be followed by peritonitis than any of the other methods, due apparently to the ligature becoming contaminated in the wound and acting as a septic foreign body, maintaining infection therein, whence it spreads along the cord to the peritoneal cavity. This accounts for the method not being much in vogue.

The Covered Method

INDICATIONS.—When scrotal hernia is present or has been in existence previously, or for ordinary castration, as being the safest of all methods, ensuring, when the clams are used, absolutely against hæmorrhage, descent of the bowel, and peritonitis.

PROCEDURE.—As in the uncovered method as far as grasping the testicle. Then incise the skin, dartos, and subdartos, exposing the tunica vaginalis, which is left intact. Enucleate the testicle enclosed in the tunica vaginalis to a point above the level of the epididymis. Sever the cord by one of the methods mentioned. The emasculator is not convenient in this case on account of the volume of tissue to be included in its jaws. Procedure with the ecraseur is slow and causes a great strain on the chain, which may be sufficient to break it. The full advantage of this method is only obtained when the clams are used. They are applied as described, but outside the tunica vaginalis. It facilitates adjusting the clams to incise the tunica vaginalis after enucleating it, as recommended by Degive (Fig. 148).

As already stated, this is undoubtedly the safest of all methods of castration. The clams are usually left in position for forty-eight hours. If a hernia is present or suspected, they are not removed until a week after the operation or are allowed to fall off.

Whatever method of operation has been adopted, make sure that the scrotal wound is well open. If the incision has not extended

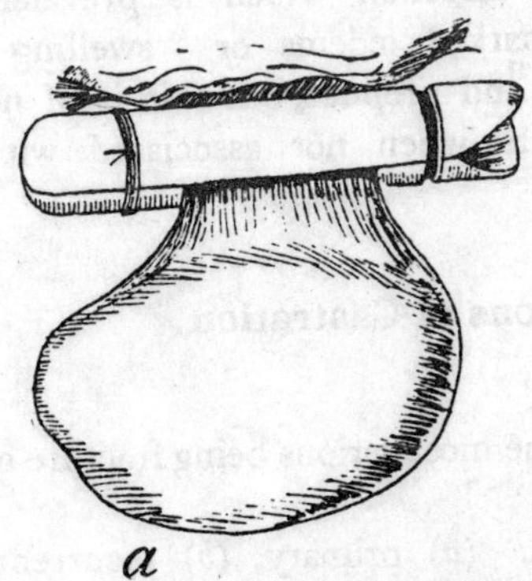

Fig. 147.—Castration with Testicle Covered.

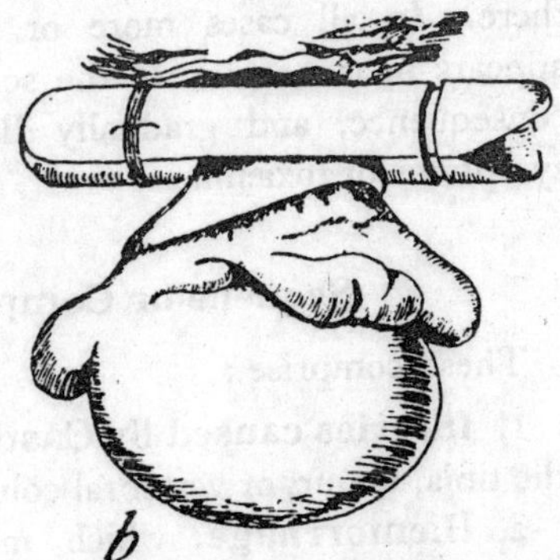

Fig. 148.—Castration with Testicle Uncovered and Cord Covered.

from one end of the scrotum to the other, enlarge it forwards by means of a straight scissors or the knife. This is important to prevent a pocket forming in front, where discharge will accumulate and interfere with the healing process and favour complications.

Having completed the operation, it is advisable to pour a mild antiseptic preparation into each scrotal wound. A lubricant has the advantage of preventing possible adhesion of the edges of the skin before the wound is closed beneath. Fluid B.I.P. or acriflavine emulsion is very suitable for the purpose. Mop up any blood in the vicinity of the wounds to prevent its getting into the latter and contaminating them. Immerse the hands in an atiseptic solution before touching the wounds with the fingers.

After-Treatment.—In the country put the horse to grass

immediately after the operation, and then no further treatment will be required. If the operation has been done in the town, or if it is inconvenient to turn the horse out, put him in a hygienic loose box and keep him on laxative diet. Splash an antiseptic solution on the wounds once or twice daily. If the borders of the wound become adherent, preventing the escape of discharge, separate them with the fingers after careful disinfection of the latter. Do not allow the groom to do this. Let the horse have gentle walking exercise once or twice a day for half an hour. A little magnesium sulphate and potassium nitrate in the drinking water is advisable.

RESULT.—Generally speaking, the fatality after the operation is nil, but in exceptional cases the patient may die from one of the complications mentioned below. Occasionally several colts die in the same district from some form of infection which is prevalent there. In all cases more or less marked œdema or "swelling" appears in the region of the scrotum and prepuce, but this is of no consequence, and gradually disappears when not associated with symptoms of toxæmia.

Sequelæ or Complications of Castration

These comprise :

1. **Injuries caused by Casting,** the most serious being fracture of the tibia, femur, or vertebral column.

2. **Hæmorrhage,** which may be: (*a*) primary, (*b*) recurrent, (*c*) secondary, (*d*) internal.

(*a*) *Primary hæmorrhage* occurs at the time of operation, due to failure of the method adopted to produce hæmostasis. The bleeding may be from cutaneous veins or the artery in the posterior part of the cord, or from the spermatic artery. In the two former cases it is not serious, and soon stops spontaneously Hæmorrhage from the spermatic artery may be slight and cease after a while, but when the artery is spurting it is serious and requires immediate attention. It is often difficult to see the source of the hæmorrhage, but when it is severe it may be assumed to be from the spermatic artery.

TREATMENT.—When the bleeding is slight, keep the animal under observation for a while, and it may become arrested spontaneously. A wet sack over the loins favours hæmostasis. If the hæmorrhage is fairly profuse, take a pledget of cotton-wool, tie a piece of tape thereto, saturate it in an antiseptic solution, and push it into the scrotal sac, leaving the tape protruding. Insert more wool until the cavity is tightly packed or preferably tampon it with sterilised or medicated gauze. Suture the lips of the wound to keep the plug in position. Remove the latter in twenty-four hours. Cut the stitches, apply traction on the string or gauze and the whole plug will come away. Do not interfere with the clot for fear of renewing the hæmorrhage. It will disintegrate and fall away. Dress the wound with an antiseptic solution.

If the bleeding is very severe, cast the animal, get up the cord, and arrest the hæmorrhage by crushing the vascular part with the emasculator, or searing it with the hot iron, or by applying a ligature. A long spring forceps is very useful for grasping the cord to get it out of the wound. It is difficult to hold the cord with the fingers. Apply B.I.P. to the wound afterwards. Never go away from a place leaving an animal bleeding.

(*b*) *Recurrent hæmorrhage* takes place within a few hours after the operation, due, perhaps, to a very small artery in the wound continuing to bleed and leading to an accumulation of clotted blood in the scrotum, which falls out when the patient moves, followed by an escape of liquid blood. This may recur at intervals, causing alarm to the owner, but usually it is not serious. Or the hæmorrhage may be from the spermatic artery, and escape in a constant stream from the wound.

TREATMENT.—As in the case of primary hæmorrhage.

(*c*) *Secondary hæmorrhage* occurs some days afterwards, due to septic disintegration of the thrombus in the vessel or to sloughing of the occluded end of the latter. This case is serious on account of the septic infection of the wound as well as the hæmorrhage. Peritonitis is apt to supervene and cause death after arrest of the hæmorrhage.

TREATMENT.—As in (*a*) above and administer penicillin in the usual manner.

(*d*) *Internal hæmorrhage* rarely supervenes.

SYMPTOMS.—Nothing may be noticed until the animal is found dead, except it has been under constant observation, when the symptoms of internal hæmorrhage may be detected. It is generally due to rupture of the spermatic artery inside the abdomen as the result of excessive traction thereon during the operation.

TREATMENT.—If the case is seen in time, apply a cold wet rug over the loins and administer adrenaline hypodermically.

3. **Descent of the Bowel or Omentum.**—The latter is more common than the former. The accident may occur during or

immediately after the operation, but more frequently within some hours afterwards. It is usually unilateral, but may be bilateral.

Symptoms.—The prolapsed omentum appears as reddish tissue protruding a variable distance from the wound. The exposed bowel consists of a loop of small intestine, which may be only just outside the wound or protruding much further, and perhaps in contact with the ground.

Prognosis.—Prolapse of the omentum is not serious, but that of the bowel frequently proves fatal, owing to peritonitis supervening.

Treatment.—In the case of the omental prolapse, draw the protruding omentum out a little further to expose a clean portion, cut it off there, and dress the wound antiseptically. If only a small portion of bowel is exposed and it is returned immediately after it has been prolapsed, there is a good chance of recovery.

The procedure consists in chloroforming the horse in the standing position with a large dose of chloroform, so that he will go down without a struggle ; fixing him in the dorsal position with the hind-quarters raised ; cleaning the prolapsed bowel with sterilised normal saline solution, gradually pushing it back into the abdomen, as in a case of hernia ; and applying a clam or a ligature on the cord, including the tunica vaginalis. When there is much of the bowel out it may be impossible to return it, and then the patient must be destroyed. Even if returnable the patient should be painlessly destroyed on the grounds of humanity, especially if the bowel has been even slightly soiled. If the bowel appear during the operation, return it at once and perform the covered method of castration, using a clam.

4. Œdema or Swelling.—There is always some œdema of the sheath and scrotal region. Even when it is very marked, causing paraphimosis, due to great swelling of the penis, the condition is not serious provided that there is no evidence of toxæmia, the patient continuing to feed, having a good pulse, a temperature not much above normal, and a clean conjunctiva. The patient is more or less stiff in movement, but not so much so as in a case of severe inflammation of the cord. The condition may be due to the edges of one or both scrotal wounds adhering and imprisoning the normal serous discharge. Neglect of daily exercise favours it. Infection, although not of a serious nature, is probably the chief source of the trouble. It is most marked about the fifth day, and gradually subsides afterwards, to disappear about the tenth day.

Treatment.—Taking strict antiseptic precautions, separate the lips of the wounds well with the fingers; exercise the animal at a walk twice daily; give laxative and diuretic medicine, and prescribe potassium iodide in bad cases; hot stupes to the swelling, combined with gentle kneading or massage thereof, may be used.

If the swelling is slow to subside, the skin may be punctured here and there with the knife to permit of the escape of serum. This is rarely indicated and should be avoided as much as possible, on account of the risk of infection through the wounds.

5. **Malignant Œdema.**—Infection by the malignant œdema bacillus rarely supervenes. It is characterised by symptoms of profound toxæmia, and terminates fatally within a week after its onset. There is marked swelling locally and a fœtid discharge due to liquefied putrid tissue. It is obviously different from ordinary œdema. Death may occur from invasion of the peritoneal cavity by this organism, without the usual characteristic local symptoms.

TREATMENT.—Prior to the clinical introduction of penicillin treatment was useless, but now there is some hope of recovery when it is promptly administered in massive and frequent doses. Other treatment consists of local antisepsis and drainage, and in adopting the usual measures for severe febrile disturbance.

6. **Peritonitis.**—When this supervenes, its symptoms are apparent within a week after the operation. Fortunately it is not a common complication, but it has been known to appear as an enzootic in certain districts, killing a large percentage of the colts operated upon.

7. **Tetanus** is a complication that is always to be feared after castration, more so in some districts than others. It appears several days after the operation, when the wound is granulating or almost cicatrised. It can be prevented by the use of antitetanic serum.

8. **Abscess in the Cord,** characterised by great stiffness and lameness in the corresponding hind-limb and intense inflammation in the cord, revealed by a hard, hot, painful swelling extending up into the inguinal canal. After a few days the abscess bursts, and recovery then gradually ensues.

TREATMENT consists in frequent hot fomentations to mature the abscess, and opening it if it points within reach.

9. **Gangrene,** indicated by sloughing of the lining of the scrotal wound and a very fœtid odour therefrom, and more or less febrile disturbance, rarely occurs. This is not of a malignant type, and is usually followed by recovery after separation of the slough.

10. **Abscess in the Sublumbar Lymphatic Glands.**—This is a

rare complication. It is characterised by remittent fever and by the patient losing condition. It is generally of a subacute nature, the animal "hanging fire" for weeks, perhaps, after the operation, and eventually succumbing from toxæmia. The abscess may be felt on rectal examination as a distinct swelling in the sublumbar region. On post-mortem examination the abscess, which may be of huge dimensions, is discovered.

11. **Scirrhous Cord.**—This is a fibrous thickening of the spermatic cord, due to its invasion by micro-organisms, usually the botriomyces. As a rule, the condition is slow in manifesting itself, and may not be detected or brought to the notice of the veterinary surgeon until weeks, months, or even years have elapsed since the operation. Occasionally it is of a more acute nature, appearing before the castration wound has healed, and revealed by hardness and pain along the course of the cord, and by marked stiffness and lameness in the corresponding hind-limb.

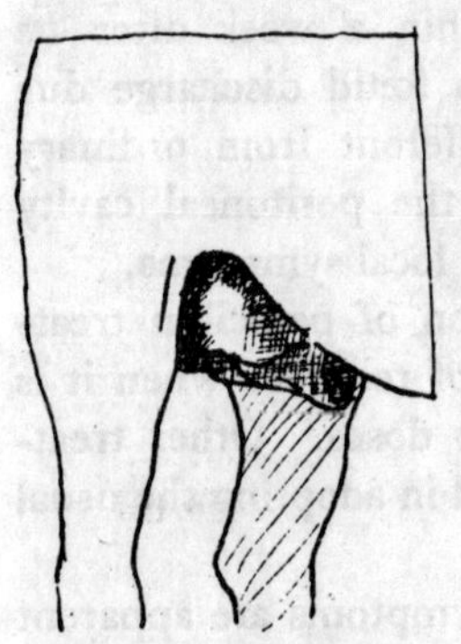

FIG. 149.—SCIRRHOUS CORD IN THE HORSE.

SYMPTOMS.—The typical scirrhous cord is characterised by a hard swelling on the end of the cord, varying in size from a fist to a man's head, and extending a variable distance upwards. In bad cases it may be felt *per rectum* involving the abdominal portion of the cord, but this is very unusual. There is a sinus extending more or less deeply into the swelling through which a probe can be passed. It discharges the typical granular pus when due to botriomycosis. The horse may be lame in the corresponding hind-limb, which is then abducted during progression.

TREATMENT.—A recent acute inflammatory case may respond to local antiseptic and antiphlogistic measures, including irrigation of the wound by tincture of iodine, but even in this case recovery is more quickly brought about by excision of the affected portion of the cord. Some practitioners have obtained a cure in recent subacute cases by injecting tincture of iodine into the substance of the cord by means of a hypodermic syringe (Imrie, Glasgow). Potassium iodide internally may have a beneficial effect, but it is not a specific.

42. Operation for Scirrhous Cord

INDICATION.—In all well-established forms of the disease. Even in very recent cases operation is the surest and quickest method of effecting a cure.

Control.—Cast and fix in the dorsal position as for castration and administer chloroform.

Procedure.—Having taken a position behind the patient, make an elliptical incision in the skin over the base of the swelling, enclosing the orifice of the sinus. Pass a piece of tape by means of a seton needle beneath the isolated portion of skin to serve as a handle for the operator or an assistant to hold during the progress of the operation. Reflect the skin all round the periphery of the tumour, exposing the tunica vaginalis, which encloses and is adherent to the swelling, and is recognised by its glistening aspect.

Continue the dissection, keeping close to the tumour, until the normal part of the cord is reached. There is usually more or less profuse hæmorrhage, but except a large vessel can be seen bleeding, and can be secured with a forceps or ligature, the hæmorrhage may be ignored and the operation quickly proceeded with. Divide the cord as in the covered operation for castration. The ecraseur and emasculator are suitable for the purpose, especially the former, as the loop of chain can be pushed up far on the cord if necessary. The strain, however, may be too much for the chain, and cause it to break. Moreover, neither the ecraseur nor the emasculator may be sufficient to prevent hæmorrhage, particularly when the part cut through contains hard fibrous tissue. Fatal hæmorrhage has ensued after the use of the ecraseur in such cases. A ligature is a sure method of arresting hæmorrhage, but it may be slow to come away or difficult to remove, and as long as it remains *in situ* it prevents healing of the wound. One end of the thread should be left protruding from the wound to facilitate its removal, although doing so favours sepsis. The safest plan, if possible, is to apply a clam. A short metal one is suitable for pushing up high on the cord when it is required to sever it there. The ordinary retention clam may be left on the cord for 24 hours, its handles being tied together by cord to secure it in position.

If the tumour extend into the abdominal cavity it cannot be satisfactorily operated upon. All that can be done is to remove it as close to the external inguinal ring as possible. If there are no suppurating centres in the remaining portion of the cord recovery will ensue. If there is much general hæmorrhage from the wound, plug the cavity and suture the skin.

After-Treatment.—Next day cut the sutures and remove the plug when present. When a clam has been employed, leave it in position for forty-eight or seventy-two hours. Otherwise deal with the case as one of castration.

Result.—Complete recovery usually ensues.

Complications.—The chief complication to be feared is hæmorrhage, as already alluded to. The wound may become fistulous owing to the persistence of ligatures therein when used to occlude bleeding vessels. Hence they should be avoided.

Cyst on the End of the Cord

This is a form of hydrocele due to an accumulation of serum inside the tunica vaginalis. It forms slowly and is not noticed until a few months after the operation, when the scrotal sac has the appearance of still containing the testicle.

Symptoms.—A fairly circumscribed, elastic, painless swelling in the scrotum, and varying in size from a hen's egg to a fist. It does not incommode the animal in any way, but depreciates his value for sale.

Diagnosis.—Distinguish it from scrotal hernia and scirrhous cord, neither of whose characteristic features are present. Puncture with a fine trocar and canula will cause the escape of an amber-coloured liquid.

Treatment.—Control as for castration in the dorsal position. Dissect out the lower end of the cord, which is always adherent to the skin at the level of the scar therein, separating the tunica vaginalis (recognised by its glistening aspect) from the surrounding tissues, and apply a clam above the affected part, or sever the cord with the emasculator or ecraseur.

Cutting a Horse " Proud "

Some owners like to have their horses " cut proud "—that is, to have the testicle removed below the level of the epididymis, leaving the latter in position, the idea being to enable the horse to retain more of his virility. Occasionally, when this is done, the horse behaves like a rig, retaining all his stallion propensities.

Vasectomy

It has been suggested that merely cutting the vas deferens (vasectomy) would have practically the same effect as removing the testicle, while the subject would have the advantage of retaining the beneficial effect of the endocrine secretion of the gland. Experience, however, has shown that this is not the case in connection with rig castration, for the horse continues " to rig " after mere removal of the epididymis. In rare cases a horse continues to show the propensities of a sire after ordinary castration (see Rig Castration).

Castration without Incision of the Skin

The horse may be castrated by compression of the spermatic cord through the intact skin with a special forceps invented by Burdizzo, whose use is described in connection with castration of the ox Its application to the cord in the horse is rather difficult. It is facilitated by having the hock drawn outwards.

43. Castration of the Ox

INDICATIONS.—To render the animals docile and manageable and to improve the quality of the flesh.

AGE.—Calves are castrated at from six weeks to six months old, but frequently the operation is necessary on adult bulls that are no longer required for the stud.

SEASON.—The autumn and spring as a rule, but the operation may be done any time provided that extremes of weather are avoided.

CONTROL.—Suck calves may be operated upon in the standing or cast position. When cast, a convenient attitude is with the animal resting on its buttocks and held between a man's knees, the man being seated on a stool and grasping each hind-limb by the hamstrings. When standing, it is simply held against a wall or paling.

The bull is more conveniently operated upon in the standing position, being securely held against a wall or a partition in a stall, or alongside a paling, with a " bulldogs " or ring in the nose and a rope round the horns or neck fixed by a slip knot to a ring or post. A kicking-strap may be applied above the hocks, as the vigorous young bull sometimes " lashes out " violently backwards. Or the beast may be fixed in a sort of creel or stocks with sufficient opening behind for the operator.

PROCEDURE—*Standing Position.*—Let an assistant hold the tail out of the way. Apply a little tincture of iodine on the scrotum. Inject a local anæsthetic into the substance of the gland. Stand behind the animal, grasp the right testicle with the left hand and draw it backwards, making the skin over it as tense as possible; incise the scrotum on its posterior aspect from the upper to the lower extremity of the gland, making sure to go right through the base of the sac, completely exposing the testicle. Remove the testicle by any of the methods described for the horse.

In the young calf, scraping the vascular portion of the cord or traction thereon is sufficient. Even in adult bulls rupture of the vascular part of the cord by traction has the desired effect, and is often practised. An objection to it is that it favours pelvic hernia or "gut-tie" by sometimes causing rupture of the ligament of the cord in the abdomen, leaving an opening therein in which the bowel becomes strangulated.

The emasculator is very convenient and, in the writer's opinion, reliable for cattle, although some authorities say that it occasionally proves disappointing.

An alternative method of opening the scrotum is to cut off the base of the two scrotal sacs by one bold horizontal incision, exposing the two testicles simultaneously, enclosed in their vaginal sheaths. The wound thus made tends to close in too soon, interfering with drainage before the discharge has ceased, and leading perhaps to accumulation of the latter and the formation of a "serous abscess." A better "cod" is formed after the method of incision first mentioned.

Complications are even more rare than in the horse, but most of those mentioned for the latter have occurred in the ox from time to time. A large chronic abscess with thick fibrous walls, simulating a scirrhous cord, has been seen in the ox, and successfully removed in the same manner as that adopted for scirrhous cord, the pus cavity not being opened.

44. Castration without Incision of the Scrotum

1. **Bistournage.**—Briefly, this means manipulation of the testicle and cord within its coverings, whereby the spermatic artery becomes thrombosed and the gland consequently undergoes atrophy. It was formerly much employed in France for bulls. It has fallen into disuse, and does not merit a detailed description.

2. **Crushing the Testicle** by applying a clam on the scrotum and then striking the gland with a wooden hammer, an old-fashioned and barbarous method which was uncertain in its results.

3. **Crushing the Spermatic Cord (Martelage).**—The neck of the scrotum is included in wooden clams, which are hammered for several minutes with a mallet. It was practised in India to avoid making an open wound, with its consequent risks, especially in a hot climate. It is not in vogue with veterinarians.

4. **Burdizzo's Method.**—Burdizzo has invented a special forceps for crushing the spermatic cord through the skin without solution of continuity of the latter.

Procedure.—Have the beast securely held. Stand behind; draw one of the testicles backwards; isolate the cord, pressing it outwards against the skin, and hold it there with the fingers and thumb of the left hand. Take hold of the forceps, with its jaws open, by one of the handles in the right hand; rest the other handle on the knee, held slightly flexed; push the cord in between the middle parts of the jaws of the forceps with the left hand, and hold it there until it is crushed by closing the forceps by pressure between the right hand and the knee. Take care that the cord does not slip out of the jaws before it is crushed. To ensure the success of the operation it is

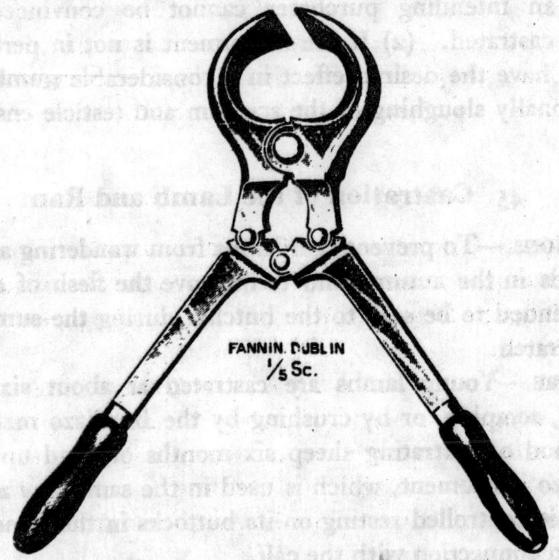

Fig. 148.—Burdizzo's Castrator.

advisable to crush the cord in two places. It facilitates the procedure considerably to let an assistant use the forceps while the veterinarian holds the cord in position. A curved attachment to one of the handles to adapt it to the knee has been introduced, and greatly facilitates performing the operation single-handed. A special forceps to grasp the cord and hold it in position between the jaws of the castrator has been invented by Pomeroy (Cork), and proves of great assistance.

Result.—When the genuine Italian instrument is employed and properly used, the desired result is obtained in practically every case, the testicles gradually undergoing atrophy and completely disappearing in the course of two or three months, the animals at the same time losing all the propensities of the entire.

Advantages.—(1) All risk of infection is avoided. (2) It can be performed during any kind of weather without endangering the life of the animal. (3) It does not interfere with the animal's thriving or put it back in condition in the least, an advantage which is greatly appreciated by owners and dealers. (4) A plump scrotum or "cod" is left after the operation. (5) It is expeditious. When the animals are tied up in a close rank the operator can pass from one to another in quick succession. Some operators claim to have done upwards of sixty per hour in this way.

Disadvantages.—(1) If the animals are to be sold soon after the operation an intending purchaser cannot be convinced that they have been castrated. (2) If the instrument is not in perfect order it will fail to have the desired effect in a considerable number of cases. (3) Occasionally sloughing of the scrotum and testicle ensues.

45. Castration of the Lamb and Ram

Indications.—To prevent ram lambs from wandering and breaking out of fields in the autumn and to improve the flesh of adult sheep. Lambs intended to be sold to the butcher during the summer should not be castrated.

Procedure.—Young lambs are castrated at about six weeks old by traction, scraping, or by crushing by the Burdizzo method. The safest method of castrating sheep six months old and upwards is by the Burdizzo instrument, which is used in the same way as in the ox. The sheep is controlled resting on its buttocks in the same manner as described in connection with the calf.

Castration of the sheep by removal of the testicles is dangerous by every method except the use of the wooden clams or hot iron. Experience has shown that the application of caustic clams is the safest of all the open methods, and that when using them it is important not to apply traction on the testicle after opening the scrotum, and not to put the clams high up on the cord, but rather to include the tunica vaginalis—that is, in fact, to perform a modification of the covered operation. The operation should be done when the weather is mild, although it has been observed by some that sheep are more likely to die after castration in October than in December. They should be kept in a clean, dry place, upland sheltered pasture being best. Practitioners of the old school have said that if a drop of blood is left in the scrotum the sheep will die. Cases are recorded in which over 90 per cent. of the sheep operated upon have succumbed after operation by methods other than the clams. The cause of death was not always clear. Infection of the wound by the organisms of tetanus and malignant œdema has accounted for many of the fatalities, but in a large number of cases death has supervened within twenty-four hours, before evidence of infection had time to be manifested. Shock would appear to be the cause of the fatal result in these instances. Hence it may be concluded that the ideal method of castrating sheep six months old and upwards is by means of Burdizzo's instrument.

46. Castration of Swine

INDICATIONS.—To enable the animals to fatten better and to improve the quality of the flesh, which in the boar emits an unpleasant odour. The operation is usually done at about six weeks old, but is often deferred for some months. Occasionally the adult boar is castrated.

CONTROL.—The young pig may be held in a variety of ways to suit the convenience of the operator—*e.g.*, in the arms of an assistant, who holds the two hind-limbs above the hocks or slung between his legs, while he grasps the hind-limbs with his two hands, or the pig may be placed on a table and held in a suitable position there. Strong pigs require to have their legs tied together with a piece of soft rope Big boars must be controlled in the usual way with a rope round the upper jaw, and cast and fixed with thin ropes or hobbles above the fetlocks. Chloroform or ether and oxygen may be administered.

The operation is performed in the usual way. Scraping and traction are the most suitable methods for suck pigs. For stronger subjects any of the methods mentioned for the horse may be used, the emasculator being particularly convenient for the purpose. Many young pigs are found to be affected with scrotal hernia at the time of castration. It is usually sufficient to suture the scrotal sac in these cases, but a safer procedure is to put a ligature on the covered cord.

RESULT.—Complications are rare, but the pig may die from septic infection if the operation has been carelessly performed, making the incision too small or neglecting antisepsis, or if the pig has been put in a dirty place afterwards.

47. Castration of the Goat

The goat is castrated in the usual way, being secured in the recumbent position for the purpose. The emasculator, torsion forceps, etc., are suitable for the operation.

48. Castration of the Dog

Indications.—Diseased testicle, to prevent wandering and undue sexual excitement, and enlarged prostate.

Control.—Fix in the dorsal position on the table and administer a general anæsthetic.

Procedure.—As usual—severing the cord by torsion by means of two artery forceps, by crushing with the emasculator, or by ligation. Healing by first intention may be aimed at and attained by suturing the skin, but the majority of operators leave the wounds open and allow them to heal by second intention.

After-Treatment.—Dress the wounds daily with an antiseptic solution until covered by granulations. If sutured, apply tincture of iodine daily and remove the sutures in about a week.

Results.—The operation is practically always successful. It has the desired effect as regards allaying sexual desire, but otherwise it rather spoils the dog, which tends to become lazy and too fat.

49. Castration of the Cat

Indications.—To make the animal a "house cat," to prevent its wandering and fighting, and the unpleasant smell caused by the urine of the tom-cat.

Control.—General anæsthesia is compulsory in the cat over six months old. (See p. 195). When it is not employed, the cat can be held as described on p. 170. Have the tail drawn out of the way, and avoid the stream of urine which the cat emits in a straight line backwards. The animal may also be rolled up tightly in a cloth with its head and tail protruding, or fixed in the ventral position on the table.

When a general anæsthetic is used, it may be administered in the ordinary way, or under a bell-jar, or in a box provided with a glass window. The latter method is often adopted thus: Put the cat in the box, introduce chloroform on a couple of pledgets of cotton-wool, and observe its effects through the window. When the animal has ceased to struggle and lies quietly, take it out of the box quickly and operate at once. When general anæsthesia is not employed a local anæsthetic should be used.

Procedure.—In Persian cats always clip the fur in the region of the scrotum, or it may get into the wound and interfere with healing. Open the scrotum in the usual manner, using a very sharp knife or a safety-razor blade. The testicle does not come out so freely as in other animals. Remove it by scraping or by torsion with two artery forceps, one being used as a clam while the other performs the torsion, or by ligation or by a hot iron. The ligature is not advisable, as it may become septic and cause trouble. Mr. Henry Gray, of London has seen so many cases of hæmorrhage after castration by torsion and scraping in adult cats that he recommends the use of a special clam and hot iron which he has invented for the purpose and which ensures against bleeding. Holding the cord with one artery forceps and searing it across on the distal side of the instrument by grasping it with another artery forceps, made almost red hot in a gas flame, is another method of using the actual cautery to perform bloodless castration in cats of every size and age.

50. Castration of the Monkey

INDICATION.—The operation is sometimes done with a view to obtaining more control over the animal when mischievous or wicked.

PROCEDURE.—Fix the animal on the table, administer a general anæsthetic, and operate as usual, the emasculator being very suitable for removing the testicle.

RESULT.—The patient recovers well from the operation.

51. Caponing of Fowl

INDICATIONS.—To increase the size of the birds, to hasten their development and improve the quality of the flesh, to prevent young cocks from crowing and fighting.

SEASON.—August to November inclusive is said to be the best time " when cockerels are cheap and unruly, and worry the pullets."

AGE.—Usually when the cockerels are three to four months old.

PREPARATION.—Have the birds fasting for thirty hours before the operation. This is essential, so that the intestines will be empty and collapsed to enable the testicles to be seen and grasped, and also to avoid wounding the bowel.

PROCEDURE.—Tie the two legs together and attach a weight thereto. A local anæsthetic is advisable. Stretch the bird on its side on a support or table in the sunlight, if any. Have the wing held forward. Pluck the feathers from the site of the operation—the space between the last two ribs. Have a small electric torch to illuminate the abdominal cavity, if necessary ; it is a great help when the visibility is not good. Make an incision between the last two ribs about 1½ inches long, incise the peritoneal membrane to the same extent, insert the dilator, and allow the light to shine into the abdomen. The testicle is recognised as a small, yellowish, sausage-shaped body immediately in front of the kidney in the sublumbar region opposite the last intercostal space. In the young bird it is not unlike a short whitish maggot, but in the adult it is massive and easily seen and felt. Do not use any sharp-pointed instrument in the vicinity of the testicle, for fear of wounding the vena cava and causing immediate death. Grasp the testicle with the special forceps, and by gentle traction and torsion remove it. If firmly compressed, it may break down and fall away inside the abdomen. This will not interfere with the effect of the operation. Both testicles may be removed through the same opening, but it is easier and safer to operate on the two sides separately. It is not usual to suture the wound.

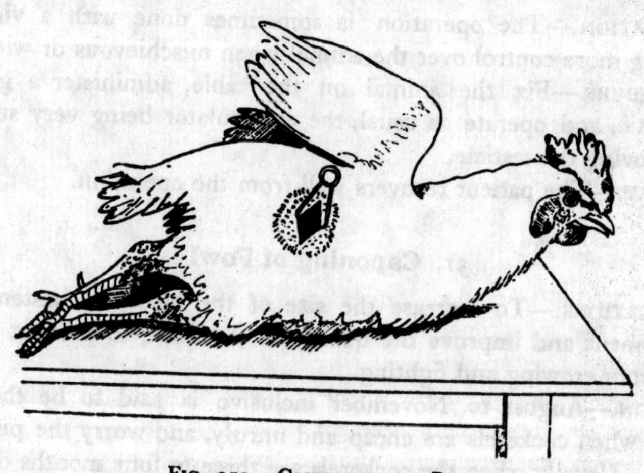

FIG. 151.—CASTRATION OF BIRD.

RESULT.—Good, the birds suffering no ill-effects from the operation, as a rule. All the desired objects of the operation are not always obtained.

COMPLICATIONS.—The chief complications to be feared are hæmorrhage and wounding the bowel. These are fairly common accidents with the novice. If the bird is not well starved, the bowel may easily be snipped with the scissors when it is used to enlarge the abdominal incision. Emphysema of the surrounding tissues may ensue, but it is not serious. The air escapes on pricking the part. It may recur after pricking, but eventually disappears.

AFTER-TREATMENT.—Feed the birds on bread and milk for a while.

52. Castration of Pullets

The ovaries are sometimes removed from pullets through an opening in the last intercostal space, as in the male.

Caponing of ostriches is an important operation in South Africa, and was fully described and illustrated in an article by Mr. Stanley Elley, M.R.C.V.S., in the *Veterinary Journal*. August, 1913.

53. Castration of the Rabbit and Guinea-Pig

The difficulty with the rabbit is that when the animal becomes frightened it can draw the testicles up so far that they can hardly be grasped. In both these animals the testicles may be removed by scraping, torsion, or traction. Catching the rabbit by the hind-legs and swinging it in a circle at arm's length causes the testicles to descend after they have been drawn up.

54. Castration of Cryptorchids

INDICATION.—To render the horse docile and capable of being worked in the company of other horses. Occasionally the rig is quiet and gives no trouble, but as a rule he is more troublesome than the ordinary entire horse (see chapter on affections of the male genital organs).

PREPARATION.—Administer a purgative or strong laxative a few days before the operation, and keep the animal on short laxative rations in the meantime and allow no food for twenty-four hours beforehand. This preparation is very important in order to diminish the volume of the intestines as much as possible, and thus facilitate finding the testicle in the abdominal cavity. If not so prepared, the operation may be extremely difficult or impossible. For the same reason an enema may be given before casting and the horse walked about until it is ejected. If the coat and feet are dirty, have them cleaned.

AGE.—It is not advisable to operate on a horse under two years old. As a rule the horse is two to four years of age when presented for operation. In the yearling the tissues of the abdominal wall are delicate and easily broken down, so that the abdominal opening may become too large and be followed by prolapse of the bowel. Moreover, the inguinal canal is comparatively narrow in the young animal, hampering the operator, and necessitating more force to pass the hand through it, with a consequent greater risk of making the abdominal opening too large, apart from the greater delicacy of the tissues.

SEASON.—The operation may be done at any time of the year with the same prospect of success, but for preference the autumn or spring is chosen, as for ordinary castration.

Condition.—The patient must be in perfect health. A horse in hard-working condition is the best subject for operation. A big soft colt is more susceptible to infection than the adult hard-fed animal and more likely to bleed.

Environment.—As for ordinary castration.

Methods of Operating comprise:

(1) The inguinal method.
(2) The flank method.

(1) The Inguinal Method

Control.—Cast, anæsthetise, and fix the horse in the dorsal position, with the hocks well flexed and separated, so as to expose and dilate well the inguinal region (see (*b*) on p. 156). If the ground is sloping, have the horse's head down the hill. It is advisable to have a damped clean sack of hay or straw tightly packed ready in case of need, to put under the hind-quarters.

Preparation of the Site.—Withdraw the penis from the sheath, remove loose bits of smegma, paint the scrotal and preputial regions with tincture of iodine, or alternatively thoroughly wash out the prepuce with soap and water, and then dry the skin with a perfectly clean towel and apply tincture of iodine. This latter procedure takes considerable time, and is not necessary except the sheath is very dirty. Fix cloths wrung out of an antiseptic solution on the feet to prevent dirt therefrom falling on the site of operation, having the cloths on the hind-feet coming back over the hocks to prevent soiling from these parts. A window cloth covering the abdominal, scrotal, and inguinal regions is also desirable. Have an assistant prepared with clean hands to give assistance if required.

Procedure.—Taking every aseptic precaution, as mentioned under "Operative Technique," and having examined the inguinal region to ascertain if any portion of the testicular apparatus can be felt, take up a transverse fold of skin at the level of the external inguinal ring, hold one end of it with the left fingers and thumb, and let an assistant hold the other end with an artery forceps; incise it so as to make an antero-posterior incision about 5 inches long. Cutting the skin in this way avoids the risk of wounding large veins that are often present in this region in the rig. An enlarged vein has been mistaken for a testicle and cut into, with fatal results. Tear through the areolar tissue with the thumbs and fingers, pushing vessels aside, into the inguinal canal. Form the fingers into a cone and, using the right hand for the right side (cast position), pass it into the inguinal canal with a rotary movement, and explore the passage carefully for the testicle, epididymis, or vas deferens. If any of these structures is present in the canal, it will be enclosed in the tunica vaginalis. In this case incise the latter, and if it contain the testicle proceed as in ordinary castration. If only the vas deferens or epididymis is found, apply traction thereto

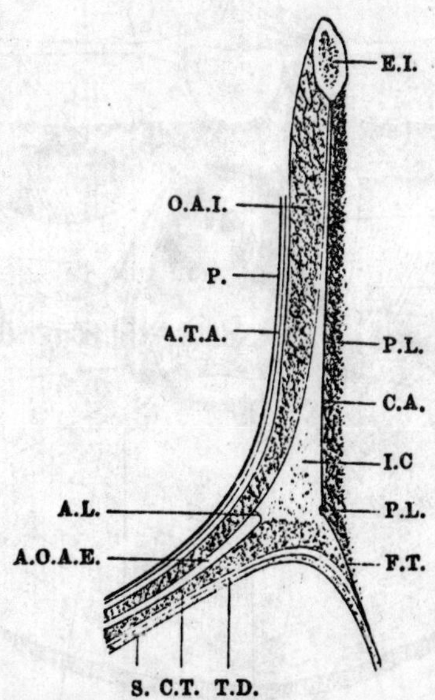

FIG. 152.—SECTION THROUGH THE WALLS OF THE LEFT INGUINAL CANAL.

The section is through a line drawn from the centre of the lower abdominal ring to the antero-external angle of the ilium.

S, Skin ; C.T., connective tissue and fascia beneath the dartos ; T.D., tunica dartos ; A.O.A.E., aponeurosis of the obliquus abdominis externus muscle ; A.L., anterior lip of the lower abdominal ring ; P.L., posterior lip of the lower abdominal ring ; I.C., inguinal canal and its contained connective tissue ; O.A.I., obliquus abdominis internus muscle ; A.T.A., aponeurosis of the transverse abdominal muscle ; P., peritoneum ; P.L., Poupart's ligament ; F.T., fascia of the thigh ; C.A., crural arch ; E.I., external angle of the ilium.

with the object of drawing out the testicle. This procedure generally fails, the fibrous sac being too narrow and unyielding to allow the testicle to pass through. It is necessary then to proceed as for a complete abdominal rig, as follows. Perforate the anterior wall of the inguinal canal according to the Danish or Belgian method. Sometimes, however, the testicle is felt in a process of peritoneum without any fibrous thickening, in the top of the canal protruding through the internal inguinal ring and can be released by rupturing the membrane with the fingers and thumb and then brought into view.

1. *Danish Method*.—Make the perforation through the thick muscular part of the internal abdominal oblique—that is, far out from the middle line of the body. To facilitate this being done, incise the outer commissure of the external ring for a distance of

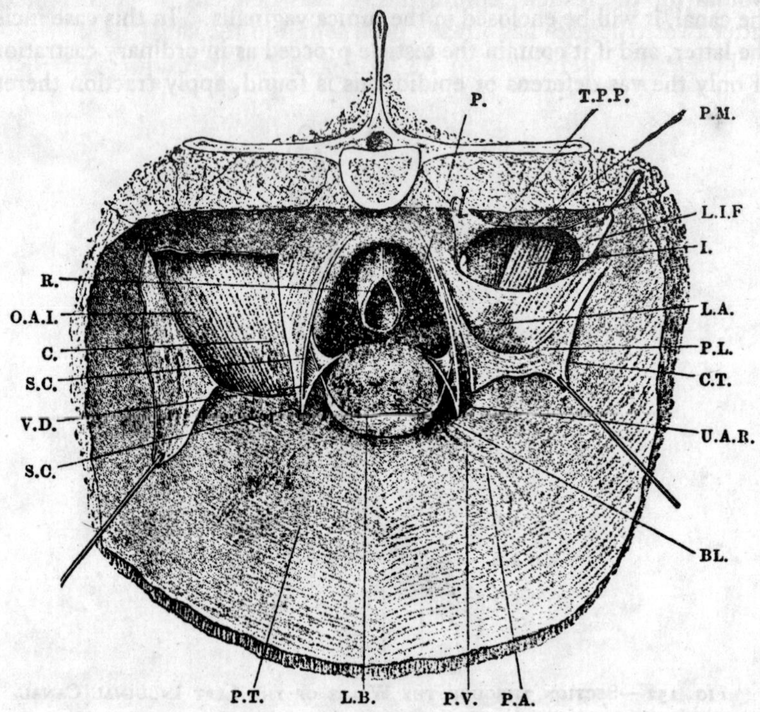

FIG. 153.—TRANSVERSE SECTION IN A PERPENDICULAR PLANE THROUGH THE POSTERIOR ABDOMINAL REGION, TOGETHER WITH A PART OF THE SUPRALUMBAR, ILIAC, AND PREPUBIC REGIONS (NORMAL).

P.T., Peritoneum; P.A., branch of prepubic artery; P.V., branch of prepubic vein; U.A.R., upper abdominal ring; S.C., spermatic cord; V.D., vas deferens; P.L., Poupart's ligament turned downwards, the deep surface visible; L.A., long adductor of the thigh; L.I.F., lumbo-iliac fascia; I., iliacus; P.M., psoas magnus; T.P.P., tendon of the psoas parvus; P., pelvis; R., rectum; BL., bladder; L.B., lateral ligaments of the bladder with the obliterated umbilical artery; O.A.I., internal oblique abdominal muscle; C., cremaster; C.T., layer of connective tissue which surrounds the upper border of Poupart's ligament, the posterior margin of the internal oblique abdominal muscle, the cremaster, and the peritoneum.

2 or 3 inches. Make the perforation with the fingers, or a blunt seton needle, or a long narrow forceps, during an inspiration, when the abdominal wall is tense. As a rule, all the structures give way at once, but sometimes the peritoneum remains intact and requires renewed intervention to puncture it. An instrument is better than

the fingers for the purpose. An advantage of the forceps is that it can be used to dilate the opening by separating its handles. Make the opening sufficiently large to admit the two first fingers. Introduce them into the abdominal cavity and search in the vicinity of the wound for the testicle, epididymis, or vas deferens, if neither of the latter two structures has already been found in the canal.

The testicle is recognised by its feel and shape, and by its being

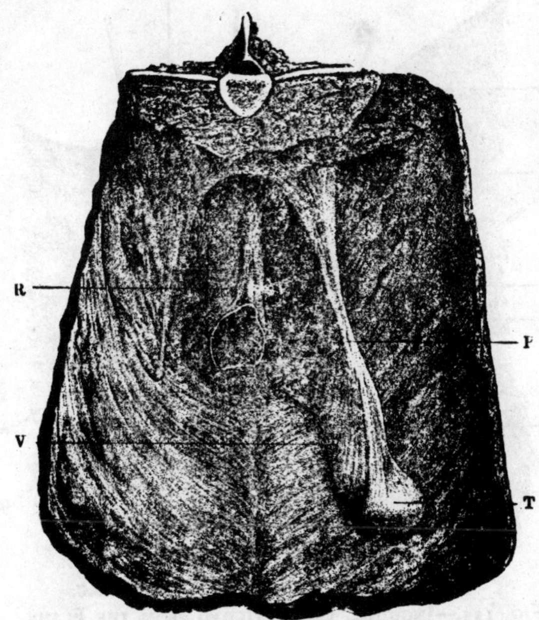

FIG. 154.—A CASE OF ABDOMINAL CRYPTORCHIDISM.
T., Testicle ; P., fold of peritoneum surrounding the spermatic cord ; V., vas deferens ; R., rectum.

isolated. The epididymis gives the sensation of a corrugated substance beneath a smooth surface. The vas deferens feels like a piece of wet cord about the thickness of a crow's quill. Traction on the cord or epididymis usually brings the testicle into view or within reach of the fingers, but sometimes it fails to do so, owing generally to the gland being large and cystic and held in position by coils of intestine.

Having found the cord or epididymis, grasping it with a long forceps and applying traction thereon with the hand outside the abdomen will assist the other hand in securing the testicles. If none of these structures is found at once, pass the fingers backwards towards the site of the internal inguinal ring, recognised as a depression in the abdominal wall, and identify there the fold of peritoneum attached to the supero-lateral wall of the pelvis, forming part of the suspensory ligament of the gland, and carrying on its inferior border the gubernaculum testis. Following the latter may bring the testicle within reach.

If the foregoing measures fail, enlarge the opening gradually, introduce the whole hand into the abdomen, pass it backwards to

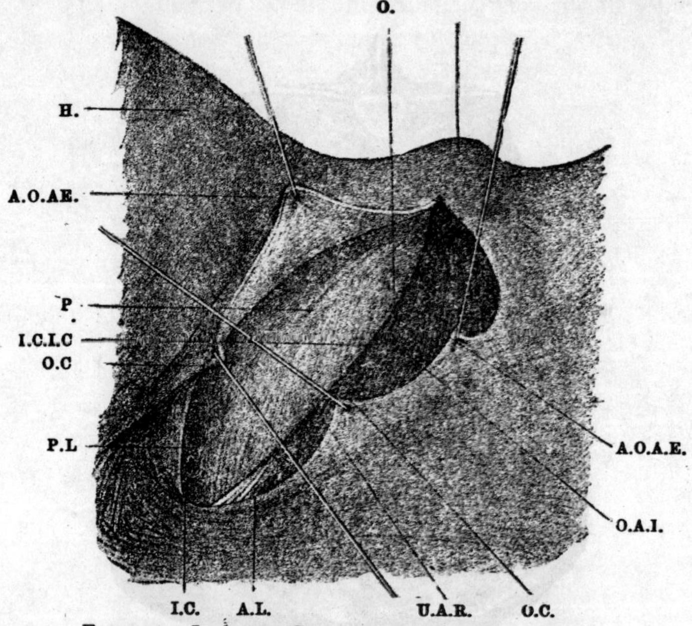

FIG. 155.—INGUINAL CANAL VIEWED FROM THE FLANK.

The external lip of the left inguinal ring has been removed; the aponeurosis of the external oblique abdominal muscle has been cut through a little in front of the spot where it divides; the inner oblique abdominal muscle has been separated from Poupart's ligament to a point near the inner commissure of the inguinal canal.

P., Poupart's ligament; O.A.I., obliquus abdominis internus muscle; I.C.I.C., inner commissure of the inguinal canal; A.O.A.E., aponeurosis of the obliquus abdominis externus muscle divided and reflected; I.C., inner commissure of the lower abdominal ring; O.C., outer commissure divided; A.L., anterior lip; P.L., posterior lip; U.A.R., indicates the position of the upper abdominal ring; O., indicates the position in which the opening is made in operating for abdominal cryptorchidism; H., hind-limb adducted.

the upper surface of the bladder, and recognise there Douglas's fold and the vas deferens. Follow the latter until the testicle is reached. Great care must be exercised during this stage of the operation to avoid leaning against the commissures of the opening, especially the inner one, for fear of making the aperture too large and leading to prolapse of the bowel during or following the operation. If the bowel persist in protruding during the operation, get the hind-quarters raised by means of a sack of hay or straw, as mentioned.

Having found the testicle, draw it outside the abdomen and remove it by means of the emasculator or ecraseur. Having removed the testicle put a liberal quantity of sulphanilamide powder into the canal. When the whole hand has been in the abdomen or if the opening made with the fingers is large, suture the wound in the muscle by means of a special curved needle mounted on a handle and plug the inguinal canal

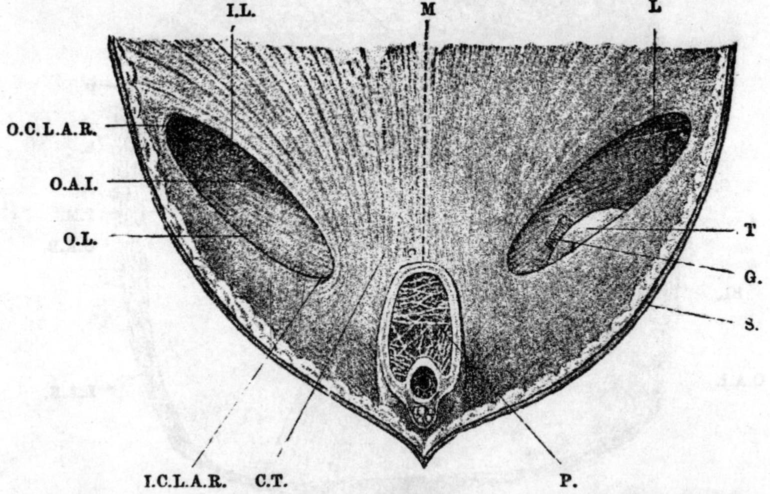

Fig. 156.—The Prepubic and Inguinal Regions seen from Below.

On either side of the middle line is visible the lower abdominal ring and the entrance to the inguinal canal.

I.C.L.A.R., Inner commissure of the lower abdominal ring; O.C.L.A.R., outer commissure of the lower abdominal ring; I.L., inner lip; O.L., outer lip; O.A.I., obliquus abdominis internus muscle; T., testicle covered with the tunica vaginalis propria; it has descended as far as the lower abdominal ring (inguinal cryptorchidism); G., fibrous band representing the gubernaculum testis; L., the dotted line shows the position and direction of the opening made in the obliquus abdominis internus muscle when operating by Bang and Möller's method; C.T., common tendon of the abdominal muscles; P., section through penis; S., skin; M., median line.

with sterilised gauze kept in position by cutaneous sutures. Suturing the muscle wound is not necessary when the canal is well packed with gauze. A lubricant preparation, such as a weak solution of lysol made with boiled water or thin B.I.P. or acriflavine emulsion, facilitates greatly the introduction of the gauze.

During the course of the operation scrupulous care must be taken against contamination of the hands and of the wound. The hand and arm should be bathed with the non-irritant antiseptic solution every time before inserting them into the peritoneal cavity, and no blood or lotion from the outside should be allowed to pass into the operation wound. Blood accumulating in the groin should be made to escape by an assistant pressing on the abdomen there or removed by mopping.

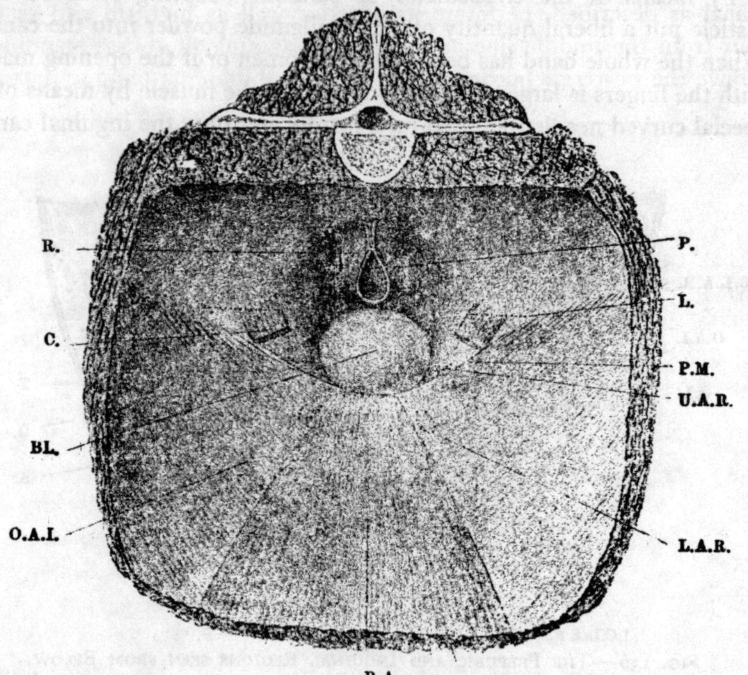

FIG. 157.—TRANSVERSE SECTION OF THE POSTERIOR ABDOMINAL REGION IN A VERTICAL PLANE.

This figure shows the insertion and arrangement of the obliquus abdominis internus and the cremaster. The peritoneum and transverse abdominis muscle have been removed.

O.A.I., Obliquus abdominis internus ; P.M., posterior margin of same ; C., upper portion of the cremaster muscle (divided) ; R.A., rectus abdominis muscle ; L.A.R., the dotted line shows the position of the lower abdominal ring ; U.A.R., the dotted line indicates the upper abdominal ring ; L., the dotted line shows the point at which the hand pierces the peritoneum in the operation for abdominal cryptorchidism ; P., pelvis ; R., rectum ; BL., bladder.

Advantages of the Danish Method.—(1) It is a convenient site and affords room for searching for the testicle without cramping the arm ; (2) the abdominal opening is made in strong muscular tissue ; (3) the wound, being made parallel to the muscular fibres, tends to close spontaneously, and besides can be sutured if necessary.

Yet this method is not much in vogue in Great Britain and Ireland, but it is extensively practised on the Continent. It might be objected to on the ground that the opening is rather dependent and favourable to prolapse of the bowel when it is large.

2. *The Belgian (Degive's) Method.*—Having explored the inguinal canal as described, perforate its anterior wall as high up and as far out from the middle line as possible (imagining the horse standing), above the posterior border of the internal abdominal oblique muscle,

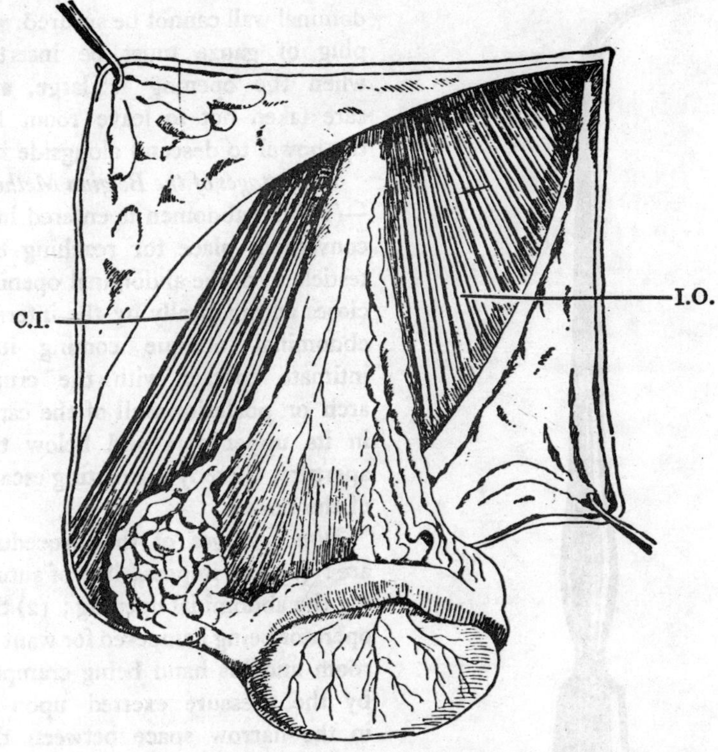

FIG. 158.—RIG CASTRATION BY DANISH METHOD.

The external inguinal ring has been enlarged by incising its outer commissure. C.I., internal commissure ; I.O., internal abdominal oblique muscle.

where the coils of intestine can be felt through the peritoneal membrane. Form the fingers into a cone, and pass the hand into the inguinal canal, using a gentle rotary movement and keeping it close against the posterior wall of the canal. Separate the fingers occasionally to help to rupture the areolar tissue occupying the inguinal interstice. Perforate the abdominal wall as described. If the peritoneum is relaxed, it may be torn by the nail between the finger and thumb. It requires great care to make this opening properly and to avoid breaking down the delicate tissue in its vicinity, especially towards the inner commissure. The peritoneal cavity is entered close to the pelvic border, between the tendon of the psoas parvus and the middle of the inferior aspect of the psoas magnus. The remaining part of the operation is the same as in the Danish method. The wound in the abdominal wall cannot be sutured. A plug of gauze must be inserted when the opening is large, and care taken not to leave room for the bowel to descend alongside it.

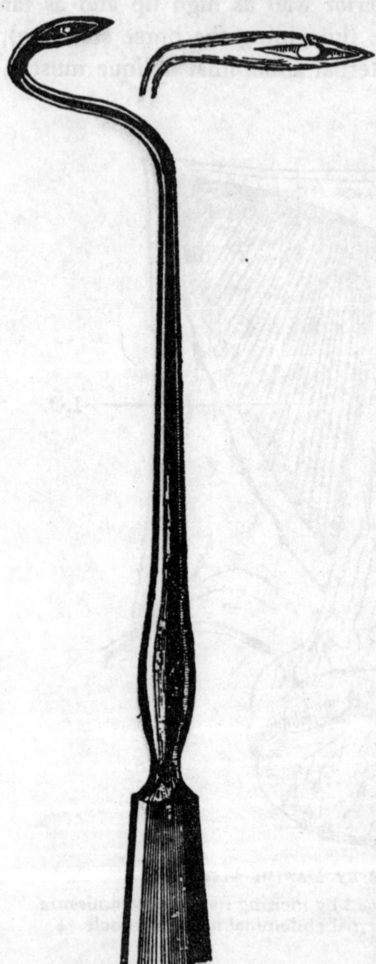

FIG. 159.—CURVED NEEDLE FOR SUTURING MUSCULAR WOUND (DANISH METHOD).

Advantages of the Belgian Method.—(1) The abdomen is entered in a convenient place for reaching the testicle; (2) the abdominal opening closes automatically by the internal abdominal oblique coming into intimate contact with the crural arch or posterior wall of the canal in its upper part and below the aperture, thereby preventing escape of the bowel.

Disadvantages of the procedure are: (1) The impossibility of suturing the abdominal opening; (2) the operator being hampered for want of room and his hand being cramped by the pressure exerted upon it in the narrow space between the two walls of the inguinal passages, sometimes rendering it powerless; (3) the danger of the tissue being broken down excessively and the bowel descending.

Many operators have no particular landmark for entering the abdomen except the site of the internal inguinal ring, which may be felt as a depression in the anterior wall of the canal about a long finger's length up from the external ring. They make the puncture higher up and further out than this point (assuming the standing position). The important point is to avoid making the opening large and dependent.

Even when a plug in the canal has not been considered necessary it is advisable to suture the scrotal wound closely to avoid the bowel escaping should it happen to pass into the canal. It is, in fact, a sound practice to insert a plug in every case when the abdomen has

FIG. 160.—CASTRATION OF CRYPTORCHID BY DANISH METHOD.

been entered. It is surprising how the small intestine can escape through a very small opening between cutaneous sutures after it has entered the inguinal canal.

The retained testicle is always abnormal, being usually small and flabby, and other times greatly enlarged from the presence of a cyst or teratomatous tissue, such as bone, teeth, or hair. It may contain both a liquid cyst and some of the abnormal tissues mentioned.

CYSTIC TESTICLE.—When the testicle is cystic it may be possible to draw it out carefully through the abnormal opening. If not, puncture it to allow the liquid to escape. This may be done with the thumb-nail inside the abdomen, where the liquid, being aseptic, will do no harm. It is better, however, to draw the testicle close to the wound and puncture it with a long, fine trocar and canula, and allow

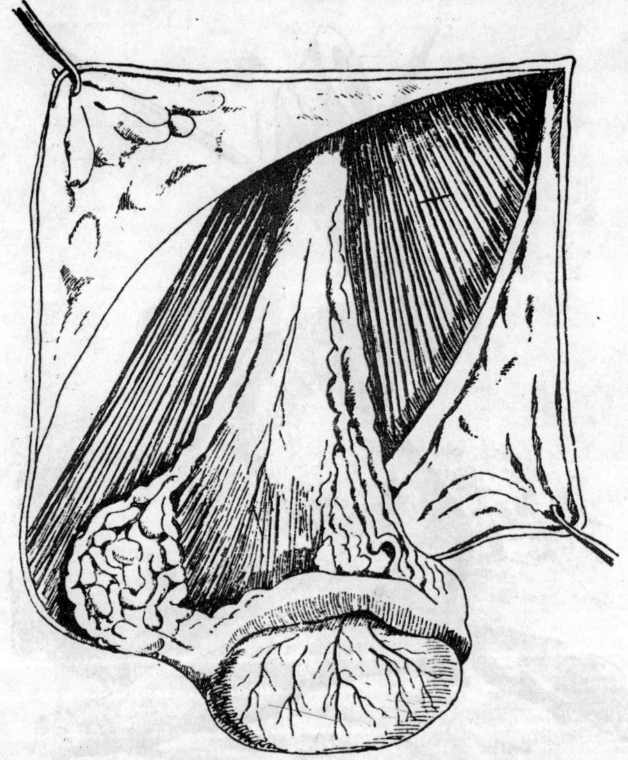

FIG. 161.—ILLUSTRATION SHOWING THE TESTICLE RELEASED IN THE DANISH METHOD OF RIG CASTRATION.

the liquid to escape outside by turning the horse on his side. Or a piece of rubber tubing may be attached to the canula and the fluid allowed to escape through it. The testicle distended with the fluid may be the size of a child's head, or even larger.

TERATOMATOUS TESTICLE.—There may be great difficulty experienced in removing a testicle containing a teratoma, owing to its increased size and solidity. When not very large, it can be carefully manipulated through the opening. If it contains a liquid cyst, the latter can be punctured as described. If the solid structure is too large to extract, it may be left in the abdomen after dividing the spermatic artery and the vas deferens with the emásculator outside the abdominal opening. The writer has done this with the desired effect on two occasions. Occasionally a case is met with where the animal has a scrotal hernia and a retained abdominal testicle on the same side. The procedure in this case is to open the hernial sac, pass the fingers or hand into the abdomen, secure the testicle, withdraw it, and sever the cord in the usual way, and then proceed as in the covert operation by including the peritoneal hernial sac and the cord in a wooden clam.

The author had a case of this kind in which the testicle was the size of a child's head and contained several large fully developed molar teeth as well as some cystic fluid. The hernial sac easily admitted the hand into the abdomen from which the testicle was extracted after prolonged effort. The patient recovered.

(2) The Flank Method

This consists in performing laparotomy in the flank on the side of the retained testicle, introducing the hand into the abdomen, searching for the testicle in the vicinity of the internal inguinal ring, and, having found it, taking it outside the abdominal opening and removing it by the emasculator or ecraseur. It has been recommended to make the incision at the level of the curl in the hair, and so that its lower extremity is just above the fold of skin in the flank. It is sufficient to suture the skin afterwards.

ADVANTAGES.—(1) The operator is not hampered by compression of his hand and arm, as in the inguinal method, and by the fear of tearing the tissues and making a dangerous opening. He can move his hand with freedom inside the abdomen. (2) There is practically no danger of descent of bowel. (3) The wound can be sutured easily.

DISADVANTAGES.—The hand and arm must always be introduced in the peritoneal cavity, thereby subjecting the patient to a greater risk of peritonitis than when only two fingers are introduced, and when the testicle is in the canal it is almost ridiculous to remove it via the peritoneal cavity.

This method is not adopted by modern expert operators, with the exception of a few. It is the older method. It is quite successful when carefully done. The writer has succeeded by this method for the removal of a very large teratomatous testicle which he had failed to extract through the inguinal canal. He allowed an interval of three weeks to elapse between the two operations.

False Rig.—Sometimes a horse is presented for operation with the history that he has been behaving as a rig, becoming excited and erecting the penis in the presence of mares, and even ejecting what would appear to be semen, yet on operating and exploring both inguinal canals a cord is found in each adherent to the skin at its extremity, and with the cremaster muscle attached, clear evidence that the horse has been castrated. He may or may not have been "cut proud." If the epididymis has been left it should be removed, and the sexual symptoms may then disappear after a while. It would be foolish to proceed to search the abdomen in a case of this kind.

The author has had experience of a few such cases.

Under this heading might be mentioned recorded cases of one or both testicles in colts over one year old having descended fully into the scrotum and after a variable time being permanently drawn up the canal out of view and out of reach, *e.g.*, the case reported by Howard (*Vet. Rec.*, **13**, No. 36).

The Anorchid.—Rarely a case is met with in which one of the testicles has not been developed at all. Persevering search for the testicle in such cases with consequent excessive interference with the peritoneum has caused the death of the patient in many instances, and post-mortem examination revealed the complete absence of the gland, the end of the cord being simply attached in the sublumbar region. The Author has had personal experience of two such cases. Or the cord may enter the inguinal canal in the ordinary way and communicate with the epididymis without any evidence of a testicle, which, however, may be present, but is so rudimentary that it escapes notice.

It should be a rule with operators, if the testicle cannot be found after a reasonable amount of searching or traction on the cord, not to proceed further except to remove the epididymis when it is within reach. It is better for all concerned to fail to remove a testicle even when present than to run the risk of causing the death of the animal by protracted operation.

Double Cryptorchid.—When both testicles are retained in the abdomen, the same procedure is adopted on each side and the two testicles are removed on the same occasion. It has been advised to operate on one side only at a time, and to await the healing of the first wound before operating on the other side. This is not to be recommended. Experience (of the author and others) has shown that there is no extra risk in operating on both sides at once. If the whole hand has been introduced into the abdomen at first, the two abdominal testicles may be removed through the same wound.

After-Treatment.—Put the horse into a hygienic loose box and give him the usual hospital diet. Never allow the animal to be walked a distance to the stable, as it may lead to escape of the bowel. Keep him under observation for a couple of hours after the operation, lest the bowel might descend if the canal has not been tamponed or has been insufficiently occluded.

If the patient show symptoms of decided colicky pains, examine the scrotum, and if a loop of bowel is found protruding inside or outside the scrotal wound, administer a large dose of chloroform standing and cast the horse immediately and return the bowel and plug the canal tightly. When attended to immediately, the accident will probably have no untoward effect.

Some operators make it a rule to put the horse in a stall with its hind-part raised with turf or planks, so as to cause the abdominal organs to fall forwards away from the inguinal region. It is a wise precaution, although usually unnecessary.

Apply an antiseptic lotion to the wound morning and evening.

When a plug has been inserted, remove it in twenty-four to seventy-two hours, depending on the size of the abdominal opening, and watch the horse after its removal, lest a portion of bowel may protrude, an unlikely event.

There is no need to exercise the horse. It is better not to do so, especially when a large orifice has been made in the abdomen, as it favours descent of the bowel. Marked œdema need not cause alarm so long as the patient's health remains good. Magnesium sulphate and potassium nitrate in the drinking water are indicated. When cut grass is obtainable, it should be given *ad lib*. The animal is fit to be discharged about a fortnight after the operation but the wound will not be closed by this time. Several weeks may elapse before it is completely cicatrised.

Results of Rig Castration.—When the operation has been carefully performed and not unduly prolonged, the patient usually makes a perfect recovery. With experienced careful operators the mortality may be estimated at 1 to 5 per cent.

COMPLICATIONS.—*Prolapse of the bowel* has accounted for a considerable number of deaths. The conditions favouring it and the measures to be adopted to prevent it and to deal with it have already been referred to (see also Complications of Castration).

Peritonitis is the commonest cause of death whether it ensue from descent of the bowel or from infection otherwise contracted. It is rare nowadays. The conditions favouring it have been alluded to in the course of the operation.

Hæmorrhage taking place into the peritoneal cavity occasionally causes death within about forty-eight hours after the operation.

The symptoms are those of internal hæmorrhage.

Treatment is seldom successful. It is that for internal hæmorrhage.

Œdema.—When the normal testicle has been already removed, the swelling after rig castration is comparatively slight or almost nil; but when the normal testicle, which is usually very large, has been taken away at the same time, marked œdema ensues. It is of no consequence when the patient's health is not affected. It gradually subsides in the course of nine or ten days.

Local Infection.—Severe traumatic fever may supervene as the result of local infection of the wound. Recovery usually takes place, although a portion of the lining of the wound has undergone ordinary gangrene. The temperature may reach 105° F., but the pulse remains full and does not exceed sixty, and the animal feeds fairly well. The respirations may be very accelerated, due to the pain in the wound, especially if the animal is made to move or is exercised.

Septicæmia or a fatal toxæmia may ensue from virulent infection of the wound.

The Bull

INDICATION.—As for ordinary castration.

PROCEDURE.—Perform laparotomy in the flank of the affected side, after having the animal starved for at least twenty-four hours. Pass the hand backwards, as in the horse, to the region of the bladder, and, having found the testicle, draw it out and remove it in the usual way.

The Ram

The procedure is the same as in the ox. The opening in the abdomen is made in the upper part of the flank in front of the angle of the haunch. In both animals recovery is the rule.

The Pig

The abdomen is opened high up in the flank, and the testicle drawn out by the first and second fingers and removed by scraping or by the emasculator, according to its size. The operation is practically always successful.

The Dog

The operation is indicated when the dog shows unusual sexual appetite or becomes vicious.

PROCEDURE.—Perform laparotomy just in front of the pubis. Insert the fore or middle finger backwards towards the pelvis, and recognise Douglas's fold and the vas deferens. Follow the latter to the testicle and remove it by ligation. Finish as for laparotomy.

The Cat

Operate for preference in the flank, performing laparotomy and removing the testicle in the usual way. Make sure that the testicle is not misplaced subcutaneously before opening the abdomen.

55. Ectopia of the Testicle

Occasionally, although one or both testicles are outside the abdomen, they are not in the scrotum, but situated subcutaneously in the groin or its vicinity. This abnormality is most common in the ox. Misplaced testicles in the dog are not uncommonly affected with sarcoma or carcinoma.

The operation to remove the testicle is the same as for ordinary castration.

56. Clitoridectomy : Mare

INDICATIONS.—Nymphomania of obscure origin, hyperæsthesia, or a tumour of the clitoris.

CONTROL.—In the standing position, using a side fetter or service hobbles, and an injection of a local anæsthetic round the base of the clitoris, or cast and administer chloroform.

PROCEDURE.—Have the lips of the vulva drawn apart by retractors and the tail held out of the way. Have the mucous membrane made tense by means of two forceps, one grasping the lower commissure of the vulva and the other the fold of mucous membrane above the clitoris. Grasp the summit of the clitoris with a forceps. Encircle it by two incisions in the mucous membrane. Using a sharp scissors, isolate the body of the organ as far as its base, and then excise it by means of a bistoury. If the bleeding seems severe, arrest it by touching the wound with a hot iron. The gouge forceps with hollow sharp-edged jaws may be used to snip off the clitoris.

AFTER-TREATMENT consists in applying a mild antiseptic lotion daily for a while.

57. Ovariotomy, Oöphorectomy : Mare

INDICATIONS.—*Ovariotomy* means removal of diseased ovaries, and is indicated when they affect the animal's behaviour or temperament to such a degree that she becomes a nuisance or so vicious that she is useless. When one ovary is diseased in a brood mare that has proved

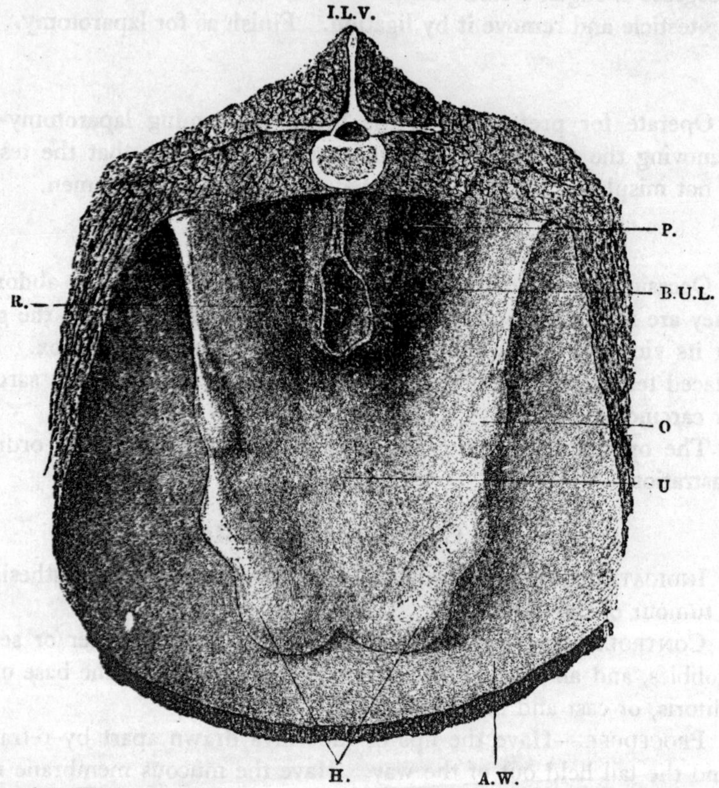

FIG. 162.—TRANSVERSE SECTION OF THE POSTERIOR ABDOMINAL REGION IN A VERTICAL PLANE.

The subject is a mare, and the section passes just in front of the first lumbar vertebra. The figure shows the position of the uterus as seen from below and that of the ovaries above the broad uterine ligament.

O., Ovary ; H., horns of the uterus ; U., uterus ; B.U.L., broad uterine ligament ; R., rectum ; A.W., abdominal wall ; P., pelvis ; I.L.V., first lumbar vertebra.

sterile, it may be removed with a view to enabling the normal one to function. This has been done with the desired effect. It is really difficult to decide by rectal examination of the ovaries, or even by their examination after removal, whether they are affected with disease. They may appear normal in a mare that has shown all the symptoms of sexual excitement and the viciousness that may accompany it. Some mares are constantly wicked and others are only wicked during the œstral period. Œstrum, however, may appear to be constantly present, judging from the mare's behaviour—squealing, everting the vulva, and squirting urine when touched or when in the presence of

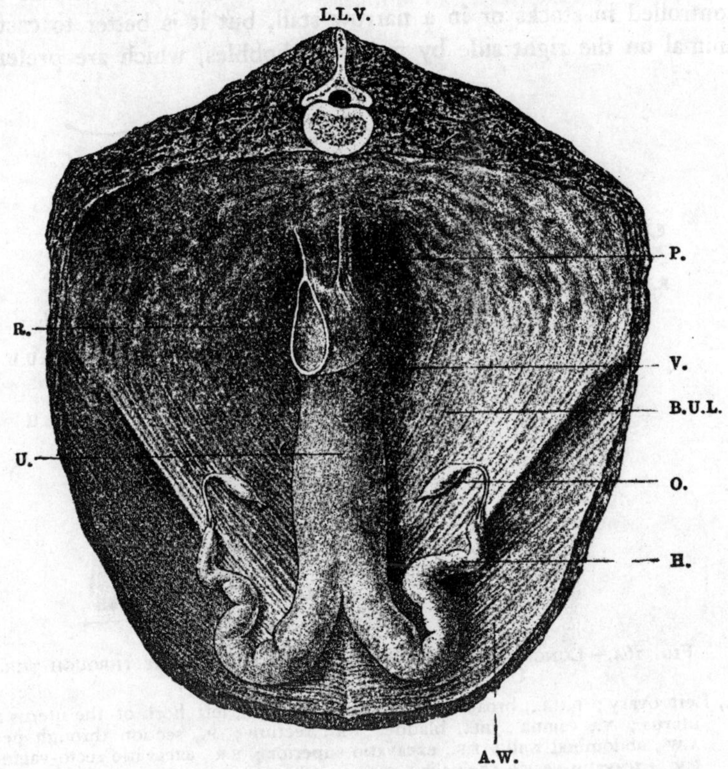

FIG. 163.—TRANSVERSE SECTION OF THE POSTERIOR ABDOMINAL REGION IN A VERTICAL PLANE.

The subject is a cow, and the vertical plane passes in front of the last lumbar vertebra. The figure shows the position of the uterus and the insertion of the ovaries in the uterine ligaments (seen from above).

O., Ovary; H., horn of the uterus; U., uterus; B.U.L., broad uterine ligament; V., vagina; R., rectum; P., pelvis; A.W., abdominal wall; L.L.V., last lumbar vertebra.

other horses. When the ovaries are large and cystic or small and cirrhotic, they are considered abnormal. Yet the ovaries may be of this nature without affecting the mare's disposition.

Oöphorectomy, or removal of normal ovaries, has been performed in racing mares to prevent œstrum interfering with their true racing form.

Preparation.—As for laparotomy. If the mare will permit it, have the rectum and bladder evacuated and the perineal region washed with soap and water before casting. If not, it must be done afterwards. It is better not to give an enema, as it may lead to soiling of the region of the operation.

Control.—The operation can be conveniently done on the mare controlled in stocks or in a narrow stall, but it is better to cast the animal on the right side by means of hobbles, which are preferable

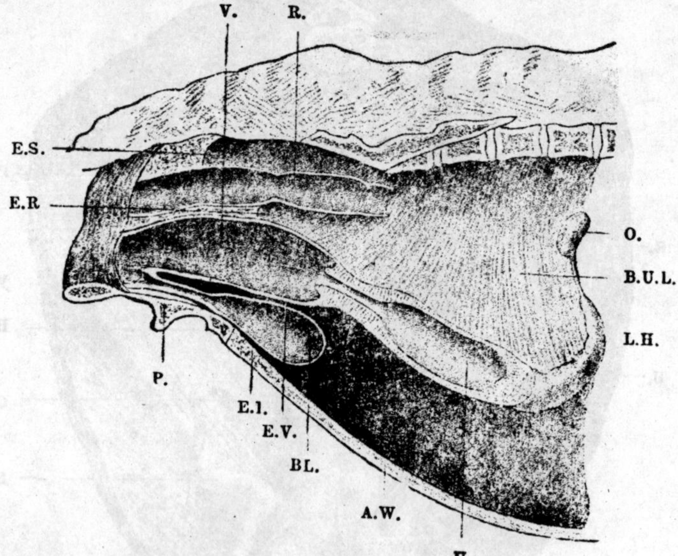

Fig. 164.—Longitudinal Section in a Vertical Plane through the Urino-genital Organs of a Mare.

O., Left ovary; B.U.L., broad uterine ligament; L.H., left horn of the uterus; U.; uterus; V., vagina; BL., bladder; R., rectum; P., section through pelvis; A.W., abdominal wall; E.S., excavatio superior; E.R., excavatio recto-vaginalis; E.V., excavatio vesico-vaginalis; E.I., excavatio inferior.

to the rope, as the latter causes the limbs to be flexed and cramped, interfering more or less with the relaxation of the vagina and thus hampering the operator. Administer a general or epidural anæsthetic.

Sites of Operation.—The site may be:

1. *The anterior wall* of the vagina (*a*) about the width of two fingers above the os uteri (mare standing), or (*b*) immediately beneath the latter. Site (*a*) is usually chosen. There is less risk of prolapse of the bowel through it; on the other hand, there is danger of wounding the iliac vessels in this situation if the puncture is not carefully made. With site (*b*) there is the danger of wounding the urinary bladder.

2. *The flank*, as for rig castration.

The vaginal site is almost universally adopted now.

PROCEDURE—*Vaginal Method*.—The rectum and bladder having been evacuated and the perineal region and dock washed, as mentioned, mop out the vagina with sterilised wool soaked in a solution of potassium permanganate (1 in 1,000) made with boiled water. Avoid prolonged douching and swabbing of the passage and the use of an irritant antiseptic solution, which would give rise to straining and do more harm than good. Normally the vaginal canal is aseptic.

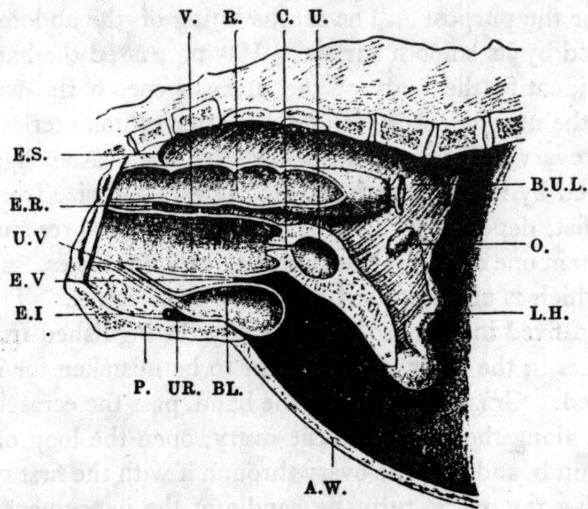

FIG. 165.—LONGITUDINAL SECTION IN A VERTICAL PLANE THROUGH THE URINO-GENITAL ORGANS OF A COW.

O., Left ovary ; L.H., left horn of uterus ; U., uterus ; B.U.L., broad uterine ligament ; C., neck ; V., vagina ; BL., bladder ; UR., urethra ; U.V., valve covering the opening of the urethra ; R., rectum ; P., section of the pelvis ; A.W., abdominal wall ; E.S., excavatio superior ; E.R., excavatio recto-vaginalis ; E.V., excavatio vesico-vaginalis ; E.I., excavatio inferior.

Should it contain a septic lesion, the operation would be contra-indicated. Cover the tail from base to tip with a sterilised bandage, and spread a sterilised cloth attached to the skin by fixation forceps across the quarters to rest the hand on during the operation. Observing all the rules of operative technique, kneel behind the animal, introduce the sharp-pointed concealed knife with the blade covered to the site of operation, press the still-protected blade firmly against the anterior wall of the vagina, stretching it as much as possible, and endeavouring at the same time to recognise if there is a vacant space in front of this part. This is possible by moving the stretched membrane from side to side and up and down with the *concealed* knife.

Hold the knife parallel to the vertebral column, or very slightly downwards, to avoid the iliac vessels.

Having decided that the point of the knife is in the proper place, expose the blade by drawing back the guard with the thumb and push it vigorously but steadily without a jerk into the peritoneal cavity, making sure that it goes right through the peritoneal membrane, otherwise the latter will recede before the finger when it is inserted into the wound. Enlarge the peritoneal opening by inserting successively two or three fingers and then the whole hand, considerable force being required for the purpose. The serous lining of the abdominal cavity is recognised by its smooth surface. Having passed the hand into the abdomen, identify the body of the uterus beneath the wound, pass from it to the uterine cornu, follow the latter to its anterior extremity where the ovary will be felt suspended by the ovarian ligament and distinguished by its peculiar features. It varies in size from a walnut to a large fist, depending chiefly on the absence or presence of cysts. It may contain one or several distended Graafian follicles. It possesses a hilum, which is an important distinguishing feature. The organ is isolated and fixed in position, and thereby distinguished from a pellet of hard fæces in the colon, which is apt to be mistaken for it if care is not exercised. Grasp the ovary in the hand, pass the ecraseur with the other hand along the arm up to the ovary, open the loop of the chain with the thumb, and pass the ovary through it with the first two fingers. Still grasping the ovary, turn the handle of the instrument, gradually tightening the chain on the ovarian ligament. Pass the fingers into the loop occasionally to make sure that no portion of bowel is included therein. Before tightening the chain completely, make sure again that it is the ovary, and it alone, that is being compressed. Remove the organ by turning the handle as slowly as possible. The ovary usually comes away in the hand rather quickly.

The upper ovary is more easily found than the lower, the mare being on her side. If there is difficulty in reaching the latter, turn the patient on to the other side. This is not likely to be necessary with an experienced operator. There may be great difficulty in getting a very enlarged ovary into the loop of the chain. The author in such a case found that putting the mare in the dorsal position facilitated the procedure, the ovary by the force of gravity being then comparatively easily made to pass through the loop when the latter was placed beneath it.

Hauptner of Berlin supplies another instrument on the same principle as the emasculator for the purpose which might prove more convenient than the ecraseur.

It is very important to be provided with a reliable ecraseur, otherwise all sorts of trouble may be encountered, such as hæmorrhage, breaking of the chain, or jamming of the latter. An extra chain and even an extra instrument are desirable. French operators find the Chassaignac ecraseur very satisfactory. Dewar's pattern, with a longer shaft than usual, answers the purpose well, the bevelled edge of the chain being applied next the ovary. The instrument in which the chain is tightened by a handle inserted on the side of the shaft is not reliable, because the horizontal threads of the handle cannot withstand the strain.

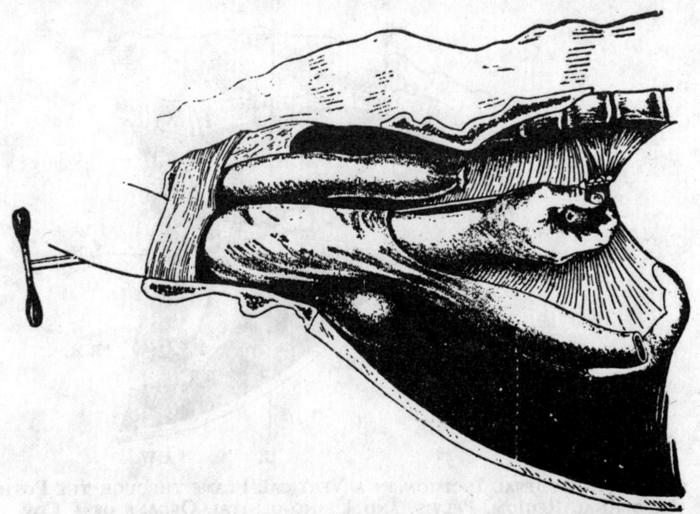

FIG. 166.—OVARIOTOMY WITH THE ECRASEUR (CADIOT'S METHOD).

Having removed the ovaries, swab out the vagina with the solution of potassium permanganate.

AFTER-TREATMENT.—Put the mare in a hygienic loose box and give her the usual laxative hospital diet. No further attention is required.

RESULT.—The mare may be dull and lie down a few hours after the operation, but the next morning she appears as if nothing had been done to her. In some cases she strains occasionally during the first twenty-four hours afterwards.

The desired effect is likely to be obtained in young mares in which the viciousness has not had time to become an established habit, and more particularly if it only appeared during the œstral period.

In aged mares that have been wicked for a long time the operation may fail to make them quiet. Occasionally the mare becomes perfectly quiet for a short period, but after a while becomes as vicious as ever. Other times weeks or even months elapse before the required effect is produced. She may improve gradually. If the mare still shows viciousness after a considerable rest, and perhaps a run at grass, an effort should be made to control her or compel her to work and she may then gradually become docile.

COMPLICATIONS.—The possible complications of the operation comprise:

1. *Fatal Hæmorrhage*, resulting from wounding the aorta or one of the iliac vessels when puncturing the vaginal wall, or from the

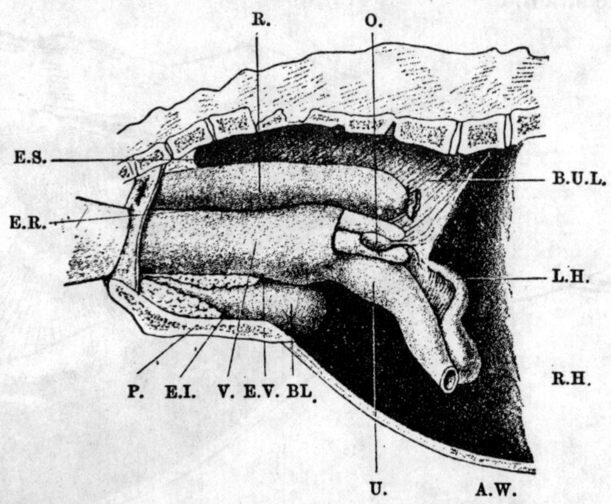

FIG. 167.—LONGITUDINAL INCISION IN A VERTICAL PLANE THROUGH THE POSTERIOR ABDOMINAL REGION, PELVIS, AND URINO-GENITAL ORGANS OF A COW.

The section is somewhat to the right side of the median plane. The figure illustrates the second stage of ovariotomy: the hand is grasping the left ovary.

O., Ovary; U., uterus; V., vagina; R.H., right horn of the uterus (cut through); L.H., left horn of uterus; B.U.L., broad uterine ligament; R., rectum; BL., bladder; P., pelvis; A.W., abdominal wall; E.S., excavatio superior; E.R., excavatio recto-vaginalis; E.V., excavatio vesico-vaginalis; E.I., excavatio inferior.

ecraseur failing to prevent hæmorrhage from the ovarian artery. If symptoms of hæmorrhage appear after the operation, little can be done except to give a hypodermic injection of adrenaline and apply cold wet cloths across the loins. If blood escapes freely along the arm or can be felt running from the ovarian artery when the hand is in the abdomen, a fatal issue may be feared. The author had a fatal result in a thoroughbred mare from this cause owing to a new ecraseur chain being used whose edges were not bevelled.

2. *Prolapse of the Bowel* into the vagina rarely occurs. If it happen

during the operation return it at once, and to prevent its recurrence afterwards keep the mare standing with the hind-quarters raised. If this is not sufficient, pack the vagina with sterilised towels.

3. *Peritonitis* rarely supervenes. It is generally the result of want of the necessary skill to perform the operation expeditiously, with due observance of the rules of asepsis. It terminates fatally.

4. *Abscess in the Vagina.*—This occasionally forms several days after the operation. The mare becomes uneasy, loses appetite, and shows a rise of temperature. Vaginal examination reveals inflammation at the seat of operation, and a fluctuating abscess may be detected. If the abscess burst into the peritoneal cavity death will ensue. It more frequently bursts into the vagina, and is then followed by recovery. When fluctuation is discovered, the abscess should be lanced.

5. *Eversion of the Rectum* may ensue from violent straining due to irritation of the vagina from an irritant antiseptic or rough handling of the passage during the operation.

Treatment consists in returning the prolapse, inserting an anal purse-string suture, and administering a sedative.

The operation should not be attempted on the living animal until proficiency in operating has been attained by practice on the dead subject.

The Heifer and Cow

INDICATIONS.—In the heifer the operation is indicated to prevent œstrum and allow the beast to settle down and fatten for the butcher. In the milch cow the operation has the effect of prolonging the milking period and of increasing the quantity and quality of the milk. It is performed at the age of six to nine months after the last calving, when lactation is at its height, but not during an œstral period. It is contra-indicated in a subject affected with chronic metritis, as peritonitis is then likely to supervene.

SITE OF OPERATION.—There are two sites of operation—viz.: (1) The left flank; (2) the anterior wall of the vagina immediately above the os uteri.

The Flank Method.—This is the better method for the heifer, in which the vagina is too narrow for the passage of the hand.

CONTROL.—Have the beast securely held against a wall and the tail kept out of the way by an assistant.

PROCEDURE.—Perform laparotomy in the upper part of the flank under the influence of paravertebral anæsthesia. Introduce the hand towards the pelvis, grasp each ovary in succession and remove it with the ecraseur. Finish as for laparotomy.

If general anæsthesia is obligatory or desirable, cast the beast on the opposite side and have the upper hind-limb drawn backwards.

Vaginal Method.—CONTROL in the standing position. Apply a solution of a local anæsthetic by means of a little cotton-wool at the site

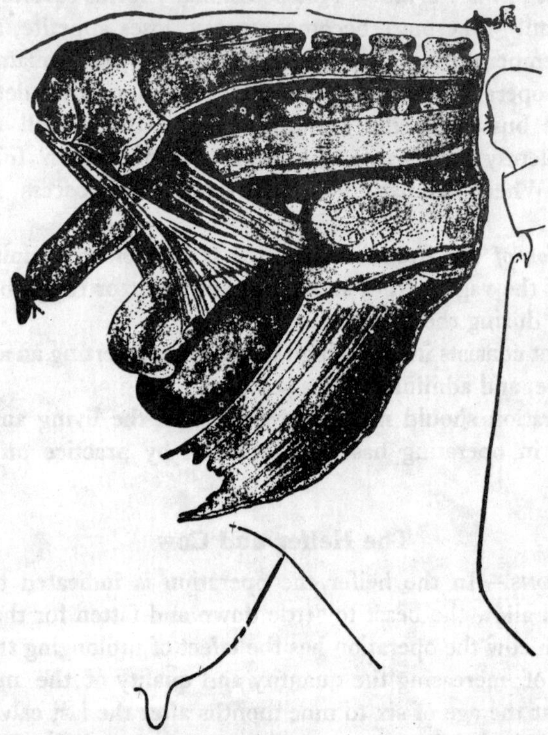

FIG. 168.—OVARIOTOMY IN THE COW: FIRST STAGE.

of the operation, and then proceed as in the mare until the abdomen is perforated. Introduce the first two fingers through the opening, search for the ovary to the inner side of the broad ligament near its anterior border, and, having found it, draw it into the vagina and remove it with the ecraseur. If there is difficulty in securing the ovary with the fingers, introduce the entire hand and the organ will be readily found.

RESULTS.—The operation is usually a complete success, but occasionally a death occurs from hæmorrhage. The desired effect of prolonging the milking period for upwards of two years is always obtained, and in heifers the quality of the flesh is invariably improved and the yield of beef is increased.

COMPLICATIONS.—The complications mentioned in connection with the mare are also possible in the cow, but are even more rare in the latter than in the former.

Flocard, a Swiss veterinarian, has operated on more than 9,000 cows, and has obtained excellent results in making use of a special

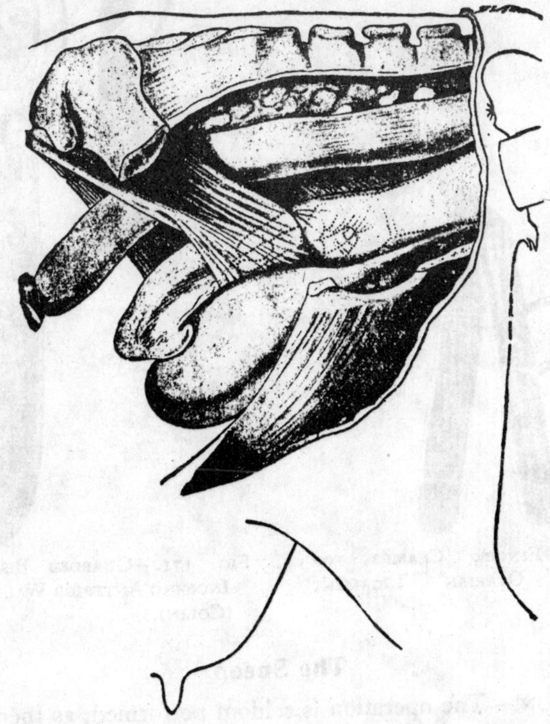

FIG. 169.—OVARIOTOMY IN THE COW: SECOND STAGE.

ecraseur which compresses forcibly the ovarian ligament before dividing it. He insists on the necessity of slow compression of the pedicle before cutting it. He operates at the rate of three cases per hour, and his mortality is nil. He maintains that owners will not be satisfied with a death rate exceeding 3 per cent. In the Argentine the operation is extensively practised through the vagina, and experts can operate on 140 to 180 cows per day, with a death rate not exceeding 2 to 3 per cent. Some operators there have reduced the mortality to 3 per 1,000.

Degive and others have practised ligation of the ovarian pedicle, thereby absolutely preventing hæmorrhage. The latter is more likely to ensue in the cow in full milk than in the heifer.

FIG. 170.—FINGER CLAMPS FOR GRASPING OVARIAN LIGAMENT (COLIN).

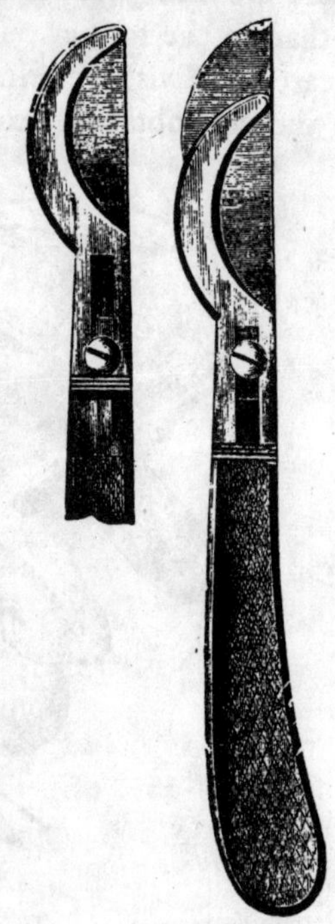

FIG. 171.—GUARDED BISTOURY FOR INCISING ANTERIOR WALL OF VAGINA (COLIN).

The Sheep

INDICATION.—The operation is seldom performed, as there is really no object for doing it except in places where they are used for milk production, to prolong the milking period.

Podasca operates as follows extraperitoneally :

1. Incises the flank vertically 4 centimetres in front of the muscles of the thigh and 3 centimetres from the extremities of the lumbar transverse processes, not including the peritoneum.

2. Separates the lips of the wound, observes the broad ligament through the peritoneum, exerts traction on the latter, bringing the ovary into view, seizes the gland still covered by peritoneum with an artery forceps, and applies a ligature to its pedicle.

3. Finishes as for laparotomy.

The advantage of this procedure is that there is little or no risk of peritonitis owing to the peritoneal cavity not being opened. Primary healing occurred in most cases. The usual precautions before, during, and after the operation were taken.

The Goat

INDICATIONS.—The operation is extensively performed in Roumania and Switzerland to prevent the hircine odour in the milk and to prolong the milking period to twelve or fifteen months. It also favours fattening, improves the quality of the flesh, and prevents the unpleasant hircine odour and taste which it usually possesses.

The operation is performed in the flank, the ovary being removed by scraping or torsion.

The Pig

INDICATION.—To prevent œstrum and hasten fattening.

PREPARATION.—Have the animal fasting for twenty-four hours.

AGE.—Six weeks to three months.

CONTROL.—Put the pig on its right side on a table or platform with the left hind-leg drawn backwards.

PROCEDURE.—The rule is to remove both uterus and ovaries—that is, to perform ovaro-hysterectomy. Make an incision immediately below the external angle of the ilium. Puncture the peritoneum with the finger, and insert it into the abdomen in the sublumbar region with its palmar surface upwards. Search for a hard, small body, the ovary, or a sinuous hard cord, the uterine cornu. Draw out the ovary and corresponding horn. Scrape through the ovarian ligament and tear through the broad ligament back to the body of the uterus. Separate the other ovary and cornu in the same way, and then scrape through the body of the uterus. Finish as for laparotomy.

Lay experts perform the operation with lightning speed, having it completed in some cases in thirty seconds, including the insertion of a cutaneous suture.

The operation may also be done through the white line in the space between the last three pairs of teats. The finger is introduced, and the ovary and cornu recognised and removed as described above.

COMPLICATIONS rarely supervene.

The Adult Sow

The adult sow is sometimes operated upon to improve the quality of its flesh.

CONTROL.—Cast on the right side and administer a general anæsthetic.

PROCEDURE.—Perform laparotomy in the left flank. Draw each ovary in succession through the wound, and remove it by means of the ecraseur or a clam and hot iron. Suture the wound.

Death rarely supervenes.

The Bitch.

INDICATIONS.—To prevent pregnancy. If done before six months old it may prevent œstrum. Otherwise, œstrum usually recurs, and copulation may ensue.

PREPARATION AND CONTROL.—As for laparotomy.

SITES.—(1) The white line immediately behind the umbilicus; (2) immediately to the inside of the fold of skin which separates the flank from the lower abdominal wall; (3) the flank.

PROCEDURE—*Site No.* 1.—Perform laparotomy. Introduce the middle finger into the abdomen and direct it backwards, seeking the uterine cornu or body. In a bitch that has been pregnant these are easily recognised, but in the virgin animal they are merely thin cords and are not detected by the feel.

The easiest and quickest way to find the ovary in every case is to introduce the first finger and thumb into the abdomen, grasp the kidney by its lateral aspects, and glide backwards from it to the ovary, which is situated almost immediately behind it. Grasp the ovary with an artery forceps and give the latter to an assistant to hold. Puncture the broad ligament beneath the ovary with an artery forceps, apply a silk ligature in front and another behind the gland, and then excise it. In a young animal that has not been pregnant it is sufficient to remove the ovary by scraping, but it is safer to make a practice of using a ligature. Finish as for laparotomy.

Site No. 2.—This site is not often chosen. Those who have adopted it find it a convenient place for reaching the ovary.

Site No. 3.—Many operators prefer the flank to the white line.

Make an incision immediately behind and parallel to the last rib, and perforate the abdominal wall as for laparotomy. Introduce the first finger into the sublumbar region of the abdomen, and, taking the kidney as a guide, recognise the ovary behind it and proceed as before.

It is possible to remove the two ovaries through the same wound, especially in a small subject, but it is more convenient to operate on both flanks. Finish as for laparotomy.

Advantages of the flank method are : (*a*) The ovary is very easily reached ; (*b*) the wound is not so likely to be soiled by contact with the bed or floor ; (*c*) escape of the bowel does not occur so easily as after the white-line operation.

Slight disadvantages of this site are a certain amount of hæmorrhage during the procedure and the fact of making two incisions as a rule.

Result.—Usually good. Exceptionally the animal succumbs, apparently to shock, within twenty-four hours after the operation.

The Cat

What has been said with reference to the bitch applies to the cat. The ovaries in the cat are naked, while those in the bitch are enveloped in fat. The flank site is preferable in the cat, as a local peritonitis seems more likely to ensue after operation at the white line, with consequent adhesion of the mesentery or bowel and interference with health, characterised by loss of condition and general vigour. The crouching position which the cat assumes is believed to favour this taking place at this point.

Hysterotomy Cæsarean Section

Indication.—The removal of the fœtus through an incision in the abdominal wall at the time of parturition when it cannot be delivered in the normal manner.

Preparation and Control.—As for laparotomy.

The Mare

The operation consists in performing laparotomy in the left flank, bringing the uterus to the abdominal opening, incising it, extracting the fœtus and fœtal membranes, closing the uterine wound by a double row of Lembert sutures, and finishing as for laparotomy. Up to the present the operation has been rarely performed and with little or no success.

The Cow

The operation has had a fair measure of success in the cow, and is being much more frequently performed now than formerly owing to the advance in surgical technique. It is sometimes preferable to prolonged embryotomy in difficult cases of dystokia.

Procedure.—Opinions differ as to the optimum site. The best site is that from which the uterus can be readily brought into the incision and maintained there without undue strain on the operator and his assistant and where the omentum and intestines come least in the way. P. M. Sutton (*Vet. Rec.*, May 24th, 1947) prefers the left side and makes the incision from immediately in front of the udder anteriorly for about 14 inches along a line 2 or 3 inches from and parallel to the milk vein. R. H. Smythe makes a right side incision extending for about 18 inches downwards and forwards; commencing 3 inches below the tuber coxæ and terminating about 4 inches in front of the stifle (*Vet. Rec.*, April 19th, 1941). Several sterile cloths are required. The pregnant horn is brought to the wound and incised sufficiently to permit of extraction of the calf. The membranes having been removed, the uterine wound is closed by a double row of Lembert sutures. Results vary according to the condition of the patient and the skill or experience of the operator. Death may occur from shock or peritonitis or general toxæmia. Many successful cases have been recorded. A very good paper by P. M. Sutton and an instructive discussion on the subject appeared in *Vet. Rec.*, May 24th, 1947.

The Sow and Bitch

The operation in the sow and bitch is carried out on similar lines ofter proceeding as for laparotomy. An effort should be made to remove the several fœti through the same uterine opening. When performed on the animal in normal health it is usually successful.

58. Hysterectomy (Removal of the Uterus): Mare

INDICATION.—When the organ is prolapsed after parturition and cannot or is unfit to be returned.

CONTROL.—Cast and anæsthetise the mare.

PROCEDURE.—Thoroughly cleanse and disinfect the uterus, especially at its neck, where the amputation is to be performed. Make sure that the bladder is not included in the prolapse and there is no protrusion of bowel into the peritoneal cul-de-sac of the uterus. If the organ is not very much damaged or very septic, a bandage may be applied to it, Esmarch fashion, to prevent the loss of blood contained in the organ. Apply a ligature round the neck of the uterus close to the vulva. The ligature may be composed of whipcord, strong silk, or india-rubber in the form of a tube or band. The rubber ligature is preferable, being elastic, but it must be of good quality. Two or three bands of rubber may be combined to increase its strength.

To prevent the inelastic cord slipping it should be applied in the form of a double ligature as follows: Insert a large needle with a handle through the neck of the uterus, pass the doubled cord through the eye of the needle and draw the latter back. Cut the cord at its centre and ligature the part in two halves. Or the Staffordshire ligature may be employed. Instead of cutting the cord as in the last case, take each end of the cord and pass it backwards through the loop formed by the doubled thread; then bring both ends in opposite directions round the whole neck of the prolapse and tie them tightly. This is equivalent to ligaturing the part in two halves and in its entirety as well. Disinfect the stump and push it back into the pelvic cavity. If some bleeding ensue despite the ligature, the hot iron may be applied to the bleeding surface.

AFTER-TREATMENT.—Apply an antiseptic lotion to the stump once or twice daily until the ligature and the portion behind it come away.

RESULT.—Not very hopeful. The operation has been seldom performed. There have been probably more failures than successes, although Lanzilotti had six cures and two deaths out of eight cases. When death supervenes, it is of course due to the toxæmia resulting from metroperitonitis contracted before removal of the organ.

The Cow

INDICATIONS.—As in the mare. The operation is more often required in the cow.

PROCEDURE.—As described in the case of the mare.

RESULT.—Good when performed before the animal is exhausted by toxæmia. Reported cases prove that the operation is frequently followed by recovery. Lanzilotti had seventy-seven cures and nine deaths in eighty-six cases. The cow is not so susceptible to metroperitonitis as the mare.

The Ewe

The operation is seldom indicated in the ewe. The prospect of recovery is about the same as in the cow.

The Sow

What has been said with regard to the cow applies, generally speaking, to the sow.

The Bitch (Ovaro-Hysterectomy: Removal of the Uterus and Ovaries).

INDICATIONS.—Dystokia which cannot be relieved by ordinary measures; pregnancy in a small bitch, as the result of mating with a bigger dog, to prevent dangerous parturition in consequence of the large size of the pups; and pyometra.

PROCEDURE.—Perform laparotomy on the median line behind the umbilicus, making the opening sufficiently large to permit of the withdrawal of each pregnant or distended horn. Draw out the latter, gradually commencing at its middle portion, taking care not to rupture it by rough handling. Apply two ligatures in front of the ovary ; cut between the ligatures ; tear through the broad ligament back to the body of the uterus. Proceed similarly with the other horn. Apply two ligatures on the cervix, place a piece of lint or cotton-wool beneath the latter to intercept any liquid that may escape from its interior, and sever it between the ligatures. If the uterine contents are septic, disinfect the stump by swabbing it lightly with tincture of iodine, and introduce a little of the tincture into its lumen through the channel of a grooved director, taking care not to allow any of the preparation to come in contact with the peritoneum. Remove the lint or wool without contaminating the serous membrane, and finish as for laparotomy.

RESULTS.—Practically always successful when performed on a healthy subject in which the uterine contents are aseptic. When toxæmia has supervened, the result will depend on its severity. If the pups have undergone putrefaction and a putrid metritis has supervened, the patient is sure to succumb.

In cases of chronic pyometra recovery frequently ensues, although the patient may have shown distinct toxic symptoms.

After removal of a septic pregnant uterus or one affected with pyometra it is necessary to seal the uterine stump so as to prevent its interior communicating with the peritoneal cavity and leading to contamination thereof. Merrilat has insisted on the importance of this indication.

Various methods of sealing the stump have been performed including the following :—

1. **Invagination of the Stump,** the procedure being as follows :

(1) Ligate the body of the uterus in the usual manner.

(2) Insert a forceps through the vagina, seize the ligatured stump and draw it back into the vaginal passage, thus invaginating it.

(3) Suture the peritoneal orifice of the stump, thereby shutting off the peritoneal cul-de-sac from the abdominal cavity. The dead portion of the stump eventually sloughs and is discharged through the vagina. In the meantime the latter is flushed daily with a suitable antiseptic lotion to remove debris and discharge caused by the necrotic tissue.

Considerable difficulty may be experienced in effecting the invagination and in some cases it proves impracticable.

2. **Peritonisation.** This consists in enveloping the stump in a layer of omentum which effectively closes the orifice of the stump and prevents the invasion of the peritoneal cavity by bacteria in its lumen. Apart from its mechanical effect, it is known that the omentum has the power of entrapping micro-organisms and preventing their diffusion on the serous membrane.

Professors McCunn and Wright have reported success by the adoption of this procedure for preventing peritoneal infection following enterectomy and hysterectomy (*Vet. Rec.*, **12**, 19).

3. **Suture of the Stump after Ligation** performed as follows as described by R. H. Smythe (Camborne).

(1) Apply a tape ligature temporarily round the vagina as close to the vulva as possible to enable the vagina to be drawn well forward.

(2) Insert a piece of cotton-wool or gauze beneath the uterus at the site of amputation.

(3) Apply a silk ligature immediately behind the cervix.

(4) Divide the organ between the two ligatures and remove it.

(5) Dress the stump inside and outside with tincture of iodine, without allowing any of the solution to enter the peritoneal cavity.

(6) Remove the gauze or wool.

(7) Insert an interrupted silk suture through the lateral borders of the stump, passing through the serous and muscular coats which on being drawn tight and firmly tied brings the lateral serous surfaces into apposition, while the upper and lower serous surfaces automatically come into contact.

Pressure on the uterine vessels is thus effected and arrests hæmorrhage therefrom.

(8) Unite the upper and lower borders by an interrupted or continuous Lembert suture.

(9) Remove the temporary ligature.

It is claimed for this method that it ensures complete closure of the stump with rapid union of the serous surfaces.

The Cat

The cat is on a par with the bitch regarding this operation. In both these animals the prolapsed uterus may be amputated as in the other subjects dealt with. Professor J. G. Wright, of the Royal Veterinary College, London, advises the following procedure in the kitten from three to five months old. It is not so suitable for older animals. Make a vertical incision ⅜-inch long on a level with the anterior border of the ilium and about the middle of the flank, the patient being in the ventral position. If a large quantity of fat is encountered, snip some of it off, and if a blood vessel is severed arrest the hæmorrhage by forcipressure. Pick up with a forceps the external abdominal oblique muscle which is very thin at this point, and puncture it, exposing the internal abdominal oblique. Grasp the latter with the forceps and draw it out of the wound, tent fashion, and make an opening in it sufficiently large to permit the points of a dressing forceps to be introduced into the abdomen.

Maintain the grip on the internal abdominal oblique muscle until the ovary has been located and secured, as the traction thus caused on the peritoneum tends to pull the uterus into the wound. If omentum protrudes, replace it immediately, pushing it towards the abdominal floor, as the ovary is dorsally situated.

Fixed fat may be found in the fold of peritoneum, running backwards from the peri-renal region to the pelvis and gentle traction on it will bring the uterine horn or ovary into view. The former may be encountered immediately on introducing the forceps into the peritoneal cavity. Draw the uppermost cornu with its ovary out of the wound. Secure the vessels with artery forceps and sever the ovarian attachment. Draw the uterine cornu upwards and backwards, thus bringing the bifurcation into view. Grasp the other cornu with a forceps and draw it carefully out of the wound. In order to bring the other ovary outside the abdomen it will be necessary to press the abdominal wall downwards with the fingers. Deal with it in the same way as the first ovary, then draw the entire uterus with ovaries attached well outside the operation wound and remove it by section of its body by scraping or after ligation. Close the wound by inserting two No. 1 silk sutures in the internal abdominal oblique muscle, one in the external abdominal oblique and two in the skin. Remove the sutures on the seventh day. Healing by first intention ensues. It requires considerable practice to operate skilfully in this fashion.

Marsupial Operation for Pyometra in the Bitch

INDICATIONS.—Closed pyometra.

PROCEDURE.—Observe the usual operative technique, administer $\frac{1}{2}$ grain morphine sulphate and $\frac{1}{100}$ to $\frac{1}{60}$ gr. stropine. Use local anæsthesia; fix the patient in the lateral position; perform laparotomy with a vertical incision in the flank; have the lips of the parietal wound moderately retracted with self-fixing retractors; cause the uterus to bulge into the abdominal opening by placing a pad under the opposite flank ; fix the uterus to the abdominal wall by a few sutures of chromicised gut parallel to the lips of the wound and close thereto; make a central puncture in the uterus, preferably with a thermocautery ; the contents may gush out ; insert into the uterus a piece of rubber tubing, about 6 inches long and fenestrated at its inner end by several holes made by snipping pieces out with a curved scissors, fix it in position by a single suture through the uterine wall ; sprinkle the wound with sulphanilamide powder and apply a thick pad of gauze to absorb the discharge. All the contents are drained away in 3 or 4 days after which the tube is removed and the wound left exposed. The fistula heals in about 21 days.

The foregoing description of the operation is based on a communication to the *Vet. Rec.*, May 10th, 1947, by R. E. Williams, B.Sc., M.R.C.V.S., Southampton, who states that the operation, devised in America, is highly successful, that animals persistently vomiting and in the last stage of toxæmia which would have surely succumbed to hysterectomy make spectacular recoveries. It is recommended to have the uterus removed after about 3 months as recurrence of the condition supervenes in a certain proportion of cases.

59. Amputation of the Penis : Horse

INDICATIONS.—Irreparable injury ; malignant tumour ; permanent paralysis.

SITE.—Above the affected part, and in the case of malignant disease or paralysis as close to the base as possible.

CONTROL.—Cast and anæsthetise, and fix in the dorsal position.

PROCEDURE.—Introduce a catheter and apply a tourniquet on the base of the organ. Attach a piece of tape in the form of a noose behind the glans to enable an assistant to keep the penis extended forwards. Make a cutaneous transverse incision on the inferior (now superior) aspect of the organ involving half its circumference. From the extremities of this incision make two others backwards, converging to meet at a point about 3 inches behind the first incision. Excise the tissues included in the triangular area thus mapped out as far as the urethra, which is left intact. Incise the latter at the level of the transverse incision. Insert a grooved director into the wound in the urethra and incise its inferior wall on the instrument up to the apex of the triangle. Suture the cut edges of the urethra to the corresponding edges of the skin. Remove the catheter and tourniquet, apply an india-rubber ligature round the penis at the level of the transverse incision, and amputate the organ about 1 inch in front of this point. There will be no hæmorrhage.

AFTER-TREATMENT.—Inject a non-irritant antiseptic solution into the sheath once daily until the ligature and the tissue in front thereof come away, which will occur about nine or ten days after the operation.

RESULT.—Good as a rule. The sutures fall out after some days. Large granulations may form where the sutures were situated, but they contract afterwards, leaving a flat cicatrix. A gaping orifice is left in the urethra, through which the horse urinates freely. Irritation of the skin on the under aspect of the abdominal wall just in front of the prepuce may be caused by the urine coming in contact with it. This, however, does

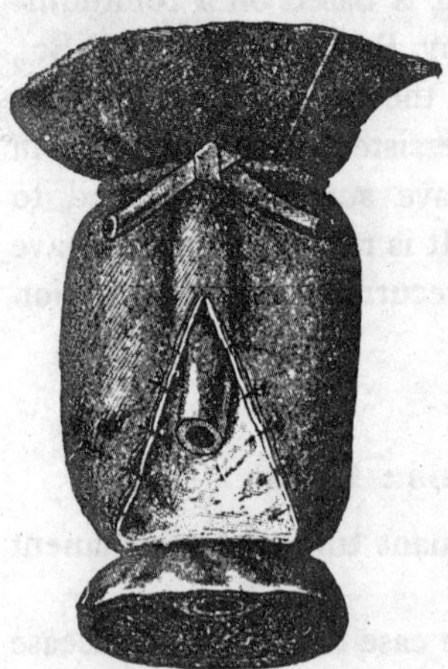

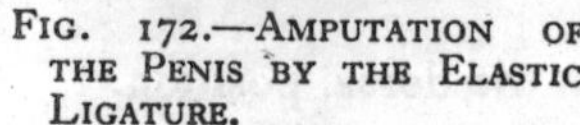

FIG. 172.—AMPUTATION OF THE PENIS BY THE ELASTIC LIGATURE.

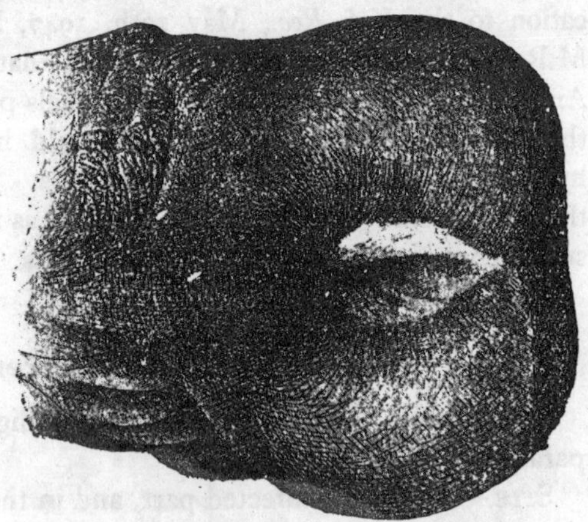

FIG. 173.—AMPUTATION OF THE PENIS, SHOWING STUMP AND URETHRAL ORIFICE.

not always ensue. When the organ has been removed at its base, the interior of the sheath may become inflamed from urination therein.

When the operation has been done for a malignant tumour, the latter may recur on the stump. Stricture of the urethral orifice does not supervene, owing to the cicatricial contraction of the wound tending to make it gape.

Excision of the Sheath—INDICATION.—In a case where the penis has been amputated at the base and urination into the sheath causes inflammation of its lining.

PROCEDURE.—Divide the prepuce in the middle line, and then remove its two lateral halves level with the abdominal wall. Arrest the hæmorrhage from the preputial plexus and suture the opposing edges of the skin.

The Ox

INDICATION.—As in the horse, but less frequently than in the latter.

CONTROL.—As in the horse.

PROCEDURE.—Divide the sheath on the middle line throughout its entire length, and suture the external and internal layers of the preputial wound. Proceed to amputate the organ on the same lines as in the horse, making the V-shaped wound and suturing the urethral borders to the integument of the penis.

Lannuse performed the operation successfully thus: Cast on the left side, fix the upper hind-limb forward to the shoulder, open up the sheath, apply a rubber ring 1 to 2 mm. thick and 1½ cms. wide on the penis a little above the point of section, amputate the organ with the knife, and introduce into the urethra a small gum-elastic or metal catheter tapering to one of its extremities. The pressure of the elastic ring will keep it in position and prevent hæmorrhage. Remove the catheter and the ring after a few days.

The Dog

INDICATIONS.—As in the horse.

PROCEDURE.—Having fixed and anæsthetised the patient in the dorsal position, divide the fleshy portion of the penis with the knife, dissect out the urethra for a short distance in front of the point of section and reflect it backwards. Saw through the bone, leave a V-shaped wound on the stump, slit up the urethra, and suture its edges to the corresponding edges of the penial integument.

RESULT.—Stricture of the urethral orifice is apt to ensue within twelve months after the operation.

60. Vennerhalm's Operation (Removal of the Integument of the Penis from a Point a Short Distance behind the Glans to the Base of the Organ).

INDICATIONS.—Paraphimosis due to a chronic thickening of the skin of the penis, forming a collar of variable depth round the organ, and paralysis of the penis.

CONTROL.—As for amputation of the penis.

PROCEDURE.—Have the penis extended forwards. It is better not to apply a tourniquet. It interferes with the procedure and is not necessary, as the hæmorrhage is of no consequence. Make a circular cutaneous incision behind the glans penis and another at the base of the organ: join these by a longitudinal incision. Dissect and remove the intervening skin, and suture the borders of the two circular incisions, thereby shortening the penis by the distance between the two circumferential incisions. If the upper cutaneous circle is larger than the lower, diminish its circumference by two or three V-shaped excisions, followed by sutures.

Healing by first intention does not always ensue, and when the sutures cut through the wound assumes its original dimensions. Yet, although several inches separate the two cutaneous borders, they gradually approach each other and meet in the course of six to eight

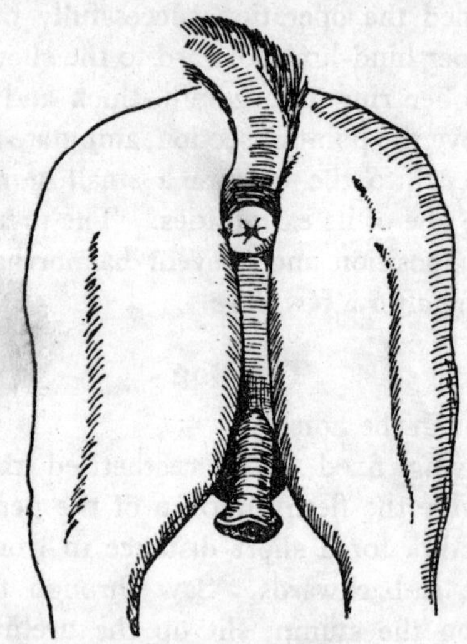

FIG. 174.—RETRO-DEVIATION OF PENIS.

weeks, when the operation will have had the desired effect of retracting the organ inside the sheath, except the organ is paralysed, when it still protrudes.

RESULT.—As just indicated. It is not satisfactory for paralysis of the penis. Amputation of the organ is preferable for this condition, and such a large excision is not necessary for the removal of a mere ridge of thickened tissue round the organ.

61. Retro-deviation of the Penis

INDICATION.—To render a stallion incapable of service while acting as a teaser in the presence of mares, for the purpose of exciting œstrum.

CONTROL.—Cast and anæsthetise on the near side, and fix the upper hind-limb forward to the shoulder.

SITE.—A hand's-breadth behind the scrotum, where the penis is only covered by the skin, a fibro-elastic membrane, and a layer of connective tissue.

PROCEDURE.—Make an antero-posterior incision about 5 inches long through the skin and subjacent fascia. Having exposed the penis, isolate it throughout the whole extent of the incision by tearing through the areolar tissue on its superior and lateral aspects, hook the index finger round the detached portion of the organ, and draw it forcibly backwards. The anterior part of the penis is now only held by adhesions to the sheath. Open the preputial cul-de-sac by a median incision, and then cut through the integument forming the cul-de-sac all round the penis. To facilitate this, instruct an assistant to introduce his hand into the sheath and push the cul-de-sac backwards. The whole anterior part of the penis remains henceforward directed backwards. Hæmorrhage is slight. Dress the wound daily with an antiseptic solution until it is uniformly granulating.

62. Lithotomy (Extraction of a Calculus from the Bladder) : Horse

CONTROL.—The most convenient position for the operator is standing, but it is better, generally speaking, to cast and anæsthetise the horse and fix him in the dorsal or lateral position.

SITE.—The perineal region in the middle line, immediately above the ischial arch.

PROCEDURE.—There are three stages in the operation—viz. : (1) Urethrotomy; (2) introduction of the forceps; and (3) extracting the stone.

(1) *Urethrotomy.*—To facilitate locating the urethra, pass a catheter or have the canal distended with boiled water introduced by a suitable syringe, and prevented from escaping by an assistant compressing the meatus. Have the tail drawn dorsally out of the way. Make a longitudinal incision 1½ to 2 inches long, going successively through the skin, retractor penis, accelerator urinæ, the corpus spongiosum, and the urethra. Stretch the skin by downward pressure with the fingers to make it tense for the incision. An alternative procedure, when the urethra is dilated with fluid, is to puncture it in the same way as an abscess and enlarge the wound on a grooved director. Hæmorrhage is slight when the internal pudic artery is avoided by keeping the incision on the middle line.

(2) *Introduction of the Forceps.*—Hold the left hand extended, with the dorsum of the fingers placed against the skin immediately below the lower commissure of the wound. Take the forceps in the right hand, with the concavity of the jaws downwards, glide it along the left

hand into the urethra, and by slight rotary movements pass it into the bladder.

(3) *Extraction of the Calculus.*—Instruct an assistant to pass his hand into the rectum and guide the stone into the open jaws of the forceps. Or, instead, the operator may pass one hand into the rectum for the same purpose. Withdraw the stone with gentle rotary movement of the instrument. It may be possible to grasp the stone with the fingers introduced in the form of a cone through the neck of the bladder. This is facilitated by the use of a lubricant such as liquid paraffin or olive oil or linseed tea, sterilised by boiling. If there be sabulous matter in the bladder, remove it with the bladder curette. If the calculus is too large to pass through the neck of the bladder, it will be necessary either to incise this part of the organ and the intrapelvic portion of the urethra (cystotomy) or break the calculus (lithotrity).

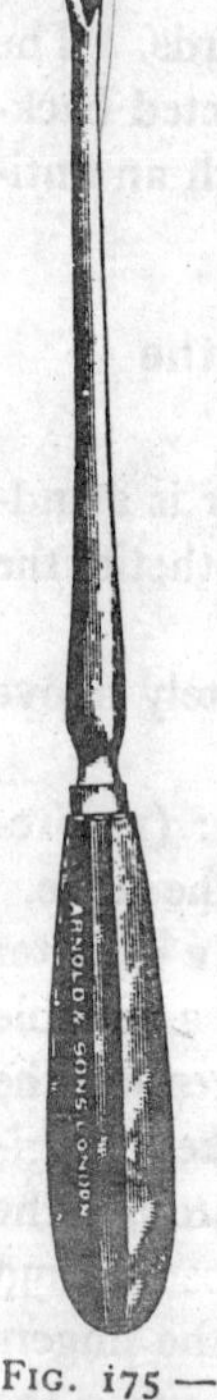

Fig. 175—Calculus Spoon.

Cystotomy.—Introduce a lithotome, a special concealed knife, or a blunt-point bistoury guided on a grooved director beyond the neck of the bladder, and in withdrawing it incise the neck in a lateral direction. If necessary, incise both sides. Then seize the stone with the forceps, or possibly with the fingers, and extract it.

Result of Cystotomy.—Although several operators have recorded successful cases, the procedure, nevertheless, is dangerous on account of the severe hæmorrhage and urinary infiltration with septic inflammation or even gangrene that may ensue. The sphincter of the bladder being inert, the urine constantly trickles from the organ, infiltrating the tissues through the operation wound.

Lithotrity (Breaking the Calculus).—Have the following requirements ready: (1) A urethral speculum to dilate the pelvic portion of the urethra and the neck of the bladder; (2) a syringe furnished with a nozzle sufficiently long to enter the bladder through the perineal wound; (3) a few quarts of boiled water containing boracic acid in solution for injection into the bladder; (4) sterilised olive oil or liquid paraffin or linseed tea to serve as a lubricant; (5) a lithotrite to crush the stone.

Procedure comprises three stages: (1) Introduction of the lithotrite and prehension of the calculus; (2) breaking the stone; (3) removal of debris.

(1) *Introduction of the Lithotrite.*—There are different patterns of lithotrites—*e.g.*, Bouley's, Guillon's, and Axe's. Pass the instrument carefully through the urethra and the neck of the bladder. Having recognised the stone, direct some of the boric solution to be injected into the bladder to distend it and prevent its walls clinging to the stone and interfering with its prehension. Grasp the stone in the jaws of the instrument, aided by a hand in the rectum, as mentioned above. If difficulty is experienced in introducing the instrument, it may be overcome by using the dilator to distend the passage, and one of the lubricants mentioned.

(2) *Breaking the Stone.*—Break or crush the stone by turning the screw on the handles of the forceps. If one of the fragments is very large, it may be necessary to crush it in the same way, although in the large animals a relatively voluminous calculus or fragment can be manipulated through the urethra.

(3) *Evacuation of the Debris.*—Insert the speculum and irrigate the bladder with the boric solution, which will flush out the debris.

The lithotrite may fail to crush a large hard calculus. This may be fractured by the use of a blunt chisel and mallet. Let an assistant with his hand in the rectum push the stone into the neck of the bladder. Introduce the chisel through the wound, place its edge against the stone, and strike it with repeated slight blows of the hammer until it gives way.

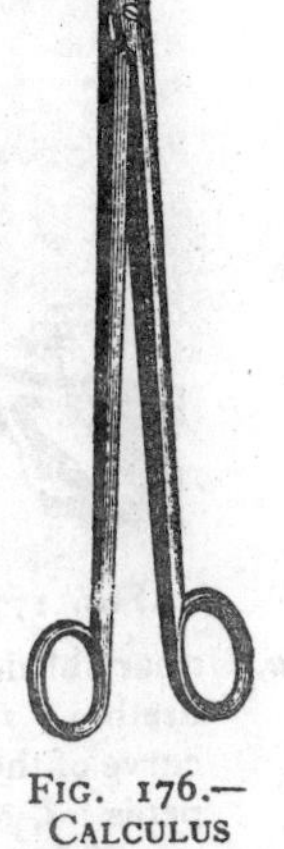

Fig. 176.—Calculus Forceps.

Treatment of the External Wound.—Either: (1) Leave the external wound open; or (2) suture the urethra only; or (3) suture the urethra and the skin, leaving an opening in the latter for drainage of urine. No. (1) is the safest procedure. Infiltration of the tissues with urine, favouring abscess formation and gangrene, is more likely to ensue if method No. (2) or (3) is adopted.

After-Treatment.—Apply a mild antiseptic solution to the wound once daily.

Results.—Complete recovery is the rule after lithotomy. The same applies to lithotrity, provided that it did not involve cystotomy or severe injury to the urethra. The urine always continues to escape through the wound for a few days, but the latter is usually completely cicatrised about four weeks after the operation; occasionally a fistula persists for a longer period, but closes eventually.

The COMPLICATIONS to be feared are cystitis and infiltration of the tissues with urine, which may be followed by gangrene. In the mare lithotomy and lithotrity can be performed through the urethra.

63. Operation for Urethral Calculus

When a calculus is lodged in the urethra, the operation consists in performing urethrotomy at its level, removing it, and treating the resulting wound as described. The usual site is the ischial region just below the arch. If the bladder is distended, it is wise to puncture it *per rectum* before casting, to prevent the risk of rupture of the organ by the fall.

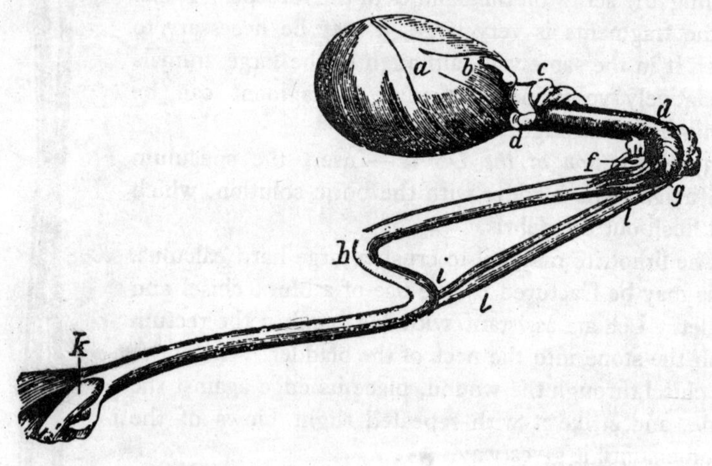

FIG. 177.—COURSE OF THE URETHRA IN THE OX. (AFTER HERING.)

a, Urinary bladder; *b*, ureter, cut off; *c*, vesiculæ seminales; *d*, *d*, pelvic portion of urethra; *f*, commencement of the corpus cavernosum of the penis; *g*, ischial curve of the urethra; *h*, first bend; *i*, second bend *k*, anterior extremity of the penis; *l*, retractor penis muscle.

The Ox and Pig

Operation for cystic calculi is rarely indicated in these animals. It is performed on similar lines to those for the horse.

64. Urethrotomy in the Ox

SITES.—(1) *Post-scrotal urethrotomy*, a hand's-breadth behind the scrotum on the middle line; (2) *ischial urethrotomy*, the median line just below the ischial arch.

Post-Scrotal Urethrotomy—INDICATION.—To remove a urethral calculus situated at the level of the S-shaped curve of the penis, usually the first curve.

CONTROL.—Cast and anæsthetise and fix on the left side with the upper hind-limb drawn forward to the shoulder.

PROCEDURE.—Make a longitudinal incision 3 to 4 inches long, introduce the left index finger into the wound, and, using it like a hook,

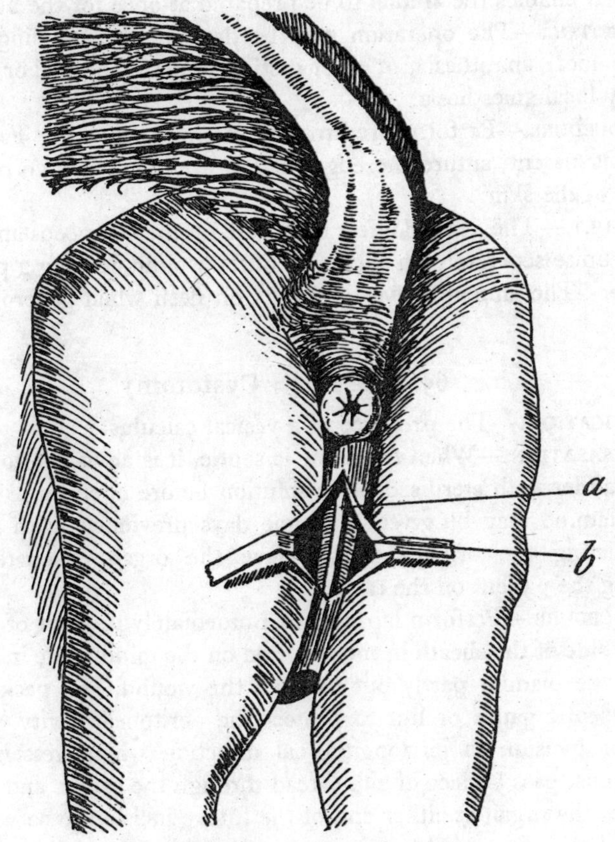

FIG. 178.—ISCHIAL URETHROTOMY.
a, Retractor penis ; *b*, accelerator urinæ.

draw out the curved portion of the penis, locate the seat of the calculus, incise the urethra at its level, and remove it. It is a question whether it is better to suture the urethral wound or leave it open. There will probably be less infiltration of the tissues with urine when it is sutured in this case.

RESULT.—Variable. In a fat subject infiltration of the tissues round the wound with urine and consequent gangrene are apt to supervene and terminate fatally, although recovery may ensue after sloughing of the dead part.

Ischial Urethrotomy—Indication.—To make an exit for the urine behind the urethral obstruction, instead of removing the latter, operation by this method being much safer than that by the post-scrotal site. It enables the animal to be prepared at once for the butcher.

Control.—The operation may be done in the standing position, under local anæsthesia, or after casting under epidermal or general or simply local anæsthesia.

Procedure.—Perform urethrotomy, as in the horse. To keep the opening patent, suture the edges of the urethra to the corresponding edges of the skin.

Result.—The desired effect is obtained ; the cutaneous and mucous edges unite separately on each side of the wound, leaving a permanent orifice. The animal thrives and puts on flesh when generously fed.

65. The Dog : Cystotomy

Indication.—The presence of a vesical calculus.

Preparation.—When the urine is septic, it is advisable to wash out the bladder with sterilised boric solution before operating. A course of hexamine may be given for some days previously with a view to disinfecting the urinary tract. Have the organ evacuated before putting the patient on the table.

Procedure.—Perform laparotomy immediately in front of the pubis to one side of the sheath in the dog, and on the middle line in the bitch. Draw the bladder partly out through the wound, and pack it round with aseptic gauze or lint to protect the peritoneal cavity. Select a site for incision in its longitudinal direction where vessels are not numerous, pass a piece of silk thread through the serous and muscular coats of the organ at either end of the future incision to serve as loops for an assistant to hold it in position, make an incision sufficiently large for the exit of the calculus, and take out the latter with a suitable forceps, taking care not to allow any urine to drop on the serous membrane. Suture the vesical wound closely, Lembert fashion, with fine specially prepared catgut. Return the bladder to its position, and finish as for laparotomy. For a few days give only milk, and administer some alkaline medicine (bicarbonate or benzoate of soda).

Results.—Recovery is the rule, even when the urine has been offensive and rich in bacteria.

66. Urethrotomy in the Dog

INDICATION.—The presence of a urethral calculus or calculi, which are usually situated just behind the os penis or lodged in its groove.

CONTROL.—Fix in the dorsal position and administer a general anæsthetic; or morphia may be used instead, associated with a local anæsthetic. The latter alone is generally sufficient.

SITE.—The seat of lodgment of the obstruction ascertained by passing a probe or metal catheter into the urethra.

PROCEDURE.—Grasp the penis through the skin with the left finger and thumb and lift it upwards. Having the catheter in position, make a longitudinal incision through the skin and urethra, exposing the catheter *in situ*, and remove the calculi. When the urethra is cleared, the urine will escape freely. Pass the catheter up and down the urethra to make sure that it is clear. Exceptionally it is necessary to make another incision farther back to reach a calculus fixed there. Leave the urethral and cutaneous wounds unsutured.

AFTER-TREATMENT.—As for cystotomy. Dress the wound daily with a mild antiseptic solution.

RESULTS.—The operation is usually successful. Possible complications are infiltration of the tissues round the wound, and gangrene thereof as a consequence. A sequel to be feared is stricture of the urethra at the seat of operation as a result of cicatricial contraction, but it does not always ensue.

67. Urethrotomy in the Bitch

Urethrotomy in the bitch is rarely indicated. It consists in incising the urethral orifice for the purpose of removing a large calculus from the bladder or from the urethra itself.

68. Lithotrity in the Dog

Perform urethrotomy midway between the scrotum and the anus. Pass the lithotrite through the wound into the bladder, carefully search for and secure the stone in the jaws of the forceps, and crush it. Remove the fragments by means of the forceps or by irrigation with boric or other mild antiseptic solution.

AFTER-TREATMENT as for urethrotomy.

In the *bitch* the operation is done through the vagina. First dilate the vagina with a vaginal speculum, then withdraw it and introduce a urethral dilator to dilate the urethra sufficiently to admit the little finger. Insert the lithotrite through the dilated urethra and crush the stone. Remove the fragments as before. Take care not to include the mucous membrane in the forceps.

69. Puncture of the Bladder : Horse and Ox

INDICATION.—Retention of the urine due to urethral obstruction, or when passing the catheter is difficult or impracticable.

SITE.—*Per rectum* on the upper surface of the bladder on the middle line as close to the neck as possible. This site avoids injury to the vesiculæ seminales, the vas deferens, and the prostate.

PROCEDURE.—Take a trocar and canula about 10 inches long and not more than $\frac{1}{8}$ inch in diameter. Introduce it, guarded by the point of the finger, to the operation site, and push it forwards and downwards until a sensation of resistance overcome is experienced. Withdraw the trocar, and the urine will flow through the canula. It is a harmless operation, and may be repeated several times.

In the ox the puncture is transperitoneal, owing to the bladder being completely covered by serous membrane, whereas in the horse the posterior portion of the organ is devoid of a serous covering, and the puncture is consequently outside the peritoneal cavity.

70. The Dog and Cat

INDICATIONS.—As stated for the horse.

CONTROL the animal in the dorsal position.

PROCEDURE.—Insert a fine trocar and canula beneath the skin a short distance behind the pubic brim, and then thrust it downwards and forwards into the bladder. In the male cat the operation is often indicated for obstruction of the urethra by sabulous deposit, to relieve the pressure behind it, and enable it to be displaced backwards to clear the passage. The dog and cat must be gently handled to avoid rupture of the distended bladder. It is inadvisable to completely evacuate a very distended bladder in the dog as the patient is apt to collapse soon afterwards. It is better to empty it gradually.

71. Amputation of the Mammary Gland : Cow

INDICATIONS.—Severe suppurative and gangrenous forms of mastitis and malignant disease of the gland, the latter being a rare condition. The whole gland or one lateral half of the organ may be amputated as required but not one quarter.

Control.—Cast and fix on the opposite side, or in the dorsal position, and administer chloroform or an epidural anæsthetic.

Procedure.—If only one half of the organ is to be removed, make a cutaneous incision, enclosing the two teats; dissect out the gland, following the fibro-elastic membrane, which separates the right and left halves of the organ; ligature the inguinal vessels, which enter the gland at the junction of its middle and posterior thirds near the middle line, and the mammary vein; and arrest hæmorrhage from small vessels by torsion. Tampon the wound with gauze and wool and suture the skin. Remove the dressing in twenty-four to forty-eight hours, and apply an antiseptic solution twice daily until the wound is granulating, when a daily application of dry dressing is sufficient.

Result.—Recovery ensues and the wound cicatrises rapidly, provided that the patient has not been exhausted from toxæmia before the operation was performed, when death supervenes.

If the whole gland is to be extirpated, a similar procedure is adopted.

The Sheep

Indications, control, and procedure as in the cow.

The Mare

Indications.—Chronic mastitis; a neoplasm of the gland.

Control.—Cast and chloroform, and fix in the dorsal position.

Procedure.—Dissect out one half or the whole of the gland, as in the cow. It is a much simpler operation in the mare than in the cow.

72. Amputation of the Tail (Docking): Horse

Indications.—Irreparable injury; malignant tumour; to prevent the horse getting the tail over the reins; and to improve the appearance of the hind-quarters. It is the fashion to dock hackney horses. Except for the first two indications, the operation should be strongly condemned as it is cruel to deprive a horse of the use of this ornamental appendage as a protection against flies about the hind parts of the body.

Preparation.—Turn back the hairs at the site of operation, and maintain them in position by a string tied round the tail. Clip the hairs below this point.

Site.—In case of a malignant disease or injury, at a point well above the seat of the lesion or at the base of the appendage. Otherwise, leave sufficient tail to cover the vulva in the mare and about the same length in the horse. Aim at performing the section through an inter-vertebral joint.

CONTROL.—If the docking knife is to be used, have a twitch applied and a fore-foot held up, or a side fetter or service hobbles put on. Inject a local anæsthetic solution hypodermically in four places equidistant round the tail just above the seat of operation.

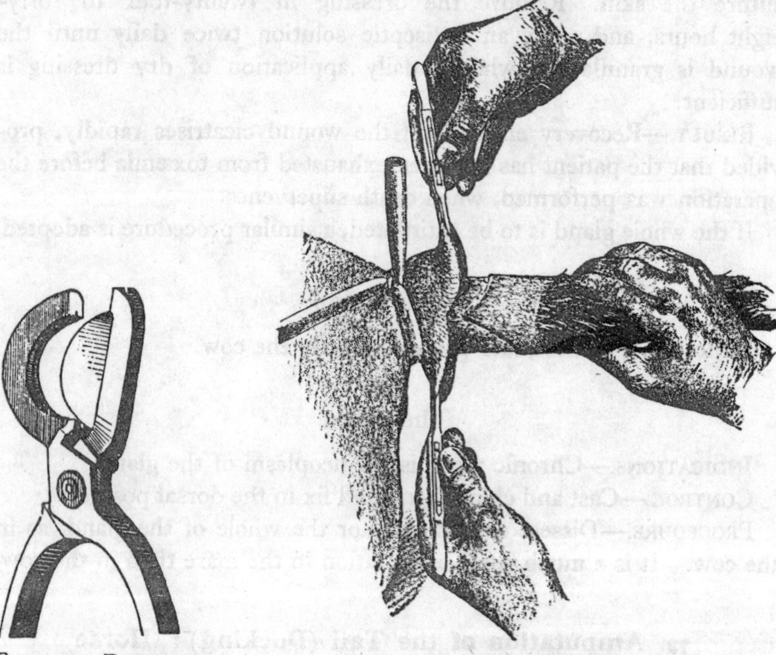

FIG. 179.—DOCKING KNIFE.

FIG. 180.—AMPUTATION BY THE FLAP METHOD.

Alternative precautions are : (1) to have the horse standing in a stall close to the near trevis with the tail held out behind the heel-post, while the operator stands to the left of the latter ; and (2) to have the tail held over a half-door, which serves as a protection against a kick from the patient.

PROCEDURE.—To use the docking knife, have the tail held fully extended and stretched backwards in a straight line with the body. Place the knife in position, and with a vigorous movement sever the tail with one stroke. Blood spurts in a fountain from the four main arteries in the stump. Arrest the hæmorrhage either by (1) applying a tape ligature round the tail and leaving it in position for twenty-

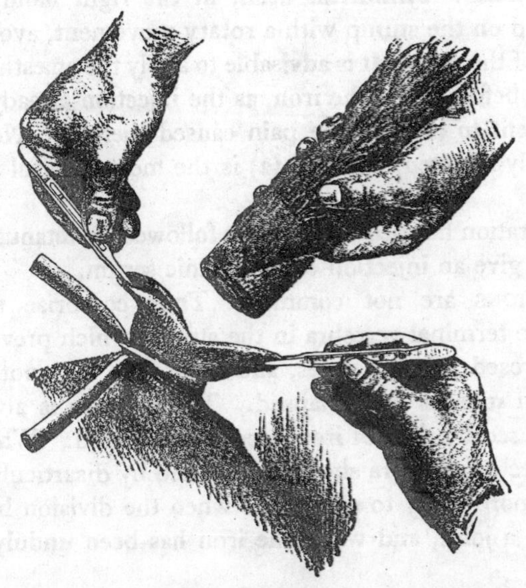

Fig. 181.—Shewing the Cutaneous Flaps after Amputation of the Tail.

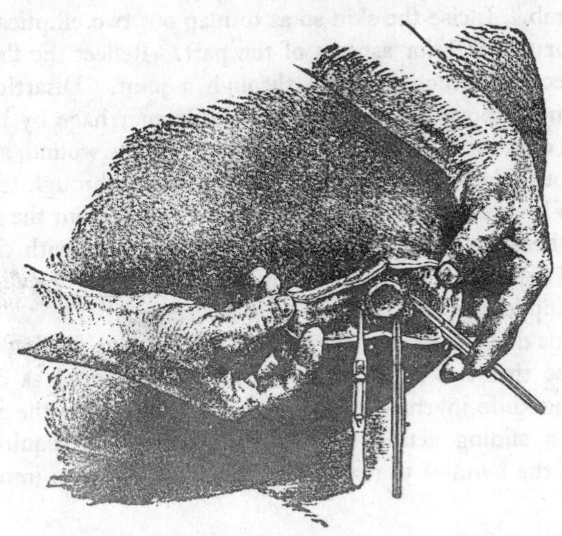

Fig. 182.—Shewing Severed Bloodvessels Secured by Forceps.

four to thirty-six hours ; or (2) applying an antiseptic pad of cotton-wool on the stump, and fixing it in position by a bandage wound tightly round the tail ; or (3) by searing the bleeding surface with the hot iron. Turn the end of the tail upwards with the left hand, take the iron, which has a hollow cylindrical head, in the right hand, and apply its circular end on the stump with a rotary movement, avoiding excessive burning of the part. It is advisable to apply the anæsthetic solution to the wound before using the iron, as the injection already given may not be sufficient to prevent the pain caused thereby. No. (3) is the method usually adopted, but No. (2) is the most surgical and rational method.

As this operation has been frequently followed by tetanus, it is a wise precaution to give an injection of antitetanic serum.

COMPLICATIONS are not common. They comprise tetanus and necrosis of the terminal vertebra in the stump, which prevents healing until the necrosed part separates, and separation may not occur until weeks or even months have elapsed. The necrosis is always due to the eschar caused by the hot iron becoming infected. When it supervenes, the affected vertebra should be excised by disarticulation. The condition is more likely to supervene when the division has not been done through a joint, and when the iron has been unduly applied to the part.

When operating at the base of the tail, proceed as for the amputation of a limb. Incise the skin so as to map out two elliptical flaps on the superior and inferior aspects of the part. Reflect the flaps to the point of section, which is made through a joint. Disarticulate the vertebræ and remove the tail. Arrest the hæmorrhage by ligation of the vessels, dust some sulphanilamide powder on the wound, and suture the cutaneous edges. Insert also Halsted sutures through the base of the flaps to keep their surfaces in apposition and prevent the formation of a space between them. Paint the lines of sutures with tincture of iodine, and apply a protective dressing of cotton-wool. Healing ensues without complication as a rule. (See Figs. 180—2.)

As regards docking knives, they all act in guillotine fashion and some are made so that two flaps are left, which are sutured as described. The docking knife invented by McKenny (Dublin), has the advantage of having a sliding action of the blade, and only requires steady pressure of the handles to make it cut through the part immediately.

The Ox

In the ox docking may be indicated for some incurable lesion, and can be done with the docking knife as in the horse, and the hæmorrhage can be arrested in the same way, or the flap operation may be performed.

Lambs

Lambs are docked at three or four weeks old. When intended for early slaughter, a little more than half the tail is removed, a common procedure with shepherds being to grasp the tail near its base with the left hand and by a vigorous twist with the right hand remove the part below. It may also be cut with a knife or a strong scissors. This method must be adopted when the tail is to be cut short, as in lambs intended for breeding. The hæmorrhage stops spontaneously. When using the knife, it is advisable to apply traction on the skin towards the base of the tail, in order to ensure the stump being covered.

The Dog

INDICATIONS.—In certain breeds it is done to have the dog *à la mode*. Otherwise, the indication is an incurable lesion of the tail—*e.g.*, an ulcer on its extremity, a necrotic vertebra, or a malignant tumour.

Puppies are done when a few days old by simply snipping off the required length of tail with the scissors, or cutting it across on the table with the knife. Bleeding is insignificant, but may be arrested by tying a piece of string round the tail and leaving it on for a while.

CONTROL.—In the adult dog, inject a local anæsthetic subcutaneously in three or four places round the tail above the seat of operation. No special control is required, as a rule, but if necessary the dog may be fixed in the ventral position on the table.

PROCEDURE.—Amputate the tail by the flap method, as described for the horse. In young dogs of medium size, the tail may be simply cut across with a sharp knife at the level of a joint after pushing the skin forwards, and the bleeding can be arrested by a tape tied round the tail and left on for a few hours.

RESULTS.—In normal cases recovery is uneventful. When an ulcer or malignant disease has been present, the condition is apt to recur in the stump, the former being usually caused by biting or rubbing the wound. An adhesive bandage or a leather encasement may be applied on the tail over the dressing until the wound is completely cicatrised (Fig. 184). It is necessary to include almost the whole tail in the bandage.

An apparently simpler and more effective protective dressing for a lesion on the dog's tail is the device described by E. O. Longley, M.R.C.V.S. (*Vet. Rec.*, Nov. 26th, 1949) consisting of a stainless steel cylindrical tube of an appropriate short length which is fitted snugly and directly over the stump of the tail or the tail itself protecting the lesion whatever it may be. The tube is as light as is consistent with strength and has been found to resist all attempts of the patient to bite it off. The tube or sleeve is acutely flared at one or, better, at both ends to facilitate application and prevent any possible fretting by the metallic edge (which has never occurred). It projects slightly beyond the tip of the tail. One used successfully on an Irish terrier was 8 cm. long and 2 cm. in diameter, projected about 2·5 cm. beyond the tip of the tail and weighed 24 grams. The tube is fixed in position by a couple

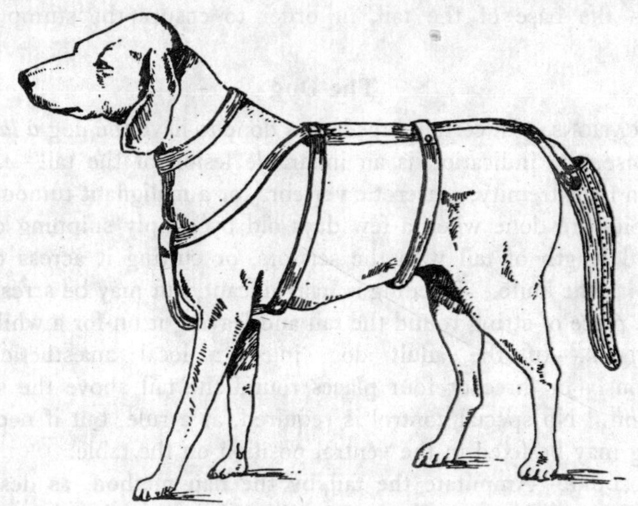

FIG. 183.—TAIL GUARD FOR DOG.

of turns of an elastoplast bandage carried forward on to the tail itself. "Staybrite" stainless steel is employed, the same as is used in permanent arterial anastomoses in human surgery. The tube is supplied by Mayer and Phelps Ltd., Tabard Street, London, S.E.1. (See Fig. 183).

73. Myotomy, or Nicking : Section of the Depressor Muscles of the Tail

INDICATION.—To improve the carriage of the tail, to make it assume the horizontal or extended position when the horse insists on keeping it depressed.

PREPARATION.—In order that the operation may have the desired effect, it is necessary to keep the tail raised a little beyond the horizontal position for a few days after the operation. The contrivance for this purpose must be ready for use. It consists of a cord passed over a pulley fixed above the horse at the level of the tail, with one end of the cord attached to the latter and the other end carrying a weight of about 1 pound.

CONTROL.—As for docking, in the standing, or if necessary in the cast position.

SITE.—The width of two or three fingers from the base of the tail on its under aspect.

PROCEDURE.—This consists in dividing the two depressor muscles in one or several places through punctured wounds made at the level of the external border of the muscles. Have the tail raised approaching the vertical position. To operate on the right muscle, stand on the right side of the horse at about an arm's length from the tail. Take a sharp-pointed knife in the right hand and puncture the skin at the outer border of the ridge formed by the muscle ; pass the knife flatwise beneath the latter, cutting through the coccygeal aponeurosis. Withdraw this instrument, and in doing so introduce the blunt-pointed tenotome until its extremity is felt near the middle line ; turn the edge towards the muscle, and, holding the knife in the full hand and the thumb outside on the skin, cut the muscle from within outwards towards the thumb, taking care not to incise the skin. Proceed similarly for the other muscle, operating from the left side with the left hand.

If there be hæmorrhage from the wound, cover it with an antiseptic pad and bandage ; otherwise, it will be sufficient to seal it with collodion and iodoform, or compound tincture of benzoin. Place the animal in the stall, and fix the tail in position as described. Remove the dressing in twenty-four to forty-eight hours.

The wounds heal quickly by first intention when proper aseptic and antiseptic precautions have been observed. So long as the wounds are not healed, keep the tail raised and prevent the animal from lying down. When they suppurate, dress them antiseptically twice daily. Healing in this case will take ten to twelve days. It is advisable to give an injection of antitetanic serum at the time of operation.

RESULT.—The desired effect is usually obtained.

COMPLICATIONS.—Possible complications are : (1) Necrosis of a coccygeal vertebra or intervertebral disc, causing a sinus and interfering perhaps with the object of the operation ; (2) gangrene of the tail as the result of raising it too high or of excessive tension thereon ; (3) faulty position of the tail, owing to irregularity or inequality of the incisions. This may be remedied by renewed incision and keeping the tail tied round to the side opposite to that to which it is deviated.

Sometimes it happens that the tail is carried too high. This, however, is usually only temporary, the tail being lowered as cicatrisation advances.

When the tail is carried crooked, it may be straightened by section of the lateral curvator coccygis of the side to which it is turned and keeping the tail fixed to the opposite side until cicatrisation has been completed.

74. Caudal Tenectomy in the Dog: Section of the Tendons of the Elevator Muscles of the Tail

INDICATION.—Too high carriage of the tail in the large breeds, including Alsatians and sheep-dogs, etc.

CONTROL.—In the ventral position on the table.

PROCEDURE.—Make an incision on the middle line of the dorsum of the tail 2 to 3 inches long; separate the lips of the wound with retractors; remove the subcutaneous fatty tissue, exposing the aponeurosis; puncture the latter, and incise it on a grooved director to the same extent as the skin. Insert the tenotome beneath the tendons of the long elevators at one end of the incision, and cut them by turning its edge upwards. Seize the tendons with a forceps, and detach them to the opposite end of the wound and remove them. Flush the wound with normal saline solution and suture the skin. If tenectomy is not sufficient, myectomy of the same muscles may also be performed.

75. Median Neurectomy

INDICATIONS.—All aseptic, incurable, chronic inflammatory conditions between the seat of operation and the fetlock inclusive—*e.g.*, certain forms of splint, carpitis, sesamoiditis, "bobba bone," and sprained tendons. It may also be done for similar conditions below the fetlock in preference to double plantar neurectomy, such as ringbone and navicular disease, since it has proved sufficient for these conditions in some cases, and is not so liable to untoward sequelæ as double plantar, there being still some innervation provided by the internal plantar nerve through the portion of it formed by the continuation of the ulnar.

CONTROL—(1) *Standing Position.*—Inject a local anæsthetic hypodermically and deeply over the nerve at the site of operation, using ½ to 1 drachm of the solution in each situation. A twitch may be applied if the horse is uneasy, although not feeling pain. If for some reason the local anæsthetic is not having the desired effect, it is not advisable to proceed with the standing method. As a rule, however, it acts well, enabling the operation to be easily performed and without risk to the horse.

(2) *Cast Position.*—Cast with hobbles on the side of the affected limb; fix the upper fore- to the upper hind-limb above the knee and hock by cross-hobbles or by a soft rope or web; attach a rope to the pastern of the under fore-limb, release it from the hobble, and have it drawn forwards and well outwards from the body. General or local anæsthesia may be used, the former being more suitable in this position as it prevents movement of the limb.

SITE.—There are various ways of defining the site, the best probably being: (1) The inner aspect of the forearm immediately below the lowest point at which the nerve can be felt, and immediately behind the inner border of the radius—that is, between the latter and the flexor metacarpi internus. Other ways of locating the site are: (2) At the junction of the belly and the tendon of the posterior superficial pectoral muscle and just behind the bone; (3) at a point equidistant from the point of the elbow, the anterior extremity of the fold of skin in the axilla, and the antero-inferior aspect of the chestnut and immediately behind the bone.

The nerve can always be easily felt through the fleshy part of the posterior superficial pectoral muscle, but the disadvantages of operating here are: (1) A deep wound is necessary to reach the nerve, which will take a comparatively long time to heal; (2) there is considerable hæmorrhage; (3) considerable œdma of the limb supervenes; (4) the nerve is divided before important branches are given off to the flexor muscles.

PROCEDURE.—Make a longitudinal incision about 2 inches long, going successively through the skin and the tendon of the posterior superficial pectoral muscle. Have the lips of the wound drawn apart by retractors, exposing the strong aponeurosis binding the muscles to the bone. Puncture the aponeurosis with the point of the knife close to the radius at the lower end of the wound, or preferably push the grooved director through it. Introduce the director beneath the aponeurosis in the long axis of the incision and cut it on the instrument to the same extent as the other tissues.

The nerve and vessels may now be in view. If not, separate the internal flexor from the bone and search for the nerve on the deep face of the former. It is usually more superficially situated than the vessels. Having recognised it, pass the tenaculum beneath it, isolate it, and draw it out of the wound. Examine it carefully to make sure it is the nerve. The following points aid in identifying the nerve:

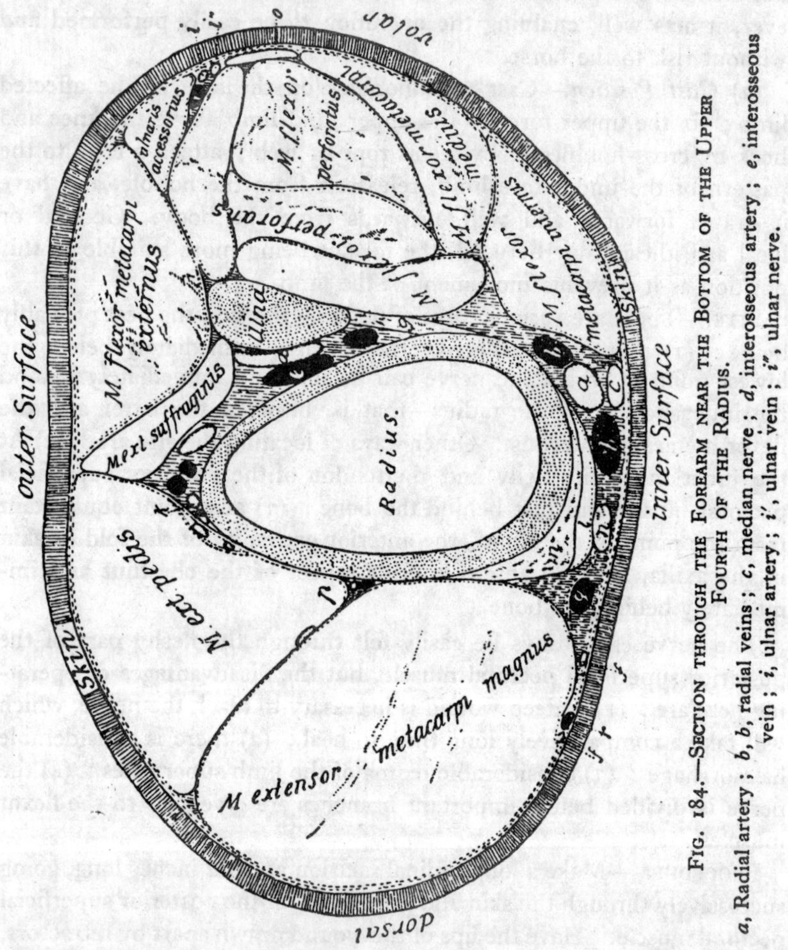

FIG. 184.—SECTION THROUGH THE FOREARM NEAR THE BOTTOM OF THE UPPER FOURTH OF THE RADIUS.

a, Radial artery; *b*, *b*, radial veins; *c*, median nerve; *d*, interosseous artery; *e*, interosseous vein; *i*, ulnar artery; *i′*, ulnar vein; *i″*, ulnar nerve.

(1) It is striated longitudinally by its fibres; (2) it can be stretched far outside the wound, and on being released it fails to go back to its place, remaining limp in the incision; (3) it has a pale yellow colour; (4) when the point of the knife is drawn flatwise across the nerve a grating sound is produced; (5) if anæsthesia is not profound, the horse winces when the nerve is touched; (6) pulsation can be felt in the

artery, and when it is drawn out and let go it promptly returns to its place; (7) the vein is blue in colour, but if stretched with the tenaculum it will become pale.

Cut the nerve with a sharp scissors or knife at the level of the upper commissure of the wound. Catch the distal end of the nerve with an artery forceps and remove about ½ inch thereof. Suture the musculo-cutaneous wound after dusting it with sulphanilamide, and paint the line of sutures with tincture of iodine.

After-Treatment.—When the operation has been done where the nerve is comparatively superficial and without much searching or interference with the tissues, healing by first intention may ensue. In

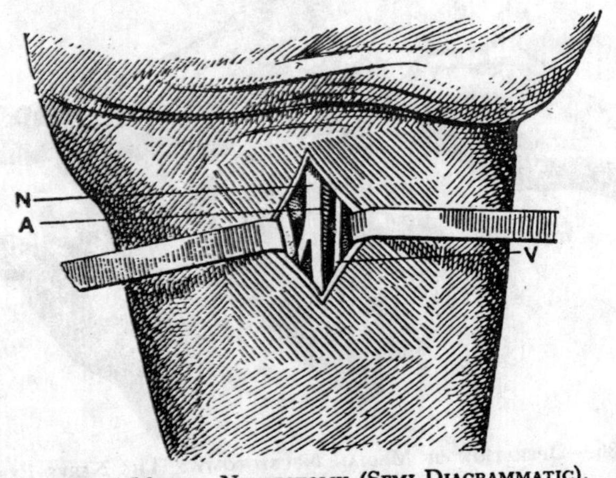

Fig. 185.—Median Neurectomy (Semi-Diagrammatic).

N, Median nerve; A, posterior radial artery; V, one of the post-radial veins.

this case leave the sutures *in situ* for a few days, painting the wound and its vicinity in the meantime once daily with dilute tincture of iodine. If the wound has been deep and subjected to considerable interference, it is much better to remove the sutures the next day and irrigate the wound with a mild antiseptic solution and dress it with an antiseptic powder. This treatment should be repeated once daily until the wound is almost healed. Whenever suppuration supervenes, the sutures must be taken out and the wound dressed as described.

Results.—When first intention ensues, the wound is healed within a week. Otherwise, it is completely cicatrised in a fortnight or three weeks after the operation. The horse may trot sound or almost so immediately after the operation, but becomes lame again, due to the inflammation in the wound.

After the wound has healed the lameness gradually disappears, provided that innervation has been removed from the affected part. Weeks may elapse before the horse goes quite sound. If after a reasonable time there is no evidence of improvement, it will be necessary to perform ulnar or external plantar neurectomy, depending on the seat of the lesion. As a rule median neurectomy gives very satisfactory results, enabling horses that were useless to give good service for years afterwards. Experience has shown that horses can be safely hunted after the operation.

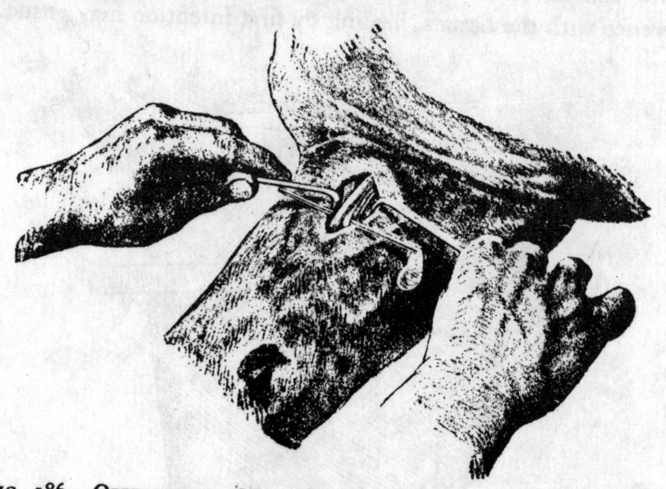

FIG. 186.—OPERATION OF MEDIAN NEURECTOMY: THE NERVE EXPOSED.

UNTOWARD SEQUELÆ are not common, but degeneration of the tissues below the seat of operation occasionally ensues. The flexor tendons may undergo gelatinous degeneration and give way, or the hoof may be shed at a variable time after the operation. If some softening of the tissues and oozing of serum appear at the coronet, it is usually a sign that the hoof is about to separate, but not always. If the foot be immersed in an antiseptic bath for half an hour twice daily the process may be arrested. In some cases at a variable period after the operation a neuroma forms on the proximal end of the nerve, causing severe lameness and pronounced pain locally. The only remedy for this is to repeat the operation above the site of the tumour.

Fatal hæmorrhage from wounding the radial artery is a possible complication which can be avoided by careful use of the knife, avoiding bold incisions and making use of the grooved director. There may be more or less profuse venous hæmorrhage from wounding one of the many veins in the region. When it interferes with the procedure, it can be controlled by a tourniquet below the wound. It usually stops soon after the wound is sutured.

76. Ulnar Neurectomy

INDICATIONS.—Conditions for which median neurectomy was indicated and performed without the desired effect.

CONTROL.—The operation can be easily done in the standing position under the influence of a local anæsthetic.

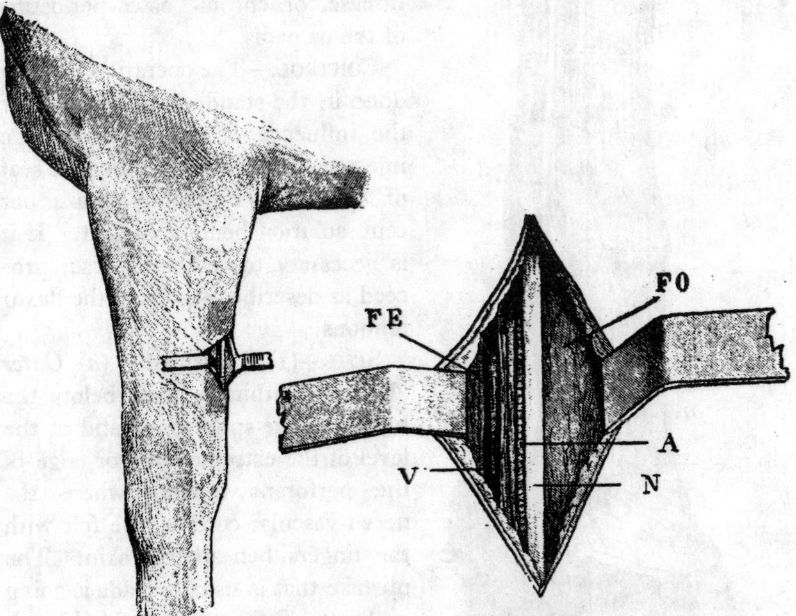

FIGS. 187 AND 188.—NEURECTOMY OF THE ULNAR NERVE.
FE, Flexor metacarpi externus; FO, flexor metacarpi obliquus; N, ulnar nerve; AV, ulnar artery and nerve.

SITE.—A hand's-breadth above the upper border of the pisiform bone and on the straight line between it and the point of the elbow—that is, in the groove between the flexors metacarpi externus and medius.

PROCEDURE.—Make a longitudinal incision through the skin and aponeurosis about 1½ inches long. The nerve will be found immediately beneath the latter on one side or the other of the wound. Do not mistake the glistening tendon of the flexor accessorius for the nerve. Having found the latter, isolate it and proceed as for median neurectomy. Avoid wounding the accompanying artery and vein.

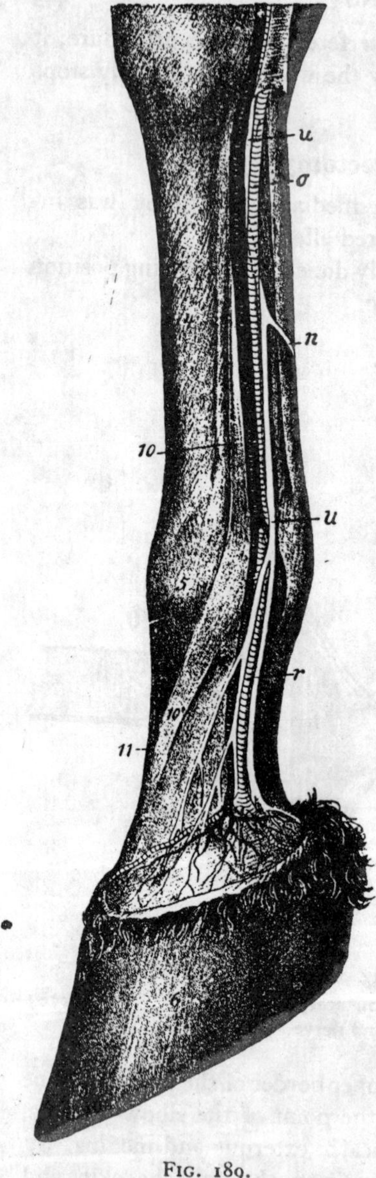

FIG. 189.

u, Internal plantar nerve, which, below the fetlock, divides into the anterior, middle, and posterior digital nerves; *n*, oblique branch from internal to external plantar nerve; *o*, large metacarpal artery; *r*, digital artery.

RESULTS.—The wound heals without complications. Degeneration of the tissues below the seat of operation is very apt to supervene after the double operation, which is only performed as an absolute last resource.

77. Plantar Neurectomy

INDICATIONS.—Incurable lameness due to ringbone, navicular disease, or chronic osteo-periostitis of the os pedis.

CONTROL.—The operation is easily done in the standing position under the influence of a local anæsthetic injected over the nerve above the seat of operation, 1 drachm of a 4 per cent. solution being sufficient. If it is necessary to cast the horse, proceed as described for firing the flexor tendons.

SITES—(1) *Fore-Limb : (a) Outer Aspect.*—Within ½ inch below the button of the splint-bone and at the level of the extreme anterior edge of the perforans tendon, where the nervo-vascular cord can be felt with the fingers beneath the skin. The mistake that is usually made is going in front of the tendon. A branch from the inner nerve joins the outer one at the level of the button of the splint-bone, and each plantar nerve divides to form the digitals ½ inch below the button. Hence the necessity for confining the site of operation within the limits mentioned, in order to obtain the desired effect.

(*b*) *Inner Aspect.*—The same as (*a*), except that it is not necessary to go below the button of the splint-bone.

(2) *Hind-Limb.*—The branch from the inner nerve often joins the outer one within ½ inch below the button of the splint-bone. Hence it is necessary here to operate ½ inch below the button to ensure cutting the nerve after it has received the branch and before it divides into the digitals.

PROCEDURE.—Make a cutaneous longitudinal incision about 1 inch long; incise the subcutaneous tissue covering the nerve and expose the latter. Pass the tenaculum beneath it, and having made sure of it by observing its characteristic features, as in median neurectomy, proceed as usual. Suture the wound with an ordinary interrupted suture or a Halsted suture, and apply an antiseptic pad and bandage. Both nerves are usually operated upon.

AFTER-TREATMENT.—Some operators remove the sutures the next day to make sure of drainage, should sepsis of the wound ensue. In this event it certainly proves a wise procedure. The more common procedure is not to disturb the dressing for about a week, except evidence of inflammation is evinced.

RESULTS.—The horse usually goes quite sound immediately after the operation. Separation of the hoof is always to be feared within days, weeks, or months after the operation, although in many cases it never supervenes, the horse remaining permanently sound. This may be due to regeneration of the nerve to a sufficient extent to prevent degeneration, and yet not sufficient to cause lameness. Nocard advised that not more than 1 centimetre of the nerve be excised, to enable this regeneration to take place.

78. Digital or Low Plantar Neurectomy

INDICATIONS.—Navicular disease and chronic osteo-periostitis of the os pedis. The operation is usually sufficient for these conditions, but sometimes after the horse has gone sound for a while he goes lame again, due, it would appear, to the inflammation from the foot extending above the seat of operation. For this reason, and because it is easier, high plantar neurectomy is often preferred.

CONTROL.—The operation can be easily performed in the standing position under the influence of cocaine injected over the plantars. Otherwise, control as for firing the pastern in the cast position.

SITE.—The upper extremity of the lateral aspect of the pastern in the depression between the flexor tendons and the tuberosity on the supero-latero-posterior aspect of the os suffraginis, where the nervo-vascular cord can be felt beneath the skin.

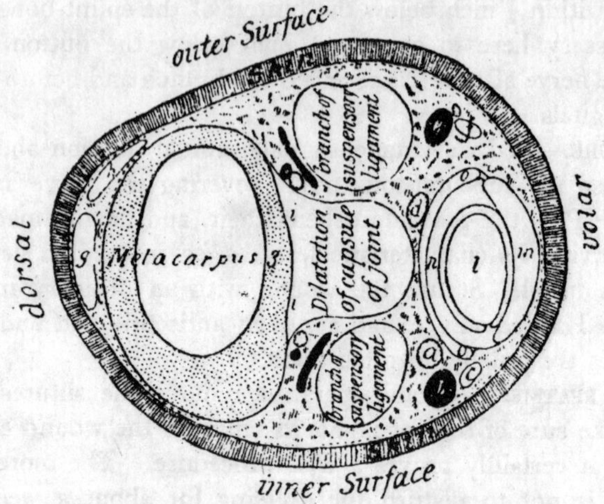

FIG. 190.—SECTION THROUGH THE METACARPUS ABOUT 3 TO 4 INCHES ABOVE THE FETLOCK-JOINT.

a, Digital artery; *b*, digital vein; *c*, digital nerve; *l*, flexor pedis perforans tendon; *m*, flexor pedis perforatus tendon; *o*, tendon sheath.

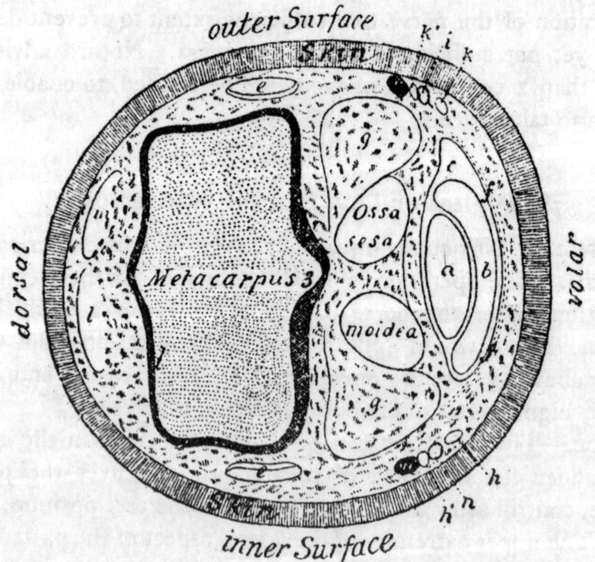

FIG. 191.—SECTION THROUGH THE FETLOCK-JOINT.

a, Flexor pedis perforans tendon; *b*, flexor pedis perforatus tendon; *c*, tendon sheath; *d*, capsule of the fetlock-joint; *h* and *h'*, *k* and *k'*, branches of the posterior digital nerves; *i*, *n*, digital arteries.

PROCEDURE.—Make an incision in the skin parallel to the nerve, and proceed as described for high plantar neurectomy.

RESULTS.—Already alluded to under the heading of indications. Separation of the hoof is not so likely to ensue as after high plantar neurectomy.

79. Anterior Tibial Neurectomy

INDICATIONS.—The usual aseptic incurable conditions between the site of operation and the hock inclusive, usually spavin. It may be

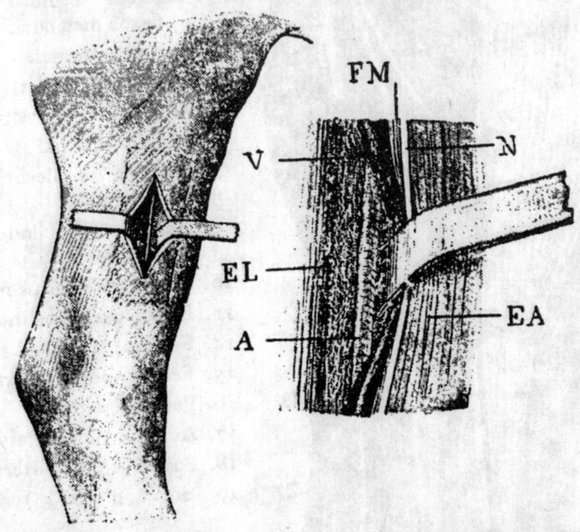

FIGS. 192 AND 193.—NEURECTOMY OF THE ANTERIOR TIBIAL NERVE.

EA, Extensor pedis muscle ; EL, tendinous portion of flexor metatarsi ; FM, muscular portion of flexor metatarsi ; N, anterior tibial nerve ; V, anterior tibial vein ; A, anterior tibial artery. The operation should be performed a little nearer the hock than indicated on Fig. 192.

sufficient in some cases of spavin, but probably in most cases it requires to be associated with posterior tibial neurectomy.

SITE I.—Recognise the anterior tuberosity of the tibia and pass outwards from it to the external tuberosity. Within a distance of about 2 inches below the latter, and on a level with the groove between the extensor pedis and peroneus muscles, the external popliteal nerve will be felt passing downwards and forwards to enter the space between the two muscles. At this point it divides into the anterior tibial and the musculo-cutaneous. The former passes deeply between the peroneus and extensor pedis.

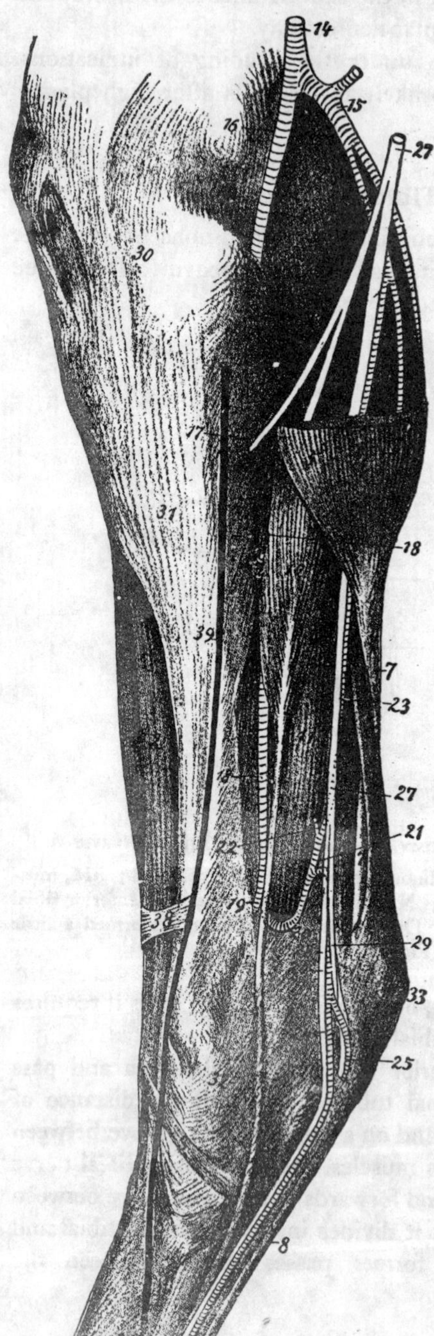

FIG. 194.

1. Extensor pedis muscle.
2. Muscular portion of the flexor metatarsi.
3. Internal terminal tendon of flexor metatarsi.
4. Popliteus muscle.
5. Inner head of gastrocnemius.
6. Outer head of gastrocnemius.
7. Tendo Achillis.
8. Tendon of flexor perforatus muscle.
9. Reinforcing band of flexor tendons.
10. Flexor accessorius muscle.
11. Flexor perforans muscle.
14. Femoral artery.
15. Femoro-popliteal artery.
16. Popliteal artery.
17. Anterior tibial artery.
18. Posterior tibial artery.
19, 20, and 21. Its S-shaped curve.
22 and 23. Anastomosing twigs.
24 and 25. Internal and external plantar arteries.
27. Internal popliteal nerve (continued lower towards the hock as the posterior tibial nerve).
28 and 29. Internal and external plantar nerves.
30. Stifle-joint.
31. Tibia.
32. Hock.
33. Point of hock.
38. Annular band of hock.
39. Saphenous vein.

CONTROL.—(1) Standing, under the influence of cocaine injected over the nerve, using a twitch and a side-line in addition if necessary.

(2) Cast with hobbles on the opposite side, and employ local or general anæsthesia.

PROCEDURE.—Incise the skin parallel to the course of the external popliteal nerve, distinguish the anterior tibial from the latter and from the musculo-cutaneous nerve, isolate it, and proceed as usual.

SITE 2.—About 6 inches above the hock on its outer aspect in the groove between the extensor pedis and peroneus muscles.

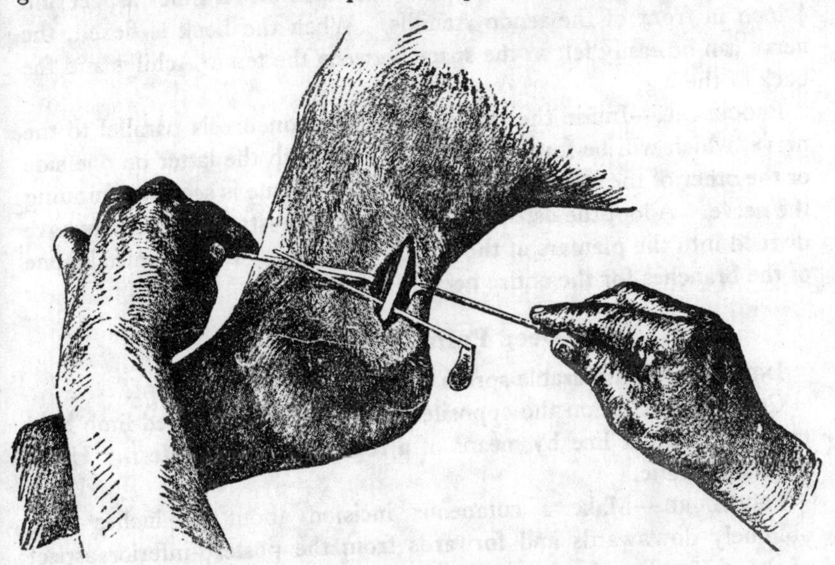

FIG. 195.—NEURECTOMY OF THE POSTERIOR TIBIAL NERVE.

PROCEDURE.—Make the cutaneous incision; separate the extensor pedis from the peroneus. Recognise the line of junction between the extensor pedis and the flexor metatarsi, separate them for a short distance, and the nerve will be seen as a thin white streak on the fleshy surface of the latter. Pass the tenaculum beneath it and proceed as usual.

RESULTS.—The operation has been seldom performed alone, but it has been reported as having had the desired effect in some cases of incurable spavin lameness.

80. Posterior Tibial Neurectomy

INDICATIONS.—All incurable chronic aseptic inflammatory conditions between the seat of operation and the fetlock inclusive, comprising chiefly spavin, chronic sprained tendons, and sesamoiditis.

CONTROL.—A docile horse can be operated upon standing under the influence of local anæsthesia, and with the aid of a side-line on the opposite limb to control it and keep it forward out of the way. A twitch may also be required. Most operators prefer to cast the horse with hobbles on the side of the affected limb, and employ local or general anæsthesia. It facilitates the procedure considerably to have the hock moderately flexed. Hence it is advisable to attach a rope to the pastern of the affected limb, pass it beneath the body towards the dorsal region, and apply traction on it in order to flex the hock. Have the other hind-limb taken forward and fixed to the shoulder.

SITE.—About 5 or 6 inches above the hock on its inner aspect and ½ inch in front of the tendo Achillis. When the hock is flexed, the nerve can be easily felt in the space between the tendo Achillis and the back of the leg.

PROCEDURE.—Incise the skin and strong aponeurosis parallel to the nerve, which will be found immediately beneath the latter on one side or the other of the incision. Yellow adipose tissue is seen surrounding the nerve. Adopt the usual procedure. The posterior tibial may have divided into the plantars at the site of operation. Do not mistake one of the branches for the entire nerve.

81. Deep Palmar Neurectomy

INDICATION.—Incurable sprain of the suspensory ligament.

CONTROL.—Cast on the opposite side. Have the affected limb held taut in a straight line by means of a rope round the pastern. Use a local anæsthetic.

PROCEDURE.—Make a cutaneous incision about 1½ inches long obliquely downwards and forwards from the postero-inferior aspect of the pisiform to the posterior border of the head of the small splint-bone (Fig. 197). Afterwards incise to the same extent the carpo-metacarpal aponeurosis and keep the edges of the incision apart. Displace successively the external palmar nerve and vein. The palmar branch to be operated upon will be found beneath the vein. Isolate it and remove a portion thereof. Finish as usual.

82. Supracarpal Tenotomy: Section of the Tendons of the Flexors Metacarpi Externus and Medius above the Knee

INDICATION.—Bending forward of the knees, due to contraction of the tendons mentioned, especially when congenital.

CONTROL.—Cast on the opposite side, apply two ropes or webs on the limb, one on the upper part of the forearm directed backwards and the other on the hoof directed the opposite way.

Section of the Flexor Metacarpi Externus—SITE.—The anterior border of the tendon about 2 inches above the pisiform.

PROCEDURE.—Make a puncture in the skin and aponeurosis. Push

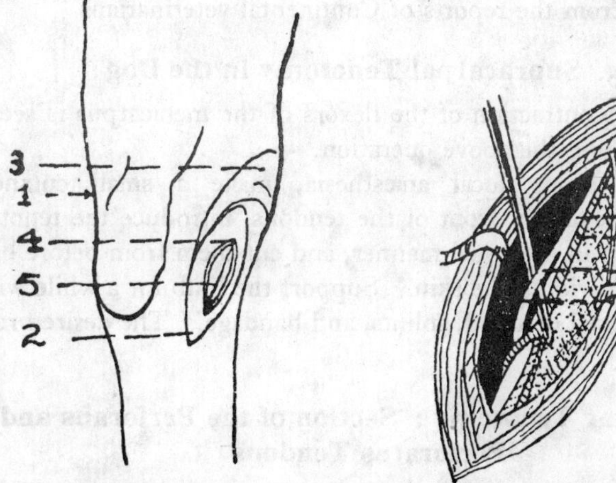

FIGS. 196 AND 197.—ILLUSTRATING DEEP PALMAR NEURECTOMY.

1. Anterior aspect of the knee.
2. Head of internal splint bore.
3. Prominence of the pisifora.
4. Upper extremity of extraneous incision.
5. Line of incision in aponeurosis.

1. Cutaneous incision.
2. Section of aponeurosis.
3. External palmar nerve.
4. Deep palmar branch.
5. Branch of ulnar artery.
6. External palmar vein.

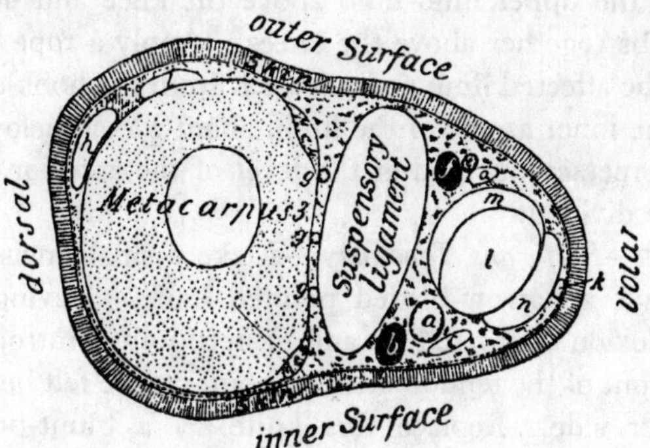

FIG. 198.—SECTION THROUGH THE CENTRE OF THE METACARPUS.

a, Large metacarpal artery ; *b*, metacarpal vein ; *c*, inner plantar nerve ; *d, e, f*, corresponding external structures ; *g, g, g*, interosseous arteries ; *k*, oblique branch from internal to external plantar nerve ; *l*, tendon of flexor perforans ; *m*, its reinforcing band ; *n*, tendon of flexor perforatus.

the curved tenotome flatwise beneath the tendon as far as its posterior border, and then turn the edge towards the tendon. Whilst the assistants pull on the ropes, cut the tendon from before backwards without incising the skin. Operate on the medius in the same way through a narrow incision at its anterior border.

RESULTS.—The operation has been performed several times successfully, judging from the reports of Continental veterinarians.

83. Supracarpal Tenotomy in the Dog

Occasionally contraction of the flexors of the metacarpus is seen in the dog, indicating the above operation.

PROCEDURE.—Using local anæsthesia, make a small cutaneous incision immediately in front of the tendons, introduce the tenotome in front of them in the usual manner, and cut them from before backwards without dividing the skin. Support the limb for a while with a dressing composed of a pad, splints, and bandage. The desired result is obtained.

84. Plantar Tenotomy: Section of the Perforans and Perforatus Tendons

INDICATIONS.—Contraction of one or both tendons, causing deformity due to more or less permanent flexion of the fetlock or interphalangeal articulations.

CONTROL (FORE-LIMB).—Cast with hobbles on the side of the affected limb. Use a general or a local anæsthetic. Fix the upper fore-limb to the upper hind-limb above the knee and hock. Fix the two fore-limbs together above the knees. Apply a rope or web round the hoof of the affected limb and release it from the hobble.

SITE.—The inner aspect of the limb, about ½ inch below the midway point of the metacarpus and at the level of the anterior border of the tendon to be divided.

PROCEDURE—*Perforans Tenotomy.*—Make a small incision just sufficient to admit a narrow-bladed pointed knife. Having the tendons relaxed by flexion of the fetlock and pastern joints, introduce the knife flatwise in front of the tendon until its point can be felt beneath the skin on the other side. Replace this knife by a blunt-pointed curved tenotome; turn the edge of the latter towards the tendon, and having it made taut by extension of the joints mentioned, divide it from before backwards by a restricted to-and-fro and seesaw movement of the knife. At the moment of its division a smacking noise may be hard, the gap between the ends can then be felt, and the deformity disappears. If the fetlock still remains flexed, the perforatus must also be divided in a similar manner, cutting from behind forwards. Suture the wound and apply an antiseptic pad and bandage.

Perforatus tenotomy alone is sufficient when the fetlock-joint only is involved in the deformity. Great care must be exercised when operating on the perforans tendon not to cut the large metacarpal artery. The operation is performed on the inner aspect of the limb, so as to cut away from the vessel. In order to avoid the vessel it is essential to insert the tenotome as close to the tendon as possible. An alternative procedure with a view to ensure leaving the artery intact is to make an incision in the skin large enough to enable the vessel to be seen. Should the latter be accidentally divided, the bleeding may be arrested by a tight pad and bandage, or the wound may be enlarged and the vessel exposed and ligatured, a tourniquet being used to control the hæmorrhage in the meantime.

CONTROL (HIND-LIMB).—Cast on the opposite side. Fix the two hind-limbs together above the hocks. Attach a rope to the hoof of the upper hind-limb, release it from the hobble, and draw it backwards.

SITE.—The midway point of the metatarsal region on the outer aspect of the limb at the level of the lateral border of the tendon. The operation is performed on the outside of the limb, because it is a convenient place and there is no important vessel to avoid on the inside, as in the fore-limb.

PROCEDURE.—As in the fore-limb, except that the perforans may be safely cut from behind forwards. Both fore- or hind-limbs may be operated upon on the same occasion.

AFTER-TREATMENT.—In order that the operation may have the desired effect, it is essential that the horse puts weight on the limb afterwards ; otherwise, the condition will quickly recur. Consequently, if the tendons are the seat of pain at the time of operation, preventing weight being borne, it will be necessary to perform neurectomy at the same time, median being indicated for the fore-limb and posterior tibial for the hind-limb. The former is much more likely to be successful than the latter. Möller has enabled horses to work in the streets of Berlin five weeks after performing perforans tenotomy and median neurectomy.

The horse should be kept in a loose box or exercised slowly every day to ensure weight being placed on the affected limb. There is nc need to support the tendons by a high-heeled shoe or other device even after double tenotomy. Although the fetlock pad be near the ground at first, it will gradually ascend to the normal level, and the trouble is that it may go farther and cause renewed deformity.

RESULTS.—The wound in the skin usually heals by first intention. If not, it is generally closed by second intention within a fortnight.

The space between the tendons gradually becomes filled with embryonic tissue. The horse may prove useful for months or years after the operation. The result is always better after single than after double tenotomy and in the fore- than in the hind-limb. Occasionally, however, the deformity rapidly returns, or the horse remains lame, rendering the operation useless. Exceptionally the fetlock fails to ascend and the pastern remains in an almost horizontal direction. Necrosis of the tendon may ensue from infection through the wound, necessitating destruction of the horse.

85. Operation for Blemished Knee

This is an autoplastic operation which may be performed in a valuable horse that has accidentally wounded his knee, with the result that a large scar or blemish is left.

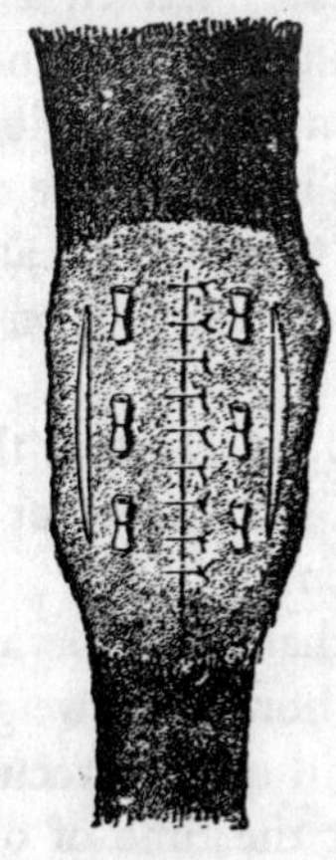

FIGS. 199 AND 200.—AUTOPLASTIC OPERATION FOR BLEMISHED KNEE.

CONTROL.—The best method of control is on the operating table. Failing this, cast with hobbles and fix the affected limb to a rigid bar leashed to the limb above and below the knee. Administer chloroform.

PROCEDURE.—Take the strictest possible aseptic and antiseptic precautions. Having shaved and disinfected the whole knee, envelop it in a sterilised cloth with a window in front corresponding to the site of operation. Make an elliptical incision with its long axis parallel to the limb, enclosing the scar. Dissect out the latter along with the portion of skin included within the incision, taking care not to wound the synovial sheaths or joint capsule. Make two other longitudinal incisions, one on either side of the wound, about equal in length to the latter and about $\frac{3}{4}$ inch therefrom to facilitate its edges being brought together. Suture the central wound with silk-worm gut. Envelop the knee in an antiseptic dressing composed of iodoform gauze, cotton-wool, and a bandage, and immobilise the joint by means of a gutter splint applied at the back of the limb from the fetlock to the elbow region, with plenty of padding beneath. Keep the horse in slings until the wound is cicatrised. If there be no evidence of severe inflammation in the wound, leave the dressing undisturbed for eight to ten days, when the dressing should be renewed. Remove the sutures in fifteen to twenty days. Maintain the immobilising dressing in position for at least three weeks to avoid rupture of the cicatrix.

RESULT.—When the operation has been done with scrupulous care and the limb perfectly immobilised afterwards, primary healing ensues and the desired effect is obtained, scarcely any trace of the wounds

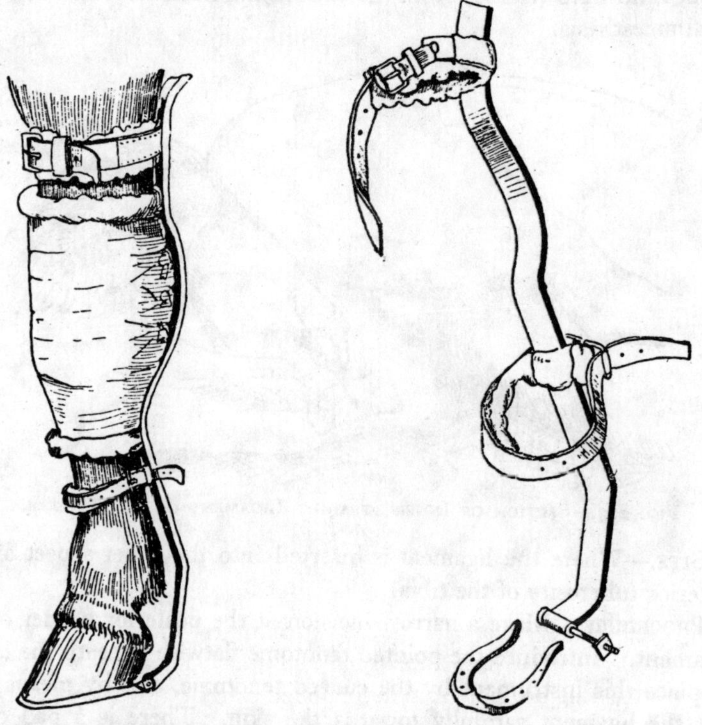

FIGS. 201 AND 202.—APPARATUS FOR IMMOBILISING THE KNEE AFTER OPERATION.

being visible on the knee. It is extremely difficult, however, to obtain primary healing. Although cicatrisation by second intention ensues, the result may be satisfactory.

A special apparatus has been devised for immobilising the limb for the purpose of this operation, but a blood horse would hardly tolerate its application. It is in the form of an iron splint extending upwards from the heels of the shoe and embracing the limb above and below the knee by means of straps and buckles. It is simple and effective.

86. Section of the Inner Straight Ligament of the Patella

INDICATION.—Pseudo-luxation of the patella in the horse, whereby the patella becomes fixed above the trochlea of the femur and the ordinary measures have failed to reduce it.

CONTROL.—Cast on the side of the affected limb and fix the upper hind-limb forward at the shoulder. It is an advantage to have the lower hind-limb released from the hobble and drawn backwards. Use local anæsthesia.

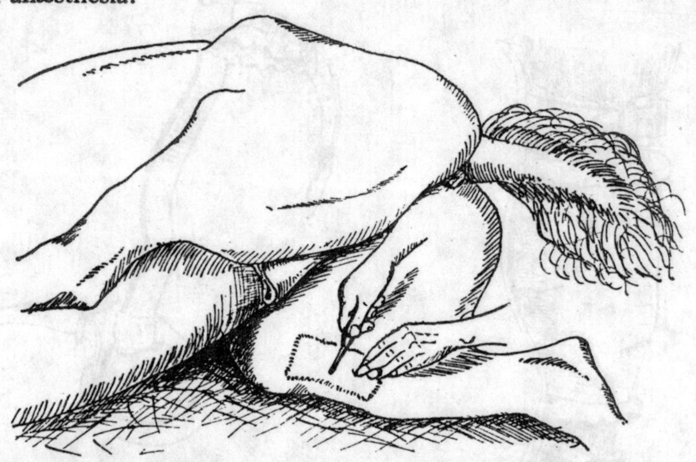

FIG. 203.—SECTION OF INNER STRAIGHT LIGAMENT OF THE PATELLA.

SITE.—Where the ligament is inserted into the inner aspect of the anterior tuberosity of the tibia.

PROCEDURE.—Make a narrow incision at the posterior border of the ligament. Introduce the pointed tenotome flatwise beneath the latter. Replace this instrument by the curved tenotome, and by means of it cut the ligament carefully towards the skin. There is a pad of fat between the ligament and the synovial capsule of the joint, serving to protect the latter. Suture the wound.

RESULT.—The desired result is obtained. Several operators have performed the operation successfully.

87. Cunean Tenotomy and Periosteotomy

INDICATION.—Lameness due to spavin.

CONTROL.—Cast with hobbles on the side of the affected limb. Fix the upper hind-limb forward to the shoulder. Use local or general anæsthesia. The former is injected subcutaneously at the seat of operation.

SITE.—Pass the fingers downwards over the true hock-joint, and the cunean tendon will be felt as a band crossing its lower extremity to become inserted into the small cuneiform. Follow the tendon inwards and backwards, and operate at its level on the inner aspect of the hock clear of the true hock-joint. The site is on a line with the chestnut.

PROCEDURE.—Make a small transverse incision—in fact, a mere puncture—in the skin. Introduce a curved blunt-pointed scissors into the wound, and by means of it separate the skin from the subcutaneous tissues over all the small bones on the inside of the hock. Withdraw the scissors and pass the blunt-pointed convex periosteotomy knife beneath the skin flatwise, turn its edge towards the tendon, and with a pressing and sawing movement cut through the tendon and other tissues down to the bone until the knife grates thereon. Make several such incisions in a radiating manner from the cutaneous wound, taking care not to penetrate the tibio-astragaloid joint or the tarsal sheath. Suture the wound. There is no need for a protective dressing. Healing without suppuration usually ensues.

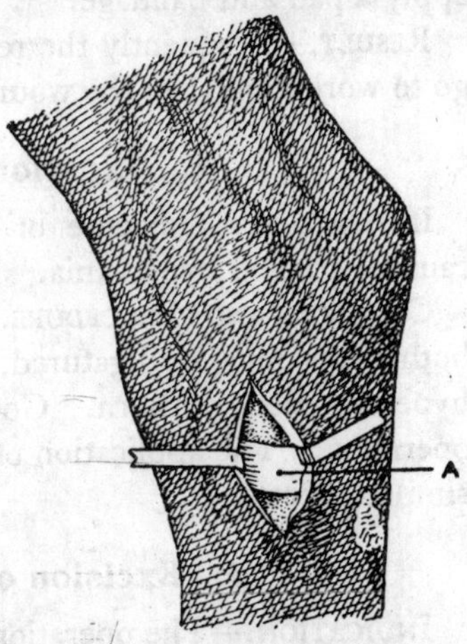

FIG. 204.—OPERATION FOR DIVISION OF THE CUNEAN TENDON OF THE FLEXOR METATAPSI MUSCLE.
A, The tendon.

Should the wound become purulent, no harm will supervene. In fact, the desired effect may be more readily attained when suppuration takes place consequent on the increased inflammation which accompanies it. The object of the operation is to cause acute inflammation in the affected gliding articulations in the hope that it will be followed by anchylosis of these joints. Complete rest for a period of upwards of six to eight weeks is essential to enable the desired effect to be obtained.

The operation is usually successful. Occasionally the improvement is only temporary, the horse going lame again after being a while at work. Exceptionally a chronic painful ostitis persists after the operation, making the patient lamer than he was originally.

88. Ligation of the Digital Artery

INDICATION.—Subacute laminitis, when the horse remains lame despite all other measures of treatment.

CONTROL.—Inject a solution of cocaine over the corresponding plantar nerve and operate in the standing position. If necessary, cast and fix as for plantar neurectomy.

SITE.—The outer aspect of the fetlock-joint, where the nervo-vascular cord can be felt on a line with the anterior edge of the perforans tendon.

PROCEDURE.—Make a longitudinal incision about 1 inch in length. Recognise the artery, whose position is " van " from before backwards. It is distinguished by its pulsation. Apply a silk ligature in two places, and cut the vessel between the ligatures. Suture the wound, and apply a pad and bandage.

RESULT.—Frequently the result is good, the horse being enabled to go to work soon after the wounds have healed.

89. Ligation of the Digital Vein

INDICATION.—Subacute or chronic laminitis, for the purpose of causing passive hyperæmia.

CONTROL AND PROCEDURE.—As for ligation of the artery. One or both veins may be ligatured. The venous stasis is said to cause a hypersecretion of horn. Good results have been claimed for the operation. The application of a rubber band on the limb should have similar effects.

90. Excision of the Lateral Cartilage

INDICATION.—The operation is indicated for " quittor " when other measures have failed, or in preference thereto.

CONTROL.—Cast with hobbles on the side opposite to that of the coronet on which the lesion is situated. Administer chloroform. If it is a fore-foot that is affected, take a piece of webbing about 30 feet long, wind it round the upper hind-limb above the hock a few times, and make a reef knot, leaving the two ends of equal length. Apply a hobble provided with a D or a pulley on the affected limb above the fetlock. Take one end of the web, pass it between the two hind-limbs from before backwards, then bring it forwards over the hind-limb and pass it through the D or pulley in the hobble on the fore-limb. Release the latter from the hobble, and have it drawn backwards by means of the web. Fix it above the upper hock by the aid of the two ends of the web passed in opposite directions round the limb and securely tied.

PREPARATION OF THE FOOT.—Before casting the horse, have the hair clipped on the pastern and the hoof scraped, thoroughly washed with soap and water, and disinfected.

PROCEDURE: CLASSICAL METHOD.—Apply a tourniquet round the pastern and proceed as follows:

1. *Removing the Horn.*—Remove the horn from the quarter and heel corresponding to the affected cartilage either by a process of thinning or by stripping. Thinning is done by means of the rasp until only a thin layer of horn is left covering the laminæ. Stripping is performed thus: Make a groove right through the wall from the coronet to the plantar aspect at the anterior extremity of the cartilage and directed somewhat obliquely backwards. Make a similar, perpendicular, groove at the posterior extremity of the heel, and join the two grooves by a third groove at the white line extending to the sensitive tissues. Seize the isolated piece of horn at its lower border with a pincers, and pulling forcibly upwards strip it right off the laminæ and the coronary band. This method is more expeditious than thinning, but exposes the laminæ unnecessarily.

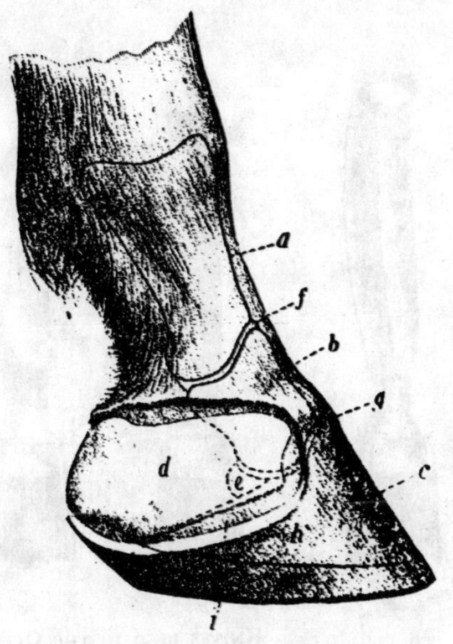

FIG. 205.—SHOWING THE LATERAL CARTILAGE AND ITS RELATIONS.

a, Os suffraginis; *b*, os coronæ; *c*, os pedis; *d*, lateral cartilage; *e*, os naviculare; *f*, pastern-joint; *g*, coronet-joint; *h*, horny wall; *i*, sensitive laminæ.

2. *Incision of the Podophyllous Membrane.*—Make an incision through the podophyllous membrane between the coronary band and the sensitive laminæ extending from the anterior to the posterior extremity of the cartilage.

3. *Separation of the Coronary Band.*—Take one of the sage knives, insert it into the incision already made, and separate the coronary band from the cartilage throughout the entire length of the latter.

4. *Separation of the Skin from the Cartilage.*—Insert a retractor beneath the coronary band and give it to an assistant to hold. Pass the double-edged sage knife beneath the band, and sweeping it backwards and forwards separate the skin from the outer surface of the cartilage without wounding the latter or cutting through the skin.

5. *Excision of the Cartilage.*—Take the right or left sage knife according as the horse is lying on the right or left side, pass its blade

round the posterior border of the cartilage, and, cutting vigorously from within outwards, excise the posterior portion of the structure. Remove the superficial portion of the remainder by slicing it with the sage knife and the deep portion by means of the loop knife and curette. Great care must be taken when operating anteriorly where the synovial membrane of the corono-pedal joint comes into contact with the cartilage. Have the joint rigidly extended so as to stretch the synovial membrane and diminish the risk of its being perforated. In using the curette, cut from within outwards. Keep the cut edge of the cartilage

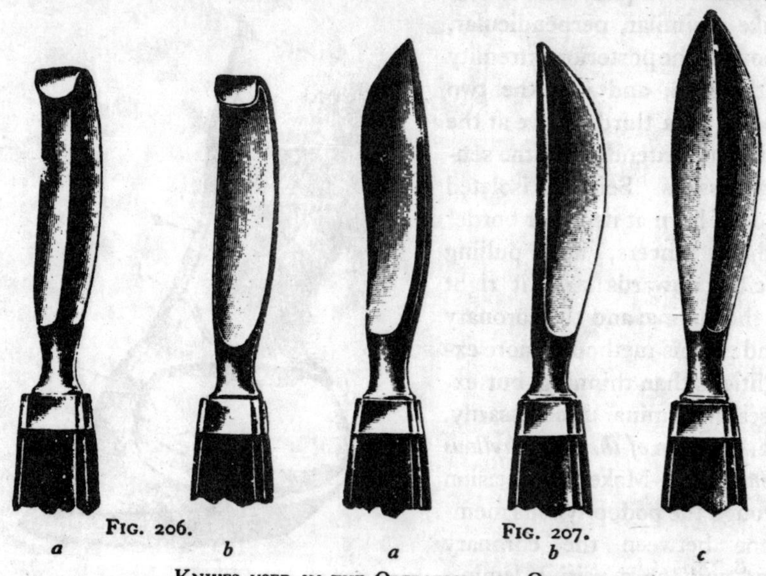

FIG. 206. *a* *b* — FIG. 207. *a* *b* *c*

KNIVES USED IN THE OPERATION FOR QUITTOR.

Fig. 206, *a* and *b*, Double- and single-edged knives for thinning the horn ; Fig. 207, *a*, *b* and *c*, left-handed, right-handed, and double-edged knives for removing the lateral cartilage (French models).

in view as a guide to the depth of the wound. During the procedure pass the probe occasionally to show the direction and depth of the sinus in whose course the green necrotic cartilage will be found. Make sure of removing every particle of necrotic cartilage. Should the joint be accidentally opened, the synovia will be seen escaping. If strict antiseptic precautions are taken, arthritis will not supervene. Do not leave particles of semidetached cartilage *in situ*, as they may undergo necrosis afterwards and cause a recurrence of the condition.

6. *Dressing the Wound.*—Flush out the wound with an antiseptic solution by means of a syringe to remove tissue debris ; then paint it with tincture of iodine, and dress it finally with sulphanilamide powder.

Replace the flap of skin and coronary band in position. Cover the wound with a dressing of gauze, cotton-wool, and bandage, tightly applied to arrest the hæmorrhage. Enclose the foot in a leather boot or in one improvised from straw as follows: Make two thick plaits of straw about 3 feet long. Intercross them at their centre and tie them there. Place the foot in the centre of the cross and fix the plaits longitudinally on the limb by means of a bandage. This can easily be renewed as it gets soiled or worn. Fairly profuse hæmorrhage may ensue through the dressing, but it stops in the course of an hour or so.

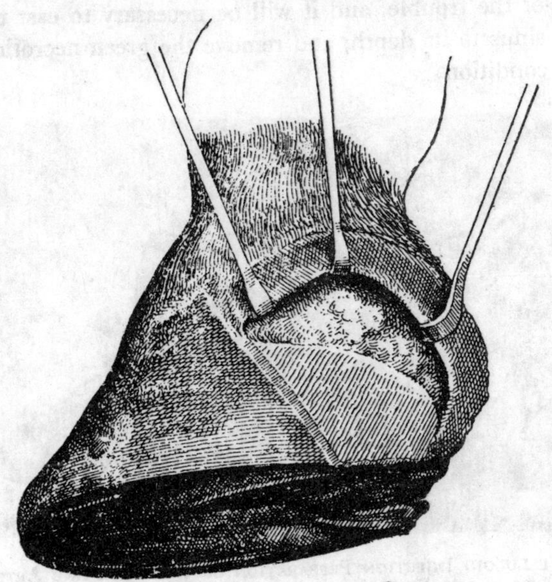

FIG. 208.—OPERATION FOR QUITTOR.
The whole of the lateral cartilage has been removed.

AFTER-TREATMENT.—Renew the dressing the following day, as it is usually saturated with blood. Afterwards redress the wound occasionally. If doubtful about the condition of the wound or if the joint has been opened during the operation, put the foot in a hot antiseptic bath for half an hour once or twice daily. Perchloride of mercury solution 1 in 1,000 is very suitable for the purpose. New horn forming on the coronary band should be kept pared until the wound beneath is quite healed. Otherwise it may interfere with drainage or wound the delicate granulations and give rise to an abscess beneath the flap.

RESULT.—Although the case is progressing favourably, there may be a considerable purulent discharge from the wound after about a week,

This should gradually diminish and practically cease about the fourth week after the operation. The pain and lameness should diminish accordingly. If the discharge continues beyond the period mentioned, it is an indication, as a rule, that there is still some necrotic cartilage *in situ* or that a portion of the healthy cartilage left has become infected and undergone necrosis.

The wound may appear to be going on well for about a fortnight and an abscess then form. This may heal on bursting or being opened, or be followed by a sinus. In the latter case necrotic cartilage is at the bottom of the trouble, and it will be necessary to cast the horse, explore the sinus to its depth, and remove the green necrotic material causing the condition.

FIG. 209.—CELLULOID INJECTION PREPARATION OF THE VEINS AND ARTERIES OF THE FOOT PREPARED BY MACERATION.
The veins are light in colour, the arteries dark.

The rule, however, is that the wound is completely cicatrised within five weeks after the operation. When the new wall has grown down after the lapse of some months there is usually no deformity left, but occasionally a space persists between the coronary and laminal horn, into which sand and dirt may gain entrance and cause lameness by pressure on the sensitive laminæ. In this case it will be necessary to thin the parietal horn and remove the foreign matter beneath.

SHOEING.—When the horse is sound, put on a three-quarter shoe with a leather sole, tar and tow, and cover the breach in the wall with a dressing of tar and tow kept in position by a short bandage, whose outer surface should also be smeared with tar.

COMPLICATIONS.—(1) The chief complication to be feared is arthritis, due, as a rule, to the joint being opened during the operation and infection gaining entrance, but it might be the result of sloughing of the antero-lateral ligament owing to its being involved in the disease.

(2) If the skin is separated too thinly from the cartilage, the former may undergo necrosis from insufficient blood supply, accompanied by that of the coronary band, leaving a permanent false quarter.

If the coronary sinus is due to a diseased side-bone, proceed similarly until the ossified cartilage is exposed; then, using a fine sharp saw, cut through the base of the side-bone. Insert the edge of a chisel into the groove made by the saw and prise the bone upwards. Separate it from its fibrous attachments by the knife and remove it. If the digital artery has been severed, apply a ligature on the vessel. Dress the wound as before. The case almost invariably does well, the affected tissue being excised in one piece.

When a hind-foot is affected, the limb is fixed similarly to the upper fore-limb above the knee.

Modifications of the Classical Method—(1) *Section of the Coronary Band.*—Proceed as described until the coronary band and skin have been separated from the cartilage; then divide the flap by a mesial incision into anterior and posterior halves in order to facilitate excision of the cartilage. Remove the latter as described. Suture the cut edges of the skin. Owing to the hollow beneath, it is difficult to keep the edges in accurate apposition; consequently, the ends of the band do not always unite evenly, but sometimes leave a deformity. A permanent fissure is formed in the wall at the level of the division in the coronary band.

(2) *Bayer's Method.*—Strip the horn from a semicircular area of the wall at the level of the cartilage, the concavity of the semicircle being directed upwards. At a short distance from the edge of the cut horn and parallel thereto make an incision in the coronary band and podophyllous membrane, and continue it in the skin to a point a little above the band in front and behind. Reflect the flap thus marked out, completely exposing the outer aspect of the cartilage, which can then be easily excised. After excision, replace the flap in position and suture the edges of the skin and of the podophyllous membrane. Apply a compressive dressing.

RESULTS.—Healing by first intention has been obtained in a number of cases. Owing to the coronary band having been cut in two places, two fissures are left in the wall, but they are of little or no significance. The method has the disadvantage of interfering with the coronary band and laminæ, more than other methods.

(3) *Perrier's Method.*—Make an elliptical incision on the coronet extending almost from the anterior to the posterior extremity of the cartilage through the skin and subcutaneous tissues, and enclosing the orifice of the sinus. Remove the tissue included in the incision, taking away a piece like a section of an orange or a slice of melon. Separate the remaining skin from the outer surface of the cartilage. Excise the cartilage piecemeal, making use chiefly of the loop knife and the curette. Follow the probe to the depth of the sinus to make sure that a particle of necrotic cartilage is not left there to set up a renewal of the condition. The wound is so deep and narrow it is difficult to see clearly its depth. A small electric torch proves very useful to illuminate it.

Having excised the cartilage, irrigate the wound with an antiseptic solution, paint it with tincture of iodine, and pack the cavity with a powder composed of sulphanilamide or of a mixture of boric acid (1 ounce) and biniodide of mercury (10 grains), or with iodoform and boric acid, or with thick B.I.P.P. Apply a pad and bandage. No boot is required, the ordinary shoe being left in position.

RESULTS.—Although there is no drainage from the wound, it usually heals without interruption. The method has the advantage that there is no interference with the wall or coronary cushion, and that when the wound has cicatrised in four or five weeks after the operation the foot has a perfectly normal appearance.

(4) *Excision from the Plantar Aspect of the Foot.*—It is possible by the aid of the searcher, special loop knife, and curette to remove the cartilage from the plantar aspect of the foot, operating in the posterior angle of the sole, between the wall and the bar. It is not easy to reach the extreme antero-inferior region of the cartilage by this method, whose advantages are as follows: (1) The operation can be done standing when cocaine is injected over the plantar nerves; (2) there is free dependent drainage from the wound; (3) the wall and coronary cushion are not disturbed; (4) the wound is reduced to a minimum and the period of idleness is less than when other methods are adopted; (5) the operation is rapidly executed.

Irrigate the wound with an antiseptic solution and insert into it a tampon of gauze saturated with B.I.P.P., and apply a pad, bandage, and boot. Renew the dressing every three or four days. Remove the new horn, which tends to encroach on the orifice of the wound before its depth is closed. The animal is usually fit to return to work in twenty to twenty-eight days.

The advantages claimed for this method are almost outweighed by the difficulty of operating through such a narrow confined space, and of keeping the depth of the wound in view. If the retrorsal process of the os pedis is well developed, it will be necessary to remove it to enable the portion of cartilage in its vicinity to be excised. The method is not much in vogue.

Experience during the First World War and since has proved that the method introduced or revived by Perrier has given most satisfaction. It is consequently so much in vogue now that all the other methods described may almost be considered obsolete except perhaps for the removal of a diseased side-bone.

91. Resection of the Plantar Aponeurosis

INDICATION.—Necrosis of the plantar aponeurosis as the result of a deep punctured wound of the plantar aspect of the foot, usually caused by a " picked-up nail."

PREPARATION of the foot and CONTROL of the patient as for quittor.

PROCEDURE—(1) *Removal of the Horn.*—Pare away all the horn of the frog and thin the horn of the sole and bars.

(2) *Excision of the Plantar Cushion.*—Have the foot extended by an assistant, and make a transverse incision in the plantar cushion near its base by means of the double sage knife. As the incision gets deeper, let it have a slightly oblique direction from behind forwards, so that when it is continued through the aponeurosis it will abut on the posterior border of the navicular bone. Grasp the anterior part of the cushion with a hook or sharp retractor or a spring forceps, and separate it from its attachments with one of the sage knives. As a rule the deep part of the cushion is left in contact with the aponeurosis. Dissect it away with the knife and forceps.

(3) *Excision of the Plantar Aponeurosis.*—Take the sage knife and cut the aponeurosis transversely from one lacuna to the other at the level of the posterior border of the navicular bone, having the instrument under good control to avoid wounding the important structures beneath. Divide the distal portion of the severed aponeurosis by a mesial incision into two lateral halves ; excise successively each portion, making first a semicircular incision at its periphery, and then dissecting it from the semilunar crest.

(4) *Curetting the Surfaces of the Bones.*—If the posterior surface of the navicular bone is ulcerated, scrape the affected part with the curette. In like manner curette the surface of the semilunar crest if the remains of the aponeurotic fibres in contact therewith are necrotic or the bone itself is diseased. Should the terminal fibres of the aponeurosis be

healthy, do not remove them, as they will granulate freely and hasten the healing of the wound.

DRESSING.—Irrigate the wound with an antiseptic solution, swab it with tincture of iodine, fill it with sulphanilamide powder, and pack it with sulphanilamide gauze. Cover the plantar aspect of the foot with a pad of cotton-wool kept in position by a bandage and put on a leather boot. An alternative method of dressing is to apply a shoe and and maintain the material in position by means of strips of hoop-iron inserted between the hoof and the shoe. Renew the dressing occasionally.

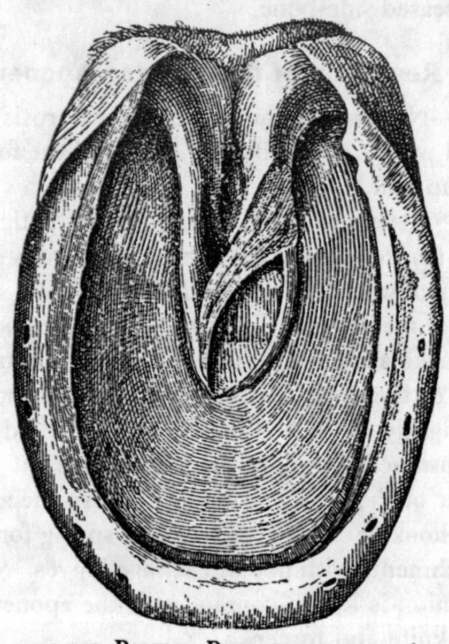

FIG. 210.—OPERATION FOR PARTIAL RESECTION OF THE APONEUROSIS OF THE FLEXOR PEDIS PERFORANS TENDON.

It is advisable to put the horse in slings, as no weight can be borne on the affected limb until two or three weeks after the operation. When the wound is healed, put on a shoe with a dressing of tar and tow and a leather sole.

RESULTS.—The case usually does well, the wound gradually closing in to be completely cicatrised and covered with new horn in five or six weeks. About fourteen days after the operation the animal commences to bear weight on the limb, and is quite sound on it in the course of six to eight weeks after the operation. A depression takes the place of the prominence formerly formed by the frog, and the foot usually remains more or less contracted.

COMPLICATIONS.—If a piece of necrotic tissue be left in the wound, the inflammation and suppuration will continue and the patient will still show evidence of great pain. An abscess may form in the hollow of the pastern. Renewed intervention is then necessary. A seton passed through the wound and hollow of the pastern may be required to drain an abscess in the latter situation. The antiseptic foot-bath for half an hour once or twice daily is indicated until the discharge diminishes. The interosseous ligament may have been already perforated, leading to arthritis and rendering the case hopeless. The

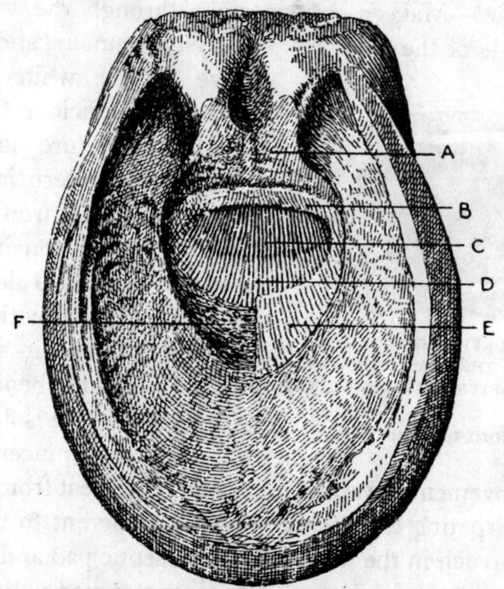

FIG. 211.—OPERATION FOR COMPLETE RESECTION OF THE APONEUROSIS OF THE FLEXOR PEDIS PERFORANS TENDON.

A, Cut surface of frog and plantar cushion ; B, section of the aponeurosis of the flexor tendon ; C, postero-inferior surface of the navicular bone ; D, interosseous ligament ; E, oblique section of the aponeurosis of the flexor tendon ; F, tendinous surface of the navicular bone cleaned by curetting.

navicular bone may have been fractured by the picked-up nail. In this case cure is out of the question.

Sometimes, although the wound has healed perfectly and is covered with horn, the lameness persists, due apparently to contraction of the hoof or to hyperæsthesia in the cicatrix. Thinning the new horn at the seat of operation or grooving the hoof may get rid of the lameness. If not, low plantar neurectomy is indicated.

The plantar aponeurosis is not involved in every case of plantar sinus. The necrosis may be confined to the plantar cushion. Opening up the sinus and curetting the diseased surface will be sufficient in this case. The operation can be done standing after injecting a local anæsthetic over the plantar nerves.

92. Operation for the Removal of a Keratoma

INDICATION.—A keratoma or horny tumour situated on the inner aspect of the wall of the hoof.

CONTROL.—As for quittor. It is possible to operate standing under the influence of a local anæsthetic injected over the plantar nerves.

PROCEDURE.—Make a groove right through the wall immediately on either side of the part occupied by the tumour, and join these by a groove at the white line. A sharp searcher is sufficient for the purpose, but the procedure is facilitated by making the superficial part of the grooves with a hot iron. Cut the layer of horn next the sensitive tissues with the sage knife passed along the border of the groove formed by the isolated horn, and held so that it will not wound deeply the tissues beneath. Seize the lower border of the isolated horn firmly with a strong pincers, and with a vigorous movement towards the coronet separate it from its attachments, thereby extirpating the tumour which is adherent to its inner surface. Cover the breach in the wall with an antiseptic pad and bandage. The exposed band and laminæ soon become covered with a thin layer of horn, when a dressing of tar and tow should be applied. When the horse is going sound, put on a shoe having no bearing in the immediate vicinity of the affected region and let the animal go to work. Keep the laminal horn thinned until the new wall has grown down to the plantar aspect of the foot, and maintain it supple by the application of Archangel tar.

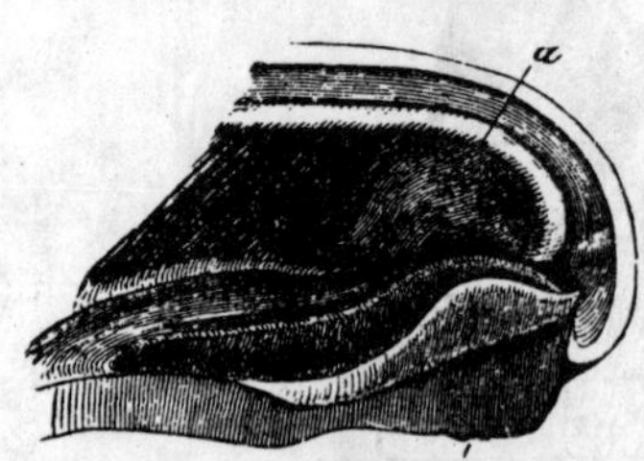

FIG. 212.—PORTION OF THE INNER SURFACE OF THE WALL, SHOWING CHANGES AFTER OLD-STANDING CORN.

a, Horn tumour.

The above operation may require to be supplemented by the removal of necrotic laminæ and curetting of the ulcerated surface of the os pedis in a case complicated by infection of these structures.

RESULT.—The desired effect is obtained, the horse being rendered sound and fit for work as indicated. The cicatricial tissue does not possess in its superficial layer the morphological characters of the podophyllous membrane, the laminæ are not regenerated, and the adhesion of the new horn to the sensitive parts is less intimate. Occasionally there is a recurrence of the tumour after a variable period.

93. Operation for Contracted Hoof (Smith's Operation)

Indications.—Contracted hoof, associated or not with sidebones and causing lameness.

Control.—No special control is required, the operation being confined to the horn, and therefore painless.

Site.—The quarter and heel regions of the wall, limited anteriorly by a vertical line let fall from the anterior extremity of the lateral cartilage.

Procedure.—Make a vertical groove right through the wall at the level of the anterior border of the lateral cartilage from the coronary to the plantar border, and a similar one obliquely downwards and forwards at the posterior part of the heel. Between these make two other grooves parallel to the posterior one. At the white line make a groove down to the sensitive tissues, joining the parietal grooves. Shorten the lower ends of the isolated portions of the wall by means of the rasp or drawing knife, so that they will not bear on the shoe when applied.

The operation is easily performed by means of a hot iron and a sharp searcher. Special instruments, however, may be used for the purpose in the form of a hoof plane, or hook-shaped knife and a hoof saw. The foot may be rested on the edge of a pedestal of any kind or lifted in the flexed position during the procedure. Fill the grooves with Archangel tar. Have a bar shoe applied with the bar resting on the frog, and no bearing on the portions of wall operated upon. A leather sole with a dressing of tar and tow is also indicated. Let the horse have daily exercise to cause pressure on the frog, and thus promote expansion of the posterior region of the hoof. It is advisable to blister the coronet at the same time.

Results.—Decided expansion of the hoof in the regions grooved is observed three weeks after the operation. The lameness is much improved as a rule by this time, and in the majority of cases the horse goes sound soon afterwards. Many of the cases in which the operation has failed to cause improvement are affected with navicular disease. Horses which have been lame for months have been made sound by this procedure. Sir Frederick Smith practised the operation extensively in the army, and brought its utility so prominently before the veterinary profession that it has been called "Smith's operation." Most practitioners speak highly of its advantages.

Complications.—There are really no complications, but the laminæ are sometimes wounded when completing a groove, causing a certain amount of hæmorrhage and giving rise to a localised transient laminitis. Large granulations may form at the wounded part.

A hot antiseptic bath will dispel local inflammation in a day or two, and the application of formalin will soon remove the excessive granulations. The operation may be repeated with perhaps good effect when the first intervention has not given the desired result.

94. Removal of Side-Bones

INDICATIONS.—When the side-bones are very prominent and depreciating the value of the animal, or when the inner one is being struck by the opposite foot during progression, causing inflammation and lameness.

CONTROL.—As for quittor.

PROCEDURE (1) *Partial Operation.*—Make an incision between "hair and hoof" from the anterior to the posterior extremity of the side-bone. Bisect this by an incision extending to the upper border of the side-bone. Reflect the two cutaneous flaps thus marked out. Saw through the bone at the level of the first incision. Insert a chisel into the groove caused by the saw and lever up the piece of bone. Separate it from the soft tissues with a knife and remove it. If one of the branches of the digital artery is severed, secure it by ligation, otherwise alarming hæmorrhage may supervene. Suture the wound and apply an antiseptic pad and a long tight bandage.

RESULT.—Recovery from the operation is uneventful, and the unsightly enlargement is removed.

(2) *Complete Operation.*—The procedure here is the same as that described for quittor due to a diseased side-bone, and is only indicated in such a case, it being sufficient in ordinary cases to remove the enlargement at the level of the coronet.

95. Amputation of the Digit in the Ox

INDICATIONS.—Any incurable affection of the digit causing constant lameness, chiefly arthritis, compound fracture, and necrosis of one of the phalanges.

CONTROL.—Cast and anæsthetise the beast, and have the limb held in a convenient position for the operation.

PROCEDURE—*The Terminal Phalanx.*—Having thoroughly prepared the foot by clipping, washing, and disinfecting, and applied a tourniquet above the fetlock, thin the horn on the outer and anterior aspect of the claw by means of the rasp until only a thin pellicle is left. Recognise the level of the first interphalangeal joint by palpation and by movement of the claw. Disarticulate the joint by an incision A, B, C

(Figs. 213 and 214), made with the sage knife a little below the coronet, so as to leave the coronary band intact. Continue the incision through the ligamentous and tendinous tissue until complete section is effected, the navicular bone being left *in situ* if not diseased. If any of the remaining soft tissues show evidence of necrosis, remove the affected parts. If the articular surface of the os corona is ulcerated, scrape the ulcerated surface with the curette or, better, excise the articular end of the bone with a sharp saw. Release the tourniquet to recognise the bleeding vessels, and secure them by torsion or ligature. Bathe the wound with an antiseptic solution, dust it with iodoform or smear it with B.I.P.P., and cover it with gauze, cotton-wool, and bandage. Envelop the whole foot in strong canvas or sacking covered by a leather or straw boot, and keep the patient in a clean place. If the season permits, put the animal on grass, as it is cleaner than a house. Change the dressing occasionally, as seems indicated.

FIG. 213.—AN OX'S CLAW.
The letters *a* to *d* show the position of the pedal joint.

RESULT.—The wound heals without complication, and is completely cicatrised and covered with horn about six weeks after the operation. A certain amount of lameness still remains, but in the course of three months it generally disappears. The patient is greatly relieved by the operation and soon commences to thrive.

If the suffragino-coronal joint is involved in the disease, make the first incision as described; then make another incision upwards on the mesial anterior aspect of the digit to the level of the first interphalangeal joint. Reflect the skin to expose the region of the articulation. Disarticulate the latter and proceed as before. An alternative procedure for the removal of the third phalanx is that practised by

Gould (Southampton), which is as follows. Having taken the necessary preliminary measures saw through the hoof and bone immediately below the coronary band. Then separate the band from the structures beneath and remove the remnant of the pedal bone by disarticulating it from the second phalanx. Dress the wound as described. This procedure facilitates and expedites the operation.

Gold (Redditch) in " Some Aspects of Bovine Surgery," published in *Vet. Rec.*, April 12th, 1941; describes what in his experience is the best

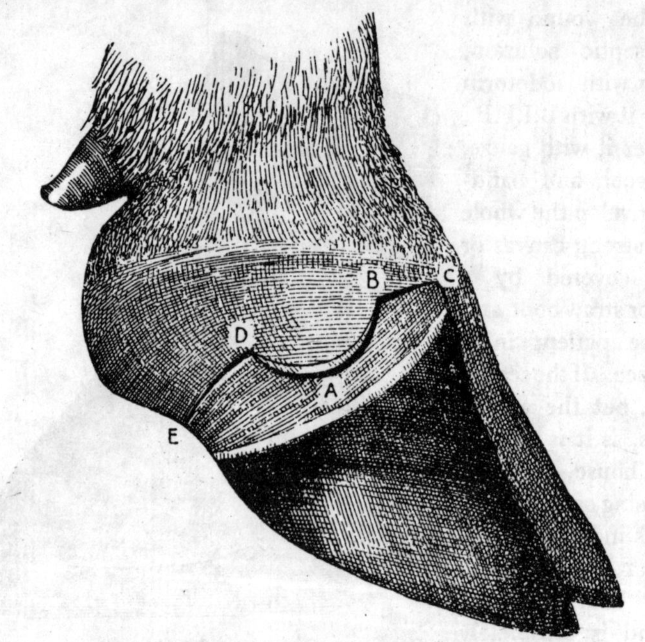

FIG. 214.—DISARTICULATION OF THE OX'S CLAW: PRIMARY INCISION.

method of amputating the bovine digit. In all cases he performs the operation through the os suffraginis, making the following incisions :

(1) In front of the pastern on the middle line, from the anterior end of the interdigital space to about the level of the dew claws.

(2) A similar incision on the posterior aspect of the pastern.

(3) A vertical incision on the middle line of the lateral aspect of the pastern from the coronet to the level of the dew claws.

(4) An incision parallel to and a little above the coronet joining the ends of the other incisions.

(5) Having reflected the two flaps thus marked out, he makes an incision in the interdigital space connecting the lower ends of incisions

(1) and (2) and carries it upwards between the digits, keeping as close as possible to the bone of the affected side, as far as the middle of the os suffraginis. He now saws through the latter about its middle, releases the tourniquet and ligates the bleeding vessels, he then re-applies the tourniquet and sutures the flaps of skin at their distal ends and to the skin of the opposite digit at the distal ends of the anterior and posterior incisions, thus forming a short sleeve into which is put a piece of gauze soaked in 1 to 1,000 acriflavine solution and the cavity is tightly packed with cotton wool soaked in this solution. A pad of cotton wool also saturated with that same antiseptic is applied and covered with a tight calico bandage. A clean bag is put over the foot and the dressing left on for four days and renewed then and at weekly intervals afterwards. The result in each case was excellent, the patient going sound on the affected limb about six weeks after the operation.

He disapproves of the methods above described whereby a stump is left with the coronary band *in situ* for the purpose of covering it with horn, on the ground that this stump being therefore longer it sometimes becomes injured from contact with the ground, causing inflammation and lameness.

96. Amputation of the Terminal Phalanx in the Dog

INDICATIONS.—Chronic sprain or dislocation of the second inter-phalangeal joint, rupture of its lateral ligaments, fracture of one of the phalanges forming the joint, or serious injury to the claw, conditions which do not respond to treatment and result in intermittent or permanent lameness. It is chiefly in greyhounds that the operation is required.

CONTROL.—Quiet animals can be operated upon without any special control under the influence of local anæsthesia, but refractory subjects may require to be narcotised by a hypodermic injection of morphia. General anæsthesia by an intravenous injection of pentothal sodium or nembutal may be preferred to the latter owing to its quicker action.

PROCEDURE.—Inject the local anæsthetic on the dorsum of the digit a little above the base of the nail, continuing to push on the needle until it touches the second phalanx, thus making a wheal.

Make a series of wheals in a fan-shaped manner round the upper part of the articulation only, partially withdrawing the needle before reinserting it, and then anæsthetise the inferior and lateral aspect of the joint in a similar manner, always keeping the needle close to the bone, so as to include the periosteum.

When the anæsthesia is complete grasp the toe with the finger beneath the pad and the thumb on the dorsum of the nail and flex the joint to make it prominent and thus facilitate dissection.

Make an incision just behind the nail parallel to and co-extensive with its rim thereby opening the joint and severing its lateral ligaments and the flexor tendons which are attached to the inferior aspect of the phalanx, taking care not to cut through the pad which is then carefully dissected away from the bone by cutting close to the surface of the latter.

Having removed the claw, close the wound by two or three sutures through the skin and pad, and apply a dressing of antiseptic powder, gauze and cotton-wool, kept in position by a bandage.

RESULT.—The wound heals rapidly by second intention, and in the course of a few weeks the dog goes sound and is fit to resume racing or coursing. The loss of the claw seems to have little or no appreciable effect in diminishing the speed of the animal.

97. Amputation of the Second and Third Phalanges

INDICATIONS.—Similar to those mentioned for amputation of the third or (terminal) phalanx, but most frequently for chronic arthritis or periarthritis of the first interphalangeal joint resulting from sprain of the joint, and constituting what is known as "sprung toe."

CONTROL as in No. 96.

PROCEDURE.—Having injected the local anæsthetic all round the digit above the first interphalangeal joint and disarticulated the terminal articulation, make a longitudinal incision exposing the former joint, disarticulate it and then dissect the two phalanges from the skin and pad and finish the operation by arresting hæmorrhage from any bleeding vessel and by suturing the transverse and longitudinal wounds. Apply a protective dressing as before.

RESULT.—The wound heals without any complication, and the desired effect is obtained, the animal going sound, and being able to race after an interval of a few weeks. Sometimes after this operation on the left outside digit, leaving the first phalanx in position, tipped with a modified horny pad, the dog goes lame as the result of its coming in contact with the ground during the gallop, and the lameness disappears when the phalanx along with the remains of the pad is removed. It would appear, therefore, that the better procedure in this case would be, in the first instance, to remove the entire digit.

98. Excision of the First Interphalangeal Joint in the Dog

INDICATIONS as mentioned in No. 97.

PROCEDURE.—Produce local anæsthesia as already described.

Make a longitudinal incision exposing the first interphalangeal joint. Dissect out the ends of the two bones forming the joint and remove the articular end of each by means of a bone forceps and suture the cutaneous wound. Apply a protective dressing.

RESULT.—This method has not as far as the writer knows been extensively practised, but was brought to his notice by Pierse (Listowel) who has performed the operation successfully in a few cases. The writer has operated on two cases in this manner with the desired effect in removing the lameness.

The advantage claimed for the method is that the nail is left *in situ*, and although of little or no use as regards its functioning, it renders the paw less unsightly and makes the dog more saleable than when the two phalanges have been completely removed.

99. Spinal Puncture and Injection

Lumbar puncture of the spinal canal is a well-known operation in the human subject, in which it is practised both for diagnostic and for therapeutic purposes and for producing spinal anæsthesia. It is performed in the lumbo-sacral space by means of a trocar and canula or a hollow needle, which is inserted into the subarachnoid space. A certain quantity of cerebro-spinal fluid is withdrawn, and then an anæsthetic or specific serum or other agent is injected.

INDICATIONS.—Anæsthesia of the hind-quarters, injection of anti-tetanic serum, or some medicament for the treatment of specific cerebro-spinal affections, and examination of the cerebro-spinal liquid.

CONTROL.—The horse may be operated upon standing, with a twitch applied and the fore-limb held up or a side fetter in position ; but it is more convenient to have the animal cast with the back kept in the arched position, so as to facilitate entering the neural canal and the escape of the cerebro-spinal fluid. The diffusion of the liquid injected through the spinal canal is favoured by raising the hind-quarters.

SITE.—The space between the last lumbar and the first sacral vertebræ, the point of the instrument being inserted at the point of intersection of the median line with that joining the internal angles of the ilia. The conical extremity of the spinal cord reaches the level of the first or sometimes even that of the second sacral vertebra, while the dura mater is prolonged as far as the third or fourth vertebra.

PROCEDURE.—Take up a position at the level of the croup or the back, according as the animal is cast on the left or right side. Make a small cutaneous incision with a sharp scalpel. Take a trocar and canula about 6 inches long and $\frac{1}{16}$ to $\frac{1}{12}$ inch in diameter, hold it perpendicular to the surface of the region with its point in the wound, push it towards the cord to a depth of 4 to 6 inches, depending upon the size

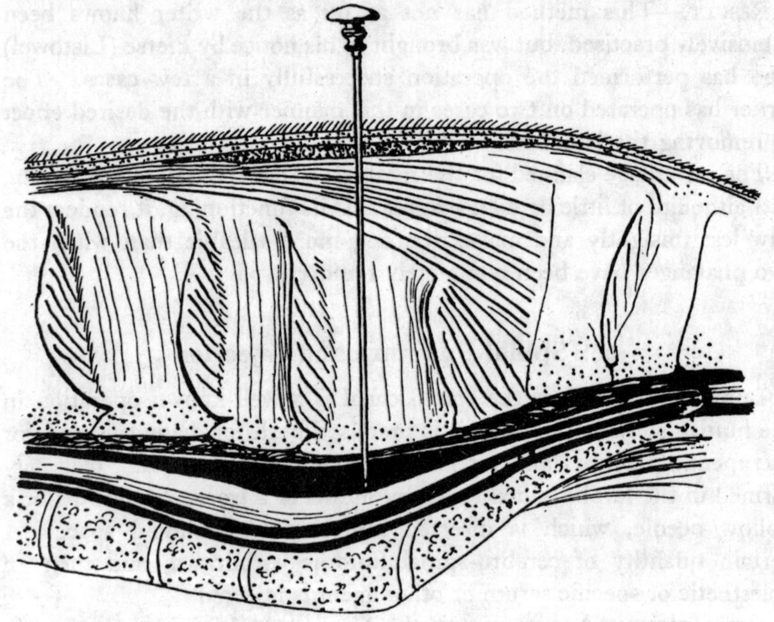

FIG. 215.—SPINAL PUNCTURE.

Vertical antero-posterior section of the lumbo-sacral region.

of the patient. Slight resistance may be encountered when the instrument is passing through the periosteum of the neural canal and through the dura mater, and when it reaches the subarachnoid space the animal may wince, due to pricking of the terminal portion of the cord. Withdraw the trocar, and if the spinal canal has been penetrated the spinal fluid will escape, slightly tinged with blood, as a rule, at first, but afterwards limpid. The amount which can be drawn off varies; it may attain 2 to 4 drachms. When an anæsthetic or therapeutic injection is to be made, a quantity of fluid about equal to that to be introduced should be withdrawn. The latter should be sterilised, raised to the body temperature, and injected slowly into the subarachnoid space, one or two minutes being occupied for the purpose. The operation is fairly delicate, and is not much in vogue with veterinary surgeons. A danger of the procedure is that the spinal cord may be injured by the trocar.

100. Operation for Gid

INDICATION.—Brain symptoms, due to the presence of the *Cœnurus cerebralis* on the brain.

The Ox

CONTROL.—Fix the patient in the cast position, and use local or general anæsthesia.

SITE.—At the level of the cyst, whose location may be marked by a soft swelling or simply a soft spot. When this landmark is absent, there is no definite indication as to the situation of the cyst, but experience has shown that it is commonly found to one side of the middle line about half-way between the base of the horn and the supra-orbital process. It is advisable to postpone operation until the case is well developed, when the cyst may become subcutaneous from absorption of the overlying bone.

PROCEDURE.—The operation may be performed by means of a trephine, or of a borer, trocar and canula, and a syringe. The latter is the method most in vogue at present, and is performed thus : Incise the skin, insert the point of the borer in the wound perpendicular to the bone, having the travelling screw which it carries arrested at the point to which it is intended to insert the instrument. Push the latter through the cranial bone. Introduce the trocar and canula through the opening thus made, and insert it into the cyst or brain as the case may be. Withdraw the trocar, and if the cyst has been penetrated some of its liquid contents will escape through the canula. Introduce the nozzle of the syringe through the latter into the cyst and aspirate the remainder of the fluid. In doing this the wall of the cyst is generally sucked into the orifice where it can be grasped with a forceps and carefully removed. If the cyst wall is not taken away the cyst will generally reform, but a sufficient interval of relief may be afforded by the mere removal of the liquid to enable the animal to be prepared for the butcher. Brain matter may protrude through the cranial orifice without any harmful sequel. As the frontal sinus covers the whole of the cranium its inner and outer walls have to be penetrated to reach the brain, but both may be in contact or absent at the level of the cyst due to the pressure caused thereby.

If trephining is adopted, the procedure is the same as that for trephining the sinus, care being taken not to have the centre piece projecting beyond the level of the edge of the trephine and not to insert the latter into the brain. The crown of the trephine should not be more than $\frac{1}{3}$ inch in diameter.

The AFTER-TREATMENT consists in suturing the wound and protecting it with a dressing, which may be in the form of a pad and bandage or a smear of tar or a pitch plaster, the first-mentioned being probably the best. The patient should not be allowed out in the rain until the wound has healed.

RESULTS.—When the operation succeeds in removing the cyst recovery is the rule, but when the cyst cannot be exactly located and its situation is merely guessed at the procedure is apt to fail. Fatal hæmorrhage may ensue from puncturing the venous sinus. When the operation is carefully performed by a experienced operator in a suitable subject with definite local symptoms, the percentage of recoveries may be estimated at about 95 per cent.

Sheep

In the sheep the procedure is on the same lines as in the ox, with equal prospect of success in similar circumstances. Rams, in which the frontal sinus is well developed, are difficult subjects, except the cyst is very large and has caused the inner and outer walls of the sinus to come into contact and form a superficial bulging. When no direct evidence of the site is available, most operators select a spot about $\frac{3}{8}$ to $\frac{3}{4}$ inch behind the horn core on the side to which the head is turned. To avoid puncturing the sinus longitudinalis, the cranium should not be entered nearer than $\frac{3}{16}$ inch from the middle line.

101. Amputation of Limb

INDICATIONS.—Irreparable injury involving the greater portion of the thickness of the limb, and malignant disease and gangrene for which there is no hope of cure.

CONTROL.—In a suitable position under a general anæsthetic.

SITE.—A point above and well clear of the lesion to ensure operating in normal tissue.

PROCEDURE—(1) *Elliptical Flap Method.*—Apply a tourniquet above the site of operation. On opposite sides of the limb make an elliptical incision, mapping out a flap which will be of sufficient size along with its fellow of the other side to cover the stump after removal of the limb. First incise the skin and then the other soft tissues, the latter being cut so as to form a somewhat smaller flap than that formed by the skin. Reflect all the soft tissues from the bone back to the base of the flap on both sides. This dissection is best performed by holding the blade of the knife perpendicular to the bone while the flaps are being drawn towards the proximal end of the limb. Take a sharp saw and sever the bone at the level of the base of the flaps. Release the tourniquet and secure the bleeding vessels. Apply some sulphanilamide powder and unite the flaps over the stump by interrupted sutures, and apply a protective antiseptic dressing. When an artificial limb is to be worn, it is better to have the cicatrix laterally situated than in the centre of the stump.

This is effected by making a long and a short flap so that the former covers the end of the stump and meets the latter at one side thereof.

RESULTS.—Healing by first intention may take place. If not, suppuration will ensue and healing will not be completed until about a fortnight after the operation. Occasionally necrosis of the bone supervenes, when cicatrisation is delayed until the sequestrum has come away or is removed.

The operation is practically unknown in the horse, in which it serves no useful purpose. But in the bovine it has often been performed successfully, allowing the beast to be prepared for the butcher or to complete its milking period. An artificial limb is supplied in these cases, enabling the subject to bear weight on the stump. In small animals like the dog and cat amputation is a common operation, and always gives satisfactory results, the patient suffering little or no inconvenience from the loss of one limb. An artificial limb may be fitted, but it is rather a disadvantage to the animal.

(2) *Circular Flap Method.*—In this method a circular incision is made through the soft tissues at a point corresponding to the free extremity of the elliptical flap. Dissection is carried out as in No. (1) back to the point where the bone is to be divided. The edges of the skin are united by sutures over the stump. The resulting puckering at the extremities of the wound may be cut off with a sharp scissors, and the cut edges then brought together with sutures.

No. (1) is the better method.

102. Hæmatoma in the Dog's Ear

INDICATION.—A hæmatoma on the inner or outer aspect of the flap of the ear.

CONTROL.—In the ventral position on the table. Local or general anæsthesia is advisable to avoid the pain of suturing.

PROCEDURE.—Incise the swelling from its lower to its upper extremity on the middle line. Evacuate its contents completely and swab its lining with tincture of iodine. Insert a series of interrupted sutures right through the concha across the incision, tying them on the outside, assuming that the lesion has been on the inner aspect of the flap, as is usually the case or alternatively insert Halsted sutures right through the ear, on either side of the wound and parallel thereto. Turn the tip of the ear back over the poll and immobilise it there by means of a pad and bandage or cap, avoiding excessive pressure for fear of causing necrosis of the part pressed upon. The dressing should be removed daily for a while, and any discharge from the wound mopped with sterilised pledgets of cotton-wool. The sutures are to be removed after some days when adhesion has occurred between the skin and the cartilage.

RESULTS.—When the operation has been successful, adhesion occurs

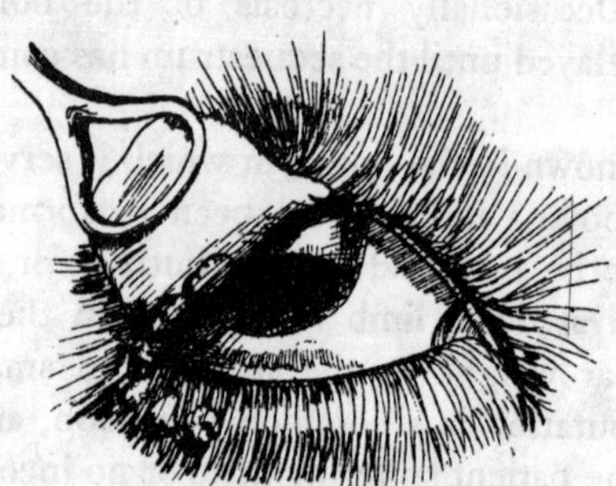

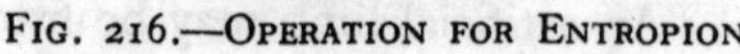

FIG. 216.—OPERATION FOR ENTROPION.

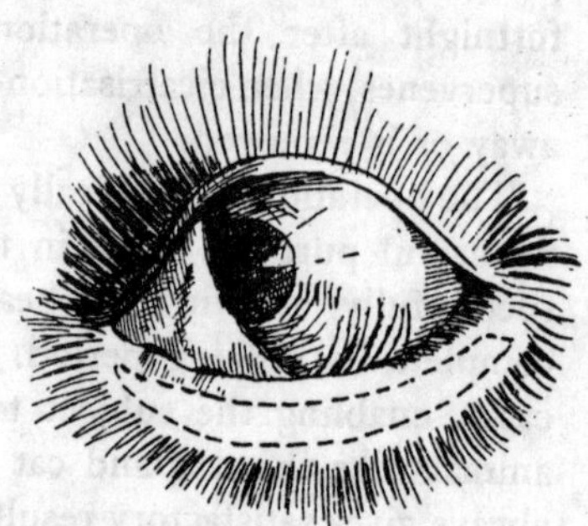

FIG. 217.—OPERATION FOR ENTROPION. The portion of skin to be excised is marked by the dotted line.

at once between the separated skin and cartilage with a minimum of cicatricial contraction and deformity. The desired effect, however, is not always obtained, the adhesion mentioned failing to take place. Then the result is the same as if the hæmatoma was treated in the ordinary way.

103. Operation for Entropion

INDICATION.—Turning in of the palpebral border, so that the eyelashes irritate the conjunctiva and the cornea, setting up conjunctivitis and keratitis.

CONTROL.—Puppies may be held in the arms of an assistant and larger dogs may be controlled standing or fixed in the ventral position on the table.

PROCEDURE.—Inject a few drops of a solution of eudrenine subcutaneously at the seat of operation. Take up a fold of skin parallel to and a short distance from the palpebral border by means of a special wide-jawed forceps or an ordinary dressing forceps, the depth of the fold being sufficient to bring the eyelid into its normal position by everting the border. Remove the fold of skin by cutting it with a sharp scissors and suture the wound with fine silkworm gut.

RESULTS.—Healing by first intention generally ensues ; otherwise it occurs rapidly by second intention. The desired effect is always obtained, the eye clearing up and resuming its normal appearance in a short time.

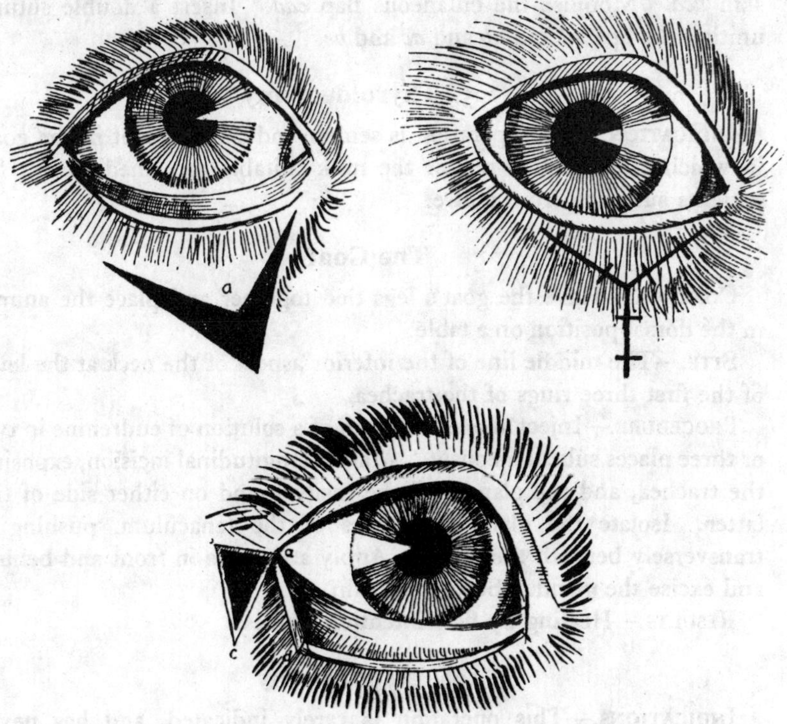

FIGS. 218 TO 220.—OPERATION FOR ECTROPION.

104. Operation for Ectropion

INDICATION.—Eversion of the eyelid, as the result of a scar on its cutaneous surface, exposing the conjunctiva to irritation.

CONTROL.—As in No. 103.

PROCEDURE.—Having injected eudrenine at the site of operation. make a V-shaped incision including the scar, with the opening of the V next the palpebral border. Separate the V-shaped flap from the underlying tissue from its apex to its base in order to mobilise it. Push the separated flap towards the palpebral border and suture the cut edges in a Y-shaped manner (see Fig. 219). It is usually the lower eyelid that is affected. Another procedure indicated when the condition is due to chronic inflammatory contraction of the lid is to excise a triangular piece from the entire thickness of the lid near the external canthus and suture the borders of the wound, or to adopt the method of Dieffenbach and Graefe as follows:

Incise the external commissure, following the line *ab*. Excise part of the everted palpebral border *ad*. Excise the triangular piece of skin *bca*. Mobilise the cutaneous flap *cad*. Insert a double suture, uniting the lips *ad* and *ab* and *ac* and *bc*.

105. Thyroidectomy

Indication.—The operation is seldom indicated except in the goat, in which it is done to render the milk suitable as a medicament for patients suffering from goitre.

The Goat

Control.—Have the goat's legs tied together and place the animal in the dorsal position on a table.

Site.—The middle line of the inferior aspect of the neck at the level of the first three rings of the trachea.

Procedure.—Inject about 1 drachm of a solution of eudrenine in two or three places subcutaneously. Make a longitudinal incision, exposing the trachea, and the glands will be easily found on either side of the latter. Isolate the gland by means of the tenaculum, pushing it transversely beneath the organ. Apply a ligature in front and behind and excise the gland. Suture the skin.

Results.—Healing by first intention ensues.

106. Nephrotomy

Indications.—This operation is rarely indicated, and has never been performed in the large animals. It has often been practised successfully and experimentally in the dog. It is indicated for renal calculi, when they cause persistent or recurrent renal colic or give rise to pyelonephritis.

Control the patient in the lateral position and administer a general anæsthetic.

Site.—There are two sites: (1) In the lumbar region, and (2) on the lower abdominal wall. No. (1) site is usually chosen, and is the only one suitable for the large animal, the incision being made in the angle between the posterior border of the last rib and the transverse process of the first lumbar vertebra, the organ being reached without penetrating the peritoneum.

PROCEDURE.—Make a cutaneous incision 2 to 4 inches long in the dog and proportionally longer in the horse. Divide the muscles carefully to the same extent. Introduce the index finger through the wound and gently push the peritoneum aside, separating it from the psoas muscles without perforating it. Enucleate the organ with the first finger and draw it outwards. Hold it between the finger and thumb, and incise it on the middle line parallel to its long curvature, exposing its pelvis. The latter may be washed out if necessary. Bleeding is fairly profuse, but does not persist as a rule in the dog. Compressing the two halves of the cut organ one against the other is generally sufficient to arrest the bleeding. Suturing the renal wound is not necessary. Finish as for laparotomy.

107. Nephrectomy : Removal of the Kidney

INDICATION.—Pyelonephritis affecting one kidney, the other one being normal.

SITE.—As in No. 106.

PROCEDURE.—As in No. 106 until the organ is exposed. Separate the kidney from its capsule, enucleating it therefrom. Draw it outwards, ligature the ureter and the renal vessels and then remove the organ. Finish as in the last operation.

In the case of a very enlarged kidney, the abdominal method of operating is more convenient in the small animals. Having removed the kidney in this way, the breach in the peritoneum should be sutured.

RESULT.—Experience has proved that the loss of one kidney causes no inconvenience to the patient, the remaining organ performing the functions of both.

108. Operation for "Crib-Biting"

INDICATION.—Loss of condition and strength of the horse consequent on the vice.

CONTROL.—Cast, chloroform, and fix in the dorsal position with the head moderately extended on the neck, making an angle of about 40° with the horizontal plane. Further extension might have the effect of rupturing the inferior laryngeal nerves by causing excessive tension thereof after section of the sterno-maxillaris muscles.

SITE.—The inferior aspect of the neck on the middle line from the body of the hyoid bone to a point about half-way down the neck, or about 12 inches from the starting-point.

PROCEDURE.—Shave the site and its vicinity on either side. Take precautions to prevent soiling and infection of the wound by having a sterilised cloth spread on the ground or bed beneath the head and neck and another cloth covering the neck with an outcut in its centre corresponding to the site of incision. Have several artery forceps ready, as the hæmorrhage will be profuse. (1) Incise the skin and subcutaneous tissue ; (2) dissect the skin from the muscles on either side as far as the upper border of the jugular furrow, taking care not to wound the jugular or submaxillary vein ; (3) divide the muscles longitudinally on the middle line to the same extent as the skin, and then proceed to resect the following muscles on each side successively : the sterno-maxillaris, the omo-hyoid, and the sterno-thyro-hyoideus ; incise the fascia sufficiently to enable the finger to be passed round the belly of the sterno-maxillaris to hold it while it is being cut transversely at the posterior extremity of the wound. Separate the severed muscle from the jugular vein by traction towards its insertion, aided if necessary by the cautious use of the scalpel. Strong forward and upward traction will expose its tendon clear of the parotid gland and the vessels in the vicinity, and enable it to be cut with safety. Deal with each of the other muscles in a similar fashion. Suture the skin. A continuous wire suture has been recommended.

RESULTS are said to be good, the desired effect being obtained in most cases.

109. Peroneal Tenotomy (Boccar's Operation)

INDICATION.—Stringhalt.

CONTROL.—It may be done standing, under local anæsthesia, using a side-line or side-fetter to control the affected limb or having the corresponding fore foot held up, but if necessary cast the horse on the opposite side with hobbles or the casting rope.

SITE.—The outer aspect of the limb below the hock, where the peroneus tendon joins that of the extensor pedis.

PROCEDURE.—Make a cutaneous incision about 1½ inches long at the level of and parallel to the tendon. Having exposed the latter, pass a tenaculum beneath it and raise it out of the wound. Sever the tendon at the upper and lower commissures of the incision, thereby excising a portion of the tendon and ensuring against reunion of its cut ends.

An alternative method is to make two short incisions over the tendon a couple of inches apart, cut the tendon at the level of each wound, and then remove the intervening portion, the advantage being that a long piece of the tendon can thus be removed without making a large cutaneous incision.

RESULT.—The desired result is obtained in the majority of cases. Recovery may be immediate or gradual, usually the latter. Daily exercise at the trot is necessary to get the best results. If it is neglected, the operation is apt to be a failure.

110. Stenson's Operation for Stricture of the Cow's Teat

INDICATION.—Stricture confined to the tip of the teat, and usually the result of direct injury.

CONTROL.—Have the cow held by the horn and nose against a paling, and have her kept close to the latter by means of a rope passed round the body and the bars of the paling in the form of a noose, or simply have her pushed against a wall.

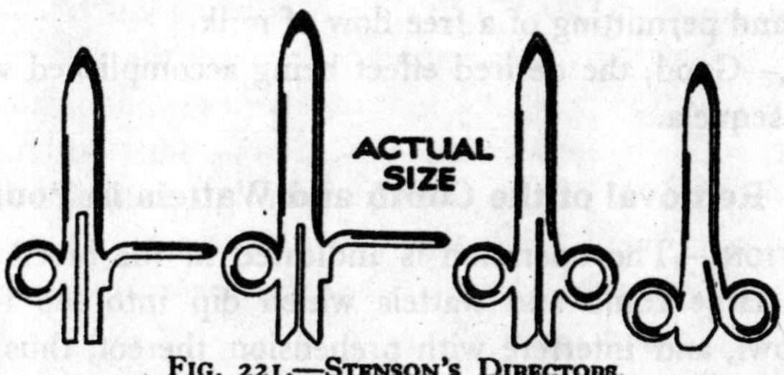

FIG. 221.—STENSON'S DIRECTORS.

PROCEDURE.—Take strict aseptic precautions. Having cleaned the teat, spray the affected part with ethyl chloride, which will act as a local anæsthetic lasting for a couple of minutes. Insert the special director into the lumen of the teat and make an incision to the depth of its groove by means of a small razor blade. Push the director into the incision, and then increase the depth of the latter by again incising in the groove of the instrument. Having completely cut the stricture in one direction, incise it to the same extent at right angles to the first incision, thus making a crucial wound across the tip of the teat. Milk the teat, and if the stricture has been properly severed the milk will be felt and seen to flow freely in a wide stream. If the milk does not flow sufficiently freely, the incision will require to be continued more deeply. When the bleeding has ceased, apply a little carbolic ointment on the wound.

RESULT.—Good, the desired effect being obtained without any complication. Mastitis does not supervene, and the stricture does not recur. Should the cow be put dry soon after the operation, the orifice may close owing to the absence of the milk flow. In such a case the operation may be repeated.

McLean of Belfast (Ireland) has invented a more convenient and simpler instrument for operating on this form of stricture. It makes the same sort of incision on being pushed through the teat orifice.

111. Hudson's Operation for Stricture of the Teat

INDICATIONS.—A membranous partition across the duct a little below the lower extremity of the galactophorous sinus, with a thickening in its centre which feels nodular when the duct is being drawn.

CONTROL.—As in last case.

PROCEDURE.—Taking the usual aseptic precautions, pierce the centre of the partition with the trocar. Pass the corkscrew instrument through the opening thus made until its convoluted part has cleared the stricture ; then draw it back sharply through the opening, thereby enlarging the latter and permitting of a free flow of milk.

RESULT.—Good, the desired effect being accomplished without any untoward sequela.

112. Removal of the Comb and Wattels in Poultry

INDICATION.—The operation is indicated in the breed of poultry with very large comb and wattels which dip into the food in the feeding bowl, and interfere with prehension thereof, thus preventing the birds thriving.

PROCEDURE.—Inject a non-toxic local anæsthetic such as eudrenine beneath the base of the comb or wattel, insert a series of Halsted sutures close together at the base of the appendage, and excise it with a sharp knife on the distal side of the sutures which have the effect of preventing hæmorrhage which would otherwise be profuse and sufficient in some cases to cause the death of the patient.

PART III

REGIONAL SURGERY

AFFECTIONS OF THE HEAD

AFFECTIONS OF THE EYE AND ITS APPENDAGES

THE EYE

Examination of the Eye

1. **Examination of the Exterior of the Eye,** using natural light and without the aid of an instrument, enables obvious abnormalities to be recognised. Take the horse to the stable door facing outwards, but not in the direct sunlight. Stand at one side of the head, looking in the same direction, and observe the general appearance of the eye. To examine it for opacities of the cornea and lens, hold a black object—a hat or a piece of felt, etc.—opposite the eye to prevent the reflection of surrounding objects and look at the organ from various angles. The animal may be blind, although the eyes appear normal. Ordinary tests for blindness are : (1) Walking the animal towards an obstacle and observing whether he tries to avoid it or walks into it ; (2) using threatening movements with the hand or an object at some distance from the eye, after awakening his attention by striking him lightly with the fingers on the face, and observing whether the gesture causes reflex movement of the eyelids ; (3) observing the effect of light on the pupil. The animal may hesitate when being walked into a house or strike against the door-posts, and shows rapid movements of his ears in his endeavour to hear what he cannot see.

2. **Exploration of the Conjunctival Culs-de-Sac** is indicated in recent inflammatory affections of the eye to ascertain if the cause of the trouble is there.

(*a*) *The Inferior Cul-de-Sac.*—Place the first two fingers on the outer aspect of the lower eyelid and draw it gently downwards.

(*b*) *The Superior Cul-de-Sac.*—This is a difficult procedure. Take hold of the ciliary border of the lid between the thumb and index finger of the left hand and draw it gently downwards and forwards, whilst the point of the right thumb depresses the middle part of the cutaneous surface of the eyelid, thereby turning the border upwards. A few drops of a 1 to 2 per cent. solution of cocaine in the eye will greatly facilitate the procedure. An eyelid dilator may be used to keep the lids apart.

3. **Examination of the Pupil** as to its response to light and the action of mydriatics and myotics. Cover the two eyes with the hands ; after a few seconds remove one hand, still keeping the other eye closed, and if the organ is normal the pupil which was dilated when in the dark will contract under the influence of the light Its dilatation and contraction will be observed on alternately closing and opening the eye for a few seconds in most animals but not in the horse. Artificial light causes dilation in the latter animal and this is taken advantage of in ophthalmoscopic work (Smith's *Vet. Phys.*). In direct sunlight the pupil of the horse is a mere narrow chink, but in ordinary diffused light it barely responds. Even when light is concentrated on

FIG. 222.—EXAMINATION OF THE EYE WITH LATERAL ARTIFICIAL LIGHT.

the eye by means of either a mirror or a lens the iris practically remains unchanged. Under the influence of artificial light it actually dilates. In all herbivora the pupil is relatively sluggish in response to the stimulus of light (Smith's *Vet. Phys.*). Atropine and cocaine are usually employed as mydriatics, and pilocarpine and eserine as myotics. A 1 per cent. aqueous solution of atropine instilled into the eye causes rapid and uniform dilation of the normal pupil. If the dilatation is irregular, adhesions are present between the iris and the cornea or the lens. It is advisable to use the atropine on one eye only at a time to avoid the possibility of its causing acute glaucoma, which, however, has so far only been observed in the human subject. Myotics are seldom employed for examination purposes.

4. **Examination of the Eye by Lateral Light** permits of the observance of even slight abnormalities in the outer structures of the eyeball which could not be detected by ordinary examination. Put the horse in a dark box and examine the eye by the aid of artificial light and a biconvex lens of about 15 diopters. The Priestly Smith or Rolland lamp may be used for the purpose. It has the advantage of combining the light and the lens in one instrument. If this lamp is not available, let an assistant hold a candle or ordinary bull's-eye lamp 12 to 20 inches from the eye to be examined, at its level and a little behind it, moving it in different directions as indicated by the observer. If the eyelids are held closed, separate them with the dilator. Stand in front of the horse and a little to one side, interpose the lens between

FIG. 223.—EXAMINATION OF THE EYE WITH DIRECT ARTIFICIAL LIGHT, USING THE OPHTHALMOSCOPE.

the light and the eye so that the distance between it and the cornea is a little less than its focal distance, thereby concentrating the luminous rays on the anterior aspect of the globe. The smaller the angle formed between the axis of the beam of light and the antero-posterior diameter of the eyeball, the more deeply does the light penetrate.

Another procedure is to simply illuminate the eye by having the light held close to it, and to interpose the lens between the horse's eye and the observer's eye, thereby magnifying opacities that may be present on the cornea or crystalline lens. A still more effective method is to use two lenses, one between the light and the horse's eye and the other between the latter and the observer's eye.

5. **Examination of the Depth of the Eye with the Ophthalmoscope**—(1) *Examination by Direct Light*—(*a*) *Using Artificial Light.*—Take the horse into a dark box, have the light held at the level of the

opposite ear, stand on the production forwards of a line from the base of the opposite ear to the supra-orbital process of the eye to be examined. Hold the rim of the ophthalmoscope resting on your eyebrow, and by means of it project the light through the pupil into the depth of the eye, which is then brilliantly illuminated. Opacities of the crystalline lens and floating bodies in the vitreous humour are readily recognised. Opacities intercepting the rays of light at their

FIG. 224.—EXAMINATION OF THE DEPTH OF THE EYE BY DIRECT DAYLIGHT WITH THE OPHTHALMOSCOPE.

level appear as dark spots on the perfectly clean field formed by the illuminated retina. The nearer the instrument is held to the patient's eye, the better for detailed examination. A more convenient way of examining the depth of the eye with artificial light is by means of a special ophthalmoscope carrying an electric bulb which provides the illumination.

(*b*) *Using Natural Light*.—Take the horse to the stable door, or under an awning, or in the shade of a tree, so that there is a comparatively dark background. Stand at the side of the horse's neck, turn his head towards you so that the eye to be examined is in the shade, looking backwards. Use the ophthalmoscope or retinoscope as in (*a*), reflecting the light from the sky into the eye and avoiding direct sunlight. It is an advantage to instil a few drops of atropine into the eye about an hour beforehand in order to dilate the pupil, and thus facilitate the examination. Both (*a*) and (*b*) are good practical methods of examining the eye, the former affording a clearer definition of its depth.

(2) *Examination by Indirect Light.*—Proceed as in No. (1) (*a*), but in addition interpose a biconvex lens between the horse's eye and the ophthalmoscope. This method is not suitable for veterinary practice.

Examination of the eye by lateral light with the lens and by direct light with ophthalmoscope constitute two good methods of examining the eye for cataract, corneal opacities, etc.

Appearance of the Depth of the Eye.—*In the horse* there are seen :

(1) *The tapetum lucidum*, recognised by its brilliant colouring, varying in tint in different subjects, being usually greenish or bluish, the former being commonly the case in old and the latter in young horses. The colour, however, may be clearer, or yellowish, or variegated, with spots of a deeper green or blue, or, more rarely, pink hue.

(2) *The tapetum nigrum*, situated inferiorly, and separated from (1) by a horizontal line.

(3) *The papilla*, appearing just below the line of separation between (1) and (2). On the sides of and just above the papilla the pigment of the tapetum nigrum is less dense, and allows the green or bluish tint to appear through it. In the papilla there are three zones—viz. : (1) A peripheral whitish zone, representing the sheath of the optic nerve ; (2) a central yellowish-white zone, having the appearance of a star-shaped cicatrix, and showing near its centre two or three small red spots in which can be distinguished a network of capillaries ; (3) an intermediary zone traversed by fine capillaries.

The vessels of the retina, which generally emerge from the periphery of the papilla, are most numerous on its lateral aspects. They are flexuous, often double, and branched, but they do not anastomose.

In the ox the tapetum lucidum is of a beautiful green colour and devoid of all spots. The tapetum nigrum is not so dark as in the horse, and is situated very low down. The papilla is small, whitish, irregular, and not well circumscribed. The bloodvessels emanate from its centre in three groups, the veins being large and blackish and the arteries less voluminous and clearer in colour.

In the dog the tapetum lucidum varies in tinge. Usually it is yellowish in the centre and green at its periphery, but it may be blue or red with green spots. The tapetum nigrum is of a more or less deep brown colour. It may be marbled in its upper part, showing in parts tints of the tapetum lucidum. Sometimes the pigmentation is slight, and allows the red colour and the vessels of the choroid to be seen. The papilla may be situated in the tapetum lucidum or nigrum, or between the two. It varies in form, and the retinal bloodvessels come from its centre.

Refraction

When the refracting media of the eye are at fault, the subject is affected either with short sight (*myopia*), due to the image being formed in front of the retina, or long sight (*hypermetropia*), due to its being formed behind the retina. These defects can be remedied in the human subject by means of spectacles. Normal vision is known as *emmetropia*, and abnormal vision as *ametropia*.

Astigmatism is an abnormal condition of the eye, due to the refracting surfaces of the cornea and lens not having the same curvature in all their meridians.

These errors of refraction are probably the cause of shying in horses whose eyes appear quite normal.

Congenital Anomalies

These comprise :

1. **Anophthalmia.**—Complete absence of eyeballs, although the eyelids may be present.

2. **Cryptophthalmia.**—Incomplete development of the organs, with or without a palpebral fissure.

3. **Cyclopia.**—The presence of one eye only, situated on the middle line of the head.

Exophthalmia (Abnormal Protrusion of the Eyeball)

Etiology.—Any swelling occurring behind the orbit and tending to push it out of its cavity—*e.g.*, a hæmatoma, abscess, or tumour developing behind the eyeball. Pekingese and Japanese spaniels have normally very protruding eyes.

Treatment consists in removing the cause as far as possible.

Enophthalmia (Retraction of the Eyeball in the Orbital Cavity)

This may be congenital or the result of the absorption of the fat at the back of the orbit. It occurs spasmodically in tetanus, accompanied by protrusion of the membrana nictitans. Hamilton Kirk records a case (*Vet. Rec.*, Oct. 18th, 1947) of a greyhound that was brought to his notice as having lost an eye as the result of an accident at a stadium. There was no sign of an eye in one of the orbits, its floor showing only the membrana nictitans, and he inserted his thumb into the apparently empty orbit. As the eyeball could not be found and there was no hæmorrhage, he lifted the membrana with a forceps, and about $\frac{1}{8}$ inch of the cornea could be seen in the post-orbital fat. In 36 hours, the eye came forward, and after 2 days it was normal. There was no untoward sequel.

Applications for the Eye

The following applications are suitable for the various inflammatory conditions of the eye :

1. Antiseptic Lotions :

(1) Boric acid, 2 to 3 per cent.
(2) Perchloride or cyanide of mercury, 1 in 5,000.
(3) Chinosol, 1 in 2,000.
(4) Collargol, 2½ to 5 per cent.
(5) Dakin's solution.
(6) Argyrol.
(7) Cod liver oil which has been found to be a wonderfully effective application for traumatic lesions and those due to burns by sparks. (See *Vet. Rec.*, May 22nd, 1937.)
(8) Solution of penicillin.

2. Astringent Lotions :

(1) Zinc sulphate, 2 to 4 grains to the ounce.
(2) Nitrate of silver, same strength.

An excellent prescription for an inflamed eye is :

℞ Zinc. sulph.	grs. ii. to iv.
Extract. belladon. vir.	grs. x. to xx.
Aquæ	ad ℥i.

Lotion may be introduced into the eye by means of cotton-wool soaked therein, or by means of a pen-filler or small syringe, or it may be splashed in from a bottle. The salts of mercury used on the eye are incompatible with iodides given internally, the iodide being partly excreted by the tears and forming with the mercurial salt, especially calomel, an iodide of mercury which is extremely irritant and painful, and capable of perforating the eye.

3. **Mydriatics :**

   (1) Sulphate of atropine, 2 to 6 grains to the ounce.
   (2) Cocaine hydrochloride, 1 to 2 per cent.

4. **Myotics :**

   (1) Salicylate of eserine, 1 to 2 grains to the ounce.
   (2) Nitrate of pilocarpine, 1 to 2 grains to the ounce.

5. **Local Anæsthetics :**

   (1) Cocaine, 1 to 2 per cent.
   (2) Eudrenine.
   (3) Phenolaine No. (1) is the best.

Numbers 3, 4, and 5 are applied in small quantity or in the form of drops.

6. **Ointments :**

   (1) Yellow oxide of mercury, 1 in 50 to 1 in 25 of vaseline.
   (2) Oculentum iodoformi B.P. 1932 (4 per cent. sterile base).
   (3) Penicillin ointment.

7. **Anodynes :**

   (1) Green extract of belladonna, 10 to 20 grains to the ounce.
   (2) Warm decoction of poppy-heads which is soothing for an acutely inflamed eye.

Protection of the Eye

It is necessary to take precautions against an animal rubbing or scratching its eye when inflamed or wounded. The horse can be tied on the pillar reins, and in the horse and dog a special shield fitting over the eye may be used.

Traumatic Lesions

LUXATION and AVULSION of the eyeball—*i.e.*, displacement forwards from its socket.

ETIOLOGY.—Violent pressure exerted on the organ from its supero-posterior aspect—*e.g.*, a foreign body insinuated between the eyeball and the posterior wall of the orbital cavity. In dogs with prominent eyes it occurs easily—as the result of a scratch from a cat, fighting with other dogs, or pressure with the hands on the head when holding the animal while it struggles.

The term *avulsion* is applied when the optic nerve is ruptured, and *luxation* when it is merely stretched.

TREATMENT.—When called early before the eye is much altered, endeavour to reduce it. Bathe the organ gently with a suitable warm antiseptic lotion, separate the eyelids, and by methodical pressure on the globe in the direction of its antero-posterior axis return it to its place. A little castor oil or liquid paraffin applied on the surface of the eye facilitates its reduction. It may be necessary to incise the external canthus or to anæsthetise the patient.

To maintain the organ in position, unite the palpebral borders by one or two sutures and leave them in position for twenty-four to forty-eight hours. Sometimes the eye regains its normal condition rapidly; at other times severe inflammation ensues, for which treatment proves of no avail, and then the organ must be extirpated. Extirpation is always indicated immediately when the eyeball is hopelessly injured.

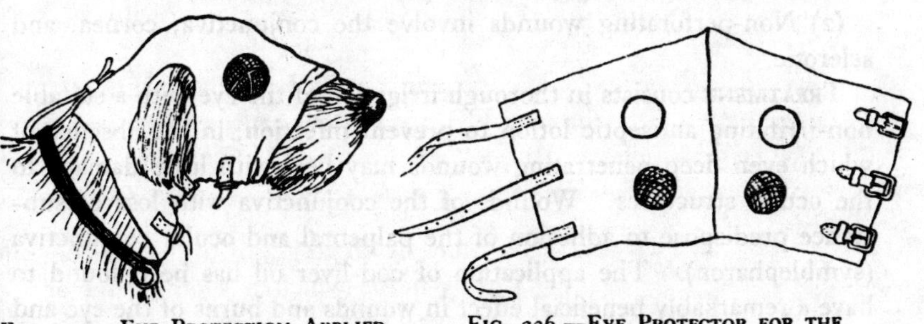

FIG. 225.—EYE PROTECTION APPLIED ON THE DOG.

FIG. 226.—EYE PROTECTOR FOR THE DOG.

Contusion of the Eyeball

ETIOLOGY.—Blows inflicted thereon.

SYMPTOMS vary according to the severity of the injury. The most constant lesion is subconjunctival ecchymosis, which gradually disappears in ten to fifteen days after giving rise to the usual diversified coloration as seen in the non-pigmented skin. Blood may accumulate in the anterior chamber, constituting hypohæmia. Erosions of the cornea, rupture of the iris, luxation of the lens, and tearing of the choroid and retina are possible results. The sclerotic or, more rarely, the cornea may be ruptured, allowing escape of the aqueous humour, the lens, and the vitreous body.

TREATMENT consists in applying the usual antiseptic and antiphlogistic eye lotions, which should be used cold at first to favour hæmostasis, and warm later to promote absorption of extravasated blood and exudate. In slight cases, blood in the anterior chamber becomes absorbed.

Puncturing the cornea to effect its removal is seldom indicated. It might open the way for infection to set up panophthalmia. When the coats of the eyeball are ruptured, strict antisepsis is necessary to prevent this septic complication. In such cases the organ is disorganised and ceases to function.

Open Wounds of the Eyeball

These may be (1) penetrating or (2) non-penetrating.

ETIOLOGY.—Injuries by pointed or sharp bodies, barbed wire, nails, glass, sharp stones, shot, etc.

(1) Penetrating wounds involve the iris, lens, choroid, or retina, and may be accompanied by hypohæmia, escape of the aqueous humour, or hernia of the iris (staphyloma). The worst form of injury is penetration of a foreign body into the depth of the eye.

(2) Non-perforating wounds involve the conjunctiva, cornea, and sclerotic.

TREATMENT consists in thorough irrigation of the eye with a suitable non-irritating antiseptic lotion to prevent infection, in the absence of which even deep penetrating wounds may heal with little damage to the ocular structures. Wounds of the conjunctiva with loss of substance predispose to adhesion of the palpebral and ocular conjunctiva (symblepharon). The application of cod-liver oil has been found to have a remarkably beneficial effect in wounds and burns of the eye and its appendages and has the advantages also of being protective and lubricant, preventing symblepharon in the case mentioned. In its absence castor oil or olive oil is a good substitute. Incised wounds of the sclerotic may be sutured with fine needle and thread. If the iris is prolapsed, the treatment is that for staphyloma.

Burns

Burns are caused by flames, sparks, and by caustic agents.

TREATMENT.—Wash the eye immediately with cold water and afterwards apply the usual antiseptic lotions. Cod liver oil is specially recommended. When caused by an acid, use a 1 per cent. cold solution of bicarbonate of soda ; and when due to an alkali, employ a slightly acidulated lotion. Burns by lime may be treated with a solution of sugar to dissolve any lime in the eye, as well as by repeated irrigation with boiled water.

Foreign Bodies in the Eye

These comprise hay seeds, chaff, grains of sand, hair, insects, and grains of shot, etc. Usually they are located in one of the conjunctival culs-de-sac or embedded in the cornea. Sometimes they are situated deeply in the eye—in the anterior chamber, the iris, lens, or vitreous humour.

Diagnosis.—It is often difficult to detect a foreign body in the eye, owing to the resentment of the animal to its examination, its retraction, and the obstacles offered by closure of the lids and the protrusion of the membrana. The instillation of an anæsthetic, eversion of the lids, the use of a dilator, and controlling the membrana by a piece of silk passed through it, serving to hold it, are methods of aiding the procedure. The use of lateral and direct light by means of the lens and ophthalmoscope may enable foreign bodies in the back of the eye to be recognised, provided that they are not concealed by the iris.

Treatment consists in extracting the foreign body and applying an eye lotion afterwards. The foreign body may be extracted as follows, after anæsthetising the eye with a 2 to 4 per cent. solution of cocaine or other anæsthetic:

1. Use a small blunt instrument such as a probe to dislodge it.

2. Flush out the foreign body with warm sterilised water or boric solution.

3. When a piece of chaff is fixed on the surface of the cornea, it may be extracted with a dissecting forceps, when it comes into view, but this is often difficult owing to the movements of the eyeball. It may be more easily removed by passing the ball of the index finger over the eyeball and exerting gentle pressure on it, the piece of chaff coming away on the finger or being pushed out between the eyelids. A curved suture needle may be used to rupture the film covering a piece of chaff on the cornea and to lift it out.

4. If the offending body is more or less deeply embedded in the cornea, it may be possible to extract it with a forceps. If not, the cornea may be incised slightly at the level of the object with a Graefe knife, and the corneal needle then introduced and used to push the body from within outwards and make it project, so that it can be grasped and removed. This is a delicate operation not likely to be undertaken by the average veterinarian. It would be necessary to have the animal cast and anæsthetised for the purpose.

5. When the foreign body is lodged in the anterior chamber, it is necessary to make a small incision towards the inferior border of the cornea with Graefe's knife, when it may escape with the aqueous humour, or be extracted with a forceps, or drawn out with a blunt curette. A foreign body in the iris may be removed with a portion of the latter by performing iridectomy. When the sclerotic is the seat

of lodgment, extraction may be easy. When the lens or vitreous body is the part involved, an oculist might incise the sclerotic and take out the foreign body with a forceps, but the ordinary practitioner would not attempt such an operation. In any case, where a foreign body is so deeply embedded that it cannot be reached it is usual to leave it alone. If aseptic, it may be tolerated and do no harm; but if suppuration ensues, the eyeball must be either evacuated or removed unless the foreign body is comparatively superficial in situation, when it may be extruded with the pus.

6. Metallic objects may be removed by the use of a magnet.

Any of the applications recommended may be used daily until the traumatic inflammation has subsided. Protection from the light by keeping the patient in a dark place is also indicated.

Conjunctivitis (Inflammation of the Conjunctiva)

Etiology comprises (1) *external injury* (open wounds, contusion, foreign bodies, smoke, gases, dust, etc.); (2) entropion and ectropion, leading to injury and exposure of the conjunctiva; (3) bacterial disease, the condition occurring in the course of influenza in the horse and distemper in the dog; a diphtheritic conjunctivitis is common in birds.

Conjunctivitis has often been seen in an enzootic form in horses of a troop, where it may be contagious or the result of all the animals being exposed to the same cause, such as dust, when on the march.

Symptoms.—The following forms have been distinguished:

1. *Catarrhal conjunctivitis*, the commonest form, and characterised by a mucoid or muco-purulent discharge and congestion of the blood-vessels. The swollen mucous membrane may extend above the level of the cornea, constituting *chemosis* and that of the eyelids may protrude beyond their borders.

2. *Diphtheritic conjunctivitis*, recognised by the presence of false membranes adherent to the ocular mucous membrane.

3. *Purulent conjunctivitis*, in which the inflammation is more severe and the discharge distinctly purulent. Chemosis may be very marked.

4. *Follicular conjunctivitis*, seen occasionally in the dog, and whose characteristic lesion is hypertrophy of the lymphatic follicles, indicated by the presence of small, red, round swellings most marked on the inner aspect of the membrana nictitans.

5. *Granular conjunctivitis*, met with in warm countries, and especially in marshy districts, characterised by the development of yellowish granulations containing the *Filaria irritans*, and by the presence of

ulcers, both lesions being most numerous in the conjunctival culs-de-sac, especially the upper one.

6. *Vesicular conjunctivitis*, occurring in eruptive diseases—*e.g.*, horse-pox, aphthous fever.

7. *Parasitic conjunctivitis*, affecting the horse, ox, camel, and dog, but rarely seen, and due to a nematode (Thelazia); also a form in birds caused by oxyspirum.

TREATMENT comprises:

1. *Suppression of the Cause.*—This is obviously the first indication.

2. *The application of warm antiseptic eye lotions*—*e.g.*, boracic acid 1 to 2 per cent., perchloride of mercury 1 in 4,000 or 5,000, two or three times daily, which have an excellent effect. Thorough flushing of the conjunctival culs-de-sac is indicated to remove ocular discharge or any foreign matter that may be present.

For *chronic conjunctivitis* the following applications are indicated: Zinc sulphate, 2 to 4 grains to the ounce; silver nitrate, 2 to 4 grains to the ounce; yellow oxide of mercury ointment in the proportion of 2 per cent. of vaseline, or the latter containing 2 per cent. cocaine.

3. The use of *silver nitrate* in 1 to 2 per cent. solution for the purulent form of the affection, on which it has an excellent effect. Having washed the eye with an ordinary mild lotion, the eyelids are everted and the silver solution is painted on the conjunctiva. The excess is then neutralised with saline solution. When the pain is severe, cocaine may be instilled.

4. Astringent lotions—sulphate of zinc, silver nitrate—are indicated for follicular conjunctivitis.

5. Excision of the membrana nictitans is indicated for follicular conjunctivitis when it has failed to respond to other measures. In some cases in which the condition is confined to hypertrophy of the Harderian gland, which then appears as a red bead in the inner canthus, excision of the latter is sufficient (see Tumours of the Membrana).

6. In granular conjunctivitis, cauterisation of the granulations with a crystal of copper sulphate every other day is indicated, the eye being frequently bathed with boric solution in the meantime. When the case is of long standing, the larger granulations may be removed with a curette under the influence of cocaine. This form of the disease is practically unknown in veterinary practice.

7. *Diphtheritic conjunctivitis* is treated by removal of the false membranes and by the application of a solution of corrosive sublimate or cresyl. Prophylactic measures are necessary to prevent spread of the disease.

8. Verminous conjunctivitis is treated by flushing out the worms with an antiseptic solution.

9. *Protection from the light* is always indicated by keeping the patient in a dark place or covering the eye by a shade. The latter requires a contrivance in the form of a head-piece provided with a wire shield over the eye, which can be covered with green baize.

10. See Applications for the eye (p. 497).

Non-Inflammatory Conditions

1. **Chemosis** disappears with the inflammation which accompanies it. Scarification is seldom necessary.

2. **Pterygium,** thickening of the conjunctiva, and encroachment thereof on the cornea in the form of a triangular process with its apex towards the centre of the cornea, is occasionally met with in the dog.

TREATMENT consists in instilling eudrenine into the eye, catching the process with a forceps, and shaving it off carefully by means of a Graefe knife or a razor-blade. If it has not reached the level of the pupil, it causes no inconvenience and need not be interfered with. The author has seen a form of this condition affecting both eyes in a 5 years old thoroughbred brood mare without any evidence of inflammation and cresentic in shape, which responded to a course of treatment with binoidide of mercury, internally.

AFFECTIONS OF THE CORNEA

Keratitis (Inflammation of the Cornea)

ETIOLOGY.—The causes are the same as those mentioned for conjunctivitis, with which it is frequently associated.

Varieties of Keratitis.—1. *Superficial keratitis*, confined to the epithelium and the superficial layers of the cornea, with faint blurring of its surface.

2. *Vascular keratitis, or pannus*, characterised by the formation of capillaries between the epithelium and Bowman's membrane.

3. *Spotted keratitis*, characterised by blurring of the cornea and the appearance of greyish- or yellowish-white spots here and there on the corneal surface capable of undergoing ulceration.

4. *Parenchymatous keratitis*, recognised by diffuse infiltration of the layers of the cornea with leucocytes, giving it a whitish, greyish, or yellowish appearance, and by a new formation of capillaries radiating from its periphery towards its centre.

5. *Deep keratitis*, or descemetitis, associated with iridocyclitis, in which an inflammatory deposit is formed on Descemet's membrane.

6. *Suppurative keratitis*, characterised by the formation of ulcers on and abscesses in the cornea. There may be complete purulent infiltration of the structure, or the abscess may be circumscribed and rounded in form or in the shape of an arc of a circle (onyx). It generally opens externally, but may burst into the anterior chamber, constituting one form of *hypopyon*.

SYMPTOMS comprise photophobia (fear of light), closure of the eyelids, weeping, pain on exploration, alteration of the appearance of the cornea, depending on the form that is present. There is always more or less opacity of the cornea, and when it has become vascular the superficial vessels can be seen growing in from the conjunctiva and the deep vessels from the sclerotic.

TREATMENT comprises :

1. The use of *warm antiseptic lotions*, as recommended for conjunctivitis.

2. *Insufflation of calomel* after the acute symptoms have subsided. Its object is to stimulate absorption of the cellular exudate, and thus clear up the cornea.

3. The introduction of *yellow oxide of mercury ointment* 1 in 20 for the same purpose as No. 2.

4. Syndectomy or circumcision of a narrow band of conjunctiva round the periphery of the cornea, which has been recommended for pannus, the operation being performed under the influence of cocaine. The application of an infusion of jequirity or paternoster bean has been recommended to set up irritation and bring about absorption of the pannus.

5. Warm moist antiseptic lotions or compresses, indicated for the purulent form of the disease. Hydrogen peroxide 1 in 4 or 5 may be employed. Dionine, a morphine derivative in 5 per cent. solution, has been recommended. It causes vascular dilatation with chemosis and a flow of lymph. It is instilled on alternate days.

6. *Instillation of atropine* in 1 per cent. solution, to be used when iritis is present or suspected, and when an ulcer is situated towards the centre of the cornea, in order to keep the iris away from this region, and thus ward off anterior synechia (adhesion of the anterior surface of the iris to the cornea) and possible protrusion of the iris should the ulcer perforate the cornea. Atropine causes increase in the intraocular tension and may thus be objected to in case of deep ulceration on the ground that it favours rupture of Descemet's membrane.

7. Instillation of eserine or pilocarpine when a marginal ulcer is present, for the same reason. Avoid the prolonged use of eserine as it favours iritis.

8. Puncture of an abscess with a Graefe knife or hot needle.

A contagious form of keratitis associated with conjunctivitis of a severe nature has been met with on the Continent affecting chiefly bovines. Prophylactic measures are very important when dealing with an outbreak.

Ulcers of the Cornea

Ulcers of the cornea may be (1) atonic or non-inflammatory, (2) inflammatory.

(1) Atonic ulcers arise from lack of nutrition in the cornea, and may be seen in old dogs apart from any inflammation.

(2) Inflammatory ulcers have already been alluded to as a result of keratitis.

Ulcers vary in depth from mere desquamation of the epithelium to deep outcuts which may eventually involve Descemet's membrane and lead to perforation into the anterior chamber. It is sometimes difficult to make out exactly the area of an ulcer. The instillation of a little solution of fluorescine will colour the ulcer a vivid green, and enable its full extent to be easily recognised.

Possible COMPLICATIONS of corneal ulcers are:

1. *Opacity of the cornea.*—This ensues when the ulcer has destroyed some of the corneal fibrous tissue, the latter being always replaced by white fibrous tissue, which causes a permanent opacity.

2. *Keratocele*—that is, a protrusion of Descemet's membrane beyond the surface of the cornea, owing to erosion of the superficial layers of the latter.

3. *Corneal fistula*, which ensues when Descemet's membrane ruptures. This may heal without complication or be followed by the next conditions mentioned.

4. *Anterior synechia*, or adhesion of the iris to the cornea at the seat of rupture.

5. *Staphyloma*, or protrusion of the iris through the ruptured cornea. When only a portion of the iris protrudes the staphyloma is partial, but when it occupies the whole corneal region it is complete.

TREATMENT OF CORNEAL ULCERS AND THEIR COMPLICATIONS.—1. The recent ulcer is to be treated with the usual warm antiseptic eye lotions. Warm boric solution applied every three hours and followed by one application at night of collargol (1 in 30 or 40) has a good effect.

2. The insufflation of calomel is a well-known effective remedy for most ulcers that are slow to heal.

3. Atropine is indicated when there is iritis, as it keeps the organ

at rest and favours resolution, and when the ulcer is central, as described before (see Keratitis). Eserine must be employed when the ulcer is marginal.

4. Cauterisation of the surface of the ulcer with silver nitrate often has the desired effect, but it has the disadvantage that it may cause perforation when the ulcer is deep. The excess of caustic must be neutralised with normal saline solution.

5. Touching the ulcer with a hot needle has been practised by oculists in the human subject with good results. It has the same objection as No. 4.

6. Puncturing the cornea through the ulcer with a special needle or an ordinary surgical needle held in a forceps seems to have a beneficial effect in promoting healing. It also diminishes the pressure behind the ulcer by the removal of the aqueous humour, and thus lessens the risk of keratocele (protrusion of Descemet's membrane) and rupture thereof. The puncture closes spontaneously, but may be reopened with an ophthalmic probe if necessary. Strict aseptic precautions are essential.

7. When keratocele is present, continue the antiseptic lotions and instil atropine or eserine according as the lesion is central or marginal. Stimulate healing by insufflating calomel. Puncture the swelling formed by the keratocele as described in No. 6 to prevent its rupture.

Staphyloma

When the staphyloma is small, perform iridectomy of the protruding portion and instil atropine or eserine according to its situation. Iridectomy is performed by grasping the protruding iris with a forceps, and cutting it off on a level with the corneal surface. An alternative procedure, which often proves satisfactory, is to cauterise the protrusion with silver nitrate. Continue the use of a solution of sulphate of zinc and belladonna extract until the inflammation subsides. An opacity of the cornea always ensues at the seat of the lesion known as adherent leucoma.

Opacities of the Cornea

Opacities of the cornea may be congenital, but they usually result from some form of keratitis or of a wound of the cornea. There are three degrees of opacity: (1) Nebula, a slight blurring of the surface; (2) albugo, a more dense opacity; and (3) leucoma, a very dense opacity.

TREATMENT consists in applying an irritant to the eye to stimulate the circulation and promote the absorption of the exudate causing the opacity. The daily insufflation of calomel for a few days is very efficacious. When the opacity is due to the formation of new fibrous tissue, no treatment will have any effect. The white colour may be got rid of by tattooing the opacity with china ink, which is performed, after cocainising the eye, by pricking the part with needles dipped in the ink.

Formston (London) has used, with success in the dog, the following subconjunctival injections advised by Nesfield for leucoma and other corneal opacities :

Phenolaine ♏II
Sterile tap water ad ℥I

20 to 40 minims of the solution being injected by means of an intradermal syringe carrying a fine Schimmel's needle.

The technique consists in gripping the conjunctiva by a fixation forceps to steady the eyeball and inserting the needle beneath the conjunctiva after instilling a solution of cocaine. It is repeated at intervals of ten to fourteen days if necessary, until the desired effect is obtained. Under this treatment, dense opacities of some months' standing have disappeared. It is difficult to understand how this could effect the removal of fibrous opacities.

A certain amount of success in the restoration of sight has been attained in human surgery by excision of the opaque corneal tissue, and its replacement by a graft of transparent corneal tissue taken from a human eye which had just been removed from another patient on account of an ocular lesion, the graft being kept in position above and below and on either side by sutures inserted in the cornea of the affected eye and tied over the graft.

Corneal grafting has been done successfully in experiments on rabbits.

AFFECTIONS OF THE IRIS AND THE CHOROID

Persistence of the Pupillary Membrane has been seen in the horse, ox, and dog in the form of threads, bands, or plaques of greyish tissue attached to the iris. It may cause interference with vision. It may become absorbed and disappear. If necessary, proceed as for iridectomy and remove it.

Enlarged Corpora Nigra.—Rarely these are so large that they cause amblyopia. This is proved by instilling atropine, when the symptoms of defective vision disappear owing to the dilatation of the pupil.

Iritis

The choroid, ciliary body, and iris are usually affected simultaneously, but iritis is generally the predominating lesion.

ETIOLOGY.—The condition is usually the result of the action of the toxin of a bacterial disease from which the patient is suffering (influenza in the horse, distemper in the dog, and gangrenous coryza in the ox). The commonest cause, however, in the horse is specific ophthalmia. It may, of course, be a sequel to severe injury to the eye.

SYMPTOMS.—There is intense inflammation of the eye. The iris is altered in colour, becoming yellowish or brownish ; the aqueous humour becomes opaque, or seems replaced by inflammatory exudate, due to the migration of leucocytes from the vessels of the iris, constituting *hypopyon*. The pupil is contracted and adhesions are present between the iris and the cornea (anterior synechia), and between the iris and the lens (posterior synechia). A subacute or chronic form of the disease may be met with, causing only slight symptoms. There is a tendency to recurrence of the condition, and after repeated attacks the animal's vision is impaired or lost altogether. One severe attack might be sufficient to have this effect.

TREATMENT.—Prompt intervention is necessary to prevent synechia, by the frequent instillation of a solution of atropine. If this becomes irritant, solutions of duboisine or scopolamine (1 in 200) may be tried. If the pupil fails to dilate under the influence of atropine, it is an indication that firm adhesions have formed. The use of the drug must be continued until all inflammatory symptoms have disappeared, being instilled at increasing intervals as the disease improves during a period of several weeks. Nicolas advises subconjunctival injections of cyanide of mercury (1 in 200) in addition to treatment with atropine. Internally salicylate of soda and quinine may be administered. Calomel by the mouth and pilocarpine hypodermically are also indicated to promote absorption of inflammatory exudate.

OPERATIVE TREATMENT comprises (1) puncture or paracentesis of the cornea, (2) iridectomy.

(1) **Puncture of the Cornea** is performed to permit of the escape of inflammatory exudate from the anterior chamber. The most convenient site in the horse is the periphery of the cornea at the level of the inner or outer canthus, but in the dog the inferior border of the cornea can be easily reached, and is the best site, being dependent.

PROCEDURE.—Anæsthetise the eye and separate the eyelids with the speculum. Taking strict aseptic precautions, seize the conjunctiva with a forceps at the site of operation in order to steady the eyeball. Introduce the special narrow-bladed knife through the cornea parallel to the iris, and the contents of the chamber will then escape. Protect the eye with a dressing for a few days.

(2) **Iridectomy, or Partial Excision of the Iris**—INDICATIONS. To form a new pupil in cases of corneal opacity, occlusion of the pupil. and cataract ; and also as a remedy for glaucoma, iritis, and irido-choroiditis, and for rupturing a synechia.

SITE.—Usually towards the upper third of the cornea, where the incision will be hidden by the eyelid, or in the case of synechia at the level of the latter.

PROCEDURE.—Use local or general anæsthesia, and separate the eyelids with the dilator. Incise the cornea with the Graefe knife, introduce the iridectomy forceps, and seize the iris ; draw it gently outside the wound, and remove a portion of it by means of the iridectomy scissors. Apply a suitable lotion, and cover the eye with a protective dressing for twenty-four hours. Apply an antiseptic lotion and instil atropine daily for a few days. A posterior synechia may be ruptured by traction by means of a Weber hook inserted between the posterior aspect of the iris and the lens.

Choroiditis

Choroiditis is recognised by the aid of the ophthalmoscope by changes in the depth of the eye, where a dirty yellowish exudate appears scattered over its surface. This is known as diffuse choroiditis. Another form designated as disseminated choroiditis is characterised by the presence of vari-coloured spots on the tapetum nigrum, but chiefly below and on the sides of the papilla. Some authorities believe that this disease gives rise to shying in horses, while others are of opinion that it causes no interference with vision.

TREATMENT consists in promoting absorption by the administration of laxative and absorbent medicine, including the subcutaneous injection of pilocarpine. Salicylate of soda and iodides are indicated.

Periodic, Specific, or Recurrent Ophthalmia (Moon Blindness, Fluxion Périodique)

The occurrence of the disease was once believed to have some relation to certain phases of the moon, hence the term " moon blindness." It is a disease affecting all the structures of the eye, but characterised chiefly by iritis or iridocyclitis. The condition is common in the horse, but rare in other animals. It seems to be favoured by bad hygienic surroundings.

Etiology.—The exact cause of the disease has not been discovered. It occurs most commonly in marshy, low-lying districts. Heredity has been blamed. It has also been looked upon as a rheumatoid affection. One recent investigator claimed to have discovered the cause of the malady in the form of a bacillus present in the optic nerve, and which he called the *Bacillus nervi*, but this has not been accepted as correct. Specific ophthalmia has often appeared as an enzootic in cavalry regiments, affecting from 5 to 35 per cent. of the horses and terminating in blindness in most cases. It was very prevalent in France during the First World War.

Symptoms.—The disease follows a course which may be arbitrarily divided into three periods.

First Period.—This is characterised by acute inflammation—weeping, photophobia, swelling of the eyelids, injection and infiltration of the conjunctiva, turbidity of the aqueous humour and of the cornea. The onset of the disease is sudden. The horse may be perfectly normal, say, at night, and found in the morning showing the symptoms mentioned, giving the impression that the eye had met with some severe accident in the meantime. There may be a slight febrile reaction.

Second Period.—The acute symptoms of the first period have attenuated, the turbidity of the anterior chamber becomes more marked, yellowish flakes of fibrin appear in the aqueous humour and gravitate towards the lower part of the chamber, forming hypopyon. The deposit may be tinged with red, due to the presence of red blood corpuscles. The eye now becomes more transparent, but the iris shows a greyish or dead-leaf appearance and remains contracted.

Third Period.—During this period there is some recurrence of the acute inflammation, with renewed cloudiness of the aqueous humour, but the deposit in the chamber gradually becomes absorbed. After a few days the eye clears up and the inflammation disappears. The attack has terminated after a duration of about three weeks.

The course of the trouble varies in intensity in different cases, and does not always show all the features depicted in the three periods. An almost constant sequel of the disease, irrespective of the acuteness of the attack, is adhesion of the iris to the lens (posterior synechia).

Repeated attacks of the affection cause lesions of the lens, choroid, and retina, and eventually atrophy of the eye accompanied by deformity of the eyelids, especially the upper one, which becomes wrinkled. The commissures of the eyelids become more acute and the eyeball looks smaller. The lesion of the lens is in the form of a cataract or opacity. The two eyes are usually affected alternately, but sometimes both are attacked simultaneously.

Diagnosis depends on the suddenness of the attack without any evidence or history of an external injury to the eye ; the exudate in the anterior chamber ; the alterations in the iris ; contraction of the pupil and its resistance to the action of atropine. Pressure on the upper part of the orbit may cause sudden and violent reaction on the part of the patient. During the intervals between attacks the aftermath of previous occurrences of the affection may be seen in the changes already alluded to. Although posterior synechia may ensue from iritis of traumatic or toxic origin, one is always justified in suspecting periodic fluxion as the cause of the condition, the other causes rarely having this sequel.

Prevention consists in avoiding what has appeared to be the cause of the trouble.

Treatment.—There is no specific remedy for the disease. The measures to be adopted comprise those already mentioned in connection with conjunctivitis, keratitis, and iridocyclitis. Good results have been claimed for the administration internally of calomel and iodide of potassium, the latter being repeated daily until iodism appears.

Locally, chief reliance is placed on the instillation of atropine to prevent synechia and closure of the pupil.

AFFECTIONS OF THE LENS

Dislocation of the Lens

This has been seen in the horse, ox, dog, and cat, but most frequently in the horse. Generally speaking it is not a common condition, but Wright recorded fifteen cases in the dog during twelve months in the free clinique of the Royal Veterinary College, London.

It is usually unilateral but may be bilateral. It was bilateral in six of Wright's cases.

The congenital form is always bilateral and symmetrical, the lens being diverted upwards and slightly outwards.

The presence of fibres still connecting the displaced lens with its suspensory ligament or zonula of Zinn is characteristic of the congenital deformity, these fibres being absent as the result of their rupture when the displacement is of traumatic origin.

Etiology.—It is the result of external violence or of an iridocyclitis. It may be congenital.

Incomplete Dislocation.—The lens is still fixed between the iris and vitreous body, having only undergone slight displacement.

Complete Dislocation.—The lens occupies the anterior chamber, or a situation beneath the conjunctiva or in the vitreous humour.

SYMPTOMS.—*Incomplete Dislocation* is characterised by a slight displacement round its vertical or horizontal axis. The anterior chamber is not the same depth throughout; the pupil is deformed and the iris seems relaxed. Slight displacement of traumatic origin may disappear, but generally it leads to cataract.

Complete Dislocation.—Dislocation into the anterior chamber is easily recognised. When it occurs into the vitreous humour, the lens assumes a greyish aspect. Vision is, of course, greatly impaired.

TREATMENT.—No useful treatment can be adopted.

Cataract

Cataract, or opacity of the lens, occurs in all animals, but is most commonly seen in the horse and dog. There are:

1. **Capsular or false cataract,** due to a lesion on the capsule of the lens.
2. **Lenticular or true cataract,** resulting from an alteration in the lens itself.
3. **Capsulo-lenticular or mixed cataract,** in which both the lens and its capsule are involved.

ETIOLOGY.—From this point of view cataracts may be classified as follows:

1. *Congenital Cataract.*—This has been seen in the horse, ox, goat, and dog.
2. *Acquired Cataract* may be due to:

(*a*) *External injury*, such as a contusion or open wound of the eye, or even a contusion in the vicinity of the orbit.

(*b*) *Advanced age* (senile cataract), not common in the horse, but fairly frequent in the dog.

(*c*) *Diabetes*, not uncommon in the dog.

(*d*) *Heredity*, or predisposition to cataract.

(*e*) *The toxin* of some bacterial disease.

(*f*) *Parasites* in the anterior chamber.

(*g*) *Specific ophthalmia*, which is the most frequent cause of cataract in the horse.

Sometimes cataract appears without any apparent cause, even in young animals in which there has never been any acute affection of the eye. Whatever the exciting cause may be, the actual cause of the condition is desiccation of the lens. Cataract has been caused experimentally in animals by injections of pilocarpine. It has been produced in the frog by extracting water from the blood.

Symptoms and Diagnosis.—Cataract varies in size from an almost imperceptible spot to an opacity covering the entire anterior surface of the lens. It is usually pearly white when viewed with the naked eye assisted by a black object, as described on p. 491. When a cataract completely covering the lens is seen with the ophthalmoscope, it has the same appearance as by reflected light; but when a considerable portion of the lens is clear, the light reaches the depth of the eye, and on returning therefrom is intercepted at the level of the opacity, which then appears as a smudge or dark speck or area on an otherwise clean illuminated field. When the opacity is very thin the light may pass through it, causing it to escape notice if the ophthalmoscope alone is relied upon to detect it. Examination of the eye by lateral light is a well-known method of procedure for ascertaining if a cataract is present.

In a case of doubt, every method of examination should be tried. Skill in examination of the eye requires much practice, otherwise mistakes may easily be made. Shadows and reflections in a normal eye may be mistaken for opacities. Cataract always causes defective vision, and may be a cause of shying.

Prognosis.—Recent deposits on the surface of the lens may become absorbed, but once the structure of the capsule or of the lens itself is affected, the opacity remains permanently.

Treatment is only of use to promote absorption of an inflammatory deposit on the capsule of the lens, which, however, is not a true cataract. The operations performed for cataract in the human subject are of no benefit for the horse. Operation in the dog, however, will enable the animal to find its way about in a case where it has been completely blind from cataract involving the entire lens in both eyes. It is not indicated except in a case of total blindness.

Operation is so rarely indicated that it is hardly necessary to describe the procedure, which can be best obtained in a work devoted to the eye. The three principal methods of operation may be mentioned:

1. *Displacement* of the lens consists in rupturing the capsule above and below, and then applying pressure backwards on the upper part of the lens so as to push it backwards and downwards out of the line of vision.

2. *Discission.*—Suitable for cataracts in young animals and for soft

cataracts in aged subjects. It consists in slightly incising the capsule of the lens with the object of allowing the aqueous humour to infiltrate the lens and thus lead to its dissolution and eventual absorption.

The technique is as follows :

(1) Prepare the eye by thoroughly flushing it with a suitable antiseptic lotion.

(2) Anæsthetise the patient, for preference by nembutal introduced intravenously.

(3) Immobilise the eyelids by means of the eye speculum or by special retractors.

(4) Fix the eyeball by grasping the conjunctiva to the side of the cornea with a forceps.

(5) Holding the discission needle like a pen, make it perforate the cornea in its upper half at a few millimetres from its border, into the anterior chamber, parallel to the iris.

(6) Direct the point of the needle towards the upper part of the pupil.

(7) Incise or scratch the anterior surface of the lens capsule for a variable extent without penetrating the substance of the lens, which might lead to its subluxation. The incision may be crucial in form occupying about two-thirds the surface of the lens.

(8) Withdraw the needle in the same direction in which it entered, to avoid enlarging the corneal wound.

It is not necessary to cover the eye with a dressing. Instil atropine into the eye daily for a while. Several repetitions of discission at intervals of some weeks may be necessary before the desired effect is obtained.

3. *Extraction of the Lens.*—The operation consists in incising the capsule of the lens in the form of a triangle and then forcing the lens out through the corneal wound.

AFFECTIONS OF THE RETINA AND OPTIC NERVE

Hæmorrhage from the Retina may ensue as the result of a contusion of the eye, or during the course of infectious diseases. It causes an abnormal appearance in the depth of the eye when examined by the ophthalmoscope. Treatment by absorbent medicine is indicated *e.g.*, iodide of potash.

Separation of the Retina and the collection of liquid between it and the choroid may be traumatic in origin or complicate choroiditis from any cause. It causes blindness.

Inflammation of the Retina and of the Optic Nerve generally coexist. They are rare in animals and are usually secondary to some toxic affection. On examination by the ophthalmoscope undoubted changes are observed in the depth of the eye. The usual sequel is atrophy of the retina and of the optic papilla.

Treatment is rarely effective. The administration of iodide of potassium is the most likely to give some good result.

Atrophy of the Optic Nerve and of the Papilla may occur without any apparent cause or follow neuro-retinitis. The papilla becomes blanched from atrophy of its capillaries.

Treatment is practically hopeless. Potassium iodide may be tried. Antipyrine and hypodermic injections of pilocarpine in large doses may be administered.

Amaurosis.—This term is applied to blindness occurring without any apparent lesion of the eye, even on examination by the ophthalmoscope. It may be temporary or permanent, the former being probably due to toxæmia of some sort and the latter to some affection of the brain.

The only treatment is to deal with the cause, if it can be ascertained.

Glaucoma and Hydrophthalmia

Both these conditions are due to an increase in the intra-ocular fluids. When the eyeball does not become distended, but simply shows increased tension, the affection is called *glaucoma*. It is rare in veterinary patients. When the coats of the eye dilate, causing a great increase in its volume, the term hydrophthalmia is employed. This condition is occasionally seen in the horse, dog, and cat, but is rare in other animals. It is the dog which is most frequently affected. It may develop slowly or rapidly.

ETIOLOGY.—Glaucoma has been ascribed to rheumatism, contusions of the eye, iritis, etc. It has also been attributed to hypersecretion of the ocular liquids or to some obstacle to the normal filtration of the liquids through the ocular membranes. Hydrophthalmia must arise in a similar way, but it may also result from anterior luxation of the lens, leading to pressure on the Spaces of Fontana and thus obstructing the filtration of the aqueous humour through the Canals of Schlemm.

SYMPTOMS.—Hydrophthalmia is recognised at once by the great increase in size of the ocular globe. Excessive tension of the eyeball on palpation is the chief symptom of glaucoma. This leads to dilatation of the anterior ciliary veins. Dilatation of the pupil, slight opaqueness of the cornea, and hypoæsthesia or anæsthesia of this membrane are other symptoms. Touching the cornea may not cause any reflex. Examination by the ophthalmoscope shows the veins of the retina dilated and sinuous, and the papilla pushed backwards or excavated by the pressure of the intra-ocular fluid.

TREATMENT.—In the early stages of glaucoma, repeated instillations of eserine ($\frac{1}{2}$ to 1 per cent. solution) are indicated. If the eye become irritated by its constant use, it should be replaced by pilocarpine (1 per cent.). When the case is well established, iridectomy or sclerotomy may be performed. The latter consists in scarifying very superficially the sclerotic to promote the filtration of liquid through it from the interior of the organ.

Hydrophthalmia is treated by repeated puncture of the anterior chambers or by iridectomy, but neither procedure is sure to effect a cure. When the eye becomes very large and shows no improvement after treatment, its excision is indicated.

Sympathetic Ophthalmia

This term is applied to ophthalmia affecting one eye as the result of transmission of the disease from the other eye by way of the optic nerve and the optic chiasma. The condition is rare, and when it occurs it is probably due to infection following the course mentioned, the organisms migrating in this way from one eye to the other—hence the name migratory ophthalmia has also been given to the affection. The chief lesions are iridochoroiditis and neuro-retinitis. Six weeks or more may elapse before the second eye becomes affected.

PREVENTION consists in careful antiseptic treatment of the eye in which the disease has commenced. This, however, can hardly have any effect on the posterior part of the eye, so that the only sure preventative measure is to perform early removal of the eyeball, incising the optic nerve as close to its foramen as possible. It is difficult to decide when this step should be taken.

TREATMENT.—When the second eye has become affected, it must be treated for iridochoroiditis as mentioned. Should a painful neuroma form on the end of the severed optic nerve, it must be excised.

Panophthalmia

Panophthalmia is the name given to accumulation of septic pus in the eyeball.

ETIOLOGY.—Injury and infection of the eye, sometimes following accidental and operation wounds of the organ. It may be a sequel to ulceration of the cornea.

Symptoms.—There is intense inflammation of the eye and a perforation of the cornea is usually present, discharging pus. Staphyloma is frequently an accompanying lesion.

Treatment.—A free exit must be given to the pus by incising the cornea, and the eye should then be bathed repeatedly with a warm antiseptic solution. An alternative procedure is removal of the eyeball. This operation has been objected to on the ground that the wound made at the back of the eye may become infected from the purulent lesion, and that the infection may extend along the optic nerve and give rise to meningo-encephalitis. Incision to evacuate the pus is a simpler and safer procedure.

Tumours of the Eye

Tumours affecting the eye may be benign or malignant, the former involving chiefly the conjunctiva and the latter the deep structures of

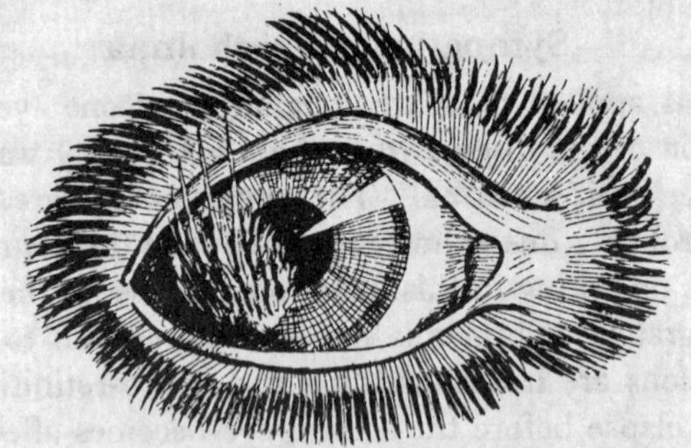

Fig. 227.—Dermoid Cyst in the Conjunctiva.

the organ. Tumours on the conjunctiva comprise dermoid cysts, polypi, lipomata, and melanomata.

Dermoid cysts are the most common, especially in the dog. The condition is in the form of a plaque of tissue showing the characters of skin developed on the conjunctiva only or partly encroaching on the cornea. A tuft of hair from the cyst protrudes between the eyelids and is a source of irritation to the eye. Malignant tumours are occasionally encountered, including carcinoma, sarcoma, and melanosarcoma.

Treatment (Dermoid Cyst).—Anæsthetise the eye with cocaine or eudrenine, seize the cyst with an artery forceps and excise it by little snips of a narrow-bladed sharp scissors. If the cyst extends deeply into the cornea, it is better not to attempt to remove it completely on account of the risk of perforating the globe and leading to complications. Apply antiseptic eye lotions for a few days. The operation leaves hardly any scar.

For malignant tumours the only chance of cure lies in extirpation of the eye as soon as possible. Even then the growth may recur in the orbit.

Tuberculosis of the eyeball has been seen in the ox and in the cat.

Parasites in the Eye

Parasites in the eye are rare. The *Filaria oculi* has been found in the eye of the horse, mule, ass, ox, sheep, and dog. It is a common affection of the horse's eye in India, but rare in Europe and America.

SYMPTOMS.—The usual symptoms of inflammation of the eye are observed, and in addition the filaria may be seen moving about like an eel in the aqueous humour. The presence of the parasites may cause little or no alteration in the eye, or it may give rise to keratitis, iritis, and cataract. The worm eventually dies and then disappears.

TREATMENT.—The only effective intervention consists in puncturing the cornea as described (see p. 507) to allow the aqueous humour, and along with it the parasite, to escape. It might be necessary to take the worm out with a forceps. When the filaria has been removed, the lesions caused by it soon disappear. The usual eye lotions are afterwards indicated. Collargol administered internally and used locally (1 in 100) is said to have had satisfactory results in the ox, in which the parasite seems less virile than in the horse.

THE APPENDAGES OF THE EYE

AFFECTIONS OF THE EYELIDS

Functional Affections

Tonic Spasm of the Eyelids (Tonic Blepharospasm).—Contraction of the orbicularis palpebrarum may be permanent or occur periodically.

ETIOLOGY.—It is usually a symptom of some painful condition of the eye, but occasionally the cause is not apparent.

SYMPTOMS.—The condition is easily recognised.

Clonic Spasm, Nystagmus, Involuntary Winking may be provoked by some ocular lesion or be due to some obscure nerve affection It has been seen in the early stage of hydrophobia in the dog.

Paralysis of the Orbicularis may result from injury to the facial nerve. It is recognised by inability to close the eyelids, the absence of winking, and relaxation of the lower eyelid, which appears somewhat everted.

Drooping of the Upper Eyelid (Ptosis or Blepharoptosis)—Etiology.—The cause of the drooping may be swelling of the lid or section of its tendon, but the chief cause is paralysis of the levator palpebræ, which may be more or less complete.

Treatment of the foregoing conditions must be directed against the causal agent. When paralysis of the levator of the eyelid is permanent and complete, impeding vision, the eyelid may be partially excised to expose the eyeball.

Trichiasis (Turning in of the Eyelashes)

Etiology.—The condition may be hereditary or the result of a chronic inflammation of the eyelid.

Symptoms.—Conjunctivitis and keratitis. The eyelashes are seen in contact with the eyeball.

Treatment.—(1) Pull out the offending eyelashes. This only gives temporary relief, as the hairs grow again.

(2) Operate as for entropion (see p. 482). This effects a permanent cure.

Distichiasis

A double row of eyelashes, the supernumerary row being in the form of fine hairs inside the normal row, and impinging on the eyeball and irritating it, with the usual consequences. It is occasionally seen in the dog.

Treatment.—The operation for entropion is again indicated.

Entropion

Turning in of the palpebral border may affect one or both eyelids of one or both eyes. It may involve only a part or the whole of the palpebral border.

Etiology.—The condition may be congenital or acquired. The latter may be spasmodic or organic. The spasmodic form results from acute conjunctivitis or keratitis and the organic form from chronic inflammatory lesions of the eyelids—follicular conjunctivitis, eczema, and mange. The congenital variety may affect a whole litter of puppies.

Symptoms comprise those of conjunctivitis and keratitis caused by the eyelashes and the hair of the skin encroaching on the conjunctiva and cornea. The deformity of the lid or lids is observed.

Treatment.—The spasmodic form of the affection requires treatment of the inflammation which has given rise to it. Organic entropion is treated by performing the operation already described for the condition (see p. 482).

An American veterinarian has treated entropion successfully by the injection of a few minims of a heavy oil into the muscular tissue of the affected part of the eyelid, taking care not to introduce it beneath the conjunctiva. A very fine needle like that used for the intradermal injection of tuberculin is required for the purpose. Formson (London Veterinary College) has followed his example, but has used liquid paraffin instead of oil, and has had success with the treatment in the few cases in which he practised it. The injection causes swelling of the lid which prevents turning in of its border. Although the swelling disappears after some days, a permanent cure is usually effected. A possible explanation offered by Formson is that the temporary relief afforded by the injection allows the eyeball to come forward in its orbit, thus preventing recurrence of the condition after the swelling has subsided.

Ectropion

Turning outwards of the free border of the eyelids may be complete or partial, single or double, and uni- or bilateral. The condition is normal in bloodhounds and St. Bernards. Otherwise it is not common.

Etiology comprises œdema of the conjunctiva and cicatricial lesions on the outer aspect of the eyelids.

Symptoms.—The exposed conjunctiva is red and congested, but apart from this the eye suffers little ill-effects. There is a flow of tears from the affected eye.

Treatment.—When the abnormality is due to œdema of the conjunctiva it is only of temporary duration, and may be quickly remedied by incision of the membrane. If the result of chronic thickening of the latter, the best procedure is to excise an elliptical piece of conjunctiva with its long axis parallel to the palpebral border. One of the plastic operations described is indicated when the cause is a cicatrix on the cutaneous surface of the eyelid (p. 483).

Traumatic Lesions

Contusions and open wounds of the eyelids are on a par with those in other parts. The most serious open wounds are those going right through the eyelid either perpendicularly or obliquely to its free border. There is more gaping in the case of the perpendicular fissure. The eyelid might be completely torn away. Wounds may be caused by falls, blows, or catching in hooks or nails, or by bites.

Treatment is on general principles, but a particularly important point here is to conserve as much tissue as possible. The wound should be carefully sutured, if practicable. Pin sutures are best, as they keep the edges of the wound in rigid apposition. Primary healing frequently occurs. When the borders of the fissure are granulating, the granulations should be cut off with a scissors and the wound then sutured. A small portion of the upper eyelid, which is the one usually involved, can be dispensed with without the eye suffering in consequence. The horse should be tied on the pillar-reins until the wound is healed, to prevent its being rubbed against the manger or wall.

Ciliary or Marginal Blepharitis

Inflammation of the palpebral borders is occasionally seen in the dog, and seems to be associated with general debility.

Treatment.—Bathe the eyelids frequently with warm boric lotion and afterwards smear their borders with diluted yellow oxide of mercury ointment or with that of the red oxide (1 in 100 to 1 in 20) and give tonic medicine internally—Fowler's solution, cod-liver oil, or iodide of iron.

Tumours

Tumours of the eyelids may be benign or malignant. Of the former, warts or papillomata are the most common, while the latter may be sarcoma, carcinoma, or epithelioma.

Treatment.—Excise benign tumours and suture the resulting wound. The operation may be done standing in the horse or ox, under the influence of local anæsthesia. Malignant tumours necessitate complete removal of the affected lid and extirpation of the eyeball, and even then recurrence of the tumour usually takes place.

Tumours on the Membrana Nictitans.—The membrana nictitans is occasionally the seat of a new growth, which is most commonly carcinoma.

Treatment.—Have the horse well controlled in the standing position, instil a local anæsthetic into the eye and inject it subconjunctivally in the region of the membrana, seize the membrana with an artery forceps, and excise it completely. Recurrence is always to be feared.

Hypertrophy or Tumour of the Harderian Gland requires excision of the organ, which is effected by grasping it with a forceps and cutting it away with a curved scissors after anæsthetising the eye. The resulting hæmorrhage soon ceases. Adrenalin solution may be used to produce hæmostasis.

AFFECTIONS OF THE LACHRYMAL APPARATUS

Inflammation of the Lachrymal Gland (Dacryoadenitis) is rarely observed. It is usually accompanied by a hypersecretion of tears (epiphora). Treatment is antiphlogistic.

Lachrymal Fistula may be cutaneous or conjunctival. Cauterise its orifice with silver nitrate or with a hot needle to effect its closure.

The **Caruncula** may be affected with a tumour and require removal.

Obstruction of the Lachrymal Ducts and Lachrymal Canal

This is characterised by a constant flow of tears from the inner canthus of the eye, depilating and irritating the skin beneath. Exploration of the lachrymal passages will reveal the seat of obstruction. Take a syringe provided with a suitable nozzle, and by means of it inject a little warm water into the lower lachrymal duct. If the water escape through the nostril, all the lachrymal courses are clear; if it escape only by the upper lachrymal duct, the two ducts are permeable, but the sac or canal is occluded; if the liquid return by the duct into whose orifice it was injected, that duct is occluded. It is, however, a very delicate procedure to make an injection by the orifice of the lachrymal duct, and to do it without risk of injury to the eye it is necessary to cast the horse. A more practical method of ascertaining whether the canal and ducts are clear is to inject liquid from the nasal orifice, as this can be easily and safely done in the standing position, as a rule.

Etiology.—Occlusion of the lachrymal ducts is not common, but it may be congenital or the result of inflammatory thickening of their lining. The upper end of the lachrymal canal may be occluded as the result of inflammation in the sac. Closure of its lower portion may be congenital or follow from inflammation of its lining or from obstruction by dust, as sometimes used to happen in cavalry horses on the march in dry weather.

Symptoms.—There may or may not be evidence of ophthalmia, but there is always constant weeping from the eye of the affected side.

Treatment.—When occlusion of the ducts accompanies conjunctivitis, it may be sufficient to treat the latter. If not, and they or the canal are blocked by inflammatory exudate or foreign material, the injection of liquid through the nasal orifice of the canal may be sufficient to dislodge and eject the cause of its stoppage. The passage of a long, fine, smooth-pointed stilette through the canal from below is another method of clearing it. In a case of permanent closure of the ducts, it is necessary to make an opening into the lachrymal sac.

When the lachrymal canal is definitely obstructed or devoid of a nasal orifice, an artificial opening must be made in the nasal chamber. The following procedure may be adopted : Pass a stilette through the upper duct and make it bulge at the level of the inferior extremity of the patent part of the canal, where it may be felt, by the finger, beneath the nasal mucous membrane, and cut down on it here, thereby making a counter-opening. To ensure the orifice remaining open, pass two or three silk threads through the canal and leave them in position for about twenty days. If the stoppage is in the bony part of the canal, it will be necessary to trephine the bone to make an opening into the nose.

If the foregoing measures fail or are impracticable, it has been advised to extirpate the lachrymal gland. The wisdom of this procedure, depriving the eye of its natural liquid protection, is doubtful.

Inflammation of the Lachrymal Sac (Dacryocystitis)

Etiology.—Inflammation of the lachrymal sac may be acute or chronic. Both forms may be associated with corresponding inflammation of the conjunctiva and lachrymal ducts or with catarrh of the nasal mucous membrane. The affection may be caused by strangles in the horse and by distemper in the dog.

Symptoms.—The first symptom noticed is a profuse flow of tears. After a few days a prominent swelling is observed in the inner canthus, formed by distension of the sac. It may suppurate and burst, giving rise to a *lachrymal fistula*, which shows little tendency to heal. In the dog, lachrymal fistula generally results from the osseous lachrymal canal being involved in disease of the superior maxilla, associated with dental fistula.

Treatment for inflammation of the sac consists in frequent bathing with a warm, non-irritant, antiseptic solution. When an abscess forms, it is opened either by way of the upper lachrymal duct or through the skin.

Lachrymal fistula requires in the first instance clearance of the lachrymal passages and then cauterisation of the wound to promote its cicatrisation.

AFFECTIONS OF THE MUSCLES OF THE EYEBALL

Strabismus, or Squint

Strabismus, or squint, is the term applied to all abnormal deviations of the eye.

Etiology.—The condition may be due to : (1) Want of balance of power in the antagonistic muscles of the organ ; (2) paralysis of some of these muscles ; (3) adhesions of the ocular globe to the orbit ; (4) tumours of the orbit.

The SYMPTOMS are obvious, the eyeball being deviated inwards (convergent) or outwards (divergent), or upwards or downwards.

TREATMENT.—When due to muscular contraction, the treatment is operative, as follows : Use general or local anæsthesia, separate the eyelids with a dilator, seize the conjunctiva close to the cornea, and incise it with a curved scissors ; introduce a strabismus hook beneath the tendon to be severed, and cut it with the scissors. Treat the eye afterwards with an eye lotion. When the condition is due to other causes, treat it according to their nature.

Ocular paralysis may be peripheral or central in origin. Paralysis of the motor oculi is characterised by (1) drooping of the upper eyelid, (2) deviation outwards of the eyeball, and (3) dilatation of the pupil.

Treatment will vary according to the origin of the paralysis. Iodide of potash internally, a counter-irritant on the periorbital region, and the electric current are the agents usually employed.

AFFECTIONS OF THE ORBIT

Contusions and Open Wounds of the orbit are of a similar nature to those in other parts, and are dealt with on general principles. A penetrating wound at the back of the orbit may become infected and lead to destruction of the eyeball.

Fracture of the Supra-orbital Processs is a common lesion in the horse as the result of direct violence. It is easily recognised by the deformity of the region and by the mobility of the fragment. It is often compound, when the broken bone may be seen.

Treatment is on general principles for fractures. When the fragment is displaced downwards, it may be reduced by inserting a smooth spatula beneath it to lever it into position. Recovery is the rule.

Tumours of a benign or malignant nature may affect the orbit. Carcinoma is fairly often seen in the horse, ox, and dog. Melanoma occurs in grey horses. Exophthalmia is a common result of the development of a neoplasm on the wall of the orbit.

Treatment is generally unsatisfactory, and usually involves extirpation of the eyeball.

AFFECTIONS OF THE EAR

Examination of the Ear

The external ear can be examined without any special device. The horse may require the twitch and the dog to be muzzled. An aural speculum is useful to facilitate examination of the depth of the organ.

THE EXTERNAL EAR

Open wounds and contusions of the external ear do not require any special description, being of the usual nature and dealt with on general principles. There may be trouble in obtaining healing of any open wound owing to necrosis of the cartilage having supervened. A difficulty with them in regard to the dog in particular is the constant shaking of the ear, which often prevents cicatrisation. An essential feature of the treatment of an open wound in the dog's ear, therefore,

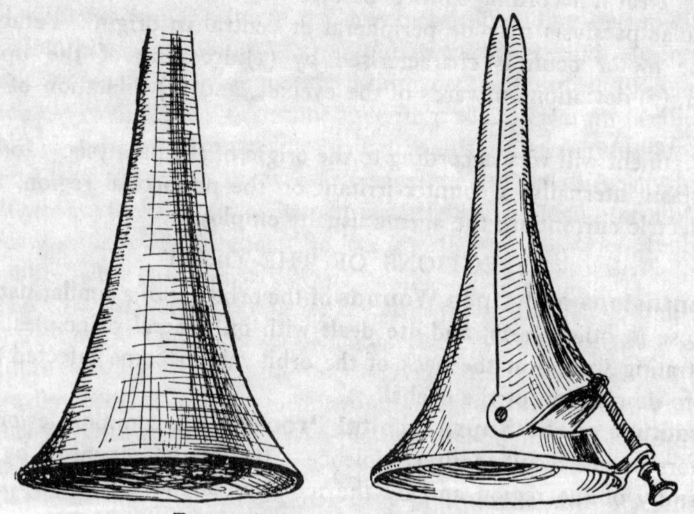

FIGS. 228 AND 229.—EAR SPECULUM.

is the application of a cap to immobilise the appendage. This precaution is indispensable after suturing a fissure in the concha. The best suture to employ is the pin suture. It keeps the edges of the cartilage in rigid apposition. The pins are inserted through the cartilage, or two series of cutaneous sutures may be used, one on the inner and the other on the outer aspect of the ear.

Hæmatoma, or Othæmatoma

Hæmatoma, or othæmatoma, of the flap of the ear is common in the dog, especially in the long-eared varieties. It is usually situated on its inner aspect, but in rare cases it is on the outer aspect, and more rarely still in both places. The blood is accumulated between the perichondrium and the cartilage.

ETIOLOGY.—It is nearly always traumatic in origin, being caused by a contusion, or by scratching, or repeated shaking of the ear in subjects affected with mange or otorrhœa.

SYMPTOMS.—An ovoid or roundish, tense, and more or less voluminous swelling, uniformly fluctuating and accompanied by pain, appears

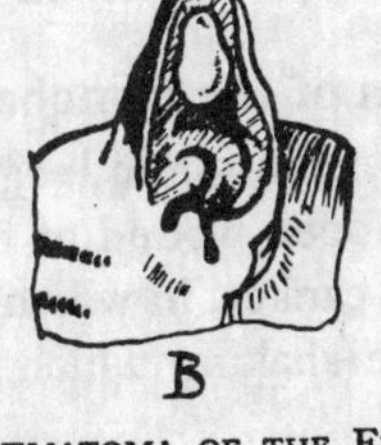

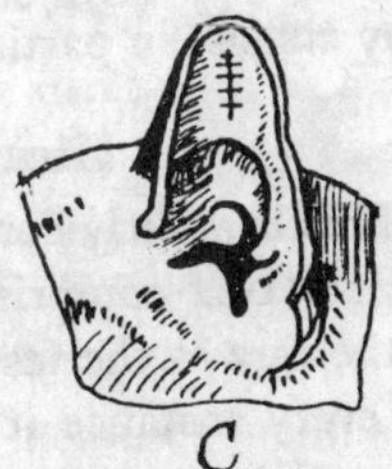

FIG. 230.—HÆMATOMA OF THE EXTERNAL EAR.

A. Crinkled condition of the ear following opening of the hæmatoma without suturing the wound.

B. Hæmatoma before operation.

C. Appearance of the ear after operation for hæmatoma (Hobday).

in one of the situations mentioned. The acute inflammatory symptoms subside after a while, but the collection of fluid remains. If infection gain entrance, suppuration will ensue.

TREATMENT consists in opening the swelling at its centre by an incision extending from its base to its apex, evacuating its contents, and swabbing its lining with tincture of iodine. Dressing with iodine is renewed a few times until the lining of the cavity is in the form of a granulating surface. The ear is immobilised by a well-fitted cap until healing has occurred. A certain amount of puckering or deformity of the flap ensues from cicatricial contraction, most noticeable in small ears, *e.g.*, those of the cat. It is, of course, necessary to deal with the primary cause of the trouble when still present—mange or otorrhœa. A special operation for hæmatoma has been described (p. 481).

FIG. 231.—EAR BANDAGE APPLIED ON THE DOG.

Necrosis of the Conchal Cartilage

Necrosis of the conchal cartilage in the horse has been seen as the result of open wounds and infection.

The SYMPTOMS are those of a sinus abutting on the cartilage. The gradual destruction of the cartilage, in a case of some standing, leads to deformity of the ear as a consequence of cicatricial contraction.

TREATMENT is as usual for a sinus. It aims at getting rid of the necrotic cartilage by the application of caustics or by operation, which may consist in partial or complete excision of the pavilion (see p. 293)

Ulceration of the Conchal Cartilage

This is a fairly common condition in long-eared dogs.

ETIOLOGY comprises an open wound of the ear or repeated shaking of the ears as the result of canker, in which case it is usually bilateral. In every instance it is the shaking which is the actual cause of the ulceration.

SYMPTOMS.—The presence of a small wound with a bleeding surface or covered by a scab and having tumefied red borders. It gradually

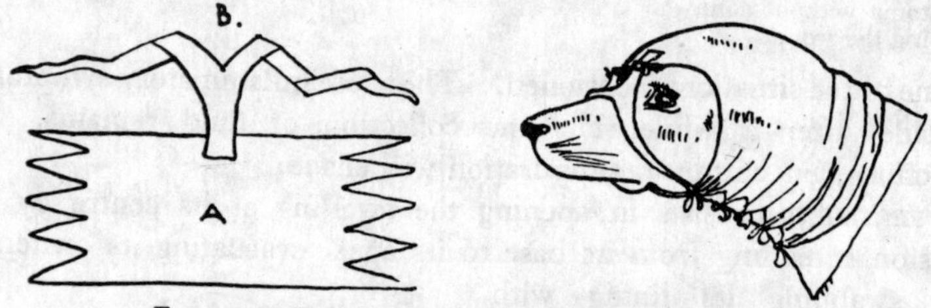

FIG. 232.—EAR BANDAGE FOR THE DOG (HOBDAY).

increases in area and depth, and is very tender on manipulation. It is frequently itchy, and is then scratched or rubbed by the animal, thus helping, along with the shaking of the head, to perpetuate the condition.

TREATMENT consists in cleaning and disinfecting the wound, cauterising it if indolent, freshening and suturing it when in the form of a fissure, and immobilising the ear with a pad of cotton-wool covered with a cap securely fixed in position. When brought about by canker or otorrhœa, the latter must be treated.

Foreign Bodies and Parasites in the Ear

Foreign matter in the ears may consist of inspissated cerumen, sand, small pebbles, bits of wood, or grass seeds, and the parasites infesting them comprise fleas and acari.

SYMPTOMS.—Constant shaking of the head due to the irritation caused by the presence of the material in the ear. On careful exploration the cause of the trouble is detected.

TREATMENT.—The forcible injection of hot water with a syringe is generally sufficient to dislodge and remove foreign matter from the ear. If a quantity of hard wax is fixed in its depth, it can be softened by a few injections of glycerinated carbonate of soda composed of :

Carbonate of soda	1
Glycerine	20
Water	20

A forceps or blunt curette may also be cautiously used to remove a foreign body. Parasites may be expelled by a liquid injection or killed *in situ* by an injection of olive oil or the use of an anti-parasitic ointment, and then extracted or flushed out.

Otitis of the External Ear—Inflammation of the Lining of the Concha—Otorrhœa—Canker

This is very common in the dog and rare in other species. It is of two kinds—viz. : (1) Simple, (2) parasitic.

SIMPLE OTORRHŒA may be acute or chronic. It is particularly common in long-eared dogs, and one or both ears may be affected.

ETIOLOGY.—The disease may be caused by constitutional debility of an obscure nature or associated with distemper, and is then often accompanied by eczema in other parts of the body. Want of exercise and improper feeding may concur in its production. It may be classified in the dog as follows :

1. Otorrhœa of distemper.
2. Eczematous otorrhœa.
3. Glandular otorrhœa.
4. Otorrhœa due to inspissated cerumen.

No. 1 only persists during the course of the disease, and occurs in about 50 per cent. of cases. The secretion is more liquid than in the other forms.

No. 3 is an affection of the sebaceous and ceruminous glands characterised by inflammation and by hypersecretion, and sometimes by ulceration. The glands may afterwards atrophy and be replaced by a new formation of fibrous tissue in the form of hypertrophied papillæ or excrescences which may close the auditory meatus. This is the chronic form of the disease.

SYMPTOMS.—In the ordinary acute otorrhœa, the interior of the ear is red, hot, and painful, and secretes a purulent fœtid fluid. The dog frequently shakes the head, rubs the ear along the ground, or scratches it with the paw. When the condition is confined to one ear, the head is held towards the affected side. In rare cases there is vomiting or some other reflex symptom.

The disease is seldom met with in other animals, but occasionally the horse is affected with uncontrollable shaking of the head at intervals during work, and on treating the interior of the ears with an emollient and antiparasitic ointment (equal parts of zinc and sulphur ointment) the symptoms sometimes disappear. In such cases there is generally evidence of the ear being affected by the horse yielding the head when the interior of the ear is rubbed with the finger or the base is squeezed with the finger and thumb. An accumulation of cerumen may be the cause of the trouble in the horse.

TREATMENT comprises the following measures :

1. Clip the hairs at the entrance to the ear and clean the part thoroughly with soap and water.

2. When the lesion is very painful, introduce an anodyne or emollient preparation into the interior of the concha—a decoction of poppy-heads, aqueous tincture of opium, chloral hydrate (1 in 200), cocainised glycerine.

3. An antiseptic powder may be applied as an absorbent or desiccant of the aural discharge, but it has the disadvantage of forming concretions if left long *in situ*—subnitrate of bismuth, starch, oxide of zinc and boric acid, tannin and iodoform, or a perfumed toilet powder for ladies' pets. They may be applied for the night and removed in the morning.

4. Smearing an antiseptic emollient ointment over the affected part is often efficacious—zinc ointment or resinol ointment. The latter is particularly useful.

5. When the very acute symptoms have subsided, the ear should be thoroughly but gently syringed out with a warm, mild, antiseptic solution and then dried with pledgets of cotton-wool wrapped round the end of a director or other suitable instrument which can be introduced to the base of the concha. Hydrogen peroxide is an excellent detergent agent for the purpose. Methylated spirit (1 part) and warm water (4 parts) make also a good cleansing preparation. Except the lesion is very painful, it is best to commence the treatment by cleaning the affected part.

6. After cleaning the ear, an astringent preparation may be employed —sulphate of zinc 1 to 2 per cent., or glycerine and tannin 1 in 20, permanganate of potash 1 in 1,000, when an offensive odour is present.

7. Petrol has proved to be an excellent detergent and curative agent, one or two applications being sometimes sufficient. Magee (Ireland)

speaks highly of its efficacy. It should not be used more frequently than once per week as it is irritant.

8. A solution of iodoform in ether (1 to 20 or 1 to 10) is a simple and effective way of introducing the former as a fine deposit into every part of the interior of the external ear, where it produces a marked good effect as an antiseptic and an anodyne, its only drawback being the penetrating odour of the iodoform.

The disease requires careful daily attention until improvement occurs.

INTERNAL TREATMENT.—Laxative medicine is always indicated. The diet requires to be regulated. Vegetable soups and milk foods are generally best, with a moderate allowance of flesh meat. Alkaline medicine—magnesia and soda bicarbonate—may be beneficial. If the patient is debilitated, a course of arsenic should be prescribed.

Treatment of Chronic Otorrhœa is on similar lines, but it may be necessary to use for a while some comparatively strong or irritant agent to overcome infection and excite a healthy reaction—*e.g.*, tincture of iodine or 2 to 5 per cent. solution of carbolic acid. Carbolised glycerine (1 in 20 or 40) is anodyne and antiseptic. Resinol ointment or petrol is also useful in this form of the affection. Odylin is also a good application and may be combined with a course of aricyl hypodermically.

When vegetations have formed in the lumen of the concha, more or less occluding it and causing deafness, excision of the growths under general anæsthesia is necessary. Liquor arsenicalis internally should be prescribed. (See amputation of the conchal cartilage, p. 293.)

Parasitic Otorrhœa (Otacariasis)

In the dog, cat, rabbit, and ferret this is caused by the *Symbiotes auricularum*, and in the horse, ass, mule, sheep, goat, and rabbit by the *Psoroptes communis*.

SYMPTOMS.—The symptoms are those of otorrhœa with pronounced irritation, causing the patient to continually scratch or rub the ear, to shake the head, and hold it to the side. There is a profuse secretion of cerumen, usually of a brownish or blackish and pasty nature. Epileptiform symptoms may supervene.

PROPHYLAXIS.—The ordinary prophylactic measures are indicated and are important, as otacariasis may be the source of an outbreak of psoroptic mange.

TREATMENT.—The condition responds quickly to antiparasitic treatment. Probably the best applications are hot solutions of sulphate of potash (1 per cent.) and cresyl (2 to 3 per cent.), repeated two or three times at intervals of a week to destroy new generations for the eggs remaining *in situ*. Sulphur and other antiparasitic ointments are also efficacious.

Tumours

Tumours of the ear in the various animals comprise papillomata, sebaceous cysts, polypoid fibromata, and sarcomata. Papillomata in the dog are often in the form of cauliflower-like growths, more or less obliterating the entrance to the meatus.

TREATMENT.—Benign tumours may be successfully excised, but the removal of malignant growths is usually followed by recurrence. Prompt amputation of the concha is the only chance of cure when the lesion is confined to it (see p. 293).

THE MIDDLE EAR

Inflammation of the tympanum and of the middle ear may result from external injury or be due to infection extending from the external ear. The condition is rare.

The SYMPTOMS vary according to the severity of the attack. The collection of pus in the middle ear is always very painful, and causes complete deafness. Epileptiform symptoms may ensue. The disease may extend to the internal ear and to the brain.

TREATMENT.—Remove a foreign body, if present. Flush out the cavity gently with warm sterile solution of normal saline. Catarrh or purulent inflammation of the part demands irrigation with a mild antiseptic solution. Puncture of the tympanum for the evacuation of pus is a delicate operation not likely to be undertaken in veterinary practice.

THE INTERNAL EAR

Lesions of the internal ear may ensue from severe external violence or by extension from the middle ear. They usually involve the brain, giving rise to cerebral disturbance and terminating fatally. Purulent inflammation of the internal ear has been seen as an enzootic affection in a flock of sheep in Co. Dublin, giving rise to symptoms simulating sturdy, but affecting a larger proportion of the flock, and proving more rapidly fatal. Diagnosis was confirmed on post-mortem examination. The origin of the infection could not be traced, and nothing could be done to prevent or cure the disease.

AFFECTIONS OF THE EUSTACHIAN TUBE AND OF THE GUTTURAL POUCHES

I. THE EUSTACHIAN TUBES

The Eustachian tubes, owing to their situation, are not subject to mechanical injury, but their lining may be affected by inflammatory conditions extending from the pharynx. Their mucous membrane may become thicker as the result of chronic inflammation and occlude the entrance to the guttural pouches. When the lumen of the tube is obstructed, deafness always supervenes owing to the air being thus prevented from entering the middle ear to balance the pressure of the external air on the tympanum, and thereby enable the proper impulses to be conveyed through the medium of the chain of small bones of the ear to the lymph in the labyrinth. Convulsive, epileptoform, or vertigoid symptoms may supervene from irritation of the nerves of the labyrinth.

II. THE GUTTURAL POUCHES

Before considering affections of the guttural pouch, the student or veterinarian should master its anatomy, as the pouch has very important relations.

Catarrh of and Collection of Pus in the Guttural Pouch

ETIOLOGY.—The condition is usually secondary to an acute pharyngitis, and in this way may be a sequel to strangles, but it may also accompany infectious parotiditis or a subparotid or retropharyngeal abscess. It may be associated with a neoplasm on its walls (*e.g.*, melanoma in the grey horse). Food material may enter the pouch through the Eustachian tube (a rare occurrence), and give rise to suppurative inflammation. Once inflammation is produced in the pouch it becomes chronic, owing to the want of complete dependent drainage for the inflammatory products. The accumulated material perpetuates the abnormal condition. The solid portion of the exudate may become fashioned into chestnut-like bodies, called chondroids, which remain in the pouch and act as foreign bodies.

SYMPTOMS.—The symptoms comprise:

1. *An intermittent discharge*, which only appears during feeding or when the head is lowered to eat from the ground, or to take the bit or during exercise. It is generally inodorous, and in the form of a liquid containing yellowish-white flocculi of variable size. It does not adhere to or become inspissated on the nostrils. Although only one pouch is

affected, the discharge may be bilateral. Rarely it is blood-stained, due to ulceration of the lining of the pouch.

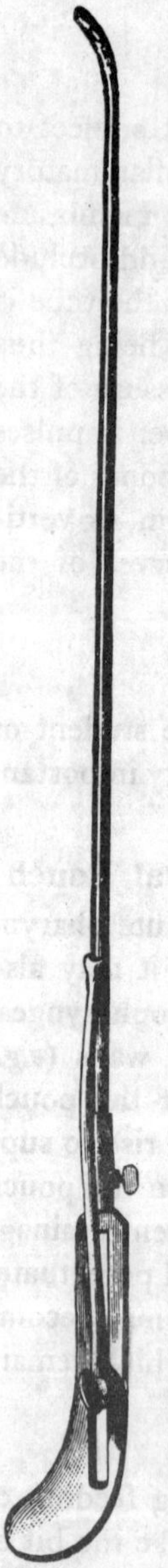

2. *Swelling of the submaxillary lymphatic glands.*—They become enlarged, as in empyema of the sinuses, and are not adherent to the jaw.

3. *Swelling in the parotid region*, only noticed when the pouch is much distended. Pressure on it will then cause an escape of discharge through the nose. It may be abnormally hot and slightly painful.

4. *Interference with swallowing and respiration*, observed when the pouch becomes greatly distended owing to stenosis or partial obstruction of the Eustachian tube, allowing the escape of a much smaller quantity of the contents than usual. The patient has difficulty in swallowing, makes a respiratory noise, and shows more or less dyspnœa during exercise, due to the swelling encroaching on the pharynx and larynx.

5. *Rupture of the pouch*, due to excessive distension to repeated efforts of swallowing, and to snorting. It is a rare occurrence.

6. *Holding the head towards the sound side* when the horse is being ridden, observed in some cases.

7. *A rattling noise* in the pouch during exercise, sometimes produced, due to agitation of the contents.

Diagnosis is based on (1) the intermittency of the discharge; (2) its consistency and non-offensive nature; (3) the local swelling; (4) enlargement of the submaxillary glands; (5) the absence of characteristics of other conditions which cause a nasal discharge.

When in doubt, Günther's catheter may be passed through the inferior meatus of the nasal chamber and through the Eustachian tube into the pouch, whence the fluid, if present, will escape through the catheter. The instrument is composed of metal, and is slightly curved at its distal extremity. The pharyngeal entrance to the Eustachian tube is at the same level as the temporal canthus of the eye, and the distance from this point is measured on the instrument and marked by a runner for the purpose. The catheter is introduced into the nose, and when it has entered as far as the point indicated by the marker the level of the Eustachian opening is reached, and the proximal end

Fig. 233.—Günther's Catheter.

of the instrument must then be held close to the septum nasi so as to direct the other end outwards and enable it to enter the orifice, which is on the outer wall of the pharynx. To facilitate the passage of the instrument and to diminish the resistance of the horse, it should be immersed in warm water and smeared with vaseline before using it. It requires considerable practice and skill to make the instrument enter the tube.

PROGNOSIS.—There is no chance of spontaneous cure, but when the pus becomes inspissated and the quantity of fluid is diminished the functional disturbance is relieved. Death rarely supervenes from hæmorrhage due to ulceration of the mucous membrane and the opening of a bloodvessel, or to gangrenous pneumonia caused by alimentary matter gaining entrance to the lungs. The author had a case of this kind in a valuable nine years old thoroughbred mare in which the preliminary and only symptom was food returning through the nostrils during feeding. This extended over a period of 14 days. Then some blood and pus were noticed in the nasal discharge and chiefly from the left nostril, and the mare was heard to cough occasionally when taking food. Eventually profuse nasal hæmorrhage ensued, the animal became distressed and very dejected and died. Post-mortem examination revealed ulceration of the left pouch wall involving a small area of the petrous temporal bone. It was from this lesion that the hæmorrhage originated. There was also evidence of foreign body pneumonia.

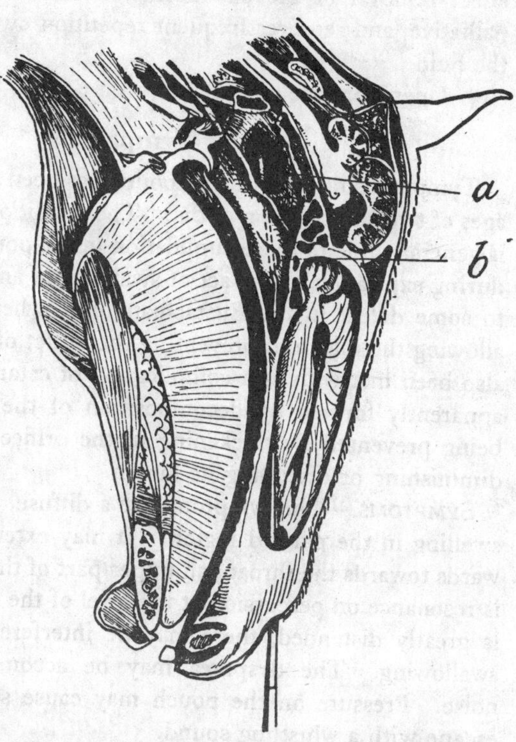

FIG. 234.—GÜNTHER'S CATHETER PASSED INTO THE GUTTURAL POUCH.

TREATMENT.—The treatment comprises:

1. *Antiseptic inhalations*, which may be of some use in a recent case by allaying inflammation of the mucous membrane, but once pus has accumulated in the pouch they have no beneficial effect.

2. *The passage of Günther's catheter*, to evacuate the fluid contents and to enable the cavity to be irrigated with an antiseptic lotion introduced through the catheter by means of a syringe. As it does not effect removal of the chondroids, this method of treatment is only palliative, and requires frequent repetition owing to reaccumulation of the fluid.

3. Operation (see p. 296).

Tympanitis

Tympanitis of the guttural pouch has been seen in foals between the ages of two and twelve months. The condition is usually bilateral, and is generally due to the accumulation in the pouches of air, which enters during expiration or the act of swallowing, and cannot gain exit owing to some defect in the Eustachian tube, whereby it acts like a valve, allowing the inlet and preventing the outlet of air. The condition has also been met with as a complication of catarrh of the pouches, being apparently formed by decomposition of the exudate, and its escape being prevented by thickening in the orifice of the Eustachian tube, diminishing or occluding its lumen.

SYMPTOMS.—The symptoms are a diffuse, painless, elastic tympanic swelling in the parotid region. It may extend downwards and backwards towards the throat and upper part of the jugular furrow. There is resonance on percussion at the level of the pouch. When the cavity is greatly distended, there may be interference with respiration and swallowing. The dyspnœa may be accompanied by a respiratory noise. Pressure on the pouch may cause some of the air or gas to escape with a whistling sound.

TREATMENT.—The application of counter-irritants or other topics to the skin over the pouch has no beneficial result. Puncturing the sac gives only temporary relief, as it rapidly refills. When the condition is due to deformity of the Eustachian tube, preventing the exit of the gas, it is necessary to open the pouch, by Dieterich's method for preference, introduce a grooved director into the tube, and passing a narrow-bladed bistoury along its groove, incise the lower part of the tube in an anterior direction. Even this procedure may not have the desired effect, and then the only course to adopt is to open the pouch externally in two places, above and below, and insert a drainage tube to afford an exit for the air. When the openings close, however, the condition will recur except the gas was due to decomposition of the exudate. If the condition be associated with pus in the pouch, treat for this condition.

AFFECTIONS OF THE SALIVARY GLANDS

THE PAROTID GLAND

Open Wounds

When the parotid gland is wounded, there is an escape of saliva through the wound. The latter heals in the ordinary way as a rule, a fistula seldom persisting.

TREATMENT is on the usual lines. Arrest the hæmorrhage by appropriate measures. If some of the large vessels are severed, they must be promptly secured by artery forceps and ligatured. If this cannot be done through the wound, the vessel should be isolated at some distance from it and the ligature applied there. Even ligation of the carotid may not stop persistent hæmorrhage from the internal carotid on account of the latter anastomosing with the corresponding artery on the other side. Suture and seal the wound.

Stenson's Duct

Wounds of the duct may be transverse, longitudinal, or oblique, and partial or complete. During feeding there is a copious discharge of saliva from the wound. It is more difficult to obtain healing of the lesion here than in the gland, on account of the greater quantity of saliva flowing through the opening in the canal. Consequently, when the wound is not promptly treated, or is incapable of healing by first intention, a fistula frequently results. Rarely the proximal portion of the duct becomes obliterated, when atrophy of the gland ensues.

TREATMENT.—Aim at healing by first intention. To promote this, perforate the cheek at the level of the wound, when the latter is near the mouth, to provide another passage for the saliva. Suture the cutaneous wound and seal it with collodion and iodoform. Do not give the patient any solid food for twenty-four hours, and avoid putting him in the company of horses that are feeding, in order not to excite salivation.

Salivary Fistula

Salivary fistula may be due to a wound of the parotid, or submaxillary salivary gland, or of Stenson's or Wharton's duct.

ETIOLOGY.—The fistula is usually from Stenson's duct, where it may be caused by an open wound or an abscess involving the canal.

PROGNOSIS.—A fistula of the gland usually responds to treatment, and has a tendency to close spontaneously within a few weeks. It is much more difficult to effect closure of the orifice in the wall of Stenson's duct. But when there is a clear passage for the saliva into the mouth, suitable treatment of the external wound generally has the desired effect.

TREATMENT.—When the condition is due to a recent incised wound of the gland or duct, endeavour to get healing by first intention, as stated above. If the fistula has been in existence for some time, cauterisation of its edges or freshening thereof and suturing will be necessary. The application of silver nitrate, or of pure nitric acid with a glass rod, or of the hot iron, or of a blister, or freshening the lips of the wound and inserting a purse-string suture is often successful provided that there is no obstruction to the flow of saliva.

If the foregoing methods fail, one of the following procedures may be adopted for a fistula of Stenson's duct situated on the cheek :

1. *Clearing the Lumen of the Distal Portion of the Duct.*—Pass a probe from the fistular orifice through the duct into the mouth. A few strands of thread may be attached to the instrument and drawn through the canal two or three times to clear it of inspissated mucus that may be present. The external opening is then treated as described by cauterisation, or by suturing after freshening its borders.

2. *Making an Artificial Opening into the Mouth.*—(*a*) Perforate the cheek with a trocar at the level of the fistula, pass a few strands of silk thread through the passage, and fix them in position by tying their two ends at the commissure of the lips. Leave them *in situ* for a few days until a permanent fistula into the mouth is formed. Then proceed to bring about closure of the cutaneous opening.

(*b*) Make a double perforation into the mouth, pass a seton through both passages, and tie its two ends together in the mouth. By this method the external opening can be closed at once.

(*c*) Perforate the cheek in two directions—viz., inwards to the mouth and outwards through the skin from the fistula. Pass a seton through the two perforations, one end being in the mouth and the other outside the cheek, and close the cutaneous orifice of the fistula immediately. Remove the seton after a few days. Method (*a*) is simple and effective, and probably the most suitable for animals.

Destruction of the Function of the Gland

This is indicated when closure of the fistula cannot be effected. It may be brought about by:

1. **Injection of irritants** through the upper part of the duct into the gland, such as tincture of iodine, pure or dilute, liquor ammonia (10 per cent.), or Labat's preparation of iodine, composed of tincture of iodine (20 or 40 parts), potassium iodide (1 part), and water (60 to 80 parts). Several injections may be necessary before atrophy is produced.

2. **Ligation of Stenson's duct** (see p. 293).

Fistula of the submaxillary gland or of Wharton's duct is a comparatively rare condition, and responds to treatment by a blister or by cauterisation.

Foreign Bodies in the Salivary Ducts

Small particles of hay or awns of grass or oat hairs may gain entrance to the main salivary ducts, usually Wharton's duct, and set up inflammation or suppuration. Occasionally the foreign body causes little or no irritation, and simply serves as a nucleus round which salts are deposited to form a calculus.

SYMPTOMS.—When inflammation arises, it is revealed by swelling and redness of the buccal orifice of the duct, from which a fœtid whitish pus may be oozing. There is excessive salivation.

TREATMENT.—Endeavour to expel the foreign body into the mouth by pressure on the course of the duct. If this fail, the oral orifice of the canal may be enlarged by an incision, or Wharton's duct may be incised where it is distended behind the barb. Prescribe an antiseptic mouth lotion to be used for a few days.

Salivary Calculi

Salivary calculi usually occur in Stenson's duct; rarely in Wharton's duct. The size of the calculi varies; they are usually small, but exceptional cases of concretions weighing individually 7 to 12 ounces have been recorded. There may be several present, and then they are faeeted from attrition. An isolated calculus is usually oval in shape, smooth on its surface, and yellowish-grey in colour. The composition of the deposit is 80 to 90 per cent. carbonate of calcium and 9 to 10 per cent. organic matter, comprising salivary corpuscles and bacteria.

ETIOLOGY.—The condition is usually caused by a small particle of foodstuff getting into the duct and carrying with it bacteria, which cause fermentation in the saliva and consequent deposition of lime on the foreign body. The latter may be a spicule of hay or grass, or an awn of oats or barley, or rarely a bit of dental tartar.

SYMPTOMS.—The symptoms are a hard, painless swelling on the course of the duct, distension of the latter behind the obstruction and of the gland, and a grating noise when the skin is pierced with a needle at the level of the enlargement. There may be swelling round the buccal orifice of the duct when the stone is situated there. The calculus may be a long time present without causing apparent inconvenience. Rarely an abscess forms in its vicinity.

TREATMENT.—If possible, force the calculus into the mouth and then remove it. If it bulge into the oral cavity and cannot be pushed into it, incise the mucous membrane covering the calculus and take it away. If the foregoing procedures are not practicable, operate as described (p. 295).

Tumours

The parotid gland may be the seat of benign or malignant tumours or of cysts. The commonest tumours in this region are melanomata, which often contain sarcomatous elements, and are found chiefly in grey horses.

TREATMENT.—If the tumour be benign and circumscribed, remove it, taking care not to wound the important vessels and nerves in the vicinity. If it be malignant or diffuse, it is better not to intervene. The removal of a wide-based tumour, to be radical in effect, would necessitate extirpation of the gland, a rather delicate operation which is rarely indicated. It is not usual to intervene for melanotic tumours.

Subparotid Abscess

An abscess may form in the subparotid region, usually as the result of strangles in the horse and tuberculosis in the ox. It causes a diffuse painful inflammatory swelling. If not opened, it will burst outside or inside, or in both situations, in the course of eight to fourteen days. Septic pneumonia may supervene from the pus entering the larynx and bronchi, or a fistula of the pharynx may result. The inflammation is more diffuse and more deeply situated than that caused by parotiditis.

TREATMENT consists in opening the abscess in the manner described for opening a deep-seated abscess in the region of important vessels and nerves (see p. 10). It may be possible to open the abscess with the finger after incising the skin.

AFFECTIONS OF THE NASAL CAVITIES AND FACIAL SINUSES

Exploration of the Nasal Cavities

The entrance to the nasal chambers can be readily examined without the aid of an instrument; their middle portion can be fairly well illuminated and explored by reflecting natural or artificial light into it by means of a plain or concave mirror, or by means of a small electric torch, but the depth of the cavities can only be viewed by means of a special, rather complicated electrical apparatus known as a rhino-laryngoscope. Probably the best instrument is Leiter's.

Affections of the Nostrils

Contusions of the nostrils are the result of direct violence, such as that caused by a fall or a blow.

SYMPTOMS.—The symptoms are those associated with contusions in general, and, usually, epistaxis. In severe cases there may be fracture of the nasal bones or of the septum nasi, and the formation of a submucous hæmatoma.

TREATMENT.—Apply cold and astringent antiseptic lotions to check hæmorrhage and limit extravasation and inflammatory exudate. Recovery is the rule in a few days.

Open Wounds

The wings of the nostrils in the horse are often wounded by being torn by projecting nails against which the animal rubs its nose, and by bites from other horses when standing together in lines or in stables with low partitions, especially at feeding time. The wound may be superficial or deep, perforating the nostril. In the latter case, if the lesion is in the form of a cleft its edges will gape widely, and if not sutured will heal separately, leaving a permanent fissure in the nostril. If the cartilage is involved, it may undergo necrosis.

TREATMENT.—Clean and disinfect the wound and bring its edges into accurate contact with sutures, the pin suture being very useful, as it keeps the lips of the wound immobile and in rigid apposition. Interrupted stitches going right through the wings of the nostril are necessary for perforating wounds. If the edges of the wound are uneven as the result of laceration, causing shreds of dead tissue, remove the latter with a scissors, and if the lesion is not recent, but granulating, freshen it by snipping off the granulations before suturing. Primary union may occur in wounds that have been in existence for several days if they are freshened and sutured, the rich vascularity of the part being very favourable to cicatrisation, which always takes place rapidly, despite movement and soiling of the part. Apply an antiseptic sealing topic over the line of sutures.

Necrosis of the Cartilage of the Wing of the Nostril

Necrosis of the cartilage or of the septum nasi of the nostril is indicated by a hard swelling on the inner aspect of the orifice, uni- or bilateral according as one or both nostrils are involved, and containing a sinus discharging a greyish pus which may be streaked with blood. The submaxillary lymphatic glands of the affected side are swollen and more or less indurated. On casual examination the case is suggestive of glanders, but on close investigation diagnosis of the lesion is easy.

PROGNOSIS.—There is no tendency to spontaneous cure, and the condition may resist ordinary antiseptic treatment indefinitely.

TREATMENT.—Aim at removal of the cause by extirpating the necrotic portion of the cartilage by the use of caustics or by operation. Open up the sinus to its depth and swab it with tincture of iodine or a solution of chloride of zinc (1 in 10). This is generally sufficient. The surest procedure is to curette or cut out the piece of necrotic cartilage. If the hæmorrhage be profuse, it may be arrested by plugging the nostril or by the hot iron. There may be more than one sinus requiring attention.

Œdema of the Head

Œdema of the head affects chiefly the nasal region.

ETIOLOGY.—It may be the result of a wound and infection, giving rise to simple or malignant œdema or to erysipelas, or it may be a symptom of a specific disease such as purpura hæmorrhagica in the horse, or malignant catarrh in the ox. A dependent position of the head favours the condition.

SYMPTOMS.—The œdema is easily recognised by the great increase in the size of the head. There is more or less dyspnœa from encroachment of the swelling on the lumen of the nose, and even asphyxia may supervene.

TREATMENT.—Treat the condition from which the symptoms arise. In simple œdema resulting from injury, raising the head above the level of the body may be sufficient. This may be effected by putting a platform covered with a sack of hay in front of the horse and allowing him to rest his lower jaw on it. Pricking the swelling here and there, with antiseptic precautions, may have a good effect by allowing some of the serum to escape. If suffocation be threatened, perform tracheotomy.

Fracture of the Nasal Bones and of the Septum Nasi

Fractures of the nasal bones are fairly common in the horse, and are always due to direct violence, such as falling on the face, colliding with a fixed object, or a kick from another horse.

Symptoms.—The symptoms are those of traumatic inflammation or contusion, with bleeding from the nose and perhaps deformity. When the lesion is subcutaneous and the swelling is not marked, displacement

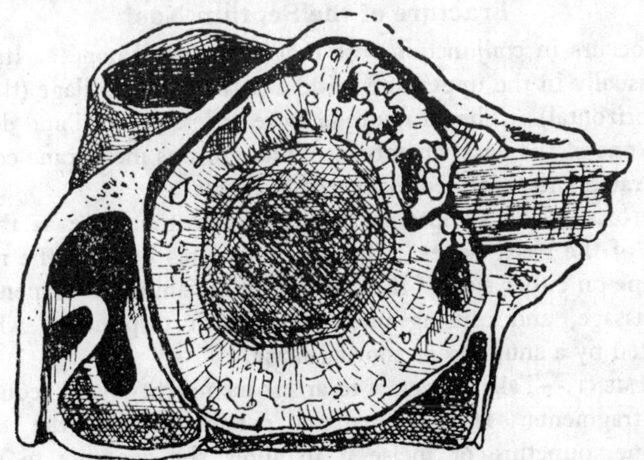

Fig. 235.—Facial Œdema after Injury.

of the fragments may be noticeable, but fracture may occur without displacement. When there is comminution of the bone, crepitation can be detected. If the fracture be compound, the broken bone is visible. The condition may be complicated with crushing of the turbinated bones, which may afterwards undergo necrosis as the result of infection of the seat of injury. The septum nasi may be damaged and displaced. In these bad cases there may be dyspnœa from occlusion of the nasal chambers. Emphysema may ensue in the surrounding tissues, but is never extensive. Necrosis of the nasal bone may be a sequel to infection in compound fracture.

Treatment.—When there is no displacement, treat as a contusion and give antiseptic inhalations to allay inflammation of the nasal mucous membrane. Use cold douches on the face to combat epistaxis, which is usually easily arrested. To reduce a displaced fragment near the nasal orifice, introduce a piece of wood guarded with a small pad on its end into the nostril, and using it as a lever of the first order endeavour to raise the depressed piece of bone. If it be higher up, trephine the bone in its vicinity and perform leverage through the opening, or the lever may be inserted through an incision at the level of the fracture, but the fragment may be so firmly fixed in the displaced position that its reduction is impossible. An immobilising dressing is not necessary. If the fracture be compound, treat accordingly. Remove loose spicules of bone, replace attached portions that are displaced, and apply an antiseptic lotion and powder. Treat complications according to their nature. Perform tracheotomy if necessary.

Fracture of the Septum Nasi

This occurs in conjunction with that of the nasal bones. Its situation is usually in the upper and middle part of the cartilage (the head being horizontal). The structure is more or less crushed and deviated towards one of the nasal chambers. The mucous membrane covering it is lacerated and separated to a variable extent.

SYMPTOMS.—The symptoms are practically the same as those of fracture of the nasal bones. Blood accumulates beneath the mucous membrane on either side of the septum, diminishing the lumen of the nasal passage, and causing interference with respiration, which is manifested by a snuffling or snoring noise.

TREATMENT.—Take measures to arrest hæmorrhage and reduce displaced fragments. If a hæmatoma persist beneath the mucous membrane, puncture or incise it to allow the contents to escape. Necrosis of the cartilage may result from infection, and must be treated as described.

Tumours of the Nostrils

Papillomata or warts, which are common on the skin of the muzzle in the horse, are generally multiple and of small dimensions. When very small, they frequently disappear spontaneously. Large ones usually persist.

TREATMENT.—The application of a solution of caustic potash or potassium chlorate or salicylic acid ointment causes small warts to wither and drop off. Larger ones may be snipped off with the scissors. Those that are too large to be removed in this way can be dissected out with the knife, the operation being easily done in the standing position under the influence of local anæsthesia, the resulting wound being sutured. When very numerous and of considerable size, treatment cannot be undertaken.

Other tumours are rare in the region of the nostrils, and when they are present must be extirpated. Malignant growths are usually incurable. Polypoid fibromata occasionally occur in the horse just inside the anterior nares. They may be multiple, and then interfere with breathing, causing a respiratory noise, and when bilateral more or less dyspnœa, depending upon the amount of obstruction of the air passages. They may be removed by the ecraseur or a snare, or by the knife. When in clusters they cannot be completely taken away, and the cicatricial contraction which follows this partial excision causes increased and permanent stenosis of the nasal orifice, and if both sides are affected, the dyspnœa will be so marked that tracheotomy and the insertion of a tube will be necessary to enable the horse to work.

FIG. 236.—ATHEROMA OF THE FALSE NOSTRIL.

Cyst or Atheroma in the False Nostril

A sebaceous cyst may form in the false nostril in the horse, causing a local swelling and perhaps a nasal respiratory noise due to encroachment on the nasal passage.

TREATMENT.—Incision of the swelling, evacuating it, and swabbing its lining with tincture of iodine or any irritant or stimulating topic, such as ammonia or turpentine liniment, constitute an effective method of treatment, care being taken that the irritant does not come in contact with the mucous membrane of the nose. The surest procedure is dissecting out the cyst as if it were a new growth.

Paralysis of the False Nostril

Temporary paralysis of the false nostril due to loss of function in the dilator naris lateralis muscle is occasionally seen in the horse. When both sides are affected, severe dyspnœa or threatening asphyxia may result from the wing of the nostril falling in towards the lumen of the respiratory passage instead of being drawn outwards during inspiration. It is only during exercise that the distressed breathing is observed. The condition is probably due to injury of a branch of the facial nerve.

The TREATMENT is that for paralysis. When the nerve recovers from the injury its function returns.

Traumatic Lesions of the Nasal Chambers

Traumatic lesions of the nasal cavities are associated as a rule with those described in connection with the nasal bones, but in rare instances they are due to the penetration of foreign bodies through the floor of the nasal passage. Injuries of the lower part of the chambers can be recognised through the nostrils, but those of the upper part are only revealed by epistaxis and by a nasal respiratory noise. When the turbinated bones or septum nasi are involved, necrosis of these structures may supervene.

TREATMENT.—Treat the lesion according to its nature. Wounds of the nasal cavities usually heal rapidly. Irrigate the passage with a gentle stream of a non-irritant antiseptic liquid like potassium permanganate (1 in 1,000). The liquid may be introduced by gravity through a funnel and tube via the other nasal chamber, whence it reaches the affected side through the posterior nares. Avoid the use of irritant solutions and take care not to use great force with the syringe for fear of causing the liquid to enter the larynx and bronchi and set up broncho-pneumonia. Insufflation of iodoform is advisable to assist in counteracting infection and preventing necrosis.

Epistaxis (Bleeding from the Nose)

This may be (1) idiopathic, primary, or essential; or (2) symptomatic or secondary. The hæmorrhage may be from one or both nostrils. The mucous membrane of the nasal chambers is very richly supplied with blood, being fenestrated with small vessels superficially situated and liable to be ruptured on comparatively slight provocation.

ETIOLOGY.—(1) *Idiopathic hæmorrhage* occurs without any lesion of the nasal cavity, and the only apparent cause is congestion of the blood-vessels resulting from violent exertion such as racing, especially in warm weather. Appearing under other circumstances, it can only be ascribed to some affection of the blood or of the small bloodvessels (hæmophilia, leucæmia).

(2) *Secondary hæmorrhage* is symptomatic of some lesion in the nose, usually of traumatic origin, or due to an ulcerating tumour or to glanders. In the dog it may be due to the presence of the *Linguatula tænioides* in the nasal fossa. It may also be caused by irritating dust getting into the nasal cavities, such as that from musty hay, and it has been seen in horses working in limekilns, when it is due to finely powdered lime suspended in the air having a corrosive effect on the bloodvessels of the Scheiderian membrane. A foreign body or parasites in the nose may cause the condition.

If the hæmorrhage be very profuse or prolonged, or repeated frequently at short intervals, it may prove fatal. Bleeding due to a morbid condition is frequently of a recurrent nature.

DIAGNOSIS.—Epistaxis is distinguished from hæmoptosis or bleeding from the lungs by the blood in the latter case being foamy and always coming from both nostrils, and from the mouth as well in some cases. Moreover, the hæmorrhage in the lungs causes accelerated respiration and dyspnœa, and gives rise to hissing or mucous râles, which can be heard on auscultation of the chest. Hæmatemesis, or bleeding from the stomach, occurs through the mouth and nose, and the blood appears clotted and blackish, like coffee-grounds. When the seat of the hæmorrhage is far up the nose it may be difficult to ascertain the cause of the condition. The rhino-laryngoscope would be useful for the purpose. Mallein can be employed when glanders is suspected.

TREATMENT.—Apply cold douches to the face, and inject hot water or a solution of vinegar or alum or tannin into the nasal cavity. Keep the patient quiet with the head raised, but not to a sufficient extent to enable the blood to flow into the larynx. If the bleeding be from one nostril only and be very profuse, plug the cavity at the level of the bleeding part as described on p. 273. If the hæmorrhage be bilateral, both nasal cavities, of course, cannot be plugged without first performing tracheotomy and inserting an ordinary tube or a tampon canula, the stem of the latter being enveloped in lint or gauze, which prevents the blood passing alongside it into the lungs. Internal treatment is also indicated, giving cold or acidulated drinks, subcutaneous, intravenous, or rectal injections of normal saline, or atropine, ergotine, or adrenaline hypodermically. The last mentioned has given good results in race-horses, but is often disappointing. The administration of normal horse serum is said to have proved highly effective as a cure for epistaxis in race-horses in India. (See Jugular Phlebotomy, p. 317.)

Necrosis of the Turbinated Bones

This occurs occasionally in the horse, but is rare in other animals.

ETIOLOGY.—The lesion is generally due to strangles, with an accumulation of pus in the folds of the bones, but it may also be the result of a wound inflicted directly through the nostril or through the nasal bones followed by infection of the seat of injury, or it may be a complication of disease of the root of a molar tooth in its vicinity.

SYMPTOMS.—The symptoms consist of a fœtid purulent discharge, usually unilateral, interference with respiration, manifested by a snuffling or roaring noise, a swelling in the nasal chamber, which may or may not be visible or palpable from the nostril, ulceration and discoloration of the bone, which may be felt rough by the finger if within reach, dullness on percussion of the affected region, and swelling of the submaxillary lymphatic glands.

PROGNOSIS.—When the necrotic portion can be entirely removed cure supervenes.

TREATMENT consists in operating as described (see p. 274).

Abscess on the Septum Nasi

Occasionally an abscess forms on the septum nasi, especially in the horse, due to an open wound and infection and causing a nasal respiratory noise. If it can be reached with the finger, fluctuation can be detected in it and it will be visible from the nostril. Otherwise diagnosis will be difficult. The abscess may extend through the cartilage, forming a swelling in each nasal chamber. It may be acute or chronic.

TREATMENT.—Open the abscess if possible; if not, prescribe inhalations of steam to hasten its maturation, and wait until it bursts.

Cyst in the Nose

Sometimes in the colt or filly a cyst containing a syrupy liquid is found in one of the nasal cavities. It causes a noise during inspiration, and may be felt and seen through the nostril. Its wall is thin and may rupture on pressure with the finger. It has been associated with a similar cystic condition in one of the maxillary sinuses. When largely opened by incision or by excision of a portion of its wall and its lining is swabbed with tincture of iodine it disappears permanently.

Foreign Bodies in the Nose

There are many cases on record of foreign bodies being found in the nasal chambers, gaining entrance through the anterior or posterior nares or through an abnormal communication between the mouth and the nose. Food material may be coughed into the nasal chambers from the pharynx or return this way in a case of dysphagia, during an attack of pharyngitis, or in a case of paralysis of the pharynx. Alimentary matter may also reach the nose via the maxillary sinus when a dental fistula opens into the sinus after the affected tooth has been removed. The writer has reported a case in which the fifth upper molar tooth became displaced into the nasal fossa in an aged carriage-horse (*Vet. Jour.*, 1906).

In the horse, various things have been found in the nasal chambers which were apparently introduced through the nostrils accidentally or intentionally, such as particles of hay or straw, a piece of sponge, a bit of wood, and strands of tow or wool. Pus may become inspissated in the turbinated bones after a case of strangles and remain *in situ* indefinitely. A concretion may escape from the guttural pouch through the Eustachian tube and lodge in the nose.

SYMPTOMS.—If the foreign body be large, there will be symptoms of nasal obstruction characterised by a respiratory noise. The patient may reveal nasal irritation by snorting or rubbing the nose against objects, and when the body has been in position for some time it will give rise to a muco-purulent unilateral nasal discharge. There may be epistaxis. Swelling of the submaxillary glands is absent unless the case is of long standing. There is no deformity on the face. When the object is near the nostril it can be seen, but when it is in the upper part of the chamber it requires the use of the rhinoscope to recognise it.

TREATMENT.—Remove the foreign body as soon as possible through the nostril, if within reach, by means of a forceps. If this cannot be done, localise as far as possible the seat of the object, trephine the bone at its level, and extract it through the trephine opening, or insert a sound through the latter and, if practicable, push the foreign body towards the nasal orifice. Particles of hay, straw, wool, or tow must be picked out individually with a forceps. A gentle stream of lukewarm boiled water directed up the nose or downwards after introduction through the other nasal chamber by means of a tube and funnel may serve to dislodge material fixed therein. In small animals procedure is much more difficult, on account of the small size of the anterior nares. It may be necessary to operate by trephining the nasal cavity.

Parasites in the Nasal Chambers

The only parasite with which the veterinarian is familiar in the nasal chambers is the *Linguatula tænioides*, which is almost confined to the dog, being very rarely found in the horse, mule, sheep, and goat. It is very common in the dog in some places, whilst in others it is rarely met with. The parasite may take up its abode in any part of the cavity, but most commonly in the convolutions of the ethmoid and in the cul-de-sac of the middle meatus. The dog becomes infested by eating the viscera of herbivora, usually the sheep and rabbit, containing the larvæ of the parasite.

SYMPTOMS.—Frequently the number of parasites does not exceed two, and then there may be no objective symptoms. When they are more numerous, their presence may be revealed by agitation of the host, the dog scratching his nose with his paws, sneezing frequently, and sometimes showing aberrations simulating rabies. Epileptiform fits may supervene. There may be a mucoid discharge from the nose, occasionally streaked with blood. The parasites remain for months in the nose, eventually die, or are expelled, when the symptoms to which they have given rise disappear.

Diagnosis is arrived at by finding the parasites or their eggs, the latter being discovered on microscopic examination of the nasal discharge. The condition may be confounded with nasal catarrh, distemper, or rabies. On post-mortem examination, exploration of the nasal chambers is indicated when diagnosis of the cause of death is required under the circumstances mentioned.

Treatment.—Treatment of the symptoms is of no avail while the linguatula remains *in situ*. An errhine such as snuff may be used to make the dog sneeze, with a view to causing expulsion of the pest. It seldom has the desired effect. If the case is alarming, the only thing to do is to trephine the nose and remove the worms. Slightly irritating injections have been used with some success—for example, dilute solutions of ammonia or benzine. These may be introduced through the nostril or through an artificial opening, their object being to dislodge or destroy the parasites.

Tumours of the Nasal Chambers

Most of the common tumours of the body affect the nasal chambers in the domesticated animals, but probably the commonest neoplasms of this region are fibrous polypi. The principal subjects are the horse, ox, and dog. The following new growths have been found in the nose: papillomata, angiomata, lipomata, myxomata, sarcomata, carcinomata, and adenomata. Dentigerous cysts may be met with bulging into the nasal cavity from the bones of the jaws. Botriomycotic tumours may develop in the nasal fossæ of the horse, but they are very rare. Actinomycotic enlargements frequently encroach on the nasal passages in the ox.

Diagnosis.—Diagnosis is easy when the tumour is well developed. The following symptoms are usually observed: a mucoid or mucopurulent discharge, epistaxis, occasionally more or less complete obstruction of the nasal passage causing a respiratory bruit, and deformity of the face due to bulging of the nasal bones. If the neoplasm be malignant it may be ulcerating externally, and the submaxillary lymphatic glands may be enlarged by the formation of secondary growths when the primary one is carcinoma.

Treatment.—Malignant tumours are incurable. It is useless to operate to remove them. Benign tumours, if fairly circumscribed, are amenable to treatment. They may be excised through the nostril, or through an opening to the inner side of the false nostril, or through a breach in the upper part of the nasal bones, depending upon the situation of the neoplasm. Pedunculated tumours can be extirpated by means of the ecraseur or by ligation, the tumour being cut off on this side of the ligature. The procedure for operation is similar to that described in connection with diseased turbinated bones (see p. 274). If benign tumours are multiple and bilateral and their removal is impracticable, the usefulness of the horse may be prolonged by tracheotomy.

AFFECTIONS OF THE SINUSES

Traumatic lesions, including contusions, open wounds, and fractures of the bones of the facial sinuses, are almost identical with those of the nasal bones, and must be dealt with accordingly. Lesions of the sinuses and nasal cavities often coexist. Rarely the cranium and brain are involved in injuries of the frontal sinus. The prognosis of these affections, without complications, is usually good. The accumulation of blood in the sinus favours the proliferation of organisms therein, which may cause suppuration and a collection of pus in the cavity, necessitating further intervention as described below.

Figs. 237 and 238 illustrate a plastic operation performed by Bayer to remedy loss of skin in two carriage-horses which had run away and damaged the bone to such an extent as to necessitate removal of considerable portions. The skin having become adherent to the mucous lining of the sinus, it was necessary to dissect considerable flaps in order to cover the defects. The parts were carefully shaved and disinfected, and a slender paring removed from the edges of the wound to ensure fresh surfaces for union. In the first case an incision was carried from *d* successively to points *f*, *g*, *h*, and the flap dissected free from adjacent tissues, leaving it connected with the rest of the skin only at *a*, *h*. The prolongation to *f* and the large size of the flap were necessitated by the knowledge that contraction would occur. The edges *a*, *e*, *d*, *f* were then brought in contact with *a*, *b*, *c*, and *f*, *g* were united to *c*, *d* with closely placed sutures. Healing of the flap was perfect, and the exposed surface *h*, *d*, *f*, *g* soon granulated and was finally covered by skin. When in consequence of injuries in the neighbourhood of the neck or withers large indolent wounds are left, healing can often be effected by incising the skin and subcutaneous tissues on either side of the wound, dissecting the skin free so as to form flaps, and uniting these in the middle line as indicated in Figs. 239 and 240.

Pus in the Sinuses

ETIOLOGY.—The causes of pus in the sinuses may be primary or secondary.

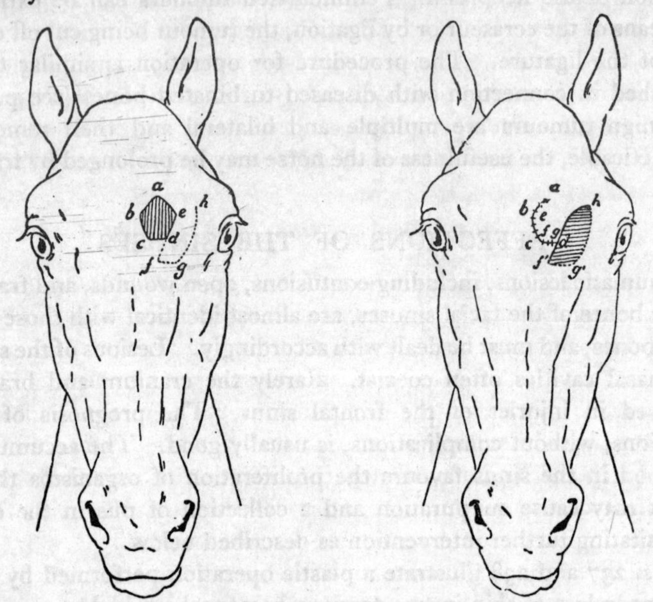

FIGS. 237 AND 238.—PLASTIC OPERATION TO REMEDY LOSS OF SKIN RESULTING FROM FRACTURE OF THE SINUS.

Primary Causes.—The primary causes are injuries of the walls of the sinuses—viz., contusions and open wounds—causing bleeding into

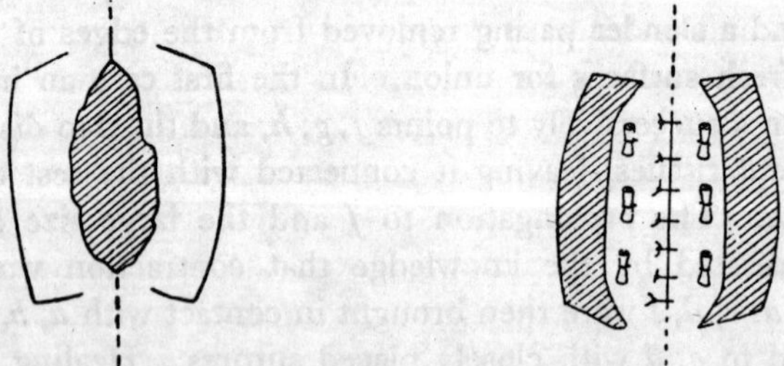

FIGS. 239 AND 240.—OPERATION TO PROMOTE HEALING OF LARGE INDOLENT WOUNDS OF THE NECK OR WITHERS.

the cavities, where pyogenic organisms may multiply and cause suppuration, the pus accumulating for want of a dependent orifice. The prolonged sojourn of pus in the sinus brings about chronic inflammation of its lining, and may lead to necrosis of the inner plates of the bones and of the turbinated bones, which then act as a secondary cause. A spicule of bone in a case of comminuted fracture may fall into the sinus and act as a foreign body, or the latter may gain entrance from the nasal cavity in the form of alimentary matter coughed up from the pharynx.

Secondary Causes comprise dental affections with suppuration of the alveoli of the teeth and perforation of their walls into the sinus, malignant tumours involving the sinuses, *Œstrus ovis* in the frontal sinus of the sheep, and injuries of the horns in cattle, as described.

SYMPTOMS.—The first symptom to attract attention is a nasal discharge, which at the commencement of the affection is of a mucopurulent, non-offensive nature, but when it is well established it is purely purulent and fœtid. The pus is greyish, often contains yellowish-white coagula, and may occasionally be streaked with blood, which may be an indication that the bone is ulcerated. The discharge is usually unilateral, one sinus only being affected as a rule, and it is constantly escaping. It is more copious during exercise, due to the movements of the head and the increased respiration causing currents of air to pass through the sinus and force out more pus. The submaxillary lymphatic glands become swollen after some time, but remain movable under the skin. If the sinus be distended with contents there will be a swelling at its level, and when the cavity is full of fluid there will be dullness on percussion, which may also cause a little pain, as shown by the resentment of the animal. There is seldom constitutional disturbance, but when the affection is of long standing the subject is generally somewhat unthrifty and more easily sweated and tired than usual. There may be some lachrymation of the eye of the affected side, and a clot of mucus may lodge at its inner canthus.

DIAGNOSIS.—The condition must be distinguished from affections of the nose, which are usually accompanied by a respiratory noise, due to swelling therein, and from glanders, which can be eliminated by the mallein test. Positive diagnosis can be made by exploration of the sinus through an opening made by a gimlet or a trephine, preferably the latter, as it makes a larger aperture. When the gimlet is employed, the pus may be seen in the groove of the instrument. The absence of the characteristic features of pus in the guttural pouches and of tumours of the nose, dealt with elsewhere, will serve to exclude them in considering the nature of the case.

PROGNOSIS.—The prognosis should generally be guarded, for although the condition is not dangerous, it is often difficult to say whether it will recur or not after apparent cure. When the result of an injury which has not damaged the bones to an appreciable extent, rapid cure is the rule by appropriate treatment. When due to secondary causes recovery depends on their removal, and when this is not thorough there is sure to be a recurrence of the malady.

TREATMENT consists in operating as described on p. 274.

Foreign Bodies

Foreign bodies in the sinuses are not common. They may be inspissated pus, spicules of broken bone, alimentary matter gaining entrance through a breach in the floor of the sinus following the repulsion of a molar tooth or through a dental fistula communicating with the mouth, bits of wool or tow which had been used as plugs in trephine openings, and bits of shrapnel or shell casing. Smooth, clean, foreign bodies that have entered the sinus without causing much damage to the tissues may remain *in situ* without detection, as they only give rise to a little mucous discharge from the nose. Otherwise they set up the condition of " pus in the sinus," when the treatment for it must be adopted and the foreign body removed. When the sinus becomes filled with alimentary matter which has come from the mouth through the empty alveolus which is communicating with the air cavity, it will be necessary to evacuate the sinus and plug the alveolus with gutta-percha to prevent recurrence of the condition. (See p. 288.) If the abnormal passage between the two cavities be recent, it may be sufficient to plug its upper part with gauze until its oral portion is almost closed by granulations.

Parasites

The parasites found in the sinuses are the linguatula in the frontal sinus of the dog and the larvæ of the *Œstrus ovis* in that of the sheep. The favourite habitat of the linguatula is the nasal chamber of the dog, but occasionally it develops in the frontal sinus. The latter cavity is the predilection site of the *Œstrus ovis*, but in rare instances it infests the maxillary sinus. The number of larvæ present in the sinus of the sheep is ordinarily two to six, but upwards of fifty have been found in it. Except a large number exists in the sinus, there may be no symptoms betraying their presence. When they cause trouble there is a mucoid discharge from the nose, sneezing and snorting, and the animal rubs the nose with the claws or against a fixed object. Phenomena resembling those of sturdy may supervene.

PREVENTION.—Preventative measures comprise the use of agents for keeping the flies at bay, such as tar smeared on the nostrils, and the destruction of the larvæ.

TREATMENT.—Treatment is not very satisfactory. Drugs are of little use in destroying or dislodging the parasites except introduced directly into the sinus after trephining it. Benzine diluted with water and injected into the sinus is sometimes successful. Those that can be reached may be removed mechanically with forceps. The method of dealing with the linguatula in the dog has been described in connection with affections of the nasal chambers (p. 549).

AFFECTIONS OF THE JAWS

Fracture of the Superior Maxilla

Fracture of the superior maxilla is caused by direct violence, as may result from a fall, or collision, or the animal striking the head violently against a hard fixed object. It may be accompanied by fracture of other bones of the skull. The seat of fracture may be the palatine plate or the alveolar border.

SYMPTOMS.—The following symptoms may be observed : deformity due to inflammation and displacement of the fragments, hæmorrhage from the mouth and nose, crepitation, salivation, and interference with mastication.

PROGNOSIS.—When the fracture is simple, rapid cure usually takes place ; when compound, it may also heal without complication ; or infection of the wound may lead to pus in the maxillary sinus or necrosis of the bone, and if the alveolus of a tooth is involved a dental fistula may supervene. General infection or toxæmia may arise when the wound is contaminated by very virulent organisms.

TREATMENT.—The treatment is that for contusions or open wounds, and fractures in general. If there be neither a wound nor displacement no special intervention is required. Loose teeth may become fixed in a few days, and therefore should not be removed until suppuration occurs in their alveoli. Semi-liquid diet should be given to limit the masticatory movements. If there be a wound in the mouth, the cavity should be washed after feeding to prevent food material lodging in the wound.

Trephining may be required to allow of leverage of a depressed fragment. An immobilising dressing is not essential as a rule, but strips of plaster or bands of calico smeared with pitch may be applied across the face to maintain fragments in position. The head-collar should be left off, and to prevent the horse knocking the injured part against the manger he may be kept in a stall, tied by the pillar reins fixed to a strap round the neck, and fed from a trough or pail placed at a convenient level and removed after feeding, when a tight nose-band may be used to keep the jaws at rest. Complications are to be treated according to their nature.

Fracture of the Premaxilla

The premaxilla may be fractured by direct violence, falling forward on the nose, or by a kick or blow. The fracture may be transverse or longitudinal, or both, uni- or bilateral, and simple or compound, usually the latter. It may also be fractured in the horse by his seizing hold violently of a fixed object.

TREATMENT.—Treatment is on general principles for wounds and fractures. A stout piece of stick may be used to push the displaced fragment into position, holding it by the two ends, and pressing its middle part against the bone, the horse being in the cast position. When the displacement is inwards towards the mouth, the stick may be used as a lever of the first order to raise the depressed bone.

Retention is best effected by means of silver wire wound round the teeth of the two premaxillæ, whether the fracture be transverse or longitudinal. When the fracture occurs in front of the canine tooth, the latter proves a very useful *point d'appui* for affixing the wire. When there is displacement upwards of both bones, wire may be attached to the incisors and to the first molar on each side, a hole being bored by means of a drill between the latter and the second molar to accommodate the wire. A niche should be made in the corner incisor to prevent the wire slipping.

If fixation of the teeth be insufficient or impossible owing to loss of teeth, the bones may be sutured with wire passed through holes made by the drill. The wound in the mucous membrane should be sutured and care taken that a portion of it does not become insinuated between the fragments and prevent their union. The wound should be thoroughly cleaned with a solution of potassium permanganate before performing reductions and any loose spicules of bone should be removed.

Some of the incisors may be broken, and projecting points thereon should be removed with a file. Loose teeth should not be removed at once. They may become fixed again after a few days; if not, they should then be extracted. The mouth should be washed after meals. Diet requiring little mastication is indicated. The case usually makes a good recovery. Should necrosis of the bone supervene and union fail to occur, the loose fragment may be removed. Fracture in small animals is dealt with on similar lines.

Fracture of the Inferior Maxilla

The inferior maxilla may be fractured by kicks, falls, or direct violence of any kind, and also, though rarely, by violent muscular effort, as has been known to occur from excessive contraction of the masseter muscles when a gag was placed in the mouth of the horse. Repulsion of a tooth may cause the bone to fracture. In the dog it may be fractured by the vigorous movement of the hind-limb of a beast or stag which it has seized in its jaws. Occasionally the lower jaw of the fœtus is fractured as the result of severe traction on a hook fixed in it during delivery.

FIG. 241.—INCOMPLETE UNION OF FRACTURE OF THE BODY OF THE LOWER JAW.
(From a photograph.)

The site of the fracture may be the body, one or both rami, the condyle, or the coronoid process. The direction of the fracture in the body may be longitudinal, transverse, or oblique. The fracture may be simple or compound, usually the latter. In either case it may be comminuted.

TREATMENT.—Treatment is on similar lines to those adopted for fractures of the premaxilla.

1. *Fracture through the Symphysis.*—Most common in young animals. Replace the fragments in their normal position and maintain them there by joining the teeth on either side by wire. An alternative but less satisfactory procedure in the dog is to fix the two jaws together by a bandage, and feed the animal artificially with liquid food introduced at the commissure of the lips or through an œsophageal tube.

2. *Fracture through One Side of the Body.*—After reduction, wire the teeth as in No. 1, if those of the affected side are sufficiently intact for the purpose ; otherwise the bones may be united by wire sutures

3. *Transverse Fracture through the Body or through Both Rami near the Symphysis.*—In this case the separated fragment is displaced downwards and it is difficult to keep it in place after reduction. Wiring the incisors to the first molars may be useful in conjunction with an apparatus in the form of a V fixed to the lower jaw, the apex of the V being spoon-shaped to support the chin and its branches being grooved to adapt themselves to the horizontal rami. The parts in contact with the skin are padded and the apparatus is kept in position by padded

straps over the face and poll. For small animals a device of this nature made in gutta-percha may answer the purpose. The objection to all these dressings is that they become displaced, cause excoriation of the skin, and interfere with mastication. A false joint may supervene, owing to fibrous union taking place between the fragments. Wire sutures through the bone are probably the best means of immobilising the seat of fracture. Should every method fail to bring about union or necrosis of the loose pieces of bone ensue, the latter may be amputated. The operation has been done successfully in the horse and dog.

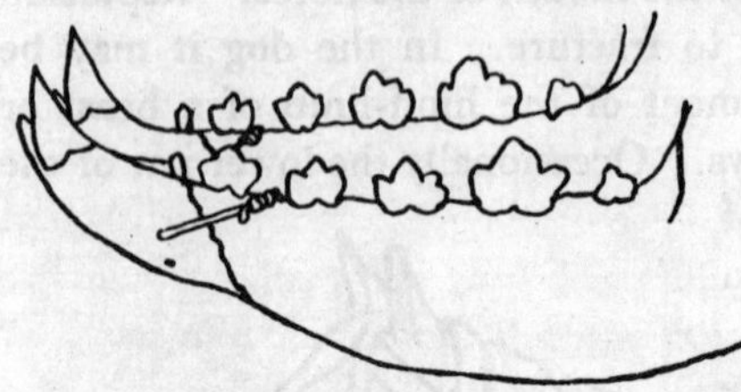

FIG. 242.—WIRE SUTURE INSERTED IN THE FRACTURED INFERIOR MAXILLA IN THE DOG.

4. *Fracture of One Ramus*.—This requires no treatment, there being practically no displacement. Even when compound and comminuted, recovery usually takes place. The vertical ramus may be fractured along with the horizontal ramus, and healing ensue in both places. If the latter ramus is broken in two places with a loose intervening fragment healing may not supervene especially if the fracture is compound.

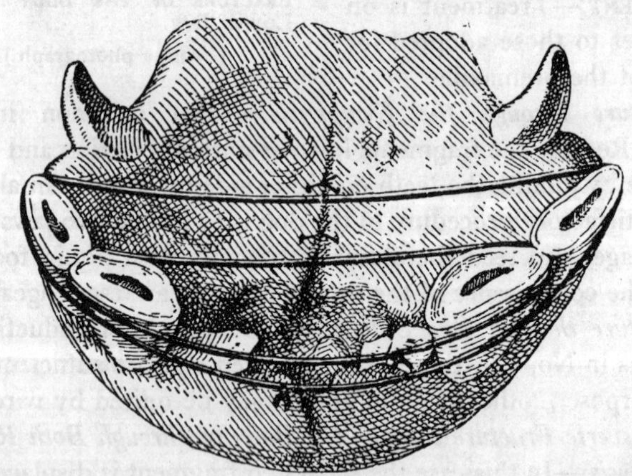

FIG. 243.—FRACTURE OF THE LOWER JAW UNITED BY WIRING.

A common treatment with practitioners is to apply a blister or pitch plaster on the skin at the level of the fracture. The blister causes increased inflammation and swelling, which have an immobilising effect and bring about additional hyperæmia, which may hasten the healing process. If the fracture be compound or comminuted, treat accordingly. Loose bits of bone may be felt through the wound in the mouth, and should be removed if free from attachment. The oral wound must be cleaned after meals.

In all cases of fractures of the jaws, soft easily masticated food is indicated. Fracture of the coronoid process or of the condyle is rare. Fibrous union occurs in the former case and anchylosis of the joint is apt to supervene in the latter.

Contusion, Sinus, Fistula

Contusions of the jaws are inflicted in the same way as fractures. They may give rise to osteo-periostitis. A common seat of injury is the inferior maxilla, where it is usually due to striking the jaw against the manger. The lesion in this case is not of an acute nature, as a rule, being gradually produced by repeated slight knocking of the posterior border of the bone against the edge of the manger and assuming the form of an exostosis. It may also be caused by the constant use of a head-collar with a tight nose-band. Should infection gain entrance into the injured part, necrosis of the bone may supervene and purulent osteomyelitis may extend to a variable depth. The sinus which results may abut on the root of a tooth, constituting a form of dental fistula. The floor of the mouth may be injured by the bit, the bone becoming affected with acute osteo-periostitis, which frequently becomes septic from organisms penetrating through the abraded mucous membrane and causing necrosis of a thin layer of bone, which soon becomes separated and extruded. The disease may extend through the bone, causing a fistula opening on the posterior border of the jaw.

SYMPTOMS.—The symptoms are those of acute or chronic traumatic inflammation, or of a sinus or fistula in the bone. When an exostosis is present on the posterior border of the lower jaw it is easily recognised. A sinus in the bone is characterised by a suppurating orifice surrounded by a hard inflammatory enlargement. A probe passed into it comes in contact with the rough bone, and may reveal a loose portion, or it may abut on the root of a tooth, or it may be passed into the mouth when there is another opening there. There may be a cavity in the bone filled with thick pus.

TREATMENT.—Alter the manger, which is usually too narrow, or cease feeding from it. Discontinue the use of the bit until the oral lesion heals, and afterwards use a rubber bit if the horse "pulls." Adopt antiphlogistic measures for inflammation. Remove a sequestrum when it is loose. When a sinus in the mouth persists unduly, open it up and remove loose bone, if present, or curette the bone which may be affected with superficial caries. It may be necessary to make a counter-opening externally at the level of the inferior border of the bone. When there is an external sinus into the bone, remove an elliptical piece of skin round its orifice. Enlarge the latter by means of a trephine, bone forceps, or sharp chisel, if necessary. Remove loose pieces of bone and curette the cavity throughout, irrigate it with tincture of iodine, dust it with iodoform or dress it with B.I.P.P., and plug it with gauze. Remove the plug the following day, and treat subsequently as an open wound, continuing the application of the iodine and iodoform until the cavity is found to be closing, when dry dressing will be sufficient. Although an offensive discharge persists for some days after the operation, cure is usually uninterrupted even in cases where the root of the tooth has been exposed, provided that alveolar periostitis has not supervened in the latter case. Should the alveolar membrane become involved, extraction of the tooth will be necessary.

FIG. 244.—CANCER OF THE INFERIOR MAXILLA.

If the exostosis on the border of the jaw is small and has a narrow base, it can be easily removed with a chisel and mallet or a fine saw. If it be large it is better to leave it alone. It is only a blemish.

Open Wounds

Open wounds of the jaws are only of special interest, in that they may be complicated by infection and necrosis of bone, as just described.

Tumours

What has been said about tumours of the sinuses applies in a general way to those of the upper jaw, which is more commonly affected than the lower jaw. Neoplasms of the jaws are fairly frequently met with in veterinary practice, especially in the horse and dog. In the ox actinomycotic tumours are very common.

The following varieties of new growths may be found affecting the maxillary bones :

1. **Dentigerous Cysts,** which are slow in development and may persist for a long time without causing inconvenience, but occasionally they suppurate, leading to necrosis of the bone and the formation of a sinus.

2. **Fibromata.**—Most common in the dog, growing on the surface of the alveolar border. They may undergo calcification or ossification.

3. **Chondromata.**—Hard subperiosteal tumours, uniform or bosselated on their surface, slow in development, and having little tendency to spread to surrounding parts.

FIG. 245.—BOTRIOMYCOSIS OF THE LOWER JAW.

4. **Sarcomata,** developing in the substance of the bone or beneath the periosteum, growing and extending rapidly, accompanied by ulceration of the skin and mucous membrane, and interfering with respiration or mastication, or both, according to their situation. They often cause loosening or shedding of the teeth and hæmorrhage from the mouth or nose, and may become generalised, causing cachexia and death in a short time. The submaxillary lymphatic glands are seldom involved. They affect animals of every age, and are most common in the dog.

5. **Carcinomata** are almost confined to adults, and especially aged subjects. They are more common than sarcomata in the horse. They are characterised by the rapidity of their evolution, by a fœtid and purulent nasal discharge when the upper jaw is affected, by destruction of the bone, its place being taken by the tissue of the tumour, by ulceration of the skin in the later stages of the disease and a discharge of a

very offensive liquid of a dark red colour mixed with pus from the centre of the growth, by loosening and eventually shedding of the teeth in the affected region, and ultimately by enlargement of the submaxillary glands due to invasion by the neoplasmic elements. When some of the teeth are shed, there is also a stinking discharge from the mouth. When the swelling has burst or is opened, fungoid granulations form in the wound.

TREATMENT.—If benign tumours are small and circumscribed, extirpate them completely as described (Tumours of the Sinuses). It is useless to intervene for malignant neoplasms. Actinomycotic enlargements are treated by the administration of potassium iodide.

AFFECTIONS OF THE TEMPORO-MAXILLARY ARTICULATION

Contusions

Contusions of this joint are the same as those of other articulations. They may cause synovitis, which interferes with mastication, owing to the pain caused by movement of the joint. They respond to the ordinary methods of treatment. Rarely an osteo-periostitis supervenes, causing the formation of an exostosis and anchylosis of the articulation.

Open Wounds

The prognosis of penetrating wounds of the joint must be guarded, as there is always the risk of infection gaining entrance and causing septic arthritis and destruction of the articulation, with fatal consequences, owing to the patient being unable to masticate.

The TREATMENT of penetrating wounds, recognised by the escape of synovia, is on the same lines as those recommended for synovial fistula in general. When the case is chronic and the fistula shows no tendency to close, cauterisation of its borders or the application of a blister of biniodide of mercury (1 in 8) to the wound and its vicinity, or point firing the latter, may have the desired effect. A little powdered perchloride of mercury applied to the wound is often very effective, causing a scab, under which healing takes place. Easily masticated food should be given. During the intervals between feeds, a fairly tight nose-band may be applied to limit movement of the joint.

Arthritis

Dry arthritis of this joint has been seen in the horse and dog. Möller records a case in the dog in which both articulations were affected.

Symptoms.—There is difficulty in mastication, and a hard swelling is usually formed at the level of the joint. Occasionally there is little alteration externally. Crepitation may be detected due to friction of the ulcerated surfaces of the bones. The mouth cannot be properly opened, so that the condition may be confounded with trismus, from which it is distinguished by the local symptoms.

Treatment is useless when the joint is disorganised. Counter-irritation by blistering or needle-point firing may be tried in the hope that repair is possible, and that the lesion has not gone beyond the stage of chronic synovitis.

Dislocation

Dislocation of the joint is not common, even in carnivora. It would seem to be impossible in herbivora without fracture of the long coronoid process, yet cases of it in the horse and ass have been recorded by Continental veterinarians. In this country we are only familiar with the condition in the dog. The displacement is almost always forward. It occurs as the result of the dog seizing a large object in its jaws, in the staghound from the stag violently snatching its hind-limb from the grasp of the dog's mouth, and in the sheep-dog similarly from biting the hind-limb of the ox.

Symptoms.—The mouth remains wide open, the lower jaw being dropped and fixed rigidly in this position. Saliva trickles from the mouth and the tongue is pendulous. Prehension is impossible. There may be exophthalmia owing to displacement of the coronoid process into the orbit. If the luxation is unilateral, the jaw will be depressed and deviated from the affected side.

Diagnosis.—It is distinguished from paralysis by the jaw in the latter case not being fixed, but capable of being passively lifted. If the paralysis be rabiform, there will be other symptoms or a history to guide the clinician.

Treatment.—Reduction of the dislocation is effected by two movements : (1) Pushing the inferior maxilla downwards so as to bring the opposing articular surfaces on a level, and (2) pushing the bone backwards into its normal position. It can be done by placing a stout piece of stick crosswise in the mouth as far back as possible between the molars, and then forcibly bringing the jaws together. In the dog it can be accomplished by the hands alone by grasping the lower jaw with each hand, with the thumb, protected by a glove finger or cloth, resting on the alveolar border and the fingers grasping the horizontal ramus, and first depressing the jaw posteriorly and then pushing it backwards. The operation is facilitated by general anæsthesia, which is best effected in the dog by an intravenous injection of nembutal. To prevent recurrence, give soft or liquid diet only for a few days.

AFFECTIONS OF THE MOUTH

Exploration of the Mouth

In order to explore the horse's mouth proceed as follows:

1. **Without the Aid of an Instrument.**—Put a halter on the horse and have him backed into a corner or stall with plenty of light in front. Pass the left hand into the interdental space on the right side, and catching the tongue gently but firmly, draw it out at the right side of the mouth. Pass the thumb of the right hand inside the left cheek at the commissure of the lips, and draw it outwards so as to expose the gums and teeth on this side. Reversing the hands, examine the other side of the mouth in the same way. To make the horse open the mouth wider for a general view of the cavity, press on the hard palate with the thumb of the right hand while the left hand holds the tongue.

In the ox a similar procedure is adopted, the beast being securely held by the horn and nose.

In the dog, held by an assistant and prevented from going backwards, pass the right hand under the throat, with the latter between the fingers and thumb, and grasp the lower jaw, in order to steady the head. Pass the left hand gradually down the face and grasp the upper jaw with the fingers and thumb, and releasing the hold with the right hand, use it to depress the lower jaw by placing the thumb on the inner aspect of the incisor teeth.

In the cat the mouth is opened by separating the jaws by means of the two index fingers applied to the upper and lower incisors.

2. **Using an Instrument.**—To keep the jaw separated in the horse use a speculum oris or mouth gag, of which there are various patterns on the market—*e.g.*:

(1) *Varnell's gag* (Fig. 246), which is simple and useful for most purposes.

(2) *Haussmann's gag* (Fig. 252), in which the parts in the mouth are in the form of plates adapted exactly to the upper and lower incisor teeth, on which all the pressure is borne without discomfort to the patient or injury to the jaw. A raised border on the plate in front prevents its slipping off the teeth. The upper and lower parts move

on a horizontal axis and are fixed in any required position by a ratchet. It is fixed in position by straps over the poll and round the jaws. Special plates covered with leather or rubber to rest behind the incisor teeth can be used when it is necessary to have the latter exposed, or when the instrument is employed for the ox. A more serviceable and much stronger gag on the same principle as No. 2 is made by Mr. Robert Mitchell, M.R.C.V.S., Glasgow. Its utility has been proved by the writer.

(3) *Bayer's gag* (Fig. 247) is useful for a cursory examination of the

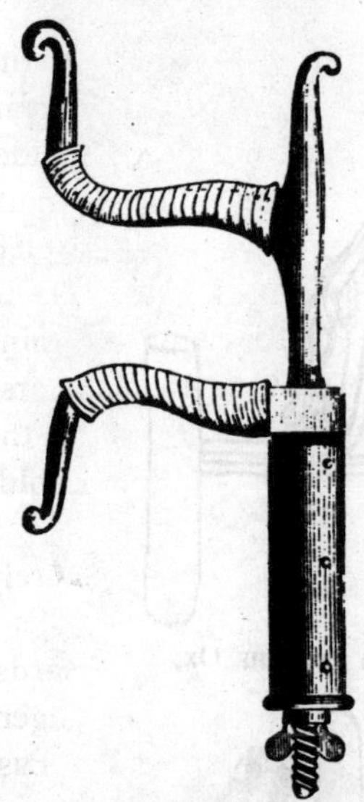

Fig. 246.—Varnell's Mouth Gag.

Fig. 247.—Bayer's Mouth Gag for Horses and Oxen.

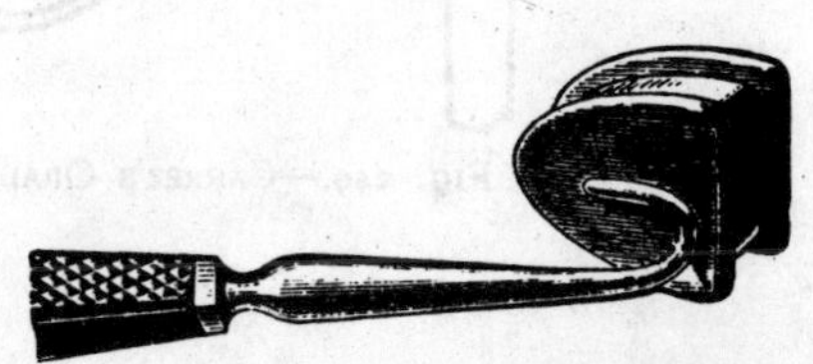

Fig. 248.—Bayer's Mouth Gag for Dogs.

mouth and for simple dental operations. It is inserted between the upper and lower rows of molars.

(4) *Carrez's gag* for the ox seems very effective and reliable. The opening O affords ample room for the insertion of the hand. The arch A fits over the face. The poll strap B and the forehead strap C fix the gag securely in position. The handles D afford good grips for assistants holding the beast.

For the dog the following patterns are useful: Gray's (Fig. 251), Woolf's, Kirk's and Hobday's which is very simple and effective. In small dogs and cats a piece of tape applied round each jaw behind the canine teeth and pulled in opposite directions answers the purpose admirably, and is often preferable to the speculum. A piece of wood placed transversely in the mouth between the molar teeth, pressing back the commissures of the lips, and fixed by a string from either end behind the ears is useful for a refractory subject, provided that it is not in the way of operative procedure. The oral cavity can be illuminated by the aid of a mirror and artificial or natural light, or by

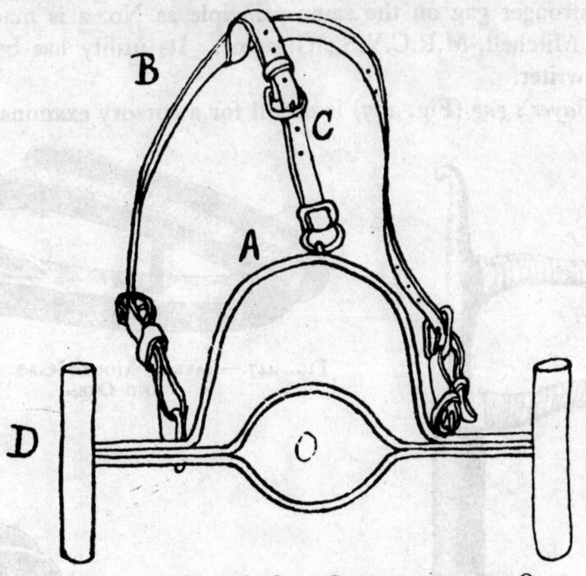

FIG. 249.—CARREZ'S ORAL SPECULUM FOR THE OX.

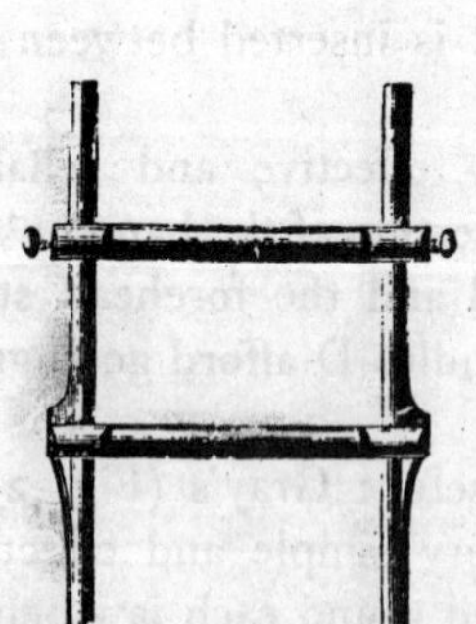

FIG. 250.—JOGER'S MOUTH GAG FOR HORSES.

This apparatus can be dismounted and packed in a very small space.

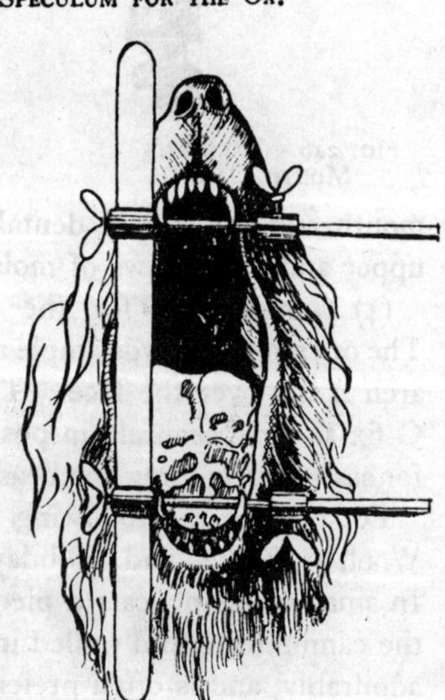

FIG. 251.—GRAY'S MOUTH GAG FOR THE DOG.

an electric torch. The molar teeth and alveolar borders of both jaws can be explored on their outer aspect by drawing the cheek outwards at the labial commissures by means of the finger or a smooth blunt

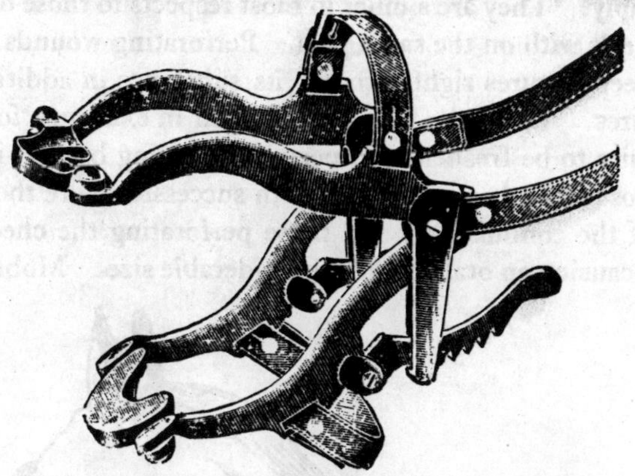

FIG. 252.—HAUSSMANN'S MOUTH GAG (OPEN).

instrument, even when the jaws are closed by a tape muzzle. Mr. Mitchell has also made a gag for the dog which can be fixed securely in position leaving the whole interior of the mouth and throat exposed,

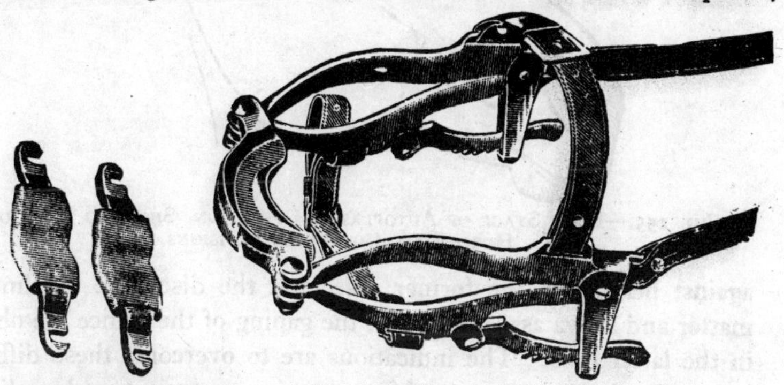

FIG. 253.—RUBBER-COVERED PLATES FOR OPERATIONS ON INCISOR TEETH.

FIG. 254.—HAUSSMANN'S MOUTH GAG (CLOSED).

facilitating all surgical procedures therein, no part of the instrument being in the way of the operator. It can be supplied only by the maker.

AFFECTIONS OF THE LIPS AND CHEEKS

Open wounds of the lips and cheeks are common in the horse, and are caused by bites, nails or sharp hooks, by falls, and by kicks from other horses. The commissures of the lips may be excoriated by the pressure of the bit. Despite the mobility of the part, the soiling of the wounds by alimentary matter and their contamination by the organisms of the mouth, they cicatrise rapidly on account of their rich blood supply. They are similar in most respects to those of the nostrils and are dealt with on the same plan. Perforating wounds of the cheek require deep sutures right through its substance in addition to cutaneous sutures. When the lesions have been in existence for some time they require to be freshened to permit of healing by first intention.

The most difficult cases to deal with successfully are those involving section of the commissures and those perforating the cheek, with loss of tissue, causing an oral fistula of considerable size. Mobility militates

FIG. 255.—FIRST STAGE OF AUTOPLASTIC OPERATION, SHOWING POSITION OF HORIZONTAL CUTANEOUS INCISIONS.

against healing in the former case, and the discharge of alimentary matter and saliva associated with the gaping of the orifice are obstacles in the latter case. The indications are to overcome these difficulties by appropriate measures. After dressing, suturing, and sealing the wound, give liquid diet only for a few days, fix the jaws with a nose-band when the animal is not feeding, and tie him on the pillar reins. If the loss of tissue prevents intimate approximation of the lips of the fistulous wound, an autoplastic operation may be performed as follows (Fig. 255): Make a horizontal incision (head being horizontal) at a tangent to the wound above and below, extending a short distance to either side of it, mapping out rectangular flaps of skin separated by the original wound. Mobilise each flap by dissecting it from the subcutaneous tissue, freshen the borders of the fistula, unite all the opposing edges with interrupted sutures, seal the wound with collodion and iodoform, and take the steps mentioned to favour the healing process. Loss of substance in the labial borders will prevent the horse drinking by suction in the ordinary way, and will necessitate his immersing the muzzle below the commissures.

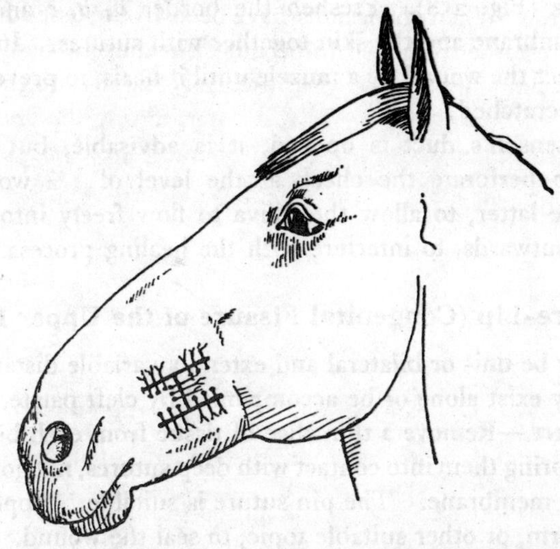

Fig. 256.—Second Stage of the Operation; Opposing Edges Sutured.

If there be much loss of tissue, their function as prehensile organs may be interfered with. Small loss of substance may be remedied by Syme's autoplastic operation for the same condition in man, thus: Prolong the two borders of the wound upwards to form a V-shaped

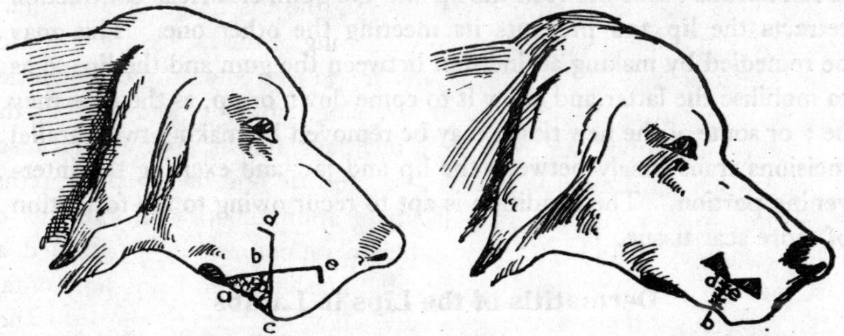

Figs. 257 and 258.—Syme's Autoplastic Operation for a Wound with Loss of Substance.

incision, *d*, *b*, *e* (Fig. 257). From the extremity of each branch of the V make another short incision to enable the skin to be drawn down afterwards to bring the edges *d*, *b* and *e*, *b* into apposition. Mobilise the skin between the incisions and the borders of the wound by dissecting it from the underlying tissue, and suture the edges *d*, *b* and *b*, *e*. The two little triangular areas above the sutured wound will heal by granulations (Fig. 258). Freshen the border *a*, *b*, *c* and bring the mucous membrane and the skin together with sutures. In the case of a dog, protect the wound by a muzzle until it heals, to prevent its being rubbed or scratched.

When Stenson's duct is opened, it is advisable, but not always essential, to perforate the cheek at the level of the wound before suturing the latter, to allow the saliva to flow freely into the mouth instead of outwards, to interfere with the healing process.

Hare-Lip (Congenital Fissure of the Upper Lip)

This may be uni- or bilateral and extend a variable distance into the lip. It may exist alone or be accompanied by cleft palate.

TREATMENT.—Remove a thin slice of tissue from each border of the fissure and bring them into contact with deep sutures, not going through the mucous membrane. The pin suture is suitable. Apply collodion and orthoform, or other suitable topic, to seal the wound. The lower lip may be affected in a similar way and associated with a bifid inferior maxilla. If confined to the lip, operation will prove successful.

Retraction of the Lip

Sometimes as the result of injury, and consequent development of much fibrous tissue between the lip and the gum, cicatricial contraction retracts the lip and prevents its meeting the other one. This may be remedied by making an incision between the gum and the lip, so as to mobilise the latter and allow it to come down or up, as the case may be; or some of the new tissue may be removed by making two parallel incisions transversely between the lip and jaw and excising the intervening portion. The condition is apt to recur owing to the formation of more scar tissue.

Dermatitis of the Lips in Lambs

A vegetative dermatitis has been seen affecting the borders of the lips in lambs due, in the opinion of Megnin, to sarcosporidia. It is a contagious affection beginning in the form of excoriations on which granulations or vegetations afterwards develop. Excision of the vegetations and the application of a mild antiseptic solution (boric acid or potassium permanganate) effect a cure.

Ulceration of the Lip in the Cat

This condition is occasionally met with, the ulcer sometimes extending gradually until a considerable portion of the lip is destroyed, exposing the teeth and gums. It commences at the free border, in the centre, or to one side of the middle line. It may eventually become arrested and be followed by recovery, or it may remain progressive, causing pain and toxæmia, followed by emaciation and death. The lesion may be tuberculous, and microscopic examination for the tubercle

FIG. 259.—ULCERATION OF THE LIP IN THE CAT.

bacillus should be made. If not due to this, the application of tincture of iodine or the stick of lunar caustic usually effects a cure. The patient should be isolated and generously fed.

Tumours

Papillomata or warts are common on the lips of the horse and are less frequently seen on those of the ox. They have been dealt with in the section on "Tumours of the Nostrils." Multiple papillomata are often found on the buccal mucous membrane and gums in the dog, and appear to be of a contagious nature, as all the animals in a kennel usually become affected one after another.

SYMPTOMS.—The tumours form in clusters and are of various dimensions. They cause salivation and usually an offensive smell from the mouth.

PROGNOSIS.—The warts may disappear spontaneously. They respond readily to treatment.

TREATMENT.—Excise the large warts and apply an astringent mouth wash (solution of alum or potassium chlorate), or apply to the remaining warts tannic acid (1 part) and glycerine (8 parts). Administer saline laxative medicine internally, such as magnesia or sodium bicarbonate.

Malignant Tumours

These are not common as primary growths on the lips of the large animals, but epithelioma frequently develops on the lips of the dog.

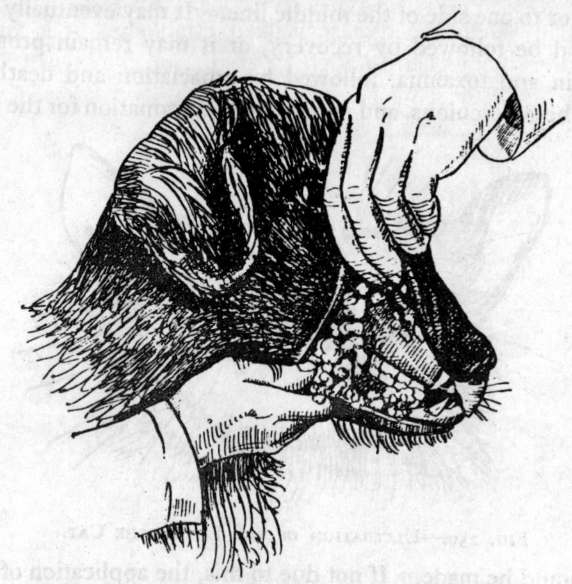

Fig. 260.—Papillomata in the Dog's Mouth.

Fig. 261.—Epithelioma of the Lip, with Enlargement of the Cervical Lymphatic Glands.

It commences as a small hard swelling, which soon ulcerates and rapidly extends in area and depth, involving the bone. Its surface becomes red and angry, and presents a mulberry-like appearance. The neighbouring lymphatic glands are usually affected. There is an offensive odour from the mouth due to the decomposition of food, which adheres to the diseased surface, and to the discharge which comes from the latter.

TREATMENT.—When the disease is well established it is futile to interfere, as the tumour cannot then be eradicated. When it is small and confined to the lip it may be excised by a V-shaped incision, the base of the V corresponding to the border of the lip, the resulting wound being deeply sutured, the stitches going right through the lip, except the mucous membrane. If necessary, Syme's autoplastic operation may be performed (see p. 569). Radiotherapy or radium therapy may be tried for malignant lesions in the mouth (see p. 269), and may prove successful when they are localised.

Cysts

A mucoid retention cyst, due apparently to obstruction of the duct of a mucous gland, sometimes forms on the inner aspect of the lips. When opened, a clear viscid fluid escapes.

The TREATMENT consists in removing a portion of its wall and destroying its lining by the application of tincture of iodine, or in complete extirpation of the cyst.

FIG. 262.—RIGHT-SIDED FACIAL PARALYSIS (CENTRAL).
The protrusion of the tongue is accidental; it does not necessarily occur in facial paralysis.

Paralysis of the Facial Nerve

Paralysis of the facial nerve is fairly common in the horse and rare in other animals. In the ox the horns protect it from external injury. It may be uni- or bilateral, and its origin may be peripheral, intratemporal, medullary, or cerebral.

ETIOLOGY.—The cause may be :

1. *Traumatic*, a contusion or wound involving the nerve where it turns round the inferior maxilla below the temporo-maxillary articulation.

2. *Toxic*, occurring during the course of an infectious disease, like influenza or strangles.

3. *Physical* or rheumatoid, from exposure to severe cold, a rare occurrence.

4. *A tumour* in the parotid region pressing on the nerve.

5. *Inflammation* in the duct of Fallopius, causing pressure on the nerve.

SYMPTOMS.—In unilateral paralysis the lips are drawn towards the sound side. When it is bilateral, they are incapable of prehension and the lower lip is pendulous; the animal is unable to drink without immersing its muzzle above the level of the commissures; the nostrils are contracted; and the respiration, which is normal at rest, is noisy during exercise. When the nerve is injured behind the origin of the anterior auricular branch there is paralysis of the orbicular sphincter muscle, and the patient is unable to close its eyelids. If the lesion be

FIG. 263.—DOUBLE-SIDED FACIAL PARALYSIS (PERIPHERAL).

FIG. 264.—POSITION OF NOSTRILS AND NOSE IN DOUBLE-SIDED (PERIPHERAL) FACIAL PARALYSIS. (From a photograph.)

intratemporal, there is paralysis of the ear of the affected side, the tongue may be involved, some deafness may be present, and there may be slight dysphagia. When the medulla is the seat of the cause, the limbs of the opposite side of the body may also be paralysed. When the origin of the condition is in the cerebrum, there is usually paralysis of the limbs of the same side of the body.

TREATMENT.—The treatment is that for paralysis in general. The first indication is to ascertain the cause of the condition and remove it, if possible. Peripheral paralysis is usually followed by recovery in the course of five or six weeks. Persistence of faradic irritability is a sign of early cure. When the cause is a contusion, treat accordingly. If there be a tumour pressing on the nerve, remove it, if possible.

When the lesion appears to be in the brain, prescribe potassium iodide. Electric therapy is also indicated, using a continuous current of feeble power for five to ten minutes daily. Care must be taken to supply food to the horse in such a way that he can grasp it with his teeth, and water so that he can immerse the muzzle above the level of the labial commissures, when both sides of the face are paralysed. To relieve dyspnœa during exercise, the nostrils may be kept dilated by means of wire fixed across the nose.

Traumatic Lesions

The mouth may be wounded by the penetration of sharp or pointed bodies entering through the cheek or jowl ; by sharp molar or incisor teeth lacerating the cheeks and lips respectively ; by fragments of bone in fracture of the jaw ; by the bit affecting the bars ; by foreign bodies taken in with the food, such as nails, needles, pins, fish-hooks, etc. ; and by laymen burning or lancing the palate for lampas. These wounds are only serious when an important vessel or nerve is involved.

TREATMENT.—Ordinary wounds of the mouth heal rapidly. It is only necessary to clean them after feeding. A foreign body must be removed and the use of an offending bit must be discontinued. Food requiring little mastication should be given. If necrosis of the lower jaw ensue from injury by the bit, treat as already described (*vide* Lower Jaw).

Hæmorrhage from the palato-labial artery is generally most conveniently arrested by the hot iron. The vessel is usually wounded on the line joining the corner incisors, where it turns round on either side to meet its fellow. In this situation the bleeding can be stopped by tying a cord tightly round the upper jaw and beneath the upper lip, and leaving it in position for a few hours ; or a pad soaked in tinct. benzoin. co. may be applied over the wound and compressed by a cord as described, or by a bandage over the face. A suture is often sufficient to arrest fairly profuse hæmorrhage from a wound on the buccal aspect of the lips. Ligation may be performed on a severed vessel in the soft parts of the mouth when within reach.

Foreign Bodies in the Mouth

Foreign bodies lodged in the mouth are most common in the ox and dog, but are found in all animals. They may be a needle embedded in the tongue or cheek, a piece of wood across the palate or floor of the mouth, or between the teeth and the cheek, a fish-hook in the dog's or cat's cheek, and a piece of bone fixed on the molar teeth in carnivora.

Cattle are very prone to pick up foreign bodies, especially when pregnant.

Symptoms.—The animal is unable to feed. Saliva trickles from the mouth, which may be half open ; the patient appears more or less distressed ; the dog rubs his paws against the jaws in an effort to dislodge the object, may hide in dark corners or beneath furniture, and give the owner the impression that it is affected with rabies. The cause of these symptoms is often overlooked by the person in charge, with the result that he treats it for something else, and when the veterinarian sees the case the patient is weak and more or less emaciated for want of food. On careful examination of the mouth the foreign body is discovered, and there is usually an offensive odour from the cavity when the object is of considerable size, due to food material adhering to it. This is most noticeable in the dog.

Treatment.—Extract the foreign body with a forceps or the hand. A needle usually has a piece of thread attached to it, and is generally inserted with the point forwards. Hence to remove it draw the thread backwards. Fish-hooks in the cheek are usually most readily taken out by pushing them outwards through the skin, the barb preventing their being drawn towards the mouth.

Scalds

The mouth may be scalded by too hot drinks or mashes, or by caustic drugs or agents such as turpentine or ammonia in concentrated solution or lime.

Symptoms.—The symptoms are those of stomatitis : tenderness in the mouth, salivation, inability to eat coarse food, or difficulty in doing so. Sloughing of the borders of the lips to a varying degree may ensue from the use of inhalations with too hot steam associated with quick-lime, sometimes prescribed by laymen who put hay soaked in boiling water and sprinkled with quick-lime in a bag which is fixed over the animal's head, in the treatment of respiratory affections.

Treatment.—The case responds to expectant treatment, or to the use of astringent mouth washes, alkaline solutions such as those of soda bicarbonate or lime or magnesia being indicated when the condition is due to an acid, and acidulated solutions such as those of vinegar or tartaric acid when the lesion is caused by an alkali. Antiseptic lotion (*e.g.*, thymol 1 in 1,000, potassium permanganate 1 in 1,000) should be used afterwards to prevent the propagation of organisms. Sloppy diet is indicated until recovery supervenes.

AFFECTIONS OF THE TONGUE

The tongue is frequently wounded in various ways—for example, by needles, bits of glass or flint taken in with the food, by sharp teeth, by excessive traction on the organ when manipulating it in administering a bolus to a horse, by a cord tied round the lower jaw including the tongue, or by being bitten during anæsthesia. The nature of the wound varies in different cases. It may be superficial or deep, affect the frænum or the tongue proper, or involve loss of a portion of the organ. Hæmorrhage is usually slight. Although practically the whole of its free portion has been removed by section or by gangrene, recovery usually takes place. If severed above the frænum, its function in assisting mastication by keeping the food between the teeth is lost and the herbivorous animal succumbs to inanition. Loss of the anterior part of the tongue prevents the dog lapping, but after a while it acquires the power of drinking by suction.

Treatment.—In most cases washing out the mouth with a suitable lotion is sufficient. If the hypoglossal artery is cut, it can be ligatured, after casting the horse, if necessary. When the organ is partially severed, it should be sutured by strong silk going right through its thickness. Even if only held by a thin band of tissue, the semi-detached and main portions may unite by first intention when they are kept in intimate contact with sutures.

Primary healing sometimes occurs after the wound has been in existence for some days when its surfaces are freshened and sutured. A portion of the side of the organ may be destroyed and be followed by recovery without any loss of function. When the free portion of the tongue is lost in the horse or ox, mastication is difficult for a while, but eventually becomes normal except that the process is slower, the animal taking longer to finish its feed. Cutting the frænum renders the stump more mobile, and thus more adaptable for performing its function, but the resulting cicatricial contraction may again restrict its movement.

Strangulation

Strangulation of the free portion of the tongue has been caused in the horse by tying a string round it as a means of control when the animal is vicious, or by including it in a cord fixed and left in position round the lower jaw. The organ becomes swollen and cyanotic from venous engorgement in front of the ligature and remains normal behind it. If relief is not forthcoming within about twenty-four hours, the distal portion will undergo necrosis from arrest of the blood supply.

The TREATMENT is to remove the ligature and scarify the swelling on the dorsum of the organ to prevent pressure necrosis by the engorgement even after the ligature has been removed. There is no danger of wounding the hypoglossal artery by superficial incisions, as it is deeply situated. Venous hæmorrhage resulting from this procedure or other causes may be arrested by applying a thick layer of flour on the dorsum linguæ and keeping the jaws strapped together by a tight nose-band for a few hours. Strangulation of the tongue in the dog may be caused by a rubber ring being slipped over it or by section of a large bloodvessel, such as the aorta of the ox, or of the trachea becoming fixed round it.

Cysts

Mucoid, dermoid, serous, and glandular cysts have been found on the base of the tongue, chiefly in the horse. When of considerable size, they interfere with mastication and deglutition and may cause dyspnœa or even asphyxia.

The treatment is as usual for a cyst—incision or partial excision and destruction of the lining of the cyst. Owing to the difficulty in reaching it, complete removal is generally impossible. The hot iron has been used successfully to cauterise the interior of the cyst after puncturing and iodine injections had failed.

Tumours

Neoplasms, including fibromata, lipomata, and angiomata, are recorded as affecting the tongue in rare instances. Carcinoma confined to the tongue is probably unknown in the domesticated animals. Epithelioma affecting the fauces usually involves the tongue, and in the dog contagious papillomata of the mouth usually appear thereon.

SYMPTOMS.—Tumours cause difficulty in mastication, characterised by the usual signs of trouble in the mouth, salivation and quidding—that is, partially chewing the food and allowing it to drop from the mouth soaked with saliva. Dysphagia is also present. When the tumour is ulcerated there may be a bloodstained discharge from the mouth.

TREATMENT.—Malignant tumours should not be interfered with, except they are confined to the anterior part of the organ, when prompt amputation of the whole of the free portion of the tongue should be performed. The disease usually recurs.

Ranula—Honey Cyst

Ranula is a cystic swelling which sometimes forms at the side of the frænum linguæ, due apparently to obstruction of a mucous gland or of one of the ducts of the sublingual salivary gland. It has been seen in all veterinary patients, but most frequently in the dog. It interferes with mastication and swallowing, but is not inflammatory. Its size seldom exceeds that of a hen's egg.

TREATMENT.—Open it largely or remove a portion of it and paint its interior with tincture of iodine to cause inflammation, granulation, and cicatrisation. Other agents which may be applied to its interior are chloride of zinc (10 per cent.) or silver nitrate (10 to 20 per cent. or the pure stick). The caustic should not be allowed to touch the mucous membrane. Excess of the agent should be mopped up with a little cotton-wool moistened with boiled water.

A cyst of a similar nature and origin, but larger, and sometimes called a honey cyst, appears externally on the under aspect of the throat in the dog, causing a remarkably large, painless, pendulous swelling in this region. Treat it in the same way as the cyst in the mouth. It may be necessary to dissect out and remove its fibrous lining. There may be profuse hæmorrhage after the operation necessitating plugging of the cavity.

Paralysis of the Tongue (Glossoplegia)

Paralysis of the tongue may be peripheral or central in origin, usually the latter when it is the result of meningitis or hydrocephalus, or some other lesion of the brain. It is the first symptom of labioglosso-laryngeal paralysis. It may occur during the course of an infectious disease, such as influenza, distemper, contagious pleuro-pneumonia, or rabies. It may be of traumatic origin, resulting from a wound or excessive traction of the organ.

SYMPTOMS.—In a case of unilateral paralysis (monoplegia) the tongue is deviated towards the non-affected side. When diplegia is present the organ hangs inert, protruding more or less from the mouth. When monoplegia has been in existence for some time, the affected side of the tongue atrophies to such a degree that its dorsal and ventral mucous membranes come into contact.

PROGNOSIS.—Occurring during an infectious disease, the condition is usually temporary, disappearing in the course of seven to ten days. The same may be the case when it is due to traumatism, provided that the nerve is not severed. In monoplegia the tongue is able to perform its function, but in diplegia it is functionless.

TREATMENT.—Treat as for paralysis in general. Nux vomica and potassium iodide are always indicated internally. If improvement does not occur within a reasonable time, destruction will be necessary in the case of diplegia.

Glossitis (Inflammation of the Tongue)

This may be *acute* or *chronic*, and *superficial* or *deep*.

Acute Glossitis—Etiology.—The condition may be the result of injury, as already described, or of some specific disease (foot and mouth disease, horse-pox, black-quarter), or of extension from an inflammatory lesion in the vicinity.

Symptoms.—The tongue becomes swollen and inert, attaining twice to four times its normal size, and protrudes from the mouth, which is held partly open and discharges saliva. The soft palate is pushed upwards and backwards. Respiration is interfered with and noisy, and death may ensue from asphyxia. In ruminants acute glossitis has been seen in the form of an enzootic. In such cases partial gangrene of the tongue is a common occurrence.

Treatment comprises scarification of the tongue on the middle line of its ventral aspect, frequent irrigation with an antiseptic mouth lotion, and in cattle protecting the protruding tongue by enveloping it in a bag suspended from the horns. When due to a specific disease, the latter must be dealt with according to its nature.

Chronic Glossitis (Macroglossia)—Etiology.—The condition may be (1) a sequel to the acute form, (2) due to a foreign body, or (3) the result of actinomycosis, or tuberculosis, or, more rarely, psorospermosis.

Symptoms.—The tongue becomes larger and thicker, and eating and breathing are rendered difficult.

Treatment is unsatisfactory, as a large amount of new fibrous tissue has been formed between the muscle fibres, causing atrophy of the latter, and more or less arresting the function of the organ. When due to actinomycosis, it must be treated as such.

Gangrene of the Tongue

This is seen accompanying gangrenous stomatitis in the dog, and as a complication of distemper, and of Stuttgart disease. It is characterised by a very offensive odour from the mouth and alteration in the appearance of the organ, which becomes greenish and shrivelled in the affected part. The disease is confined to the anterior region of the tongue. If the patient survive, the gangrenous portion will be separated after five to ten days.

Treatment consists in frequent irrigation of the mouth with hydrogen peroxide or potassium permanganate until the dead part is cast off, assuming that the animal does not succumb to the cause of the trouble, which is usually the case.

Sublingual Abscess

Occasionally an abscess is found beneath the tongue, causing a swelling on the floor of the mouth in the intermaxillary space, and giving rise to the usual symptoms of trouble in the mouth.

TREATMENT consists in opening the abscess in the intermaxillary space.

Fracture of the Hyoid Bone

This is not common.

ETIOLOGY.—In horses and cattle it has been caused by horn thrusts and by kicks, and by violent traction on the tongue. In the dog it has been produced by rough seizure by the throat, as is sometimes done by police in securing stray animals.

SYMPTOMS comprise salivation, prolapse of the tongue, difficulty in eating and especially in swallowing, accumulation of food in the mouth, and swelling in the throat. There may be bleeding from laceration of the hypoglossal artery or other vessel. Crepitation on moving the tongue can seldom be detected.

PROGNOSIS.—Union of subcutaneous fracture is usually complete in four weeks. Intense inflammatory swelling may ensue, preventing mastication and swallowing, and causing death from inanition or necessitating slaughter. Fatal hæmorrhage may ensue, but even cases complicated by exfoliation of large pieces of the hyoid bone may recover in from six to eight weeks.

TREATMENT.—In simple fracture give semi-liquid diet. At first nutrient enemata may be given instead of food by the mouth. If there is a wound in the mucous membrane, clean it thoroughly after meals. Remove loose spicules of bone.

AFFECTIONS OF THE PALATE

Fissure

Congenital fissure of the soft palate has been seen in the horse, ox, and dog. It may exist alone or accompany some other anomaly in a "monster" fœtus. It often coexists with hare-lip. Fissure of the soft palate interferes with swallowing, and some of the milk or food material is returned by the nasal passages. The affected animal gradually wastes and, if not relieved, dies.

TREATMENT is not often undertaken in veterinary practice, but it may be possible to perform one of the following operations:

1. *Staphylorrhaphy*.—Suturing the edges of the fissure, very difficult to perform in the large animal owing to the depth of the mouth.

Anæsthetise the patient, and fix him in the dorsal position with the head and neck extended. Have the mouth opened widely by a speculum. Freshen the edges of the fissure by means of long scissors or a knife, and unite them by interrupted silver wire sutures. If it be impossible to keep the edges of the cleft in contact owing to their being far apart, make an incision on either side of and parallel to the fissure of sufficient extent to relieve the tension on the sutures.

2. *Uranoplasty.*—Make a longitudinal incision on either side of the hard palate, keeping close to the teeth to avoid the palatine artery. Separate the mucous membrane and its fibrous foundation from the palatine bone between the fissure and the incision, and then proceed as in No. 1. A strip of bone is thus left denuded, but as a rule necrosis thereof does not supervene.

Paralysis of the Muscles of Mastication—Paralysis of the Lower Jaw—Paralysis of the Trifacial Nerve

This condition is rare in the horse and ox, but fairly common in the dog. It may be uni- or bilateral, partial or complete, and peripheral or central in origin.

ETIOLOGY.—The commonest cause of the affection is rabies, but it may be the result of some other toxic lesion. Central causes operate in the brain between the point of origin of the nerve in the bulb and the cortical layer of the cerebral hemisphere of the opposite side, and may be in the form of pressure by extravasated blood, inflammatory exudate, or a tumour. Peripheral causes affect the nerve near its origin or anywhere along its course, such as tumours, extravasations, direct injury, or the toxin of an infectious disease, most frequently distemper in the dog. The paralysis is on the same side as the lesion in this case. Trifacial paralysis may be accompanied by labio-glossal or facial paralysis. Of the three branches of the trifacial nerve, one, the inferior maxillary nerve, is mixed, the other two, the ophthalmic and superior maxillary nerves, are purely sensory.

SYMPTOMS.—Paralysis of the inferior maxillary division of the fifth nerve is characterised by loss of power in the muscles of mastication. When the paralysis is unilateral, the lower jaw is deviated towards the affected side by the unbalancing effect of the action of the pterygoid muscles on the sound side. Prehension and the movements of the tongue are normal, but mastication is interfered with; to facilitate it, the patient holds the head low and towards the sound side, so that the food is directed towards the corresponding molars.

Bilateral paralysis may be incomplete and characterised by slow intermittent masticatory movements. Complete paralysis is manifested by absolute loss of power in the muscles of mastication on both sides. The lower jaw remains dropped, but can be easily raised by the hand. The tongue is dry and may protrude from the mouth. The dog is able to lap and swallow liquid diet and partake of solid food when placed in its mouth. The animal is normal in disposition. Sensibility to touch is abolished in the temporal regions, the cheeks, the lower gums and teeth, the lips, and the chin.

PROGNOSIS.—When the paralysis is due to lesions pressing on or destroying the motor branch of the nerve it remains permanent, and the muscles of mastication undergo atrophy. The condition is nearly always incurable in such cases. A temporary form of paralysis of these muscles in the dog may result from rheumatism, lasting five to ten days.

Paralysis of the ophthalmic branch is recognised by loss of sensation in the eye, especially in the cornea, and by the lodgment of foreign matter therein, causing conjunctivitis and keratitis. Paralysis of the superior maxillary division is indicated by anæsthesia of the infra-orbital region, of the nose, cheek, upper gums and teeth, and of the upper lip as far as the middle line. In peripheral paralysis sensibility of the mucous membrane may be preserved, the anæsthesia being confined to the skin.

DIAGNOSIS from dislocation of the lower jaw and from rabies is easy when one is familiar with the symptoms of the latter conditions.

TREATMENT.—If any doubt exists as to the animal being rabid, it should be isolated for a few days to observe whether rabies is developing. Otherwise the treatment is that for paralysis in general. If the condition is rheumatoid, treat accordingly.

AFFECTIONS OF THE CRANIUM

Contusions of the Cranium

Contusions of the cranium are not common in veterinary patients, owing to the small area of its surface exposed to injury, and the protection afforded to it by the sinuses in the horse and ox and the massive temporal muscles in the dog.

SYMPTOMS.—The symptoms are those of acute local inflammation. There is more or less extravasation of blood, which may be in the form of a subcutaneous, subfascial, or subperiosteal hæmatoma. If the violence has been severe, the bone itself will be crushed with ecchymosis into its substance, and even some of the meningeal vessels may be ruptured. Should infection gain entrance into the injured part an abscess may form in the soft tissues, and if the organisms pass through the damaged bone a subdural abscess may ensue, followed by meningo-encephalitis. The latter is manifested by cerebral excitement, stupor, or vertigo.

DIAGNOSIS of the condition is easy, but it is difficult to estimate the depth of the lesion.

PROGNOSIS depends on the nature of the injury. When the brain is not involved recovery is uneventful, but when brain symptoms supervene the condition is grave, and when infection of the organ occurs the case is hopeless. Symptoms of compression of the brain may gradually disappear when they are the result of slight effusion, but if it be copious fatal coma is apt to ensue.

TREATMENT.—The treatment is that for a contusion or hæmatoma or abscess, as the case may be. When brain symptoms are present, they must be treated according to their nature. Trephining may be performed as a last resort to relieve compression, but it is rarely practised in our patients, and usually proves futile. Laxative medicine and potassium iodide internally are always indicated.

Open Wounds

Open wounds of the cranium are only of special interest when associated with fracture of some of its bones and involving injury to the brain. Concussion may be caused by the violence producing the wound, although the brain has not been penetrated. When the cerebral tissue is wounded death is the usual sequel, but in exceptional cases, even after protrusion of brain matter, recovery ensues, provided that sepsis has been excluded.

Cure, however, may be incomplete, the patient remaining more or less paralysed or stupefied. Potassium iodide should be prescribed to promote absorption of effusion on the surface of the brain. If a sinus is formed from the presence of necrotic bone or from caries thereof, it must be treated accordingly.

Fractures

Fractures of the cranium are probably most common in the horse, due to the frequency of fracture of its base from rearing and falling back on the poll, or striking this part violently against the top of a doorway or a low ceiling, the seat of the lesion being either the body of the sphenoid or the basi-occipital. The number of foramina in this region of the cranium predisposes it to fracture.

SYMPTOMS AND DIAGNOSIS.—If the fracture affects one of the bones of the vault of the cranium it may be recognised by the deformity of the part when displacement of the fragments has occurred, or the broken bone may be seen when an open wound is present. When no displacement has supervened, it is impossible to diagnose the condition except by the aid of X-rays. The inner table or the outer table of the bone only may be fractured, more frequently the former, the explanation being that it forms the arc of a smaller circle than the outer plate, and therefore cannot withstand the same amount of pressure without giving way. Symptoms of concussion may be apparent without direct injury to the brain, or the function of the latter may be more or less interfered with by the pressure of a depressed fragment or by the penetration of a spicule of bone into its substance. Fractures of the base of the cranium can only be inferred from the symptoms, bleeding from the nose and ears being practically diagnostic when it occurs in conjunction with coma following violent impact of the poll on the ground or against a fixed object.

Prognosis.—The prognosis is usually grave on account of the brain being commonly involved in the injury. Fracture of the base of the cranium generally causes immediate death. Rarely the animal recovers sufficiently to rise and stagger about in a dazed condition for a while, after which it collapses and succumbs. Whe.. the coma has been merely due to shock, without direct injury of the brain, complete recovery may ensue.

Treatment is out of the question for fracture of the base. In fracture of the vault, local treatment comprises : (1) Cold applications to the head to arrest bleeding, diminish inflammation, and help to ward off meningitis and encephalitis ; (2) trephining the cranium in the region of the fracture to enable a lever to be introduced to raise a depressed fragment when indicated by symptoms of compression.

When an open wound is present, direct leverage may be performed through the wound. Operative interference is contra-indicated except as an extreme measure to relieve symptoms of cerebral compression. A certain amount of compression may be tolerated by the brain. Trephining the cranial cavity is carried out in the same way as that of the sinuses, with the additional precaution of avoiding injury to the meninges and brain. If the venous sinus is opened, the bleeding may be arrested by a pad and bandage. Strict asepsis is essential to prevent septic meningitis and encephalitis. The operation wound should be sutured and protected by an antiseptic dressing.

Hernia of the brain tissue may occur through the trephine opening. It cannot be pushed back, and experience has shown that it is better to let it slough off than to remove it by ligation or excision. It should be protected by a moist antiseptic compress until it separates. Recovery may supervene.

General Treatment consists in :

1. Isolating the patient, keeping him in a quiet place.

2. Bleeding from the jugular vein when the patient is robust and the pulse is strong. This is not a routine procedure, but may be performed with advantage.

3. The administration of a purgative to act as an eliminative and febrifuge, and to diminish the risk of meningitis and encephalitis.

4. Adopting appropriate measures for brain affections when they arise, cerebral excitement requiring the exhibition of nerve sedatives, and coma the application of the usual methods of resuscitation.

The most serious fractures of the vault are those of the parietal, temporal, and upper part of the frontal bones. Fracture of the occipital crest is not dangerous, as it does not involve the risk of injury to the brain.

Tumours

Tumours of the cranial region are not common, but papillomata, fibromata, sarcomata, melanomata, and cysts may occur there, and must be treated on general principles. Osteomata projecting into the cranial cavity rarely develop, and are most frequent in the ox. They cause no disturbance, and are only recognised on post-mortem.

Tumours of the Brain are of comparatively rare occurrence, and are most frequently found in the horse, affecting as a rule the choroid plexus. They may be present for a long time without causing any disturbance of function, but when they assume considerable size they give rise to cerebral excitement or stupor or paralysis of different parts of the body, according to their situation. When developing on the cerebellum, they interfere with the co-ordination of movement.

Treatment is impossible, but as the diagnosis is always doubtful at first it is usual to treat the symptoms for a while on the assumption that the disturbance may be temporary, and, when it proves useless, to destroy the animal.

Dentigerous Cyst

A dentigerous cyst is one containing a tooth growing from the bone over which it is situated. It is occasionally seen in the horse, and more rarely in the ox, sheep, and dog. It develops soon after birth, simultaneously with the eruption of the normal teeth, and is usually first noticed at about two years old.

SYMPTOMS.—At first a soft painless swelling is observed towards the front of the base of the ear, occupying a variable position between the mesial line of the head and the zygomatic process of the squamous temporal bone. After some time the wall of the cyst ulcerates and then ruptures, allowing the liquid contents to escape, forming a glairy discharge which continues indefinitely if the cyst is not removed. The fistulous orifice varies in its situation. It is usually over the centre of the swelling, but may be found on the border of the concha near its base, or more rarely on its inner aspect. A probe passed into the fistula comes in contact with the tooth, which usually abuts on the petrous temporal bone, but may be growing from the squamous temporal bone. The tooth is not firmly fixed as a rule, but exceptionally it is deeply embedded in the bone, and more rarely protrudes into the cranial cavity. Several teeth may develop successively, a new tooth appearing after removal of its predecessor. There may be more than one tooth present in the cyst.

TREATMENT consists in operating as described (p. 290).

Dermoid Cysts

More rarely a dermoid cyst may appear in the temporal region of the horse or other animal, presenting similar symptoms to those of a dentigerous cyst, except that it contains dermoid tissue instead of a tooth.

The TREATMENT consists in dissecting out the lining of the cyst so as to cause an open wound, which will heal in the ordinary way.

Cœnurus Cerebralis (Study, Gid)

The *Cœnurus cerebralis*, or cystic form of the *Tœnia cœnurus* of the dog, develops on the brain of the sheep, ox, goat, and rarely other animals. The condition is very common in the ox and sheep in certain districts and practically unknown in others. This form of the parasite enters the host as the result of the latter partaking of grass or food contaminated by the fæces of the dog containing segments of the *Tœnia cœnurus*. The disease is perpetuated by dogs consuming the brains of animals infested with the cystic form of the worm. It is usually yearling or two-year-old cattle and sheep that are affected.

SYMPTOMS.—The symptoms are local and general.

Local symptoms may be absent or quite distinct. In the latter case a swelling can be detected due to the cyst causing pressure, atrophy, and bulging of the bone at its level. The bony tissue may have disappeared, when fluctuation can be felt.

General symptoms comprise those of disturbances of brain function characterised by abnormal movements of the patient, varying according to the situation of the cyst as follows : (1) When the crown of the head is held on one side, with the corresponding ear held at a lower level than the other one, and the animal keeps turning in a circle towards this side, it is a sign that the lesion is situated on the cerebral hemisphere, which corresponds to the centre of the circle described. (2) When the animal trots with the head high, the cyst occupies the anterior part of the brain, the olfactory lobe, or the corpus striatum. (3) If localised in the cerebellum or posterior part of the cerebrum, the animal has a staggering gait and frequently falls. (4) If developed on the pons Varolii, the subject rolls round the long axis of the body. (5) If the eyes roll and lose the power of sight, the optic tract is affected. These movements, however, are not sufficiently regular to be of much practical assistance in determining the exact site of the hydatid. Besides, there may be more than one cyst present affecting different parts of the brain.

PREVENTION consists in keeping dogs free from tape-worm by the administration of vermicides and preventing them from eating brains containing the cysts.

TREATMENT.—The only satisfactory treatment is operation to remove the hydatid (p. 479). Continuous cold irrigation of the head is said to have caused rapid improvement and even complete cure in some cases.

AFFECTIONS OF THE HORNS

Separation of the Horn in the Ox

ETIOLOGY.—It may be caused by direct violence—for example, when cattle are fighting in an enclosed place, the beast striking its horn against that of its antagonist or against a paling or wall. It may also be caused by repeated injury by the yoke in working oxen, setting up a chronic inflammation of the keratogenous membrane, whereby the sheath of the horn becomes loose and easily detached by striking it against a fixed object.

PROGNOSIS.—The accident is not serious ; the resulting hæmorrhage is easily arrested, and the lost horn is regenerated, although not to so perfect a degree as the original horn.

TREATMENT.—Clean and disinfect the exposed horn core, and protect it with an antiseptic pad and bandage. A dressing of Archangel tar smeared over the wounded surface and outside the bandage is very suitable in the summer, as it tends to keep away flies. Despite this, however, maggots may form beneath the dressing.

Fracture of the Horns

Etiology.—The fracture may be caused by a blow or by striking the horn against a fixed object. It may be incomplete, only partly severing the bone, or complete, right through the structure. It may be situated near the point of the horn, in its middle part, at its base, or in the frontal bone beneath the skin. The direction of the fracture is usually oblique and the broken surface is always more or less irregular.

Fig. 265.—Splint for Fracture of Horn Core.

Treatment—(1) *Fracture of the Distal Third of the Horn*—(a) *Incomplete Fracture*, the horn and its core being partially severed. The usual procedure in an ordinary beast is to amputate the horn just below the seat of fracture with a fine sharp saw and protect the wound with an antiseptic pad and bandage, the latter being made secure by fixing it to the normal horn. The stump may be further protected by a pad placed on its free extremity and kept in position by a cross-shaped bandage, whose centre is placed over the pad and whose ends are applied longitudinally on the horn and fixed by another circular bandage.

In the case of a pedigree animal, or one required for the yoke, an attempt should be made to bring about union between the fragments by an immobilising dressing, the best one being in the form of a splint shaped to adapt itself exactly to the two horns and to the space between them. It is applied from behind, and is concave to accommodate the horns. It is grooved transversely here and there to receive the wire used to bind it to the horn. Coculet's splint answers this description, and is the one usually employed. Failing this contrivance, plaster or pitch bandages may be used.

(*b*) *Complete Fracture.*—If the fractured surface is irregular, amputate it and proceed as in (*a*).

(2) *Fractures of the Middle and Lower Thirds* of the horn are dealt with in the same way as that of the distal third, but it is more difficult to immobilise the seat of fracture here, on account of the leverage thereon by the long distal fragment.

(3) *Fracture in the Frontal Bone.*—If necessary, an attempt may be made to bring about healing here by the aid of the special splint. If it fail, or it is not required to conserve the horn, the latter and loose piece of bone should be removed. In all cases the wound must be treated antiseptically.

COMPLICATION.—The complication that may arise is pus in the frontal sinus following the accumulation of blood therein consequent on the fracture.

Fissures in the Horn and Horn Core

A fissure may form in the horn or horn core only, or in both, as the result of direct injury, and appear on its convexity parallel to its long axis.

SYMPTOMS.—Those of inflammation in the affected part, and when there is a fissure in the covering horn blood may ooze therefrom.

TREATMENT consists in applying cooling, astringent, antiseptic lotion with a view to arresting hæmorrhage.

COMPLICATION.—When the core is fissured, bleeding may occur into the frontal sinus and the blood accumulating there may lead to purulent sinusitis.

AFFECTIONS OF THE TEETH

The affections of the teeth may be classified thus :

I. Abnormalities of development.
II. Irregular wear of teeth.
III. Alterations in the substance of the teeth.
IV. Affections of the periosteum lining the alveolus.

I.—ABNORMALITIES OF DEVELOPMENT

These comprise: (*a*) Abnormal number of teeth; (*b*) irregularities in the shedding of the temporary teeth; (*c*) abnormalities of the position and direction of the teeth.

(*a*) **Abnormal Number of Teeth.**—Supplementary incisor, canine, and molar teeth may be present. A double row of incisors is occasionally seen in the horse. This is usually due, however, to the temporary incisors being retained after eruption of the permanent teeth. The supernumerary incisors always belong to the permanent dentition. Additional canine teeth seldom occur, but increase in the number of molars is fairly common, the extra teeth being usually found in the upper jaw in front, behind, outside, or inside, the normal teeth, most commonly behind. Diminution of the number of teeth in the horse is a rare condition. In the dog the number of molar teeth varies, the short-jawed varieties having fewer molars than those belonging to the long-jawed breeds.

FIG. 266.—SUPERNUMERARY TOOTH (HORSE).

(*b*) **Irregularities in the Shedding of the Teeth.**—Sometimes the milk teeth persist for an unusual time, with the result that the permanent teeth take an abnormal course. On the other hand, the persistence of the temporary teeth may be due to the permanent teeth not erupting immediately beneath them, and extruding them as they develop. It is the incisors that are most commonly involved.

(*c*) **Abnormalities of the Position and Direction of the Teeth.**—The incisor teeth may be found overlapping, or taking a transverse or oblique direction, or rotated on their long axis. Unequal length of the upper and lower jaws prevents their incisors coming into contact, with the result that they become excessively long from want of wear, and that those of the shorter jaw may penetrate the soft tissues opposite. When the upper incisors overhang the lower the condition is called "parrot mouth," and when the lower protrude beyond the upper it is spoken of as "pig or sow mouth."

Sometimes the teeth are not close together, but have spaces between them in which food material lodges, irritating the gum and perhaps leading to separation of it from the teeth, and opening the way for infection into the alveolus to cause alveolar periostitis.

Symptoms.—Many of the foregoing abnormalities may exist for a long time without causing inconvenience, but interference with mastication or prehension may ensue, depending upon the nature of the condition. A pronounced " parrot " or " sow " mouth will interfere with grazing owing to the incisors not coming into apposition. A tooth abnormally situated may wound sensitive structures, causing pain and difficulty in mastication. Spaces between the teeth have the effects mentioned. Just before shedding of the temporary teeth food material may become insinuated between a partly separated tooth and the gum, causing irritation and symptoms of trouble in the mouth, the gum appearing red and swollen.

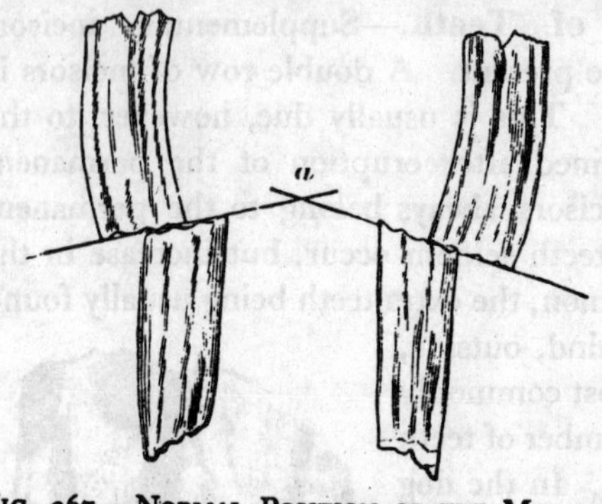

Fig. 267.—Normal Position of the Molars in the Horse.

Treatment consists in shortening or extracting offending teeth. When a narrow space exists between two teeth in which foodstuff lodges, the remedy is to remove one of the teeth. If it occur between the third and fourth molar, the latter will be the easier to extract, being the older tooth, and having consequently a shorter root.

II.—IRREGULARITIES OF WEAR

Irregularities of wear in the molar teeth are common in the horse, and comprise the following examples.

1. Sharp Teeth

The outer border of the upper and the inner border of the lower row of molars become sharp. The explanation of this occurrence is as follows : (*a*) The upper jaw being wider than the lower, the inner aspect of the tables of the upper molars and the outer aspect of those of the lower molars are subjected to most wear, the movement of the jaws being from side to side ; (*b*) normally the tables of the upper and lower molars slope slightly downwards and outwards (the head being horizontal) ; (*c*) restricted lateral movements of the jaws from any cause, such as weakness of the masseters or painful lesions in the mouth, will accentuate the slope of the teeth and eventually cause the sharp borders mentioned. When the condition becomes well marked, the overlapping of the upper and lower teeth further restricts lateral movement and aggravates the abnormality.

Symptoms.—The symptoms include:

1. *Interference with mastication*, due to laceration of the cheeks or tongue, or both, by the sharp teeth during movement of the jaws. It is manifested by (*a*) *quidding* the food—that is, partially chewing hay or corn and letting it drop from the mouth saturated with saliva; (*b*) *salivation*, the escape of saliva from the mouth, with the formation of foam at its borders, the manger and food being moistened by the fluid; (*c*) imperfect grinding, recognised by the absence of the normal grinding sound during feeding and by cautious limited movement of the jaws; (*d*) holding the head to one side when chewing; (*e*) food collecting between the teeth and the cheeks in the intervals between the feeds.

2. *The presence of the sharp edges* on the teeth, detected on manual and visual examination.

3. *Wounds of the cheeks or tongue*, or both, caused by the sharp teeth.

4. *Loss of condition*, resulting from indigestion and insufficient nourishment following imperfect mastication.

Treatment.—Have the horse backed into a stall or corner and securely held with a slip or head-collar, or the bridle with the bit taken out of the mouth. Have the nose-band slackened and the tongue held out of the mouth at the interdental space by an assistant. Apply the rasp to the outer border of the upper and the inner border of the lower molars, running it freely from one extremity of the row to the other, taking care not to hurt the soft tissues.

There are different patterns of rasps. The ordinary hand rasp may be large or small to suit the size of the patient. For yearlings and two-year-olds the small rasp, which can be used with one hand, is suitable. For large animals the full-size rasp or the power rasp is indicated. The latter has a spherical head and is made to rotate by means of a wheel in the same manner as a clipping machine is worked. Another form of this instrument fits over the row of teeth and functions with a to-and-fro movement. It was invented by Mr. Nolans (Ireland).

The teeth require periodical attention for this condition, but the rasp should not be used to excess, and thereby render the teeth too smooth to have a grinding effect. This mistake is occasionally made. " Quidding " the food is not always due to abnormalities of the teeth. It may be the result of debility of the muscles of mastication, or insufficient secretion of saliva, or the cause may be obscure. In the latter case the condition is called " dry mouth." D. E. Wilkinson, M.R.C.V.S., in a letter published in the *Vet. Rec.*, Vol. 13, No. 20, says he has treated " dry mouth " and " non-sweating " in chasers and polo ponies by the administration of ½ lb. of glucose dissolved in hot water and given in the last meal before playing or racing, and has never found it to fail.

2. Overlapping Molars (Shears Mouth)

The upper and lower molars overlap like the blades of shears. The condition is an exaggerated form of sharp teeth. It may attain such a degree that some of the upper teeth wound the gum of the lower jaw, while those of the lower row may injure the inner gum above, or the palate. It is mostly horses advanced in age that are affected, but occasionally the abnormality is found in a young animal.

TREATMENT.—Treatment is unsatisfactory as a rule, as it is impossible in most cases to bring the teeth into proper apposition again. When the overlapping is confined to two or three teeth, the use of the shears to remove the overlapping portions may have the desired effect, as in the next condition dealt with. When most of the teeth are involved, the repeated use of the rasp may produce sufficient improvement to enable mastication to be tolerably well performed, and thus prolong the period of utility of the patient.

3. Individual Irregularities

The first superior molar may overhang the corresponding lower molar in front, and the last inferior molar may project behind the sixth superior molar to a varying degree. The projecting part not undergoing wear forms a hook, which may lacerate the cheek or tongue. The irregularity may be on one of the teeth towards the centre of the row, most commonly on the outer border of the upper row.

TREATMENT.—Remove the projection on the tooth with the tooth shears or tooth chisel. It may not be possible to grip it with the shears ; then the use of the chisel is indicated. The shears must be made of the best steel, so as not to bend or break under the great force sometimes required to cut through an entire tooth. The power may be obtained by bringing the handles together by means of a screw, or by a series of levers, as in Squair's shears. Any ordinary long blunt-edged chisel or even a hoof rasp may be employed to remove a projection on the last molar where it is difficult to apply the shears or for knocking off an irregularity which is too narrow to be gripped by the instrument. The edge of the chisel is placed against the projection and struck a short blow with a heavy hammer or hoof rasp.

To use the shears or chisel, it is necessary to have the mouth gag inserted and the tongue held out of the way in the usual manner. When an entire tooth offers great resistance to the shears, its cutting may be facilitated by grasping one half of the tooth at a time, with one jaw of the instrument on the centre of its table and the other on the side of the tooth. When the tooth is severed a loud report is heard, and if the separated part does not fall out of the mouth it should be removed by the hand. Any sharp border left on the tooth is filed with the rasp. Efforts to cut a tooth in an aged horse may cause it to come away in the jaws of the shears.

If the horse is too restive in the standing position, he should be cast on the side opposite to the affected tooth. The muzzle is then turned upwards and the mouth gag introduced as before, care being taken to prevent the animal beating the head against the ground, especially when the gag is in position. Slight projecting spicules may be knocked off by jabbing them in a restricted fashion by the end of the rasp, particularly when situated on the inner aspect of the lower row. This is much more easily and satisfactorily done in the cast position.

4. Wave-Formed Mouth

This is due to a variation in the plane of the wearing surface of the teeth. It is generally bilateral, the fourth lower molar being the shortest and the corresponding upper tooth being the longest in their respective rows. Sometimes the reverse is the case. The molars in front and behind become gradually longer or shorter respectively. The condition usually depends on unequal durability of the individual teeth, and sometimes on disease of the alveoli. Slight inequalities cause little trouble, but when well developed, and especially if the alveoli are involved, mastication is greatly impaired and the sharp points and edges wound the opposing soft parts. Certain teeth may be worn level with the gum, rendering mastication exceedingly painful and leading perhaps to alveolar periostitis.

Treatment.—Remove sharp points and edges, shorten or extract too long teeth, and give suitable diet. Treat alveolar periostitis if present.

5. Step-Formed Mouth

The neighbouring molars vary suddenly in height. Spaces resulting from loss of opposing teeth may be the cause of the condition, but it often exists apart from this, due apparently to unequal resistance of individual teeth.

Symptoms.—The irregularities generally cause the usual symptoms of interference with mastication by impeding lateral movement of the jaws and wounding the soft tissues.

Prognosis depends on the degree and extent of the irregularity. It is gravest, of course, in the young animal.

Treatment is merely palliative. It consists in removing irregularities as far as possible and giving suitable diet. The shears or chisel may be used as described.

6. Premature Wear of the Teeth

Etiology.—Defective resisting power in the teeth, appearing in herbivora and carnivora. In bad cases the crowns become worn to the level of the gums at any early age, leading to infection of one or more of the alveoli and terminating the career of the horse

Treatment is of no avail except to deal with alveolar periostitis when it supervenes, and retard the wear of the sound teeth by feeding mostly on soft diet.

7. Smooth Mouth

This is due to equal wearing of the enamel and dentine of the teeth, causing an absolutely smooth surface on their tables instead of the normal rough grinding surface. In old age this always occurs when the crown becomes worn down to the root of the tooth where the enamel is absent. Appearing in young horses, it is due to a defect in the dental structure. The condition may be confined to two opposing teeth on one or both sides, and then it is of little consequence, as mastication is not materially interfered with. If most of the teeth are affected, proper mastication will be impossible and the animal will suffer from lack of nutrition, rendering it unserviceable.

Treatment is palliative, consisting in giving crushed oats and mashes, and allowing a longer time for feeding.

8. Ruminant's Mouth

The opposite to No. 7, the grinding surfaces being unusually rough. This is normal in the virgin teeth, and seldom persists or proves troublesome.

III.—ALTERATIONS IN THE SUBSTANCE OF THE TEETH

Fractures

Fractures of the teeth are fairly common in the horse, especially of the incisors, and result from direct violence, usually caused by falls. The fracture may be complete or splintered, and involve the crown only or include the root, opening the pulp cavity and leading to alveolar periostitis. In the molars the fissure or fracture is usually caused by some hard substance in the food—a nail or a piece of flint—which the animal unexpectedly chews. Difficult mastication may ensue from the sharp borders of a splintered tooth lacerating the soft tissues. A fissured fracture may not be detected until alveolar periostitis has supervened.

TREATMENT.—If the fracture be partial, involving only a portion of the crown, smooth the rough surface left with the rasp. If the root is affected, extract the tooth.

Dental Tartar

Dental tartar is a greyish-brown deposit on the teeth formed from the fluids of the mouth and composed of carbonate and phosphate of lime, magnesium carbonate, and organic matter, comprising bacteria and mucus.

ETIOLOGY.—The condition is very common in house dogs getting little exercise and receiving food that requires no tearing or gnawing, which keeps the teeth clean. The presence of a leptothrix organism in the mouth causes a deposit of lime salts on the teeth. It is less frequently seen in the cat, and is rare in herbivora. When present in the latter, it is of no consequence as a rule.

Symptoms in the Dog.—At first the only symptom is the presence of the deposit on the teeth. It appears on the incisors, canines, and molars, mostly at the base of the teeth and on their outer aspect. After a while it tends to encroach on the fangs, causing gingivitis and separating the gum from the teeth, thus opening the alveoli and allowing alimentary matter with bacteria to gain entrance and set up alveolar periostitis or pyorrhœa, which is usually present, affecting one or more teeth, when the patient is brought for treatment. In an advanced case of this kind the tartar appears in thick greyish-yellow deposits at the base of the teeth, especially the molars, encroaching on and accompanied by inflammation of the gums. There is an offensive odour from the mouth. In most instances the symptoms of alveolar periostitis are present, as described later.

PREVENTION consists in keeping dogs under natural conditions, giving them flesh to tear and bones and crusts to gnaw, restricting their meals to once or twice daily, allowing them plenty of exercise, examining their mouths occasionally, and brushing their teeth with precipitated chalk or some dentifrice, if any deposit is present thereon. By this means their teeth will be kept clean and their general health will be preserved.

Treatment is carried out as follows :

1. Have the dog controlled, fixing it in the ventral position on the table if necessary. If the animal is wicked, a tape muzzle may be applied. Most of the teeth can be reached with the mouth thus closed by retracting the lips and cheeks. If the patient is very violent, a hypodermic of morphia is indicated.

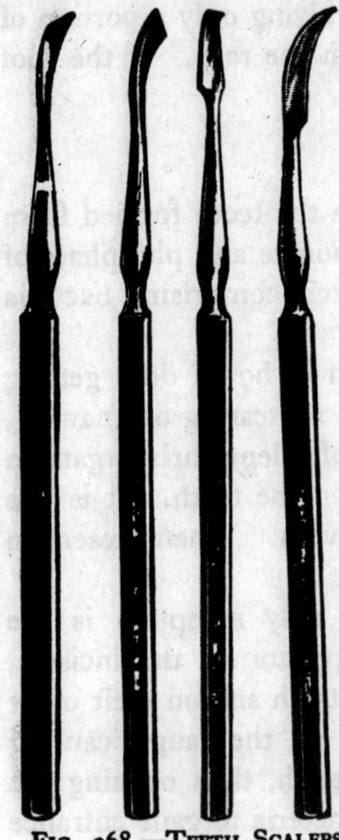

Fig. 268.—Teeth Scalers for Dogs.

2. Scrape off the tartar by means of scalers for the purpose, or a curette, or one of the limbs of a dressing forceps from the base towards the table of the teeth.

3. Brush the teeth afterwards if they are not sufficiently clean.

4. Wash the mouth with a suitable mouth wash, such as 1 in 1,000 potassium permanganate, or hydrogen peroxide 1 in 5, or dilute hydrochloric acid 1 in 100 parts of water. The latter is particularly good for cleaning the teeth.

5. If alveolar periostitis is present, treat it as described below.

Dental Caries (Caries Dentium)

This term is applied to the destruction or decay of the cement, dentine, and enamel of the teeth, the enamel being more slowly destroyed. The condition is comparatively rare in veterinary patients. It is believed to commence in the osteo-cement cavity on the table of the tooth formed by the involution of the enamel. When this is not filled by cement substance, food material lodges therein and decomposes and harbours bacteria, which proliferate and have a destructive effect on the tooth, resulting in a hole being formed which gradually increases in size, forming the typical caried or diseased tooth. When the disease is advanced the pulp cavity becomes involved, and then alveolar periostitis is set up.

Symptoms.—The condition may not be suspected until the symptoms of alveolar periostitis draw attention to the mouth, when the changes in the affected tooth are observed. If noticed early, the disease is indicated by the appearance of a dark spot on the tooth. When the excavation is sufficiently advanced to expose the nerve, the usual signs of trouble in the mouth are observed, " quidding " being the chief feature. An offensive odour is exhaled from the mouth, and the dental cavity is found filled with stinking decomposed food-material. Alveolar periostitis may be present at the same time. The tooth may fracture in consequence of its weakened condition by the force of mastication. The disease most commonly occurs at nine or ten years of age, being less frequent at a later period.

Prognosis.—When the disease appears, it usually necessitates removal of the affected tooth or teeth, as filling is seldom resorted to.

Treatment consists in extracting the diseased tooth or teeth (see p. 281).

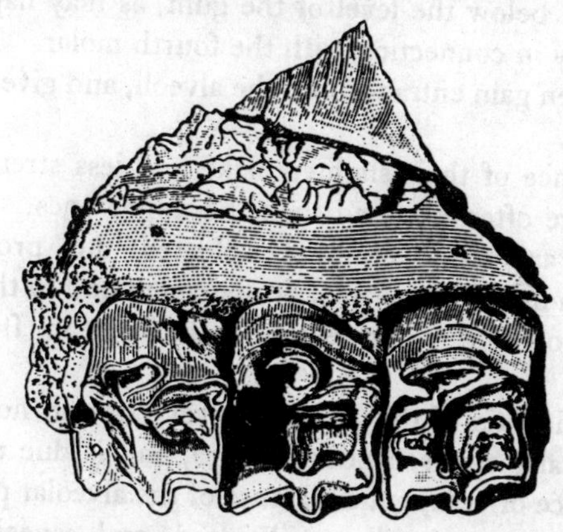

Fig. 269.—Central Dry Caries of a Horse's Upper Molar (Kitt).

IV.—DISEASES OF THE ALVEOLI

Alveolar periostitis (periostitis alveolaris) is by far the commonest dental disease of herbivora and carnivora, especially of dogs.

Alveolar Periostitis in Herbivora

Two forms are distinguished—viz.: (1) Chronic ossifying and (2) purulent alveolar periostitis.

(1) **The chronic ossifying form** is characterised by the formation of exostoses at the root of the tooth, which appears either roughened or covered with flat or knob-like masses of new bone, the latter greatly hindering the extraction of the tooth.

(2) In the **purulent form** the periosteum is usually thickened and extremely vascular; at points it is covered with granulations and

separated from the wall of the alveolus or root of the tooth by a quantity of grey offensive bone pus. Opposite these points the bone or root of the tooth is often eroded to the extent of $\frac{1}{16}$ inch or more. In occasional cases, especially in the lower jaw, necrosis of the bone and purulent osteomyelitis supervene.

Etiology.—Anything which leads to exposure of the alveolus will give rise to the disease, such as (1) separation of the gum from the teeth by the insinuation of coarse food material between them, or by tartar; (2) compound fracture of the jaw involving an alveolus; (3) opening of the pulp cavity as the result of caries or a deep fissure; (4) a tooth, becoming worn below the level of the gum, as may happen in an old horse, especially in connection with the fourth molar. Foreign matter and bacteria then gain entrance into the alveoli, and give rise to alveolar periostitis.

In consequence of their slighter make and less strength, the lower molars are more often diseased than the upper ones. The third and fourth molars are most commonly affected, due probably to their central position in the fan-shaped arrangement and to their consequent exposure to powerful compression both from in front and from behind.

Alveolar periostitis of the incisors is very rare in horses and ruminants, is generally of a secondary nature, and is due to injury of the interdental space or compound fracture of the alveolar process. When several neighbouring alveoli are diseased, and especially where the teeth are very loose, a suspicion of some new growth is always justified.

Symptoms.—Mastication is slow, interrupted and one-sided with rolling of the tongue, slobbering, and dropping of food from the mouth. From the outside it may be discovered that a tooth is displaced. The cheek may be distended with masses of food. On manipulation of the tooth through the mouth, it may be found to be loose and painful. The peculiar repulsive " carious " smell emanating from the mouth, and very pronounced in the retained masses of food, is characteristic of alveolar periostitis. The gum in the vicinity is found inflamed, bathed in pus, and receding from the tooth. The affected tooth may be displaced out of line with the normal teeth, or lie deeper than their level. The upper molars are naturally displaced outwards and the lower inwards, in accordance with the direction of the wearing surfaces.

Treatment consists in removing the affected tooth or teeth (see p. 281).

Alveolar Periostitis in Carnivora (Pyorrhœa)

Dogs, especially those kept in the house, are the most frequent sufferers.

ETIOLOGY.—The chief cause of the condition is dental tartar, as already described, but it may occur apart from this. If dogs are injudiciously fed, receiving mostly soft food instead of that requiring tearing and chewing, the teeth become practically functionless, the gums become soft, and micro-organisms remain in contact therewith without disturbance, and eventually set up a gingivitis. The infection extends from the gum to the periodontal membrane, and thence to the surrounding bone, giving rise to a varying degree of toxæmia, manifested by different forms of constitutional disturbance. Many of the cases of obscure affections in dogs, characterised by inappetence and general loss of vigour, are believed to be due to pyorrhœa.

It has been proved in the human subject by the aid of radiography that the bone of the jaw may be affected with ostitis originating in the alveolus of a tooth before obvious symptoms of pyorrhœa are observable in the mouth.

SYMPTOMS.—In a typical case in the dog, the teeth are covered with tartar as described. The gums are swollen, more or less reddened, and bleed easily. At points where the tongue cannot reach, as along the external borders, the gums are moist with a grey slimy fluid of a particularly penetrating odour. The masses of tartar usually present are found intruding under the gum in the direction of the alveolus, loosening the tooth, which may eventually fall out if not extracted. Where the disease is extensive, the animals salivate freely, eat badly, and either avoid gnawing bones or whine occasionally when doing so, whilst the mouth emits a most offensive smell. Sometimes single teeth become displaced, preventing the animal closing the mouth, and giving rise to suspicion of rabies. The condition was formerly regarded as systemic in origin, and received such names as scurvy, mouth-rot, etc. There is no febrile disturbance as a rule. When the affected teeth are removed, the local symptoms disappear and the general health and vigour of the patient are restored. Most of the teeth, including the incisors, canines, and molars, may be affected.

PREVENTION consists in avoiding the causes enumerated, and chiefly in adopting the measures mentioned to prevent the deposit of tartar on the teeth.

TREATMENT.—Remove the affected teeth, scrape away the tartar from those not involved, and prescribe a mouth wash as recommended when dealing with dental tartar. Paint ulcers on the gums with tincture of iodine.

Dental Fistula

This is a fistula abutting on the root of a tooth.

ETIOLOGY.—The cause may be :

1. *Alveolar periostitis*, giving rise to purulent osteomyelitis and the formation of an abscess in the bone, which bursts externally, or into the maxillary sinus, or into the nasal cavity.

2. *External injury*, followed by osteomyelitis extending into an alveolus. Occurring in this way, the condition is most commonly found in the lower jaw in connection with the first and second premolars, seldom the third, and usually in young horses, in which the roots of the teeth are long and close to the inferior border of the horizontal ramus, which is the usual seat of injury, caused by striking the bone against the manger or other fixed object. Although the sinus abuts on a tooth in this case, alveolar periostitis may not ensue, or may remain localised and be followed by recovery. The root of the tooth may become thickened, being surrounded by actively growing granulation tissue, which becomes covered with fresh cement ; a periostitis alveolaris ossificans results, with the formation of an exostosis, which renders extraction difficult or impossible.

SYMPTOMS.—There is a little funnel-shaped orifice in the skin in the affected region. There may also be an opening into the mouth alongside the affected tooth, and the probe may be passed through into the oral cavity, and fluid injected through one orifice will escape through the other. Round the external opening and over the course of the canal the bone is rarefied and swollen ; mastication is not always impeded. Examination of the mouth may reveal nothing wrong with the corresponding tooth when the condition is the result of external injury.

When the fistula opens into the sinus or nasal chamber, there is an offensive purulent discharge from the nostril of the affected side. Diagnosis in this case is based on evidence of alveolar periostitis in connection with one of the superior molars. When opening into the nose, a catheter passed up the nasal chamber may come into contact with a rough uneven patch caused by the fistulous orifice.

TREATMENT.—When the fistula is the result of external injury, it may not be necessary to remove the tooth, the treatment then consisting in opening up the fistula and removing loose bone and curetting its lining. As a rule recovery ensues rapidly. When it fails to supervene, it is usually an indication that the root of the tooth is diseased and that the latter must be removed.

In the dog dental fistula is nearly always in connection with the fourth upper molar, and has its orifice a little below the lower eyelid. A probe passed into it strikes the root of the tooth. The condition is also spoken of as pus in the antrum. As long as the tooth remains *in situ* the fistula will persist. The orifice may close for a while and then open again, discharging a purulent fluid.

FIG. 270.—DENTAL FISTULA IN THE DOG.
A. Orifice of Fistula.

The only treatment in this case is extraction of the tooth involved, which is usually the fourth molar, but sometimes the fifth. Recovery follows immediately. Little or nothing may be noticed abnormal in connection with the tooth viewed from the mouth.

Neoplasms of the Gums and Alveoli (Epulis)

Under the common title of epulis are grouped all tumours originating in the gum or alveolus. They are included in "tumours" of the jaws, and have been dealt with.

Dental Tumours

True dental tumours, odontoma, have been rarely described as occurring in the domesticated animals. The condition may be present without causing trouble, and then is not detected. It may be associated with alveolar periostitis, and extraction of the tooth may then be very difficult. Winter (Limerick) removed a tooth affected in this way, causing fracture of the jaw during the procedure.

AFFECTIONS OF THE NECK

AFFECTIONS OF THE POLL

Contusions

CONTUSIONS occur in the usual way. The actual cause may be striking the poll against the top of a low doorway or ceiling, or the roof of a pit, or the manger ; a blow from a stick or whip-handle ; falling over on the poll ; or the constant use of a heavy bridle, or having the poll strap of the latter too tight, or the pressure of a tight overcheck.

SYMPTOMS.—The symptoms are those of traumatic inflammation. If a hæmatoma form its characteristics will be manifested, and if the bursa over the atlas is involved there will be evidence of bursitis. A horse may prove " poll shy " following injury to the poll, apparently due to hyperæsthesia, resenting the poll being touched or the bridle being put on, although all inflammation has disappeared.

TREATMENT consists in adopting the measures recommended for acute aseptic inflammation, cold and astringent applications being indicated at first, followed by hot applications and absorbent topics. If a hæmatoma does not become absorbed it must be opened aseptically, and the resulting wound treated with antiseptic solution until it is uniformly granulating. A chronic bursitis is treated by counter-irritation, needle-point firing being most effective. If the bursa contain riziform bodies, it will require to be opened, evacuated, and irrigated with tincture of iodine with a view to causing it to fill up by granulation tissue or the lining of the cavity may be excised. The application of a blister of biniodide of mercury has proved successful for hyperæsthesia of the poll.

COMPLICATIONS.—Possible complications are :

1. *Direct or indirect fracture of the cranium*, caused by severe violence.

2. *Pressure on the bulb* through the thin occipito-atlantoid ligament, due to the presence of a large bursal swelling, and giving rise to respiratory or circulatory trouble, or to coma, or to partial or complete paralysis of the trunk and the limbs.

Open Wounds

Open wounds are dealt with on general principles, their gravity depending on their depth and the degree of infection which ensues, the complication to be feared being necrosis of the ligamentum nuchæ.

Abscess

An abscess may form as the result of direct injury and infection. The symptoms at first are those of intensely acute inflammation, followed by the characteristic features of an abscess. The animal shows evidence of great pain, holding the head stiffly at a lower level than usual, with the nose poked out, and resents interference with the lesion.

Recovery may ensue on opening the abscess, or a sinus may supervene, owing to the ligamentum nuchæ being necrosed.

Poll Evil

Poll evil is the name given to a sinus or purulent fistula abutting on the poll, and due to necrosis of the ligamentum nuchæ, and perhaps of some of the other structures as well, including the tendon of the complexus, the occiput, atlas, and axis.

ETIOLOGY.—The condition is due to injury and infection of the region of the poll. It is usually a sequel to an abscess. (See Fistulous Withers.)

SYMPTOMS.—The symptoms are those of a sinus or purulent fistula on the poll, accompanied by pronounced inflammatory swelling, causing great pain, manifested by the position of the head and by the resentment of the patient to interference with the lesion, as in the case of an abscess mentioned above. The swelling is most prominent on the sides of the middle line, and may be more marked on one side than on the other. The tense funicular portion of the ligamentum nuchæ prevents distension of the mesial aspect of the region. The discharge is more or less profuse, depending on the amount of necrosis in the depth of the lesion. A probe passed into the fistula will enable its extent to be ascertained.

PROGNOSIS.—The condition is usually troublesome to deal with, on account of the difficulty of getting rid of all the necrotic tissue, which is essential for recovery. Possible incurable complications are extension of the infection through the occipito-atlantoid or atlanto-axial ligament to the cord, causing paralysis, and arthritis of the occipito-atlantoid articulation, followed by anchylosis of the joint and immobility of the head on the neck.

Treatment.—The lesion being a typical example of a sinus or purulent fistula, the measures described for that condition are indicated. In this case the method to be chosen is either (1) the use of solid caustics to slough out the interior of the cavity, and thus bring about the separation of the necrotic tissue ; or (2) operation to excise the diseased structures. The caustic most in favour, being very effective, is perchloride of mercury. Arsenic paste has also been successfully employed. It is very drastic in its effects. In a well-established case, operation is the most satisfactory method of treatment. Whatever form of local treatment is adopted, the inoculation of a polyvalent vaccine is always advisable. Some practitioners claim to have had rapid cure from its effects, with little or no local intervention.

AFFECTIONS OF THE CERVICAL REGION

The cervical region comprises many important structures and organs, including, in addition to the parts dealt with as belonging to the " poll," the larynx, trachea, œsophagus, carotid artery, jugular vein, etc., any of which may be involved in traumatic lesions of the neck. The various affections of these organs are dealt with separately ; consequently, only those of the muscles, bones, and ligaments remain for consideration.

Contusions, Open Wounds, and Abscesses of these tissues require no further description than that given for these conditions in general. The gravity of deep wounds consists in the risk of necrosis of the ligamentum nuchæ, or supraspinous ligament, or one of the vertebræ ensuing and causing a sinus. If the carotid is wounded, make a longitudinal cutaneous incision above the jugular vein. Use blunt disection until the trachea is reached ; recognise on its supero-lateral aspect the carotid, which can be felt pulsating. Isolate it from its accompanying nerves and ligature it.

Fistula of the Neck

This condition, which is really a sinus, is due to necrosis of the funicular or lamellar portion of the ligamentum nuchæ, or of both. In more advanced cases necrosis of the supraspinous ligament or the bone may also be present.

Etiology.—The condition is caused by an open wound extending to the ligament and becoming infected, or results from an abscess involving the structure. It may be a complication of strangles, or an extension forwards of " fistulous withers."

SYMPTOMS.—The lesion is characterised by the presence of a more or less painful and indurated swelling in the affected region, containing one or more fistulous orifices discharging copious offensive pus. In neglected cases the suppuration may reach the cervical vertebræ, causing necrosis of the bone, or it may even extend as far back as the dorsal spines, associated throughout with necrosis of the cervical ligament and perhaps with that of the other ligamentous and osseous structures.

PROGNOSIS.—The condition may undergo spontaneous cure by separation and escape of the dead tissue. This separation, however, may take weeks to be accomplished.

Treatment in a well-established case is always tedious and troublesome. The tendency in most cases is for the necrosis to spread.

Treatment is on the same lines as those recommended for poll evil. It consists in opening up the sinus largely so as to expose completely its depth and enable all the dead tissue to be removed, followed by antiseptic irrigation of the wound and the application of B.I.P.P. This procedure, combined with the use of a vaccine, usually has the desired effect. Sometimes, however, it fails, the disease continuing to spread through the ligament. To arrest the invasion of the latter, the operation known as cervical desmotomy is indicated. It is performed thus: Having taken the usual precautions, make a longitudinal incision in the skin at a point about 2 or 3 inches in front of the anterior boundary of the lesion and at the level of the funicular portion of the ligament just large enough to admit the tenotome beneath the latter. Turn the edge of the knife towards the structure, and sever it with a to-and-fro and seesaw movement.

The effect of the operation is to form a barrier of embryonic vascular tissue, which will arrest the progress of bacteria through the ligament when they have reached this point. When this wound has healed, the sinus may be opened up and the portion of ligament behind the cicatrix removed. It is better, however, to await the separation of the affected part, while continuing the antiseptic treatment. The operation has had the desired effect.

Pustular Eruption

Sometimes, especially in entire horses used for draft work, a painful lesion forms on the crest where the collar is in contact with it. It is formed of a number of nodules, which may be felt like grains of shot in the thickness of the skin. Some of them are suppurating, while others are cicatrised spots. The condition is evidently due to infection through abrasions caused by the collar, and is sometimes spoken of as " sore chine." The affection appears to be a variety of eczema or acne localised in the skin of the mane.

SYMPTOMS.—The affected part appears corrugated and thickened, is very sensitive to the touch, and presents the characteristics mentioned above.

TREATMENT consists in clipping the hair, cleaning the region thoroughly with soap and warm water, drying it, and then applying mercurial or oleate of mercury ointment, or a blister of biniodide of mercury. After a week or ten days the part should be again washed and dried. Complete recovery is the rule.

Injuries caused by the Collar

An ill-fitting collar, or one whose lining is dirty and hard from a dried mixture of sweat, dandruff, and hairs, is often a source of injury to the parts on which it lies. The collar should be parallel with the scapula, without touching it, which it is apt to do if too wide, producing excoriation of the skin over the scapular region. Most frequently the upper groove causes injury; if too narrow it bruises, and if too wide the skin is rubbed. As a rule, when the collar is in position there should be sufficient room to pass the fingers between it and the top of the neck. It should fit the shoulder so that it is neither pushed towards the left nor the right. Injuries caused by the collar are in all essentials similar to those caused by the saddle, which are considered in detail elsewhere (p. 637).

Shoulder Abscess or Tumour

The point of the shoulder is a fairly common seat for an abscess in the horse. It may be (1) superficial or (2) deep.

(1) The superficial abscess is of the ordinary variety, and runs the usual course.

(2) The deep abscess is usually of a chronic nature, forming slowly and presenting the external features of a neoplasm, owing to the thickness of its fibrous walls.

ETIOLOGY.—The cause of the condition is the entrance of pyogenic organisms into the deep tissues of the region, the mastoido-humeralis muscle being the chief structure involved. The causal organism may be the ordinary staphylococcus or a streptococcus, but in more than 70 per cent. of cases the specific cause is the *Discomyces equi*. It is a question how the infection gains entrance. The most likely port of entry is through the skin, due to abrasions produced by the collar, which, however, may be so slight as to escape notice. This theory is borne out by the fact that the lesion is most common in draft-horses. In some cases it may be due to irregular strangles. It might be the result of infection carried by the lymphatic vessels from a septic wound lower down on the limb, the prepectoral lymph glands being the seat of the abscess in this case.

SYMPTOMS.—A hard tumour-like swelling is observed in front of the point of the shoulder, gradually increasing in size and seldom displaying acute inflammatory symptoms. The horse may continue working

FIG. 271.—MULTIPLE ABSCESS FORMATION IN THE SHOULDER REGION DUE TO BOTRIOMYCES.

for weeks without showing evidence of pain from pressure on the lesion by the collar. It seldom comes to a point and bursts. The area occupied by the enlargement varies in different cases. It may have the dimensions of an orange, or be much larger. It may spread to the jugular furrow and even into the axilla. When the abscess bursts it rarely heals without treatment, a sinus persisting until the cavity is properly evacuated. There may be a crop of small abscesses in the vicinity of the main tumour resembling the lesions of acne. The swelling is usually sensitive on firm manipulation.

DIAGNOSIS is generally easy. The affected region is seldom the seat of a neoplasm, and the latter would be more circumscribed and non-inflammatory in character.

TREATMENT.—The obvious aim of treatment is to remove the cause of the trouble—viz., the bacteria in the centre of the lesion. The procedure may be:

1. *Incision and evacuation of the cavity.*

2. *Complete or partial excision* of the fibrous enlargement, with its purulent centre.

1. *Incision.*—A knife is inserted through the centre of the swelling into the purulent cavity, whose penetration is revealed by the escape of thick pus through the wound. Should the pus not appear at once, introduce a blunt instrument instead of the knife, and manipulate it in different directions until the purulent fluid escapes. An artery forceps or a strong grooved director answers the purpose. Then continue the incision so as to open the tumour from its upper to its lower extremity. If hæmorrhage is profuse, arrest it by firmly plugging the cavity with cotton-wool or tow kept in position by sutures. Afterwards treat the interior of the cavity with tincture of iodine, so as to substitute a granulating surface for its smooth lining.

Should puncture with the knife and sound fail to reach the purulent centre, a blister may be applied, which will cause acute inflammation, resulting in the abscess bursting into the track of the instrument after a few days, when the cavity can be opened up as described. Some practitioners open the abscess by means of the thermo-cautery. The cavity may be slow to fill up and considerable thickening may remain; yet many veterinarians prefer this treatment to excision, maintaining that it ensures more rapid recovery on account of the smaller size of the wound, that there is less risk of reinfection of the tissues, and that the fibrous thickening practically disappears as if fibrolysis had ensued.

2. *Excision.*—Complete excision is indicated when the tumour is well circumscribed and not very extensive in area. It consists in making an elliptical vertical incision over its centre and dissecting it out cleanly from the surrounding tissues, and dealing with hæmorrhage as it arises. Care must be taken not to cut into the purulent cavity and allow pus to escape and infect the operation wound. Should this happen, extra antiseptic precautions will be necessary. If the tumour encroach on the jugular vein, carotid artery, and the accompanying nerves, blunt dissection must be practised in their vicinity to avoid cutting them. It may be possible, when the greater portion of the tumour has been dissected, to grasp it in the hands and tear it away from contact with these vessels.

An alternative procedure is to first divide the tumour into two parts by a mesial incision, and then dissect out each half separately. This method is safe when there are no important structures beneath it, and enables the depth of the tumour to be ascertained at once, but has the serious disadvantage of allowing pus to escape into the wound, and for this reason should not be practised.

Partial excision is advisable when the tumour is very extensive and complete removal would necessitate a very large wound which would take a long time to cicatrise. In this method a thick slice of the tumour is removed on either side of the cutaneous wound extending into the abscess cavity, which is then curetted and swabbed with tincture of iodine. Further portions of the tumour may be removed if so doing does not involve the risk of wounding the large vessels in the jugular furrow.

In both methods the operation wound is dressed with tincture of iodine and an antiseptic powder, and packed with antiseptic gauze, wool, or tow kept in position by sutures. If the bleeding is not severe and the cavity of the wound not deep, it is not necessary to plug the latter. In this case its lips are brought into apposition by sutures, an orifice being left at its lower part for drainage. The following day the plug is removed, and the wound irrigated with an antiseptic solution and dressed with antiseptic powder. Healing takes place without interruption, and is completed in two to four weeks, depending on the size of the wound. After complete excision, with careful antiseptic precautions, the condition seldom recurs, but in some instances, even when the operation has been carefully performed, the abscess reforms after the lapse of a few months. The writer had a case in which the shoulder abscess was tuberculous.

Jugular Phlebitis

Jugular phlebitis answers the description of phlebitis in general (p. 92). It usually follows jugular phlebotomy, when infection of the vein may be brought about as follows: (1) By neglect of aseptic and antiseptic precautions; (2) by making the incision in the vessel transverse to its long axis, whereby it gapes, allowing the entrance of bacteria; (3) by not making a clean incision in the vessel wall, so that the wound therein fails to heal by first intention, thus favouring infection.

SYMPTOMS.—The symptoms are those already described for phlebitis, appearing on the course of the jugular vein. The operation wound fails to heal and shows a purulent discharge. The lumen of the vessel above this point is filled with a thrombus, giving it a corded feel. The lower part of the vein is collapsed. An œdematous swelling forms in the jugular furrow and in the parotid region. When the suppurative form of the disease occurs, abscesses form here and there in the affected part of the vein, and after bursting cause so many fistulæ.

PROGNOSIS.—Recovery is the rule at the expense of the vein, which remains impervious to the circulation. Within six months afterwards the collateral circulation is sufficiently developed to prevent œdema of the head when the animal is grazing. Hæmorrhage or general infection seldom supervenes.

TREATMENT is on the principles already laid down. It comprises:

1. Disinfection of the operation wound.
2. Keeping the patient quiet and avoiding disturbance of the thrombus.
3. Opening abscesses when they appear, and injecting an antiseptic solution into the suppurating part of the vein through a piece of rubber tubing introduced through one of the orifices in the vessel.
4. Applying a blister of biniodide of mercury over the suppurating region when the case becomes chronic, having failed to respond to the treatment in No. 3. This has often proved successful in obstinate cases.
5. Opening up the suppurating vein, removing its septic contents, and treating the lesion as an open wound.
6. Excising the affected part of the vein by ligaturing it in a normal part above the level of the thrombus, and dissecting it out as far down as the sepsis extends. When the operation is done with careful aseptic and antiseptic precautions, healing of the wound made for isolating the vein and applying the ligature thereon occurs by first intention, and the excision wound heals in due course by granulations.
7. Ligation of the vein above the thrombus when severe hæmorrhage ensues.

COMPLICATIONS.—Possible complications are: (1) Fatal hæmorrhage from complete breaking down of the clot in the vessel; (2) septic embolic pneumonia from passage of a portion of the septic clot into the circulation; (3) septicæmia from invasion of the blood stream by organisms in the lesion.

AFFECTIONS OF THE THYROID GLAND

Thyroiditis

Thyroiditis has been seen affecting cattle from six to eighteen months old, coming on suddenly, characterised by inflammation and enlargement of the gland, and by febrile disturbance. It usually disappears after a few days, but occasionally persists. The swelling may be so great as to cause dyspnœa and necessitate tracheotomy. The cause of the condition is obscure.

TREATMENT consists in applying tincture of iodine to the swelling and administering potassium iodide internally.

Goitre

This term is applied to non-inflammatory enlargement of the thyroid gland.

ETIOLOGY.—The condition has been seen affecting the horse, mule, ox, and dog in districts where it is common in the human subject. The cause has been ascribed to an organism conveyed through the drinking water, to an insufficiency or absence of iodine in the soil, to functional hypertrophy, and to infectious diseases, especially distemper in the dog. Various forms of enlargement of the gland have been described and designated as follows—viz.; parenchymatous, colloid, fibrous, cystic, vascular, etc. Calcification and ossification of the gland have been seen. The dog is the most frequent sufferer from enlarged thyroid. Generally speaking, goitre is not common in veterinary practice. Exophthalmic goitre is very rare in animals.

TREATMENT varies according to the nature of the abnormality in the gland.

In soft or parenchymatous goitre iodine medication has often had good results, potassium iodide in daily doses of 2 to 3 drachms in the horse and 5 to 20 grains in the dog being prescribed, while the surface of the gland is painted with tincture of iodine. About 50 per cent. of cures have been obtained by this treatment.

For cystic goitre incision and evacuation of the cyst, followed by the injection of iodine, has often had the desired effect in dogs. Aspiration of the contents with a fine trocar and canula and injection of tincture of iodine generally proves successful in dogs when the cyst is recent and its wall thin.

In fibrous goitre injections of tincture of iodine into the centre of the gland are indicated, 20 to 30 minims being used for the horse and about 5 minims in the dog. If the swelling is lobulated, the injection should be distributed between the lobes. When the resulting inflammation has subsided the injection is repeated. Cure, as a rule, takes months.

When the foregoing measures have failed, thyroidectomy may be considered. Complete thyroidectomy usually causes death in the dog, but has no bad effect on the horse. Provided that not more than two-thirds of each gland is removed in the dog, the animal will survive. If the parathyroids are left intact no untoward effect may be produced. (For operation, see p. 484.) In the human subject the administration of fresh thyroid gland or of thyroid extract has caused improvement in a fair percentage of cases.

DISEASES OF THE LARYNX AND TRACHEA

Exploration

Alterations in the exterior of the larynx can be detected by viewing and palpating it externally. Its interior cannot be satisfactorily examined in the horse without the aid of a laryngoscope, owing to the length of the soft palate and the distance of the organ from the oral orifice. The rhino-laryngoscope made by Lester of Vienna, referred to when treating of the nasal chambers, affords a comprehensive and clear view of the inside of the larynx. In the ox the fingers can be inserted into the larynx through the mouth. In the dog and cat a complete view of the laryngeal orifice can be obtained through the mouth on widely separating the jaws, and drawing the tongue forwards and depressing its base with a spatula. A small torch is very useful to illuminate the part.

Injuries

Contusions of the larynx and trachea are occasionally met with. Their effects vary from mere subcutaneous or submucous rupture of capillaries to fracture of the cartilage. Loss of consciousness, with cardiac and respiratory syncope, as the result of injury inflicted on the front of the neck is very rare in animals. Epistaxis may ensue.

Open Wounds of the larynx and trachea may be surgical or accidental. The latter vary much in their nature and gravity. When the cutaneous wound is not directly in line with that into the air passage, emphysema will ensue. Intratracheal or interlaryngeal hæmorrhage may lead to dyspnœa, and even cause asphyxia. Broncho-pneumonia is a possible complication.

TREATMENT.—Contusions are dealt with in the usual way. Open wounds are also treated on general principles, care being taken not to allow any antiseptic lotion to enter the larynx and trachea through perforating wounds, and thereby cause inflammation of their lining, or perhaps fatal broncho-pneumonia. If the wound in the skin does not communicate directly with the perforating wound, it should be made to do so by enlarging the superficial wound. If the perforation is in the form of a clean incision, immediate suture may be followed by primary healing. Even extensive wounds of the organs in question usually cicatrise rapidly. If there be much bleeding into the trachea, threatening asphyxia, tracheotomy below the affected part and the insertion of a tampon canula are indicated. The latter is a form of tracheotomy tube all in one piece, with a bent cylindrical stem (Fig. 272). It prevents blood passing into the bronchi, while respiration occurs freely through the tube.

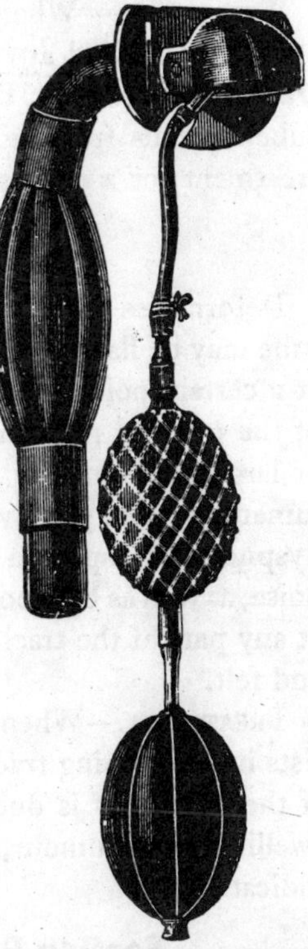

FIG. 272.—TAMPON CANULA OR TRENDELENBURG CANULA.

Fracture of the Larynx

Fracture of the larynx is a very rare lesion. It is caused by external violence, and may or may not be accompanied by an open wound.

SYMPTOMS.—The chief symptom is dyspnœa, due to narrowing of the lumen of the larynx following inflammation of the mucous membrane, and perhaps displacement of the fractured cartilage. There may be hæmorrhage through the mouth and nose, and dysphagia may supervene. External evidence of inflammation and deformity may be observed.

TREATMENT.—If asphyxia is threatened, tracheotomy is indicated. Otherwise the treatment is that for a contusion or open wound.

Reduction of displaced fragments might be performed through the tracheal opening, or through an incision made in the crico-thyroid ligament. If there is bleeding into the trachea, it may be necessary to insert a tampon canula.

Fracture of the Trachea

The trachea may be fractured by direct violence, such as kicks, bites, and falling against fixed objects.

SYMPTOMS.—The symptoms are those of a contusion or open wound, associated with emphysema, extending a variable distance beyond the seat of injury, and in rare cases becoming generalised. Dyspnœa and a respiratory noise are caused by the submucous inflammation and extravasation. Asphyxia may supervene if relief is not forthcoming. Septic pneumonia is a possible complication.

The fracture, which may be transverse or longitudinal, can be felt on manipulation when the inflammatory swelling has subsided, a deformity being present due to displacement of a portion of one or more rings.

TREATMENT.—When danger of asphyxia is present, the seat of injury should be incised at once to expose the trachea, and insert therein a tracheotomy tube or, better, a tampon canula. Simple cases involving subcutaneous fracture of one or two rings only require the ordinary treatment for a contusion.

Deformities of the Trachea

Deformities of the trachea may be congenital or acquired. The tube may be flattened from before to behind, or laterally, or constricted at a certain point, or even twisted on its long axis. The ends of some of the tracheal rings may be incurved or overlapping. A hæmatoma or large inflammatory swelling may so press upon the trachea that its lumen becomes greatly diminished, or even obliterated, causing severe dyspnœa or asphyxia. Dyspnœa is characterised by a respiratory noise, as well as by laboured breathing. The deformity may be situated at any part of the trachea. When in the cervical region it can be seen and felt.

TREATMENT.—When the affected part is accessible, treatment consists in performing tracheotomy below this point and inserting a tube. If the deformity is due to pressure by a hæmatoma, or inflammatory swelling, or a tumour, appropriate measures for these conditions are indicated.

Foreign Bodies in the Trachea and Larynx

In cases of pharyngitis, tumours, or paralysis of the pharynx, or any condition causing dysphagia, food material may pass into the larynx and trachea during feeding. Medicine administered by drenching in such cases is also apt to encroach on the respiratory passage. Except a large amount of the material takes the wrong course it is ejected by coughing. Other foreign bodies have been found in the larynx and trachea in large and small animals, including needles, pins, fish-hooks, onions, pebbles, a piece of cartilage when performing tracheotomy, a portion of a tracheotomy tube, etc.

SYMPTOMS.—When foreign matter enters the larynx or trachea coughing ensues immediately, and may or may not be sufficient to dislodge it. If a considerable quantity gains entrance coughing is insufficient to eject it, and a fatal broncho-pneumonia then generally supervenes. Should the object be large enough to obstruct the lumen of the passage, death from asphyxia is sure to occur.

DIAGNOSIS without a history is difficult. Even when it is known that a foreign substance has gained entrance, it may be very hard to say at what point it is located. Its position may be changed by the act of coughing.

TREATMENT consists in removing the foreign matter immediately, if possible. In the ox and the small animals it may be possible to detect the foreign body in the larynx through the mouth, and remove it with the hand or by the aid of a forceps or hook ; or in the horse it might be extracted after performing laryngotomy.

When asphyxia is threatened, tracheotomy must be performed at once below the seat of obstruction if the latter can be located, and it may be possible to remove it through this tracheal opening, or through another one made at its level. A long forceps or a piece of wire with its end formed in the shape of a hook may be used for the purpose.

Tumours of the Larynx and Trachea

Neoplasms are not common in the larynx or trachea, but are more frequently found in the former than in the latter. Papillomata are the variety most frequently met with, and are usually polypoid.

SYMPTOMS AND DIAGNOSIS.—Laryngeal and tracheal tumours cause interference with respiration, giving rise to dyspnœa and producing a noise during expiration and inspiration, but usually more marked during the former, especially in the case of the trachea. Exploratory laryngotomy may be necessary to diagnose a tumour in the interior of the larynx in the large animals. A tracheal tumour may cause a distension of the tube. Compression of the trachea at the level of the growth may increase or decrease the dyspnœa by occluding still more the lumen of the tube, or by dilating it, according to the position of the tumour.

TREATMENT.—In the small animals, and perhaps in the ox, benign tumours may be removed through the mouth by grasping the tumour with a forceps and excising it with a scissors or knife, or the galvano-cautery may be used for the purpose. In large animals, laryngotomy is generally necessary to enable the tumour to be reached. When the epiglottis is the site of the new growth, it may be removed through the mouth even in the horse. A tumour in the trachea can be removed through a tracheal opening made at its level. In all cases where the tumour of the larynx or trachea is sessile and wide-based, complete extirpation is impracticable ; and then all that can be done is to relieve respiratory distress by performing tracheotomy below the seat of the lesion. Intervention for malignant tumours is useless, except to perform tracheotomy lower down for the purpose of prolonging the life of the patient for a while.

Parasites in the Larynx

The larvæ of the *Gastrophilus equi* have been found in the larynx of the horse by Continental veterinarians, causing dyspnœa and even asphyxia in some cases.

DIAGNOSIS is difficult, and can only be confirmed by performing laryngotomy and examining the interior of the larynx, when the parasites can be easily removed.

Surgical intervention is the only effective treatment for the condition. Leeches have also been known to attach themselves to the interior of the larynx, with similar symptoms (see Affections of the Pharynx).

Roaring (Paralysis of the Larynx)

Roaring, due to paralysis of the intrinsic muscles of the larynx, is only of interest surgically from the point of view of operation for the relief of the condition, and this has been already described (see p. 302).

AFFECTIONS OF THE PHARYNX

Examination of the Pharynx

To examine the pharynx satisfactorily in the horse, it is necessary to cast the animal and to have the mouth kept open by a mouth gag. To make a manual exploration of the cavity, introduce the hand, palm uppermost, along the roof of the mouth as far as it will reach, raising the soft palate when it is encountered. Even with the patient thus controlled it is impossible to explore the whole interior of the pharynx in the horse, as its posterior part in most cases is out of reach. The use of a torch will enable the anterior region of the organ to be seen. In the ox a more thorough examination of the part can be made.

When the patient is suffering from respiratory distress due to some obstruction in the region of the pharynx or larynx, it is advisable to perform provisional tracheotomy to prevent the risk of asphyxia during the process of examination. In the small animals the pharynx can be readily examined through the mouth by keeping the jaws apart and having the tongue drawn forward and depressed, and by illuminating the region with a small torch. It may be necessary to grasp the tongue transversely with a long-jawed forceps.

Wounds of the Pharynx

The pharynx may be wounded in a variety of ways—for example, by dental instruments, a sharp-pointed stick used to administer a ball, a probang, and by sharp foreign bodies taken in with the food. In the large and small animals sharp bodies like pins, needles, fish-hooks, etc., may become embedded in the pharyngeal walls, and eventually escape externally through the bursting of an abscess to which they have given rise. Wounds inflicted from the exterior are rare.

SYMPTOMS.—The symptoms are those of pharyngitis. There may be bleeding from the mouth due to wounding of a pharyngeal vessel. When an abscess bursts externally and internally a pharyngeal fistula may ensue, with the escape of alimentary matter and saliva through it, and persist for a variable time. General infection and death may ensue from virulent sepsis of the wound.

TREATMENT is on the same lines as for pharyngitis, and consists in giving only liquid diet and irrigating the oral cavity and pharynx with a weak saline solution once or twice daily, followed by the exhibition of an antiseptic electuary.

Foreign Bodies in the Pharynx

Foreign bodies have been found in the pharynx in all animals, but most commonly in the dog and cat, in which the object may be a pin, needle, fish-hook, a bone, or piece of cartilage. In the pig a potato or piece of turnip may be lodged in the pharyngeal pouch. The pharynx in the ox is fairly frequently the seat of lodgment of a foreign body.

SYMPTOMS comprise coughing, dysphagia, salivation, and attempts at vomiting in the dog. The condition is diagnosed on careful exploration of the pharynx. Asphyxia has been seen as the result of an onion occluding the entrance to the larynx.

TREATMENT consists in removing the foreign body by the aid of a forceps through the mouth, a simple procedure in the dog and cat when the animal is properly controlled. It can generally be removed by the hand in the ox, but in the horse the hand cannot reach beyond the level of the epiglottis.

Parasites in the Pharynx

The chief parasites invading the pharynx are the larvæ of the *Œstrus equi* and certain varieties of leeches. Horse leeches have been found in the pharynx of the horse, ox, and dromedary. They are taken in with the drinking water, and become attached to the mucous membrane of the mouth and pharynx. They become distended with blood extracted from their host, and may eject some of it, causing hæmorrhage from the mouth and nose. Eventually they give rise to anæmia and consequent debility.

PREVENTION consists in (1) placing eels in the drinking ponds, which will devour the leeches ; and (2) in filtering the water before giving it to the animals.

TREATMENT to remove the parasites comprises (1) administering solutions of vinegar or common salt, (2) fumigation with pitch or tobacco twice daily, and (3) mechanically separating the parasites with the hand, or by the aid of a stick whose end is covered with a cloth securely fixed in position and impregnated with ether. If asphyxia is threatened, tracheotomy is indicated. It is between October and April that the *Œstrus equi* invades the pharynx of the horse, causing symptoms of pharyngitis, including dysphagia, salivation, coughing, and dyspnœa.

Its presence is discovered on exploration of the pharynx, and its removal is effected in the same way as that of leeches.

Pharyngitis

Pharyngitis, except when traumatic in origin or accompanied by abscess formation, belongs to the domain of medicine, and as such is not dealt with here.

Abscesses in the Pharynx

Abscesses may occur in the posterior or lateral wall of the pharynx.

ETIOLOGY.—The cause may be direct injury and infection of the pharyngeal wall, or the passage of pyogenic organisms from the mucous membrane of the pharynx through the lymphatic vessels to the lymphatic glands of the region in a case of pharyngitis, as during an attack of strangles. Abscesses arising in these ways are usually acute. Chronic or subacute abscesses may be tuberculous in cattle, or a sequel to strangles in the horse.

SYMPTOMS.—The symptoms are those of acute pharyngitis in the case of recent abscesses. Cold pharyngeal abscesses are not accompanied by acute inflammation, but interfere with swallowing and give rise to snoring. The abscess may burst into the pharynx or into the larynx, causing death in the latter case from asphyxia or from septic pneumonia. On careful examination of the interior of the pharynx, a swelling more or less inflammatory according to the nature of the abscess may be detected. In the ox and small animals, the abscess can be diagnosed by manual examination through the mouth.

TREATMENT.—Treatment is as usual for abscesses. When the abscess is detected fluctuating externally it is opened, the method described for opening a deep-seated parotid abscess being adopted (see p. 10). To open a pharyngeal abscess in the ox proceed thus : Have the animal securely held and the mouth kept open by means of a speculum. Take a concealed bistoury or an ordinary sharp-pointed knife guarded with tow to near its point in the right hand, introduce it into the pharynx, and puncture the abscess ; withdraw the hand quickly, and let the animal's head drop at once to allow the pus to escape outside instead of entering the larynx. It is often possible to open the abscess by means of the finger. The condition being usually tuberculous in the ox, it is advisable to prepare the animal for the butcher as soon as possible, owing to the abscess being likely to recur. Rarely a pharyngeal abscess bursts externally and internally, causing a pharyngeal fistula, already referred to.

Paralysis of the Pharynx

Paralysis of the pharynx has been most frequently seen in the horse.

ETIOLOGY.—The cause of the condition is often obscure, but it may be due to some form of toxæmia interfering with the function of its nerve supply. The upper two-thirds of the œsophagus, having the same innervation, is involved along with the pharynx.

SYMPTOMS comprise inability to swallow, food and drink being returned through the nose, and coughing during attempts at deglutition owing to alimentary matter entering the larynx. There is no evidence of inflammation in the pharyngeal region. When the hand is introduced into the pharynx, there is no contraction felt in its walls or in the soft palate. The patient becomes thin and debilitated for want of food, and death usually supervenes in the course of two to four weeks from inanition, or from foreign-body pneumonia due to food material gaining entrance into the lungs. Rarely the paralysis is temporary, occurring during an attack of an acute bacterial affection and disappearing with convalescence.

TREATMENT is usually of no avail. The animal's strength may be maintained, in the hope of eventual recovery, by feeding through the œsophageal tube passed through the nose, or by administering nutrient enemata. Potassium iodide and nux vomica may also be given by the tube, and strychnine may be injected hypodermically. Counter-irritation over the pharynx and electrotherapy are also indicated. A seton passed subcutaneously from one side to the other over the throat is generally considered to be the best counter-irritant for the purpose.

Actinomycosis of the Pharynx

The pharynx is a common site of actinomycosis in the ox. The lesion may be in the form of polypoid or sessile tumours. It most frequently affects the posterior wall of the pharynx.

TREATMENT consists in removing the tumour if possible, and, if not, in administering potassium iodide.

Tumours of the Pharynx

Apart from actinomycotic enlargements in the ox, tumours are not common in the pharynx in animals. The following neoplasms have been found therein: papillomata, polypoid fibromata, sarcomata, and epitheliomata.

SYMPTOMS comprise (1) dysphagia; (2) dyspnœa, often accompanied by snoring; (3) hæmorrhage from the nose in some cases, due to ulceration of the tumour; (4) attempts at vomiting in the dog. A pedunculated tumour may become displaced during feeding and obstruct the entrance to the œsophagus, giving rise to a fit of coughing and the ejection of alimentary matter through the mouth and nose. It might also fall into the lumen of the larynx, and cause death from asphyxia if not promptly dislodged by coughing.

DIAGNOSIS is confirmed by manual examination of the pharynx through the mouth in the manner described.

PROGNOSIS depends on the nature of the tumour. Malignant growths are incurable. Polypoid benign tumours can be successfully removed, but wide-based neoplasms are inoperable.

TREATMENT.—The only practicable way of removing a pharyngeal tumour is through the mouth. This is only possible in the horse when the tumour has a long pedicle, allowing it to come within reach; but in the ox all pharyngeal tumours can be reached in this way. Procedure is as follows: (1) Perform provisional tracheotomy if the tumour is large and there is danger of asphyxia ensuing during the operation; (2) have the beast controlled in the cast position with the mouth held widely open by means of the mouth gag; (3) seize the tumour either with the fingers or a forceps and remove it by tearing and torsion, or extirpate it by means of the ecraseur. Other methods of operating very rarely employed are the performance of laryngotomy or pharyngotomy to enable tumours to be excised that could not otherwise be reached.

Pharyngotomy is performed thus: Make an incision parallel to the jugular furrow a little below the inferior extremity of the wing of the atlas, going through the skin and subparotid connective tissue, making a wound sufficiently large to admit the hand. Introduce the fingers beneath the parotid gland, pushing it outwards and the carotid artery upwards. Push the hand forwards, and the posterior aspect of the larynx and pharynx will be reached at once. Incise or puncture the pharyngeal wall, introduce the fingers into the pharynx, explore its cavity, and having recognised the tumour remove it if possible.

AFFECTIONS OF THE ŒSOPHAGUS

Exploration of the Œsophagus

The œsophagus, owing to its deep situation, is not visible in outline except it is distended by a bolus or an obstruction, or by a dilatation of its lumen, and then only in the cervical region. Any swelling of the tube in this part of its course can be felt by manipulation in the jugular furrow. The passage of a probang or an œsophageal catheter into the lumen of the œsophagus will afford information as to its patency from the mouth to the stomach.

Passing the Probang

The Horse—Control.—The probang may be passed in the standing or cast position, more easily in the latter.

Standing Position.—Have the horse backed into a stall or corner. Insert the oral speculum, and have the head extended so as to obliterate the angle at the throat. Smear the end of the probang with vaseline, pass it gently along the roof of the mouth into the pharynx, and allow the animal to swallow it. Continue its passage firmly but gently until it reaches the stomach ; slight points of resistance are encountered at the level of the soft palate, at the entrance to the œsophagus, and at the cardiac extremity of the tube.

Cast Position.—The procedure is similar in the cast position, which has the advantage that the horse can be more easily controlled and the head more readily extended.

If the movements of the tongue interfere with the passage of the instrument into the pharynx, it should be held out of the mouth to one side, but the objection to doing this is that it interferes somewhat with the act of swallowing. The probang for the horse is usually made of gum-elastic, about 7 feet long, $\frac{3}{4}$ inch in diameter, and fitted with a cup-shaped attachment on its gastric end not more than 2 inches in diameter. Great care must be exercised not to use violence in the passage of the instrument, and thereby rupture the mucous lining of the organ or its muscular coat as well. When this accident happens, blood or a shred of membrane may be seen on the end of the probang when it is withdrawn, but it may occur without this symptom being observed.

The Ox.—The probang is usually passed in the standing position in the ox, but if the beast is very refractory it is much more convenient to pass it in the cast position. When the animal is standing it must

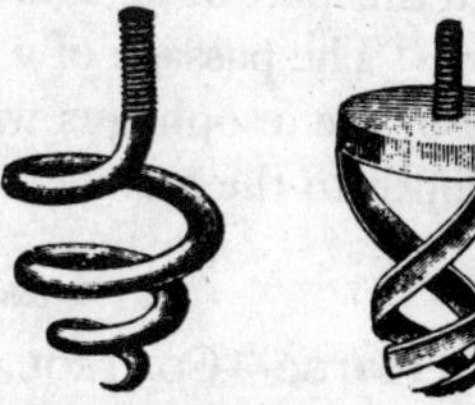

FIGS. 275 AND 276.—ŒSOPHAGEAL SCREWS.

be securely held with plenty of room in front, as it always goes forwards when the probang is passed into the œsophagus. A wooden gag is used (Fig. 273), fixed on each side by a piece of cord to the horn, or merely held by two assistants. The probang is passed in the same way as in the horse, but with greater facility.

The stomach tube for the horse can be used as a probang in that animal, passed through the inferior meatus of the nose, a procedure which is more easily carried out than the passage of the probang through the mouth.

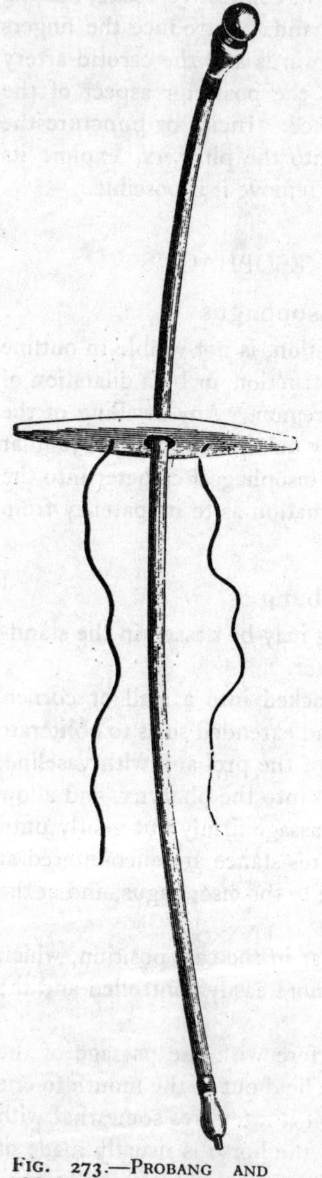

FIG. 273.—PROBANG AND MOUTH GAG FOR CATTLE.

FIG. 274.—DELVOS AND HERTWIG'S ŒSOPHAGEAL FORCEPS.

The œsophageal catheter is passed in the dog or cat with the animal fixed in the ventral position on the table and the mouth gag in position. In the absence of a catheter made for the purpose, the urethral catheter for the horse may be used instead for a large dog. Should the œsophageal tube be passed by mistake into the larynx, a fit of coughing usually ensues immediately, but not always. The tube can be felt in the œsophagus through the skin more easily at the upper part of the neck above the trachea.

Passing the Stomach Tube through the Nose has come much into vogue within recent years. Its utility was popularised by Mr. W. W. Lang who has on many occasions demonstrated the procedure.

Indications for its Use.—Exploration of the œsophagus for obstruction or stricture, the dislodgment of an œsophageal obstruction in a case of choking; the administration of large draughts or of medicine which would be irritant to the mouth if allowed to come in contact with its mucous membrane; the relief of gastric tympany and the introduction into the stomach of liquid diet when the animal is unable to partake of food in the ordinary way.

Procedure—1. *The Horse.*—Have the horse backed into a corner or stall. Take the tube, with its proximal end lubricated with liquid paraffin, in the left hand while the assistant holds the other end in a straight line in front of the horse. In the absence of an assistant this end of the tube is passed over the shoulder of the operator. Stand looking in the same direction as the animal, evert the inner wing of the left nostril by means of the right thumb, place the end of the tube on the floor of the nasal orifice with the left hand, and keeping it well pressed against the floor of the chamber with the middle finger of the right hand pass it with a continuous steady movement along the inferior meatus, and when it has reached the level of the pharynx, watch for a swallowing movement and then pass it on until it has reached the stomach. It often becomes arrested at the upper extremity of the nasal chamber by striking the bone there instead of passing through the posterior nares. In this case withdraw the tube for a short distance and pass it on again—a repeated to and fro movement may be required before the obstacle is cleared. Torsion of the tube may have the desired effect, or lowering or raising the head may overcome the difficulty. If failure occurs after a few attempts, it is advisable to try passing it through the other nostril, which often succeeds at the first attempt. Frequently the trouble is that the tube repeatedly enters the trachea instead of the œsophagus.

The following are indications that the tube has or has not entered the œsophagus.

1. A certain amount of resistance to the passage of the tube is felt when it enters the œsophagus, whereas if it enters the trachea no resistance is offered.

2. A gurgling sound is heard when the ear is put to the end of the tube if it is in the œsophagus, whereas when it enters the trachea breathing occurs through its lumen, which is at once detected by holding its end against the cheek.

3. The tube can generally be seen bulging the skin over the œsophagus as it passes towards the stomach.

4. When air is blown into the tube after it has cleared the pharynx and entered the œsophagus it causes a swallowing movement and bulges out the œsophagus as it passes down.

5. When the tube enters the trachea, the subject usually coughs, but not always, so that the absence of a cough must not be relied upon as a sign that the trachea has not been entered.

6. The tube can be felt in the œsophagus just behind the pharynx by means of the fingers of both hands pressed firmly on opposite sides of the neck above the trachea, but when the neck is thick and short it may not be felt here.

7. When the tube is in the trachea, and the latter is grasped with the hand and moved from side to side the tube can be felt and heard impinging against the walls of the trachea.

Sometimes, although the tube has entered the œsophagus, fluid poured into it does not pass on to the stomach, but remains in the funnel in the end of the tube. This is due to the end of the tube buckling in the œsophagus and is apt to occur when the tube is too soft and flexible. The tube after bending may pass into the mouth and be chewed by the horse. It can be prevented by passing a stilette made for the purpose through the tube. Fluid can be introduced into the tube through a funnel or by means of a pump.

It is advisable to pour a little water into the tube before administering oil or irritating liquid this way in case a mistake might have been made by passing the tube into the trachea instead of into the œsophagus. Coughing would indicate that the water had entered the trachea, and that the tube should be withdrawn.

The tube employed may be ordinary white hose-piping, 14 feet long, $\frac{5}{8}$ inch in diameter, $\frac{1}{2}$ inch in bore, and having the edges of the proximal end rounded to prevent this wounding the mucous membrane. This tube is very suitable and can be passed in a donkey or pony as well as in a large horse. It is sufficiently rigid to prevent its bending.

Or a tube made for the purpose may be used composed of red india-rubber, oval and blind at its proximal end, but having an orifice at the side of this extremity. It is more flexible than the hose-piping, and is provided with a cane stilette which, however, is only necessary when there is some obstacle to the passage of the tube, causing its end to buckle.

As a rule the tube is passed without difficulty, and is not resented, even by thoroughbred horses, but in exceptional cases repeated attempts at passing it are required before succeeding, and then the nasal mucous membrane is apt to be wounded, causing profuse but temporary hæmorrhage, which, although not serious, is objectionable and makes a bad impression on the owner when present.

Occasionally a horse offers stern resistance to the tube.

The author has passed the tube repeatedly, in one instance, to feed a horse affected with acute tetanus which could not otherwise partake of food. The patient recovered. Attempts, however, to use the tube in this way on subsequent cases of tetanus failed owing to the impossibility of passing the tube into the œsophagus.

Generally speaking the stomach tube is the most convenient way of giving a large draught of medicine or liquid nourishment.

In the ox, the stomach tube of the same dimensions as those for the horse can be easily passed through the nasal chamber. The procedure consists in having the head held steady with the muzzle raised while the practitioner passes the tube in the same manner as in the horse.

Wounds of the Œsophagus

The œsophagus is seldom wounded from the outside, but in exceptional cases it is injured by kicks, horn thrusts, or bites. If struck by a blunt body at a point where it is distended by a passing bolus, its walls may be more or less damaged, and even ruptured, without solution of continuity of the skin. The œsophagus is more frequently lacerated by foreign bodies obstructing its lumen or embedded in its walls, or by the rough usage of a probang.

Symptoms.—When the œsophagus has been ruptured subcutaneously, the affected part becomes the seat of an inflammatory swelling which eventually fluctuates at its centre. There may be diffuse œdema in the pectoral region. Incision of the swelling gives exit to pus mixed with alimentary matter.

Wounds of the lining of the gullet are characterised by dysphagia and salivation. When perforation occurs through the skin, saliva and alimentary matter escape thereby, an œsophageal fistula persisting for a variable time. If there is not a free exit for the food material after escaping from the œsophagus, it will accumulate in the subcutaneous tissues and perhaps give rise to gangrene. When perforation takes place in the thoracic portion of the tube, food material gains entrance into the chest and causes a fatal pleurisy. Ordinary slight wounds of the œsophagus usually heal without giving rise to stricture or dilatation of the tube as a sequel, but when they are extensive and when there has been loss of tissue an œsophageal fistula is slow to heal and stenosis of the tube usually results owing to the large cicatrix which ensues.

TREATMENT.—Treatment is to a large extent expectant. When there is merely laceration of the lining of the œsophagus, it is sufficient to give semi-liquid diet, which can be more easily swallowed than solid food. If the wound is perforating externally, the solution of continuity in the œsophageal wall may be sutured or left open, as described in connection with œsophagotomy (p. 315). Subcutaneous rupture of the tube with accumulation of alimentary matter beneath the skin requires incision of the latter to allow of escape of the foreign matter and treatment of the œsophageal wound. When the tube is perforated in the thorax or abdomen, treatment is out of the question. When an œsophageal fistula is slow in healing, its edges may be cauterised with the thermo-cautery, or, if this is insufficient, the tube may be isolated and the perforation freshened and sutured.

Obstruction of the Œsophagus : Choking

Obstruction of the œsophagus occurs in all animals, but is most common in bovines, which are very prone to pick up foreign bodies and bolt them, especially during pregnancy. The cause of the lodgment of the obstruction may be (1) its large size ; (2) its having sharp projections, which get fixed in the œsophageal wall ; (3) stricture of the œsophagus or spasm of its muscle ; (4) a tumour in or pressing on the œsophagus—a rare condition. The inferior third of the œsophagus in the horse, being normally comparatively constricted, is a common seat of obstruction ; whilst in the ox the lower part of the cervical region of the tube is most frequently obstructed, due to its compression between the trachea and the first rib. This is also the case in the dog. Just behind the pharynx is also a common seat of choking in all animals.

The Horse.—In the horse, choking may be caused by (1) a foreign body, such as a piece of wood, an extracted tooth swallowed by accident, or a portion of balling gun broken off and swallowed when the instrument was being used, etc. ; (2) a piece of carrot, turnip, or potato ;

(3) food material bolted, and consequently impacted in the gullet—for example, chop, bran, linseed meal or dry sugar-beet pulp; (4) a hen's egg.

SYMPTOMS.—The symptoms appear suddenly, and comprise the following:

1. *Cessation of feeding* and return by the nose of any food material or drink partaken of or administered.

2. *Restlessness*, pulling back in the stall, and showing an anxious expression.

3. *Vain efforts at swallowing*, making gulping movements.

4. *Attempts at vomiting*, arching the neck and bringing the muzzle in towards the chest.

5. *Salivation*, when the obstruction is near the pharynx.

6. *Coughing*, when the object is large and pressing on the trachea.

7. *Dyspnœa*, which may supervene in the latter case.

8. *A swelling* observed at the seat of obstruction when in the region of the neck.

If the site of the choking cannot be ascertained from outward appearances, it can be located by means of the œsophageal tube passed through the mouth or nose. In rare cases there may be œdema of the head due to compression of the jugular vein.

PROGNOSIS.—In most cases the obstruction is of such a nature that it usually responds to treatment.

TREATMENT comprises:

1. *Injecting pilocarpine and eserine or arecoline, and awaiting the spontaneous passage of the obstruction into the stomach.* This method should be always adopted when the animal is not much distressed. It succeeds in the majority of cases of choking by roots, tubers, apples, or soft food material, the œsophagus becoming cleared within twelve hours, as a rule. The injection may be repeated about this time, if necessary. The eserine increases the peristaltic movement of the œsophageal muscle, and the pilocarpine induces a copious secretion of mucus, which acts as a lubricant. An injection of arecoline is an alternative procedure which also proves very efficacious in many cases by the increased salivation which it causes. Gentle manipulation of the œsophagus at the seat of obstruction favours its dislodgment. In the case of impaction with soft food material, the administration of a small quantity of water will help its disintegration.

2. *Extraction of the object by the mouth with the hand.* The procedure in this case consists in pushing the obstruction by external manipulation from the œsophagus into the pharynx and removing it thence by the hand. This is a difficult procedure in the horse, owing to the

length of the soft palate and the distance of the pharynx from the oral orifice. To attempt it, it is necessary to cast the animal and to have the mouth kept open by a speculum. One person is required to maintain pressure on the œsophagus behind the object to prevent its being re-swallowed, while another passes the hand into the pharynx to extract it.

3. *Extraction by means of an œsophageal forceps or screw.* Removal of an obstruction from the œsophagus in the horse by one of these instruments would be difficult and is rarely indicated. The procedure is similar to that described for passing the probang, but is more difficult, and is apt to be followed by severe injury to the gullet.

4. *Using the probang* to propel an obstruction into the stomach when it is of the nature of a piece of root, tuber, or an apple ; but in the case of impaction with dry food its use is contra-indicated, as it would tend to impact the mass still more, instead of dislodging it. The operation consists in passing the instrument as described until the obstruction is reached, when steady pressure is exerted upon it. When the object is displaced, it is followed at once by the probang to continue its passage into the stomach. Care must be taken not to use violence, and thereby rupture the œsophagus. When this method is carefully carried out it is quite safe, and has the advantage of giving prompt relief when it proves successful.

5. *Dislodgment of the obstruction by direct manipulation of the œsophagus.* This consists in exposing the œsophagus through an incision and manipulating it directly, at the level of the obstruction with the object of displacing the latter and causing it to be swallowed. This method has succeeded where passage of the probang had failed to dislodge the obstruction.

6. *Incision of the object.* Incision of a piece of turnip, or carrot, or similar material may be practised through a narrow opening in the œsophagus immediately below the obstruction, so as to divide it into smaller portions which can be readily swallowed. This procedure is seldom necessary. It consists in performing œsophagotomy on a small scale.

7. *Œsophagotomy* is indicated as described (p. 315).

8. *Lavage*, indicated for dry impacted material like beet pulp, etc., as described by Scott (*Vet. Rec.*, Vol. 13), and which consists in introducing into the œsophagus by means of the stomach tube sufficient warm water to cause the patient to show some distress, then lowering the head until retching is induced, causing the vomition of a certain amount of the impacted food ; and repeating the procedure until the passage is clear. Care is required to perform the lavage slowly with

about a cupful of water at a time to avoid the risk of regurgitated matter entering the larynx and lungs. Hours may elapse before the desired effect is obtained, intervals being allowed between periods of intervention. The lavage has a threefold purpose, viz., (1) to soften the impacted mass, (2) to permit of siphonage of the softened material, and (3) to induce vomition or regurgitation. Gentle massage externally helps the process.

The Ox.—Choking, by all sorts of objects, is a frequent occurrence in the ox, but the most common cause of obstruction is a piece of turnip, mangold, potato, or apple.

SYMPTOMS.—The symptoms are the same as those described for the horse, with the addition of gastric tympany, which constitutes a dangerous complication. The distension of the rumen becomes very marked, and if relief is not promptly forthcoming asphyxia will ensue from pressure on the diaphragm and the absorption of carbonic acid gas.

TREATMENT.—The first indication in the ox is to relieve the tympany. This may be done by passing the probang immediately and propelling the obstruction into the stomach. If this procedure is not suitable or would involve too much delay, the rumen should be punctured at once and the canula left in position until the lumen of the œsophagus is cleared. Having done this, any of the methods mentioned for the horse may be adopted. The removal of the gas from the rumen, relieving the pressure behind the obstruction, favours its descent to the stomach. The injection of eserine and pilocarpine or of arecoline has often proved very effective in the ox. Repulsion of the object into the pharynx and its removal through the mouth is more easily performed in the bovine than in the horse. It can usually be done with the animal well controlled in the standing position, the operator standing on the left side of the patient with the right hand over the neck and the two thumbs pressing behind the obstruction so as to push it into the pharynx.

The beast's head may be held and lowered within about 18 inches from the ground or in an extended position. Alternating these positions may be necessary before the desired effect is produced. In the former position the object may drop out of the mouth, but it is generally necessary to have the hand of the operator or an assistant passed into the pharynx to extract the obstructing body behind which pressure must be maintained to prevent its being reswallowed. A mouth gag is necessary to protect the hand in the mouth, although an experienced practitioner can dispense with it and merely use an old glove to prevent wounding of the hand by the teeth. When a gag is not employed, the left hand is used to grasp the tongue and depress it while the other hand is inserted quickly into the pharynx. Care is required to avoid obstruction of the glottis during manipulation of the body. Hence the importance of rapid procedure.

Cattle grazing in orchards often become choked by taking apples from the trees. On the Continent special muzzles are used to prevent prehension of the apples from the trees, while they permit of eating from the ground. When a foreign body is lodged in the abdominal portion of the œsophagus and cannot be dislodged by the probang, it may be removed via the rumen after performing rumenotomy and evacuating the viscus. The œsophageal groove can be recognised and a forceps passed along it into the œsophagus to grasp and remove the obstruction.

The Sheep.—Choking in the sheep is similar to that in the ox.

The Pig.—Choking in the pig from œsophageal obstruction occasionally occurs, the offending body being usually a piece of tuber or root. The usual symptoms are observed. The condition may respond to expectant treatment, aided or not by a hypodermic injection of pilocarpine or arecoline, or vomiting and ejection of the obstruction may be induced by administering apomorphia subcutaneously. It may be possible to push the body into the pharynx, and have it removed thence by a hook or forceps. A suitable probang carefully passed may have the desired effect. If, however, much trouble is experienced with the case, it is usual to have the animal slaughtered, especially if in good condition. Œsophagotomy might be performed successfully in a thin subject.

The Dog and Cat.—In the dog and cat œsophageal obstruction is usually caused by a piece of bone or cartilage, more commonly the former, whose fixation is generally due to sharp points or projections thereon becoming fixed in the mucous membrane.

The SYMPTOMS are similar to those evinced by the large animals, comprising inability to swallow, or dysphagia, salivation, attempts at vomiting, swallowing movements, and an anxious expression. If the obstruction cannot be felt externally in the cervical region, it can be located by means of the probang. Occasionally it is difficult to locate it exactly even by this means. The instrument may pass alongside a small spicule of bone embedded in the wall of the tube, or the object may be so close to the stomach that it is hard to say whether the probang has reached the latter. Th. X-rays would ensure a correct diagnosis in an obscure case.

TREATMENT is on the same lines as in the pig, but it is a mistake to attempt to propel a piece of bone into the stomach, as it would probably aggravate the condition by lacerating or rupturing the œsophagus. Apomorphia may be administered, but this is also contra-indicated in the case of an obstruction embedded in the œsophageal wall. It is generally best to wait twenty-four to forty-eight hours in the hope that the object may be swallowed, and, if not, then to perform œsophagotomy if it is the cervical region that is involved. The œsophagoscope often proves effective for extracting an object from the œsophagus provided that it is not embedded in its wall. When the body is situated near the stomach, it might be removed through the latter after performing gastrotomy. When an obstruction in the thoracic portion of the tube cannot be removed by any of the ordinary methods mentioned the case is hopeless, as operation is out of the question in this region.

Stricture of the Œsophagus

Stricture or stenosis of the œsophagus results from cicatricial contraction following an injury or a severe inflammatory condition of its lining.

SYMPTOMS.—The first symptom noticed is difficulty in swallowing, which gradually becomes more marked as the lumen of the tube gets narrower. The passage of the œsophageal catheter will locate the site of the stricture. It is usually followed by dilatation of the part immediately above it.

PROGNOSIS.—The condition is usually incurable.

TREATMENT comprises (1) dilatation, and (2) incision.

(1) *Dilatation* is effected by passing bougies of gradually increasing diameter at intervals through the constricted part. Gum-elastic sounds are generally employed, and are passed every two or three days. The same catheter or bougie is passed five or six times before the next size is used. It is left in position for about five minutes. If improvement ensues, the bougies are passed at longer intervals—about once per month—to maintain the part dilated. The procedure is disappointing, as a rule.

(2) *Incision* consists in cutting the stricture by a special knife introduced into the œsophagus, or by operating from the outside. The continued passage of sounds is required afterwards to prevent recurrence, which, however, usually ensues in an aggravated form, despite this precaution, rendering the operation useless.

Dilatation or Ectasia and Diverticulum of the Œsophagus

Dilatation of the œsophagus affecting its entire circumference is usually the sequel to stricture, being caused by the accumulation and stagnation of food material above the seat of the latter. Diverticulum is a dilatation occurring on one side of the tube only, and due, as a rule, to rupture of the muscular coat and protrusion of the intact mucous membrane through the opening after the manner of a hernia. The rupture must be preceded by some injury to the muscle, whereby it becomes weakened and gives way before the pressure exerted upon it during deglutition, or the rupture may be caused directly by violence, as by the awkward use of a probang. The condition has been called œsophagocele, and from its resemblance to the crop in a bird it has been called "jabot" in France. It may occur in any part of the tube, but more commonly in the thoracic than in the cervical region. It most frequently appears in the horse and ox, but it has also been seen in the dog.

The extent of the diverticulum varies in different cases. It may have a capacity of several pints in the horse or ox, and that of a small teacup in the dog.

Symptoms.—Diverticulum and dilatation usually develop gradually, but the former may appear suddenly as the result of violence. Both conditions are characterised by the same phenomena. When the animal partakes of solid food, the dilatation or diverticulum becomes gradually impacted with the alimentary matter until the lumen of the tube is obstructed, when symptoms of choking supervene, any additional food taken being regurgitated and ejected through the mouth and nose mixed with saliva, so that the stall in front of the patient is always bespattered with the regurgitated material.

When the cervical region is affected, the swelling caused by the impaction can be seen and felt. Pressure upon the part will cause some of the contents to be regurgitated, and may give rise to dyspnœa by compression of the trachea. The enlargement is painless, and varies in its dimensions according to the degree of impaction. The contents of the swelling pass into the stomach by degrees, and constitute the only solid nourishment the animal receives. The patient is always hungry, and when the dilatation is emptied starts again to eat greedily until the impaction recurs. Liquid food can be swallowed without difficulty. Except the animal is generously fed on semi-liquid diet, it soon loses condition and becomes debilitated.

Prognosis.—In a well-marked case where impaction is frequently occurring there is no object in keeping the patient alive, as there is no effective treatment for the condition. Foreign-body pneumonia may ensue.

Treatment in most cases is palliative, consisting in giving suitable semi-liquid diet. Surgical interference is rarely successful even for diverticulum. If, however, the latter is recent and due to a direct injury of the normal œsophageal wall, the following operation may be successful: Proceed as for œsophagotomy, and having isolated the tube, remove a portion of the protruding mucous membrane and suture its cut edges, and those of the rent in the muscle if its borders will permit of suturing.

As a rule, the muscle is so damaged or weakened that it gives way again, rendering the procedure useless. Nevertheless, complete success of this operation has been recorded by several Continental veterinarians.

The writer has reported a case of diverticulum affecting the terminal portion of the œsophagus in a dog. The animal lived for six months on liquid diet, and then died from distemper. A piece of bone 1½ inches by 1 inch was found in the diverticulum, which had the capacity of a small teacup. When solid food was swallowed, the symptoms mentioned appeared.

Tumours of the Œsophagus

The œsophagus is rarely the seat of tumours, but papillomata, fibromata, cysts, sarcomata, and carcinomata have been found there growing on its mucous coat or in the muscular wall or in the peri-œsophageal tissue. Papillomata may be isolated or multiple.

SYMPTOMS.—The symptoms are those of stricture or obstruction of the tube. When affecting the cervical region, deformity is observed at the level of the new growth. A tumour in the lumen of the gullet may be located by the aid of the probang or stomach tube. A peri-œsophageal tumour causes compression of the tube and the same symptoms as stricture.

TREATMENT.—Operation is only practicable for isolated, benign, circumscribed tumours, which can be dissected out without leaving a breach in the œsophageal wall. A small growth on the mucous membrane may be removed after performing œsophagotomy at its level, care being taken to excise as little of the membrane as possible.

Parasites in the Œsophagus

The larvæ of the *Œstrus equi* have been found in the œsophagus of the horse, and the *Spiroptera sanguinolenta* in that of the dog. The latter parasite causes the formation of a cyst, and when several of them are present they cause fits of coughing and repeated vomiting, and may give rise to cachexia, terminating in death. This condition in the dog has been reported as common in parts of Tunis. If the host survives the parasitic invasion, the cysts eventually burst and the worms are discharged by the mouth and anus.

There is no satisfactory treatment for these conditions. Anthelmintics are of little avail, as a rule.

Paralysis of the Œsophagus

This condition is rare, and is usually associated with paralysis of the pharynx, already described. Swallowing is impossible, and food or water partaken of is returned by the mouth and nose.

IMPACTION OF THE CROP IN BIRDS

Impaction of the crop in poultry and pigeons is a fairly common occurrence, due to the consumption of a large quantity of indigestible material, such as grass, or an excessive amount of wheat, oats, etc. The condition has also been ascribed to a parasite, the *Trichosomum contortum*, which perforates the œsophageal mucous membrane, paralyses the muscular coat, and thus causes indigestion.

SYMPTOMS.—The bird is off its feed and dull, its beak is open and may discharge a sour or fœtid liquid, and its crop is abnormally distended.

TREATMENT.—Try massage of the crop and the administration of a little stimulating medicine, coffee, or tea, with a little whisky added. Zurn advises hydrochloric acid (2 to 5 per 1,000). If this fails, open the crop with a longitudinal incision, evacuate it, and suture it and the skin separately.

Recovery is the rule, if treatment is not delayed too long. Pigeons, especially during the breeding season, are not good subjects for the operation, on account of the vascularity of the organ.

AFFECTIONS OF THE WITHERS AND BACK

THE withers and back are frequently the seat of injury caused by the saddle, but it may ensue from other causes. The nature of the lesion varies according to the depth of the injury and the degree of infection when it gains entrance. The condition may be:

1. **Excoriation of the skin,** common in young horses when first put to work. The epidermis becomes softened by the sweat, and is rubbed off by the movements of the saddle, exposing the Malpighian layer, which appears bright red. A serous discharge occurs, which afterwards becomes dried to form a thin scab on the denuded surface. The affected spot is very sensitive.

2. **A gall,** or œdematous condition of the skin or subcutaneous tissue, due to infiltration with serum and inflammatory exudate. The lesion is brought about by the saddle becoming adherent to the moist skin and the latter being dragged upon by the movements of the former, causing laceration of the connective tissue, with the result mentioned. The condition is characterised by the presence of one or more circular swellings, varying in size from a shilling to a five-shilling piece, recognised by passing the hand over the seat of the saddle. They are sensitive, and pit on pressure. When the saddle-bed is wet, these parts dry first. They may also be caused by direct pressure concentrated on the affected area.

3. **A hæmatoma,** due to excessive pressure by the saddle on a particular part, as may result from unequal distribution of the weight of the rider or uneven padding of the saddle. A hot, soft, fluctuating swelling forms rapidly. Later it becomes firmer and crepitates, owing to the blood therein having coagulated. An exploratory puncture will confirm the diagnosis.

4. **A sit-fast,** an area of dry gangrene due to arrest of the blood supply by pressure of the saddle. The depth of the lesion varies. It may be confined to the skin or extend into the subcutaneous tissues. It is cone-shaped in form, the surface corresponding to the base of the cone. Spontaneous separation of the dead part occurs, a line of demarcation forming at its periphery.

5. **A hygroma or bursal enlargement,** due to distension of the bursa, which usually exists on the top of the anterior dorsal spines, and sometimes to an accumulation of serum in the connective tissue space beneath the trapezius or rhomboideus. The condition presents the features of an acute abscess, from which it can be distinguished by capillary puncture.

6. **An abscess,** due to injury and infection of the injured part. It might be due to strangles. It may be superficial or deep, and be situated laterally or centrally. Diagnosis is easy, and may be confirmed by exploratory puncture. It may be associated with necrosis of the deep tissues and constitute the first stage of "fistulous withers."

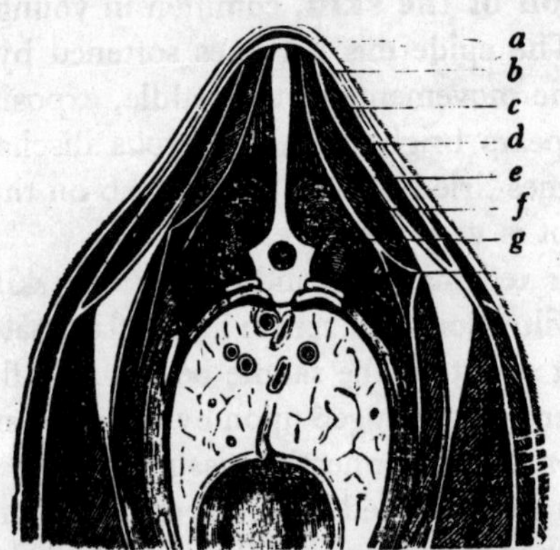

FIG. 277.—TRANSVERSE SECTION THROUGH HORSE'S THORAX (SEMI-DIAGRAMMATIC, AFTER FRANCK).

a, Skin ; *b*, fascia of panniculus ; *c*, dorsal fascia ; *d*, muscular layers ; *e*, external fascia of withers ; *f*, muscular layers ; *g*, subscapular fascia.

7. **An open wound,** caused in various ways by pointed, sharp, or blunt bodies or fire-arms. Their gravity depends on the risk of infection of the ligaments, cartilage, and bones in the region of the withers, setting up necrosis thereof, and consequently "fistulous withers."

8. **Fracture of the dorsal spines,** which has occurred from falling on the back over an embankment and given rise to symptoms of a severe contusion in the region, in which crepitation could be detected by placing the hand on the part whilst the animal was being moved. Stiffness of the shoulders may be evinced during progression. The fracture may be simple or compound. In the former case, recovery ensues without complication. This may also obtain in the latter case, but there is always a risk here of the complications mentioned in No. 7 supervening.

9. "**Fistulous withers,**" the term applied to a sinus or blind purulent fistula developed in the region of the withers. Its cause has already been indicated as being due to injury and infection, followed by necrosis of some of the deep-seated tissues. It is usually preceded by an abscess, but may be a sequel to a deep "sit-fast." The tissue most commonly affected by necrosis is the ligamentum nuchæ, but any of the following structures may be involved : the supraspinous ligament, the cartilages of the dorsal spines, the spines themselves, the cartilage of prolongation of the scapula, the bone itself, and the ribs. The lesion on the bone may be superficial caries, in the form of an ulcer. Cases of fistulous withers and poll evil appearing without any external exciting cause have been ascribed to the presence of *Bacillus abortus* or a filarial parasite (*Onchocerca reticulata*) owing to either of these organisms having been found in the lesion in such cases. It is believed, however, that their presence is not sufficient to cause the condition except there is some constitutional defect such as avitaminosis, especially that of Vitamin E.

The Symptoms of fistulous withers are always well marked, and are those of a sinus associated with an inflammatory swelling varying in size according to the extent of the lesion, and always very sensitive on manipulation. There is one or more orifices discharging pus, which is very copious when there is a large area affected with necrosis. The disease generally advances from behind forwards and from above to below. The suppuration spreads easily in the intermuscular spaces, and pus may collect in the connective tissue spaces in this region. It may also collect behind the scapula or reach the costo-vertebral groove, and even penetrate the neural canal or the chest cavity. Septicæmia may ensue.

The condition is always serious, but the deeper and the more anterior the lesion, the worse the prognosis. In the latter case, the necrosis tends to spread through the ligamentum nuchæ and lead to "fistula" of the neck. A lesion on the summit of the spines in high withers responds more readily to treatment than that on a low withers on account of the isolated position of the former and the better drainage therefrom.

Treatment of the foregoing conditions is carried out on the principles laid down in the sections dealing therewith in general surgery. The first indication is to remove the cause by discontinuing the use of the offending saddle. When this is attended to early, resolution of the inflammation will ensue spontaneously, or aided by the ordinary measures prescribed for this condition. An excellent article on this condition of Poll Evil by Professor J. G. Wright appears in the *Veterinary Record*, March 2nd, 1946.

Excoriations are treated with astringent lotion, dry dressing, or antiseptic ointment.

Cold applications and astringent lotions are indicated for galls in their early stages, followed later by hot stuping and massage. A small hæmatoma may also respond to this treatment, but when it is large it will be necessary to incise it, remove its contents, and apply tincture of iodine, etc., to the lining of the cavity.

A sit-fast is dealt with as described under the heading of "Dry Gangrene." Its separation is hastened by a vesicant applied at its periphery, and when the line of demarcation is well marked, the dead part should be cut away.

A hygroma is treated on the general principles for this condition. It is important to distinguish it from an abscess, and refrain from incising it and opening the way for infection until the usual antiphlogistic remedies have failed to have the desired effect. On the assumption that the condition may be due to the *Brucella abortus* the use of *Brucella abortus* vaccine is indicated. H. Sumner (*Vet. Rec.*, June 27th, 1942) observed alarming reactions in a young cart gelding in which he had injected the *Brucella abortus* shock vaccine in the treatment of Poll Evil ascribed to this organism. He records having had another success with the employment of Nator B *Brucella abortus* dead vaccine in several cases of purulent sinuses (quittor, etc.).

Abscesses are dealt with in the ordinary way. When being opened the incision should not be transverse to the long axis of the back, and thus leave a gaping wound which would be slow to cicatrise. Counter-openings may be necessary on one or both sides of the withers.

An open wound requires careful antiseptic treatment to prevent septic complications.

Simple fracture of the dorsal spines heals after the patient has been rested for a few weeks. It is advisable to apply an antiseptic solution on the skin to prevent the risk of infection through a hidden abrasion on its surface. When the fracture is compound, frequent antiseptic irrigation of the wound is essential.

"Fistulous withers" constitutes a typical example of a sinus. and must be treated accordingly (p. 17). The principles of treatment are: (1) to provide drainage for the escape of pus, and (2) to promote the separation and removal of necrotic tissue. The methods of carrying these out have been described. Well-established cases require drastic treatment. it being necessary to make extensive incisions to expose thoroughly the diseased parts, so that they may be acted upon by antiseptic applications frequently applied, or by liquid or solid caustics, or excised. Necrotic ligament should be severed in a healthy part and completely removed. This will be of little use if infection of the wound cannot be prevented, for then the condition will recur in the healthy part.

When the tops of the spines have undergone necrosis or caries, the affected part may be removed with a fine saw, chisel, or gouge forceps, or a sharp curette. The curette is generally the most suitable instrument for the operation. The curetting should always extend well into the bone to make sure of leaving a healthy surface. When this is done, and careful antiseptic precautions are taken afterwards, the wound heals rapidly.

When the bone has been operated upon, it is essential to protect the wound afterwards with a sterilised dressing composed of a pad of cotton-wool covered by gauze and sewn on to a cloth kept in position by strings tied to a roller and underneath the neck. The worst cases are those in which necrosis has invaded the ligamentum nuchæ. Even after excision of the dead ligament and careful antisepsis, the disease may continue to spread and prolong recovery for months. A vaccine is always indicated in such cases. In some instances it appears to have a surprisingly good and rapid effect, whilst in others it is disappointing.

When pus has burrowed beneath the scapula, it will be necessary to make a counter-opening at its postero-inferior aspect. This involves making a deep wound through the thick muscles of the region, between which infection may spread and give rise to abscess formation and necrosis of the intermuscular areolar tissue. The scapula may undergo necrosis, and recovery ensue after the lapse of months, when the sequestrum has been removed.

Prevention of Saddle Injuries.—Prevention of these injuries is effected by careful attention to the fitting of the saddle, keeping its lining clean, having it evenly stuffed, seeing that the weight on the back is equally distributed and evenly balanced, avoiding long journeys with young horses, keeping horses in good working condition, as debility and emaciation greatly favour injuries by harness. Leaving the saddle on for about half an hour after work is believed to prevent the formation of cutaneous galls, the explanation being that when certain areas have undergone excessive pressure by the saddle, the arterioles therein are deprived of blood and paralysed, and if the pressure of the saddle be suddenly removed, the blood rushing into the paralysed vessels will cause them to dilate excessively and rupture, leading to infiltration of the tissue with blood, whereas if the saddle is left in position, the circulation in the affected vessels will be gradually restored. Under this heading may be mentioned the administration of wheat germ oil as a preventative where several cases are appearing in an enzootic form in a locality and possibly due to deficiency in Vitamin E, allowing the *Bacillus abortus* or a filaria to set up the fistulous lesions. Moussu claims to have proved the efficacy of this treatment in preventing contagious abortion in cattle.

Filariasis of the Withers

This condition has been described by Robson in Australia as a common affection of horses in that country. It is due to invasion of the ligamentum nuchæ and of the muscles in the vicinity of the withers by a filarial worm, which may be present in large numbers. Most cases are characterised by a uni- or bilateral swelling, persisting for months, and then followed by atrophy of the affected tissues, causing " dropped neck " or hollow withers. In other cases a sinus is established, due to infection and necrosis of the deep tissues following the parasitic invasion.

TREATMENT consists in applying parasiticides and dealing with a sinus when it appears. Arsenical preparations internally have been found very efficacious, especially the intravenous injection of arsenobenzol.

AFFECTIONS OF THE LOINS

Traumatic Lesions

Traumatic lesions of the loins are similar to those of the withers and back, but not so serious as a rule, owing to the greater complexity of the latter region. A deep punctured wound here, however, may be difficult to cure when infection has reached its depth owing to the impossibility of making a counter opening for drainage.

Sprain of the Longissimus Dorsi

Myositis resulting from sprain of this muscle may ensue in the horse from violent struggling when cast. One or both muscles may be affected.

SYMPTOMS.—There is evident stiffness of the back, the head is extended on the neck, there is difficulty in walking, most marked on turning, the back may be slightly arched ; there may be an anxious expression, groaning on movement, and accelerated pulse and respiration. Pain, swelling, and hardness may be revealed on palpation of the muscle. There may be even a rise in temperature. The foregoing are the possible symptoms in a case of severe sprain, and they appear in a few hours or the day after the accident. Milder cases are met with in which the symptoms are not noticed until a few days afterwards, and are much less marked.

Recovery generally ensues in the course of a couple of weeks. Cases of abscess formation in the muscle, due apparently to pyogenic organisms carried there by the blood stream, have occurred. Degeneration and atrophy of the muscle is another possible sequel.

TREATMENT.—Hot, moist compresses in the form of a blanket or rug soaked in hot water applied over the back and loins are indicated, and should be frequently renewed. Later a stimulating liniment should be rubbed in over the affected part. Laxative medicine is indicated in the drinking water. If an abscess is present, it is treated as usual.

Rheumatism of the Lumbar Muscles

The muscles of the lumbar region, including the longissimus dorsi, may be affected with rheumatism, constituting a form of lumbago.

SYMPTOMS.—There is evidence of inflammation on manipulation of the loins, and the gait indicates an affection of the lumbar region. The fugitive and recurrent nature of the condition suggests rheumatism.

TREATMENT consists in prescribing for rheumatism locally and internally.

AFFECTIONS OF THE VERTEBRAL COLUMN AND SPINAL CORD

The chief significance of injury to the vertebral column is that it may involve the spinal cord, whose function is consequently more or less interfered with. When the cord is altered, all the parts innervated from a point behind the seat of injury are paralysed.

Distortion of the Neck (Torticollis)

Various forms and degrees of torsion of the neck, or crooked neck, have been recorded in veterinary literature at home and abroad. The condition may be congenital or acquired. When it is acquired, it may be due to one of the following causes :

1. **Incomplete dislocation of an intervertebral articulation.** Cases have been reported in which the oblique articular processes were displaced and the intercentral joints more or less altered.

2. Fracture of the articular processes or other parts of a vertebra.

3. Paralysis of the muscles on the convex side of the bent neck.

4. Contraction or spasm of the muscles on the concave side.

5. A combination of the foregoing causes.

FIG. 278.—SUBLUXATION OF THE THIRD CERVICAL VERTEBRA, AS SEEN FROM THE LEFT SIDE.

FIG. 279.—SUBLUXATION OF THE THIRD CERVICAL VERTEBRA, AS SEEN FROM THE RIGHT SIDE.

A common history of the case is that the horse fell with the neck in the bent position, usually as the result of the shoe of the hind-foot becoming fixed in the head-collar, as may occur when the horse scratches the head with the hind-foot.

SYMPTOMS.—The patient is usually found in the recumbent position, and it may be difficult to get him to rise. The head is turned to the right or to the left, perhaps as far as the corresponding shoulder. One side of the neck is convex and the other side correspondingly concave. The summit of the convexity is usually at the level of the fourth or fifth cervical vertebra. The animal cannot walk in a straight line, but moves in a circle. Frequently the neck is not only bent to one side, but is also deviated downwards.

PROGNOSIS.—Most cases are followed by recovery, even when the condition appears grave from the marked degree of deformity. In some instances, however, one or both vertebræ at the seat of the injury are fractured through the neural canal, and the spinal cord afterwards becomes affected, causing fatal paralysis. Occasionally the deformity persists, despite treatment.

FIG. 280.—DISTORTION OF THE NECK (TORTICOLLIS) IN CONSEQUENCE OF THE CALKIN OF A HIND-SHOE BECOMING CAUGHT IN THE HEAD-COLLAR.
(Redrawn from a photograph.)

TREATMENT comprises: 1. *Antiphlogistic remedies*, as for traumatic inflammation or contusions.

2. *Measures* usually adopted for paralysis, when it appears to be associated with the condition, including the electric current, whose efficacy, however, has not been clearly demonstrated.

3. *Manipulation*, indicated when there is dislocation with marked deformity not likely to disappear spontaneously. It includes (*a*) reduction and (*b*) retention.

In a recent slight case it may be possible to perform reduction in the standing position by pressing the convexity with one hand whilst the other hand draws the head towards the convex side. As a rule, the horse resents the intervention and offers stubborn resistance; consequently, it is generally necessary to cast and anæsthetise the patient. The procedure may be to cast the horse with either the convexity or the concavity upwards. In the former case, firm pressure is exerted on the prominence with the knees and hands, while extension and counter-extension are applied by ropes on the neck. In the latter case, reduction is attempted by forward traction on the head. There should be a large baton of straw beneath the head and neck. Several assistants may be required to produce the desired effect. A dull sound is usually heard when the displaced parts revert to their normal position.

Reduction having been effected, the neck has a tendency to return to the abnormal position as if actuated by a spring. Hence the necessity for a retention apparatus. This may be in the form of: (1) A sort of rigid cradle fitted closely to the neck, such as Knudsen's iron splint. It is not easy to fit accurately, and may become displaced and wound the soft tissues. (2) A roller provided with two rings on the side of the convexity, to which are fixed two ropes going from the same side of the head-collar. Nocard improved on this by substituting a stout rubber tube for the ordinary cords and passing it, well stretched, five or six times from the ring in the head-collar to that of the roller. Its tension was slightly increased every day It proved successful in some cases, but failed in others.

Ricked or Jinked Back

The above term is applied to an affection of the back and loins, the nature of which is often obscure. The condition would appear to be most frequently due to a lesion of the intervertebral joints or of the spinal cord. Post-mortem examination, however, of fairly typical cases often fails to reveal anything to account for the symptoms.

Etiology.—Sometimes there is no history to indicate how the case originated, but often it can be traced to an accident such as a fall or violent slipping of both hind-limbs, as may happen when a horse galloping stops suddenly and the hind-limbs go forward under the body, or to the pressure of a heavy weight on the back or loins such as that of a large animal jumping on a smaller one. It has also been seen as a sequel to toxic diseases like influenza and strangles. The ox is subject to it as well as the horse, while in the dog a similar condition follows injuries to the loins and appears as a sequel to distemper.

Symptoms.—There is obvious weakness of the hind-quarters, over which the animal seems to have lost control to a varying degree in different cases. Even at rest an abnormal attitude may be assumed, the hind-limbs being forward beneath the body or carried to the right or to the left, or widely separated. The quarters may be swayed from side to side by pressure with the hands on the haunch, or by slight traction on the tail. The animal may have difficulty in rising, and when he has succeeded in doing so the quarters move from one side to the other for some time. When the patient walks, the dorso-lumbar part of the vertebral column seems to have lost its rigidity, allowing the quarters to "wobble" and strike against the door-post when entering or leaving the stable. There is a want of co-ordination of movement in the hind-parts resembling locomotor ataxia. At the trot the hind-limbs intercross and may strike one another. During turning the symptoms are more marked, and if done hurriedly the animal may almost fall. Backing and movement in a circle are also difficult, and should be used as tests when examining a suspected case.

As already indicated, the pathology of the affection is not always clear. In a fair number of cases it is due to a chronic myelitis or meningo-myelitis, but probably the most common lesion found on post-mortem examination is arthritis of some of the dorsal or lumbar intervertebral joints. The intervertebral disc may have disappeared and anchylosis may have taken place.

PROGNOSIS is generally unfavourable, the condition usually persisting, despite treatment. Exceptionally, however, recovery ensues, the spinal cord or intervertebral joints being probably not affected in such cases.

TREATMENT is usually of no avail. When of a toxic nature, repeated large doses of sodium salicylate and potassium iodide are indicated, and sometimes have a good effect. When the condition is the result of an accident, complete rest is essential. Slings are advisable for the horse, and side-to-side movement should be prevented by making the stall narrow by placing a beam alongside the animal extending from the manger to an upright post behind the stall.

Antiphlogistic remedies should first be tried, followed by counter-irritation, blistering, or needle-point firing. Experience has shown that a sheepskin, removed immediately after death, applied over the back and loins with the fleece outside is probably the most effective form of treatment. It is left in position for a couple of weeks. It has a blistering effect. A prolonged course of arsenic or strychnine is indicated, associated with potassium iodide. Hot baths, electro-therapy, and the hypodermic injection of oxygen over the loins are worth trying in the dog. A course of arsenic in the form of "Aricyl," a Bayer preparation, is also indicated.

Recovery, when it ensues, is often slow. It may be incomplete, but sufficient to enable an animal to do light work.

Dislocation of the Intervertebral Joints

Owing to their intimate dovetailing and firm union by powerful ligaments and muscles, the dorsal and lumbar intervertebral joints can hardly be dislocated without fracture. Although the same applies largely to the cervical region, there are several cases on record of dislocation of the anterior cervical vertebræ occurring alone or associated with fracture, resulting usually from falling on the head when galloping or jumping. Complete dislocation always involves injury to the spinal cord, causing general paralysis or immediate death. In small animals the condition is generally the result of direct violence, such as a kick or a wheel of a vehicle passing over the part.

TREATMENT is out of the question.

Fracture of the Vertebral Column

The Cervical Vertebræ.—The fracture may be confined to the processes or involve the neural arch or body of the vertebræ. The transverse processes may be fractured by direct violence, but the arch and body are generally broken as the result of bending of the neck when the animal falls on the head, or of violent impact of the head against a fixed object. In small animals fracture is caused by being run over, usually by motor vehicles.

SYMPTOMS.—In simple fracture of the transverse processes there is evidence of contusion associated with crepitation. When the fracture is compound the broken bone is seen through the wound. Fracture through the body or neural arch causes sudden death from laceration of the spinal cord. Occasionally the fracture is deferred, displacement occurring at a variable time after the accident, when immediate death ensues.

TREATMENT.—Fracture of the transverse processes is treated as a contusion or open wound, according as it is simple or compound. If a sinus ensue due to necrosis of the exposed fractured bone, removal of the necrotic portion is indicated. If fracture of the body is suspected or proved by X-ray examination an immobilising dressing on the neck is indicated. When paralysis has supervened after injury to the cord, the case is hopeless.

Dorsal and Lumbar Vertebræ.—The site of fracture may be the transverse or spinal processes, or the arch or body of the vertebra, or a combination of these parts. The last three or four dorsal and the first two or three lumbar vertebræ are most commonly fractured, but any of the bones in these regions may be involved.

ETIOLOGY.—The cause of complete fracture may be :

1. *Struggling* when cast.

2. *Falling* when jumping, the animal coming down on its head after clearing a fence, or the hind-limbs slipping backwards into a ditch on the landing side.

3. *Pressure* by a low, rigid bar beneath which the animal attempts to escape.

4. *Violent muscular* effort during galloping.

Prolonged rest in the stable predisposes to fracture, as does also anchylosis of the intervertebral joints. Fissured fracture of the bodies of the dorsal vertebræ without displacement is not uncommon in animals, as is proved by the frequency with which callous formation is seen on the bodies of these bones in the slaughter-house and knacker's yard. The lateral support afforded by the ribs is instrumental in preventing displacement. In small animals fracture through the lumbar and dorsal regions is a common occurrence, and is usually the result of being run over.

The cause of broken back, when it occurs after casting, has often been discussed. It has been ascribed to the shock of the fall, but

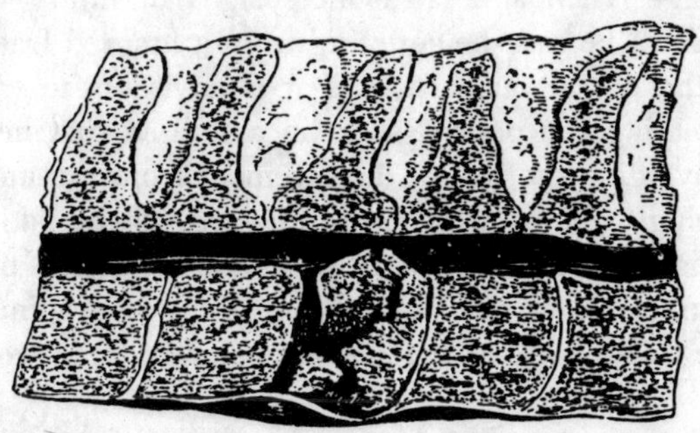

FIG. 281.—FRACTURE (BY CRUSHING) OF THE BODY OF A VERTEBRA.

there is no doubt that the chief cause is muscular contraction arching the spine or bending it laterally. By these actions the centre of the force is the posterior dorsal and anterior lumbar regions, where the fracture under these circumstances almost invariably occurs. Two or three vertebræ are usually involved, and the bone is often broken into numerous fragments. There is a combined tearing and crushing of the bone. Deferred fracture of the dorsal vertebræ has often been met with, the displacement taking place hours or days after the accident.

DIAGNOSIS of broken back is generally easy when the history of the case is forthcoming, as it may be inferred from it that the paraplegia is due to fracture of the vertebræ—for example, when it supervenes during casting or follows a fall in the hunting field or race-course. There is complete paralysis behind the seat of fracture, where no response is given to pricking with a pin, while usually an involuntary passage of fæces and urine occurs due to relaxation of the sphincters.

In the large animals crepitation cannot be detected, as a rule. Radiography removes all doubt, and can be easily practised in small patients. Crepitation can often be elicited in the latter.

Fracture of the dorsal spines in the horse may ensue from falling over an embankment or from a heavy weight falling on the withers, and the symptoms produced are those of a contusion. Crepitation may be discovered in some cases on manipulation of the part.

PROGNOSIS.—When paraplegia is present the case is hopeless. Fracture of the dorsal spines is usually followed by recovery. When it is compound, fistulous withers may supervene, owing to the entrance of infection.

PREVENTION.—For method of prevention when casting the horse, see p. 159.

TREATMENT.—When a horse evinces signs of injury to the back after an accident, he may be suffering from a fissured fracture of one or more of the dorsal vertebræ, and it is advisable to treat for this condition by tying the patient short in a stall so that he cannot lie down, thus avoiding the risk of displacement from the movements of lying and rising. Slings are contra-indicated, as the patient may sit in them, thus disturbing the seat of fracture. When paraplegia is present, treatment is of no avail. When the dorsal spines alone are involved, the treatment is that for a contusion or open wound, as the case may be.

In fracture of the vertebral laminæ in the dog the cord may retain its function, although partly encroached upon. When recovery ensues in this case paralysis may supervene later from the callus pressing on the cord. In human surgery, "laminectomy" has been successfully performed for this condition. It consists in opening the neural canal by removing a portion of its dorsal wall and excising the offending portion of the callus. Fibrous tissue fills the breach in the spinal canal.

Injuries to the Spinal Cord

As indicated, the spinal cord may be injured as the result of fracture or dislocation of the vertebræ, but it may also be damaged apart from these lesions—for example, by grains of shot in sporting dogs.

The SYMPTOMS are the same as those mentioned in connection with fracture.

Concussion of the Cord

Concussion of the spinal cord may result from a shock received by the vertebral column, due to a fall or severe blow. Paralysis supervenes, and is more or less complete according to the violence of the shock and the region affected. The paralysis, however, is of a temporary nature. When it persists, it indicates that the cord has been actually injured.

TREATMENT consists in keeping the patient at rest in a comfortable box or kennel, and if it seems excited administering sedative medicine (chloral or chloretone). Potassium iodide may be prescribed to promote absorption of any effusion that may be present on the cord.

Diseases of the Vertebral Column

Diseases of the vertebral column comprise chiefly (1) tuberculosis, and (2) streptococcic infection. The former is common in the ox, and the latter is a rare sequel to strangles in the horse. When the bovine, even in good condition, shows symptoms of spinal trouble, tuberculosis of the body of one of the vertebræ should be suspected.

TREATMENT is out of the question.

Tumours of the Spinal Column

These are not common. They comprise :

1. *Exostoses* of variable size occupying the infero-lateral aspect of the vertebral centra, including sometimes the intervertebral joints and more rarely the costo-vertebral articulations. They are a sequel to osteo-periostitis or an arthritis ossificans of the joints mentioned, and are most common in race-horses, where they appear to be due to severe exertion, coexisting with bony formations on the limbs which occur during training. They may be simply the result of a bony diathesis, making their appearance along with exostoses on other parts of the body without any apparent exciting cause.

In exceptional cases the exostosis encroaches on the spinal cord, causing symptoms of "ricked" back or paralysis. Exostoses may form over one or more of the spinal processes in the dorsal or lumbar region, due in some instances, perhaps, to pressure of an ill-fitting saddle, but occurring most frequently apart from any exciting influence, e.g. behind the seat of the saddle. They are of no consequence when devoid of inflammatory symptoms.

2. Sarcomata, which have been recorded in the horse and dog.
3. Melanomata, observed in the horse.

When these tumours have developed sufficiently to press on the spinal cord, the usual symptoms of such pressure are observed. Nothing can be done in the way of treatment.

Curvature of the Spine

There are three well-known forms of curvature of the spine—viz. :

1. Upward curvature, or *kyphosis* or roach back.
2. Downward curvature, or *lordosis* or hollow back.
3. Curvature to one side, or *scoliosis*.

Nos. 1 and 3 may be combined, constituting kypho-scoliosis.

ETIOLOGY.—The abnormalities may be congenital or acquired. In some cases the curvature is so marked at birth that the young animal is destroyed, but many horses work for years affected with kyphosis or lordosis, the deformity causing no interference with their utility. The deformities as acquired conditions are not often met with. Kyphosis has been ascribed to violent muscular effort arching the spine. Lordosis may ensue from constant heavy pressure on the back, as of a heavy rider or pack saddle. It follows rupture of the prepubic tendon in the mare. A long back favours the condition. Rickets predisposes to all these deformities.

TREATMENT is rarely required. In a young animal a roach back may be improved by fixing a rigid bar along the spine from the withers to the croup, compressing the curvature through the medium of a pad, the ends of the bar being attached to other pads kept in position by straps and a crupper. Removal of the cause, if still operating, is always indicated.

Paraplegia

Paraplegia has been referred to as a sequel to injury to the spinal cord following fracture or dislocation of the spinal column. It is characterised by loss of power in the hind-quarters, and usually by loss of sensation as well. The tail is flaccid and without resistance. In the male the penis hangs limp from the sheath. There is an involuntary escape of fæces and urine owing to paralysis of the sphincters of the anus and bladder. Pricking with a pin or needle of the paralysed region causes no voluntary response, but occasionally it produces an aimless reflex movement of one of the hind-limbs. Paraplegia must be distinguished from other affections of the hind-quarters, owing to which the patient is unable to rise, but in which the spinal cord is intact.

The dog frequently suffers from loss of power in the hind-quarters which is often only temporary, resulting from an injury to the loins, such as may be caused by a collision with another dog, or from being struck by a vehicle, or from constipation. In such cases there is no loss of sensation in the hind-parts and the sphincters still perform their functions. When paraplegia is not of traumatic origin it is usually the result of some toxic affection, such as distemper in the dog.

PROGNOSIS depends on the cause of the condition. When the spinal cord is only temporarily injured recovery ensues, but when its structure has been disorganised by traumatism, or has undergone degeneration as the result of toxæmia, return to the normal is impossible.

Diagnosis of the exact cause of the condition being often doubtful, a guarded prognosis should be given.

TREATMENT consists in keeping the patient comfortable in a hygienic box or kennel and prescribing suitable treatment for the restoration of nervous function, assuming that the case has not been pronounced hopeless. The measures to be adopted are those described for paralysis in general (see p. 105). The hypodermic introduction of oxygen over the loins has given good results in the dog. The bed must be kept dry and the patient turned periodically to prevent bed-sores. It is usually necessary to evacuate the rectum and draw off the urine. The large animal should be propped with batons of straw, and frequent attempts should be made to get the subject on its feet. The dog moves about freely, dragging the hind-legs on the ground. When the paralysis is permanent in the dog, he may acquire the power of walking and running on the fore-limbs while balancing the hind ones in the air, or he may be supplied with a spinal carriage to which he can be yoked and whose wheels enable him to move about (*Vet. Rec.*, **57**, 17). When the horse regains sufficient power to stand he should be put in slings. Sometimes, when unable to rise himself, he will stand when lifted.

AFFECTIONS OF THE CHEST

Contusions

Contusions of the chest wall are caused in various ways—by kicks, falls, collisions, etc.

Symptoms —The symptoms are those of contusions in general, except the injury is deep-seated and involving some of the thoracic organs, when they will vary according to the nature of the lesion. In the event of a deep contusion, the following conditions may arise :

1. *Concussion of the thoracic organs.* Several cases have been recorded of rupture of the heart and of the lungs as the result of severe violence being inflicted on the chest wall without fracture of the ribs.

2. *Laceration of the lung* may ensue from the fragment of a fractured rib penetrating the organ. The visceral pleura being ruptured, air escapes from the lung into the pleural sac, causing pneumothorax and infiltrating the tissues round the parietal wound. The emphysematous swelling thus caused is evident on the outside of the chest wall. There may be hæmoptysis, characterised by the escape of frothy blood from the nose. Blood may accumulate to a varying degree in the pleural cavity, hæmopneumothorax being then produced. The lung may be ruptured without division of the visceral pleura by the force of a blunt object reaching the organ without perforating the thoracic wall. In this case, pulmonary emphysema extends by the root of the lung to the base of the neck, and may spread thence for a variable distance and even become generalised.

3. *Rupture of the heart and large thoracic vessels* may be caused in the same way as that of the lungs. The present author has seen both these accidents happen in horses as the result of casting.

Prognosis.—Ordinary contusions respond to treatment. Rupture of the lung, accompanied or not by that of the visceral pleura, is frequently followed by recovery ; but if the lesion is extensive, death may ensue from hæmorrhage or from asphyxia caused by the pressure of hæmopneumothorax. Cardiac injuries and rupture of large vessels are always fatal.

Treatment consists chiefly in keeping the patient at rest. The usual local applications for traumatic inflammation are indicated.

When the lung has been penetrated, nothing further can be done except to inject adrenalin hypodermically with a view to arresting hæmorrhage, and applying cold compresses or ice bags to the chest wall.

Fracture of the Ribs

Fracture of the ribs is not common, and when it occurs often escapes notice, as is proved by the number of cases of healed fractures recognised after death in the slaughter-house and the dissecting-room that were not suspected during life.

ETIOLOGY.—The usual cause is direct violence, such as a fall, a blow, or a collision, but the ribs covered by the shoulder may be fractured by muscular violence.

SYMPTOMS.—The commonest site of fracture is the ribs between the sixth and the eleventh, which are the most exposed to injury. The fracture may be incomplete or complete, simple or compound. There may be only two or three fragments in the fracture, or it may be comminuted. Simple subcutaneous fracture without displacement is denoted by inflammatory swelling at the seat of injury. Crepitation may be detected by placing the hand on the affected part and causing the animal to cough.

When displacement is marked, it is revealed by deformity of the rib in the shape of a depression or flattening of the affected region. Several adjacent ribs may be involved, and then the flattening of the chest wall is very noticeable. The breathing may be shallow and painful, owing to laceration of the parietal pleura. In the absence of crepitation and much displacement diagnosis is difficult, but of little importance. In compound fracture the broken bone may be seen and felt through the wound.

The following complications may arise :

1. *Perforation of the lung*, heart, or thoracic vessels by one of the fragments, as described under the heading of Contusions.

2. *Perforation of the chest wall* from without by the violence which caused the fracture. This is dealt with under Penetrating Wounds.

3. *Radial paralysis* in case of fracture of the first rib caused by laceration or rupture of the nerve by one of the fragments.

4. *Hæmorrhage* from division of an intercostal artery.

TREATMENT of simple fracture even with considerable displacement is chiefly expectant, consisting in keeping the patient at rest until union ensues. The measures recommended for a contusion are indicated. Complications are dealt with as described elsewhere. Compound fracture is treated on general principles. A depressed fragment may be raised by inserting a blunt hook beneath its anterior border if exposed. It might be necessary to incise the soft tissues to enable this to be done. In so doing, great care is required to avoid perforating the pleura. It is generally better not to take this risk.

Hæmorrhage from an intercostal artery may be difficult to stop, owing to the trouble in isolating the vessel for ligation. The bleeding may be more easily stopped by crushing the vessel against the bone by means of a blunt instrument.

" Costal fistula " may ensue from necrosis of the rib or from a loose septic piece of bone remaining *in situ*. Visceral complications are dealt with according to their nature (see Penetrating Wounds).

Fracture of the Costal Cartilages

This may occur in much the same way as that of the ribs, with analogous symptoms and requiring similar treatment. Union takes place by ossification. Crepitation is absent in fractured cartilage.

Fracture of the Sternum

This occurs occasionally as the result of a fall or collision against a fixed object. It may be simple or compound, and complete or incomplete.

The SYMPTOMS are those of a contusion or open wound.

DIAGNOSIS is often difficult, owing to the thick muscular covering of the bone. Crepitation may be detected on movement of the patient or during respiratory movements. When compound, the fractured bone may be felt. In this case a sternal fistula usually results, owing to infection of the wound in the bone.

TREATMENT is that for a contusion, open wound, or a sternal fistula. When a hæmatoma is present without solution of continuity of the skin, opening of the swelling should be avoided as far as possible, as it will probably lead to infection of the bone and the formation of a sinus.

Open Wounds

The infero-lateral aspects of the chest wall may be excoriated by the girths. Other open wounds are caused in various ways, and may be non-penetrating or penetrating. The former present no special features except that when the wound is deep and in the axillary region it may be complicated with emphysema, or that an oblique deep wound on the chest wall may open and close alternately by the respiratory movements, causing the air to be aspirated into it and expelled alternately with a hissing noise, as if the pleural cavity were perforated, and producing local emphysema.

SYMPTOMS AND DIAGNOSIS.—The ordinary symptoms of open wounds are observed. When a penetrating wound is very narrow it is impossible to see the opening into the chest, and the only indication that the latter is open is the hissing noise caused by the passage of air between the pleural sac and the exterior. Probing to assist diagnosis is contra-indicated on account of the risk of introducing infection from the outer part of the wound into the thoracic cavity, or of perforating the pleura if still intact. When the penetrating wound is large, the interior of the cavity may be visible.

PROGNOSIS.—The prognosis of penetrating wounds is always grave, on account of the more or less dangerous complications that may ensue—viz.:

1. *Collapse of the lungs*, which may occur from obliteration of the pleural vacuum and the entrance of air therein through the external wound. When the perforation is small, this does not always happen, the explanation probably being that the affinity between the two serous surfaces, similar to that between two moist plates of glass when in contact, prevents their separation. When air gains entrance into the chest in the horse, it invades both pleural sacs through the communication in the posterior mediastinum, rendering a perforating wound more dangerous in this animal than in those in which the two sacs do not communicate. Sudden death takes place when both lungs collapse. The frequency of penetrating wounds, in the horse, however, without death ensuing from this cause, proves that collapse is not a constant sequel to perforation of the chest wall, although there is evidence of pneumothorax.

2. *Pneumothorax*, which ensues from entrance of air into the chest as mentioned. Air enters the cavity during inspiration when the chest expands, and escapes during expiration when it contracts. If the wound is oblique and acts like a valve, preventing the escape of air, the latter will accumulate and compress the lung. The latter can tolerate a certain amount of air pressure on its surface, and when the air ceases to enter the cavity, what remains therein becomes absorbed, recovery supervening.

3. *Pneumohæmothorax*, due to the presence of blood and air in the pleural sac, the significance of which is the lung compression which it causes. The extravasated blood soon becomes coagulated. When its quantity is not great it does no harm, and eventually undergoes absorption. It favours the growth of bacteria, should they gain entrance.

4. *Pleurisy*, which is the chief danger to be feared. It is a common

complication, and always proves fatal. It is sometimes slow to supervene, weeks, and even months, elapsing in some cases before its presence becomes evident. In such instances the progress of infection is gradual through a narrow opening. In the majority of cases, however, its onset is rapid.

5. *Penetration of the lung, heart, or large vessels.* Recovery may ensue after wounds of the lung, provided that infection does not supervene, but it is very exceptional. Perforation of the heart or large vessels is always fatal.

6. *Hæmorrhage from opening of an intercostal artery*, already referred to in connection with contusions.

7. *Penetration of the abdominal cavity* through the diaphragm. A fragment of broken rib or cartilage may be displaced with this effect, and if the stomach or bowel is perforated, fatal peritonitis will ensue. Notwithstanding the dangers of penetrating wounds, many cases are recorded of recovery in the horse, ox, and dog, even after the lung was wounded.

TREATMENT.—Treatment is on the same lines as those recommended for wounds in general, care being taken not to introduce any lotion into the pleural sac. Suturing may be indicated, but drainage must always be provided for. An antiseptic pad over the wound kept in position by a body bandage is advisable.

Little can be done for internal complications, such as injury to a thoracic organ or hæmopneumothorax, except to keep the patient quiet, and hope that nature's methods of repair may have the desired effect. Protrusion of a portion of lung, if recent, may be successfully reduced, and if it is unfit to return, it may be ligatured and excised, and be followed by recovery.

When purulent pleurisy supervenes, cure is out of the question. The only treatment for it is to perform pleurotomy—that is, to open the chest by an incision between two ribs in a dependent position, evacuate the pus, and irrigate the cavity with a warm solution of boric acid in concentrated solution. The operation can only be performed on one side at a time, as it involves collapse of the lung. The administration of penicillin is indicated.

Costal Fistula

This is a sinus or purulent fistula on the thoracic wall, due to necrosis or caries of one of the ribs or to the presence of a foreign body embedded deeply in an intercostal space, such as a piece of wood or glass, or shrapnel.

Symptoms.—The symptoms are those of a sinus. A probe passed into it abuts on hard resistant bone when the condition is due to necrosis of a rib, and on soft spongy bone when due to caries thereof. When a foreign body is the cause of the trouble, it may be fairly large and easily discovered, or very small and difficult or impossible to locate until the bottom of the fistula is exposed.

Treatment consists in getting rid of the cause of the sinus. The surest way of doing this is to open it to its depth, remove a sequestrum or foreign body when present, or curette a caried surface. The foreign body may be very small, such as a tiny spicule of wood or a little bit of glass, and require careful searching to find it. It may be in contact with the pleura, puncture of which must be avoided. The subsequent treatment is that of an open wound.

Should the foregoing treatment fail in the case of extensive disease of a rib, costectomy—*i.e.*, resection of the affected portion of the latter—is indicated. The operation may be briefly described as consisting in exposing completely by careful dissection the diseased section of the rib, removing its periosteum in front and behind withoutwounding the intercostal vessels, separating the bone cautiously from the pleura, and detaching it by means of a fine saw or costotome. The operation is delicate, but has been performed successfully by several operators. The inflammatory thickening of the pleura in the vicinity of the lesion diminishes the risk of penetrating it, and also acts as a barrier against infection of the pleural cavity. For the latter reason the condition is not often followed by pleurisy, even when existent for months. After the operation the wound is sutured and protected with an antiseptic pad and bandage, and dealt with subsequently on general principles. It is usually healed within five weeks.

Sternal Fistula

This is a sinus abutting on the sternum, and due to necrosis thereof following injury and infection of the bone or cartilage. It may be a sequel to compound fracture of the structure or it may be due to a foreign body lodged in its vicinity. There is no mistaking the lesion. The prominent inflammatory swelling, the persisting purulent orifice or orifices, and the probe, inserted through the latter, coming in contact with the bone are characteristic. The fistula is usually very deep, traversing the thick pectoral muscles. When the cariniform cartilage is the part involved, the lesion is superficial. The suppuration may burrow beneath the muscles and give rise to an enormous abscess under the breast. There may be an abscess in the bone itself. The disease may reach the pleural cavity and cause purulent pleurisy.

PROGNOSIS must be guarded. Although the patient is seldom in danger of death from the condition, it may not be an economic proposition to treat it, owing to the length of time required to effect recovery or to the impossibility of attaining this object in some cases. Sometimes there is no evidence of pain being suffered by the animal, and no interference with its gait ; so that it may be allowed to work while simple treatment is adopted for the sinus.

TREATMENT is as usual for such conditions. Liquid and solid caustics may be tried at first. If these fail, the hot iron inserted into the depth of the lesion may be employed with success. Operation to open up largely the sinus or sinuses and remove diseased tissue offers the best chance of success. It sometimes fails, however, even when thoroughly and carefully performed. Owing to the great depth of the wound, it is difficult to keep it under observation throughout and to ensure that it is healing from the bottom. Vaccine therapy is indicated as is also a course of treatment by penicillin.

Hernia of the Lung (Pneumocele)

Hernia of a portion of the lung has been seen appearing in an intercostal space enclosed in a sac formed by the skin and parietal pleura. It presents the symptoms of a hernia with soft, spongy contents. It may persist indefinitely without complication, or gangrene may supervene from strangulation of the contents. It is a rare condition, and is not interfered with, as a rule, except strangulation exists or is threatened, when the operation advised for abdominal hernia is indicated. It is possible for hernia of the bowel to appear intercostally after passing through a rupture in the diaphragm.

AFFECTIONS OF THE ABDOMEN

Contusions

CONTUSIONS of the abdominal wall are typical of contusions in general, and are commonly met with. When caused by severe violence, they may be complicated with rupture of an abdominal organ or organs, the liver and spleen being most frequently involved. The stomach and intestines are predisposed to injury in this way when very distended, and such cases have been seen after violent impact of the abdomen against fixed objects. Rupture of abdominal organs in the dog is common as the result of being run over by vehicles. The dog may be comatose from the shock of the accident and gradually regain consciousness, afterwards appearing to be recovering from the effects of the injury. Nevertheless, he may succumb within twenty-four hours later from internal hæmorrhage due to a rupture in the spleen or liver.

PROGNOSIS.—The internal injuries mentioned always prove fatal. The contused area constitutes a weak spot in the abdominal wall, which may give way later, producing a hernia.

TREATMENT requires no further description than that given for contusions in general. Intervention to deal with rupture of internal organs may be said to be hopeless. Rare cases of spontaneous recovery from rupture of the bowel and that of the rumen, and escape of alimentary matter through the agency of adhesion of the organ to the abdominal wall, and the formation of a stercoral abscess bursting externally have been recorded.

Abscesses

The abdominal wall is a common seat of abscesses brought about in the usual way by trauma and infection.

DIAGNOSIS may be hesitating when the abscess is deep-seated, but may be made certain by an exploratory puncture. It may be confounded with a recent hernia accompanied by inflammatory swelling, and when chronic it is similar in appearance to a tumour or cyst.

PROGNOSIS is usually favourable, but exceptionally a deep-seated abscess opens into the peritoneal cavity. The pus of such an abscess is sometimes extremely fœtid, and produced by a combination of organisms, including coli bacilli, staphylococci, and streptococci. Abscesses developed in the thickness of the abdominal wall diminish its resistance and predispose to hernia, especially in its lower part. A hernia may even accompany the abscess.

TREATMENT is as usual for an abscess. The important point is to make sure of the diagnosis before inserting the knife to open the "abscess." It is advisable in many cases to proceed cautiously, cutting the tissues layer by layer for fear of opening the abdomen or perforating bowel that might be present in the swelling. Occasionally an abscess that has burst is followed by a sinus, due to the want of a dependent opening and the presence of necrotic aponeurotic tissue. Removal of the necrotic tissue and the formation of a counter-opening are then indicated.

Tumours

The abdominal wall is not a common site for tumours, but papillomata, lipomata, fibromata, cysts, and malignant growths are occasionally found there. Papillomata are the most frequently met with, and usually appear on the sheath and its vicinity.

TREATMENT is as described in the section on tumours.

Open Wounds

Open wounds of the abdominal wall may be (1) non-perforating, or (2) perforating.

(1) Non-perforating Wounds.—These may be caused in various ways—by falls, collisions, blows, by being staked when jumping, etc. They vary in depth and extent in different cases. Layers of tissue may be separated, abscess formation may ensue, or a sinus may supervene from the presence of necrotic tissue or a foreign body, or for want of drainage. A punctured wound involving the mammary vein in the ox may lead to the formation of a large hæmatoma. In the case of a deep narrow wound it may be difficult to say whether it is penetrating. Probing for the purpose of ensuring diagnosis is contra-indicated, on account of the risk of introducing infection into the abdomen if it is intact. Large, deep wounds of the abdominal wall predispose to hernia by causing a weak spot in the affected region, the cicatricial tissue being never so strong as the original tissue.

TREATMENT is on the usual lines, every wound being dealt with according to its nature. Avoid using a syringe for narrow, deep, punctured wounds, owing to the danger of forcing material into the peritoneal cavity should the latter be perforated. Provide for drainage and take strict antiseptic precautions to overcome sepsis. Sutuer extensive wounds whose edges are even and capable of being approximated, leaving an orifice in a dependent part to ensure drainage. Should an abscess or fistula ensue, deal with it as described in connection with these lesions.

(2) **Perforating Wounds.**—These are caused in a variety of ways, the offending body penetrating the abdominal cavity to a variable distance in different cases. They may be classified as follows: (*a*) Perforating wounds without injury or prolapse of abdominal organs; (*b*) perforating wounds with injury of some abdominal organ; (*c*) perforating wounds with prolapse of a portion of bowel; (*d*) perforating wounds, as in (*c*), with injury and perforation of the prolapsed organ.

(*a*) *Perforating Wounds without Injury or Prolapse of Abdominal Organs.*—The perforation of the abdomen may be obvious or doubtful, as already mentioned. The prognosis of such wounds must be guarded and on the grave side, as there is always the danger of fatal peritonitis ensuing. Yet treatment should always be adopted, as recovery frequently supervenes.

TREATMENT is the same as for non-penetrating wounds, taking the precaution not to irrigate the wound with a syringe for the reason stated. Wounds unaccompanied by prolapse are usually narrow, and do not require to be sutured.

(*b*) *Perforating Wounds with Injury of an Abdominal Organ.*—It is usually the bowel that is perforated, and except the perforation is made by a sterile pointed instrument of small calibre, such as a trocar and canula, death from peritonitis uniformly follows, due to escape of intestinal matter into the peritoneal cavity.

DIAGNOSIS is not easy immediately after the accident, except the escape of alimentary matter is observed through the wound. Within twenty-four hours after the occurrence, symptoms of peritonitis will have developed, indicating the nature of the lesion.

PROGNOSIS.—In rare cases, where the opening in the bowel has been small and very little intestinal matter has escaped, a local peritonitis may ensue, with adhesions which form a barrier to the spread of infection throughout the peritoneal cavity. A stercoral abscess may then form, burst externally, and be followed by recovery. When peritonitis has developed the condition is hopeless.

TREATMENT.—As a rule treatment is of no avail. The only chance of success would be the immediate performance of laparotomy, suturing the opening in the viscus, and removing the foreign material from the abdominal cavity. Frequently the case is too far gone for this procedure, which in any case, especially in the large animals, is practically certain to fail.

(*c*) *Perforating Wounds with Prolapse of a Portion of Bowel.*—Prolapse of the bowel through an abdominal wound may occur in the course of a laparotomy, or follow an accidental perforation of the abdominal wall, as when an animal is staked in jumping.

SYMPTOMS.—A portion of bowel is seen protruding from the wound, varying in size in different cases. Small intestine escapes with greater facility than the larger bowel, owing to its smaller calibre and greater mobility. It may be more or less altered, depending on the duration of its exposure and the amount of soiling it has undergone. When the wound in the abdominal wall is very oblique, a loop of protruded bowel may be concealed between the muscles, constituting intraparietal prolapse. If it is insinuated between the peritoneum and the deep face of the muscular wall it is properitoneal prolapse.

PROGNOSIS.—The condition is dangerous, death ensuing in the majority of cases from peritonitis following soiling and infection of the exposed peritoneal surface. However, when the case is attended to early, before the organ has been altered from exposure, recovery usually takes place. Even in cases where the bowel has been visibly contaminated, treatment may prove successful. The case should be seldom abandoned as hopeless. Prolapse of the omentum only is usually harmless.

TREATMENT consists in cleaning the prolapsed mass with boiled water, or sterile normal saline solution, or a non-irritant sterilised antiseptic lotion, returning it to the abdominal cavity, and closing the parietal wound, as in laparotomy. The first step in the procedure is to prevent the further escape of the intestine by applying a wide body bandage, which will also protect the prolapsed mass during the controlling of the patient. In the large animals it is generally advisable to administer chloroform in the standing position, giving a large dose, so that the patient will go down without a struggle. If there is a difficulty in returning the bowel, it may be overcome by puncturing the latter if it is distended with gas or liquid, or it may be necessary to enlarge the wound slightly to permit of its reduction. The process may be assisted by taxis *per rectum* by the hand of an assistant. Raising the hind-quarters facilitates reduction of a prolapse in the posterior region of the abdomen. If these measures should fail, another opening may be made into the abdominal cavity in the vicinity of the original wound and direct taxis performed from the interior of the abdomen. To prevent protrusion of the bowel during the suturing of the wound, spread a folded piece of aseptic lint or a sterilised towel over the intestines beneath the opening. When the prolapse consists only of omentum and it has been contaminated, draw the latter out slightly to expose a clean portion, ligature it there, remove the distal portion, and return the stump into the abdomen. After the operation, treat as described for a case of laparotomy.

(*d*) *Prolapse as in* (*c*), *with Injury and Perforation of the Bowel.*—This case is more serious than the one just described, owing to the injury inflicted on the bowel. Recovery, however, may ensue by proceeding as in (*c*) after suturing the wound in the viscus. Should the exposed portion of bowel be too much damaged to be returned, it will be necessary to resect it (see p. 353). In all cases of contamination or suspected contamination the administration of penicillin is indicated.

Bowel Fistula—Anus Preternaturalis

A bowel or stercoral fistula and an anus preternaturalis are abnormal orifices discharging intestinal matter. The anus preternaturalis gives exit to the greater part of the intestinal contents, while the bowel fistula only gives passage to a small quantity thereof. In the former condition a whole loop of intestine has been destroyed, the two ends of the bowel opening on the skin, whereas in the latter only a portion of the circumference of the organ is involved.

ETIOLOGY.—Either of the lesions may arise as follows :

1. A perforating wound of the abdominal and intestinal walls may be followed by adhesion of the visceral and parietal peritoneum in the affected region, and persistence of the perforation owing to the passage of intestinal matter through it. The wound may be inflicted from without or from the lumen of the bowel by the penetration externally of a sharp foreign body present therein. The fistula is more likely to ensue in the latter case.

2. A hernia may undergo gangrene as the result of strangulation or the application of a caustic, adhesion taking place between the bowel and the abdominal walls round the gangrenous part and preventing diffuse peritonitis. When the gangrenous part sloughs, the intestinal matter escapes and continues to pass through the opening for a variable time. The epithelium of the mucous membrane may eventually unite with that of the skin, making the opening permanent.

SYMPTOMS.—The condition is easily recognised by the passage of stercoral matter through an abnormal opening in the abdominal wall. When a drink of water is taken by the patient, some of it passes out through the fistula a few minutes after being swallowed. The health of the animal appears to be quite normal, and its general condition may remain good. The horse and ox may be able to work as usual.

PROGNOSIS.—The fistula may close spontaneously within a few days after its appearance, but when there is much intestinal matter passing through it the opening usually persists. The animal is not likely to die from its effects, but may fail to thrive or to do useful work owing to malnutrition resulting from the interference with function in the alimentary tract. It may or may not respond to treatment.

TREATMENT.—When the case is recent leave it alone, and spontaneous recovery may ensue in the course of five to fifteen days, or in certain cases after some months. If the skin is being soiled or excoriated by the discharge, keep it clean and protect it by a dressing of vaseline or an antiseptic powder. When the case is of long standing and treatment is required, some of the following measures may be adopted :

1. *The use of irritants* applied to the lining of the passage and to its periphery, such as tincture of iodine, to promote inflammation, granulation, and cicatrisation of the fistula.

2. *The application of a blister*, as in No. 1.

3. *Cauterisation of the walls of the fistula* by a caustic agent such as silver nitrate, or by the actual cautery in the form of a red-hot wire rapidly applied, the object being to destroy the smooth lining of the passage and replace it by granulation tissue.

4. *Suturing the orifice* after dissecting away the lining of the fistula, a purse-string suture being the most effective.

Care must be taken not to open the abdominal cavity during the process. Nos. 2 and 3 are the simplest and probably the most useful methods. They may require to be repeated. Should these measures fail, the intestine may be liberated from its attachment to the abdominal wall and have its fistulous opening closed by Lembert sutures. This is a rather delicate operation, which is not likely to succeed in veterinary practice. It would not be wise to attempt it.

When an entire loop of bowel is in the fistula, its afferent and efferent ends are separated by a ridge or spur due to the folding in of the bowel wall opposite to the perforation. This prevents the free passage of ingesta into the distal portion of the tube. This ridge of tissue may be grasped by an artery forceps, which is left in position until the tissue between its jaws separates by sloughing, when some of the measures mentioned may be adopted to close the fistula.

An intestinal fistula may open into the uterus, vagina, bladder, or urethra instead of on the skin. Measures similar to those mentioned above may be employed as far as practicable to close the abnormal opening. In most cases it is impossible to apply these remedies satisfactorily, and except spontaneous cure ensues the fistula persists.

HERNIA

Abdominal hernia is of two kinds :

I. External abdominal hernia.

II. Internal abdominal hernia.

I.—EXTERNAL ABDOMINAL HERNIA

DEFINITION.—An external abdominal hernia is the protrusion of a portion of the abdominal contents through an accidental or normal physiological opening in the abdominal wall to lie beneath the skin, which remains intact.

PARTS OF THE HERNIA.—The hernia is composed of (1) the hernia, opening or ring, (2) the hernial swelling.

(1) *The hernial opening* may be an accidental rupture in the abdominal wall (ventral hernia), or a persistent prenatal opening (umbilicus), or a normal passage (inguinal canal). Its size, as a rule, varies from that which will admit one finger to that into which four fingers of the extended hand can be inserted. In exceptional cases, however, it may be much larger. Its shape may be round, oval, slit-like, or irregular. It may be a simple opening, or in the form of a passage with an upper and a lower opening, as in inguinal hernia.

(2) *The hernial swelling* varies in size from that of a grape to that of a man's head or, rarely, a much larger object. Its shape may be somewhat hemispherical, cylindrical, or conical. It comprises (*a*) the hernial sac, and (*b*) the hernial contents.

(*a*) *The hernial sac* encloses the hernial contents, and is formed from without inwards of skin, perhaps a few muscular fibres, fibrous tissue, and parietal peritoneum. The peritoneal layer may be absent in ventral hernia, owing to the peritoneum having been ruptured by the accident causing the hernia. Some authors confine the term " sac " to the peritoneal layer, when it is present. There may be a large amount of thickening in the fibrous portion of the sac, particularly in an old hernia, and in the latter case it may be calcareous. On palpation, this condition may give the impression that there are adhesions between the sac and the contents. The sac has a neck, a body, and a fundus. The neck is the portion nearest the ring, the fundus the lowest part, and the body the intervening region. The inner surface of the serous sac is exquisitely smooth, and thus greatly favours the passage of abdominal viscera into the cavity. It is thrown into folds at its neck, and these may become adherent by a fibrinous deposit caused by local inflammation. Cicatrisation may ensue here, constricting or actually closing the mouth of the sac.

(*b*) *The hernial contents* usually comprise a loop of bowel with its ingesta and mesenteric attachment (enterocele), or omentum (epiplocele), or both (entero-epiplocele), or rarely the stomach (gastrocele) or bladder (vesicocele), or more rarely still some other abdominal organ (spleen, liver). The sac may also contain some serous fluid (hernial fluid). In subjects like the mule and ass, in which there is a thick layer of subperitoneal fat, the sac of a small hernia may be filled entirely with subserous adipose tissue. This may also be the case in puppies.

VARIETIES OF HERNIAS.—Hernias may be classified according to their situation—viz., umbilical hernia (omphalocele, exomphalos), inguinal hernia (bubonocele), scrotal hernia (oscheocele), ventral hernia, crural hernia, femoral hernia, and perineal hernia; or according to the nature of the hernial contents—viz., enterocele, etc.—or according to the condition of the contents, as follows:

1. *Reducible hernia*, in which the contents can be returned into the abdominal cavity through the hernial orifice.

2. *Irreducible hernia*, in which the contents cannot be completely returned to the abdomen.

Irreducible hernia comprises (1) incarcerated hernia, (2) strangulated hernia, (3) hernia with adhesions.

(1) *Incarcerated Hernia*.—In this case the contents have become too voluminous to pass through the hernial ring.

(2) *Strangulated Hernia*.—Here the incarcerated contents are so compressed by the hernial ring or by the neck of the sac, or by both, that their circulation is arrested and the lumen of the bowel is obstructed, causing them to undergo death or gangrene within twenty-four hours, if relief is not forthcoming, micro-organisms passing from the interior of the viscus through its weakened or mortified walls into the peritoneal cavity, and giving rise to a fatal peritoneal septicæmia. The cause of the strangulation is a sudden increase of the contents of the herniated loop of bowel, producing obliteration of its efferent end by compressing its walls against the border of the ring. Eventually the mutual pressure of the two parts of the loop completely closes its entrance and its exit, causing fæcal stasis and arrest of the circulation in the part. The double dovetailing of the mesentery, attached to the affected parts of the bowel, between the abdominal cavity and the hernial sac acts as a wedge in the opening, and helps in producing strangulation. The intestinal mucous membrane at the

constricted part acts like a valve, gliding on the other coats of the organ, and tending to further occlude its passage and imprison its contents. Venous congestion of the hernial contents occurs, owing to the blood continuing to flow in through the arteries for some time after the veins have become occluded, the constriction affecting the latter first on account of their thin walls. There may be hæmorrhage, due to the rupture of congested capillaries, and a variable amount of fluid collects in the hernial sac as the result of the venous engorgement. The bowel may be much altered in colour, appearing blackish from ecchymosis and cyanosis, and yet retain sufficient vitality to regain its normal condition. On the other hand, although the alteration may not appear serious, the herniated piece of bowel on being returned to the abdomen may undergo necrosis and cause death from peritonitis.

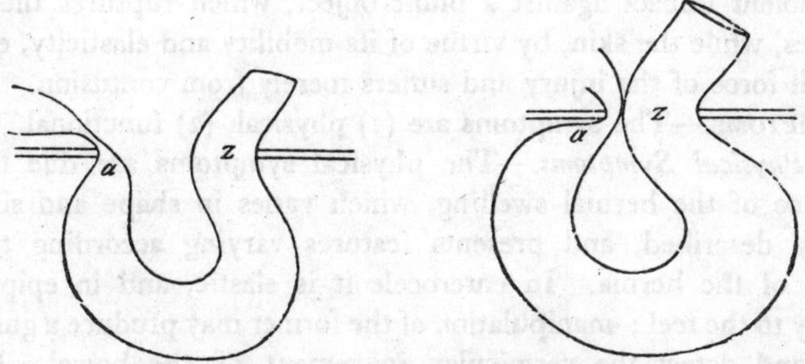

FIGS. 282 AND 283.—SHOWING MECHANISM OF INCARCERATION OF INTESTINE.
(*a*) Efferent, (*z*) afferent, portion of intestinal loop.

When strangulation has been in existence for some time, the signs of death in the affected bowel are obvious. It becomes blackish, greyish, or yellowish, and may be ulcerated or perforated. In entero-epiplocele the omentum, swollen and hyperæmic, supports part of the pressure, relieving to some extent the bowel, in which the lesion is slower in forming and less marked than in a case of enterocele. When the strangulation is not very acute, adhesions form between the contents and the sac, especially at its neck, and may be sufficient in exceptional cases to protect the peritoneal cavity from infection ; while perforation of the bowel and sac takes place externally, giving rise to an intestinal fistula, as already described (p. 665).

(3) *Hernia with Adhesions*.—Inflammatory adhesions have united the contents to the lining of the sac. When recent, the adhesions are fibrinous and easily ruptured, but when old they are fibrous and resistant. They may be in the form of bands or plaques. They

prevent complete reduction of the hernia, and may cause strangulation by constricting the bowel.

Etiology.—Hernia occurring through a natural passage may be congenital, as is often the case with umbilical and inguinal hernia. The etiology of acquired hernia comprises (1) predisposing causes, and (2) exciting causes.

(1) *Predisposing causes* include heredity and conditions which give rise to weak points in the abdominal wall, such as imperfect occlusion of the umbilicus, deep wounds, contusions, or abscesses, or which bring about increased intra-abdominal pressure, such as straining from constipation or diarrhœa or parturition, fits of coughing, or intestinal tympany.

(2) *Exciting causes* are increased intra-abdominal pressure, which tends to force the viscera through weak spots in the abdominal wall, and violent impact against a blunt object, which ruptures the rigid muscles, while the skin, by virtue of its mobility and elasticity, evades the full force of the injury and suffers merely from contusion.

Symptoms.—The symptoms are (1) physical, (2) functional.

(1) *Physical Symptoms.*—The physical symptoms are due to the presence of the hernial swelling, which varies in shape and size, as already described, and presents features varying according to the nature of the hernia. In enterocele it is elastic, and in epiplocele doughy to the feel; manipulation of the former may produce a gurgling noise and detect the vermicular movement of the bowel. If the herniated portion of intestine is distended with gas it will be tympanitic on percussion, and if it contains a quantity of fluid it will fluctuate on palpation. It may be tympanitic in its upper and contain fluid in its lower part. In entero-epiplocele there is a combination of the foregoing characters. In reducible hernia the swelling can be obliterated by pushing the contents into the abdomen, and the edges of the ring can then be felt by two or three fingers inserted through the opening. During manual reduction of the hernia the bowel slips back suddenly into the abdominal cavity, accompanied generally by a gurgling sound, while the omentum is more gradual in its disappearance, and may transmit a slight sense of crepitation to the hand, due to friction against the walls of the sac. When both are present, the bowel is reduced first. If the patient makes a sudden effort or is made to cough, the swelling can be seen and felt increasing in size. When adhesions are present, the swelling can be pushed through the hernial ring, but the sac cannot be separated from the contents. When the hernia is incarcerated, the contents cannot be reduced and the ring cannot be easily felt. When a

reducible hernia becomes strangulated, well-marked symptoms are observed. The swelling increases in size, becomes hard and tense, painful and irreducible, and fails to convey an impulse to the hand during coughing. These symptoms may coincide with the production of the hernia, and then the condition is spoken of as *acute hernia*. When gangrene supervenes, the inflammatory phenomena disappear and the hernia becomes cold and insensitive.

(2) *Functional Symptoms*.—In ordinary reducible hernia these symptoms are practically absent. It may cause slight indigestion and an occasional mild attack of colic. Incarcerated hernia is more likely to cause such disturbance. Strangulation is usually associated with severe and continuous abdominal pain, a febrile reaction, and evidence of intestinal obstruction. The patient may lie on its back in an effort to relieve the pain. When gangrene has occurred the pain subsides, and the animal becomes dull and listless, with perhaps a subnormal temperature and an almost imperceptible frequent pulse and cold extremities, being, in fact, moribund. The temperature, however, may remain high up to the point of death. Deceptive cases are occasionally met with in which, although the local inflammation and abdominal pain are not very marked, gangrene and death supervene if treatment is too long delayed.

Diagnosis of reducible hernia is based on its reducibility, the presence of the hernial ring, and the expansion of the swelling against the hand during coughing. It is more hesitating with incarcerated hernia, but is generally arrived at after careful examination. Conditions with which it may be confounded are abscess, tumour, hæmatoma, cyst, and aneurism, but any person familiar with these lesions is not likely to confuse them with hernia. In strangulation, the diagnostic symptoms are the local phenomena and the general disturbance associated with the history of the case. When doubt exists, it may be removed by rectal examination and by exploratory puncture with a fine trocar and canula or an exploratory needle.

Prognosis.—Congenital hernia (inguinal, umbilical) may disappear spontaneously within one year after birth. When it is a portion of large bowel which forms the hernia, its spontaneous reduction is favoured by the organ becoming distended by dry food. Nutritious diet always promotes recovery, which is therefore more likely to ensue when colts are housed and hand-fed during the winter. If it does not supervene within this period, the hernia is likely to persist and may increase in size. After some time the sac may become much thickened by fibrous tissue. The contents are always more or less exposed to external injury, especially in a large hernia, owing to the prominence of the swelling and the inadequate protection afforded by the hernial sac. A big hernia may interfere with a horse's usefulness. A horse with a hernia may work throughout its life without suffering inconvenience, but there is always the danger of strangulation taking place, and from this point of view recent hernia is more serious than old hernia, and irreducible hernia more dangerous than reducible hernia. When the hernial swelling is large compared with the size of the hernial ring, strangulation is more likely to supervene. It is more apt to occur in horses doing hard than in those doing slow work, and the small intestine is more easily strangulated than the colon or omentum.

Treatment consists in adopting measures which will have the effect of returning the hernial contents into the abdomen and causing cicatrisation in, and consequent closure of, the neck of the sac, and therefore obliteration of the hernial orifice. Its details will be given in connection with the different forms of hernia.

Umbilical Hernia

Synonyms.—Omphalocele, exomphalos.

Etiology.—Umbilical hernia may be congenital, or acquired during the first few weeks after birth, as the result of straining from diarrhœa or constipation, or from exertion of the abdominal muscles when playing or gambolling, or some other effort. Viscera appearing in a dilatation of the cord without a cutaneous covering is a prolapse of the bowel, and must not be confounded with hernia. The hernial contents may be bowel (cæcum or colon) or omentum, or both. The hernial sac is composed of skin, fibrous tissue, and parietal peritoneum. The fibrous tissue is in the form of a fibrous membrane, which is often very much thickened at the fundus of the sac.

Symptoms.—The symptoms are those of a hernia at the umbilicus, the swelling and hernial orifice varying in size and shape, as stated.

Prognosis.—Incarceration or strangulation seldom occurs, probably on account of the nature of the contents. It frequently disappears spontaneously within six or twelve months of age, as the result of the bowel becoming filled with solid food and the abdominal muscles developing and filling up the opening in the abdomen as the animal grows. Adhesion between the sac and contents is rare.

Treatment.—When the animal is under one year old and the hernia is reducible and not threatened with strangulation, nature may be depended upon to effect a cure of her own accord, or aided by the use of a truss, blister, or caustic agents, which are of little or no avail in older animals. A truss is a pad which retains the hernial contents in the abdomen, and thus favours closure of the hernial opening. It is kept in position by a roller. It requires to fit accurately and to be well adjusted, otherwise it may become displaced or cause chafing, or even necrosis of the skin. The patient may resent its use and fret and fail to thrive from the irritation which it causes. When of a good pattern and properly applied it is undoubtedly a useful contrivance. A blister applied to the hernial sac will cause a certain amount of inflammatory swelling, which will tend to push the contents of the hernia into the abdomen and give rise subsequently to the formation of cicatricial tissue, which will help to reduce the size of the sac and that of the hernial opening.

The application of a caustic will cause an eschar and the same results as a blister, but to a more marked degree. Sulphuric acid, 1 part to 3 parts of water, applied daily for five to eight days, is reported as having been used with success. Pure nitric or sulphuric acid applied in lines with a glass rod not more than twice may have the desired effect. The hair should be clipped before applying these dressings. The action of the caustic must be carefully watched, for if used too often or rubbed in for too long a time a deep slough may separate and be followed by prolapse of the bowel. Chromic acid, bichromate of potash, and the actual cautery have also been employed, with similar results.

Bandaging and blistering combined, although more effective than either alone, constitute a method which is apt to cause chafing and great irritation. These irritant and caustic topics frequently fail in their object, and may, when repeatedly applied, cause great thickening of the sac, blemishing of the skin, and inflammatory adhesions between the sac and the contents, which render subsequent operative intervention more difficult and dangerous. Subcutaneous injection of 1 to 2 ounces of a 15 per cent. solution of common salt is another form of treatment, with results similar to those of the caustics mentioned, but it has been known to cause too severe sloughing. The injection of a few drops of a 10 per cent. solution of zinc chloride has, according to a French authority, Launelangue, given remarkably good results in the treatment of chronic hernia in man.

All the foregoing forms of treatment, however, are of doubtful benefit. The surest way of curing the condition is by operation (p. 324).

Inguinal and Scrotal Hernia

Inguinal hernia (bubonocele) and scrotal hernia (oscheocele) are practically the same thing, the latter being merely an extension of the former from the inguinal canal into the scrotum. The hernial sac is formed by the skin, dartos, subdartos, and tunica vaginalis. The contents may be small intestine or omentum, or both.

Etiology.—It may be congenital or acquired in the same way as umbilical hernia. In adults it may be caused by the hind-leg slipping outwards and backwards, thus dilating the inguinal canal; by heavy testicles, which tend to dilate the internal abdominal ring; and by too vigorous copulation, which has the same effect, and further favours it by the erect position throwing the chief weight of the abdominal viscera on the inguinal region. Dragging on the cord or the use of too heavy clams in the operation of castration may lead to it in the gelding.

Symptoms.—When the contents do not extend outside the external inguinal ring the hernia is not suspected, except strangulation has occurred. A common situation for the hernia is towards the antero-internal aspect of the spermatic cord, and usually at about the level of the epididymis. A large scrotal hernia may reach as far as the hock. In chronic cases in the stallion the corresponding testicle becomes atrophied from pressure. When the hernia is recent or acute, there is interference with the animal's gait, as well as symptoms of more or less severe colicky pains. The limb of the affected side is abducted and the toe dragged. These symptoms may pass off or become intensified, due to strangulation supervening.

Prognosis.—When congenital it may disappear spontaneously, as stated. Occurring suddenly in adult stallions, it is usually strangulated and in all cases is more prone to strangulation than other forms of hernia. When large, it may incommode the animal's movements.

Diagnosis depends on the characteristic symptoms of a hernia appearing in the region mentioned, and which are usually easily distinguishable from sarcocele, a hard tumour in the testicle, and hydrocele, which always occupies the floor of the scrotum, and can be displaced from one part of it to another, while in the gelding it is not likely to be confounded with scirrhous cord but may be confused at first sight with a cyst on the end of the latter. Drawing up of the testicle of the affected side, when accompanied by symptoms of continuous abdominal pain, is looked upon as an almost pathognomonic sign of strangulation of a hernia confined inside the inguinal canal. Otherwise diagnosis of the latter condition can only be arrived at by careful rectal examination, when a piece of bowel or omentum may be detected extending into the inguinal passage. Strangulation of an inguinal hernia is revealed by the symptoms already described for hernia in general.

TREATMENT—(1) *Reducible Inguinal Hernia.*—The measures that may be adopted comprise :

(*a*) *Expectant Treatment*, which is indicated in animals under one year old, and consists in helping nature to effect a spontaneous cure by generous feeding and good hygiene.

(*b*) *Periodic Reduction.*—Putting the patient in the dorsal position and reducing the hernia at least once daily is believed to favour cure of the condition.

(*c*) *The Use of Irritants* rubbed into the skin at the level of the spermatic cord, with the object of causing inflammation and consequent adhesion between the cord and the tunica vaginalis.

(*d*) *Applying a Woollen Cord* round the scrotal sac, after reducing the hernia, and leaving it in position for eight hours, being sufficiently tight to prevent return of the contents without arresting the circulation. It has the same effect as (*c*).

(*e*) Operation as described (p. 332).

A truss is not applicable for inguinal hernia in animals.

(2) *Strangulated Inguinal Hernia.*—It may be possible to reduce the hernia by local manipulation (scrotal taxis), the contents being gradually returned by pressure towards the neck of the sac, violence being avoided for fear of damaging further the already altered and weakened bowel. For this procedure it is necessary to have the animal in the dorsal position, with the hind-quarters raised and the hind-limb of the affected side drawn outwards and backwards, or the hocks fully flexed and spread wide apart. General or epidural anæsthesia will aid the procedure. Taxis on the herniated bowel *per rectum* will help reduction. A little sterilised oil injected into the sac will serve as a lubricant and help the process. If the bowel is distended with gas or liquid, capillary puncture will reduce its volume and favour its return to the abdomen. It is a mistake, however, to lose much time by these methods. It is better to perform the radical operation at once (p. 335).

False Inguinal Hernia—Interstitial Inguinal Hernia—Peritoneal-Scrotal Hernia

Here the hernial contents are in the inguinal canal or scrotum, but outside the tunica vaginalis. The hernial ring is in front of the internal inguinal ring. The sac may or may not be lined by peritoneum. The swelling appears higher up and closer to the abdominal wall than true inguinal hernia, and it has been described as having the appearance of a peaked nightcap.

TREATMENT.—If it is not strangulated, it is better not to interfere. In a case of strangulation, operation consists in opening the sac, reducing the contents after incising the ring outwardly, if necessary, and suturing the muscle and skin separately. If the peritoneal sac can be isolated, it may be ligatured before suturing the ring.

Crural Hernia

This is a hernia through the crural arch, and is very rare in veterinary practice. It causes a swelling on the inner aspect of the thigh between the sartorius and gracilis, where the saphena vein passes between these muscles, and may lead to a straddling gait.

If treatment is required, proceed as for other forms of hernia and suture Poupart's ligament to the sartorius muscle. In case of strangulation, avoid cutting the femoral artery when enlarging the opening.

FIG. 284.—PERITONEAL-SCROTAL HERNIA (HERING).

Perineal Hernia

Perineal hernia is most common in dogs, and will be dealt with when considering hernia in the dog and cat.

Ventral Hernia

Ventral hernia is a hernia through any part of the abdominal wall except through the umbilicus or inguinal canal. It is usually caused by external violence, such as the impact of blunt bodies, but may result from overstretching of the abdominal muscles by a sudden unexpected effort or by violent straining during parturition. Great distension of the abdomen, as during the later stages of pregnancy, favours the condition. The contents may be intestine, omentum, or both. When the condition is recent, the symptoms of a contusion are present in addition to those of a hernia, and the former may mask the latter more or less. Its most common situation is close to the last rib on the left side, but it has also been seen in front of the inguinal region and in the vicinity of the flank. Its size varies from that of a fist to a man's head, or rarely something larger.

PROGNOSIS.—Ventral hernia seldom becomes strangulated, and it may exist throughout an animal's lifetime without causing inconvenience.

FIG. 285.—VENTRAL HERNIA IN A MARE.
(From a photograph.)

When it is situated close to the ribs, treatment is not likely to be successful; but when farther back and of moderate size, operation generally succeeds (p. 338).

Hernia in Ruminants

What has been said about hernia in the horse applies in practically every detail to the same condition in the ox and sheep, in which, however, it is less common. The veterinary surgeon may not be called in to treat it except it has become strangulated or is causing digestive disturbance. Occasionally, in umbilical hernia in calves the contents become adherent to the sac and the patients suffer from diarrhœa, which terminates fatally after weeks or months.

Inguinal hernia is not common in the ox, but is frequently met with in the ram. Ventral hernia in the ox is more common on the right than on the left side, close to the last rib. Hernia of the rumen may occur on the left side. The fourth stomach may be herniated in the lower part of the right flank between the hypochondrium and the white line.

Hernia in Small Animals

Hernia as it occurs in the dog and cat and other small animals is similar to that in the larger animals. Vomiting is an important symptom of strangulation in carnivora. In umbilical hernia, the size of the swelling generally varies from that of a hazel-nut to that of a walnut. The contents are small intestine or omentum, or both. It is usually congenital, and generally diminishes with age, to disappear soon after weaning. Ventral hernia is similar to umbilical and is dealt with in the same way.

TREATMENT comprises :

1. *Subcutaneous injection of a* 10 *per cent. solution of chloride of zinc* ; seldom adopted.

2. *Use of a bandage*, comprising a pad applied over the orifice after reducing the hernia, but this is seldom satisfactory, as it is difficult to maintain in position.

3. *Radical operation* (see p. 339).

Sometimes a case is met with in which the umbilical opening has closed, incarcerating a piece of omentum in the sac, where it undergoes degeneration.

Inguinal and Scrotal Hernia

Scrotal and inguinal hernia are rare in the dog, and still more rare in the male cat, but inguinal hernia is common in the bitch and much less frequent in the female cat. The condition may be congenital in the dog and disappear as the animal grows, but inguinal hernia in the bitch is usually acquired, and shows no tendency to undergo spontaneous cure.

SYMPTOMS.—In the dog the symptoms are those of a hernia in the scrotal region. In the bitch the condition causes a more or less voluminous swelling in the groin, varying in size approximately from a hen's egg to a child's head, and is fairly often bilateral. It is generally reducible in the dorsal position. Pregnancy favours its occurrence, but it may occur apart from it. The contents are, as a rule, one or both horns of the uterus, with its broad ligament, which gives a sort of corrugated feel to the swelling when manipulated. Sometimes they are formed by the intestine or the bladder, and in the latter case urination is generally interfered with owing to bending of the neck of the organ. The uterus may be pregnant or distended by pyometra, and is then more likely to become strangulated. Otherwise strangulation is rare. Even in reducible cases the patient may evince occasionally a little pain or signs of discomfort, especially when the hernia is large. The vagina is dragged forward by the presence of the uterus in the sac, and consequently feels somewhat tense and stretched on digital examination. The condition may be confounded with a mammary tumour, a cyst, a hæmatoma, or an abscess, or it may be associated with one of these conditions. When the hernia is reducible diagnosis is easy, but when incarcerated it is hesitating. Exploratory puncture will assist diagnosis. A hernia may be concealed beneath a tumour in the inguinal region.

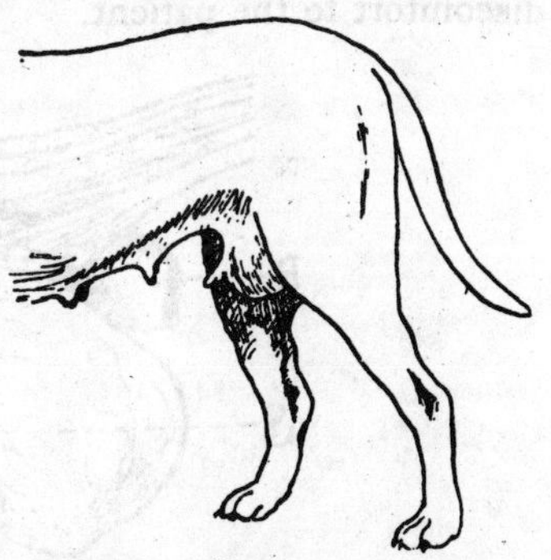

FIG. 286.—INGUINAL HERNIA IN THE BITCH.

PROGNOSIS.—The hernia is more likely to increase in size than to disappear. It may exist for years without endangering the life of the patient, and when the uterus is pregnant the fœtuses may be delivered without difficulty, or those in the hernia may be too large to pass through the hernial ring, necessitating surgical interference to remove them.

TREATMENT.—The only successful treatment for inguinal and scrotal hernia is operation, as described (p. 340).

Perineal Hernia

Perineal hernia is fairly common in old dogs, usually as the result of straining from constipation or enlarged prostate gland. It is characterised by the symptoms of a hernia at the side of the anus or vulva, between the base of the tail and the tuber ischii. These orifices are deviated laterally by the pressure of the hernia, which is usually reducible. The sac is formed by skin, subcutaneous tissue, and sometimes peritoneum. The latter is usually ruptured, leaving the contents practically b[illegible] the skin. The hernia is produced by the protrusion backwards [illegible] ne of the abdominal contents through the recto-vesical or r[illegible]al cul-de-sac, pushing the peritoneum before them or more frequently rupturing it. It is usually the bladder that is contained in the hernia, and being more or less bent on itself, there may be stoppage of micturition, causing abdominal pain, vain efforts at urination, and increased tension and pain in the hernial swelling. Diagnosis may be confirmed by exploratory puncture if reduction cannot be effected. The return of the contents to the abdomen is facilitated by raising the hind-quarters, while lifting the fore-part increases the volume of the hernia.

Prognosis.—The patient may live for years with the hernia without suffering ill-effects, but when symptoms of interference with micturition are present the condition will be a constant source of pain and discomfort to the patient.

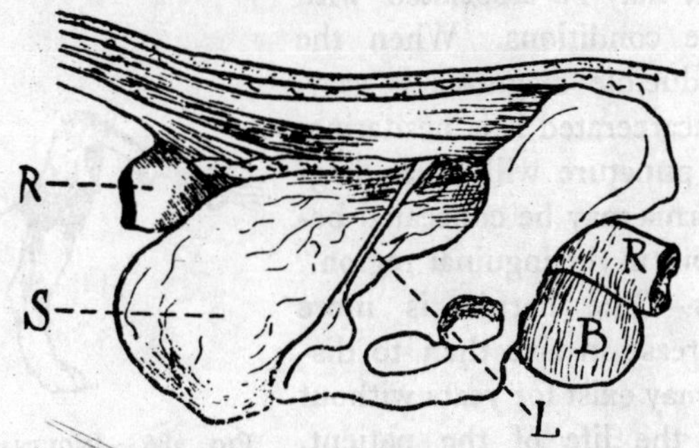

Fig. 287.—Perineal Hernia in the Dog.

S, Hernial sac; L, Sacro-sciatic ligament; R, Rectum; B, Bladder.

Treatment is generally unsatisfactory. Radical operation affords the only chance of cure, and it is often impracticable owing to the frequent absence of a peritoneal sac to be ligatured to obliterate its cavity. Plugging of the intrapelvic space occupied by the hernial contents, after their reduction, by sterilised gauze until it fills up in front by cicatricial tissue is not likely to succeed. Merely removing the greater portion of the cutaneous sac and suturing the cut edges of the skin is not sufficient to obliterate the hernial passage, and is apt to be followed by infection of the peritoneal cavity and death (see p. 342).

II.—INTERNAL ABDOMINAL HERNIA

An internal abdominal hernia is the passage of an abdominal organ through an orifice in a membrane or partition inside the body. The chief forms of internal abdominal hernia are: (1) Diaphragmatic hernia, (2) pelvic hernia.

Diaphragmatic Hernia

Diaphragmatic hernia is the passage of an abdominal organ or organs through an opening in the diaphragm into the chest cavity. The opening is usually the result of an accidental rupture of the tendinous or muscular portion of the structure, such as may result from a horse falling in a violent manner on the ground, or throwing himself recklessly thereon during an attack of colic ; or the accident might be due to a fragment of a broken rib perforating the diaphragm.

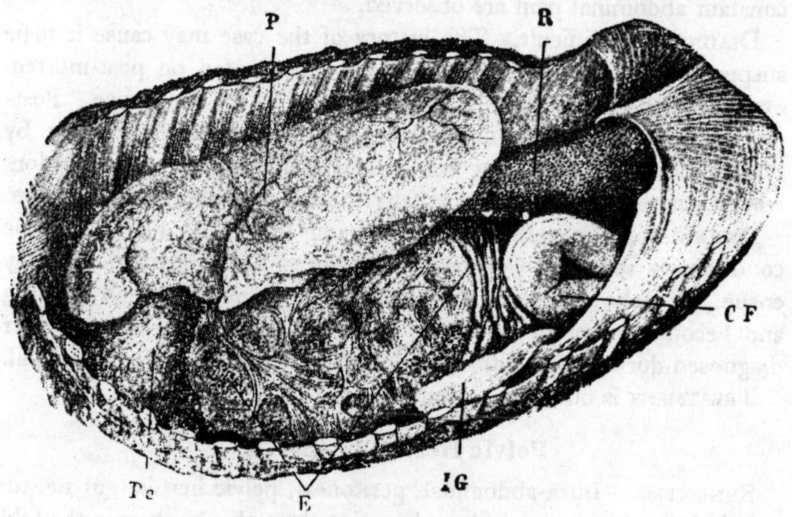

FIG. 288.—DIAPHRAGMATIC HERNIA.
E, Epiploon ; IG, loop of small intestine ; CF, floating colon ; R, spleen ; P, lung; Pe, pericardium.

Rarely the hernia occurs through the foramen sinistrum ; in such a case the condition may be congenital. Violent contraction of the abdominal muscles or anything causing great pressure of the abdominal organs against the diaphragm may be an exciting cause of the lesion. The size of the rupture varies in different cases. It may only admit the passage of a portion of omentum or a knuckle of small intestine, or many of the abdominal organs may pass through it—viz., bowel, omentum, liver, stomach, or spleen.

SYMPTOMS.—The symptoms are not very characteristic. They comprise more or less severe dyspnœa from pressure on the lungs, and tympany on percussion and intestinal sounds on auscultation of the thorax. When the protrusion into the chest cavity is slight there may be little or no interference with health, and exceptional cases have been seen in which a large portion of the abdominal contents had passed through a wide opening in the diaphragm without causing obvious respiratory distress. Raising the fore-quarters may relieve and raising the hind-quarters may increase the dyspnœa, thus accounting for the patient sometimes sitting up like a dog when suffering from the affection. Palpation of the abdomen may give a sensation of emptiness, due to more or less of the viscera having passed into the chest cavity. When incarceration or strangulation occurs, the usual symptoms of constant abdominal pain are observed.

Diagnosis is difficult. The history of the case may cause it to be suspected, but in many cases it is only discovered on post-mortem examination. Exploratory puncture might be of assistance. Post-mortem rupture of the diaphragm often occurs from pressure by tympanitic bowel, the rent being usually in the muscular portion, whereas ante-mortem rupture usually appears in the tendinous portion.

Prognosis.—When the hernia is causing functional disturbance the condition is serious. Collapse of the lungs and instant death may ensue. If only a piece of omentum passes through a small opening and becomes adherent thereto, it is of no consequence and is never diagnosed during life. Strangulation of the hernia is, of course, fatal.

Treatment is out of the question.

Pelvic Hernia in the Ox

Synonyms.—Intra-abdominal, peritoneal, pelvic hernia, gut-tie.

It is formed by a loop of bowel passing through a rupture in the fold of serous membrane which suspends the spermatic cord in the sublumbar and supero-lateral pelvic regions, or by constriction of the intestine caused by the spermatic cord returning to the abdomen after castration and becoming adherent to the floor of the abdomen, with a portion of bowel caught between it and the abdominal wall. The condition occurs on the right side, being prevented on the left side by the presence of the rumen.

Etiology.—Castration by violent traction on the cord may rupture its membrane, or sever the cord high up and allow the end to recede to the abdomen and behave as described. The hernia is most common in hilly districts, the ascent of heights throwing the abdominal contents backwards, and thus favouring its formation. Abnormal distension of the rumen is also a predisposing cause by increasing the intra-abdominal pressure on the right side. Castration by traction on the cord, as already indicated, has been proved to be the cause in many cases, the hernia appearing some months after the operation, when firm adhesions have been formed. The condition prevails in districts where this method of castration is practised. It is well known in some parts of England, is prevalent in Germany and Switzerland, and rare in France and Italy.

Symptoms.—When not strangulated it is not suspected, but when strangulation takes place it is manifested by abdominal pain and by signs of intestinal obstruction, the animal becoming uneasy, lying down and getting up, looking towards the affected side, and making vain efforts at defæcation, passing only small particles of fæces or simply mucus. In some cases these symptoms appear immediately after the accident, and subside after about twelve hours, to reappear during the next few days. If enemata are used they are expelled at once. Pain may be evinced on pressure of the right flank.

Diagnosis is formed on rectal examination, which reveals the presence of a soft, doughy swelling at the entrance to the pelvis on the right side near the sacrum when due to a perforation in the serous membrane, and lower down when caused by the free end of the cord. The swelling is generally about the size of a man's head, and may be slightly painful on pressure. Towards the middle line it is bordered by the tensely stretched cord.

Prognosis.—If relief is not afforded within a few hours after the symptoms have appeared, gangrene of the bowel will ensue, and death will take place on the fourth or fifth day. Rarely it may be delayed until the second week after the accident.

Treatment comprises: (1) Jumping the animal from a height or making it descend rapidly a steep incline; (2) applying taxis *per rectum* to draw the bowel out of the orifice; (3) performing laparotomy to rupture or cut the spermatic cord and release the incarcerated viscus. No. (1) is worth trying in a recent case, as it may succeed when the constriction is slight and firm adhesions are absent. It offers no safeguard against recurrence of the condition. No. (2) may be successful if the hernia is small and not tightly wedged in the opening. It is facilitated by having the hind-quarters raised. No. (3) is the best treatment, and should be practised at once, before the animal is exhausted or gangrene has set in (see p. 341).

SURGICAL AFFECTIONS OF THE STOMACH AND BOWELS

Foreign Bodies in the Digestive Tract

CASES of foreign bodies in the digestive tracts of the domesticated animals have been frequently recorded, most commonly in the ox, dog, and cat, the horse being rarely affected in this way.

The Horse may swallow nails, tacks, etc., accidentally mixed with the food.

Cattle are very prone to pick up and swallow foreign bodies of various kinds, including cloth, hair, leather, twine, needles, pins, pieces of iron, wire, umbrella ribs, etc. It is astonishing how some of the long sharp objects found in the stomach could have been swallowed. Balls of hair or binder twine are a common cause of trouble in the stomach of the calf.

The Sheep is not often affected, but young lambs frequently die from wool-balls obstructing the pylorus.

Dogs often swallow stones, corks, balls, or coins, which have been thrown for them to fetch or which they have picked up. Dogs bolting their food frequently swallow foreign bodies contained therein, chiefly skewers and fish-hooks.

SYMPTOMS.—*Horses* seldom betray symptoms of having swallowed foreign matter. It is only when a calculus has formed round a nail or tack or piece of wire, and has caused the death of the animal, that evidence of the accident is disclosed on post-mortem examination and section of the calculus through its centre, but occasionally a sharp body (nail, wire) swallowed penetrates the stomach or bowel, causing fatal peritonitis.

Cattle usually show signs of indigestion at a variable time after swallowing foreign bodies, including periodic colic and tympanites. When the object is metallic it is usually lodged in the reticulum, but when composed of cloth it passes into the rumen. Sharp bodies in the reticulum almost invariably pierce the diaphragm and enter the pericardium, setting up traumatic pericarditis, which is manifested by dyspnœa, irregularity of the heart's action, pericardial murmurs (tinkling, rubbing, scraping, or buzzing sounds), œdema of the dewlap and jugular furrow, a jugular pulse, and usually a grunt, on pressure in the region of the ensiform cartilage and that of the heart.

Sucking calves exhibit symptoms of abomasal indigestion, are listless, with a temperature of 103 to 105° F., breathing heavily and groaning, the symptoms being aggravated after sucking. Milk may return through the nose. Death supervenes when obstruction of the intestine is caused by a hair or twine ball.

Dogs and cats suffering from intestinal obstruction by foreign bodies vomit all kinds of nourishment, even pure water, soon after receiving it, become affected with extreme weakness, and die in the course of eight to ten days. Febrile symptoms indicative of acute gastritis are absent. Foreign bodies not causing obstruction may remain in the stomach for years unaccompanied by evidence of constitutional disturbance. Light foreign bodies are apt to obstruct the pylorus or, if they pass into the intestine, to cause stoppage at the ileo-cæcal valve. Bottle corks are particularly dangerous on account of their swelling in the bowel.

DIAGNOSIS of trouble due to foreign bodies in the digestive tract is always difficult in the absence of a history indicating that the symptoms dated from the time when the patient was seen to swallow a foreign body. The symptoms are not so characteristic as to exclude the possibility of their being due to some other cause. The most satisfactory method in diagnosis in small animals is by means of the X-rays, but every kind of object is not revealed upon the plate, *e.g.*, a rubber ball.

In the dog and cat an object of moderate size, like a cork, a ball, or pebble, in the alimentary tract can be felt through the abdominal wall, but a tumour in the abdomen, hard fæces in the bowel, or the kidney may be mistaken for a foreign body. To perform palpation in the dog, place it on its hind-legs ; when in this position, grasp the body from behind with the two hands, and allow the viscera to glide between the fingers by moving them with slight pressure from the under portion of the abdomen towards the vertebræ. This may require to be done repeatedly before the body is felt ; when it is far forward the ribs prevent its being grasped. Contraction of the abdominal muscles interferes greatly with palpation of abdominal organs, but it can be overcome by morphia narcosis or by general or epidural anæsthesia. The discharge of needles, hair-pins, and portions of wire has often been observed in cattle, and usually occurs on the left side close behind the elbow. Similarly needles and pins may be seen protruding through the abdominal or thoracic wall from the digestive tract of the dog or cat. When pericarditis is well established in the ox it is easily recognised, and is practically always due to a foreign body penetrating from the stomach.

PROGNOSIS.—As already indicated, foreign bodies may be present in the alimentary canal without causing any trouble, but when constitutional disturbance ensues recovery will not occur until the foreign body is removed. Spontaneous cure supervenes when a sharp foreign body gains exit through the medium of an abscess in the abdominal wall, adhesion having taken place between the wall of the viscus and the abdominal parietes as the result of local peritonitis in the affected region. When the perforation is through the chest wall a local pleurisy has also supervened, shutting off the rest of the pleural sac.

TREATMENT often fails to have the desired effect. When a dog is seen to swallow a foreign body, it should be offered a feed of flesh with a view to distending the stomach, and a dose of apomorphia or other emetic should then be given to cause vomiting and ejection of the foreign substance. When the object has reached the intestine, its passage towards the anus may be favoured by an oleaginous purgative or by a hypodermic injection of eserine, after giving solid food to surround the object, the latter drug being always indicated when medicine given by the mouth is vomited. Recovery occasionally takes place owing to the foreign body being passed out with the fæces ; an india-rubber hand-ball was discharged in this way by a retriever. Pieces of bone and needles, with or without thread, are often arrested in the rectum of the dog, whence they can be extracted with the fingers or a forceps.

Rumenotomy has often been performed in the ox for the purpose of removing foreign bodies from it or from the reticulum. Obich cured four cases out of thirteen in this way. To reach the reticulum, the hand is directed downwards and forwards through the rumen, towards the right of which it lies. The chief difficulty is the impossibility of certain and early diagnosis.

For hair or binder-twine balls in sucking calves Brown (Invergordon, N.B.) performs laparo-gastrotomy, operating through the abdominal floor immediately behind the sternal cartilage. The incision is made in the middle line. The abomasum is readily distinguished from the intestine by its colour, and is drawn into the wound and opened by a 3-inch incision. If the stomach contains much milk it is emptied by means of a syringe, then a finger is inserted to remove the hair-ball, which is found usually near the pylorus. The gastric wound is closed by Lembert sutures, the abdomen is flushed with warm saline solution, and finally the external wound is sutured and protected with a pad and bandage.

The lamb has been operated upon successfully for wool-ball in the stomach (see p. 332).

Gastrotomy or enterotomy is indicated in the dog and cat when other methods of treatment are of no avail (see pp. 352 and 353).

Intussusception or Invagination of the Bowel

The etiology, symptoms, diagnosis, prognosis, and medicinal treatment of this condition belong to the domain of medicine. However, the only chance of undoing the invagination and curing the patient is by surgical intervention. The procedure consists in performing laparotomy (p. 343) and directly reducing the invagination, or if this is impossible owing to firm adhesions having formed between the two serosa, or if gangrene has supervened, resecting the affected portion of the bowel. To effect reduction, the bowel is taken through the operation wound and laid on a sterilised cloth covering the abdominal wall, and the invaginatus is released by careful and gradual pressure by the fingers and thumbs behind the affected part. Traction on the invaginatus will have little or no effect in performing reduction, and may tear the bowel.

To prevent recurrence of the intussusception, ventro-fixation of the bowel is performed by suturing its mesentery, where the invagination commenced, to the abdominal wall by two or more catgut or kangaroo tendon sutures. This procedure has often proved effective in the dog and cat in cases of invagination of the intestine appearing as a prolapse behind the anus (see p. 701). Direct reduction has also been performed with success in the ox.

Resection of the affected portion of the viscus is recorded as having been successfully performed by different operators in the ox. Taccoen operated on two cows, from one of which he removed 10 inches of bowel. Both animals recovered. Moussu has operated successfully by making a longitudinal incision in the *invaginans* near the commencement of the invagination, severing and removing the *invaginatus* through this incision.

Twist or Rotation of the Colon in Horses

In 1890 Jelkmann announced his views on twist of the colon, and his successful method of dealing with it. He says twist is usually towards the right, and is produced by distension of the upper portion of the colon and its displacement from the left lower wall of the belly at the same time that portions of the rectum are forced towards this spot. If the animal rises after lying on the right side, the upper portion of the bowel, which has been displaced towards the middle line of the belly, is thrust downwards and finally twisted around its long axis This explains many cases, but just the opposite sometimes occurs, twist taking place towards the left, as is shown by the reports of post-mortem examinations in the Pathological Institute of the Berlin College. Sometimes the upper layer of the colon is displaced towards the centre line, sometimes towards the left abdominal wall. The comparatively great length of the portion of bowel filled with food and its freedom to move explain the frequent occurrence of rotation. (For the normal position of the abdominal contents, see Figs. 139 to 141.)

SYMPTOMS.—The usual symptoms indicative of twist or stoppage of the bowel are evinced. Rectal examination reveals twist of the colon when it is the cause of the trouble. In front of the anus one feels the distended colon, which may for the moment be mistaken for the over-filled urinary bladder, but careful examination reveals its real nature. The longitudinal muscular bands can be distinctly felt, and show not only that we have colon to deal with, but also in what direction torsion has occurred. When the bowel is in its proper position, the bands run nearly parallel to the long axis of the body ; but in twist a change in their course is distinctly appreciable. In torsion towards the right they run backwards and inwards ; in torsion towards the left. backwards and outwards.

According to Jelkmann, the rectal mesentery, whose fixed border can be felt towards the lumbar vertebræ, appears greatly stretched, and in right rotation does not pass perpendicularly downwards, but towards the left, and pressure on it causes the animal pain. Careful examination of the bands of the colon seems of more importance in diagnosis, and no doubt can exist either as to the presence or direction of the torsion if they can be discovered ; but the posterior bands of the cæcum, which can be distinctly felt when the latter is distended with food, must not be mistaken for those of the colon. Such an error is avoided by remembering that normally the cæcum runs from the outer angle of the right ilium in a bow directed backwards, and ends near the left side.

PROGNOSIS.—In very exceptional cases torsion may be reduced by the animal rolling, but as a rule the only chance of recovery lies in early manual treatment.

TREATMENT—(1) *Jelkmann's Method.*—Proceed as follows : Having cleared out the rectum by the aid of a clyster, insert the left hand, press it forwards towards the left abdominal wall, and endeavour to thrust the left portion of the colon with the convolutions of the rectum forwards from this point towards the middle line of the abdomen. Once the bowel is brought into this position, pass the hand slowly upwards, when the colon will fall back over it into its normal position. The convolutions of the rectum displaced towards the left lower abdominal wall, having been thrust upwards, leave room for the colon to return to its normal position.

(2) *Müller's Method to replace a Left Rotation of the Colon.*—Proceed thus : Empty the rectum, introduce the right hand, and recognise the bands of the colon running from in front, backwards and outwards, or towards the left ; then make use of the bands of the colon lying above to bring about reposition. With the hand in the rectum, place its volar surface or the fingers against the bands and endeavour to draw these so far towards the right that the colon will again take up its position parallel with the middle line of the body. The possibility of carrying out these manœuvres was proved by experiments on the dead subject.

In torsion towards the left it was shown that the bands of the lower section of the bowel offered a purchase for retroversion. After effecting replacement of the bowel in a case of colic due to twist of the colon, the pelvic flexure, until then filled with gas, at once collapsed, the symptoms of pain disappeared, peristaltic action was resumed, the pulse improved, and eventually recovery ensued.

It requires much experience with these methods of procedure and a good deal of physical strength and perseverance to carry them out successfully. Puncture of the bowel to allow the escape of gas facilitates the operation.

SURGICAL AFFECTIONS OF THE POSTERIOR PORTIONS OF THE RECTUM AND OF THE ANUS

Exploration by the Rectum and Anus

THIS affords useful information, not only of the condition of these regions, but of all the parts within reach inside the abdomen, and students should practise it frequently in order to become familiar with the procedure and with recognition of the parts felt. To practise it in the horse, have the animal controlled by holding up a fore-foot or by a side-fetter, lubricate the hand and arm with soap and water, have the tail held to one side, form the fingers into the shape of a cone, introduce the hand slowly but forcibly past the sphincter ani, evacuate the rectum of fæces, and then pass the hand forward gently and make a methodical examination of all the parts within reach, applying your knowledge of anatomy to recognise the various points and structures of practical interest. Great care must be exercised to avoid wounding or rupturing the intestinal wall. Perforation of the bowel followed by fatal peritonitis has occurred from neglect of this precaution. When it happens blood appears on the hand and arm after they are withdrawn.

Congenital Malformations

Congenital malformations of the rectum and anus are fairly common in all animals. The ano-rectal passage is developed from two distinct centres in the embryo. Normally the two tubes coalesce to form a single conduit. It sometimes happens, however, that one of the parts, or both, is insufficiently developed.

The following anomalies may be met with : (1) Neither the rectum nor the anus is fully formed. (2) The rectum is fully developed, but the anus is absent. (3) The anus and rectum are only separated by a thin partition. (4) The partition between the rectum and anus is partially removed, leaving a constriction of the rectum. (5) During early embryonic life the rectum and bladder are one cavity. As development proceeds it becomes divided into two compartments, the lower one forming the bladder and urethra. If the separation is incomplete, a recto-vesical or a recto-urethral fistula results. In the female the abnormal passage is between the rectum and the vagina, forming a recto-vaginal fistula.

Symptoms.—In cases of complete obstruction, attention is usually first called to the animal within a few hours after birth by its showing symptoms of abdominal pain, a distended abdomen, straining without expulsion of the meconium, and no inclination to suck. Local examination of the perineal region reveals the nature of the condition. In No. (1) there is no evidence of bowel contents beneath the skin in the anal region, and it is impossible to say how far forward the rectal cul-de-sac is situated. In rare cases the colon has been arrested in its development, ending blindly in front of the pelvis at about the level of the flank. In No. (2) the skin is usually bulged backwards by the meconium when the animal strains. In No. (3) the membrane between the parts, with the meconium fluctuating in front of it, can be felt on examination by the finger or a sound; and in No. (4) the stricture can be recognised in the same way. If an exit is not made for the fæces, the patient will die within four or five days after birth.

Fig. 289.—Congenital Malformation: Atresia Ani et Recti in the Bitch (Semi-Diagrammatic).

When one of the fistulæ mentioned is present, the animal will live and thrive as long as it is on milk diet and the fæces remain fluid. If the orifice becomes obstructed by solid matter, signs of stoppage of the bowel will appear, and death will ensue if relief is not promptly afforded.

Treatment must be prompt when there is no orifice for the escape of the meconium, although exceptional cases are recorded of young animals living several weeks without passing fæces. The rectum may become paralysed or ruptured from over-distension. Then treatment is useless. The procedure varies according to the nature of the abnormality.

1. *When the Anus alone is Absent.*—Remove a disc of skin corresponding to the normal size of the anus. The meconium will then escape. Suture the borders of the mucous membrane to those of the skin.

2. *When the Anus and Rectum are not Fully Formed.*—Proceed as in No. 1 until the piece of skin has been removed; then dissect

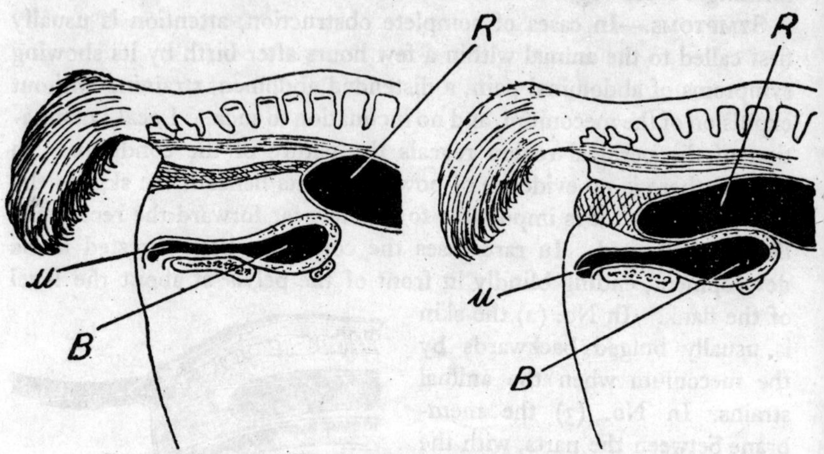

FIGS. 290 AND 291.—ABNORMALITIES OF THE ANUS AND RECTUM.
R, Rectum; B, bladder; *u*, urethra.

further forwards until the ampulla of the rectum is discovered. Separate it from its attachments for a short distance, and draw it gently backwards to the level of the skin; open it by removing a small circular piece from its blind extremity, and unite the cutaneous and mucous borders with interrupted sutures. As a rule the end of the rectum is situated within 2 or 3 inches from the perinæum, and can be fairly easily reached, but in some cases a fruitless search is made for it, owing to its being far forward in the pelvis or in front of the latter. A cord of fibrous tissue may be found in the place which the rectum should occupy, and serves as a guide in finding it. A sound passed through the urethra in the male and into the vagina of the female will indicate the direction of the dissection to reach the bowel, and prevent these passages being encroached upon by the knife.

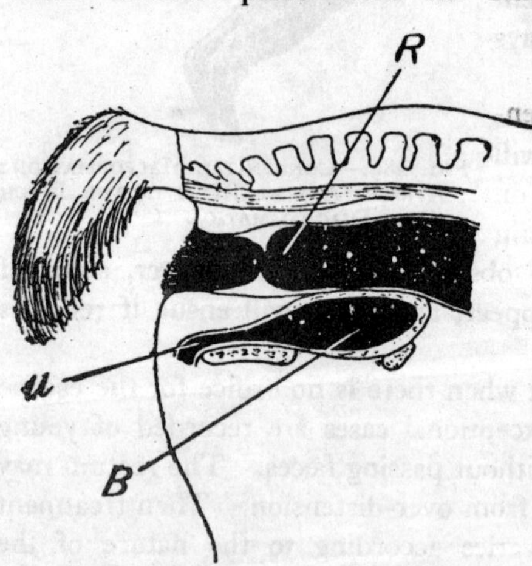

FIG. 292.—ABNORMALITIES OF THE ANUS AND RECTUM.
R, Rectum B, bladder; *u*, urethra.

When the intervention succeeds the case usually does well afterwards, although a sphincter may fail to develop, the anal orifice remaining patent, causing fæcal incontinence and the production of a noise during movement due to the passage of air through the opening. If this operation cannot be effected, the case may be considered hopeless. The only alternative is to perform laparotomy in the flank, bring the blind end of the bowel through the wound, fix it to the borders of the latter, open it, and unite the edges of the skin and mucous membrane by interrupted sutures. This might be of some use to enable a calf to be prepared for the butcher as veal. The rule, however, in such cases is to have the animal destroyed.

Treatment of recto-vaginal fistula is described later.

Injuries to the Rectum and Anal Region

Injuries of the rectum and anus are met with in all animals, but occur most frequently in the horse and dog. Wounds may be (1) *superficial*—that is, confined to the mucous membrane; or (2) *deep*, perforating the rectal wall into the perirectal tissue or into the peritoneal cavity.

Etiology.—The injuries may be caused from (1) the outside, or (2) from the inside.

(1) *Injuries from the outside* may be caused by animals backing against a shaft or a projecting pole or bar, by a horn thrust, the nozzle of a clyster syringe, awkward rectal examination by the hand, the penis of the stallion, and a piece of wood such as a broom-handle passed into the rectum, maliciously, or in the practice of sadism. The entrance of the penis into the rectum during service instead of into the vagina rarely occurs except in the mare. Cases of the penis having passed into the rectum of the horse or gelding have also been recorded. Several instances of a number of animals in one place being killed by the insertion of a stick into the rectum in the practice of sadism have been met with.

(2) *Wounds inflicted from the inside* may be due to fragments of a fractured pelvis, or to needles, pins, pieces of wood, hard fæces, bones, etc., lodged in the rectum, or to a limb of a fœtus penetrating the wall of the rectum during parturition.

The rectum may rupture spontaneously in the horse as the result of severe straining when cast, or in the mare from the same cause when foaling. Violent expulsion efforts on the hand during a rectal examination may cause tearing of the bowel wall.

SYMPTOMS.—The symptoms vary according to the nature of the lesion. Superficial wounds may only be revealed by hæmorrhage from the anus or by blood appearing on the hand after its withdrawal from the rectum. After a while symptoms of rectitis supervene. Deep wounds through the intrapelvic portion of the rectal wall may lead to severe cellulitis of the perirectal tissues, or to the formation of an abscess or fistula. Those perforating the peritoneal cavity soon give rise to a fatal peritonitis. Injuries by the penis of the horse are usually of this nature. The mare may die within twenty-four hours following a false service, after showing signs of pain and general depression. When there is much fæces in the rectum, they may prevent rupture of the peritoneal portion of the organ by this accident.

DIAGNOSIS is formed on rectal examination, which is greatly facilitated by the use of a speculum and a torch. But before proceeding thus to determine the seat and extent of the injury, it should be ascertained whether manipulation of the parts has already been practised, and the owner should be informed of the possible existence of a fatal injury, so that the operator may not be suspected of having caused it. External lesions of the anus are readily recognised.

PROGNOSIS.—All wounds of the rectum and anus heal rapidly, as a rule, except those perforating the peritoneum, which are practically always fatal, due to the entrance of fæcal matter into the abdominal cavity. When the sphincter ani is severed it ceases to function until the wound is healed.

TREATMENT of external wounds is on the usual principles, comprising suturing, antisepsis, and drainage; and that of superficial internal wounds includes evacuation of the rectum and its irrigation two or three times daily with a non-irritant, warm, antiseptic solution (biniodide of mercury 1 in 5,000, potassium permanganate 1 in 1,000), When bleeding is severe, cold-water clysters are indicated, or a bladder may be introduced into the rectum and inflated so as to arrest the hæmorrhage by pressure on the blood-vessels.

Deep wounds of the pelvic region of the bowel require the same attention, but in those involving the peritoneal cavity rectal injections are contra-indicated, and little can be done except to administer opium to check the movement of the intestinal contents towards the perforation in the bowel. Even in non-perforating wounds this drug may be employed to diminish the frequency of the defæcation and straining and thus favour the healing process. Rupture of the perinæum is dealt with on p. 760.

Inflammation of the Rectum (Rectitis) and Anus (Proctitis)

Etiology includes direct injury by rough handling of, or the presence of foreign bodies, or hardened fæces, or parasites in, the rectum ; by rubbing the anus along the ground in the case of pruritus ani in the dog ; by the use of irritating clysters ; and diarrhœa due to some irritant or toxin in the bowel. In long-coated dogs the hairs may get matted with soft fæces and cause irritation and inflammation in the anal region. The anal glands may become infected and inflamed. When the anus or rectum is prolapsed and long exposed it becomes inflamed. The inflammation is usually confined to the mucous membrane, but it may involve the other coats of the organ or spread to the perirectal and periproctal tissues. Suppuration, ulceration, or sloughing may ensue in exceptional cases.

Symptoms.—The symptoms are those of acute inflammation. Constipation and tenesmus are present and defæcation is accompanied by severe pain. A sero-purulent or sanguinolent discharge appears on the fæces. The mucous membrane of the rectum is hot, swollen, and painful, and during defæcation the everted anus appears as a deep red œdematous swelling. Prolapsus ani et recti may result from the straining caused by the condition.

Treatment.—Ascertain the cause of the trouble and take measures to remove it ; otherwise the local treatment consists in the introduction into the rectum of demulcent clysters, providing semi-liquid diet, and the administration of mild laxative medicine in order to facilitate defæcation and relieve the pain which it causes. Warm injections of a solution of soap, or boric acid, or poppy-heads, or linseed tea are indicated. Suppositories of opium or extract of belladonna and the smearing of cocainised vaseline or belladonna ointment on the inflamed parts have a soothing effect. The rectal injection of liquid paraffin acts as a demulcent and laxative. In chronic rectitis, injections of alum or tannic acid have a beneficial astringent action. Ulcers should be touched with a mild caustic such as tincture of iodine or nitrate of silver.

Inflammation of the Anal Glands in the Dog

These glands are ordinarily filled with their own secretion, which is composed of a brownish fœtid material. They are frequently the seat of a purulent inflammation which is favoured by constipation and by closure of their orifices, and excited by some of the causes mentioned as producing rectitis and proctitis.

Symptoms.—The animal rubs its anus on the floor and frequently licks the part. Symptoms of proctitis are observed. The affected gland or glands are found swollen, bluish, fluctuating, and very painful. On squeezing the anus from side to side between the finger and thumb, a purulent very fœtid liquid is discharged from the suppurating glands. If not attended to early, an abscess may burst through the skin and an anal fistula may then persist. Sometimes the pain caused by the condition prevents the animal walking upstairs.

Treatment consists in evacuating the glands by compression of the anus and applying the remedies recommended for inflammation of this region. It may be necessary to open the gland to effect its evacuation. If the trouble is recurring frequently, dissect out and excise the glands. The dog appears to suffer no ill-effects from their removal. Obliteration of the glands as recommended by Auchterlonie (*Vet. Rec.*, Jan. 24th, 1942, p. 51) can be effected by injecting into them the following preparations :

Ferric chloride	ʒi.
Glacial acetic acid	1 c.c.
Absolute alcohol	6 c.c.
Chloroform	3 c.c.

by means of Horrock's fine blood canula attached to a 5 c.c. all-glass syringe by a rubber adaptor, under pentothal sodium anæsthesia. This treatment has been reported as rapidly and completely successful (*Vet. Rec.*, Aug. 11th, 1945) not only for this condition but also for sublingual cyst in the dog, after partial excision. It is claimed to be much simpler than and just as effective as the operation of excision of the glands.

Abscesses in the Ano-Rectal Region

These are fairly common in the horse, occupying the peri-anal tissue, or more commonly the walls of the rectum, or the surrounding connective tissue, or the partition between the rectum and vagina.

Etiology.—They are generally caused by injury and infection of the part, but they may be due to a specific disease, most commonly strangles. A melanotic or botriomycotic abscess may be found in this region.

Symptoms.—The abscess may be superficial or deeply situated towards the roof, floor, or lateral walls of the rectum at a distance of from 2 to 6 inches in front of the anus. The typical symptoms of acute rectitis are manifested, and the abscess is diagnosed on rectal examination by its fluctuation.

Prognosis.—The case is only serious when the abscess is anteriorly situated, and liable to burst into the peritoneal cavity and cause peritonitis.

Treatment.—Facilitate defæcation as advised for rectitis, and when the abscess is fluctuating open it, evacuate its contents, and irrigate its cavity with a mild antiseptic solution. An abscess pointing inside the rectum may be opened by the finger or a guarded knife, and if it fluctuate in the vagina in the female it should be opened there. The deep-seated abscess cavity can be irrigated by the aid of rubber tubing attached to a syringe and introduced through the anus. The injections are continued until it is evident that the wall of the abscess is uniformly granulating, when they are no longer required. The melanotic abscess usually refuses to heal owing to the presence of melanotic tissue in its lining, and a fistula then ensues.

Ano-Rectal Fistulæ

Ano-rectal fistula occurs in all animals, but is most common in the dog.

Varieties.—(1) *Complete fistula*, having a cutaneous and an intestinal opening (Fig. 294).

(2) *Incomplete or blind fistula*, opening on one surface only (Figs. 293 and 295).

(3) *External blind fistula*, when the orifice is on the skin (Fig. 295).

(4) *Internal blind fistula*, when it is on the mucous membrane (Fig. 293).

(5) *Simple fistula*, when it is in the form of a single passage.

(6) *Complex fistula*, when the main passage has tributaries or side passages.

The cutaneous orifice is usually in the vicinity of the anus, and the fistula may pass inside the sphincter (subsphincteral), or outside it (extrasphincteral), or through it (intersphincteral).

Etiology.—The condition is usually a sequel to an infected wound or abscess in the ano-rectal region, the septic lesion persisting owing to the presence of necrotic tissue, or inspissated pus, or insufficient drainage. When the case is of long standing, the smooth callous lining of the passage is an obstacle to healing. Less frequently the fistula is the result of carcinoma, tuberculosis, purulent prostatitis, or necrosis of the ischium or coccygeus.

Symptoms.—A purulent discharge is observed in the neighbourhood of the anus, and on further examination the orifice is discovered, into which a probe can be passed for a varying distance. The hand or finger inserted into the rectum will ascertain whether the instrument has reached its lumen. Although the fistula is complete, the probe may not penetrate into the rectum on account of the fistulous passage being tortuous or branched, but in all cases of complete fistula a coloured liquid injected through the cutaneous orifice will be seen escaping through the anus. The opening of the anal gland in the dog must not be mistaken for a fistula. A blind internal fistula is not so readily recognised. Attention is drawn by the appearance of pus on the fæces and by the dog licking the anus. Rectal exploration will

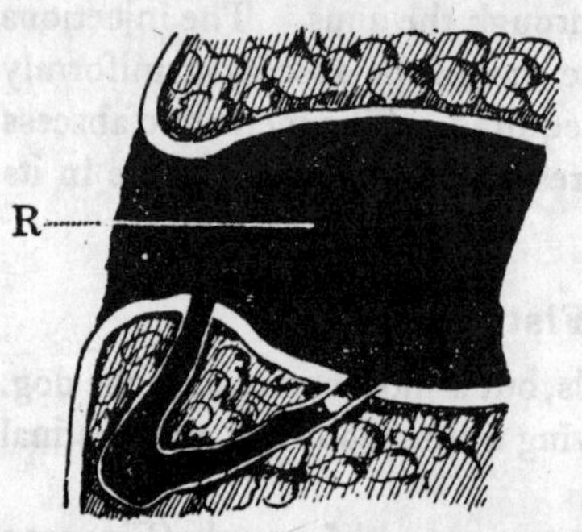

FIG. 293.—BLIND INTERNAL FISTULA.

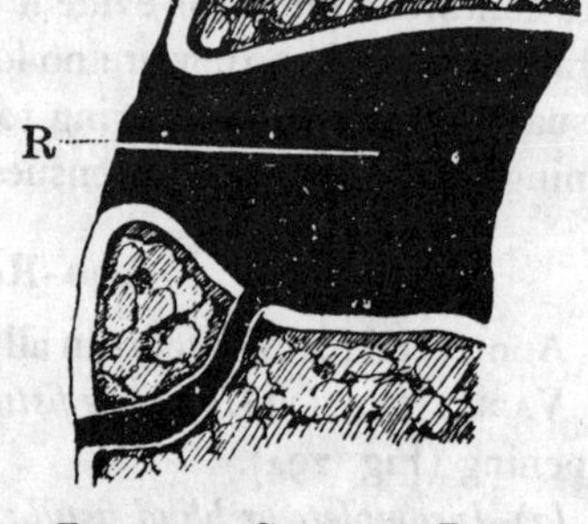

FIG. 294.—COMPLETE FISTULA.

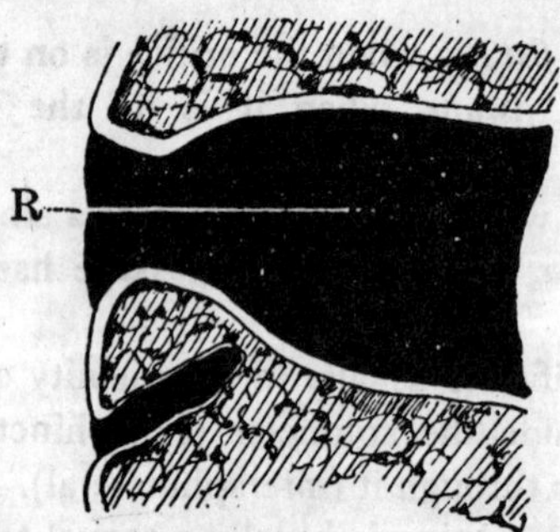

FIG. 295.—BLIND EXTERNAL FISTULA.
R, Rectum.

reveal a rough spot corresponding to the orifice of the fistula. The use of a speculum and a torch will facilitate diagnosis.

TREATMENT.—Treatment of the fistula aims at removal of its cause, and comprises :

1. *The injection of an irritant or caustic solution* into a blind external fistula to disinfect its passage and promote the removal of its callous or necrotic lining. Tincture of iodine, or 5 to 10 per cent. solution of chloride of zinc, or copper sulphate, or liquor Villati (cupri sulph. 1, zinc. sulph. 1, plumb. acet. 2, vinegar 12) may have the desired effect.

It is generally advisable to enlarge the orifice to facilitate the introduction of the preparation.

2. *The application of a solid caustic* suitable for a complete or incomplete fistula—for example, the silver nitrate stick, or copper sulphate, or zinc sulphate powdered and introduced by means of a little cotton-wool rolled round a sound and smeared with vaseline to make the powder adhere to it.

3. *Operation* as follows : Pass a suitable cylinder of wood into the rectum and insert a probe or sound into the fistula through its cutaneous orifice, and incise the tissues included between the two instruments, thereby laying open the passage without risk of injury to the opposite wall of the rectum. If there are secondary sinuses, open them up also.

An alternative procedure when the fistula is complete is to pass a flexible probe through it into the lumen of the bowel, bring its extremity out through the anus, and incise the tissues between the two parts of the instrument. When the case is an internal blind fistula, introduce the flexible probe into its lumen and make its extremity bulge beneath the skin, cut down on it there, and thus convert the blind into a complete fistula and deal with it accordingly. When an external fistula is superficial it can be opened up without any special precaution. After operation it is generally advisable to cauterise the lining of the tract with silver nitrate to stimulate granulation and cicatrisation.

4. *Removal of a sequestrum or curetting a caried surface* after opening up the fistula, when the condition is due to disease of bone.

Prolapse of the Anus and Rectum

The following forms of prolapse of the bowel may appear behind the anus :

1. **Prolapsus ani, mucous prolapse, or partial prolapse of the rectum,** in which the mucous membrane has glided backwards on the muscular coat to form a circular protrusion behind the anus in the same way as the loose lining of a sleeve may project beyond the cuff (Fig. 296).

2. **Prolapsus ani et recti, or complete prolapse of the posterior non-peritoneal portion of the rectum,** in which the entire rectal wall has glided backwards from the perirectal tissue to form a larger protrusion than that occurring in No. 1 (Fig. 297).

3. **Prolapse as in No. 2, with invagination of the colon into it** (Fig. 298).

4. **Invagination of the anterior part of the rectum or of the colon** into the posterior part, and appearing as a prolapse extending for a variable distance behind the anus (Fig. 299).

The foregoing conditions are met with in all the domesticated animals, but most frequently in the horse, pig, and dog.

ETIOLOGY comprises predisposing and exciting causes. The former include loss of tone in the sphincter ani, loose attachment of the mucous membrane to the rectal wall or of the latter to the peri-rectal tissue, and the presence of any condition giving rise to straining, which is the exciting cause of the trouble—for example, constipation, diarrhœa, and rectitis. These prolapses are most common in very young and

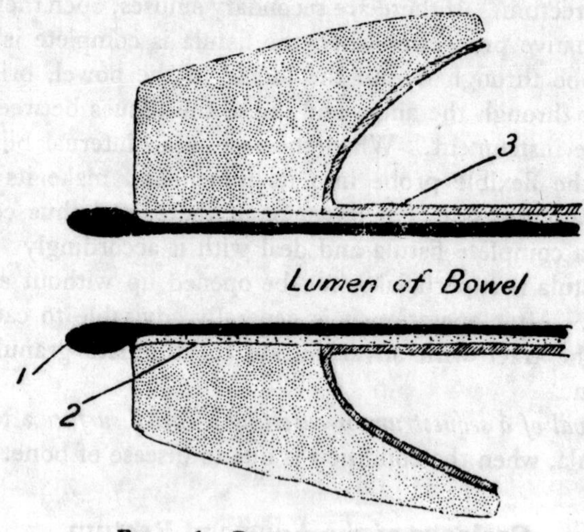

FIG. 296.—PROLAPSE OF THE ANUS.
1, Mucous coat; 2, muscular coat; 3, peritoneum.

in very old debilitated subjects, although violent straining may cause them in a young vigorous animal. They may result in the large animal from straining when cast for an operation. Invagination of the bowel, appearing as a prolapse behind the anus, sometimes results in the mare from violent straining during parturition.

SYMPTOMS.—No. 1, or partial prolapse, appears as a red hemispherical swelling behind the anus, with its surface thrown into transverse folds and showing at its centre an orifice corresponding to the lumen of the bowel. No. 2, or complete prolapse, is of a similar nature, but more voluminous and extending farther back in the form of a cylinder. In No. 3 the swelling is firmer and thicker than in No. 2, owing to the anterior part of the bowel being invaginated inside the prolapsed posterior part. If the finger can be passed into the lumen of the prolapse, it will feel the invaginated part telescoped into it or projecting therein like a tap into a barrel.

In the first three forms of inversion mentioned the mucous membrane of the prolapse is continuous with the skin at the anus. In No. 4 there is a trench surrounding the prolapse inside the anus extending for a variable distance forwards, depending on the length of the invagination. A gum-elastic catheter or probe passed into this space will give an idea of its depth. The protruding mass in this case may extend backwards for a distance of 4 to 12 inches in the dog, and of several feet in the horse. It may be twisted upwards, owing to the tension of the mesentery.

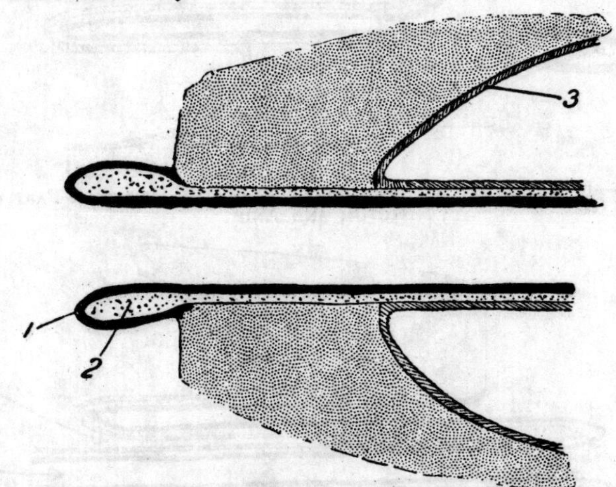

Fig. 297.—Prolapse of the Anus and the Posterior Part of the Rectum.
1, Mucous coat; 2, muscular coat; 3, peritoneum.

Prognosis depends on the nature of the prolapse, the duration of its exposure, and on the presence or absence of complications. In form No. 1 recovery ensues even when the prolapse is allowed to slough off. No. 2 is usually treated successfully when attended to early, or even when necrotic, but death may supervene in the latter case from toxæmia, especially in weakly subjects. The forms Nos. 3 and 4 are of the same gravity as intussusception of the bowel inside the abdomen. Reduction of the invagination is often difficult, and may be impossible, and when it cannot be effected death is almost certain to follow. In rare cases, chiefly in the pig and ox, spontaneous cure may result from the invaginated part becoming separated and being passed out with the fæces.

Treatment comprises (1) reduction and retention, (2) amputation.

In all recent forms of the condition it is generally easy to push the prolapse forward inside the anus, but in Nos. 3 and 4 reduction of the invagination is also necessary, and this is often difficult or

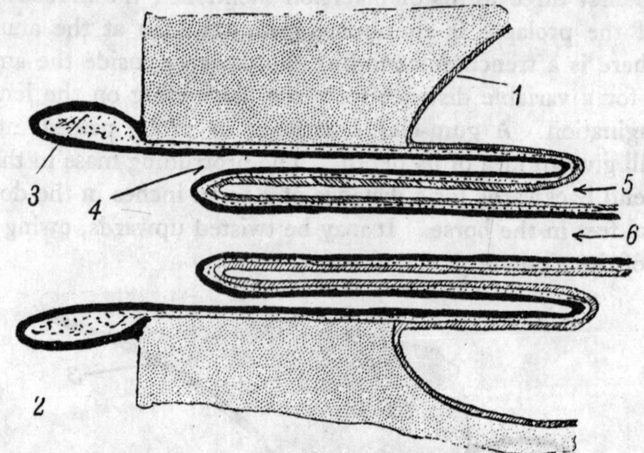

FIG. 298.—INVAGINATION WITHIN A PROLAPSE OF THE POSTERIOR PART OF THE RECTUM AND ANUS.

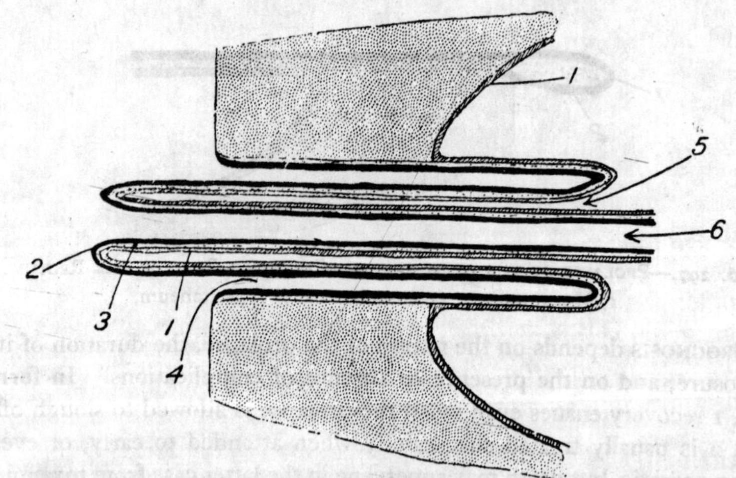

FIG. 299.—INVAGINATION OF THE BOWEL, FORMING A PROLAPSE BEHIND THE ANUS.

1, Peritoneum ; 2, mucous coat ; 3, muscular coat ; 4, trench surrounding the invagination ; 5, entrance to peritoneal cul-de-sac ; 6, lumen of bowel.

impossible to accomplish. Long exposure, causing inflammation and swelling of the affected part, makes reduction difficult. Severe straining is an obstacle to the operation, but it can be overcome by the use of an anæsthetic, if necessary.

Procedure.—Have the hind-quarters raised, clean the prolapsed mass, smear it with vaseline or liquid paraffin, and by careful manipulation gradually replace it in its normal position. Complete reduction is essential, otherwise the prolapse will recur. To reduce an invagination in the large animal, push the hand as far forward *per rectum* as the arm will reach. If this is not sufficient, a repeller in the form of a stick with its end covered by a pad and wash leather may be cautiously employed for the purpose. In the dog a tallow candle or a gum-elastic catheter may be used. A safer and more satisfactory procedure is to give a rectal injection of warm water. Holding up the hind-legs in the dog helps its action. These measures, however, frequently fail to have the desired effect, and then the only remedy is to perform laparotomy, reduce the invagination directly, and prevent its recurrence by ventro-fixation of the bowel. To perform reduction, compress the bowel with the fingers and thumb immediately behind the invagination, thus causing the invaginatus to emerge anteriorly. Drawing on the invaginatus has little effect and may tear the bowel.

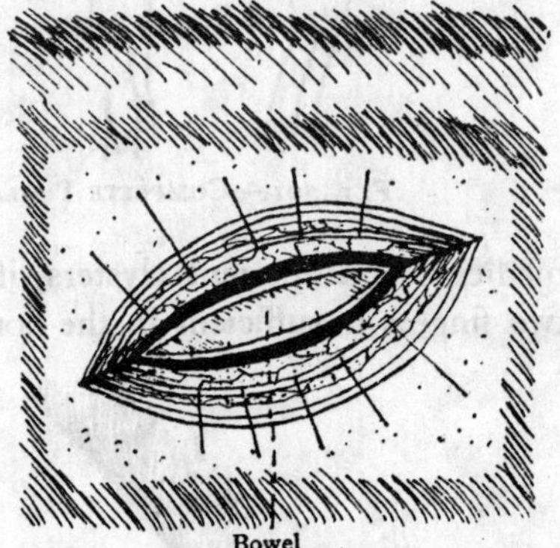

Fig. 300.—Ventro-fixation of the Bowel.

Having effected reduction, fix the bowel to the abdominal wall at the side of the parietal wound by a couple of catgut sutures passed through the comesentery close to the bowel at the part where the invagination commenced and through the parietal peritoneum and abdominal muscles (Fig. 300). This operation is likely to succeed in the dog and cat when performed early before firm adhesions have formed between the sercus surfaces.

When it is the volume of the prolapse which is the obstacle to reduction, it may be diminished by bathing with cold water and an astringent lotion (2 to 5 per cent. solution of alum), or by hot fomentations when the swelling is hard, or by compression with an Esmarch's bandage; or when these methods have failed, by scarification of the mucous membrane, which has a marked effect by relieving the vascular congestion.

1. *Retention* may be effected as follows by :

(1) *Anal Suture.*—By means of a stout needle insert a purse-string suture of tape or strong silk through the skin all round the anus at

about ½ iuch from its border, leaving an orifice sufficiently large for the passage of fæces, kept semi-solid by the administration of laxative

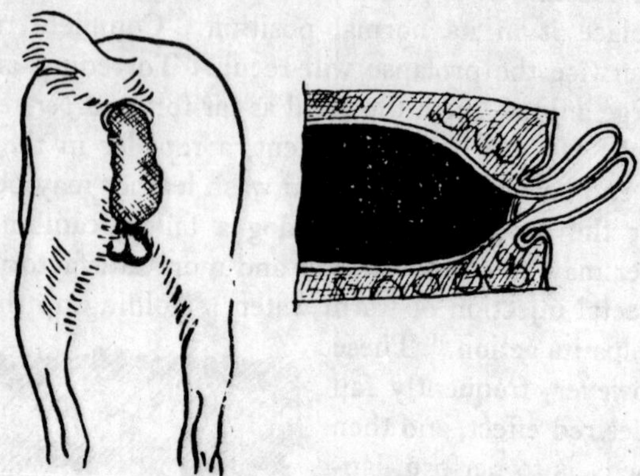

Fig. 301.—Complete Prolapse of the Rectum in the Dog.

medicine and aperient clysters, if necessary. An opening admitting two fingers is sufficient in the horse. The suture may be tightened

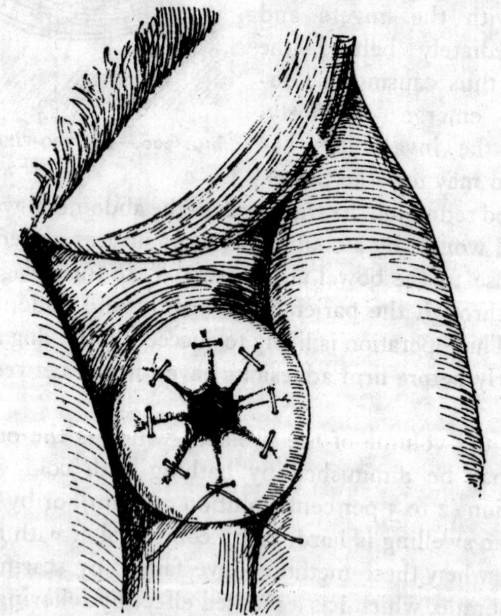

Fig. 302.—Anal Suture.

or loosened at will. This method is very effective except violent straining ensues, when the suture material may cut through the skin.

(2) *A Truss*, similar to that recommended for prolapse of the vagina and uterus, but compressing the anus. The tail drawn forwards between the hind-legs and fixed to a roller might be used to compress a pad over the anus. These methods have the disadvantage of interfering with defæcation.

(3) *The Submucous Injection of Melted Paraffin Wax*, introduced by Gersuny. Having melted the paraffin, inject a little of it beneath the mucous membrane at equal intervals all round the prolapse close to the anus. Then reduce the prolapse. The paraffin will soon solidify and form antero-posterior pillars, which will prevent eversion of the bowel. This method has been frequently adopted with success in the dog.

(4) *Cauterisation* of the mucous membrane by means of the thermo-cautery in a case of prolapsus ani, making lines about 1 inch apart parallel to the long axis of the bowel. The cicatricial contraction which ensues binds the mucous membrane to the rectal wall and prevents its prolapse. This procedure has been adopted in persistent cases of prolapse of the anus in children. It would be rarely required in veterinary practice. The same result may be obtained by the excision with the scissors of longitudinal folds of mucous membrane close to the anus.

(5) *Ventro-fixation*, which has been already alluded to, and is the only effective method for prolapse with invagination.

In all cases steps must be taken to remove the cause of the trouble by treating the conditions which have favoured or excited it, such as diarrhœa, debility, etc. A general sedative and sedative clysters or suppositories are generally indicated to allay tenesmus. Chloral hydrate may be administered and a cocaine suppository may be inserted in the rectum. When straining has ceased, the anal suture or truss is no longer required.

2. *Amputation* is indicated when the prolapse has existed for several days and reposition is impossible, and when the tissue is torn or gangrenous. In a case of prolapsus ani it is not necessary to interfere, as spontaneous recovery will ensue after sloughing of the exposed mucous membrane. It may, however, be dealt with as a prolapse of the posterior part of the rectum, in which one of the following methods of amputation may be employed :

(1) *Excision and Suturing the Cut Edges of the Bowel.*—Operate on one half of the prolapse at a time. Having cut through one half of the cylinder, suture the cut edges of the mucous membrane or of the rectal wall, as the case may be. Then proceed in the same fashion with the

other half. There may be hæmorrhage, necessitating the use of artery forceps.

(2) *Excision by Means of the Thermo-cautery*, in order to avoid hæmorrhage.

(3) *Ligation.*—Divide the prolapse into four longitudinal sections and apply a silk ligature on each at its base. The ligatured parts will slough off in four or five days, and recovery will ensue.

(4) *Möller's Method.*—Pass a needle furnished with silk thread vertically through the centre of the prolapse close to the anus. Pass another thread horizontally through its centre. Cut away the portion of bowel behind the threads. Draw out each thread from the lumen of the anus and cut it, thereby making two sutures. Tie the ends. If necessary, insert additional sutures between the others (Figs. 303 and 304). This is a good practical procedure.

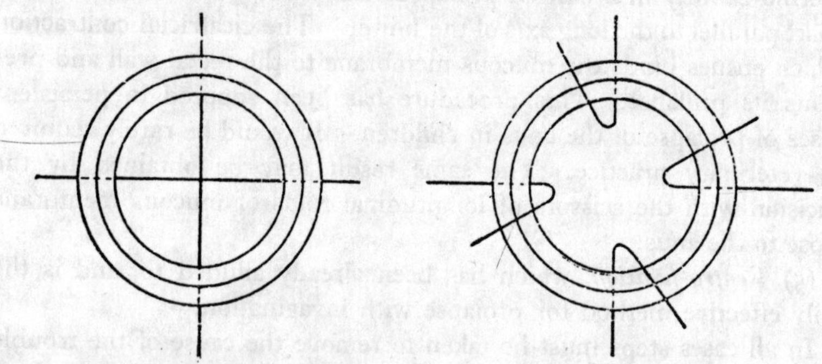

FIGS. 303 AND 304.—METHOD OF LIGATION IN PROLAPSUS RECTI.

(5) *Hobday's Method for the Dog.*—Pass a thermometer case into the lumen of the prolapse as far as the anus to serve as a guide. Insert a series of sutures transversely through the bowel close to the anus, passing the needle down to the instrument. Excise the prolapse, behind the sutures, and then unite the cut edges by another set of stitches.

Nos. (4) and (5) might be adopted for amputation of an intussusception appearing behind the anus, but there would be the risk in each case of transfixing a loop of bowel that might be present in the peritoneal cul-de-sac between the invaginans and the invaginatus. A safer procedure in this case is as follows: Draw out the prolapse as far as it will come, so as to operate on a clean part and as far forward as possible. Cut through one half of the external cylinder into the peritoneal cul-de-sac. If there be a loop of bowel there return it into the abdomen. Unite the two serous surfaces by Lembert sutures. Then proceed similarly with the remaining half of the prolapse, and afterwards join the borders of the mucous membrane with ordinary interrupted sutures. Reduce the remaining invagination by pushing the bowel towards the abdominal cavity. If adhesions have already formed in this part of the invagination, reduction will be impossible and the case will be a failure. It may be said that there is very little chance of this operation succeeding, and that it is not worth while performing it.

Fig. 305.—Stockfleth's Wooden Ring.

An alternative method of procedure is the following: Divide the prolapse into two lateral halves by a careful median incision, looking out for a portion of bowel in the serous cul-de-sac. Insert a cylinder of wood into the lumen of the bowel (Fig. 305). Apply an elastic ligature close to the anus including the cylinder. Sever the prolapse a couple of inches behind the ligature, suture the borders by two series of sutures as before, and then remove the ligature and cylinder. The after-treatment consists in giving enemata three or four times daily, for about a week, of a warm, mild, antiseptic solution through a rubber tube attached to a syringe or funnel.

Stenosis of the Rectum and Anus

Etiology.—Stenosis of the rectum and anus may be the result of cicatricial contraction following wounds or inflammatory affections, or of tumours or abscesses in the region. Chronic diarrhœa in young dogs and pigs has been known to cause the condition, the epithelium becoming desquamated and the raw opposing surfaces of the mucous membrane uniting to more or less obliterate the lumen of the passage. Congenital stenosis is rare.

Symptoms.—There is more or less marked difficulty in defæcation, and the patient may evince signs of colic. The nature of the condition is discovered on local exploration.

Prognosis is unfavourable when the stenosis is due to cicatricial contraction or a malignant or diffuse tumour, as these conditions are incurable.

Treatment.—An attempt may be made to overcome cicatricial contraction by the passage of gum-elastic bougies of gradually increasing diameter, or by the use of a forceps. The result is disappointing as a rule. A circumscribed benign tumour can be successfully removed, and abscesses and acute inflammatory lesions respond to the usual treatment. An abnormal membrane or bands partly occluding the passage may be excised. Incision of a cicatricial constriction, followed by dilatation, will give temporary relief.

When the stricture is extensive, linear rectotomy—that is, section of the tissues comprised between the ano-rectal passage and the tail—may be performed as follows: Have the animal suitably controlled, evacuate the rectum, introduce therein a cylinder of wood, and plunge a red-hot knife horizontally into the tissues beneath the tail. When the knife is felt to have passed the stricture withdraw it, complete the perforation by a flexible sound, bring the end of the latter out through the anus, and then sever the intervening tissue by the thermo-cautery or the ecraseur. This operation, however, will only be of temporary benefit, as cicatricial contraction will ensue, rendering the condition as bad or worse than it was before. To postpone recurrence as far as possible it is necessary to pass bougies at intervals.

Dilatation of the Anus and Rectum

The anus may be dilated as the result of diarrhœa or of a prolonged rectal examination. The anus remains open and the air which streams in and out during breathing produces a loud noise. Except the condition is due to the congenital absence of a sphincter or permanent paralysis, recovery ensues without special treatment.

The entire pelvic portion of the rectum may be dilated in the horse. It is common in old horses fed on bulky food and in dogs suffering from habitual constipation. The dilatation is characterised by the animal defæcating at longer intervals and in larger quantity than usual.

Tumours of the Anus and Rectum

Warts, cysts, lipomata, myxomata, sarcomata, adenomata, and carcinomata may be found in the ano-rectal region of the domesticated animals. Cysts, polypoid myxomata, and fibromata are the most common tumours of the rectal mucous membrane. The cysts are usually polypoid. Melanotic tumours are fairly common in the perirectal and periproctal tissue of grey horses.

Symptoms.—The symptoms vary according to the volume and site of the tumour. When it is of considerable size defæcation becomes difficult, and when it is ulcerated blood and pus may be seen in the fæces. The patient may evince signs of colic. A tumour inside the rectum may protrude through the anus during defæcation. Deformity caused by the new growth may be evident on inspection. Rectal examination will afford further information on the lesion.

Prognosis.—Benign tumours can usually be successfully removed, but malignant growths are nearly always incurable.

Treatment is carried out on the lines laid down for tumours in general. Polypoid growths may be removed by the ecraseur or by ligation, while sessile tumours are carefully dissected out. A sharp-pronged retractor or a forceps with pronged jaws is very useful to hold the tumour while being dissected. After excision of an anal tumour between the skin and mucous membrane, the edges of these two structures may be united with sutures. Recent small epitheliomata, most common in the dog, may not recur after extirpation. The patient's life may be prolonged for some time by repeated excision of a recurring tumour. When removal of the enlargement is out of the question, temporary relief may be afforded by rectotomy (p. 708), but it is not advisable. Cysts may be treated effectively by puncture and injection of tincture of iodine, but incision or excision is preferable.

Hæmorrhoids

Hæmorrhoids, or piles, are rare in veterinary patients, but are occasionally seen in the dog. They are due to varicosity of the hæmorrhoidal veins of the rectum. They are classified as *external* when situated in the anal orifice, and *internal* when present inside the rectum in front of the sphincter. Hæmorrhoids are favoured by constipation, want of exercise, and by cardiac and hepatic affections. Neighbouring varicosities may be confluent, forming a lobulated mass.

SYMPTOMS.—The symptoms comprise constipation, difficulty and pain in defæcation, and perhaps bleeding from the rectum due to forcible expulsive efforts. Local examination will reveal the nature of the condition.

TREATMENT may be (1) constitutional and (2) local.

(1) *Constitutional treatment* includes moderate exercise, laxative and tonic medicine, and laxative nutritious food.

(2) *Local treatment* comprises clysters of warm water and glycerine, or of liquid paraffin or olive oil, the application of an astringent or anodyne ointment (gall, resinol, cocaine, belladonna, or sulphur ointment), and surgical removal, which consists in dilating the anus, incising the mucous membrane round the varicose vein, and applying a ligature round the swelling.

If the condition is not attended to early, it may be complicated with ulceration, fissure, or fistula of the anal region.

Paralysis of the Rectum

Paralysis of the rectum is most common in the horse and dog, and is frequently associated with paralysis of the tail, or of the bladder and hind-limbs.

ETIOLOGY includes lesions of the spinal cord or of the nerves supplying the rectum. Fractures and severe injuries of the sacrum, tumours of the sacral region, the toxins of infectious diseases, such as strangles, hæmoglobinuria, and thrombosis of the hæmorrhoidal artery, and old age are the usual causes of the condition. The paralysis may be complete or incomplete.

SYMPTOMS.—The walls of the rectum become distended by the accumulation of fæces, which they are powerless to expel. Colicky symptoms may supervene. The tail is limp and powerless, and the anus is open. Urine may escape involuntarily, due to accompanying paralysis of the bladder. There may be atrophy of the muscles of the hind-quarters.

PROGNOSIS depends on the cause of the trouble, which in the majority of cases is incurable.

TREATMENT.—The treatment is that for paralysis in general, including the administration of strychnine, or arsenic, and potassium iodide, and the use of the electric current. The rectum must be evacuated by the hand at intervals during the day. The paralysis, however, is usually progressive, and shows no response to treatment.

Spasm of the Anus

Spasm of the anus is a rare condition, but has been recorded as occurring in the ox, characterised by difficulty in defæcation and in passing the hand through the anal orifice. When the hand is in the rectum, the firm pressure of the sphincter on the arm can be felt.

Cure has been effected by cutting the sphincter subcutaneously.

Parasites in the Rectum

The larvæ of the *Œstrus equi* and the oxyures (*Oxyuris curvula*) adhere to the rectal and anal mucous membrane of the horse, and cause irritation, evinced by pruritus, stamping the ground with the hind-feet, rubbing the dorsum of the tail against the wall or side of the stall, straining, and slight colic, and by a varying degree of rectitis and proctitis. When the oxyures are present, the anus, the perinæum, and the inferior aspect of the tail are soiled by a viscid deposit, which gradually becomes dried to form a whitish scum containing the eggs of the parasite. The affected animals may lose condition.

TREATMENT.—For the larvæ of the gastrophilus, treatment consists in removing the parasites by the hand, or in giving rectal injections of soapy water or of a slight emulsion of petroleum or benzine (½ ounce to a gallon of water), while that for the oxyures comprises enemata of acidulated water (½ ounce of vinegar to the quart of water), or of thymol (1 in 1,000), or of perchloride of mercury (1 in 2,000).

AFFECTIONS OF THE URINARY ORGANS

AFFECTIONS OF THE KIDNEY AND URETER

SURGICAL intervention for kidney affections is seldom resorted to in veterinary practice. To ascertain when it is indicated requires a precise diagnosis, which can only be arrived at by careful local exploration and by an examination of the urine. Exploration includes inspection and palpation. Inspection may recognise a deformity in the costo-iliac space of the lumbar region caused by enlargement of the kidney or by a swelling in the perirenal tissue. Palpation may be practised externally and, in the large animals, *per rectum*. To perform palpation in the small animal, have it held in the standing, dorsal, or lateral position, and pass the fingers beneath the false ribs in the sublumbar region, where the organ will be recognised by its contour and consistence. In the large animal, the posterior border of the kidney may be reached by inserting the hand as far forward as possible *per rectum*. When it is enlarged it is more easily felt. Examination of the urine will reveal the various changes caused by disease in the structure of the kidney, and the presence or absence of bacteria in the liquid. The diagnosis of the various affections of the kidney is dealt with in works on medicine, and it is only those which may require surgical treatment that are referred to here.

Floating Kidney (Ectopia)

Floating kidney as a congenital or acquired condition is rare in veterinary patients except in the cat, in which both kidneys are normally of this nature. The displacement of the organ is recognised in the small animal on palpation through the abdominal wall.

SYMPTOMS.—When ectopia of the kidney occurs in the dog, pain may be evinced during exercise, caused by the tension exerted by the displaced organ on its pedicle.

TREATMENT, if necessary, consists in performing either nephropexia —fixation of the kidney by suturing its capsule to the abdominal wall— or nephrectomy.

Contusions of the Kidney

Contusions of the kidney are rare except in dogs as the result of being run over by motor-cars, when this and other internal organs may be badly injured.

SYMPTOMS comprise colicky pains, hæmaturia, alteration in the quantity of urine passed, there being oliguria at first, followed by polyuria in some cases, and perhaps a swelling in the lumbar region. If the ureter is ruptured or obstructed by a blood clot, hæmaturia may be absent.

PROGNOSIS.—Slight contusions are followed by recovery, but when the organ is seriously damaged death is likely to ensue from hæmorrhage or from pyelonephritis.

TREATMENT comprises rest, cold applications on the lumbar region, the hypodermic injection of ergotine, and, if the hæmorrhage persists, operation to suture the rupture in the gland or to perform nephrectomy, which is also indicated in pyelonephritis if the condition of the patient justifies it.

Open Wounds of the Kidney

Open wounds of the kidney may be caused by any sharp body penetrating the abdominal wall at its level, such as a bullet, or a trocar wrongly inserted in a case of tympany, or by the end of a broken rib.

SYMPTOMS.—There is more or less profuse hæmorrhage from the wound in the kidney. Urine rarely exudes therefrom. Hæmaturia is a constant symptom.

PROGNOSIS.—Slight wounds generally heal without complications, but there is always the risk of pyelonephritis or peritonitis ensuing. Hæmorrhage seldom proves fatal.

TREATMENT consists in adopting strict antiseptic precautions with regard to the open wound, taking measures to arrest hæmorrhage, suturing the renal wound when necessary, and performing nephrectomy when the condition of the organ indicates it. Packing the external wound with antiseptic gauze is a good means of excluding infection. Should a renal or perirenal abscess form, it must be opened and drained.

Renal Calculi (Renal Lithiasis)

The term *renal lithiasis* means the deposit in the kidney of salts from the urine in the form of :

1. *Sabulous material*, or fine sand.
2. *Gravel*, or small concretions resembling coarse sand.
3. *Small calculi*, or stones capable of passing through the ureter into the bladder.

4. *Large calculi*, incapable of passage through the ureter.

The number of stones varies. When small, they may be very numerous. There may be only one large calculus present, occupying the whole pelvis of the kidney and assuming its shape. In the horse the calculus may attain a weight of 4 pounds. In the ox it seldom exceeds the volume of a hazel-nut. A large calculus in the dog may weigh 3 ounces.

ETIOLOGY.—An excessive proportion of certain salts in the food or water may be followed by a deposit of some of these salts from the urine. The correlation existing between the frequency of calculi in the ox, composed of phosphate and carbonate of lime and magnesia, and the large proportion of these salts in the soil has often been noticed. Urinary calculi are common in districts where the soil is of a chalky nature. Sheep and cattle fed on roots and fodder grown on land heavily dressed with artificial manure or grazed on fields top-dressed with lime or basic slag frequently suffer from lithiasis. A too large proportion of nitrogenous material in the ration, especially if accompanied by insufficient exercise, favours the condition. For this reason sheep and lambs and young bovines fattened on cake, grains, and bran are often affected with calcareous urinary deposits. In old age the diminution of the consumption of mineral matter required for the upkeep of the bones predisposes to calculi formation. Catarrh or inflammation of the renal mucous membrane, with desquamation of its surface, leads to the production of small foreign bodies composed of epithelia or inflammatory exudate, on which lime salts become deposited.

SYMPTOMS.—Renal calculi may be present without causing any apparent trouble, and frequently are only detected incidentally on post-mortem examination. In some cases, however, decided symptoms are observed—viz., colic, hæmaturia, and stiffness of the loins and hind-quarters during movement. Renal colic has been most frequently met with in the dog, the animal being uneasy, showing an anxious expression, whining, making frequent attempts at micturition and passing urine in drops, and moving with the back arched and all the limbs gathered under the body. The patient in such cases refuses to feed, and death usually ensues. Local examination in the dog may enable the calculus to be felt, and pressure over the kidney may cause pain. Hæmaturia is excited or aggravated by movement and by straining. Anuria, hydronephrosis, and pyelonephritis are possible complications.

DIAGNOSIS is made out from the symptoms, which, however, are not always characteristic. When hæmaturia results from bleeding in the kidney, the blood is intimately mixed with the urine, which is thus coloured red from the beginning to the end of micturition, and when there is no history of an accident this is suggestive of renal calculus. Diagnosis can usually be confirmed by the use of X-rays, but it may be hard to interpret the photograph of a small calculus on the plate.

TREATMENT.—Medicinal and hygienic treatment usually have the desired effect in cases of sabulous deposit or gravel, but nephrotomy or nephrectomy is indicated when a calculus or calculi are causing trouble. Food too rich in salts of magnesium and calcium must be withheld, and more suitable food substituted. Linseed, barley, green food, and turnips may replace bran, oats, and beans. When cattle suffering from lithiasis are put to grass in the spring after being dry-fed during the winter the malady disappears. Bicarbonate of soda mixed with the food and a plentiful supply of water are advisable.

In the dog, as in the human subject, there are an acid lithiasis and an alkaline lithiasis. The former indicates diminution of nitrogenous food and that rich in oxalates, and the administration of alkalines and diuretics. Alkaline lithiasis is usually the result of pyelitis, and points to the treatment of that condition. If renal colic persist or suppuration of the kidney is evident, nephrolithotomy or nephrectomy is indicated (p. 485).

Calculi in the Ureter

Rarely a calculus in its passage from the kidney towards the bladder becomes arrested in the ureter, causing obstruction of the duct and leading to dilatation of its lumen by the accumulation of urine behind the seat of lodgment of the stone. Eventually the corresponding kidney ceases to secrete urine, and should both ureters be involved, or should the other kidney have already ceased to function as the result of disease, anuria will ensue, followed by uræmic poisoning and death.

SYMPTOMS of urinary colic may have been produced by the movement of the stone in the ureter; otherwise there is little to draw attention to the condition. On rectal examination in the large animal, the stone may be felt and the fluctuating ureter recognised in front of it. Some cases recorded in the ox were only discovered on post-mortem examination. When both ureters are occluded, the symptoms of uræmic poisoning will be observed.

DIAGNOSIS is very difficult and TREATMENT still more difficult. Nephrotomy would be indicated to enable a probe or sound to be passed into the ureter in the hope of dislodging the stone and allowing it to pass on to the bladder, a procedure not at all likely to succeed.

Pyelonephritis

Pyelitis means inflammation of the pelvis and calices of the kidney. It is usually associated with nephritis, constituting pyelonephritis. When pus is retained in the organ the condition is termed pyonephrosis.

ETIOLOGY.—The disease is duc to the entrance of pathogenic bacteria into the gland, which they may reach by way of the ureter (ascending infection) or through the blood stream (descending infection) or lymphatic system. In this way it may be the result of a general infection, of traumatic lesions of the kidney, or of septic affections of the bladder, urethra, vagina, or uterus.

In cases of coprostasis the colon bacillus may pass into the blood and become eliminated by the kidney. The lymphatics of the cæcum and colon anastomose with those of the renal capsule, and the latter with those of the gland itself, so that bacteria from the intestine may gain access to the kidney directly through the lymph stream.

Retention of the urine in the bladder, causing stasis of the liquid in the ureters and pelvis or its reflux towards these parts, favours very much the ascent of infection to the kidney in a case of cystitis or urethritis. The female is more often affected than the male, owing to the disease being frequently a sequel to parturition.

SYMPTOMS.—The symptoms, which are not always very definite, are local and general. The local symptoms comprise pyuria, pain, and swelling.

1. *Pyuria*, or the presence of pus in the urine, is the most constant symptom. It varies in quantity in different cases and at different times in the same case. Polyuria is also present. Pyelitic urine is nearly always alkaline and contains albumin, pus cells, blood corpuscles, renal casts, and epithelial cells. The urine is thick and whitish or lactescent, and clarifies slowly but incompletely when allowed to stand, the pus being gradually deposited on the bottom of the vessel.

2. *Pain* may be evinced on external palpation in the lumbar region in small animals and on rectal palpation in large animals. It may also be manifested by stiffness on movement.

3. *Swelling* may also be detected by manipulation, as in No. 2. In the large animal the ureter may be felt dilated, with the thickness of a child's arm.

The general symptoms indicate digestive disturbance, comprising anorexia and loss of condition. The skin is dry and the coat harsh and staring. The patient urinates more frequently than normal. In acute cases there is febrile disturbance, and renal colic may be observed.

PREVENTION consists in avoiding the causes as far as possible—*e.g.*, by careful treatment of septic lesions of the genital tract after parturition and by strict asepsis when passing the catheter.

TREATMENT.—Once the disease is established, treatment is of little or no avail. Milk diet, diuretics, and antiseptics to the urino-genital tract are indicated (salol, borate or benzoate of soda, hexamine). When pus has accumulated in the kidney, surgical intervention is necessary—viz., puncture of the organ, nephrotomy, or nephrectomy, which are only practicable in the small animal. Puncture would only give temporary relief. The administration of penicillin is indicated here as for all septic conditions which may be caused by gram positive organisms.

A strangles abscess may form in the kidney, with symptoms similar to those just described for pyelonephritis. It almost invariably proves fatal. The abscess may burst externally in the lumbar or inguinal region, and give rise to a fistula persisting for months or indefinitely.

Hydronephrosis

Hydronephrosis, or dropsy of the kidney, whereby it is distended by aseptic urine, may be partial or complete and congenital or acquired.

ETIOLOGY.—The condition results from some obstruction in the urinary tract causing stasis of the urine in the kidney. Abdominal and pelvic tumours, calculi in the ureters, and hypertrophy of the prostate are possible causes of the trouble. Congenital hydronephrosis is due to a fault of development, the ureter being absent or imperforate. When the obstruction is situated in the bladder, prostate, or urethra, both kidneys and both ureters are dilated.

DIAGNOSIS is seldom effected during life. The dilated kidney may be recognised as a fluctuating tumour in the abdomen, when puncture of the swelling will confirm the diagnosis. Intermittent hydronephrosis may be met with due to temporary obstruction of the ureter by a renal calculus on its way to the bladder.

TREATMENT consists in removing the cause, if possible, and, failing this, puncture of the kidney, nephrotomy or nephrectomy. Puncture only gives temporary relief, and the other operations are seldom performed and rarely successful in veterinary practice.

Tumours of the Kidney

Primary tumours of the kidney may be malignant (sarcomata, epitheliomata) or benign (fibromata, osteomata, myxomata, angiomata).

SYMPTOMS comprise hæmaturia, colic, and the presence of a more or less voluminous swelling inside the abdomen. The hæmaturia is spontaneous, occurring independently of movement. Cylindrical clots of blood may be found in the urine, representing casts of the ureter. One of these clots may obstruct the urethra, causing retention of the urine. The tumour can often be felt on rectal examination in the large animals and on external palpation in the small animals.

Nephrectomy is the only effective treatment.

Parasites in the Kidney

The *Eustrongylus gigas* infests the kidney of the dog in certain countries. It is reported as being common in sporting dogs in Tuscany.

SYMPTOMS comprise hæmaturia, dullness, loss of appetite, and in some cases more or less constant whining. Some patients display symptoms simulating rabies. Microscopic examination of the urine will reveal the eggs of the parasite when the female is present.

The PROGNOSIS is grave. Rarely the parasite is expelled spontaneously in the urine.

The only effective TREATMENT would be nephrotomy or nephrectomy. In some instances the parasite, after leaving the kidney, becomes fixed in the connective tissue in the perineal region, where it forms a swelling which, on being opened, will give exit to the worm.

AFFECTIONS OF THE BLADDER

The diagnosis of affections of the bladder is based on (1) functional disturbance, (2) local symptoms.

(1) **Functional Disturbance** includes interference with micturition and changes in the character of the urine.

Frequent micturition (sychuria) is indicative of a vesical calculus or cystitis.

Difficult micturition (dysuria) is due to feeble muscular contraction of the organ or to some obstruction to the flow of urine (stricture or calculus of the urethra or enlarged prostate). The patient makes frequent efforts at urination, but the liquid is only passed in drops or in a thin stream.

Painful micturition (strangury) accompanies cystitis and urethritis.

Incontinence and retention of urine usually point to vesical, urethral, or prostatic lesions. Hæmaturia, due to bleeding in the bladder, is the result of hæmorrhagic cystitis, or laceration of its lining by calculi, or of ulcerating vesical tumours.

In hæmorrhage occurring at the neck of the bladder the urine, as a rule, is only coloured red at the beginning of micturition, whereas, when arising from other parts of the organ, it is only observed towards the end of the process.

(2) **Local Symptoms** are revealed by palpation of the bladder and by passing the catheter. In the large animals palpation is performed *per rectum* in the male and *per vaginum* in the female. In the small animals palpation can be effected through the abdominal wall, or *per rectum* or *per vaginum* by means of the finger. Rigidity of the abdominal muscles may render external palpation difficult or impossible, but it can be overcome by general or epidural anæsthesia. Distension of the bladder and pain therein are readily recognised in the dog or cat by gentle pressure with the palm of the hand on the abdomen in front of the pubis when the animal is in the dorsal position and the muscles of the abdomen are relaxed. Digital vaginal or rectal examination may be combined with external manipulation.

Passing the Catheter

The Horse.—The catheter employed is usually of gum elastic, but it may be of rubber or coiled wire. It is about 3½ feet long and a little less than ½ inch in diameter, and provided with a stilette.

PROCEDURE.—Sterilise the instrument and take care not to allow it to become soiled. Have the horse held in the standing position, backed into a corner, with a fore-foot held up and a twitch applied if necessary. Stand at the level of the near flank, pass the right hand into the posterior extremity of the sheath, grasp the head of the penis firmly, and by gradual traction draw out the organ and extend it fully. Take the catheter, lubricated with pure vaseline or sterilised oil, in the left hand, introduce it through the meatus, push it gently towards the bladder, using a to-and-fro movement occasionally to overcome folding of the mucous membrane. When it has reached the level of the ischial arch, draw out the stilette for a distance of about 8 inches to facilitate the instrument turning round the curve in this region. When it has entered the pelvic portion of the urethra, reintroduce the stilette and continue the passage of the catheter into the bladder.

If there is difficulty in clearing the ischial curve, it can be overcome by an assistant exerting slight pressure on the instrument here so as to direct its extremity towards the pelvis. Evacuating the rectum before proceeding facilitates the operation. When the catheter has entered the bladder, withdraw the stilette and the urine will flow. Pressure on the bladder *per rectum* may be practised to promote the escape of the urine, but it is rarely necessary. For ponies and foals a catheter of smaller dimensions is required.

The Mare.—A gum-elastic or metal catheter about 10 inches long and ½ to ¾ inch in circumference is used.

PROCEDURE.—Have the animal controlled standing. Taking aseptic precautions, pass the hand into the vagina, and recognise the urethral orifice on the floor of the passage about 4 or 6 inches from the entrance to the vulva beneath a transverse fold of mucous membrane. Pass the finger into the meatus and glide the catheter along the former into the bladder.

The Ox.—In the ox, owing to the S-shaped curve on the penis, the catheter cannot be passed from the meatus into the bladder. The urethra can be sounded from its orifice as far as this curve after exposing

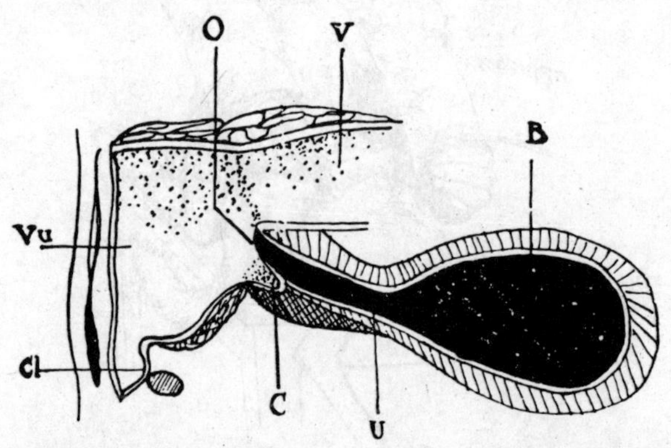

FIG. 306.—THE URINARY SYSTEM IN THE COW.
C, Cul-de-sac beneath meatus urinarus; V, vagina; Vu, vulva; B, bladder; U, urethra; O, orifice of urethra; Cl, clitoris.

the penis. After performing ischial urethrotomy the catheter can be passed into the bladder. A fine gum-elastic instrument is necessary to correspond to the narrow lumen of the urethra.

The Cow.—The procedure is similar to that for the mare, but rendered somewhat difficult by the lower wall of the urethra projecting backwards in the form of a valve, over which the catheter must be passed to enter the meatus. The instrument is apt to be arrested in the cul-de-sac beneath the valve posteriorly. Pass the finger first into the cul-de-sac, then glide it forward over the valve downwards into the urethra. Introduce the catheter alongside the finger into the bladder. A metal catheter about 8 inches long and ⅜ inch in circumference, with its anterior extremity bevelled like a flute, is the most suitable, but a narrow gum-elastic catheter answers the purpose admirably.

The Ram.—The urethra in the ram, owing to its filiform appendix and the curve on the penis, cannot be explored without a cutting operation to permit of the introduction of the catheter.

The Ewe.—The passage of the catheter of suitable size is a simple procedure.

The Dog.—Have the animal held in the dorsal position on the table, stand to the right of the patient with the left hand next the tail, and use a gum-elastic catheter whose diameter corresponds to that of the urethra. The human male catheters are suitable. Press forward the penis with the left hand and push back the prepuce with the right.

FIG. 307.—PASSING THE CATHETER IN THE DOG.

Introduce the lubricated sterilised catheter into the meatus, and pass it gently with a slight to-and-fro movement into the bladder.

The Bitch.—Have the animal standing or fixed in the ventral position on the table. Separate the lips of the vulva, and the meatus will be seen on the floor of the passage at a fair distance from its orifice. In a small animal it is not easily recognised without the aid of a speculum or forceps to dilate the vulva and vagina; a torch is useful to illuminate the passage. It may be felt with the finger inserted into the vagina. The catheter used for the male or one of larger calibre may be employed. It is easily passed into the bladder once the opening is observed.

The Male Cat.—The finest human metal catheter is suitable when straightened out. The instrument must be rigid and not thicker than a fine probe; about 6 inches is a convenient length. Have the cat in the dorsal position, extrude the penis, insert the catheter, sterilised, warmed, and lubricated, into the urethra perpendicular to the long axis of the body, bend the penis with the catheter *in situ* backwards, and push the latter forwards into the bladder.

The Female Cat.—The procedure is the same as in the bitch, but more difficult on account of the narrowness of the vagina.

Intravesical Exploration or Endoscopia of the bladder may be practised by external or internal light. By the former method light is reflected from outside through a tube introduced into the bladder and illuminates the small area of mucous membrane in front of the extremity of the tube. In the latter method a small electric lamp is carried into the interior of the reservoir and illuminates the greater part of its lining, and a series of lenses conveys an image of the illuminated region to the eye of the observer.

Disinfection of the Urinary Tract is indicated in many affections of the urinary apparatus, and is effected by the administration of certain agents which are eliminated by the kidneys—for example, benzoate of soda, salol, terebene, balsam of Peru, urotropine, helmitol (antiseptic and analgesic), and hexamine—and by the direct introduction of antiseptic solutions into the bladder, such as nitrate of silver (1 in 500), protargol (1 in 200), collargol (1 in 100). The bladder and urethra may be flushed out with weak antiseptic preparations—for instance, boric acid (3 to 4 per 100), silver nitrate (1 in 1,000), collargol or protargol (2 to 3 per 1,000).

Wounds of the Bladder

The bladder may be wounded by a foreign body penetrating it through the abdominal wall or *per rectum*, or from the perineal region, or by way of the urethra. It may be perforated by projectiles, or by splinters of bone in case of fracture of the pelvis. The wound may be extra- or intraperitoneal.

DIAGNOSIS is easy when the urine is seen flowing through the external wound. Otherwise the condition is suspected from the history and symptoms of the case, the situation of the external lesion, and the presence of blood in the urine.

PROGNOSIS.—Intraperitoneal wounds are almost invariably fatal. Those not involving the peritoneum may heal readily or result in the formation of a vesico-rectal, or vesico-vaginal, or vesico-cutaneous fistula.

TREATMENT.—For wounds perforating the wall of the bladder the only chance for recovery consists in performing laparotomy and suturing their borders. To succeed, this should be done early, before peritonitis has set in. The procedure, however, may be said to be hopeless in the large animals and to have little prospect of success in the small animals. The administration of an antibiotic may ward off peritonitis when done before the infecting organisms have proliferated. With regard to extraperitoneal wounds, the treatment aims at preventing infection of the wounded tissues, which are more or less infiltrated with urine and prone to become gangrenous if invaded by pathogenic bacteria. It may be advisable to leave a catheter in position to afford constant drainage for the urine, and thus prevent its infiltrating the tissues. When the latter has occurred, scarification is indicated where practicable, followed by frequent antiseptic irrigation. If a fistula ensues, it must be treated accordingly.

Foreign Bodies in the Bladder

Ulceration of the partition between the bladder and vagina or rectum may allow foreign matter to enter the former, such as fæcal matter, intestinal worms, embryonic debris, etc. Foreign bodies have been introduced into the organ maliciously and by the practice of sadism.

SYMPTOMS.—Foreign material in the bladder is soon followed by the deposit thereon of lime salts, causing the formation of calculi. Cystitis also ensues, as a rule, and symptoms of this condition and of vesical calculi are then observed.

TREATMENT consists in adopting the procedure used for the removal of stone from the bladder and the remedies advised for cystitis.

Rupture of the Bladder

Rupture of the bladder may be (1) traumatic or (2) spontaneous.

(1) **Traumatic rupture** is favoured by distension of the organ, and results from violent contusion of the abdominal wall in the antepubic region, as may be caused by a heavy blow or by falling on a projecting object. Even the force of an ordinary fall, as in casting, may rupture the viscus when it is over-distended. The rupture may be caused by the feet of the fœtus in the large animals during parturition. Pressure with the hands on the abdominal wall may be sufficient to cause rupture of the distended bladder in the dog or cat.

(2) **Spontaneous rupture** is usually a sequel to obstruction of the urethra by a calculus or a stricture, and is seen most often in the ox.

SYMPTOMS.—When the accident is due to retention of the urine, the pain thus caused suddenly subsides and the patient seems relieved, although no urine has passed through the urethra. On rectal examination the bladder is found to be empty. If the catheter is passed, a little blood may escape through it. After a while the expired air exhales an odour of urine.

Diagnosis.—When there is no history of urethral obstruction and consequent distension of the bladder diagnosis is difficult.

Prognosis is very grave, death ensuing, as a rule, in a few days, exceptionally after some weeks. Rare instances of spontaneous recovery in the ox have been recorded.

Treatment, as a rule, is useless. If the rupture is observed early in a small animal, immediate laparotomy and suture of the rupture may be followed by recovery.

Cystitis

Cystitis is due to invasion of the bladder by various pathogenic organisms (staphylococci, streptococci, and the colon bacillus, etc.). Predisposing causes of the condition are retention of the urine and injuries of the vesical mucous membrane. Infection may gain entrance through the urethra or by way of the blood or lymph stream. The excretion of irritant or toxic substances in the urine may cause cystitis, such as cantharides, turpentine, etc. The inflammation may be acute or chronic, and varies in character in different cases. It may be catarrhal, purulent, diphtheritic, gangrenous, ulcerative, or hæmorrhagic. The last mentioned is characterised by vegetations or fungoid patches on the mucous membrane, and is common in cattle in certain districts, the cause being unknown. It is of a chronic nature.

Symptoms of acute cystitis comprise frequent and painful micturition and the passage of purulent urine, which may be fœtid. There may be evidence of slight colic. Some pain is evinced on pressure of the bladder *per rectum*. The urine contains albumin, mucus, white blood corpuscles, and desquamated epithelium. It may also include false membranes, or separated gangrenous portions of mucous membrane, or red blood corpuscles (hæmorrhagic cystitis).

Prognosis.—Catarrhal cystitis is usually followed by recovery. The other forms are more serious, and require a guarded prognosis. The hæmorrhagic form peculiar to cattle defies treatment.

Prevention consists in avoiding the causes, including aseptic precautions when using the catheter.

Treatment.—The first indication is to deal with the cause of the trouble (calculi, toxins). Two other principles of treatment are: (1) to render the urine less irritant and disinfect the urinary tract by administering suitable agents (milk, soda bicarbonate, etc.), as mentioned before; (2) direct disinfection of the bladder through the urethra. The organ can be flushed out in the mare by the aid of a tube with an inlet and exit channel. The preparations suitable for action on the bladder have already been mentioned (p. 721)

Vesical Calculi

Vesical calculi are met with in all animals, but are most common in the horse, ox, and dog.

Etiology.—The general causes of urinary calculi have been discussed in connection with renal lithiasis. Primary vesical calculi form without any apparent lesion of the bladder, while secondary calculi are associated with some infection of the organ. Retention of urine, foreign bodies, and cystitis favour the deposit of salts.

Vesical calculi vary in number, volume, weight, form, and chemical composition. There may be one, a few, or a great number present (as many as 500 in the dog). In the horse a weight of 40 pounds may be reached. Their composition in herbivora is chiefly carbonate of lime and phosphate of lime and magnesia in varying proportions. In carnivora they are composed mostly of urate, oxalate, and phosphate of lime. As a rule they are free in the bladder, but occasionally a stone is fixed in the neck of the reservoir or embedded in its mucous lining.

Symptoms.—Sabulous matter in the bladder is ejected with the urine, and forms a deposit on the ground after evaporation of the liquid. In the ox and ram it is precipitated on the hairs at the preputial orifice. In the female it appears on the skin in the perineal region. A stone or stones too large to pass through the urethra may be tolerated for a long time in the bladder, but as a rule they give rise to colic, frequent micturition, and hæmaturia. There is often difficulty in urination, and evidence of pain during the process. Hæmaturia is most marked after exercise. There may be rectal straining, causing eversion of the anus. On rectal exploration the calculus can be felt. In the dog it can be palpated through the abdominal wall and *per rectum*.

Treatment.—The only effective treatment is operation to remove the calculus or calculi (see p. 425).

Prolapse of the Bladder

The bladder may be prolapsed in two different ways—*e.g.*:

1. It may escape through a rent in the floor of the vagina which has occurred during parturition, when it appears as a tumour inside the vulva or protruding between its lips, and is recognised by its relations and its smooth serous surface. It becomes distended with urine, and handling the organ causes escape of some of the liquid. The wound in the vagina can be felt. The condition is most common in the cow and sow.

The Prognosis is grave, as peritonitis and death usually ensue.

Treatment consists in returning the bladder to its normal position and suturing the rupture in the vagina, a difficult or impossible task.

2. It may be associated with prolapse of the vagina, the organ being turned back on itself and forming a swelling beneath the prolapsed vaginal wall varying in size according to the amount of distension with urine. The condition is distinguished by the fluctuation of the swelling, the pedicle attaching it to the vaginal floor, and by its communicating with the meatus urinarius, which is discovered on raising the prolapse, which also causes the escape of urine. Recovery is the rule with appropriate treatment.

Treatment consists in proceeding as for prolapsed vagina, returning the displaced organs to their normal position, and retaining them there by the usual methods of retention. The procedure is facilitated by evacuation of the bladder by the passage of the catheter, if possible, or by puncture of the viscus with a fine trocar and canula.

Inversion or Invagination of the Bladder

Here the bladder becomes invaginated through the meatus like a pocket turned inside out. It is not a common condition. It has been most frequently met with in the mare.

Etiology.—Relaxation or distension of the neck of the bladder and of the urethra must precede the inversion, which is brought about by violent straining, usually during parturition.

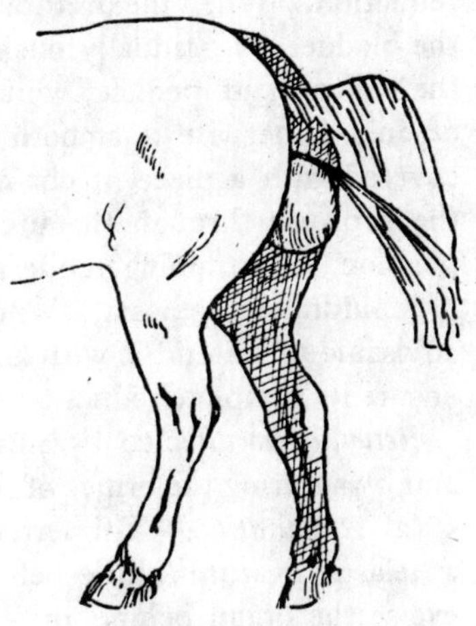

Fig. 308.—Inversion of the Bladder in the Mare.

Symptoms.—The condition appears as a reddish, round, or pyriform swelling, with a moist mucous surface, between the lips of the vulva, varying in size from that of a fist to that of a man's head. On its upper aspect and towards its anterior extremity are seen two little nipple-like projections formed by folds of the mucous membrane, and representing the orifices of the ureters. Urine exudes from the latter drop by drop, or escapes in squirts from the distended tubes when the organ is manipulated or the patient moves. The walls of the bladder become gradually infiltrated and thickened, and when it has been exposed for a long time the mucous membrane becomes dry and soiled and may undergo necrosis. The constant flow of urine causes dermatitis on the inside of the thighs.

DIAGNOSIS is easy from the nature of the swelling, its continuity with the meatus, and the presence of the two ureteral orifices.

PROGNOSIS is only serious when the organ has been torn or injured severely. The veterinarian may not be called in until days or weeks after the accident. Recovery may ensue, even after prolonged exposure, by suitable treatment.

TREATMENT comprises (1) reduction and retention, and (2) amputation, which is indicated when reduction is impossible or when the bladder is so altered that it is unfit to be returned.

(1) *Reduction and Retention.*—When the accident has occurred before parturition is accomplished, it is generally useless to perform reduction until after the event, as the straining during the process causes recurrence of the condition. To effect reduction, proceed as follows: Secure the animal in the standing position with the hind-quarters raised. Clean the mucous membrane with a warm, mild antiseptic solution (boracic acid, potassium permanganate), and in order to diminish the volume of the organ compress it gently with the fingers through an aseptic cloth or by means of an Esmarch bandage. The longer the prolapse is in existence, the more difficult is reduction. When the urethra is widely dilated, it is possible to return the bladder by gradually pushing it with the fingers of both hands in the region of its pedicle, while the thumbs compress the base of the organ. Otherwise a smooth cylinder of wood, with its extremity covered with a piece of chamois leather, may be used to invaginate the prolapse through the urethra, and thus return it to its normal position. If straining renders the operation difficult, induce general or epidural anæsthesia. When the organ has been replaced, it is advisable to distend it with an injection of sterilised boric solution to ensure its complete reduction.

Retention is effected by administering a narcotic to allay straining, and by suturing the orifice of the urethra if considered necessary.

(2) *Amputation.*—To perform amputation proceed thus: Apply an elastic ligature a little behind the orifices of the ureters, and then excise the organ behind the ligature or allow it to slough off. The ligature has a tendency to slip forward and include the ureters. To prevent this, either (*a*) make a groove in the mucous membrane to accommodate the ligature, or (*b*) apply a piece of tape longitudinally over the organ with one end on its upper and the other on its lower aspect, include the two parts in the ligature, and then unite their ends

by a knot after meeting them over the fundus of the prolapse ; the part behind the ligature falls away after about ten to fifteen days, and cicatrisation quickly follows. As the result of the operation the animal is deprived of a reservoir for the urine, which consequently dribbles over the thighs, causing a painful dermatitis. Notwithstanding this, Gaullet's patient worked for four years after the operation. A certain amount of urine accumulates in the anterior part of the vagina during rest, and is afterwards expelled by straining.

Another method of amputation is to dissect out the ureters for a distance of about 2 inches, rendered easy by inserting a rubber sound into the ureter. Suture the ureters to the vaginal wall after incising the mucous membrane at their level, and apply a ligature about ½ inch behind the point where the dissection of the ureters terminated. Coquat adopted this procedure, with excellent results, the urine being voided afterwards without coming in contact with the skin.

Tumours in the Bladder

Tumours affecting the bladder are rarely met with in animals. The dog is probably the most frequent sufferer. Papillomata and epitheliomata are the varieties that most commonly affect the organ, but it may also be the seat of fibromata, myxomata, lipomata, myomata, sarcomata, and carcinomata.

Symptoms comprise colicky pains, hæmaturia, and interference with micturition, as well as alterations in the walls of the bladder, recognised on vaginal or rectal examination. In the mare and cow it may be possible to feel the tumour directly through the urethra. The condition may be accompanied by a purulent cystitis. The use of the cystoscope would be a valuable aid to diagnosis, but is seldom necessary.

Treatment.—The only effective remedy is extirpation of the tumour, which is seldom practicable. If the growth is malignant the case is hopeless. It may be possible to operate through the urethra in the large animals, after performing ischial urethrotomy in the case of the male. In small animals prepubic cystotomy is indicated. Traction on the tumour through the urethra may cause eversion of the bladder and facilitate excision of the neoplasm. When a large portion of the bladder is involved or the disease is malignant, cystectomy and transplantation of the ureters may be practised, the ureters being anastomosed with the origin of the urethra. This delicate procedure is not likely to be adopted or worth while in veterinary practice.

Paralysis of the Bladder (Cystoplegia)

Paralysis may be confined to the sphincter, causing incontinence of urine, or affect the entire organ, when micturition is impossible and the urine is retained in the bladder.

ETIOLOGY.—Paralysis of the sphincter is most common in the dog and cat, and may be a consequence of old age, cystitis, prolonged retention of the urine, dilatation of the neck of the bladder by a calculus or a tumour, or an affection of the spinal cord. Complete paralysis of the bladder is a sequel to lesions of the brain or spinal cord ensuing from fracture of the vertebræ, medullary hæmorrhage, and cerebral tumours. It often coexists with paralysis of the rectum and tail. It may occur temporarily after castration or during an attack of colic or hæmoglobinuria in the horse, or post-partum paralysis in the cow or other animal.

The PROGNOSIS depends on the cause. Except it is due to some temporary indisposition, the condition is usually incurable.

TREATMENT is as usual for paralysis, consisting in administering potassium iodide and nux vomica internally, or strychnine hypodermically, and practising electrotherapy and massage of the bladder in addition to evacuating the organ at intervals by gentle pressure thereon or by passing the catheter.

AFFECTIONS OF THE PROSTATE

The prostate may be involved in traumatic injuries of the urethra, rectum, and perinæum. The lesion is dealt with on general principles.

Prostatitis

Prostatitis may be acute or chronic, and is rare in the horse and ox, but comparatively common in the dog. It is frequently purulent, and then generally terminates fatally.

ETIOLOGY.—The cause may be a calculus or calculi arrested in the pelvic portion of the urethra, repeated careless passage of the catheter, injury by a foreign body in the rectum, or the condition may accompany cystitis or urethritis, or be the sequel to the administration of irritating drugs which are excreted through the urine (cantharides, etc.).

SYMPTOMS.—There is interference with defæcation and micturition. The former is performed with difficulty, and is usually painful. Obstinate constipation may be present. There is a constant desire to urinate. The urine may be passed freely and with little pain, or there may be dysuria or ischuria, and marked pain during micturition. There may be febrile disturbance.

DIAGNOSIS.—The condition simulates cystitis and urethritis, but on rectal palpation the prostate is found to be swollen, tense, and painful. The swelling may be confined to one of the lobes of the gland.

TREATMENT comprises:

(1) *Warm enemata.*

(2) *Hot fomentations* and *compresses* in the perineal region. Anodyne agents may be associated with (1) and (2), such as the green extract of belladonna or liquor opii or a hot decoction of poppy heads.

(3) *Hypodermic injections* of morphia to relieve pain.

(4) *Evacuation of the bladder*, when there is retention of urine, by the use of the catheter, or, if its passage is difficult, by puncture with the trocar and canula.

(5) *Laxative medicine* and *milk diet.*

(6) *Opening an abscess* when present. It may burst into the urethra or rectum, or in the perineal region. It should be opened where it is felt fluctuating. When fluctuation is in the rectum, evacuate the latter and wash it out with a solution of boric acid or potassium permanganate and open the abscess with a concealed bistoury in the large animal, and with a trocar and canula in the small animal.

Hypertrophy of the Prostate

Hypertrophy of the prostate is common in dogs, especially in old subjects. It would appear to be due to a chronic prostatitis, showing little evidence of inflammation except a hyperplasia of its stroma and a proliferation of its epithelial cells.

SYMPTOMS.—The first indication of its presence is constipation. Then micturition becomes frequent and eventually difficult. This difficulty is most marked at the commencement of the act. It is only after considerable effort that urine is passed.

DIAGNOSIS is arrived at by rectal exploration, when the abnormal condition of the gland is revealed. When the hypertrophy is of long standing and the gland much enlarged, retention of urine may ensue. Perineal hernia and hydronephrosis are possible complications.

PROGNOSIS is unfavourable, as the condition is incurable except castration is performed.

TREATMENT consists in adopting the measures recommended for prostatitis. These, however, have only a palliative effect. It is best to perform castration at once. Hobday had striking success with this treatment.

Tumours of the Prostate

Tumours of the prostate are rare in all animals. Sarcoma and carcinoma have been seen affecting the gland in the horse, ox, and dog.

The SYMPTOMS are similar to those of hypertrophy. There may be cachexia. Rectal palpation confirms the diagnosis.

TREATMENT.—R. H. Smythe (*Vet. Rec.*, March 10th, 1945) records remarkable success in the treatment of tumours affecting glandular tissue in the dog by the injection of *large* doses of stilbœstral dipropionate, including a case of a large tumour of the prostate which caused great difficulty in defæcation and urination with prolonged straining and fits of screaming.

Prostatectomy is impracticable without performing cystectomy, which would necessitate dissecting out the ureters and putting them into communication with the rectum, a troublesome, delicate, and difficult operation.

At the Annual General Meeting of the British Empire Cancer Campaign in London in 1943 attention was drawn to "the dramatic and striking results obtained by the treatment of malignant disease of the prostate with synthetic œstrogens."

AFFECTIONS OF THE URETHRA

Congenital Deformities

Congenital deformities comprise:

1. Constriction of the meatus and a variable portion of the tube.
2. Imperforate uretha.
3. Hypospadia.
4. Epispadia.

1. **Constriction** is recognised by the narrow stream of urine which escapes through the meatus. The remedy is to incise the canal as far as the stricture extends.

2. **Imperforate Urethra** has been seen in all species of animals. The imperforation may be due to an adhesion between the lips of the meatus, or to the presence of a membrane stretching across some part of the canal, or to a complete absence of the latter, its place being taken by a fibrous cord. In the last case there may be an orifice posteriorly through which the urine escapes, or the only exit for the liquid may be a pervious urachus.

TREATMENT.—Open an occluded meatus with the knife and rupture an abnormal membrane with the catheter. When the urethra is blind for a long distance, nothing can be done except to enlarge an existing orifice if necessary. The skin in the scrotal region may be inflamed from the passage of urine over it from the abnormal meatus. Smear the affected part with vaseline as a protection against the irritation.

3. **Hypospadia** is a fissure in the lower wall of the urethra and penis at a variable distance behind the glans. When the fissure is in the scrotal or perineal region, the anterior part of the penis is atrophied and the animal appears to be hermaphrodite. Dermatitis ensues in front of the orifice from irritation by the urine.

TREATMENT.—The only treatment adopted in veterinary practice is to enlarge the fissure if it is too small for the free exit of the urine. The operation performed on the human subject might be tried on an animal. It consists in making a new canal in the lower aspect of the penis from the fissure to its free extremity, and then closing the two lips of the fissure by sutures, after freshening their borders.

4. **Epispadia.**—Epispadia is an abnormal opening or fissure on the upper wall of the urethra and penis. Like hypospadia, it interferes with the proper discharge of the urine and prevents impregnation in the sire by diverting the course of the semen. It is treated similarly.

Injuries of the Urethra

The urethra may be wounded accidentally, especially in the dog. A urinary fistula persists for a variable time, but healing eventually ensues. There is always the danger of stricture ensuing from cicatricial contraction. If there is not a free exit for the urine through the wound, the tissues may become infiltrated and gangrene may ensue. It is best to treat the wound as recommended after urethrotomy—viz. to leave it open and dress it antiseptically.

Rupture of the Urethra

The urethra may be ruptured as the result of a severe contusion of the perineal region. The rupture may be partial, confined to the mucous membrane, or complete, involving all the coats of the duct.

SYMPTOMS.—The first symptom observed is bleeding from the urethra. There may be retention of urine. Later the tissues in the vicinity become infiltrated with urine, and then gangrene usually supervenes, with perhaps a fatal result. When recovery occurs, stricture of the urethra is a common sequel.

DIAGNOSIS is made from the history, the presence of a perineal swelling, and bleeding from the urethra. If a catheter is passed, it is arrested at the seat of the rupture.

TREATMENT.—When the rupture is complete, cut down on the lesion, pass a catheter into the urethra, and leave it in position. If the tissues are not badly damaged, the edges of the wound may be sutured over the catheter; otherwise leave it open and apply an antiseptic solution. When the mucous membrane only is affected, treatment is expectant.

Urethral Abscesses

A urethral or periurethral abscess may result from injury and infection of the duct. The abscess may open into the lumen of the canal and be followed by recovery or by urinary infiltration and the subsequent formation of urinary fistulæ through gangrenous tissue, or it may burst externally. An abscess may occlude the urethra and cause retention of the urine. A catheter passed for the purpose of diagnosis may rupture the abscess, and be followed by a discharge of pus and a flow of urine.

TREATMENT consists in providing drainage for pus and infiltrating urine, and applying antiseptic solutions to the breaches of surface. When urine is retained, puncture of the bladder may be necessary. When gangrene is threatened or present penicillin should be administered.

Urethritis

Urethritis is rare in veterinary patients. Balano-posthitis has been mistaken for it in the dog.

ETIOLOGY.—It is generally traumatic in origin, following wounds and contusions of the duct. Gonorrhœa has never been demonstrated in the domesticated animals. A granular urethritis has been observed in the horse in hot climates during the summer, causing gradual stenosis of the urethra.

SYMPTOMS are a muco-purulent discharge from the urethra, swelling and redness of the lips of the meatus, and pain during micturition.

DIAGNOSIS is confirmed by observing that the discharge escapes through the meatus, and is therefore not due to inflammation of the prepuce.

TREATMENT is (1) internal and (2) local.

(1) *Internal treatment* comprises the prescription of demulcent drinks, diuretics, and antiseptics to the urinary tract.

(2) *Local treatment* consists in injecting into the urethra suitable astringent antiseptic lotions (potassium permanganate 1 in 1,000,

etc., and in chronic cases 2 per cent. silver nitrate), and in the granular form the removal of the granulations by curetting or by excision of the free end of the urethra, when the disease is confined thereto.

Urethral Calculi

Urethral calculi occur in all the domesticated animals. They comprise :

1. **Calculi** which originate in the urethra as the result of stagnation of the urine behind a constriction, and are of rare occurrence.

2. **Migratory calculi** which have originated in the bladder and become arrested in the urethra. In the latter situation they become increased in volume by further concentric deposits from the urine. The urethra becomes dilated above the obstruction.

There is usually only one calculus, but there may be several present. The terminal portion of the urethra in the male may be occluded by material composed of mucus and urinary sediment.

The Horse.—The usual seat of urethral calculi in the horse is the intrapelvic portion of the tube in the ischial region. The navicular fossa may be filled with a concretion, compressing and obstructing the meatus.

SYMPTOMS.—There is more or less obstruction to the flow of urine, which may be in drops or a thin stream, or completely arrested. It may be blood-stained. Symptoms of more or less violent colic are observed. When the urethra is occluded, the bladder will be found on rectal examination to be distended. The occlusion might be due to spasm of the neck of the bladder, stricture of the urethra, or a urethral calculus. If the terminal portion of the urethra is obstructed, waves of urine may be noticed behind the obstruction caused by contraction of the accelerator urinæ and of the muscular walls of the bladder, and the stone may be felt here by compressing the tube with the fingers, or a hypodermic needle inserted into the swelling will grate on the calculus, and when the catheter is passed it will be arrested at its level. Small calculi may be expelled with the urine. A large one causing complete obstruction will be followed by rupture of the bladder if relief is not promptly forthcoming.

TREATMENT.—Extraction of the calculus is the only treatment. This may be effected (1) by the meatus, or (2) through an artificial opening.

(1) *Extraction by the meatus* is easy when the stone is near the anterior extremity of the urethra. It may be possible to grasp it

through the meatus with a forceps or to force it out with the pressure of the fingers and thumb. An injection of oil into the tube facilitates its displacement.

(2) *Extraction through an artificial opening* (see pp. 428 and 429).

The Ox is the most frequent sufferer from urethral calculi, due in great part to the fact that the urethra gradually diminishes in calibre from behind forwards, and that the penis forms an S-shaped curve behind the scrotum. Calculi which escape from the bladder become arrested and undergo increase in volume at the level of the curve. The most common seat of lodgment is the first or anterior curve, but sometimes they reach the second or posterior curve.

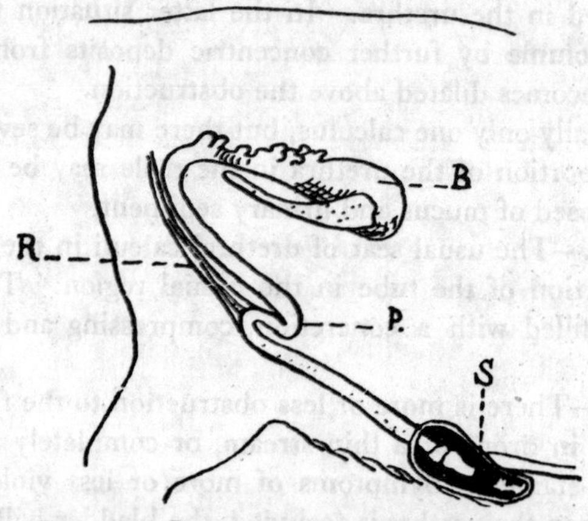

FIG. 309.—PENIS AND SHEATH OF THE BULL.
P, Penis at sigmoid curve; B, bladder; R, retractor penis; S, sheath.

SYMPTOMS.—When the urethra is not completely obstructed there is merely dysuria, but later when the calculus becomes increased in volume and totally occludes its lumen there are ischuria and retention of the urine, causing colic, agitation of the tail, stamping with the hind-feet, and vain efforts at micturition. The animal may lift the hind-limbs almost perpendicularly in attempting to kick at the abdomen in the prepubic region. Waves of urine in the urethra may be observed in the perineal region. On rectal examination the voluminous, hard, spheroidal, distended bladder is felt. When the calculus is at the level of the curve it may be felt through the skin in a thin subject, while in a fat animal pain only may be revealed on pressure in this region. Rupture of the bladder is a common complication.

Treatment is palliative or curative, the former consisting in providing an artificial opening for the urine by performing ischial urethrotomy or puncturing the bladder, while the latter is carried out by operating and removing the stone as described (p. 428).

The Ram.—A sabulous deposit is common in the vermiform appendix of the urethra in the ram, especially in the highly-bred animals, whose diet is rich in phosphates of ammonia and magnesia.

SYMPTOMS.—The usual symptoms of urethral obstruction are observed. The patient is dull and restless, breathes quickly, stands with the back arched, or lies down more than usual, and makes vain efforts to micturate, a few drops of urine only being passed. If not relieved promptly death will ensue, as in the ox.

TREATMENT.—Preventative treatment consists in avoiding the cause (see Renal Lithiasis). Curative treatment consists in clearing the urethra of the deposit or calculi. Warm fomentation and gentle massage of the appendix may succeed in removing the obstruction there. If these measures fail, either remove the appendix, as is often done by shepherds, or, if there is a calculus at the S-curve or other part of the urethra, perform urethrotomy and remove it.

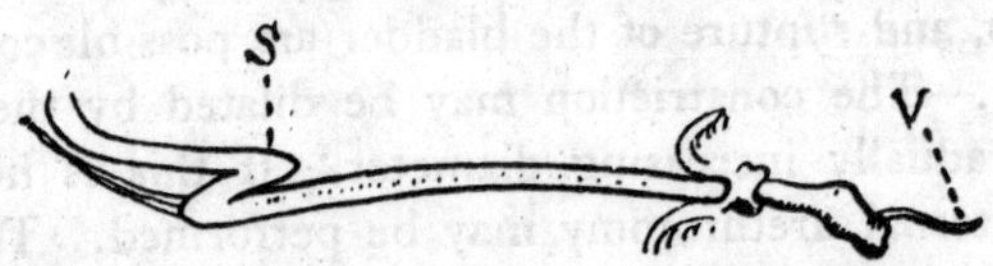

FIG. 310.—PENIS OF THE RAM.
V, Vermiform appendix; S, sigmoid curve.

The Pig.—Urethral calculi in the pig cause symptoms similar to those mentioned for the ram. Surgical removal is the only effective treatment.

The Dog.—Urethral calculi are fairly common in the dog, especially in aged subjects. The usual seat of lodgment is the gutter of the os penis or immediately behind the bone.

SYMPTOMS.—There are obvious symptoms of obstruction to the flow of urine—frequent attempts at micturition, with passage of urine in drops, and eventually evidence of uræmic poisoning. The catheter will locate the obstruction.

TREATMENT.—Operate and remove the obstruction (p. 431).

The Cat.—The castrated male suffers fairly often from a sabulous obstruction of the terminal portion of the urethra, causing retention of urine and marked distension of the bladder.

TREATMENT.—It may be possible to dislodge the material by pressure with the fingers on the penis or by means of a fine metal catheter. Immediate puncture of the bladder is advisable to prevent its rupture and to facilitate displacement of the deposit by removing the pressure behind it. It may be necessary to incise the urethra.

Urethral Calculi in Females

Urethral calculi in the female are rare in all species of animals. Gray has recorded a case in the bitch in which he successfully removed a stone the size of a marble by an incision in the meatus, under chloroform.

Stricture of the Urethra

Stricture of the urethra is the result, as a rule, of cicatricial contraction following a wound or severe inflammation of the duct. Rarely it is congenital.

SYMPTOMS.—Micturition is slow and performed with difficulty, the urine appearing in a thin stream or only in drops. Urination is frequent, as a rule. The passage of the catheter will reveal the site of the stricture.

PROGNOSIS.—The condition becomes gradually worse. Cystitis, pyelonephritis, and rupture of the bladder are possible complications.

TREATMENT.—The constriction may be dilated by the passage of bougies of gradually increasing diameter. If this is not sufficient, internal or external urethrotomy may be performed. The former is done by a special instrument, which is passed into the urethra beyond the stricture, which it incises on being withdrawn, while the latter is performed, as described (p. 425), to cut the stricture from the outside. In each case it is necessary to continue passing the catheter at intervals to prevent recurrence of the condition, which, however, usually ensues, despite this precaution. Ischial urethrotomy may be performed as a palliative measure when the stricture is below the ischium.

Tumours of the Urethra

Tumours of the urethra are not common, but some cases have been recorded. They are more frequent in the female than in the male, and are usually pedunculated.

SYMPTOMS are those of chronic urethritis or stricture.

DIAGNOSIS is not always easy in the male, as the tumour cannot be seen or felt directly except it is near the meatus. In the large female it is comparatively easy.

TREATMENT.—If the tumour is near the meatus it may be removed through the latter, and if farther back it can be excised after opening the urethra. Stricture is apt to follow excision.

Retention of the Urine

Retention of the urine has already been referred to as a complication of conditions obstructing the urethra, and as the result of paralysis of the bladder. It may also be due to spasm of the neck of the organ. Sometimes the retention is incomplete, a small quantity of urine being emitted after severe efforts to micturate.

Diagnosis of the condition has been dealt with (see Paralysis of the Bladder).

Treatment consists in (1) evacuating the bladder at once by passing the catheter or puncturing the organ, the latter being generally the better and easier procedure (see p. 432); and (2) removing the cause of the trouble, if possible. Spasm of the neck of the bladder has been overcome by injecting into it an aqueous solution of atropine *per rectum*, also by a hypodermic injection of cocaine beneath the anus.

Incontinence of Urine (Enuresis)

The impossibility of retaining the urine has also been referred to as occurring in conditions which interfere with the function of the sphincter vesicæ. The urine escapes drop by drop, and causes an acute eczema of the skin of the hind-limbs by constantly trickling over it.

Treatment consists in removing the cause of the trouble, when possible. The treatment for paralysis is usually indicated.

Infiltration with Urine and Urinary Abscess

Infiltration with urine and urinary abscess are due to a solution of continuity in the urinary tract, whereby the urine escapes into the surrounding tissues. When the liquid is discharged in small quantity it tends to become encysted, forming a urinary abscess, but when the quantity is large the tissues are infiltrated.

Symptoms.—The urinary abscess causes a circumscribed fluctuating swelling, while infiltration gives rise to a diffuse engorgement of an œdematous nature, which pits on pressure. In the latter case the overlying skin soon sloughs in patches, leaving ulcerated areas, discharging a greyish fluid containing gas and fragments of dead tissue. Symptoms of uræmic poisoning and bacterial toxæmia ensue, and death may supervene.

Treatment.—The principles of treatment are to (1) provide an exit for the infiltrating urine, (2) clear the normal course of the urine if it is obstructed, and (3) administer penicillin.

(1) To carry out the first indication, scarify the infiltrated area with

the knife or thermo-cautery and dress the wounds with an antiseptic solution (eusol, hydrogen peroxide, Lugol's solution, penicillin solution).

(2) This is effected according to its nature. It is advisable to leave a catheter *in situ* for some time to prevent further escape of urine through the wound in the urethra.

Urinary Fistulæ

Urinary fistulæ may be congenital or acquired. The former are due to a vice of development, and the latter to an accidental breach in the urinary tract, and are referred to in connection with wounds of the urethra, kidney, etc. A congenital fistula of the bladder opens at the umbilicus or into the intestine.

Pervious Urachus.—The urinary fistula at the umbilicus is due to non-closure of the orifice of the urachus at birth. The condition is fairly common in the foal, but rare in other animals.

ETIOLOGY.—The fistula may be due simply to failure of the urachal orifice to close, or the latter may be forced open by the pressure of the urine, due to atresia or congenital occlusion of the urethra. It has also been attributed to the cord being ruptured too close to the abdominal wall.

SYMPTOMS.—The urine is observed escaping at the umbilicus in drops or in a stream immediately after birth, or in some cases not until a few days afterwards. The fistulous orifice is in the centre of a swelling varying in size from a nut to a hen's egg. When the urethra is patent, a certain amount of urine passes through it also.

PROGNOSIS.—When the urethra is normal, spontaneous closure of the fistula generally ensues, otherwise it will persist. Although recovery is the rule when the urethral passage is clear, there is always the risk of urinary infiltration of the tissues, with its possible consequences, in the umbilical region.

TREATMENT.—The first indication is to ascertain if the urethra is clear by observing the animal during urination or by passing a catheter. If it is permanently occluded the case is incurable, and the fistula is left open while the animal is being prepared for the butcher, if it is a calf or a lamb, provided that no complication ensues. If the urine is being voided freely through the urethra, adopt some of the following measures to bring about closure of the fistula :

(1) *The application of a blister* round the orifice.

(2) *Needle-point firing* the surrounding tissues.

Both (1) and (2) cause inflammatory swelling which promotes closure of the opening, the latter being much more effective than the former.

(3) *Ligation* of the urachus. This is effected by passing a strong pin through the lips of the urachus and applying a ligature above the pin, or by passing a strong needle furnished with thread in the same way through the tissues, cutting the two parts of the thread close to the needle and ligaturing the part in two halves.

(4) *Inserting a pin suture* through the skin and urachus.

Nos. (3) and (4) are the surest methods of causing obliteration of the opening.

Other urinary fistulæ are dealt with on general principles, which are to ensure a clear flow of urine through the urethra to treat the wound antiseptically, and take steps to promote the escape of urine from the tissues if they are infiltrated.

AFFECTIONS OF THE MALE GENITAL ORGANS

Anomalies of the Testicle

ANOMALIES of the testicle comprise :

1. *Anomalies of development* with regard to (*a*) the number, and (*b*) volume of the glands.

2. *Anomalies of migration*, including (*a*) abnormal arrest of the organ in some part of its course towards the scrotum (cryptorchidism), and (*b*) its passage outside its normal course to occupy an abnormal situation (ectopia testis).

1. **Anomalies of Development**—(*a*) *Abnormal Number.*—The existence of more than two testicles (polyorchidism) has not been definitely established. Recorded cases are not authentic. The epididymis and the testicle have been mistaken for separate glands, and the presence of a hard cyst on the cord has been diagnosed as an extra testicle.

The absence of one testicle (monorchidism), or of both (anorchidism) is a rare but well-known occurrence. It has been frequently proved on post-mortem examination of the cryptorchid horse in which operation had failed to discover the missing testicle.

(*b*) *Anomalies of Volume.*—*Hypertrophy* of one testicle is generally observed when the other testicle has been arrested in development, which is usually the case in ectopia and retention of the organ. Both organs are rarely hypertrophied. The retained testicle is often much enlarged from the presence therein of a cyst or teratoma.

Atrophy of the testicle is, as a rule, unilateral and congenital. The affected organ may be in the scrotum, but it is more frequently retained in the abdomen or inguinal canal. It may be so rudimentary that it is not recognised when an attempt is being made to remove it, and may then be considered as practically absent. The condition, however, may be acquired from pressure on the organ by hydrocele or inguinal hernia.

2. **Anomalies of Migration.**—One or both testicles may be arrested in their course before reaching the scrotum, constituting (*a*) *inguinal or incomplete retention*, when the testicle is situated in the inguinal canal ; and (*b*) *abdominal or complete retention*, when it is retained inside the abdomen. In some cases of retention the

epididymis or the vas deferens alone, or both, are in the canal, while the testicle is in the abdomen. This is spoken of as incomplete abdominal retention. In each instance there is a tunica vaginalis enclosing the portion of the apparatus in the canal.

There is ectopia of the testicle when the organ is outside the abdomen, but not in the scrotum. This abnormality is probably most common in the ox, in which the testicle is often found beneath the skin on the abdominal wall, and usually alongside the prepuce. In the dog it is sometimes found anterior to the scrotal region.

The terms *monorchid* and *cryptorchid* are loosely applied. The former may mean an animal in which there is absence or simply retention of one testicle, and the latter one in which one or both testicles are retained. They may be also used in connection with animals affected with ectopia testis. The popular terms for horses and cattle affected with these abnormalities are rig and rigling.

The cause of retention of the testicle is not always very clear. Improper functioning of the gubernaculum testis, or insufficient length of the fold of peritoneum suspending the testicle, or a too narrow inguinal orifice, or abnormal size of the gland, due to the presence of a cyst or a teratoma, may account for the organ failing to enter the inguinal canal or scrotum. There is an hereditary predisposition to the abnormality.

The Horse.—In the foal the testicles are generally in the scrotum at birth or arrive there before the tenth month after birth. Rarely they are not fully down until the twelfth or fifteenth month. Retention is usually unilateral, but occasionally it is bilateral. In the former case statistics have shown that the frequency of retention is about equally divided between the right and left sides. In most cases the retained testicle is more or less abnormal in size and consistency; it is generally small and flabby, as in the fœtus. Its tissue is greyish or pinkish, and contains no spermatozoa. Its weight may not exceed 1 ounce, or it may be so rudimentary that it is hardly recognisable. On the other hand, the retained testicle may be greatly enlarged, due to its being cystic or teratomatous, when it is also much altered in shape.

The teratoma may be composed of cartilage, bone, teeth, or hair, or a combination of these structures, or, rarely, it may be sarcomatous or carcinomatous. Its weight in such cases greatly exceeds the normal, and may even attain 100 pounds. One or several sclerostomes may be found in the centre of the abnormal organ.

In the abdominal cryptorchid the tail of the epididymis is widely separated from the testicle. There may be a distance of 4 to 6 or even

8 inches between them, the intervening portion being in the form of a flexuous cord. The gland is suspended by a roughly triangular fold of peritoneum stretching from the sublumbar region to the bladder, its upper fixed border being parallel to the long axis of the body, while of its two free borders the antero-inferior carries the spermatic vessels and the postero-inferior the vas deferens. From its outer aspect another fold of peritoneum passes outwards, to be fixed to the lateral border of the pelvis, and having along its inferior border the abdominal portion of the gubernaculum testis, which extends from the region of the internal inguinal ring to the tail of the epididymis and to the testicle. The membrane may be only slightly developed.

The testicle is usually free and movable in the abdomen, and generally rests on the abdominal floor in the inferior region of the flank, just in front of the pelvis, but it may be mixed up with coils of intestine, or situated in the sublumbar region, or on the upper aspect of the bladder. In exceptional cases it is adherent to the wall of the abdomen or to an abdominal organ.

DIAGNOSIS of cryptorchidism is generally easy when the animal has been under observation for some time, for then he usually displays all the propensities of the stallion, although the testicles are absent from the scrotum. He may show a greater sexual appetite than the entire, and be consequently more difficult to control, especially in the presence or vicinity of other horses, particularly mares. He may chase and kill sheep by worrying them. Occasionally, however, the rig is as docile as the gelding. He may have the appearance of a stallion, showing a well-developed neck and crest, or there may be nothing in this respect to suggest that the subject has not been castrated.

On the other hand, a gelding may behave like a rig, and be operated upon as such, but when the inguinal canals are opened, each is found to contain the stump of the severed cord and the cremaster muscle attached thereto. This behaviour of the gelding has been ascribed to cutting the horse " proud "—that is, leaving the epididymis—but it occurs apart from this. Rigs are often sold and resold as geldings, their condition not being detected until they have been in the buyer's possession for some time. On exploring the inguinal region of the cryptorchid, there is no evidence of the testicle or cord in the scrotum of the affected side.

When the testicle has been removed, a well-formed scar marks the site of the operation and the skin is depressed and decidedly puckered or thrown into folds at this point. The stump of the cord is adherent to the skin at the level of the scar, and if the extended fingers be pressed backwards and forwards and laterally over the integument in this region, the cord will be felt rolling beneath it and can be followed upwards into the inguinal canal. When a scar is present as the result of an unsuccessful attempt at castration of the rig, it is not accompanied by puckering of the skin and the cord cannot be felt. In the standing position the scar is best seen from behind after having the limb of the same side taken forward.

If the testicle is in the inguinal canal, it may be felt by pushing the fingers up the interstice through the external inguinal ring. The easiest way to find the latter, when the horse is standing, is to place the palmar surface of the fingers on the abdominal wall alongside the sheath and pass them backwards until the ridge of fibrous tissue extending from the inside of the thigh and continuous with the external border of the ring is felt, and then glide them into the canal immediately to the inside of this point. Rectal exploration will reveal the cord entering the internal inguinal ring in the inguinal cryptorchid, and may enable the testicle to be felt if retained in the abdomen. This method of diagnosis, however, is seldom necessary, and is not very reliable.

When the horse is put in the dorsal position, an inguinal testicle may appear outside the external inguinal ring or be more easily felt than in the standing position. The action of the cremaster muscle may draw it out of reach occasionally.

CASTRATION.—See p. 385.

The Ox is seldom affected with cryptorchidism. The condition is similar to that in the horse. (See p. 400.)

The Ram.—Retention of the testicle is occasionally met with in the ram, and should be borne in mind when examining the animal for stud purposes. (See p. 400.)

The Pig.—Non-descent of the testicle is fairly common in the pig. (See p. 400.)

The Dog.—One or both testicles may fail to reach the scrotum in the dog. In such cases the animal is generally treacherous and more troublesome sexually than the normal subject. (See p. 401.)

DIAGNOSIS can only be confirmed by performing laparotomy and exposing the organ or organs.

The Cat is fairly often affected with cryptorchidism.

Ectopia of the Testicle

In all cases where the testicle is absent from the scrotum, a careful search should be made for it in other parts of the inguinal region and on the abdominal wall before deciding that it is retained in the abdomen.

Traumatic Lesions of the Scrotum and Testicle

Contusions and open wounds of the scrotum and testicle may be caused in various ways and give rise to the usual local symptoms of these conditions. A varying degree of inflammation ensues, accompanied by œdema, causing a swelling in the vicinity of the affected part. Narrow punctured wounds are dangerous when they penetrate all the coverings of the gland, as they may be followed by infection of the serous membrane, and consequently by peritonitis. The testicle may be released from its coverings by a deep extensive wound. This is often the case in dogs as the result of fighting.

TREATMENT is on general principles, consisting in the employment of antiphlogistic, antibiotic, and antiseptic agents. In the horse a suspensory bandage may prove beneficial to support and relieve the pain in an inflamed testicle. When the testicle or tunica vaginalis has been penetrated castration is generally indicated, but if the wound is incised, recent, and apparently aseptic, an attempt may be made to conserve the gland by dusting the wound with sulphanilamide powder and suturing it, thus aiming at healing by first intention.

Inflammatory Affections of the Scrotum and Testicle: Orchitis and Vaginalitis

Superficial inflammatory conditions are confined to the skin of the scrotum, and comprise excoriations, eczema (common in the dog), and dermatitis caused by cold, mostly seen in the ox as the result of the scrotum coming in contact with snowdrifts. They are treated on general principles. The dog affected with acute scrotal eczema has a peculiar straddling gait.

Deep lesions include orchitis and vaginalitis, which may be primary or secondary, and acute or chronic.

The term *sarcocele* has been applied to all abnormal enlargements of the testicle, but there is a tendency now to confine it to acute and chronic inflammation of the gland and its coverings.

Vaginalitis, epididymitis, and orchitis may exist separately or conjointly, but vaginalitis is usually a sequel to inflammation of the testicle or epididymis.

ETIOLOGY.—The cause of the inflammation may be traumatism, an irritant applied in the scrotal region, or the toxin of an infectious disease such as glanders, tuberculosis, dourine, or chronic pyæmia, or the presence of the *Strongylus armatus* in the testicle. A case was recorded in the *Veterinary Record* of a six-year-old Clydesdale stallion being rendered sterile as the result of a blister applied on the hocks being transferred to the scrotum by the tail and causing intense inflammation of the testicles, followed by atrophy of the glands.

Orchitis has been seen apparently resulting from infection from the intestinal tract, when it usually follows an attack of colic. This form of the disease has been studied by Vallée and others under the title of infectious epididymo-vaginalitis of the horse, the causal organism being a streptobacillus.

SYMPTOMS.—When the condition is toxic in origin, febrile disturbance is generally the first symptom noticed, the animal being dull, off its feed, and showing a rise of temperature. The patient is stiff in the loins and moves with difficulty, and the limb of the affected side is abducted. There is well-marked local inflammation, the testicle and cord being swollen and painful. Pus may collect in the vaginal sac and a diffuse œdematous swelling may form in the vicinity.

In the specific form alluded to above one or both glands may be involved. Vaginalitis is practically always secondary to epididymitis or orchitis. As the result of fibrinous exudation adhesion occurs between the two serous surfaces, and at castration the testicle is found adherent to the tunica vaginalis.

TREATMENT consists in applying the local remedies for inflammation and administering alkaline, laxative, and absorbent medicine internally. Rest and warm moist compresses, kept in position by a suspensory bandage, are indicated, and should be frequently renewed. Soda bicarbonate and potassium iodide should be given daily in the drinking water. The inflammatory phenomena subside, as a rule, in the course of eight to ten days, but a chronic form of the condition may ensue for which the application of mercurial or iodine ointment may be prescribed, with, however, little chance of effecting a cure. When suppuration has occurred in the vaginal sac an abscess will form there, and burst externally if it is not opened. When the substance of the testicle is not involved, recovery, with conservation of the gland, may ensue in the course of four to six weeks after evacuating the pus and dressing the cavity antiseptically but when the animal is not of much value as a sire it is better to remove the affected organ.

In the specific form of epididymo-vaginalitis the usual prophylactic measures for a contagious disease are indicated. Fodder suspected of carrying infection should be withheld and intestinal antiseptics administered. The serum of horses recovered from the disease has a prophylactic and curative effect when injected subcutaneously into a susceptible or affected subject, the dose being about 100 c.c. once daily for five days. The simplest and most effective treatment, when the animal is not required for the stud, is castration, both testicles being removed in the infectious form of the malady.

Hydrocele—Hæmatocele

Hydrocele, or the accumulation of serous fluid in the sac of the tunica vaginalis, is usually the result of a chronic vaginalitis following an injury to the scrotum, but in the gelding it is most commonly a sequel to castration (see p. 376). It may accompany ascites. When blood is mixed with the fluid it is called hæmatocele, and when fluid is collected in the folds of the tunica vaginalis propria it is spoken of as spermatocele.

SYMPTOMS.—The condition is characterised by the presence of a non-inflammatory, soft, fluctuating swelling in the scrotum, anterior to the testicle in the entire, the gland being fixed to the tunica vaginalis posteriorly.

DIAGNOSIS from other conditions in this region is easy, and all doubt can be removed by exploratory puncture, which causes the escape of a serous, amber-coloured liquid. The quantity present varies from a few ounces to a couple of quarts. There may be false membranes present, causing the condition to assume the nature of a multilocular cyst. It is most likely to be confused with inguinal hernia (see p. 674).

PROGNOSIS.—In the stallion the pressure of the liquid causes atrophy of the testicle, otherwise it has no ill-effects.

TREATMENT.—The local application of absorbents or irritants and the internal exhibition of diuretics have little or no effect. Simple aspiration of the liquid is soon followed by a recurrence of the affection, but when associated with an injection of freshly prepared tincture of iodine it may have the desired effect. The injection causes acute inflammation, which gradually disappears in ten to twelve days. There is a risk, however, of peritonitis ensuing from the irritant reaching the peritoneum. Occurring in an ordinary colt, the best treatment is castration by the covered method, placing the clams high on the cord, so as to remove as much as possible of the tunica vaginalis.

Scirrhous Cord (Champignon, Funiculitis)

The above terms are applied to a chronic inflammatory condition of the spermatic cord following castration. It has been dealt with as a complication of the latter operation (see p. 374).

Varicocele or Cirsocele

This is due to a varicose condition of the veins of the spermatic cord. It is not common in animals, although well-marked cases of it have been found in the horse and ox. It may be congenital, or develop at any age. The cord assumes the nature of a soft, knotty, elongated tumour of varying size in different cases. It causes no inconvenience, as a rule, but in rare instances the enlarged cord becomes strangulated in the inguinal canal, giving rise to all the symptoms of strangulated inguinal hernia, from which it may not be diagnosed until the operation for the latter is attempted.

TREATMENT is seldom required except the enlargement is great or strangulation has ensued. It consists in performing castration by the clams or ligation method as the surest means of guarding against hæmorrhage from the dilated vessels.

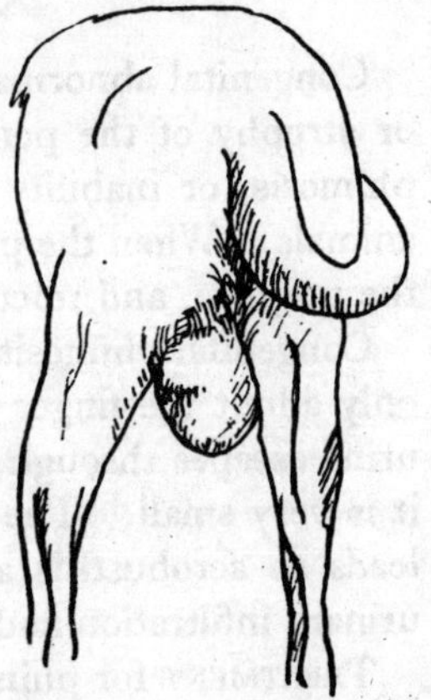

FIG. 311.—CARCINOMA OF THE TESTICLE IN THE DOG.

Aneurismal Varix

This is an aneurism in the cord, caused by the spermatic artery opening into the spermatic vein. It is similar to varicocele, and dealt with as such.

Tumours of the Testicle

Tumours of the testicle are fairly common in the horse, ox, and dog, carcinoma and sarcoma being the varieties most frequently met with. Lymphadenomata, chondromata, myxomata, fibromata, osteomata, and dermoid and dentigerous cysts have also been found affecting the organ.

SYMPTOMS.—The symptoms are as usual for a new growth. The testicle is enlarged, hard, often nodular, and devoid of inflammation.

DIAGNOSIS is easy.

PROGNOSIS is grave when the tumour is malignant, as recurrence is usual after excision of the testicle, and the operation may precipitate metastasis. When the lymphatic glands in the vicinity are involved, operation is contra-indicated.

TREATMENT consists in performing castration as high up on the cord as possible. The horse may work for a year, or even longer, after excision of a cancerous testicle.

Tuberculosis of the Testicle

Tuberculosis of the testicle has been observed in the bull, pig, dog and cat, and at least one case has been recorded in the horse.

The SYMPTOMS are those of orchitis and epididymitis associated with hydrocele. The disease is nearly always secondary in this situation, and does not call for treatment. Rarely it is localised in the cord as the result of inoculation through the castration wound, and is then dealt with as scirrhous cord.

AFFECTIONS OF THE PENIS AND SHEATH

Congenital Abnormalities

Congenital abnormalities of the penis and sheath comprise absence or atrophy of the penis, its torsion, its adhesion to the sheath, and phimosis, or inability to protrude the organ. They rarely occur in animals. When the penis is rudimentary it is situated in the depth of the prepuce, and micturition occurs into the latter.

Congenital phimosis is due to a narrow preputial orifice, which may only admit the finger in a large animal or a probe in the dog. The urine escapes through this opening in a thin stream or in drops when it is very small. The constant irritation of the prepuce by the urine leads to acrobustitis and balanitis, which may be complicated with urinary infiltration and with ulceration or gangrene of the sheath.

Treatment for phimosis consists in enlarging the preputial opening by excising a portion of the sheath inferiorly and suturing the edges of its internal and external layers on each side where the excision has been made. It is best to make the excision anterior to the orifice when the sheath extends in front of this point. It may be possible to separate adhesions between the penis and prepuce, and prevent their recurrence by the repeated application of a lubricant.

In a case of atrophy of the penis, the only remedy is to excise a sufficient portion of the inferior region of the sheath to permit of micturition without the urine coming in contact with its lining, the two layers of the skin being sutured on each side as above. A mesial incision may first be made and then a portion on each side excised, or a V-shaped outcut may be made in the lower wall of the sheath. The lower wall of the sheath may be incomplete in the pup, leaving an orifice through which the penis may protrude and perhaps become strangulated if not relieved. The treatment is to freshen the edges of the opening and bring them together with sutures. An autoplastic operation may be necessary on the same principle as that for blemished knee (see p. 456). Excise the edges of the orifice and then proceed as indicated. The ordinary preputial opening is normal in this case.

Traumatic Lesions of the Penis

When the penis is exposed, and particularly in the state of erection, it is subject to contusions and open wounds, which are dealt with on general principles and are usually followed by recovery. When the erectile tissue is involved, copious hæmorrhage may ensue even from a small punctured wound. A hæmatoma resulting from a contusion may be slow to disappear.

The penis in the horse may be wounded by the whip. It has been mistaken in the sheath in the scrotal region by the lay castrator for a testicle, and included in the clam, with fatal results from occlusion of the urethra and rupture of the bladder.

The bull may fracture the penis against the ischium of the cow.

In the dog the organ is most frequently injured during coitus by violent separation or by bites from other dogs. Rarely the bone is fractured. As the result of injury, the penis may become more or less distorted and paraphimosis may ensue. The urethra may be concerned in the lesion (see Affections of the Urethra).

TREATMENT varies according to the nature of the lesion, and is on the usual lines for a contusion or open wound. Suturing may be sufficient to arrest slight hæmorrhage, and if an artery is seen bleeding it should be ligatured. The thermo-cautery may be required to arrest hæmorrhage from a deep punctured wound. Erection excites hæmorrhage, and should be avoided by isolating the patient and administering potassium bromide. A suspensory bandage is useful as a support and protection to the organ when it is outside the sheath. Incision of a hæmatoma is contra-indicated here on account of the risk of severe hæmorrhage and the danger of infection in this region. When irreparable injury has been inflicted on the penis its amputation is necessary. Adhesion of the penis to the sheath has been seen as the result of injury and ulceration of the opposing surfaces.

Strangulation of the Penis

Strangulation of the penis arises from the application of a ring or cord round the organ, and is most common in the dog. In the bull the repeated protrusion and withdrawal of the penis may cause the preputial hairs to become twisted round the organ a few inches behind its extremity. When the organ is forcibly protruded the hairs may rupture or become embedded in its surface, acting as a ligature and causing necrosis of the part in front. The gangrenous end of the organ is easily recognised. The urine may escape through several holes in the dead tissue.

Treatment.—In all cases remove the cause of the trouble, prescribe antiseptic lotions for the wounded part, and fomentations and gentle massage to diminish the swelling. Cure is the rule when the urethra has not been occluded. When the end of the penis in the bull becomes necrotic the dead portion sloughs off and recovery follows.

Acrobustitis—Balanitis—Balano-Posthitis

Acrobustitis, or inflammation of the prepuce, and balanitis, or inflammation of the surface of the free portion of the penis, may occur independently, but usually they are associated, constituting balano-posthitis. The conditions affect all the domesticated animals, but are most common in the ox, which is predisposed to them by the peculiarities of the sheath. The long, narrow prepuce of the ox, lined by a mucous membrane rich in sebaceous glands, favours inflammation, as does also the fact that the penis is not protruded during urination, thus allowing the urine to come in contact with the preputial lining and smegma to accumulate in the front of the passage. The bull is less liable to these affections than the bullock, owing to the greater calibre of the prepuce and the more frequent protrusion of the penis in the former.

The Horse—Etiology.—The causes of the trouble in the horse comprise urinating into the sheath, lying in dirty, wet litter, the accumulation of smegma in the sheath, the secretion becoming fœtid and irritant, tumours and swelling of the sheath, and anything which prevents extension of the penis therefrom. In some districts horses suffering from colic or showing difficulty in urination are treated by rubbing the penis with an irritant like pepper, which leads to inflammation, ulceration, and sometimes necrosis of the affected parts. Sometimes a large amount of smegma accumulates around the corona glandis, filling up the urethral sinus and interfering with or preventing urination by pressure on the urethra.

Symptoms.—The inflammatory condition of the sheath is obvious. When the urethra is occluded by smegma in the suburethral sinus, the horse evinces the same symptoms as in a case of urethral calculus. Examination of the sinus reveals the cause of the trouble. The accumulated smegma may be as hard as a stone. Phimosis or paraphimosis may be present.

Treatment consists in removing the cause of the condition as far as possible. When it is due to an accumulation of smegma, the horse must be cast, the penis withdrawn from the sheath, and the latter washed with hot water and soap, and then treated with an astringent lotion or an antiseptic emollient powder. When there is ulceration of the affected region, an antiseptic emollient ointment or, better, B.I.P.P. is indicated as a lubricant and protective. When the suburethral sinus is filled with smegma it must be extracted. If the material is in the form of a concretion, it may be necessary to break it with a forceps or dig it out with a stout director. Whenever a horse shows difficulty in urination this sinus should be examined.

The Ox.—In the ox the cause may be some foreign matter gaining entrance to the sheath, such as the head or portion of the stem of grass, or particles of sand ; or an injury, due to direct violence, followed by infection of the injured part ; or a specific infection of the same nature as contagious vaginitis in the cow, and usually contracted during service. The contagion, however, may also be conveyed through the bedding.

SYMPTOMS.—A longish, hot, painful swelling first appears in front of the sheath, and may extend as far as the scrotum. Urination is difficult, and the urine is passed in drops or in a fine stream. The prepuce cannot be drawn back over the penis. Phimosis exists. In the prepuce a grey-black smegma is found, the removal of which gives pain. On rectal examination the bladder may be felt distended and painful on pressure. Colic soon sets in, the patient ceases to feed, and if relief is not promptly afforded will die from rupture of the bladder. Infiltration of the tissues round the prepuce may ensue, and be followed by sloughing of the latter, and perhaps of the penis as well. Recovery may take place even after a portion of the penis has sloughed off.

TREATMENT.—The first indication is to ensure that there is a sufficient exit for the urine. If the sheath is completely occluded, the bladder must be punctured *per rectum* at once.

The next procedure is to clean out the sheath as follows : Cast the animal and fix it in the left lateral position, with the right hind-limb fixed to the shoulder ; cut the hairs at the entrance to the prepuce, and wash the part with hot water and soap. Smear the index finger with vaseline, pass it into the prepuce, and extract the sebaceous matter collected there, or, if necessary, introduce a blunt curette for the purpose. Irrigate the sheath with warm solution of boric acid or potassium permanganate. Repeat the injections for a few days. In a case of long standing the preputial opening is constricted, and it may be necessary to incise the sheath inferiorly to enable its interior to be cleaned as described.

An alternative procedure in the latter case is to open the sheath at the level of the extremity of the penis, evacuate it of the accumulated material as before, and pass a seton or drainage tube through the anterior portion of the passage. The urine will escape through the two openings while the seton is in position, but when it is removed after a few days the incision will heal.

If the anterior part of the prepuce is permanently occluded, excise a V-shaped piece of the sheath at the level of the point of the penis.

Baldoni advises section of the retractor penis, so that the glans penis will be situated at the level of the entrance to the sheath, and thus avoid urinating into the latter. The operation is performed in the same way as post-scrotal urethrotomy until the penis is exposed, when the retractor is severed behind its insertion into the second curve.

The Pig.—The umbilical pouch in the upper wall of the sheath and close in front of its opening may become distended by its own sebaceous secretion, especially in the castrated animal. The material may become hard, forming preputial calculi.

SYMPTOMS.—Swelling and inflammatory symptoms are observed in the affected region, and local examination reveals the nature of the condition.

TREATMENT consists in cleaning out the sheath in the same way as in other animals.

The Dog.—Acrobustitis in the dog is more of the nature of a catarrh than an inflammation. It is characterised by a greenish, purulent discharge, which moistens and agglutinates the hairs at the preputial opening. The dog frequently licks the part. There may be no evidence of inflammation. It has been erroneously called gonorrhœa, for the urethra is not involved. The catarrhal condition is very common. In well-marked chronic cases the follicles of the mucous membrane become swollen, and the latter undergoes thickening and induration, and may show granular enlargements or vegetations on its surface.

TREATMENT.—Slight cases do not require treatment, but when the discharge is comparatively copious it may be diminished by astringent injections into the sheath such as sulphate or sulphocarbolate of zinc (1 to 2 per cent.), or tannic acid (3 to 5 per cent.), or potassium permanganate, or chinosol (1 in 1,000).

Phimosis

Phimosis, or inability to protrude the penis from the sheath, may be congenital or acquired. The congenital abnormality has been dealt with (p. 748). Phimosis is caused by anything which obstructs or constricts the preputial orifice, such as inflammatory or œdematous swelling, or a neoplasm or cicatricial contraction.

SYMPTOMS.—The symptoms of the cause of the trouble are observed.

TREATMENT consists in dealing with the lesion which has given rise to the condition.

Paraphimosis

Paraphimosis, or inability to withdraw the penis into the sheath after protrusion, occurs occasionally in all animals, but is most common in the dog.

ETIOLOGY comprises inflammatory or œdematous swelling, paralysis, or a new growth affecting the penis. In the dog it may appear after coitus, when it is favoured by the circular erectile swelling round the penis in front of the prepuce. When the organ is being retracted into the sheath some of the preputial hairs may be drawn with it into the preputial opening, forming a wedge between the penis and the sheath,

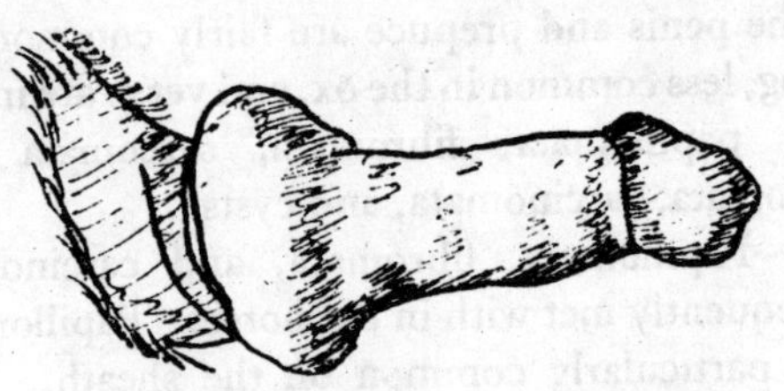

FIG. 312.—PARAPHIMOSIS IN THE DOG.

and tending to prevent complete return of the organ. The swelling which ensues from this constriction aggravates the condition. In the horse a ridge of fibrous tissue may form round the penis as the result of chronic balanitis, and prevent its entrance into the sheath.

TREATMENT.—The obvious treatment is to remove, if possible, the cause of the condition by the adoption of appropriate measures. When it follows coitus in the dog, steps should be taken immediately to return the penis to the sheath as follows: Place the dog in the dorsal position on the table. If the organ is soiled, bathe it with warm water and apply liquid paraffin on its surface as a lubricant. If the preputial hairs are turned in, clip them off. Push the penis backwards with one hand while the other endeavours to draw the sheath forwards over the organ. If the penis is much swollen, use cold or hot applications to reduce its volume. If these measures are insufficient, incise the sheath at its orifice to relieve the stricture and enable the penis to be returned.

When due to chronic balanitis in the horse, Vennerholm's operation is indicated (see p. 423).

After service in the bull there has been observed a protrusion of the membrane covering the penis, forming a reddish-brown tumour about the size of a fist in front of the prepuce, with an orifice in its centre through which the urine is passed. The mucous membrane of the sheath at the point of its reflection on the penis does not follow the movement of the organ on its withdrawal after copulation in this case, but becomes detached from it, forming the swelling mentioned. Astringent lotions may be sufficient to reduce the prolapse ; if not, it must be excised after inserting a series of ligatures through the periphery of its base. The writer operated in this way on a yearling Aberdeen-Angus bull in which the tissue removed was found to contain a tuberculous lesion.

Tumours of the Penis and Prepuce

Tumours of the penis and prepuce are fairly common in the horse, mule, ass, and dog, less common in the ox, and very rare in other species. They comprise papillomata, fibromata, sarcomata, melanomata, myxomata, adenomata, carcinomata, and cysts.

The Horse.—Papillomata, fibromata, and carcinomata are the varieties most frequently met with in the horse. Papillomata, warts, or angleberries are particularly common on the sheath. They may be isolated or multiple. They often occur in clusters, and when infiltrated with urine round the preputial orifice give rise to a fœtid odour. Maggots may appear between them in the summer. Fibromata are subcutaneously situated in the form of " apple " or " potato " tumours, which escape when an incision is made over them, or fall out spontaneously in some cases through sloughing of the overlying skin. Carcinoma is usually confined to the penis, forming an angry, fœtid, granular-looking mass round the glans.

TREATMENT.—Complete excision is the only effective remedy. Papillomata may be so numerous and so close together that radical operation would involve the removal of too much skin ; then the operator must be content with excision of them on a level with the latter, and repeat the operation when they recur. Carcinoma or any malignant growth on the penis necessitates amputation of the organ.

The Ox.—Papillomata may form a cluster round the preputial orifice. They may be attached inside and only protrude when the penis is extended ; occasionally the organ itself is involved.

The chief difficulty in removal of growths on the penis is to get the organ exposed for the purpose. It, however, protrudes spontaneously under the influence of epidural anæsthesia (see p. 208). If it cannot be protruded after casting and anæsthetising the beast, it is best to incise the sheath at the level of the tumour, draw the penis partly through the wound with the finger, and then excise the growth. The thermo-cautery may be lightly used to arrest hæmorrhage. When the beast is completely anæsthetised, it is generally fairly easy to protrude the penis from the sheath if spontaneous protrusion does not occur.

The Dog.—Venereal tumours, sometimes called infective sarcomata, are common in the dog, affecting the surface of the penis and more or less of the lining of the sheath. The commonest seat of the growths is the base of the penis and the sheath in this vicinity, but any

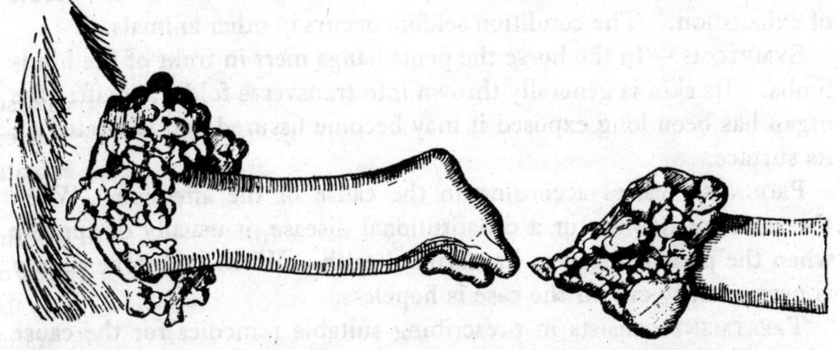

FIGS. 313 AND 314.—VENEREAL TUMOURS OF THE PENIS IN THE DOG.

part of the organ may be affected, and in some instances it is practically covered with them. The disease also affects the vulva and vagina of the female, and is transmitted from one sex to the other by copulation. The condition would appear to be of bacterial origin, but no causal organism has been found in connection with it.

SYMPTOMS.—The first symptom observed, as a rule, is a sanguinolent discharge from the prepuce. When the new growths are well developed, they cause a swelling of the sheath at their level. On exposing the penis, the cauliflower-like enlargements are readily recognised.

TREATMENT consists in complete excision of the tumours. When practicable, it is advisable to suture the membrane over the site of excision. When the tumours are very numerous, successive operations at intervals of a week may be necessary. If there is a suspicion of recurrence in the operation wound, the latter should be cauterised with silver nitrate. It is usually possible to operate even on the base of the penis after protruding it from the sheath, but if necessary the latter may be incised at its depth to facilitate removal of a tumour in that region, the preputial wound being afterwards sutured. Care must be exercised in examining stud animals, lest they be affected with this disease.

Paralysis of the Penis

Etiology.—Paralysis of the penis may be the result of an injury causing more or less damage to its nerves, or it may be of toxic origin, accompanying some bacterial disease, such as influenza in the horse. The penis in the horse may hang limp as if paralysed when the animal is debilitated from any cause. Numerous cases of this kind were observed in military horses during the First World War as the result of exhaustion. The condition seldom occurs in other animals.

Symptoms.—In the horse the penis hangs inert in front of the hind-limbs. Its skin is generally thrown into transverse folds, and after the organ has been long exposed it may become fissured and ulcerated on its surface.

Prognosis varies according to the cause of the affection. When the result of debility or a constitutional disease, it usually disappears when the patient recovers its normal health. When the nerve supply is permanently cut off the case is hopeless.

Treatment consists in prescribing suitable remedies for the cause of the trouble, when it is apparent, and adopting the usual measures for combating paralysis, including massage of the retractor penis between the anus and scrotum, and electrotherapy. When the paralysis appears without obvious cause or is associated with progressive paralysis of the hind-quarters, treatment is of no avail. If the horse is able to work, the penis may be supported and protected by a leather sling or, preferably, it may be amputated. In the case of the stallion, excitement of sexual desire by bringing the horse into the presence of a mare in season may stimulate innervation and favour recovery.

AFFECTIONS OF THE FEMALE ORGANS OF GENERATION

Exploration.—Diagnosis of affections of the genital organs may require careful and methodical exploration. It comprises *inspection* and *palpation.*

Inspection.—To inspect the interior of the vulva and vagina, and the os uteri, insert a vaginal speculum and illuminate the parts by means of an electric torch. Simply everting the lips of the vulva by the hands or fingers will enable a considerable portion of its interior to be viewed.

Palpation may be external or internal. Internal palpation may be vaginal or rectal. It is performed by the hand in the large animals, and by the index finger in the small animals. The patient being suitably controlled and aseptic precautions being taken, the hand or finger, lubricated with vaseline or liquid paraffin, is gently introduced into the vaginal passage.

Rectal examination in the large animal affords valuable information as to the condition of the uterus, ovaries, and Fallopian tubes. In small animals the uterus can be palpated through the abdominal wall by putting the patient on its back and compressing the abdomen with the fingers and thumb between the umbilicus and the pubis. To examine the cervix uteri in the cow, it is drawn backwards outside the vulva by means of a special forceps grasping the lip of the os.

Vaginal Irrigation may be effected by means of a syringe or india-rubber tube and funnel. The solution employed should be made with boiled water and used at the body temperature. Suitable lotions for the purpose are potassium permanganate (1 in 1,000), boric acid (4 in 100), lysol (1 in 100), carbolic acid (1 or 2 in 100), hydrogen peroxide (1 in 4 or 5), perchloride of mercury (1 in 2,000 or 5,000) containing 0·5 per cent. tartaric acid, acriflavine (1 in 1,000), solution of penicillin, etc. Any of these preparations used morning and evening will disinfect the vagina and os uteri when suffering from ordinary infection.

Uterine Irrigation is best performed by means of a rubber tube and funnel, the former being carefully introduced into the uterine cavity. A special bifurcated tube may be used with advantage having an inlet and an outlet portion, so that the fluid escapes from the uterus according as it is introduced instead of accumulating in the organ and requiring to be removed afterwards, as with the ordinary tube. It does not always work satisfactorily. The double-acting pump is also suitable when not worked too forcibly. It can be employed as an injector, and as an aspirator to remove the fluid from the uterus. The solution used should never be allowed to remain in the uterus. If it is not expelled by the expulsive force of the organ, it should be siphoned off or withdrawn with the aspirating syringe.

Toxic irritant preparations should be avoided. The following lotions used at the body temperature are suitable: potassium permanganate (1 in 1,000), biniodide of mercury (1 in 5,000 or 10,000) containing sufficient potassium iodide to ensure its solution, boric acid (3 to 4 in 100), lysol (1 in 100), hydrogen peroxide (diluted with 1 to 4 parts of water), iodine in weak solution (1 in 1,000 or 2,000) or in strong solution (2 or 3 in 1,000), carbolic acid (½ to 1 in 100). Perchloride of mercury (1 in 5,000) may also be employed, but it is not advisable for cattle, on account of their susceptibility to mercurial poisoning. Iodine solution is the antiseptic agent most in vogue at present for chronic cervicitis and metritis.

When the uterus contains much septic material, it should be first flushed with boiled water or normal saline until the liquid comes out clear; then one of the agents mentioned can be introduced. Four or five gallons of water may be required to thoroughly wash out the uterus in the mare or cow.

R. H. Smythe (*Vet. Rec.*, July 25th, 1942) draws attention to the facility with which rupture of the bovine uterus can be caused by uterine injections, basing his remarks on experimental injections of methylene blue by means of a Higginson's rubber enema syringe into twelve healthy non-gravid uteri immediately after their removal from the warm carcases. His findings were:

(1) The fluid passing through the rupture does not enter the peritoneal cavity but goes between the double peritoneal folds of the broad ligament.

(2) The minimum amount of fluid to cause rupture was 6 ounces in Guernsey heifers and 10 ounces in young cows which had borne two calves.

(3) The margin of safety would appear to be 3 to 4 ounces in heifers and 6 ounces in multiparous cows.

He concludes that rupture in this way must have occurred in the past not by puncture, but by the force of the fluid. He has observed on several occasions that, using the quantities of liquid usually recommended, pain, straining, loss of appetite, and prolonged cessation of lactation ensued.

AFFECTIONS OF THE VULVA

Contusions

Contusions of the vulva are rare except as the result of injury during parturition. They present the usual features of a contusion, and are dealt with accordingly. A hæmatoma may result similar to that of the vagina.

Open Wounds

Open wounds are usually caused by injuries inflicted during delivery of the fœtus, but occasionally they are caused by external violence. The rig sometimes bites the vulva of the mare.

TREATMENT is on general principles, with the same precautions as for vaginal wounds when following parturition.

Rupture of the Perinæum

Rupture of the upper commissure of the vulva and a varying portion of the perinæum is occasionally caused during parturition, especially in primiparæ. The rupture may be :

1. *Incomplete*, in which the sphincter ani is intact ; or
2. *Complete*, involving the sphincter ani and the ano-rectal mucous membrane, and causing the vaginal and rectal cavities to become confluent, with the result that fæces and urine escape through a common orifice.

In both cases the separation of the lips of the wound and their constant soiling by excrement prevent their union. During progression the entrance of air through the solution of continuity into the vulva or vulvo-rectal cavity causes a noise, and the mare affected with the condition is consequently spoken of in some places as a " fluter." The edges of the wound are often jagged, and after cicatrisation form a fringe inside the vulva. Cicatricial bands may also be formed across the cavity. When the vagina and rectum are in communication, the former will contain fæces and its mucous membrane will be inflamed. The general health of the patient is not affected, but in the case of complete rupture the animal is hardly fit for work. Even when the rupture is incomplete, the " fluting " noise is objectionable and impregnation is likely to be interfered with.

TREATMENT.—Antiseptic lotions are indicated when the case is recent, to prevent septic complications. Immediate suturing of the wound is generally impracticable on account of its very uneven and damaged borders. If attempted, it would be necessary to first excise the damaged tissues and make the borders even. When cicatrisation has already ensued, the following procedure may have the desired effect in a case not involving the anus or rectum : Separate the mucous membrane from the underlying tissue for a distance of about ½ inch from the edge of the rupture and throughout its whole extent. Bring the raw surfaces of the skin into apposition, and maintain them there by Halsted sutures inserted through the base of the flaps. Unite the free borders of the latter by ordinary interrupted sutures. Paint the lines of sutures with tincture of iodine or collodion, and iodoform or tinct. benz. co. (Fig. 315).

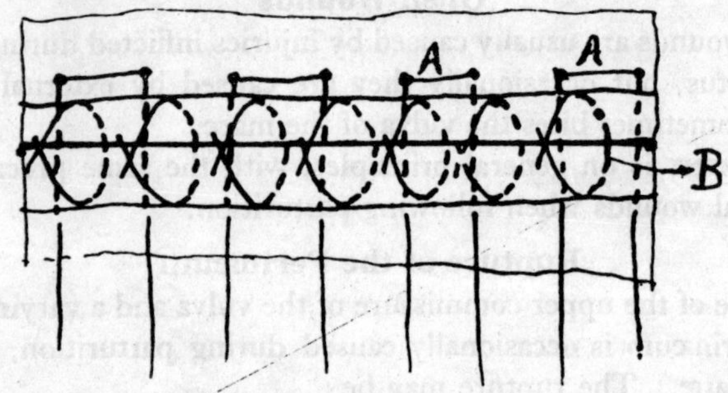

Fig. 315.—Perineal Suture.
A, Halstead suture through base of skin flap ; B, interrupted cutaneous suture.

When the recto-vaginal partition has been divided it is more difficult to obtain healing, but it may be effected by the above method after first uniting the freshened borders of the divided partition by closely applied interrupted sutures.

Vulvitis

Vulvitis may be the result of an injury caused by the penis, when the vulvar orifice is very narrow, or by violence of any kind. It coexists with vaginitis, and may be symptomatic of a specific disease such as horse-pox, dourine, or " foot and mouth disease."

The symptoms are those of inflammation or of the disease from which it arises and the treatment is carried out accordingly.

AFFECTIONS OF THE VAGINA

Imperforate Hymen—Occlusion of the Vagina

Occasionally in the mare and more frequently in the heifer the hymen remains imperforate. It is usually white or roan heifers that are affected, but the condition is also met with in others. Occlusion of the vagina may also ensue from cicatricial adhesion of its opposing walls, following some inflammatory condition, causing desquamation of its epithelial surface. In either case, the mucous secretion in front of the obstruction accumulates and distends the vaginal cavity.

SYMPTOMS.—Attention is usually first attracted by the animal making violent expulsive efforts. In the case of persistent hymen, this generally occurs at the first œstral period or after being served by the bull for the first time. On rectal examination the fluctuating distension of the vagina is detected, and when the hand is introduced into the latter a partition, varying in thickness in different cases, can be felt traversing the cavity in front of the meatus urinarius, and fluctuation of the retained fluid may be recognised through the membrane. In some instances the hymen bulges outside the lips of the vulva when the patient is recumbent, and then simulates prolapse of the vagina. When the obstruction is due to adhesion between the walls of the vagina, the hand is arrested at this point. Defæcation may be difficult, owing to compression of the rectum, and cause further straining.

TREATMENT consists in giving exit to the retained fluid by incising or excising a portion of the persisting membrane or puncturing the occluded part by a stout, slightly curved trocar and canula about 15 inches long and $\frac{3}{8}$ inch in diameter and flushing out the cavity with an antiseptic solution. It is advisable to fatten the heifer for the butcher at once, as she is not fit for breeding, and, moreover, the condition may recur. The fluid present is generally thick and yellowish, but it may be blackish or reddish, and it is always very fœtid. Its quantity varies ; it may amount to a couple of gallons. Straining continues for some time after the operation, but when the irritation caused thereby passes off it ceases. Vestiges of the hymen in the form of bands stretching across the vagina may persist and interfere with parturition. It is generally sufficient to sever them with the knife or scissors to allow delivery to be effected. The resulting hæmorrhage is insignificant.

Wounds of the Vagina

Wounds of the vagina are most common in the large animals, and are usually produced during parturition by extraction of a fœtus in a malposition or by obstetrical instruments. Occasionally the vagina is ruptured by the penis during service, and several cases have been recorded of sadism in which the passage was more or less severely wounded by the insertion of a stick or some rough instrument, the wounding body in several instances penetrating the peritoneum, bladder, or rectum.

Prognosis.—The possible complications of vaginal wounds comprise:

1. *Hæmorrhage*, which may prove fatal. Post-partum bleeding is usually from the vagina.

2. *Prolapse of the bladder* through a rent in the vaginal floor.

3. *Prolapse of the bowel* through a perforation in the recto-vaginal cul-de-sac.

4. *Abscess formation* in the perivaginal tissues, the abscess bursting, as a rule, into the vagina, or rarely into the abdominal cavity.

5. *Peritonitis*, due to perforation of the peritoneal cavity in the first instance, or to an abscess opening into it, or to extension of vaginal infection, via the uterus and Fallopian tubes.

6. *Occlusion of the vagina* by inflammatory adhesions between its walls.

7. *Recto-vaginal or vesico-vaginal fistula.*

Treatment.—Wounds of the vagina which do not perforate the peritoneum are treated by antiseptic irrigations and by the introduction into the cavity of antiseptic pessaries. When the peritoneal cavity has been opened these measures cannot be adopted, as the agents employed would gain entrance thereto, and probably give rise to a fatal peritonitis. It is inadvisable to forcibly inject antiseptic solutions into the vagina for the treatment of vaginal wounds following parturition, as the force of the injection might drive septic material into the uterus. Gentle irrigation or swabbing of the affected part should be adopted, followed by the insertion of a pessary.

Recto-vaginal and vesico-vaginal fistulæ are usually the result of dystokia, in which one of the fœtal limbs traverses the vaginal wall. These fistulæ usually persist indefinitely, suturing of the orifice being impracticable except when the fistula is near the vulvar orifice. The author had such a case in a thoroughbred mare after foaling, on which suturing by means of a fully-curved needle was followed by closure of the fistula. It has been suggested to incise the tissues between the anus and the recto-vaginal fistula, and then perform the suturing advised for ruptured perinæum, but the procedure is not to be recommended.

Hæmatoma in the Vagina

A hæmatoma is sometimes formed in the connective tissue of the vaginal wall as the result of vascular rupture caused by forcible extraction of the fœtus when it is abnormally large or in malposition. When the extravasation is slight the blood is absorbed after a few days but when it is copious the hæmatoma persists and may become infected, terminating in suppuration, gangrene, or general infection. It is the dilated vaginal veins which are ruptured. Isolated cases of the vulvar and vaginal veins being in a varicose condition and bursting spontaneously during pregnancy have been recorded.

TREATMENT.—Cold antiseptic injections are indicated at first, with a view to arresting the hæmorrhage and preventing complications. If, after a couple of weeks, the hæmatoma shows no tendency to become absorbed, it should be incised and evacuated and washed out with an antiseptic lotion. Puncturing the swelling with a trocar and canula is not so satisfactory. Early opening of the hæmatoma, before the bleeding into it had completely ceased, might be followed by profuse and perhaps uncontrollable hæmorrhage.

Hæmorrhage from the Vagina

This usually results from wounds inflicted during parturition, but may be a sequel to the incision of a hæmatoma, as mentioned. It may be arrested by cold or hot douches, or by packing the vagina with sterilised towels, associated with a hypodermic injection of adrenalin or pituitrin.

Vaginitis

The various forms of vaginitis are acute or chronic, simple or specific, and sporadic or contagious. They are also classified, according to the nature of the lesion, as catarrhal, purulent, croupous, phlyctenular, ulcerative, phlegmonous, and follicular. Vaginitis may be primary or secondary to vulvitis or metritis. It may be a symptom of a specific disease, such as horse-pox, glanders, or dourine. In all cases the cause is bacterial.

Simple Vaginitis is commonly the result of injuries received during parturition, but it may also be caused by sadism or the use of irritating vaginal injections.

SYMPTOMS comprise a muco-purulent discharge from the vulva, swelling of its lips, and evidence of pain during micturition and defæcation. On manual examination the vagina is found to be hot, swollen, and painful, and when viewed by the aid of a speculum and torch its mucous surface is seen to be red and perhaps desquamated, or even ulcerated, depending upon the stage of the disease. In the croupous form its lining is covered by a yellowish-grey exudate, associated with necrotic areas and ulcerated spots.

PROGNOSIS.—The inflammation may rapidly undergo resolution, or it may become chronic. Bad cases may be complicated with gangrene which may terminate fatally from toxæmia or septicæmia.

TREATMENT consists in irrigating the vagina with warm, emollient, antiseptic solutions and administering laxative medicine. Any of the agents already mentioned may be employed (see p. 757). Liquid paraffin or linseed tea may be injected into the vagina as emollients. In the croupous form the false membranes must be removed and the affected areas swabbed with a comparatively strong antiseptic agent (hydrogen peroxide, potassium permanganate, etc.). Penicillin is indicated in bad cases, locally and parenterally.

Chronic Vaginitis is only characterised by a continuous or intermittent muco-purulent discharge which adheres to the lower commissure of the vulva. On examination by the aid of the speculum, the mucous membrane is found palish, thickened, and sclerosed, and perhaps ulcerated here and there. In cases following acute forms of the disease, in which there has been loss of substance, there may be stenosis or atresia of the vagina.

TREATMENT.—Astringent and antiseptic injections are indicated, such as sulphate of zinc or alum in 2 to 4 per cent. solution, or iodine (2 or 3 per 1,000), repeated daily until the discharge ceases. If much irritation and straining ensue, they should be discontinued for a while and pessaries used instead.

Contagious Vaginitis may be acute or chronic, and is variously spoken of as infectious vaginitis, exanthematous vaginitis, and granular vaginitis. A similar condition affects the covering of the penis and the lining of the sheath in the male, and the disease is transmitted from one sex to the other by copulation. The disease is dealt with in detail under the heading of " Contagious Diseases " in works on medicine and in those on obstetrics.

Prolapse (Eversion) of the Vagina

There are two forms of prolapse of the vagina, one in which there is merely stretching of the ligaments or tissue binding the vagina to the pelvic walls, and another in which these structures are ruptured. The former usually occurs during pregnancy and the latter during parturition. The condition is met with in all animals, but is most common in the cow and sheep.

ETIOLOGY.—The following are factors in bringing about the prolapse :

1. *Distension of the abdomen* by bulky food or a gravid uterus, or both, causing pressure on the pelvic region and tendency to push the vagina backwards.

2. *Lying in sloping stalls*, which, associated with No. 1, is the usual cause of the trouble in the cow. When the animal is recumbent, the lips of the vulva are everted and the mucous membrane of the vagina is protruded in the form of a pink enlargement of variable size in different cases. At first it only appears during recumbency, disappearing when the animal rises, but eventually it persists, and when it becomes irritated from exposure the patient strains and aggravates the condition.

3. *Expulsive efforts* during a difficult parturition rupturing the attachments between the vagina and the pelvis.

SYMPTOMS.—The prolapse is readily recognised. Occurring during gestation, it usually appears towards the end of the period (seventh or eighth month in the cow) in the form of a reddish tumour between the lips of the vulva, with a depression in its centre corresponding to the lumen of the passage. The mucous membrane is more or less inflamed and secretes a viscid exudate which agglutinates the hairs on the lower commissure of the vulva. The swelling is often soiled by excrement, and may be excoriated from contact with foreign matter. The form appearing during or subsequent to parturition is usually more voluminous and more serious than that accompanying pregnancy. The prolapsed mass may hang down between the thighs, and the opening of the urethra may be seen on its inferior aspect, and its bent position may prevent the escape of urine, distending the bladder and increasing the volume of the prolapse. The part becomes inflamed and painful from injury and exposure, causing the patient to strain incessantly. The os uteri may be visible in the centre of the prolapse. There may be evidence of febrile disturbance. The absence of cotyledons on the surface of the tumour in the ruminant shows that it is not a case of prolapse of the uterus.

PROGNOSIS.—Most cases of prolapse, when attended to early, are treated successfully. The longer the case is in existence, the more difficult it is to deal with. When there has been laceration of the perivaginal tissues and the prolapse is of long standing, new cicatricial tissue will have formed, rendering reduction of the mass difficult or impossible. In rare instances gangrene of the prolapsed part ensues, and sometimes leads to the death of the patient.

TREATMENT consists in cleaning the prolapsed part, returning it to its normal position, and maintaining it there, or if reduction is impossible amputating it. To perform reduction, have the animal with the hind-quarters on a higher level than the fore, push the prolapse gradually forwards, beginning at the part next the vulva, and when it has been returned inside the latter, pass the hand into the vagina and press the fist against the os uteri so as to stretch the vaginal mucous membrane and obliterate its folds, thereby ensuring complete reduction. A possible accident during the procedure is rupture of the anterior vaginal wall and escape of the bowel, especially in the mare, due to violent straining. General or epidural anæsthesia is indicated when the expulsive efforts are difficult to overcome. If the bladder is distended, evacuate it by puncturing or by passing the catheter. One of the following methods of retention is required to maintain the vagina in position until straining has ceased :

1. *A truss*, by means of which the lips of the vulva are so compressed by a rope that eversion of the vagina is impossible.

2. *Wire sutures* in the form of two stout pieces of copper or galvanised wire, with bayonet points inserted through the lips of the vulva and crossing the passage about 4 inches in from the vulvar orifice, the ends of the wire being then turned with pliers into the shape of rings to keep it in position. This method answers the purpose well and causes no discomfort to the patient. Two bicycle spokes with one end sharpened to a point and passed through the vaginal walls and fixed by an ordinary coat button on either end, as used by F. Daly, M.R.C.V.S.(Dublin), suit the purpose admirably. One piece of galvanised wire passed through the lips of the vulva and having its ends twisted one round the other has been used successfully in the sheep.

3. *Tape sutures* passed deeply through the lips of the vagina, as in No. 2, a simple and effective method.

4. *West's clam*, whose sharp teeth grasp the vulvar walls. Its application is very painful, and is strongly resented by the patient, but once it is in position it is well borne and proves very effective. It is made in sizes to suit the cow, sheep, and bitch.

5. *Tying the wool* across the vulvar orifice usually has the desired effect in the sheep.

In all cases care is taken that urination is not interfered with. The animal should be placed in position with the hind-quarters on a higher level than the fore-quarters, and a sedative draft should be administered to allay straining.

In the bitch, *hysteropexia* may be performed in a case of chronic prolapse of the vagina when other measures have failed. It consists in performing laparotomy immediately in front of the pubis, drawing the uterus forwards in the abdominal cavity so as to stretch the vagina into its normal position, and then fixing it in this situation by suturing the body of the uterus to the abdominal wall. The sutures are passed through the serous and muscular coats of the body of the uterus and of the lips of the parietal wound. The latter is closed in the usual way (Fig. 316).

Partial amputation of the prolapsed vagina is indicated in a chronic case which has resisted other methods of treatment and which would not be suitable for hysteropexia. It is effected by applying a ligature round the base of the prolapse, taking care not to include the urethra, and cutting off the portion behind the ligature. The latter may be of silk or india-rubber, the former being more convenient and quite effective. It is generally advisable to ligature the mass in two sections. The operation is most commonly required in the bitch, in which the prolapse usually involves only a portion of the circumference of the passage.

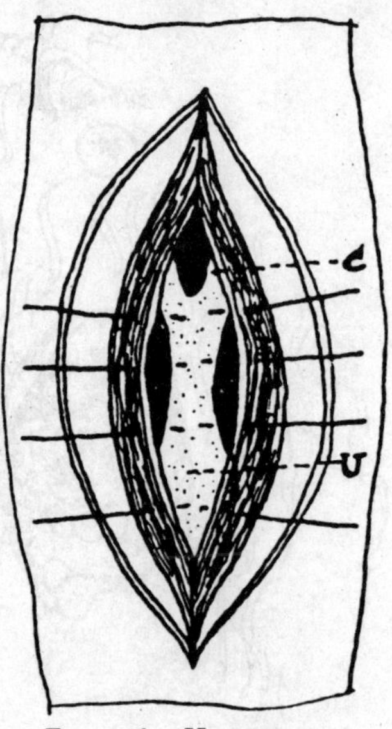

FIG. 316.—HYSTEROPEXIA.
U, Body of uterus;
C, Uterine horn.

Tumours of the Vulva and Vagina

Tumours affecting the vulva and vagina comprise fibromata, sarcomata, carcinomata, lipomata, adenomata, and cysts. Generally speaking, neoplasms of these passages are rare. Cysts occur in the mare and cow. They may be congenital or the result of a hæmatoma. They vary in volume, are usually pedunculated, and contain a clear or yellowish serous fluid in which some flakes of fibrin may be floating.

The commonest vaginal growths in the bitch are venereal sarcomata of the same nature as described in connection with the prepuce and penis of the dog, and transmissible from one animal to the other by copulation. They cause a sanguinolent discharge from the vulva, and are readily recognised on digital examination covering more or less of the lining of the passage. A vaginal speculum is useful to enable the passage to be inspected to confirm diagnosis by palpation or to show up a suspicious spot that might not thus be detected. Polypoid fibromata are fairly common in the bitch. Carcinoma of the vulva is occasionally met with in the mare and cow, and appears to be more common in ponies than in larger horses. It involves the lips of the vulva and the clitoris. The surface of the tumour is ulcerated and angry, and emits a very offensive odour. Papillomata affect the same region, but do not present the features of the malignant growth. Polypoid cysts or neoplasms may remain undetected until the time of parturition, when straining causes them to appear between the lips of the vulva or protrude behind it.

TREATMENT.—Cysts in the large animals can be removed by the ecraseur when pedunculated. If sessile, they should be largely incised or partially excised, and their interior should then be treated with tincture of iodine, or 5 per cent. carbolic, or 5 to 10 per cent. chloride of zinc to destroy the lining of the cyst and promote granulations. Ligation is an alternative method of dealing with polypoid growths, and the most suitable one for the bitch.

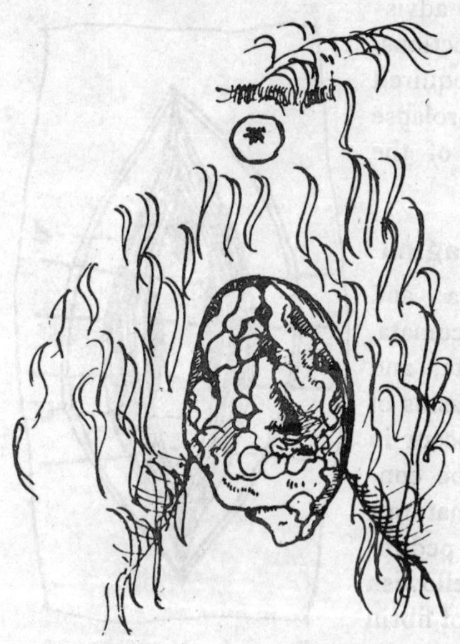

FIG. 317.—POLYPOID TUMOUR IN THE VAGINA OF THE BITCH.

Venereal tumours of the bitch require complete excision, adopting the following procedure. Use epidural or nembutal anæsthesia. Evert the lips of the vulva by means of artery forceps and by use of the scissors remove the tumours in the posterior part of the passage. Then grasp the wall of the vagina anteriorly with mouse-teeth artery forceps and evert it so as to bring the tumours there within reach and remove them in the same way. The curette may also be used to scrape away small granulations. The operation may be supplemented by the application of powdered copper sulphate to the affected parts. It is repeated occasionally as seems necessary. After operation the vagina is irrigated with a suitable antiseptic lotion. The daily injection of liquid paraffin into the passage, as an emollient, is indicated until the wounds are nearly healed. Malignant neoplasms of the vulva and vagina are incurable, but benign growths can be successfully extirpated.

AFFECTIONS OF THE UTERUS

Most of the affections of the uterus are dealt with at length in text-books on obstetrics, and will consequently be only briefly referred to here.

Atresia or Occlusion of the Os Uteri

This condition may be due to a neoplasm or cicatricial contraction. It renders impregnation difficult or impossible. It is diagnosed on digital examination.

TREATMENT.—When the opening is not completely obliterated, it may be dilated with the fingers or special dilators. The latter are essential for the bovine, in which the walls of the cervix are more rigid than in the mare.

Wounds of the Uterus

Wounds of the uterus may be confined to its mucous membrane or extend more deeply and perforate the abdominal cavity in some cases. It is only during pregnancy, when the uterus is distended and close to the abdominal wall, or at the time of parturition that the organ is liable to injury. The gravid uterus may be ruptured by violent impact of the abdominal wall against a fixed object. Wounds by the feet of the fœtus or by instruments or ropes may be caused during delivery in cases of dystokia. The organ may also be wounded when prolapsed, from a neighbouring animal treading on it, or by bites from dogs or pigs, or it may be ruptured in the act of reducing it.

SYMPTOMS.—Uterine wounds are accompanied by more or less severe hæmorrhage, which may be sufficient to cause death within a short time. When the rupture extends through all the coats of the organ, prolapse of the bowel or omentum may ensue, and death from peritonitis usually follows. Rarely, and most frequently in the bovine, recovery takes place after perforating wounds occurring during parturition. The womb in the bitch is very apt to be ruptured by obstetric forceps if great care is not exercised. When the patient vomits, it is usually a sign that rupture has taken place.

PROGNOSIS.—Death may ensue from hæmorrhage or peritonitis, as indicated. Even superficial wounds at parturition may lead to a fatal metritis. Perforating wounds of the upper wall of the uterus are less serious than those of the floor.

TREATMENT.—In a case of rupture during gestation, all that can be done is to treat for internal hæmorrhage. Non-perforating wounds inflicted at the time of parturition are treated by antiseptic irrigation and antiseptic pessaries. If there is any suspicion that the uterus has been perforated, irrigation should not be adopted for fear of the liquid entering the peritoneal cavity. When the organ is perforated, there is no effective treatment for the condition. The administration of sedative medicine to allay straining may help to bring about spontaneous recovery. When hæmorrhage is profuse, measures to arrest it are indicated.

Metrorrhagia

Hæmorrhage from the uterus is usually the result of a wound inflicted during parturition, as mentioned, or it may be a sequel to the tearing away of maternal cotyledons when removing the placenta in the cow.

PROGNOSIS is always grave when the hæmorrhage is profuse, death supervening in the majority of cases. If due to a perforating wound death will ensue from peritonitis.

TREATMENT comprises: (1) Cold douches over the loins; (2) injections of cold or very hot water into the uterus; (3) packing the uterus and vagina with sterilised cloths and injecting normal saline subcutaneously or intravenously when the hæmorrhage is very profuse; (4) the hypodermic injection of ergotin or pituitrin or adrenalin, pituitrin being probably the most effective. The packing material should be removed after twenty-four hours, and the uterus should be subsequently irrigated with a suitable antiseptic solution. Generous diet and the administration of tonics are indicated to recoup the animal's strength.

Metritis

Metritis will be only briefly alluded to as inflammation of the uterus due to the presence in its cavity of pathogenic bacteria, and characterised in the acute form by febrile disturbance, local inflammation, and an offensive muco-purulent discharge from the vagina, and in the chronic form by loss of condition and a constant or intermittent purulent uterine discharge unaccompanied by inflammation.

TREATMENT consists in each case in repeated irrigation by antiseptic solutions, and in the use of antiseptic pessaries, and in administering suitable medicine internally, including penicillin. An autogenous vaccine is indicated in chronic cases. Metro-peritonitis usually proves fatal. The condition is almost invariably a sequel to parturition.

For "Torsion of the Uterus," "Prolapse of the Uterus," and "Retention of the Fœtal Membranes" the reader is referred to standard works on obstetrics.

AFFECTIONS OF THE MAMMARY GLAND

Congenital Abnormalities

Congenital abnormalities of the mammary region comprise absence of the glands, supernumerary glands, absence of teats, supernumerary teats, and imperforate teats.

Absence of the Mammary Glands is exceedingly rare, and only occurs in cases of hermaphrodism.

Supernumerary Glands.—It is only in multiparous animals that the number of mammæ varies.

Absence of Teats is extremely rare, but isolated cases in which the teats were only represented by slight eminences have been met with.

Supernumerary Teats.—It is not uncommon to find one or two supernumerary teats in the cow. The extra teat may be alongside a normal teat or in the form of an outgrowth therefrom. It may interfere with the ordinary process of milking, or when the normal teat is being drawn milk may escape outside the pail from the accessory one.

TREATMENT consists in excising the supernumerary teat before the gland becomes active, and suturing the wound. The operation should not be done during lactation, owing to the risk of infection of the udder supervening and the difficulty or impossibility of obtaining healing of the wound on account of the milk constantly passing through it.

Imperforate Teats.—Imperforation of one or more of the teats is occasionally met with in the cow. As a rule, only one teat is involved. The obstruction is usually at the lower extremity of the duct, but it may be in the form of a membrane between its upper part and the galactophorous sinus.

SYMPTOMS.—When it is the lower orifice of the duct that is imperforate, the condition is revealed after the first parturition by the affected teat being abnormally distended, shining, and sensitive on palpation, and by pressure thereon failing to express the milk. On examination of its tip the orifice is found to be absent. When the obstruction is at the origin of the duct, the teat is undistended and feels more or less solid.

TREATMENT.—The obstruction of the orifice may be cleared by the insertion of a milk siphon or, if this is insufficient, of a suitable trocar and canula, the latter being left in position for some time. When the occlusion is due to a membrane traversing the upper part of the duct, it may also be punctured by a trocar and canula. In either case Morier's special curette may be employed (see Obstruction of Teats). It will be necessary to pass the milk siphon occasionally or to leave a wax bougie in position in the intervals between milking to prevent cicatricial contraction and stenosis. The strictest aseptic precautions are essential to prevent infection of the gland. The siphon should always be boiled immediately before use.

Contusions of the Udder

When the udder is distended or pendulous, it is subject to contusions from various causes. In the cow it may be trodden upon by a neighbour during recumbency. It may also be injured by the head of the suckling. In all animals the pendulous udder is apt to be struck against projecting objects.

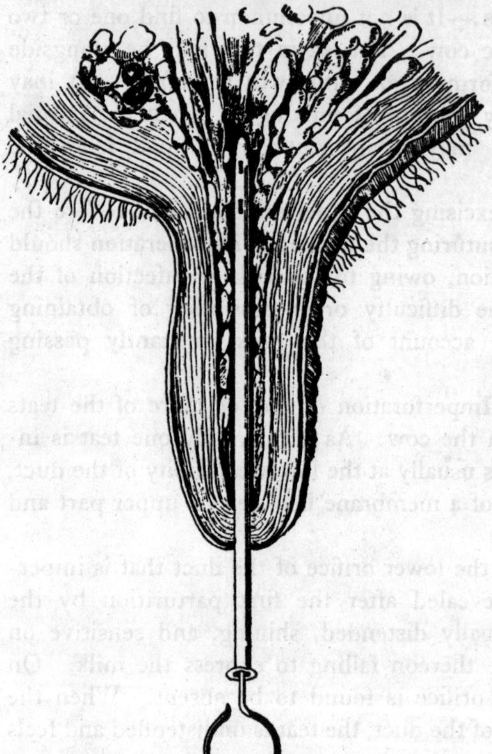

Fig. 318.—Teat Siphon passed into Milk Duct.

Symptoms are as usual for a contusion—viz., local inflammation and more or less extravasation of blood. There may be a subcutaneous hæmatoma or hæmorrhage into the substance of the gland, characterised by the presence of blood in the milk. When the bruise is severe, gangrene may supervene. The injured part is prone to become infected, resulting in mastitis of the quarter affected or the formation of an abscess.

Treatment.—In slight cases the extravasated blood becomes absorbed, and the inflammation soon undergoes resolution. Cold applications are indicated immediately after the occurrence, to be followed by hot applications later. A thick layer of hot antiphlogistine, covered by a layer of cotton-wool kept in position by a suspensory bandage, is very beneficial. Antiseptic agents must be used to ward off infection through abrasions on the injured region. It is advisable to milk the affected quarter at frequent intervals. Massage, aided by the use of a stimulating liniment, will promote absorption of exudate and extravasate.

Open Wounds of the Mammary Gland

The large distended udder of the cow is very exposed to injury, and is apt to be wounded by coming in contact with sharp or pointed bodies. Barbed wire is a frequent cause of lacerated wounds of the teat and gland, which may also be bitten by dogs, while goring by the horn of another beast also occasionally occurs. Even superficial wounds are serious when the organ is active, owing to the risk of the glandular tissue becoming infected therefrom, while deep wounds of the parenchyma are almost invariably followed by mastitis, and when accompanied by much contusion, give rise to gangrene. The escape of milk through open milk ducts retards or prevents healing, a milk fistula usually persisting when a large duct, especially that of the teat, has been penetrated. Very narrow punctured wounds of the teat duct only give exit to milk during milking. Wounds of the gland, when it is not secreting, are of no more consequence than those of ordinary tissue, except in so far as some of the parenchyma is replaced by a cicatrix.

TREATMENT.—Superficial wounds of the gland and teat are treated on general principles. Perforating incised wounds should be sutured and sealed with collodion, with a view to obtaining primary healing, but those accompanied by bruising must be left open and frequently irrigated with an antiseptic solution in the hope of securing healing without infection of the quarter, not forgetting the virtues of penicillin against gram positive bacteria. For perforating wounds of the teat two series of sutures are indicated (see Milk Fistula). When the lesion is on the teat, milking may be performed by compressing the teat with the finger and thumb without touching the wound ; if not, the milk must be drawn off with a milk siphon under the strictest aseptic precautions. The application of cocained vaseline on the teat may enable it to be milked without resentment by the patient.

Milk Fistula

A milk fistula may originate as follows : (1) Rarely it is congenital when it is usually found on the postero-internal aspect of a hindquarter, where a supernumerary teat is commonly found ; (2) it may be due to excision by the owner of a supernumerary teat in a calf without suturing the wound ; (3) the most common cause of the condition is a perforating wound of the gland or teat during lactation.

PROGNOSIS.—A fistula in the gland involving some of the small ducts usually heals spontaneously, but a fistula on the teat is exceedingly difficult to close during lactation, owing to the large amount of milk constantly passing through it. The chief gravity of the condition is that it favours mastitis by (1) leaving a way open for infection of the gland, and (2) keeping the organ and the floor of the shed wet and dirty through the constant escape of milk, when the opening is large. If the fistulous orifice in the teat is very small, milk will only escape when the gland is fully distended or during process of milking. In the latter case it is generally impossible to direct the two streams of milk into the pail.

TREATMENT comprises one of the following methods: (1) The application of a blister round the orifice; (2) cauterisation of the edges of the opening by the actual cautery or a potential caustic; (3) suturing the borders of the fistula after freshening them, if necessary, taking care not to include the mucous membrane in the suture, which would prevent union of the cutaneous edges. Nos. (1) and (2) may be said to be useless for a fistula on the teat, and even No. (3) usually fails in this case.

The following method of operation, recommended by Moussu, may prove successful: (1) Having injected a local anæsthetic, pare

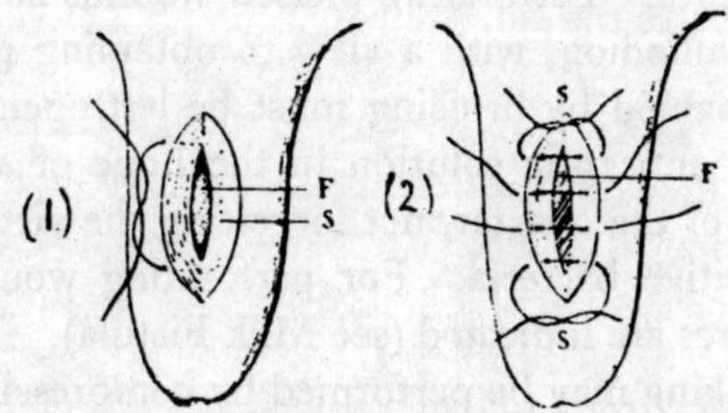

FIG. 319.—Milk fistula. (1) deep suture—schema showing the course of the suture; F, base of the fistula; S, suture; (2) superficial interrupted suture.

away the callous surface of the fistula: (2) using fine nylon thread insert a Halsted suture through the deep part of the wound, penetrating the skin only on the side of the wound on which the two ends of the thread are tied; (3) bring the edges of the skin into contact with ordinary interrupted sutures; (4) seal the wound with collodion; (5) insert a milk tube and fix it in position by strips of plaster, to allow the milk to escape through the teat orifice instead of entering the fistula. The operation must be performed with strict aseptic precautions. As a rule, however, it is hardly worth while operating until the animal has gone dry. The application of penicillin to the wound, and its introduction into the quarter through the teat duct, are indicated to ward off an attack of mastitis.

Gold (*Vet. Rec.*, Oct. 2nd, 1943) excises the callous borders of the fistula, removing a piece of tissue like the segment of an orange and then sutures as follows, using silkworm gut. The needle and thread is passed through the lips of the wound thus: (1) through the skin ½–1 centimetre from its edge down to but not including the mucous membrane; (2) the same course reversely on the opposite side; (3) through the skin on this side 2–3 millimetres from its border; (4) through the skin on the opposite side 2–3 millimetres from its border thereby everting the skin and ensuring close apposition of the deep and superficial parts of the lips of the wound. He removes the sutures in 10–14 days, the wound having been left intact in the meantime.

Fissures or Cracks in the Teats

Fissures or cracks in the teats are common in bovines, young cows and fine-skinned animals being particularly liable to them.

Etiology.—When the teat is very distended in the newly calved cow its epithelium is apt to crack, especially when the skin is left wet after milking or sucking, and exposed to the effects of cold, frosty weather. The friction caused by the hands of the milker or the mouth of the suckling aggravates the condition, and the cracks become deeper and very sore.

Symptoms.—The cracks appear parallel to the circumference of the teats, and vary in width and depth according to the length of time they are in existence. Their borders may be thickened, raised, and callous, and their depth is of a greyish or red colour, and contains a certain amount of whitish, greasy material. The lesions are very painful, and the animal becomes fidgety and restless when they are touched. She will not allow the teat to be milked or sucked. The milk consequently accumulates in the quarter, which becomes uncomfortably distended, and acute mastitis may thus be a sequel of the condition. When the tip of the teat is involved, the inflammatory exudate may seal its orifice and prevent the flow of milk.

Treatment.—Preventative treatment comprises drying the teats when they are wet, and protecting the animal from inclement weather. Smearing a little glycerine, lard, or a mixture of lard and glycerine on the teat after drying it has a protective effect. When cracks are present, the teat should be immersed in an antiseptic bath for a while, then carefully dried and smeared with boric or ichthyol ointment, or with one of the following preparations: Liquor plumbi subacet. ℥iii. and glycerine or olive oil ℥xvi., or carbolic acid ℥i. and glycerine O.i. Deep indolent cracks require to be cauterised with the silver nitrate stick. It is usually necessary to draw off the milk with the siphon, as milking by the hand prevents healing of the cracks, and will not be tolerated by the patient. For the same reason the suckling must be weaned or put on a foster-mother. When the point of the teat is covered by a scab or exfoliated epithelium, the latter should be softened with a little glycerine or vaseline to favour its removal. A wax bougie should be inserted to keep the opening patent.

Obstruction of the Teats

Acquired obstruction of the teats may be complete or incomplete. It is most common in milch cows. The obstruction may arise from : (1) Inflammation and thickening of the mucous lining of the duct ; (2) a polypus or polypi in its interior ; (3) a partition across the duct ; and (4) milk calculi more or less occluding its lumen. When there is complete occlusion of the duct, the galactophorous sinus and the teat above the point of obstruction are distended with milk, which cannot be made to flow by the act of milking. If the occlusion is partial the milk can be forced out in a thin stream, and the cow is difficult and tiresome to milk. The additional force required to expel the milk may irritate the mucous membrane and promote the formation of new fibrous tissue, which further diminishes the lumen of the duct. In this way contraction or spasm of the sphincter may be followed by fibrous thickening and increased obstruction to the flow of milk.

Papillomata, or polypi, occupy a variable position inside the teat. A small wart may protrude through the meatus and coexist with other warts on the skin of the teat. When higher up the duct, it can be felt as a nodosity or kernel between the finger and thumb. Inflammatory thickening with obstruction of the teat canal also varies in its situation and extent. It may be in the form of a circumscribed nodule or a cord-like structure involving the greater part of the duct. The former is usually in the middle part of the teat, and feels like a pea, which can be displaced somewhat upwards and downwards. More than one teat may be affected in this way. The latter is cylindrical in shape and rigid on palpation. When recent it is sensitive or painful on pressure, but when chronic it is painless. These lesions would appear to be of bacterial origin.

Obstruction by a partition or septum between the sinus and the canal is produced during the period when the gland is inactive, towards the end of gestation, affecting teats which up to that time were easy to milk. It appears to be due to hypertrophy of and adhesion between the folds of mucous membrane developed at the region mentioned. When the occlusion is complete, the sinus is distended and the teat is flaccid ; but if there is a slight orifice, milk will pass drop by drop into the duct and escape in a normal jet when the teat is milked, after which the duct will be slow to fill again.

Treatment.—The following are methods of dealing with obstruction of the teats :

1. When the duct is merely constricted at a point, it may be dilated by the repeated insertion of a metallic sound or bougie, and by keeping an antiseptic wax bougie in position in the meantime. Even when this is done with aseptic precautions, there is a risk of the quarter becoming infected and acute mammitis ensuing.

2. When dilatation is insufficient, the stricture may be incised by a special knife introduced into the duct, an antiseptic bougie being left *in situ* in the intervals between milking. A very narrow-bladed tenotome may be used to make the incision, or Guilbert's teat knife may be employed for the purpose (Fig. 320). This procedure is even more risky than No. 1, owing to the greater tendency of mammitis to ensue from infection of the operation wound. Moreover, the cicatricial contraction which follows the healing of the incision usually increases the stricture, despite the use of dilating bougies. When the constriction is confined to the tip of the teat, Stinson's method of operating by a crucial incision proves almost invariably successful (see p. 487).

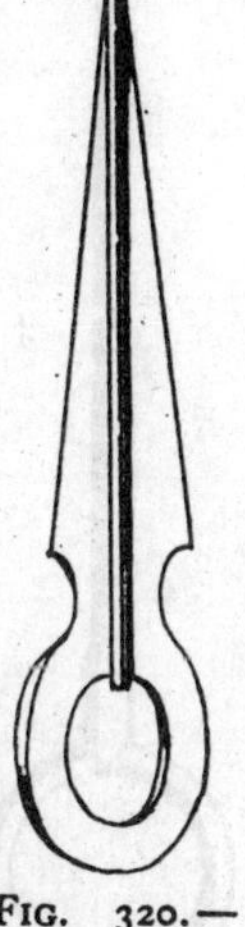

Fig. 320.—Guilbert's Teat Knife.

3. When the obstruction is in the form of a partition between the sinus and the duct, it may be recognised as a circular thickening at the base of the teat. If a small opening still remains, it may be dilated as in No. 1 ; but if this is not sufficient, multiple incisions may be made in the thickened tissue by means of a *bistouri caché* made for the purpose. Good results have been reported after the use of this instrument. Nevertheless, the sequelæ mentioned are to be feared. Operation by Hudson's method has proved very successful for this condition (see p. 488).

4. Fibrous callosities and polypi on the mucous membrane of the milk duct may be pierced by a trocar and canula, or removed. Removal may be effected by a cone-shaped instrument pushed up and down the duct (Fig. 321), or by a knife after making an incision into the duct at the level of the lesion. The special instrument referred to is composed of a metal rod about $\frac{1}{12}$ inch in diameter, terminated at one end by a ring and at the other by a hollow cone with a sharp-edged periphery, by means of which the excision is performed. Different sized cones may be screwed on to the handle. When the knife has been employed, the wound is sutured by the method described for closing a milk fistula.

5. When the foregoing methods have failed and the stricture occurs in the lower part of the teat, but too high for Stinson's method, the teat may be amputated above the affected part. The operation is facilitated by grasping the teat by Kühn's special forceps. The resulting hæmorrhage is slight. The escape of milk is prevented by the application of a rubber band on the stump, exerting moderate pressure. After a few weeks a new sphincter will have developed, when the milk will again be retained or only allowed to escape in drops. The band is then dispensed with, and the teat is milked in the ordinary way.

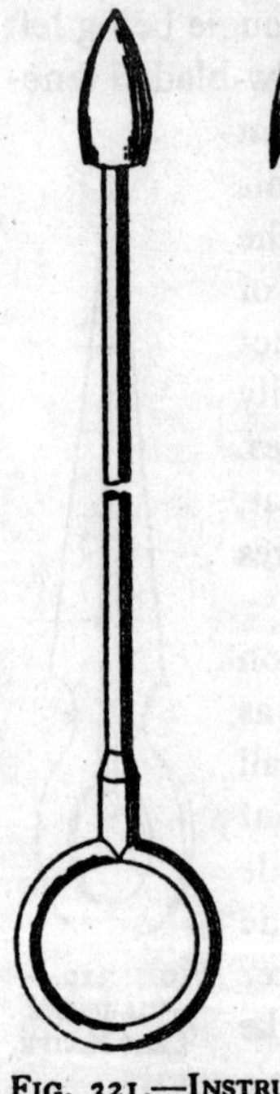

FIG. 321.—INSTRUMENT FOR REMOVAL OF POLYPI FROM THE MILK DUCT.

6. When the induration of the duct is recent, it may possibly be cured by ceasing to milk the quarter by "stripping" the teat, using the milk siphon instead, and by gently massaging the teat three or four times a day after smearing it with a little belladonna ointment. When the condition is chronic, the case is incurable.

Notwithstanding the occasional success of the above forms of treatment, it is a wise rule to follow the example of many experienced practitioners and refrain from adopting them on account of the serious risks involved. It is better to allow complete occlusion of the duct to supervene, when the pressure of the milk in the affected quarter will bring about atrophy of its secreting structure, and cause the quarter to go dry, without endangering the health of the animal. A certain amount of compensatory hypertrophy will ensue in the normal quarters. The introduction of penicillin into the teat after operation should materially help to prevent the development of gram positive bacteria in the gland.

7. Milk calculi are not common. They are composed of 60 per cent. organic matter and 40 per cent. inorganic matter, chiefly phosphate of lime. They vary in size from a pea to a nut. As a rule, only one calculus is present, but there may be several. They may be situated in the small ducts of the gland or in the teat canal. It may be possible to force the calculus down as far as the teat orifice by compression with the fingers and thumbs, as in the act of milking, and it may then be extracted by a fine forceps, or it may be possible to expel it through the opening when the latter is kept dilated by an assistant.

Eruptions on the Gland and Teats

A vesicular and pustular eruption appears on the gland and teats during attacks of foot and mouth disease, cow-pox, gangrenous coryza, and cattle plague, but it may also be the result of local infection by common organisms. The vesicles of foot and mouth disease have distinctive features, being greyish in colour, and containing a clear liquid. They occur simultaneously in the mouth and on the feet, and are accompanied by febrile symptoms. The pustules of cow-pox form chiefly on the teats, are of a pale yellow colour, and are umbilicated. The buccal cavity is not affected, and there is no general disturbance. Three or four pustules are commonly found on each teat, and on bursting leave ulcers which are slow to heal. Malignant catarrh and cattle plague are readily recognised by their characteristic symptoms. A moist eczematous condition or a dermatitis of the skin of the udder, where it comes in contact with the inside of the thighs, is fairly common in newly calved cows, especially those with very large glands. It is due apparently to the constant contact of the two cutaneous surfaces, and of the friction between them during movement. The condition is excited by excessive exercise and by the parts becoming soiled by dirt or grit. When the inflammation is well marked, it is revealed by the animal being disinclined to move, by a straddling gait, and by the appearance of an offensive blood-stained discharge in the affected region. The cow is apt to remain in the recumbent position.

TREATMENT of the foregoing conditions is on general principles, The contagious diseases must be dealt with as such. The eruptions on the teats are treated with mild, warm antiseptic lotions and emollient ointments. Prophylactic measures are essential to prevent the spread of the disease to other members of the herd. The inflamed surface in the region of the groin must be cleaned with a mild, warm antiseptic solution (boracic acid), dried with gauze, and then smeared with zinc ointment or dusted with a mixture of boric acid and starch.

Congestion of the Gland

Congestion of the mammary gland is observed chiefly in the cow sheep, and goat immediately before or just after parturition.

SYMPTOMS.—The gland is abnormally distended, hot, and slightly painful, due to vascular congestion. There is no evidence of constitutional disturbance. The milk withdrawn from the organ is not altered except that it may have a pink or reddish tint, due to the presence of blood from ruptured capillaries. Rarely pure blood drips from the teat. The congestion usually disappears in the course of a few days, but it may be followed by mastitis, which is favoured by the distended condition of the gland.

TREATMENT.—Frequent milking of the gland is indicated, and is generally sufficient. Cold and astringent applications are useful. Bleeding from the jugular may be performed, but is rarely indicated. Leeches may be applied to the gland in small animals to relieve congestion.

Mammitis

Inflammation of the mammary gland (mammitis or mastitis) is observed in all animals, and is very common in the cow and sheep, particularly the former. It is popularly known in these animals in various districts as sore elder, garget, blast or flagging of the udder, udder clap, and downfall of the udder.

CLASSIFICATION.—Mammitis may be classified in various ways, as follows :

1. Acute, subacute, and chronic mastitis.
2. Parenchymatous, catarrhal (confined to the milk ducts), interstitial, and paramammitis. All three, however, are usually present, owing to the rapidity with which the disease spreads from one part of the organ to the other.
3. Purulent and gangrenous mastitis.
4. According to the method of infection—viz., *hæmatogenous*, by the blood stream ; *lymphogenous*, by the lymph stream : *galactophorous*, by the milk ducts.

For clinical purposes, the classification of acute, subacute, and chronic mammitis is the most suitable.

ETIOLOGY.—The cause of mammitis is the entrance of pathogenic organisms into the gland. These may be streptococci, staphylococci, most frequently, or bacilli. The infection may be monomicrobic or polymicrobic. The acuteness of the attack depends on the virulence of the organism or organisms present. The variety of the sources of infection accounts for the different degrees of gravity of the disease. Anything which favours the entrance into or development of bacteria in the organ is a contributory cause—for example :

1. *Secretory activity of the gland*, the disease being practically confined to the organ in the state of lactation, and being most common soon after parturition, when milk secretion is at its height. Even when the disease appears in a heifer it is usually associated with an abnormal secretion of milk.

2. *Retention of milk in the gland.* This is a fruitful source of trouble. Bacteria entering by the teat orifice find the accumulated milk in the duct and sinus a suitable medium for development, and consequently multiply there, and thence invade the rest of the gland and set up their pathogenic effects. Mere retention is not sufficient to cause the disease, as is proved by the fact that it does not ensue when a teat is blind after parturition, although the quarter is greatly distended with milk.

3. *Open wounds and eruptions on the gland and teats*, from which infection is very apt to spread into the interior of the organ.

4. *Retention of the fœtal membranes*, causing a septic discharge from the vagina which may contaminate the gland.

5. *Bad hygiene*, including dirty bedding and insufficient ventilation.

6. *Want of cleanliness on the part of the milkers*, milking the cows with dirty hands or contaminated with the discharge from an infected gland, and the careless use of teat siphons.

7. *Exposure to cold and wet, over-driving, and general maltreatment* after calving, lowering the animal's powers of defence, and allowing bacteria already present in the gland and ordinarily harmless to assume virulent characters.

8. *Moist warm atmosphere*, which favours the development of bacteria.

In veterinary patients, infection nearly always occurs by way of the teat duct. Hæmatogenous and lymphogenous infection are rare, especially the former. The latter may occur directly from septic lesions on the surface of the organ. The fact that the milk is in practically every case altered at the very onset of the disease indicates that the bacterial invasion took place through the galactophorous ducts.

SYMPTOMS.—Acute mammitis is always sudden in onset. The constitutional disturbance may be the first to attract attention, the animal being found shivering, straddling, and restless, with a staring coat, an anxious expression, quick, short respirations, suspended appetite and rumination, and a temperature which may attain 106° or 107° F. There is usually constipation, and sometimes gastric tympany. The secretion of milk is diminished or almost arrested in the healthy quarters of the gland.

The local symptoms are those of intensely acute inflammation. The affected quarter or quarters, including the teats, are enormously swollen, hot, hard, painful, and red in colour. The teat stands out prominently, hard and shining. The least interference with the affected region causes pain, and is resented by the patient. On drawing the diseased quarter, a yellowish or reddish-yellow serosity escapes. This is afterwards mixed with clots of casein, and becomes more or less purulent and fœtid. There may be subcutaneous œdema in front of and behind the gland.

When gangrene supervenes, the teat and affected part of the quarter become cold and insensitive, and purple or green in colour. If the teat is not obstructed, stripping it will cause the discharge of a port-wine-coloured putrid liquid. Crepitation may be detected on manipulation, due to the presence of gas. In many cases death ensues from septic intoxication, but sometimes the patient withstands the attack until sloughing of the dead part has occurred, when recovery rapidly ensues, although a considerable time will elapse before the animal regains the condition which it lost in fighting the disease. The first indications of recovery are the cow becoming brighter and commencing to feed.

Abscess formation in the gland is more frequent than gangrene, and of course much less serious. Although it is destructive of the gland tissue, it represents successful defence of the part against general infection. However, when several quarters are affected with diffuse suppuration, the patient is apt to succumb from the accompanying toxæmia.

When mammitis arises from infection through the lymphatic system on the surface of the gland, the constitutional symptoms are much the same as those described, but the local changes are confined for a while to the perimammary and interstitial tissue, the secretion showing little or no alteration. The parenchymatous tissue soon becomes involved, and then the secretion is profoundly affected. The most marked local symptom at first in this case is a painful œdematous swelling of the gland extending anteriorly and posteriorly well beyond the limits of the organ.

Suppurative mammitis may be accompanied in its later stages with synovitis, affecting chiefly the hock and fetlock joints, and characterised by stiffness, lameness, and local inflammation.

Cows that have been put dry in the late spring and put on to rich grass during the summer often become attacked with acute mastitis of one or more quarters during July or August. The hind-limbs become so stiff in some of these cases that the beasts are hardly able to rise. In all cases of acute mammitis the patient rapidly loses condition.

PROGNOSIS.—Acute mastitis is always serious, because the best that can be hoped for is that the animal will recover from the general effects of the disease, the affected quarter or quarters being lost for the production of milk. There is a constant risk of infection of the healthy quarters from the affected one. During subsequent lactation there may be a certain amount of compensatory hypertrophy of the quarters that were not affected. Although evidence of infection has left a diseased quarter and it has undergone atrophy, organisms may remain latent therein during the period when the cow is dry and become active again after the next parturition, setting up a fresh attack of acute mammitis. Gangrenous mastitis is more frequently followed by death than by recovery.

PREVENTION consists in avoiding as far as possible the causes of the trouble. Mr. F. T. Harvey, F.R.C.V.S., and others, following his example, have succeeded in preventing "summer mastitis," occurring during the period when the cow is put dry prior to the next parturition, by injecting into the galactophorous sinuses and teat ducts a mixture of bismuth subnitrate and liquid paraffin, with due aseptic precautions. It prevents the entrance of infection through the teats, remaining *in situ* until milked out after the next parturition.

TREATMENT is very unsatisfactory, as little can be done to counteract the effects of the bacteria hidden in the small ducts and acini of the gland. The ideal treatment would be to remove, destroy, or inhibit the growth of the causal organisms, but this is impossible. The clinician must be contented with palliative rather than curative measures, including those indicated for febrile disturbance and local inflammation as follows:

1. *Internal treatment* comprises the administration of:

(1) *A purgative* to promote the elimination of toxins. The more promptly it acts the better, and for this reason some prescribe eserine or arecoline, but magnesium sulphate is most commonly employed.

(2) *Laxative medicine* in repeated small doses when the patient is too weak for purgation, or after the effects of the latter have passed off. Magnesium sulphate combined with potassium nitrate as a diuretic is usually prescribed.

(3) *A diffusible stimulant*, indicated when the beast is shivering.

(4) *An internal antiseptic*, the best being sulphanilamide powder administered in the usual way with large commencing and gradually diminishing doses for a period of 5 or 6 days at 3 or 4 hourly intervals. (See p. 222.) It has a more or less bacteriostatic effect on certain strains of staphylococci which are commonly the cause of acute mastitis. Other drugs that have been used are quinine, salicylate of soda, and formalin, the last mentioned appearing to be the most efficacious in daily drachm doses well diluted with water. It is believed to have some local effect

in being excreted by the gland. The other agents have a general febrifuge effect. Salicylate of soda is particularly indicated when synovitis is present.

(5) *Antitoxic serum or vaccine.* A polyvalent serum might be useful, but a vaccine would probably cause an insupportable reaction in a patient already profoundly affected by the disease. Serum and vaccine treatment have, however, so far proved disappointing. The latter is more useful for chronic forms of mammitis. A serum and vaccine employed simultaneously should be more efficacious than either alone.

2. *Local treatment* includes :

(1) *Frequent stripping of the affected quarter* to remove as much as possible of the septic contents. This is an important indication.

(2) *The injection of an antiseptic solution*, which is only of benefit when the quarter has been well evacuated, and even then its effects are very disappointing. Acriflavin (1–1000), boric acid (4 per cent.) and hydrogen peroxide (1 to 4 or 5) are suitable for the purpose. The solution is diffused as far as possible through the quarter by gentle massage before being withdrawn. The inefficacy of the treatment is doubtless due to the solution's failure to reach the small tubes and acini of the gland. Even the infusion into the organ of a solution of penicillin is of no avail in this form of mastitis. If it is not carried out with strict aseptic precautions, it may aggravate rather than improve the condition. Schmidt, of Denmark, claimed good results from the infusion into the quarter of 4 ounces each of alcohol and glycerine, the preparation being left *in situ* for three days before being milked out. If more than one quarter is affected, only one quarter is dealt with at a time. A little normal saline solution may be added to the liquid.

A preparation known as Aureomycin Hydrochloride Ointment issued by the American Cyanamide Company, New York, has been found to be an effective bacteriostat against many gram positive and gram negative organisms invading the mammary gland of the cow. The ointment is infused from a tube with strict asceptic precautions after milking out the quarter. One infusion with the entire contents of the tube has been found to be sufficient to clear up an infected quarter. If not a repetition of the infusion on two subsequent occasions at 48 hours interval had the desired effect. The author has seen it used in one case of sub-acute staphylococcic mastitis with striking effect, the milk becoming normal and sterile after two infusions at 48 hours interval.

(3) *Hot fomentation of the gland* at least two or three times daily, accompanied by gentle kneading of the organ. This has a somewhat soothing effect, and seems to favour resolution.

(4) *Hot poultices* of bran, spent hops, or marsh-mallows, which constitute a favourite popular remedy, having much the same effect as No. (3).

(5) *A cataplasm of glycerine and kaolin* or " antiphlogistine " applied in a thick layer over the udder and covered by cotton-wool or flannel kept in position by a bandage tied over the loins, openings being left for the teats to enable them to be drawn out at frequent intervals. The dressing should be renewed every twelve hours. It seems to afford relief to the patient. The support given by the suspensory bandage has a comforting effect if it does not become displaced.

(6) *The application of an anodyne ointment or liniment*, such as green extract of belladonna, camphor, and glycerine, or belladonna liniment rubbed in with gentle massage after fomenting.

(7) *The use of a counter-irritant* in the form of a stimulating liniment or blister rubbed into the quarter, but kept clear of the teat, which should be protected by smearing it with vaseline. If an abscess is forming, its maturation will be accelerated and the pus will be brought nearer to the surface. Ammonia liniment, tincture of iodine, and biniodide of mercury ointment are the agents usually used. This treatment is only adopted, as a rule, after the very acute stage of the inflammation has passed.

(8) *Massage*, which is always associated with the application of ointments and liniments, and believed by many to account for the apparent good effects of these applications. It is condemned by some practitioners on the ground that it breaks down granulation tissue in the gland, thereby weakening its defence and facilitating the bacteria in extending their invasion of the organ. It should be practised lightly and superficially.

(9) *Opening of an abscess.* When deep-seated, the method described for opening a deep-seated abscess in a vascular region should be adopted ; otherwise profuse hæmorrhage may ensue. An alternative procedure is to use a pointed hot iron for the purpose. Exploratory puncture with a trocar and canula may be necessary to verify the presence or location of an abscess. A sinus may persist after the bursting of a chronic abscess for want of a dependent orifice or due to a callous lining in the cavity. When there is no systemic disturbance it is not advisable to operate to provide a counter opening or excise the callous tissue because the open wound thus produced may lead to acute or gangrenous mastitis, probably the death of the patient. This however may now be prevented by the administration of penicillin.

(10) *Amputation of the teat at its base or incision of its duct from top to bottom* to provide constant drainage for the septic material in the

gland. This is the most rational, and probably the most effective remedy. In a case of gangrene extending beyond the base of the teat, it is always indicated, to allow the putrid liquid to escape.

(11) *Scarification*, indicated in cases of diffuse purulent mastitis to allow the escape of pus from suppurating centres. It may also be employed for a gangrenous lesion to provide exits for the toxic liquid, but there is a risk in its use here of simultaneously wounding the living tissue and opening the way for inoculation thereof by the putrefactive bacteria.

(12) *Pyropuncture*, which may be adopted for gangrenous mastitis or the interstitial form of the disease, the affected region being penetrated here and there by a hot iron to make openings for the escape of septic liquid. Moussu claims good results from it in cases of interstitial mastitis. He punctures the œdematous area in the postero-superior region of the organ.

(13) *Amputation of the gland* (see p. 432).

Subacute Mammitis

Subacute mammitis is a mild form of the disease due to the presence of bacteria of feeble virulence, which only cause slight changes in the gland structure. The mode of infection is usually by way of the galactophorous ducts, and it is the latter which are chiefly involved, being affected with a catarrhal inflammation, causing desquamation of their lining. In well-developed cases the parenchyma of the gland is affected to a varying degree.

Symptoms.—There is not much constitutional disturbance, and the function of the gland is only slightly impaired. If the condition arises on the surface of the gland, there is merely redness of the skin accompanied by a little œdema, and the milk is quite unaltered. When there is catarrh of the ducts, there is slight swelling of the teat and of the quarter at the base of the latter, with more or less tenderness on manipulation. At first the milk does not appear to be altered, but after a while it loses its whiteness, and consists of yellowish serum and clots of casein mixed with cast epithelial cells. With suitable treatment the inflammatory symptoms disappear, and the milk gradually returns to the normal. A considerable time should be allowed to elapse after cure of the condition before making use of the milk for dairy purposes. Although it appears normal it turns more quickly than usual, and may spoil good milk if mixed with it. The reduction in milk-secreting capacity depends on the number of secreting cells that have been destroyed by the disease. There is always a certain amount of atrophy and consequent loss of milk production subsequent to an attack.

TREATMENT is carried out on the principles laid down for acute mammitis.

Chronic Mammitis

Chronic mammitis arises independently or follows the acute form. Infection usually occurs by the secretory ducts, rarely by way of the blood or lymph stream.

SYMPTOMS.—Nodular hardness or diffuse induration is detected in the gland, slightly painful or painless on pressure. On milking the affected quarter, a serous liquid mixed with clots of casein is expelled. Occasionally an abscess or abscesses form in the affected region, and may burst externally or into the milk ducts.

DIAGNOSIS is easy when there is an abnormal secretion from the gland. Otherwise the condition might be confounded with a tumour.

PROGNOSIS.—The disease may undergo resolution, leaving a certain amount of induration in the organ, or it may continue to extend with increased sclerosis and additional destruction of parenchymatous tissue. The life of the animal is not endangered, but when more than one quarter is involved she is useless for dairy purposes, and is often difficult to fatten for the butcher.

TREATMENT is purely local, and consists in the application of iodine ointment or a biniodide of mercury blister. Antiseptic injections through the teat are not of much value, and if carried out carelessly may do more harm than good by setting up acute mastitis. When an abscess is detected, it is opened and evacuated. A vaccine is indicated when the case is persistent.

Contagious Mammitis.—There are various forms of chronic mammitis of a contagious nature affecting the cow due to streptococci of different degrees of virulence. One form studied in France by Nocard and Mollereau responds to prophylactic measures, including the injection of a warm 4 per cent. boric solution into the affected quarter, after milking, at intervals of a week. After three or four injections the disease is arrested. The injection of " Entozon," a Bayer preparation, nto the udder has given good results in the treatment of chronic streptococcal mastitis in cattle.

This disease may be present without causing clinical symptoms and without apparent alteration of the milk except when examined by the fore milk container (strip cup). Diagnosis may be verified by laboratory methods. The other measures are those usually adopted to prevent conveyance of the virus from one animal to another.

Two other forms occurring in Switzerland have been investigated by Tschokke, one being caused by a streptococcus in long chains, defying treatment, and the other by a streptococcus in short chains, quite amenable to treatment.

The commonest form of contagious mammitis in dairy cows is that due to the streptococcus agalactiæ, and this and certain other forms of streptococcic mammitis are promptly cured by the introduction into the affected quarter or quarters of penicillin either as an aqueous solution or incorporated in a non-irritant base of arachis oil with 4·5 per cent. white beeswax in single-dose tubes of 100,000 units of penicillin, the latter securing a steady and prolonged action of the drug in the udder. It is now generally agreed that a single dose of 100,000 units into each affected quarter is sufficient to effect a cure. The advantages of the tube method are that it is safe, simple, and convenient, the trouble of preparing the solution and the provision and sterilisation of teat-tubes being eliminated. Each tube is provided with a nozzle which fits into the teat duct and it is only necessary to have this and the teat sterilised to ensure that no infection is carried into the quarter during the procedure. There is, however, a certain amount of doubt with some practitioners as to whether this method is as efficacious as the injection of the aqueous solution. The writer has found the tube method quite successful. When the aqueous solution is employed meticulous care must be observed as to aseptic precautions, a different sterilised teat siphon being used for each quarter.

Bacillary mammitis, caused by a pyogenic bacillus, has been seen as an enzootic in dairy herds, assuming the catarrhal, parenchymatous, and interstitial forms of the disease, the two last mentioned being characterised by the presence of multiple purulent foci in the gland, destroying its function.

Tuberculous mammitis is usually of a chronic nature, causing induration of the gland. It can only be diagnosed by laboratory methods. According to Bang, about 3 per cent. of tuberculous cows have lesions in the udder. The supramammary gland may or may not be enlarged.

Actinomycosis of the mammary gland has been seen in the cow and sow, and *botriomycosis* in that of the mare. The lesions are of a chronic nature, and are diagnosed by microscopic examination of their discharges. Amputation is the most effective remedy.

Mammitis in the Sheep

Mammitis in the sheep is similar in most respects to that in the cow, but the gangrenous form in this animal deserves special mention. It is ushered in by hyperacute inflammation. The gland becomes voluminous, hard, hot, and painful, and bluish-red in colour, simulating erysipelas, and death of the organ soon supervenes. The swelling extends rapidly along the abdominal wall into the groin and upwards in the perineal region. Death of the patient may occur in the course of twenty-four to forty-eight hours. The disease is due to a specific micrococcus which is found in the interstitial as well as in the parenchymatous tissue of the gland, so that antiseptic liquid introduced into the ducts is powerless in counteracting its effects. The disease is not transmissible to the cow or goat by inoculation.

TREATMENT.—Notwithstanding the rapidly fatal nature of the disease, cure is reported to have followed the injection into the gland of ½ per cent. solution of carbolic acid throughout the periphery of the gangrenous area. The best treatment, however, is prompt extirpation of the gland (see p. 433).

Prophylactic measures are essential to prevent the disease spreading through a flock. Bridré has carried out successful vaccination with an attenuated culture of the micrococcus, and found that the serum of hyperimmunised sheep possessed protective properties.

Mammitis in Goats

There are two recognised forms of mammitis in goats—viz., purulent and gangrenous.

1. **Purulent mastitis** is characterised by acute inflammation and abscess formation. It is usually seen soon after parturition, and is believed to be due to a diplococcus.

2. **Gangrenous mastitis** is almost identical with that described in the sheep, but due to a different organism.

Prophylaxis and treatment are carried out on the usual lines.

Mammitis in the Mare

Mammitis is not common in the mare. The gland is comparatively small, far from the ground, and not so exposed to contamination as that of the cow. The disease may occur prior to parturition, or even to pregnancy, but as a rule it appears during lactation.

ETIOLOGY.—The etiology is infection of the gland, the causal organism being usually a streptococcus. Early weaning of the foal when the organ is in full activity is a predisposing cause. Septic discharges about the mouth and muzzle of the foal may cause the disease, as in a case of strangles or stomatitis in the young animal.

DIAGNOSIS is easy, the symptoms being similar to those described in the cow. The condition frequently terminates in abscess formation and induration. Gangrene occurs occasionally. The disease often becomes chronic when a large amount of fibrous tissue is formed giving the lesion the appearance of a neoplasm or of botriomycosis.

PROGNOSIS.—When gangrene occurs, the mare usually dies. The gland is always lost as a secretory organ, and the mare will not be able to rear a foal.

PREVENTION consists in avoiding as far as possible the predisposing and exciting causes of the disease. If the mare is long separated from the foal, as during working, some of the milk should be drawn off with the hand. It may be necessary to do this at weaning time, if the gland is very full of milk. Purgation and the local application of vinegar or extract of belladonna or alum favour drying of the organ.

TREATMENT is on the same lines as in the cow. When the gland becomes enlarged and fibrous, with pus in its centre, amputation is indicated (see p. 433).

Mammitis in the Bitch

Mammitis is occasionally met with in the bitch, in which it is caused in the same way as in other animals, and characterised by the same systemic disturbance and local phenomena. The disease may affect one or more glands. In diffuse virulent forms of the affection, death usually ensues. A chronic mastitis may follow the acute forms recognised by enlargement and hardening of two or more glands, resembling mammary tumours.

PREVENTION consists in observing hygienic measures in kennels, and weaning the pups gradually.

TREATMENT is on the principles laid down for the cow, the local measures to be adopted comprising *hot bathing*, having the patient standing in a bath for the purpose ; *cataplasms* of " antiphlogistine " ; *stripping affected glands*, *removing the offspring*, and milking the healthy glands ; *gentle massage* with an anodyne ointment or liniment ; opening of abscesses when present ; and the excision of fibrous enlargements in chronic forms of the disease.

General treatment consists in administering a purgative, a sulphonamide preparation or penicillin together with good nursing.

Mammitis in the Sow

Mammitis is rare in sows that are well cared for. It occurs in those exposed to hardship and living in dirty surroundings or in places where the gland may come in contact with projecting objects—

sticks, stones, barbed wire, etc. In snowy weather it may become frost-bitten from contact with the snow, and infection may spread from the surface lesions into the gland. The disease is very similar to that occurring in the bitch, and is dealt with accordingly.

Tumours of the Mammary Gland

Tumours of the mammary gland are rare in the mare. Papillomata are extremely common on the teats in cows, but, apart from these, the bovine mammary gland is seldom the seat of a neoplasm. Pigs and sheep are singularly free from mammary growths, but the bitch is very subject to them.

The following varieties of tumours have been found in the mammary gland in the domesticated animals: papillomata, fibromata, myxomata, lipomata, sarcomata, carcinomata, and adenomata.

Papillomata on the Teats

Papillomata, or warts, occur frequently on the teats of cows of all ages, but most commonly on those of young cows. They may be isolated or multiple, and are usually in the form of small papillary processes. Rare cases have been seen where the warts attained a length of 2 to 4 inches, and were so numerous over the teats and glands that they gave to the organ a cauliflower-like appearance. Sometimes the warts in clusters ulcerate and assume an angry appearance. Occasionally, also, the warts become cracked at their base. Warts may be present on the teats without causing any trouble during milking, being non-inflammatory and causing no pain when compressed by the hand; but if they are ulcerated or cracked, they are very painful on pressure, and the patient will not tolerate drawing of the affected teats.

TREATMENT.—Warts should be removed at such a time before parturition that the wounds will be healed when milking or sucking is commenced. They can be readily snipped off with a scissors after controlling the cow in the standing or cast position, according to the nature of the case. If present during the milking period, and ulcerated or cracked, antiseptic precautions must be taken to prevent mammitis, and the milk must be drawn off with the teat siphon until the warts are removed and the resulting wounds healed. Touching isolated warts with nitric acid without burning the surrounding skin is an effective way of enucleating them without making a fresh open wound. The repeated application of an ointment made with salicylic acid and vaseline may cause them to separate and fall off. As there is evidence of warts being contagious, affected cows should be isolated.

Mammary Tumours in the Bitch

These comprise all those mentioned already. Chondromata, fibromata, and carcinomata are probably the most common forms met with. In some cases the apparent tumour would appear to be the result of a chronic mastitis.

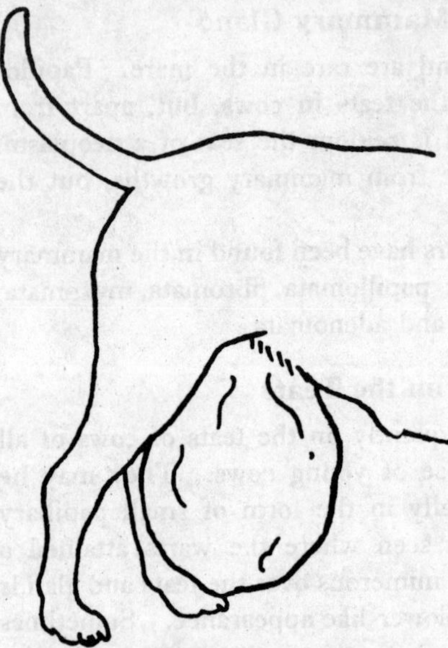

Fig. 322.—Large Mammary Tumour in the Bitch.

Symptoms.—The tumour varies in size from a walnut to a man's head. The large growth is pendulous, and may almost reach to the ground. The chondroma sometimes becomes ossified. Frequently the tumour, although non-malignant, has a necrotic centre, leading to the formation of a sinus. A tumour in the groin may conceal an inguinal hernia or appear alongside it.

Treatment consists in complete excision of the tumour, taking care to look out for a hernia when the inguinal region is involved. Although the operation wound may be very extensive, cicatrisation is rapid, and complete recovery ensues provided that the growth was not malignant.

AFFECTIONS OF THE TAIL

Open Wounds of the Tail

Open wounds of the tail are caused by direct violence (blows, crushing, etc.), rubbing the appendage against fixed objects in pruritic affections of the region (mange, oxyuridæ, and bots in the rectum and anus), and by friction or pressure of the crupper.

Treatment consists in removing the cause, if still operating, and applying antiseptic preparations to the wounds.

Rupture of the tail is occasionally met with in the ox, due to the appendage getting caught between two rigid objects and the animal pulling violently to release it, the separation usually taking place near its base. When the wound is irregular, it should be made even and then dressed antiseptically. It may be necessary to remove the remnant of a fractured vertebra.

Fractures of the Sacrum and the Tail

Fracture of the sacrum is rare. It most commonly occurs in the ox, due chiefly to its prominent position. It is usually caused by falling over an embankment.

Symptoms.—When the anterior region of the bone is broken, with laceration of the spinal cord, paraplegia ensues. When the lesion is posteriorly situated, the tail is limp and powerless. In most cases there is deformity, characterised by a prominence or a depression. On rectal examination crepitation can be detected, and if there is depression of a fragment it can be felt as a swelling inside the rectum. There may be injury to pelvic organs (the rectum, bladder, vagina) or to important bloodvessels.

Treatment.—If paraplegia is present, the case is hopeless; otherwise treatment comprises reduction and retention. The former may be effected by means of the hand *per rectum* or by the aid of a lever protected by a pad inserted through the anus and supported on an upright post behind the patient to serve as a fulcrum. A charge placed over the sacrum will help to immobilise the seat of fracture. Supporting the tail by a crupper with a well-padded dock may prove useful in keeping the fragments in position. The deformity resulting from this fracture in the female may cause difficulty in parturition.

Fracture of the Tail

The tail, by virtue of its flexibility, is seldom fractured, but one of the first coccygeal vertebræ may be broken by direct violence. The lower part of the appendage may be fractured by crushing, especially in the dog. In the horse, the accident may occur through the tail being caught between the two cross-bars of a tip-cart.

Symptoms comprise abnormal mobility, deformity, and crepitation. When the base is fractured, the tail is paralysed.

Treatment.—The padded crupper referred to above is suitable for a fracture at the base. Lower down an adhesive bandage answers the purpose. It must include the tip of the tail, otherwise necrosis of the latter may supervene. A plaster-of-Paris bandage may be applied over it, if necessary, in a large animal. In the dog, a leather sheath enclosing the tail will help a dressing to immobilise the seat of fracture. It is fixed forwards by a strap along the spine attached to a strap round the body and to one round the neck. When several vertebræ are crushed, amputation is indicated. This operation is also advisable in cases that have been neglected, and in which healing has occurred with the tail deviated from its normal direction. In the greyhound, every effort should be made to conserve the tail. When crooked after formation of the callus, it may be refractured and set straight.

Dislocation may accompany fracture. It is dealt with on similar lines. When the fracture is compound, it is treated on general principles.

Tumours of the Tail

The tail is not a common seat of tumours. Fibromata, sarcomata, and carcinomata have been seen affecting it in the horse. In grey horses, melanotic growths sometimes appear on the tail, involving it to a variable extent. They usually ulcerate and give rise to a blackish fœtid discharge.

Treatment.—If the tumour or tumours are benign and not interfering with the usefulness of the animal, it is generally better to leave them alone, as operation usually necessitates a large wound, encroaching on the vertebræ, which is slow to heal. If malignant, or ulcerated, or a source of pain to the animal, amputation should be performed.

Botriomycosis occasionally affects the tail in the horse. If not encroaching on the sacral region, the best treatment is amputation. If the latter is involved to a considerable extent the prognosis is grave, and all that can be done is to administer potassium iodide internally and use tincture of iodine locally, with little hope of success.

Dermatitis of the Tail

The horse's tail may be affected with dermatitis consequent on rubbing it against some fixed object when suffering from a pruritic affection, as mentioned in connection with open wounds. The injured part is devoid of hair, and more or less inflamed.

TREATMENT consists in dealing with the cause of the trouble.

The ox also may suffer from cracks or fissures in the skin of the ail as the result of symbiotic mange, whose treatment is indicated.

The dog is frequently affected with eczema of the tail, and the irritation which it produces causes the dog repeatedly to bite the part aggravating and perpetuating the condition, so that it assumes the nature of an ulcer. The chief treatment consists in preventing the dog from biting the tail. The best way to effect this is by applying the tail guard mentioned (see p. 794) or the steel tubular device advised by Longley (see p. 438). It may be necessary to amputate the ulcerated part.

AFFECTIONS OF THE LIMBS

Lameness

DEFINITION.—Percival's definition of lameness is generally accepted as applicable to most cases—viz., " lameness is the manifestation in the act of progression by one or more limbs of pain, disease, weakness, deformity, or impediment." It may be maintained, however, that an animal evinces lameness when at rest by holding up a limb or allowing it to bear only a portion of its normal weight.

ETIOLOGY.—The etiology is manifest from the definition, and several examples of exciting causes of the condition will be dealt with in the succeeding pages.

DIAGNOSIS.—In many cases the diagnosis of the seat of lameness in a limb is obvious, but in others it is exceedingly difficult. It requires careful and prolonged observation of sound and lame horses in motion to become expert in locating the cause of obscure lameness. The novice may have difficulty in deciding whether a horse is sound or lame, or which limb is affected. To arrive at a diagnosis in a case of lameness it is necessary to ascertain (1) which limb is lame, (2) the seat of the lameness, and (3) the nature of the lesion.

1. *The Lame Limb*.—In order to recognise the affected limb, the animal should be examined at rest and in motion. When the lameness is well marked, the limb is held in an abnormal position during rest. The fore-limb is carried forward or partly flexed at the knee or fetlock. When the foot is kept in an advanced or backward position, it is said to be " pointed." In certain cases the limb is adducted or abducted.

The horse is in the habit of resting the normal hind-limbs alternately when standing by taking the weight off one hind-limb and holding the fetlock semi-flexed, but he never does this with the fore-limb except it is suffering from some painful condition. Frequent lifting of a hind- or fore-limb is an indication of lameness. Repeated shifting of the weight from one foot to the other is a sign of lameness in both limbs. When a lame horse is made to come over in a stall he treads lightly on the lame limb, and in a case of stringhalt or shivering lifts it spasmodically or in an awkward manner.

The subject, having been observed at rest, is then exercised at the walk and at the trot. When the lameness is pronounced it is detected at the walk, but when slight it can only be seen at the trot. Rarely a horse walks lame and trots apparently sound. It is advisable to watch the horse carefully when first trotted out, as ephemeral lameness may pass off with exercise. To facilitate the observer as much as possible, the horse should be trotted slowly in hand, without excitement, on level hard ground, pavement for preference, and in a halter or snaffle bridle, the rein being held about 18 inches from the cheek, so that the head will be free to oscillate with the movement of the limbs and yet be under control. There should be no trappings or clothing on the horse. A rider on the animal would impede the observer and interfere with the head movements of the subject. When the lameness is doubtful, it is advisable to have the horse ridden to increase the weight on the limbs, and thereby intensify the pain and make the lameness more evident when the horse is again trotted in hand. It may be necessary to gallop a horse, then rest him in the stable for upwards of half an hour, and trot him again in hand to bring out a latent or intermittent form of lameness, which becomes marked after rest following severe exercise.

The sound of the shod feet on pavement is a guide as to the presence of lameness, the lame limb being put down more lightly than the others, the sound caused when it comes to the ground is not so loud as that caused by the normal limbs. When the lameness is confined to one fore- or one hind-limb, there is a striking contrast between the sound of the lame limb and that of its fellow.

In fore-limb lameness, the movement of the head is an important indication as to the limb affected. When the lame limb bears weight the head is raised, and when the sound limb comes to the ground the head drops or "nods."

In hind-limb lameness, the movement of the head is not so noticeable. It is raised when the affected hind-limb bears weight. When a horse very lame in a hind-limb is walked, the head falls when the corresponding fore-limb reaches the ground.

The movements of the croup and haunch are also affected by lameness. In hind-leg lameness, at the trot, the croup is raised when the lame limb bears weight and lowered when the weight is transferred to the sound limb. In cases of severe fore-limb lameness, the croup is lowered during the trot when the hind-limb of the opposite side bears weight. At the walk it is different; the lowering referred to occurs when the corresponding hind-limb is in support. The difference is explained by the limbs moving diagonally at the trot, while at the walk each fore-limb bears weight at the same time as the corresponding hind-limb. Therefore, to recognise lameness in front, the observer should watch the horse carefully when being trotted towards him, while for lameness behind he should pay particular attention to the animal's quarters as he is being trotted away from him.

Lameness is frequently accentuated on turning, owing to the extra pressure put on the lame limb when being used as a pivot in the turning movement. For this reason the horse should always be turned fairly sharply and observed closely when doing so. Stringhalt, shivering, and spavin lameness are most apparent at this time. It is also desirable to have the horse trotted past the observer, so that he may have a side view of the movement of the limbs.

Exercise up or down a gradient is better for revealing certain forms of lameness than exercise on the level. An uneven surface will aggravate swinging leg lameness (difficulty in taking the limb forward), owing to the impediment it offers to forward movement of the limb. Backing the animal is indicated to examine for shivering.

When both fore-limbs are suffering equally from some painful condition, the horse goes level and appears sound to the inexperienced observer. His gait is, however, " pottering," short strides being taken and the feet being placed on the ground in a stilty fashion. The patient appears stiff rather than lame. This is well shown in navicular disease affecting both fore-limbs. In double hind-leg lameness, both limbs are moved stiffly and the gait is suggestive of injury to the loins, particularly in well-marked cases, when the animal assumes a crouching gait. Backing is difficult in this case.

Diagnosis may be difficult when there is a combination of hind- and fore-leg lameness. Lameness in two legs of the same side causes an up-and-down movement of the head and quarters, due to the jerking up of the head as the affected fore-limb reaches the ground and dropping of the quarter as the sound hind-limb touches the ground. This, of course, does not apply to pacers. If the latter are lame in both legs of the same side, the body drops when the sound limbs bear weight and rises when the lame limbs come to the ground.

In a case of diagonal lameness—say near fore and off hind—the body rises as the lame limbs are put on the ground, and the head and quarter drop as the off fore and near hind reach the ground. Ordinarily, a horse lame in a hind-limb appears at first sight to be lame in the opposite fore-limb, and *vice versa* when trotted, due to both limbs contacting with the ground at the same time. This is spoken of as cross-lameness. To avoid an error, it is necessary to watch the fore and hind extremities separately, especially when lame in both places. It is well to watch the way each limb is brought to the ground, and then it will be seen that the lame limb is put down with less force than the sound one of the other side, for in slight cases of lameness the movement of the head is hardly perceptible. It is interesting to remark that a horse may be quite lame at the walk and sound at the trot. Griffin (Curragh, Kildare) had three such cases (two in the same place), in each of which the seat of lameness was obscure.

Peculiarities of gait such as the following must not be mistaken for lameness :

(1) *Bridle lameness*—that is, the horse appearing to be lame on the side from which he is led, especially when trotted in a circle with the leading leg inside. When it is suspected, the animal should be led from the other side or trotted in a halter instead of a bridle.

(2) *Rolling gait*, seen in wide-breasted cart-horses, the horse rolling from side to side in the trot.

(3) *Dishing*—that is, winding outwards of the fore-feet after flexing the knees during the trot.

2. *The Seat of Lameness.*—When the seat of lameness is not obvious, a systematic procedure is necessary in order to locate it, as follows :

(1) Ascertain the history of the case and question the owner on all points that may assist diagnosis.

(2) Have the horse standing square if possible, and walk round him at a distance of a few paces, so as to inspect the limb from every angle. Compare corresponding parts of the sound and lame limbs. Note the attitude of the limb at rest, and look out for peculiarities of gait at the trot and during turning and backing, which may help to reveal the affected part.

(3) Palpate the limb methodically in front, laterally, and behind from the withers or croup to the foot several times, examining different individual structures on each occasion, paying particular attention to the tendons and ligaments, and examining specially all the common seats of lameness. In applying compression for the detection of pain, do the same on both limbs, lest when the animal winces he may do so from being naturally irritable. Complete reliance is not to be placed on apparent flinching, in every case.

(4) Make a special and thorough examination of the foot, despite the fact that there may be some other obvious inflammatory lesion in the limb.

(5) Try passive movements of various parts to ascertain if they cause pain of certain structures, including extension, flexion, adduction, abduction, and rotation of joints. When suspicious of inflammation

in a joint, flex it forcibly for a couple of minutes and then send the horse on at a trot, when the lameness will be intensified if the joint is affected. This is called the " spavin test " when applied to the hock.

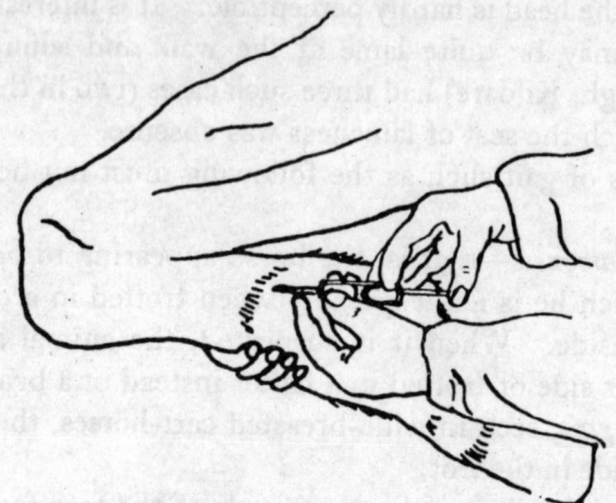

FIG. 323.—BLOCKING THE PLANTAR NERVE.

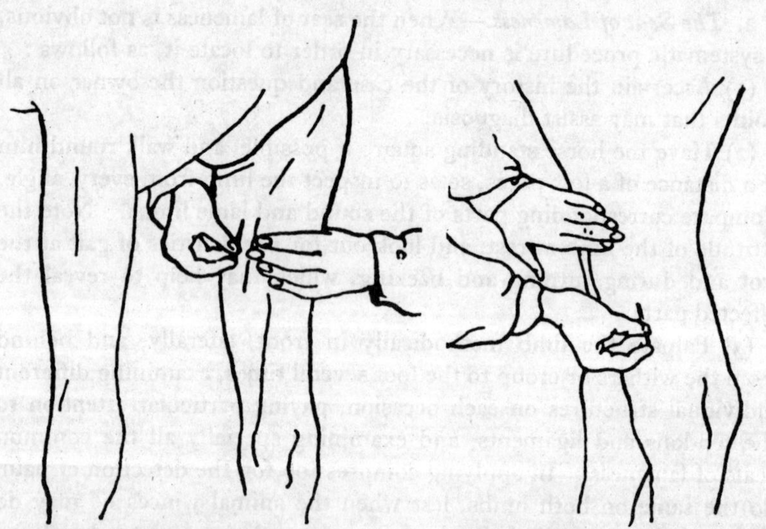

FIG. 324.—BLOCKING THE MEDIAN NERVE.

FIG. 325.—BLOCKING THE ANTERIOR TIBIAL NERVE.

The results obtained from passive movements are often doubtful. It is not always easy to say whether the animal resents them or whether his apparent resentment is due to pain or to his disposition. The same movements should be practised on the sound limb.

(6) If the foregoing examination fails to disclose the seat of lameness,

resort to the injection of a local anæsthetic over certain nerves, so as to arrive at a diagnosis by a process of exclusion thus :

FORE-LIMB.—(*a*) Inject a solution of cocaine hydrochloride, stovaine, novocaine or other local anæsthetic, over each plantar nerve and wait for ten to thirty minutes for its effect to be produced (Fig. 323). If the horse goes sound the seat of lameness is below the point of injection, and if he remains lame it is above this point.

(*b*) Inject the solution over the median (Fig. 324) and ulnar nerves, and interpret the result in the same way.

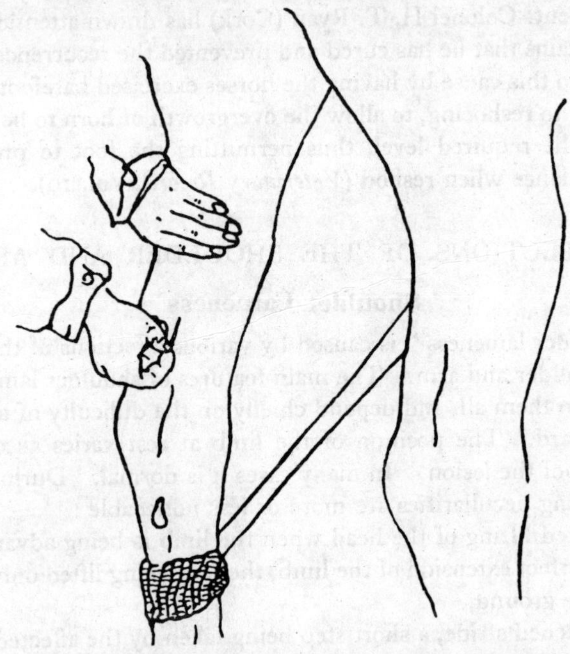

FIG. 326.—BLOCKING THE POSTERIOR TIBIAL NERVE.

It must be remarked that the injection of cocaine may possibly have a misleading effect by exciting the horse and causing him to forget about his lameness, irrespective of its seat.

HIND-LIMB.—Proceed similarly, injecting the anæsthetic over the anterior (Fig. 325) and posterior tibial (Fig. 326) nerves after the plantar.

(7) Radiography may be adopted to reveal obscure lesions below the elbow and stifle in large animals which are capable of being shown on a skiagraph, such as fractures, bony deposits, or foreign bodies lodged in the tissues.

(8) Examination *per rectum* must not be forgotten for hind-limb lameness (see p. 690).

3. *The Nature of the Lesion.*—Consideration of the lesions causing lameness will be dealt with in the following pages, but it may be stated here that lameness may be due primarily to the injudicious fitting of shoes on abnormal feet—*i.e.*, not adapting the shoe to the form of the particular foot, but rather endeavouring to alter the latter by paring it to make it approach the normal, thus interfering with the natural balance of the foot and predisposing to sprain of the lower joints of the limb. Lieut.-Colonel H. T. Ryan (Cork) has drawn attention to this, and maintains that he has cured and prevented the recurrence of lameness due to this cause by having the horses exercised barefooted on the road prior to reshoeing, to allow the overgrowth of horn to be naturally worn to the required level, thus permitting the foot to preserve its natural balance when reshod (*Veterinary Record*, Vol. 10).

AFFECTIONS OF THE SHOULDER AND ARM

Shoulder Lameness

"Shoulder lameness" is caused by various affections of the regions of the shoulder and arm. The main features of shoulder lameness are common to them all, and depend chiefly on the difficulty of taking the limb forward. The position of the limb at rest varies according to the nature of the lesion. In many cases it is normal. During motion the following peculiarities are more or less noticeable :

1. Marked lifting of the head when the limb is being advanced.
2. Imperfect extension of the limb, the foot being lifted only slightly clear of the ground.
3. Shortened stride, a short step being taken by the affected limb.
4. Stumbling due to the limb being insufficiently raised to clear slight obstacles.
5. Fixation of the scapula and humerus, recognised by their being held stiffly during progression, with restricted movement of the shoulder-joint.
6. Increased lameness on rough or uneven ground and uphill.
7. Indifference as to the hardness of the ground, provided that it is level. Soft ground is more likely to impede movement, as its surface is apt to be irregular.
8. Circumduction of the limb in the effort to overcome the difficulty in advancing it.

Passive movement of the upper part of the limb causes the animal to evince pain, care being taken that the limb is grasped above the knee, and that the movement is practically confined to the shoulder region. Compression and palpation of the latter may reveal evidence of inflammation. Comparison of the two shoulders may lead to the recognition of an abnormality. Atrophy of the shoulder muscles does not necessarily indicate shoulder lameness. Causes of shoulder lameness will now be dealt with.

Contusions of the Shoulder

Contusions of the shoulder answer to the description of contusions in general. It is only those that are deep-seated which give rise to lameness.

Sprain and Rupture of the Muscles and Tendons of the Shoulder

ETIOLOGY.—The muscles of the shoulder or their tendons may be sprained or more or less completely ruptured by accidents which cause over-stretching of the structures, such as slipping or unexpected movements when jumping or galloping, or during heavy draft, or from falling on the shoulder. Exaggerated muscular effort may also give rise to the lesions. Severe contusions may cause these ruptures directly.

SYMPTOMS.—Generally speaking, the symptoms are those of acute local inflammation and shoulder lameness. When a bundle of muscle fibres or an entire muscle is ruptured, a gap is formed between the ends, and blood accumulates there to form a hæmatoma.

TREATMENT.—The treatment is that described for inflammation, and comprises rest, cold and astringents followed by hot applications, massage with liniments, and, in the later stages, counter-irritation. When weight cannot be borne by the limb, slings are indicated. Should a hæmatoma persist after the prolonged use of absorbent topics, it will be necessary to open and evacuate it, and treat its lining with tincture of iodine or other stimulating antiseptic solution.

Sprain and Rupture of Individual Muscles : The Biceps—(Coraco-radialis, flexor brachii) Bursitis Intertubercularis

This muscle contains much tendinous tissue throughout its length, and is subject to sprain like a tendon from slipping backwards, over-stretching the muscle, or from violent efforts to extricate the limb when fixed. Rarely it is completely ruptured. Local inflammation and shoulder lameness characterise the condition. When the muscle is ruptured, evidence thereof is observed, and there is complete inability to take the limb forward, the toe being dragged along the ground during progression.

Probably the commonest seat of injury in connection with this muscle is its bursa over the bicipital groove in the humerus. Inflammation of this bursa is known as ***bursitis intertubercularis***. It is associated with sprain of the muscle, and is manifested by typical shoulder lameness. It is an exceedingly painful lesion, which prevents

FIG. 327.—LAMENESS FROM BURSITIS INTERTUBERCULARIS. The horse is being led.

any weight being borne by the limb, and completely inhibits its forward movement. During rest, the foot is placed behind its neighbour. There are marked local inflammatory symptoms just below the level of the shoulder-joint. The acute condition may become chronic, with abrasion of the cartilage, the formation of exostoses on the humerus, and even ossification of the muscle, as recorded by Williams and Dieterich. The gliding surface of the biceps is often roughened from friction against the ulcerated bicipital groove.

The local SYMPTOMS are not very obvious at first, but usually some deformity is noticed, such as a diffuse swelling on one or both sides of the tendon, or muscular atrophy. A chronic bursitis (which may be bilateral) has been seen in tramway and omnibus horses, caused by half-falls or slipping in rapid driving. The disease may be of toxic origin, occurring as a sequel to some infectious disease. When both limbs are involved, the animal seems "tied at the shoulder." Atrophy of the shoulder muscles ensues from the prolonged lameness.

PROGNOSIS of sprain of the biceps depends on its severity. When slight, recovery ensues within six weeks; otherwise it may take months, and chronic bursitis is incurable.

TREATMENT is that already described for sprains in general.

Purulent Bursitis

Purulent bursitis following an open wound and infection of the bursa causes intense lameness, and may be associated with ulceration of the bicipital groove, when cure is impossible.

TREATMENT is on general principles.

The Pectorals

The pectoral muscles may be sprained or ruptured from slipping outwards or violent abduction of the limb, causing the usual local anflammatory symptoms and lameness, characterised by marked abduction of the shoulder, whose point is widely separated from the thorax.

Rupture or Sprain of the Anterior and Posterior Spinati Muscles—Suprascapular Paralysis—"Shoulder Slip"

One or both muscles may be involved. In case of rupture of the interior spinatus, the scapulo-humeral joint is abnormally flexed; during the walk, lifting of the limb is difficult or impossible, the toe trailing on the ground. On local examination, a transverse depression is felt a little above the level of the joint. Similar symptoms are observed when the posterior spinatus is affected. Many cases that were formerly described as sprain of these muscles were probably due to paralysis thereof resulting from injury to the suprascapular nerve, which will now be dealt with under the heading

Suprascapular Paralysis

ETIOLOGY.—The nerve may be directly injured as it comes round the point of the shoulder as the result of impact against a fixed object, such as a tree or a vehicle, or it may be over-stretched and rendered functionless by the limb being forcibly pushed backwards when off the ground, as Möller has known to occur during collisions in cavalry charges. Williams described a condition in young horses first put to plough which seemed almost identical with suprascapular paralysis, but which he ascribed to pathological changes in the spinati muscles, affecting chiefly the bursa of the post-spinatus. He believed it was caused by awkward turning of the horses at the headlands. He called the condition " shoulder slip."

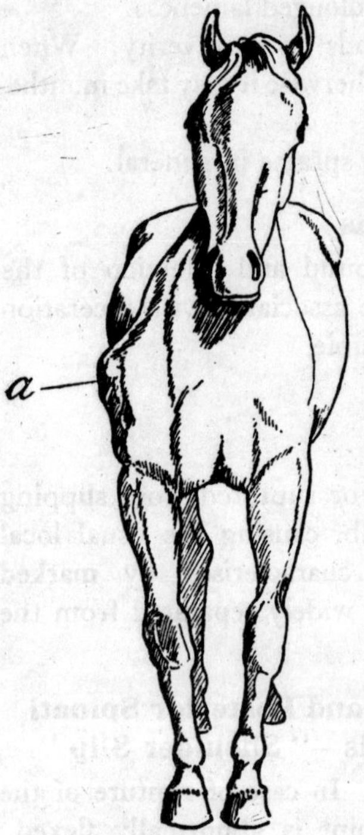

Fig. 328.—Suprascapular Paralysis.
a, The bulging shoulder-joint.

Symptoms.—The symptoms are due to loss of power in the muscles, which is characterised by difficulty in extending the shoulder-joint, and by a marked bulging outwards of the articulation when weight is placed on the limb for want of the binding effect of the muscles. The shoulder-joint appears to slip outwards at each step, thus accounting for the term " shoulder slip." This is best seen when the horse is coming towards the observer. Atrophy of the muscles is well marked when the condition has been in existence for some weeks, causing the spine of the scapula to become very prominent. The anterior spinatus may show more atrophy than the posterior.

Prognosis must be guarded. Recovery may ensue within six weeks or the paralysis may persist for months or become permanent, depending on the nature of the injury to the nerve. Rapid atrophy of the muscles is an unfavourable symptom. In some cases, although the horse eventually goes sound, the muscles never regain their normal volume. Although animals affected may not become quite sound, they may be able to do slow work in a breast collar.

Treatment is that given for paralysis in general. Electrotherapy is indicated. The local hypodermic injection of veratrine (1 grain of the insoluble form in 75 minims of water) may have a good effect also in preventing atrophy. Strychnine injected beneath the skin in the affected region and repeated daily for several days has given good results. The most common treatment is the application of a blister over the affected muscles and the administration of nux vomica and potassium iodide internally, the latter being discontinued for a while if symptoms of iodism appear. A prolonged course of arsenic or its preparations is an alternative treatment which may have a good effect. Exercise is indicated during convalescence.

Inflammation of the Tendon of the Postero-Spinatus Muscle and of its Bursa

This may be caused by contusion or by strain of the tendon. When horses with narrow chests and closely placed fore-legs are used for fast-trotting work, this tendon may become strained on account of increased abduction of the shoulder necessitated by the special conformation.

SYMPTOMS.—There is abduction of the entire limb, with supporting leg lameness. The foot is placed outwards to relieve tension on the inflamed tendon. Local inflammation is detected on palpation, pain being evinced on pressure, and crepitation (tendo-vaginitis crepitans) may be felt by the hand.

PROGNOSIS.—Recovery is the rule after four to eight weeks' rest.

TREATMENT is as usual for acute or chronic inflammation, as the case may be. The writer had a case in which subcutaneous section of the tendon was followed by disappearance of the lameness which, however, reappeared when reunion of the ends occurred, but the pony eventually went sound after needle-point firing.

The Subscapularis

Slipping outwards has caused rupture of this muscle. Lameness is characterised by deviation outwards of the upper part of the limb. It may be accompanied by rupture of the pectorals and serratus magnus.

The Serratus Magnus (Serratus Ventralis)

Rupture of the serratus magnus has been recorded. When it is present, the trunk is lowered between the two shoulders, the withers being some inches below the level of the croup, while the upper part of the shoulder surpasses the summit of the dorsal spines. The lower margin of the sternum may reach as low as the chestnut. If the trapezius is also ruptured, the anterior part of the cartilage of prolongation of the scapula bulges the skin upwards. The shoulder on the other side is directed obliquely forwards and outwards. Walking is painful, and the animal is reluctant to move. Local inflammatory symptoms are evident.

PROGNOSIS of complete rupture is bad, as perfect recovery is not likely to ensue.

The Mastoido-Humeralis (Brachiocephalicus, Levator Humeri)

This muscle is more subject to contusion or direct injury than to sprain. It is usually caused by the collar when the horse is engaged at heavy draft, and is brought about by some unexpected obstacle to the load which stops the animal and causes the collar to be jerked against the muscle. It may occur in this way during ploughing from the plough being stopped by a root or large stone. Pain is evinced on manipulation of the affected part, and if the horse is put to work he refuses the draft.

The Triceps Extensor Cubiti (Triceps Brachii)

This extensor of the elbow may be sprained or ruptured from violent slipping forward of the fore-limb. Sprain is revealed by difficulty in extending the elbow and by local inflammatory symptoms. During progression, the horse is apt to knuckle forward at the knee. If completely ruptured, the space between the ends will be detected. The tendons may be torn from the bone, or a portion of the latter may be separated.

Prognosis.—Ordinary sprain responds to treatment, but complete rupture causes permanent lameness and may necessitate slaughter. Osteo-periostitis and the formation of exostoses at the seat of rupture on the bone are always to be feared.

Treatment in all the foregoing cases is on the same lines, and comprises the measures mentioned under the headings of " Inflammation " and " Contusions."

Shoulder Rheumatism

Muscular rheumatism of the shoulder region is not infrequent in the horse and ox. It is favoured by prolonged exposure to cold and wet.

Symptoms comprise shoulder lameness and more or less evidence of pain on manipulation of the affected muscles. The spinati muscles seem to be the most frequently affected. When the condition is chronic, muscular atrophy may be noticed as well as some diminution of electric contractility. During the walk, the limb is held stiffly and lifted with difficulty. The lameness varies in intensity, and usually diminishes with exercise as the horse becomes " warmed up " or sweats, to reappear after a few minutes' rest. The lameness is often intermittent, and may pass from one limb to the other. If both limbs are affected at the same time, the horse is " tied in " at the shoulders.

When the mastoido-humeralis is the seat of the disease, it becomes swollen, tense, and painful, the neck is curved towards the affected side, and during progression there is marked difficulty in taking the limb forward and the head is more or less lowered. Backing is difficult.

DIAGNOSIS is often doubtful. The diagnostic features are the intermittency and fugitive and shifting nature of the lameness, and its diminution on exercise, associated with the absence of other evidence to account for the condition. When both limbs are involved, the affection may be confounded with laminitis and navicular disease. Young horses, when first put to work, may suffer from simple myositis resembling rheumatism. It is the result of fatigue.

PROGNOSIS varies with the intensity and duration of the lameness. Recent cases receiving appropriate treatment often recover in a few days. Sometimes, however, weeks, and even months, elapse before lameness disappears. There is always the fear of the condition recurring.

TREATMENT.—The treatment is that for inflammation and rheumatism. In recent cases, local applications comprise moist heat, anodyne and stimulating liniments, associated with massage. In chronic lesions, counter-irritation is indicated. Internal treatment includes the administration of sodium salicylate, antipyrine, and iodide of potassium. Success has been claimed for subcutaneous injection of either (1) morphia 4 grains, atropine ½ grain, and water ½ ounce ; or (2) a solution of strychnine in doses of ½ to 1 grain repeated daily for five or six days. This treatment may be renewed several times if necessary.

In obstinate cases other special treatments may be tried, including :

1. *Hypodermic injection of veratrine*, which may be repeated daily for a while if the reaction is not too severe. The dose is about 1 grain in 1¼ drachms of water (a suspension) or alcohol (solution).

2. *Subcutaneous injection of a saturated solution of common salt* in five places round the point of the shoulder, 5 c.c. of the solution being used for each injection. It causes great inflammation, and may lead to abscess formation or sloughing.

3. *Subcutaneous injection of the essence of turpentine*, 15 minims of the liquid being injected in four different places equidistant from the point of the shoulder. It causes intense inflammation with diffuse swelling, which increases for some days until it extends as far as the knee, after which it gradually disappears. Some remarkable cures of chronic cases have been claimed for this treatment.

4. *Luchow's treatment*. Ammonia, turpentine, and soap liniment is rubbed into the shoulder, producing a lather. The animal is clothed in a sheet and hood and exercised in the ring with the lame leg outside

until the body is bathed in sweat. He is returned to the stable, and cold compresses are applied to the affected part and renewed every two hours. The last compress put on at night is left in position until the next morning. On the following days the horse is exercised at the walk for half an hour. Cure may be effected in the course of three or four weeks. Two Continental authorities, Hertwig and Delwort, have reported success with this treatment, which, however, is rarely practised.

Fig. 329.—Fracture of the First Rib, in which the Union was Fibrous (Hunting's Case of Radial Paralysis).

Radial Paralysis (Dropped Elbow)

The radial or musculo-spiral nerve is the largest branch of the brachial plexus. It supplies the extensors of the forearm, the extensors and external flexor of the metacarpus, and the extensor pedis and extensor suffraginis. Radial paralysis has been frequently seen in the horse, ox, and dog, but most commonly in the horse.

Etiology.—The usual cause of the condition is some traumatic injury to the nerve whereby it becomes functionless. It has occurred in the following ways:

1. From casting the horse on hard ground, the underneath limb being affected. When Möller practised casting horses on a mattress, the accident ceased to occur.

2. From fixing the under fore-limb to the upper hind in the cast position, thus compressing the nerve between the shoulder and the thorax, or overstretching it. It has often occurred in this way following operations on the foot.

3. Accompanying fracture of the first rib, the nerve being lacerated by the fragments of the bone or being compressed by the extravasation or inflammatory exudate associated with the fracture. Willis, Rogers, Hunting, and others have drawn attention to the frequency with which it occurred in this way. Hunting has proved its occurrence in this manner in horses working in double harness, the fracture ensuing in one of the horses as the result of plunging forward into the collar when starting while the other horse hesitates. Post-mortem examination of cases which he followed up confirmed his diagnosis (Fig. 329).

Two interesting cases came to the notice of the writer recently resulting from a head-on collision between two thoroughbred yearlings galloping in a field in opposite directions. At the moment of contact the two animals fell and rose with difficulty showing the characteristics of radial paralysis in the off fore limbs which failed to respond to fairly prolonged treatment. Post-mortem examination of one of them revealed fracture of the first rib, that of the other was not reported.

4. Suddenly during a journey, without any apparent exciting cause.

SYMPTOMS.—Owing to the paralysis of the extensor muscles mentioned there is flexion of the elbow and all the joints beneath it, and the animal is unable to extend the limb. The scapulo-humeral angle is very open, the triceps is flaccid and less in relief, and the elbow is

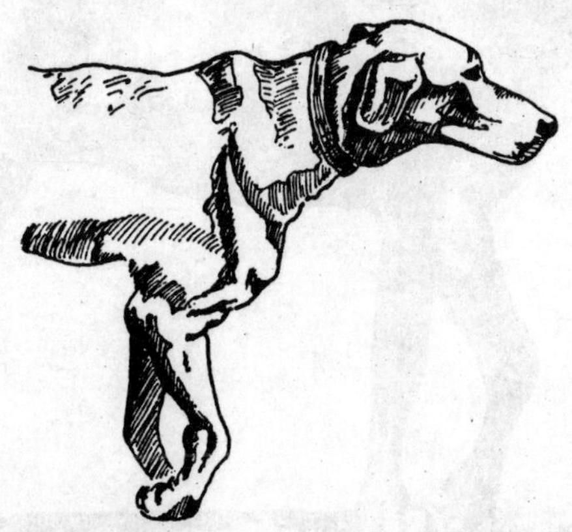

FIG. 330.—RADIAL PARALYSIS IN THE DOG.

dropped. The leg appears too long for the body. The toe or front wall of the hoof is in contact with the ground and placed a little in front of or behind the perpendicular line. The animal moves forward with difficulty, and drags the toe in doing so, but backs with comparative ease. If the knee is firmly supported in front, weight can be borne by the limb.

The foregoing symptoms are those of complete paralysis. In some cases the paralysis is not complete. Then the affected limb can bear weight, but the caput muscles may show tremors. During progression the limb is taken forward in a semi-flexed condition, and if the pace is accelerated the animal stumbles and may fall. Möller met with a number of cases of radial paralysis in 1887 which seemed to be of specific origin, occurring suddenly without any obvious exciting cause. In many of these the paralysis was partial, the caput medium and muscles in front of the forearm being unaffected. When weight was placed on the foot, these contracted in the ordinary way, giving rise to a peculiar gait characterised by a jerking forward of the shoulder during progression.

When the radial nerve is over-stretched, the twigs supplying the caput medium and parvum and extensors of the digit may escape injury because they are longer and less subject to tension than those supplying

FIG. 331.—COMPLETE PARALYSIS OF THE RADIAL NERVE.

the other muscles. This accounts for some of the cases of incomplete paralysis. Loss of sensation does not always accompany paralysis. Muscular atrophy invariably ensues when the condition has been in existence for a considerable time.

DIAGNOSIS presents no difficulty to an observer conversant with the symptoms of the condition. It is easily distinguished from rupture of the extensor pedis and fracture of the olecranon, which would give rise to somewhat similar symptoms, the local lesion being obvious in each case.

PROGNOSIS.—In some cases occurring after casting, the paralysis is of a very temporary nature, disappearing suddenly in a few minutes, a few hours, or after three or four days, but in the majority of cases it lasts five or six weeks, when recovery gradually ensues. Certain severe cases, possibly due to fractured first rib, persist for six to nine months when the patient is allowed to live so long. Uncertainty of movement sometimes remains after disappearance of the lameness, but disappears in time. In exceptional cases there is no sign of improvement after the lapse of six or more weeks, and by this time the muscular atrophy is very marked. Except the horse is very valuable, it is seldom considered worth while to pursue the treatment further.

TREATMENT is that for paralysis in general. Slings are advisable for the horse when the paralysis is complete, except it is a light animal which can lie and rise on three legs. When they are not employed, short bedding like peat moss should be provided. The measures mentioned for suprascapular paralysis may be adopted. Frequent massage of the muscles is always indicated. The routine procedure, when the case does not respond to the use of liniments and massage, is to apply a blister on the affected muscles and give potassium iodide and nux vomica internally or strychnine hypodermically. When the use of the limb is being regained, exercise should be prescribed (see Suprascapular Paralysis, p. 805).

Fracture of the Scapula

On account of its position and slight mobility, the scapula is comparatively seldom fractured in the domesticated animals.

ETIOLOGY.—The usual cause is direct violence, the result of a blow, collision, kick, tread, or fall. It may also be due to violent slipping outwards of the fore-limb. The neck of the bone has been fractured from forcibly reining-up animals.

SITES comprise the acromion process, one of the superior angles of the body, the neck, and the articular cavity.

1. *The Acromion Process.*—Fracture of this is characterised by an inflammatory swelling at its level. Crepitation may be detected and the loose bone may be felt.

2. *The Superior Angles.*—The muscular attachment at the angles causes displacement of the fragments, which can be felt in a new situation.

3. *The Body, Neck, and Articular Cavity.*—These are the commonest sites of fracture, the direction of which may be longitudinal, transverse, or oblique. There is acute local inflammation, and crepitation may be detected by placing the hand on the scapula and moving the limb in different directions. When the neck is broken, abnormal mobility

may be discovered on manipulating the olecranon, which can usually be pushed farther outwards than normally.

There is severe lameness in each case, but it is most marked in No. 3, in which the animal walks on three legs.

DIAGNOSIS.—Sometimes it is difficult to elicit crepitus, and then diagnosis is uncertain, and can only be suspected from the history of the case and the great lameness.

PROGNOSIS.—In No. 1 complete recovery ensues. When compound, there may be trouble from infection giving rise to necrosis or caries of the bone, or necrosis of the fascia in the region. In No. 2 fibrous union takes place between the fragment and the main bone, but the subject eventually goes sound. In No. 3 the case is serious in large animals, and the nearer the fracture to the lower end of the bone the graver the condition, there being less displacement of the fragments in the upper part. Destruction of the horse is usually necessary.

Exceptional instances of perfect recovery from such fractures in large animals have been recorded. As a rule, treatment is only attempted in valuable subjects. When the articular cavity is involved, arthritis and anchylosis are the usual sequelæ. Cattle sometimes make a good recovery even without treatment. In small animals treatment is always successful, except when the joint is involved and anchylosis supervenes. When sepsis ensues in compound fracture, extensive necrosis of the bone may follow.

TREATMENT is carried out on general principles. Having reduced the fracture as far as possible, an attempt may be made to immobilise the seat of fracture by making use of:

1. *Slings*, which are always indicated in the horse if the patient will olerate them.

2. *A special apparatus* in the form of an iron band riding across the withers and compressing, by means of a plate and pad at either extremity, the scapular region.

3. *A pitch bandage* enveloping the shoulder, forearm, base of the neck, and girth. Continental veterinarians had several successes in the horse by such a dressing, even without the aid of slings. It is difficult, however, to apply it satisfactorily in the large animals. In the small animals its application is easy, and in these it is advisable to include the paw, for fear of the possibility of the circulation being arrested therein if omitted.

In light cattle a charge is sufficient while the animal is left at liberty. Compound fracture is treated on general lines.

Fracture of the Humerus

Fracture of the humerus in large and small animals is usually due to direct violence, but rarely it occurs from muscular contraction. The inner or outer condyle may be broken by a violent rotary movement at the elbow-joint. The condyles are the commonest seat of fracture in the dog and cat. Falling or jumping from a height is a common cause of the condition in these animals.

SYMPTOMS.—The symptoms are as usual for a fractured bone.

DIAGNOSIS is generally easy, as displacement and crepitation can usually be detected.

PROGNOSIS of complete fracture in the large animals is bad, as it is usually oblique in direction and accompanied by marked displacement, rendering accurate reduction and retention impossible. When displacement is slight or absent, recovery may ensue, as recorded by Meredith, Warnecke, etc. In stud animals, recovery with deformity and mechanical lameness may be sufficient. In small animals cure is the rule, although when the fracture involves the articular surface of the bone anchylosis of the joint may follow.

TREATMENT is on general principles, and on the same lines as those advised for fracture of the scapula. It should be attempted in valuable horses, especially those of the light breeds and of docile temperament. Light cattle are generally good subjects for treatment, the application of a charge usually having the desired effect. When union has taken place, exercise and massage are important indications. Months may elapse in large subjects before lameness disappears.

Dislocation or Luxation of the Shoulder-Joint

Luxation of the shoulder-joint is more rare in animals than in man, due to the joint being more firmly braced by muscles in the former than in the latter. Yet numerous cases of the condition have been recorded by veterinarians as occurring in the horse, ox, and dog. Luxation can generally be ascribed to excessive flexion of the joint. The humerus is then always thrust forwards and upwards, the head of the bone being discovered in front of and above the glenoid cavity of the scapula. As the biceps antagonises this movement, displacement can only occur when this muscle is partially relaxed, as it would be, for instance, during simultaneous flexion of the elbow-joint. For this reason luxation of the shoulder-joint results most frequently from falls in jumping. A sudden check to the movement of the lower portions of the leg may also bring it about. Excessive abduction may result in the head of the humerus being displaced inwards beyond the glenoid cavity. Luxation in other directions is seldom met with.

Symptoms comprise sudden and severe shoulder lameness ; difficulty in passive flexion and extension of the joint, while abduction and adduction are abnormally easy ; shortening of the leg ; and local deformity, associated with inflammation.

Possible Complications include fracture of the scapula and humerus, most commonly the border of the glenoid cavity, and rupture of vessels and nerves in the axillary region.

Prognosis.—The results of many observations seem to indicate that even complete luxation, if early reduced, can be cured in two to three weeks. Reduction and retention are sometimes impossible, and permanent lameness may ensue from irreparable injury to the articular ends of the bones. In working horses, if there is no improvement within about fourteen days after reduction the case is hopeless. Reduction is easier in small animals.

Treatment is carried out in the manner described (see Dislocations, p. 136). In large, quiet animals, reduction may be attempted in the standing position thus : Let one man hold the animal's head, another draw the leg forward, and a third press on the knee-joint to extend it whilst the operator tries to press the head of the humerus into position. It is generally necessary to cast and anæsthetise the patient, and then perform extension and counter-extension by means of ropes applied on the pastern and round the girth, and pulled in opposite directions parallel to the long axis of the limb by assistants, while the operator endeavours by means of the hands and knees, or by standing on the shoulder, to replace the head of the bone. Successful reduction is indicated by a loud click, and by restoration of the free movement of the limb. When dislocation is lateral, abduction or adduction of the limb is necessary to lever the head of the humerus into place. When the head of the humerus lies in front of the glenoid cavity, strongly flexing the elbow-joint helps reduction, and this should be tried when the method mentioned above fails.

After-Treatment consists in keeping the joint at absolute rest to avoid recurrence until the articular ends are safely fixed in position. Bandaging is not necessary, and would be of little use. A charge is sometimes used. A blister may have some good effect in bracing up the shoulder muscles. Eventually, exercise is essential to promote mobility of the joint and prevent stiffness therein.

AFFECTIONS OF THE ELBOW AND FOREARM

Fracture of the Ulna

In the large animals, the usual site of fracture is the olecranon process commonly between its beak and the upper extremity of the radius, or at the level of the radio-ulnar arch. The usual cause is direct violence, such as a kick, but it may be the result of muscular contraction. In the dog, the shaft is often fractured along with that of the radius.

SYMPTOMS.—In transverse fracture of the olecranon, the fragment is drawn upwards by the triceps, causing a gap between the broken ends. The elbow is dropped, as in radial paralysis. The forearm assumes an oblique direction downwards and forwards, while the metacarpus is in a vertical position. When the fracture is at the level of the radio-ulnar arch, the ends of the fragments are in apposition. Crepitation can be detected when the fragments are in contact, and abnormal mobility is revealed on manipulating the olecranon.

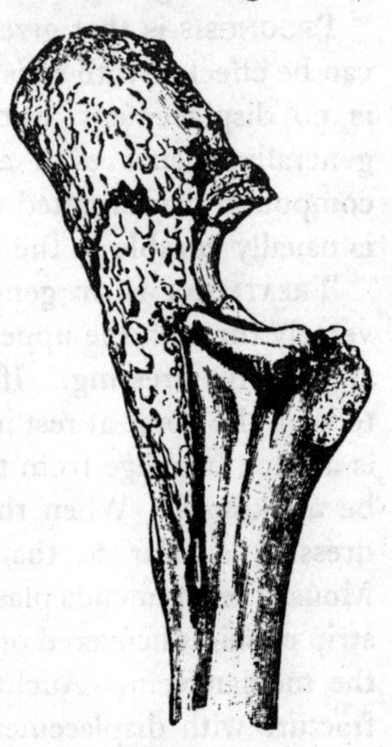

FIG. 332.—FRACTURE OF THE ULNA IN A HORSE.

PROGNOSIS in the large animals is unfavourable, as it is impossible in most cases to keep the fragments in apposition. In small animals, recovery is the rule. When arthritis of the elbow-joint supervenes, the gravity of the case is increased. Fibrous union of the fragments is a good enough result in cattle intended for the butcher and in brood mares, as it enables them to bear weight on the limb and to get about.

TREATMENT is on general principles. In transverse fracture of the olecranon, it is generally impossible to immobilise it in the proper position. When the fragments are in apposition, rest in slings may be sufficient to ensure healing. An effective dressing is impracticable in the region of the olecranon, although the bandage recommended for fracture of the scapula may be tried. In the pig, dog, and cat, the ulna, apart from the radius, may be fractured. In this case the radius acts as a splint to keep the fragments of the ulna in position, and allows union to occur even without a dressing.

Fracture of the Radius

The radius in the horse is often fractured by direct violence, such as a fall or a kick, and rarely by muscular violence. The fracture may be in the form of a fissure, which may or may not be followed by displacement later (deferred fracture). In the dog, the fracture is frequently the result of being run over, and is usually accompanied by that of the ulna.

SYMPTOMS.—The cardinal symptoms of fracture are usually observed rendering diagnosis easy.

PROGNOSIS is that given for fractures of the limbs in general. Cure can be effected with satisfactory results in the large animals when there is no displacement, but in case of the latter, permanent lameness generally ensues even after callous formation has occurred. Even compound comminuted fracture of the radius and ulna in both limbs is usually curable in the dog and cat.

TREATMENT is on general principles. When the fracture is transversely through the upper extremity of the bone, it is difficult to apply an effective dressing. If there is no displacement, it will be sufficient to keep the horse at rest in slings. In other situations the best dressing is a pitch bandage from the foot to the elbow, with which splints may be associated. When the fracture is in the vicinity of the elbow, a dressing similar to that used for fractured humerus is indicated. Moussu recommends plaster-of-Paris splints in the ox, leaving a narrow strip of skin uncovered on the inner aspect of the forearm at the level of the median vein. Auchterlonie has reported successful treatment of fracture with displacement of the lower third of the radius in a six-years-old Dutch funeral horse by the use of slings and of splints and bandages (*Vet. Rec.*, 49, No. 49).

Luxation of the Elbow

Luxation of the elbow-joint is rare. To enable it to occur, there must be rupture of one or both lateral ligaments. The author has seen it occur in a hackney horse from falling on the side with the affected limb bent inwards beneath the body. The force of several assistants applying extension and counter-extension with ropes, with the patient anæsthetised, failed to dislodge the bones from their displaced position. It may also be caused by violence in the dog, but it is more commonly congenital in this animal

PROGNOSIS.—The case is usually hopeless in the horse, but may be treated successfully in the dog except it is congenital, when it is impossible to keep the bones in apposition.

TREATMENT is carried out on general principles.

Inflammation of the Elbow-Joint

The elbow-joint is particularly prone to traumatic septic arthritis, owing to its exposed and superficial situation. The sheath of the flexor metacarpi externus communicates with the synovial capsule of the joint, and when it is wounded and infected, the infection frequently spreads into the joint. A wound has often been inflicted in this region by kicks, falls, and prods of forks. The bone is apt to be involved in the primary injury, aggravating the prognosis. Even careful antiseptic treatment often fails to exclude infection from the joint, and then septic arthritis usually supervenes, necessitating destruction of the animal.

The SYMPTOMS are as usual for synovitis or arthritis.

TREATMENT is that described for joints in general.

Capped Elbow—Hygroma of the Elbow—Shoe Boil

Under this heading there will be discussed all inflammatory conditions of the elbow involving the subcutaneous bursa and its vicinity at the supero-posterior aspect of the olecranon—viz.: (1) Acute bursitis and parabursitis; (2) chronic bursitis and parabursitis; (3) purulent bursitis or abscess formation in the elbow region; (4) a sinus or fistula of the elbow.

ETIOLOGY.—1. *Acute Bursitis and Parabursitis* are usually the result of direct injury, which may be caused in various ways as mentioned below in connection with No. 2. Occasionally it is of toxic origin, occurring as a complication of an infectious disease like influenza or strangles.

2. *Chronic Bursitis and Parabursitis.*—This constitutes the typical capped elbow, and is brought about by repeated slight injury of the elbow, which may be caused as follows by:

(1) *The heel of the shoe* repeatedly coming in contact with the elbow when the horse is lying. This is more likely to happen when the animal goes down on the knees, like a cow, or when the heels of the shoe are very long. Cart-horses shod with long-heeled shoes provided with calkins are most liable to injury in this way, and are the most frequent sufferers from capped elbow. It is difficult to explain, however, why individual horses are so subject to this injury. Ordinarily the heels of the foot are not in contact with the elbow during recumbency. The relative lengths of the forearm and the

metacarpophalangeal regions may have something to do with it, or it may be a habit acquired by the horse.

(2) *The elbow frequently coming in contact with the bare floor.* The horse, when rising in the ordinary way, sometimes slips or purposely drops back on his elbows, and when this occurs on hard ground they are more or less contused thereby. Horses with prominent elbows are most likely to get them capped in this way. With this conformation the olecranon processes may reach the ground before the sternum, and bear weight during recumbency.

Large dogs sometimes show bursal distensions on their elbows as the result of dropping on them when assuming a recumbent position. When this is done repeatedly, the enlargements take the form of callosities.

(3) *The heel of the shoe or hoof of the corresponding foot during galloping.* Cagny, a French veterinarian, has stated that he has known it to occur in this way in race-horses, the injury giving rise to lameness, which appears after a race and lasts for some hours.

Symptoms.—The symptoms vary according to the nature of the lesion, being those associated with acute or chronic bursitis, or an abscess or fistula, as the case may be. In a case of acute inflammation there is lameness. The typical capped elbow is a chronic lesion unaccompanied by pain or lameness. The enlargement in this case is mostly fibrous, due to the walls of the bursa becoming thickened by new fibrous tissue. When fairly recent the condition is cystic, being in the form of a fluctuating painless swelling. In cases of long standing it is practically a fibroma behind the point of the olecranon. Occasionally the chronic swelling becomes infected, an abscess forming and bursting, and refusing to heal owing to the cavity having a smooth or callous vegetating lining, and thus giving rise to a purulent bursal fistula. Sometimes the liquid contents of the cystic form become absorbed, leaving an empty cutaneous sac hanging below the point of the elbow.

Prognosis.—The condition is not serious, but is often difficult to get rid of owing to the cause persisting.

Prevention.—Preventative measures comprise :

1. *Using tan for litter*, which experience has shown to have the desired effect in some cases where the condition was due to the elbow coming in contact with the bare floor.

2. *Applying a pad* over the heel of the foot to prevent the heels of the shoe injuring the elbow.

3. *Fixing a sheaf of straw* longitudinally on the limb below the knee,

preventing the heel of the foot reaching the elbow when the horse is lying.

4. *The use of a special pad*, which adapts itself to the elbow in the standing and recumbent positions. It is obtainable from veterinary instrument makers.

TREATMENT is that for the various forms of acute or chronic bursitis. When the case is acute, measures include cold and astringent applications, followed by hot fomentations and absorbent topics. Iodine preparations usually prove effective in dispelling inflammatory swelling, provided it is not fibrous. Biniodide of mercury ointment (1 in 8) rubbed into a chronic enlargement may reduce it considerably. When the condition is cystic, the best treatment is to incise the bursa, evacuate its contents, and treat its lining with tincture of iodine or other irritant preparation, which will set up inflammation followed by granulation and obliteration of the cavity. When the lining is callous or vegetative it is best to dissect it out, although searing it with a hot iron is an alternative procedure. Inserting a seton through the cyst from above to below is another procedure which acts as in "capped knee." When the lesion is in the form of an abscess, it is treated as such ; and if in that of a tumour, it must be extirpated.

Extirpation may be performed by means of the knife or by ligation. When the knife is employed, the tumour must be dissected out without cutting into its structure or exposing the bone. The cutaneous incision should encircle a considerable piece of skin, to be removed with the tumour, so that the edges of the wound will meet evenly when brought together afterwards. Although primary healing need not be expected, suturing has the advantage of bringing the lips of the wound into contact and hastening cicatrisation. When the wound is extensive and there is much bleeding, a plug of wool or gauze or tow kept in position by sutures is indicated. The plug is removed the next day, and the wound then left open or drawn together by fresh sutures. The horse should be tied up short until the wound is permanently cicatrised, as the movement of lying and rising causes it to gape and retards the healing process. Some veterinarians use slings, but they are not necessary.

The use of the ligature is preferred by many, even for large wide-based tumours. A piece of good quality catapult rubber is passed round the base of the swelling and drawn as tight as possible after cutting the hair and disinfecting the skin. The ends of the ligature are tied together with string. In four to ten days the tumour is sloughed off, leaving a granulating wound which soon closes in. It is a simpler method than excision, and quite as effective. Sometimes the rubber breaks and has to be replaced by cord. When the tumour is large, it may be necessary to remove and reapply the ligature after three or four days. During the process of separation, a disinfectant should be applied daily to the affected region, potassium permanganate being very suitable on account of its deodorant qualities. No form of treatment will be satisfactory if preventative measures are neglected.

Treatment in the dog is on similar lines. When the bursa is cystic and the lesion is not very chronic, aspiration of its contents and the injection of tincture of iodine sometimes effects a cure in a short time. When the enlargement is callous, it must be removed surgically. The wound should be protected with an antiseptic pad and bandage, the latter being carried round the body and base of the neck to keep it in position. Primary healing may be obtained when the operation is carefully performed.

Contusions and Open Wounds of the Forearm

Contusions present no special features except that when inflicted on the inner aspect of the forearm, where the bone is superficial, cutaneous ostitis may supervene or a fissured fracture may be produced. They are dealt with on general principles. Open wounds transverse to the long axis of the limb gape considerably, but nevertheless heal in due course. When infected and involving the aponeurosis, pus may burrow beneath the latter, necessitating a counter-opening and the insertion of a seton to keep the passage patent until discharge has ceased. When the bone is implicated, necrosis or caries thereof may ensue, setting up a sinus, which will not heal until the sequestrum has been taken away, or the diseased surface has been removed with a curette.

Hygroma, or Distension (Hydarthrosis) of the Elbow-Joint

Distension of the synovial capsule of the elbow-joint is rarely observed, yet several cases of it have been recorded.

The Etiology is not always apparent. There may be little or no inflammation accompanying the condition, but the distension causes a certain amount of mechanical stiffness which impedes free movement of the limb. The abnormality is recognised by the presence of a bilobed swelling at the lower border of the triceps at the level of the tendon of origin of the flexor metacarpi externus, with its long axis directed obliquely downwards and forwards. Its inferior lobe is in front of the tendon mentioned, while the other lobe is behind it.

The surest TREATMENT is aspiration of the swelling and the injection into the cavity of tincture of iodine (pure or diluted with one to two parts of sterilised water), associated with needle-point firing and the light application of a biniodide of mercury blister. Several weeks may elapse before the desired effect is obtained. Strict asepsis must be observed. (See Synovitis, p. 79.)

AFFECTIONS OF THE KNEE

Contusions of the Knee

Contusions of the knee are common in the horse and ox, and are most frequently situated on its anterior aspect, where they are generally caused by falls or by striking the knee against fixed objects. The horse may injure the front of the knee in the stable by going down and getting up on the knees like the ox. The inner aspect of the joint may be bruised by " speedy-cutting "—that is, by striking this region with the inner branch of the shoe of the opposite foot during progression Cattle injure the front of the knee from constantly lying on bare floors and from striking it against the trough when rising.

SYMPTOMS.—The symptoms, generally speaking, are those of acute traumatic inflammation. Bursitis of the subcutaneous bursa in front of the knee or synovitis of the extensor sheaths in this region may supervene.

TREATMENT is as usual for contusions. Bursal and synovial distensions will be dealt with separately.

Capped Knee—Hygroma, or Distension of the Subcutaneous Bursa in Front of the Knee

This condition is fairly common in the horse, but is most frequently met with in the ox.

ETIOLOGY.—It may be a sequel to a sudden direct injury, as mentioned in the previous section, but it is most frequently the result of repeated contact of the part with the floor, wall, or manger in the shed or stable. It is very common in housed cattle provided with little or no bedding. Horses sometimes lie down and rise like an ox and suffer in consequence. It may also be caused in the ox by the animal repeatedly striking the knee against the trough when rising, and in the horse it may be the result of hitting the manger with the knee when pawing during feeding.

SYMPTOMS.—*In the horse* the lesion is in the form of a diffuse, usually indolent swelling, extending over the whole anterior face of the knee, which is œdematous, fluctuating, or indurated according to the stage of its development. When it is of long standing, its walls become thickened and indurated. It may become infected, and then show the symptoms of an abscess. Its diffuse character distinguishes it from other synovial distensions.

In the ox the hygroma may be in the form of (1) *an acute bursitis*, which is not common ; (2) *a chronic serous bursitis* or typical hygroma ; (3) *a suppurating swelling*, due to infection of the injured part ; (4) *a diffuse fibrous enlargement*.

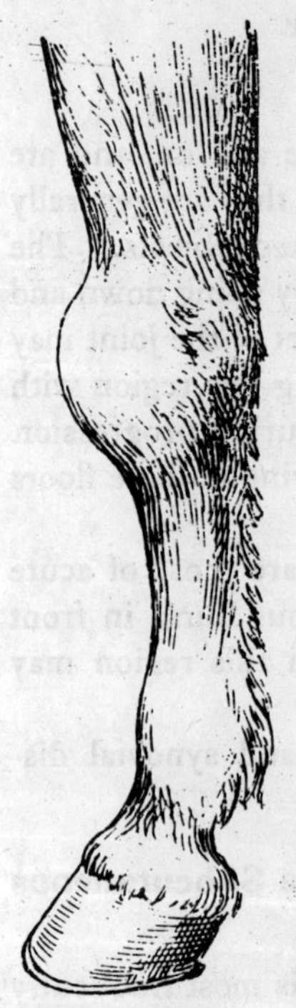

Fig. 333.—Hygroma of the Knee resulting from Bruising.

Rarely the lesion is due to botriomycosis or tuberculosis. The swelling may assume enormous dimensions and contain upwards of 10 pints of liquid. The skin over the part may be more or less excoriated. In old-standing cases the whole mass becomes indurated with a thick horny covering, and rarely ossification occurs in its substance.

Treatment is that described for bursitis in general, the measures to be adopted comprising :

1. *Removal of the cause* as far as possible.

2. *Antiphlogistic applications* when the condition is recent.

3. *Counter-irritation* with a liniment or blister, which may have the desired effect when the swelling is small.

4. *Puncture* with a trocar and canula to remove the liquid, followed by an injection of tincture of iodine, which is diffused through the cavity and then withdrawn as far as possible, although leaving it in the bursa is harmless. This method is only useful when the enlargement is purely serous, and even then it may require repetition and prove tedious in its results (see p. 84).

5. *A seton* passed vertically through the swelling, thus providing for the escape of the liquid contents. An antiseptic lotion is injected into the cavity through one of the openings. This is a good method of treatment when the lower opening has been made sufficiently large to allow of the evacuation of riziform bodies. Cicatrisation occurs round the seton, which is removed after a few days.

6. *Incision* of the swelling in a dependent part, complete evacuation of its contents, and the injection of tincture of iodine or other stimulating antiseptic solution. Turpentine or turpentine liniment is a suitable agent to apply to the lining of the cavity. In a case of considerable

standing the bursa contains a lot of loose fibrous tissue, which must be dissected out with the knife. It is generally advisable to plug the cavity with gauze, wool, or fine tow saturated with the antiseptic solution, and leave it in position for twenty-four hours, after which the lesion is treated as an open granulating wound. This is undoubtedly the best treatment for a typical chronic capped knee in the ox.

7. *Needle-point firing*, which may be found efficacious in the horse, provided that much fibrous thickening is not present.

8. *Extirpation*, which is indicated

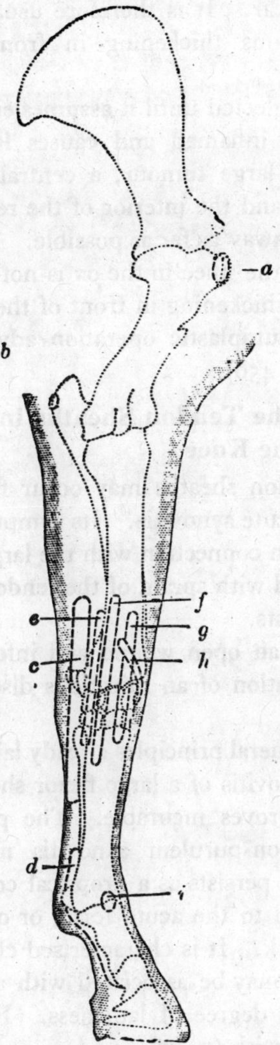

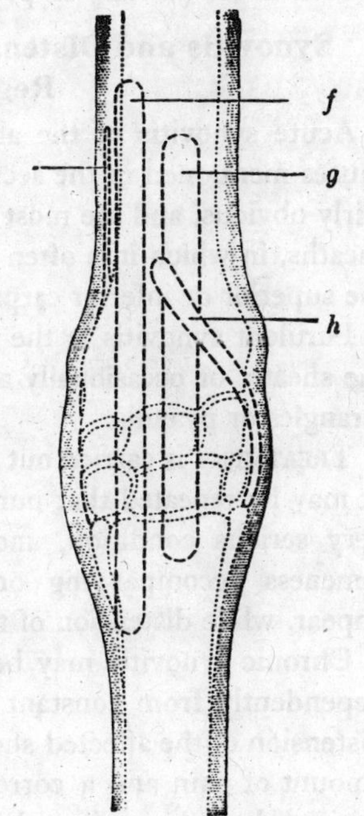

FIG. 334.—SCHEMA OF THE MORE IMPORTANT TENDON SHEATHS AND BURSÆ OF THE FORE-LIMB, SEEN FROM IN FRONT AND WITHOUT.

FIG. 335.—THE SAME, AS SEEN FROM THE FRONT.

a, Bursa intertubercularis ; *b*, bursa olecrani ; *c*, upper tendon sheath of the flexor pedis muscles (carpal sheath) ; *d*, lower tendon sheaths of the flexor pedis muscles (metacarpo-phalangeal or great sesamoid sheath) ; *e*, sheath of the flexor metacarpi externus ; *f*, upper sheath of extensor pedis ; *g*, sheath of extensor metacarpi magnus ; *h*, sheath of extensor metacarpi obliquus ; *i*, bursa of extensor pedis.

when the condition is in the form of a small fibroma and incapable of being reduced by other methods. If the enlargement is diffuse the operation is rather drastic, causing an extensive wound that will take a long time to heal and leave a large scar. It is therefore usual not to interfere with an old chronic fibrous thickening in front of the knee in the horse.

Capped knee in the ox is often neglected until it assumes enormous dimensions or becomes septic and inflamed and causes lameness. Instead of completely extirpating a large tumour, a central wedge-shaped piece may be taken out of it and the interior of the remaining halves of the swelling then dissected away as far as possible. Excision of a horny swelling on the front of the knee in the ox is not practicable or advisable. A small fibrous thickening in front of the knee in the horse may be treated by the autoplastic operation advised for broken knees (Cherry's operation, p. 456).

Synovitis and Distension of the Tendon Sheaths in the Region of the Knee

Acute synovitis of the above tendon sheaths may occur from the causes mentioned in the section on acute synovitis. Its symptoms are fairly obvious, and are most marked in connection with the large flexor sheaths, in which it is often associated with sprain of the tendons or of the superior or inferior carpal ligaments.

Purulent synovitis is the result of an open wound and infection of the sheath, or occasionally a complication of an infectious disease like strangles or pyæmia.

TREATMENT is carried out on the general principles already laid down. It may be repeated that purulent synovitis of a large flexor sheath is a very serious condition, and often proves incurable. The pain and lameness accompanying ordinary non-purulent synovitis may disappear, while distension of the sheath persists as a dropsical condition.

Chronic synovitis may be a sequel to the acute form, or occur independently from constant hard work. It is characterised chiefly by distension of the affected sheath. It may be associated with a certain amount of pain and a corresponding degree of lameness. Its prognosis and treatment have been dealt with (p. 79).

Distension or Dropsy of the Carpal Sheath

This is characterised by the presence of three swellings, two above the knee, oblong in shape, one of which is on the outside and the other on the inside of the limb between the back of the radius and the flexor muscles, the former being usually more voluminous than the latter and

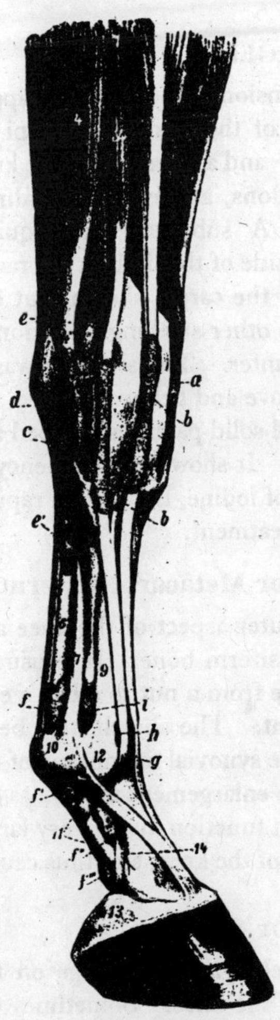

Fig. 336.—Outer Surface of the Fore-Limb, to show Synovial Sheaths.

a, Tendon sheath of extensor metacarpi magnus (extensor carpi radialis dorsalis); *b*, tendon sheath of extensor pedis (extensor digitalis Communis, anterior extensor of the phalanges; *c*, tendon sheath of extensor suffraginis (extensor digitalis lateralis, lateral digital extensor); *d*, tendon sheath of flexor metacarpi externus (extensor carpi ulnaris, ulnaris lateralis); *e*, *e'*, superior and inferior pouches of the synovial membrane of the carpal sheath; *f*, *f'*, *f''*, and *f'''*, superior, middle, and inferior pouches of the synovial membrane of the metacarpo-phalangeal sheath; *g*, bursa beneath the extensor pedis tendon; *h*, bursa beneath the extensor suffraginis tendon; *i*, protrusion of the synovial capsule of the fetlock-joint.

Fig. 337.—Inner Surface of the Fore-Limb, to show Synovial Sheaths.

a, Tendon sheath of the extensor metacarpi obliquus; *b*, tendon sheath of flexor metacarpi internus (flexor carpi radialis, radialis volaris); *c*, carpal sheath; *d*, *d'*, *d''*, *d'''*, superior, middle, and inferior pouches of the metacarpo-phalangeal (great sesamoid) sheath; *e*, bursa beneath the extensor pedis tendon in front of the fetlock; *f*, distended synovial capsule of the fetlock-joint.

more diffuse than the swellings due to distension of the synovial capsule of the radio-carpal joint or of the sheath of the flexor metacarpi externus, which appear in the same situation ; and a third below the knee, cylindrical in shape, surrounding the tendons, and extending almost half-way down the metacarpal region. A subcutaneous acquired bursal enlargement has been seen on the inside of the limb in the radio-metacarpal region simulating distension of the carpal sheath, but distinguished therefrom by the absence of the other swellings mentioned. The author had a case of this kind in a hunter. The swelling was of long standing and extended for 3 inches above and below the knee. It was opened at the lower part and serum and solid particles escaped and there was a calcareous deposit on its walls. It showed no tendency to heal after repeated irrigation with tincture of iodine, but healed rapidly after the adoption of the Bier hyperæmia treatment.

Distension of the Sheath of the Flexor Metacarpi Externus

This is indicated by a swelling on the outer aspect of the knee and the lower part of the forearm above the pisiform bone. It is usually rounded or ovoid in form, and varies in size from a nut to a hen's egg. It is tense when the limb is bearing weight. The sheath may be in communication with the carpal sheath or the synovial membrane of the radio-carpal joint. In exceptional cases the enlargement may be as big as a fist. As a rule it does not interfere with function, but if very large, or indurated, or calcified, it impedes flexion of the knee, and thus causes lameness.

Distension of the Extensor Sheaths

This is recognised by the presence of elongated swellings on the courses of the extensor tendons in front of the knee. Sometimes the swelling is bilobed, with a lobe on either side of the tendon. They are very distinct from one another when of small dimensions, but, when large, they seem almost confluent. Their form and depth distinguish them from distension of the subcutaneous bursa, while anterior dilatations of the synovial membrane of the knee-joint are hemispherical in outline.

Prognosis.—Mere distension, even of the carpal sheath, not being a painful affection, does not cause lameness. Mechanical stiffness may ensue from a dilated carpal sheath or flexor metacarpi sheath interfering with free movement of the joint. Distension of the extensor sheaths has not this effect.

Treatment to get rid of the unsightly swellings is that described in connection with chronic synovitis (p. 79). Care must be exercised

with the carpal sheath to avoid infection thereof if puncturing or needle-point firing is adopted, and on no account should a knife be inserted therein.

FIG. 338.—DISTENSION OF THE SHEATH OF THE FLEXOR METACARPI EXTERNUS.

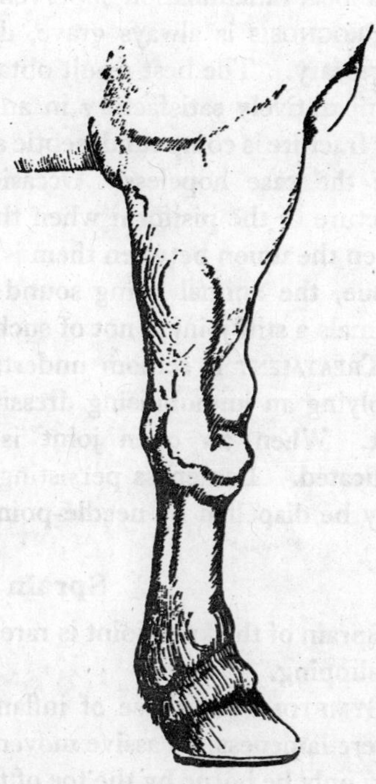

FIG. 339.—DISTENSION OF THE EXTENSOR TENDON SHEATHS IN FRONT OF THE KNEE.

Fractures of the Carpus

Fracture of the carpus is rare, and is usually confined to one or two bones, but occasionally all the bones of one of the rows is involved, and more rarely most of the bones of both rows are broken.

ETIOLOGY.—The fracture may be simple or compound. The former is due to concussion of the bones when a false unexpected step is made during jumping, and is consequently most common in hunters and chasers. The latter results from falling on the knee, and is usually complicated with open joint. The pisiform is generally fractured by muscular contraction during jumping or galloping, or as the result of slipping forwards.

Symptoms.—There is sudden and severe lameness, no weight being borne by the affected limb, and the joint is incapable of flexion or extension. Crepitation can generally be detected. Acute inflammatory swelling supervenes later. In fracture of the pisiform, the fragments are usually separated by muscular contraction. Intense lameness and local inflammation supervene, as in the case of the other bones.

Prognosis is always grave, destruction of the horse being usually necessary. The best result obtainable is an anchylosed joint, which is comparatively satisfactory in an animal suitable for the stud. When the fracture is compound, septic arthritis commonly supervenes, rendering the case hopeless. Occasionally complete cure is obtained in fracture of the pisiform when the fragments are not displaced. Even when the union between them is only of a fibrous nature, recovery may ensue, the animal going sound in some cases. Of course, in small animals a stiff joint is not of such importance as in the horse.

Treatment is seldom undertaken in large animals. It consists in applying an immobilising dressing and keeping the patient at perfect rest. When an open joint is present, the treatment therefore is indicated. Lameness persisting after healing of a fractured pisiform may be dispelled by needle-point firing.

Sprain of the Knee

Sprain of the knee-joint is rare. It may result from jumping, falling, or slipping.

Symptoms are those of inflammation associated with more or less severe lameness. Passive movement of the joint causes pain. Weight may only be borne by the toe of the foot.

Treatment is as usual for inflammation. Recovery ensues after prolonged rest.

Dislocation of the Knee-Joint

Dislocation of the knee-joint is a rare occurrence, and is usually incomplete. It is caused in the same way as sprain.

Symptoms.—In complete luxation the animal goes on three legs, and there is marked deformity and inflammation in the affected joint, which is also abnormally mobile, as a rule, especially when fracture is present, which is not infrequently the case. When the dislocation is incomplete, the lower part of the limb is deviated from the normal, and there is a concavity on the inner or outer aspect of the knee according as the deviation is inwards or outwards. Some of the carpal bones may be felt displaced from their normal position.

PROGNOSIS.—Complete dislocation is hopeless. Partial dislocation may be followed by recovery, as in the case recorded by Flynn in the *American Veterinary Review*. When there is an open wound, the case is still more grave.

TREATMENT consists in reduction and retention and, in the case of the horse, rest in slings.

Synovitis—Arthritis—Distension of the Synovial Capsule of the Joint

Inflammation of the joint may be confined to the serous membrane (*synovitis*) or affect the articular ends of the bones as well (*arthritis*). The causes of synovitis and arthritis have been mentioned in the sections in general surgery dealing therewith. They are often rheumatoid in the dog.

The SYMPTOMS are those of inflammation in the joint and lameness varying in degree according to the acuteness of the affection. At rest the limb is held in an advanced position with the knee semi-flexed. During progression the joint is held stiffly. Dry arthritis affecting this joint was first described by Cherry in 1845, who spoke of it as " chest founder," from the horse giving the sensation of foundering under the rider, and also as " knee spavin." He ascribed the condition to constant hard work, violent exertion, and slipping.

Horses with narrow, imperfectly formed knees, short forearms, and upright shoulders appear most predisposed to the condition, possibly on account of the peculiarly exaggerated movement of the knee-joint which such formation favours. Russian trotters with this form and action often suffer from chronic carpitis. Not infrequently the disease is bilateral ; it is certainly more common in coarse than in well-bred animals. The knee becomes swollen, and the swelling is usually hard, consisting principally of new connective tissue and, later, of exostoses. Free movement of the joint is interfered with. At rest the animals lean forward, and during progression move stiffly. Passive flexion of the knee causes pain and intensifies the lameness, and reveals a varying degree of anchylosis in the joint. Lameness is characterised by the limb being advanced slowly and the stride shortened, whilst the knee-oint is imperfectly flexed and the limb abducted when weight is placed upon it.

Chronic carpitis is incurable. Sometimes a horse has a stiff knee from the development of periarticular fibrous tissue, and is capable of doing moderately hard work.

TREATMENT is useless when the joint is diseased, but when the inflammation is only periarticular, counter-irritation may have a good effect. Median neurectomy may be tried as a last resort. Möller had several successes after this operation.

Distension of the Radio-Carpal Joint

This is characterised by (1) a swelling confined to the upper part of the front of the knee beneath the extensor tendons, and sometimes by (2) a round, firm swelling, varying in size from a walnut to a fist, situated on the outer aspect of the knee above the pisiform bone between the posterior face of the radius and the flexor metacarpi externus, the bulging taking place in the space between the posterior common ligament of the carpus and the carpo-metacarpal ligament. It is sometimes confounded with distension of the sheath of the flexor metacarp externus. The latter is practically irreducible, while the distension of the joint is compressible, and, when pressed upon, increases the tension of the pericarpal swelling.

Distension of the Intercarpal Joint

This is revealed by the presence of two or three small hemispherical swellings on the middle region of the anterior aspect of the knee. These are tense and hard when weight is placed on the limb, and soft and fluctuating when the latter is lifted, except in very chronic cases, when the walls of the swelling may be indurated or calcified. The carpo-metacarpal joint cannot become distended owing to the close union of the bones by ligaments.

The DIAGNOSIS of the various synovial enlargements of the region of the knee is easy when the characteristics of each are remembered. Ordinary articular distensions, unaccompanied by inflammation, do not cause lameness, but may produce a certain amount of mechanical stiffness of the joint varying in degree according to the size of the swelling and the induration in its walls.

TREATMENT, when required, is that described for chronic synovitis.

An exostosis on the pisiform bone associated with more or less ossification of the tendons which are inserted into it is sometimes seen in race-horses, resulting, as a rule, from a partial rupture of the tendons at their points of insertion or more rarely from fracture of the bone. It gives rise to prolonged or permanent lameness. Needle-point firing and blistering are indicated, and if this treatment fails, the only resort is median neurectomy.

Broken Knee—Open Knee-Joint—Traumatic Arthritis

The front of the knee is a common seat of wounds caused chiefly by falls. They may involve the skin only or extend into the joint, and be associated with fracture of some of the carpal bones. All wounds, superficial and deep, on the front of the knees are spoken of as "broken knees." Once a knee is deeply "broken," the horse is generally prone to fall on it again, owing to the cicatrix diminishing the freedom of movement in the joint, and probably to the animal's knee action being naturally defective. The posterior aspect of the carpus is sometimes wounded by the horse getting the limb over the tying-up chain and making efforts to release it.

Superficial wounds on the front of the knee do not cause severe lameness, but those on its posterior aspect cause much pain during movement, being more affected by flexion and extension of the joint. Synovial discharge from the wound may be due to a tendon sheath or the joint being opened. Probing should not be practised to ascertain the antero-posterior depth of the wound.

Prognosis depends on the nature of the wound. When the joint is open, there is always danger of a fatal septic arthritis supervening. When the bones are damaged, exostoses may be formed, causing anchylosis of the joint. Penetrating wounds of the posterior aspect of the carpus are generally more serious than those in front, due to the complex anatomy of the back of the carpus, comprising tendons and ligaments, wounds of which are slow to heal. Nevertheless recovery may eventually ensue.

Treatment is carried out on general principles. There is frequently a "pocket" beneath the skin requiring a counter-opening. Suturing is seldom indicated, but it may sometimes be useful to keep a displaced flap in position. When it is employed it is necessary to apply a gutter splint, with padding beneath, at the back of the knee; otherwise, the movement of the joint will soon cause the sutures to cut through the skin. It is generally best to leave the wound open and uncovered, having it repeatedly irrigated with an antiseptic solution until it is uniformly granulating, when a dry astringent dressing should be applied.

It must be remembered that when the front of the knee is wounded as the result of a fall, the deep tissues that came in contact with the ground become hidden by the skin when the animal is standing, the cutaneous wound being displaced upwards owing to the skin reverting to the situation it occupied before flexion occurred. It is for this reason that there is usually a pocket beneath the skin containing bruised tissue and foreign matter in its depth necessitating perhaps the making of a counter opening to ensure draining and cleansing of the wound. The same applies to a wound on the outside of the hock caused by contact with a sharp object on the ground in the recumbent position —the cutaneous part of the wound being at a higher lèvel than that in the deep tissues when the standing position is resumed.

When the joint is open, some of the remedies recommended for that condition are indicated. When the synovial fistula is slow to heal, the application of a blister of biniodide of mercury often hastens its closure. Should the articulation become septic, the case is generally incurable. If the infection has not gone beyond the synovial membrane, there is a possibility of recovery ensuing under the influence of the Bier treatment, penicillin, and antisepsis. The blemish caused by a large cicatrix in front of the knee may be removed by an autoplastic operation (see p. 456).

Bent Knees

The knees may be overflexed as the result of contraction of the tendons of the flexor metacarpi muscles, chiefly the externus and medius. The condition may be congenital, or acquired soon after birth, or later in life, apparently as the result of constant hard work. When the deformity is so marked as to interfere with function, tenotomy is indicated (see p. 454).

AFFECTIONS OF THE METACARPUS

Supernumerary Digit—Fissured Digit

Occasionally a foal is born with a supernumerary digit on a hind- or fore-limb corresponding to the index digit of the human limb, and situated to the inner aspect of the normal digit. It is always smaller than the latter, and rarely assists in bearing weight. The plantar aspect of its hoof looks towards the ground, or backwards or upwards It results from abnormal development of the inner splint bone, which becomes furnished with three phalanges and two sesamoids. Rudimentary extensor and flexor tendons detached from those on the normal digit may also be present. It is endowed with very limited movement, and its vascular system is feebly developed.

Another form of congenital deformity sometimes met with is fissure of a digit, involving as a rule the terminal phalanx and os corona.

TREATMENT.—A supernumerary digit has often been successfully removed. The operation consists in making a longitudinal (cutaneous) incision from the upper to the lower extremity of the abnormal metacarpal or metatarsal along its mesial free surface, dissecting back the skin from the bone, separating the latter from the normal bone, removing it, and suturing the skin over the wound, which is then protected by an antiseptic pad and bandage. The union between the lower parts of the bones is fibrous, and can be divided with the knife; but in the upper part the bones are fused, and can only be separated by the use of a fine saw. Healing by first or second intention usually occurs without complication, the wound being completely cicatrised within two or three weeks.

The foregoing procedure involves making a large wound in the main bone, which may consequently become rarefied and fracture subsequently, as in a case recorded by the writer, after apparent complete cure. To avoid this, it is better to remove only the lower third or half of the abnormal metacarpus. This is done by cutting the bone obliquely downwards and inwards with the saw, and then resecting the distal portion by means of a bone forceps or a chisel and mallet.

Supernumerary digits in small animals are dealt with on similar lines.

Traumatic and Inflammatory Lesions of the Metacarpal Region—Section of the Tendons

The above lesions of the metacarpal regions are in accordance with those dealt with in general surgery. Open wounds penetrating the flexor synovial sheaths or the joints are serious, as stated in the sections devoted to these structures. Those involving the tendons are apt to be followed by necrosis thereof, and when it is a flexor tendon that is affected the case may prove incurable. When the bone is wounded a sinus may ensue, due to necrosis or caries of the osseous tissue.

TREATMENT is carried out on general principles for ordinary wounds, open synovial sheaths or joints, or a sinus, as the case may be.

Section of the Tendons

Section of the tendons deserves special mention. Complete division of the tendons gives rise to well-marked symptoms. When it is the extensors of the phalanges that are divided, extension of the digit is impossible, and during progression the front of the wall of the hoof trails on the ground, but weight can be borne on the foot as usual. When the flexors are involved, it may be the perforatus or perforans, or the suspensory ligament, or a combination of these structures that is severed.

The accident is most common in the hind-limbs, where it is often caused by kicking the limb against a sharp object or by the horse backing against the blade of a mowing machine. One or both tendons may be partly or completely divided by an "overreach," or by being struck by the shoe of a following horse during a race. The deformity resulting from these accidents is characterised by more or less descent of the fetlock and abnormal extension of the phalanges, depending on the structures affected. When the perforatus only is severed, there is noticeable lowering of the fetlock, and this is more marked when the suspensory is divided. When the perforans is cut across, there is excessive extension of the interphalangeal joints, causing the toe of the hoof to be turned upwards and its plantar aspect to look forwards. If there is complete section of all the structures, the fetlock pad is down on the ground and the pastern is horizontal.

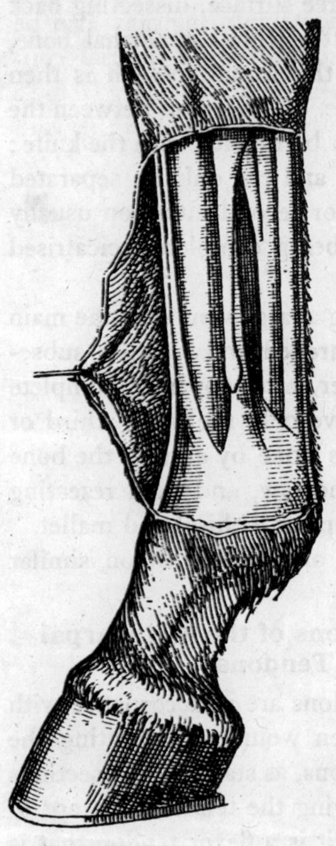

FIG. 340.—SHOWING RELATIVE POSITIONS OF TENDONS, ETC., IN THE METACARPAL REGION.

Immediately behind the metacarpus lies the suspensory or superior sesamoid ligament; the short band extending from behind the knee half-way down the metacarpus is the check ligament; behind it lies the perforans tendon to which it is connected; the hindmost of the tendons shown is that of the flexor pedis perforatus muscle.

PROGNOSIS.—Section of the extensor tendons is much less serious than that of the flexors, and, of course, section of two or all of the latter structures is more grave than that of one only. In all cases there is the danger of necrosis and its consequences supervening, and when one of the flexor sheaths is opened, there is grave fear of purulent synovitis ensuing. Apart from these complications, healing may be imperfect, being followed by elongation of the tendons, and consequent deformity and interference with function. Many cases of complete recovery from division of the flexor tendons and of the suspensory ligament have been recorded. Divided extensors generally heal without difficulty.

TREATMENT comprises antisepsis of the wound and immobilisation of the limb in such a position that the ends of the divided structure or structures are brought as close together as possible. In small animals suturing the tendon and the application of an antiseptic pad and bandage are sufficient. In the horse suturing may also be practised, and in addition to bandaging support by a special contrivance is necessary, such as the swan-necked shoe, or Defoy's apparatus, or that of Brogniez, each of which acts as a prop beneath

FIG. 341.—RUPTURE OF THE FLEXOR PEDIS PERFORANS AND PERFORATUS TENDONS.

the fetlock. Slings are also indicated to keep the horse stationary if of a docile disposition. Healing usually occurs within four weeks when the case takes a favourable course. After it has taken place in the horse, a shoe with thick heels or calkins is advisable in many cases to take the strain off the cicatricial tissue and prevent elongation of the tendon. After about two months the patient is able to put weight on the affected limb. The fetlock may be abnormally low for a considerable time, but eventually cicatricial contraction usually raises it to its normal level.

Rupture of the Extensors of the Phalanges

Rupture of the extensor tendons is rare. It has been seen as a congenital condition in the foal. Rarely it is caused in the adult horse by a false step during galloping. There is inability to extend the

FIG. 342.—RUPTURE OF THE FLEXOR PEDIS PERFORANS BEHIND THE FETLOCK IN CONSEQUENCE OF SUPPURATION IN THE TENDON SHEATH.

FIG. 343.—RUPTURE OF THE FLEXOR PEDIS PERFORANS TENDON. (From a photograph.)

phalanges and the gap between the ends of the ruptured tendon can be felt. Immobilisation of the part associated with antiphlogistic remedies effects a cure when the tendon is healthy. When of congenital origin there is no effective remedy.

Rupture of the Tendons of the Perforatus and Perforans

(see p. 77)

This condition has been frequently observed. The rupture may be primary or secondary and partial or complete. Primary rupture occurs as the result of violent stretching of the healthy tendon, as may occur during galloping or jumping. It is predisposed to by a period of idleness or a debilitating disease. When the muscles become tired during severe or prolonged exertion they cease to afford active support, and then extra passive strain is thrown on the tendons, which may give way in consequence. Secondary rupture is a sequel to degeneration or necrosis of the tendons. It is fairly common, following double plantar neurectomy. In a case of severe lameness in one limb, whereby it is unable to bear weight, the other limb may suffer from rupture of one or both flexor tendons from the constant unremitting strain thrown upon them, especially when the patient is debilitated or showing signs of lack of nutrition. Mares and cows affected with puerperal metritis have been known to suffer from complete rupture of the flexor tendons. A common seat of rupture is at the level of the fetlock.

SYMPTOMS.—The deformity caused by rupture of the tendons is the same as that resulting from section thereof, being characterised by hyperextension of the fetlock or phalangeal joints, as already described. When the accident is recent, the empty space between the ends of the divided tendon may be felt ; but at a later period it is filled by extravasated blood, and then the local evidence of rupture is not so clear. The subcarpal or subtarsal ligament may be ruptured and evince symptoms of severe strain, so that diagnosis of the exact nature of the lesion is difficult.

PROGNOSIS.—When the ruptured tendon has been the seat of disease or degeneration the case is hopeless. Complete rupture of a healthy tendon or tendons may be followed by recovery. When rupture is confined to one tendon, the prognosis is more favourable than when both are involved. Incomplete rupture of the perforatus and perforans or of their check ligaments is not uncommon, and varies in degree in different cases. It is characterised by marked inflammatory symptoms and severe lameness. Its diagnosis may be difficult.

TREATMENT.—Incomplete rupture is treated as a severe sprain. Immobilisation with a bandage is the chief indication. Complete rupture is dealt with on the same principles as those adopted for section of the tendons. Healing in the case of a healthy tendon occurs in the course of about six weeks if the ends are not too far apart. Two or three months at least will elapse before the animal is fit for use.

Ruptured tendons are more easily treated in small than in large animals. Suturing the ends of the tendon may be practised in the former, in which there is more chance of operating aseptically than in the latter. It is better not to attempt the operation in large animals, on account of the risk of infection and necrosis supervening.

Inflammatory New Growths on the Metacarpus and Metatarsus

Occasionally an open wound in these regions becomes the seat of a chronic inflammatory enlargement, an enormous amount of fibrous tissue being developed, presenting the appearances of a fibroma. It may be wide-based or fungiform in shape.

TREATMENT consists in excising the enlargement level with the surrounding parts and checking the recurrence of excessive granulation by the use of caustic and astringent dressings, formalin (1 in 40) having an excellent effect in this respect.

Rupture of the Suspensory Ligament

The suspensory ligament may be ruptured in much the same way as the flexor tendons. It is usually the result of violent effort in jumping and galloping, and is commonest in racehorses, in which it most frequently occurs towards the end of a race, when the muscles are more or less exhausted and an extra passive strain is thrown on the ligament as well as on the tendons.

SYMPTOMS.—The horse goes suddenly lame, stopping, as a rule, and holding up the affected limb. When weight is momentarily placed on the limb the fetlock comes down to the ground. Local examination reveals a solution of continuity in the ligament, usually just above its bifurcation. This is generally the condition in the racehorse when he is said to have "broken down." It may be accompanied by rupture of one or both flexor tendons or by fracture of the sesamoids. In some instances only one of the branches is ruptured, most frequently the inner one.

PROGNOSIS.—If the rupture occurs in two limbs or is complicated by that of other structures the case may be looked upon as incurable. As a rule treatment is not undertaken for complete rupture except it is unilateral and affecting a very valuable animal. The case is not quite so serious in a hind- as in a fore-limb.

TREATMENT is carried out on the same lines as those laid down for rupture of the flexor tendons, comprising immobilisation of the affected region with a plaster bandage and support of the fetlock by one of the devices mentioned. Several months, amounting often to a year or more, must elapse before work is possible.

Sprain of the Flexor Tendons—Tendinitis

The term "sprained tendons," or "sprain of the flexor tendons," includes sprain of the perforatus and perforans tendons and their check ligaments and of the suspensory ligament. The condition is much more common in the fore- than in the hind-limbs, due undoubtedly to the fact that in all classes of animals the former bear the greater part of the body-weight and in saddle-horses the greater proportion of the weight of the rider. The lesion is particularly common in hunters and chasers, the nature of whose work exposes most of the structures in question to over-distension. The mechanism of sprain has been explained by Barrier and Siedamgrotzky by the aid of instantaneous photography of the various phases of movement of the limbs. Working independently, they arrived at the same conclusions. They found that the moment the foot is placed on the ground there is flexion of the corono-pedal joint, and also, but to a less extent, of the suffragino-coronal joint, whereby the distances between the points of origin and insertion of the perforans and perforatus tendons are diminished, thus relaxing these tendons and leaving all the strain at this moment to be borne by the suspensory ligament, which stretches, allowing the fetlock to descend. After this descent has gone a certain distance the perforatus is put on the stretch, and helps the suspensory ligament to support the bodyweight. It follows from this that if the foot is brought to the ground with great violence the suspensory and the perforatus are liable to be sprained, thus explaining why sprain of these structures is most common in horses doing fast work. They also found that just prior to the foot leaving the ground there is extension of the corono-pedal joint, increasing the distance between the points of origin and insertion of the perforans; so that if an unusual effort is made at this time, its tendon and check ligament are apt to be sprained. The above findings are in accordance with experience in practice, the facts being that sprain of the perforatus and its check or supracarpal ligament and of the suspensory ligament is most common in galloping and fast-trotting horses, while that of the perforans and the subcarpal ligament is most frequent in draft-horses, in which the greatest effort is made just before the foot is lifted from the ground.

Etiology.—The etiology of sprained tendons comprises predisposing and exciting causes, which may be taken together as follows:

1. *Unfit Condition*, sprain being much more likely to occur in horses put to severe exertion after a term of rest or idleness than in those kept at regular work.

2. *Conformation.*—Any conformation which puts the " tendons " at a disadvantage favours sprain thereof, such as long sloping pasterns, a very oblique hoof, or one whose toe is long or heels very low, which increase the resistance to the action of the flexors. Also the more slender the fetlock when viewed from the side, the greater the mechanical disadvantage to which the tendons are placed. Horses with " tied-in " knees generally have this type of fetlock. The greater the muscular development of the hind-quarters, the greater the shock produced on the tendons in the fore-limbs by the violence with which the weight of the body is thrown forward on to them. In a horse with " calf-knees," the back tendons are at a disadvantage and predisposed to strain. A heavy body compared with the limbs also favours the condition.

3. *Temperament.*—When a horse is very high-spirited, he is more apt to over-exert his tendons than when of a phlegmatic temperament.

4. *Fast Work.*—Tendons are obviously more likely to be strained during fast work, like galloping, jumping, and fast trotting, than during slow work.

5. *Heavy Draft*, which, as already explained, predisposes to sprain of the perforans and the subcarpal ligament in the cart-horse.

6. *The Nature of the Ground.*—A slippery surface leads to slipping and unexpected movements, which often involve strain of ligaments and tendons, while irregular or yielding ground has the same effect, and in the case of cart-horses makes draft more difficult and irregular and necessitates occasional extraordinary efforts to overcome obstacles.

7. *Muscular Fatigue*, which occurs towards the end of a race or a tiring journey, is a fruitful source of strain, whose occurrence under such circumstances is well known. The muscles, being exhausted, cease to act, with the result that an increased passive strain is thrown on the tendons.

8. *The Quality of the Tendons.*—Soft " gummy " tendons are easily sprained, while " fine " hard tendons are able to withstand prolonged and violent exertion without ill-effects.

Tendinitis, apart from sprain, is caused by contusion and by the toxins of bacterial diseases like influenza and pneumonia, being accompanied in the latter case by synovitis. Invasion of the suspensory ligament by the *Filaria reticulata* occurs in Austria, Russia, and the South of France. It excavates galleries, which are afterwards represented by nodular enlargements. The ligament is predisposed to injury. The perforatus is less frequently affected.

Symptoms.—The symptoms of sprained tendons vary according to the extent and acuteness of the lesions. In a recent case there is evidence of acute inflammation at the seat of sprain. The swelling may be very marked and diffuse, extending over the entire metacarpal region, or circumscribed, confined to a portion of the tendon or to one of the check ligaments, or to the suspensory ligament or one of its branches. The swelling may not be pronounced until two or three days after the accident. Palpation reveals the swelling and the abnormal heat, and pressure with the fingers causes the patient to evince pain. The latter is most marked in the early stage of the condition. Later it is not always in accordance with the gravity of the lesion, which may be very persistent, although the pain and lameness are not very pronounced. Lameness is always severe after the onset of acute tendinitis. It is most intense when the lesion is in the region of the knee or fetlock, or at the back of the pastern. At rest the horse may hold the fetlock flexed.

In cases of chronic sprain the lameness is comparatively slight, and may be intermittent. In some instances the mass of tendons is voluminous and indurated, the chief cause of enlargement often being a thickening of the aponeurosis ensheathing the tendons. In others the lesion is confined to one of the tendons or its ligament, or to the suspensory ligament, or to a part of one of these structures. Individual exploration of the latter reveals any abnormality that may be present. Sometimes the tendinitis is gradual in its development, commencing with stiffness or intermittent lameness, and becoming acute when the horse is put to severe exertion. When sprain occurs at the level of one of the sheaths it is accompanied by synovitis. As regards the incidence of sprain in each of the structures in question, the following chief sites may be mentioned :

1. *The perforatus*, the level of the superior carpal ligament, the upper and middle parts of the tendon, and its branches of insertion. A fairly common lesion is a thickening of the peritendineum in the middle part of the metacarpus resulting from slight and repeated strain. It gives the tendon a bowed appearance, and is known as " bowed tendon."

2. *The perforans*, the level of the check ligament, the middle part of the tendon, and the back of the pastern.

3. *The suspensory ligament*, one of its branches, just above its bifurcation, and the middle part of the body of the ligament.

Diagnosis.—In an acute case in which the swelling is diffuse the diagnosis of the exact structure or part thereof involved may be difficult. The region in which most pain is evinced on compression with the fingers and thumb generally represents the chief seat of sprain. Each structure is best examined with the knee flexed. Filariasis of the ligament is characterised by a nodular, diffuse, painless swelling in the body of the structure, which persists in spite of rest and treatment.

PROGNOSIS.—" Sprained tendons " is always a more or less serious condition, because the injured part never completely regains its normal condition and is predisposed to recurrence of the affection. The prognosis varies with the situation, extent, and intensity of the lesion. Perforatus and suspensory sprains are less serious than those of the perforans and check ligament. When both the latter are affected at the same time, the case is more grave than when one only is involved. In any particular case the gravity of the lesion is in accordance with the degree of injury to the structure—that is, with the number of fibres ruptured or distended. Severe sprains suddenly produced are of a more serious nature than those occurring gradually, and may prove incurable, while the latter usually respond to appropriate treatment. Repair of ruptured fibres is brought about by the organisation of granulation tissue, and torn peritendineum and interfascicular fibrous tissue are repaired in the same way. The contraction of the new fibrous tissue shortens the tendon involved, and may be so great as to cause excessive flexion of the fetlock or interphalangeal joints, and consequent " knuckling over." When the sprain is chronic this is more likely to ensue, owing to the greater amount of new fibrous tissue formation. The prognosis is rendered more grave by the presence of complications, such as chronic synovitis of the great sesamoidean or carpal sheath, or ostitis of the phalanges, which is not an uncommon accompaniment of the lesion.

TREATMENT.—In a general way preventative treatment consists in avoiding as far as possible the predisposing causes mentioned. Cold bathing, massage, and bandaging, combined with regular exercise, tend to keep the tendons in good condition. Careful shoeing, ensuring equal distribution of the weight on the foot and preserving the normal slope of the digit, is an important point in protecting the tendons from sprain.

Curative treatment, generally speaking, consists in adopting the measures described for the treatment of acute or chronic inflammation, as the case may be. The usual routine of treatment is as follows :

1. *Rest* is the first essential, to give Nature an opportunity of healing the injured part ; without it other measures are useless. It should be prolonged even after the horse has become sound, as the damaged part of the tendon remains weak and predisposed to sprain until the new tissue is well developed. Under this heading may be included

the application of a plaster bandage to immobilise the fetlock and pastern, a method of treatment, however, not often adopted. The patten or skate shoe with high calkins joined by a bar at their free extremities has been recommended to rest the tendons by preventing the limb bearing weight. It raises the foot 3 or 4 inches from the ground, and is in contact with the latter on a skate-like edge, rendering the foot unstable and unfitted to bear weight. It is of very doubtful advantage, and is rarely employed. Raising the heels of an ordinary shoe relaxes the tendons and relieves tension thereon, and on this ground may be justifiable ; but it has the objection when its use is continued for a considerable time of favouring contraction of the tendons. When it is the suspensory ligament that is affected a shoe with low heels is indicated, as it relieves the strain upon it and throws more on to the tendons.

2. *Cold and Astringent Applications* in the form of constant cold irrigation, cold baths, or cold compresses, and the usual cooling lotions have a very beneficial effect in the early stages of the condition, when the pain is severe and the swelling well marked.

3. *Hot Moist Applications* may be employed at once, but usually after No. 2, to promote absorption of inflammatory exudate and prevent thickening in the part. They must be frequently repeated. Hot moist compresses applied over the tendons and renewed every half-hour have an excellent effect. A hot poultice of kaolin or antiphlogistine applied over the inflamed region to a depth of about ½ inch, and covered by a layer of cotton-wool and a bandage exerting slight pressure, is considered by many to be the best form of hot application. It retains the heat for a long time and is certainly very efficacious.

4. *Massage* is always indicated after the acute stage has passed. Its good effects are incontestable. It should be practised for five to ten minutes twice daily in the manner described (see Massage, p. 263).

5. *Compression* by wadding or cotton-wool and bandage is good to promote the reduction of inflammatory swelling, and is always indicated after massage. The late Mr. Wm. Hunting advised the use of cotton-wool and a linen bandage during the day and of a woollen bandage alone during the night. In chronic cases support and compression may be effected with plaster bandages such as Burgess's plaster bandages or those made by spreading roboreous plaster liquefied by heat over strips of calico. These are left in position for six to eight weeks, provided no complication ensues in the form of inflammation of the skin caused by the bandage.

6. *Counter-irritation* by liniments, blisters, or the actual cautery is

frequently resorted to in subacute and chronic forms of sprains. The massage associated with the application of a liniment or mercurial ointment probably accounts for the greater part of its beneficent action. Blistering, or firing and blistering, often has the desired effect, but some chronic cases are met with which defy all kinds of treatment. Superficial firing in the form of transverse lines or of the herring-bone pattern is usually adopted. Deep needle-point firing is the most efficacious, but has the objection that the deep-seated cicatrices to which it gives rise predispose somewhat to shortening of the tendons. (See Objections to Firing, p. 258.)

Other special forms of treatment comprise :

1. *The Insufflation of Air* into the subcutaneous connective tissue of the region, introduced by Joly. A rubber tourniquet is applied above the knee. The air is slowly pumped in through several layers of iodoform wool, which acts as a filter, sufficient being injected to distend the skin moderately over the tendons. The puncture made by the needle is dressed with tincture of iodine, and the tourniquet is removed. The horse is left loose in a box. The insufflated air spreads to the forearm. On the following days cold douches and massage are employed. This treatment is said to be particularly useful for peritendinous thickening. A couple of weeks after its adoption the affected tissues become supple, painless, and free from peritendinous induration. It has been claimed for this treatment that it has cured cases in which firing had failed.

2. *Subcutaneous Injection of the Essence of Turpentine*, as recommended by Cagny, a French veterinarian. One gramme of the preparation is injected on the inner and outer aspect of the limb, below the knee, between the suspensory ligament and the tendons. On the following days a large inflammatory swelling forms at the seat of injection. It is a very severe form of treatment which most practitioners would hesitate to adopt.

3. *Use of Radio-active Muds.*—These are described as having antiphlogistic, analgesic, tonic, and stimulating properties, and have been recommended for tendon sprains in the form of baths, plasters, and dressings. To form the bath, 7 or 8 ounces of radio-active mud are added to 2 or 3 gallons of water at a temperature of 113° to 122° F. It is used once daily for one hour after morning exercise. Slight massage is practised at the same time. After the bath a poultice of the radio-active mud is applied in a thick layer extending beyond the affected part, and covered with a layer of cotton-wool and bandage without pressure. This treatment is to be continued for weeks, when

gradual progressive improvement will be noticed. Cases in which firing followed by prolonged rest at grass had failed were much improved in ten days and cured in six weeks after the commencement of the radio-active treatment. Even a case which had resisted ordinary measures for two years is said to have been cured in fifteen days by this method, the swelling and lameness having disappeared.

As soon as lameness has disappeared, regular daily walking exercise is to be prescribed, if the horse is not at grass. When the animal is put to work the shoeing must be carefully attended to, lest the affected tendon be placed at a disadvantage by an unsuitable shoe.

When all forms of treatment have been exhausted and lameness persists, the only resort is median neurectomy for the fore-limb and posterior tibial for the hind one (see pp. 440 and 451).

Knuckling at the Fetlocks—Contracted Flexor Tendons

Knuckling at the fetlock is due to retraction or contraction or shortening of the flexor tendons. There may be said to be three degrees of the condition :

1. The phalanges are almost vertical.

2. A perpendicular let fall from the front of the fetlock strikes the front of the hoof.

3. The perpendicular referred to in No. 2 reaches the ground in front of the hoof.

This deformity must be considered separately in (1) young animals, and in (2) aged or adult subjects.

1. **Young Animals.**—In these it is most frequently congenital, but may be acquired within the first three or four years of age, usually during the first year.

The Cause of the condition is not very clear. The fact that recovery frequently ensues spontaneously would go to show that it is generally due to mere shortness or tension of the tendons. It has, however, been ascribed to insufficient nutrition of the dam, to muscular debility induced by confinement in the stable, especially when it is cold and damp, to insufficient food, to digestive troubles, to muscular rheumatism, and to rickets. In cases of muscular weakness the patient seeks to relieve the muscles by " standing over " on the joints. Foals, calves, and lambs suffer from the abnormality, and except for it they may be perfectly developed and in normal health. Among foals it is the coarser breeds which most frequently suffer. Usually both fore-limbs are involved. Less frequently the knuckling is in the hind-limbs.

Symptoms.—The young animal shows one of the degrees of knuckling mentioned or complete flexion of the affected joint or joints, the front of which is on the ground bearing weight. In the latter case an open wound is soon produced, which may extend into the joint and lead to septic arthritis. In the other cases the animals are apt to stumble when trotted. On palpation the tendons seem normal.

Fig. 344.—Double-Sided "Knuckling" in a Two-Year-Old Colt. (From a photograph.)

Prognosis.—When the condition is congenital or appears a few days after birth and is attended to before complicated by open joint, recovery is the rule; but when the deformity is acquired later it is more likely to be due to some systemic defect, and the case is not so hopeful.

Treatment.—When the condition is congenital the tendency is for the normal position to be assumed, and it is brought about spontaneously if weight can be borne on the foot. The aim of treatment is to get the toe of the foot, at least, to bear weight. Splints or a plaster-of-Paris bandage may be required to maintain the foot in this position, care being taken not to damage the tender skin with the hard dressing.

The young animal is inclined to lie down when the dressing is applied, defeating its object. Slings often succeed in such cases in keeping the animal standing for a sufficient time to obtain the desired effect. At a later period, when the foal's or young horse's foot is capable of being shod, a special shoe may be applied which tends to throw the fetlock back into position. In slight cases it is sufficient to lower the heels and put on a shoe with the toe thickened and projecting in front. In more pronounced cases Friebel's apparatus (Fig. 345) or that of Brogniez is indicated. If these measures fail, tenotomy is necessary; but then the case is not very promising. Occasionally a case is met with in which the fetlock remains fixed in the flexed position after cutting the tendons.

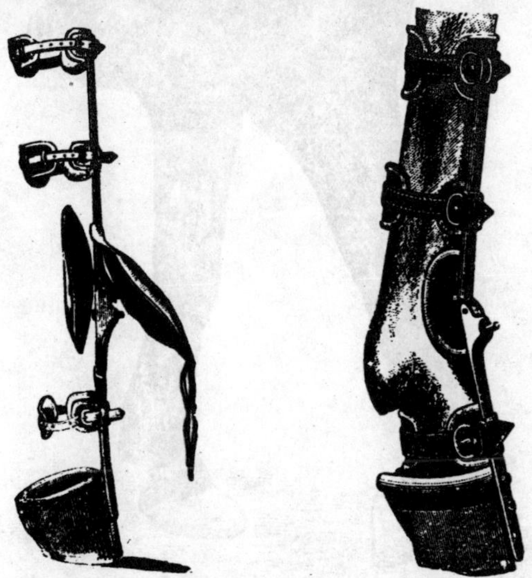

FIG. 345.—FRIEBEL'S EXTENSION APPARATUS.

2. **Adult Subjects.**—Excessive volar flexion in adults may be due to cicatricial contraction of the tendons following chronic tendinitis, or shortening of these structures may be secondary to other lesions, such as ringbone or diffuse osteo-periostitis of the pastern, chronic synovitis, dry arthritis of an interphalangeal joint, corns, or contracted foot. All these conditions interfere more or less with the normal support of weight on the limb, causing the fetlock to assume a permanent degree of flexion, so that the flexors, being no longer subjected to the antagonism which they experience under normal conditions, contract gradually, causing the pastern to become upright or directed slightly downwards and backwards, and the fetlock-joint to project forward.

SYMPTOMS.—The deformity, varying in degree, as stated, is very obvious, and local examination reveals the cause of the trouble—viz., one of the lesions mentioned above. The lameness or interference with gait is in accordance with the nature of the affection. When the contraction is very marked and confined to the perforatus tendon the fetlock-joint only shows excessive flexion, the foot remaining flat on the ground ; but when the perforans is much contracted, the fetlock and interphalangeal joints are over-flexed and the heel of the foot

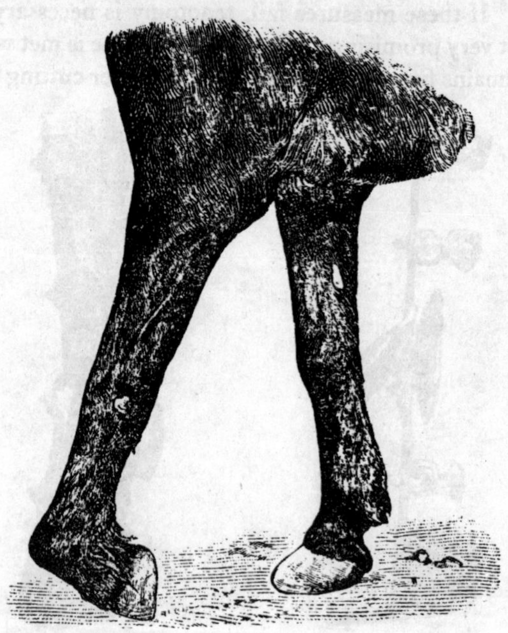

FIG. 346.—EXCESSIVE "KNUCKLING" IN A HORSE.
(From a photograph.)

cannot be placed on the ground, and weight may be borne by the front of the wall. When the knuckling is less marked, the lameness is characterised chiefly by a tendency to stumble. When the abnormality is of the first degree, the affected fetlock becomes straightened or normal in appearance when forced to bear weight by lifting the other limb ; but in the more advanced degrees of flexion the latter is aggravated when the weight on the limb is increased.

PROGNOSIS is always more or less grave, its degree of gravity depending on the nature of the lesion with which the condition is associated. The only case likely to be improved by treatment is that due to cicatricial contraction of the tendons.

Treatment consists in adopting measures appropriate to the cause, but is not likely to be successful except for mere contraction of the tendons, for which tenotomy may have the desired effect (see p. 454). Horses which are "knuckled" if worked slowly and on soft ground may be made useful for a long time by applying a long-toed shoe, though this will not cure or even improve the original disease.

Fracture of the Metacarpus and Metatarsus

The metacarpus or metatarsus may be fractured by direct violence, such as a kick or by bending of the bone, as when the horse puts the foot in a hole during galloping. Occasionally the fracture occurs mysteriously when the horse is cantering on level ground.

Symptoms and Diagnosis.—The symptoms are as usual for complete fracture, and the diagnosis is always easy except for a fissured fracture, which is not common. Fracture of one of the splint-bones alone may result from direct injury, and is characterised by acute inflammation, which may be hard to distinguish from osteo-periostitis if crepitation cannot be detected.

Prognosis.—In light animals of the large type there is a good chance of recovery, especially if of a docile disposition. But in heavy horses a cure is not likely to be effected, and treatment is seldom undertaken. Cure is the rule in cattle, and almost invariably ensues in small animals.

Treatment is carried out on general principles already described, and consists in accurately replacing the fragments in their normal position and maintaining them there by an immobilising dressing extending from the knee (exclusive) to the foot. Plaster-of-Paris bandages form a very convenient and suitable dressing applied over an even layer of padding. Carefully adjusted splints will also have the desired effect. Light horses do not require slings, but they are essential for heavy subjects. As regards dogs and cats, nothing need be added to what has been said in connection with fractures in general. Many cases of cure of fracture of the large metacarpal bone in the horse have been recorded. In a valuable animal treatment should always be undertaken. Fracture of the splint bone is dealt with as a contusion or open wound as the case may be.

Splints

The typical splint is an exostosis situated on or contiguous to one of the splint-bones, but the term splint is often applied to an exostosis on the large metacarpal or metatarsal bone quite clear of the splint-bone. The commonest site of splint is the inner aspect of the fore-limb.

When splint appears in the hind-limb it is usually on its outer aspect. The upper and middle thirds of the cannon region are the usual levels of the exostosis.

Varieties of Splint.—The recognised forms of splint are:

1. *Simple splint*, a simple exostosis at the usual seat of splint.

2. *Knee splint*, in which the exostosis involves the head of the splint-bone or actually encroaches on the knee-joint.

3. *Rod or peg splint*, an exostosis on either side of the cannon-bone connected by an abnormal ridge of bone beneath the suspensory ligament.

4. *Chain splint*, consisting of several small bony excrescences arranged in a row along the course of the small splint-bone.

ETIOLOGY.—The etiology of splint may be discussed under the following headings:

1. *Heredity.*—There is undoubtedly a hereditary predisposition to splints, and they may appear in this way in young unbroken horses without any apparent exciting cause, not being accompanied by pain or lameness. It may be a predisposing conformation which is inherited, such as small knee-joints or bad quality of bone which nature endeavours to strengthen by a new osseous deposit, or an abnormal shape of the limb whereby the weight is unequally distributed, causing a strain of the carpal or interosseous ligaments which may lead to osteoperiostitis and the formation of an exostosis.

2. *Sprain of the Interosseous Ligament.*—Splint usually makes its appearance in a horse under five years of age when first put to work, and is due in many cases to sprain of the interosseous ligament which has not yet become ossified. This occurs more frequently on the inner aspect of the fore-limb, due probably to the fact that the lower surface of the trapezoid articulates almost entirely with the small metacarpal bone, thus transmitting to the latter most of the weight which it bears, whereas the unciform articulates chiefly with the large metacarpus, so that little strain is put on the interosseous ligament on the outer aspect of the limb. The periosteum and the bone become involved in the inflammation, osteoperiostitis and the formation of an exostosis ensuing. Sprain of this ligament affords the most satisfactory explanation of splint of inflammatory origin occurring in young horses first put to work.

3. *Sprain of the Carpal Sheath.*—Traction of this sheath on the periosteum, where it is attached, may give rise to an exostosis at the usual seat of splint, or at the back of the large metacarpus.

4. *Sprain of the Suspensory Ligament* at its origin may be the cause of splint at the back of the metacarpus below the knee.

5. *Concussion* of the bone itself by fast work on hard ground may be sufficient to cause osteo-periostitis and a consequent exostosis.

6. *Traumatic Injury.*—An exostosis on the inner side of the metacarpal bone below the knee may be caused by the horse striking the part by the other foot during progression, as in "speedy-cutting." On the other hand, an exostosis may appear first from some other cause, and owing to its prominence it may be struck as mentioned.

A blow of any kind on the metacarpus may give rise to an exostosis at the injured part. Such an enlargement clear of the splint-bones is commonly called a "bump" rather than a splint.

SYMPTOMS.—When a splint appears without prior inflammation, the only symptom is the presence of the exostosis. When it is of inflammatory origin, there are local symptoms of acute inflammation and lameness. Before the exostosis is formed, the inflammation is marked chiefly by pain on pressure and abnormal heat in the affected part. The swelling is at first of an œdematous nature. When the splint is developed, it can be easily felt as a bony enlargement varying in size generally from a pea to a walnut. The following are methods of examining the limb for splints (say the near fore):

1. Stand on the near side of the horse, looking in the same direction; pass the fingers of the right hand down the inner aspect of the limb from the knee to the fetlock along the course of the splint-bone and its junction with the large metacarpus.

2. Stand looking in the opposite direction, lift the foot and flex the knee, hold the pastern in the right hand, pass the left thumb over the inner splint-bone from its upper to its lower extremity, pushing the tendons aside at the same time. To search for a splint at the back of the bone, examine deeply in front of the tendons to ascertain if the suspensory ligament is bulged backwards by an exostosis. To examine the outside of the limb reverse the hands.

3. Stand as in No. 1, but lift the foot and flex the knee, and examine the limb inside and outside as in No. 2, taking care to avoid being hit should the horse strike backwards with the lifted foot.

Splint lameness presents the following features:

1. There is a striking contrast between the degree of lameness at the walk and at the trot; the horse may walk practically sound, but trots decidedly lame.

2. The lameness is more marked on hard than on soft ground, and is worse down-hill than on the level.

3. There may be imperfect flexion of the knee and the limb may be abducted in its forward movement.

4. The lameness does not improve with exercise ; it rather becomes more marked.

Diagnosis.—The diagnosis of splint lameness depends on (*a*) the age of the horse, it being rarely present in a horse over five years old ; (*b*) the local symptoms of acute or subacute inflammation ; and (*c*) the features of the lameness mentioned above. Cases of doubt of course arise, which may necessitate the use of local anæsthesia to aid in arriving at a diagnosis (see Lameness, p. 796).

Prognosis.—A splint devoid of inflammation is of no consequence, except it is so large that it is liable to be struck by the other foot during progression. Then it is serious, as the horse may fall when he strikes it. When the acute inflammation associated with the development of a splint has run its course, the pain and lameness disappear and the exostosis remains as a harmless blemish, except it is very large. Splint involving the knee-joint may be called knee spavin, and is an incurable lesion. If it is quite close to the articulation, but not interfering with its articular surface, it is serious on account of the possibility of its encroaching thereon. A peg splint often causes persistent lameness, which may be ascribed to the pressure of the suspensory ligament on the exostosis or to the latter causing distension of the ligament. Exostoses of a longish form occurring on the small metacarpus in young horses are apt to be troublesome. The chance of recovery is less if in consequence of defective formation of the limb the affected region is likely to be struck by the other foot. In exceptional instances even a simple splint causes prolonged lameness in spite of treatment. In rare cases the exostosis disappears, being apparently removed by the osteoclasts.

Treatment.—The treatment of splint is on the same lines as that for all inflammatory conditions, and comprises :

1. *Rest*, which is the great essential when the lesion is acute.

2. *Cold and astringent applications*, as advised for inflammation in general. They are continued until the acute inflammation has subsided.

3. *The application of a blister* to the affected region, biniodide of mercury 1 in 8 being the most effective. Perchloride of mercury 1 to 4 or 8 of spirit carefully rubbed in with a burnt cork or a tooth-brush is recommended by some veterinarians, but its action may be too severe. This method is indicated after No. 2 has had its effect.

4. *Needle-point firing*, which is the most effective form of treatment for chronic splint lameness, the points being inserted into the exostosis.

5. *Pressure* with a piece of flat lead or of leather, associated with repeated massage, which has been recommended for the purpose of

causing absorption of the exostosis. It may require to be practised for months before its effect is shown, or it may fail entirely.

6. *Periosteotomy* performed over the splint in the same manner as described for spavin (see p. 458). This may be done, however, before the exostosis appears, and may prevent its production by releasing the exudate beneath the periosteum and promoting its absorption before it undergoes ossification. Its practice has not given better results than No. 4.

When after point firing and repeated blistering along with rest extending over months or a year lameness continues, median neurectomy is indicated. When the splint is very large and being struck by the other limb during exercise, the only remedy is removal of the exostosis as follows: Cast and anæsthetise the horse, prepare the site in the usual way, apply a tourniquet on the upper and lower extremities of the cannon-bone, surround the limb with a calico cloth with an opening opposite the exostosis, and make an incision through the skin and periosteum parallel to the long axis of the tumour. Reflect the periosteum or remove it over the exostosis. By means of a sharp chisel and mallet excise the latter level with the bones. Suture the wound and apply an antiseptic pad and bandage. Strict asepsis is essential to avoid the risk of infection and necrosis of the bone. The operation should not be lightly undertaken, owing to the risk mentioned.

In a case of persistent chronic splint lameness cure of the latter has been obtained by repeated fast exercise on the road. It is the opinion of some experienced horse owners that forced exercise is better than rest for persistent splint lameness, the concussion of the bone thus produced apparently acting as a counter-irritant intensifying the local inflammation which on subsequent rest is followed by resolution and consequent recovery from the lameness.

"Sore Shins"

The term "sore shins" is applied to an inflammatory condition of the metacarpal and less frequently of the metatarsal regions, commonly met with in young racehorses in training. It is particularly common in horses from one year and a half to two years old. It seldom affects three-year-olds, and is rare in aged animals.

ETIOLOGY.—The predisposing cause apparently is the immature condition of the animals, while the exciting cause is concussion, the affection being very prevalent when the "going" is hard, although it may also occur when the going is soft. The nature of the lesion has been disputed, but there is no doubt that the commonest source of the trouble is an osteo-periostitis of the cannon-bone, affecting chiefly its lower third. In some cases the inflammation is confined to the extensor tendons and the peritendinous tissue, constituting *pseudo-sore shins.*

Symptoms.—The first symptom observed is lameness, usually in both fore-limbs, although it may be more pronounced in one than in the other. There is a diffuse painful swelling on the anterior aspect of the cannon-bone. Eventually the bone becomes thickened and assumes a more convex shape in front. In aggravated cases the ligaments of the fetlock become ossified, causing anchylosis of the joint.

Prognosis.—The prognosis is favourable when the horse is rested on the first appearance of lameness, but if work is continued the case may become incurable, owing to the formation of exostoses involving the fetlock-joint.

Treatment comprises rest and the usual antiphlogistic applications. Iodine ointment has been found useful. Massage is always advisable when the acute symptoms have subsided. Later blistering is indicated. Firing is seldom necessary. Periosteotomy has been advised, but it is better not to practise it on account of the risk of infection and necrosis of the bone.

Rheumatoid Ostitis

Sometimes an intermittent form of lameness is met with, due apparently to a rheumatoid ostitis of the large metacarpus, characterised by pain on pressure in certain regions of the bone, most commonly in its upper part and chiefly below and behind the carpus.

The Treatment is that for rheumatism.

AFFECTIONS OF THE FETLOCK AND DIGIT

The fetlock and digit, owing to their situation, are much exposed to traumatic lesions, which vary in gravity from excoriation of the skin to deep wounds involving the bone or tendons or ligaments, or penetrating into the great or small sesamoidean sheath or into the fetlock or one of the interphalangeal joints. They present symptoms in accordance with their nature, and the prognosis depends on the character of the lesion. The only dangerous conditions are open wounds of the flexor synovial sheaths and of the joints.

Treatment is carried out on general principles.

Special mention may be made of lesions on the inner aspect of the fetlock caused by striking it with the other foot during progression. They vary in character, including excoriation, contusion with subcutaneous extravasation of blood and serum, an abscess, an area of necrosis, and an open wound. The front of the fetlock may be excoriated or contused as the result of knuckling over when asleep in the standing position.

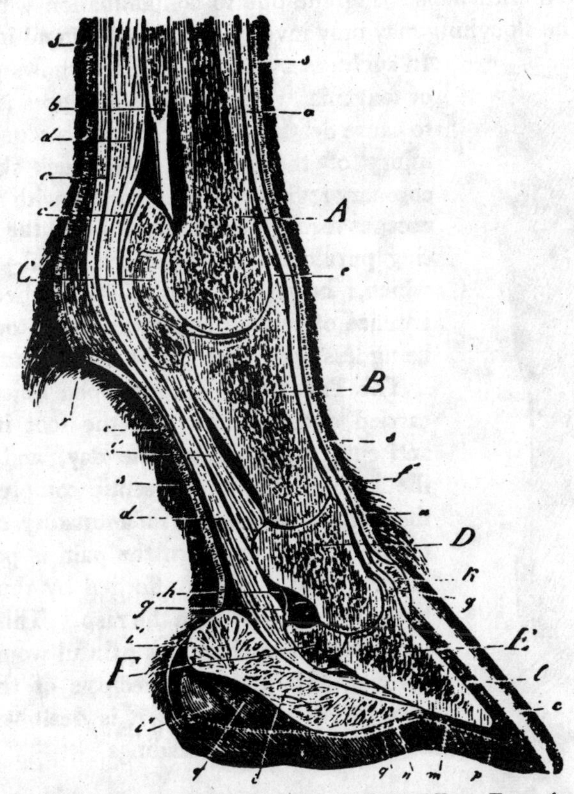

Fig. 347.—Perpendicular Mesial Section of Right Fore-Foot (the Position of the Lower Bones is shown rather too Upright).

A, Lower end of great metacarpus; *B*, suffraginis or first phalanx; *C*, inner sesamoid bone (to render the bone visible, a portion of the intersesamoid ligament has been removed); *D*, coronet bone; *E*, pedal bone; *F*, navicular bone; *a*, extensor pedis tendon; *b*, superior sesamoid or suspensory ligament; *b′*, inferior sesamoid ligament; *c*, flexor pedis perforatus tendon; *c′*, great sesamoid sheath; *d*, flexor pedis perforans tendon; *e*, capsular ligament of the fetlock-joint; *f*, capsular ligament of pastern-joint; *g* and *g′*, capsular ligament of coffin-joint; *h*, bursa of flexor pedis perforans; *i*, plantar cushion; *i′*, portion of plantar cushion forming the bulbs of the heel; *k*, coronary band; *l*, sensitive wall; *m*, sensitive sole; *n*, sensitive frog; *o*, horny wall; *p*, horny sole *q*, horny frog; *r*, ergot at base of fetlock; *s*, skin.

Treatment of these lesions is preventative and curative. Brushing may be prevented by appropriate shoeing, and the part subjected to injury may be protected by a boot.

The worst injuries to the coronet are caused by treads, and when produced by sharpened calkins during frosty weather they may penetrate deeply into the tissues, involving the lateral cartilage and even the synovial capsule of the corono-pedal joint. These wounds are often complicated with moist gangrene due to contamination with freezing mud. The sloughing may only involve the skin or extend into a joint. In such cases the patient often shows symptoms of toxæmia, which in some instances is sufficient to cause death. Quittor may be a sequel to deep injury of the coronet. The thick skin in the coronary region may be underrun with pus, which escapes through openings here and there, simulating purulent arthritis of the pedal-joint, from which, however, it is distinguished by the absence of synovia and by the symptoms of pain being less acute than in the latter condition.

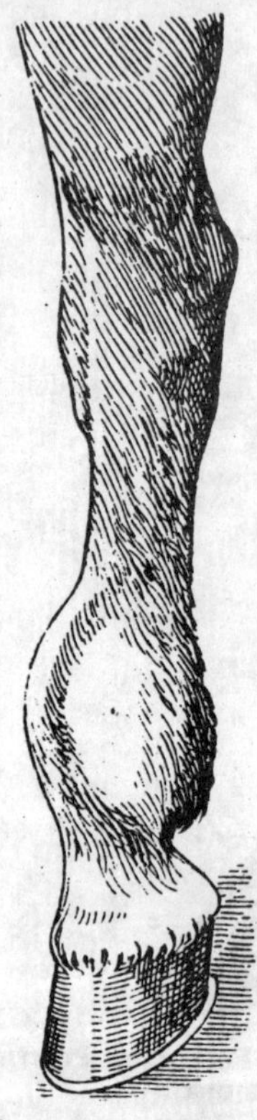

FIG. 348.—ENLARGEMENT OF THE BURSA OF THE EXTENSOR PEDIS TENDON.

See also Figs. 336 and 337.

The TREATMENT of these open lesions is best carried out by immersing the foot in a warm antiseptic bath during the day, and covering the lesions with an antiseptic compress during the night. When the inflammatory region extends beneath the horn the pain is particularly intense, and relief is afforded by thinning the horn over the part with the rasp. This is always indicated when there is a painful wound on the coronet. If quittor or necrosis of the plantar aponeurosis supervenes, it is dealt with as described under these headings.

Capped Fetlock—Distension or Hygroma of the Subcutaneous Bursa in Front of the Fetlock

This condition is equivalent to capped knee, and occurs in the same way from repeated injury. It has been seen in cavalry stables as the result of horses knuckling over on bare flagged floors. The bursa may become distended suddenly from a contusion, and then show acute inflammation, otherwise it is of a chronic nature and devoid of inflammation. It is not a serious affection, but forms a blemish that may be difficult to get rid of.

TREATMENT is the same as that for hygroma in front of the knee. Needle-point firing gives the best results in the chronic cystic condition, but when the walls of the bursa are fibrous a permanent thickening remains.

Synovitis and Distension of the Sheath of the Extensor Pedis Tendon in Front of the Fetlock

Acute synovitis supervenes from the usual causes, but is not common. Chronic synovitis or mere distension of the sheath is more frequently met with, and its cause is not always apparent. It is characterised by a soft, fluctuating, painless swelling, occupying the antero-lateral aspects of the fetlock and inferior part of the cannon region. When large it is very markedly bilobed, being divided into two halves by the extensor pedis tendon, which can be felt on palpation. The condition is much more common in the hind- than in the fore-limb. It is devoid of inflammatory symptoms, and does not cause lameness, but is difficult to remove.

The TREATMENT is as usual for chronic synovitis. Incision should not be resorted to, on account of the risk of infection of the joint with whose synovial sac the sheath sometimes communicates.

Acute and Chronic Synovitis of the Great Sesamoidean Sheath—Windgalls

Acute closed synovitis of the sheath arises from the causes given for synovitis in general. It accompanies tendinitis in this region. Purulent synovitis is common here as the result of septic penetrating wounds of the sheath, and requires no further description than that given in general surgery. Lifting of the limb, as in chronic gonitis, is characteristic of this condition. The limb is carried further forwards than in chronic gonitis.

Chronic synovitis here is also in accordance with the condition as dealt with generally. It is sometimes associated with sesamoiditis, or sprain of the sesamoid ligaments or of the flexor tendons, and its prognosis depends largely on these lesions. A simple chronic synovitis will respond to treatment.

Occasionally a case of subacute synovitis of the great sesamoidean sheath is met with, characterised by an extremely tense distension of the sheath and by severe lameness. The sheath may burst through the skin under the great tension of the liquid, giving rise to a synovial fistula. When this occurs at the upper part of the sheath the fistula closes after a while, to be followed, perhaps, by another at a lower level, and so on until the lowest part of the sheath is reached, the swelling continuing to subside gradually and eventually disappearing, when the animal usually goes sound The application of a blister of biniodide of mercury is generally effective in promoting resolution and dispelling the lameness in the course of six to eight weeks. Suppuration of the sheath rarely ensues in such cases.

Windgalls are mere distensions of the great sesamoidean sheath. They appear just above the sesamoids at the level of the inferior third of the tendons in the form of two roundish or ovoid swellings, one on either side, between the tendons and the suspensory ligament.

Fig. 349.—Position of the Limb in Suppurative Inflammation of the Great Sesamoidean Sheath.
(From a photograph.)

They are described as tendinous windgalls, to distinguish them from articular windgalls, which are due to distension of the synovial membrane of the fetlock-joint, and appear one on either side just above the fetlock between the suspensory ligament and the back of the cannon-bone. The tendinous windgalls vary in size in different cases, but the inner and outer swellings are usually of the same dimensions.

The Cause of windgalls is not very clear. They may be a sequel to chronic synovitis, but most frequently they arise spontaneously as a dropsical condition of the sheath. They may appear as such in young horses that have never worked, especially of the draft type, but they are most common in aged horses, most of which are affected to some degree. The ordinary windgall found in the working horse is devoid of inflammatory symptoms, does not cause lameness, and is of no practical significance. Sometimes the windgall continues to increase in size, and when of long standing its walls may become much thickened and even calcareous. In this case the action of the tendons may be interfered with, causing the horse to be stiff in action and go on the toes.

TREATMENT of windgalls is seldom indicated. In young horses their disappearance is desirable, as they deteriorate their value. Constant bandaging reduces or dispels them. Plaster-of-Paris bandages are the most effective. If it is wished to reduce or get rid of old tense windgalls, they may be treated as chronic synovitis by aspiration and in-injection or by needle-point firing, or by a combination of the two methods.

Sprain of the Fetlock-Joint

The fetlock is said to be sprained when the flexor tendons or suspensory ligament at its level or its own lateral ligaments have been over-distended. When the joint is moved beyond its physiological limits some of these structures are over-stretched or sprained. The situation of the sprain may be anterior or posterior and external or internal. Anterior sprain ensues when the body-weight is thrown on the fetlock in the flexed position, which may occur when the foot slips backwards; while posterior strain is caused by over-extension of the joint, as may supervene during heavy draft or fast exercise. Lateral sprains are due to a false step or inward or outward slipping.

SYMPTOMS.—In a recent sprain there is more or less intense lameness and acute local inflammation. At rest the fore-limb is held forward with the fetlock partly flexed, while the hind-limb rests only on the toe. During the walk and the trot the weight is only supported by the toe of the affected limb, and is quickly transferred to the other limb. The inflammation is characterised by heat, pain, and swelling. Pain is evinced on compression and on passive movement of the joint. To examine the joint the limb is held flexed by an assistant, who grasps the lower end of the cannon-bone while the surgeon catches the pastern in his hand and moves the joint in different directions.

Chronic sprain may succeed the acute form or appear gradually. At rest the fetlock is very upright or slightly "knuckled" over in front, although the back tendons are not contracted. There is a variable amount of thickening in the vicinity of the joint. During trotting the fetlock remains upright or partly knuckled. Anterior and posterior sprains are common, but lateral sprains are rare.

PROGNOSIS depends on the severity of the sprain. It is not favourable in a chronic case with " overshot " fetlock—that is, with the joint in a state of semi-flexion (" knuckling ").

TREATMENT is that for acute or chronic inflammation. In an acute case it comprises complete rest, cold and hot applications (antiphlogistine) in the order mentioned, followed by massage and compression. Massage is very important, as it is effective in reducing subacute inflammatory swellings. The same applies to compression. Firm pressure by a lead plaster bandage or a Burgess's plaster bandage has given excellent results, due to its supporting and immobilising effects. In chronic cases counter-irritation by blistering or firing, or both, is indicated, and if this fails median or posterior tibial neurectomy must be resorted to.

Sprain of the Corono-Pedal Joint

Sprain of the corono-pedal joint is a common condition. It is the result of slipping or making a false step or of violent effort. Irregularity of tread may cause it, or it may be a consequence of faulty shoeing interfering with the normal distribution of the weight on the foot.

SYMPTOMS.—There is a variable degree of lameness depending on the severity of the injury to the ligaments. Its characteristics are similar to those of fetlock lameness. It may come on suddenly during work or be first noticed when the horse is going out in the morning.

The local symptoms include heat, pain, and swelling in the region of the coronet. Pain is evinced on pressure over the coronet and on passive movement of the joint, especially rotation. The horse may be fidgety when being shod, owing to the pain caused by the movement of the joint.

TREATMENT is the same as for all sprains or inflammatory lesions, and as mentioned for sprains of the fetlock. When the case is incurable, median or posterior tibial neurectomy is indicated.

Sprain of the Inferior Sesamoidean Ligaments

Sprain of these ligaments ensues on hyperextension of the first interphalangeal articulation, as may result from slipping or a violent effort during heavy draft or when jumping. Sloping pasterns and long toes or low heels predispose to the condition. The degree of injury may be slight or severe. The sprain is more common in the

fore- than in the hind-limbs. Only a few or most of the ligamentous fibres may be involved.

SYMPTOMS.—When the lesion is suddenly produced, there is severe lameness and pronounced local inflammation, characterised by swelling

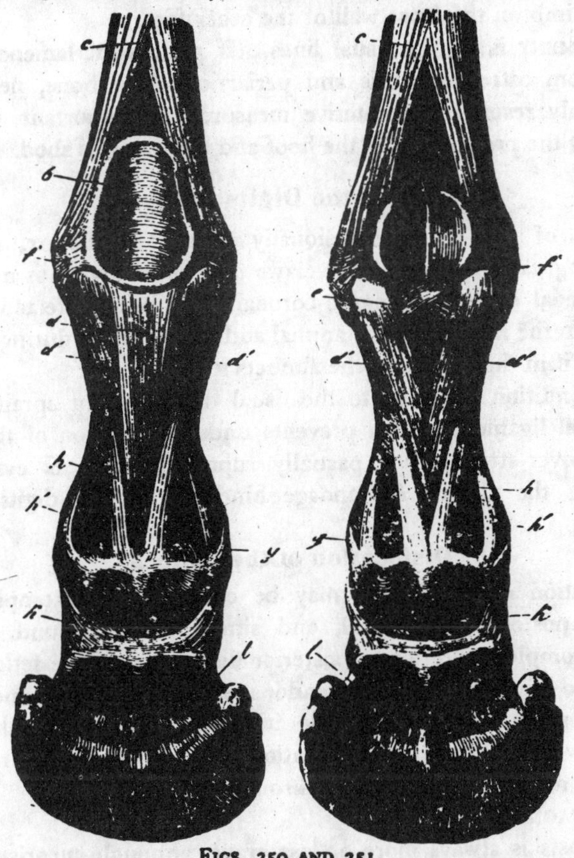

FIGS. 350 AND 351.

a External lateral ligament of pastern-joint; b, intersesamoidean ligament; c, superior sesamoidean ligament; d, middle limb of inferior sesamoidean ligament; d', lateral limb of inferior sesamoidean ligament; e, cruciate ligament; f, lateral sesamoidean ligament; g, outer lateral ligament of the coronary-joint; h and h', posterior corono-suffraginal ligaments; i, outer lateral ligament of pedal-joint; k, postero-lateral ligaments of navicular bone; l, fibrous sheath of synovial membrane of coffin-joint.

and by pain on pressure and on movement of the phalanges. The condition, however, may be slow and insidious in onset, with little or no local manifestations. The lameness in this case is slight, and may not be very noticeable until the horse goes on hard ground or is made to bear extra weight on the limb. In all cases there is a tendency to go on the toe. When the lesion is chronic, exostoses may eventually form at the insertion of the ligaments, constituting posterior ringbone. It may also be accompanied by distension of the great sesamoidean sheath. At rest the animal often places the heel of the foot of the affected limb on the front wall of the other foot.

TREATMENT is on the usual lines. If permanent lameness supervenes from osteo-periostitis and periarticular ringbone, neurectomy is the only resort. Preventative measures are important, in superintending the preparation of the hoof and the way it is shod.

Sprain of the Digits in the Ox

Sprain of the digits occasionally occurs in the ox, especially in working cattle. One of the claws only is involved, as a rule, the corono-pedal or the suffragino-coronal joint being affected. If the lesion is in the inner claw the animal adducts the limb during progression, and if in the outer claw he abducts it.

The condition responds to the usual treatment for sprains. The interdigital ligament, which prevents undue separation of the digits, may be over-stretched or partially ruptured. Pain is evinced on separating the claws. A bandage binding the two digits favours recovery.

Dislocation of the Fetlock

Dislocation of the fetlock may be complete or incomplete, and anterior, posterior, or lateral, and simple or compound. Several cases of complete anterior or posterior dislocation of the fetlock, with little or no injury to the flexor tendons and suspensory ligament, have been recorded. Incomplete dislocations are usually lateral. Many cases, however, of complete dislocation are compound, with the metacarpus or metatarsus protruding through the skin.

The DIAGNOSIS is obvious.

PROGNOSIS is always more or less grave, although surprising cases of perfect recovery after simple complete dislocation have been recorded.

TREATMENT consists in reduction and retention (see Dislocations, p. 134). A special apparatus may be employed to support the joint.

Inflammation of the Fetlock-Joint

Acute synovitis usually results from a sprain of the articulation, but it may be due to some bacterial disease. It is characterised by acute local inflammation, with distension of the culs-de-sac of the synovial membrane, as in articular windgalls, and by lameness.

Treatment is on the principles prescribed for inflammation and for sprains in general.

Dry arthritis is occasionally met with in aged horses, apparently as the result of constant hard work, although it may be rheumatoid. It is associated with ossific deposits round the joint, and sometimes with distensions of its synovial capsule. It causes chronic lameness, for which the only relief is neurectomy. " Cab-horse disease," or " bobba bone," is sometimes associated with arthritis of this joint.

Articular Windgalls

These have already been alluded to as resulting from distension of the synovial capsule of the fetlock-joint, appearing on either side above the sesamoids between the suspensory ligament and the back of the cannon-bone. They are tense when the limb is bearing weight, and soft and fluctuating when it is lifted. There has been observed in racehorses a distension of this capsule appearing below the fetlock on either side of the pastern and extending down almost to the first interphalangeal joint. The swelling here may reveal abnormal heat on palpation, and be more or less painful on pressure. This form of distension is serious. It may disappear with rest, but reappears when the horse is put to work and gives rise to lameness. The ordinary synovial enlargement above the fetlock is usually of a chronic nature, and does not cause lameness as a rule.

Treatment is that prescribed for chronic synovitis.

Inflammation of the Interphalangeal Joints

This is rarely observed except as a chronic arthritis in conjunction with ringbone, under which it is dealt with.

Open Wounds of the Fetlock-Joint

The fetlock-joint is very exposed to open wounds, especially in its lateral aspects, at the points where the distensions of its synovial membrane appear, and in front, where its capsule is only supported at the level of the extensor pedis and, in the fore-limb, that of the extensor suffraginis. The articulation may be injured in various ways: by prods of forks, kicks, falls, barbed wire, by the blade of a mowing machine, and by other means. When the synovial membrane has been penetrated there is a copious discharge of synovia, which is increased by movement of the joint. The situation of the fistula distinguishes it from that of the great sesamoidean sheath.

The **Prognosis** is always guarded, on account of the risk of infection and septic arthritis supervening; but when severe infection is excluded recovery is the rule. Many cases of cure of open fetlock-joint have been recorded.

TREATMENT is carried out on the principles mentioned in the section on "Open Joint." Suturing is indicated when the wound is comparatively extensive. Bier's hyperæmic treatment is always advisable to help to control infection and promote rapid healing.

Fractures of the Phalanges—Split Pastern

Fractures of the pastern are common in the horse, the os suffraginis being the bone most frequently affected. The fracture may be complete, with more or less displacement, or in the form of a fissure or crack in the bone. Fissured fracture occurs mostly in the first phalanx, and is known as "split pastern." The fissure usually commences in the depression on its upper articular surface, and extends straight through the length of the bone or takes an oblique course towards its lateral aspect, terminating at its lower articular extremity or at a variable distance above this point. Sometimes the fracture is comminuted. Fracture of the os corona is usually vertical in direction and often comminuted.

ETIOLOGY.—The most common cause of fractured pastern is concussion, the accident occurring during galloping or jumping. It also results from violent slips and sudden turns. It seems to take place with little provocation on some occasions—for example, during the trot or canter. Some of these cases are accounted for by the bone being affected with a rarefying ostitis or osteomalacia. Neurectomy is a well-known predisposing cause. Direct violence is the cause in exceptional instances—for example, a heavy cart-wheel passing over the coronet, fracturing the os corona or os pedis. Several cases have been recorded of simultaneous fracture of both fore-pasterns during ordinary fast exercise on level ground. The accident occurs in fore- and hind-limbs, but more frequently in the former. The pedal bone may be fractured by the penetration of a sharp hard object through the sole.

SYMPTOMS.—The first symptom is sudden and severe lameness during work or fast exercise, causing the horse to stop and hold up the affected limb or rest it only on the toe. Inflammatory swelling appears quickly when the fracture is complete, but is slow in onset when it is a fissure. When displacement is present, mobility and crepitus are easily recognised, especially in the first phalanx. They are not always so apparent in the second phalanx, and in the os pedis they cannot be detected.

In fissured fracture the chief local symptom is evidence of pain on pressure with the finger over the front of the bone, especially on the line of fracture. A local periostitis would be detected in the same way,

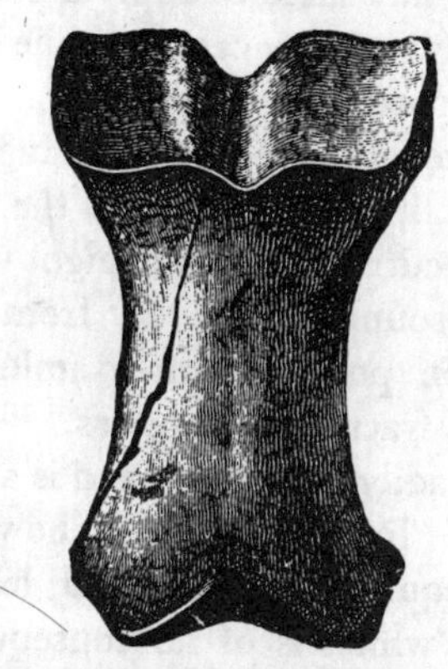

FIG. 352.—FRACTURE OF OS SUFFRAGINIS.

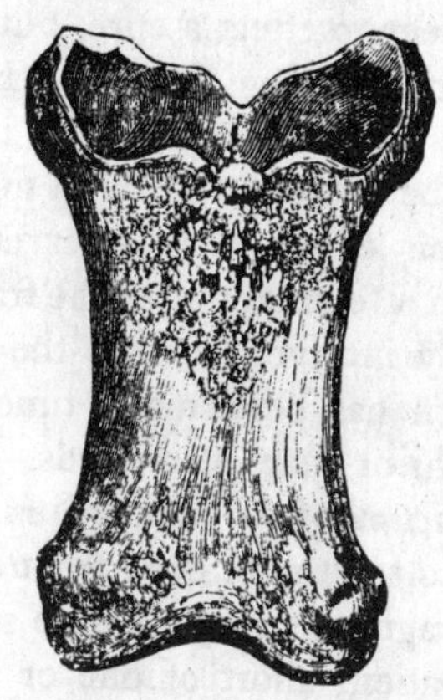

FIG. 353.—FRACTURE OF OS SUFFRAGINIS WITH FORMATION OF EXOSTOSIS.

but the history of the case and the more marked and more prolonged nature of the lameness in the case of fracture generally enable a correct diagnosis to be made. The X-rays may be used to confirm the diagnosis

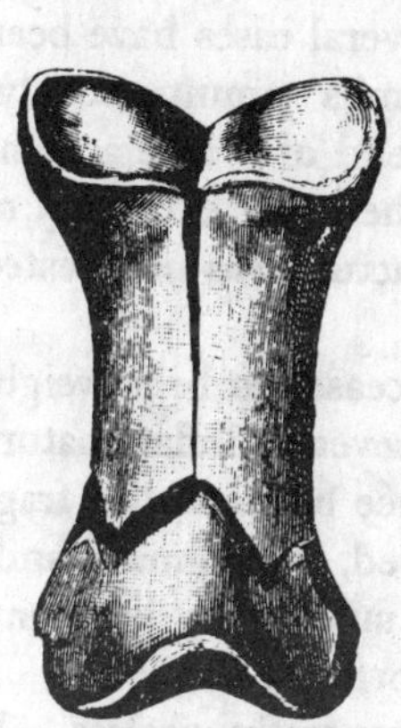

FIG. 354.—TRANSVERSE FRACTURE OF OS SUFFRAGINIS.

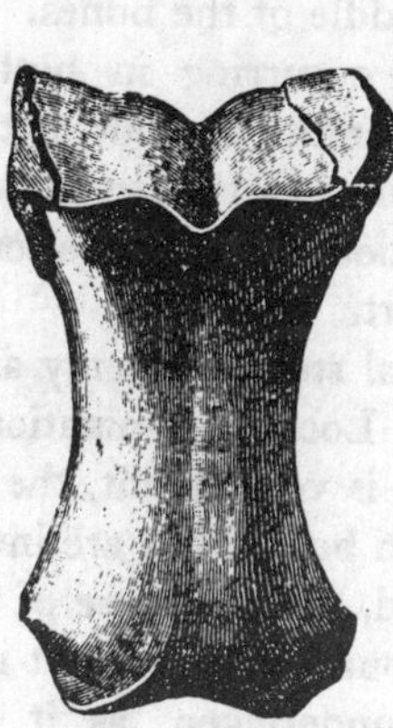

FIG. 355.—DOUBLE FRACTURE OF UPPER END OF OS SUFFRAGINIS.

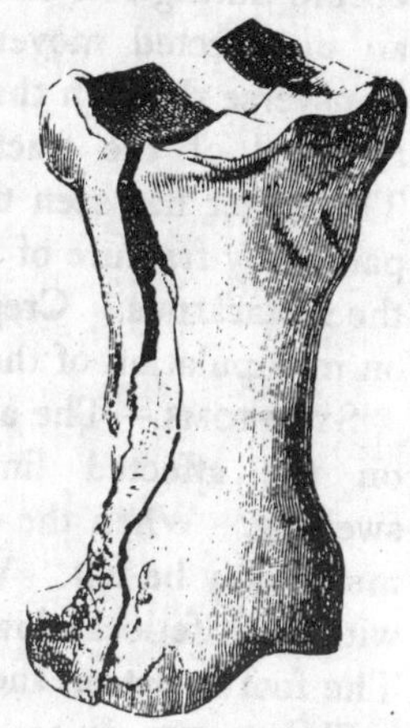

FIG. 356.—LONGITUDINAL FRACTURE OF OS SUFFRAGINIS.

TREATMENT.—Treatment of fracture with displacement is seldom indicated. Although union of the fragments ensues, a deformity in the shape of a large exostosis is produced, which generally causes permanent lameness, for which the only remedy is neurectomy. When there is little or no displacement, as in the case of split pastern, recovery is the rule. In such cases rest in slings or in a box is generally sufficient to effect a cure, but it is always advisable to apply a plaster-of-Paris bandage from the hoof half-way up the cannon-bone after filling up the hollow at the back of the pastern with padding. Care must be exercised to avoid undue pressure with the hard dressing, lest necrosis of the skin supervene. Weight may be borne on the limb within a fortnight after the fracture has occurred, but six to eight weeks usually intervene before the horse goes sound. Recovery from split pastern has been many times verified on post-mortem examination months or years afterwards. Compound fracture is hopeless.

Fracture of the phalanges in the dog is readily diagnosed, and is amenable to treatment even when compound. In the latter case, however, the fragments may become septic and require to be removed, leaving the patient short of one or more digits which is of no consequence except for a racing dog, and even the latter can dispense with one digit without material impairment of its speed.

Fracture of the Sesamoids

Fracture of the sesamoids has been frequently recorded. It generally occurs during fast exercise, and may be the result of a slip or fall, or an unexpected movement of the fetlock. The fracture is usually transverse through the middle of the bones. Several cases have been reported of the fracture occurring in both limbs simultaneously. The writer has seen the condition occur at the end of a race accompanied by fracture of the inner articular half of the lower extremity of the metacarpus. Crepitation due to the latter fracture was manifested on manipulation of the part.

SYMPTOMS.—The animal stops suddenly and ceases to bear weight on the affected limb. Local examination reveals inflammatory swelling. When the case is very recent, the space between the fragments may be felt. When both limbs are involved, the animal stands with both fetlocks lowered, as in rupture of the suspensory ligament. The foot is flat on the ground when weight is borne by the limb.

TREATMENT is rarely undertaken, as it is generally useless. If adopted, it is on general principles.

Sesamoiditis

The sesamoids in the horse may be affected with acute or chronic inflammation, associated with ulceration of their anterior or posterior surface, usually the latter.

Etiology.—The condition may arise from the same causes as those producing sprain of the flexor tendons. It is predisposed to by long, sloping pasterns, especially under a heavy body. It is commonest in "weedy" hacks and hunters, and in draft-horses, affecting chiefly the fore-limbs. It may be the result of jumping, especially from a height, or from suddenly reining-up. In this case the disease may set in with acute inflammation, but as a rule it develops slowly, the flexor sheath being often simultaneously affected at a point close to the fetlock-joint.

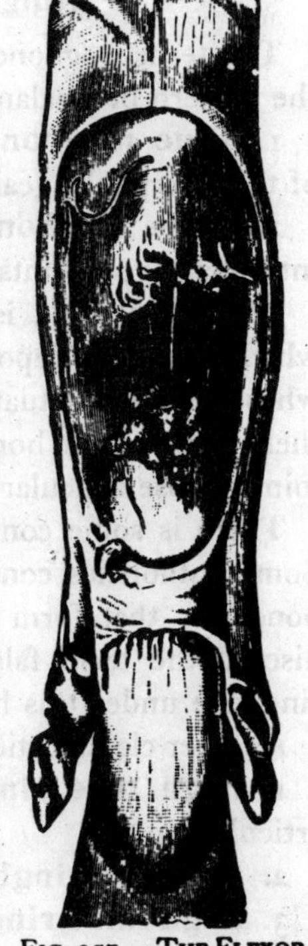

Fig. 357.—The Flexor Pedis Perforans Tendon in a Case of Sesamoid Lameness. At the point where it passes over the sesamoid bones the perforans tendon is fibrilated. (After Brauell.)

Symptoms comprise lameness and local inflammation. Pain is most marked when weight is placed on the limb. Lameness decreases, and may disappear, with exercise. It is decreased by long rest and increased by work, is more marked on rough hard ground than on sand or grass, and is sometimes so slight as only to be detected by carefully watching the animal whilst trotting, though in severe cases it is apparent at a walk. Pain may be evinced on local manipulation. After some time the sesamoid bones become enlarged and the fetlock assumes a square appearance when viewed from behind. If it is the anterior surface of the sesamoids that is ulcerated, the enlargement is close to the metacarpus—*i.e.*, at the side of the joint; in disease of the posterior surface it is farther back on the volar aspect of the joint. After a further variable period the flexor tendons become swollen in the neighbourhood of the sesamoid bones, though such swelling may occasionally appear before the other symptoms. The acute form is distinguished by local heat, etc., which is absent in chronic cases. During the later stages there is knuckling at the fetlock-joint from thickening of the tendons. Movement of the fetlock-joint is often distinctly limited. Crepitation can rarely be detected. The course is chronic, the inflammation seldom subsiding, so that cure is usually out of the question.

Diagnosis is based on the symptoms mentioned. It may be doubtful until enlargement of the sesamoid bones is evident, but it must be said that exostoses sometimes occur on the sesamoid bones, particularly on their lateral surfaces, without causing lameness.

TREATMENT is that for acute or chronic inflammation. It is of no avail in established chronic cases, in which median neurectomy is indicated.

Ringbone—Phalangeal Exostoses

The term ringbone is the popular name for bony enlargements on the pastern or phalangeal bones. It has been classified as follows:

1. **True ringbone,** in which the exostosis occurs at the level of one of the interphalangeal joints.

2. **False ringbone,** in which the exostosis is quite clear of the interphalangeal joints.

TRUE RINGBONE is subdivided into (1) ARTICULAR RINGBONE, in which the bony deposit is associated with an arthritis of the joint at whose level it is situated; and (2) PERIARTICULAR RINGBONE, in which there is merely a bony deposit at some part of the periphery of the joint, whose articular surfaces are intact.

There is some confusion about the terms true and false ringbone. Some authorities confine the term "true ringbone," or even "ringbone," to that form of the disease associated with arthritis. Some discard the term false ringbone, while others include periarticular ringbone under this heading.

Another classification is the following:

1. **High true ringbone,** at the level of the suffragino-coronal articulation.
2. **Low true ringbone,** at the level of the corono-pedal articulation.
3. **High false ringbone,** affecting the os suffraginis.
4. **Low false ringbone,** affecting the os corona.

The tendency in practice is to make use only of the term "ringbone" for any phalangeal exostosis, and explain its significance according to its situation. The foregoing classifications, however, are useful for descriptive purposes.

ETIOLOGY.—*False ringbone* is the result of osteo-periostitis, which is usually of traumatic origin, such as a blow or a knock, but it may be due to concussion. The inflammatory exudate becomes ossified to form the exostosis.

Articular ringbone is a form of dry arthritis whose cause is often obscure. It has been ascribed to concussion without any definite reason. If due to this cause, it should be more prevalent. There may be an hereditary predisposition to the condition. The exciting cause may be rheumatism, or it might possibly be a remote sequel to navel infection. The lesion may ensue from sprain of the joint, but this is more likely to give rise to periarticular ringbone.

Periarticular ringbone most commonly occurs at the lateral aspects of the suffragino-coronal joint, where it arises in many cases from sprain of the lateral ligaments. Therefore, anything favouring sprain of these structures predisposes to the condition, such as malconformation of the limbs, unequal distribution of the weight on the foot, and uneven footing. Improper shoeing, interfering with the normal

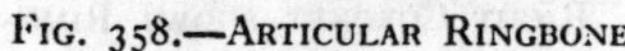

FIG. 358.—ARTICULAR RINGBONE.

FIG. 359.—PERIARTICULAR RINGBONE.

slope of the digit or the balance of weight on the foot, causes a strain on the ligaments of the interphalangeal joints, and favours the production of ringbone. The prevalence of this form of the disease in heavy draft-horses has been ascribed to the fact that they are usually shod with calkins and work on roads sloping from the centre towards the sides, a combination of circumstances which predisposes to sprain of the lateral ligaments of the first interphalangeal joint. The condition may occur, however, without any history of local inflammation or lameness and is then probably due to a hereditary tendency to the formation of exostoses in this class of horses. Appearing in young unbroken horses, periarticular ringbone may be of rachitic origin, the lower end of the os suffraginis and upper end of the os corona becoming enlarged without any evidence of inflammation.

The low variety of this ringbone is usually due to direct injury, such as may be caused by a weight falling on the coronet or a cart-wheel passing over it. Sometimes a phalangeal exostosis is the result of a fissured fracture of the os suffraginis or os corona. Hard work in young horses, before the bones are mature, predisposes to ostitis and periostitis and the formation of ringbone.

SYMPTOMS.—*False ringbone* may appear mysteriously without any evidence or history of inflammation, but it usually commences as an osteo-periostitis with lameness and local symptoms of acute inflammation. When the exostosis is completely developed, the local inflammation and lameness disappear and the horse remains sound. Should the enlargement be on the inner aspect of the pastern, it may be struck by the other foot during progression and be a constant cause of lameness. The exostosis varies in size in different cases; it may be hardly perceptible or very prominent.

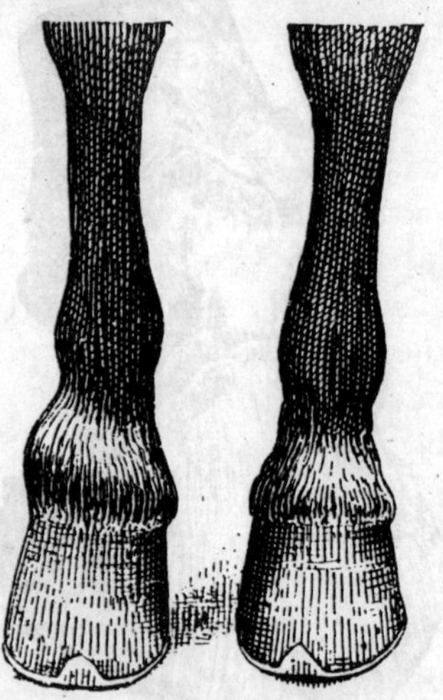

FIG. 360.—THE OUTSIDE OF THE RIGHT CORONET SHOWS RINGBONE FORMATION; THE LEFT IS NORMAL.

Articular ringbone causes permanent lameness, which is often present before the exostosis appears, being due to the inflammation in the joint. The bony deposit may form on any aspect of the joint or all round it (hence the term "ringbone"), but most commonly in front. It may be so small that it is hardly perceptible, or it may be quite obvious to sight and touch. An enlargement in front is best seen by standing at the side, and one at the side by standing in front. There is supporting leg lameness. Pain is evinced on passive movement of the joint. Anchylosis of the joint may supervene from fusion of the articular surfaces, and then the absence of movement can be detected on manipulation.

Periarticular ringbone may or may not be accompanied by lameness. Lameness is present during the acute inflammatory stage of the condition following sprain of the ligaments and the osteo-periostitis which results therefrom. The lameness may persist after the complete development of the exostosis, but it usually disappears when this stage is reached. The most common site of the ringbone is on the lateral aspects of the first interphalangeal joint, where it is best seen by standing in front. When well marked or confined to one side of the joint or to one limb, it is easily detected by comparison with the normal joint. When the joints of both limbs are unusually large and of the same size, it is difficult to decide whether the condition is normal or abnormal. These joints may be normally very prominent in the draft-horse, and must not then be condemned as being affected with ringbone.

The exostosis in this form of ringbone is sometimes enormous, and may extend all round the pastern, and even then the horse may go sound. Anchylosis may ensue from fusion of the ossific deposits on the os suffraginis and os corona, causing mechanical lameness, which may not be very noticeable. The writer has seen a case in which the exostosis formed a sheath for the perforans tendon, and yet the horse was working sound. The nature of the condition was seen on post-mortem examination. The rachitic form of the disease in young horses is not accompanied by lameness, and may disappear as the animal grows. Low ringbone, whether articular or periarticular, is characterised by the presence of a hard bony swelling at the level of the coronet, and in either case causes lameness, the pressure of the horn on the exostosis being sufficient to cause pain apart from the presence of an arthritis.

Diagnosis of ringbone is difficult in its incipient stages, before the exostosis appears, and sometimes the latter is so small that it is difficult to detect. When lameness is present it is impossible to say whether true ringbone is articular or periarticular, but when lameness is absent it is certainly not articular.

Prognosis.—False ringbone is of no consequence when the inflammatory stage has passed, except it is large and situated internally, when it may be struck by the other foot during progression. The same is true, as a rule, of periarticular ringbone, but exceptionally it causes more or less anchylosis of the joint, as mentioned. Articular ringbone is incurable. Low ringbone is always more serious, owing to its being partly beneath the wall of the hoof.

Treatment.—During the acute inflammatory stage of the condition the treatment is that for acute inflammation, the chief indication being rest. When the ringbone is developed and lameness is present, the treatment consists in blistering or firing the enlargement, needle-point firing being undoubtedly the best. No form of treatment will have any good effect on articular ringbone, and the only thing to be done in such a case is double plantar neurectomy. Should persistent lameness ensue from false or periarticular ringbone, median neurectomy should first be tried, and if it proves insufficient, external plantar neurectomy should then be performed.

Bobba Bone—Cab-Horse Disease

Lameness due to osteo-periostitis, and a consequent exostosis affecting the supero-antero-internal aspect of the os suffraginis in the fore-limb, is fairly common in horses doing fast work in cities. Its frequency in cab-horses in London accounts for the condition being spoken of as cab-horse disease. It is of the same nature as ringbone, but is usually described as a separate condition. It is often accompanied by a dry arthritis of the fetlock-joint.

Etiology.—The lesion is apparently brought about by concussion resulting from rapid work on paved streets.

Symptoms.—The affection is insidious in origin. The late Mr. William Hunting was very familiar with the disease. He said that its first indication was intermittent lameness. The horse would be noticed lame one day, but the next morning would be sound and continue so while going on the macadamised road, but when brought on to the pavement lameness would reappear. Eventually lameness is constant. At first there is no local evidence of the lesion, which does not appear until lameness has been in existence for some time. The enlargement is not preceded by obvious local inflammation, thus rendering early diagnosis difficult.

When the exostosis is present it can be seen and felt. It is recognised by standing in front of the horse and comparing the two fetlocks. It is situated as mentioned, and is on a level with the tuberosity which can be easily felt on the supero-postero-lateral aspect of the os suffraginis.

Prognosis.—The lesion, being usually associated with arthritis of the fetlock-joint, is incurable in most cases. That this is not invariably the case, however, is proved in some instances by the horse going sound after treatment.

Treatment.—Needle-point firing and blistering should be tried, and if it has not the desired effect median neurectomy is indicated.

Sprain of the First Interphalangeal Joint in the Dog

Sprain of the first interphalangeal joint is common in track greyhounds characterised by lameness and by inflammatory swelling at the level of the articulation. The degree of injury to the periarticular structures varies in different cases. Some acute cases respond to antiphlogistic remedies followed by prolonged rest to prevent recurrence of the condition. Many cases, however, assume a chronic character with a fibrous thickening round the joint and enlargement of the articular ends of the phalanges and usually defy treatment, although an occasional case is cured by counter-irritation in the form of repeated rubbing in of tincture of iodine or an iodine ointment or a blister of biniodide of mercury or line or needle-point firing, followed by a long period of rest. In a typical case of this kind, it is best to excise the affected joint or remove the second and third phalanges (see p. 476). This chronic form of the lesion is popularly known as "Sprung toe."

Arthritis of this joint is not uncommonly met with causing permanent lameness and characterised by crepitation on manipulation of the affected phalanges and which renders diagnosis from fracture difficult without the use of X-rays. Excision of the joint or amputation of the two terminal phalanges is the only effective remedy (see p. 475).

Dislocation of the Phalanges in the Dog

Dislocation of the phalangeal articulations is very rare in large animals, but is common in sporting dogs, especially track greyhounds.

It is usually accompanied by rupture of the ligaments of the joint, and although reduction is easy in such cases, recovery seldom supervenes, the condition recurring under fast exercise. Sometimes although the articular ends of the bones are in apposition, the joint appears lax from stretching or rupture of its ligaments. In both cases it is usually necessary to amputate the second and third phalanges or excise the affected joint (see p. 476).

The terminal phalangeal joint is often deformed in the greyhound as the result of rupture or stretching of the flexor tendon at its insertion into the third phalanx. The nail projects beyond the level of those on either side and the joint cannot function properly, the displaced nail being an impediment and source of discomfort during fast paces. This condition is also referred to as "knocked-up toe." Amputation of the terminal phalanx enables the dog to race to his usual form.

Dislocation of the First Interphalangeal Joint in the Dog

TREATMENT.—When the joint is loose owing to rupture of its lateral ligaments the bones can be kept in apposition by means of wire. The procedure as demonstrated by Formston (London Veterinary College) at the Congress of the National Veterinary Medical Association at Bournemouth, 1937, consists in incising the skin so as to expose the ends of the two phalanges on each lateral aspect of the joint, drilling a hole transversely through each bone, passing a piece of German silver wire through the holes and twisting its two ends round each other by means of two artery forceps, one for each end of the wire. Grasping both ends with one forceps is apt to result in the wire breaking before it is sufficiently twisted. Having made the wire taut, flatten the twisted end against the lateral aspect of the bone, suture the skin with silkworm gut and apply a protective dressing of gauze, cotton-wool and bandage.

The wound usually heals by first intention and the desired effect is obtained, the dog going sound and being fit to race in the course of five or six weeks.

AFFECTIONS OF THE HIND-LIMB

Hip Lameness

HIP lameness is due to various affections of the hip region, including those of the coxo-femoral and sacro-iliac joints, the bones, muscles, tendons, nerves, and bloodvessels, which are dealt with under special headings.

SYMPTOMS.—Although the various forms of hip lameness, being due to different causes, exhibit important peculiarities in their symptoms, yet taken as a whole they show certain features of general agreement. Thus in all there is difficulty in advancing the limb (swinging leg lameness), retardation of movement, and shortening of the forward stride, and in many cases a tendency to stiffen the limb during movement and to drag the toe. When the hip-joint itself is diseased there is supporting leg lameness, and the animal tries to avoid throwing weight on the affected side—symptoms which are usually absent in the purely muscular forms. Lameness is marked when turning and backing, and appears in an aggravated form after severe exertion. Sometimes it is most distinct when commencing work and gradually decreases ; sometimes the reverse. Though rheumatic lameness usually wears off with exercise, the continuance or aggravation of lameness under such circumstances by no means points to a traumatic origin. Mechanical lameness is a much more common cause of lameness than rheumatism. Sometimes anatomical changes, such as muscular atrophy, swelling, and increased warmth, which can be detected, assist diagnosis and render it approximately exact. The more thorough and complete the examination, the less common will be the diagnosis " hip lameness." The injection of a local anæsthetic over the anterior and posterior tibial nerves will serve to eliminate the hock and the parts below in arriving at a diagnosis.

AFFECTIONS OF THE QUARTER

Traumatic Lesions

1. **Contusions** of the hip, thigh, and leg are common in the horse, caused by falls, blows, and kicks, and by getting the leg over a bar. The nature of the lesion depends on the violence with which the injury is inflicted. The symptoms are those described for contusions in

general. A superficial or deep hæmatoma may be produced, or a collection of serum may be formed beneath the skin or between muscles. When the inside of the leg and thigh are injured by being caught over a beam or board, the skin is severely abraded and a diffuse hæmatoma is frequently produced.

The angle of the haunch is frequently contused by falls and by striking against door-posts, and in cattle it is often injured by repeatedly knocking against the sides of wagons in long train journeys. In many cases of direct injury fracture of the bone results. Should infection gain entrance to any of the bruised parts alluded to, an abscess will ensue and must be dealt with accordingly. When the angle of the ilium or tuber ischii is involved necrosis of the bone may supervene, giving rise to a sinus which will persist until the sequestrum is removed.

2. **An abscess** of obscure origin or due to strangles sometimes forms in the psoas magnus, accompanied by febrile disturbance and causing severe lameness, characterised by stiffness of the joints in the corresponding limb and by arching of the loins. The abscess may point in the groin or in the hollow of the flank, or at the level of the transverse processes of the lumbar vertebræ. Rectal examination will reveal the true seat of the abscess. The latter may burst internally, causing the death of the patient, or externally and be followed by recovery. An abscess (in the same situation) sometimes occurs in the ox,

3. **Open wounds** of the regions mentioned are frequently met with; and are treated as described in general surgery. Pus may burrow deeply beneath the fascia, necessitating a counter-opening and the insertion of a seton to ensure drainage. When bone is involved a sinus may ensue, due to necrosis thereof, and will require to be treated as such. A foreign body may be embedded in the tissues of the quarter, and necessitate incision to remove it.

4. **Bed-sores** in the form of dry gangrene may form over the angle of the haunch and the great trochanter of the femur as the result of prolonged decubitus. Prevention of these lesions should be aimed at by supplying plenty of litter and keeping it dry, as moisture favours their occurrence.

Treatment of the foregoing conditions is on general principles as described under the respective headings in General Surgery.

Bursal Enlargements

A hygroma may form over the external angle of the ilium in the horse and ox from repeated slight injury. It is more common in the latter animal, which is more subject to knocks passing through doorways. Prolonged decubitus is a fruitful source of the condition. It is of the same nature as a collection of serum. A hygroma may also appear over the great trochanter of the femur, due to distension of the gluteal bursa following direct injury. The tuber ischii is occasionally the seat of a bursal enlargement. It is probably most common in the large breed of dogs, especially deer-hounds and wolf-hounds, as the result of contact with hard ground.

TREATMENT is that given under the heading of " Bursitis." Removal of the cause is always indicated as far as possible. Aspiration and injection should be tried in the dog before resorting to the knife, as there may be difficulty in obtaining healing of the wound caused by the latter. A biniodide of mercury blister has succeeded in healing a callous bursal wound on the tuber ischii in the dog after other applications had failed.

Sprain and Rupture of Muscles

The muscles of the croup, hip, and thigh may be sprained or ruptured in various ways : slipping, jumping, falling, violent effort.

Sprain and Rupture of the Psoas Muscles.—The psoas muscles may be sprained or ruptured from over-stretching as the result of the hind-limbs slipping backwards—for example, into a ditch, which the animal has failed to clear in jumping, or of violent struggling when cast, or of forcible extension backwards of the hind-limbs.

SYMPTOMS.—The condition is spoken of as sprain of the loins. There is stiffness of the dorso-lumbar region and difficulty in moving the hind-limbs, especially in the act of backing. The gait is straddling, and there is a tendency to drag the toes and to knuckle at the fetlocks. The horse finds it difficult to assume the position for stalling. There may be blood in the urine, due to over-stretching of the ureters and rupture of capillaries therein. Pain is evinced on pressure over the muscles *per rectum*. When the horse is lying he may have difficulty in rising. The severity of the symptoms, however, depends on the degree of injury. When it is slight they are not very noticeable, but when there is complete muscular rupture the above well-marked symptoms are observed, and even death may ensue from hæmorrhage or peritonitis.

PROGNOSIS.—Complete recovery seldom follows rupture of these muscles. An abscess has been seen, apparently as a sequel of the condition, pointing in the groin under Poupart's ligament some weeks after the accident to the muscles, recovery ensuing rapidly after bursting of the abscess. Repair is brought about by fibrous tissue, whereby the muscle loses much of its power.

The Gluteal Muscles may be ruptured in the region of the hip-joint, causing local symptoms of inflammation and hip lameness, characterised by a shortened stride and by dragging the toe. There may be adduction of the limb during its forward movement.

Rupture of the Biceps Femoris.—This muscle may be ruptured as the result of violent contraction, as may occur when a horse struggles vigorously in hobbles, or during heavy draft. The rupture usually occurs at its upper attachment, where it causes a well-marked, slightly painful swelling. Lameness is characterised by difficulty in taking the limb forward, and by a movement of circumduction when attempting to do so.

Rupture of the Tensor Vaginæ Femoris has been seen near its origin from the external angle of the ilium. It is manifested by a swelling a little below the latter point, and by a depression between the bone and the enlargement. The hip is lowered, and the limb is carried somewhat diagonally towards the opposite fore-limb. When bearing weight, the limb is not completely extended. The horse may have difficulty in rising from the recumbent position.

Rupture of the Adductor Muscles Inside the Thigh.—Rupture of some of these muscles, most frequently the semi-membranosus and semitendinosus, occurs occasionally from excessive contraction when struggling in the cast position, or more rarely when galloping. The accident is apt to occur in vigorous thoroughbred stallions when cast for operation. The author had such a case in an aged thoroughbred stallion cast for castration.

SYMPTOMS.—A hot, painful swelling forms at the seat of injury, due to extravasation of blood, and severe lameness supervenes. Both limbs may be affected, and then the horse is almost powerless in the hind-limbs. When the animal is able to walk or stand the limb is abducted. If there is only partial rupture of one or two superficial muscles, the extravasation of blood is slight and becomes absorbed after some time, leaving a depression corresponding to the space between the divided fibres.

PROGNOSIS of complete rupture is bad, a perfect recovery seldom or never ensuing.

Rupture of the Quadriceps rarely occurs. It is characterised by the usual local symptoms of inflammation and extravasation. Lameness is manifested by inability to extend the stifle-joint, and it, as well as the hock, is held in a state of flexion, as in crural paralysis.

A partial rupture of the muscles may occur, characterised by lameness, which is more or less severe according to the nature of the lesion. The local symptoms in this case may not be very obvious.

TREATMENT of all the foregoing lesions is carried out on general principles as laid down for inflammation and contusions. In cases of complete rupture, when the case is worth treating, slings are necessary to support the patient and to keep him at rest. The danger of rupture of the thigh muscles should be considered when about to cast a "blood" horse, and to prevent the accident chloroform should be administered in the standing position.

Displacement of the Biceps Femoris

In cattle the biceps femoris or longus vastus muscle glides on the great trochanter of the femur by means of a large serous bursa, and its anterior border is firmly embraced by the double laminæ of the fascia lata. This fascia may become fissured, allowing the muscle to slip backwards off the trochanter, which passes into the fissure, and flexion of the femur is then impossible. The accident happens particularly in emaciated animals with prominent trochanters and in mountain cattle with sloping quarters, and is caused by slipping with the limb extended backwards in the cowshed, at work, or during coitus.

SYMPTOMS.—The condition is usually confined to one leg. Immediately the muscle becomes fixed behind the trochanter, flexion of the thigh is impossible and lameness is at once developed. The limb is fixed in an extended position, similar to that in upward displacement of the patella, or is thrust outwards and forwards with a kind of mowing movement, the claws scraping the ground. On local examination, the trochanter appears very prominent and situated directly above a rigid cord, which extends parallel with the anterior margin of the luxated muscle. The limb is not so firmly fixed in the extended position as in luxation of the patella. Sometimes the dislocation is only momentary, the muscle immediately returning to its normal position, so that the animal goes sound for a few steps, but soon falls lame again. When the muscle becomes fixed in the abnormal position it appears tense and its outline is more distinct, whilst a depression appears in front of the trochanter.

COURSE AND PROGNOSIS.—Spontaneous recovery is never permanent, and, unless operation be resorted to, habitual luxation results—*i.e.*, the lameness continually recurs or becomes lasting. Prognosis is only grave in working animals. The accident is now less common than formerly, probably because cattle are better fed and better managed.

Treatment.—When the displacement is due to stretching of the fascia, rest and good feeding favour the deposition of fat, and soon alter the conditions responsible for the accident. Counter-irritation may be employed with advantage in cases where spontaneous reduction occurs. If, however, the fascia lata is ruptured and the " trochanter " firmly fixed in the fissure, operation becomes necessary to release the trochanter and restore the function of the limb. To operate, proceed thus: At a point about 3 inches below and in front of the trochanter,

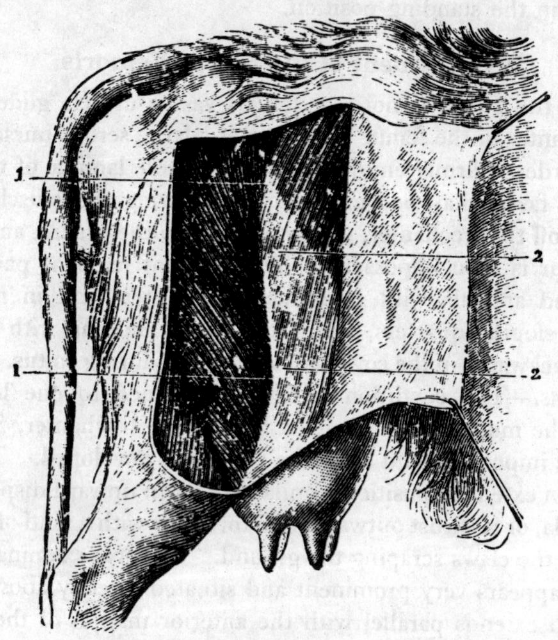

Fig. 361.—Biceps Femoris Muscle.
1, Anterior margin of muscle; 2, fascia lata.

in the direction of the muscle, make an incision about 2 inches long through the skin and aponeurosis, separate the anterior border of the muscle from the subjacent tissues by using a spatula, pass a director transversely beneath it, and divide it from within outwards. It may be necessary to plug the wound to arrest the hæmorrhage. The wound usually heals in ten to eighteen days. The condition is rare in the horse, in which the displaced muscle passes in front of the trochanter. In fracture of the ischium the tuber ischii may be displaced by the pull of this muscle, resulting in deformity of the buttock.

Ossification of the Aponeurosis of the Hip or Thigh

This lesion is rarely met with. It may occur without any apparent cause, or be the result of direct injury. Its most common site is the outer aspect of the hip.

Symptoms.—There is slight lameness or mere stiffness in the limb. Locally a hard painless swelling is detected, regular or irregular in outline.

Treatment consists in excision of the ossified tissue, the resulting wound being sutured in its upper part. Complete cure is usually effected.

Inflammation of the Gluteal Bursa

Inflammation of the gluteal bursa, which facilitates the gliding of the gluteal tendon over the convexity of the great trochanter, is occasionally met with, associated with more or less inflammation of the tendon itself.

Etiology.—The tendo-synovitis is the result of violent contraction of the gluteal muscles, or of stretching of their tendons when the horse falls with the limb underneath the body. It might be of toxic origin occurring during the course of an infectious disease like rheumatism, influenza, or strangles.

Symptoms.—There is hip lameness, characterised by a crooked or oblique configuration of the quarter, the body being slightly curved inwards, with the convexity on the lame side. A short step is taken by the affected limb. At rest the latter is held flexed and in a state of adduction, with its foot in advance of that of the other limb. During the trot there is marked lowering of the affected hip. These features of the lameness are not of themselves diagnostic of the condition, but when associated with local inflammatory symptoms there can be little hesitation about the nature of the lesion.

The local symptoms consist of a swelling, which is at first hot and painful, but afterwards cold and indolent, when crepitation, due to synovitis, may be detected on passive movement of the limb. Eventually atrophy of the muscles ensues.

Treatment is that for acute or chronic inflammation according to the age of the lesion. When there is marked atrophy of the muscle, there is little chance of recovery. The condition may be complicated with periostitis of the great trochanter, and the consequent production of exostoses, causing permanent incurable lameness

Fractures of the Pelvis

The site of fracture may be the ilium, pubis, ischium, or cotyloid cavity, and several of these bones may be involved at once.

Fractures of the Ilium

The External Angle—ETIOLOGY.—The fracture is due to direct violence, such as falling on the haunch or striking it violently against a post or corner of a wall. In young animals it is believed that

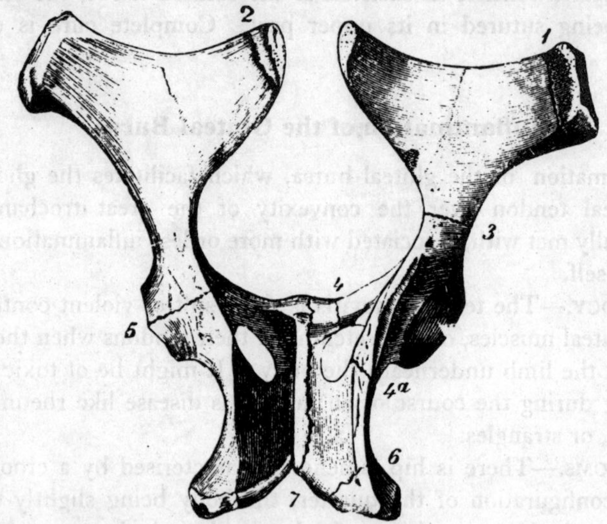

FIG. 362.—SCHEMA ILLUSTRATING FRACTURES OF THE PELVIS IN THE HORSE. Fracture of: 1, external iliac angle; 2, internal iliac angle; 3, shaft of the ilium 4, transverse portion of the os pubis; 4*a*, external portion of the ischium 5, cotyloid cavity; 6, tuber ischii; 7, symphysis pubis.

the angle may be detached by muscular exertion, especially in two-year-old racehorses. Occasionally only one of the tuberosities of the angle is fractured, and usually remains attached to the bone, causing little or no deformity, but capable of being diagnosed by slight crepitation on manipulation. As a rule, however, the whole angle is fractured, and the fragment is pulled downwards by contraction of the tensor vaginæ femoris, causing marked deformity.

SYMPTOMS.—The deformity is readily detected on standing behind the animal and comparing the two hips. Locally there is evidence of a contusion, and the displaced fragment can be felt as a hard substance in the hollow of the flank below its normal situation.

When the fracture is compound the broken bone can be seen and felt, and a hollow wound is observed at the seat of the lesion. Crepitation is absent, owing to the space between the fractured surfaces. The animal affected is said to be " hipped " or " down of its hip." There is distinct lameness at first, but when the local inflammation subsides it disappears, and the only bad result of the accident is the blemish caused by the deformity. When there is an open wound there may be trouble, due to infection, causing necrosis or caries of the bone. Apart from this, however, the horse is usually fit to return to work in three or four weeks.

FIG. 363.—FRACTURE OF THE EXTERNAL ANGLE OF THE ILIUM.

The Body.—Sometimes the fracture involves the body of the bone, extending from its anterior to its lower border. In this case there is not so much displacement, and crepitation can be detected. Fracture of the angle and of the body may occur at the same time. The lameness is more marked and the sinking of the quarter more pronounced when the body of the bone is broken, while the width of the two sides remains the same. The lameness is very marked, little or no weight being borne, and great difficulty being evinced in taking the limb forward. Crepitation may be heard when the animal moves, and is usually easily detected on external and rectal manipulation. It is generally more easily felt than heard by placing the hand flat on the hip while the patient is made to walk, or by grasping the external angle of the ilium in one hand and the tuber ischii in the other, and pushing the animal gently from side to side. It is recognised *per rectum* during movement of the patient or passive movement of the limb. Rectal examination reveals the swelling and deformity caused by the lesion, and confirms the diagnosis.

The PROGNOSIS is more serious, for if union of the fragments does not occur, permanent lameness ensues. A possible complication of both fractures is the penetration of spicules into the peritoneal cavity, resulting in the case of compound fracture in peritonitis and death.

The Internal Angle of the Ilium is rarely fractured. It is generally caused by falling over an embankment and landing on the croup. Crepitation may be detected on external and rectal palpation.

The Shaft of the Ilium—ETIOLOGY.—The fracture is usually caused by falling on the hip, but cases of its occurring during exercise, without any obvious exciting cause, have been recorded. Rarely the fracture is bilateral.

SYMPTOMS.—On comparing the quarters from behind, the absence of symmetry is at once observed, the whole of the gluteal region on the affected side being gradually lowered from the middle line towards the external angle of the ilium. Crepitation can be detected as in fracture of the body. Sometimes displacement of the fragments is deferred, and the diagnosis is difficult at first. The history of the case and the sudden and severe lameness are aids to diagnosis, although the degree of lameness is not always in proportion to the gravity of the lesion.

PROGNOSIS.—The prognosis must be guarded. It depends largely on the amount of displacement and the quietude of the patient. Complete recovery, except for a varying degree of persisting deformity, ensues in some cases, while in others union of the fragments fails to occur. The resulting constriction of the pelvis after healing of the fracture may render the mare unfit for breeding, but even marked deformity of the hip does not interfere with the animal's utility for work. Death may rapidly supervene from internal hæmorrhage, due to laceration of an iliac artery or vein by one of the fragments.

Fracture through the Cotyloid Cavity results from direct violence, usually from falling on the great trochanter of the femur, the force being transmitted to the head of the latter, and thence to the bones forming the cavity. It may be associated with fracture of the head of the femur.

SYMPTOMS.—There is sudden and severe lameness, and the patient evinces pain on the least movement of the affected region. Crepitation can usually be detected. There is not much deformity of the quarter. On palpation *per rectum*, the inflammatory swelling caused by the lesion is not always evident. Crepitation may be perceptible when the animal is made to walk or the limb is passively moved. Occasionally diagnosis of the exact condition is only confirmed on post-mortem examination, owing to the absence of characteristic symptoms during life.

PROGNOSIS.—The case is incurable.

Fracture of the Floor of the Pelvis

Etiology.—Fracture of the pelvic floor is caused by falls and by slipping outwards of the hind-limb or limbs. It usually occurs through the obturator foramen, and generally involves the pubis and ischium.

Symptoms.—The animal goes suddenly lame. When the accident results from falling, the patient may be unable to rise without assistance. The lameness is characterised by stiffness in the hind-quarters, and by circumduction of the limb on the affected side. There is no deformity of the quarters, but in a recent case there is swelling at the level of the tuber ischii and œdema may be noticed in the perineal region. In the mare ecchymosis may be observed in the mucous membrane of the vagina. Crepitation can be detected by placing the hand firmly against the tuber ischii while the patient is being slowly walked. Rectal, or in the mare vaginal, examination reveals deformity, crepitation, and mobility in the region of the fracture, rendering diagnosis easy. The fracture may be overlooked at first, the lameness in some cases being apparently not sufficiently well marked to warrant the existence of a fracture. In all cases of marked hind-leg lameness the pelvis should be carefully examined before giving a definite opinion as to the seat of lameness.

When the condition has been in existence for some time, atrophy of the muscles of the hip and thigh is observed, and paralysis of the adductors of the thigh may ensue from a callus pressing on or overstretching the obturator nerve, giving rise to symptoms of "obturator lameness." Death may result from hæmorrhage, due to rupture of the obturator vessels by one of the fragments. The callus may be so large that it causes pelvic constriction, precluding the use of the female for breeding. This, however, is seldom the case.

Prognosis.—The prognosis must be guarded. It depends on the degree of displacement and the amount of mobility of the fragments. In many cases complete recovery is obtained.

Treatment of the foregoing pelvic fractures is carried out on general principles. In simple fracture of the external angle of the ilium rest and antiphlogistic applications are sufficient. In the course of a few weeks the animal will go sound. When the body of the bone or its shaft is fractured, it is generally advisable to put the horse in slings to restrict movement and prevent the patient lying and rising. They do not always have the desired effect in these respects, as the horse may sit on the slings and thus disturb the seat of fracture more so than by ordinary movements. In all cases the stall should be made narrow to prevent side-to-side movements. A charge over the affected quarter is usually applied to diminish mobility there. A fair percentage of recoveries occurs, but the issue is always in doubt. The deformity persists after healing of the fracture, but even when it is marked it does not interfere with the utility of the animal for work.

For fracture of the pelvic floor treatment is on the same lines. Strapping the two hind-limbs together above the hocks helps to keep the fragments in apposition, but it may not be tolerated by every patient. A charge over both quarters may also be used with advantage. Some cases make good recoveries, while others prove incurable. Mares have been known to breed successfully after healing of the fracture. Fracture of the tuber ischii is dealt with in the same way as that of the external angle. In each case fibrous union occurs between the detached fragment and the bone.

Separation through the symphysis pubis and ischii occurs in cattle from violent slipping outwards of the hind-limbs and from powerful traction on a large fœtus during parturition. The animal goes down in the spread-eagle position, and is unable to rise. Vaginal examination reveals the space where separation has taken place. The case is incurable.

Fractures of the Pelvis in Small Animals

Fractures of the pelvis in the dog and cat result from falling from a height and from being run over by vehicles. Diagnosis is easy, crepitation and mobility being readily detected. Digital examination *per rectum* reveals the exact seat of the lesion and the degree of displacement. Peritonitis and death may ensue from perforation of the anterior part of the rectum, or fatal hæmorrhage may supervene from laceration of the iliac vessels. Otherwise recovery is the rule, provided that the displacement of the fragments is not very marked.

Treatment consists chiefly in keeping the patient confined in a small kennel, so as to restrict movement as much as possible. Further immobilisation, however, may be effected by a pitch plaster over the quarters. When there is great displacement of the fragments bone-pinning will be necessary to bring about their alignment and immobilisation (see p. 120).

Fracture of the Femur

Etiology.—The fracture may be caused by external or muscular violence. It is comparatively rare in large animals, but is very common in the dog. In the former it results from falling on the hip, and from struggling when cast and fixed with ropes, or when a back strap is used after casting with hobbles. In the latter it is caused by falling from a height, by kicks, and by being run over.

SITES.—The site of fracture may be the shaft, the lower epiphysis the neck, the head, or one of the trochanters. The commonest site is the shaft, particularly its lower third. Fracture of the neck is probably more common in the dog than in the horse.

SYMPTOMS.—When the shaft is involved, the characteristic symptoms of fracture are observed—viz., abnormal mobility, crepitation, inability to bear weight, and local inflammation and deformity. The limb can be bent outwards almost at right angles to the body. Some hours after the occurrence of the fracture a large swelling may be formed, due to extravasation of blood. When the line of fracture is very long and oblique, abnormal mobility is not so evident. Fracture at the level of the condyles is indicated by similar symptoms, and on careful manipulation crepitus can always be detected.

When the lesion is in the head or neck of the bone, diagnosis may be difficult, the symptoms being similar to those due to dislocation. Sharp crepitation is a distinguishing feature, as is also the greater mobility of the limb in the case of fracture. When fracture of the neck has been in existence for some weeks, considerable weight may be borne on the affected limb, and in this case there is marked prominence of the great trochanter, which is displaced upwards, and a rude noise rather than a crepitation is produced by rubbing of the femur against the ilium, the head of the femur remaining in the cotyloid cavity. Separation of the articular head of the femur has been observed in colts (males) under three years old that have been running at grass, resulting from slipping or from muscular effort when first put to work, with symptoms similar to those just described. It has been reported as fairly common in Belgium.

Fracture of the great trochanter is characterised by local acute inflammatory swelling, crepitation, and severe lameness. The fragment may be movable on manipulation. Little weight is borne on the limb, which is held in a state of abduction, and during progression it is taken forward with difficulty and directed somewhat outwards. When there is an open wound communicating with the broken bone, necrosis of the latter may ensue, causing a fistula, which persists until the diseased tissue is removed. When the third trochanter is fractured, similar local symptoms are observed, but the lameness is not so severe.

In many cases of complete fracture of the femur in the horse and ox the animal is lying and unable to rise when the veterinarian arrives, and it is necessary for him to have the animal turned over to make a diagnosis when it is the under side that is affected.

PROGNOSIS of complete fracture of the femur in the large animals is grave, and slaughter is usually advised for the horse and large bovine. In light cattle and sheep spontaneous recovery may ensue, and cure is helped by treatment. Even a false joint in these animals does not prevent their getting about and being prepared for the butcher. In dogs and cats fracture of the shaft and condyles almost invariably heals under suitable treatment, but that involving the head and neck or lower articular surface is incurable. Fatal hæmorrhage is a possible complication in all animals from laceration of the femoral artery.

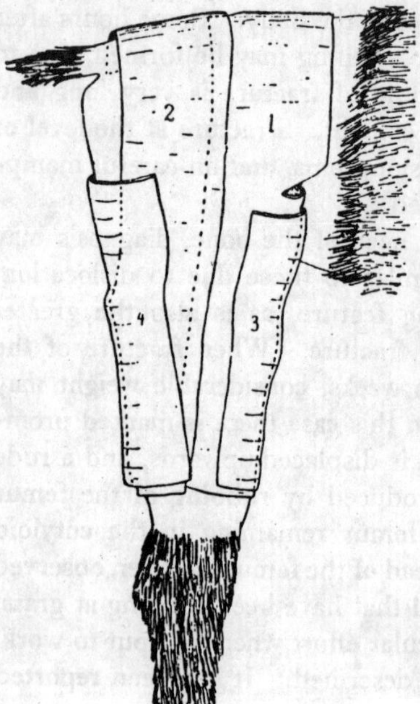

[*Vet. Rec.*

FIG. 364.—PLASTER CAST APPLIED FOR FRACTURE OF THE FEMUR IN THE DOG. Shaft and lower third femur.

TREATMENT.—As indicated, treatment in the large animals is unsatisfactory, as reduction and immobilisation cannot be properly effected, and even if healing were obtained in the horse, the deformity resulting from defective reduction would render the animal useless except for the stud, when suitable for breeding. Treatment in all classes of patients is on the usual lines for complete fracture. In the small animals a pitch bandage applied from the foot to the croup always has the desired effect for fracture of the shaft and of the condyles. It immobilises the whole limb. The ordinary calico or tarlatan bandage is commenced on the lower part of the limb and carried up to the croup, where it is made to adhere by means of pitch. It is then folded in different directions over the outer aspect of the thigh and hip, and made to encircle the former, with a layer of pitch between each fold and turn of the bandage, the skin on the inside of the thigh being protected by a layer of cotton-wool. A single turn is brought down over the lower part of the limb, to which it is made adherent by a layer of pitch. The patient is kept in a cool place, and if it attempts to bite the dressing an Elizabethan collar is applied. Portions of the dressing may become separated now and again, but can be readjusted by a fresh application of pitch. Burgess's plaster bandage is very suitable for the purpose, and for small dogs an ordinary adhesive bandage has the desired effect. This treatment has been followed by complete recovery even when both femurs were fractured. Unpadded plaster splints have also proved very suitable for immobilising the seat of fracture (Fig. 364) (see p. 123). Keeping the patient confined in a small kennel would probably effect a cure in the majority of cases, but if the animal is allowed to move about without a dressing a false joint is very likely to result. In the event of this happening, a cure may be obtained by cutting down on the seat of fracture, scraping the ends of the fragments, and uniting them with plates and screws, or applying an external rigid dressing. The Stadar Splint is the best means of reducing and immobilising the fragments.

Dislocation of the Ilio-Sacral Joint

This is a rare condition, and occurs more frequently in the bovine than in the horse. It may be complete or incomplete, and is usually observed in the cow as the result of a difficult parturition, being due to the forcible extraction of a fœtus which offers unusual resistance to delivery.

SYMPTOMS.—There is difficulty in moving, but weight can usually be borne on the affected limb. When the beast is down, she has great difficulty is rising. The ilio-sacral region is swollen, hard, and slightly painful. When the dislocation is complete there is marked deformity, the sacrum being depressed and the internal angles of the ilia being abnormally prominent. The depression of the sacrum is confirmed on rectal examination. In this case the patient is down and unable to rise, and the condition is apt to be confounded with post-partum paralysis.

PROGNOSIS.—Complete dislocation is incurable.

TREATMENT.—If the symptoms warrant treatment, the horse should be rested in slings and the bovine left at liberty, a charge being applied over the croup in each case.

Dislocation of the Hip-Joint

Dislocation of the coxo-femoral articulation is fairly common in the dog and ox, less frequent in the sheep and goat, and rare in the horse. It may be complete or incomplete. The former is distinguished as follows : (1) Anterior or precotyloid ; (2) posterior or postcotyloid or ischiatic ; (3) internal pubic or obturatoral ; and (4) outward or supracotyloid. Experience has shown that the accident can occur without fracture, although the latter is a common complication. The comparative frequence of the condition in the ox and the small animals is due to the absence of the pubo-femoral ligament in these animals.

Etiology.—The dislocation is due to violent movement of the joint beyond its physiological limits, as may result from a fall or from slipping outwards. In the dog it is commonly the result of a severe contusion, caused by a kick, blow, or fall from a height or the passage of a wheel of a vehicle over the region. Spontaneous luxation as a sequel to chronic arthritis is rare, as is also that due to tubercular arthritis. Bilateral dislocation may occur in the ox from both hind-limbs slipping outwards. The surrounding muscles are more or less ruptured.

Symptoms.—Severe lameness follows the accident. The toe of the foot only may be in contact with the ground, or some weight may be borne on the whole plantar aspect. During progression the affected limb is deviated outwards and is taken forward stiffly, without flexion of its joints, by a movement of circumduction. The great trochanter becomes very prominent in outward dislocation, whereas when the latter is inwards the tuberosity can hardly be recognised. The length of the limb is diminished or increased according as the head of the femur is displaced upwards or downwards. In the former case the projecting upper extremity of the bone moves backwards and forwards during progression, and the movement can be felt by placing the hand on the prominence. When the head of the bone occupies the obturator foramen, it can be felt there on rectal examination. A rocking noise may be heard during progression, due to the displaced femur rubbing against the ischium.

Diagnosis is based on the differences between fracture and dislocation described in General Surgery. The condition may be confounded with fracture of the neck of the femur, as mentioned when dealing with that condition.

Prognosis.—The obturator or sciatic nerve may be compressed or crushed by the displaced bone, causing temporary or permanent paralysis. Reduction of the dislocation in the large animals is often impossible, and when it is effected, even in small patients, retention may be impossible on account of the damage done to the surrounding tissues, including rupture of the round and capsular ligaments. In bovines the veterinarian is generally satisfied with the formation of a false joint, which is sufficient to enable the animal to bear weight on the limb while being prepared for the butcher or being used as a milker or for breeding. In the dog the false joint may be so well formed that lameness is hardly noticeable.

TREATMENT is carried out on the lines mentioned in General Surgery. Extension and counter-extension and local manipulation are practised under general anæsthesia, the lower portion of the limb being used to lever the head of the femur into its socket. In the large animals a rope passed through the groin and its two ends attached to a fixed point will serve as a fulcrum. A large cylindrical object placed between the limbs in the perineal region also answers this purpose. After reduction, the horse should be put in slings and kept there for some weeks. A pitch plaster over the joint may have some immobilising effect, but some practitioners prefer the application of a blister on the ground that it stimulates the process of repair.

Inflammation of the Hip-Joint

ETIOLOGY.—Inflammation of the hip-joint is a rare occurrence in all animals. It is caused in the following ways: By—

1. *Direct injury* following heavy falls on rough, hard ground.
2. *Excessive movement* of the joint, spraining its ligaments or even causing its dislocation.
3. *Rheumatism*, which is most common in cattle and may cause chronic arthritis.
4. *Joint-ill* in young animals.

The chronic inflammation termed malum coxæ senile, so common in men, is not met with in veterinary practice.

SYMPTOMS.—Lameness is more or less severe, depending on the degree of inflammation. In cattle the diseased limb is extended with the toe turned outwards. The gait is of a rolling character, the limb being directed outwards and carried forward in a semicircle. It is apt to collapse under the animal, especially when turning on the diseased side. In the horse the symptoms are similar. As a rule the quarter is tilted and atrophied, the animal moves diagonally or away from the lame side, the limb is abducted, and in harness work the leg and shaft on the sound side show marks of friction. Suppuration is notified by great increase of lameness and by cellulitis in the region of the joint.

PROGNOSIS.—Simple traumatic synovitis of the joint responds to treatment, but arthritis is incurable.

TREATMENT comprises rest and the use of the usual antiphlogistic agents or that for rheumatism or joint-ill if due to one of these affections. Counter-irritation by blistering, firing, or the insertion of a seton is indicated in chronic cases.

Paralysis of the Obturator Nerve

ETIOLOGY.—The paralysis may be due to:

1. *Laceration of the nerve* by a fragment of a fractured pubic bone.
2. *A callus*, following fracture of the pubis, compressing the nerve.
3. *The pressure of a fœtus* during delivery in a case of fœtal dystokia.
4. *A tumour* on the course of the nerve, compressing it, such as a melanotic tumour in a grey horse.

SYMPTOMS.—The characteristic feature of the condition is marked abduction of the limb during progression, due to loss of power in the adductor muscles supplied by the obturator nerve—viz., the adductors parvus and magnus, the pectineus, and the gracilis. The abduction is accompanied by more or less difficulty in taking the leg forward. The limb is lifted as in stringhalt. Gradual atrophy of the affected muscles supervenes, although it is not so noticeable as in other forms of paralysis.

PROGNOSIS.—When the condition is due to extravasation or effusion following temporary compression of the nerves, it disappears when they become reabsorbed. But when caused by a tumour, or by rupture of the nerve, it is incurable. When a callus decreases in size, diminishing the tension on the nerve, the function of the latter may return.

TREATMENT is of no avail when the cause cannot be removed. When due to a temporary condition, recovery is favoured by the administration of potassium iodide and nux vomica, and by regular exercise.

Crural Paralysis

Crural paralysis is indicated by loss of power in the quadriceps extensor cruri muscles—viz., the vastus externus, the vastus internus, the rectus femoris, and rectus parvus—situated in front of the femur.

ETIOLOGY.—The cause may be:

1. *Over-stretching* of the nerve, as may ensue from slipping backwards of the hind-limb or from violently kicking backwards, or from a great effort during heavy draft.
2. *Hæmoglobinuria*, in which the muscles supplied by this nerve as well as other muscles of the hind-quarters may become powerless and rapidly undergo atrophy.
3. An *abscess*, *tumour*, or *exostosis* compressing the nerve, or ***toxic neuritis***.

No. 1 is the commonest cause of simple crural paralysis.

SYMPTOMS.—During rest the limb is held with the stifle **and the** joints below it in a semi-flexed position. Extension of the stifle is impossible. Consequently, when the horse attempts to put weight on the limb there is sudden flexion of the stifle and hock. There is marked dropping of the stifle, simulating dropped elbow in the fore-limb. If the condition persists for some time, gradual atrophy of the quadriceps supervenes. At first sight the limb appears to be fractured on account of its loose, powerless appearance.

FIG. 365.—PARALYSIS OF THE ANTERIOR CRURAL NERVE.

DIAGNOSIS is easy from the characteristic symptoms mentioned. It can only be confounded with rupture of the muscles concerned, a rare condition accompanied by local inflammatory symptoms.

PROGNOSIS.—In most cases the injury to the nerve is of a temporary nature, and recovery ensues within six weeks, occasionally in a few days, but exceptionally months elapse before cure is effected. Resulting from hæmoglobinuria, the prognosis is unfavourable.

TREATMENT is that described for paralysis in general. Counter-irritation over the muscles affected and the administration of potassium iodide alone or along with nux vomica or strychnine hypodermically constitute the chief curative measures. When power returns to the muscles, gradually increasing exercise is indicated. The other methods of treating paralysis may also be employed. In a valuable subject hope should not be abandoned until at least six months have elapsed since the accident.

Sciatic Paralysis

The sciatic nerve is not much exposed to injury, being well protected by the overlying muscles, yet several cases of paralysis of the muscles supplied by it have been reported in the horse, ox, and dog.

ETIOLOGY.—The condition may be caused by:

1. *Excessive extension* of the hind-limb from slipping or from its being fixed in this position when the animal is cast.

2. *Falling* on the corresponding quarter.

3. *Toxœmia*, following strangles, pneumonia, or purpura, or distemper in the dog.

4. *Compression* by a tumour.

SYMPTOMS.—There is paralysis of all the muscles of the hind-limb, except those supplied by the crural nerve—viz., the quadriceps. During progression the patient is powerless to lift the affected limb forward, and it is dragged with the front of the foot in contact with the ground. The stifle is jerked forward by the action of its extensor muscles. Backing is difficult.

In the dog the skin on the anterior part of the paw becomes excoriated from friction against the ground, and in the horse and ox the front of the fetlock may be similarly affected. If by manipulation the limb is placed in its normal position, it is able to sustain weight in the usual way, because the extensors of the stifle fix that joint, and with it the other joints of the limb. Anæsthesia of the skin of the lower part of the limb accompanies this condition.

TREATMENT is as usual for paralysis. When the result of direct injury, antiphlogistic remedies are indicated, and if due to a tumour the latter must be removed. Slings are advisable for the horse until the muscles regain some power, when exercise should be prescribed.

Paralysis of the External Popliteal Nerve

This belongs rather to the region of the leg, but may be conveniently dealt with here in company with the other forms of paralysis affecting the hind-limb.

ETIOLOGY.—The cause of the paralysis may be:

1. *Direct injury*, such as may ensue from a fall, a blow, or a kick inflicted over the nerve where it passes downwards and forwards over the supero-external aspect of the tibial region. This is the usual cause of the condition.

2. *Toxic*, ensuing in the course of an infectious disease like strangles or purpura. It very rarely occurs, however, in this way.

SYMPTOMS.—When the paralysis is complete, there is total loss of power in the extensor pedis and the flexor metatarsi muscles, which are innervated by this nerve. At rest, the limb may appear normal, bearing weight with the foot resting naturally, or the stifle may be dropped, the hock extended, and the fetlock and front of the pastern

FIG. 366.—PARALYSIS OF THE EXTERNAL POPLITEAL NERVE.

resting on the ground. In advancing, the limb appears to dwell, becoming rigidly extended backwards, and then dragged forwards, renewing contact with the ground by the flexed fetlock or the plantar surface of the foot. In backing, at first the fetlock is straightened and the heels come to the ground, then the foot is drawn stiffly backwards, the fetlock is suddenly shot forwards, and the heels are raised from the ground. At liberty in a field the patient can canter, trailing the defective limb, which touches the ground by the front of the fetlock and the toe-wall of the foot.

PROGNOSIS.—Recovery is the rule in a few days or a few weeks when the lesion is the result of injury.

Treatment is the same as that described for the other forms of paralysis.

Internal Popliteal Paralysis

The muscles at the back of the tibia are affected.

Symptoms.—The hock cannot be extended nor the foot flexed, but as flexion of the hock causes automatic flexion of the interphalangeal joints, these joints remain in a state of flexion. The limb can bear weight because the Achilles tendon fixes the hock. The limb is advanced with all the joints excessively flexed, the foot being lifted very high and set down with a hesitating (" tapping ") movement, the action, as a whole, bearing some resemblance to stringhalt. The gastrocnemii are unable to extend the hock while the flexor metatarsi is passive, and only affects movement through the medium of the peculiar tendinous apparatus. Trotting is impossible. The muscles affected, especially the gastrocnemii and flexor pedis perforans, are relaxed, and afterwards become atrophied. The nerve would appear to be affected in its course between the gastrocnemii muscles.

Fig. 367.—Paralysis of the Internal Popliteal Nerve.

Treatment.—As usual for paralysis.

Thrombosis of the Posterior Aorta and of its Branches

Arterial thrombosis and its consequences have been dealt with under the heading of Affections of Arteries. The commonest seat of the disease, giving rise to clinical symptoms, is the termination of the posterior aorta, the vessel itself or one or more of the iliac vessels being involved.

Etiology.—The etiology is sometimes obscure, but in a general way it may be said that the condition arises from an arteritis which roughens the intima of the vessel, on whose lining a thrombus then forms. The commonest cause of this in the horse is the presence of sclerostomes in the blood stream, which become arrested at the double bifurcation of the posterior aorta. The thrombosis may also be due to an embolus arrested here after separation from a thrombus in an aneurism of the anterior mesenteric artery, which is almost invariably present as the result of sclerostomes located there. Bacteria in the circulation may have the same effect. The condition has also been ascribed to over-stretching of the affected vessels from slipping backwards of the hind-limbs, as may possibly occur in a stallion during vigorous service.

Symptoms and Diagnosis.—The symptoms and diagnostic features of the disease may be briefly stated as follows:

1. The patient is perfectly normal at rest and at walking exercise, or perhaps during light work.

2. When the animal is made to trot, functional disturbance ensues after the lapse of about five to fifteen minutes, affecting one or both hind-limbs.

3. The lameness is characterised by gradually increasing powerlessness of the limb or limbs, which are carried stiffly with little or no flexion of the hocks. If the exercise is continued when both limbs are affected, the patient will fall as if affected with paraplegia.

4. The affected limb or limbs are cold compared with the rest of the body, and when the latter is bathed in sweat they remain dry.

5. When the lameness appears, the animal evinces signs of pain, which become intensified as the exercise continues. The expression is anxious and the respirations hurried, and the animal stops, if not forced to go on. Sweating occurs over the body, except in the affected region. The patient sometimes behaves as if affected with colic for some time after forced exercise.

6. After a period of rest, the normal appearance of the animal is restored.

7. On rectal examination the thrombus may be detected, and the feeble pulsation or entire absence thereof may be recognised on the distal side of the thrombus, or a vibratory tremor may be felt, due to the blood percolating through the stenosed vessel.

When the thrombus is small no functional disturbance may ensue. Stallions are sometimes unable to serve mares. Möller saw one in which erections occurred, but were not followed by ejection of semen. The post-mortem of such animals shows emphysema of the lungs and dilatation of the heart. The pain caused by the condition during exercise is comparable to that occurring in man during temporary obstruction of an artery in a limb from pressure—viz., a feeling of painful stiffness and severe burning (" pins and needles ").

Prognosis depends on the degree of interference with movement, but the tendency is towards aggravation of the symptoms, and only in slight cases can the development of an efficient collateral circulation and recovery be looked for. Sometimes, however, the stallion improves sufficiently to be fit for service.

TREATMENT is unsatisfactory. The administration of potassium iodide and alkaline carbonates, formerly recommended, is of little value. Massage *per rectum* is dangerous. It has led to increased thrombosis and death. The only treatment likely to have some good effect consists in exciting collateral circulation by regular work. The animal is exercised until the first symptoms of lameness appear, and then rested, or it may be put to continued light work. The increased blood circulation thus excited favours development of collateral circulation, but too much is not to be expected from this treatment. The writer had a case in a racehorse which recovered sufficiently to be used successfully at the stud.

Tumours

The hind-quarters may be the seat of various kinds of tumours, including papillomata (common on the inside of the thighs in the horse and ox), fibromata, botriomycomata (affecting the croup and tail), sarcomata, melanomata round the anus and extending into the pelvis in grey horses, osteomata in the aponeurosis already mentioned (see p. 883), and cutaneous epitheliomata (fairly common in dogs). The inguinal lymphatic glands may be affected with primary or secondary malignant growths. Chondromata and osteosarcomata of the femur have been reported in the dog.

TREATMENT is as described for tumours in general.

AFFECTIONS OF THE STIFLE AND OF THE LEG

Contusions and open wounds of these regions do not require description except to mention some special features as follows :

1. **Hæmatoma or Collection of Serum,** which is a common condition in the regions of the stifle and lower part of the buttock, being situated inside or outside the former, or in both or in all three situations. It is usually the result of a fall, and forms almost immediately. It presents the characteristic symptoms already described in Part I.

TREATMENT is that given when dealing with the lesion in general.

2. **Sinus abutting on the Tibia.**—Occasionally, as the result of an open wound of the tibia following a blow or a kick, the bone undergoes necrosis and gives rise to a sinus, which persists until the sequestrum is removed.

3. **Fissure of the Tibia.**—When violence, as from a kick, is inflicted on the tibia where it is subcutaneous, it may be fissured without displacement.

The SYMPTOMS are those of acute local inflammation due to osteoperiostitis and well-marked lameness.

The DIAGNOSIS can only be conjectured from the history and severe local inflammation and lameness, except radiography is resorted to. Displacement of the fragments is prevented by the periosteum and by the strong fascia in the region.

TREATMENT is that for acute inflammation associated with complete rest of the patient to avoid disturbance of the seat of fracture. Slings are indicated for this purpose. Some veterinarians advise the application of a blister to effect hyperæmia, limit movement of the limb, and enforce general rest. Or a charge or pitch plaster bandage may be applied to immobilise the part. If the patient is exercised or put to work before union has had time to take place, displacement of the fragments will ensue, giving rise to a "deferred fracture," which has often occurred in this way.

Distension of the Subcutaneous Bursa in Front of the Patella

The subcutaneous bursa in front of the patella may become affected with an acute or chronic bursitis as the result of injury, and display the usual symptoms of either of these conditions. Lameness is present in an acute case, but may be absent when the lesion is chronic. The swelling may be confounded with distension of the femoro-tibial articulation, which, however, is situated beneath the patella, while the bursal enlargement is in front. Both conditions might coexist. The lesion in the joint is more serious, and is always associated with lameness.

TREATMENT comprises the measures described for bursitis in general. In an obstinate chronic case the best method to adopt is to incise the bursa, evacuate its contents, and irrigate its lining with tincture of iodine or other irritant antiseptic solution.

Sprain of the Flexor Metatarsi

This was first described by M. V. Robin and M. G. Lesbouyries (*Revue Générale de Médecine Vétérinaire*, Vol. xxxvi, No. 430). They had seen it several times in heavy horses.

ETIOLOGY.—The history of the case never gives reliable information as to its cause, but simply indicates that the lameness appeared suddenly during work. It must be due to some movement which puts an extra strain on the muscle without being sufficient to rupture it.

Symptoms.—During rest weight is borne normally by the limb, and at the walk nothing unusual is observed. During the trot, however, the characters of the lameness are well shown as follows: (1) The length of the stride is the same for both limbs; (2) the foot is placed flat on the ground without flexion of the joints; (3) there is difficulty in lifting the foot clear of the ground, owing to imperfect flexion of the hock, the toe striking its surface during the movement, and in a case of protracted lameness causing excessive wear of the front of the shoe, especially when the trot is hurried; (4) backing is difficult, the plantar aspect of the foot being trailed on the ground during the act; (5) turning the animal sharply with the affected limb inside aggravates the lameness.

In all the affected subjects pressure exerted on the anterior aspect of the inferior part of the tibial region caused the animal to wince, and in one case the antero-external aspect of the stifle-joint at the level of the outer straight ligament of the patella was the seat of pain and slight swelling. Forced extension of the hock before trotting does not exaggerate the lameness, doubtless because it is difficult to perform this extension without opening at the same time the angle of the stifle-joint. The lameness is continuous, being neither diminished nor increased during work.

Diagnosis.—Diagnostic features are: (1) Imperfect flexion of the hock; (2) pain on pressure above the angle of flexion of the joint; and (3) the pathognomonic symptoms of rupture of the muscle being absent. The lameness may be confounded with that of spavin, especially when the latter is occult; but in sprain of the muscle the lameness is not intermittent, and is not affected by passive flexion of the hock. The symptoms also simulate those of external popliteal paralysis, but in the latter the phalangeal joints cannot be extended, the front of the pastern may be in contact with the ground, and during backing the foot is more decidedly dragged over its surface.

Prognosis.—Complete recovery is the rule. The intensity of the clinical symptoms is no guide to the time required for recovery. It usually takes weeks, but may take months.

Treatment consists in prolonged rest, accompanied by the use of antiphlogistic applications and massage on the anterior aspect of the leg. Blistering or firing may be necessary, taking care to avoid the angle of flexion of the hock

Rupture of the Tendinous Portion of the Flexor Metatarsi Muscle

This condition has been frequently observed in the horse, and less frequently in the ox. Rupture of the tendon, which extends from the internal surface of the tibia to the bones of the tarsus (in the dog), has been recorded.

FIG. 368.—RUPTURE OF THE FLEXOR METATARSI.

ETIOLOGY.—Rupture of the tendon results from over-extension of the hock, due to the animal kicking violently or struggling in hobbles, or to the limb slipping or being violently drawn backwards, as in shoeing in the trevis, or drawn upwards by means of a cord passed through a ring, especially if the animal fall while thus fixed. Efforts to withdraw the foot when fixed in railway points or in soft ground and getting the limb over a bale may also give rise to it. It seldom follows external violence, but rupture of the corresponding tendon in the dog may be caused in this way. It is rarely bilateral.

SYMPTOMS.—There is lameness, characterised by marked flexion of the stifle-joint and excessive extension of the hock-joint. As the fibrous band stretching between the external condyle of the femur and the metatarsus is no longer able to transmit the movements of the femur to the metatarsus, and as the flexor metatarsi muscle itself is powerless to make up for the deficiency, the cannon-bone is no longer flexed on the limb, but hangs inertly, and all the lower joints of the limb follow suit or are slightly flexed. That portion of the limb below the hock is not properly advanced, while the relaxation of the tendon favours excessive flexion of the stifle-joint. The want of harmony in the function of both joints produces an uncertain movement of the limb, which may give the impression of a broken bone, which is disproved, however, by the fact that the limb still supports weight. At rest nothing unusual is observed, but during movement the diagnostic features of the condition are very evident. When the foot is lifted off the ground, the absence of the antagonism of the tendon of the flexor metatarsi is revealed by relaxation of the tendo Achillis, which becomes flaccid and thrown into a fold, constituting a pathognomonic symptom of the lesion. This relaxation is very marked when the limb is taken backwards, as in the

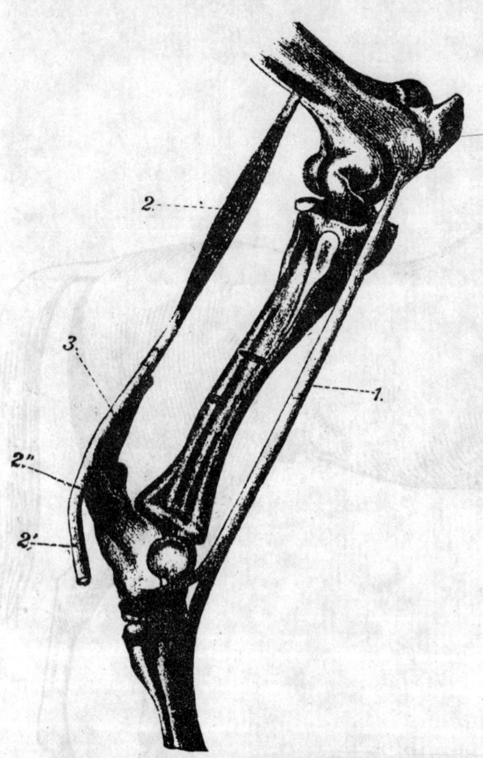

FIG. 369.—SHOWING THE MECHANISM OF THE HOCK AND STIFLE JOINTS.

The tendons of the flexor metatarsi and gastrocnemius muscles unite the bones forming the joints in such a way that they are unable to move independently. 1, Tendinous division of the flexor metatarsi muscle; 2, 2′, and 2″, flexor perforatus; 3, gastrocnemius tendon.

act of shoeing. As a rule, nothing is observed in the front of the limb to indicate the exact site of the rupture.

Prognosis.—Recovery is the rule within a period of four to eight weeks, but occasionally it is delayed for three or four months, and in rare cases does not ensue at all. When the tendon is divided in the bursa at its origin, or is torn away from this point, recovery is less assured, because formation of new tissue remains incomplete, the paratendineum essential to union being absent from the tendon sheath and bursa. When cure supervenes in this case, it takes

Fig. 370.—Rupture of Flexor Metatarsi Muscle.
(From a photograph.)

months before it is complete. Insufficient rest militates against recovery. If the horse is put to work too soon, the newly-formed cicatricial tissue gradually becomes strained and the tendon lengthened, necessarily causing permanent lameness.

Treatment consists in keeping the patient perfectly quiet for four to six weeks. Recovery is favoured by keeping the limb in a forward position by means of a rope attached to a hobble on the pastern, or better to a ring in the toe of the shoe and fixed round the neck. A blister applied over the level of the affected muscle will not have much effect, except to enforce rest. It is, however, a measure which is usually adopted. When the lameness disappears the horse may be gradually put to work.

"Track-Leg" in the Greyhound

The term "track-leg" in the greyhound is applied to an inflammatory swelling on the inner aspect of the left tibial region and a little below its midway point, at about the level of the insertion of the tendon of the semimembranosis. The condition is evidently due to a strain of the structures of the affected region, with vascular rupture and extravasation of blood and the formation of an inflammatory exudate. The symptoms are those of acute inflammation with a well marked swelling which may or may not fluctuate according as it contains much or little fluid exudate or extravasate. The treatment is that for acute or chronic inflammation, as the case may be. When the case is slow to respond to hot stuping and the use of absorbent topics, and the enlargement is distinctly fluctuating incision is advisable to permit of the escape of the fluid and thus hasten recovery, careful antiseptic precautions being taken and the wound being protected by a pad and bandage. When the lesion is in the form of a fibrous thickening causing persistent lameness line or needle-point firing is indicated, followed by prolonged rest and gradual return of the dog to fast exercise. Recovery is the rule.

Rupture of the Tendo Achillis

Rupture of the gastrocnemius muscles or of the Achilles tendon is oftenest seen in cows, and sometimes in both limbs at once. Rupture generally occurs at the lower point of insertion of the tendon, a portion of the os calcis being at the same time torn away. It also takes place where the muscle becomes continuous with the tendon. Rupture of the muscle itself has been seen in horses and cattle.

Etiology.—Rupture results from excessive strain thrown on the tendon, as may ensue from cattle jumping on one another. In horses it may occur during jumping or during heavy draft. External violence may produce the lesion. In dogs it has been caused by the animal being caught in a door. In exceptional cases the rupture is secondary to necrosis or suppuration of the tendon, and it has been reported by Uhlic as a sequel to influenza.

Symptoms.—There is inability to bear weight on the affected limb and flexion of all the joints. The hock and stifle joints can no longer be fixed to support the body-weight, and there is consequent collapse of the limb, allowing the back of the hock to approach or come in contact with the ground. The excessive flexion of the hock increases the distance between the points of origin and insertion of the flexor pedis, and the phalanges take up a position of excessive plantar flexion. As a rule, a depression can be noted in the course of the tendon or swelling in the gastrocnemii muscles; the tendon appears relaxed even when the limb touches the ground.

Prognosis depends almost entirely on whether the uninjured leg

Fig. 371.—Rupture of the Tendo Achillis.

can sustain weight until union occurs. Small animals like dogs and cats almost always do well, but larger animals are less favourably circumstanced. They sometimes succumb to the continued standing or lying, for union takes from four to six weeks, and under some circumstances may be protracted for several months. Oxen do best lying, but as horses are obliged to stand, it becomes a question whether laminitis may not supervene in the other foot. Nevertheless, a considerable number of recoveries have been recorded in the horse. The hind-foot is more subject to laminitis from bearing undue weight than the fore-foot. As a rule, the more marked the degree of flexion, the slighter the chance of recovery, which is often protracted by elongation of the tendon and consequent lameness.

TREATMENT consists in keeping the hock in a state of extension, so as to have the ends of the ruptured tendon as close together as possible, and thus favour their union. This can be effected by a plaster bandage in small animals. The horse is generally put in slings, while the hock is kept in extension by an immobilising dressing, which may be in the form of two wooden splints applied laterally from the region of the

FIG. 372.—RUPTURE OF THE TENDO ACHILLIS. (AFTER STOCKFLETH.)

stifle to the foot and shaped to correspond exactly to the normal conformation of the limb. Ample padding is applied beneath the splints, which are fixed by straps and buckles above and below the hock. In the dog, suturing the ruptured tendon has been successfully performed. The dressing advised for fracture of the os calcis in the dog is indicated here (see p. 926).

Section of the Gastrocnemius and Perforatus Tendons

This has been seen in the horse, ox, pig, and dog as the result of cuts by sharp bodies. It has often been done maliciously, when the animals are said to have been "hamstrung." The nature of the condition is obvious, and it renders the limb quite powerless. Recovery is not likely to ensue in the large animals. It may be obtained in small patients by suturing the severed tendons and immobilising the limb with the hock fully extended.

Fracture of the Tibia

In the horse, fracture of the tibia ranks next in point of frequency with that of the pelvis.

Etiology.—The cause may be :

1. *Direct violence*, usually a kick from another horse, inflicted on the internal face of the lower fourth of the tibia, which lies directly under the skin. In many cases the bone is at first only fissured, separation taking place later during such acts as rising, lying down, or passing urine or fæces. It is seldom postponed more than a week or ten days from the date of original injury, although cases have occurred where separation did not take place until four or five weeks afterwards. Displacement at first is prevented by the periosteum and fascia, which are intact. When they become softened and weakened by inflammation, displacement occurs more readily. The injury to the bone may only cause ostitis at first. This produces rarefaction of the bone, which may then fracture during severe exertion. The fracture may also be caused by a fall or a collision.

2. *Muscular violence*, most commonly when struggling in hobbles, but also as the result of slipping.

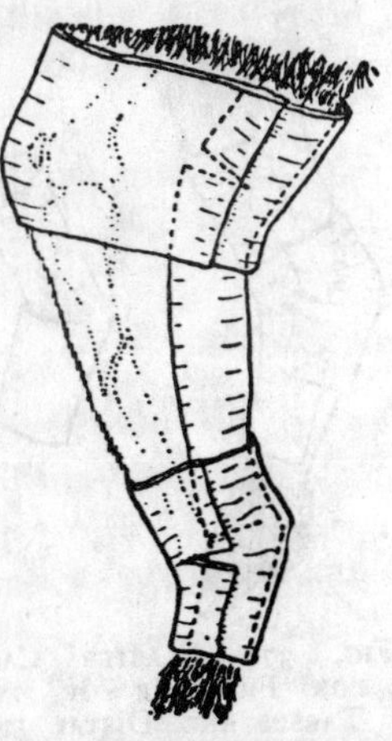

Fig. 373.—Plaster Cast on Mid-Shaft of the Tibia with Window. (*Veterinary Record.*)

The accident is very common in dogs, due to kicks, blows, and being run over. Parrots and canaries are not uncommon sufferers from fracture of the tibia. Fenimore describes a case of fracture of the tibia in a fœtus ; the fracture had been caused by a kick received by the mother (a cow) whilst pregnant, and when the calf was born the fracture was healed.

Symptoms.—The symptoms of complete fracture are typical, and cannot be mistaken. Fissured fracture can only be guessed at from the history of the case and the seat of the inflammation. The more severe the latter and the greater the lameness, the more likely is fracture present. X-rays will reveal the fissure.

Prognosis.—The prognosis in large animals is grave, recovery seldom supervening. There is always the risk of laminitis affecting the other foot from the constant excessive weight thereon. In light horses, ponies, and foals, especially the latter, there is a good chance of obtaining a cure by the usual methods of treatment. In dogs and cats complete cure is almost invariably effected. When the seat of fracture is in the lower part of the bone, the prognosis is more favourable than when it is higher up. In France a number of cases are reported where complete fracture of the tibia in horses has been treated successfully, but they extend over many years, and must be regarded as exceptional.

TREATMENT.—As already stated, all serious injuries of the tibia should be regarded as possible fractures, and dealt with as such, the horse being rested for at least four weeks to enable a fissured fracture to heal, and to prevent displacement. The horse should be placed in slings or tied up short in order to restrict movement as much as possible. Complete fracture is treated on general principles. An immobilising dressing from the foot to the stifle is necessary. A pitch bandage, which can be made adherent to the skin in the stifle region, is the most suitable; it may be associated with splints, with padding beneath to prevent wounding of the soft tissues by the latter. A charge or pitch dressing is commonly applied in cattle. Light beasts often recover without treatment of any kind. The dressings recommended for fracture of the femur in the dog are very suitable for fractured tibia, also the unpadded plaster cast described on p. 124.

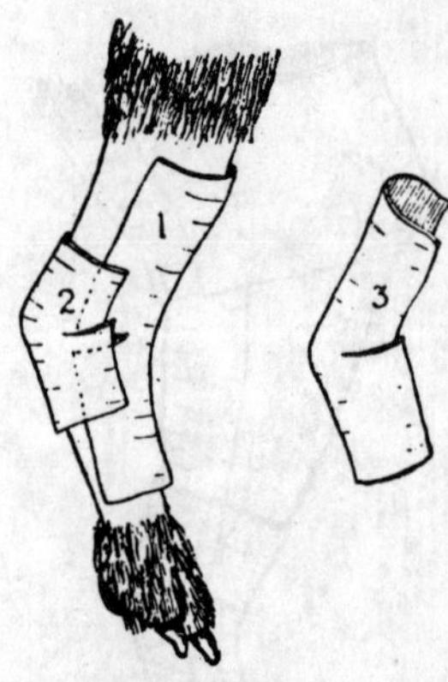

FIG. 374.—PLASTER CAST FOR FRACTURE OF THE TARSUS AND DISTAL END OF THE TIBIA.

Fracture of the fibula usually accompanies that of the tibia. Rarely it occurs alone, and then usually at its upper part. It is not a serious lesion, and heals under ordinary antiphlogistic treatment.

Fracture of the Patella

Fracture of the patella is rare, and up to the present has only been seen in horses.

ETIOLOGY.—Kicks, collisions, and falls with the stifle-joint strongly flexed are the principal causes, especially of vertical fractures. Those horizontal in direction may be caused by violent muscular contraction.

SYMPTOMS.—There is inability to bear weight on the limb, and intense inflammation at the seat of injury. When the fracture is vertical there is no evidence of displacement, which is prevented by the fibrous covering on the anterior aspect of the bone, but when it is horizontal a portion of the bone may be drawn upwards by the muscles attached thereto. Diagnosis is confirmed when crepitation and mobility of the fragments can be recognised. The limb is usually held in a state of flexion, and may be pendulous. Crepitation resembling that of fracture may occur in a case of arthritis affecting the trochlea of the femur, but in this case weight can be borne by the limb and acute local inflammation is absent.

PROGNOSIS is grave. Even when union of the fragments occurs permanent lameness is apt to ensue. When the fracture is comminuted or compound, exposing the joint, the case is hopeless.

TREATMENT, from what has been said, is not likely to be successful. It is carried out on general principles, slings being necessary for the horse. The joint should be kept as far as possible in a state of extension. Removal of the fractured bone is indicated in the dog after dissecting back its periosteum, which is afterwards sutured. A slight limp will remain, which is preferable to stiffness and pain in action (Craven, N. S., *N. Amer. Vet.*, **19**, 12, 55).

Contusion and Sprain of the Stifle-Joint—Acute Gonitis

ETIOLOGY.—Contusion is caused by external violence. Sprain is not common. It is more often met with in working oxen than in horses. It is fairly common in greyhounds, as the result of over-exertion of the joint in some particular direction when racing or coursing, especially in the act of turning shortly. In any animal it may be due to violent slipping when the joint is extended.

SYMPTOMS.—The symptoms are those of acute synovitis and periarthritis. There is well-marked local acute inflammation, and the lameness is very pronounced and characterised by stiffness of the stifle-joint, and consequent shortening of the stride, the animal going on the toe.

TREATMENT is as usual for a sprained joint or for a contusion. If more than one patellar ligament is ruptured, there is little chance of recovery. When the sprain has been severe, recovery may be very protracted. A chronic synovitis may succeed the acute form. A long rest is always necessary before returning the animal to work or racing.

Open wounds of the stifle-joint are of the same nature as those of joints in general. When septic arthritis supervenes it is incurable.

Chronic Inflammation of the Stifle-Joint—Chronic Gonitis

This condition is most common in heavy draft-horses, but is also seen in other breeds, and in the ass and mule as well as in the ox. The typical arthritis is not common in the dog, but it is occasionally met with in the larger coursing and working breeds. The disease may be bilateral in the horse.

ETIOLOGY.—The etiology of the lesion is obscure. Heavy haulage appears to be a predisposing factor, as the disease is certainly most common in horses doing heavy draft work. Shunters are particularly liable to it, and farm-horses are often affected. It may be rheumatoid. It is sometimes present in young unbroken horses, and may then be looked upon as of toxic origin, following navel infection.

FIG. 375.—LEFT-SIDED CHRONIC INFLAMMATION OF THE STIFLE-JOINT (GONITIS CHRONICA).

FIG. 376.—BILATERAL CHRONIC INFLAMMATION OF THE STIFLE-JOINT (GONITIS CHRONICA BILATERALIS). (From a photograph.)

SYMPTOMS.—At the outset the lameness is slight or intermittent, and where the disease is bilateral may for a long time be overlooked. Well-known features of the disease may be briefly stated as follows :

1. The lesion is of a chronic nature, defying treatment.

2. During rest the horse repeatedly flexes the stifle and hock, and holds the limb suspended for a while. On exercise at a walk the animal shows well-marked lameness, and may go on the toe or put the foot flat on the ground. When made to trot he keeps the joint

extended, and may go on three legs with the joint locked in this position.

3. The stifle-joint is enlarged, due to periarticular fibrous thickening and the deposit of osteophytes round the articular ends of the femur and tibia, as well as to synovial distension of its capsule. The synovial distension is recognised as a boggy swelling behind and between the anterior straight ligaments of the patella.

4. Pain is usually evinced on pushing the fingers deeply into the

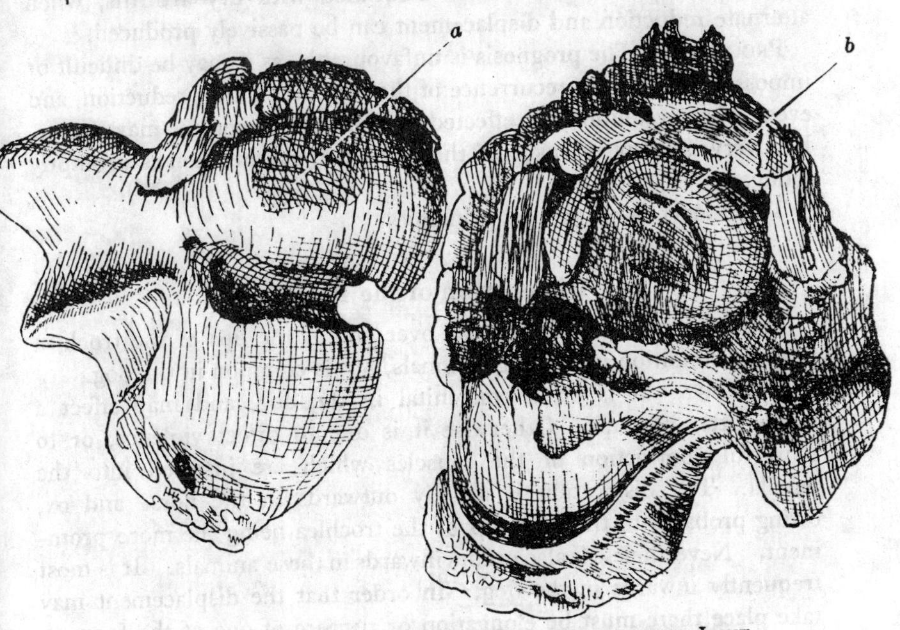

FIG. 377.—CHRONIC ARTHRITIS OF THE FEMORO-TIBIAL JOINT.
a and *b*, Eroded surfaces on the tibia and femur.

boggy swelling and on passive forcible movement of the joint, and sometimes from compressing it laterally.

5. Crepitation is sometimes heard on flexion and extension of the joint, due to friction between the eroded articular surfaces.

DIAGNOSIS is easy when the disease is well established, but in its early stages it may be hesitating.

PROGNOSIS.—The condition is incurable.

TREATMENT is useless, but firing and blistering are sometimes practised when the diagnostic features are not pronounced, in the hope that the condition is curable. The fact of their having no good effect confirms the diagnosis when it is doubtful.

Post-mortem examination reveals the typical lesions of a chronic arthritis. Erosion of the articular surfaces is most marked around the tibial spine and the inferior surface of the condyles.

Dislocation of Femoro-tibial Articulation

This is a rare occurrence. It is most common in the dog, especially the racing varieties, and is brought about by over-exertion of the joint. It has taken place during galloping. The condition is easily recognised. It may be of a chronic nature associated with dry arthritis, when alternate reduction and displacement can be passively produced.

PROGNOSIS.—The prognosis is unfavourable, as it may be difficult or impossible to prevent recurrence of the dislocation after reduction, and even when retention is effected permanent lameness may ensue. Recovery is likely to ensue in the dog when the luxation is promptly reduced.

TREATMENT is on general principles.

Dislocation of the Patella

True dislocation of the patella over one of the lips of the trochlea is a rare condition in the large animals, but is common in the dog.

ETIOLOGY.—It is often congenital in the dog, and may affect a whole litter of pups. Otherwise it is due to direct violence, or to powerful contraction of the muscles which are inserted into the patella. The dislocation is usually outwards in the horse and ox, owing probably to the inner lip of the trochlea being the more prominent. Nevertheless it also occurs inwards in these animals. It is most frequently inwards in the dog. In order that the displacement may take place there must be elongation or rupture of one of the femoro-patellar ligaments. In the dog it results from a fall or a jump, or a blow inflicted in the stifle region. A chronic form of the condition has been seen in young coarse bred horses, apparently due to chronic arthritis, the patella slipping in and out with a clicking noise during progression.

SYMPTOMS.—In the case of outward dislocation the stifle is in a semi-flexed position, and appears deviated outwards with the toe only touching the ground. The nature of the condition is ascertained on palpation : the patella is felt in an abnormal situation, and the patellar ligaments are found directed upwards and outwards. During progression the limb is carried stiffly, the stride is shortened, and the movements of the patella are observed.

When the dislocation is inwards the stifle can be neither flexed nor extended, and the straight ligaments and the quadriceps are directed inwards. In all cases the vacant trochlea of the femur may be recognised. In the dog it is generally easy to replace the patella, but it immediately becomes displaced again. In some instances the luxation is associated with a chronic arthritis.

PROGNOSIS is generally unfavourable, as it is often impossible to retain the patella in its normal position after reduction. Congenital cases and those due to chronic arthritis are hopeless.

TREATMENT comprises reduction and retention. To effect reduction, apply a rope to the pastern of the affected limb, let assistants pull the limb forwards by means of the rope, and at the same time push the patella into its normal position. To prevent recurrence of the condition, tie the horse up short and apply a blister over the patellar region. When the luxation occurs suddenly in the dog, without rupture of the lateral patellar ligaments, and is promptly reduced, it may not recur. If reduction prove difficult in the horse in the standing position, he may be cast and chloroform may be administered to overcome muscular resistance.

Bénard claims to have cured congenital cases in the ox as follows: Take a linen bandage about 6 inches wide and long enough to go four times round the stifle, make a hole in its centre sufficiently large to accommodate the patella, and 4 to 6 inches from this make a transverse slit in the bandage. Arrange the bandage so that the patella is lodged in the central opening, pass one of the ends through the other opening, and pull it tightly. Cross the two ends first above and then below the patella, and tie them. It is usually impossible to keep the patella in position in the dog after reduction. Section of the tendons of insertion of the vasti muscles relieves the tension on the patella and improves somewhat the animal's gait. It is easily done subcutaneously.

Fixation of the Patella above the Trochlea

This has been described as upward dislocation of the patella, but it hardly deserves this name, as the patella is not out of line with the trochlea, and the condition is not associated with rupture or severe injury of the ligaments which keep the bone in position. It is much more common in horses and oxen than the true dislocation above described.

ETIOLOGY.—The accident occurs suddenly without any extraordinary effort, in the stable or outside. It sometimes happens when the horse stretches the leg rigidly backwards, thereby fully extending the stifle. It has been seen taking place in this way in the young horse tired after a hard day's ploughing the day before. The condition is favoured by debility and poor condition and consequent absorption of the fat between the straight ligaments and the joint.

Symptoms.—The affected limb is rigidly extended backwards and cannot be flexed. On palpation the straight ligaments are felt to be tensely stretched, the trochlea of the femur is free from the patella, and the latter is found fixed beyond its upper extremity. When the animal is walked, the front of the hoof trails on the ground. During backing the limb is also rigid. The fetlock can be passively flexed, but all attempts at flexion of the hock and stifle are in vain.

Sometimes the symptoms disappear as suddenly as they came. When the animal is made to move on, or more frequently when backed, the patella may be released, and then the limb regains its normal position, the joints being at first spasmodically flexed as in stringhalt, but afterwards flexed normally. A dull sound may be heard when the patella slips back on the trochlea. In many cases, however, the displacement continues for hours or days until it is reduced by manipulation.

Treatment.—Reduction may be effected as follows :

1. By local manipulation, pushing the patella forwards while the horse moves on a step or two in the loose box or stall.

2. Make the animal walk forward with the head high, and if he is too slow in his movements flick him with the whip. After a few steps the patella may return to its place.

3. If No. 2 has not the desired effect, forcing the animal to back may succeed.

4. When Nos. 2 and 3 fail, apply a rope to the pastern of the affected limb, have the latter drawn forwards by an assistant pulling on the rope after passing it through a collar on the patient's neck or through a ring in the wall in front of the animal, and at the same time push the patella downwards and inwards.

5. If No. 4 prove difficult, cast the patient and draw the limb forward to the shoulder by means of a side-line. As a rule reduction is easily accomplished, but the displacement may recur after a variable interval. The application of a blister over the joint will cause inflammatory swelling, which will help to prevent recurrence. Giving the animal nutritious diet and moderate work or regular exercise will also aid in this respect.

In many cases the displacement recurs repeatedly after easy reduction, and they seem hopeless, but experience has shown that eventually, in most instances, the normal condition is restored. These cases would appear to be due to loss of tone in the muscles which bind the stifle joint accompanying a sort of general debility following severe work such as racing, and when the normal condition is regained the abnormality disappears. Recovery is undoubtedly favoured by applying a high heeled shoe and by bedding the horse with peat moss or sawdust. The author has knowledge of cases of this nature in race horses in which this procedure has proved successful. Should these measures fail to prevent recurrence the operations for section of the internal straight ligment of the patella is indicated (p. 458).

Henry Taylor, Haywards Heath, published a good article on " Luxation of the Patella," *Vet. Rec.*, May 4th, 1946 ; and the *Indian Veterinary Journal*, July, 1944, contains one on " Luxation in Bovines." Sir Frederick Smith in his *Physiology* states that the condition is usually due to cramp of the muscles attached to the patella, owing to their being affected with maintained contraction known as " contracture."

AFFECTIONS OF THE HOCK

Contusions and Open Wounds of the Hock

The hock, being much exposed to injury, is a common seat of traumatic lesions. Contusions vary in gravity ; they may involve fracture of one or more of the bones of the joint, or cause displacement of the perforatus tendon. When slight and repeated at the level of the os calcis they cause capped hock. Open wounds are of various kinds, the most serious being those penetrating the true hock-joint or one of the gliding articulations.

The SYMPTOMS are in accordance with the nature of the condition, and treatment is carried out on general principles.

A guarded PROGNOSIS must be given in connection with punctured and contused wounds of the hock, when recent, as there is always the risk of the joint or the tarsal sheath being involved, and the results of infection thereof will not be apparent for some days, and all such wounds must be treated with meticulous care on the principles laid down in General Surgery.

Large open wounds in the front of the hock or encroaching thereon from its lateral aspect are often difficult to cure, owing to the persistence of excessive granulations due to the irritation caused by the frequent flexion of the joint. Excision followed by the use of formalin (1 in 40) may have the desired effect.

Capped Hock—Hygroma or Distension of the Superficial Bursa on the Point of the Hock

This is a common condition in the horse, and it varies in character according to the age of the lesion.

ETIOLOGY.—Contusion of the point of the hock will always give rise

FIG. 378.—EXUBERANT GRANULATION IN FRONT OF THE HOCK.

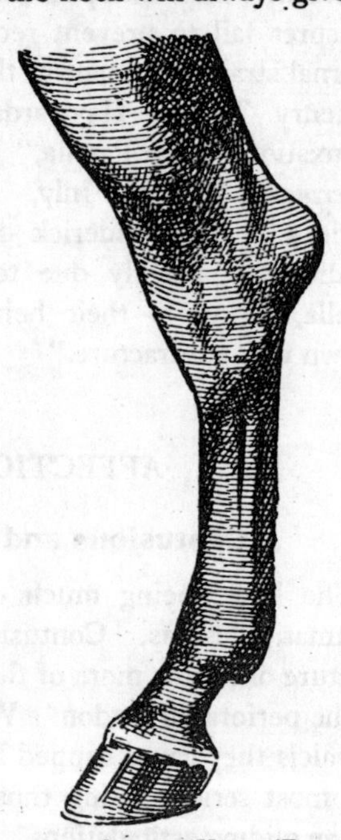

FIG. 379.—CAPPED HOCK (DROPSY OF THE SUBCUTANEOUS BURSA OF THE HOCK).

to a swelling there, which, however, is only temporary when the cause is not renewed. Typical capped hock is caused by repeated injury of the part from kicking in the stable or in harness, or from lying on bare floors. Sudden effort of a horse in rising may cause the point of the hock to be injured against the floor. When a severe injury is inflicted there, the swelling forms quickly. Distension of the bursa may occur during an attack of lymphangitis or purpura hæmorrhagica.

SYMPTOMS.—When the case is recent and the result of a definite contusion, an acute inflammatory swelling appears on the point of the hock. If it become infected an abscess will form. Otherwise, if the injury is not repeated, it will gradually subside and perhaps disappear entirely. Chronic cases resulting from inveterate kicking or frequent friction against the ground or wall of the stable are characterised by the presence of a painless, more or less prominent swelling, due to a chronic bursitis associated with a varying degree of fibrous thickening. Occasionally this becomes acutely inflamed and infected as the result of more severe injury, and when the resulting abscess bursts it may refuse to heal, owing to the presence of a smooth, non-granulating lining. Lameness, even in acute cases, is rarely present.

PROGNOSIS.—The condition in itself is not serious, but it is an unsightly blemish which may be difficult or impossible to get rid of, chiefly due to the fact that the cause cannot be removed.

TREATMENT consists in adopting measures to arrest the cause of the trouble, and applying the usual remedies for acute or chronic bursitis, as the case may be.

Prevention may comprise padding the sides of the stall; providing an increased amount of litter, peat moss or tan being the most suitable; the use of a good kicking-strap in harness; and the application of hock-caps in horses travelling by boat or train.

The details of curative treatment are those described in connection with bursitis in general. Nothing will succeed in dispelling an old fibrous enlargement. The best results are obtained by the repeated application of a slightly stimulating absorbent preparation, such as a combination of iodine, potassium iodide, and Archangel tar, as is found in the proprietary preparation known as "Reducine." Painting the swelling with ordinary gas tar at intervals for a prolonged period is said to be very effective. French veterinarians have great faith in a liniment composed of goudron de Norvège 450 parts, savon vert 450, poudre de tan tamisée 100. It is applied daily with a brush, and is said to remove even a voluminous capped hock in the course of a few weeks. When the condition is cystic, aspiration and the injection of tincture of iodine associated with needle-point firing is a very effective form of treatment. The use of the knife for incision or excision of the swelling is generally contra-indicated, as the resulting wound might be very difficult to heal and cause more trouble than the original lesion, suppuration and increased fibrous thickening ensuing. Lanzillotti, however, reports having operated successfully. To excise a fibrous enlargement, he made a crescentic incision on the inner aspect of the hock, reflected a flap of skin, and after excising the tumour sutured the cutaneous edges and obtained healing by first intention.

Strict asepsis and antisepsis and protection of the wound afterwards from outside interference are essential.

The ox may also be affected with capped hock in the same way as the horse and requires similar treatment.

The dog occasionally shows slight capping of the hocks, especially amongst the larger breeds, from repeated contact with hard ground, the best treatment for which is the application of iodine preparations.

Dislocation of the Perforatus Tendon

Dislocation of the perforatus tendon, from the summit of the os calcis to the outside or inside of the process, is not a common condition, but several cases of it have been recorded in the horse. It is much more rare in other animals. Outer dislocation is the more common.

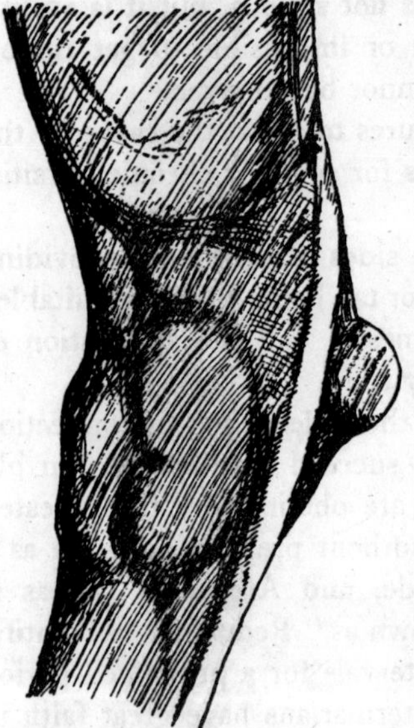

FIG. 380.—DISLOCATION OF THE PERPORATUS TENDON.

ETIOLOGY.—The cause may be :

1. *External violence*, such as a kick or a severe knock against the point of the hock.
2. *Powerful muscular contraction* when the hock is in a state of flexion.
3. *Rearing and falling on the hock.*
4. *Slipping during a gallop.*

In all cases there must be rupture of one of the lateral ligaments which bind the tendon to the os calcis. The inner ligament is the weaker, and gives way more readily than the outer.

SYMPTOMS.—When the case is recent, there are well-marked lameness and acute local inflammation. The tendon is seen to be displaced from its normal position. When the animal is made to move, the tendon may slip laterally to and from its normal situation, and the slipping is sometimes accompanied by a slight noise. There is excessive flexion of the hock and stifle. The horse may carry the affected limb during progression, or take it forward with difficulty, dragging the foot along the ground.

PROGNOSIS.—Treatment usually fails to keep the tendon in its normal position. Nevertheless, the function of the limb is completely restored in most cases, the tendon operating in a new channel to the side of the os calcis. Occasionally, instead of doing this, the tendon continues to glide on and off the os calcis, causing a permanent interference with gait. As a rule outward is more hopeful than inward luxation.

Treatment.—All efforts at keeping the tendon in place on the summit of the os calcis usually fail. Reduction is always easy in a recent case. Section of the tendon at the level of the base of the hock has been advised to permit of its upper part being kept in position on the os calcis. Drouet and others suggest suturing the tendon to the tendo Achillis and calcaneo-metatarsal ligament. It is better, however, to trust in recovery ensuing without these operations. Otherwise the treatment is that for acute or chronic inflammation, according to the age of the lesion. Counter-irritation by blistering or firing, or both, may be practised when

Fig. 381.—Tendon Sheaths and Bursæ of the Hind-Limb of the Horse seen from Without (Semi-Diagrammatic).

a, Trochanteric bursa; *b*, prepatellar bursa; *c*, tendon sheath of the extensor pedis; *d*, bursa calcanea; *e*, tendon sheath of the flexor pedis perforatus tendon; *f*, tendon sheath of the peroneus tendon.

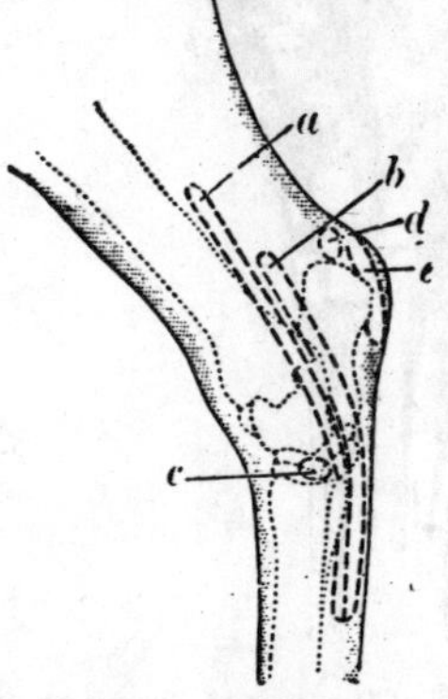

Fig. 382.—Tendon Sheaths and Bursæ of the Hock-Joint seen from Within (Semi-Diagrammatic).

a, Tendon sheath of the flexor accessorius tendon; *b*, tendon sheath of the flexor pedis perforans tendon; *c*, bursa of the internal division of the flexor metatarsi tendon; *d*, bursa calcanea; *e*, tendon sheath of the flexor pedis perforatus on the point of the hock.

lameness persists and is apparently due to chronic inflammation in the part.

Synovitis of the Tarsal Sheath

Acute Synovitis of the tarsal sheath may be the result of a contusion or of a sprain of the perforans tendon at its level, or it may be due to the toxin of an infectious disease like influenza, pneumonia, or rheumatism.

SYMPTOMS.—The symptoms are those of acute synovitis in general. The acute inflammation and distension of the sheath are very pronounced, and the lameness is severe.

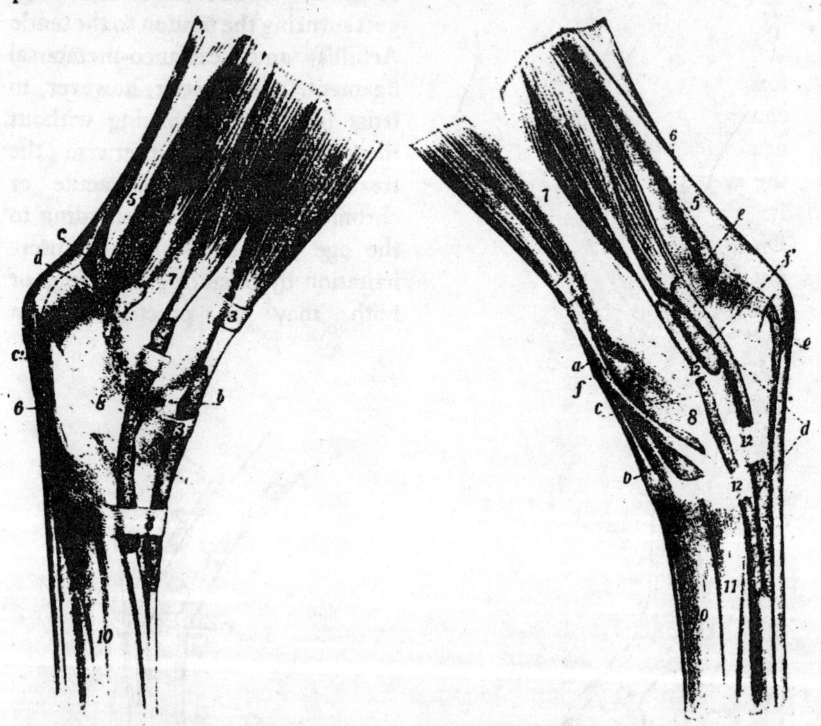

FIG. 383.—EXTERNAL SURFACE OF THE HORSE'S HOCK, TO SHOW SYNOVIAL SHEATHS.

a, Tendon sheath of the extensor pedis muscle; *b*, tendon sheath of peroneus muscle; *c*, *c′*, tendon sheath of flexor perforatus and gastrocnemius muscles; *d*, protrusion of the synovial capsule of the true hock-joint.

FIG. 384.—INTERNAL SURFACE OF THE HORSE'S HOCK, TO SHOW SYNOVIAL SHEATHS.

a, Tendon sheath of flexor metatarsi muscle; *b*, tendon sheath under inner terminal tendon of flexor metatarsi; *c*, tendon sheath of flexor accessorius; *d*, tendon sheath of flexor perforans; *e*, *e′*, tendon sheath of flexor perforatus and gastrocnemius muscles; *f*, *f′*, distended synovial capsule of the true hock-joint.

Treatment.—The treatment is that already described for all cases of acute synovitis.

Purulent Synovitis of this sheath is a dangerous condition. It may be complicated with necrosis of the tendon, and prove incurable. It causes intense pain and lameness.

Treatment is on general principles including drainage and antiseptic irrigation of the sheath (see p. 81). It is usually the result of an open wound. More rarely it is due to strangles.

Chronic Synovitis, or Distension of the Sheath—Thoroughpin

Chronic synovitis may follow the acute form, or occur independently as the result of constant hard work. The pain and lameness which arise from it vary according to the degree of chronic inflammation present. It may be very slight or well marked. Distension of the sheath often occurs without any inflammation or lameness. In either case the condition is known as thoroughpin, and is characterised by two swellings above the hock, one on the inside and the other on the outside, filling up the hollows on either side of the tendo Achillis, and sometimes by a third swelling below the hock on the inside at the level of the seat of curb, and spoken of by some authors as soft curb. Mere distension of the sheath occurs without any apparent cause, being of the nature of a dropsy. It is often present in young horses that have never done any work. Straight hocks favour distension by tending to relax the sheath. It occurs in all breeds of horses, but draft-horses are most subject to it. The swellings vary in size in different cases, and the inner of the two superior ones is generally the larger. Sometimes, however, the outer enlargement is more prominent than the inner. Exceptionally the inner swelling above is so great that it is rubbed by the other limb during progression.

Fig. 385.—Distension of Sheath of Flexor Pedis Perforans.
(From a photograph.)

Prognosis.—Where there is merely distension of the sheath lameness is absent, and the condition may disappear as mysteriously as it came without any treatment; but when it is associated with chronic synovitis the lameness may be difficult to get rid of, especially when the inferior swelling is present.

TREATMENT to dispel the swellings is often tedious, and sometimes disappointing. It consists in adopting some of the measures advised for the treatment of chronic synovitis and synovial distensions in general, including the following:

1. *Expectant treatment*, indicated in young horses in which the sheath is merely distended, and there is no evidence of pain or lameness. The swellings often disappear spontaneously in such cases in the course of a few months.

2. *Pressure* constantly applied by several layers of cotton-wool and a bandage, or by means of a thoroughpin truss. The former method is probably the better, as it distributes the pressure more evenly over the hock. The truss cannot be always easily adjusted, and it may not be tolerated by the horse. The rubbing in of a mild liniment is advisable before applying the cotton-wool. The condition may recur when the pressure is discontinued.

3. *Blistering*, which is generally disappointing in its results. It may have some effect in relieving chronic inflammation.

4. *Line firing* and blistering, more effective than No. 3, but often failing to have the desired effect.

5. *Needle-point firing*, which often proves efficacious, but is by no means infallible.

6. *Aspiration of the sheath and the injection of* (*a*) *tincture of iodine*, pure or diluted with one or two parts of boiled water; or (*b*) of *Dean's preparation*; or (*c*) of *Collinson's preparation*; or (*d*) *Cagny's injection of antipyrine* (see p. 84). This is better than any of the foregoing methods of treatment; (*b*), (*c*), and (*d*) have given excellent results. The operation must be done with strict asepsis. Its beneficial effects are frequently not shown until several weeks or even some months have elapsed after its performance. The sheath remains swollen in the meantime, but eventually the distension gradually subsides until it disappears altogether. It is probably an advantage to repeat the aspiration once or twice when the swelling is slow in its disappearance.

7. *A combination of No. 5 and No.* 6 is better than either alone, and if there is no objection to the slight marks of the iron is the best method of treatment to practise. It may also be slow in producing its good effect.

8. *Synoviotomy*, opening the sheath with the knife, the only efficacious method of removing riziform bodies. It has been done successfully by some veterinarians, including Williams of New York. It is a dangerous procedure, because if very strict asepsis is not

observed purulent infection of the sheath may ensue, with fatal results. When this complication does not occur, cure is said to be obtained in the course of three or four weeks. The ordinary practitioner would be well advised to avoid this method.

To the foregoing may be added the repeated rubbing into the swelling of equal parts of rectified spirits of tar and linseed oil, which the late Mr. James Daly, F.R.C.V.S., of Dublin, claimed as an almost certain cure when patiently persisted in, perhaps for months. The same good result is claimed for " Reducine," a preparation of iodine, potassium iodide, and Archangel tar.

Distension of the Sheath of the Cunean Tendon

This is rarely seen. It is recognised as a small, oval, fluctuating, painless swelling at the level of the tendon. It constitutes a blemish on the inner aspect of the hock, but does not incommode the animal, although when very tense it might cause a little stiffness in flexion of the joint. The surest way to get rid of it is to incise the sheath and treat its lining with tincture of iodine.

Distension of the Perforatus Bursa on the Point of the Hock—Deep-Capped Hock

Distension of this bursa between the perforatus and gastrocnemius tendons at the point of the hock is occasionally met with. Its cause is not always apparent, and it is seldom accompanied by pain and lameness. It appears on either side of the tendons just above the point of the hock.

The best TREATMENT is either needle-point firing and blistering or aspiration and injection, or a combination of these measures. Incision with the knife is contra-indicated, owing to the risk of infection, which might be followed by necrosis of the tendons. It has been called " deep-capped hock."

Distension of the Sheaths of the Extensor Pedis and Peroneus Tendons

The distension is recognised by the presence of a fluctuating cylindrical swelling at the level of the tendon involved. One or both sheaths may be affected, but distension of the peroneal sheath is more common than that of the extensor pedis, and has been noticed most frequently in horses doing fast work. Lameness seldom accompanies the condition in either sheath.

TREATMENT is the same as in the preceding case, but if necessary the sheath may be incised and its interior then treated with tincture of iodine, as there is less risk of complications here.

Fractures of the Tarsal Bones : Fracture of the Os Calcis

ETIOLOGY.—The fracture may be caused by external violence or by muscular contraction. Falls and kicks are common causes in all animals, and in dogs it may be the result of being run over. It is a fairly common accident in racing greyhounds. It has occurred in the horse when jumping.

SYMPTOMS.—There is inability to extend the hock, as in the case of rupture of the tendo Achillis; but the local inflammation is more painful in the case of fracture. Abnormal mobility of the os calcis is readily recognised. Crepitation is not evident when the upper fragment is drawn upwards by the action of the gastrocnemius muscle; but when the line of fracture is inside the ligamentous attachments and the fragments are in contact, it may be heard and felt.

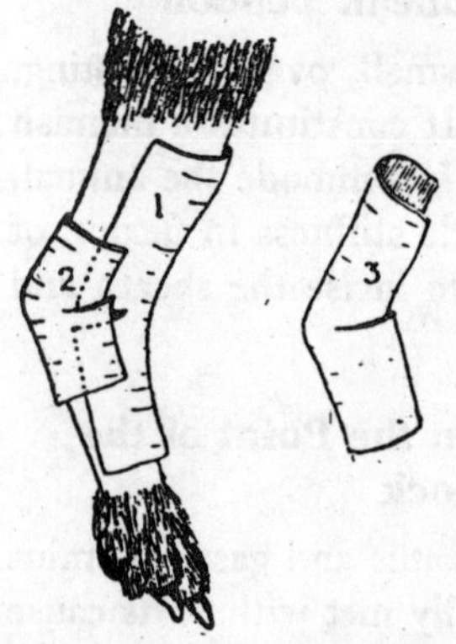

[*Vet. Rec.*

FIG. 386.—UNPADDED PLASTER CAST FOR FRACTURE OF TARSUS IN THE DOG.

PROGNOSIS.—The condition is practically hopeless in the large animals, although exceptional cases of successful treatment in the ox have been recorded. Cure is more likely to be obtained in small animals like the dog and cat.

TREATMENT consists in immobilising the hock in the state of extension. This may be effected in the small animals by the use of one of the dressings recommended in the chapter on Fractures. A gutter-shaped splint fitted to the anterior aspect of the limb, and reaching from the middle of the metatarsus to the middle of the tibia, with padding beneath, and fixed with straps and buckles above and below the hock, is a suitable contrivance for the horse and ox, should treatment be attempted.

The following method of immobilisation of the seat of fracture (recommended by Elam (Liverpool)) has proved completely successful in the greyhound when applied before displacement of the os calcis has occurred.

Apply a splint at the back of the limb extending from the paw to a point about 4 inches above the summit of the os calcis. Bind the projecting part of the splint to the limb above the hock by several turns of a bandage, thereby keeping the tendo Achillis completely relaxed and taking all strain off the bone into which it is inserted.

If displacement has occurred, this treatment is not likely to succeed, although the os calcis has been replaced into what appears to be its normal position before application of the dressing.

The unpadded plaster dressing (Fig. 386) is suitable for this fracture.

Fracture of the Astragalus

The astragalus is not so exposed to fracture as the os calcis, but the bone has been broken by violent torsion of the hock when the foot was bearing weight and fixed, and also by direct violence.

Symptoms.—There are sudden and severe lameness, with inability to bear weight, and intense local inflammation. The whole hock is swollen and very painful on manipulation. Its synovial capsule is distended, as in acute synovitis. Crepitation may be detected by placing both hands around the joint and moving the lower part of the limb. It may, however, be masked by the great swelling, and then the diagnosis is hesitating until the latter has subsided. Abnormal mobility and deviation of the inferior portion of the limb are generally observable.

Treatment.—There is no chance of treating the lesion successfully in the horse. When treatment is undertaken, it is the same as that for the os calcis. When healing ensues a stiff joint is apt to result.

Fractures of the other bones of the hock may be caused by direct violence, such as a kick or from lashing out and striking the hock against a fixed object. The writer saw simple fracture of the scaphoid in a pony from striking the back of the hock against the step of a van to which it was yoked. If the fracture is compound, there is little hope of recovery. Otherwise, and when confined to one bone, it may ensue, but even then permanent lameness may supervene. Sudden and severe lameness, with inability to sustain weight, is observed after the accident. The local symptoms are those of a severe contusion. On careful manipulation, some abnormal mobility and crepitus can generally be detected.

Sprain of the Hock-Joint—Sprung Hock

Sprain of the hock is fairly common as the result of over-exertion of the joint, as may ensue when jumping or during heavy draft, or from slipping at this or some other time. The ligaments may in this way be more or less severely stretched and injured. The surfaces of the bones where they are inserted also become inflamed, and a synovitis of the true hock-joint may also be set up. When the whole hock is thus involved, the condition is spoken of as "sprung hock." Lameness is always well marked. At rest, weight is only placed on the toe of the foot, the hock being in a state of semi-flexion. Pain is evinced on passive movement of the joint. During progression the hock is carried stiffly, little or no weight is borne by the limb, and the toe of the hoof may only touch or be trailed along the ground. The local inflammatory swelling is very obvious, and is most pronounced at the chief seat of sprain. When the hock is "sprung," it is swollen all round.

The SYMPTOMS, of course, vary according to the severity of the sprain.

PROGNOSIS.—Recovery is the rule, but sometimes a chronic inflammation ensues, causing permanent enlargement of the joint and protracted lameness. The horse, however, may go sound, while the hock remains enlarged. Spavin and curb are possible sequels of the accident.

TREATMENT of the acute case comprises rest and the application of the usual remedies for acute inflammation, while the chronic form requires counter-irritation by blistering or firing, or by both. The cautery should be used all round the hock, except in the angle of flexion.

Sprain of the hock is not uncommon in sporting dogs, and must be treated on lines similar to those for the horse. Rubbing in tincture of iodine or iodine ointment often has a good effect on the dog. When the case is chronic, needle-point firing is indicated.

Dislocation of the Hock

Dislocation of the hock has been recorded by various observers as occurring in the horse, ox, sheep, dog, and cat, being produced in most cases by violent contusion or extraordinary muscular effort, as may occur in an endeavour to release the foot when fixed between two objects. The seat of dislocation varies. It may be the tibio-tarsal joint or one of the gliding articulations. It is not infrequently accompanied by rupture of ligaments and fracture or crushing of some of the tarsal bones. The symptoms are those of dislocation and of acute inflammation.

PROGNOSIS.—The prognosis is very grave. Perfect cure is seldom or never obtained, and the rule is to destroy the large animal wher affected with the condition. In small animals even imperfect recovery may satisfy the owner.

TREATMENT is carried out on general principles.

The writer had a case of dislocation of the tibio-tarsal joint in a greyhound with overlapping of the bones and found it impossible to reduce the dislocation, under complete nembutal anæsthesia, until he cut the tendo Achillis subcutaneously when reduction was easily effected. The case did well afterwards except that slight thickening remained at the seat of the tenotomy.

Synovitis and Arthritis of the Hock-Joint—Distension of the Tibio-tarsal Articulation—" Bog Spavin "

Synovitis may ensue from a contusion or sprain of the joint, or be a complication of a bacterial affection like influenza.

Purulent Synovitis or Arthritis is usually the result of a penetrating wound, or it might be due to strangles.

Symptoms, Prognosis, and Treatment of these conditions are in accordance with what has been said in the general articles thereon.

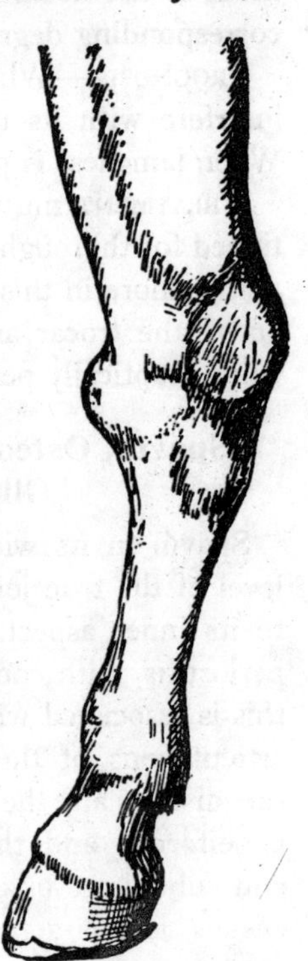

Fig. 387.—Distension of the Synovial Capsule of the True Hock-Joint.

Bog Spavin, or distension of the synovial capsule of the tibio-tarsal joint, is characterised by the presence of three uniformly fluctuating swellings, one situated antero-internally at the level of the inner lip of the trochlea of the astragalus, and one on either side of the joint posteriorly at the level of the malleolus of the tibia, in the lower part of the hollow of the hock, and above the lateral ligaments. The swellings vary in size in different cases. Those laterally situated are small compared with the one in front, which constitutes the typical bog spavin. The former have been described as *articular thoroughpin.* Pressure on any one of the swellings causes increased distension of the others. One of the lateral distensions may be more prominent than the other. When the swelling in front is not well marked, those at the sides are hardly perceptible. Nevertheless, pressure at their level can be felt going through to the distension in front. Sometimes it is only one of the lateral swellings that is noticeable. Then the condition is not called " bog spavin," but merely " articular thoroughpin."

Etiology.—The distension may be due to chronic synovitis, or merely to dropsy of the joint, the latter being often present in young unbroken horses, in which it is frequently accompanied by tendinous thoroughpin and windgalls. Bent hocks relaxing the synovial capsule of the joint favour its occurrence. It has been ascribed to constant hard work in aged horses. Aged stallions and breeding mares are frequently affected.

SYMPTOMS.—In the absence of synovitis, the only symptom is the presence of the swellings mentioned. If the distension is very prominent, there may be some mechanical interference with the movement of the hock. When synovitis is more or less severe, there is a corresponding degree of lameness.

PROGNOSIS.—When the horse is not lame the condition does not interfere with its usefulness, but is a blemish and an unsoundness. When lameness is present it may be difficult to get rid of.

TREATMENT must follow general principles. The measures mentioned for thoroughpin may be adopted here, but one hesitates perhaps a little more in this case to perforate the cavity by needle-point firing, or by the trocar and canula, although the operations are quite safe when aseptically performed.

Spavin, Osteo-periostitis, and Chronic Arthritis of the Gliding Articulations of the Hock

Spavin in its widest sense is an exostosis on the hock below the level of the true joint, but in the vast majority of cases it is confined to its inner aspect. The lesion may be merely a superficial osteo-periostitis, with consequent exostosis formation. As a rule, however, this is associated with a chronic arthritis of one or more of the gliding articulations of the joint. The bones most commonly involved in the disease are the large and small metatarsals, the large and small cuneiforms, and the scaphoid, but in rare instances the astragalus and cuboid are involved. Anchylosis of the affected joints frequently ensues, and is a favourable termination, as then the pain caused by movement of the ulcerated bones on one another disappears and the horse goes sound, provided that a chronic ostitis does not persist.

Arthritis may occur without any exostosis, constituting "*occult spavin*." It may be said that all true cases of spavin are due to a chronic arthritis of some of the gliding articulations of the hock. The terms "dry arthritis" and "arthritis ossificans" are also applied to the condition.

The origin of the disease has often been discussed, and various theories have been put forward with regard to it, but the prevailing belief is that it starts as an ostitis and that the articular and periostea surfaces become affected subsequently. The idea of Dieckerhoff anc others, that the disease begins in the bursa of the cunean branch of the flexor metatarsi, cannot be sustained. It must be mentioned that fusion of the small bones of the hock consequent on anchylosis of the gliding articulations is not uncommon in old horses that have never shown hock lameness. The interosseous ligament may become ossified, while the articular surfaces remain intact. It is possible that permanent lameness may supervene in such cases from chronic ostitis alone, which is favoured by the loss of the articular movements. A bony deposit may occur at the seat of spavin in young horses affected with rickets. In this case there is neither inflammation nor lameness, and the condition is usually accompanied by enlargements on the inferior extremities of the radius and cannon-bone. As the animal grows, these exostoses diminish or disappear.

ETIOLOGY.—The causes are predisposing and exciting.

Predisposing causes comprise :

1. *Heredity.*—Experience has proved that there is an hereditary predisposition to the disease.

2. *Defective conformation*, including *small hocks* ; " *tied-in* " *hocks* in which the joint is not " well let down," but becomes constricted at its base ; *sickle-shaped hocks* ; and " cow hocks." Such conformations constitute weaknesses, rendering the joint liable to inflammation under the stress of work.

3. *Youth.*—A young horse put to hard work is more liable to develop spavin than a mature animal.

4. *Severe exertion* of the hock, as occurs in heavy draft and in galloping and steeple-chasing.

Exciting causes comprise :

1. *Violent movements* of the hock, as may occur in starting or drawing heavy loads, in rearing, jumping, and slipping.

2. *Rheumatism*, setting up a rheumatoid arthritis, as in chronic carpitis and articular ringbone.

3. *Rickets*, giving rise to exostoses or osteophytes at the seat of spavin, apart from osteo-periostitis and arthritis. The enlargement, however, in this case is not true spavin, there being no arthritis present.

In galloping horses the injury caused by exertion is of the nature of concussion, which sets up a central arthritis, while in draft-horses the injury is caused by laceration of the ligaments and gives rise to a marginal osteo-arthritis.

Symptoms.—Under this heading there are to be considered (1) local symptoms, and (2) spavin lameness.

1. *Local Symptoms.*—Spavin may be classified as follows:

(1) *Visible spavin*, in which there is an exostosis as well as an arthritis.

(2) *Occult spavin*, in which there is only an arthritis.

(3) *Anterior spavin*, situated towards the anterior aspect of the joint.

(4) *Posterior spavin*, situated postero-internally.

(5) *High spavin*, located close to the true hock-joint.

Fig. 388.—Spavin Formation on Left Hock seen from in Front.

Fig. 389.—Spavin Formation on Right Hock seen from Behind. A, Spavin.

The popular term "jack spavin" is applied to a very prominent spavin. Visible spavin can be seen and felt. The following are recognised methods of viewing the hocks in an examination for spavin:

(1) Hold the cheek of the bridle standing at an arm's length therefrom, and facing in the opposite direction to that of the horse, and look obliquely at the inner aspect of the hock. If there is an enlargement at the seat of spavin it will catch the eye.

(2) Stand in front of the horse, stoop, and compare the two hocks, looking between the forelegs.

(3) View and compare the two hocks from behind. This is the best way to see a posterior spavin.

The exostosis can be felt by passing the fingers lightly over the small bones of the hock from above downwards. It requires much experience and oft-repeated manipulation of hocks to appreciate the difference in some cases between sound and spavined hocks. When the exostosis is very slight, it is difficult to recognise. It is important to bear in mind the normal prominences on the antero-internal aspect of the joint, and not to mistake them for spavin—viz., the ridge on the large cuneiform and the tuberosity on the supero-antero-internal aspect of the large metatarsus. These prominences are more marked in some horses than in others, and may even differ in size on the two hocks of the same animal.

Coarse Hock.—When these normal enlargements are very pronounced the horse is said to have a coarse hock, and as they are rather a sign of strength than of weakness, such a hock is perfectly sound. It is the tuberosity on the large metatarsus which is most likely to be mistaken for spavin. The coarse hock is most common in the horse under five years old. It becomes finer with age. In the normal hock the following grooves may be made out:

(1) A vertical groove between the large and small metatarsal bones, always very evident.

(2) A vertical groove between the large and small cuneiforms, not so distinct as No. 1, but still appreciable and situated immediately above and slightly in front of No. 1.

(3) A transverse groove between the large metatarsal and the large cuneiform.

(4) A transverse groove between the large cuneiform and the scaphoid.

Therefore, when one or more of these grooves are absent or replaced by an exostosis the hock may be said to have spavin.

2. *Spavin Lameness.*—A spavin may be present without lameness, as in the case where anchylosis has ensued and ostitis is absent. On the other hand, spavin lameness may occur in the absence of an exostosis, as in occult spavin and in cases in which the exostosis has not yet developed. The following features are usually associated with spavin lameness:

(1) *Imperfect Flexion of the Hock.*—During progression the hock is not well flexed, and there is a tendency to drag the toe. In some cases the wall at the toe of the foot is worn in this way.

(2) *Going on the Toe.*—The horse puts most weight on the toe of the foot, especially on starting, with the result that the toe of the shoe is excessively worn.

(3) *Diminution of Lameness on Exercise.*—The lameness is always worse on starting after resting, but gradually diminishes with exercise, and in some cases almost entirely disappears. However, when the lesion is extensive, and in case of occult spavin, the lameness continues.

(4) *Lowering of the Hip.*—When the horse is made to trot, the hip of the affected side is lowered in taking the limb forward.

(5) *Exaggeration of the Lameness on Passive Flexion of the Hock.*—If the hock be forcibly flexed for about one minute and the horse then made to trot on, the lameness is intensified. This has been called the "spavin test." Flexing other joints affected with arthritis would have the same effect. Care must be taken in practising this on aged horses, as it might cause the animal to fall over on the other side.

(6) *Spasmodic Flexion of the Hock.*—In some cases the horse, when at rest, repeatedly flexes the hock in a spasmodic manner. Exceptionally the hock is excessively flexed during exercise. When the horse is made to come over in the stable, the lameness is more marked on moving towards the sound side than towards the affected side. When both limbs are affected, the horse has a peculiar short stiff gait, as if suffering from an injury to the loins.

When a horse affected with spavin lameness is kept at work, atrophy of the gluteal muscles of the lame limb ensues; whereas if the horse is left idle, the atrophy does not occur. Hunting, of London, explained this phenomenon as follows: When the horse has been working all day he suffers pain at night, and consequently rests the limb all the time, throwing the muscles out of action, and thus leading to atrophy thereof; while the idle horse suffers no such pain, and hence does not rest the limb.

Diagnosis.—From the symptoms described it is evident that the diagnosis may be easy or difficult. The X-rays might be employed in a case of doubt to locate exostoses, and to ascertain whether prominences are abnormal. Cocaine injected over the tibial nerves may be used when there is indecision as to whether the lameness is in the hock or higher up. In cases of dispute, veterinarians often differ in their opinions as to the existence of spavin.

Prognosis.—It has been estimated that approximately two-thirds of the horses suffering from spavin go sound eventually, owing to anchylosis having taken place in the affected joints and ostitis having disappeared. Occult spavin is not likely to result in anchylosis, and is therefore often incurable. Anterior is more serious than posterior spavin, as it interferes most with movement of the joint and is subjected to more disturbance, which hinders fusion of the affected bones. For the same reason a high is more serious than a low spavin. The longer the horse is kept at work before being treated, the less favourable the prognosis, as anchylosis is not likely to supervene after prolonged exertion of the affected hock. As a rule, when a horse with spavin is sound he remains sound, but lameness from the condition may recur, especially if the animal is put to heavy work.

TREATMENT of spavin aims at bringing about anchylosis in the affected joints. The chief essential for this is complete rest, which usually must extend over a period of six to eight weeks. Other measures favouring this result are:

1. *Blistering*, which has some effect in hastening anchylosis by counter-irritation and in enforcing rest of the joint. Its action, however, is too superficial to be of much benefit.

2. *Line Firing*, which is better than No. 1, but still not deep enough in its action.

3. *Puncture Firing*, inserting a sharp-pointed iron into the exostosis, and only through the skin in its vicinity. If the exostosis is large this procedure is without danger, but if it is small there is a risk of opening the joint and setting up an incurable septic arthritis. When the spavin is small, the iron should only be inserted once into the bone. This method has often proved effective.

4. *Needle-point Firing*.—This is the best form of counter-irritation, being safe and producing a deep-seated inflammation which greatly favours anchylosis. A blister should be applied after firing in each case.

5. *Cunean Tenotomy and Periosteotomy*.—See p. 458.

6. *Anterior and Posterior Tibial Neurectomy*, indicated when all the foregoing measures have failed (see pp. 449 and 451).

Curb

DEFINITION.—Curb is an enlargement at the postero-inferior aspect of the hock, causing a backward curvature of the normal straight line between the point of the hock and the fetlock. It may be hardly perceptible or very distinct.

STRUCTURE INVOLVED.—The structure involved may be either:

1. *The Aponeurosis*.—Post-mortem examination in some cases, in young horses that have not shown lameness, has revealed a thickening confined to the aponeurosis and apparently of no consequence.

2. *The Perforatus Tendon*.

3. *The Perforans Tendon*.

4. *The Check Ligament*.—Nos. 2, 3, and 4 are rarely affected.

5. *The Calcaneo-Cuboid Ligament*.—It is generally accepted that this is the structure usually involved when the curb is inflammatory in origin—that is, the result of sprain following over-distension of the ligament. When the lesion arises in this way it constitutes the

most serious form of the condition, and has been spoken of as true curb, in comparison with the forms due to other causes.

6. *The Head of the Outer Small Metatarsal Bone.*—The head of the outer small metatarsal bone may be so prominent that it answers the definition of curb, but when it can be definitely shown that the enlargement is not pathological, but merely due to well-marked development of the bone, it is not a curb. It must, however, be remembered that the calcaneo-cuboid ligament is partly inserted into this bone, and that the apparent enlargement of the latter may be due to a thickening of the ligament. It is not always easy to say whether the thickening is in the bone or in the ligament.

An exostosis may form on the postero-external aspect of the hock, involving the head of the outer splint-bone, associated with an arthritis of the gliding articulations in the region. When the enlargement encroaches on the straight line referred to in the definition it simulates curb, but the condition is really spavin affecting the outer side of the hock.

The French use the terms *jarde* and *jardon* for enlargements about the seat of curb, but are not unanimous as to the signification of each term. *Jardon* generally means an enlargement on the postero-infero-external aspect of the hock, due as a rule to an enlarged head on the outer splint-bone, and not projecting behind the straight line mentioned; whereas, when this projection does occur, the term *jarde* is applied. When the swelling is bony it is called *jarde osseuse*, and when fibrous *jarde fibreuse*.

Formerly in France *courbe* had the same signification as the present-day *curb* in English-speaking countries, but it has been replaced by *jarde*, and is now applied to an exostosis on the internal aspect of the lower extremity of the tibia, where it is rarely associated with arthritis of the tibio-astragaloid articulation.

A cutaneous thickening does not constitute a curb.

Etiology.—The causes of curb are predisposing and exciting. Predisposing causes include:

1. *Mal-conformation of the Hocks*, as is represented by—

(*a*) *Sickle-shaped or curby hocks*, in which the os calcis, instead of being vertical, is inclined slightly forwards, thus favouring sprain of the calcaneo-cuboid ligament by the pull of the gastrocnemius muscle in extension of the hock-joint.

(*b*) *Tied-in hocks*, in which the lower row of tarsal bones and the upper end of the large metatarsal are too slight, putting the ligament at a disadvantage by increasing the strain thereon. Curb, however, is not confined to such hocks, for it may appear in those that are well shaped.

2. *Powerful Quarter Muscles*, whose action during severe exertion is apt to sprain the ligament.

3. *Violent Exertion*, as jumping and heavy uphill draft-work.

4. *Hereditary Predisposition.*—This has been often illustrated in the progeny of certain mares or sires. The predisposition may be in the form of the hock or apart therefrom. In such cases the curb may appear without any apparent exciting cause, arising insidiously in young animals, without inflammation or lameness, and before being put to work.

EXCITING CAUSES comprise movements which result in great exertion of the hock-joint—viz.:

1. *Violent Attempts at Extension* at moments when the limb is flexed and bearing weight, as in jumping, or heavy or uphill draft-work.

2. *Suddenly throwing a Horse on his Haunches.*—When a curb occurs suddenly in either of these ways, with local inflammation and lameness, the horse is said to have sprung a curb.

But a curb may form without any apparent exciting cause, and can then hardly be ascribed to sprain of the ligament, the enlargement in such instances appearing without inflammation or lameness and being probably due to a thickening of the subcutaneous aponeurosis, as was observed by the writer on post-mortem examination of two subjects affected with typical curbs.

SYMPTOMS.—When a curb forms without any local inflammation or lameness, the only symptom is the presence of the curb, which can be seen and felt. In order to recognise a curb, the observer must stand at right angles to the vertical line between the point of the hock and the fetlock. If he stands obliquely, he may mistake the normal outward curvature at the level of the head of the external splint for a curb.

The enlargement is usually bow-shaped, shading off gradually upwards and downwards from its centre, which is about on a level with the chestnut. It must be on the straight line at the back of the hock to answer the definition of curb.

The swelling can be felt by passing the fingers or thumb firmly and horizontally down the back of the limb from the point of the hock towards the fetlock. If it is very small it feels like a button beneath the skin. When the curb has been sprung, its formation is accompanied by acute local inflammation and lameness of varying intensity in different cases. In the hunter it may be first noticed in the morning after a day's hunting.

The lameness is characterised by the horse tending to go on the toe, and to rest the limb with the heel off the ground, so as to relieve tension on the inflamed part. It does not diminish with exercise. These symptoms of pain generally disappear in from one to three weeks, but the swelling persists.

DIAGNOSIS.—The diagnosis is usually easy. Doubt arises when the backward curvature is due to enlargement of the head of the outer small metatarsal, and a careful examination is required to ascertain whether the swelling is entirely bony or partly fibrous.

Distension of the tarsal sheath may cause a swelling to the inner aspect of the seat of curb, and gives to the eye the appearance of the latter, but manipulation will reveal its true nature. Möller has called this condition *soft curb.* Cutaneous thickening can be recognised by its being movable along with the skin.

PROGNOSIS.—When the hock is well formed, curb is not a serious condition, as it rarely causes recurrent lameness. even under severe exertion; but when its conformation is bad, lameness may repeatedly ensue if the horse is put to hard work. It is a common belief that when the curb has been fired, lameness is less likely to supervene. It is always a blemish, is hereditary, and in every case constitutes, at least, technical unsoundness.

TREATMENT.—When there is acute local inflammation with lameness, treatment comprises:

1. *Rest* of the patient.
2. *Cold and astringent* applications.
3. *The application of a high-heeled shoe*, with a view to relieving tension on the structures at the back of the hock. It is not essential, and is not always employed.

In a chronic case, with or without lameness, treatment includes:

1. *The use of absorbent topics*, rubbed well into the overlying skin, and repeated, if necessary, with a view to promoting resolution of inflammation, when present, and diminishing or removing the enlargement, such as:

(*a*) *Preparations of iodine*, including a mixture of iodine, potassium iodide, and Archangel tar, as represented by "Reducine," iodine ointment ("Vetiod"), and linimentum iodi. These topics require to be repeated several times, and even then generally prove disappointing.

(*b*) *A solution of perchloride of mercury in spirit* (1 in 10), rubbed in once with a tooth-brush.

(*c*) *A blister of biniodide of mercury.*

All the foregoing applications, however, usually fail to diminish or dispel the curb.

2. *Firing* in the form of :

(*a*) *Horizontal, oblique, or vertical lines* covering the curb and extending a little beyond it. When the vertical pattern is adopted, five lines are made, one long centre line and two gradually shorter on either side, thus : ||||| One pattern is just as effective as the other.

(*b*) *Penetrating points.*

(*c*) *Needle points,* which is the most effective and leaves least mark.

(*d*) *A transverse cutaneous incision* in the centre of the curb made with a sharp-edged hot iron, the edge of the iron being directed upwards and forwards. The writer was informed that the late Mr. Bell, M.R.C.V.S. (Clonmel, Ireland), found this procedure very successful in the removal of small curbs. The writer proved its efficacy in one case.

(*e*) Passing a red-hot needle transversely through the curb is also said to have proved effective in some cases.

Occasionally curbs vanish spontaneously from young horses as they become older. Lieut.-Colonel Ryan, in an article on curbs, and referring chiefly to horses four and five years old, says : " If an animal has a good broad hock with a large os calcis, and he is lunged four or five times a week over a low wall or pole, or both, and if the height of the jump be increased each day by 1 inch till it is $3\frac{1}{2}$ or 4 feet high, it is extraordinary how quickly some curbs vanish " (*Veterinary Record*, Vol. 10). A horse with curbs should be put to severe work gradually. If made to do it suddenly, lameness is more likely to ensue.

Stringhalt

Stringhalt is an involuntary spasmodic lifting of one or more of the limbs during progression. It is a common condition in the hind-limbs, but rarely affects a fore-limb. It differs from chorea in that it only occurs when the animal is made to move.

ETIOLOGY.—Temporary or symptomatic stringhalt often appears as the result of some irritation in the lower part of the limb, such as a cracked heel, a sandcrack, a bandage or blister on the hock, or even the straw bed (straw cramp). The exaggerated flexion of the limb in these cases is evidently due to reflex action. It has been noticed that in some cases the stringhalt persisted after the obvious cause had disappeared. In the great majority of cases of stringhalt nothing can be detected to account for the condition, and many theories have been put forward as to its etiology, including the following, ascribing it to:

1. *Articular Lesions of the Hock or Stifle.*—It has been seen accompanying arthritis of the true hock-joint and chronic gonitis, but was probably only a coincidence, as it does not always accompany these lesions. Pastureau looked upon it as a modified form of fixation of the patella above the internal lip of the trochlea, the bone becoming momentarily fixed there, and offering only a temporary resistance to the flexor muscles, which overcome the resistance by a sudden convulsive flexion, causing the limb to be lifted excessively.

2. *Muscular Tendinous and Aponeurotic Lesions.*—Lafosse ascribed it to spasmodic contraction of the muscles which flex the metatarsus, the cause of the contraction being some obscure reflex irritation. Boccar and Brogniez believed the abnormal movement was due to shortening of these muscles or their tendons, particularly the peroneus. Colour is given to this belief by the fact that section of the peroneus tendon, as recommended by Boccar, sometimes cures the condition. The spasmodic lifting of the limb has also been ascribed to shortening of the fascia lata. Cutting the fascia, however, has failed to arrest the abnormal movement.

3. *Nervous Lesions.*—Youatt and Spooner were of the opinion that stringhalt was due to lesions of the great sciatic nerve, causing overstimulation of the flexor muscles, while Percivall attributed it to an affection of the spinal cord or of the nerves of the hind-limb, whereby excessive muscular contraction was produced.

4. *Affections of the Feet.*—Flexion of the hock brings about flexion of the digit by putting its flexors into action. If there is any obstruction to the latter movement, an extra effort will be made to overcome it. Should the resistance disappear suddenly, there will be excessive flexion of the hock, or stringhalt. Hence, any lesion, painful or mechanical, which would retard digital flexion would favour stringhalt. Watrin, Weber, and others have upheld this theory, which is feasible enough in some cases.

Symptoms.—When stringhalt is present it is generally easily recognised. It may be so slight as to be hardly noticeable, or so marked that the hind-foot almost touches the abdomen. It is best seen when the horse is walked after resting, or when turned in short circles. It is often intermittent, disappearing for variable periods. When the horse is worked hard, rested for a while, and then exercised, the stringhalt is aggravated. It is also worse as a rule after a journey by train, and after an attack of influenza. In some cases the foot, after being spasmodically lifted, is brought to the ground with great force, whereas in others it is brought down normally. The former constitutes the more serious form of the affection.

Diagnosis.—The only difficulty about diagnosis is that the stringhalt might be absent at the time the horse was being examined, in a case where it was intermittent.

Prognosis.—As a rule stringhalt does not interfere with a horse's usefulness, but occasionally the spasm is so acute or convulsive that it impedes a horse galloping and jumping. A temporary stringhalt due to an apparent lesion disappears with the latter, but the ordinary stringhalt, whose cause is obscure, shows no tendency to spontaneous recovery, and is unsatisfactory to treat.

Treatment.—The only treatment that has given a fair measure of success is peroneal tenotomy (see p. 486). Section of the tensor vaginæ femoris, of the fascia of the leg, and of the cunean tendon, has been done without success. Anterior and posterior tibial neurectomy have been recommended when the condition appears of nervous origin, but the result of these operations might be worse than the disease.

Shivering

"Shivering" is the name applied to a peculiar neuro-muscular disease, characterised by involuntary spasmodic muscular contraction, with consequent irregular movements, generally affecting one or both hind-limbs and the tail; sometimes only a fore-limb, or occasionally the limbs, lips, cheeks, eyelids, and neck.

Shivering is often regarded as hereditary, but the cause has not been ascertained. Frequently its occurrence is preceded more or less remotely by an attack of strangles, influenza, or pneumonia; and this fact has led many observers to suggest that shivering is connected with neuropathic lesions produced by infection, or toxins derived from antecedent disease. Shivering is sometimes attributed to accidental injuries, falls, fright, etc.

It occurs at all ages, and while principally affecting draft-horses, it is frequently seen in light harness-horses, hunters, and hacks, and occasionally in thoroughbreds. It is very rare in ponies. It has also been observed in cattle.

Symptoms and Diagnosis.—Shivering varies very much in degree or manifestation. The symptoms may be constant and easily seen, or intermittent, occasional, or latent, and very difficult to discover. Many shivering horses only exhibit the symptoms when being shod, or when moving over in the stall; others while standing in harness constantly attract attention by frequently raising and abducting the shivering hind-limb. In well-marked bilateral posterior shivering the horse in advancing may give no sign of the disease, or the symptoms may be restricted to the first two or three steps; but on lifting a hind-foot, or in backing the horse, the limb is suddenly raised, semi-flexed and abducted, shaking or shivering in suspension, the superficial muscles of the thigh and quarter quivering, while the tail is elevated and tremulous. In a few moments the spasms cease, the limb is slowly extended and the foot brought to the ground. In severe cases the horse exhibits symptoms on every occasion he is set back, turned round, or moved from side to side. He may be unable to move backwards or to lie down, and if he should fall, unable to rise without assistance.

Diagnosis of cases in which the symptoms are slight or intermittent usually requires patient observation of the animal in the stable or the forge. Hammering the foot or shoe, allowing the horse to drink from a pail placed on the ground, forcibly backing the horse uphill over rough setts or slippery pavements, or puncturing the pastern with a pin may reveal the symptoms. Repeated testing of the horse at longer or shorter intervals, after prolonged exercise or hard work, or watching the horse rising in the early morning, may be necessary before a positive opinion can be formed in a doubtful case.

In anterior shivering, which seldom interferes with the animal's capacity for work, on attempting to lift the foot the limb is thrust forwards in full extension, the foot barely touching the ground, or the limb with the knee flexed is elevated and abducted, the extensors above the elbow quivering while the spasm lasts or until the foot returns to the ground. When affecting the head, the lips exhibit twitching with spasmodic retraction of the commissure, rapid blinking of the upper eyelid, and sometimes the ear of the same side is in constant motion.

Prognosis.—Usually shivering is a chronic or very slowly progressive affection, but it may develop rapidly under constant hard work, or during an attack of intercurrent debilitating disease. This is particularly noticeable in the intermittent and latent forms, when, owing to the excitement of a railway journey, or the pain produced by wounds, injuries to the feet, or arising from colic, influenza, or other systemic disease, the symptoms become much aggravated. Hunting-horses that are known to be occasional shiverers may hunt and jump for several seasons without hindrance or complaint, but eventually they lose power behind, and, though able to gallop and willing to jump, are unable to clear the obstacle with the hind-feet or to rise sufficiently to jump a moderate fence. Rest in the stable or on pasture for six or eight weeks will produce considerable modification in the symptoms of most well-marked cases, and it may enable an affected horse successfully to pass an examination as to soundness. Horses that are slight shiverers, and even those that offer no difficulty in diagnosis, may work satisfactorily for many years, but in time their usefulness becomes greatly impaired; the spasms increase both in frequency and in severity, the hind-quarters become atrophied, and the limbs more or less stiff or rigid. Animals so affected sleep standing, and their fore-fetlocks and knees are much bruised and disfigured by frequent half-falls. There is no curative treatment for shivering.

AFFECTIONS OF THE FEET

Examination of the Foot

As already indicated, the foot should be thoroughly examined in all cases of lameness, even when there is a lesion in some other part of the limb sufficient to account for the lameness. The procedure usually adopted in the examination of the foot comprises:

1. **Inspection.**—That is, viewing the foot from different aspects, and comparing it with the other foot. Various abnormalities may be noted in this way.

2. **Palpation,** applying the palmar surface of the fingers and hand over the wall of the hoof to ascertain if the heat of the foot is greater than normal or than that of the other foot, and over the coronet to find out whether it is swollen or abnormally hot. Lifting the foot and holding the wall resting on the two hands is another method of palpating it.

3. **Percussion** of the hoof with the hammer to ascertain if there is a tender spot indicating the presence there of some inflammatory lesion. The percussion is performed by smart, but not heavy taps with the hammer, using the foot of the sound limb as a control. When the horn is thick and the inflammation slight, it is possible for the latter to escape notice, little or no evidence of pain being exhibited by the animal. The tapping is done all over the hoof from heel to heel on the wall and on the sole, and at the level of the frog. Pain is shown by the horse attempting to draw the foot away when it is struck. When in doubt, the other foot should be percussed in the same way to compare the effects.

4. **Compression** with a pincers with large jaws, so that when the foot is grasped between them one can be made to reach the centre

of the sole and the frog. When the inflamed part is squeezed, the horse shows resentment by drawing away the foot. The ordinary farrier's pincers answers the purpose well enough. Compression of the coronet with the fingers will cause pain when it is inflamed.

5. **Paring** the horn in a place where inflammation is suspected to see if its deep layers are discoloured from extravasation of blood, or whether pus is imprisoned beneath it. The junction of the wall and sole is the proper place to search for pus beneath the latter. The deep layers of the horn in this case are yellowish and infiltrated with moisture. When the horn has been thinned, pain is more readily manifested on pressure, and may be evident on compression with the thumb.

6. **Mensuration** by the aid of the calipers or a tape measure to compare the dimensions of two fore- or two hind-feet to ascertain if one has undergone contraction, which might be the cause or the effect of lameness.

Affections of the Horn : Sandcrack—Fissure in the Wall

A sandcrack is a fissure in the wall of the hoof, parallel to the horn tubules, commencing at the coronet and extending a variable distance down the wall, usually to its plantar aspect. It may occur at any part of the wall, and even in the bar, but its commonest situations are the toe of the hind-foot and the inner quarter of the fore-foot. The following varieties of cracks are distinguished :

(1) **Complete,** extending from the coronet to the plantar border of the wall.

(2) **Incomplete,** extending downwards through part of the height of the wall.

(3) **Superficial,** only going through part of the thickness of the wall.

(4) **Deep,** extending as far as the sensitive tissues.

(5) **Straight or sinuous** in direction.

(6) **Recent,** (7) **old,** (8) **simple,** (9) **complicated,** with more or less damage to the sensitive tissues beneath.

Etiology.—The causes of sandcrack comprise :

1. *Heredity,* an inherent weakness in the horn being transmitted from parent to offspring, rendering it liable to crack.

2. *Alternate moisture and dryness* of the horn, causing it to become brittle and easily cracked.

3. *Thinness of the horn.*

4. *Violent extension* of the corono-pedal joint, whereby the os corona comes to press forcibly against the coronet, causing the horn

to split at its origin in the region of the toe. It has often occurred in this way in the hind-foot of heavy draft-horses in cities and in tram-way horses. It is more apt to occur when the animal's hind-foot slips from one pavement block against another. A crack at the quarter is most common in contracted feet, and in those low at the heels. In the case of out-toed or in-toed horses it is the surcharged quarter which is usually affected.

5. *Excessive rasping of the wall*, removing its periople and superficial fibres, and exposing its deeper layers to evaporation, rendering them brittle and easily ruptured.

SYMPTOMS.—The fissure in the wall may be hardly perceptible or well marked. When the crack is simple it is the only local symptom, but when it is complicated there may be an escape of blood when the condition is recent, due to rupture of the laminæ from the violence which caused the fissure or from their being pinched between the lips of the latter, or an oozing of serum or pus when the sensitive tissues are inflamed or suppurating. When the inflammation is severe the coronet is swollen and painful. When necrosis of the laminæ or caries of the os pedis has supervened there is diffuse inflammatory swelling of the digital region.

Lameness is absent when the crack is superficial, but is usually present when it is deep, due either to laceration of the laminæ when the case is recent and the result of violence, or to inflammation of the sensitive structures when the crack has been in existence for some time, and they have undergone repeated irritation from the movement of the lips of the fissure, or have been subjected to injury from the presence of foreign matter and invasion by micro-organisms. When suppuration has supervened the lameness is very marked. Lameness from sandcrack at the toe of the hind-foot is characterised by the horse lifting the foot spasmodically, as in stringhalt, taking it well forward, and putting it carefully on the ground heel first. When the crack is in the quarter, the foot is also lifted smartly. When weight is placed on the foot, the sensitive tissues are compressed by closure of the crack, and relief is obtained by rapidly removing the weight from the foot.

DIAGNOSIS is generally easy, but the crack may be concealed by the presence of mud on the wall, or it may be skilfully filled with wax or gutta-percha. Hence the necessity of washing muddy feet before examining them. Scraping the wall at a suspected point will reveal whether a fissure extends through the horn. A crack in the bar is detected on lifting the foot and paring the horn. It may be difficult to determine the exact nature of complications when present, but the more pronounced the lameness and the greater the inflammatory swelling the more serious is the lesion.

PROGNOSIS varies according to the nature of the condition. When the crack is simple and properly treated recovery ensues eventually. When it is complicated with necrosis of the sensitive tissue, the case requires special treatment, and is more or less protracted. When the horn is brittle, cracking is apt to recur.

TREATMENT.—1. *Sandcrack at the Toe—Simple Crack without Lameness.*—The indications in this case are to (1) immobilise the lips of the crack, and (2) promote the secretion of new horn to fill the crack at its origin in the coronary band.

(1) *Immobilisation of the Crack* may be effected by:

(*a*) *A Special Shoe* divided in the inner half of its width at the toe, and provided with quarter clips and with special clips at the heels, one at the inner aspect of the branch on each side fitting into the lateral lacuna. When the shoe has been applied its branches are forcibly separated at the heels by the aid of a sort of vice, thereby bringing the lips of the fissure into contact and maintaining them there. The shoe however, is not much in vogue.

(*b*) *Bandages*, either in the form of an ordinary bandage or of a tar rope wound round the hoof from the coronet to its plantar aspect. They really have little or no effect in keeping the edges of the crack in apposition, but are efficacious in preventing the entrance of foreign matter into the fissure.

(*c*) *Clasps.*—These are inserted by the aid of two instruments made for the purpose, an iron and a forceps. The iron is made red hot and used to form a groove to receive the clasp, which is fixed in position by means of the forceps in much the same way as a ring is inserted into a pig's nose. The uppermost clasp is applied about $\frac{1}{2}$ inch below the coronet, and two others below this about $\frac{3}{4}$ inch apart. It is advisable to fill the crack with gutta-percha or Archangel tar. These clasps look well and are fairly effective, but are apt to become loose or fall out under severe exertion.

(*d*) *Horseshoe Nails* driven transversely through the lips of the crack sufficiently deeply to get a good hold without compressing the sensitive tissues. A little transverse groove is first made on either side of the fissure with the searcher, or more conveniently with the iron used in connection with the clasps to accommodate the nail, which is then driven carefully through the horn, its point being afterwards cut off and the stump clenched towards the crack. For the sake of appearance the head may also be filed off to enable a second clench to be made. This is the best method of fixing the lips of the crack, but it requires care and skill to carry it out properly without wounding the sensitive laminæ. The insertion of the nail may be facilitated and rendered more safe by first boring a hole in the horn with a drill. A good farrier can drive the nail safely through the horn.

(e) *A Piece of Wood* inserted into the crack. A slot is first made to receive the wood, which is then tapped into position like a lid on a chalk-box. It prevents pinching of the tissues by the edges of the crack, and excludes dirt from the latter. The method was much in favour with Greaves, Pritchard, Sowerby, and other London practitioners. Filling up the crack with gutta-percha 2 parts and gum ammoniac 1 part has also been recommended for the same object, but its chief effect is the exclusion of mud and dust.

(2) *Promotion of the Secretion of New Horn* is effected by counter-irritation of the coronary band by means of a blister or the actual cautery. A common method of using the latter was to make three transverse lines at the level of the crack—one on the coronet, another ½ inch above it, and a third ½ inch below. Another procedure is to make two transverse grooves across the crack in the wall, and a third on the coronet. Those in the wall have the effect of intercepting pressure transmitted to the lips of the crack.

Instead of adopting the above devices for preventing movement of the lips of the crack, the edges of the latter may be thinned for a short distance on either side to prevent pinching of the tissues between them. The shoe should have side toe-clips, or quarter clips instead of a toe-clip, and the wall should be slightly shortened with the rasp in the vicinity of the crack to prevent bearing on the shoe in that region.

2. *Sandcrack accompanied by Lameness.*—The indications here are to remove the shoe and immerse the foot in a warm antiseptic bath for at least half an hour morning and evening. If the horse becomes sound the measures prescribed in No. (1) can be adopted. If the lameness persists after the lapse of a few days it will be necessary to thin the horn on each side of the fissure to relieve the pressure on the inflamed tissues and permit of the escape of inflammatory exudate or pus, if present, and if this procedure fails to have the desired effect an operation will be required to strip off completely the overlying horn, to expose the necrotic tissue which is probably the cause of the trouble, and to enable it to be removed. It may be necessary to curette the os pedis.

3. *Sandcrack at the Quarter.*—When lameness is absent the treatment is on the same lines as those for sandcrack at the toe, except that

clasps or horseshoe nails cannot be employed with safety owing to the comparative thinness of the horn in this region. The usual procedure, which gives satisfactory results, is to make a transverse groove across the crack in its upper third, to put on a flat shoe having no bearing in the vicinity of the crack, and to apply a vesicant on the coronet. When the condition is accompanied by lameness, the measures to be adopted are exactly the same as those advised when it is situated at the toe.

When there is a crack in the bar the surrounding horn should be thinned, and a leather sole with tar and tow applied along with a flat shoe if the horse is sound. If lameness is present, the treatment prescribed for other situations must be adopted.

Transverse Cracks

These may be superficial or deep. They follow injury to the coronet and separation of the horn in this region. As the horn grows down the separation becomes a crack. If they go right through the wall, lameness will ensue from injury of the sensitive laminæ.

TREATMENT consists in paring the lips of the crack to relieve pressure on the subjacent structures, and thus prevent or remove lameness.

Seedy Toe

This is characterised by separation of the wall from the subcorneal tissue, and the formation in the interspace of crumbly pumice-stone-like horn secreted by the sensitive laminæ. This abnormal horn does not completely fill the space beneath the wall, which is consequently more or less hollow.

ETIOLOGY.—The cause is not clear, but the condition would appear to be the result of a chronic local laminitis following traumatic injury, such as might be caused by a too-closely-driven nail, or by the pressure of a large clip. Wide-spreading feet are most subject to it.

SYMPTOMS.—The condition is often first recognised by the farrier when preparing the hoof for shoeing. The foot appears normal when resting on the ground, but if the wall be struck on its outer aspect with a hammer a hollow sound will be emitted opposite the affected part. The extent of the lesion varies in depth and peripheral area. It may occupy any region of the circumference of the wall, and may affect only the lower portion of the latter or extend as far as the coronet. Lameness is absent when the area involved is small, but when there is considerable separation of the horn the sensitive laminæ are insufficiently protected from concussion, and, moreover, foreign matter accumulates in the space, causing pressure on the laminal surface, giving rise to more or less well-marked lameness. The abnormal horn is easily broken down with the knife.

Prognosis depends on the depth and area of the lesion. When circumscribed it is not of much importance, not causing lameness, and allowing the horse to work during treatment. When a large part of the foot is affected to a great depth, causing lameness, months may elapse before the horse is fit to work.

Treatment.—Remove the new formation of horn to diminish the pressure on the sensitive structures, pack the cavity with tar and tow, and apply a shoe having no bearing on the affected region and a leather sole to keep the dressing in position. If the disease extend far beneath the wall, it will be necessary to remove a portion of the latter at the level of the lesion in order to expose it and enable the abnormal horn to be pared away. A bar shoe with a breach in the iron opposite the affected part is suitable. A blister on the coronet will promote the growth of normal horn.

Keratoma

Keratoma is a horn tumour growing from the inner aspect of the wall. It varies considerably in volume, form, and extent. Its diameter may be ½ inch to 1 inch. Its shape may be cylindrical, conical, pyramidal, or irregular, and it may be bifurcated at its upper extremity. It may extend up a portion or the full height of the wall, or even bulge into the cutigeral groove. Exceptionally it is only adherent at its lower part. It may be solid or fistulous, the fistula terminating in the tumour or passing through it to abut on the laminæ, and having its lower orifice at the white line.

Etiology.—The condition is apparently due to hyperactivity of the laminæ or coronary band, caused by some irritant or injury, whereby an abnormal quantity of horn is secreted. In this way it may result from mechanical injury of the wall or coronet, or from a close-driven nail compressing or penetrating the laminæ, or from dirt gaining entrance through a sandcrack, or a separation between the wall and the sole. There is another and rare form of keratoma which appears independently of inflammation or irritation of the horn-secreting structures. It may be adherent or free, and of similar dimensions to the one just described.

Symptoms.—The tumour may develop insidiously and be present for a considerable time before being detected. Its presence is recognised on examination of the plantar aspect of the foot by the abnormal appearance of the horn at the place corresponding to the lower end of the growth between the wall and the sole, the white line being deviated inwards here. If fistulous, a probe can be passed into it, and the fistula may be discharging pus. The pressure of the tumour on the laminæ and os pedis may cause inflammation and lameness. The former is indicated locally by pain on percussion at the level of the lesion, and by abnormal heat on palpation. The latter varies in degree. The abnormality of gait may be of the nature of stringhalt. The wall may bulge over the tumour. When the sensitive tissues become affected through the fistula, the laminæ may undergo necrosis and the os pedis may become affected with caries. The pressure of the new horn causes atrophy of the laminæ, which eventually disappear, preventing further increase in size of the tumour. The pedal bone may also undergo atrophy and become weakened in consequence, and fracture on slight provocation.

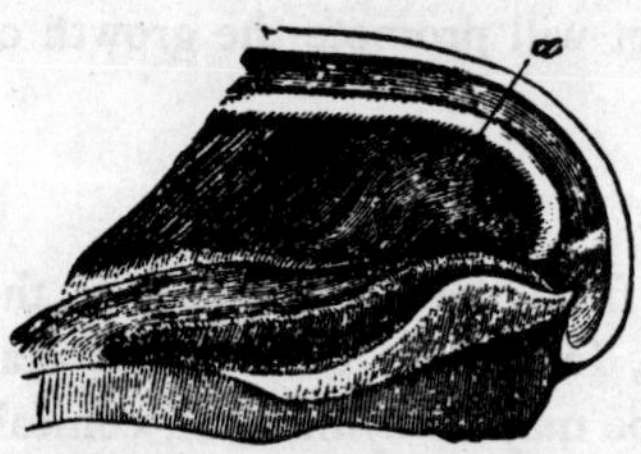

Fig. 390.—Portion of the Inner Surface of the Wall, showing Changes after Old-Standing Corn.

a, Horn tumour.

Diagnosis is easy, owing to the characteristic appearance of the horn at the lower end of the tumour or to the presence of the fistula, into which a probe can be passed to abut on the tumour or pass through it as mentioned.

Prognosis, generally speaking, is unfavourable, there being no tendency to spontaneous cure and no means of effecting the latter, except by operation, after which the tumour may recur.

Treatment.—If there be neither pain nor lameness, it is sufficient to regulate the shoeing so as to have a minimum amount of bearing on the affected region. When lameness supervenes, palliative or curative measures may be adopted. Palliative treatment comprises rest and antiphlogistic applications, which may cause temporary improvement, and if these fail, paring out the tumour from below with a searcher or boring it with a drill to allow it to collapse on itself, and thus diminish the pressure on the sensitive tissues until the tumour increases in size, when this procedure will require repetition. Curative treatment consists in performing the operation described (see p. 470).

Keratoma on the Sole

A keratoma may be found on the deep face of the sole in flat or convex feet, in which it may arise from circumscribed chronic inflammation resulting from contusion. It is hemispherical in shape, its base being flush with the sole. The velvety tissue becomes atrophied through its pressure, and the os pedis may become excavated from the same cause. It is diagnosed by pain confined to the region affected, revealed on percussion, and by the dry, hard consistence of the horn of the tumour, which retains these characters after deep paring, while that of its periphery, when cut to the same extent, causes wounding of the sensitive tissues. Infection of the lesion rarely occurs.

TREATMENT.—Thin or hollow out the tumour to diminish its pressure or remove it radically. If necrotic tissue is present, excise it. Cover the wound until healed with an antiseptic dressing and a leather or metal sole fixed under the shoe.

Thrush

Thrush is the term applied to an affection of the frog characterised by an offensive greyish discharge from the central lacuna, and sometimes from the lateral lacunæ as well, and associated, as a rule, with more or less disintegration of the horn.

ETIOLOGY.—Constant moisture of the frog favours the condition, which is thus brought about by prolonged standing on dirty wet litter, especially peat moss, or running in a marshy pasture. The moisture softens the horn, which then becomes broken and ragged, and emits the characteristic discharge from the lacunæ. Atrophy of the frog from disuse favours the trouble, and for this reason contracted feet are very subject to it. Hind-feet are more often affected than fore ones, due to the fact that the former are more frequently in contact with wet bedding, and their frogs are more often prevented from bearing weight. Neglecting to pick out the feet regularly naturally favours the onset of the condition.

SYMPTOMS.—The local symptoms are the conditions of the frog, as described. There is no evidence of inflammation or lameness, except the greater portion of the horn has been shed, and the insufficiently protected sensitive tissue suffers from contusion or from the action of a caustic dressing.

DIAGNOSIS.—Thrush is distinguished from canker by the horn being separated from the sensitive tissues in the latter case, and by the ready response of the former to appropriate treatment.

Contusion, Crushing, and Open Wounds of the Foot

Contusion or crushing of the foot is generally caused by direct violence inflicted from above downwards on the upper part of the foot in the region of the toe, quarters, or heels, the offending body being usually the wheel of a heavy vehicle passing over the coronet. The

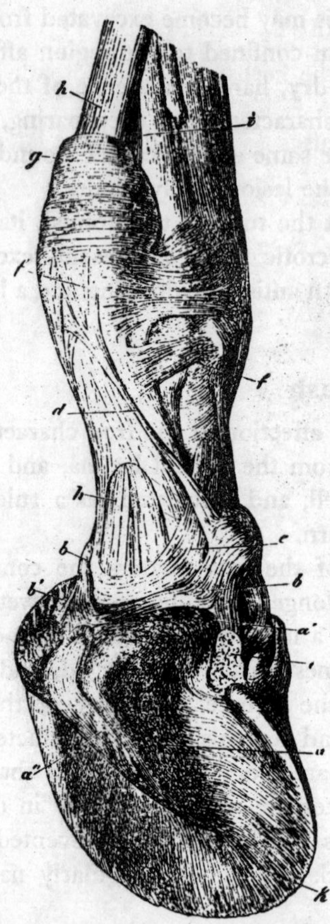

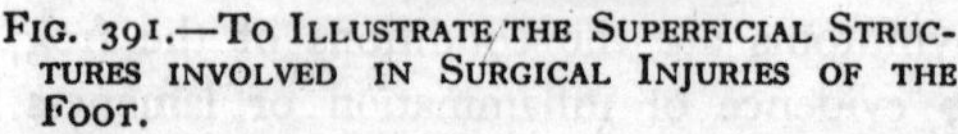

FIG. 391.—TO ILLUSTRATE THE SUPERFICIAL STRUCTURES INVOLVED IN SURGICAL INJURIES OF THE FOOT.

The outer lateral cartilage and the tissues covering the lower surface of the pedal bone (sensitive frog and sensitive sole) have been removed. *a*, Plantar cushion; *a'*, bulbar portion of plantar cushion; *a"*, cleft of the frog in which rests the "frog stay"; *b*, origin of the so-called "suspensory ligament of the bulbs"; *b'*, small elastic band passing towards the lateral cartilage; *c*, elastic band arising from lateral cartilage and becoming inserted into pastern bone—it unites with *b*; *d*, small tendon which arises from the skin and becomes attached, in common with *b* and *c*, to the pastern bone; *e*. fibro-elastic supporting sheath of flexor pedis perforans; *f*, fibro-elastic supporting sheath of flexor pedis perforatus; *g*, flexor pedis perforatus tendon; *h*, flexor pedis perforans tendon; *i*, suspensory ligament; *k*, lower surface of pedal bone, to which the flexor pedis perforans tendon is attached.

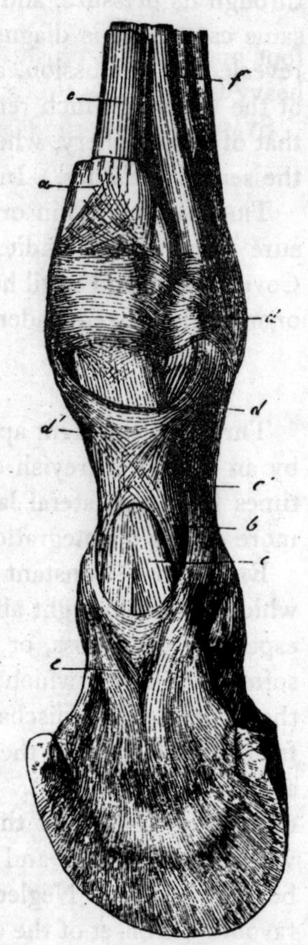

FIG. 392.—TO ILLUSTRATE THE DEEPER-SEATED STRUCTURES INVOLVED IN SURGICAL INJURIES OF THE FOOT.

Right fore-foot seen from behind and slightly from one side. *a*, Flexor pedis perforatus tendon; *b*, two limbs formed by its bifurcation; *c*, flexor pedis perforans tendon; *d*, fibrous reinforcing band of great sesamoid sheath; *d'*, fibrous supporting sheath inserted into suffraginis bone by four heads; *d"*, upper insertions (the lower not visible in figure); *e*, fibro-elastic plate covering the lower surface of flexor pedis perforans and inserted into suffraginis bone at *e'*; *f*, suspensory ligament.

foot may also be crushed between the kerbstone of a footpath and a heavy wheel.

SYMPTOMS.—A slight contusion causes a varying degree of lameness,

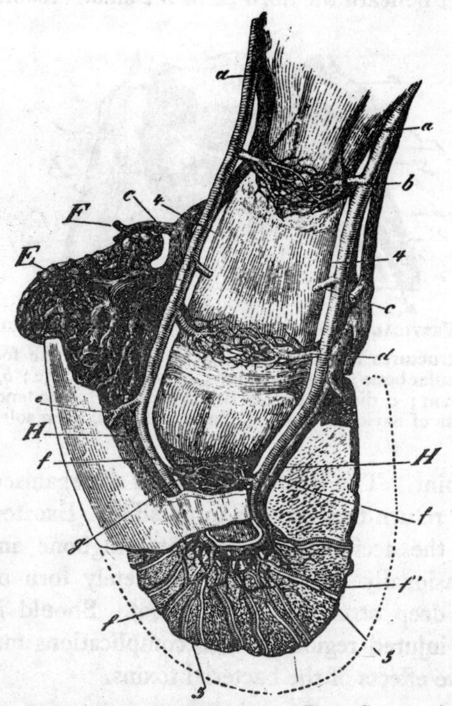

FIG. 393.—TO ILLUSTRATE THE JOINTS AND DEEP-SEATED ARTERIES, VEINS, AND NERVES INVOLVED IN SURGICAL INJURIES OF THE FOOT.

Right fore-foot seen from below, behind, and somewhat from one side. The outer lateral cartilage is removed, together with sufficient of the pedal bone to render visible the vessels, etc., in its interior. The nerves accompanying arteries *f'* are shown too thick; they should be less than half as broad as figured. *a*, Digital artery; *b*, posterior suffraginal artery; *c*, artery of plantar cushion (cut through); *d*, posterior artery of coronary circle; *f*, plantar artery, which anastomoses with its fellow within the pedal bone and gives off twigs *f'*, which pass to the anterior surface of the pedal bone just above its lower edge; *g*, twigs of plantar artery supplying coffin-joint; *E*, deep lateral layer of coronary plexus clothing inner surface of lateral cartilage; *F*, divided ends of superficial part of coronary plexus. From these arise the digital vein (not shown), *H*, plantar vein; 4, posterior branch of digital nerve accompanying vessels into pedal bone; 5, twigs of posterior branch passing towards sensitive laminæ.

which disappears in the course of a few days. There is slight hæmorrhage or ecchymosis in the bruised tissues. When the contusion is caused by severe violence, or when the foot is actually crushed, the animal becomes extremely lame. If there be no breach in the horn there will be no obvious local symptoms, but in many instances some trace of the accident is left on the horn or the coronet reveals evidence of a contusion, with heat, pain, and swelling. The damage done to the foot varies according to the severity of the injury. Extravasated blood may collect beneath the horn or in the small sesamoidean sheath,

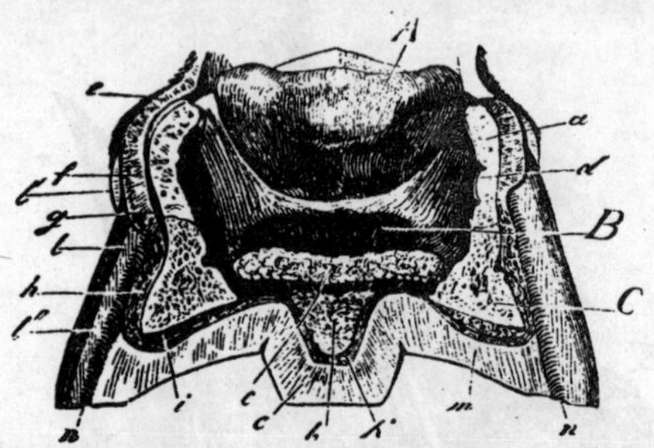

FIG. 394.—VERTICAL CROSS-SECTION OF A FOOT SEEN FROM BEHIND.

To illustrate the structures involved in surgical injuries of the foot. *A*, Coronet bone; *B*, navicular bone; *C*, pedal bone; *a*, lateral cartilage; *b*, anterior portion of plantar cushion; *c*, divided part of flexor pedis perforans tendon; *d*, postero-lateral ligaments of navicular bone; *l*, horn wall; *m*, horn sole; *n*, white line; *o*, horn frog.

or even in the joint. The tissues may be so disorganised by the contusion that their return to normal is impossible. Exostoses may form as a sequel to the accident, causing low ringbone and permanent lameness. Occasionally the hoof is completely torn off, with little damage to the deep structures of the foot. Should infection gain entrance to the injured region, serious complications may ensue, due to the destructive effects of the bacterial toxins.

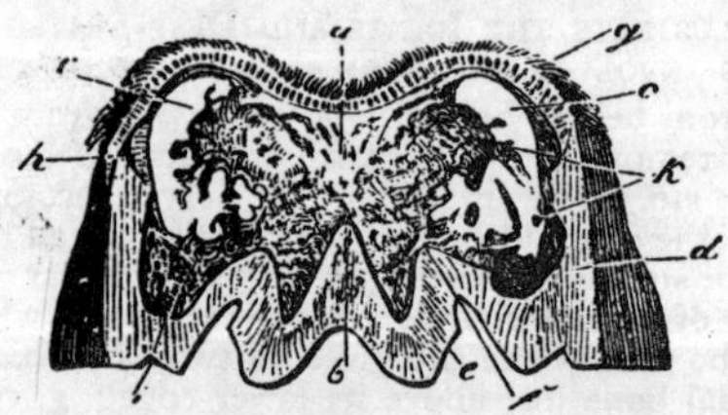

FIG. 395.—VERTICAL CROSS-SECTION OF FOOT SEEN FROM BEHIND (THIS SECTION HAS BEEN MADE NEARER THE HEELS THAN FIG. 394).

To illustrate the structures involved in surgical injuries of the foot. *a*, Posterior part of plantar cushion; *b*, median ridge of frog; *c*, lateral cartilage; *d*, horn wall; *e*, lateral face of frog; *f*, point of union between the bars and frog.

When an open wound is present, its seat will be a guide to the parts likely to be involved—lateral cartilage, bones, or joint. Crepitation on manipulation of the foot will reveal fracture, and a synovial discharge from a wound on the coronet will be proof of an open corono-pedal joint.

Diagnosis may be difficult when there is no history to the case and no mark of injury to the hoof. When the horn of the plantar region is pared, ecchymosis may be seen at the white line. These symptoms, associated with severe lameness and the acute pain evinced on percussion or compression, generally lead to a correct conclusion, although

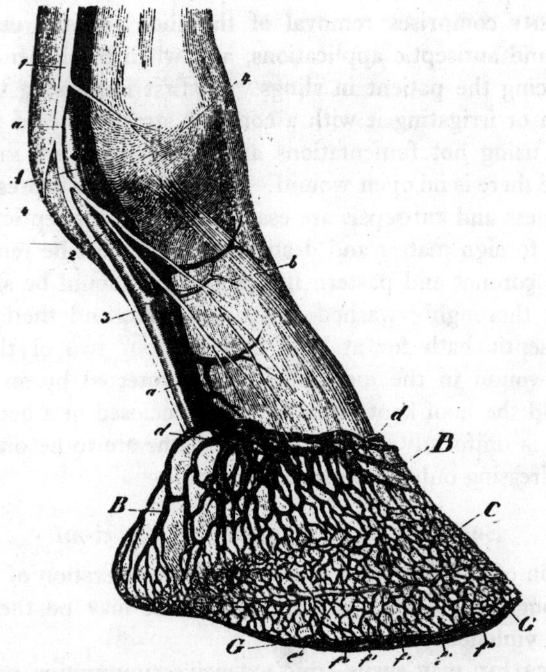

Fig. 396.—Lateral View of Fore-Foot, with Nerves and Injected Vessels, showing Some of the Structures involved in Inflammation of the Sub-coronary Connective Tissue and its Complications.

a, Digital artery ; *b*, perpendicular artery ; *e'*, preplantar artery ; *f'*, twigs from the plantar artery which escape through the foramina just above the lower margin of the os pedis, and by their anastomosis form *f''*, the circumflex artery of the toe ; *A*, digital vein ; *B*, coronary venous plexus ; *C*, laminal plexus ; *G*, circumflex vein ; 1, digital nerve ; 2, anterior terminal branches of digital nerve ; 3, posterior terminal branches of digital nerve ; 4, cutaneous branches.

it is not always easy to give a definite opinion as to the exact nature of the lesion or the extent of the injury inflicted.

Prognosis.—In cases of moderate contusion cure is effected in a few days, but when the tissues are severely damaged there is always the danger of secondary changes occurring, such as the formation of exostoses, or anchylosis of the pedal-joint, causing incurable lameness. It is important to bear this in mind from the point of view of jurisprudence. These changes may not supervene until months after the accident. Injury to the anterior or middle regions of the foot is more likely to have serious consequences than that confined to the region of the heel. Deep-seated septic conditions are always serious and may defy treatment. Infected open joint is, of course, hopeless, as is also complete compound fracture of the os pedis or navicular bone.

TREATMENT comprises removal of the shoe and the use of antiphlogistic and antiseptic applications, and when the lameness is very severe, placing the patient in slings. At first immersing the foot in a cold bath or irrigating it with a constant stream of cold water, and afterwards using hot fomentations and compresses, are indicated in cases where there is no open wound. When the latter is present, rigorous cleanliness and antisepsis are essential to prevent septic complications. All foreign matter and destroyed tissue must be removed, the skin of the coronet and pastern in the vicinity should be shaved, the whole foot thoroughly washed and disinfected, and then kept in a warm antiseptic bath for at least half an hour two or three times daily, the wound in the meantime being protected by an antiseptic dressing and the hoof kept clean by being enclosed in a boot. When the wound is uniformly granulating, the baths are to be discontinued and a dry dressing only employed.

Separation or Evulsion of the Hoof

Separation of the hoof may be caused by degeneration of its attachments through the agency of infection, or it may be the result of mechanical violence.

Degeneration may ensue from extensive suppuration beneath the horn, and it is favoured by ordinary poultices, which have no antibacterial effect, but rather promote the growth of bacteria. It is, however, most frequently a sequel to neurectomy.

Mechanical violence is a cause when all muscles of the limb are violently contracted in an effort to extricate the foot which has become fixed between two resistant objects, or when the foot is crushed from above downwards by a heavy weight such as a wagon wheel passing over it, and the pain thus caused makes the animal endeavour to snatch it away suddenly.

SYMPTOMS.—The sensitive tissues are all exposed and more or less injured when the result of violence. Evidence of pain is not always marked. It is surprising how slight it is in some cases. Instances are recorded where the horse continued to trot fairly well after losing one or two hooves.

PROGNOSIS.—When the condition is the result of degeneration and sloughing after neurectomy it is hopeless. But if the case be noticed when separation is commencing at the coronet, it may be possible to arrest it by keeping the foot for prolonged periods in an antiseptic bath. When the loss of the hoof is due to mechanical violence, the chances of recovery depend on the amount of injury suffered by the tissues. In every case it will take about nine months for the new hoof to grow down from the coronet. Sometimes the newly formed horn is deformed, and occasionally, although the regenerated hoof is fairly normal in shape, lameness persists from hyperæsthesia in the subcorneal tissues. The hoof, however, may be perfectly reproduced, and even in cases where a piece of bone has been torn away with a portion of the horn-secreting membrane recovery may occur to an extent sufficient to enable the animal to go to work.

TREATMENT comprises the removal of shreds of dead tissue, thoroughly cleaning and disinfecting the foot after clipping or shaving the pastern, and applying a dressing of iodoform or sulphanilamide covered with gauze and several layers of cotton-wool kept in position by a bandage and protected from the dirt of the stable floor by a boot. The frequency of renewal of the dressing will depend on the progress of the case. It should be renewed whenever it becomes moistened from discharge. When the sensitive tissues are covered with horn, it will be sufficient to keep them covered with tar until the new wall is formed. If the hæmorrhage after the accident is severe, a tourniquet should be applied above the fetlock until the foot is enveloped in the compressive dressing.

Chronic Coronitis or Villitis—Chronic Dermatitis of the Perioplic Band and of the Coronary Cushion

ETIOLOGY.—The etiology is often obscure. The condition may accompany skin affections or be associated with a febrile condition. Its typical form often appears without any apparent cause, but it may result from repeated injury or irritation of the coronet. In all cases there may be an hereditary predisposition to the affection, which may be of a rheumatoid nature. It most commonly affects light horses, those engaged in fast work. It is particularly common in the ass and mule. The disease affects chiefly the toe and quarters. The perioplic band appears to become more active, secreting a horny material, disposed in irregular masses, separated by narrow fissures, resembling somewhat the bark of an old tree.

The coronary cushion in the affected part produces thickened abnormal horn of the same appearance as that formed by the perioplic ring. The skin in the vicinity may also be covered by a horny formation, fissured in every direction and sometimes discharging from the cracks a purulent fluid. In old-standing cases there may be separation of the horn at the coronet. The subcutaneous tissue becomes thickened at the level of the lesion in typical old cases, causing a swelling which projects over the hoof. Sometimes an ulcer forms between the swelling and the horn. In the subacute form accompanying a febrile disease or skin affection, the whole of the coronet is involved and reveals slight symptoms of inflammation, chiefly abnormal heat. In this case there is more or less marked lameness, characterised by a shuffling gait something like that of subacute laminitis. In the ordinary chronic form of the disease, with local changes as described, lameness may or may not be present. When the new formation of horn on the coronet is thick or cracked or when the wall is separated from the coronary band, lameness supervenes.

TREATMENT.—When apparently of constitutional origin, treat the general affection from which the animal is suffering. Apply cold swabs to the coronet to counteract local inflammation. Afterwards rub on the coronet an ointment composed of equal parts of Stockholm tar and mutton suet boiled together, or a preparation consisting of one part of coal tar and six parts of fish oil, in order to promote the growth of good horn and to render it supple and elastic. A blister on the coronet may have a good effect in an old-standing case. When the growth of new horn is thick it should be thinned to a pellicle, and the weeping cracks therein should be treated with an antiseptic lotion. Ulceration should be combated by the use of a wound stimulant or caustic, to excite a healthy reaction and bring about granulation and cicatrisation. In all cases the horn beneath the affected part of the coronet should be made as thin as possible with the rasp to diminish the pressure and pain in the inflamed part. Delpérier, a well-known French authority on the horse's foot, recommends washing and drying the affected part every five days, and then applying rapidly over its surface the flat portion of a red-hot iron, and passing its edges into the fissures. Slight repeated application of nitric acid more or less dilute, or of chloride of zinc (5 to 10 per cent.), or of pyrogallic acid, or of picric acid in saturated aqueous solution or as an ointment (1 to 10 of vaseline) has often had good results.

Gangrenous Coronitis

Gangrenous coronitis, or sloughing of a portion of the coronet or subcorneal tissues, may result from an open wound and infection by the bacillus of necrosis or other virulent organism. The condition is fairly common in horses constantly standing in mud, especially during very cold frosty weather, the severe cold diminishing the vitality and resistance of the tissues. The lesion was very prevalent in army horses during the winter months of the First World War.

SYMPTOMS.—There is intense inflammation in the region of the coronet and severe lameness. An extremely painful swelling more or less diffuse is formed; the skin, if not pigmented, becomes dark red, and serum oozes from its surface, which becomes clammy, owing to the desquamation of the epithelium, which can be scraped off with the nail. The affected part then becomes insensitive, and a line of demarcation is observed between the dead and healthy tissues. If infection has not extended beneath the horn, the lameness attenuates when the eschar is formed. When the subcorneal tissue is involved the pain is more excruciating, owing to compression of the inflamed part by the resistant horn, and it does not subside with separation of the slough, which cannot be cast off on account of being confined beneath the horn, the result being that the bacteria continue to exercise their pathogenic effects, causing further necrosis of the sensitive parts, including the laminæ, or extensor pedis tendon, or the lateral cartilage or pedal bone. A general toxæmia generally ensues which may prove fatal.

TREATMENT.—Thoroughly clean the extremity of the limb, clip or shave the hair in the affected region, thin the horn to a pellicle beneath the lesion, and keep the foot immersed in a warm antiseptic bath, which will have a hyperæmic and softening effect, promoting separation of the slough and facilitating the penetration of the antiseptic solution. When the bath is not being used, envelop the foot in moist antiseptic compresses. When the slough has separated healing ensues rapidly, provided that the joint has not been opened, when the case is incurable.

Fracture of the Os Pedis

ETIOLOGY.—Fracture of the os pedis may be caused by violent concussion, or by crushing of the foot by a heavy object failing on or by the wheel of a heavy vehicle passing over it. Rarefying ostitis of the bone predisposes to the accident. Partial fracture may result from the penetration of a nail or other sharp rigid substance through the sole of the foot.

SYMPTOMS comprise sudden and severe lameness and evidence of severe inflammation in the foot, characterised by pain on palpation of the coronet, percussion of the hoof, as well as on torsion of the terminal phalanx. When there is an open wound with exposure of the bone the fracture may be obvious, but otherwise the diagnosis cannot be certain without the aid of X-rays, although the history of the case is strong evidence in favour of fracture. Crepitation can seldom be detected.

TREATMENT is that for a contusion, comprising rest and antiphlogistic applications. When there is an open wound with partial fracture of the bone, operation is indicated to remove the loose separated portion of bone.

Fracture of the Navicular Bone

Fracture of the navicular bone may be caused also by violent concussion, as may occur in jumping or prancing. Navicular disease is a predisposing cause, rendering the bone more brittle, and when neurectomy has been performed the fracture is still more prone to occur The bone has often been broken by a nail penetrating it through the plantar aspect of the foot.

SYMPTOMS are on a par with those mentioned for fracture of the os pedis.

DIAGNOSIS can only be guessed from the history of the case. Radiography is the only means of confirming it.

TREATMENT is useless, as a rule. Nothing can be done except to wait and see if recovery will supervene. When associated with a punctured wound of the foot, the case is incurable.

Wounds of the Plantar Aspect of the Foot—Picked-up Nail

ETIOLOGY.—An open wound in the plantar aspect of the foot is usually in the form of a puncture, caused by the penetration of a nail or some other sharp-pointed resistant object, such as a piece of iron, wood, or bone, or the clip of a shoe, or a piece of shrapnel, or a fragment of shell casing. The point of entrance may be in the sole or frog. When the sole is hard, concave, and free from cracks, the offending object may glide from it into the lateral lacuna and enter the foot there. In the frog the commonest seat of puncture is near its point. The bar is seldom penetrated, owing to its obliquity and hardness. The thinner and softer the horn, the greater the risk of sharp bodies passing through it into the sensitive tissues. The direction of the wound depends on the angle at which the foot meets the projecting point, and on the deviation which the latter may undergo by the weight exerted upon it. The lesion is one of the commonest affections of the foot, and is particularly frequent in horses working in places where rubbish of every kind is strewn. In military horses on active service it is the chief cause of foot trouble.

SYMPTOMS.—When the foreign body enters the horn it may not at once penetrate the sensitive tissues. This may occur from repeated force applied to it by the foot striking the ground during progression. Attention is generally first attracted by lameness, and when the foot is examined the cause of the trouble is usually discovered at once by finding the foreign body more or less firmly embedded in its plantar region. It may require a pincers to remove it from the foot. The object may, however, be broken on a level with the horn, when its situation may be recognised by a dark or abnormal spot corresponding to its distal extremity, or it may have become divided at some distance in from the surface of the horn, and require to be searched for with the hoof knife before being discovered. When it is removed the lameness may disappear; the resulting perforation in the horn may be so small that it is hardly visible. There may be some blood on the object when withdrawn, or a little hæmorrhage may appear at the orifice after its removal. When the wound is slight, it may heal at once without further symptoms. If not, and the condition has existed for some days, infection will have supervened, and there will be a purulent discharge from the wound, blackish or whitish in colour, or mixed with blood. The deep layers of the horn in the affected part will be infiltrated with moisture, yellowish, and separated from the sensitive tissues. There is severe local inflammation, causing great pain and lameness. At a later stage the tissues will be more altered, owing to the prolonged action of the organisms, causing more or less necrosis of the velvety sole or plantar cushion, and the purulent discharge will be more copious, a sinus being present.

When important deep-seated structures are involved in the necrotic or septic lesion, special symptoms are manifested according to the nature of the complication. If the os pedis undergoes necrosis, there will be a profuse escape of blood-stained pus, and a probe passed into the sinus will come in contact with the bone. The plantar aponeurosis may become necrotic, causing a constant purulent discharge until the affected portion is removed. Should the synovial sheath be opened, there will be a purulent synovial discharge and an inflammatory swelling will form in the hollow of the heel at the level of the sheath. The navicular bone may be ulcerated on its tendinous aspect or completely fractured. The interosseous ligament may be destroyed, allowing infection into the joint, setting up arthritis, which becomes evident by a prominent coronary swelling, with perhaps abscesses, which, on bursting, discharge offensive purulent synovia and persist as fistulæ until the horse dies from septicæmia or toxæmia, or is destroyed, the case being hopeless. Lameness is always well marked in connection with these deep-seated complications, which may prevent any weight being borne by the affected limb.

DIAGNOSIS is easy after removing the shoe and paring the foot.

PROGNOSIS depends on the part affected and on the nature of the injury. Taking the plantar region of the foot as being composed of an anterior, middle, and posterior region, the most serious part to be perforated in a more or less upright direction is the middle region, because most of the important structures of the foot are situated directly above it. After it comes the anterior region, in which the os pedis may be injured. The posterior region is made up practically entirely of the plantar cushion, lesions of which are comparatively benign, being always followed by recovery when rationally treated. When the case is seen early, before complications have arisen, the latter may be prevented by careful treatment. All the septic lesions of the foot arising in the manner described respond to treatment, except arthritis, extensive disease of the os pedis, and fracture of the navicular bone. The degree of lameness and the temperature of the patient are guides as to the gravity of the condition. The lameness, however, may be extremely severe, no weight being borne by the affected limb, and yet the case may be amenable to treatment—for example, septic synovitis of the small sesamoidean sheath causes alarming lameness, but when it is properly treated recovery ensues. When arthritis supervenes or when the navicular bone is fractured the case is incurable, but superficial ulceration of the cartilaginous surface of the bone may be treated successfully.

TREATMENT.—An injection of antitetanic serum is indicated at once. The treatment in a recent case, before suppuration has had time to ensue, is that of an ordinary open wound. Having extracted the wounding body, thin the horn round the orifice of the wound over an area of the diameter of half a crown or a crown to facilitate the escape of discharge should it form, to relieve pressure on the injured region, and to allow the antiseptic lotion to come into contact with the wound. It is a good and common practice to pour into the latter a little pure carbolic acid or pure creolin, which ensures the destruction of any bacteria that are present, and causes no ill-effects from the superficial destruction of tissue which it produces. Afterwards protect the wound with an antiseptic dressing of iodoform and cotton-wool, or a moist antiseptic compress kept in position by a bandage and boot, or by strips of hoop-iron or a metal plate inserted between the shoe and the hoof. Remove this dressing the following day, and immerse the foot for at least half an hour in a warm antiseptic bath, after which reapply the dressing. Continue the foot-baths daily until the horse goes sound. Should the wound be fairly large and the sensitive tissues exposed, excessive granulations are likely to form from the irritation caused by the edges of the surrounding horn, and it will be necessary to remove them with the knife, if large, or, if smaller, by the application of a caustic, such as powdered sulphate of zinc, perchloride of mercury, or sulphate of copper, or formalin 1–40. When the wound is cicatrised and covered by horn, put on a dressing of tar and tow covered with a leather or metal sole.

In slight cases where the wound is superficial, one or two applications of an antiseptic dressing are generally sufficient. When the lesion is of some standing and discharging pus, it must be treated as a sinus by adopting measures to provide for drainage, to remove necrotic tissue, and destroy the bacteria which have invaded the affected part. Paring the horn round the seat of injury and removing it entirely where it is underrun, followed by the use of the antiseptic foot-bath once or twice daily and an antiseptic dressing in the meantime, often prove effective in the course of a few days. Should this procedure fail, it may be concluded that there is necrotic tissue in the wound requiring removal. This may be effected by the use of a caustic, or the hot iron, or by surgical interference (see p. 467).

Sprain of the Corono-pedal Joint

Sprain of this joint ensues when its lateral ligaments are distended as the result of a false step, slipping, or falling.

SYMPTOMS.—There is a varying degree of lameness, appearing suddenly after the accident mentioned. During rest the foot is held forward in a state of semi-flexion. To examine the joint, let an assistant lift the foot and hold the pastern firmly and horizontally while the examiner practises torsion of the joint by grasping the hoof in the two hands. In the case of sprain this causes the horse to evince pain, which is also revealed on pressure of the coronet in the region of the quarters. Afterwards abnormal heat can be detected in the foot and at the coronet, and the latter may be more or less swollen. In slight cases the lameness gradually subsides, and recovery may be complete in the course of a month. When the joint is very severely sprained synovitis and the formation of exostoses may ensue.

TREATMENT is as usual for sprains in general.

Osteo-periostitis of the Pedal Bone

This may ensue from a trauma, but a primary form of the condition also occurs affecting chiefly the fore-feet, where it would appear to be the result of repeated concussion, to which they are more subject than the hind-feet. Anything favouring concussion is therefore concerned with its etiology, such as fast work on hard ground, boxy contracted feet, absence of frog pressure, and the use of high-heeled shoes. To these may be added an inherent defect in the bone, whereby it is predisposed to inflammation. It may also occur during the course of an infectious disease. The lesion is characterised at first by the bone becoming rarefied, appearing more porous than normally. Later, the bone may become denser and harder than normal, and little conical excrescences appear on its surface and penetrate the overlying tissues. The most constant change in the bone is rarefaction, affecting chiefly its antero-inferior portion. The phalanx eventually becomes deformed, undergoing atrophy to a varying extent. Its solar aspect may become flat or convex, and its articular surface lowered. Osteo-periostitis involving the pyramidal process is seen chiefly in the hind-foot, and predisposes to fracture of the eminence. It may be associated here with the formation of osteophytes, invading the tendon of the extensor pedis, where they are recognised by the hard swelling to which they give rise.

When the malady is localised at the level of the semilunar crest, the nodosities formed there penetrate the plantar aponeurosis, interfering with its movement, and causing symptoms similar to those of navicular disease, which in some cases is an accompanying lesion Beneath the velvety sole the disease may cause a bony enlargement. The wings of the os pedis are probably the commonest seat of bony deposits, causing increase in size of the basilar and retrosal processes. From these the process of ossification may extend to the lateral cartilages, which then also become enlarged and constitute "*side-bones*." When these osseous excrescences form beneath the heels, they cause compression of the soft tissues between the bone and the horn, producing ecchymotic spots or staining of the horn, which is known in the heel region as a "*corn*." In the same way the parietal horn may be found discoloured on paring into its depth.

Symptoms.—There is lameness, which at first is intermittent, disappearing when the horse is rested, and returning when the animal is put to work on hard ground, being due to compression of the soft tissues between the bone and the hoof. The local symptoms include abnormal heat, pain on percussion, staining of the horn in certain regions as mentioned, and swelling, due to enlargement of the pyramidal process, or of the alæ of the os pedis when those parts are involved. When work is continued, the heels gradually increase in height, the coronet becomes horizontal, and the horse commences to knuckle at the fetlock. Sometimes the hoof becomes elongated antero-posteriorly, as in a case of chronic laminitis. Many cases of obscure lameness are due to the condition under consideration, and its diagnosis is not easy, as the local symptoms are not always obvious or characteristic. Although the use of a local anæsthetic confines the lesion to the foot, it does not distinguish it from navicular disease, with which it has many points in common.

PROGNOSIS.—The disease is generally incurable.

TREATMENT is that for acute or chronic inflammation, according to the duration of the affection. Smith's operation always deserves a trial (see p. 471). Neurectomy is usually necessary.

Navicular Disease

Navicular disease is due to chronic ostitis of the navicular bone, associated usually with chronic synovitis of the navicular bursa and inflammation of the plantar aponeurosis. The condition is practically confined to the fore-feet, affecting both as a rule. The hind-feet are rarely affected. The most noticeable change in the navicular bone is the presence of ulcers on its tendinous aspect, appearing as outcuts in the cartilage thereon. Osteophytes may also form on this surface, especially near its extremities. The articular aspect remains intact. Owing to the rarefaction of the bone, it becomes weak and brittle, and may fracture under the body-weight, especially if the foot is brought violently to the ground. Adhesion may occur between the bone and the tendon as the result of fibrinous synovitis. The tendon sometimes becomes fibrillated from friction against the roughened posterior surface of the bone.

ETIOLOGY.—The real exciting cause of the disease is obscure, but the circumstances under which it most commonly occurs are well known. It is most common in light horses, especially those doing fast work on hard roads, particularly when they are not getting regular exercise, but are subjected to rapid work occasionally after more or less prolonged rest in the stable. Cart-horses are rarely affected. An hereditary tendency to the malady is believed to exist in certain breeds of horses of the roadster type, but it is also common in hunters.

The disease usually attacks the horse when he is in his prime, about seven years old, but it may appear even at the age of two years, before the animal has been put to work. The conformation of the foot has been looked upon as a factor in the production of the disease, which most commonly occurs in narrow, upright, or contracted feet. The cause in this case, however, may be confounded with the effect, for when the disease has been in existence for some time it tends to produce this conformation. The disease is usually gradual in its onset and insidious in its appearance, being generally well established before the symptoms are sufficiently developed to attract the serious attention of the owner. Rarely it appears suddenly as the result of shock on the foot, as may occur during jumping, or prancing in a fresh horse, or from making a false step. The cause might be of a toxic nature, resulting from rheumatism or some infectious disease like strangles or influenza. The absence of frog pressure, preventing the action of the anti-concussion mechanism of the foot, is undoubtedly a contributing cause of the affection. Hence a defective system of shoeing, such as the application of thick-heeled shoes or those furnished with calkins, on horses engaged in fast work on hard ground favours the onset of the condition, as does also a long toe and a sloping pastern by throwing excessive weight on the posterior region of the foot.

SYMPTOMS.—The first symptom, as a rule, to attract attention is the horse pointing his foot when at rest, and as both feet are usually involved he points them alternately. Afterwards the animal is observed to go tender occasionally, but when given a rest for a few days he goes sound again. As time passes the lameness becomes decided, and is characterised by the horse taking a short stride, going on the toe, with a tendency to stumble when the toe strikes the ground. The gait is pottering or groggy, and the seat of lameness appears to be the shoulders, on account of the shortened stride. The lameness is most marked on starting after resting for a while, and diminishes with exercise. It is more pronounced on hard than on soft ground, and is intensified by frog pressure and by the use of thin shoes, which have not the same effect in breaking the shock on the feet as thick shoes. When the disease is well established the lameness is continuous. When the horse is turning, he screws round on his fore-feet instead of lifting them. Hence probably the term " Screw " sometimes applied to such a horse. The local symptoms comprise the alterations in the form of the foot, which becomes " boxy "—that is, contracted and high at the heels, with a very concave sole—deep lateral lacunæ and an atrophied frog, some swelling in the hollow of the heel due to distension of the navicular bursa—not a constant symptom—some pain perhaps, on percussion of the frog, and abnormal heat on palpation, only noticeable, as a rule, after a long journey. The form of the foot is not always altered. It may be perfectly normal in shape.

In rare cases in which the affection is sudden in appearance the lameness is severe from the beginning. When the hind-foot is affected the horse rests it more than usual, and during progression goes on the toe. If both hind-feet are affected, the lameness is characterised by stiffness of the posterior limbs. When the condition has been in existence for some time, the muscles of the shoulder undergo atrophy and the foot becomes more contracted, both changes being due to the prolonged restricted use of the limb.

Diagnosis is made from the case history, the changes in the foot, and the nature of the lameness. It must be remembered, however, that the foot may be perfect in form, and yet affected with navicular disease. Local anæsthesia may be used to locate the seat of lameness.

Pryer and Oxspring in England have done much good work in the use of X-rays in the diagnosis of navicular disease and have demonstrated their reliability in this respect in the hands of an expert. The ordinary practitioner, however, would often have difficulty in deciding whether the shadows depicted on the plate represented lesions of navicular disease or were due to other effects.

Prognosis is bad, because once the disease is established it is incurable, and the best that can be hoped for is that the horse will prove useful, for a reasonable time after the performance of neurectomy. Adhesion of the perforans tendon to the navicular bone has been spoken of as a favourable termination to the disease by arresting the movement of the tendon on the roughened surface of the bone. Despite this, however, the lameness persists.

Treatment.—Veterinarians of the old school claimed that they cured navicular disease by bleeding from the jugular, by purgation, by applying poultices to the feet, and by giving prolonged rest, especially on a marshy pasture; also by the insertion of a frog seton passed through the plantar cushion from the hollow of the heel to the point of the frog just behind the plantar aponeurosis, and left in position for about three weeks and cleaned daily, its object being to favour union between the navicular bone and the perforans tendon. Grooving the contracted hooves and applying light shoes are said to have a good effect. The former usually has a palliative effect by relieving pressure on the inflamed region, but the light shoes can only be beneficial in favouring frog pressure and acting as a preventative rather than a curative agent. Many of the so-called cures were cases of temporary improvement or mistaken diagnosis, for it is now universally admitted that in a true case of the disease cure is out of the question, and that the only means of rendering the horse workable is to perform neurectomy. Digital neurectomy is usually sufficient, but sometimes at a variable period afterwards lameness recurs, due apparently to inflammation spreading above the seat of operation, when it is necessary to do either double plantar or median neurectomy. The latter frequently has the desired effect, and should therefore be tried first, as it does not deprive the foot entirely of its innervation (see p. 444).

Canker

Looking upon the integument of the foot as a modified portion of the skin, canker may be defined as a chronic, hypertrophic, moist, eczematous dermatitis, a definition which answers the description of the disease in its most typical form. The condition is not so common now as formerly, owing apparently to the advance of hygiene in connection with the care of horses, for it is generally admitted that the affection is greatly favoured by dirty surroundings, keeping horses in dirty, ill-drained stables with the feet constantly in contact with litter soiled with fæces and saturated with urine, which macerates the horn and exposes the sensitive tissues to injury and infection, which may be a predisposing, if it is not an exciting, cause of the disease. This theory is also borne out by the fact that it is the hind-feet which are most commonly affected. Marshy localities seem to have a determining influence on the malady, as it is certainly more often found there than in upland districts. It is more common in the East Midlands of England than in other parts of the country. It occurs more frequently in coarse-bred, phlegmatic subjects than in the finer breeds.

It is generally believed that there is an hereditary tendency to the disease, and it is looked upon by many as a local manifestation of a constitutional affection, like other skin eruptions. The disease presents features which are suggestive of its being of an infectious nature, but so far no specific organism has been found in connection with it. Spirochætes and various forms of bacteria have been found in the lesions, but the disease could never be set up experimentally by any of them. Canker may remain localised on one foot for a long time, and then attack successively the other feet, and after being apparently cured it may break out again. It begins either as a sort of " grease " or moist eczema in the skin at the back of the pastern or beneath the horn. In the former case the affection gradually encroaches on the subcorneal tissue, whilst in the latter case it commences insidiously, and may remain unsuspected for a long time, until the separated horn is removed with the farrier's knife or is worn by use. It is the middle lacuna of the frog which first shows symptoms of the disease, as a rule, the affection spreading from there with more or less rapidity beneath the branches of the frog to the lateral lacunæ, and thence to the sole, from which it may extend under the wall to the coronet.

Symptoms.—When a considerable area of the foot is involved and the disease is well established, the symptoms are very characteristic. The horn overlying the affected part is separated (under-run), more or less ragged, and sodden with moisture, having the appearance in the case of white horn of having been soaked in oil. In an advanced case the horn is absent and the lesion of the sensitive tissues is exposed. They appear to be affected with chronic inflammation, being covered with a whitish caseous exudation having a very fœtid odour, and showing in places vegetations or hypertrophied papillæ or finger-like processes, which in old-standing lesions may be capped with horn, constituting what are known as ergots. The foul-smelling caseous material also forms between the vegetations and ergots. There is evidently no acute inflammation, as a rule, because lameness is frequently absent even in a well-marked case, and when it is present it may be the result of a contusion of the exposed sensitive structures. In bad cases where the os pedis is exposed, either as the result of the disease or injudicious treatment, the lameness is very pronounced, and when the laminæ are involved it may also be well marked.

Diagnosis is generally easy. The appearance of the lesion is diagnostic—viz., the underrun and sodden horn, the discharge, the vegetations, the ergots, and the very penetrating offensive odour. Wherever the horn is adherent the disease is absent.

Prognosis depends on the extent of the disease and the number of feet affected. It has no tendency to undergo spontaneous cure; on the contrary, it is progressive in its course. Except treatment is carried out with great pains and very thorough measures are adopted it will fail to have the desired effect. Sometimes, when it is almost cured, discontinuing the treatment causes it to break out afresh. When all the feet are badly affected, it is hardly worth treating. Nevertheless, when the malady is not too extensive or far gone, does not extend beneath the wall, and the os pedis is not exposed, proper treatment generally effects a cure within an average period of six weeks, and within two or more weeks of this time the horse may be working.

Treatment.—The exact cause not being known, the veterinarian is at the disadvantage of not being able to remove it, but he can avail himself of his knowledge of the admitted predisposing causes to avoid them as far as possible in combating the affection. Experience has shown that the principles of treatment which have given the best results are as follows :

1. After removing the loose horn, thoroughly cleansing and disinfecting the affected foot by enveloping it in antiseptic compresses for twenty-four hours, excise the ergots and vegetations, when present.

2. Apply to the affected part a caustic, an astringent, or merely an antiseptic, according to the nature of the lesion.

3. Exert firm pressure on the affected region by means of twisted pledgets of tow firmly compressed by the aid of a metal sole fixed to the shoe or by strips of hoop-iron inserted between the shoe and the hoof.

4. Attend to the general health of the patient and prescribe arsenic or one of its preparations, to be administered daily for a while at intervals until the disease is cured.

5. Removal of the vegetations and ergots is necessary to bring the affected part on a level with the normal tissues. Care must be taken in so doing not to expose the pedal bone, and in operating on the frog to follow its configuration, and not mutilate it unnecessarily. It is also advisable to thin the normal horn for a short distance beyond the periphery of the affected region to facilitate equalising the distribution of pressure, and to prevent irritation of the sensitive tissues by the edges of the horn.

6. Nearly all the common caustic and astringent drugs in the pharmacopœia have been recommended by different authorities for application to the diseased surface. Probably any of these is as efficacious as another, success depending rather upon the method of application than upon the agent employed. The following applications have been lauded by different practitioners : Nitric acid, sulphuric acid, pure or mixed with alum (Plasse's paste), hydrochloric acid, butyr of antimony, carbolic acid, acetate and sulphate of copper, creosote, salicylic acid, formalin, Czerney's solution (arsenic 1, methylated spirit 40, water 40), a mixture of carbide of calcium, iodoform, acetate of copper, and starch, a mixture of the three sulphates of copper, zinc, and iron, and powdered chinosol, etc.

With each of the foregoing topics success has been obtained, while failure has also been recorded, and one can hardly be said to possess more virtues than another. The hot iron is also strongly recommended by many veterinary surgeons as having an excellent effect when its edge is passed lightly over the affected region before applying an astringent dressing, such as the three sulphates as recommended by Malcolm and others. After the diseased surface has been sloughed away apply an antiseptic powder, such as iodoform, or a mixture of it with starch and oxide of zinc, or powdered chinosol. As the cases progress favourably, avoid the frequent use of caustics, and depend chiefly on antiseptic powder associated with pressure.

7. In arranging for pressure, take precautions to have it firm and equally distributed. The pledgets of tow should be in the form of hard cords of assorted sizes for adaptation to the different parts of the foot, care being taken that the lacunæ of the frog are well packed with rolls of corresponding shape and size. Apply a series of large thick pledgets on the outside. Bring pressure on the tow either by means of pieces of hoop-iron bent in the form of a bow to permit of their ends being introduced beneath the foot surface of the shoe, where they are driven in by striking the convexity with a hammer, or by a metal sole driven in from behind between the shoe and the hoof or screwed on to the sole of the shoe. The strips of iron are more satisfactory than a metal sole. To carry out these measures thoroughly it is generally necessary to have the horse fixed in stocks or cast, and when vegetations have to be removed general anæsthesia is advisable. The case should be dressed daily for a while until considerable improvement occurs, when the intervals between the dressings are gradually extended until once per week proves sufficient, the surgeon being guided by the state of the lesion. If lameness be absent it is an advantage to keep the horse working. During the early stages of the treatment, the severity of the dressings and the great pressure exerted on the exposed sensitive tissues may cause some lameness and necessitate keeping the horse idle for a while. Working on dry clay favours recovery, and may be sufficient of itself to effect a cure should it be possible to continue it for a long period.

8. The administration of arsenic has long been known as beneficial in the treatment of the affection, and comparatively recently the late Major Holmes, R.A.V.C., found, when treating surra in India with a course of arsenic, that those animals which happened to be affected with canker at the same time were cured of the latter disease by this treatment. In the United Kingdom, however, it has not proved a specific.

Nairn (Blairgowrie) claims to have got excellent results with the following application in the form of a paste :

Creta Prep.	℥iii.
Plumbi Nit.	℥i.
Formalin	ʒii.
Ol Rapii	qs.

He has found cases affecting the perioplic ring causing a "groggy" gait and effected a cure by rasping down the separated horn at the coronet and applying the paste (*Veterinary Record*, Vol. 11, No. 6). He insists that the dressing must be thoroughly carried out.

Corns

A corn is a contusion of the sensitive tissues at the heel in the angle between the wall and the bar, the structure affected being the sensitive tissue of the sole, wall, or bar. The condition is most common in horses working in cities. In an ordinary recent or dry corn there is merely an escape of blood from the injured vessels, causing more or less staining or ecchymosis of the overlying horn in a punctiform, linear, or diffuse manner. If the cause be repeated, the condition becomes aggravated and the inflammation becomes more severe, but remains aseptic so long as there is no breach in the horn to allow the entrance of infection. When the contusion is severe, the horn in the affected part becomes infiltrated with serum or the latter may accumulate beneath the horn, giving rise in either case to a "*moist corn.*" When infection ensues through an accidental fissure in the horn, or as the result of excessive paring of it, the lesion suppurates, and a *suppurating* or *festered* corn is produced. The corn is said to be *complicated* when it is accompanied by necrosis of any of the tissues in the vicinity, such as the laminæ, the plantar cushion, the plantar aponeurosis, or the lateral cartilage.

Etiology.—Corns are very rare in unshod feet. Consequently, shoeing is blamed as the primary cause of the affection. Any defect in shoeing which results in excessive pressure being brought to bear on the seat of corn favours the latter. Fitting the shoe very close on the inside to avoid the risk of brushing may have this effect, and the frequency with which this is done probably accounts for corns being more common in the inner heel. Faulty conformation of the limbs, causing unequal distribution of weight on the foot, is a predisposing cause, and it is for this reason that a corn is more often present in the outer heel when the toe is turned in. Interference with the anti-concussion mechanism, such as is caused by atrophy of the frog, high-heeled shoes preventing the frog reaching the ground, high contracted heels preventing expansion of the posterior region of the foot, upright pasterns causing increased concussion on the bony column of the limb, favours the production of the lesion. Fast work on hard roads, especially in the case of heavy horses, is a fruitful source of contusion of the heels if the shoeing is not carefully attended to.

That concussion is a prime factor in producing corns is proved by the fact that they are very rare in the hind-feet, while they are very common in the fore-feet, where concussion is greater. Wide spreading feet with low weak heels are very likely to become affected, owing to the horn affording insufficient protection to the sensitive tissues of the region where the shock is greatest. Leaving the shoes on too long causes them to be drawn forwards by the growing wall, and may thus result in their heels being brought to bear on the seat of corn and to give rise to the affection. A stone accidentally fixed between the heel of the shoe and the frog may cause a bruise in this situation.

SYMPTOMS.—A corn during the acute stage is characterised by local symptoms of a contusion, with more or less acute inflammation, and by a varying degree of lameness. The local phenomena are in accordance with the nature of the lesion. Pain is evinced on percussion and compression of the affected heel. Abnormal heat is revealed on palpation. In the case of a dry corn, paring the horn in the affected region discloses the staining of its deeper layers, varying from a glassy yellowish appearance to a deep red tinge, occupying an area of varying dimensions in different cases. In a moist corn the overlying horn is infiltrated with serum, which makes it moist in its deeper parts, or the liquid may accumulate beneath it and escape when an exit is made with the knife. When suppuration supervenes the inflammation is very intense, and if the pus is not allowed to escape by removing the horn which confines it, it will extend upwards to the coronet and become discharged through the medium of an abscess. The pain is very acute until the pus gets an outlet, when it is greatly relieved. When a sinus persists it is due to necrosis of some of the tissues in the region, caused by the bacteria present, and a probe passed into it will give an idea of the depth of the lesion and of the part affected.

Quittor is a common sequel to suppurating corn, and is very likely to ensue after the pus has reached the coronet, and when it does supervene in this case the orifice of the first abscess between hair and hoof does not constitute the opening of the quittor, which forms at a higher level by the bursting of a secondary abscess after the primary one has healed. The sinus may also abut on the plantar aponeurosis or on the os pedis. The lameness varies in degree, according to the nature of the local lesion. In a well-marked case the horse goes on his toe with the heels clear of the ground, and when standing points the affected foot, resting it only on the toe. When both feet are involved the animal has a pottering gait, and at rest points the two feet alternately. In " suppurating " corn the lameness is extreme until vent is given to the pus. In an old-standing case of corn in which the pain and lameness have disappeared, the only indication of the lesion will be the discoloration revealed on paring the horn.

DIAGNOSIS is easily made out from the symptoms. The changes in the horn at the seat of corn are characteristic.

PROGNOSIS.—A simple contusion is of little or no consequence, lameness being slight or perhaps absent. When the contusion is more severe the case is more serious, causing pronounced lameness, which may persist for a considerable time. Purulent corn is serious on account of the troublesome complications to which it may give rise. Once a corn is established, recurrent lameness is apt to ensue. Hence it is an unsoundness.

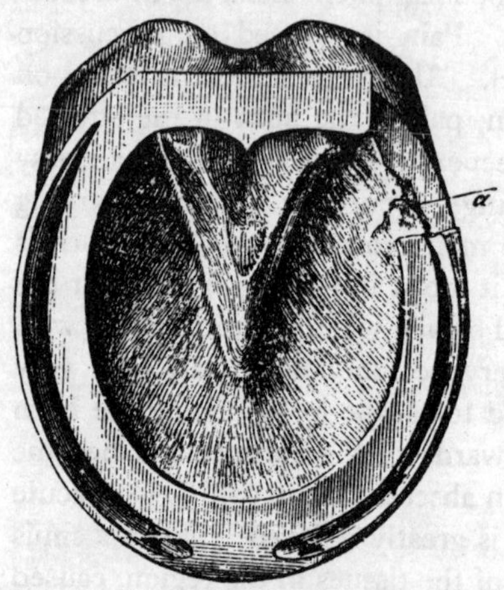

FIG. 397.—THREE-QUARTER BAR SHOE. *a*, Seat of the corn.

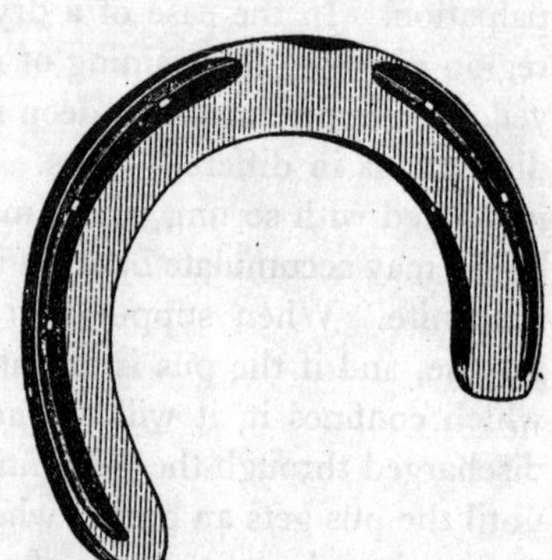

FIG. 398.—ORDINARY THREE-QUARTER SHOE.

TREATMENT consists in removing the cause and adopting the usual methods for dealing with inflammation, or an abscess, or a sinus, as the case may be. Removal of the offending shoe may be all that is necessary. Paring the horn over the corn has a decidedly good effect in relieving tension on the affected part, but care must be exercised not to overdo it by wounding the sensitive tissues and causing the risk of infection. When suppuration supervenes, a free exit must be made for the pus by removing the underrun horn, and the foot should be immersed in an antiseptic bath for half an hour to an hour morning and evening until the discharge ceases, the lesion being protected in the meantime by an antiseptic compress or a dry dressing. The wound in the sensitive tissues usually granulates excessively, owing to the irritation caused by the edges of the cut horn. The exuberant granulations must be removed with the knife or caustic, the wound being afterwards treated with an astringent or slight caustic to prevent recurrence. When suppuration has extended upwards beneath the wall, it is advisable to remove a ʌ-shaped portion of the wall to ensure the escape of the pus. Complications must be treated according to their nature, the principles of treatment being those of a sinus. When the wound following a suppurating corn has healed and is covered with horn, and in all cases where the horse is going sound, a shoe having no bearing on the affected region and a leather sole with tar and tow should be applied. An ordinary shoe with the wall shortened so as not to bear on it at the affected heel, or a shoe truncated or excavated on its foot surface, or a bar shoe with the bar resting on the frog, or a three-quarter bar shoe, the iron being omitted opposite the seat of corn, may be used.

Pricks in Shoeing

A prick or wound caused by driving a nail into the sensitive tissues in the act of nailing on a shoe is of two kinds—viz., (1) where the offending nail is withdrawn immediately after being driven, and (2) where it is not withdrawn. Another variety of the lesion similar to the second one is caused by an old stump remaining in the wall since the previous shoeing, being driven into the subcorneal tissues by the force of the newly-driven nail, which comes in contact with it.

ETIOLOGY.—The accident is favoured by several circumstances, such as:

1. *Contraction of the hoof*, rendering the wall less oblique, and thereby making the nail more likely to take an inward course.

2. *Thinness of the horn*, which accounts for pricking being more common in the inner than in the outer quarter of the foot.

3. *Want of skill* on the part of the doorman in failing to drive the nail properly.

4. *Faulty workmanship* in making the shoe, stamping the holes too coarse or too oblique, causing the nails, when driven, to be diverted towards the sensitive laminæ.

5. *Badly-shaped nails*, the malformation making the nail take a wrong course.

6. *Restiveness* of the horse, resulting in the animal violently snatching his foot from the shoer when the nail is only partly driven, and stamping the foot with great force on the ground and forcing the nail into the flesh. The lesion is more common in hind- than in fore-feet, due

probably to the fact that the horn is more upright behind than in front, and that the hind-foot is often more difficult to control than the fore-foot.

During the busy time when horses are being roughed for frost, the hurried way in which shoes are put on after being removed may lead to pricking. The amount of damage done by the nail will, of course, vary according to the depth of the injury and the part affected. The nail may merely touch the sensitive laminæ, or it may wound or even fracture the pedal bone.

SYMPTOMS.—During the process of shoeing it may be recognised that the nail is being wrongly driven by (*a*) the sound of the hammering, which, instead of becoming clearer, becomes duller, due to the nail entering the soft tissues ; (*b*) the nail meeting with less resistance

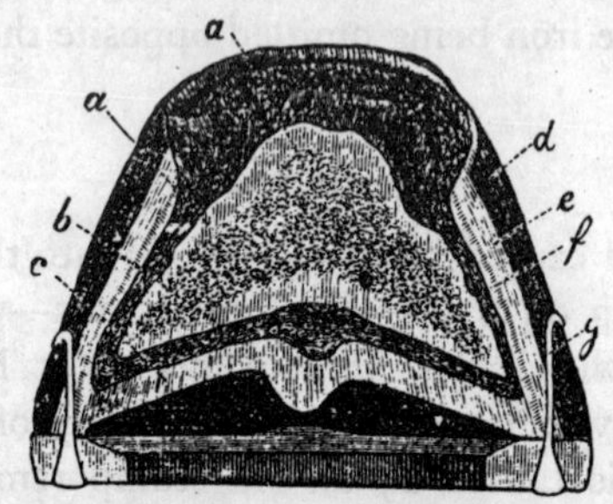

FIG. 399.—CROSS-SECTION OF A SOUND AND WELL-SHOD HOOF, SHOWING THE PROPER POSITION OF THE NAILS.

a, Pedal bone ; *b*, sensitive sole ; *c*, horny sole ; *d*, horn wall ; *e*, dark-coloured outer layer of wall ; *f*, laminal sheath ; *g*, nails.

as it penetrates deeply, showing that it is not taking an outward course towards the hard surface of the wall ; (*c*) resentment of the horse, which snatches away the limb suddenly ; (*d*) blood appearing on the nail when it is withdrawn or oozing from the orifice in the horn. The blood, however, may be wiped off the nail in its passage through the horn, and the hole in the latter may close by its walls falling into contact, thus preventing the escape of blood. The flinching of the horse may be prevented by the use of a twitch or ascribed to temperament in a fidgety animal. A simple prick, where the nail is immediately withdrawn and the nail-hole left vacant, is usually of no consequence, but when the nail is left more or less embedded in the soft tissues, lameness supervenes immediately or may be delayed for a day or perhaps several days.

The DIAGNOSIS of the cause of the lameness is easy. The horse having been recently shod, irregularity of the clenches, one or more being unusually high, and perhaps the absence of a nail, arouse suspicion which is confirmed by examination of the foot revealing symptoms of inflammation at the seat of injury. Pain is evinced on percussion, and abnormal heat is felt on palpation. Cutting the clench of the offending nail and traction on the corresponding branch of the shoe in removing it are resented by the patient. When the nail which caused the injury is withdrawn, it is seen to be black from the action of the sulphur of the horn on the iron. A greyish-whitish or blackish discharge escapes from the hole in the horn. When the nail-bed is pared out it is found to be surrounded by soft, blackish horn, infiltrated with the purulent discharge, and more or less separated from the subcorneal tissue.

PROGNOSIS.—A simple slight prick of the sensitive tissues in which the nail is at once extracted and omitted is usually of no consequence, neither pain nor lameness supervening. The other form of prick caused by the nail being left inserted in the sensitive laminæ may have serious consequences, such as diffuse inflammation of the foot, or necrosis of the horn-secreting structures, the os pedis, or the lateral cartilage.

TREATMENT.—When the prick has been discovered during the shoeing it is usually sufficient to leave the corresponding nail-hole vacant, but to prevent the possibility of infection a little antiseptic solution may be poured into the orifice, or the latter may be closed by collodion, or a red-hot nail may be passed rapidly into the hole in the horn and quickly withdrawn to act as a germicide. This is a common practice with farriers. Should a severe wound be inflicted, the horn all round the track of the nail should be thinned to favour the exit of discharge in case any may form as the result of infection of the wound, which should be prevented as far as possible by antiseptic applications, such as a little pure or strong solution of carbolic or creolin passed into the orifice, or the use of a foot-bath. No lameness may ensue; if it does, the treatment should be continued, and the horse kept at rest until it disappears. In the case where inflammation and suppuration have taken place before the condition is detected, or as a sequel to infection in the first case, the shoe must be removed, the horn thinned in the vicinity of the affected region, and the foot immersed in an antiseptic bath for half an hour to an hour morning and evening until the discharge ceases and the lameness disappears, the part being protected in the meantime by an antiseptic dressing kept in position by a boot or poultice bag. When suppuration is extensive beneath the wall, it is advisable to remove a portion of the latter to provide free drainage and relieve pressure on the inflamed area. There is usually no difficulty with the case when treated on these lines, provided that some of the complications mentioned have not arisen, when special measures may be required according to the case, as described elsewhere. When the horse is sound, a dressing of tar and tow should be applied over the seat of the lesion, and kept in position by a leather sole. The animal is then fit to go to work.

Nail Binding

The condition known as " nail binding " is that caused by driving a nail or nails too close to the sensitive laminæ without wounding them, but causing more or less pain or discomfort by pressure thereon. It most commonly occurs in feet with a thin crust.

SYMPTOMS.—The affection is manifested by cramped action or lameness, which is usually slight, and by symptoms of mild local inflammation—viz., pain on percussion or compression, and some abnormal heat on palpation of the affected part.

TREATMENT.—Removal of the shoe and the application of cold or hot compresses for two or three days have the desired effect. A prick is generally suspected, and if care is not exercised in searching for it the sensitive tissues may be wounded and infected, complicating the condition.

Bruised Sole

Contusion of the sole may be caused by treading heavily on a projecting or loose stone, or by a badly-fitting or displaced shoe. The bearing surface of the hoof on the shoe should be confined to the wall, the white line, and a narrow strip of the sole where it adjoins the wall.

The SYMPTOMS and TREATMENT are similar to those described for " corns."

Contracted Hoof

A contracted hoof is one whose wall has become contracted or shrunken in one or more situations, usually in the regions of the quarter and heel on one or both sides of the foot. The condition is more common in the fore- than in the hind-foot.

ETIOLOGY.—Anything causing dryness or brittleness of the horn, or which prevents expansion of the hoof, favours its contraction—for example :

1. *Injudicious use of the rasp*, filing the outer surface of the wall, and thereby removing the periople, which prevents evaporation and consequent dryness and shrinking of the horn, and also removing some

of the superficial horn fibres, thus exposing the deeper ones to the action of the air, and allowing them to become dry and contracted.

2. *Chronic lameness*, diminishing the activity of the foot, and consequently its expansion.

3. *Excessive paring of the frog*, causing it to become dry and contracted, and preventing its coming in contact with the ground to promote dilatation of the heel region of the foot.

4. *Mutilating the bars*, and in this way removing or weakening the buttresses or stays of the wall, and permitting it to fall inwards at the heels.

5. *Shoeing with calkins* or thick-heeled shoes, absolutely preventing the frog bearing on the ground. This want of frog pressure is probably the chief cause of the abnormality.

SYMPTOMS.—When the foot is on the ground and viewed from in front the deformity is noticed, and when unilateral the contrast between the two sides of the hoof is very striking. When looked at from the plantar aspect, the marked difference in length of the antero-posterior and transverse diameters of the hoof is observed, the former being decidedly in excess of the latter, whereas a normal fore-foot is about as broad mesially as it is long. The narrowness is most noticeable in the posterior part of the quarters and at the heels. The normal length of the hoof is not altered. The bars are less divergent posteriorly than usual, having a tendency to approach each other behind. The frog is always more or less atrophied, and the lateral lacunæ are abnormally deep. Frequently the horn is dry and brittle. Lameness may be present as the result of the contraction alone, or of the disease which gave rise to it.

PREVENTION of the deformity consists in avoiding the causes mentioned, and above all in maintaining frog pressure as far as possible by shoeing with tips or thin-heeled shoes, or by the Charlier system, even temporarily, by leaving the frog intact when preparing the hoof, and by the use of rubber pads, causing bearing on the frog when the latter is insufficiently developed to reach the ground with an ordinary shoe applied.

TREATMENT comprises: (1) Improvement of the method of shoeing, (2) the use of dilating or expanding shoes, and (3) grooving the wall to permit of its expansion.

(1) Improvement in the method of shoeing may be sufficient in slight cases, such as substituting flat shoes for those with calkins, or adopting some of the measures mentioned under the heading of prevention.

(2) The use of mechanical means to cause expansion of a contracted foot is not much in vogue, although several special shoes have been invented for the purpose, especially on the Continent. None of them is of sufficiently proved merit to deserve description. A shoe whose bearing surface, instead of being horizontal, is made to slope downwards and outwards is believed to have some effect in expanding the hoof.

(3) When the hoof is decidedly contracted, and especially if lameness is present, the best treatment is to groove the horn as described (p. 471).

Side-Bones

A side-bone is an ossified lateral cartilage.

Etiology.—The actual exciting cause of side-bones is not always clear. The ossification of the cartilage may be due to:

1. *Heredity*, as apparently obtains in draft-horses, in which side-bones are very common, without any visible external cause to account for them.

2. *A natural tendency for cartilage continuous with bone to become ossified*, as occurs in the development of bone.

3. *Concussion*, causing shock or inflammation of the bone at the base of the cartilage, stimulating proliferation of the osteoblasts, which then invade the cartilage. The prevalence of side-bones in heavy horses, their comparative rarity in light horses, and the fact that they are seldom associated with inflammation do not support this theory as a common cause of their occurrence. Anything which favours concussion would act as a cause under this heading—*e.g.*, interference with the anti-concussion mechanism of the foot, such as contracted heels and absence of frog pressure. Side-bones being practically confined to the fore-feet is evidence in favour of the concussion theory, as is also the fact that cart-horses are usually shod with calkins in front, which increase the shock on the region of the heels.

4. *Direct violence*, such as a blow, a tread, or a weight falling on the foot. Side-bone has often occurred in this way on the outer side of the inner limb of horses working in pairs.

Symptoms.—When the lateral cartilage becomes ossified it also increases in size, and in some instances assumes enormous proportions. The presence of ossification is revealed by the absence of flexibility in the structure, recognised by compressing the two structures at the same time with the fingers and thumb from above with the foot on the ground and by grasping each with the finger and thumb and trying to bend it with the foot on and off the ground. The entire cartilage is usually involved. In the early stages of the process its upper portion may not be affected. The condition is non-inflammatory, there being no evidence of pain, heat, or exudation. Side-bones *per se* are therefore not likely to be a cause of lameness, although indirectly they may act as such, especially in horses doing fast road work and in those with contracted feet, owing to their favouring concussion by preventing expansion of the posterior part of the foot, and leading to corns or compression and pain of the sensitive tissues beneath the hoof. A side-bone may be present on the inside or outside of the foot, or in both situations, and in one or both fore-limbs. It is rare in a hind-foot.

DIAGNOSIS is easy when the whole cartilage is transformed into bone, but there is sometimes difference of opinion as to whether it is partially ossified or normal, or in the former event whether it should be classified as a side-bone or not. When there is a doubt, one is justified in giving the horse the benefit of it.

PROGNOSIS.—Side-bones in horses with good open feet doing slow work are of no consequence. They are present in a large proportion of cart-horses without causing lameness. In animals intended for fast work on the road and in those with contracted feet they are serious, for the reasons stated.

TREATMENT.—If side-bones are not associated with pain or lameness no treatment is indicated. Nothing can be done to get rid of the side-bone except operation (p. 472), which is seldom desirable, and can have little or no beneficial effect except the removal of an unsightly enlargement when the structure is very prominent. Counter-irritation by blistering or firing, or both, is sometimes done on the assumption that lameness, when present, is due to chronic inflammation in the new bone. When the hoof is contracted, grooving it is indicated to permit of its expansion and relieve pressure on the subcorneal tissues (see p. 471).

Quittor

Quittor is a sinus opening on the coronet at the level of the lateral cartilage, and due to necrosis of this structure.

ETIOLOGY.—The cause of the condition may be :

1. *Injury and infection* of the cartilage, such as may result from a tread on the coronet, causing a contused or punctured open wound, which is more likely to occur when the shoes have calkins, and especially when the latter are sharpened for frost.

2. *Necrosis of the skin* in the affected region from the combined effects

of cold and septic mud, the infection spreading subsequently to the cartilage.

3. *A suppurating corn or sandcrack*, or lesion resulting from *a punctured wound or a picked-up nail*, from which suppuration extends to the cartilage.

The cartilage may be involved in an open wound without undergoing necrosis, but the latter is very likely to ensue owing to the feeble vascularity of the part, making it an easy prey to the organisms invading the wound. Once necrosis begins in the cartilage, it has a great tendency to gradually affect the whole structure on account of its poor blood supply and the close continuity of the dead and healthy parts. Spontaneous separation of the necrotic piece of cartilage may, however, take place, and should it escape with the discharge natural cure will result. This is much more likely to occur posteriorly than anteriorly, because in the former situation the cartilage is more interspersed with fibrous tissue, separating it into islets, which are comparatively easily detached.

SYMPTOMS.—The symptoms are those of a sinus, with a combination of more or less acute and chronic inflammation in its vicinity. The inflammatory swelling varies in size according to the extent of the disease. It may correspond only to a part or the whole of the cartilage. It projects beyond the level of the hoof, and bulges it outwards at the coronet. It generally begins at the heel and spreads thence forwards. It is more or less painful on manipulation, the pain being usually most marked when the antero-inferior extremity of the cartilage is affected, and being always very acute when an abscess is being formed. When the skin is unpigmented the redness due to the inflammation is noticeable, and varies in intensity according to the acuteness of the condition. The sinus has usually only one orifice on the coronet, but rarely it has two or more openings here, and they all communicate with the necrotic centre. The entrance to the sinus may be only large enough to admit a probe, and is often obscured by a mass of granulations, but it may be infundibuliform in shape. It is constantly weeping or discharging a greyish purulent fluid, which may be streaked with blood, due to rupture of some of the capillaries in the granulation tissue of the part. The calibre of the sinus varies in different cases. It may be branched. Its course is usually oblique, a common direction being downwards and forwards, terminating on the wing of the os pedis in well-established cases. When the condition is a complication of a corn or sandcrack, there may be a plantar or parietal sinus respectively, in addition to that of the coronet, or rarely the latter may be absent until the disease has been in existence for a considerable time. There may be one or more cicatrices on the skin over the swelling, representing orifices that have healed after the pus had gained exit in a new situation through the medium of a secondary abscess. Afterwards some horizontal rings or rugæ form on the wall beneath the affected part, due to the latter interfering with the secretory function of the coronary band in this region. By noticing the depth to which these extend and remembering that the horn grows at the rate of $\frac{1}{4}$ to $\frac{3}{8}$ inch per month, one can estimate approximately the duration of the affection. The degree of lameness varies according to the nature of the lesion. When the superior or posterior part of the cartilage is only affected it is slight or absent, but when the disease is in the vicinity of the antero-lateral ligament, or when the latter is involved, it is very marked. If arthritis supervene, its symptoms will be manifested.

COMPLICATIONS.—The complications which may arise are:

1. *Necrosis of the antero-lateral ligament*, which may in consequence become ulcerated, thus exposing the joint to infection.

2. *Septic arthritis* resulting from No. 1 or from perforation of the cul-de-sac of the synovial membrane of the articulation where it comes in contact with the antero-internal aspect of the cartilage, allowing infection of the joint.

3. *Necrosis of the os pedis.* Infection may spread from the cartilage to the os pedis, causing necrosis or caries thereof. If this occur near the articular surface, septic arthritis may supervene.

4. *Necrosis of the sensitive laminæ or plantar cushion*, or *plantar aponeurosis*, the latter being rare. The plantar aponeurosis is more likely to be affected when the quittor results from a suppurating corn than when it arises in some other way.

5. *An abscess*, which forms at the inner side of the cartilage and bursts on the skin.

6. *Gangrene of the skin* over the affected region.

DIAGNOSIS is generally easy on account of the circumscribed swelling at the level of the cartilage and the presence of the sinus. A probe passed into the sinus abuts on the hard cartilage. Wounds of the coronet and abscesses not involving the cartilage heal easily.

PROGNOSIS.—Quittor is an obstinate affection having practically no tendency to spontaneous cure, and often resisting ordinary therapeutic measures for months. The condition is not so serious when confined to the superior or posterior part of the cartilage, as already explained. Operative treatment is nearly always successful. Great depth of the sinus and a copious discharge of pus indicate that treatment other than operation is not likely to succeed. The presence of complications, of course, aggravates the affection. The lesion is perhaps more easily dealt with in the hind- than in the forelimb, because the cartilage is less dense and more vascular in the former.

TREATMENT.—The principles of treatment are those of a sinus, and comprise measures for the removal of the necrotic tissue, the provision of drainage for the pus, and the destruction of bacteria, with the object of causing a healthy granulating wound which will heal and bring about recovery. The method of procedure may be:

1. *The Injection of an Antiseptic Liquid* by means of a syringe with a long narrow nozzle into the depth of the sinus two or three times daily in order to flush out loose necrotic tissue, arrest the development of bacteria, render the lesion sterile, and thus allow healing to take place. This may succeed in a recent case where the sinus is not deep and the necrotic cartilage is near the surface—that is, affecting its upper or posterior border. Otherwise it is generally a failure, the affected part being too deep-seated to be effectively acted upon by the injection or to permit of the escape of necrotic material. To obtain the best result, it is necessary to enlarge the entrance to the sinus in order to facilitate reaching the affected area with the germicidal agent. The patient resents this treatment, and it is generally disappointing in its results.

2. *The Injection of a Caustic Liquid.*—This is more effective than No. 1, the agent being a more powerful germicide and having an escharotic effect, which brings about separation of necrotic tissue and the removal of the lining of the sinus, thereby opening it up and facilitating the escape of necrotic debris and purulent matter. It is carried out in the same way as No. 1, and when thoroughly done it often effects a cure within two or three weeks, the discharge becoming gradually less and the inflammation and lameness disappearing by degrees. It is, however, by no means infallible, and is contra-indicated when the sinus is deep and anteriorly situated, on account of the risk of sloughing the thin layer of tissue protecting the joint in this region and causing arthritis. Various preparations have been used with more or less success, including the following: (*a*) Corrosive sublimate 1 and alcohol 10; (*b*) corrosive sublimate 17, methylated spirit 140, hydrochloric acid 2 to 4, acetate of lead 34; (*c*) sulphate of zinc 5 to 10 per cent. solution; (*d*) chloride of zinc 5 to 10 per cent. The result depends not so much on the agent used as the manner in which it is applied to ensure its reaching the affected part. It is a painful procedure which is strongly resented by the patient.

3. *The Use of Solid Caustics*—that is, the introduction into the bottom of the sinus of a caustic in the form of a powder, or pencil, or plug, the one most commonly and successfully employed being corrosive sublimate. To allow of its deep insertion it is necessary to open up the sinus with a knife. The powder may be enveloped in blotting paper to enable it to be passed into the sinus. It has the effect of causing an eschar or slough, which comes away in the course of ten to fifteen days, carrying with it the diseased cartilage in favourable cases, and leaving a gaping granulating wound, which rapidly heals. A second application of the caustic may be necessary in some cases where a portion of the necrotic cartilage remains *in situ* after the separation of the eschar. This procedure is spoken of as the coring treatment, on account of the formation of the eschar or "core." It often fails, owing to the agent employed not "touching the spot." Used in the vicinity of the joint, it may lead to opening of the latter, with fatal consequences.

4. *The Use of the Thermo-Cautery.*—A red-hot iron rapidly plunged into the lowest part of the sinus and rapidly withdrawn has often proved effective in sloughing out its lining, including the necrotic cartilage, while at the same time it acts as a powerful bactericide. Its use is dangerous in the vicinity of the joint, on account of risk of penetrating it with the instrument, which must be inserted more or less blindly without any reliable guide as to its exact course or depth which it reaches. If not inserted deeply, it will not have the desired effect when the sinus is deep.

5. *A Combination of Nos.* 3 *and* 4, which is often employed, and proves more successful than either alone. All these caustic preparations cause severe inflammation, rendering interference with the part very painful and provocative of resentment on the part of the horse, which may become very restive and difficult to control.

6. *The Use of a Seton* or piece of tape passed into the sinus above and brought out through the wall of the hoof at the level of the bottom of the suppurating tract to ensure drainage through a counter-opening and to enable a caustic applied on the seton to be brought into contact with all parts of the lesion, a method of treatment which has often proved efficacious.

7. *The Bier Treatment* alone or combined with one of the foregoing methods. Very favourable reports have been given of its efficacy. It should always be tried (see p. 260).

8. *Operation to remove the Cartilage.*—See p. 460.

Acute Laminitis

Acute inflammation of the sensitive laminæ may occur in all the feet or in both fore- or both hind-feet, or in one foot, but never in only two diagonal or two lateral feet.

Etiology.—This comprises (1) predisposing causes, (2) exciting causes.

(1) *Predisposing Causes.*—These include :

(*a*) *Heavy Body-Weight*, big, heavy horses or those whose bodies seem too heavy for their limbs, like fat ponies and idle heavy stallions, being likely subjects.

(*b*) *Unfit Condition.*—Horses being left in the stable for days, without or with insufficient exercise, and then made to go a long journey, often become affected at the end of the latter. Young horses put to work for the first time are apt to suffer from the disease if made to do more work than their immature condition is fitted to bear.

(*c*) *Plethora.*—Plethoric subjects are more susceptible than those in moderate hard condition.

(*d*) *Hot Weather* favours the onset of the malady.

(*e*) *Abnormal Conformation of the Feet.*—Flat, spreading feet and narrow, contracted feet are more often attacked than normal feet.

(2) *Exciting Causes.*—The exciting causes may be :

(*a*) *Errors in Diet*, such as overfeeding, especially on nitrogenous food—for example, oats, rye, barley, wheat, peas and beans—or taking a big feed of any stuff to which the animal is not accustomed. Too much green food may give rise to it, such as lucerne, sainfoin, and vetches. Horses eating too much of the gleanings in the harvest field sometimes become affected.

(*b*) *Overwork.*—Horses doing long fatiguing journeys by road frequently become affected in consequence of the prolonged concussion on the feet. When (*a*) and (*b*) are associated, the condition is still more likely to supervene.

(*c*) *Exposure to Cold and Damp*, which has been blamed as a cause on the Continent, but in Great Britain and Ireland it does not seem to have a predisposing or exciting effect in producing the disease. When it does appear under these circumstances, it seems to be of a rheumatoid nature.

(*d*) *Excessive Weight on One Foot*, which, owing to the presence of a painful lesion in the other limb, may cause laminitis in the former.

(*e*) *Toxæmia*, resulting from an infectious disease, such as purpura, pneumonia, or metritis, or from the absorption of toxins from the alimentary tract following an attack of colic. It is a very common complication of simple metritis in the mare.

SYMPTOMS.—The symptoms vary according as the disease affects one or two or four feet, and according to the acuteness of the attack. They are general and local.

General Symptoms.—The general symptoms are those of pain and fever. Pain is evinced by the attitude and expression of the patient. When the two fore-feet or all the feet are affected, the horse stands with the fore-limbs in front of the body and the hind-limbs well under it, his object being to let most of the weight fall on the heels. If the hind-limbs only are affected, he keeps all the feet under the body to make the fore-feet bear most of the weight, and so that the heels will bear most of the pressure on the hind-feet. The animal stands persistently and is very unwilling to move, and when forced to do so groans. When recumbent, he lies stretched out and is very reluctant to rise, being afraid of the pain caused by putting weight on the feet. During progression the gait is of a peculiar crouching character, the heels being put to the ground first and the feet lifted quickly, as if they were burned by contact with the earth. When only one foot is affected, weight is alternately placed on it and the other foot, which is always suffering from some other painful lesion. The expression is anxious and indicative of suffering. Fever is manifested by the usual symptoms of febrile disturbance. The temperature is 103° to 106° F.; the pulse is frequent and strong in the early stages of the affection before exhaustion supervenes, when it becomes weak. It may be 70 to 120 per minute. The respirations are accelerated, due chiefly to the pain. The conjunctiva is injected.

The *Local Symptoms* are those of more or less acute inflammation. Abnormal heat is readily detected by placing the hand on the hoof, and throbbing can be felt in the digital arteries. Pain is evinced on the slightest percussion of the foot by the animal snatching it smartly from the ground. In the course of four to twelve days these symptoms usually subside and resolution sets in, the horse gradually regaining its normal condition. Sometimes, however, they become intensified, due to hæmorrhage or exudation taking place beneath the horn. Hæmorrhage is due to rupture of the inflamed and weakened laminæ by the pressure of the body-weight exerted through the os pedis. The blood accumulates between the wall and the os pedis, and its pressure on the sensitive laminæ causes excruciating pain, the patient lying prostrate groaning and bathed in sweat. Occasionally some of the blood escapes at the coronet through a separation between the horn and the coronar band. Death soon follows in a bad case of this kind. The collection of inflammatory exudate in the same situation causes similar symptoms, and some of it may ooze out between hair and hoof. Gangrene may supervene in one of the latter conditions, due to infection gaining entrance to the inflamed region. Its onset is characterised by suppression of the intense symptoms of inflammation and pain, giving the owner the impression that the patient is better, but the cold sweat over the body, the feeble, frequent, or imperceptible pulse, and the cold extremities indicate that death is approaching.

DIAGNOSIS is generally easy after careful examination of the case, which prevents the condition being confounded with tetanus, coronitis, sprained back, or rheumatism.

PROGNOSIS.—The prognosis varies according to the nature of the attack. It is more serious when all the feet are affected than when two or only one foot is involved. The condition is generally more grave in horses that have been doing fast work than in those that have been engaged in slow work, in highly-strung nervous animals than in those of lymphatic temperament, and in big than in small animals. If a cure is not obtained within fourteen days, the affection is apt to become chronic or still more acute and to terminate in death. When the symptoms are alarming in the beginning, the prognosis is generally gloomy.

PREVENTION consists in avoiding the causes mentioned and in keeping animals under good hygienic conditions.

TREATMENT.—Having put the horse in the roomy loose box with short bedding (*e.g.* peat-moss) prompt and energetic treatment should be adopted. Its general principles are those recommended for fever and acute local inflammation.

Constitutional Treatment comprises:

1. *Jugular Phlebotomy*, removing 1 to 2 gallons of blood in a sthenic subject. This has undoubtedly a good effect when promptly performed soon after the commencement of the attack. The objection to it is the risk of phlebitis.

2. *Purgation.*—Prompt purgation is decidedly beneficial. Consequently the administration of eserine or arecoline or other quick-acting drug hypodermically is indicated on account of its rapid effect. Pilocarpine may be combined with the eserine. Arecoline is particularly efficacious, and is looked upon by some authorities as a specific, its action being so frequently followed by immediate amelioration of the disease. It is not, however, invariably successful.

3. *The Administration of Febrifuges*, such as tincture of aconite,

salicylate of soda, quinine sulphate, spts. ether. nit., liq. ammon. acet., or sodium hyposulphite. Tincture of aconite is probably the most effective febrifuge in the early stages of an acute attack, but neither it nor any of the others has much influence on the course of the disease.

4. *Counter-irritation.*—On the Continent, counter-irritation of the upper part of the limbs, the chest, and abdominal walls by rubbing in a rubefacient application is done in order to cause a deviation of blood thereto from the feet, so as to relieve the congestion of the laminæ.

5. *Intravenous injection of " Anthisan "* (*Mepyramine Maleate*) a recently introduced chemo-therapeutic substance described as the most potent and least toxic of the synthetic antihistaminic agents. It is also indicated for other conditions including serum sickness and anaphylactic shock, hoven and lymphangitis. Reports indicate that it is an efficacious remedy for acute laminitis.

Local Treatment comprises :

1. *Cold Applications* in the form of a foot-bath, moist compresses, or constant irrigation. The foot-bath may be provided by a stream or pool, or by digging a hole in a clay floor in the stable or in the open, or by a thick bed of sawdust or sand saturated with cold water, the patient being allowed to stand in the bath for the greater part of the day or constantly. Cold swabs applied round the pastern and overhanging the hooves may be used in the interval between the baths, or instead of them, especially when the patient is recumbent. They should be kept cold by frequent or constant application of cold water. Continuous irrigation through a perforated rubber bracelet round the limb above the fetlocks, communicating with a rubber tube from a tank of water above the level of the horse, is a very effective means of carrying out this method of treatment. Ice-bags applied over the coronets would prove more beneficial than cold water.

2. *Astringent Applications*, to be used alternately with the cold applications, and including the usual refrigerant lotions, such as liquor plumbi subacetatis and white lotion.

3. *Bleeding from the Toe.*—Paring the horn of the sole at the toe and drawing blood from the sensitive tissues in this region has had considerable vogue, and is certainly a good method of relieving congestion in the inflamed part ; but it has the serious objection that it opens the way for infection and its dangerous sequelæ, suppuration and gangrene. When it is done, antiseptic precautions are essential.

4. *Hot Applications.*—Hot poultices or hot, moist compresses are favoured by some practitioners, but they are probably not so useful as the cold treatment.

5. *Hypodermic Injection of Adrenalin.*—The hypodermic injection of adrenalin in a dose of 20 to 30 minims diluted with an equal quantity of normal saline solution over each digital artery may have a marked beneficial effect, causing a rapid fall in the temperature and a decided and prompt improvement in the animal's gait. Nevertheless, it is not an infallible agent for bringing about a cure, and sometimes it is followed by sloughing of the skin at the seat of injection.

6. *Hypodermic Injection of a local anæsthetic* over the plantar nerves, removing sensation for a while from the feet, gives the patient some intervals of ease, allowing him to rest and recover to some extent from the exhaustion caused by suffering, and facilitates exercise, which has a good effect in dispelling the congestion by stimulating the circulation in the foot.

7. *Bier's Treatment*, the explanation of the good effect in this case being that the venous congestion increases phagocytosis, and leads to an outpouring of serum containing antibodies which act beneficially in counteracting the effects of bacteria and their toxins, which may be present at the seat of the lesion.

8. *Grooving the Hoof* at the junction of the wall and the sole at the toe to permit of the escape of inflammatory exudate. This has the same objection as No. 3, otherwise it has the good effect of relieving pain.

9. *Ligation of the Digital Artery.*—See p. 459.

Exercise is an important indication recognised by most practitioners as having a marked effect in favouring resolution. It should be continued for twenty minutes to half an hour twice daily on soft ground. If the hoofs are strong, the horse may go bare-footed or wear ordinary shoes ; but if they have dropped soles, rocking shoes should be applied —that is to say, shoes thin at the toe and heels and thick in the centre, with a wide, well-seated-out web. Exercise is most efficacious when practised early in the attack. When the disease is well established its utility is doubtful. It has been observed during military marches that when affected horses are kept moving slowly behind the column recovery usually ensues, whereas if they are left at a station many cases prove fatal.

Diet.—Soft laxative diet should be prescribed, such as linseed and bran mashes, and grass if in season. A little magnesium sulphate and potassium nitrate in the drinking water has a febrifuge effect, and keeps the excretory organs active. When pain is very severe, a hypodermic injection of morphia may be given.

Chronic Laminitis

Chronic laminitis is a sequel to the acute form or appears spontaneously. It is characterised locally by changes in the form of the foot. It becomes elongated antero-posteriorly, narrow transversely, and somewhat flattened in front. The heels are higher than normal, and the wall approaches the horizontal direction in the region of the lower part of the toe, while in its upper part it is inclined to the vertical direction, so that its centre portion appears depressed or constricted. Rings or rugæ form on the wall parallel to the coronet, comparatively widely spaced behind and almost confluent in front. The sole is convex or flat anteriorly; the lateral lacunæ are abnormally deep, more so than in an ordinary flat-foot. The sole may be perforated in front of the frog, exposing the sensitive tissues, which become inflamed, emitting a serous, sanguinolent, or greyish purulent discharge, and may also undergo necrosis. The wall becomes separated from the laminæ in front, receding from the sole at the white line, the interspace being empty or filled with abnormal horn secreted by the laminæ. The space is widest at the centre of the toe, where it may measure 2 to 3 inches. When the condition follows the acute form, the symptoms of the latter have disappeared, but a certain amount of hypersensitiveness persists in the affected feet. The degree of lameness varies. It may be absent, but the gait is always abnormal, being characterised by the horse going decidedly on the heels. If an antero-posterior section of a chronic laminitic foot be made, the alterations in its conformation will be very evident. The wall is thicker than normal, projected forwards at the toe, and not parallel to the anterior surface of the os pedis, which is more vertical than usual.

Between the wall and the sensitive laminæ in front the space already mentioned is seen filled with homogeneous laminal horn or practically vacant, except for a small deposit of horn covering the laminæ. In a recent case there may be osteophytes on the bone, but in an old case it may show signs of atrophy. The mechanism by which these changes occur is probably as follows: The sensitive laminæ in front rupture, while those at the heels, being much less involved, remain intact, and in consequence the os pedis tends to descend anteriorly under the body-weight, and the perforans muscle, asserting its superiority over its antagonist, the extensor pedis, causes the bone to swing backwards on the horizontal axis formed by the intact laminæ at the sides, thus bringing the anterior plantar border of the bone to press on the sole, causing it to bulge downwards and become flat or convex. In consequence of this pressure, the sensitive sole undergoes atrophy and ceases to secrete horn. When the existing horn becomes worn away perforation takes place. The descent of the os pedis causes stretching and bending of the papillæ on the coronary band, so that the horn formed by them is more vertical than usual and thicker than normal, on account of their secretory activity being stimulated by this interference. This accounts for the prominence and upright direction of the horn near the

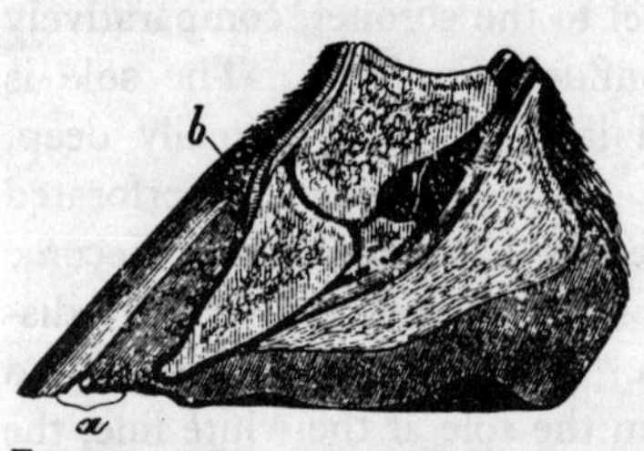

FIG. 400.—LONGITUDINAL SECTION OF HOOF THREE MONTHS AFTER ATTACK

a, Pathologically modified horn of the white line; *b*, distortion of the horn tubules in consequence of sinking of the os pedis.

FIG. 401.—LONGITUDINAL SECTION OF HOOF ONE YEAR AFTER SEVERE ATTACK OF LAMINITIS.

FIG. 402.—HOOF AFTER LAMINITIS.

coronet. During progression the horse puts most weight on the heels, thus pushing the separated wall at the toe forwards and making it approach the horizontal direction.

DIAGNOSIS is usually easy, even when the toe is shortened and the rings removed by the rasp, the convexity of the sole, the deep lacunæ, and the space between the wall and sole being characteristic.

PROGNOSIS.—The prognosis is unfavourable, the deformity and abnormal gait persisting. Recurrent attacks of subacute inflammation may supervene, especially after a long journey by road. For a long time the horse affected can only be used at slow work on soft ground.

Treatment comprises dressing of the feet and the application of appropriate shoes thus: Remove the excess of horn at the toe, but spare the horn on the sole quarters and heels. Apply a wide-webbed, well-seated-out shoe, so as to afford protection to the dropped sole without pressing on it. In order to avoid making the shoe very thick and heavy for the purpose of deep seating, a strip of leather may be interposed between the bearing surface of the shoe and the wall, so as to keep the former away from the sole. A leather plate is desirable as a protection to the sole. The horse generally goes best in long-heeled shoes whose heels project well behind those of the hooves, ensuring the posterior part of the foot striking the ground first, thus saving jar to the hypersensitive anterior laminal region. As time goes on the shape of the foot may improve. When the sole is perforated, immerse the foot in an antiseptic bath if inflammation is present, and after it has subsided dress the part with tar and tow and cover the sole with a metal plate fixed between the hoof and the shoe. When a subacute attack recurs, treat as for acute laminitis. Standing the animal in a cold bath for prolonged periods generally dispels the inflammatory symptoms.

Operative Treatment.—Removing the entire separated portion of the wall by means of the rasp has proved effective in promoting a normal growth of horn at the toe and obliterating the subparietal space in this region, and thereby causing the pedal bone to resume its normal position, with the result that the dropped sole disappeared. Mr. Baker, of Bansha (Ireland), has reported successful treatment in this way, and the writer, acting independently, has had a like experience in a racehorse in which the disease was confined to a fore-foot, causing lameness which rendered the animal unfit for racing.

AFFECTIONS OF THE FEET OF THE OX

Affections of the feet are not so common in the ox as in the horse. Even the working ox is less subject to inflammatory affections of the foot than the horse, due probably to the fact that the bovine works at a slower pace and that its digits are more mobile and elastic than those of the equine, the result being that the shock or concussion on the foot is less. Nevertheless, nearly all the diseases of the feet in the horse are met with in the ox.

Sandcrack

Sandcrack is more common in the fore-foot and in the outer aspect of the claw. The chief exciting cause is the force caused by the weight on the foot, especially during heavy draft

TREATMENT is on the same principles as in the horse, but clasps or horseshoe nails cannot be employed, the horn being too thin to bear them. Transverse cracks parallel to the coronet are fairly common in the fore-feet. They may be due to separation of the horn at the coronary band, the separation appearing afterwards as a crack when the new horn has grown down, otherwise it is due to fracture of the horn. If the crack causes trouble, its lips should be thinned as described.

Contusion of the Sole

This is caused by treading on a hard, resistant body, such as a projecting stone. A long journey by road in unshod oxen or those wearing very thin shoes is a common cause of the condition, or it may be due to the shoe being convex on its upper surface and causing too much pressure on the sole. Fat cattle driven a long distance to shows or fairs are frequent sufferers, their heavy weight being a contributory cause. It is more common in the hind-feet, owing to the horn being thinner there.

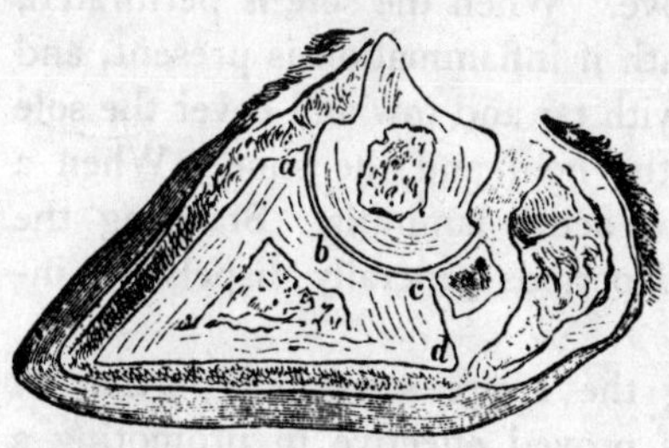

FIG. 403.—VERTICAL SECTION OF AN OX'S CLAW.

SYMPTOMS comprise lameness and local inflammation. When the animal is left at rest it lies down almost constantly, and when standing holds the affected limb in front of the other one. On examination of the foot, the seat of the lesion is detected by palpation, percussion, and paring. In a typical case the horn is ecchymosed, and may be softened and moist from infiltration with serum, and more or less separated from the underlying tissue. If the case has been neglected the separation may be extensive, involving the greater part of the sole and perhaps part of the wall, on account of the inflammation spreading and the serum or inflammatory exudate insinuating itself between the horn and the sensitive tissues, whose union is less intimate than in the horse. Should infection gain entrance, suppuration will supervene, and the inflammation will be intensified, and separation of the horn will occur more rapidly, leading in some cases to shedding of the hoof.

TREATMENT.—In slight cases, where the beasts are merely footsore or tender on their feet after walking a long distance by road, rest in the field or on soft litter is sufficient to bring about resolution. Otherwise the treatment is that advised for the same lesion in the horse.

Should necrosis supervene a sinus will develop, and must be treated accordingly by removing the dead tissue, provi ing drainage, and dressing antiseptically.

Pricks in Shoeing

These are more common in the ox than in the horse, owing to the horn of the hoof being thinner in the former. The lesion is the same as that in the horse.

Picked-up Nail or Open Wound of the Foot

The horn of the hoof being thinner than in the horse, it is more easily penetrated by sharp bodies, such as broken glass, but the commonest seat of injury in the ox is the interdigital space, where a foreign body frequently becomes lodged, such as a stone or a piece of wood.

SYMPTOMS are those of a punctured wound and of inflammation and lameness.

PROGNOSIS depends on the seat and depth of the injury. Complications which may arise are necrosis of the interdigital ligament, the tendon, or bone, and septic arthritis.

TREATMENT is the same as that described for the horse. If arthritis is present, or necrosis of the bone proves difficult to cure. the best treatment is to amputate the affected phalanx or phalanges, when healing will ensue without interruption (p. 472). A foreign body often becomes fixed between the claws, causing pain and lameness without wounding the tissues. Its removal gives immediate relief.

Separation of the Hoof

The hoof may be torn away from the foot in the same circumstances as in the horse. It will take three or four months for the new hoof to grow.

The TREATMENT is the same as in the horse.

Acute Laminitis

The condition is usually the result of walking a long distance by road. It may also be caused by long journeys by rail, the enforced standing and the shaking of the wagons accounting for the inflammation in the feet. Fat beasts, like those prepared for shows, are predisposed to the affection, owing to their great weight. One foot, or two fore- or two hind-feet, or all the feet may be affected. The inflammation may be more marked in the internal digit.

The SYMPTOMS are similar to those in the horse, the same attitude being assumed when standing, but the attack is generally less severe in the bovine. Febrile disturbance is present, with loss of appetite, and the animal loses condition rapidly.

PROGNOSIS.—Resolution is the rule, but in a severe case more or less separation of the horn occurs. Its onset is indicated by diffuse swelling of the digital region, by prominence of the coronet, which becomes dark red, and by symptoms of increased pain. About a week after the commencement of the disease a blood-stained serum escapes between the hoof and the coronet. The separation is generally confined to the posterior region of the foot, but it may extend farther and bring about shedding of the hoof. The disease seldom becomes chronic, although lameness sometimes persists from the flexor tendons becoming contracted, the abnormality being usually confined to the inner claw, with the result that excessive weight is then thrown on the other one, causing, perhaps, sprain of the ligaments of the fetlock and of the interphalangeal articulations, which may lead to periostitis and the formation of exostoses, the condition being then sometimes referred to as " big foot."

TREATMENT is on the same lines as in the horse, comprising jugular phlebotomy, purgation by sulphate of magnesia, or by the injection of arecoline, and local antiphlogistic applications. One should hesitate about bleeding, owing to the risk of phlebitis. The animal should be kept on a thick bed of short litter—peat, moss, or sawdust, or damped chaff. When separation of the horn occurs, antisepsis is necessary to prevent septic complications. When the sensitive tissues are covered by new horn, tar and tow covered by a piece of leather buckled round the pastern should be applied until the new wall is formed. After about a couple of months the animal may be fit to work on soft ground.

Simple Dermatitis of the Interdigital Region, or Scald

This condition is common. It is due to the action of an irritant on the skin, such as dirty wet bedding or mud.

SYMPTOMS.—There is inflammation in the interdigital region, the skin being red and swollen, and well-marked lameness is present.

TREATMENT.—Remove the cause by cleaning the foot and keeping the animal in a clean place, and apply some astringent, such as a 5 per cent. solution of sulphate or chloride of zinc, or sulphate of copper, or an ointment made with the latter, any of which soon effects a cure.

Toxic Dermatitis

This occasionally results from eating brewer's or distiller's grains, and may affect the digits. It is characterised by intense inflammation of the skin, and in some cases by necrosis, occurring in patches, which may extend to the deeper tissues and even involve a joint, causing septic arthritis. Constitutional symptoms of toxæmia may also be present.

TREATMENT.—The first indication is to remove the cause by stopping the grains. The local treatment is that for inflammation or necrosis, antiseptic applications being always necessary to counteract the effects of micro-organisms.

Chronic Vegetative or Verrucose Dermatitis of the Interdigital Space

This is characterised by chronic inflammation of the skin, which becomes thickened, red, and slightly painful. The thickening is noticed as a ridge or prominence appearing in front of the space between the claws. Later, owing to the persistence of the inflammation, granulations or vegetations, wart-like growths, swollen at their summits and arranged in tufts, due to hypertrophy of the papillæ of the skin, are formed. The condition is more common in the hind- than in the fore-feet. It may affect one or both feet. Occasionally both fore- and hind-feet are affected.

ETIOLOGY.—The lesion is apparently due to the constant action of an irritant on the skin of this region, as may result from an animal always standing on dirty wet bedding or in a muddy place, especially in cold weather. Frosty dew on the grass is sometimes blamed for causing the affection in animals on pasture. There is believed to be a predisposition to the malady.

SYMPTOMS.—In the early stages of the inflammation there is slight lameness, but this disappears after a while, when the condition becomes chronic, to reappear later, when acute inflammation is produced by the vegetations becoming pinched and injured between the claws during progression, causing them to ulcerate and suppurate. The digits are pushed apart by the presence of the vegetations.

TREATMENT comprises excision of the vegetations with the knife or scissors, and cauterisation of their bases with a mild caustic such as silver nitrate, or powdered sulphate of zinc, or sulphate of copper The hot iron lightly applied may also be used; it is caustic and styptic. It is necessary to have the animal well secured or fixed in the cast position to perform the operation, which must be done with the usual precautions under a local or general anæsthetic. The patient must be kept at rest in a perfectly dry, clean place until the wounds are healed. Astringent lotions, such as sulphate of zinc and acetate of lead, 1 ounce of each to a pint of water, will be necessary during the healing process to prevent the granulations becoming exuberant, which they have a tendency to do owing to the irritation caused by the movement of the claws. When they become excessive, the caustic must be applied to destroy them and make the wound level. A dry dressing of equal parts of zinc oxide and boric acid is indicated when the wound is uniformly granulating. It is astringent and absorbent, and tends to keep the granulations firm and healthy. It is kept in contact with the wound by means of a pledget of cotton-wool or tow, maintained in position by a bandage. Copper sulphate ointment is also a very useful application when a powerful astringent is required.

Foul in the Foot

Foul in the foot in its widest sense means a suppurating lesion in the interdigital region, but according to some authorities the term is confined to a necrotic lesion in this situation. In either case the condition is due to injury causing a breach of surface, and consequent infection of the part. It is often of the nature of a carbuncle or boil, with a necrotic centre or " core."

Symptoms.—The symptoms are those of severe inflammation in the digital region, and of a suppurating wound, or an abscess, or a sinus in the interdigital space, with pronounced lameness and marked loss of condition. The sinus is due to the presence of necrotic tissue. The depth of the necrosis varies in different cases ; it may be confined to the skin, or affect the interdigital ligament, or the tendons, or extend into the joint, causing septic arthritis, which is characterised by extreme lameness and by a fœtid, purulent, synovial discharge. The necrotic centre is recognised by its yellowish-greyish colour, and by being surrounded by an inflammatory suppurating zone, causing a line of demarcation or separation, at the level of which the dead part may be eventually cast off. The death of the tissue is due to the presence of the bacillus of necrosis.

Prognosis.—When the lesion is superficial, affecting only the skin and subcutaneous tissue, it responds promptly to simple treatment; but when the ligament or tendon undergoes necrosis, resolution is very tedious, the dead tissue being slow to separate, owing to its feeble vascularity, and if the joint be infected, recovery is impossible without amputation of the digit.

Treatment is as usual for a septic wound, or abscess, or sinus, as the case may be, its principles being to overcome the action of the microbes by disinfection, by providing drainage for pus, and by the removal of necrotic tissue. When the case is recent, immerse the foot in a warm antiseptic bath and apply antiseptic compresses, as advised for septic foot lesions in the horse. When an abscess is present open it, and if necrosis supervene await the spontaneous separation of the dead part while using the antiseptic applications. If the separation is too slow, operate and excise the necrotic tissue ; or if the latter is very extensive or the joint is diseased, amputate the digit (see p. 472). Since the announcement, however, of C. R. Forman (*J. Amer. Vet. Med. Ass.*, **109**, 176–7, 1946) that he had found that the intravenous injection of 60 grammes of sodium sulphapyridine in 500 c.c. of distilled water is a specific non-toxic treatment for all forms of the disease, and this has been confirmed by other practitioners, the foregoing forms of treatment will not be necessary when this drug is available. By its use marked improvement occurs within 24 hours and complete recovery in from two days to two weeks. One injection is usually sufficient. The dose mentioned may be increased for very large bovines. He found that 90 grammes in 900 c.c. of distilled water caused only slight nervous reaction immediately after injection, but he considers that this is on the border of a toxic dose. In cases of long standing however, this treatment is not always successful.

Contagious Foul

Sometimes the condition just described appears as an enzootic in a herd, and is then believed to be due to contagion, and is consequently spoken of as " contagious foul." In this case the lesion is generally necrotic. Several animals in a field or shed become affected about the same time. No specific organism other than the bacillus of necrosis has been found in connection with the disease, and this is a common saprophytic microbe which may gain entrance to any wound or breach of surface convenient to its habitat.

TREATMENT is the same as for ordinary foul, associated with the usual prophylactic measures for a contagious disease.

Deformity of the Claws

This is due to the hoof becoming overgrown as the result of prolonged housing, preventing wear of the horn.

SYMPTOMS.—The toes become excessively long and are turned inwards or outwards, often overlapping in the former case. The sole becomes convex. When the deformity is well marked and allowed to persist for some time, it causes pain and lameness by preventing equal distribution of weight on the foot, and thereby over-stretching some of the ligaments of the interphalangeal joints. The animal lies more than usual, and when standing is fidgety on its feet.

TREATMENT consists in removing the excessive growth of horn by means of a fine sharp saw or a horn-cutting forceps and finishing off with the rasp. It may be necessary to cast the beast for the operation. If the sole is very prominent, it is advisable to level it to a slight extent with the rasp. Tar should be smeared on the hoof afterwards. Deformity may also result from chronic laminitis, a rare condition, and is then characterised by rings in the wall and by convexity and thinness of the sole. It may improve with time. Little can be done to remedy it.

AFFECTIONS OF THE FEET IN SHEEP

Traumatic Affections

The sheep's foot may be wounded in the same way as in other animals. A common seat of injury is the interdigital space, where infection may give rise to suppuration or necrosis, producing in the latter case a lesion similar to foul in the foot of the ox.

The SYMPTOMS will vary according to the nature of the condition, those of more or less acute inflammation being always present and causing a varying degree of lameness. When necrosis supervenes there is an intensely inflammatory swelling in the digital region, and the animal is unable to put the foot on the ground. The redness of the skin is very noticeable when it is not pigmented, and of course the pain on manipulation is very severe. The patient is feverish, and remains lying almost constantly.

TREATMENT.—Warm, moist antiseptic applications are indicated to overcome the action of the infecting bacteria and to hasten the removal of the slough in a case of necrosis. In the event of complications such as necrosis of the phalanges or arthritis, amputation of the affected part of the digit is necessary.

Inflammation of the Biflex Canal

The biflex canal is a double blind passage which opens on either side of the middle line of the digit about ¼ inch above the entrance to the interdigital space in front, its orifice being marked with a tuft of hair. The canal is not present in the goat.

ETIOLOGY.—Inflammation of the canal is due to irritation caused by foreign matter gaining entrance to it, wounding its lining, and leading to suppuration and necrosis.

SYMPTOMS.—There is inflammation in the affected region, and a fatty fœtid discharge oozes from the canal when it is compressed by the fingers. Gangrene may supervene. Lameness is pronounced, the animal remains lying most of the time, and if both limbs are affected progresses on the knees. Complications may arise in neglected cases from infection extending to the deep-seated tissues.

TREATMENT is on the same lines as for traumatic affections.

Foot Rot

This is a specific infectious disease of the feet in sheep.

ETIOLOGY.—The disease is due to a micro-organism in the soil which gains entrance to the subcorneal tissue and there produces its pathogenic effects. A favourite habitat of the organism is wet or marshy places, especially those soiled with an accumulation of excreta, such as dirty folds. When one case of the disease appears in such a place, it rapidly spreads through the flock if preventative measures are not adopted. The disease is rare in dry, upland districts. Allowing the hoofs to become overgrown, as often occurs in sheep on rich, low-lying pastures, owing to the horn not undergoing sufficient wear, favours the onset of the affection, as the superfluous horn becomes deformed, turned up at the toes, and splits, allowing dirt and infection to gain entrance to the sensitive tissues. The virulence of the causal organism becomes increased by its sojourn in the foot, thus accounting for the rapidity with which the malady spreads after a single case is established, and explaining why it has been described as a contagious disease, although it does not spread directly from sheep to sheep or even from one foot to another in the same animal, as has been proved by putting affected sheep with those not affected in a clean, dry place.

SYMPTOMS.—Lameness first attracts attention, and it varies in degree according to the stage of the disease. It is always well marked, and in typical cases the affected foot is not allowed to touch the ground. The animal commonly rests on the knees when grazing, and always does so when both fore-feet are attacked. If the hind- and fore-feet are involved, the animal is almost always lying, only changing its position when it has consumed all the grass within reach. The disease may commence in any part of the foot, wherever the bacteria have gained entrance, but it usually begins towards its inner aspect near the heel, where the first indication of its presence is separation of the horn, exposing the sensitive tissue, which appears inflamed and covered with a whitish exudate. After a while it becomes ulcerated and angry, and excessive granulations form as the result of the irritation caused by the edges of the separated horn. The horn becomes overgrown and curved for want of wear. If the infective process is not checked, necrosis of the ligaments and tendons and arthritis may supervene.

TREATMENT.—The first indication is to take measures to prevent further spread of the disease by isolating the affected animals and moving the in-contact subjects from the infected area to a clean, dry place after disinfecting their feet by walking them through a bath containing a reliable disinfectant, such as a 2 per cent. solution of copper sulphate or Jeyes' fluid. The sheepfold must be lime-dressed before it is used again. If the feet are overgrown, they should be pared. For the sheep slightly affected, the use of the bath mentioned once or twice daily is sufficient to effect a cure. Those in which the disease is well established require individual treatment. The separated and overgrown horn must be removed, and the inflamed tissues treated with an antiseptic or slightly caustic preparation. If there be a protruding mass of granulations it should be excised. Sulphate of copper ointment is an effective application, but when cauterisation is not necessary, iodine ointment, 1 to 20 of lard or vaseline, is preferable. It is essential to keep the patients in a dry place after being dressed. To maintain the dressing in contact with the lesion and to protect the latter from dirt and moisture, it is advisable in severe cases to put on a leather or rubber boot. G. B. Lancaster (*Vet. Rec.*, May 31st, 1947) says that in his opinion the best treatment for foot-rot in sheep is a vaccine of fusiformis necrophorus, curing 90 per cent. of the cases, 50 per cent. of which require only one injection. If there are wounds he advises, locally, a solution of aloes, spirit, and linseed oil.

Dermatitis of the Interdigital Region—"Scald"

This may affect the majority of the sheep or lambs in a flock. Its cause is not always very clear. It may be due to frosty dews, when irritation from mud cannot be blamed. The inflammation is usually fairly acute, and makes the patients very lame. The pain which it causes prevents the animals thriving, and brings about loss of condition, particularly in young lambs.

TREATMENT.—Cure is rapidly effected by the use of lead lotion or other astringent solution. Dressing with boric acid has a soothing and beneficial effect, and may be sufficient to cure the condition. The cause, if evident, must be removed.

AFFECTIONS OF THE FEET IN THE PIG

The pig may suffer from sore feet as the result of being driven some distance by road, especially when the animal is fat and heavy. The degree of inflammation varies in different cases. It is manifested by the usual symptoms. The pig is lame and inclined to lie down on the road. If infection gain entrance through a breach in the horn, suppuration may supervene and may eventually cause shedding of the hoof. Then intense inflammation of the digital region and constitutional disturbance ensue.

TREATMENT.—Keep the animals at rest on soft litter, and if the inflammation is severe, apply cold water and astringent lotions to the feet. Pare away separated horn, and apply an antiseptic protective dressing to the exposed tissues. Administer laxative medicine to counteract febrile disturbance.

Affections of the Interdigital Space

The interdigital space may be affected with " scald," or a wound, or a suppurating or necrotic lesion, as in the sheep, and must be dealt with accordingly.

" Foot and Mouth Disease " is a specific disease affecting chiefly cattle, sheep and pigs, which need not be dealt with here.

AFFECTIONS OF THE FEET IN THE DOG AND CAT

Open Wounds of the Paws

The paw is frequently wounded by treading on sharp bodies—sharp stones, glass, tacks, thorns, etc.—the commonest seat of injury being one of the pads, but the interdigital region may also be wounded A foreign body may be lodged in the tissues. The lesion will vary according to the depth and extent of the injury. It causes marked lameness.

TREATMENT is on the general principles of open wounds. When the wound is punctured and small, it may be necessary to examine each pad separately to find it. A foreign body should be searched for and, if found, removed. Antiseptic lotion and powder and a pad and bandage are indicated. Occasionally the wound is callous when submitted for treatment, especially when affecting the pads. Excessive horn may have then developed at the level of the wound in the form of processes with intervening sore spaces. The abnormal horn should be excised, and the ulcerated part cauterised with silver nitrate, after which a dry antiseptic and protective dressing should be applied.

A circular wound of the paw or metacarpal or metatarsal region is occasionally met with as the result of a rubber ring or a piece of cord or a wire snare being fixed round the limb, the ring or ligature becoming embedded and hidden in the tissues and causing suppuration. The indication, therefore, in a wound of this kind is to search for a ligature and remove it when found. Healing will then rapidly ensue. It may have been in the limb for months before the case is brought for treatment.

Contused Wounds

Contused wounds caused by crushing of the paw by the wheel of a vehicle passing over it are fairly common, and are usually complicated by fracture of one or more of the digits and destruction of a considerable amount of soft tissues.

The TREATMENT is to remove shreds of dead tissue and loose pieces of bone, clip the hair in the vicinity, and immerse the foot in a warm antiseptic bath repeatedly until the wound granulates, when a dry, protective dressing will be sufficient. The latter should be renewed daily. If a digit or digits are irreparably damaged, amputation thereof must be performed.

Sinuses

A sinus may form between the digits, due to the presence of a foreign body or a piece of necrotic tendon or bone in its depth, or occasionally to the cavity left after the bursting of an interdigital abscess or cyst refusing to heal. The procedure in every case is to open up the sinus to its bottom and remove the cause of the condition. A separated sesamoid bone has been found as the cause of the trouble, and its removal was followed by immediate recovery and disappearance of the lameness, which had been in existence for months.

Burns and Scalds

The dog's or cat's paws may be burned or scalded at fireplaces, and must be dealt with as described in the section on " Burns and Scalds."

Inflammation of the Pads

Inflammation of the pads in the dog often results from the animal running a long distance by road or over rough ground, such as stubble or ploughed fields, especially in dry weather.

SYMPTOMS.—When the dog is running the inflammation may not be very noticeable, but after he has rested for a while it becomes obvious, the animal being very tender on his feet, showing general lameness, and evidently suffering pain. He lies stretched out and hesitates about putting weight on the feet. The pads are found to be hot, swollen, and painful.

TREATMENT consists in rest and the use of antiphlogistic applications, cold water and astringent topics being indicated when the case is recent. If the horn be worn down to the flesh, antiseptic foot-baths are advisable to prevent septic complications. When the pain is severe, warm solutions of belladonna or opium or a warm decoction of poppy-heads may be used as an anodyne.

Separation of the Nail

The nail may be torn off or partially separated by violence in an accident, causing intense pain and lameness. When the separation is slight, the nail may become adherent again; if not, it should be removed. If the phalanx be injured, it must be disarticulated and the resulting wound dressed with an antiseptic pad and bandage until it is healed.

Inflammation of the Nail Matrix

This may be acute or chronic. It is caused by injury—viz., a contusion or open wound—or by eczema extending from the interdigital region.

SYMPTOMS.—A painful swelling is formed at the coronet, which may also become ulcerated or the seat of small abscesses. There is marked lameness.

TREATMENT consists in applying warm antiseptic lotions, such as 1 or 2 per cent. solution of lysol or cresyl, or 1 in 1,000 potassium permanganate, and painting the ulcers with tincture of iodine, and opening abscesses and disinfecting their cavities. When the condition is due to chronic eczema, the internal administration of Fowler's solution of arsenic is indicated. In rebellious cases, amputation of the terminal phalanx is the best treatment.

Ingrowing Nails

The nail of the dew-claw, not being subjected to wear, often becomes curved and grows into the pad, causing acute pain and lameness.

The TREATMENT is to cut the offending nail with a bone forceps or rowelling scissors, applying the instrument to the sides of the nail, as its application above and below might cause splitting of the horn. This must be done periodically. An alternative procedure is to amputate the dew-claw. The dew-claws may be easily excised with the scissors during puppyhood, and the operation is often performed on whippets and greyhounds, in which the dew-claw may interfere with racing, owing to its catching the opposite limb when the dog is running. In dogs getting insufficient exercise, the ordinary claws become too long and require to be shortened, the pressure of the jaws of the forceps being applied laterally.

Horny Callosities

These sometimes form on the dog's pads, and may become fissured to form a tuft of horny processes. They cause a varying degree of lameness.

TREATMENT is not satisfactory. It consists in paring away the horn as much as possible, using warm antiseptic baths, and applying iodine and glycerine, or carbolised glycerine, or ichthyol ointment.

Interdigital Cysts or Abscesses

These are common in dogs, especially the long-coated varieties—spaniels, retrievers, and setters. The cause of the condition is evidently bacterial, but no specific organism has been discovered in connection with it, and why some individuals are more subject to it than others cannot be explained.

SYMPTOMS.—An inflammatory swelling gradually forms in one or more of the interdigital spaces of one or more feet, causing lameness, which may be very slight or well marked. The dog frequently bites or licks the affected part. The swelling, if not opened, bursts eventually, discharging a watery liquid. The resulting cavity may soon heal, or persist for want of drainage or on account of its lining failing to granulate. It may close for a while, after which the cyst or abscess reforms. Successive cysts may form in different spaces.

PROGNOSIS.—Recovery occurs rapidly in some cases on bursting or opening and draining of the cyst or cysts. Other cases are very obstinate to treat, the cysts forming repeatedly, despite the adoption of the usual surgical measures.

TREATMENT.—Rubbing in tincture of iodine over the swelling when it is forming sometimes prevents its development. When the cyst is present, treatment consists in opening it up completely and curetting its lining or destroying it by the application of silver nitrate stick. The application of tincture of iodine to the lining of the cavity may be sufficient to promote granulation and cicatrisation, and should be tried before using caustic preparations. The use of an autogenous vaccine has proved disappointing, but may have a good effect in some cases.

APPENDIX

I

EXAMINATION OF HORSES AS TO SOUNDNESS

The examination of horses as to soundness is a comparatively simple matter for the veterinary surgeon who is so well versed in the practical application of a competent knowledge of the anatomy and physiology of the horse that he has little difficulty in recognising aberrations from the normal concerning them in the course of his examination.

The newly fledged veterinary surgeon and even the matured veterinarian are not always in this happy position although they may have had a distinguished collegiate career, because they may not have taken the trouble or had the opportunities or time to apply their knowledge to the living animal by repeatedly inspecting and palpating regions subject to abnormalities or by observing at every opportunity the performance of functions liable to undergo alteration as the result of disease, for example in :

1. The locomotory system—watching the horse at rest, walking, turning, backing, trotting, and galloping.
2. The respiratory system—to listen to the respiratory sounds at rest (auscultation, using the phonendoscope), when startled ("grunting"), and during fast exercise or heavy haulage.
3. The circulatory system, including the pulse and cardiac sounds and rhythm (auscultation) at rest and after exercise.
4. The other systems as far as their functions can be observed.

Examination of the eye is not sufficiently practised by students or young veterinary surgeons to enable them to become familiar with its various structures as they appear in the living animal. Frequent practice of the use of instruments (retinoscope, ophthalmoscope, bi-convex lens) is essential to avoid mistakes in diagnosis of deep ocular affections.

The next requirement for the veterinary surgeon who wishes to become proficient in the examination of horses is to have a thorough knowledge of the pathological conditions that can be detected in the procedure and to examine all the horses that he comes in contact with to ascertain if any of these conditions are present and thus help to make himself expert in the matter.

The veterinary student is handicapped in that in the majority of colleges he has little time or opportunity for the practical application of his knowledge of the normal and abnormal animal and must rely upon himself to obtain the facilities outside the college, by spending some time with a veterinary surgeon engaged largely in equine practice and by frequenting horse shows, fairs, sale-yards, and race meetings. Notwithstanding that the veterinarian has fulfilled all the foregoing requirements, he will be by no means infallible in the art of finding whether a horse is sound or unsound, because an abnormality may be so slight (and yet serious) that it may be overlooked or be impossible to detect. This raises the point of negligence in the examination of horses for which the veterinary surgeon is liable and may be mulcted in heavy damages. It therefore behoves him to leave no loophole for this charge by exercising extreme care and omitting no detail to arrive at a correct decision. He may make mistakes and give a wrong opinion, but so long as negligence cannot be proved against him in his procedure he is not liable. There is always the danger, however, of the judge giving he verdict against him; hence the advisability of joining a veterinary defence association as a protection in this and similar contingencies.

Definition of Unsoundness

The following extract from the judgment of Baron Park (1842) is generally taken as constituting the definition of unsoundness. "The rule as to soundness is that if at the time of sale the horse has any disease which actually does diminish the natural usefulness of the animal so as to make him less capable of work of any description, or which in its ordinary progress will diminish the natural usefulness of the animal, or if the horse has either from disease or accident undergone any alteration of structure that either actually does at the time or in its ordinary effects will diminish the natural usefulness of the horse, such a horse is unsound."

Remembering this definition, the veterinary surgeon can use his judgment as to what specific conditions constitute unsoundness. From the point of view of heredity, which is important in the examination of animals for the stud, there may be differences of opinion, but there is general agreement that the following conditions are hereditary: cataract, whistling or roaring, ring-bone, side-bone, spavin, navicular disease, shivering, stringhalt, and defective genital organs.

Procedure or method of Examination

The examination of a horse as to soundness must be methodical, done in stages of the same sequence on every occasion. The following are the stages usually adopted:

(1) *At rest in the stable*, where—

(*a*) His general condition and behaviour are observed, whether he happens to show any stable vices or favours a limb by resting it or shows evidence of stringhalt or shivering on being made to come over.

(*b*) A note is taken of its description—colour, breed or class, sex, age, height, and markings, using the terms prescribed by the Royal College of Veterinary Surgeons, a list of which is obtainable from that body on application (see also pp. 1013–17). A horse that has come a distance by road to be examined should be rested and not disturbed in any way for half an hour, " until the veterinary surgeon is ready to carry out the examination," a reason for this being that the horse standing for some time after a journey may show a lameness which appears only when the animal has walked or trotted after resting (spavin, navicular disease, rheumatism), and which passes off with exercise.

(*c*) The heart and lungs are auscultated, the character of the breathing is observed (broken wind), and the temperature is taken if considered necessary.

(*d*) The eyes are examined for defective vision and opacities without and with an instrument (opthalmoscope, retinoscope, bi-convex lens) remembering that an animal may be blind although the eyes appear to be normal.

(*e*) The hearing may be tested should the horse appear to be deaf.

(*f*) If the subject is a stallion or brood mare the genital organs are carefully examined, including the mammary gland in the mare.

(*g*) The mouth, including the incisor and molar teeth (superficially at least), is examined.

(*h*) Grunting the horse, if in a safe, roomy loose box, is practised.

(2) *Having the horse taken outside in a good halter or snaffle bridle*, and—

(*a*) Walked up and down for about 40 yards, turned short in a circle, right and left, and backed for stringhalt and shivering.

(*b*) Trotted slowly up and down, without excitement, on hard, level ground in a quiet place for the same distance, watching him carefully when turning.

(*c*) Standing square on a level surface with plenty of room for the veterinary surgeon to walk round the horse at a few paces methodically inspecting every region from the head to the tail on both sides and then palpating various parts, beginning on the near side at the head—

(1) from the poll down the face, everting the inner wing of the nostril and the lips, exposing the teeth and interdental space ;
(2) the jowl and chin ;
(3) the top of the neck from the poll to the withers ;

(4) the side and under aspects of the neck and sternum, raising the jugular vein ;

(5) the back, loins, and croup ;

(6) the lateral and inferior aspects of the chest and abdominal walls ;

(7) the fore limb from the withers to the foot, anteriorly, laterally, and posteriorly, examining especially for splint, ring-bone, bobba bone, side-bone, sprained tendons, and synovial distensions, grease in hairy-legged horses, and affections of the feet ; then, having flexed the knee and supporting the fetlock with the right hand, the left hand is passed between the fore limbs from in front and the thumb pushes the back tendons aside from the knee to the fetlock feeling for splint again ; the same is done on the outside, reversing the hands ; finally the lateral cartilages and foot are carefully examined ;

(8) the fore foot having been given to the groom, the right hand is passed beneath the abdomen gradually up to the inguinal region and then along the hind limb from the angle of the haunch in front and the tuber ischii behind to the foot in a manner similar to that adopted in the fore limb, examining specially for spavin, bog-spavin, thoroughpin, curb, ring-bone, sprained tendons, and grease in hairy-legged horses in which it may be overlooked in its early stages ; the tail and dock are examined and the former raised to expose the anus, vulva, and perinæum ; the fore foot is then released to enable the examiner to lift and inspect the hind foot ; lifting the hind limb also serves now as a test for shivering.

The same procedure is gone through on the other side.

(3) *Examination of the wind*, including—

(*a*) Grunting or " bulling " the horse, which is held alongside a safe wall on good footing (not concrete or pavement), or in a place prepared for the purpose, with a large mat suspended on the wall, and the halter, shank, or reins somewhat slackened to give the animal room to spring forward when he is threatened with a stick or handkerchief to frighten him to make an expiratory effort and cause a prolonged grunt if the larynx is more or less paralysed, preventing closure of the glottis.

(*b*) " Coughing " the horse by pressure on the larynx.

(*c*) Cantering or galloping the horse either in the lunge or saddle, in a calm atmosphere if possible. The horse may be ridden by the examiner—generally considered the better way—or by another person, who rides the horse first in a large circle and then in a small circle round the examiner both ways, and finally in a long, straight gallop, preferably up an incline, to stop close to him. When lunged the horse is sent round in a ring to the right and to the left. In every case the horse is kept going until he blows distinctly. Care must be taken that the cavesson or bridle and lunging rope or rein are strong and properly adjusted. If there is wind the veterinary surgeon stands with his back to it when the horse is approaching him.

An alternative method of testing a carthorse's wind is to cause him to pull a load or a heavy vehicle with the wheel locked up a long, stiff incline until he blows. Yet another way of testing a light horse's wind is to exercise him on soft ground on three legs, a fore foot being securely strapped up, Rarey fashion. This method has been practised by dealers, being a severe test which quickly brings out a noise if present. It seems rather risky, from the danger of coming down or catching the tied-up fore foot with the hind one when plunging forward. The author has seen it adopted successfully with Army remounts before and after the " roaring " operation.

(4) The heart should be re-examined after this exercise, when its beats will be more distinct and abnormalities more easily detected. The grunting test may also be repeated.

(5) In an exhaustive examination of a horse or if there has been some doubt as to whether the animal was lame when trotted, he may be allowed to rest in the stable for a while after being tried for the wind and then jogged again, when lameness, if present, will probably be accentuated. The grunting test may also be repeated.

Vices

Vices are to be considered but cannot always be detected ; the rule is that the vendor must give a guarantee that the animal is free from same.

Blemishes

A horse may have blemishes which do not constitute unsoundness and which must be mentioned and stated as being of no consequence or not likely to interfere with the animal's usefulness.

Useful Unsound Horses

Horses may be affected with conditions for which they must be cast as unsound and yet work perfectly sound, *e.g.*, curb, spavin, peri-articular ring-bone, side-bones ; this probably accounts for so many veterinary certificates being read out at certain sales to the effect that horses are affected with some of these conditions but are " otherwise sound," never mentioning the word unsound. Another way of describing such horses in a certificate is to say they are sound except for some of the affections mentioned. Horses unsound in the wind are sometimes referred to as whistlers or slight whistlers and otherwise sound.

Certificates

Certificate is the name given to a signed statement by a veterinary surgeon that he has examined a particular horse, of which he gives a complete description, including defects, whereby the animal can be identified at home and abroad, and that he has found the said horse to be sound or unsound, without any qualification. There should be no room for doubt in the certificate as to the soundness or unsoundness of the animal. The client, or purchaser at a sale should not be left to draw his own conclusions by such phrases as "a slight whistler, otherwise sound," which a layman might take as meaning the horse is sound; "sound except for a small splint," which might be taken as meaning that the animal is unsound because of the small splint.

Fraser (Lambourn, Berks) in an excellent article on the "Examination of Horses as to Soundness" condemns the use of this ambiguous phraseology and insists that the horse should be stated to be either "Sound" or "Unsound."

Form of Certificate.—

It is convenient to have printed forms such as the following:

CERTIFICATE.

No. .... [*Name and address of the Veterinary Surgeon*]

[*Date.*]

I have this day examined at the request of [Name and address of person —description of the animal, including colour, breed or class, sex, age, and height]. *The said* [repeat the kind of animal—horse, mare, gelding, colt or filly] [has or is] [mention the form or forms of unsoundness if any] *and is in my opinion* [sound or unsound].

Identification Marks.

Signed......................M.R.C.V.S.

(If the certificate is not on a printed form it should be legibly and neatly written on good notepaper.)

II

COLOURS AND MARKINGS OF HORSES FOR IDENTIFICATION PURPOSES (as recommended by the Royal College of Veterinary Surgeons)

Colours

Black.—Where melanistic pigment is general throughout the body coat, limbs, mane and tail, with no pattern factor present other than white markings.

Black-brown.—Where the predominating colour is black, with muzzle, and sometimes flanks, brown or tan.

Brown.—Where there is a mixture of melanistic and chocolate pigment, without yellow, in the body coat, with black limbs, mane and tail.

Bay-brown.—Where the predominating colour is brown, with bay muzzle, black limbs, mane and tail.

Bay.—Bay varies considerably in shade from a dull red approaching the brown to a yellowish colour approaching the chestnut, but it can be distinguished from the chestnut by the fact that the bay has a black mane and tail and almost invariably has black on the limbs. The following three shades will suffice for description : *Bay* (includes bright bay) ; *Dark Bay ; Light Bay* (includes mealy bay).

Chestnut.—This is a whole colour of which three shades may be named : *Chestnut* (includes bright chestnut, golden chestnut, and red chestnut) ; *Dark Chestnut* (includes liver chestnut and mahogany chestnut) ; *Light Chestnut* (includes sorrel).

Blue Dun.—Where the colour of the body coat is a dilute black, evenly distributed over the body (giving a blue colour) with or without dorsal band (list) or withers stripes. Always black mane and tail. The skin is black.

Yellow Dun.—Where there is a diffuse yellow pigment in the hair with or without dorsal band (list), wither stripes, or bars on the legs. The striping is correlated with dark pigment on the head and limbs. When striping is absent the limbs will approximate to the colour of the body coat. The skin is black.

Cream.—Where the body coat is of a cream colour, with unpigmented skin. The iris is deficient in pigment ; it may even be devoid of it, giving the eye a pinkish appearance.

Grey.—Where the body coat is a varying mosaic of black and white hairs, with the skin black. With increasing age the coat grows lighter in colour. As there are many variations of grey according to age and season all of them should be described by the general term grey. In horses of this colour any distinctive hoof markings may be useful for the purposes of distinction.

Roans.—Roans are distinguished by the ground or body colours, all of which are permanent.

Blue Roan.—Where the body colour is black or black-brown, with an admixture of white hair which gives a blue tinge to the coat. The limbs from the knee and hock downwards are black.

Strawberry or Chestnut Roan.—Where the body colour is chestnut with an admixture of white hairs. The limbs are not black.

Bay or Red Roan.—Where the body colour is bay or bay-brown with white hairs which give a reddish tinge to the coat. The limbs from the knee and hock downwards are black.

Piebald.—Where the body coat consists of large irregular patches of black and white. The line of demarcation between the two colours is generally well defined.

Skewbald.—Where the body consists of large irregular patches of white and of any definite colour except black. The line of demarcation between the colours is generally well defined.

Odd Colour.—Where the coat consists of a mixture of more than two colours tending to merge into each other at the edges of the patches with irregular body markings not classifiable under the head of Piebald or Skewbald.

Note.—(1) Where there is any doubt as to colour, the muzzle and eyelids should be carefully examined.

(2) The term " whole coloured " is used (e.g. in Suffolk breeds) where there are no hairs of any other colour on the body, head, or limbs.

Markings

The variations in markings of horses are infinite and cannot therefore be comprehended by a limited number of terms without certain arbitrary groupings. In some cases a combination of the terms given below must be resorted to.

Limbs

White Coronet.—Where the hair immediately above the hoof is white. Describe the situation of the white marking as far as possible.

White Heel.—For the purpose of description of marking the heel is to be taken as the back of the pastern extending to the ergot. Where the white is confined to one or both the bulbs of the heel it must be specified.

White Pastern.—For the purpose of description of marking the term " Pastern " is to be taken as extending from immediately below the fetlock joint downwards. Any variation of the extent of the white should be specified, e.g. half pastern, three-quarter pastern.

White Fetlock.—For the purpose of description of marking the term " fetlock " is to be taken as comprising the region of the fetlock joint and downwards. Any variation of the extent of the white should be specified.

Higher White Markings.—Though the term " Sock " has been in common use for a marking extending to about half-way up the cannon, and the term " Stocking " for a marking up to the region of the knee or hock, these terms have been so loosely used that the Sub-Committee recommends for the sake of greater uniformity and certainty that for white markings extending higher than those already defined the particular height to which the white extends should be precisely stated and any variations in the upper margin noted, e.g. " White to middle of Cannon or shank " " White to Knee or Hock."

HEAD

Star.—Any white mark on the forehead. Size, shape, intensity, and position of coloured markings on the white to be specified.

Stripe.—Many terms have been used to describe the narrow white marking down the face, not wider than the flat anterior surface of the nasal bones, e.g. rase, race, rache, reach, streak, stripe, strip, etc.

The Sub-Committee recommends for the sake of uniformity that one term only be used, and they select, as being most useful for the purpose, the term " Stripe." The stripe may be a continuation of the star, or it may be separate and distinct from it. Where there is a star and a stripe and the stripe is not continuous with it the stripe should be described as " interrupted stripe " ; and where star and stripe are continuous as " star and stripe conjoined " ; where no star is present the origins of the stripe should be defined.

The termination of the stripe and any variation in breadth, length, direction and coloured markings on the white should be described, e.g. " broad stripe " " narrow stripe."

Blaze.—A white marking covering almost the whole of the forehead between the eyes and extending down the front of the face, involving the whole width of the nasal bones. Any variation in direction, termination, and coloured markings on the white should be described.

White Face.—Where the white covers the forehead and front of the face extending laterally towards the mouth. The extension may be unilateral or bilateral in which case it should be described accordingly.

Snip.—An isolated white marking, independent of those already named and situated between or in the region of the nostrils. Its position should be specified.

Lip Markings.—Should be accurately described—whether embracing the whole or a portion of either lip.

White Muzzle.—Where the white embraces both lips and extends to the region of the nostrils.

EYES

Wall Eye.—The term should be used exclusively where there is such a lack of pigment in the iris as usually to give a greyish white or bluish appearance to the eye. Any other important variations from the normal colour of the iris should be noted.

Showing the White of the Eye.—Horses which " show the white of the eye " should be so described.

BODY

Grey Ticked.—Where isolated white hairs are sparsely distributed irregularly in any part of the body.

Flecked.—Where small collections of white hairs occur distributed irregularly in any part of the body. The degree of flecking may be described by the terms " heavily flecked " " lightly flecked."

Black Marks.—The term should be used to describe areas of black hairs on white or any other colour (see " Ermine Marks ").

Spots.—Where small, more or less circular, collections of hairs differing from the general body colour occur, distributed in various parts of the body. The colour of the spots must be stated.

Patch.—This term should be used to describe any larger well defined irregular area (not covered by previous definitions) of hairs differing from the general body colour. The colour, shape, position, and extent should be described.

Zebra Marks.—Where there is striping on the limbs, neck, withers or quarters.

Mane and Tail.—The presence of odd coloured hairs in mane and tail should be specified.

Ermine Marks.—The term is used to describe black points on white, usually occurring on the coronet, but as this marking can easily be described as " Black Marks " it is recommended that the use of the word " Ermine " be discontinued.

Dappled.—The Sub-Committee recommends that this term be discontinued, as it is a seasonal and not a permanent marking.

General

Mixed.—The term " mixed " should be used to describe a marking consisting of the general colour mixed with many white or lighter coloured hairs.

Bordered.—To be used where any marking is circumscribed by a mixed border, e.g. bordered star, bordered stripe.

Flesh Marks.—Patches where the pigment of the skin is absent should be described as " Flesh Marks."

Notes

1. *Adventitious Marks.*—There are many adventitious marks (i.e. not congenital marks) which are permanent, e.g. saddle marks, bridle marks, collar marks, girth marks, and other harness marks, firing and branding marks, scars, tattoo marks. Wherever these occur they should be described. Horses that have been docked should be so described.

2. *Near and Off.*—As the terms " Near " and " Off " are not recognized abroad, it is recommended that in certificates referring to horses for export an explanatory note defining " near " as " left " and " off " as " right " should be inscribed at the foot of the certificate.

3. *Routine.*—It is recommended that the following order of examination should be adopted:

Colour.

Breed.

Sex (where the horse has a registered name it should be inserted here, followed by name of sire and dam).

Age.

Marks on head (including eyes) in the order shown.

Marks on limbs, fore first, then hind, commencing from below.

Marks on body.

Remarks on mane and tail.

Adventitious or acquired marks.

INDEX

ABDOMEN, affections of, 661
abscesses of, 661
contusions of, 661
non-perforating wounds of, 662
perforating wounds of, 663
without injury or prolapse of abdominal organs, 663
with prolapse of a portion of bowel, 664
with injury and perforation of the prolapsed bowel, 663
tumours of, 662
wounds of, 662
Abdominal hernia, 667
Abdominal section, 343
Abscess; acute, 7
anal, 664
chronic, 11
cold, 11
counter-opening for, 10
deep-seated, method of opening, 10
interdigital, in the dog, 1006
of the spermatic cord, 373
pharyngeal, 620
in the ox, 589
rectal, 696
shoulder, 608
sublingual, 581
sublumbar, after castration, 373
subparotid, 540
urinary, 737
Acid firing, 259
Acne, 58
contagious, 56
Acrobustitis in the horse, 750
in the dog, 752
in the ox, 718
in the pig, 752
Actinomycosis in the pharynx, 590
Acute gonitis, 911
laminitis in the horse, 949
in the ox, 751
Adenitis, 98
Air embolism, 91
insufflation of, for sprained tendon, 846
Albugo, 507
Alveolar periostitis, chronic ossifying, 599
in carnivora, 601
purulent, 599
Alveoli, dental, neoplasms of, 603
Amaurosis, 516
Ambrine for burns, 36
Ametropia, 496
Anæmia, traumatic, 40
Anæsthesia, epidural, 207
general, 171
in birds, 196
in the cat, 195
in the dog, 186
in the horse, 172
cast position, 173
standing position, 176
in the monkey, 196
in the ox, 185
in the pig, 186
in the sheep, 186
by anavenol, 192
by avertin, 196
by chloral, 180
by chloroform, 172
by cyclopropane, 186
by ether and oxygen, 189
by evipan, 265
by nembutal, 199
by pentothal, 206
by thiopentone (pentothal sodium), 178
by trilene, 193
local, 214
by chlorocaine, 216
by cocaine, 214
by codrenine, 216
by cold, 214
by eudrenine, 216
by locadyne and dulcine, 209
by novocaine, 216
by novo-zirol, 216
by parkane, 216
by Parsetic, (procaine) 216
by phenolaine, 216
by quinine and urea hydrochloride, 216
spinal, 207
stovaine and cocaine, 207
regional dental, in the dog, 286
Anal fistula, 697
glands in the dog, inflammation, of 695
suture, 704
Anatomy, surgical, 147
Anchylosis, 144
Aneurismal varix, 747
Aneurisms, 89
arterio-venous, 89

Angler's inhaler, 789
Anker's guarded knife, 341
Anophthalmia, 496
Anorchid, 398, 740
Ano-rectal fistulà, 696
Anterior tibial neurectomy, 449
Anthrax, 55
Anti-back-breaking apparatus, 163
Antisepsis and asepsis, 193
Antiseptic agents, 218
Anus. *See* Rectum, 690
congenital anomalies of, 690
preternaturalis, 665
spasm of, 710
Aorta (posterior), thrombosis of, 898
Aponeurosis of the hip, ossification of, 883
of the thigh, ossification of, 883
Appendages of the eye, 519
Arecoline for choking, 629
Arterial thrombosis, 90
Arterial hæmorrhage, 87
Arteries, affections of, 85
ligation of, 243
open wounds and contusions of, 85
rupture of, 88
thrombosis of, 90
torsion of, 244
Arterioles, crushing of, 244
Arteritis, 90
Artery forceps, 244
Arthritis, closed, 143
deforming, 143
dry, 143
gouty, in birds, 143
ossificans, 143
post-partum, 142
purulent, 139
rheumatoid, 141
traumatic, 139
Articular rheumatism, 141
windgalls, 865
Artificial eye, 290
hyperæmia (Biers), 260
Astigmatism, 496
Astragalus, fracture of, 927
Atheroma of false nostril, 54[illegible]
Atrophy of muscles, 72
Auto-cauteries, 254
for dividing tissues, 232
Autoplastia, 245
Avertin, 196

Bacillus of Nicolaïer, 46
Septicus, 45
Back, affections of, 637
abscess on, 638
broken, 649
galls on, 637
hæmatoma on, 637
ricked on jinked, 646
sitfast on, 637
wounds on, 638
Balanitis in the dog, 750
in the horse, 750
Balanitis in the ox, 751
in the pig, 752
Balano-posthitis, 750
Bandages, 226
Barrier and Siedamgrotzky on mechanism of sprained tendons, 841
Bees, stings by, 31
Bernadot's and Butel's apparatus for preventing broken back, 160
Biceps, rupture of, 803
(coraco-radialis), 803
sprain of, 803
femoris, rupture of, 880
displacement of, 881
operation for, 882
Bicipital bursa, inflammation of (bursitis intertubercularis), 803
purulent bursitis of, 805
Bier's hyperæmic treatment, 260
Biflex canal, inflammation of, 1000
B.I.P.P., 27, 220
Black pitch, 113
Bladder, affections of, 717
amputation of, 726
calculi in, 724
endoscopia of, 721
foreign bodies in, 722
functional disturbance of, 717
inversion of, 725
paralysis of, 728
passing catheter into, 718
prolapse of, 724
puncture of, 432
in the horse and ox, 432
in the dog and the cat, 432
rupture of, 722
stone in, 724
tumours of, 727
wounds of, 721
Bleeding. *See* Hæmorrhage
local, 321
operation for, 317
See Phlebotomy
Blemished knee, 834
operation for, 456
Blepharitis, 522
Blepharoptosis, 520
Blinds, 150
Blood stones, 94
transfusion of, 29 and 322
Bobba bone, 874
Boccar's operation for stringhalt, 486
Bog spavin, 929
Bone, affections of, 105
caries of, 129
contusions of, 105
fractures of, 107
instruments for operations upon, 232
necrosis of, 130
open wounds of, 106
pinning, 116
saws, 204
Bowed tendon, 843

Bowel, affections of, 684
  escape of, through perforating abdominal wound, 664
  fistula, 665
  foreign bodies in, 684
  intussusception of, 687
  invagination of, 687
  operations on, 353
  prolapse or descent of, after castration, 371
  puncture of (tapping), 356
  sutures, 238
  twist of, 687
  ventro-fixation of, 703
  wounds of, 665
Brain, cœnurus cerebralis on, 587
  tumours of, 586
Bridle lameness, 799
Broken back, prevention of, 160
Bruised sole, 978
Bubonocele, 673
Bull-holder, 164
  ring, 164
Burdizzo method of castration, 378
Burgundy pitch, 113
Buried sutures, 238
Burns and scalds, 38
Bursæ, affections of, 67
  atypical or acquired, 67
  deep, 67
  superficial, 67
" Bursal enlargement," meaning of, 67
Bursattee (Leeches), 62
Bursitis, acute, 67
  chronic, 67
  cystic, 67
  dry, 67
  fibrous, 68
  hæmorrhagic, 68
  intertubercularis, 803
    purulent, 805
  proliferating, 68
  purulent, 67
Button sutures, 237

Cab-horse disease, 874
Cæsarean section, 415
Cagny's injection for synovitis, 84
Calcaneo-cuboid ligament, sprain of, 935
Calcification in the aponeurosis, 883
Calculi, migratory, 733
  milk, 776
  renal, 712
  salivary, 539
  ureteral, 714
  urethral, 736
  vesical, 724
Cancer, swamp, 61
Canker of the foot, 968
  of the ear (dog), 529
Caponing of fowl, 383
Capped elbow, 819
    in race-horses, 820
  fetlock, 858
Capped hock, 918
    deep, 925
    prevention of, 919
  knee, 823
Cardiac syncope, 176
Caries of bone, 129
  of teeth, 598
Carlisle's inhaler, 173
Carpal sheath, dropsy or distension of 826
    sprain of, 852
Carpus, fracture of, 829
Cartilaginous grafting, 248
Casting, complications of, 170
  horses with hobbles, 158
    with a rope, 155
    by the Stuttgart method, 161
  oxen, using a rope, 166
    using hobbles, 168
Castration, operation for, 361
  Burdizzo's method, 378
  by bistournage, 378
  by covered method, 368
  by crushing the testicle, 378
  by crushing the cord (martelage), 378
  complications of, 370
  of cat, 382
  of cockerels, 383
  of cryptorchid, 385
  of dog, 382,
  of goat, 381
  of lamb and ram, 380
  of monkey, 383
  of ostrich, 354
  of rabbit and guinea pig, 385
  of swine, 381
Cataract, acquired, 513
  capsular (false cataract), 513
  capsulo-lenticular, 513
  congenital, 513
  lenticular (true cataract), 513
  operation for, 514
  senile, 513
Catheter for bitch, 720
  for cat, 720
  for cow, 719
  for dog, 720
  for ewe, 720
  for horse, 718
  for ox, 718
  for ram, 720
  Gunther's, 534
  œsophageal, 623
Cauterisation, 252
Cervical region, affections of, 606
    abscesses in, 606
    contusions of, 606
    fistula in, 606
    pustular eruption, 607
  vertebræ, fractures of, 648
Cervico-occipital neuralgia, 102
Chain splint, 852
Champignon, 746
Chemosis, 504

Cherry's disease, 831
Chest, affections of, 654
    founder, 831
    non-penetrating wounds of, 656
    penetrating wounds of, 656
Chime, sore, 609
Chisels, 232
Chloral anæsthesia, 180
Chlorocaine, 216
Chloroform as anæsthetic, 172
    muzzles and inhalers, 173
Choking, 628
Choroiditis, 510
Chronic abscesses, 11
    laminitis, 991
Ciliary (marginal) blepharitis, 522
Cirsocele, 746
Clams, castration, 367
    hernia, 325
    West's, 766
Claws, deformity of, in the ox, 999
    overgrown, in the ox, 999
        in the sheep, 1001
Clitoridectomy, 401
Coarse hock, 933
Cocaine, 216
Coculet's splint for horns, 589
Codrenine, 216
Cœliotomy, 343
Cœnurus cerebralis, 587
        operation for, 479
Cold abscess, 11
    water, uses of, 261
Collar galls, 608
    injuries, 608
Colon, puncture of, 356
    twist or rotation of, 687
Comb and wattels, removal of, 488
Complications of castration, 370
    of ovariotomy (mare), 408
    of wounds, 37
Conchal cartilage, amputation of, 293
        necrosis of, 527
        ulceration of, 528
Concussion of the brain, 585
    of the spinal cord, 650
    of the thoracic organs, 654
Condition of patient for operation, 147
Conjunctival culs-de-sac, examination of, 491
Conjunctivitis, 502
    diphtheritic, 502
    granular, 502
    parasitic, 503
    vesicular, 503
Contagious foul of the foot in the ox, 999
    papillomata of dog's mouth, 538
    venereal tumours in dog and bitch, 755
Contracted flexor tendons, 847
        in adults, 849
        in young animals, 847
        operations for, 454
Contracted hoof, 961
        operations for, 471
Control of the cat, 170
    of the dog, 169
    of the horse, cast, 155
        standing, 150
    of the ox, 164
    of the pig, 169
    of the sheep, 168
Contusions, 32
Cornea, affections of, 504
    opacities of, 506
    puncture of, 507, 509
    ulcers of, 506
Corneal fistula, 506
Corns, 972
    complicated, 972
    moist, 972
    suppurating, 972
Coronary cushion, dermatitis of, 957
Coronitis, chronic, 957
    gangrenous, 958
Corono-pedal joint, sprain of, 862, 927
Costal cartilage, fracture of, 656
    fistula, 658
Cotyloid cavity, fracture through, 886
Counter-opening for abscess, 10
Courbe, 936
Cox's inhaler, 173
Cracked heels, 54
Cradle, 155
Cranium, affections of, 583
    contusions of, 583
    dentigerous cyst in, 586
    dermous cyst in, 587
    fractures of, 584
    tumours of, 586
    wounds of, 584
Crib-biting, operation for, 485
Crop, impaction of, 636
Croup, tumours of, 900
Crural paralysis, 894
Crushing, operation by, 241
    arterioles, 244
Cryptophthalmia, 496
Cryptorchid, 741
    castration of, 385
Cryptorchidism in the dog, 743
    in the ox, 743
    in the pig, 743
    in the ram, 743
Culture of Reading bacillus, 27
Cunean tendon, distension of sheath of, 925
    tenotomy of, 459
Cupping, 322
Curb, 935
    true, 935
Curby hocks, 936
Curettes, 232
Curvature of the spine, 652
Cutaneous ulcers, 57
Cutting proud, after castration, 376
    and puncturing instruments, 231

Cyclopia, 496
Cyst, 50
dentigerous, 586
dermoid, 587, 708
interdigital, in the dog, 1006
in the cord after castration, 376
in false nostril, 545
in nose, 545
in sinus, 277
in the vagina, 767
sebaceous, 59
Cystic testicle, 395
Cystitis, 723
Cystoplegia, 728
Cystotomy in the dog, 430
Czerny's bowel suture, 238

Dacryoadenitis, 523
Dacryocystitis, 523
Deep-capped hock, 925
Degive's method of operating for hernia, 330
modified, 331
Dehorning of cattle, 278
Dental anaesthesia in the dog, 286
fistula, 692
Dentigerous cyst (cranium), 296
(jaw), 561
(testicle, teratoma), 741
operation for, 290
Dermatitis, 53
chronic vegetative interdigital, in the ox, 997
interdigital, in the ox, 996
in the sheep, 1002
of the perioplic band and coronary cushion, 957
toxic, in the ox, 996
verrucose, in the interdigital region of the ox, 997
Dermoid cyst (cranium), 587
Descent of the bowel or omentum after castration, 371
after laparotomy, 348
Diathermy, 263
Dieterich's operation on the guttural pouch, 296
Digit, affections of, 849
amputation of (ox), 472
(dog), 475
fissure of, 834
sprain of, in the ox, 864
supernumerary, 834
traumatic lesions of, 849
Digital artery, ligation of, 459
compression, 242
neurectomy, 447
vein, ligation of, 460
Dilatation of œsophagus, 633
Diplegia, 103
Directors, 232
Dishing, 799
Dislocations, 134
Displacement of biceps femoris, 881
operation for, 882
Distichiasis, 520
Diverticulum of œsophagus, 633
Division of tissues, 231
Dog catcher, 162
Docking, 433
Dorsal and lumbar vertebræ, fracture of, 648
Dorso-costal neuralgia, 102
Dressing materials, 225
Dropped neck, 642
Dry arthritis, 143
mouth, 593
Dysuria, 717

Ear, affections of, 525
canker of, 529
examination of, 525
foreign bodies in, 528
hæmatoma of, 526
internal, affections of, 532
middle, affections of, 532
necrosis of, 527
ulceration of, 528
tumours of, 532
wounds and contusions of, 526
Ecchymosis, 22
Ecraseur, Chassaignac's, 241
Dewar's, 241
Miles's, 241
Ectasia of œsophasgus, 633
Ectopia of the kidney, 711
of the testicle, 401, 471
Ectropion, 521
operation for, 483
Elbow and forearm, affections of, 822
capped, 819
dislocation of, 818
dropped, 810
fracture of, 817
joint, inflammation of, 819
hygroma or distension of, 822
Electrodiagnosis, 264
Electrotherapy, 265
Elephantiasis, 57
Elizabethan collar, 169
Emmetropia, 496
Emphysema, traumatic, 42
Endoscopia of bladder, 721
Enophthalmia, 496
Enterectomy, 353
Enterotomy, 353
Entropion, 520
operation for, 482
Enuresis, 737
Epididymitis, 711
Epidural anæsthesia, 207
in the cat, 214
in the dog, 213
in the goat, 213
in the horse, 211
in the ox, 208
in the pig, 213

Epidural anæsthesia in the sheep, 212
Epispadia, 731
Epistaxis, 546
Epulis, 603
Erysipelas, 44
 cutaneous, 44
 gangrenous, 44
 phlegmonous, 44
Erythema, 485
Esmarch's bandage, 240
Eudrenine, 216
Eupad, 27
Eusol, 219
Eustachian tube, affections of, 533
Eversion of the eyelids (ectropion), 520
 of the vagina, 764
Evulsion of the hoof, 956
Examination of horses as to soundness, 1007
Exomphalos, 672
Exophthalmia, 496
Exostoses, 132
 of the phalanges, 870
Extensor pedis tendon sheath, distension of, in front of fetlock, 859
 in front of hock, 889
 tendons, rupture of, 838
External angle of the ilium, fracture of, 884
 hygroma of, 878
 injuries of, 878
Extraction of teeth, 281
Eye, affections of, 491
 appearance of depth of, 495
 appendages of, 519
 applications for, 497
 artificial insertions of, 296
 astigmatism, 496
 congenital anomalies of, 496
 dermoid cyst in 518
 examination of, 491
 by lateral light, 493
 conjunctival culs-de-sac, 491
 depth of eye, 493
 the pupil, 492
 with ophthalmoscope, 493
 foreign bodies in, 500
 non-inflammatory conditions of (Chemosis, Pterygium), 504
 parasites in, 519
 protection of, 498
 refraction in, 496
 traumatic lesions of, 498
 tumours of, 518
Eyeball, affections of muscles of, 524
 burns of, 500
 contusions of, 499
 extirpation of, 289
 protrusions of, 496
 retraction of, 464
 tuberculosis of, 519
 wounds of, 500
Eyelids, affections of, 519
 clonic spasm of, 519
 drooping of (upper), 520
 tonic spasm of, 519
 tumours of, 522
 wounds of, 521

Facial neuralgia, 102
 paralysis, 573
 sinuses operation on cyst, 277
 pus in, 274
False inguinal hernia, 675
 joint, 121, 126
 nostril, atheroma (cyst), in, 545
 paralysis of, 545
 rig, 366
 ringbone, 870
Feet. *See* Foot
 affections of, in the horse, 943
 in the dog and cat, 1003
 in the ox, 993
 in the pig, 1003
 in the sheep, 1000
 examination of, in the horse, 943
Female genital organs, affections of, 757
Femoro-tibial joint, dislocation of, 914
Femur, fracture of, 888
Festered corn, 971
Fetlock, affections of, 856
 capped, 858
 distension of subcutaneous bursa in front of, 858
 knuckled, 847
 injuries of, from striking or interfering, 856
 sprain of, 861
Fetlock-joint, acute inflammation of, 864
 dislocation of, 864
 distension of, 865
 dry arthritis of, 865
 open wounds of, 865
Fever, traumatic, 40
Fibula, fracture of, 910
Filaria oculi, 519
 medinensis, 65
Filariasis of the skin, 64
 withers, 642
Firing, acid, 259
 flexor tendons, 253
 hock, 253
 irons, 254
 mixed, 257
 needle-point, 256
 objective, 252
 objections to, 258
 pastern, 253
Firing, penetrating point, 256
 superficial line, 254
 point, 255
 effects of, 257
 the dog, 259
 the ox, 259
 varieties of, 252
Fissure of digit, 799

Fissure of hoof (sandcrack), 944
of lip, 570
of tibia, 901
Fissured fracture, 107
Fistula, 17
anal, 697
bowel or intestinal, 665
complete, 17
congenital, 17
corneal, 506
costal, 658
dental, 602
excretory, 17
incomplete (blind), 17
lachrymal, 523
milk, 773
of the neck, 606
pathological, 17
purulent, 17
recto-urethral, 690
recto-vaginal, 690
recto-vesical, 690
salivary, 538
secretory, 17
Fistulous withers, 639
Fixing hind limb to tail, 153
Fleam, 318
Flexor metacarpi externus, distension of sheath of, 828
metatarsi, rupture of, 903
sprain of, 901
tendons, contraction of, 847
mechanism of sprain of, 841
rupture of, 77
section of, 835
sprain of, 841
Fluter, 759
Folliculitis, 58
Foot, boxy, 966
canker of, 968
contusion of, 978
crushing of, 978
eczematous dermatitis of, 968
foreign body in (horse), 960
(ox), 995
foul of, in the ox, 998
rot in sheep, 1001
separation of hoof from (horse), 956
(ox), 995
wounds of, 951
plantar aspect (horse), 960
(ox), 995
Forearm, affections of, 822
contusions and wounds of, 822
Fractures, classification of, 107
bone pinning for, 116
complete, 107
complications of, 121
compound, 108
deferred, 107
fissured, 107
greenstick, 107
healing of, 109
incomplete, 107
Fractures, in birds, 128
in dog and cat, 122
intermedullary pinning for 116
partial, 107
Kirschner-Ehmer splint for, 119
Stadar splint for, 116
suturing and plating for, 115
Friebel's apparatus for contracted tendons, 849
Frontal sinus operation on horse, 275
ox, 278
dog, 278
Frost bite, 38
Fulguration, 267
Funiculitis, 746
Furunculosis, 59

Galvanic cautery, 232
Gangrene, 13
after castration, 373
dry, 14
gas, 45
moist, 146
Gangrenous coronitis, 958
erysipelas, 45
mammitis (cow), 780
(ewe), 788
septicæmia, 45
Gas gangrene, 45
Gastric (chronic) tympany in the ox, operation for, 352
Gastrocnemius and perforatus tendons, section of, 908
Gastrotomy, 349
Gelding behaving like a rig, 742
inguinal hernia in, 674
Genital organs (male), affections of, 740
(female), affections of, 757
exploration of, 757
Gersuny's method of treating prolapse of rectum, 705
Gid, 587
operation for, 479
Glaucoma, 576
Glossitis, 580
Glossoplegia, 579
Gluteal bursa, inflammation of, 879
muscles, rupture of, 880
tendon, inflammation of, 880
Goitre, 613
cystic, 613
fibrous, 613
parenchymatous, 613
Gonitis, acute, 911
chronic, 911
Gouty arthritis, 143
Granulomata (infective) in the dog, 755
Grease, 54
Great sesamoidean sheath, synovitis of, 859
Grafting for corneal opacity, 508
Guilbert's teat knife, 777
Gums, epulis on, 603
neoplasms of, 603

Gunther's catheter, 534
Gut-tie, 682
operation for, 341
Guttural pouches, affections of, 533
catarrh of, 533
pus in, 533
tympanitis of, 536
operation on, 296

Hæmatocele, 746
Hæmatoma, 36
in dog's ear, 526
operation for, 481
in jugular furrow, 319
of stifle and leg, 900
of vagina, 762
Hæmaturia, 717
Hæmorrhage, 40
after castration, 370
arrest of, 240
prevention of, 239
Hæmorrhoids (piles), 709
Hæmostasis, 239
by blunt dissection, 241
by crushing, 241
by digital compression, 242
by elastic ligation, 242
by forcipressure, 244
by ligation, 242
by plugging, 245
by styptics, 245
by tearing, 241
by thermo-cautery, 241
by torsion, 244
Hair balls and binder twine in abomasum of calf, 684
operation for, 686
Hairpin clamp for bowel, 355
Halsted suture, 236
Harderian gland, hypertrophy of, 522
tumours of, 522
Hare-lip, 570
Head, œdema of, 542
shaking of, in the horse, 295, 530
Heart, rupture of, 654
Heliotherapy, 27
Hemiplegia, 103
Hernia, abdominal, 667
crural, 676
diaphragmatic, 681
external abdominal, 667
false inguinal, 675
incarcerated, 668
inguinal, 641, 673
in ruminants, 677
in small animals, 678
intercostal, 660
internal abdominal, 680
interstitial, 675
intra-abdominal, 680
irreducible, 668
of lung, 660
parts of, 667
pelvic (gut-tie), 682
Hernia, perineal, 678
peritoneal, 682
reducible, 668
scrotal, 673
strangulated, 668
umbilical, 672
varieties, 668
ventral, 676
with adhesions, 669
Herpes Zoster, 54
High ringbone, 870
Hind-limb, affections of, 877
Hip, dislocation of, 891
inflammation of, 893
lameness, 877
ossification of aponeurosis of, 883
rheumatism of, 893
Hobbles, casting, 159
cross, 159
Hobday's method of amputating prolapsed rectum in the dog, 706
Hock, capped, 918
arthritis and synovitis in, 939
coarse, 933
contusion and wounds of, 917
curby, 936
dislocation of, 928
firing, 253
fracture of, 926
sprain of, 927
sprung, 927
tied-in, 931
Hoof, affections of, 978
contracted, 942
cracks in, 978
deformity of, in the ox, 999
separation or evulsion of, 956
ox, 995
Honey cyst, 578
Horns, affections of, 588
fissure of, 590
fracture of, 589
separation of, 588
splint for, 589
Horny growths, 60
Hot water, use of, 261
Hudson's operation for stricture of teat 488
Humerus, fracture of, 815
Hydarthrosis of the elbow-joint, 822
Hydrocele, 746
Hydronephrosis, 716
Hydrophthalmia, 516
Hydrotherapy, 261
Hygroma, chronic, 67
Hymen, imperforate, 760
Hyoid bone, fracture of, 581
Hypermetropia, 496
Hypochlorous acid, 219
Hypohæmia, 499
Hypoderma bovis, 64
Hypodermic injections, 249
for shoulder lameness, 809

Hypopyon, 509
Hypospadia, 731
Hysterectomy, 416
Hysteropexia, 767
Hysterotomy, 415

Iliac thrombosis, 85, 898
Ilio-sacral joint, dislocation of, 891
Ilium, fracture of, 884
external angle of, 884
internal angle of, 886
shaft of, 886
Impaction of crop, 636
Imperforate hymen, 760
teats, 771
Imrie's inhaler, 174
Incontinence of urine, 717
Inferior maxilla, fracture of, 557
maxillary sinus, operation on, 275
sesamoidean ligaments, sprain of, 862
Infiltration with urine, 757
Inflammation, 3
causes of, 3
chronic, 6
specific, 7
symptoms of, 3
treatment of, 4
Infra-orbital nerve, section of, 295
Inguinal hernia (horse), 673
operation for 332
(ox), 697
(small animals), 678
operation for preserving the testicle in, 337
strangulated, 668
operation for, 335
(bitch), operation for, 340
Inhaler for chloroform, 173
Carlisle's, 174
Cox's, 173
Imrie's, 174
for Trilene, 193
Longley's, 190
Injections or inoculations, hypodermic, 249
intralaryngeal, 251
intratracheal, 251
intravenous, 32, 251
parenchymatous, 251
Insufflation of air for sprained tendons, 846
Instruments, 225
disinfection or sterilisation of, 229
Intercarpal joint, distension of, 832
Interdigital abscess or cyst (dog), 1006
dermatitis (ox), 996
(sheep), 1002
Internal angle of the ilium, fracture of, 886
Intermedullary pinning, 119
Interosseous ligament, sprain of, 852
Interphalangeal joints, inflammation of, 865
dog, 874
Intervertebral joints, dislocation of, 647
Intestinal fistula, 665
Intestine, foreign bodies in, 684. *See* Bowel
Intralaryngeal injection, 251
Intratracheal injection, 251
Intravenous injection, 251
Intravesical exploration, 721
Intussusception and invagination of the bowel, operation for, 687
Involuntary shaking of the head in the horse, 295, 530
Iridectomy, 510
Iris, affections of, 508
Iritis, 509

Jabot, 634, 636
operation for, 636
Jack spavin, 932
Jarde, 938
Jardon, 938
Jaw, lower, dislocation of, 563
Jaws, affections of, 555
contusions of, 559
dentigerous cyst in, 561
fistula of, 559
paralysis of (lower), 582
sinus in, 559
tumours of, 560
wounds of, 560
Jelkmann's method of treating twist of the colon, 688
"Jinked back," 646
Jobert's suture, 238
Joint-ill, 142
Joints, affections of, 133
anchylosis of, 144
contusions of, 133
dislocation of, 134
false, 121, 126
open, 137
post partum synovitis of, 142
sprain, 133
synovitis of, 141
wounds of, 137
Joly's treatment for sprained tendons, 846
Jugular phlebitis, 611
phlebotomy, 317

Keratitis, 504
contagious, 505
deep, 504
parenchymatous, 504
spotted, 504
superficial, 504
suppurative (ulcerative), 504
vascular, 504
Keratocele, 506
Keratoma, 949
on sole, 950
operation for, 470

Kicking-strap for ox, 165
Kidney, affections of, 711
calculi in, 712
contusions of, 712
dropsy of, 716
floating (ectopia), 711
parasites in, 717
tumours of, 716
wounds of, 712
Kirschner-Ehmer Splint, 116
Knee, affections of, 823
bent, 834
operation for, 452
blemished, 834
operation for, 456
broken, 833
capped, 823
contusion of, 823
hygroma or distension of subcutaneous bursa in front of, 823
joint, arthritis of, 831
Cherry's disease of, 831
dislocation of, 830
distension of synovial capsule of, 831
open, 833
splint, 852
sprain of, 830
synovitis of, 831
synovitis of sheaths in front of, 828
traumatic arthritis of, 833
Knives, sage, 461
method of holding, 232
varieties of, 231
Knuckling at fetlock, 847
Kyphosis, 652
Kypho-scoliosis, 652

Lachrymal apparatus, affections of, 523
canal, obstruction of, 523
ducts, obstruction of, 523
fistula, 523
gland, inflammation of, 523
sac, inflammation (dacrocystitis) of, 524
Lameness, 796
bridle, 799
definition of, 796
diagnosis of, 796
diagonal, 798
hip, 877
nerve, blocking for, 801
seat of, 799
shoulder, 801
spavin, 933
splint, 853
Laminitis, acute (horse), 986
(ox), 995
chronic, 991
Lancet, 318
Laparotomy, 343
Laryngotomy, 299
Larynx, affections of, 614
contusions of, 604
exploration of, 604
foreign bodies in, 616
fracture of, 615
paralysis of, 618
parasites in, 618
stenosis of, 307
tumours of, 617
Lateral cartilage excision of, 460
Lembert suture, 238
Lens, affections of, 512
discission of, 514
dislocation of, 512
displacement of, 514
extraction of, 515
Leucoma, 507
Lifting horse unable to rise, 162
hind-limb of ox, 165
Ligature, elastic, 242
Limb, amputation of, 480
Limbs, affections of, 796
Lips, affections of, 567
contagious papillomata of (dog), 571
cysts in the, 573
dermatitis of (lambs), 570
fissure of (hare-lip), 570
retraction of, 570
tumours of, 571
ulceration of (cat), 571
wounds of, 567
Lithiasis, renal, 705
Lithotomy, 425
Lithotrity, 426
Loins, affections of, 642
rheumatism of (muscles), 643
sprain of, 642
traumatic lesions of, 642
Longissimus dorsi, sprain of, 642
Longley's tail guard, 438
inhaler, 190
Loop stitch for abdominal wall, 348
Lordosis, 652
Lower jaw, paralysis of, 582
Low ringbone, 870
Lumbago, 643
Lumbo-abdominal neuralgia, 102
Lung, collapse of, 651
laceration of, 654
hernia of, 660
Lupus, 101
Luxations (dislocations), 134
Lymphangitis, 95
Lymphatic glands, tumours of, 98

McLean's knife for operation on teat, 488
Macroglossia, 580
Mal-callus formation, 121
Malcolm's treatment for canker, 970
Male genital organs, affections of, 740
Malignant œdema (gas gangrene), 745
after castration, 373
tumours, 48

Mammary gland, affections of, 770
absence of, 771
actinomycosis of, 788
amputation of, 432
botriomycosis of, 788
congenital abnormalities of, 778
congestion of, 779
contusions of, 772
eruptions on, 779
supernumerary, 771
tumours of, 791
(bitch), 792
wounds of, 740
Mammitis or mastitis, 780
acute, 780
bacillary, 780
catarrhal, 780
chronic, 787
contagious, 787
galactophorous, 780
gangrenous (cow), 780
(ewe), 788
hæmatogenous, 780
in bitch, 790
in ewe, 788
in goat, 789
in mare, 789
in sow, 790
lymphogenous, 780
parenchymatous, 780
prevention of, 783
purulent, 780
streptococcic, 788
subacute, 786
Marsupial operation for pyometra in bitch, 420
Massage, 263
and mobilisation of fractured limb, 120
Masticatory muscles, paralysis of, 582
Mastoido-humeralis, affections of, 808
Mattress suture, 236
Median neurectomy, 440
Membrana nictitans, tumours of, 522
removal of, 522
Metacarpus, affections of, 834
fracture of, 851
inflammatory growths on, 840
lesions of, 835
rheumatoid ostitis of, 856
Metatarsus. *See* Metacarpus
Metritis, 770
Micturition, difficult (dysuria), 717
frequent (sychuria), 717
painful (strangury), 717
Metrorrhagia, 770
Milk calculi, 776
ducts, obstruction of, 776
stricture of, 777
fistula, 773
Moist corn, 972
Molar teeth, overlapping of, 594
Möller's method of amputating prolapsed rectum in dog, 706
of treating twist of colon, 689
Molluscum Contagiosum, 64
Monorchid, 740, 741
Moon blindness, 510
Morphia narcosis in the dog, 195
Mouth, affections of, 564
contagious papillomata in (dog), 571
exploration of, 564
foreign bodies in, 575
gag, Bayer's, 565
Haussmann's, 564
Kirk's (dog), 565
Mitchell's, 565
Varnell's, 564
Woolf's (dog), 565
scalds of, 576
shears, 594
traumatic lesions of, 575
tumours in, 571
Mud fever, 54
radio-active, 846
Murphy's button, 353
Muscles, affections of, 69
atrophy of, 72
cramp of, or spasm, 73
in racing greyhounds, 73
inflammation of, 70
of mastication, paralysis of, 582
paralysis of, 73
rupture of, 69
spasm of, 73
tumours of, 74
Muscular rheumatism, 71
Musculo-spiral (radial) paralysis, 810
Muzzle for dog, 169
Mydriatics, 498
Myopia, 496
Myositis, 70
Myotics, 498
Mystomy of muscles of tail, 438

Nail binding, 978
ingrowing, 1005
matrix, inflammation of, 1005
separation of, in dog, 1005
Nasal bones, fracture of, 543
cavities, affections of, 541
bleeding from, 546
exploration of, 541
foreign bodies in, 548
parasites in, 549
traumatic lesions of, 546
chambers operation, 272
Navicular bone, fracture of, 960
bursa, inflammation of, 965
disease, 965
Nebula, 507
Neck, affections of, 604
distortion of, 604
dropped, 642
fistula of, 606
pustular eruption on, 607

Necrosis of bone, 130
Needles, suture, 233
Nembutal anæsthesia, 199
  dosage, 202
Nephrectomy, 485
Nephrotomy, 484
Nerves, affections of, 99
  blocking, 801
  compression of, 99
  contusion of, 100
  section of, 99
  tumours of, 101
  wounds of, 100
  wounds of, 100
Nesfield's treatment for leucoma, 507
Nettle stings, 40
Neuralgia, cervico-occipital, 102
  dorso-costal, 102
  facial, 102
  lumbo-abdominal, 102
  traumatic, 42
Neuritis, 101
Nicking, 438
Nose, bleeding from, 546
  cyst in, 545
Nostrils, affections of, 541
  necrosis of cartilages of, 542
  tumours of, 544
  wounds of, 541
Nystagmus, 519

Obturator lameness, 894
  paralysis, 894
Occlusion of anus, 690
  of os uteri, 769
  of urethra, 730
Ochromus anthropophagus, 64
Œdema after castration, 372
  malignant, 45
  of head, 542
Œsophagocele, 634
Œsophagotomy, 315
Œsophagus, affections of, 623
  dilatation of, 633
  diverticulum of, 633
  ectasia of, 633
  exploration of, 623
  obstruction of, 628
  paralysis of, 636
  parasites in, 635
  passing probang into, 623
    stomach tube into, 625
  stricture or stenosis of, 633
  tumours of, 635
  wounds of, 627
Omentum, descent of, after castration, 371
    after laparotomy, 348
  function of, 348
Omphalocele, 672
Onchocerca reticulata, 65
Onyx (keratitis), 505
Oophorectomy, 402
Opacities of the cornea, 506
Operating table for horse, 162
    for dog, 169
  theatre (horse), 148
    (dog), 149
Operation by blunt dissection, 241
    crushing, 241
    elastic ligature, 214
    tearing, 241
    thermo-cautery, 241
Operative surgery, 147
  technique, 228
Ophthalmia, specific or recurrent, 510
  sympathetic, 517
Optic nerve, atrophy of, 516
    inflammation of, 516
  papilla, 516
    atrophy of, 516
Orbicularis palpebrarum, paralysis of 519
Orbit, affections of, 525
  contusions of, 525
  fracture of, 525
  tumours of, 525
Orchitis, 744
Os calcis, fracture of, 926
  pedis, fracture of, 959
    osteo-periostitis of, 964
  uteri, occlusion of, 769
Oscheocele (scrotal hernia), 673
Ostitis, 118, 128
Otacariasis, 531
Othæmatoma, 526
Otitis, 529
Otorrhœa, 529
  ceruminous, 529
  eczematous, 529
  glandular, 529
  of distemper, 529
  parasitic, 531
Ovariotomy (bitch and cat), 414, 415
  (cow), 409
  (goat), 413
  (mare), 402
  (pig), 413
Ovaro-hysterectomy (bitch), 417
Overreach, 765
Ox, control of, 157
Oxygen and ether as anæsthetic, 189

Pads, callosities on, 1006
  inflammation of, 1004
Palate, fissure of, 581
Palmar (deep) neurectomy, 453
Pannus, 504
Panophthalmia, 517
Paracentesis thoracis, 322
Paralysis, 103
  local, 103
Paraphimosis, 753
Parasites in the eye, 519
  in kidney, 717
  in larynx, 618
  in œsophagus, 635

Parasites, in pharynx, 616
in rectum, 710
Paraplegia, 102, 652
Parenchymatous injection, 251
Parenteral injection of drugs, etc., 249
Parkane, 216
Parotid gland, affections of, 537
destruction of function of, 539
subparotid abscess, 540
Passing the catheter, 718
the probang, 623
the stomach tube, 625
Pastern, fracture of, 866
split, 866
Patella, fixation of, above trochlea (pseudo-luxation), 915
dislocation of, 914
distension of bursa in front of, 901
fracture of, 910
Patellar ligament (inner straight), section of, 458
Paw, sinus in, 1003
wounds of, 1003
Pectoral muscles, rupture of, 805
sprain of, 805
Pedal bone, fracture of, 891
osteo-periostitis of, 927
Peg splint, 852
Pelvic hernia, 650
operation for, 341
Pelvis, fracture of, 884
floor of, 887
in small animals, 888
Penicillin, 224
Penis, affections of, 748
absence of, 748
adhesion of, to sheath, 748
amputation of, 421
atrophy of, 748
congenital abnormalities of, 748
paralysis of, 756
retro-deviation of, operation for, 424
strangulation of, 749
torsion of, 748
traumatic lesions of, 749
tumours of (dog), 755
(horse), 754
(ox), 754
Perforatus bursa, distension of, 925
and perforans tendons, dislocation of, 920
rupture of, 838
section of, 835
sprain of, 841
Perinæum, rupture of, 759
Perineal hernia, 670
operation for, 342
suture, 759
Periodic (recurrent) ophthalmia, 510
Periosteotomy for spavin, 459
for splints, 855
Peritonitis after castration, 373
after laparotomy, 348
Peroneus tendon sheath, distension of, 925
tenotomy of, 486
Pervious urachus, 738
Phalangeal exostoses, 870
dislocation (dog), 875
Phalanges, fractures of, 866
amputation of (dog), 476
Pharyngitis, 620
Pharyngotomy, 622
Pharynx, affections of, 618
abscess in, 620
actinomyosis of, 622
examination of, 618
foreign bodies in, 619
paralysis of, 619
parasites in, 616
tumours of, 590
wounds of, 616
Phenolaine, 508
Phimosis, congenital, 748, 752
operation for, 748
Phlebitis, 92
jugular, 611
Phleboliths, 94
Phlebotomy (horse), 317
(ox), 320
Picked-up nail (horse), 960
(ox), 995
Piles, 709
Pilocarpine for choking, 629
Pin suture, 237
Pisiform, fracture of, 829
Place and time of operation, 148
Plantar aponeurosis, resection of, 467
neurectomy, 446
Plaster of Paris, 113
bandages, 113
splints and gutters, 114
Pleurisy, 657
Pneumocele, 660
Pneumothorax, 657
Pneumohæmothorax, 657
Poll, affections of, 604
abscess on, 605
contusion of, 604
evil, 605
operation for, 298
wounds of, 605
Polyorchid, 740
Popliteal paralysis, 896
Poroplastic felt, 115
Posterior aorta, thrombosis of, 898
spinatus, inflammation of, 807
of its bursa, 807
tibial neurectomy, 451
Posthitis, 750
Post-partum synovitis, 142
Premaxilla, fracture of, 556
Preparation of the patient 148
Prepuce, affections of, 748
tumours of, 754
Pricks in shoeing (horse), 975
(ox), 995

Probang, description of, 623
passage of (dog), 625
(horse), 623
(ox), 624
Proctitis, 695
Prolapsus ani, 699
et recti, 699
with invagination of colon into it, 699
Prolapse of invaginated rectum or colon, 699
Prostate gland, affections of, 728
hypertrophy of, 729
tumours of, 730
Prostatectomy, 730
Prostatitis, 728
" Proud ", cutting horse 376
Pseudo-luxation of patella, 915
Pseudo-sore shins, 855
Psoas muscles, rupture of, 879
sprain of, 879
Pterygium, 504
Ptosis, 520
Pupil, examination of, 492
Pupillary membrane, persistence of, 508
Pyæmia, 44
Pyelonephritis, 715
Pyorrhœa, 601
Pyuria, 715

Quadriplegia, 103
Quarter, affections of, 877
abscess of, 878
bursal enlargements of, 878
contusions of, 877
hæmatoma of, 878
sprain and rupture of muscles of, 879
tumours of, 900
Quill suture, 236
Quittor, 981
Bier's treatment for, 985
operation for, 460

Race-horses, capped elbow in, 819
sore shins in 855
Radial paralysis (horse), 810
partial, 811
Radio-active mud (for sprained tendons), 846
Radio-carpal joint, distension of, 832
Radiodiagnosis, 269
Radioscopy, 268
Radiotherapy, 269
Radium therapy, 269
Radius, fracture of, 818
Ranula, 578
Reading bacillus, culture of, 27
Rectitis, 695
Recto-urethral fistula, 690
Recto-vaginal fistula, 691, 762
Recto-vesical fistula, 690, 728
Rectum and anus, affections of, 690
abscess of, 696
complete prolapse, 699
with invagination, 700
congenital anomalies of, 690
dilatation of, 708
examination of, 690
fistula of, 697
inflammation of, 695
injuries of, 693
paralysis of, 709
parasites in, 710
partial prolapse, mucous prolapse, or prolapsus ani, 699
prolapse of, 699
stenosis of, 707
tumours of, 708
Refraction, 496
Renal calculi, 712
lithiasis, 712
Repulsion of teeth, 287
Resection of plantar aponeurosis, 467
Retention of urine, 717, 737
Retina, affections of, 515
hæmorrhage from, 515
inflammation of, 516
separation of, 515
Retractors, 204
Retro-deviation of penis, 424
Rheumatism, articular, 141
muscular, 71
of hip-joint, 893
of lumbar muscles, 643
of shoulder, 808
Rheumatoid ostitis in metacarpus, 856
Ribs, fistula abutting on, 658
fracture of, 655
Ricked back, 646
Rickets, 132
Rig or rigling, 741
castration of, 385
gelding behaving like, 742
Ringbone, articular, 870
false, 870
high, 870
low, 870
periarticular, 870
true, 870
Roaring, 618
operation for, 302
Rod splint, 852
Rumen, puncture of (tapping), 360
Rumenotomy, 349

Sacrum, fracture of, 793
Saddle galls, 637
prevention of, 641
Sage knives, 461
Salivary calculi, 539
operation for, 295
ducts, foreign bodies in, 539
fistula, 538
glands, affections of, 537
destruction of function of, 539

Salivary glands, tumours of, 540
wounds of, 537
Sandcrack, 978
at quarter, 947
at toe, 946
clasps, 946
complete, 944
complicated, 944
deep, 944
incomplete, 944
in the ox, 993
lameness from, 944
recent, 944
simple, 944,
sinuous, 944
special shoe for, 946
straight, 944
transverse, 948
Sarcocele, 741
Sarcomata (infective), 755
Scald in foot of ox, 1002
of sheep, 1002
Scalds, 38
Scapula, fracture of, 813
Scarification, 321
Sciatica, 102
Sciatic paralysis, 896
Scirrhous cord, 746
operation for, 374
Scoliosis, 619
Scrofular gummæ, 57
Scrotal hernia (horse), 673
(small animals), 646
(ox), 645
operation for, 332
Scrotum, traumatic lesions of, 744
inflammation of, 744
Section of gastrocnemius and perforatus tendons, 908
Seedy toe, 948
Septicæmia, 41
Septic dust, 42
Septum nasi, fracture of, 511
abscess on, 515
Serotherapy, 30
Serratus magnus, rupture of, 807
Service hobbles, 144
Sesamoidean sheath, synovitis of, 824
Sesamoiditis, 868
Sesamoids, fracture of, 868
Shaking of the head in the horse, 295, 530
Sharp teeth, 592
Shears mouth, 594
Sheath, affections of, 715
congenital abnormalities of, 715
tumours of, 721
Sheaths, tendon, affections of, 74
Shivering, 941
Shock, 42
Shoe-boil, 819
Shoulder abscess, 608
and arm, affections of, 802
contusion of, 803
hypodermic injection for, 809
Shoulder joint, dislocation of, 815
lameness, 801
rheumatism, 808
rupture of muscles and tendons of, 803
slip, 805
sprain of muscles and tendons of, 803
tumour, 608
Side-bones, 980
operations for, 472
Side-fetter, 152
Side-line (horse), 152
(ox), 164
Side-stick, 155
Simple splint, 852
Sinus, 17
Sinuses, affections of, 551
foreign bodies in, 554
operation on, 274
parasites in, 554
pus in, 552
Sit-fast on back, 637
Skin, affection of, 52
parasitic affections of, 64
tumours of, 62
Smith's operation for contracted hoof, 471
Sole, bruised (horse), 978
(ox), 994
Sore chime, 609
shins, 855
pseudo-, 855
Spasm of muscles, 73
Spavin, 930
anterior, 932
high, 932
jack, 932
lameness, 933
occult, 930
operation for, 459
posterior, 932
Speedy-cutting, 823
Spermatocele, 746
Spinal column, tumour of, 651
cord, affections of, 650
concussion, 650
injection into, 477
puncture and injection, 477
Spinati muscles, sprain, etc., of, 805
Spine, curvature of, 652
Spiroptera reticulata, 65
Splint lameness, 853
Splints, 851
chain, 852
knee, 852
removal of, 855
rod or peg 852
simple, 852
treatment by fast exercise, 855
Splints and bandages, 112
Split pastern, 866
Sporotrichosis, 62
Sprung hock, 927

Squint, 524
    operation for, 525
Stadar splint, 116
Staphyloma, 507
Staphylorraphy, 581
Stenson's duct, ligation of, 293
        wounds of, 537
Sterilisation of dressings, 228
    of instruments, 229
Sternal fistula, 659
Sternum, fracture of, 656
Stifle and leg, affections of, 900
    contusion of, 911
    hæmatoma of, 900
    joint, acute inflammation of, 911
        chronic inflammation of, 911
        dislocation of, 914
        sprain of, 911
    wounds of, 900
Stings by nettles, 40
    by bees and wasps, 34
Stinson's operation for stricture of teats, 487
Stocks, 153
Stomach and bowels, affections of, 684
        foreign bodies in, 684
            (dog), 685
    tube as probang, 625
Stone in bladder, 724
Strabismus, 524
    operation for, 525
Strangury, 717
Strapping up fore-limb, 151
Striking the fetlock, 856
Stringhalt, 939
    operation for, 486
    symptomatic, 939
Sturdy (gid), 587
Subcarpal ligament, sprain of, 841
Subcutaneous injection of saturated solution of common salt for shoulder lameness, 809
Sublingual abscess, 581
Subparotid abscess, 540
Subscapularis muscle, rupture of, 807
        sprain of, 807
Sulphonamides, 222
Superior maxilla fracture of, 555
    maxillary sinus, operation on, 275
Supernumerary digit, 834
    teeth, 591
    testicle, 741
Suppurating corn, 972
Suprascapular paralysis, 805
Suspensory ligament, rupture of, 840
        section of, 835
        sprain of, 840
        suprascapular paralysis, 805
Sutures, 233
    varieties of, 234
Suturing material, 225
    and plating bone, 115
Swamp cancer, 61
Sweating (non) in horses, 593
Sychuria, 719
Syncope, 42
Synechia, 473
Synovial sheaths, affections of, 79
        contusions of, 79
        wounds of, 79
Synoviotomy, 85
Synovitis, acute, 82
    chronic, 83
    closed, 82
    dry, 82
    infectious, 82
    plastic, 82
    purulent, 80
    serous, 82

Tænia cœnurus, 587
Tail, affections of, 793
    amputation of, 433
        (horse), 437
        (ox), 437
        (lamb), 437
        (dog), 437
    botriomycosis of, 794
    dermatitis of, 795
    eczema of (dog), 795
    fracture of, 793
    guard for (dog), 438
    myotomy (nicking) of, 438
    tenectomy of, 440
    tumours of, 794
    ulcer on (dog), 795
    wounds of, 793
Tampon canula, 583
Tapetum lucidum, 495
    nigrum, 495
Tapping chest, 322
    bowel, 356
Tarsal bones, fracture of, 926
    sheath, distension of, 923
        synovitis of, 922
            (purulent), 923
Tartar on teeth, 597
Teats, absence of, 771
    amputation of, 785
    calculi in, 776
    cracks on, 775
    eruptions on, 779
    fissures in, 775
    Hudson's operation for stricture of, 488
    imperforate, 771
    obstruction of, 776
    papillomata on, 791
    polypi in, 776
    Stinson's operation for occlusion of, 487
        using McLean's knife, 488
    stricture of, 777
    supernumerary, 771
    warts on, 791

Teeth. *See* Tooth
abnormalities of development of, 591
of position of, 591
abnormal number of, 591
affections of, 590
alteration in substance of, 596
alveolar periostitis in connection with, 599
caries of, 598
causing smooth mouth, 596
step-formed mouth, 595
wave-formed mouth, 595
diseases of alveoli of, 599
extraction of, 281
fistula abutting on, 602
fracture of, 596
individual irregularities of, 594
irregularities in the wear, 592
in shedding of, 591
overlapping of, 594
premature wear of, 596
repulsion of, 287
scalers for, 566
sharp, 592
shears for, 594
tartar on, 597
Temporo-maxillary articulation, arthritis of, 562
contusions of, 562
dislocation of, 563
wounds of, 562
Tendinitis, 74, 79
Tendo Achillis, rupture of, 906
Tendons, affections of, 75
contusions of, 75
inflammation of, 79
rupture of, 77
section of, 835
wounds of, 75
Tenotomy, cunean, 459
peroneal, 486
plantar, 454
supracarpal (horse), 452
(dog), 454
Tensor vaginæ femoris, rupture of, 880
Teratomatous testicle, 741
Testicle, absence of, 740
anomalies of, 740
in development of, 740
in migration of, 746
atrophy of, 740
cystic, 395
ectopia of, 401, 741
hypertrophy of, 740
inflammation of (orchitis), 744
retention of (abdominal or complete), 740
(inguinal or incomplete), 740
supernumerary, 740
teratoma in, 741
traumatic lesions of, 740
tuberculosis of, 747
tumours of, 741
Tetanus, 46
after castration, 373
Thermo-cauteries, 254
Thermotherapy, 27
Thigh, ossification of aponeurosis in, 847
Thoracentesis, 322
Thoracic organs, concussion of, 622
vessels, rupture of, 622
Thorax, penetrating wounds of, 624
Thoroughpin, 923
Three-quarter bar shoe, 975
shoe, 975
Thrombosis of iliacs, 898
of posterior aorta and its branches, 898
venous, 40
Thrush, 951
Thyroid gland, affections of, 612
removal of (thyroidectomy), 484
Thyroiditis, 612
Tibia, deferred fracture of, 901
fissure of, 901
fistula on, 900
fracture of, 909
in fœtus, 909
Tongue, affections of, 577
abscess of, 581
cyst in, 578
gangrene of, 580
inflammation of, 580
loss of free portion of, 577
paralysis of, 579
strangulation of, 577
tumours of, 578
wounds of, 577
Tooth chisel, 594
forceps, 284
Gunther's, 284
shears, 561
Squair's, 594
Torticollis, 643
Tourniquet, 239
Toxic dermatitis in the ox, 996
Trachea, affections of, 614
contusions of, 614
deformity of, 616
foreign bodies in, 616
fracture of, 615
stenosis of, 284
tumours of, 617
wounds of, 614
Tracheotome, McKenny's, 309
Spooner's, 310
Tracheotomy, 368
permanent, 308
temporary, 314
tubes, 311
"Track leg," in greyhound, 906
Transfusion of blood, 31, 322
Traumatic anæmia, 40
neuralgia, 42
Trevis, 153

Triceps extensor cubiti, rupture and sprain of, 808
Trichiasis, 520
Trichosomum contortum, 567
Trifacial paralysis, 582
Trilene anæsthesia, 193
True ringbone, 870
Tuberculosis, 61
Tumours, 48
  apple, 754
  benign, 48
  classification of, 48
  malignant, 50
  multiple, 48
  potato, 754
  skin, 62
Turbinated bones, necrosis of, 546
  operation for, 274
Twitch, 150

Udder. *See* Mammary gland
Ulceration, 15
Ulcers, 15
  cutaneous, 57
  of cornea, 566
  tuberculous, 61
Ulna, fracture of, 817
Ulnar neurectomy, 445
Umbilical hernia, 672. *See* Hernia
  operation for (dog), 329
  (horse), 324
Unpadded plaster cast, 123
Untoward sequelæ of neurectomy, 413
Urachus, pervious, 738
  ligature of, 738
Uranoplasty, 549
Ureter, affections of, 679
  calculi in, 714
Urethra, affections of, 730
  abscess in, 732
  calculi in, 733
  congenital deformities of, 730
  constriction of (stricture), 736
  fissure of, 731
  imperforate, 730
  inflammation of, 732
  injuries of, 731
  rupture of, 731
  tumours of, 736
  wounds of, 731
Urethral calculi (bitch), 736
  (cat), 735
  (dog), 735
  (horse, 733
  (ox), 734
  (ram), 735
  operation for, 428, 431
Urethritis, 732
Urethrotomy, 428
Urinary abscess, 737
  fistula, 738
  organs, affections of, 711
  tract, disinfection of, 689
Urine, blood in (hæmaturia), 717
  incontinence of, 717, 737
  infiltration with, 737
  retention of, 717, 737
Uterine irrigation, 759
Uterus, affections of, 768
  amputation of (mare), 416
  (cow), 417
  hæmorrhage from, 757
  inflammation of, 757
  irrigation of, 757
  occlusion of its os, 769
  ventro-fixation of, 767
  wounds of, 769

Vagina, affections of, 760
  abscess of, 762
  amputation of, 767
  complications of wounds of, 762
  cyst in, 767
  eversion of, 764
  hæmatoma in, 762
  hæmorrhage in, 762
  irrigation of, 757
  occlusion of, 760
  prolapse of, 764
    truss for, 766
    West's clam for, 766
    wire sutures for, 766
  tumours, 767
  wounds of, 761
Vaginalitis, 744
Vaginitis, 763
  chronic, 764
  contagious, 764
Van der Kaay's operation for chronic gastric tympany in the ox, 352
Varicocele, 746
Vasectomy, 376
Veins, affection of, 91
  air embolism of, 91
  inflammation of, 92
  varicose, 94
  wounds of, 91
Venereal tumours in dog and bitch, 755
Venesection, 317
Vennerholm's operation, 423
Venous thrombosis, 43
Ventral hernia, (horse), 676
  operation for, 338
Ventriclectomy, 302
Ventro-fixation of bowel, 705
  of uterus, 767
Veratrine, hypodermic injection of, for shoulder lameness, 809
Verrucose dermatitis of digit (ox), 996
Vertebral column, affections of, 643
  curvature of, 652
  disease of, 651
  distortion of (cervical part), 643
  fracture of, 648
Vesical calculi 724
  operation for, 425
Viborg's triangle, 296

Vibrion septique, 45
Villitis, 957
Violet rays for rickets, 133
for wounds, 31
Vulva, affections of, 759
contusions of, 759
rupture of, 759
tumours of, 767
wounds of, 759
Vulvitis, 760

Wasps, stings by, 35
Wattles, removal of, 488
West's clam, 766
Wharton's duct, foreign bodies in, 539
obstruction of, 539
Whitehouse's operation on guttural pouch, 297
Windgalls, articular, 865
tendinous, 859
Withers, affections of, 637
abscess on, 638
bursal enlargement on, 638
filariasis of, 642
fistulous, 639
galls on, 637
sit-fast on, 637
wounds of, 638
Wounds, 24
aseptic, 27
complications of, 40
Wounds, contused, 33
drainage of, 30
envenomed, 34
excision of, 26
granulation, 35
gunshot, 33
healing of, by primary adhesion, 21
by second intention, 22
by third intention, 22
by mixed intention, 22
under a scab, 22
heliotherapy for, 28
incised, 20
open, 20
poisoned, 34
primary symptoms of, 21
punctured, 20, 33
remote symptoms of, 22
secondary symptoms of, 21
septic, 26
subcutaneous, 36
suspected of infection, 25
suturing, 24, 232
thermotherapy for, 28
treatment of, 23
ulcerated wounds, 15, 21
violet rays for, 29
virulent, 34

X-rays, 268
uses of, 269